DICTIONARY OF IRISH LITERATURE

DICTIONARY OF IRISH LITERATURE

ROBERT HOGAN
EDITOR-IN-CHIEF

Zack Bowen

William J. Feeney

James Kilroy
ADVISORY EDITORS

Mary Rose Callaghan

Richard Burnham
ASSOCIATE EDITORS

 GREENWOOD PRESS
WESTPORT, CONNECTICUT

Library of Congress Cataloging in Publication Data
Main entry under title:

Dictionary of Irish literature.

Bibliography: p.

Includes index.

1. English literature—Irish authors—Dictionaries.
2. English literature—Irish authors—Bibliography.
3. Irish literature—Dictionaries. 4. Irish
literature—Bibliography. 5. Authors, Irish—
Biography. I. Hogan, Robert Goode, 1930-

PR8706.D5   820'.9'9415 [B]   78-20021

ISBN 0-313-20718-6

Library of Congress Catalog Card Number: 78-20021

ISBN: 0-313-20718-6

First published in 1979 in the United States of America by

Greenwood Press, Inc.
51 Riverside Avenue, Westport, Connecticut 06880

First published in 1980 throughout the rest of the world
under the title *The Macmillan Dictionary of Irish
Literature* by

The Macmillan Press Ltd.
London, England

Printed in the United States of America

10 9 8 7 6 5 4 3 2 1

ACKNOWLEDGMENTS

For permission to quote various published lines of verse, the editor and publisher gratefully make the following acknowledgments: to Mr. Monk Gibbon for four lines from "Microcosm," to Mr. Brendan Kennelly for several lines from several poems, to Mr. Sean O'Faolain for four lines from his translation of Donnchadh Mor O Dalaigh's "Truagh mo Thuras ar Loch Dearg," to Mr. Tom Paulin for a stanza from "Near the Christadelphians," to Allen Figgis & Co., Ltd. for Eavan Boland's poem "Requiem for a Personal Friend (On a half-eaten Blackbird)," to Mr. Seamus Heaney and Faber and Faber, Ltd. for quotations from "Digging" from *Death of a Naturalist*, "Ban Clay" from *Door into the Dark,* and "The Tolund Man" from *Wintering Out*; to Mr. Paul Muldoon and Faber and Faber, Ltd. for quotations from "How to Play Championship Tennis" and "Blemish" from *Mules*; to MacGibbon and Kee/Granada Publishing, Ltd. for quotes from Desmond O'Grady's "His Bath" and "Land," to the Goldsmith Press for a quotation from Desmond O'Grady's "Back to Our Mountains," to Victor Gollancz, Ltd. for a quotation from Eavan Boland's *The War Horse* and also from Michael Longley's *Man Lying on a Wall*; to the Estate of the late Joseph Campbell for quotations from "I Am the Mountainy Singer," "The Old Woman," and "The Key"; to Oxford University Press for quotations from *North* by Seamus Heaney, © 1975 by Seamus Heaney, from *Wintering Out*, by Seamus Heaney, © 1972 by Seamus Heaney, and from *Collected Poems of Louis MacNeice*, edited by E. R. Dodds, copyright © the Estate of Louis MacNeice, 1966, all reprinted by permission of Oxford University Press, Inc.; and to Miss Anne Yeats, Mr. M. B. Yeats, and the Macmillan Company of London and Basinstoke for quotations from W. B. Yeats' "Among School Children" and "Under Ben Bulben."

CONTRIBUTORS

Jerry C. Beasley
University of Delaware

Zack Bowen
University of Delaware

John Boyd
Lyric Players Theatre

Terence Brown
Trinity College, Dublin

Richard Burnham
Dominican College

James M. Cahalan
University of Cincinnati

Mary Rose Callaghan
Proscenium Press

Anne Clissmann
Trinity College, Dublin

Peter Costello
Dublin

Denis Cotter, Jr.
Dublin

Barbara DiBernard
University of Minnesota

James Douglas
Bray, Co. Wicklow

Paul A. Doyle
Nassau Community College

Grace Eckley
Drake University

William J. Feeney
DePaul University

John Wilson Foster
University of British Columbia

Helmut E. Gerber
Arizona State University

Christopher Griffin
Dublin

Mark D. Hawthorne
James Madison University

Jane Healy
Dublin

Richard M. Kain
University of Louisville

Colbert Kearney
University College, Cork

A. A. Kelly
Great Britain

Brendan Kennelly
Trinity College, Dublin

Frank Kersnowski
Trinity University

James Kilroy
Vanderbilt University

Thomas Kinsella
Temple University

James Liddy
University of Wisconsin-Milwaukee

Nora F. Lindstrom
Bradley University

William J. Linn
Brooklyn

M. Kelly Lynch
Boston

J. B. Lyons
Royal College of Surgeons, Dublin

Michael McDonnell
Fairfield University

Patricia McFate
University of Pennsylvania

Nora McGuinness
University of California, Davis

Alf MacLochlainn
National Library of Ireland

Bryan MacMahon
Listowel, Co. Kerry

Andrew Marsh
Irish Press

James H. Matthews
Eckerd College

D.E.S. Maxwell
York University

Donald C. Mell
University of Delaware

Thomas Merrill
University of Delaware

Liam Miller
Dolmen Press

Sven Eric Molin
George Mason University

J. H. Natterstad
Framingham State College

John Nemo
Bradley University

James Newcomer
Texas Christian University

Johann A. Norstedt
*Virginia Polytechnic Institute
    and State University*

Micheál O hAodha
Abbey Theatre

Seamus O'Neill
Carysfort Training College

Coilin Owens
George Mason University

Kathleen Danaher Parks
University of Delaware

Raymond J. Porter
Iona College

Victor Price
Great Britain

Martin Ryan
Dublin

Ann Saddlemyer
University of Toronto

George Brandon Saul
University of Connecticut

Nuala Saunders
Convent of Mercy, Callan,
  Co. Kilkenny

Bonnie Kime Scott
University of Delaware

Mary Helen Thuente
Indiana University-Purdue
  University

Jack W. Weaver
Winthrop College

Terence de Vere White
The Irish Times

Terence Winch
Washington, D.C.

CONTENTS

PREFACE

A preliminary word seems necessary about the plan of this book.

The General Introduction might really be titled "The Literary Uses of Ireland," for the principal characteristic of writing in Ireland is its Irishness. While this statement may seem obvious, it also is obvious that, since the Renaissance, nationality, as expressed in literature, has been increasingly diminished by internationality. For instance, the excellence of what D. H. Lawrence called "Classic American Literature" was considerably diluted by an international, and particularly an English, influence. The inimitable excellence of the nineteenth-century American authors Emerson, Thoreau, Poe, Hawthorne, Melville, and especially Walt Whitman appears to lie mainly in the extent to which they resisted that influence and allowed themselves to be receptive to their own native milieu. And the triumphant progression of Russian literary masters in the nineteenth century, from Pushkin to Gogol to Tolstoy and Dostoyevsky, Turgenev and Chekhov, certainly must be attributed to the backwardness, the provinciality, the isolation, and the ingrown "Russianness" of their society.

Irish society also, until the very recent past, remained surprisingly insulated from the modern world. Although in many ways pernicious, that isolation did have the effect of intensely focusing the attention of the Irish writer on the little world of his Four Green Fields. Even now, when Ireland is a much more outward-looking society, the effects remain dramatically evident. The General Introduction, then, is an attempt to chart how the Irish writer used this narrow, but rich, subject matter—the landscape, the climate, the history, the manners, the morals, the customs of his native land.

The General Introduction is not a capsule review of Ireland past and present, as any attempt to compress so much information into so little space would be to court superficiality with a vengeance. Rather, it deals with those facets of Ireland that the writers themselves have thought the most salient and that have appeared so constantly in their work. As a historical or sociological or even literary survey, the Introduction is too short and mal-proportioned to serve; but as a not wholly subjective view of how Ireland's writers have portrayed their country, and of what those writers have thought important, it may introduce the reader to at least the primary preoccupations of Irish literature.

In planning this dictionary, the most difficult editorial question to resolve has been how to treat literature written in the Irish language. Such literature is centuries-old and continues to be written, albeit in a trickle, even today. The range of that literature, from saga to satire, is broad indeed, and the quality of much of that literature is brilliant. However, the fortunes of the Irish language have been wedded to the fortunes of the Irish nation. As England's power waxed in Ireland, the old Irish culture waned and Irish as a living language progressively decayed. The year 1800 may be taken as symptomatic of the triumph of the English language in Ireland. In that year, the Act of Union abolished the separate Irish Parliament and included Irish representatives in Westminster. Irish, of course, was still spoken, but as the sole language it survived only in secluded rural pockets. An Irish language revival around the turn of the twentieth century was a harbinger of the secretly growing political revival that was to culminate in the Easter Rising of 1916, in the Irish Free State, and finally in an independent republic that comprised most of the island. However, political independence did not mean that the Irish language could be restored as the living language of the people. Ireland became nominally bilingual, but, despite great dedication and immense effort, it was impossible to go back.

Today, Irish alone is spoken in a few small sections of the country. The language is studied in the schools from an early age, and some modern books of merit have been written in Irish. Nevertheless, it remains true that the great works of modern Irish literature have been written in English. It is also lamentably true that the classic works of the Irish language are to be perceived, even by the Irish themselves, mainly through their influence on modern Irish writing in English. Whether in direct translation, adaptation, or even simply as a fecund source of allusion and inspiration, that influence is profound and pervasive, but it is an influence at one remove.

A dictionary of Irish literature assuredly must deal with writing in Irish. Apart from its own extraordinary merits, literature in Irish remains the bedrock foundation for much, if not most, modern Irish writing in English. Nevertheless, it seemed that this work must stress Irish writing in the English language. After all, W. B. Yeats, James Stephens, and James Joyce are the mirrors in which the entire world, including Ireland itself, sees reflected the old Ireland that was. Consequently, we have adopted a compromise by printing a lengthy, specially commissioned critical and historical survey of writing in Irish, from the earliest times to the present day. This survey, written by Seamus O'Neill, himself a distinguished contemporary writer who has published mainly in Irish, appears as a most necessary preliminary to the bulk of the dictionary which treats of Irish writing in English.

The bulk of the dictionary is made up of biographical and critical essays on approximately five hundred Irish authors who wrote mainly in the English language. The number of authors included could have been doubled or even trebled, but to have done so would have been to admit a flood of authors who contributed little of significance to literature and also to curtail strongly the amount of space available for discussions of more important writers.

The choice of authors to be included has been basically the decision of the editor, although he has availed himself of the oral suggestions of so many people and of the written opinions of so many more, that the final choice probably closely approaches a consensus. Most of the authors included are obvious choices, authors whose omission would have been ridiculous from the standpoint of either literature or history. Nevertheless, some will certainly question the inclusion of a minority of authors. Indeed, I fully expect to be asked (especially by the Irish), "Why did you leave out the brilliant A——— and include that poetaster X———?" The reason is probably attributable to ignorance, bias, lack of taste, and human fallibility.

Still and all, in this area of minimal excellence and excellent potential, there is no thoroughly satisfactory solution. One arbitrary solution adopted here has been to limit the entries almost exclusively to authors who have published a book, no matter how slim. Another arbitrary criterion has been to lend a tolerant ear to the new writer who is still establishing himself, even though this practice might mean skimping on or even omitting some minor authors of earlier times whom I myself valued more. Nevertheless, as the work of the dictionary progressed, the hard and fast lines of distinction increasingly blurred. How could one, for instance, defend including Congreve and Goldsmith and Sheridan and even George Darley, who hardly wrote of Ireland at all? The answer is really an intractable bias in their favor.

A few foreign authors have been included, for a few foreign authors have made a rich and lasting contribution to Irish literature. Such volumes as, for instance, Robin Flower's *The Western Island*, or Richard Ellmann's *James Joyce*, or J. P. Donleavy's *The Ginger Man*, or J. G. Farrell's *Troubles* seem classics of Irish literature, and to have omitted their remarkable authors from this company would have been jingoistic indeed.

I do not think that any author of outstanding achievement has been omitted. However, the body of Irish literature, past as well as present, is still being charted, and it is entirely possible that I am wrong. If so, I hope it will be possible to make amends at some future date.

The length of the alphabetical entries varies from about twenty-five words to about ten thousand, and obviously the length of an entry implies some judgment about the author's worth as it appears at present. However, this is only a very rough judgment, and the reader is cautioned not to regard Author A, who is discussed in two hundred and fifty words, as one-sixth less admirable than Author B, who is discussed in fifteen hundred.

The body of the dictionary also contains a handful of general articles on topics such as folklore, which have been of major importance to literature. At one time, I contemplated including a larger number of these general articles, which would deal with historical writing, travel writing, biographies, memoirs, journalism, broadcasting, and other endeavors whose best examples have strong claims to literary worth. After much consideration, however, I decided that comprehensive surveys of such fields would not only extend the book greatly, but would also dissipate its major impact by including much that was tangential or transitory. On the other hand, there are quite a few individual entries for major historians, political writers, editors, orators, journalists, and the like. The dictionary also contains a number of entries for important literary organizations or publications, such as the Abbey Theatre, the Cuala Press, and *The Nation*. The particular articles have been signed by their authors, and any unsigned articles have been written by the general editor.

Finally, whenever a name is followed by an asterisk, it is to be understood that such person or topic or organization has its own separate entry in the appropriate alphabetical place in the dictionary.

Perhaps a third to a half of this book consists of bibliographies. The bibliographies of specific writers or topics follow their individual entries. Most have been compiled by the author of the entry, although the editor is responsible for the bibliographical form of the citations and has frequently made additions and, occasionally, omissions. The individual bibliographies list all of the author's significant works, and "significant work" has ordinarily been taken to mean every individual book publication and all of the important fugitive material. In many instances, it has been possible to list practically everything an author is known to have written. However, in the case of an extremely important or prolific writer, such as Shaw or Yeats, a complete listing has been impossible. Even so, a diligent attempt has been made to list everything of primary or even secondary importance.

The individual bibliographies are divided into two sections. The first section lists the writer's works in the order in which they were published. The second, and usually shorter, section lists the major critical, biographical, and bibliographical works about the writer, and is arranged alphabetically by the last names of the authors, editors, or compilers. To conserve space, the name of the publisher has been shortened to its essential components: thus, Maunsel and Company will appear simply as "Maunsel," the Dolmen Press simply as "Dolmen," and so on. In addition, the subtitles of books usually have been omitted.

Although the limitations of space and human energy have prevented an exhaustive or complete listing, I believe that these bibliographies as a whole constitute the most comprehensive listing of Irish literature that is in print or is likely to be in print for many years.

The Chronology of historical and literary events given at the end of the dictionary is intended not as a substitute for a basic grasp of Irish history and literature but as a simple chart for the neophyte traveler in moments of occasional bafflement. For more precise knowledge, the reader is directed to the excellent volumes of history and literary history cited in the General Bibliography. The latter is a concise listing of the best general books on Ireland, its geography, its climate, its history, its economics, its architecture, its customs, and, particularly, its literature.

A dictionary or an encyclopedia does not always have an index. This volume does, and I trust that the reader will quickly appreciate its utility. Irish literature has emerged from a small and closely knit society. One Irish wit remarked that a literary movement occurred when a number of writers lived in the same place and did not speak to each other. There is a deal of justice in that remark, but in Ireland the writers do always speak about each other. They also necessarily work together, and they inevitably influence one another. For instance, the most pervasive influence in modern Irish literature is still W. B. Yeats, and he is discussed at considerable length in the article by Richard M. Kain. However, Yeats was of crucial importance for the careers of scores of writers, and additional information about him appears throughout this book. To a lesser extent, that same point is valid for many other writers. Hence, the judicious reader will not only read the article about the author he is interested in, but will also consult the Index for other citations.

To save space, there are no separate entries for individual works in the text, unless the author is unknown. Thus, a discussion of *Ulysses* or *Juno and the Paycock* will be found under the entries for their authors, Joyce and O'Casey. If the reader knows the work and not the author, he may quickly find a discussion of the work by referring to its title in the Index. An anonymous work like *The Tain*, which is not entered separately in the dictionary but is discussed in Seamus O'Neill's essay on Gaelic literature, can also be located through use of the Index. The Index does not cite information from the bibliographies, but everything cited in the text proper— both in the introductory material and in the alphabetical entries—is noted.

Not every Irish author or magazine or literary society has been thought important enough to be accorded a separate listing in the body of the work. However, a glance at the Index will indicate that many of these individuals or organizations have been discussed somewhere in the dictionary. For instance, Richard Lovell Edgeworth is cited only in the Index, but will be found briefly discussed in the notice of his very important daughter, Maria; the magazine *Threshold* is cited only in the Index but will be found in the notice of its parent organization, the Lyric Players Theatre of Belfast; the Society of Irish Playwrights, through the Index, will be found briefly discussed in the entry on its chief organizer and first chairman, John Purcell O'Donovan.

An editor of such a volume as this must feel like the captain of a ship manned by many and much more knowledgeable sailors than he. As I have that feeling quite strongly indeed, I should like to mention my particular gratitude to Richard M. Kain and William J. Feeney, without whose erudition, kindness, and generous labors this dictionary still would be far from completion. My indebtedness is scarcely less to Seamus O'Neill, Mary Rose Callaghan, James Kilroy, Zack Bowen, Sven Eric Molin, and Richard Burnham, all of whose friendships I have outrageously exploited. To them, and to the many other brilliant contributors, my deepest and most abiding thanks.

Dr. Johnson said, "A man will turn over half a library to make one book." Of the half a library that was turned over in the making of this book, there were some few volumes to which I constantly returned, and to which every student of Irish literature must remain indebted. I have particularly in mind D. J. O'Donoghue's *The Poets of Ireland,* Stephen J. Brown's *Ireland in Fiction,* Richard Best's *Bibliography of Irish Philology* and its sequel, Patrick Rafroidi's *L'Irelande et romantisme,* Brian Cleeve's *Dictionary of Irish Writers,* and Brian McKenna's *Irish Literature, 1800-1875.* Such volumes have been both an inspiration and a conscience.

My thanks also to Greenwood Press for initiating this project, and particularly to Marilyn Brownstein and Nancy J. Clements for much good and sage counsel.

Finally, I am painfully conscious that, in a work of this size and scope, errors of fact have undoubtedly crept in; and I will be most grateful if readers will bring any such faults to my attention. As for errors of judgment, let Time be the judge, for he is much more judicious than I and considerably less vulnerable.

Robert Hogan
January 1, 1979

INTRODUCTION

Ireland is a small, wet island about four hours to the west of England if you travel by the mailboat from Holyhead to Dun Laoghaire. The island was not considered important enough to conquer by Julius Caesar, but ever since then it has been thrusting itself upon the world's notice. Indeed, despite its small size and population, its negligible mineral resources, and its minor strategic value in time of war, Ireland has taken up a remarkable amount of the world's attention.

The country's richest contribution to the world has been its emigrants. Otherwise, Ireland has been, until quite recently, mainly absorbed by itself. Sometimes it has seemed to assume that the world would find that subject equally interesting, and, despite moments of exasperation with that "most distressful country," the world usually has been interested and often fascinated.

Perhaps the reason is that there is an Irish Problem. One caustic thinker shrugged the matter off by remarking, "The Irish problem—there is always an Irish problem. It is the Irish." The Irish themselves would probably say that the problem is the outsiders. For centuries, they would point out, their little bit of heaven has been overrun by outsiders who have victimized, exploited, and oppressed the inhabitants. The oppressor may have been the Danes, the Normans, the English, or American blue jeans, hamburgers, vulgarity and affluence.

The world's view is somewhat similar: Ireland is an ideal; we regard its fields as greener, its virgins purer, and its poets wittier than any others anywhere ever were. It is the repository of whimsy, charm, and geniality, and yet. . . . And yet something diabolical is always going on in that little bit of heaven. The Potato Famines of the 1840s, to take but one example, were probably the most effective decimation of a race until Hitler turned his attention to the Jews. Perhaps the Irish decimation was even worse because it happened not by madness or any overt policy, but simply by not caring. Then there have been all of the other diabolical instances—the assassinations, the wars, and the continuing petty turmoil that is a microcosm of the world's turmoil.

In our hearts we probably know that every place is a ravaged Eden, but in Ireland we seem to see more clearly our own plight, our own faults, and our own fate. Yet why do we see it there? Why has Yugoslavia, or Wales, or Chile, or Iceland not so held the attention of the world? Why have there been so many memorable and resounding voices from this country which today numbers only about four million souls?

Any answer must be speculative and subjective, and this book attempts only part of an answer. That part is concerned with why Ireland has been blessed with such a proportionately startling number of extraordinary writers. In philosophy, music, painting, sculpture, architecture, and practically every branch of human endeavor, the Irish contribution to the wealth of the world's wisdom has been, as one would expect, minor. In literature, however, in decade after decade and in century after century, this small country has produced men like Swift and Burke and Berkeley, Sheridan and Goldsmith and Wilde, Shaw and Yeats and Joyce, Synge and Fitzmaurice, O'Casey and O'Flaherty, O'Connor and O'Faolain, Bowen and Behan and Beckett, and many, many others. This volume attempts to tell something about these Irish writers and their work, but this introductory essay will attempt to suggest something more—to suggest why there were so many who were so good.

The qualities that have formed the Irish writer are the qualities that have formed the Irish man. Among them are:

GEOGRAPHY AND CLIMATE

The effects of geography and climate upon Ireland have been crucial in its history, its economy, and the character of its people.

The landscape of Ireland is often startlingly beautiful and extremely various. The weather is statistically, if not convincingly, temperate, but the perennially falling rain may at any moment be dissipated by the most dramatic appearance of blue sky to be seen anywhere in the world. The combination of mountain and bog, lake and lowland with a gentle climate and abundant rain has made the country most profitable for the growing of grass and the grazing of cattle. Hence, it has had a major effect upon the Irish economy. The combination of geography and climate upon people is perhaps even more important. Much of Ireland has a stark grandeur or a sensual beauty that can elevate or delight and that often does. However, the effect of the landscape is inevitably tempered by the weather. A good deal of the sombre and brooding character of the Irish landscape seems due to the quality of the light, to the constantly shifting and low-lying masses of clouds, and to the rain, the softly falling and ever-present rain. The psychic

effect upon people must be subliminally schizophrenic—a depressed elevation, a dull delight briefly shot through with instants of manic joy. One
might well argue that those are the tones of Irish literature.

One might almost say that those Irish novels that start off by describing a
hot and sunny day usually turn out to be either exaggerations or simple
entertainments. At any rate, one can say that descriptions of landscape in
Irish literature impart not only the striking beauty of the country, but also
even a spiritual overtone, an extra meaningfulness, much as landscape and
weather, heath and storm, enrich the meaning of *King Lear*.

THE MEMORY OF THE DEAD

When a truce was called in the Anglo-Irish war in 1921, the Irish leader
Eamon de Valera went to England to negotiate a final peace settlement with
the English prime minister, Lloyd George. A story is told about de Valera
then, which is too good to be true and yet too Irish to be basically wrong
in anything but the facts. Someone asked after several days how negotiations
were progressing, and the answer was that de Valera was rehearsing the
historical background, and so far the talks had progressed up to the battle
of Clontarf.

One Irish novel gives a quick sense of the city of Dublin merely by leap-
ing from statue to statue—from Parnell to O'Connell, to Tom Moore, to
Grattan, to Burke and Goldsmith, Davis, Tone, Emmet, and quite a few
others.

And, of course, if one is extracting symptoms, there are the innumerable
poems and ballads which still are read and sung about Owen Roe, Red
Hugh, brave Patrick Sarsfield, bold Father Murphy, and young Roddy
McCorley. Then for years there was the constant political evocation of the
past—the stirring allusion to, the rousing quotation from, and the frequent
reading of the works of Tone and Davis, of Mitchel's Jail Journal, of
Pearse's essays and speeches. Perhaps the most dramatic, or at least the
loudest, evocation of all was the memory of King Billy crossing the Boyne
on the Glorious 12th of July, celebrated by the horrific cannonade of the
Lambeg drums. Yet, the most quietly telling evocation of all was that until
very modern times the cities, towns, and countryside changed little, and so
the past was noticeably ever present; one lived in the middle of it.

Culturally, Irish legend and history have been, at least since the Literary
Renaissance, a source of pride; politically, Irish history seems remembered
as a grudge and a frustration. How deeply and how broadly the sense of
history runs through the Irish population is conjectural, but one plausible
conjecture would be that it runs more deeply and broadly than it does for
Americans. In an ordinarily peaceful time, the great mass of the Irish population probably is rather oblivious to history, but this dormant memory may
be readily roused by current events.

The Irish politician by and large uses history rather differently than does
the Irish writer. The politician has often evoked the glorious past either for

the admiration of a nobility that has come to be invested in him or for the admiration of heroism in the face of a yet unredressed wrong. No matter that the nobility is tinged by a kind of madness, or the heroism by a kind of hatred, the appeal is to the people's admiration, and the appeal has often worked.

Many novels, stories, plays, and poems have espoused this public view of history, but few of them have been of much literary merit. When the serious writer has turned to historical subjects, his primary attitude has seemed less admiring than critical, satirical, or whimsical. Even a nominally patriotic poem of great power like Yeats' "Easter 1916" when read closely is a most ambiguous statement. There is admiration for nobility and heroism, but there is also the nagging speculation of whether the nobility and heroism may not in the end have been folly.

THE LAND

The one great, pervasive, primary theme of both Irish life and literature is the land. All of the other usual themes of both life and literature—religion, love, patriotism, individual aspiration—seem in Ireland to have been amalgamated with, or attached to, some facet of love for the land.

Perhaps the reason is that the dweller in Ireland, whether Firbolg or Celt, Dane or Norman, or even modern Ulster Presbyterian, always has had good reason to fear that his hold on the land was transitory and tenuous. All of recorded Irish history, down to the Northern troubles of the present, has seemed to revolve around the ineradicable, inescapable, perhaps even irresolvable question of who owns Ireland. The ramifications of this ever different, but always same, situation have been immense, intense, far-reaching, and deep-rooted. Politically, the question for centuries has occasioned invasion, war, rebellion, murder, and violence. Economically, for the small minority it has occasioned riches, cultivation, and absenteeism, and for the large majority, poverty, backwardness, and emigration. Agriculturally, it has been a national disaster, its most horrific embodiment being the Potato Famine when the land itself seemed the nemesis and not the prize.

But if to the Irish man the land was the ultimate glittering prize, to the Irish writer it has often seemed a curse. If the land could cause physical blight and death, it could also cause psychic blight and death. Some of the most powerful Irish plays and stories are those in which a person gives his soul wholly to the land. He may be deadened and animalized by it, as is the farmer in Patrick Kavanagh's poem *The Great Hunger*; he may sell his daughter for it, as occurs in Louis D'Alton's *Lovers Meeting* or John B. Keane's *Sive* or innumerable other places; he may want it enough to murder for it, as the peasant does in T. C. Murray's *Birthright* or even in Keane's modern play *The Field*. To realistic writers, such as those above, an almost tragic pattern attaches to the theme of the land. A man so lusts for it that he struggles indomitably, hardens himself irremediably, and even casts off every other human tie or desire; but when he wins it, somehow, by death or by psychic death, he loses.

If the realistic writer most powerfully criticizes his countrymen's most ingrained desire, the romantic writer makes precisely the same criticism but makes it flippantly. The romantic writer long has idealized the landless man—even the tinker or the tramp. Even such a son of the cities as Sean O'Casey once referred to himself as a wandering road-minstrel. Synge's Nora in *The Shadow of the Glen* leaves her home to go wandering with a tramp. Colum's Conn Hourican leaves the land to his children and takes to the roads with his fiddle. Padraic Ó Conaire in reality left his office in London to wander the roads of Ireland and write short stories in Gaelic. From Synge's *Playboy* to the tinkers of Bryan MacMahon's *The Honey Spike*, there is this glorification of the shaughraun, with only an occasional demurrer like Colum's moving little poem "An Old Woman of the Roads."

Both the realistic writer and the romantic writer, however, seem deeply critical of the Irishman's love of the land, and in that criticism they may have touched the core of Ireland's tragedy.

(There is one other aspect of love for the land that should be touched on, and that is the love of the emigrant. In America or Australia, he usually has little or no hope of ever returning, and so his love for the land is entirely uncritical. Rather, he idealizes it, remembering it as better than it ever was. His nostalgia and also his money have had some economic and political effect at home. His nostalgia has had little literary effect, although it has been the basis for innumerable poems and ballads. If these usually have been mawkishly sentimental, they have been none the less deeply felt.)

RELIGION

There is a traditional story in Ireland of how Oisin, the great, truculent hero of the Fianna, returned from the Land of Youth and met with St. Patrick. One fine modern retelling of their conversations is Darrell Figgis' *The Return of the Hero*, which excellently contrasts the two utterly conflicting attitudes toward life. After many vicissitudes, the spiritual sons of St. Patrick seem finally to have triumphed in modern recorded history. And yet the triumph never has been quite total, as, indeed, the conflict never was quite thoroughgoing. It was the heroic spirit of Oisin that for centuries impelled the various armed and doomed rebellions, just as it was the same spirit that, in another way, impelled the Literary Renaissance.

For most of modern Irish history, the Roman Catholic Church has been identified closely with the people. It was the church of the people, and its priests were as oppressed as the people and sometimes much worse off. Only in quite modern times, following the Catholic emancipation of the nineteenth century, the disestablishment of the Church of Ireland, and finally the severance of the tie with Britain, did the Irish Catholic Church become publicly accepted and secure. A symptom of how recent that change is may be noticed in many towns, such as Listowel in Kerry, where the

Protestant Church is set proudly in the middle of the square and the Catholic Church is tucked unobtrusively off to one side. Nowadays, of course, the Protestant Church is most sparsely attended, a dramatic change which is well embodied in Jack White's play *The Last Eleven.*

With the formation of the Irish Free State, the Catholic Church established itself with a vengeance as a social and political force. Its favored position was written into the Irish Constitution, and that clause was only excised in the late 1970s. For the first fifty years of Irish self-government, then, the Catholic Church was probably the most powerful social force in the land. Its influence was so potent and so pervasive that it overtly or tacitly dominated every significant facet of Irish life. The government almost seemed the secular right arm of the church; and should a government, as it rarely did, oppose the views of the church, the government could be toppled. An example is the dissolution of the interparty government in 1951, after the church had opposed a mother-and-child care scheme proposed by Minister of Health Noel Browne.

How much government was a spokesman for the ecclesiastical position may be seen in various instances involving the arts. There was the rigorous book censorship which banned even innocuous references to sex (although it had no violent objections to violence). Among the thousands of books banned were many of little or no discernible merit, but the best of the banned read like a Who's Who of modern literature. The government film censorship acted with similar rigor; to take but one rather late example, *Anatomy of a Murder*, a popular courtroom melodrama of the early 1960s, was reduced to incomprehensibility when all shots of an uninhabited pair of women's panties were excised. There was also the legally unformulated but tacit censorship of the stage; one well-known example is the case of the director Alan Simpson who spent a night in Bridewell for producing Tennessee Williams' *The Rose Tattoo*. Perhaps just how enthusiastically the government supported the church's views may be seen in the Senate debates over the banning of Eric Cross's *The Tailor and Ansty* in the early 1940s. Today the remarks of the government opponents of the book seem almost satirically extravagant.

These well-known instances are merely a few among many, but they suggest a serious variance between the practices of the church and the opinions of the best writers. There was much bland popular literature that expressed the social attitudes of the church, as there was a good deal of popular hortatory literature to express the establishment political views. But the best work of the best writers either ignored the church or (as in the case of O'Casey) criticized it loudly.

It is curious that the establishment church of this century became so different from the outlawed church of the past. In the seventeenth and eighteenth centuries, and much of the nineteenth century (perhaps until the Parnell split), the church had a remarkable sympathetic union with the people. After the establishment of Maynooth, the national seminary in 1795, and the importation of Jansenistic teachers from France, the church grew more puritanical and identified ever more closely with the current political establishment. For one instance, in the Great Lockout of 1913, the workers of Dublin planned to send a shipload of their hungry children to England where they could be cared for. A line of priests barred the way on the docks, however, and the Dublin children returned to the starving tenements. In other words, when the church grew in power, it grew also to uphold power and often to diverge sharply from the opinions of many of its members.

Nevertheless, the power of the church over Irishmen, until the very recent period, has been enormous. Even when ecclesiastical opinion and popular aspiration were profoundly at odds—as they sometimes were in labor or in political struggles—the rift, though deep, was ignored by the people. Or, rather, the opinions of the church were ignored, but the church was not. In any case, the Catholic Church in Ireland became an intractable and inflexible body, bearing almost more resemblance to a fundamentalist sect in Alabama than to the Catholic Church in other European countries. The 1960s and 1970s, however, were marked by new affluence in Ireland, in the aftermath of Vatican II, and considerable upheaval in world Catholicism. As a result, the influence of the Church in Ireland seems to have waned, and its character seems to be changing.

The influence of the church upon literature generally has been to foster among the best writers an attitude of criticism and opposition. There was, of course, a morally innocuous and patriotically unctuous literature, typified perhaps at its impressive best by the novels of Kate O'Brien or the poems of Robert Farren. But, at the same time, there was the growth of an antiestablishment and frequently anticlerical literature, which contains much of the best of the most remarkable writing in modern Ireland. Probably, then, it is true to say that, if an intractable and puritanic church had not pushed the literary artist into opposition, there would be much less that is individual and exciting about modern Irish letters.

Today, when the church is a much less powerful force in society, how will literature be affected? Thus far, two stages are discernible. The first might be suggested by the early career of a writer still in his thirties, John Feeney. Feeney is old enough to have been formed by the Jansenistic 1950s and young enough to have been a leader in the pale Irish version of the university students' revolts of the late 1960s. His career reflects this division. His punch-pulling, whitewashing biography of Archbishop McQuaid is balanced by his novel outspokenly condemning the establishment, as typified by the national television service; his several-year stint as editor of the journal once called *The Catholic Standard* is balanced by his book of stories whose best pieces are strongly condemnatory of Catholic standards. The second stage might be typified by two older writers who have been exposed as people and as artists to England and America. In Brian Friel's play *Living Quarters* and in Thomas Murphy's play *Sanctuary Lamp*, the position of the modern church in Ireland is scathingly criticized by the failure of the priests in the plays to do what priests should do. It will be interesting to see how the matter develops.

DRINK

The bellicose and drunken Irishman is as irritating a cliché as was once the allegation of the pig in every parlor. In the nineteenth century, the redoubtable Father Mathew led an extraordinary temperance crusade. Its effects long since have been largely dissipated, and it has been estimated that 10 percent of all personal spending in Ireland today is for drink.

Whether that be an exaggeration, to the observant onlooker it does seem to have some basis. A sociologist or psychologist would be needed to investigate the reasons for Irish drinking, but some reasons seem fairly obvious. Ireland has always been a poor country, and drink is a prime anodyne for the frustrations of poverty, hopelessness, and boredom. The effects of a drinking culture on the country are manifold and undoubtedly pernicious, especially in a psychological sense. The toleration, even the macho glamorization of drink, seems to hold a good deal of the country in the thrall of social adolescence.

For Irish literature, the importance of drink is unquestionable as well as, like drink itself, both invigorating and enervating. Some of the greatest comic scenes of Synge, O'Casey, Joyce, and Flann O'Brien have centered around drink, and merely to list the works in which drink is significant would be well-nigh impossible. While drink is only infrequently a central theme, it seems ubiquitous as a contributory theme, and generally a source of considerable excellence.

At the same time, the tales of increasingly sodden writers whose careers are pickled in alcohol are so numerous, that the figure of the drunken Irish genius has become a cliché. For the Irish writer, drink has been a magnificent theme, but all too often a source of personal destruction.

SEX

Perhaps most great writing is in some way or another—and frequently centrally—about sex. Much literature in the Irish language, from the occasional ribaldry of *The Táin* to the inimitable *Midnight Court* of Brian Merriman is unashamedly sexual. Perhaps that fact may serve as one indicator that until modern times sex was more or less a nakedly normal part of Irish life.

Still, given the climate and geography, sex could not be too naked, for the simple reason that it usually was necessary to wear a fair amount of clothing. At the same time, economics, politics, and religion seemed to support each other mutually in inhibiting a free functioning of the sexual man. Economics may well have been the most inhibiting. Given the Irish way of life, the questions of who slept with whom and who married whom and how many children were born were of prime importance. People married carefully to remain solvent, and, when it was economic freedom versus sexual freedom, economic freedom usually won. For the mass of people, remaining solvent meant coming into a bit of land. That usually was impossible until the head of the household, the father, died or became feeble with age. Therefore, there were many late marriages, although most were prolific, perhaps partly for economic reasons again. The unfortunate younger sons tended either to emigrate or to become old bachelors, a situation reflected eloquently in M. J. Molloy's play *The Wood of the Whispering*. This situation lasted until the 1960s when the effect of relative prosperity and stronger influence from the outside world caused a gradual but considerable change.

Until recently, sex has been treated with reticence in literature. Of course, there are exceptions, the most notorious being for many years Joyce's *Ulysses*. The Catholic Church and the government, acting pretty much hand in glove, contrived to inhibit sexual expression in literature as in life. For many Irish, the effect of a sternly religious education was to extend sexual ignorance, distrust, and even antipathy well into adult years. For about the first thirty years of Irish self-government, a public puritanism was effective and thorough. The later plays of O'Casey are, among other things, simplistic satiric condemnations of this public puritanism.

In 1900, the realistic novels of George Moore were considered anathema. Thirty years later, little had changed; and when T. C. Murray in *Autumn Fire* tackled a theme bordering on incest, he had to treat the topic with a rigid dignity and a profound reticence altogether lacking in the American play *Desire under the Elms,* by Eugene O'Neill, which deals with the same situation. Since the 1960s, the Irish milieu has changed considerably, but even so the novels of the much admired John McGahern and Edna O'Brien, who dealt frankly but hardly luridly or pornographically with sex, were initially banned. (For that matter, one contemporary Irish short story has a character closely resembling Miss O'Brien, who returns to her native village and is viciously raped, the moral apparently being, "That'll show her!")

Despite such anachronistic difficulties, the Irish writer of today can write on practically any topic and from almost any point of view. There may yet be a banning or two, but the euphemizing of sex in modern Irish literature is seen as increasingly quaint.

VIOLENCE

In their popular entertainments and even their serious literature, Americans have a penchant for violence that periodically alarms even them. Although the Irish have not developed the more outré refinements of violence in their entertainments, they do have a similar tolerance for violence. Indeed, "tolerance" may be a less appropriate word than "admiration" or "glorification."

In any society, the active perpetrators of public violence are a minority, but private violence can seep into ordinary life and color opinions and attitudes. Corporal punishment in the schools and wife-beating in the homes are but two such ways; and, although the toleration of political violence waxes and wanes according to current circumstances, the potentiality for such a tolerance seems well prepared for in ordinary Irish life.

Public acts of violence have deep historical roots in Ireland. When a large majority of the population was politically, economically, socially, and culturally oppressed, any means of temporary or partial redress seemed admirable to them. For centuries, the Irish were in a weak and intolerable position, and they coped with it in two ways: by charming cunning and by covert violence. A play like Bernard Shaw's *John Bull's Other Island* is only one of innumerable reflections of the cunning guile; and the popular ballads and poems of Ireland offer hundreds of examples of the glorification of the violent hero, who stood up to the oppressors, although often dying in the attempt ("Whether on the scaffold high, or on battlefield we die . . .").

Some quite recent events also can suggest how deeply the admiration for violence runs in the Irish. In the 1960s, the country seemed to be basking in a new and uncharacteristic affluence, and the people seemed interested mainly in acquiring goods and in improving their lot in life. In 1966, the extensive and elaborate fifty-year commemorative celebrations of the Easter Rising seemed largely an empty public self-congratulation. Its rhetoric sounded hollow, and the memory of the glorious past irrelevant to the business of life. References to Ireland's lost fourth green field were lip-service to a rather remote ideal, and what was relevant was tending one's own garden in the three green fields that remained.

Yet before the decade had ended, the civil rights movement in the North had become transformed into a political movement, and the smoldering ashes of nationalism once again had erupted into flames. In the South, some prominent government ministers were involved in a notorious public scandal for supplying guns to the IRA in the North. And for a time, before the subsequent years of cumulative assassination and outrage again disillusioned people, there seemed a resurgence of the old political fervor. Although the overwhelming mass of the people in both the North and the South now seem heartily sick of the violence, the violence is unlikely to disappear, and one of the reasons is that its roots lie deeply entangled in the national psyche.

As violence has been an integral part of the Irishman's historical heritage, it predictably pervades his literature. To take but one extreme example, consider the poems and plays of W. B. Yeats. What could have been so totally unviolent as the early work of Yeats with its roses and *langours*? And who could have seemed so totally unviolent as the lissome young bard with the flowing tie and the lank lock of hair falling over his marble brow? Yet, as Yeats' work developed, it became harder, tougher, more dramatically combative. The images, the diction, even the rhythms of the late work, are both energetic and abrasive. At the same time, the poet personally grew ever bolder. His apologetic remark to the *Playboy* rioters of 1907 was, "It is the author of 'Cathleen ni Houlihan' who addresses you"; twenty years later, his first remark to *The Plough and the Stars* rioters was the inflammatory "You have disgraced yourselves again!"

From the brawls and ructions in Synge and Fitzmaurice, to the fist fights which conclude a Maurice Walsh entertainment, to the brutalities of an O'Flaherty political novel, and even to the abrasive content of many of the youngest poets and short story writers, violence is everywhere in Irish literature. It is a violence in both subject matter and diction. Synge, Yeats, Joyce, O'Casey, Samuel Beckett, and Flann O'Brien are merely the most distinctive Irish writers to have used words violently, but their uses have forced language from the traveled road of smooth convention into startling new directions. So if violence has been a political and social bane for Irish life, it has been also a major glory of Irish literature.

THE JUDGMENT OF SAINTS AND
THE LANGUAGE OF SCHOLARS

The cliché that replaced the moronic Paddy of nineteenth-century *Punch* cartoons was the ebullient Wild Irish Boy. The first figure was an amiable Handy Andy idiot; the second is a brilliantly "cute" jackeen. The first figure talked with a charming and quaint stupidity; the second talks with a wild and profane wit. Either kind of talk has an intermittent, not quite tenuous, basis in reality, but neither cliché accords well with the reality of the Irish writer.

There are two types of Irish writer. First is the serious or affirmative Man with a Cause who has a mystic, an oratorical, or a whimsical eloquence; he may be the young Yeats or the ever-young James Stephens; he may be the passionate Padraic Pearse or the dispassionate Conor Cruise O'Brien. On the other hand, the frivolous or negative Man Disillusioned with Causes has a witty, destructive, and satirical eloquence; he may be the young Myles, the middle-aged Joyce, the old O'Casey, or the infinitely ancient Beckett.

Both types talk incessantly and eloquently, and the reasons for the talk seem social, economic, political, and even geographical and climatic. If one has no money, if one is politically impotent and socially scorned, and if the rain so frequently necessitates staying indoors, the major antidote to all of these frustrations is language. In ancient Ireland, language came to be so valued that complicated codes and techniques grew up around it. In historical times, language was one of the few free entertainments in an otherwise bleak world, and so good language was admired and remembered. In other words, a sense of rhetoric grew, and judgment developed.

The language of the affirmative writer painted a world better than the existing—whether the early, idealized, pre-Raphaelite embroideries of

Yeats, or Standish O'Grady's tumultuous language of heroism, or the neo-classic order of Burke, or the whimsical fantasies of James Stephens. The language of the negative writer painted a world more extravagantly intoler-able than even the existing—whether the savage, absurd reductions of Swift, or the mad caricatures of Flann O'Brien, or the depressing exagger-ations of Samuel Beckett.

Exposed to this plethora of rhetoric, the Irishman became a connoisseur of language, a brutal but refreshingly unacademic literary critic. Even the huge sales of a bad volume of florid poems like *The Spirit of the Nation* does not refute the fact; it testifies to an enthusiasm for rhetoric so intense that it occasionally accepts fool's gold for the genuine article. But as many volumes of Great Irish Oratory suggest, the Irishman could genuinely ad-mire the genuine. Emmet's speech from the dock was not admired solely for what it said, but also for how nobly it said it; and the dull writings of a merely noble man like John O'Leary have been little read.

Nevertheless, affirmative eloquence does invite enthusiasm and does tend to squelch discrimination. Fortunately, Irish literature is fuller of negative eloquence which demands niceties of judgment. To take the language of comedy as an example, we might note that all of the great Irish dramatists, save Wilde and Synge, write on various levels of language and that their plays cannot be fully appreciated unless that fact is perceived. *The Rivals* of Sheridan, for instance, has a satire on the language of romance in Lydia, on the language of sensibility in Faulkland, on pretensions to pedantry in Mrs. Malaprop, on contemporary slang in Bob Acres, on Irish bluster in Sir Lucius, and on the inadequacies of the language of rage in Sir Anthony. The play is as brilliant for its levels of language as it is for its abundant comic situations and striking caricatures. In fact, one zealous commentator has asserted that there are potentially 327 laughs in the play arising from the audience's apprehension that a character has misused language.

It has sometimes been stated that all of Shaw's characters talk like Shaw. Actually they do not; they only talk with Shaw's fluency and energy. (See *Pygmalion*, see *John Bull*, see *Major Barbara*, see . . . etc.) It is really only a few writers, such as Wilde and Synge and the later O'Casey, who write in a uniform style, and they write to evoke admiration rather than to pro-voke criticism.

The same point of the Irishman's nice discrimination about language might be reinforced by noting how acutely the Irish have honed the destruc-tive sub-genres of invective and gossip. The poet's curse, or even the enraged layman's curse, was considered a potent, a fearful, an ultimate weapon. It demanded the full resources of rhetoric, and it worked because those re-sources were widely appreciated. The language of gossip also, which per-vades Irish literature and riddles Irish life, demands the utmost refinements and subtleties, and has a range stretching from the crudest scurrility to the gentlest (and most disemboweling) innuendo.

If this tradition of verbal dexterity and appreciation was originally motivated by frustration, it has long since become self-generated by narcissistic
delight—hence lies, hence deceit, hence the most remarkable body of
English literature in the world.

There is no such thing as the Irish Race. Generations of invaders have
become, like Behan's Monsewer, more Irish than . . . whoever the Irish
were. What there is—simply—is an Irish attitude (which is quite different
indeed from that caricature of it to be found in the second and third generation of the sea-divided Gael in Boston and New York). The Irish attitude requires that one have lived long enough in the island to be primarily
and irrationally affected by its splendors and miseries. Perhaps, too, it finally
requires that one reduce the world, as does the excellent *Irish Times*, to
the ridiculous and inappropriate and unimportant topic of how the world
affects Ireland. (In a biographical novel about Michael Collins, Constantine
Fitzgibbon manages to lug in, among many others, T. E. Lawrence, Wood-
row Wilson, and Lenin.)

One cannot write fairly or objectively about the country, for one slips
unnoticed into the national rhetorical techniques of hyperbole and prevari-
cation. And perhaps also into the snotty innuendo, the fulsome phrase, the
empty alliteration. And, worse, into the self-adulation, the pique, the hatred,
the remembrance of old hatred, the loathsome sentimentality, and all, all,
all the other disgusting techniques and attitudes. Indeed, it occurs to me
that the only Irish rhetorical devices which this essay has missed have been
wit and eloquence.

Nevertheless, one does what one can, and sometimes one does what one
cannot, but the significant point is that the language as used by the Irish,
even though it conceals more truth than it reveals, does also create. What
it creates is literature, and that in abundance, and in literature truths can
be found by those who seek them.

ROBERT HOGAN

GAELIC LITERATURE

Seamus O'Neill

The great German Celtic scholar Kuno Meyer described Gaelic literature as "the earliest voice from the dawn of West European civilization." The Romans had not brought Ireland within the empire, and consequently the native culture had not been overwhelmed by the Latin. With Christianity, however, came a knowledge of classical literature and the art of writing. As might have been expected, there was a tendency among the early Christian clerics to look askance at the vernacular and its lore as something barbaric and pagan, but from the first there were men among them who knew better. We have the two views represented in *The Life of Colmcille (Vita Sancti Columbae)*, written by Adamnan, the ninth abbot of Iona. Adamnan, who wrote in Latin, apologizes to his readers for having to use the crude Irish forms of names of people and places. Nevertheless, he tells us a story about Colmcille which reveals that his great predecessor was indeed a lover of poetry and poets. According to the story, Colmcille was sitting one day on the bank of the River Boyle when a certain Irish bard came up to him and engaged him in conversation for a while. Then when he had proceeded on his way, the monks who were in Colmcille's company asked him why he did not ask the bard for a song. Colmcille replied that he could not do so because he knew the poor fellow was about to meet his death. Adamnan quotes this story as an example of the prescient power which he attributes to Colmcille, but it also shows that the saint used to invite wandering bards and minstrels to entertain him and his company. Little wonder, for he was himself a poet and champion of poets.

We have also a delightful story of how St. Patrick, as he was listening to one of the ancient tales, was suddenly troubled in his conscience for fear that he was wasting his time. But he was assured by his guardian angels not only that there was no harm in giving ear to the old stories, pagan though they were, but also that he should have them written down because they would serve to entertain future generations until the end of time.

That is what the Irish monks proceeded to do. They adapted the Latin alphabet to the Irish language, and they committed to manuscripts the traditional literature of their ancestors. The Irish epic, the *Táin Bó Cuailnge* (*Cattle Raid of Cooley*), for example, was first written down in the ninth century, but the story belongs to the La Tène period of civilization, perhaps about 100 B.C. The monks, however, did not confine their efforts to garnering the relics of the old civilization; they used the vernacular for all the purposes of life—for prayer and instruction, spiritual and secular, for histories and poetic composition and imaginative prose. A new, written literature developed. The *Cambrai Homily,* which generally is accepted as the oldest piece of writing in the Irish language, dating from the second half of the seventh century, is in itself a reminder of this great achievement of the monks.

While the Irish language and culture were cultivated in the monasteries, classical learning was not neglected. Latin was, of course, the language of divine office and the language which the peregrini used daily. It also was used for literary composition. Some of the most important contributions to medieval Latin literature were made by Irishmen. Existing side by side, it was inevitable that the two cultures should intertwine. A new system of Irish versification grew up under the influence of Latin metrics.

OLD IRISH POETRY

We may name four distinct periods in the history of Irish poetry: (1) a period of rhythmical alliterative verse, similar to the verse of Anglo-Saxon; (2) a period of syllabic verse; (3) the period of the amhrán or stressed meters; and (4) the modern period in which there has been much experimentation with different forms.

The first period of the sixth and seventh centuries is not very important. At any rate, not much of this kind of verse has come down to us. The examples are mostly apostrophes to warriors, such as:

> Fo-chén Conall, críde lícce,
> lóndbruth lóga, Lúchar éga,
> gúss ffánd férge fo chích curad. . . .

> (Hail Conall, heart of stone,
> fierceness of a lynx, sheet of ice,
> blood-red fury of anger, under the breast of a warrior. . . .)

The second period begins in about the eighth century with the introduction of syllabic verse and lasts until the seventeenth century. A most intricate metrical system evolved during this time. Basically, the verse depended on the number of syllables in it, but in dán díreach (in perfect verse), subtle end-rhymes, internal rhymes, consonance, and alliteration were essential. The poet, however, could use looser forms of meter, called óglachas and brúilingeacht. Perfect rhyme existed between words of which the stressed vowels were identical, and all the consonants after the first stressed vowel of the same class and quality. The consonants were ranked in six classes according to kind. Thus, in syllabic meter, "mall" rhymed with "barr," "crann" with "am," "long" with "fonn." Imperfect rhyme consisted of identity of vowels, agreement of consonants in quality, but not in class, as in meas: leath; críoch: díon.

A great number of meters were devised, variation being achieved by changing the length of the verses and by manipulating the other necessary poetic artifices. The names of the most common meters were, perhaps, Rannaigheacht mhór, Rannaigheacht bheag, Deibhidhe, Séadna, Séadna mór, or Dian-mhidsheang.

As this metrical system developed, so did the subject matter of the verse. As might have been expected, the monks wrote religious verse, but as dwellers in rude beehive huts, they lived close to nature. Consequently, they were ever conscious of the physical world around them, and they have given us many nature poems of rare beauty. They delighted in the wonders of the sky, the sea, the forest, the song of the birds:

> A colonnade of trees looks down on me,
> A blackbird's lays sings to me;
> Above my lined booklet
> The trilling birds chant to me.
> In a grey mantle from the top of the bushes
> The cuckoo sings;
> Verily, may the Lord shield me!
> Well do I write under the greenwood.

Kuno Meyer pointed out that these nature poems do not contain elaborate or detailed descriptions of scenery, but rather create impressions which the poet conveys with a few swift significant strokes:

> My tidings for you: the stag bells,
> Winter snows, summer is gone.
>
> Wind high and cold, low the sun,
> Short his course, sea running high.
>
> Deep-red the bracken, its shape all gone,
> The wild-goose has raised his wonted cry.
>
> Cold has caught the wings of birds;
> Season of ice—these are my tidings.

Lines such as these remind us of Japanese *haiku*.

We have poems on every aspect of the monk's life: the joy of complete dedication to the Lord, the struggle with the flesh, the satisfaction of study, the occasional experience that enables us to see over a thousand years right into the anchorite's cell.

> All alone in my little cell, without a single human
> being along with me: such a pilgrimage would be
> dear to me before going to meet death.

One monk made his cat immortal:

> I and Pangur Bán, my cat,
> 'Tis a like task we are at;
> Hunting mice is his delight,
> Hunting words I sit all night.
>
> 'Gainst the wall he sets his eye
> Full and fierce and sharp and sly;
> 'Gainst the wall of knowledge I
> All my little wisdom try.

The terror inspired by the Viking raids is brought home to us in the quatrain

> The wind is rough tonight,
> It tosses the white mane of the waves;
> I do not fear that the Irish sea will be crossed
> By the fierce warriors from the North.

Although they certainly began the writing of the Irish language, the monks were not the only poets in the country. Indeed, they were merely amateurs. There existed a professional caste of poets from time immemorial, and if anything, they became more important with the introduction of written literature. These were the filí, or the áes dána, who, usually being of aristocratic stock, enjoyed many privileges. There were also the bards, but, although the word "bard" is used in English to denote a Celtic poet, the bards were inferior to the filí. "Bard dano; fer gin dliged foglama acht inntlicht fadesin" (A bard is a man without proper learning, but intellect, nevertheless), says one of the law tracts. To become a file, one had to spend several years at a school where poetry was studied as a craft. The highest grade of file, the ollamh, studied for twelve years. The filí were not merely poets in our sense of the term; they were also chroniclers and keepers of the genealogies of their patrons, the great lords. Giolla Bríghde Mac Con Midhe explained the importance of this function in a poem in the thirteenth century:

> Dá mbáidhtí an dán, a dhaoine,
> gan seanchas, gan seanlaoidhe,
> go bráth, acht athair gach fhir,
> rachaidh cách gan a chluinsin.
>
> (If poetry were to be suppressed, my people,
> if we were without history, without ancient lays,
> forever, but the father of each man,
> every one will pass unheralded.)

As a result of this conception of the poet's task, the profession of poetry often became hereditary in certain families. Among these families might be mentioned the O'Higginses, the O'Clerys, the O'Dalys, and the Macawards.

OLD IRISH PROSE

The Ulster Cycle: Táin Bó Cuailnge

The ancient Irish epic, the *Táin Bó Cuailnge*, has come down to us in three recensions found in several manuscripts. The oldest recension is contained in Lebor Na Huidre (LU), the Book of the Dun Cow, compiled at Clonmacnois; in the Yellow Book of Lecan (YBL); and in Egerton 1782. The second recension is contained in the Book of Leinster (LL), and the third in two late manuscripts.

The *Táin Bó Cuailnge* is the story of the great deeds of the central figure, Cuchulainn, especially in the war fought between the Ulaidh, the men of Ulster, and fir Erenn, the men of Ireland. While Cuchulainn is a mythical figure, and the tales of his exploits are fictional, the setting of the *Táin* is historical. That there was a powerful kingdom in Ulster with its capital at Eamhain Macha and that it was overthrown in the fourth or fifth century by attacks from the South are certain. The earthen rampart of Eamhain Macha (now called Navan Fort) can be seen to the present day near Armagh.

The *Táin* is the greatest of a large number of tales deriving from this era which are known as the Ulster Cycle. The *Táin* itself attracted a number of subsidiary tales called remscéla, or introductory tales, and iarscéla, or after-tales. Some of these are the remscéla of "The Revealing of the Táin," "The Debility of the Ulstermen," and "The Cattle Driving of Fraech"; and the iarscéla of "The Battle of Rosnaree," "The Death of Cuchulainn," and "The Phantom Chariot of Cuchulainn."

The hold that the Cuchulainn saga took of the Irish imagination may perhaps be inferred from the fact that, when the German traveler Kohl visited Drogheda in the year 1843, he heard a storyteller recite the tragic story of the death of Cuchulainn's son, "Aided Conlaoich." The same story was recorded by Séamus Ó Grianna in Donegal in 1915, and Yeats wrote a long poem and a play on the same theme.

The *Táin* is a typical tale of the ancient world, emphasizing the heroic deeds of the great warrior. Unlike the *Iliad,* the *Aeneid,* or *Beowulf,* however, it is told in prose, although interspersed with lyrics and verse duologues. Cuchulainn himself sets the tone of the tale when he exclaims, "Acht ropa airdirc-se, maith lem ceni beinn acht óen-láa for domun" (Provided that I be famous, I care not if I be only one day in the world). The *Táin,* then, depicts a civilization where the warrior is paramount, a world perhaps essentially like our own where the dividing line between civilization and savagery is very thin.

The most impressive episode of the *Táin* is the story of the fight to the death between Cuchulainn and Ferdiad. Cuchulainn had slain the best warriors that Maeve and Ailill, queen and king of the Connaught men, had sent against him, and they were in despair of finding a man to match him. They sought the advice of their counselors, who said there was only one man fit to do battle with Cuchulainn; that was Ferdiad, son of Daman, son of Daire, the force that could not be withstood, the rock of destruction.

But Ferdiad and Cuchulainn were foster-brothers. They had learned the use of arms from Scathach, the female-warrior of Scotland. Maeve and Ailill sent messengers to Ferdiad, asking him to come to them, but he refused, knowing why they wanted him. Then Maeve sent poets and druids to satirize him, and for fear of their scorn he went with them. Maeve and Ailill rejoiced to see him and entertained him lavishly. Finnavair, the daughter of Ailill and Maeve, sat at his side. It was she who placed her hand on every cup that Ferdiad quaffed; it was she who gave him three kisses with every cup; it was she who gave him sweet-smelling apples over the bosom of her tunic, and said he was her lover and her choice of the men of the world.

Maeve promised Ferdiad that he should have Finnavair for his wife when he had destroyed Cuchulainn; but even this bait did not tempt him. He had no wish to kill the foster-brother he loved. Then Maeve taunted him. Cuchulainn had spoken truly, she said; he did not think much of Ferdiad as a champion. That jibe struck home, and at last Ferdiad consented to meet Cuchulainn.

They still point out the ford on the River Dee, earlier Nee, on which the town of Ardee stands and where according to tradition the combat between the two friends was fought. The name Ardee comes from the Irish "Áth Fhirdia," which means "the Ford of Ferdia." Cuchulainn came down to the north side of the ford, and Ferdiad was waiting on the south side. As Cuchulainn drove up, Ferdiad's servant described his chariot; and the fact that Cuchulainn often fought from a "carbad faebrach," a scythed chariot, as did the Gauls and Britons against the Romans, is one of the features of the *Táin* that helps us to determine the period in which the great deeds of the tale are supposed to take place.

THE COMBAT

"We are too long talking thus," said Ferdiad. "What arms shall we employ today?"

"You have the choice of arms today," answered Cuchulainn, "for it was you reached the ford first."

"Do you remember the feats of arms we used to practise with Scathach and Uatach and Aife?"

"I do, indeed."

"If you do, let's try them."

So they began to try their warrior skills. They buckled on their shields, and they took up their eight javelins, their eight swords, and their eight darts that flew to and fro between them like bees on a fine day. They made no cast that did not strike, and they continued to cast at each other from the twilight of morning till the midday. Although their aiming was excellent, their defense was equal to it, and neither succeeded in wounding the other.

"Let us rest from these feats," said Ferdiad, "for we cannot reach a decision with them."

"Let us rest," said Cuchulainn, and they gave their arms to their charioteers.

"What arms shall we employ today?" asked Ferdiad.

"Yours is the choice of arms till nightfall," replied Cuchulainn, "for you came first to the ford."

"Let us try our polished smooth hardened spears," said Ferdiad.

So they began to aim their spears at each other, and, although they parried skillfully, they hurled their spears with such deadliness that each of them wounded and reddened the other.

Then they rested from the fight, and they went towards each other in the ford, each of them putting his arms around the other's neck and giving him three kisses. They brought their horses to the same paddock that night, and their charioteers to the same fire, and the charioteers made a bed of fresh rushes for the wounded men. A band of leeches came who applied healing herbs to their cuts, gashes, and many wounds.

Cuchulainn lamented. He spoke these words:

"Oh, Ferdiad, if it be you,
Death awaits you, I am certain.
You fight your comrade for a shrew."
And Ferdiad replied:
"Cuchulainn, warrior brave,
Wisely has it been decreed,

> Everyone must tread the path
> That leads onward to the grave."

Then Cuchulainn called for the gae bolga. This weapon made a wound like a single spear going into the body, but it had thirty barbs and could only be removed from the body of a man by being cut out of it. Cuchulainn hurled the gae bolga at Ferdiad, and it passed through his iron apron so his every joint and every limb were filled with its barbs. Ferdiad said:

> "Oh, Hound of great fame [Cuchulainn means the Hound of
>   Culainn],
> Unkind was that wound;
> On you falls my blood,
> On you falls the shame."

Then Cuchulainn rushed towards Ferdiad, clasped his two arms around him, and carried him northwards across the ford, so that it would be to the north of the ford that he should fall. And then a swoon came over Cuchulainn as he bent over Ferdiad.

The Book of Leinster version of the *Táin* is the fullest and most artistic that has come down to us. It is the conscious effort of a literary artist to give definitive form to the tale. With a good deal of justified self-assurance, he added a note at the end praying "a blessing on all such as dutifully recite the *Táin* as it stands here, and shall not give it any other form."

Nevertheless, a twelfth-century scribe described the *Táin* as containing "quaedam figmenta poetica, quaedam similia vero, quaedam non, quaedam ad delectationem stultorum" (some poetic fictions, some things like the truth, some things not, and some things for the delectation of fools). This judgment, to say the least, reflected a rather philistine approach to a great work of the imagination.

The Tragical Death of the Sons of Uisnech

The story of Deirdre and the Sons of Uisnech also belongs to the Ulster Cycle. It is one of the most tragic and beautiful of Irish stories and perhaps the best known of them all. It has been translated many times into English and other languages, and there are several dramatic versions of it. The most impressive version is that by Synge, although he errs a few times in putting into the mouth of King Conor language that would be more appropriate to a Connaught peasant.

Deirdre is a girl of singular beauty whom Conor has reared up for himself. But she falls in love with Naise, son of Uisnech, and she and Naise and his two brothers fly to Scotland to escape the king's wrath. When the warriors of Ulster protest that the sons of Uisnech should have to spend their lives in exile, Conor pretends to relent and invites them to return to Ireland with Deirdre, guaranteeing them safety. He breaks his bond, however, and has Naise and his brothers slaughtered and Deirdre seized. In Geoffrey Keating's version of the story (seventeenth century), she leaps from his chariot, strikes her head against a pillar-stone, and dies. In the medieval version of the tale, she leaps into the grave after Naise and expires over his body. This is the ending which Synge chose.

In this tale, as in many other Irish prose tales, we have beautiful lyric passages, such as Deirdre's farewell to Scotland:

> Ionmhain tír an tír úd thoir,
> Alba go n-a hiongantaibh;
>   nocha dtiocfainn aisti i-le,
>   muna dtíosainn le Naoise.
>
> Gleann Dá Ruadh!
> mo-chean gach fear dana dual;
>   is binn guth cuaiche ar chraoibh chruim
> ar an ndruim ós Gleann Dá Ruadh.
>
> (Dear the land, that land to the east,
> Scotland with its wonders;
> I would not have come from it here,
> Did I not come with Naoise.
>
> Glen Dá Ruadh!
> Hail to every man who is native there,
> sweet the voice of the cuckoo on the bent branch,
> on the ridge above Glen Dá Ruadh.)

Two other important cycles of tales are the Fenian, sometimes called the Ossianic, Cycle, and the Cycle of the Kings. To these some scholars would add a third, the so-called mythological cycle. But it can be argued that the *Táin* itself is basically a mythological tale. The principal character, Cuchulainn, is a mythological figure, being the offspring of Lugh, the Irish sun-god; it has been suggested that in the conflict of the bulls, around which the story is built, we have a motif from a pagan cult.

The Fenian Cycle

Like the Ulster Cycle, the Fenian Cycle has a central character, Finn mac Cumhaill, but he cuts a rather unstable figure. Unlike the Ulster tales, the Fenian Cycle is not bound to any particular historical era or place, although it certainly developed later than the Ulster Cycle. Tales of Finn and the Fianna continued to be composed and told almost down to our own day, and they were eventually to influence the whole of European literature. They supplanted almost entirely the Ulster tales in popularity. The reasons for this are, no doubt, that they possess a much greater variety of characters and lack the stark tragic quality of the Ulster cycle. There is also their romantic appeal. Finn and his companions live in a kind of Arcadia, spending their time hunting and feasting, although war sometimes interrupts the serenity of their existence.

The spirit of the Fenian tales is expressed in lines attributed to Oisin:

> Mian mhic Cumhaill fá maith gnaoi
> Éisteacht re faoidh Droma Deirg,
> Codhladh fá shruth Easa Ruaidh,
> Fiadh Gaillmhe na gcuan do sheilg.

> Sgolaidheacht luin Leitreach Laoigh,
> Tonn Rudhraighe ag buain re tráigh,
> Dordán an daimh ó Mhaigh Mhaoin,
> Búithre an laoigh ó Ghleann Dá Mhail.

> In Róis ní Ógáin's translation:
> (The desire of Cumhall's son of noble mien
> Was to listen to the sound of Drumderg,
> To sleep by the stream of Assaroe,
> To hunt the deer of Galway of the bays.

> The singing of the blackbird of Letterlee,
> The wave of Rury striking the shore,
> The belling of the stag from Magh Maoin,
> The fawn's cry from Glen-da-Máil.)

In *Agallamh na Seanórach* (*The Colloquy of the Old Men*), compiled towards the end of the twelfth century, we have a great collection of Fenian stories brought together in the form of a Dindsenchus or geographical guide. Caoilte mac Rónáin, who with Oísin is supposed to have survived the other heroes of the Fianna, journeys around Ireland with St. Patrick. At each place where they rest, Caoilte recalls for Patrick some heroic exploit of the Fianna in days gone by. But best known of all the Fenian tales is certainly "Tóraigheacht Dhiarmada agus Ghráinne" ("The Pursuit of Diarmaid and Grainne"). The story is famous because of its dramatic quality and because its chief characters are not mere legendary types, but possess an individuality often associated with modern literature. Little wonder that Micheál Mac Liammóir turned it into a successful play, *Diarmuid agus Gráinne* (1928).

The story tells how Gráinne, the daughter of Cormac mac Âirt, who is promised in marriage to Fionn, induces Diarmaid Ó Duibhne of the white teeth to carry her off. Fionn pursues the couple all over the country, but they succeed in escaping his wrath many times. To this day, hollows at the foot of many cromlechs or dolmens are pointed out as the beds of Diarmaid and Gráinne. At length Fionn catches up with them, but Aonghus an Bhrogha makes peace between them. But Fionn is not to be trusted. Diarmaid is wounded to the death by the boar of Ben Ghulban, but he may be saved by a drink of water from Fionn's hands. He implores Fionn to fetch a handful of water from a nearby spring. Fionn goes to the spring, but when returning with the water he thinks of Gráinne, and he allows the water to run through his fingers, and so Diarmaid dies.

Although the oldest extant manuscript copy of the story of Diarmaid and Gráinne is a rather late one of the seventeenth century, it is certain that the tale itself is much older. Many features of the story—the part played by Aonghus an Bhrogha, for example—show that it has its roots in the ancient mythology.

Other famous stories of the Fianna are "Cath Finntrágha" or The Battle of Ventry, "Bruildhean Chaorthainn" or The Hostel of the Rowan Tree, "Bodach an Chóta Lachtna" or The Clown of the Dun Coat, and "Cath Gabhra" or The Battle of Gabhra. The word "fian" is cognate with the Latin "vena" from which "venari," meaning "to hunt," is derived; in Ireland, however, the word came to mean a roving band of warriors. The Fenian tales became influenced by the Norse raids on Ireland, and the Fianna assume the position of a national army defending the country against the invaders. "Cath Finntrágha" is an account of how the Fianna repel the attack of the King of the World, who comes with a great fleet to Ventry. It is perhaps the most impressive of the stories in which the Fianna play this role of protecting their native land. Included in the story is the verse lament of Creidhe for her husband Caol, who is drowned in the waves while fighting against the foreigners. It is a very good example in Irish of the pathetic fallacy:

> Géisidh cuan
> ós buinne ruadh Rinn dá Bhárc,
> bádhadh laoich Locha dhá Chonn
> is eadh chaoineas tonn re trácht.
>
> Truagh an gháir
> do-ní tonn trágha re tráigh;
> ó ro bháidh mh' fhear seaghda saor
> is saoth liom a dhul 'na dháil.
>
> (The harbor moans above the rushing stream
> of Rinn da Bhárc,
> the drowning of the warrior of Loch dhá Chonn
> that is the lament of the wave against the strand.
>
> Sad the cry the ebbing tide makes on the beach,

> since it drowned my fine noble man,
> my grief that he went near it.)

The Fenian literature comprises not only the prose tales, but a great number of poems as well. Lyrics like the one quoted above are found scattered throughout the tales, as are also an immense corpus of long narrative poems, or lays, as they are commonly known. These lays are contained principally in three collections: Duanaire Finn, which was compiled by three scribes in Louvain during the years 1626-1627 for Captain Sorley MacDonnell; the Book of the Dean of Lismore (Argyllshire), which was written there by the dean, Sir James McGregory, and his brothers during the years 1512-1526; and Leabhar na Finne, compiled from many sources by J. F. Campbell and first published in 1872. The Fenian lays became as popular in Gaelic-speaking Scotland as in Ireland. In Scotland, however, the Fenian tales often mingle with those of the Ulster Cycle, this, indeed, being a feature of MacPherson's Ossian.

Among the well-known Fenian lays are "Laoi na Seilge" or Lay of the Hunt, "Cath Chnoc an Áir" or Battle of the Hill of the Slaughter, "Laoi Oisín ar Thir na nÓg" or Lay of Oisin in the Land of Youth, "Laoi Chatha Gabhra" or Lay of the Battle of Gabhair, and "Tiomna Ghoill mhic Mhórna" or Will of Goll mac Morna. These poems celebrate the great deeds in battle of the champions of the Fianna, and express regret for their passing. Many of these poems also extol the outdoor life, supposed to have been lived by the Fianna, and the beauties of nature. In the "Agallamh Oisín agus Phádraig" ("Colloquy of Oisin and Patrick"), the aged Oisin recalls all these things in order to contrast the happy days in which the Fianna roamed the land with the narrow life Patrick was proposing:

> I have heard music sweeter far
> Than hymns and psalms of clerics are;
> The blackbird's pipe on Letterlea,
> The Dord Finn's wailing melody.
> The thrush's song of Glenna-Scál,
> The hound's deep bay at twilight's fall,
> The barque's sharp grating on the shore,
> Than cleric's chants delight me more.

"Laoi Oisín ar Thir na nÓg," which tells how Oisin went with the beautiful fairy maiden Niamh Cinn Óir to the Land of Youth, is one of enduring charm because it responds to a longing set deep in the human breast. It is this bittersweet romanticism which gives the Fenian Cycle its place in Gaelic literature and which spread its influence throughout Europe.

Ossian and the Romantic Movement

In 1760, a Dr. Blair published in Edinburgh *Fragments of Ancient Poetry, collected in the Highlands of Scotland, and translated from the*

Gaelic or Erse language. The reputed collector was a Scottish schoolmaster named James Macpherson.

In 1762, Macpherson published *Fingal, an Ancient Epic Poem,* and in the next year, another epic, *Temora.* Macpherson brought out all of these poems as translations and attributed them to a Gaelic bard called Ossian. The poems of Ossian became the rage of the day and were translated into every major European language. Ossian was compared to Homer. Men of literature turned away from the arid classicism in which they had been schooled to delight in the naturalness, simplicity, and virtue of the primitive heroes of the Celtic past. It is said that Herder, the apostle of Romanticism in Germany, knew Ossian by heart. France was slower to succumb to the new movement, but was finally introduced to it by Madame de Staël and Chateaubriand during the time of the First Empire. Napoleon was an avid reader of Ossian and took a copy of the poems with him on his great campaigns, and even at the end to Saint Helena. His predilection for Ossian may perhaps be explained by the fact that he disliked the tragedies of Shakespeare, each one of which portrayed the fall of a great man. In any event, the heroic spirit of the Ossianic lays appealed to him, and he even had two Ossianic pictures painted for his chateau at Malmaison.

Macpherson's effusions were far from being translations from the original Gaelic poems and stories. Rather they are a hodgepodge of his own concoction with echoes of the Fenian and Ulster Cycles thrown together. Even the names of the warriors celebrated in them are not easily recognizable.

Nevertheless, Macpherson did a service to Gaelic literature by drawing attention to it and bringing many to study it seriously. Groups like the Scottish Highland Society and the Irish Ossianic Society were founded for that purpose. To the influence of Macpherson's Ossian may be attributed the publication in 1789 of Charlotte Brooke's *Reliques of Irish Poetry.* Unlike Macpherson, however, Brooke had a good knowledge of the language. She printed the original Gaelic poems with her translations alongside. The Irish Gaelic revival may be traced to her book.

The Cycle of the Kings

This cycle, as the title conveys, is concerned with kings. Sometimes the plural of the word "cycle" is used because in some of the stories the one king is the central figure. These tales are a mixture of fact and fiction, the creation of a world in which gods and men play a part. Few historians would deny that Cormac mac Airt and Niall of the Nine Hostages were historical figures, and it was natural that legends should grow up around such famous names. We know that the battle of Magh Rath was an historical event, and we actually know the year in which the battle was fought; but, although we should be thankful for the stories that were told about it, we would be unwise to regard them as the mere truth. Indeed, as far back as the ninth or tenth century, an Irish scribe went to the heart of this matter when he wrote: "And Suibhne Geilt having become mad is not a reason why the battle of Magh Rath is a triumph, but it is because of the stories and poems he left after him in Ireland." (Carney thinks this tale originated among the Britons of Strathclyde, but, strangely, he does not mention the traditions of Glannagalt, nor the possible origin of the Irish phrase "téighim le craobhachaibh" [I go mad; literally, I go among branches, as did Suibhne who lived in the trees].) "Buile Shuibhne" ("The Madness of Sweeney") is one of the most interesting, imaginative, and poetic of Irish tales. Incidentally, it inspired *At Swim-Two-Birds* by Flann O'Brien.

Among the most famous of the stories of the kings are "Cath Maighe Léana" or the Battle of Magh Lena, "Togail Bruidne Dá Derga" or the Destruction of Da Derga's Hostel, "Cath Maige Muccrime" or the Battle of Moy Muccruime, "Cath Crinna" or the Battle of Crinna, and "Fingal Rónáin" or the Kin-Slaying by Ronan. "Togail Bruidne Dá Derga" has an affinity with the Ulster Cycle, for several of the Ulster heroes appear in it. The story tells of the destruction of the bruidhean, the house or hostel of Da Derga, which was built over the River Dodder near Donnybrook; but the plot centers on the fate of the young king Conaire who is doomed because he unwittingly breaks his taboos or geasa. The relentless working out of these taboos lends the story its most tragic and most interesting aspect. The taboos show that the story reaches back into the dim beginnings of our civilization.

"Fingal Rónáin," which means "the murder of a kinsman by Rónán," is the story of the femme fatale who brings disaster to all those around her. The story has come down to us as little more than a synopsis, which was perhaps intended to be filled out by the storyteller.

The Mythological Cycle

The mythological cycle purports to give us an account of the early peoples who came to inhabit Ireland—the Nemedians, the Fomorians, the Firbolgs, the Tuatha Dé Danann, and others. We read also of their gods, such as the Dagda Mór, Lugh, Midir, and Angus. While most of these stories are invention, they do give a glimpse of the beliefs of pre-Christian Ireland. Indeed, it is clear that even after the coming of Christianity the people were loath to part entirely with the old gods. It was held that after a great battle at Teltown, the Tuatha Dé Danann retired into great mounds in the hills and valleys. In Irish the fairies are often referred to as "uaisle na gcnoc," or "the nobles of the hills," and a fairy mound is known as an "áit uasal," or a noble place. One of these great prehistoric figures was Balor of the Evil Eye, also called Balor Bailcbhéimneach and Balor na mBéimeann (of the Blows). Balor was the leader of the Fomorians and was defeated in a great battle, the second battle of Moytura, by Lugh Lámhfhada and his Tuatha Dé Danann. The strength of the tradition of this story is shown by the fact that it is told in Donegal to the present day. Balor was supposed to live on Tory Island and on the island Dún Bhalair, and Príosún

Bhalair bears his name. At Cloughaneely they show the stone, Cloich Cheann Fhaolaidh, on which Balor beheaded Ceann Fhaolaidh.

"Tochmarc Étaine," or the successful wooing of Etain, is the most charming of the mythological stories. It is in itself a series of stories. Etain belongs to the Other World, but she weds a mortal king, Eochaidh Airem, who discovers her washing her hair in a stream. She is so beautiful that he falls in love with her immediately. "Never a maid fairer than she, or more worthy of love, was till then seen by the eyes of men; and it seemed to them that she must be one of those that have come from the fairy mounds." This blending of the magical world of the Sidhe with the physical world of mortals gives these stories their fascination.

The Immrama

The Immrama, or Voyages, form one of the most imaginative group of tales in the whole range of Irish literature. The immram is not a voyage of discovery in the ordinary sense of the term. The motif of these tales is the quest for the Other World, the Tír Tairngire, the land of promise, or Magh Mell or the plain of honey. Among the Immrama are "Immram Brain," "Immram Maíle Dúin," "Immram Snédgusa agus Maic Riagla," and "Immram Ua Corra." These tales date from the Old Irish period, and their origins are pagan.

In "Immram Brain" (Professor James Carney would see "Immram Brain" as a Christian allegory. Professor Myles Dillon does not accept that interpretation, which would remove from the story the pagan motif of the search for Magh Mell.) we meet Manannan mac Lir, the Celtic god of the ocean, who sings:

> A n-as muir glan
> don noi brainig i tá Bran,
> is mag meld con n-imbud scoth
> damsa i carput dá roth.

> (What is a clear sea
> to the leaky vessel in which Bran is,
> is a plain of honey with many flowers
> to me in my two-wheeled chariot.)

"Immram Maíle Dúin" tells of a voyage made by Máel Dúin and his companions in early Christian times, but in both conception and detail the story is pagan. Máel Dúin visits many strange islands and meets with many strange adventures. The story incorporates much from Oriental and classical mythology; for example, we read of the Bridge of Difficulty, a Persian or Indian invention. Lord Tennyson tried his hand at making an English metrical version of the voyage of Máel Dúin (we have the story in Irish in both prose and verse), but, as Eleanor Hull has stated, he failed to capture much of the style of the original, taming it to suit Victorian taste.

"Immram Maíle Dúin" was probably the model for the Brendan legend.

"Immram Ua Corra," the voyage of the grandsons of Corra, supposedly began in about the year 540 A.D. from the coast of Connaught. This story is still remembered in the West. The Stag Rocks north of Aranmore off the Donegal Coast are called Na Mic Uí gCorra in Irish, for they are supposed to represent the grandsons of Corra who were turned into stone for their crimes and were destined to remain thus until the day of judgment.

When the spirit of extreme asceticism spread among the early Fathers of the Irish Church, they began to seek lonely places and remote islands where they could spend their lives as hermits far from the distractions of the world. Soon stories were being told of the adventures of the monks on the sea, such as the tale of Cormac Ó Liatháin's voyage northwards as recounted by Adamnan in his life of Colmcille. In this way developed the "Navigatio Brendani," which purports to be an account of St. Brendan's sea-wanderings but is actually a skillful piece of fiction, having "Immram Máile Dúin" as its prototype. But as the legend of St. Brendan's sea-wanderings was told first in Latin, it became known throughout Europe and was translated into the major vernacular languages. It was eventually regarded as a record of fact and was an important factor in inspiring the voyages of discovery of the fifteenth and sixteenth centuries. Consequently, the old Irish voyage tales have their place not merely in literature, but also in history.

BARDIC POETRY

The Bardic schools flourished from the late sixth century to the seventeenth century. Although, as we have seen, the bards were inferior in rank as poets to the filí, the poetry of the filí is best known as bardic poetry, even though the term *syllabic poetry* is also used for it. Bardic poetry does not in general conform to our conception of poetry. It was not composed to create an original emotion in the breast of the reader or listener, but rather to stir up one already there. A vast number of bardic poems are no more than eulogies of princes and great lords, their houses, and a recital of the glories of their ancestors. The bards laid great stress on pride of ancestry—sometimes too much even for their patrons. When the poets came at Christmas to Turlough Luineach O'Neill with their usual genealogical encomiums, he told them bluntly that he would prefer to hear something about his own prowess. A great deal of bardic poetry is, therefore, dul, although it has some value for social and political historians.

The file was so tightly bound by the tradition of his craft—in meter, in language, and in subject—that for four centuries, from 1250 to 1650, hardly the slightest change or development is discernible in this type of official verse. While the charge of sterility against so much of bardic poetry cannot be gainsaid, it must be admitted that the obligations which the system imposed led not merely to the development of an extraordinary metrical skill, but also to the creation of a language of classical conciseness and dignity. These are compensations for the lack of originality in themes, which the student of bardic poetry comes to appreciate and often to marvel at. And, of course, despite the restraints of the bardic system, some geniune poets succeeded in leaving us some of the great works in Irish literature.

There were two periods in which the filí burst into verse of power and beauty, and both were periods of national recovery and hope. The first was in the thirteenth century when the native Irish were rolling back the tide of Norman invasion, and the second was in the sixteenth century. The chief poet of the earlier period was Giolla Bríghde Mac Con Midhe. Although he is most widely known as the author of the lament for Brian O'Neill, king of Ulster, who fell in the battle of Down in 1260, some of his greatest poems were inspired by Cathal Crobhdhearg who was leading a revival of the Gaelic kingship in Connaught. An inaugural ode to Cathal begins, "Tabhraidh chugam cruit mo ríogh" ("Bring to me the harp of my king"). He also wrote many poems for the O'Donnells and seems to have sojourned in Scotland, for he is called Albanach. He was a much-traveled man, and one of his most interesting poems was composed during a storm at sea: "A ghiolla ghabhas an stiúir" (O lad who takes the rudder).

Another poet who earned the epithet "Albanach" was Muireadhach Albanach Ó Dálaigh, who fled to Scotland because he had killed one of O'Donnell's stewards. Muireadhach, in a poem asking his patron's pardon, expresses his surprise that O'Donnell should be angry with him over the loss of a mere servant, a sentiment which shows that these filí were aristocrats writing for an aristocratic world. Ó Dálaigh was the author of "M'anam do sgar riomsa a-raoir" (I parted from my life last night), a touching elegy on the death of his wife. Like Giolla Bríghde Mac Con Midhe, he also wrote a poem at sea, addressing it to Cathal Crobhdhearg. As the vessel was in the Adriatic at the time, he may have been going on a pilgrimage to the Holy Land. In the end he returned to Ireland, was forgiven by O'Donnell, and entered a monastery. We have a poem, "A Mhuireadhaigh, meil do sginn" (O Murray grind your knife), which purports to describe Cathal and Muireadhach about to enter the Cistercians together. The poem is not regarded as authentic, even though both king and poet did take the habit. A number of devotional poems by Muireadhach are preserved in the Book of the Dean of Lismore. He was regarded as the chief poet of Scotland in his time, Ireland and Gaelic Scotland then sharing the same culture.

Donnchadh Mór Ó Dálaigh, a brother of Muireadhach, was the greatest of the religious poets, and the Four Masters describe him as a poet who never was and never shall be surpassed. He wrote many poems to the Blessed Virgin, many on the hollowness of life, and others on repentance. The most moving of his poems is the well-known "Truagh mo Thuras ar

Loch Dearg" (Sorrowful my Pilgrimage to Loch Dearg). The poet making his pilgrimage was genuinely distressed that he could not feel true contrition for his sins:

> Yruagh mo thuras ar Loch Dearg,
> A Righ na gceall as no gclog,
> Do chaoineadh do chneadh 's do chréacht
> 'S nach dtig déar thar mo rosg.

Seán Ó Faolain's translation of this poem captures the spare beauty of the original:

> Pity me on my pilgrimage to Loch Derg!
> O King of the churches and bells,
> bewailing your sores and your wounds,
> but not a tear can I squeeze from my eyes!

Donnchadh Mór Ó Dálaigh's poems became an integral part of Irish folk tradition. Douglas Hyde met a beggarman in Connaught who could recite many of them. His poems are also known in Donegal in our day. He died in 1244 A.D.

Another eminent poet of this family was Gofraidh Fionn Ó Dálaigh, most of whose poems were addressed to the earls of Desmond. Perhaps the best known of these poems is "Mór ar bhfearg riot, a rí Saxan" ("Great our anger with you, O king of the Saxons"), a poem composed in honor of Maurice FitzMaurice, second earl of Desmond. His poem "Mairg mheallas muirn an tsaoghail" was one of the most popular religious poems in Ireland for centuries. In the verses beginning, "Filí Éireann go haonteach," he celebrated the famous festival organized for all the poets of Ireland by O'Kelly of Hy Many during Christmas 1351.

Although the poets are sometimes accused of having been cynical and self-seeking and indifferent to the national welfare, they did their best in the sixteenth century to inspire the Irish chiefs in their last great struggle against the English. It was ironic that the bardic system was to produce its greatest poetry just when it and the civilization of which it was such a distinctive part were to be overthrown. Among the principal poets of this period were Tadhg Dall ÓhUiginn, Aonghus Fionn Ó Dálaigh, Aonghus mac Doighre Ó Dálaigh, Aonghus Ó Dálaigh, i.e., Aonghus na nAor, Eoghan Ruadh Mac an Bhaird, Tadhg mac Dáire Mac Bruaideadha, and Eochaidh ÓhEóghusa.

Tadhg Dall ÓhUiginn was probably the greatest master of the dán direach* that ever lived. His metrical skill and his command of the culti-

---

*"The rules of the Irish Classic Metres (which went under the generic name of *Dán Direach* or 'Straight Verse') required a break or suspension of the sense at the end of every second line, while each idea or thought of the poet must be completed within a quatrain. Hence there could be no carrying over of the sense from one stanza to another.

vated bardic language were superb. Most of his poems, however, were conventional in subject, consisting almost entirely of odes to chieftains. He does exhort the chieftains to unite in the common cause of their country, but there is little urgency or real passion in his verses. His poem on "Inis Ceithleann," the residence of Maguire, gives us a picture of a household such as might have been lifted right out of the *Táin*.

> Buidhean cheard ag ceangal bhleidheadh,
> buidhean ghaibhneadh ag gléas arm;
> buidhean saor nách d'éanfonn uirre-
> néamhonn chaomh na mbuinne mbalbh.

> Géill dá ngabháil, géill dá léigean;
> laoich dá leigheas, laoich dá nguin;
> seóid dá síorchur inn is uadha-
> an síothbhru gh slinn cuanna cuir.

(A company of artificers binding vessels, a company of smiths preparing weapons, a company of wrights that were not from one land at work upon her—fair pearl of babbling streams.

Taking of hostages, releasing of hostages; healing of warriors, wounding of warriors; continual bringing in and giving out of treasure at the wondrous, smooth, comely, firm, castle.)

A love of nature has been a characteristic of the Celtic muse from earliest times, and the bardic poets, despite the artificiality of their training, were no exception in this respect. They knew the beauties of their country—the hills, the woods, and the streams. They appreciated, too, the use of place-names in verse. The opening stanza of "Inis Ceithleann" is a good example of this feature of their work:

> Mairg fhéagas ar Inis Ceithleann
> na gcuan n-éadrocht, na n-eas mbinn;
> guais dúinn, 'snach féadair a fágbháil,
> féagain an mhúir fádbháin fhinn.

(Alas for him who looks on Enniskillen, with its glistening bays and melodious falls; it is perilous for us, since one cannot forsake it, to look upon the fair castle with its shining sward.)

Within these narrow limits the laws governing the construction of the verse were extraordinarily complicated, alliteration, rhyme, and number of syllables being all governed by precise laws. The result of this close attention to metrical exactitude is that a great number of the poems produced under this system are unimpassioned, sententious and mechanical. It would have been impossible for them to be otherwise; the wonder is, that they ever rise into true poetry at all."—Eleanor Hull, *A Text Book of Irish Literature,* Vol. II (New York: AMS Press, 1900), p. 6.

Despite the orthodoxy of Tadhg Dall's syllabic verse, among his poems are two examples of the aisling or vision-poem, which was to become an important political device in Irish poetry in the eighteenth century. Unlike the eighteenth-century aisling, however, Tadhg Dall's vision, the beautiful lady who appears to the poet, does not reveal herself at the end as the personification of Ireland.

Aonghus Fionn Ó Dálaigh was celebrated for his poems to the Blessed Virgin, but they are inclined to be uninspired and uninspiring.

Aonghus mac Doighre Ó Dálaigh was poet to the O'Byrnes of Wicklow and one of the greatest of the patriotic poets. His stirring address to the warriors of Fiacha mac Aodha is said to have been composed before the battle of Glenmalure in which Fiacha defeated the Lord Justice. If it was, it was certainly worthy of the occasion:

> Dia libh, a laochruidh Gaoidhiol!
>   ná cluintior claoiteacht oraibh;
> riamh nior thuilliobhair masla
>   a n-am catha iná cogaidh.

> (God be with you, ye warriors of the Gael,
> Let not subjugation be heard reported of you,
> For infamy ye have never merited
> In time of battle or war.—O'Grady's translation)

Aonghus na nAor was a satirist who was employed by the English to create dissension among the leading Irish families. He finally paid for his treachery with his life, for he was foolish enough to outrage the hospitality of his host O'Meagher of Ikerrin in Tipperary, with the result that one of O'Meagher's servants avenged the insult to his master by promptly cutting the bard's throat. A fair example of his undoubted skill as a satirist is the quatrain:

> Ní fhuil fearg nach dtéid ar gcúl
> Acht fearg Chríost le cloinn Ghiobin,
> Beag an t-iongnadh a mbeith mar tá
> Ag fás in olc gach aon lá.

> (There is no anger that does not abate,
> but the anger of Christ with the Fitzgibbonses;
> little wonder that they are as they are,
> growing in evil every day.)

Eoghan Ruadh Mac an Bháird dedicated himself mostly to the service of the great Northern chiefs O'Donnell and O'Neill. Like Eochaidh Ó hEóghusa, he was in every sense a true poet. His elegiac address to Nuala O'Donnell weeping over the grave of her loved ones at Rome has the solemnity of "Venit summa dies et ineluctabile tempus/Dardaniae. Fuimus

Troes, fuit Ilium et ingens/gloria Teucrorum" (the despairing cry of Panthus in Virgil's *Aeneid* at the fall of Troy, which says, in effect, Our last day is come, Troy is no more, and we and the great glory of the Trojans passed away.):

> Do shaoileamar, do shaoil sibh
> dál gcabhra ag macaibh Míleadh
> tres an dtriar tarla san uaigh
> ag triall ón mBanba mbeannfhuair.

> (You thought and so did we that the Irish would get assistance through the three when they were leaving cool peaked Banba— the three who are now in the grave.)

This poem is well known to readers of English through Mangan's adaptation, "O, Woman of the Piercing Wail."

Tadhg mac Dáire Mac Bruaideadha was poet to the O'Briens of Thomond, and was responsible primarily for renewing the sterile controversy known as Iomarbhaidh na bhifledh, or the Contention of the Bards, about the respective merits of North and South. The folly of this academic debate had been made rather apparent by Lord Mountjoy's disastrous defeat of the Irish at Kinsale on Christmas day of 1601, and was aptly summed up by Flaithrí Ó Maoilchonaire in his lines:

> Lughaidh, Tadhg agus Torna,
> filí eólcha bhur dtalaimh,
> coin go niomad bhfeasa
> ag gleic fán easair fhalaimh.

> (Lughaidh, Tadhg and Torna,
> the learned poets of the land,
> hounds with too much knowledge
> wrangling over an empty kennel.)

Mac Bruaideadha addressed poems to his lord Donnchadh Ó Briain, fourth earl of Thomond. One of them—"Mo cheithre rainn duit, a Dhonnchaidh" or "My four verses are hereby dedicated to you, Donnchadh"— consists merely of time-worn maxims; however, his poem "A Mhacaoimh shéaas mo sheirc" (O maiden who rejects my love), has genuine feeling in it. As an old man, he met a violent death when he was hurled over a cliff by one of Cromwell's soldiers.

Eochaidh Ó hEóghusa was probably the greatest poet of this era. Despite the restrictions of the dán díreach, he was able to write poems of passion and imagination. His patron and master was Hugh Maguire, lord of Fermanagh and one of the bravest leaders in the war against Elizabeth. In the winter of 1600, Hugh O'Neill, then at the height of his power, marched into Munster, calling on the Munstermen to join him in what he knew to be a struggle for national survival. With him went Hugh Maguire. Safe at home in Fermanagh, Eochaidh Ó hEóghusa began to think of the hardships and dangers which his young master was undergoing during this winter campaign. Eochaidh composed a poem into which he poured his love for his young chief, his apprehension for his safety, and his dread of the outcome of the war for his country. It was a severe winter, and the very fierceness of the elements seemed to threaten disaster. A cloud of foreboding hung over the poet, and alas his fears were only too justified. Maguire was killed outside Cork in combat with Warham St. Leger, one of the English commissioners for Munster. St. Leger also fell in the conflict, but, as Cyril Falls, the British historian says, the death of St. Leger was small price to pay for the death of Hugh Maguire "who was one of the bravest and most determined of the rebel chiefs, and one of the most popular figures in Ulster."

Ó hEóghusa's poem begins:

Fuar leam an oidhche-se d'Aodh!
Cúis toirse truime a ciothbhraon,
Mo thruaighe sein dar seise
Neimh fhuaire na hoidhcheise.

Mangan's English version of this poem captures its air of impending doom:

Where is my Chief my Master, this bleak night, mavrone!
O, cold, cold, miserably cold is this bleak night for Hugh;
Its showery, arrowy, speary sleet pierceth one through and through,
Pierceth one to the very bone.

LOVE POEMS

Dánta Grádha, an anthology of Irish love poetry compiled by T. F. O'Rahilly, was first published in 1916. Most of the poems were composed in the sixteenth and seventeenth centuries, and some were from earlier times. As Robin Flower, then a lecturer in Irish in the University of London, said in the introduction, the subject of the poems was not the direct passion of the folk-singers or the high vision of the great poets. Rather, it was the learned and fantastic love of European tradition, the *amour courtois*, which was first shaped into art in Provence and found a home in all the languages of Christendom, wherever refined society and the practice of poetry met.

The poetry in O'Rahilly's anthology was that of high society in Ireland and in Scotland, as can be seen from the names of the authors of the poems in the volume: Gerald the Earl of Desmond, Manus O'Donnell prince of Tyrconnell, Piaras Ferriter, head of one of the chief families of Kerry, the earl and countess of Argyll, Duncan Campbell of Glenorquhy, "the good knight" who died at Flodden.

The first practitioner of this sophisticated type of verse was Gerald the Rhymer, fourth earl of Desmond and lord justice of Ireland in 1367. According to tradition, he disappeared in 1398 and sleeps under the waters of Loch Gur, whence he emerges every seven years to sweep over the lake. Piaras Ferriter, poet and soldier who was hanged at Killarney in 1653, may be said to have been the last and greatest exponent of the art.

These love poems are fanciful, extravagant, often ironic, and always elegant. As was common to this type of verse, the poet delights in describing the beauty of his mistress. One poet devotes a long poem to the praise of his favorite's hair, in this fashion:

> A bhean fuair an falachán
> do chiú ar fud do chiabh snáithmhin,
> ni as a bhfuighthear achmhasán,
> d'fholt Absolóin mic Dháibhidh.

> (All envious eyes amazing,
> Lady, your hair soft-waved
> Has cast into dispraising
> Absalon, son of David.—Robin Flower's translation)

But when the poet's compliments went unrequited, he could express himself in another mood:

> Ní bhfuighe mise bás duit,
> a bhean úd an chuirp mar ghéis;
> daoine leamha ar mharbhais riamh,
> ní hionann iad is mé féin.

> (For thee I shall not die,
> Woman of high fame and name,
> Foolish men thou mayest slay,
> I and they are not the same.)

THE RISE OF THE FOLK-POETS

With the defeat of the Irish at Kinsale in 1601 the Gaelic aristocratic order collapsed. The professional poets lost their patrons, the schools of poetry dissolved, and the classical meters and language were gradually abandoned. Irish began to be confined to the cabin, and the poets of the people came into their own. The folk-poets, like folk-poets everywhere, composed mostly songs, and their meter was the stressed or amhrán song meter.

The meters of the classical poets were syllabic and carried no regular stress. The new generation of poets sang songs of the sorrows of Éire and also songs of hope promising that help would come over the sea. While none of the poets could forget the calamity that had befallen their nation, they also sang of the sorrows and joys of everyday life. Love songs, laments, drinking songs, satire in plenty, and devotional verse have survived.

The poets who had been educated in the classical schools, and who had formed an important part of the Gaelic aristocratic civilization, looked with contempt on the new upstart, unskilled rhymers. Jack was now as good as his master. Innovators in the arts are never welcomed, but, to add insult to injury, the lot of the common people improved for a time after the Cromwellian plantation, and the poets of the old school found that boors were giving themselves airs. Dáibhí Ó Bruadair was one of these poets who resented the change. His life had covered most of the seventeenth century. He had lived through the Confederate wars (1642-1649), the Cromwellian massacres and plantations, the reigns of Charles II and James II, had seen the defeats of the Boyne and Aughrim, the complete overthrow of his country, and he had recorded it all in his poems. At the end of his days, he was reduced to utter poverty, going to the wood daily to cut faggots for his fire and seeking work as a laborer. Although he composed mostly in the new meters, Ó Bruadair used the archaic language of the classical schools. He expressed his chagrin at the way life had treated him, as follows:

IS MAIRG NACH FUIL NA DHUBHTHUATA

> Is mairg nach fuil 'na dhubhthuata,
> Ce holc duine 'na thuata,
> Ionnas go mbeinn magcuarda
> Idir na daoinibh duarca. . . .

A PITY I'M NOT A CHURL

> A pity I'm not a mere churl,
> Though it's no joke being a churl,
> So that I'd be moving about
> Like any common lout.

> A pity I'm not a stammerer,
> Among you, my good people,
> For stammerers serve you well,
> Since you know no better.

> If I could only find a buyer,
> I'd gladly sell my skill
> Of culture, for some attire;
> I'd let him have his fill.

> Less value store of mind

Than dress of any gawk,
On learning all I spent
I'd have now on my back.)

HISTORY AND ANNALS

Professor E. C. Quiggin of Cambridge University, a Celtic scholar, claimed that "No people on the face of the globe have ever been more keenly interested in the past of their native country than the Irish." Many similar statements could be quoted. Certainly the amount of historical material, fanciful and genuine, genealogical and chronical, accumulated in Irish manuscripts is astonishing.

Eoin Mac Neill believed that the writing of Irish history began in the monastery of Bangor towards the end of the sixth century when a version of the Chronicle of Eusebius was compiled, which included what purported to be a synopsis of early Irish history. The author of this *Chronicon Eusebii* was probably Sinlan or Mo Shinu Moccu Min, abbot of Bangor, who died in 609 A.D. "But," says Kenney, "it was not until the ninth, and especially the tenth, eleventh and twelfth centuries, that this historical impulse acquired full momentum." Then, many of the filí seem to have turned their energies almost entirely to the task of transmuting the national folklore into a harmonized history. A twelfth-century text declares that "he is no file who does not synchronize and harmonize all the sagas." Scholars have noted that, although the country was divided politically into a large number of small states, the particular history of these states was never written. From the beginning, the history written was the history of Ireland.

In the brief space available here, it is impossible to give an adequate summary of the amount of historical writing we possess. However, inasmuch as until recently history has been regarded as a branch of literature, some account of it is necessary. It might be helpful to classify the material under the headings chronicles or annals, particular histories, biographies, and genealogies.

Annals

The practice of keeping or compiling annals, begun by Mo Sinu moccu Min, continued until the overthrow of the old Gaelic civilization in the seventeenth century. Among the chief annals are the Annals of Tighernach, compiled in the monastery of Clonmacnois, in Latin and Irish, and continued down to 1178, although Tighearnach O Braein, whose name they bear, died in 1088. The Annals of Inisfallen were compiled in a monastery situated on the island of Inisfallen in the lower lake of Killarney. These annals cover the history of Ireland from the earliest times to the year 1326, the first part of the manuscript dating from about 1092. They are the chief source for the history of Munster in medieval times. The Annals of Ulster were compiled on Upper Loch Erne by Cathal Maguire, who died in 1498, but they were continued until 1604 by two other scribes. The title of these annals, given to them by Archbishop Ussher, is misleading, for they are not records of events in Ulster solely, although they do give prominence to Ulster affairs. Other annals are the Annals of Connacht, the Annals of Loch Cé, the Annals of Boyle, the Annals of Clonmacnois, Chronicon Scotorum, and the Annals of the Four Masters.

Of the Annals of Clonmacnois, we have only an English translation made by Conall or Conla Mageoghagan of Lismoyne, County Westmeath, in 1627. That these annals were first written in Irish we know from the comment of Mageoghagan that many leaves were missing from "the old Irish book" which he was translating. Mageoghagan uses what, no doubt, was the colloquial English of his time. These annals are so called because they give a detailed account of St. Ciaran, the founder of the monastery of Clonmacnois and of the surrounding country.

The Annals of the Four Masters are properly named *Annála Ríoghachta Éireann*, the Annals of the Kingdom of Ireland. The work was undertaken by the Franciscan friar Micheál Ó Cléirigh and his three assistants—Fearfeasa Ó Máil Chonaire, Cú-coigcriche Ó Cléirigh, and Cú-coigriche Ó Duibgennáin—on January 22, 1632, and completed on August 10, 1636, under the patronage of Ferghal O'Gara of Coolavin in County Sligo. While the work was in progress, Muiris Ó Máil-Chonaire and Conaire Ó Cléirigh, brother of Micheál, were also employed for a time. Micheál Ó Cléirigh set about this task with the approval of his superiors at a time when he feared that the ancient records of Ireland might be lost forever. While his fears did not come to pass (although a great many books perished), his work was no less valuable on that account. When the annals were finished, Micheál took the manuscript south to show it to two of the most eminent traditional scholars then living, Flann Mac Egan of Ballymacagan in County Tipperary and Conor Mac Brody of County Clare. Both expressed their appreciation of the work, saying that they had never seen its equal.

Ó Cléirigh's journey south to submit the annals to the scrutiny of the most distinguished scholars was a symbol of the unity of the Gaelic culture which once flourished throughout the whole of Ireland. Ó Cléirigh also obtained testimonials to his work from the primate of Ireland, three other bishops, and the friars of Donegal, his brethren. The annals were compiled in some shelter on the bank of the Drowes River that flows between the counties of Leitrim and Donegal, for the monastery of Donegal had been destroyed in the war against Elizabeth.

Particular Histories

These are the *Lebhar Gabhála*, or the Book of Invasions, which tells the story of the peoples who supposedly occupied Ireland in legendary times; the *Réim Rígraide*, about the succession of kings; and *Cogadh Gaedheal re Gallaibh*, or the war of the Gaels against the foreigners (the foreigners here being the Norse), which contains a dramatic account of the battle of Clontarf and of the events leading up to it. *Caithréim Toir-*

dealbhaigh, which traces the victorious career of Toirdealbhach O Briain, describes the history of Munster from the coming of the Normans to the middle of the fourteenth century.

In *Forus Feasa ar Éirinn* (History of Ireland), Father Geoffrey Keating (died 1646) attempted to write a complete history of Ireland from the earliest times to his own day. His aim was to refute the false impressions of his country given by such writers as Giraldus Cambrensis, Edmund Spenser, Richard Stanyhurst, Fynes Morrison, William Camden, and Sir John Davies. Keating's history will not stand up to modern critical examination, for he accepted much of the legendary accounts of the past as the truth, but his work is a masterpiece of Gaelic prose. Poet and classical scholar, he wrote a stately, yet limpid, narrative style which is a joy to read. Few students of modern Irish have not delighted in Bergin's *Stories from Keating's History of Ireland*. They will continue to be read when more scientific histories are dust. Such is the magic of style.

Biographies

Apart from the lives of the saints, of which we have a great number in Latin and Irish, and which are mostly hagiography, few biographies in the modern sense of the word were written until recent times. The work that most closely approaches our idea of biography is *Beatha Aodha Ruaidh Uí Dhomhnaill*, the life of Red Hugh O'Donnell by Lughaidh Ó Cléirigh. This is a most detailed account of O'Donnell's life from his birth until his death in Spain. As expected, the writer concentrates on the war O'Donnell fought alongside Hugh O'Neill for the survival of the ancient Gaelic system; hence, this work is most important for the history of that war. Indeed, the account of O'Donnell's campaigns is so detailed it is obvious that the author himself, or other members of his family, actually took notes in the field after the manner of modern correspondents. The O'Clerys were scribes and chroniclers to the O'Donnells. Valuable as this work is, it is marred by its turgid and artificial style and is difficult reading even for a person skilled in classical Irish. It was compiled before the Four Masters began their annals, for it was one of the sources they used. Strange as it may seem, another biography, written in Donegal about a hundred years before, is distinguished by the simplicity of its style. This is *Betha Cholaim Chille*, the life of Colmcille by Manus O'Donnell, prince of Tyrconnell. The O'Donnells were proud of Colmcille, for they were of the same line, and Manus decided to gather up all the information and traditions he could find about him into one book, to translate what was in Latin into Irish, and what was in hard Irish into soft Irish. This he did most admirably, and he himself dictated the text of the book. If read as folklore rather than as history, the book is charming, and it is valuable as an example of the Irish spoken at the time. It was compiled in the Castle of Lifford in 1536.

Genealogies

The Irish were very interested in history, but they seem to have been fascinated by genealogy. We have vast collections of genealogies. A book now lost, the Psalter of Cashel, compiled in about 900 A.D., contained a corpus of genealogies, as many references to them show. Other collections that have survived are contained in the *Book of Leinster*, the *Book of Ballymote*, and the *Book of Genealogies* compiled by the great antiquary Dubhaltach Mac FirBhisigh in 1650. This last is the largest collection of all, but there are many others. M. A. O'Brien has edited the pedigrees from the twelfth-century manuscripts kept in Oxford. While these genealogies may throw light on early Irish history, particularly on the history of the great septs and families, such compilations of names are scarcely the concern of the literary historian.

REFORMATION AND COUNTER-REFORMATION

The Tudor conquest of Ireland brought with it an attempt to force the Protestant religion on the people who clung to the old faith. The Irish language was to be employed towards this end. The first book in Irish to be printed in Ireland was the Protestant catechism, the *Caiticiosma lá Seaan Ó Kearnaigh*, in 1571. A font of type styled more after the Anglo-Saxon than the Irish script had been sent over from England by Elizabeth for the purpose. The catechism was followed by the New Testament translated by William Ó Domhnaill in 1602, and by the Book of Common Prayer in 1608. To counter the attempted reformation, the Irish set up colleges or seminaries on the Continent where priests were educated for the home mission. The Franciscans who had founded the college of St. Anthony at Louvain decided that they must produce Catholic books, and the first Catholic book to be printed in the Irish language was a catechism compiled by Bonaventura Ó Eodhasa, "a poor brother of the Order of Saint Francis," in 1611. The book was printed at Antwerp. After that, the friars acquired a press of their own, with a font of type based on the so-called Gaelic script, with *proprios characteres* as they claimed. This press issued a series of devotional works which were important not only in the struggle to maintain the Catholic religion in Ireland, but also in the history of Gaelic writing.

These writers wanted to get their message over to the people, and to do so they realized they must write in a language understood by the people, and not in the learned jargon of the filí. With only two exceptions, they could not have written as the filí at any rate, for they had not been trained in the bardic schools. Hugh Caughwell, also called Aodh Mac Aingil (1571-1626), explained why he wrote in Irish in his introduction to his *Scáthán Shacramuinte na hAithridhe*, or The Mirror of the Sacrament of Penance, which he published in 1618. A native speaker of Irish and a Latinist of the first rank, he felt he had to apologize for attempting to write in his native tongue, so fast were the shackles of the filí on the language. He wrote: "Da n-abarthaoi gur dána dhúinn nidh do sgríobhadh a nGaoidhilg, snár shaothruigheamar innti; As í ár bhfeagra air sin, nách do mhúnadh Gaoidhilge sgríobhmaoid, acht do mhúnadh na h-aithridhe, agus as lór linn go dtuigfidhear sinn gé nach biadh ceart na Gaoidhilge againn" (If we were to be told that it was rash of us to write in Irish, and that we had not cultivated it, our answer to that is that it is not to teach Irish that we write, but to teach penance, and we shall be satisfied if we are understood, although we might not have correct Irish).

Aodh Mac Aingil wrote beautifully clear, idiomatic Irish. He was the author of the delightful Christmas carol "Dia do bheatha, a Naoidhe naoimh!" ("Greetings to you, Holy Child!").

Many other devotional works were written by exiled Irish clerics during the seventeenth century, but from the purely literary point of view the most important was *Desiderius* by Flaithrí Ó Maolchonaire (1561-1629). This book, which began as a translation of a Catalan devotional work, ended up with more of Ó Maolchonaire in it than its Catalan author. Its principal distinction is its style. Flaithri Ó Maolchonaire, like Bonaventura Ó hEodhasa, belonged to a literary family and had studied in the bardic schools before entering the religious life. Consequently, he was a master of the learned language taught and used in them. But he realized that the highly artificial language of the schools would not serve the purpose he now had in mind. In the preface to his work, he states that he wished to express himself in Irish that was clear and intelligible, in a simple style for simple people. He could not, however, entirely suppress the effects of his early training; his grammar is inclined to be somewhat archaic, and his vocabulary literary, but this lends a dignity to his style which makes it one of the classics of Irish prose.

Desiderius was first published at Louvain in 1616. A new edition, edited by Thomas F. O'Rahilly, was issued by the Dublin Institute for Advanced Studies in 1955.

THE AISLING

As a result of the disaster of Kinsale, and of their failures in the Confederate War (1641-1649) and in the Williamite War (1688-1691), the old Irish were completely overthrown. Historians have called eighteenth-century Ireland the Protestant nation, for the Protestant planters possessed nine-tenths of the land, formed the government and Parliament, to neither of which any Catholic was admitted, controlled industry and the professions with the single exception of medicine, and enjoyed every privilege in the state. The Catholics, on the other hand, had no right in law. Their position was defined clearly by Lord Chancellor Bowes and Chief Justice Robinson, who laid it down from the bench "that the law does not suppose any such person to exist as an Irish Roman Catholic." Irish Catholics did exist, however, most of them in a lowly state.

The old Gaelic aristocratic society had perished, and with it went the profession of the filí. But poetry itself was not dead. Indeed, for a time at any rate, poetry freed from the shackles of pedantry blossomed into a new life. Poets now sang not to please a master, but to express their own hopes and fears, their own loves and hates, their own sorrows and joys. Love songs, for example, were no longer the conceits of the *amour courtois*, but the outpouring of passion from the human heart, such as "Bean an Fhir Rua" ("The Red-haired Man's Wife") and "Moll Dubh an Ghleanna" ("Dark Moll of the Glenn").

This is not to say that the poets could ignore or forget the downfall of their nation, a downfall in which they shared. Now poets were not an aristocratic caste, but poor hedge-schoolmasters who taught their informal classes out of doors, like Donncha Rua MacNamara, Peadar Ó Doirnín, and Eoghan Rua Ó Súilleabháin, or wandering minstrels like an Dall Mac Cuarta and Ó Reachtabhra, or common tradesmen and manual workers like the hackler Aodh Mhallaile, the fuller Maghnus Mhac Ardghaill, or the agricultural laborer Art Mac Cubhthaigh.

If the bardic schools were no more, schools or courts of poetry, as they were called, remained. Traditions of the old learning still survived. The hedge-schoolmaster poets were steeped in the history of their country, and many of them were first-rate Latinists. Donncha Rua Mac Conmara wrote an excellent Latin epitaph for his friend Tadhg Gaedhlach Ó Súilleabháin at the age of eighty. Tadhg Gaedhlach was himself well educated and was one of the most popular religious poets.

A new poetic convention arose in the eighteenth century, that of the political aisling, or vision-poem. Scholars are still in dispute about the origin of this aisling, some arguing that it is to be found in European literature. What is certain is that the vision-poem was not new to Gaelic literature. From earliest times we have stories in which Ireland is represented as a beautiful lady, and the myth of the lady from the síodh, the fairy-mound, uttering prophecies about the sovereignty of Éire is common. Only in the eighteenth century, however, did the aisling become a cult, especially with the Munster poets; its theme was the promise of the return of the Stuarts, or, as it has been derisively phrased, "Charly-over-the-waterism." We even know who started this fashion. It was Aodhgan Ó Raithille who composed the first political aisling when he led off with "Mac an Cheannuidhe." This poem is famous not merely because it is the first of these political vision-poems, but because of its excellence. It is a good example of the amhrán or stress meter, although it might be argued that its rhythm is too swift for its subject, as the poem does not end on a note of promise but of despair. The language is simple and direct, not excessively ornate and wordy as are his celebrated "Gile na Gile" ("Brightest of the Bright") and many of the aislingí by other poets. The opening stanzas of "Gile na Gile" read:

Gile na Gile do chonnarc ar slighe i n-uaigneas;
Criostal an chriostail a guirm-ruisc rinne-uaine;
Binneas an bhinnis a friotal nár chrion-ghruamdha;
Deirge as finne do fionnadh 'n-a gríos-ghruadhnaibh.

Caise na caise i ngach ruibe d'á buidhe-chuachaibh;
Bhaineas an ruithneadh de'n chruinne le rinn-scuabaibh,
Iorradh ba ghlaine na gloine ar a bruinn bhuacaigh,
Do geineadh ar gheineamhain di-se 'san tír uachtraig.

Mangan's translation of these lines gives a very fair impression of the style of the original to the non-Gaelic reader:

The brightest of the Bright met me on my path so lonely;
The Crystal of all Crystals was her flashing dark-blue eye;
Melodious more than music was her spoken language only;
And glories were her cheeks, of a brilliant crimson dye.

With ringlets above ringlets her hair in many a cluster
Descended to the earth, and swept the dewy flower;
Her bosom shone as bright as a mirror in its lustre;
She seemed like some fair daughter of the Celestial Powers.

Ó Rathaille was born near Killarney in the second half of the seventeenth century, in a region where some of the old noble families had survived. These families were swept away after the Williamite Wars, and most of his poems are laments for them. Despite the undoubted sincerity of these laments and their felicity of diction and rhythm, they begin to pall after a time because of the monotony of theme and of approach. But this criticism cannot be applied to one of his poems which, in my opinion, is among the greatest in the language.

Ó Rathaille, old and poverty-stricken, lay down one night in his cabin at the mouth of Castlemaine Harbor. But, wearied as he was, he did not rest, for a storm raged outside. It was one of the nights when the great waves of Ireland could be heard moaning. According to the ancient writers, the three great waves of Ireland were Tonn Chlíodhna in Glandore Harbor, County Cork; Tonn Rudhraighe in Dundrum Bay, County Down; and Tonn Tuaidh Inbhir at the mouth of the Bann. These waves, it was believed, could be heard beating the strand, ag buain re traigh, when something momentous was to happen to Ireland. Tonn Tóime is also mentioned as a wave of fateful significance, and it was Tonn Tóime that would not let Ó Rathaille sleep. It kept reminding him of his own destitution and of the sad story of his country, and it inspired him to express his grief and chagrin in words that have the passion of great poetry. The poem has been translated into English by James Stephens, who addresses the wave by the name Tonn Clíodhna because, no doubt, of its more legendary allusion and its more musical sound than Tonn Tóime.

O Wave of Cliona, cease thy bellowing!
And let mine ears forget a while to ring
At thy long, lamentable misery;

The great are dead indeed, the great are dead;
And I, in little time, will stoop my head
And put it under, and will be forgot
With them, and be with them, and thus be not.

Ease thee, cease thy long keening, cry no more;
End is, and here is end, and end is sore,
And to all lamentations be there end;
If I might come on thee, O howling friend,
Knowing that sails were drumming on the sea
Westward to Éire, and that help would be
Trampling for her upon a Spanish deck,
I'd ram thy lamentation down thy neck.

Other Munster poets of note were Seaghan (John) Clárach Mac Domh-naill (1691-1754), Eoghan Ruadh Ó Súilleabháin (1748-1784), Seán Ua Tuama (1708-1775), Seán Ó Coileáin (1754-1816?), Piaras Mac Gearailt (1709-1788?), Donnchadh Ruadh Mac Conmara (1715-1810), Tadhg Gaedhealach Ó Súilleabháin (died 1795), Brian Merrimann (c. 1747-1805), and Eibhlín Dubh Ní Chonaill (1743?-1800). Many other poets or writers of verse were living in Munster during this period, for Munster was one of the two great centers of literary activity in Ireland in the eighteenth century, the other being the eastern part of South Ulster, sometimes called Oriel.

Nearly all of these poets are sometimes called the Jacobite poets, for in their verses they expressed a desire for a Jacobite restoration, as did especially Eoghan Ruadh Ó Súilleabháin, Seaghan Clàrach Mac Domhnaill, Piaras Mac Gearailt, and, of course, Aodhagán Ó Rathaille.

Eoghan Ruadh Ó Súilleabháin was, perhaps, the most popular of all these poets, earning for himself the sobriquet Eoghan an Bhéil Bhinn, or Owen of the Sweet Mouth. "Im'Leabaidh Aréir" and "Ceo Draoidheachta," two of his most frequently printed poems, are typical aislingí, but there is more poetry in his lullaby, said to have been composed for his own illegitimate child, for there is more imagination in it. In his endeavor to soothe the child to sleep, the poet promises him a host of precious things steeped in legend and magic—Cuchulainn's gae bolga, Naise's white shield, Failbhe or Fionn's swift steed, the Golden Fleece, the nectar Hebe served to Jupiter at the table of the gods, the pipe of Pan, and so on—a cornucopia of native and classical treasures. The only fault of the poem is its great length; a tendency towards prolixity is a characteristic of all these Munster poets.

Eoghan Ruadh led an adventurous and stormy life. He was by turns a farm laborer, hedge-schoolmaster, soldier, and sailor. By a strange turn of fate, he who sang of the return of the Stuarts fought against the French in a naval engagement under the English Admiral Rodney off Dominica in 1782. Moreover, as Rodney gained a great victory, Eoghan Ruadh composed an ode in English in his praise and was invited to recite it before him on the flagship. He did so, and Rodney was extremely pleased. Surely this was a strange honor for the poor wandering Jacobite poet in whose veins ran the best blood of Munster.

Seán Ó Tuama an Ghrinn, or Seán Ó Tuama of the wit, was an innkeeper and often presided over assemblies of poets at Croom and in Limerick. Over the door of his tavern in Mungret Street in Limerick was a notice which proclaimed that any brother bard was welcome to the hospitality of the house, even if he had not the price of a drink. This invitation seems to have been accepted only too readily, so that in the end poor Ó Tuama was ruined. He wrote the usual Jacobite songs, but he well merited his name as a fellow of fun, and he was ready with a drinking song, a love song, or a satire as the occasion demanded. Among his best known pieces are "Móirín Ní Chuilleannáin" ("Maureen O'Cullinane"), which is a vision-poem, "As duine mé dhíolas liún lá" ("I am a person who sells ale"), which is a drinking song, and "Bean na Cleithe Caoile" ("Woman of the Slender Wattle"), which is a satire on the cantankerous old woman to whom the over-generous poet became servant when he had fallen on evil days.

Seán Ó Coileáin is known primarily for his poem "Machtnamh an Duine Dhoilgheasaigh" ("The Melancholy Man's Meditation"), which is a lamentation over the destroyed abbey of Timoleague. The poem conveys the sadness and loneliness which the poet feels in the ancient ruins at night.

Piaras Mac Gearailt was the author of the rousing "Rosc Catha na Mumhan" ("The Munster Battle-Cry"), which is appropriately also called "Amhrán an Dóchais" ("The Song of Hope"). Hopeful it is, promising that the waves will soon carry a French fleet to free Ireland. It is impossible to render the wonderful word music of the refrain into English:

> Measaim gur subhach don Mhumhain an fhuaim,
> 'S d'á maireann go dubhach de chrú na mbuadh,
> Torann na dtonn le sleasaibh na long
> Ag tarraing go teann 'nar gceann ar cuaird.
>
> (I feel that the news is welcome to the province of Munster,
> And to all who are eking out a miserable life:
> The sound of the waves on the sides of the ships
> Drawing boldly on a visit to us.)

What a strange twist of fortune that this song and the Orange song, "The Boyne Water," should be sung to the same air.

Donnchadh Ruadh Mac Conmara was famous as a schoolmaster. A pass from him was a qualification for admission to that lowly profession. He spent a year or more in Newfoundland, and it was probably there that he composed "Bán-chnoic Éireann Óigh" ("The Fair Hills of Holy Ireland"), which is without doubt the most beautiful of all the many Irish songs of exile.

Tadhg Gaedhealach Ó Súilleabháin, the most popular of the Munster religious poets, wrote "Pious Miscellany" which has been printed many times. His devotional verses move one by their very intensity. The directness and intimacy of his address in "Duan Chroidhe Iosa" ("Poem on the Sacred Heart of Jesus") derive from the fervor of his faith. It is, perhaps, the most beautiful of his poems:

> Gile mo chroidhe do Chroidhe-se a Shlanuightheoir,
> As ciste mo chroidhe do Chroidhe-se d'fhaghail im' chomhair;
> Ós follus gur líon do Chroidhe dom' ghvádh-sa, a Stóir,
> I gcochall mo chroidhe do Chroidhe-se fág i gcomhad.

> (You are the brightness of my heart, O Saviour,
> Since it is my heart's desire to have Yours for mine;
> And since it is clear that Your heart, my Dear, is filled with
>   love for me,
> Deep down in my heart leave Your heart in keeping.)

Brendan Behan quite rightly said that his own simple Catholicism went back to the Mass rock and to the poems of Tadhg Gaedhealach Ó Súilleabháin, not to the pious intellectualism of Newman and his ilk.

MERRIMAN

Brian Merriman was a Clareman who died in Limerick in 1805. In its death notice, the *General Advertiser and Limerick Gazette* for Monday, July 29, of that year, merely stated: "Died—On Saturday morning, in Old Clare-street, after a few hours' illness, Mr. Bryan Merryman, teacher of mathematics." Merriman is known for one poem, *Cúirt an Mheadhon Oidhche*, or *The Midnight Court*. Merriman, also called Brian Mac Giolla Meidhre and Brian MacConmara, stands apart from other Irish poets of his day because, as O'Rathaille said, "*Cúirt an Mheadhon Oidhche* is by far the most successful sustained effort in verse in Modern Irish." Merriman also seems to have stood apart in the physical sense, for there is little evidence that he had any contact with his fellow-poets. Some have claimed that he was the most original of the Irish poets, that his poem was a tour de force, being an attack on Irish Catholic puritanism as it was supposed to be practiced in the eighteenth century. An onslaught on the mores of the times it is, but, despite the enthusiasm of critics such as Piaras Béaslaí and Frank O'Connor* who saw the poet as a kind of Irish Rousseau, O'Rathaille showed that the theme was used in many other Irish verses. O'Rathaille found the poem as conventional as anything in literature and its grossness as utterly repellent. O'Connor described the poem "as classical as the Limerick Custom House, and fortunately the Board of Works has not been able to get at it." Many English versions of the *Court* have been produced; the best by far, in my opinion, being that by Frank O'Connor.

Cúirt an Mheadhon Oidhche has been edited and translated into German by Ludwig Stern.

EIBHLÍN DUBH NÍ CHONAILL

Eibhlin Dubh Ni Chonaill was an aunt of Domhnall Ó Conaill, the Liberator. She composed "Caoineadh Airt Uí Laoghaire," a lament for her husband Art Ó Laoghaire who was shot by a British soldier in a feud originating in the penal law that a Catholic could not be the owner of a horse worth more than £5. Arthur O'Leary had such a horse, and, when offered five pounds for it by a Protestant landlord named Morrison, whom he had just beaten in a race, he scornfully rejected the offer. For Arthur O'Leary was not merely an Irish gentleman, but a brave soldier who had been a captain in the Imperial army. He challenged Morrison to a duel, which Morrison refused on the basis that he could not lower himself to fight a Papist. He then had O'Leary shot down at a distance. O'Leary's riderless horse galloped home. His wife, guessing what had happened, leaped into the saddle and found her husband lying dead beside a furze bush at Carriganima, with an old woman keening over him. She then began to compose her own lament, which is remarkable for its dramatic outpouring of grief. Strangely, the inscription on O'Leary's tomb is in English, and reads:

> Lo! Arthur O'Leary
> Generous, handsome, brave,
> Slain in his bloom, lies in this humble grave.

A few words which are not a bad summing up of the tragedy.

THE POETS OF ORIEL

As mentioned above, the only other region of Ireland that could compare with Munster for literary activity during the eighteenth century was South Ulster, an area which is sometimes called Oriel and which embraced South Down, South Armagh, much of Monaghan and Cavan, much of Louth, and even extended as far as Meath. The literary tradition survived in this region for the same reason as it did in Munster: namely, economic and social conditions were not as bad there as in Connaught and in western Ulster. Courts or schools of poetry still existed in Oriel into the early years of the nineteenth century, and the copying of manuscripts and the composition of occasional verse continued until the beginning of the twentieth century.

The chief poets of South Ulster in this period were Séamus Dall Mac Cuarta (died 1753); Peadar Ó Doirnín (died 1760); Art Mac Cubhthaigh or MacCooey in English (died probably in 1773); Pádraig Mac a Liondáin (died 1733); and Cathal Buídhe Mac Giolla Ghunna (died ca. 1756).

Their death dates are known because it was the custom for the elegiast to recite the date. There were innumerable other minor poets in Ulster, some of whom composed beautiful songs but whose names must go unrecorded here.

Séamus Dall Mac Cuarta was probably the best lyric poet of his time. As he was blind from birth, he was given to introspection. Hence, much of his verse springs from his very heart and is not the product of convention as is so much of Gaelic composition.

One day Mac Cuarta heard a bird calling. It reminded him that spring had come and that the earth was about to clothe itself in finery again, finery which he would never see. His sorrow welled up in him into this lovely lyric:

> Fáilte don éan is binne ar an chraoibh,
> Labhras ar cheann na dtor le gréin,
> Damhsa is fada tuirse an tsaoil,
> Nach bhfeiceann í le teacht an fhéir.

So runs the first verse. I have translated the whole poem as follows:

WELCOME TO THE BIRD

> Welcome to the bird, sweetest on the bough,
> That sings aloft in the heat of the sun,
> I see her not in the Spring of the year,
> I nearly wish my life were done.
>
> I hear her voice, tho' I do not see
> The bird that men the cuckoo call,
> A glimpse of her on the topmost branch
> Would my very soul enthrall.
>
> All those who behold the shapely bird,
> And the land of Ireland north and south
> The flowers blooming on every side,
> For them it's easy to rejoice.
>   The song
> My sorrow that vision was never once granted to me!
> That I might gaze in quiet on the foliage growing free,
> I have no mind to be moving among the throng,
> But sit here, near the bird, at the rim of the wood alone.

This poem was composed in a form called trí rann agus amhrán in Irish, three verses and a song, a form favored by the Ulster poets. It often saved them from the vice of longwindedness, so common among Gaelic poets. Another pathetic poem of Mac Cuarta is addressed to a young girl, Róis

Ní Raghailligh, who sold stockings at fairs. On his way to a fair one day, the blind poet had the misfortune to fall into a stream, and, as he scrambled out, his bedraggled appearance caused some merriment to the onlookers. But the young girl took pity on him, brought him into the house, and dried his clothes. The poet thanked her in the best way he could— "A Chaoin Róis" ("O gentle Rose"):

> Sé d'aon phóg
> A d'fhág pian mhór
> Agus creapaill ann mo cliabh.

> (It was your single kiss
> That left a great pain
> And torment in my breast.)

In another poem, "Sgannradh an Daill" ("The Fright of the Blind Man") Mac Cuarta cries out in outraged despair when a low scoundrel steals his savings from him:

> A dhaoine, nach truagh libh mé 'mo thruaill bocht ag éagcaoin,
> Tá mé 'nocht faor ghruaim 's gan m'fhuasgailt ag aoinneach
> Fa na hocht ngeinidh dheag do bhí mé a chúdach,
> Gur fúaideadh go léir iad ón gcréatur gan súile.

> (O, people, do you not pity me, a poor wretch lamenting,
> I am tonight in gloom with no one to relieve me,
> For the eighteen guineas which I had in my keeping
> Have all been filched from the eyeless creature.)

This poem rises to a crescendo of fury.

In these poems, as in others such as "Toigh Chorr a' Chait" ("The House at Barrakit") and the "Mo Chead Mhairgneadh" ("My First Lament") Mac Cuarta speaks to us directly, at times in sorrow, at times with tenderness, at times in anger, and at times with such satisfaction that it becomes apparent that he is a true poet and not a mere versifier.

Peadar Ó Doirnín was a hedge-schoolmaster. Indeed, he died outside the little school he kept at Forkhill. The children who were playing thought he was sleeping, but when one of the older boys tried to awaken him, he found that the master "was sleeping in the sleep that would never be broke." Ó Doirnín had studied in Munster's poetry schools and was a superb artist in the Irish language. He is best known for his love song "Úr-Chnoc Chéin Mhic Cáinte" ("The freshly cultivated hill of Cian the Son of Cáinte"), which is sung to an air composed in this century by Peadar Ó Dubhda. An older air for it also exists. It must have been an easy task to set Ó Doirnín's words to music because no Irish poet has ever achieved greater musical effect than has Ó Doirnín in this song.

> A chiúin-bhean tséimh na gcuachann péarlach,
> Gluais liom féin ar ball beag,
> Nuair bheas uaisle is cléir is tuataigh i néall,
> Ina suan faoi éadaighe bána.

> (O quiet, sweet-tempered lady of the pearly tresses,
> Come along with me in a little while,
> When the nobles, the clergy, and the lay folk will be deep
> Asleep under white bedclothes.)

In Irish, the word-music is created by a marvelous interplay of assonance, by allowing the stress to fall on long vowels followed by liquid consonants, and by alternating iambic and trochaic rhythms in the succeeding verses. The sentiment of the poem is in keeping with the witchery of its music. The poet is calling on his loved one to steal away with him from the world of reality to Arcadia where they will live on mead and sweet fruits. They will find their Arcadia on "úr-Chnoc Chéin Mhic Cáinte," a hill not far from Dundalk, doubtless selected by Ó Doirnín for the musical quality of its name.

Art Mac Cubhthaigh (MacCooey) was born near Crossmaglen. He is the poet of the O'Neills of the Fews; in his poems he laments the fall of that great family and the destruction of their castle of Glasdrummond. Like the Munster poets, he composed vision-poems or aislingí, but the lady he saw wept for the O'Neills and not for the worthless Stuarts:

> Sé mo ghéar-ghoin tinnis gur theastaigh uainn Gaedhil Thír
>   Eoghain,
> Agus oighrí an Fheadha gan seaghais faol líg dár gcomhair—
> Géaga glan-daite Néill Fhrasaigh nach dtréigfeadh an céol,
> Is chuirfeadh éideadh fá Nodlaig ar na hollaimh bheadh ag géilleadh
>   dóibh.

> (It is my sharp poignant grief that we lost the Gaels of Tyrone,
> And the heirs of the Fews are near, alas! under stone,
> The bright scions of Niall that never would abandon song,
> And put raiment at Christmas on poets who round them did
>   throng.)

These lines are from "Úir-Chill a' Chreagáin," MacCooey's most popular song and one of the most haunting laments in Irish. Henry Morris, the editor of MacCooey's poems, states:

> It might be called the national anthem of South Ulster. Everyone

in the counties Louth, Armagh and Monaghan who could sing any Irish could sing "Úir-chill a' Chreagáin." Mothers sang it as they spun, and at the end wiped away a tear as they recollected how their own mothers used to sing it when they themselves skipped about as light-hearted children. It is a beautiful song, but its beauty will not altogether account for its popularity; much of the latter was due to the fact that it harmonised so fully with the national feelings of the fallen Gael, smarting under the oppression of the "Clann Bhullaigh"; it offered them a medium by which they could vocalise their own sorrow, and its suggestion of a land of promise, where the Gall held no sway, was dear to a people who seemed to live through an endless night.—*Abhráin Airt Mhic Chubthaigh agus Abhráin Eile*, ed. Henry Morris (Dublin: Gill, 1916; Dundalk: Dúndealgan, 1925).

The present writer heard it sung by the last traditional singer of Irish in South Armagh.

MacCooey was known in his own time as "Art na gCeoltaí," or Art of the songs. The story is told that one day, when working for a local farmer, the poet was carting manure to a hillside field. It was spring, traditionally the season of inspiration to poets. MacCooey lost himself in a reverie, and he began going up and down the hill with the same load of manure. This anecdote inspired Patrick Kavanagh's poem "Art McCooey."

MacCooey wrote a satire on the sister and housekeeper of the parish priest who, MacCooey believed, had slighted him. She had offered him a drink of buttermilk in the kitchen while bringing wine to another guest in the parlor. The parish priest, the Reverend Father Quinn, who had the name of a tyrant, drove the poor poet from his native district. MacCooey fled to Howth where he obtained work as a gardener and where he composed the well-known aisling "Aige Cuan Bhinn Éadair ar bhruach na hÉireann" ("At the Bay of Howth Head at the Edge of Ireland"). But Howth was in the Pale and a foreign English-speaking territory as far as MacCooey was concerned. He was homesick for the Gaelic-speaking Fews, so he decided to make peace with the Quinns. He did it in the only way he could: he wrote a song in praise of the priest's housekeeper, "Cúilfhionn Ní Chuinne" ("The blonde Miss Quinn"), and it did the trick. He was able to return to his native place where he spent the remaining years of his life. Among the other poems he wrote was the feart-laoi, or elegy, for Peadar Ó Doirnín.

It was formerly thought that Pádraig Mac a Liondáin was a native of South Down, but he was most likely a native of Armagh. His most famous poem is a lament for Owen Roe O'Neill. He was not only a poet, but also a skillful performer on the harp.

Cathal Buídhe Mac Giolla Ghunna wrote the poem "An Bunán Buidhe," or "The Yellow Bittern," which has been translated into English by Thomas

MacDonagh. Cathal Buidhe was a hard drinker and resisted all attempts to reform him. One winter's morning he found a bittern lying dead on a frozen lake, and he composed a poem in which he muses that it was the want of drink that caused the death of the bird.

> It's not for the common birds that I'd mourn,
> The black-bird, the corn-crake or the crane,
> But for the bittern that's shy and apart
> And drinks in the marsh from the long bog-drain,
> Oh! if I had known you were near your death,
> While my breath held out I'd have run to you,
> Till a splash from the Lake of the Son of the Bird,
> Your soul would have stirred and waked anew.

Goldsmith knew the bittern's cry. Readers of "The Deserted Village" will recall the couplet:

> Along thy glades, a solitary guest,
> The hollow-sounding bittern guards its nest.

The bird is now extinct in Ireland. Cathal Buidhe became a legend in his lifetime for his poetry and his dissoluteness, but like most sinners he repented towards the end. According to one tradition, he wrote his confession on the whitewashed wall of the cabin in which he lay dying with the burned ends of sticks. Although the writing of confessions was a convention among Irish poets, Cathal's has the ring of sincerity.

EIGHTEENTH-CENTURY PROSE

In the eighteenth century, Irish has little to offer in prose, for neither the novel nor the drama developed in the language. The reason was that, even though Irish was the native tongue of the majority of people, the language was gradually being supplanted by English. English had already taken over in the so-called higher walks of life. It was the language of the conquerors and, hence, the language of government, of Parliament and of civil administration. It was, and had always been, the language of the cities and towns, although many people in the smaller towns knew Irish and spoke it when necessary. Because of the predominance of English in the towns among the commercial classes and in government, Irish was almost unknown to the printing press. The only books printed in Irish in the eighteenth century were a few catechisms and devotional works. The Franciscans' seventeenth-century effort to provide Catholics with a wide range of religious works had petered out. Some prose works, such as the County Down translation of the "Imitatio," were not printed until our own time. The Catholic Church sounded the death-knell of the ancient language of the country when it succumbed to the policy of anglicization in about midcentury. After the Forty Five, it was apparent to all that the Stuart cause was lost, and the Church began to take the view that there was no hope of a restoration of the old order in Ireland and that the Catholics had no alternative but to accept the rule of the Hanoverians. The adoption of the English language was a logical corollary to such a policy.

Despite the Penal Laws, the flood of Catholic devotional books issuing from the printing presses in Dublin in the eighteenth century was astonishing. Yet, in a list of seventy Catholic works printed and sold by a Dublin house in 1777, only three are in Irish, and two of them are elementary catechisms. As O'Rahilly says in his introduction to *Irish Dialects Past and Present*, "The climax came with the foundation by the British Government in 1795 of the Royal College of St. Patrick in Maynooth, for the education of the Catholic priesthood. In Maynooth College, English from the start held a position of complete supremacy, almost as if Trinity College had been taken as the model for the new institution. Henceforth, English becomes in effect the official language of the Church in Ireland." John O'Donovan, when touring County Down for the Ordnance Survey in order to collect the place-names, tells us that the young priests just out of Maynooth pretended not to know any Irish, although O'Donovan knew that most of them had not spoken a word of English until they were twelve years of age.

It is somewhat ironic, then, that the one Irish prose work of importance printed in the eighteenth century was a book of sermons by Bishop James Gallagher of the Diocese of Raphoe, later of Kildare and Leighlin. Gallagher's sermons were first published in Dublin in 1736. They were printed in English characters because the printers had no Gaelic type and because, as Gallagher himself says in his introduction which he wrote in English, "Our mother language, sharing so far the fate of her professors, is so far abandoned, and is so great a stranger in her native soil that scarce one in ten is acquainted with her characters." These sermons became the most widely known work in the Irish language. They have been printed at least twenty times and have been translated into English. As Canon Ulick J. Bourke, who edited an edition of the sermons in 1877 said, Gallagher's sermons spoke from every fireside in three provinces. They did so not only because so few books in Irish were available, but also because of the manner in which they were written. Gallagher himself described them as written "in an easy and familiar stile," and so they were, in the language of the people. Indeed, pedants censured the author for using English words in his text which were commonly heard on the lips of Irish speakers at the time. But the popularity of the sermons was not to be attributed to these causes only. Gallagher had style. Although he used the language the people understood, he used it with great skill. He was a master of the concrete image, and there is a freshness, an originality and charm about his writing which the Irish people were quick to recognize. He could write, "Ar maidin, adeirim, an Uair a fhosglus fuinneogauidh an lae, is cóir duinn fuinneoguidh ar nanama dfoscuilt, fo chomair grasa an Tiagherna, agus a ndrud naighe gach droch rúdn, agus gach cathuidh" (In the morning, I say, when the windows of day open, we should open the windows of our souls to let in the grace of the Lord, and shut them against every evil thought and temptation), or "Chuir me cul mo laimhe ris an tsaoghal" (I gave the back of my hand to the world).

Tomas Rua Ó Súilleabháin, the Kerry hedge-schoolmaster and poet, spoke of him as "Dochtuir áluinn Gallchobhair," or "the beautiful Doctor Gallagher." In Donegal, after hearing a good sermon, someone would say, "B'fhurasta aithne gur léigh sé an Dochtúir Ó Gallchobhair" (It was easy to see that he had read Dr. O Gallagher).

THE WEST

Dr. Gallagher was a Donegal man and, as far as can be ascertained, his sermons were written while he was bishop of Raphoe and was in hiding from the British authorities on the island of Inismacsaint in Lough Erne. Nonetheless, there was little literary activity in Donegal at this time. The bardic tradition had depended on the patronage of the chiefs of Tyrconnell, and, when they fell, the bardic order fell too. The Gaelic-speaking districts of Donegal were too poor to support poets and scholars such as we find in South Ulster and in Munster. The production of great books and the copying of manuscripts ceased, but a rich folklore still survived. Storytelling and the singing of Gaelic songs continued, and local poets still composed songs which were handed down traditionally. Therefore, West Donegal is one of the remaining districts of Ireland where the Irish language is the native tongue of the people. Unfortunately, it has disappeared entirely in South Ulster and almost entirely in Munster.

The same is true of Connaught. Douglas Hyde, in his *Literary History of Ireland*, wrote:

> In Connacht during the eighteenth century the conditions of life were less favourable to poetry, the people were much poorer, and there was no influential class of native school-masters and scribes to perpetuate and copy Irish manuscripts, as there was all over Munster; consequently, the greater part of the minstrelsy of that province is hopelessly lost, and even the very names of its poets with the exception of Carolan, Netterville, Mac Cabe, Mac Govern, and a few more of the last century, and Mac Sweeny, Barrett, and Raftery of this century, have been lost. That there existed, however, amongst the natives of the province a most wide-spread love of song and poetry, even though most of their manuscripts have perished, is certain, for I have collected among them, not to speak of Ossianic lays, and other things, a volume of love poems and two volumes of religious songs, almost wholly taken from the mouths of the peasantry. This love of poetry and passion for song, which seems to be the indigenous birthright of every one born in

an Irish-speaking district, promises to soon be a thing of the past, thanks, perhaps partly, to the apathy of the clergy, who in Connacht almost always preach in English, and partly to the dislike of the gentry to hear Irish spoken, but chiefly owing to the far-reaching and deliberate efforts of the National Board of Education to extirpate the national language (605-6).

Then came the Famine, which struck hardest in the Irish-speaking areas, for they were the poorest. Thousands died, hundreds of thousands fled the country, and the Irish language suffered accordingly. Indeed, for many it became associated with poverty and suffering, and its decline was greatly hastened. Any kind of literary composition in the language eventually petered out.

A few people, especially scholars and antiquaries, deplored the abandonment of the ancient language of Ireland. As explained earlier, Macpherson's "Ossian" stimulated interest in things Celtic, and cultured men and women began to study Irish literature and Irish music. Charlotte Brooke published her *Reliques of Irish Poetry* in 1789. In addition, a great harpers' festival was held in Belfast in 1792, at which Edward Bunting was employed to write down the airs played by the harpers; it may be said that the modern Irish revival can be traced to that time. Several societies for the study of the Irish language were founded: the Irish Ossianic Society, in 1853, devoted to the study and publication of Irish manuscripts; the Society for the Preservation of the Irish Language, in 1876; the Gaelic Union, in 1880; and the Gaelic League, the most important of all these societies, in 1893.

No other organization has had as great an effect on the cultural and political history of Ireland in our time as the Gaelic League. From the first, it attracted a support that none of the other language societies had enjoyed. The reason was principally that the Parnell split had created a disgust with politics among many young people, who turned from the tiresome wrangling of the politicians to the cultural nationalism of the Gaelic League. Other factors also favored the League. The Land Acts, from the great act of 1881 on, had raised the standard of living throughout the country, as a result of which the people now had some leisure for cultural interests. The league also benefited from a renewed interest in Celtic literature and civilization on the Continent. In 1853, Zeuss published his *Grammatic Celtica* which laid the basis for the scientific study of Old Irish. The *Revue Celtique* was founded in 1870 by Henri Gaidoz and D'arbois de Jubainville, and the *Zeitschrift für celtische Philologie*, in 1896 by Kuno Meyer and Ludwig Stern. In these journals and elsewhere, a long line of European scholars, especially German, contributed to our knowledge of Celtic literature and the Celtic past. The most famous of these were Rudolf Thurneysen, Kuno Meyer, Ernst Windisch, and Heinrich Zimmer. Therefore, the Gaelic League frequently argued that, if the Irish language was worthy of the attention of foreign scholars, it merited the attention of Irishmen. Thus a new generation of Irish scholars arose.

The Gaelic League differed from the antiquarian societies that preceded it in declaring that its aims were the preservation of Irish as the national language of Ireland and the extension of its use as a spoken tongue. Moreover, it would apply itself not merely to the study and publication of existing Gaelic literature, but also to the cultivation of a modern literature in the language. Even men such as Eoin Mac Neill, who was primarily a scholar and was one of the founders of the League, stressed the importance of the creation of a new literature in the language. He realized that the language had no chance of survival unless it could produce a modern literature to satisfy contemporary tastes. Thus, as the nineteenth century drew to a close, just when it seemed that the Irish language was doomed to extinction, men began to write it again.

Although much of the writing done in the early days of the League was amateurish, it would be wrong to state that this effort was merely artificial and therefore could not produce literature. Such a notion would derive from an ignorance of the cultural excitement which the Gaelic League stimulated in the nation.

P. S. O'Hegarty was correct when he wrote:

> The language led inevitably to other things, to Irish music, Irish customs and traditions, Irish place-names, Irish territorial divisions, Irish history. It emphasized the separateness of Ireland as nothing else could; it brought with it national self-respect, a feeling of kinship with the past, the version of a persistent and a continuing tradition going back beyond human memory. Many a man and woman went casually, through curiosity, to a branch meeting, or to a concert, or a festival; and heard the language spoken, or heard Irish songs, or the Irish pipes, or a traditional air on the violin, and straightway found themselves gripped and held as if an old memory were being re-awakened; returned, and returned again, and finally became one with the others, reaching back to that Irish nation, Irish civilization, that was in the land ere ever the English came, and that was the motive force of the expressions of Irish separateness that had been made in English. The Gaelic League was not alone a re-discovery of the language, but a re-discovery of the Nation, a resurrection of the Gael.

That the Gaelic League inspired not only the writing anew of Irish, but also the creation of a new drama in English can be seen from the statement of their intentions drawn up by Lady Gregory, Edward Martyn, and W. B. Yeats when they founded the Irish Literary Theatre in 1899. "We propose," they said, "to have performed in Dublin in the spring of every year certain Celtic and Irish plays, which, whatever be their degree of excellence, will be written with a high ambition, and so build up a Celtic and Irish school of dramatic literature." The influence of the League can be gauged by the titles of the first plays presented by the new theatre. They were *The Countess Cathleen* by Yeats and *The Heather Field* by Martyn, which were staged in the Antient Concert Rooms, Brunswick Street, Dublin, in May 1899. Productions of the following year were *The Bending of the Bough* by George Moore, *Maeve* by Martyn, and *The Last Feast of the Fianna* by Alice Milligan. The third and last productions of the Irish Literary Theatre were *Diarmuid and Grania* by Yeats and George Moore, and a play in the Irish language, *Casadh an tSúgáin*, or *The Twisting of the Rope*, by Douglas Hyde. These plays were presented in the Gaiety Theatre, Dublin, on October 21, 1901. *Casadh an tSúgáin* was the first play in Irish ever to be put on the boards of a theatre. It received far more favorable notices than the more pretentious play of Moore and Yeats, and still survives.

In 1895, the Gaelic League took over the *Gaelic Journal*, the organ of the Gaelic Union, and renamed it *Irisleabhar na Gaedhilge*. Over many years much good work, especially in scholarship and folklore, appeared in it. The League also founded the weekly paper *Fáinne an Lae* in 1898 and later, *An Claidheamh Soluis;* these papers were the propaganda sheets for the League and dealt with the topics of the day.

The first writer of importance to appear in modern Irish was Canon Peter O'Leary. Although he was advanced in age when, under the inspiration of the Gaelic League, he began to write, he produced a large number of works, mostly translations and adaptations from the older language and from Latin. He even tried his hand at rendering *Don Quixote* into Irish, although he emasculated it incredibly. In 1904, however, he put all lovers of the Irish language eternally in his debt when he published *Séadna*. This was a rather unsuccessful attempt to make a novel of a folktale, but *Séadna* consists of three hundred printed pages of the Irish that was spoken in West Cork when O'Leary was a boy. While the story may not stand up to the test to which a modern psychological novel is subjected, it contains descriptive passages and dialogue that are a delight. No wonder the book became a kind of bible with revivalists, especially in Munster: three hundred pages of the living language!

When the revival began, the question that arose was what kind of Irish should be written. This was a complicated question because three main dialects were still being spoken in the country—the Munster, the Connaught, and the Ulster. Some scholars argued for a common literary language as of yore and a return to the classical language of Keating. Others argued that Keating's Irish was too far removed from the spoken tongue of our time. The publication of *Séadna* put an end to the discussion. Henceforth, "caint na ndaoine," the language of the people, was written.

Despite the great importance of Canon O'Leary's work, it may be said that modern literature in Irish begins in the writings of Patrick Pearse and Padraic Ó Conaire. Pearse, who was born in Dublin and had learned Irish well, wrote short stories, mostly about children in Connaught. Though sometimes regarded as sentimental, the stories have an enduring charm because they capture the innocent world of childhood. Pearse also wrote a small number of poems which are among the most impressive pieces of poetry to appear in Irish in this century. Even if we did not know that "Fornocht Do Chonnaic Thu" ("Naked I Saw Thee") was autobiographical and prophetic, it would still be a great poem:

> Fornocht do chonnac thu
> A áille na háille,
> Is do dhallas mo shúil
> Ar eagla go stánfainn.

> I blinded my eyes,
> And I closed my ears,
> I hardened my heart,
> And I smothered my desire.

> (Naked I saw thee,
> O beauty of beauty,
> And I blinded my eyes
> For fear I should fail.

> I turned my back
> On the vision I had shaped,
> And to this road before me
> I turned my face.

> I heard thy music,
> O melody of melody,
> And I closed my ears
> For fear I should falter.

> I have turned my face
> To this road before me,
> To the deed that I see
> And the death I shall die.)

> I tasted thy mouth,
> O sweetness of sweetness,
> And I hardened my heart
> For fear of my slaying.

This translation, which is by Pearse himself, does scant justice to the original. It does not have the original's beauty of rhyme and assonance, nor its rhythm, nor its strength of imagery. "And I blinded my eyes / For fear I should fail" is a very weak rendering of "Is do dhallas mo shúil / Ar eagla go stánfain."

Padraic Ó Conaire (1883-1928) might be described as the first and only professional writer in modern Irish. He gave up a job in the British civil service to wander the roads of Ireland with a donkey and cart, and to earn his bread by writing in Irish. He was the first Gaelic writer to come under the influence of the Russians, and some say the first Irish writer. He wrote many short stories, one novel, and one short play. Most of his stories deal with characters who have suffered much, but he frequently lapses into melo-drama, and his style sometimes reproduces some of the worst features of Victorian writing. However, he had the fertility of the truly creative writer, and through his Bohemian life, he became a legend in his lifetime. Fred Higgins wrote a very fine lament for him in English, and there is a delight-ful statue by Albert Power of his leprechan-like figure in Eyre Square, Gal-way.

The first two writers of note to appear in Ulster were the brothers Séamus and Seosamh Mac Grianna. Séamus (1891-1969) was the most prolific of modern Irish writers. Much of his later work was of little value, for he went on for years churning out short stories which were little more than anecdotes, and many of them rehashes of earlier pieces. Nevertheless, he produced many first-rate stories and some very readable autobiographical volumes. Séamus Mac Grianna (or Ó Grianna), who wrote under the pen name Máire, commanded the purest Irish written in this century. For that reason alone, his best books will always be read.

Seosamh Mac Grianna (1900-) was a more imaginative writer than his brother, but illness cut short his literary career. His best works are a picaresque autobiography and a novel set in his native Rannafast. He is also the author of two volumes of short stories, an account of some folk poets of Donegal, a narrative of a walking tour in Wales, some literary essays, and two worthless historical works.

The foundation of the Gaelic publishing firm of Sairséal and Dill, and of the Gaelic Book Club in 1947 gave fresh stimulus to writing in the lan-guage, and a new crop of writers sprang up. The government publishing agency An Gúm, set up by Ernest Blythe, was, despite many defects, of great assistance to Gaelic writers. Among them were poets, novelists, short story writers, dramatists, and historians. The standard of the work produced was high. In 1955, the periodical *Irish Writing* published a selec-tion of short stories and poems translated from the modern Gaelic revival; I translated the stories and Valentin Iremonger the poems. *The Times Lit-erary Supplement* devoted an editorial to this issue of the journal on Jan-uary 25, 1956. It stated in part: "Whether the native language can be restored is a matter of continual national controversy. . . . What is beyond dispute is the existence of a school of eager and imaginative writers and the gradual raising of critical standards." The writers who appeared in this selection were Padraic Ó Conaire, Séamus Mac Grianna, Seosamh Mac Grianna, Tarlach Ó hUid (1917-), Seán Ó Ríordáin (1917-), Máire Mhac an tSaoi (1922-), Máirtín Ó Direáin (1910-), and myself. Máirtín Ó Cadhain (1907-1970) did not contribute, although he was invited to do so. Ó Cadhain was probably the most robust of modern Gaelic writers, but he had little appreciation of form and was inclined towards the old Gaelic weakness of verbosity. It was an old jibe that Gaelic books used to be judged according to the number of difficult words in them.

The drama was slow to develop in Irish, for the older writers were not acquainted with the theatre; they were storytellers. In recent years, several competent dramatists have appeared, among them Eoghan Ó Tuairisc (1919-), Seán Ó Tuama (1926-), and Críostóir Ó Floinn (1927-). Seán Ó Ríordáin, who died a short time ago, was the best of the modern poets, although Máirtín Ó Direáin, who writes a less sophisticated type of verse, was more prolific. Máirtín is still with us, and I am glad to say that a host of young poets is hard on his heels.

Despite the number of people writing in Irish at present, I am afraid that I must finish on a pessimistic note. As the statistics show, the Gaeltachta, the Irish-speaking districts, are fast disappearing. If they die, the language is dead, and no more literature will be written in it.

a chríoch sín

BIBLIOGRAPHY

Corkery, Daniel. *The Hidden Ireland*. Dublin: M. H. Gill, 1967.

de Blacam, Aodh. *Gaelic Literature Surveyed*. New York: Barnes & Noble, 1974. (With an added chapter on the twentieth century by Eoghan O'Hanluain.)

Flower, Robin. "Introduction," *Dánta Grádha*. Thomas F. O'Rahilly, ed. Cork: Cork University Press, 1926.

Hull, Eleanor. *A Text Book of Irish Literature*. Dublin: M. H. Gill, n.d.

Hyde, Douglas. *A Literary History of Ireland*. New York: Barnes & Noble, 1967.

Jackson, Kenneth Hurlstone. *A Celtic Miscellany*. Harmondsworth, Middlesex: Penguin, n.d.

Knott, Eleanor. "Introduction," *The Bardic Poems of Tadhg Dall Ó hUiginn*. Vol. I. Dublin: Irish Texts Society [1920], 1922.

Mangan, James Clarence. *The Poets and Poetry of Munster, with Poetical Translations by James Clarence Mangan*. 4th ed. Dublin: James Duffy, 1925.

Meyer, Kuno. *Selections from Ancient Irish Poetry*. London: Constable, 1911.

Murphy, Gerald. *Early Irish Lyrics*. Oxford: Clarendon Press, 1956.

Murphy, Gerald. *Saga and Myth in Ancient Ireland*. Dublin: Cultural Relations Committee, 1955.

O'Connor, Frank. *The Backward Glance*. London: Macmillan, 1967; published in America as *A Short History of Irish Literature*. New York: Capricorn Books, 1968.

O'Neill, Seamus, ed. *Irish Writing*, No. 33. Dublin: Trumpet Books,1955.

Power, Patrick C. *A Literary History of Ireland*. Cork: Mercier Press, 1969.

Quiggin, E. C. "Prolegomena to the Study of the Poetry of the Later Irish Bards, 1200-1500," *Encyclopaedia Britannica*, 11th ed.

A NOTE ON THE HISTORY OF IRISH WRITING IN ENGLISH

In the previous essay, Seamus O'Neill traces the fortunes of literature in Irish from the earliest times to the present day, and the dictionary proper is made up largely of articles about Irish authors who have written in English. However, a brief summary of the history of Irish writing in the English language may be of use as a supplement to the chronological tables.

In modern times, say from the seventeenth century on, Ireland produced a brilliant galaxy of writers, but many of them were literary Wild Geese who looked for their subject matter and their market in England rather than in Ireland. If one were somehow to erase the contributions of Dean Swift, William Congreve, George Farquhar, Richard Steele, Richard Brinsley Sheridan, Oliver Goldsmith, Dion Boucicault, Oscar Wilde, and Bernard Shaw from English literature of the last few centuries, quite obviously the modern comic tradition in English letters would be vastly impoverished. Most of these men spent most of their writing career outside of Ireland; those, like Dean Swift, who were forced to return to Ireland did so with reluctance.

For the most part, their reasons for living in England were not unpatriotic, but economic. London was the literary marketplace of the English speaking world. It was the center of publishing and the center of theatre, and the writers followed the market. Even in modern times, this tradition of the Irish writer in exile has continued, and it may be seen in the careers of many minor writers and several major ones. For instance, although James Joyce and Sean O'Casey wrote mainly about Ireland, Joyce lived most of his writing career on the Continent, and O'Casey most of his in England. Other major figures, such as George Moore, Joyce Cary, Louis MacNeice, and Samuel Beckett, not only lived abroad, but also wrote relatively little about their own country. George Moore is a partial exception, for at one point in his career he did return to his native country and enthusiastically took up Ireland as his subject matter. In a few years, however, he was back permanently in England.

In earlier years, especially in the eighteenth century, the Irish writer who turned to Irish themes usually did so glancingly and not very seriously. In the case of Sheridan, for instance, his works contain little that is indigenously Irish. There are a few Irish references in the short farce called *St. Patrick's Day*, and there is Sir Lucius O'Trigger in *The Rivals* who might be taken as a typical example of the treatment of Ireland in literature for many years. He is an excellent stage character, but not at all a realistic portrait. He is an exaggeration of a type—bumptious, quick to anger, spoiling for a fight, impoverished—in fact, the Stage Irishman who, for English audiences, provided as good a laugh as the Stage Scotsman or the Stage Welshman.

In the late eighteenth century and throughout the nineteenth century, however, a small number of significant, and sometimes still relatively unappreciated, Irish writers looked directly and seriously to Ireland for their material. First, and possibly preeminently, among them was Maria Edgeworth (1767-1849) whose best work was superb and influenced both Scott and Turgenev. Indeed, Scott in the postscript to *Waverley* wrote that he was attempting to do for Scotland what Edgeworth had done for Ireland. *Castle Rackrent* (1802) is probably her masterpiece; in it she takes as her subject the Big House, and through the eyes of an Irish servant she depicts several generations of rackety, hard-drinking, feckless Irish landlords. Much of her brilliant novel is comedy, but her characters are not as broadly exaggerated as was Sir Lucius. She writes with sympathy about the "mere Irish," but even she was writing from outside: she was viewing the peasant from the window of the Big House.

William Carleton (1794-1869), unlike Edgeworth, had intimate and exact knowledge of his subject matter. He was the son of a peasant and a hedge-schoolmaster before he wrote of the peasantry in such volumes as *Traits and Stories of the Irish Peasantry* or *Fardorougha the Miser*. His was an astonishing talent, with a range extending from brutal realism to knockabout farce. He could have been the Irish equivalent of Dickens, except for two faults: he kept his ear cocked to the British or the Ascendancy market, and he adopted the style and manner of conventional English fiction.

The Irish subject was also greatly popularized in the nineteenth century by Charles Lever (1806-1872) and Samuel Lover (1797-1868). Despite their charms and pleasures, however, both still were basically exploiting the subject matter. Lever was a popular and prolific comic novelist, who in books such as *Harry Lorrequer* and *Charles O'Malley* wrote sprightly, picaresque tales of dashing dragoons and rackety young men. He exaggerated the Irish-

man and made him funnier, quainter, and more idiotic than any character
other than the Stage Irishman. Nevertheless, he was writing comic entertainments and not realistic or serious depictions. Lover is a lesser writer.
His most famous novel, *Handy Andy*, has as its title character a monumental boob, and for this portrayal of the Irishman Lover has sometimes
been called a literary traitor to his country. Nevertheless, the book is consistently readable and sporadically funny.

Two writers who took the Irish subject much more seriously were the
brothers John and Michael Banim, particularly in their effective series of
tales about the O'Hara family. Perhaps Gerald Griffin might also be mentioned, especially for his romantic melodrama *The Collegians*, from which
novel Boucicault fashioned his popular play *The Colleen Bawn*. Griffin's
novel still may be read with pleasure, and it has some passing authenticity
in its depiction of the rural South. Perhaps even Charles J. Kickham should
be mentioned for his sprawling and sentimental *Knocknagow*, which, for
all of its faults, is a loving portrait of the countryside.

By far the most popular Irish poet of the nineteenth century was Tom
Moore. This amiable, charming, deft, and prolific writer did not always
take Ireland for his subject, and he lived most of his adult life in England
where he was the friend of Byron and the darling of the drawing room. His
Irish Melodies, however, were vastly popular, and perhaps two dozen of
the best of them are still sung widely today. In these pieces, Moore would
write new words to traditional Irish airs, and the wedding of words to
music was often consummate. It is true that his tone was invariably nostalgic or patriotic or deeply sentimental; it is true also that the words, divorced from the melodies, are more fluent than substantial. Moore was the
great exploiter of the exile's view of Ireland, the Ireland of the smile and
the tear. But for all of that, pieces like "The Harp That Once," "The Minstrel Boy," and "Believe Me If All Those Enduring Young Charms" are
now an ineradicable, minor, but pleasant part of Ireland's literary heritage.

The two other notable Irish poets of the mid-nineteenth century were
James Clarence Mangan (1803-1849) and Thomas Davis (1814-1845),
young men of rare talent. They were both formed and harmed by the state
of their country. Mangan lived an Edgar Allan Poe-like existence of poverty and squalor, and his aspirations and assertions outran the frustrations
of his provincial milieu. He was a poet of remarkable fluency who in his
English verse occasionally reflected some of the qualities and technical complexities of verse written in Irish. His very small handful of brilliant poems
—such as "Dark Rosaleen," "Gone in the Wind," and "The Nameless One"
—can only suggest what he might have done had he lived fifty years later.
Davis was one of the leading spirits of the Young Ireland group and a
founder of its organ, *The Nation*. The nobility of his sentiments much impressed his contemporaries and many later Irishmen. His pen was as facile
as his thoughts were elevated, but he regarded writing merely as a weapon

to be used in the cause of nationalism. Little of his poetry except the "Lament for the Death of Owen Roe O'Neill" rose above the usual patriotic ditty which *The Nation* usually printed.

In the second half of the nineteenth century, Sir Samuel Ferguson (1810-1886) turned directly to Irish legendary material for several long narrative poems. Though not usually an exciting poet, he can be considered a forerunner of the Literary Revival. His best qualities and his faults may be seen in the poem "Deirdre's Lament for the Sons of Usnach."

Irish drama in the nineteenth century may be summed up mainly in the name Dion Boucicault. For most of his prolific career, Boucicault was a popular entertainer. When he and his imitators turned their attention to Ireland, they presented a never-never land of easy comedy, fulsome sentiment, and heroic patriotism. This version of Ireland was the chief literary expression of the country in the nineteenth century, and it was against this sweet simplicity that the chief writers of the Literary Renaissance were in revolt.

The beginnings of the Irish Literary Renaissance are usually traced to the publication of two volumes by Standish O'Grady: *History of Ireland: The Heroic Period* (1878) and *History of Ireland: Cuchullain and his Contemporaries* (1880). O'Grady is sometimes called the father of the Literary Revival, for his books caused much more excitement than Ferguson's poems. The two *History of Ireland* books were an exultant celebration of Irish legendary materials and, although in prose, were vibrant with poetic fervor. Of him, AE wrote in 1902: "Years ago, in the adventurous youth of his mind, Mr. O'Grady found the Gaelic tradition like a neglected antique dun with the doors barred. Listening, he heard from within the hum of an immense chivalry, and he opened the doors and the wild riders went forth to work their will." To which, W. B. Yeats added the footnote, "I think it was his *History of Ireland, Heroic Period*, that started us all. . . ."

What it started was this: in 1888, the Dublin firm of M. H. Gill published *Poems and Ballads of Young Ireland*, which included the work of most of the new poets—Yeats, T. W. Rolleston, John Todhunter, Katharine Tynan, Rose Kavanagh, and others. According to Stephen Gwynn, this book "announced the co-operative, concerted nature of the effort of the younger generation to give a new impulse to Irish poetry." In 1889, Yeats published *The Wanderings of Oisin* which treated, albeit in rather pre-Raphaelite fashion, an Irish legendary story. In 1891, at a meeting in Yeats' house in London, he, Rolleston, Todhunter, and others initiated what was to become in the next year the Irish Literary Society of London. In 1892, a sister organization, the National Literary Society, was formed in Dublin, and Douglas Hyde gave before it his influential lecture on "The Necessity of de-Anglicising Ireland." In that same year, Yeats published his play *The Countess Cathleen*. In 1893, Hyde published his beautiful translations, *The*

Love Songs of Connacht, and founded the Gaelic League for the propaga-
tion of the Irish language. In 1894, Yeats' book of folklore, *The Celtic
Twilight,* gave a popular, if misleading, title to the whole movement. In
the same year, he published another play, *The Land of Heart's Desire,* and
it was produced in March in London with Todhunter's *A Comedy of Sighs.*
In 1897, George Sigerson published his *Bards of the Gael and Gall.* In
1899, Hyde published his monumental *Literary History of Ireland* and the
Irish Literary Theatre made its first appearance. Called back to Ireland to
assist in the production was George Moore who did little for the Irish
theatre, but who wrote some stories to be translated into Irish by the Gaelic
League. And in that volume, *The Untilled Field,* may surely be seen the
beginnings of modern Irish prose fiction.

This flurry of events presaged a veritable storm of cultural activity in
Ireland. Clubs and societies were formed, and people diligently turned to
studying Irish, writing poems, producing plays, and drafting manifestos.
One underlying reason for this great ferment was probably political frustration. For generations, the Irish had been ineffectively striving for greater
freedom, and the country's political history rather resembled sharp crests
of hope and activity followed by long and deep troughs of frustration and
disorganization. One such crest was Wolfe Tone's Rebellion of 1798; another perhaps culminated in Daniel O'Connell's monster meetings of midcentury; and another in the abortive Fenian uprising a few years later. The
most recent, and perhaps most bitter attempt may be seen in the spectacular
rise and fall of Charles Stewart Parnell.

Parnell had succeeded in uniting the Irish parliamentary party and in
getting them to vote as a block in the English parliament. The Irish thus
held a powerful balance of power which Parnell was able to use as a lever
to get an Irish Home Rule bill passed. He seemed within an ace of succeeding when a personal scandal irretrievably divided the Irish party and the
country over the question of his leadership. While still attempting to reunite
the party and to regain power, he died, and the Irish cause was in effect lost.

The extinction of political hopes did not mean the extinction of nationalistic fervor; the fervor merely took another direction. Many Irishmen now
looked excitedly at the prospect of reviving Irish culture and language; at
the same time, Irishmen looked excitedly at the prospect, not of reviving,
but of creating an Irish literature.

The impulses of the Literary Renaissance were two: to send Irish writers
for their subjects either back to the Irish past or into the Irish rural present.
Behind these impulses lay the assumption that the historic past and the
rural present contained qualities that were both noble and indigenously
Irish. And certainly many made the further assumption that the past and
the present could be merged and thereby a cultural and a national r
cation could be achieved. That assumption of dying but reclaimab
underlay the folklore investigations of Hyde, Yeats, and Lady G

of whom thought that the virtues of the Celtic past were still to be discerned in the modern rural present. The further assumption, that ancient tradition and present rural virtue could be amalgamated and could transform the modern, anglicized, townbred Irishman, underlay all of the cultural fervor at the turn of the century.

Another issue was never quite faced. A literary work is composed of both matter and manner. To a certain extent, an Irish subject matter determined the Irish literary manner. Linguistically, certain Irish locutions and the faintly phonetic spelling of dialogue could bring a richness into the English. With Lady Gregory and particularly with Synge, it even seemed for a while that a new style of writing was evolving; but Lady Gregory's Kiltartan style was rural, and Synge's style was simply inimitable. Had W. B. Yeats known Irish, he might have become intrigued by the possibilities of adapting the intricate techniques of Irish verse to English. Yeats had no Irish, however, and he developed in his own indiosyncratic ways. The writers who were followed and followable were much more stylistically bland: Padraic Colum and Lennox Robinson.

Certain writers, such as Yeats, Synge, Joyce, O'Casey, and Beckett, finally developed remarkable literary strategies, but these strategies were not usable for anyone else. To this date, then, the Irishness of Irish literature resides in the primary business of an Irish subject matter and in the rich but tangential difference of English as it is spoken by the Irish.

Even the subject matter, however, raised problems. Early in the century, a writer like Synge was sent by Yeats into the rural past of the Aran Islands, and a writer like Stephens, to a certain extent, followed Yeats into the past of legend. Yeats, though, was enamored of the Irish past more for the influence it might have upon his artistry than for patriotic reasons. He was liable at any time to be diverted from his antiquarian predilections by theosophy or Noh drama or any of half a dozen other attractions. Hence, while Yeats' early work may have shown a possible direction, it did not map the road; a young Irish writer may have been startled to find his mentor not merely in another green field, but in some distant, alien, chartreuse one.

Lady Gregory, who had a more comic and prosaic mind than did Yeats, had a foot in both the past and the present. She wrote modern versions of the sagas in *Cuchulain of Muirthemne* and *Gods and Fighting Men* and treatments of recorded history in *Kincora* and *The White Cockade*. At the same time, her popular peasant plays depicted in exaggerated fashion the quirks, if not always the virtues, of the rural present.

For some years, Lady Gregory's use of the countryside proved the strongest of Irish subjects. Quite early, the staple of the Abbey repertoire became not the lyrical legendary past of Yeats, but the realistic rural present of Padraic Colum, William Boyle, T. C. Murray, R. G. Ray, Brinsley MacNamara, and George Shiels. All of these writers were good enough to temper their realism with criticism, but to the purely patriotic Irishman, such as Arthur Griffith or Maud Gonne, it soon seemed that the celebration had somehow become transformed into denigration.

Influential patriotic journalists, such as Griffith and D. P. Moran, approved the use of the rural present as the basic subject matter for the national literature, but did not want that subject matter in any way criticized. A national literature that did not basically celebrate the nation was to them anti-Irish; above all, J. M. Synge's treatment of that subject matter was to them anathema. However, a considerable body of popular literature did develop which celebrated the rural present and served the national cause by presenting the vision of Ireland that the nationalists wanted to propagate. Among such writers in the early years of the century were a gaggle of lady poets, such as Alice Milligan, Ethna Carbery, Moira O'Neill, and Lizzie Twigg, and a prolific group of fiction writers, such as Rosa Mulholland, Alice Furlong, and Victor O'D. Power. Most of their material was of little literary worth, being characterized by rampant patriotism and circumspect piety. In any event, such writers were merely treating uncritically the same basic subject matter of Synge, Lady Gregory, and Colum.

Meanwhile, the historical or legendary past was attracting far fewer writers. Of course, a number of extraordinary works with an historical background were still being produced. Among novels, some that immediately leap to mind are Joseph O'Neill's *Wind from the North*, Eimar O'Duffy's *The Lion and the Fox*, and Liam O'Flaherty's *Famine*. On the whole, however, there were few fine works in this vein, and the attitude of many writers toward that past soon came to be more whimsical or satirical than celebrative. Not until the dramatic events of the Easter Rising, and the turbulent years following it, did Irish writers in any significant numbers return to Irish history for their subject matter. And then, as in the plays of O'Casey, the novels of O'Flaherty, and the stories of O'Faolain and O'Connor, that history was so recent as to be, in effect, contemporary.

The decade following 1916 was such a dramatic time that it seemed unavoidable to writers as a subject matter, as well as much more urgent than the past of legend and history. At the same time, as many of those events occurred in the city, there was a slow shifting of literary interest from the countryside to the urban setting. Lennox Robinson and W. F. Casey turned to the town and the suburb. O'Faolain and O'Connor turned from the Old Woman of the Roads to the Young Men from the South. O'Casey and O'Flaherty, although both were capable of celebrating that Irish nostalgia which Paul Vincent Carroll called The Old Foolishness, turned to the Troubles and the tenements. Probably the most celebrated of all modern Irish works of fiction are those volumes of James Joyce, particularly *Dubliners* and *Ulysses*, which are the quintessential urban fictions.

The rural present was a tenacious subject matter, however, and did not die off. Indeed, it lingers on—and well it might, for Ireland remains basically a rural country. All the same, the attitude of writers toward rural

Ireland did begin to change. If there were fewer idealizations of the countryside, such as nostalgic Irish-Americans would enjoy, there were still some celebrations of it, among them the diverting entertainments of Maurice Walsh, and the clearly observed, warmly sympathetic, and more serious novels of Francis MacManus. Nevertheless, the attitude of many writers was becoming primarily critical. Few were as grotesque in their view as J. M. Synge or as violent as Brinsley MacNamara, and few went as far as Paul Vincent Carroll once did when he referred to rural Ireland as "a warping, killing, crookening rat-trap where the human mind and spirit are driven mad." But the best of Irish writers were beginning to take a bleak and disillusioned view of the modern countryside, such as may be found in Mervyn Wall's *Leaves for the Burning* or John McGahern's *The Barracks*.

Ireland's neutrality in World War II seems, in retrospect, the last stand of the Island of Saints and Scholars. By the late 1950s, it was abundantly clear that de Valera's attempt to preserve Ireland as an enclave of rural purities and historical integrities had not worked. The country was too poor economically to support, and too poor culturally to satisfy, many of its young people, and the emigration rate was soaring. When the Lemass government turned to woo the outside world, the long-delayed transformation of Ireland into a modern state had begun. Archbishop McQuaid might return from Vatican II and announce firmly that nothing had changed, but in actuality everything was changing very fast, even in the Church.

Television antennas began to appear on Dublin roofs in about 1960, and people avidly watched the uncensorable British programs from across the Irish Sea. The government was pursuing a vigorous campaign of attracting foreign investment. The country entered the United Nations, with an idealistic notion of being a neutral and temporizing force. Irish troops were part of the U.N. peace-keeping mission in the Congo, and an Irish writer was Dag Hammarskjöld's man in Katanga. New buildings of an incongruous and ugly modernity appeared in the capital, the tourist trade grew, and even the tide of emigration slowly receded and even turned.

All of this activity had an intense cultural and social effect on the country. Film censorship began to relax, and book censorship dwindled to such a trickle that in the 1970s John McGahern and Edna O'Brien were practically the only writers of note whose books were banned. In 1977, the banning of a book on family planning led to a court decision that may have administered the coup de grace to literary censorship. A production in 1977 at the Gate Theatre of the English play *Equus* with a naked man and a naked girl on stage, occasioned neither a police raid nor, indeed, any protest whatsoever. People began to marry earlier, traffic grew congested, the suburbs sprawled, and McDonald's ubiquitous hamburgers appeared on Grafton Street.

For the Irish writer of today, the new outward-looking Ireland has had an impact both on his subject matter and his technique. His subject matter is no longer the celebration of national virtue, but the investigation of individual faults. Few taboos and restrictions on his subject matter are left. A self-critical and disillusioned attitude remains from the previous generations, but even it seems somewhat altered. It seems to have a good deal more in common with the disillusionment of modern man anywhere in the Western world than with the native disillusionments and defeats found in the novels of the 1920s and 1940s.

This freedom of subject matter already appears to be enriching a literature that, with notable exceptions, had to resort to notable evasions in the past. One significant symptom of increased vigor in Irish writing is that at least half a dozen new publishing houses have sprung up in both the North and the South. These houses have devoted their space mainly to the publication of new writers, who have more in common with each other than with their immediate literary ancestors.

In technique, the modern Irish writer has been burdened by overwhelming examples of success. Probably the greatest experiments of modern fiction have been carried out by James Joyce. In English-speaking poetry, the experiments of W. B. Yeats have been less dramatic than those of Pound or Eliot, but they have been much more various. Samuel Beckett has been preeminent among modern avant garde dramatists, and there have been the heady and dizzying examples of Synge, O'Casey, Denis Johnston, Flann O'Brien, and the later Austin Clarke. The effect of these writers has been so enormous that only in this generation has it been assimilated, evaluated, and used. Probably it has been assimilated at second-hand, through American novelists, German playwrights, and English poets who have read Joyce, Yeats, and Beckett. The important point, however, is that the Irish writer of today has assimilated it and now has an armory of literary strategies, technical devices, and rhetorical techniques that his immediate Irish literary ancestors could not command.

How would one sum up the reaction of Irish writing to the twentieth century? Overwhelmingly, the writers seem formed by the political and social changes first of Ireland and then of the world. Politically, one might see modern Ireland falling into three periods: one of patriotic resurgence that culminated in the 1916 Rising and the Troubles; a second period of political consolidation, which began when de Valera and his followers entered the Dail and then came to dominate the country for more than a generation; and a third period of outward-looking and of economic growth which began about the time of the Lemass government in the early 1960s. To continue this considerable oversimplification, one might say that Irish writing in this century also has fallen into three basic divisions, which mirror the political ones.

The first modern literary period was launched by Yeats, Hyde, Moore, Synge, and the early modern writers of what came to be called the Literary Renaissance. The great impulse behind their work was the portrayal of Ireland—basically an idealistic and anachronistic portrayal resting on rural culture and ancient history. Although the literature of this period grew increasingly critical of details, it was fervent, patriotic, religious, and affirmative. Despite its greatest writers, Yeats and Synge, its literary manner came to be predominantly realistic and conventional.

The second period of modern Irish writing saw its greatest writers, Yeats and Joyce, increasingly concerned with formal experiment and its lesser writers increasingly content to work in established forms, but ever more critical of the Irish content. O'Faolain and O'Connor would be cases in point.

The present period of modern Irish writing may have as its John the Baptists Flann O'Brien and Austin Clarke. As yet, it is too early to discern any Messiah, but there are a multitude of promising candidates. As a group, the modern writers seem more conscious of the freedom that can come with the assimilation of formal experiments, but the question of form has so far remained secondary to the problem of statement and content. Statement and content, in turn, have grown remarkably freer than in the past.

How the Irish writer may develop is anybody's guess. It could well be that he will become increasingly less Irish, and more a citizen of the world. That development would seem inevitable as the culture of the Great World itself becomes increasingly homogeneous. Yet, if any quality has been constant in the best of Irish writing, it has been a highly critical attitude. Despite political, social, and cultural pressures to conform, the Irish writer has obdurately remained the dour and the gay, the cute and the caustic critic of society. If Irish writing continues its individual, its Irish, contribution to the civilization of the world, it will continue to be critical—and to be critical not merely of Irishmen, but of men.

THE DICTIONARY

ABBEY THEATRE (1904-), the national theatre of Ireland. Against a background of national and cultural resurgence, a new concept of dramatic writing came into existence in Ireland in the closing years of the nineteenth century. Hitherto, everything by way of actors or playwrights that Ireland had produced had enriched the English theatre. The new movement was not only nationalistic in its impetus, but also idealistic in concept and artistic in its aims. In fact, it was destined to bring back poetic imagination to the theatre in a distant outpost of Europe.

To understand how this new movement came about, it is necessary to go back to 1897 and the memorable meeting of W. B. Yeats,* Edward Martyn,* and Lady Gregory* in Duras House, Kinvara, on the shores of Galway Bay. It was then that the dramatic movement which later gave rise to the Abbey Theatre first took shape.

W. B. Yeats was born in 1865 in Sandymount, Dublin, the son of a distinguished Irish portrait painter, John Butler Yeats.* His early apprentice works in dramatic form, *The Island of Statues* and *Mosada,* were Irish neither in subject matter nor in manner. His first play on an Irish subject, *The Countess Cathleen,* published in 1892, was written long before he had gained any practical knowledge of the theatre. It was not until 1894 that Yeats had his first play produced, and that was not in Ireland but at the Avenue Theatre, London, where *The Land of Heart's Desire* was staged by Florence Farr as a curtain-raiser to John Todhunter's* *A Comedy of Sighs.* After that production, Yeats became interested in the idea of an Irish theatre, but it was not until the meeting in 1897 in Duras House that the idea began to crystallize. Yeats had become interested in the possibilities

*All names that are marked by an asterisk appear as a separate entry in this dictionary.

of giving Ireland a theatre somewhat along the lines of J. T. Grein's Independent Theatre, where Ibsen and Shaw* had their first London productions —not that Yeats was in those days an admirer of Ibsen or Shaw, except insofar as they raised a flag for the literary and artistic drama.

Ibsen's great disciple—in fact, his only disciple in Ireland at the time—was Edward Martyn, a wealthy landowner and aspiring playwright. Martyn and Yeats, in turn, succeeded in interesting the novelist George Moore* in their project. Moore had written a play, *The Strike at Arlingford*, which was produced by the Independent Theatre in 1893. Moore had lived in Paris for years and had first-hand knowledge of the precursor of all of these literary movements, Antoine's *Théatre Libre*. Yeats, Martyn, and Moore were all united in opposition to the theatrical conditions in London and, of course, in Dublin, which made impossible the production of plays whose character did not ensure immediate commercial success. Martyn and Moore thought of Ibsen as their master, and it was their intention to do for Ireland what he had done for Norway. Yeats, having already made use of a folktale as material for his verse play *The Land of Heart's Desire*, was inclined to the view that a dramatic movement in Ireland should distinguish itself from its prototypes in Bergen, Paris, and London by use of Irish legend and lore as material for poetic drama.

It was perhaps the third of the founding triumvirate, Augusta, Lady Gregory, who played the largest hand of all in the founding of an Irish theatre. The daughter of a landowning family, the Persses of Roxboro', County Galway, by the 1890s she was a middle-aged widow of comfortable means. She had as yet no ambitions as a writer and had never been particularly interested in the theatre. But she loved poetry, particularly the poetry of W. B. Yeats, and she was to exert an influence on the movement that neither Yeats nor Martyn could have foreseen. Most likely it was she who blended the oil and vinegar to launch the Irish Literary Theatre.* This occurred in May 1899, with productions in Dublin of Yeats' poetic play *The Countess Cathleen* and Martyn's *The Heather Field*, a play in the Ibsen manner.

The bills presented in Dublin by the Irish Literary Theatre in 1899 and 1900 struck a nice balance between the play of ideas and lyrical pieces based on Irish saga and legend. But in 1901 there was an unsuccessful attempt to combine continental ideas with the Gaelic mode within the framework of the same play. Yeats and Moore had written in collaboration *Diarmuid and Gráinne*, which was staged at the Gaiety Theatre, Dublin, in October 1901, with music by Edward Elgar. This production, which might have been expected to reconcile the divergent ideas of the founders, actually widened the breach and brought to almost a full stop George Moore's connection with the Irish dramatic revival. The tentative groping toward the idea of a national theatre had come up against a stone wall.

The literary ideals of the founders were admirable, but their practical knowledge of the theatre was slight. All of the six productions of the Irish Literary Theatre were played by English actors and actresses directed by everybody and nobody. Even Sir Frank Benson's Shakespearean Company, which crossed from England to stage *Diarmuid and Gráinne,* could not save this mixture of Wagnerian opera and Celtic twilight. But on the night of this debacle, October 21, 1901, the first play in Irish ever to be presented in a recognized theatre was staged on the same bill. The play was *Casadh an tSúgáin* (The Twisting of the Rope) by Douglas Hyde,* who also played the leading part, and the piece was presented by a cast of amateurs directed by a little-known Dubliner, W. G. Fay. That night the Irish Literary Theatre had both died and been reborn.

Born in Dublin in 1892, William George Fay was an electrician by trade. For a time he had traveled about Ireland as an advance-man for a circus and had played with professional "fit-up" companies on tour. (The fit-ups played short, even one-night, engagements in small provincial towns and had to set or fit-up anew their stage in each town in whatever parish hall or primitive local accommodation was available.) He made his first stage appearance in Dublin in 1891 under the name W. G. Ormonde. For several years afterwards, he appeared with his brother Frank in melodramas and sketches in various Dublin halls.

Frank Fay was a fine speaker of verse, as Yeats' dedication of *The King's Threshold* to him bears testimony. He was also an excellent teacher, and at least two generations of Abbey actors were indebted to him for the clarity and vigor of their diction. Frank Fay was also the first to advocate the formation of a national theatre in the fullest sense: the staging of plays written by Irishmen with Irish actors and actresses.

The production of *Casadh an tSúgáin* had brought Irish folklore into the theatre. The author, Douglas Hyde, a founder of the Gaelic League, had paved the way for the folk plays and rural comedies of Lady Gregory, George Fitzmaurice,* and others, which were to prove most popular with audiences in the years ahead.

Neither Yeats nor Martyn, in their preoccupation with the poetic drama and the intellectual play of ideas, respectively, had envisaged the emergence of the one distinctive strain that Ireland has contributed to world drama, the folk or peasant play. Ironically, Yeats made his own contribution to this new drama in the following year, 1902, when his first prose plays, *Cathleen Ni Houlihan* and *The Pot of Broth,* were staged by W. G. Fay's Irish National Dramatic Society. Yeats had taken the first step in a direction far removed from his own ideals for a poetic drama that would be "remote, spiritual, and ideal." In 1903, Fay's company merged with the Irish Literary Theatre as the Irish National Theatre Society. This union was both logical and desirable, but it had required considerable negotiating skill on the part of Yeats.

In 1903, Lady Gregory made her first bid for fame as a writer of folk comedy with her one-acter *Twenty-Five*, but in October of that year the presentation of *In the Shadow of the Glen* marked the arrival of a playwright of genius, John Millington Synge.* Here was an unmistakable new voice. Combining a highly developed sense of drama with a gift for poetic dialogue, Synge revealed the latent possibilities of what was and still is widely accepted as an Abbey play.

Synge was to have a decisive influence on the shaping of Irish drama. Within a few months he gave the national theatre its first masterpiece, *Riders to the Sea*. This production, in 1904, was notable also for the discovery of a new actress, Sara Allgood, who is still remembered from later productions as an incomparable interpreter of Synge. Indeed, to many older theatre-goers at home and abroad, the names of Sara Allgood and her sister Maíre O'Neill sum up the chief virtues of the "Abbey" style of acting.

Strangely, it was a generous Englishwoman, Annie Fredericka Horniman, who ensured the continuity of the company's work by purchasing and equipping the building that became known as the Abbey Theatre, and by presenting it to the Irish National Theatre Society in 1904. She is said to have arrived at this momentous decision to build and subsidize a theatre in Ireland by a reading of Tarot cards and astrological charts. She was an ardent admirer of Yeats but could not agree with his co-worker, Lady Gregory, and her attitude towards the Fays and other members of the company was condescending, when not openly hostile. She severed her connection with the Abbey in 1910, when the theatre failed to close its doors on the day of King Edward VII's death. Later, she helped Lilian Baylis to found the Old Vic, and she subsidized the Gaiety Theatre, Manchester, where an enterprising and successful repertory theatre produced the realistic Manchester plays of Stanley Houghton and others.

Like everything new, the young Abbey was bound to meet opposition from both within and outside the movement. Synge's *In the Shadow of the Glen* had aroused the ire of Arthur Griffith* in *The United Irishman*. The idea of a young wife leaving an old husband, a subject as old as folklore, was seen as a libel on the peasant women of Ireland. Maud Gonne and some of the leading actors, such as Dudley Digges and Máire Quinn, resigned from the Society in protest. Later, other members left because a propagandist, antirecruiting play by Padraic Colum,* *The Saxon Shillin'*, had been rejected. Indeed, the movement had encountered student protest from the beginning: advance denunciation of Yeats' *The Countess Cathleen* in 1899 had brought some students from the old Royal University to the Antient Concert Rooms to foment rowdyism. When, in 1906, Horniman endowed the theatre with an annual grant and the Society was registered as a limited liability company with a board of directors consisting of Yeats, Lady Gregory, and Synge, some of the leading players and members resigned in protest against what they regarded as authoritarian control.

All of these protests and secessions were in the nature of a dress rehearsal for the *Playboy* row in January 1907. The acrimonious disputes, carried on in newspapers and magazines for over a decade about Synge's *The Playboy of the Western World*, has still not quite subsided. It was an example of the eternal dispute between the mind of the artist and the mind of the mob. In those days, Synge was seen as a bogeyman, a dropout, a subversive, a degenerate who defamed the Irish people. Nationalist Ireland was on the march, believing in progress and in a utopia just around the corner. Patriotic journalists like Griffith and D. P. Moran were hypersensitive to any criticism of national failings.

Synge, of course, had his imitators but no immediate successors. His style was so vigorous and individualistic that there was an obvious danger that playwrights coming after him would be beguiled by a spurious, imitative "Synge-song." Just as artistic developments in music and painting have been accompanied, if not occasioned, by the discovery of some new instrument or medium, Synge's unique mastery of peasant idiom created a situation in which more than half the strength of what was, and still is, largely accepted as an Abbey play resided in its dialogue. If this literary quality had not developed new modes of expression appropriate to new subjects and themes, it would have been doomed to imitation or pastiche. The Abbey play remained a vital and living thing after the death of Synge largely because of his contemporaries, Lady Gregory, Padraic Colum,* George Fitzmaurice,* and T. C. Murray,* whose work, although uneven in quality, bridged the gap between Synge and the playwrights of the 1920s. Although these playwrights were influenced by Synge's mastery of poetic prose, they developed their unique styles and added a new dimension to the folk or peasant play, that "first fine careless rapture" of Abbey drama.

A London visit in May 1903 had brought the Irish national theatre to the notice of the London critics William Archer, Arthur Symons, and Michael Field. A. B. Walkley of *The Times* commented:

> As a rule they [the players] stand stock still, the speaker of the moment is the only one who is allowed a little gesture. . . . The listeners do not distract one's attention by fussy stage business; they just stay where they are and listen. When they move, it is without premeditation, at haphazard, and even with a little natural clumsiness as of a people who are not conscious of being stared at in public, hence a delightful effect of spontaneity.

For many years, the company found it hard to live down that enthusiastic notice. Captious critics even to this day are only too ready to pounce on that word "clumsiness" and to aver that the Abbey players were mere behaviorists—naturals who titillated the jaded palates of the London critics. What W. G. and Frank Fay really had done was to blend the principles of the French actor Constant-Benoit Coquelin with the production methods of Antoine at the *Théatre Libre* and to evolve a style suited to the Irish temperament. Coquelin was that *rara avis*, a fine actor who could bring a critical mind to the appraisal of his craft. Over a twenty-six year period, he created the leading roles in forty-four new plays at the *Comédie Française*. He was at his best in comic servant parts; in this respect, his interpretations influenced the Fays and, through them, Dudley Digges, Arthur Sinclair, J. M. Kerrigan, Barry Fitzgerald, and, perhaps the most versatile of them all, F. J. McCormick. But if Coquelin exerted the greatest influence on individual actors of the early Abbey, it was Antoine's *Théatre Libre* that had inspired the Fays to organize a theatre out of little more than amateur enthusiasm.

A most serious blow to the theatre was the departure of the Fays early in January 1908. W. G. Fay, the producer-manager, had asked Yeats to give him absolute control over the actors; he stipulated that Yeats should dismiss the company and let them be reengaged personally by himself. When the Abbey directors refused to make any such concession, Fay chose to resign, taking with him his wife Brigit Dempsey, his brother Frank, and one or two others.

The Irish theatre movement was not known internationally in its early years, and none of the Abbey plays was seen in America until 1911, when T. C. Murray's *Birthright* and Synge's *The Playboy of the Western World* infuriated Irish-American audiences. The Abbey's first date in the United States was at the Plymouth Theatre in Boston, a city with a large Irish community, where the company expected to be hailed as old friends. But the plays were either too modern or the audiences too ancient, and the players were booed and hissed. In fact, some weeks later the whole cast of *The Playboy* was arrested in Philadelphia and brought before a magistrate's court, charged with presenting immoral or indecent plays.

The riots and disturbances on that first American tour made it clear to intelligent playgoers that, for the first time in its history, Ireland had its own theatre and school of playwrights who had set out to mirror "the deeper thoughts and emotions of their people." That some people at home and abroad called it a distorting mirror did not matter greatly, because gradully it became clear to audiences that the Abbey was determined to correct a falsely sentimental and romantic view of the country and its people: cottages with roses round the door, mother machrees and purty colleens in old plaid shawls, swaggering boyos with caubeens and clay pipes—all this sunburstry, shamroguery, and stage Irishry was part of what the national theatre had set out to destroy. Plays like *Cathleen Ni Houlihan* and *The Rising of the Moon* not only gave inspiration to national bodies like the Gaelic League and Sinn Fein, but also foreshadowed the Insurrection of 1916. As Yeats queried, referring to *Cathleen Ni Houlihan*:

> Did that play of mine send out
> Certain men the English shot?

At home, the Abbey gradually began to find its place in the new Ireland that was taking shape after the struggle for independence. The vision of its founders and the talent and idealism of its players and playwrights were the real assets that kept the theatre open until 1925, when the Abbey became the first state-subsidized theatre in the English-speaking world. No sooner had the Abbey received a small government subsidy than its critics belabored it as part of the establishment and as "an institution as conservative as the National Gallery or the National Museum." But both the critics and the establishment were quickly disillusioned with the arrival of a new playwright of genius, Sean O'Casey.*

Sean O'Casey was born in Dorset Street, Dublin, on March 30, 1880. Though both of his parents were Protestants, they were of the lower middle class and not in any way connected with the privileged Anglo-Irish ruling class. In his youth, O'Casey identified himself with the Catholic working class and the separatist movement. Although he had severed his connection with militant labor long before the Rising, he experienced the terror and violence of the War of Independence and the grim tragedies of civil war. It is against such a background that he wrote his famed trilogy of plays in Dublin tenement settings: *The Shadow of a Gunman* (1923), *Juno and the Paycock* (1924), and *The Plough and the Stars* (1926).

In Dublin, nowadays, praise of O'Casey's early Abbey plays seems irrelevant and impertinent. As Brendan Behan*once remarked, it is like praising the lakes of Killarney. This was not always the case, however. O'Casey remained ever conscious of the fact that, when these plays were first produced, many of his fellow writers and some critics were, to say the least, rather disparaging of his great achievement. Everyone has his own favorite among the early plays, but today *The Plough and the Stars* is the most popular with audiences. It had the advantage that on its first production in 1926 it was heralded by that recipe for box-office success, an Abbey row. During the fourth performance, the stage was invaded by an organized group who considered the carrying of the national flag into a public house, in the second act, a public insult to the insurgents of Easter Week, especially when one of the onlookers was a prostitute. Fighting broke out between the cast and some of the invaders. The invaders, however, had little or no support, and the public protest was not repeated. The controversy continued in the press and in debating societies.

After this great success, O'Casey went to live in London. Most Dublin theatre-goers, despite the protests and disparagement of his works in literary circles, would have liked him to continue to write in his old vein as an ironic observer of Irish failings and hypocrisies. But he left behind his Dublin subjects to tackle a play on World War I, which he entitled *The Silver Tassie*. Irish interest in *The Silver Tassie* has centered not on this burningly sincere, if lopsided, antiwar play, but on the controversy which arose over its rejection by the Abbey in 1928. The verbal battle between Yeats and

O'Casey provided more drama than the play itself. Some newspapers published the correspondence between the two writers in dialogue form; others
reported that O'Casey had challenged Yeats to a duel.

O'Casey's trilogy had brought to the Abbey stage characters as vivid
and voluble as the country people of Synge, Colum, and T. C. Murray, but
he portrayed them against a background of city tenements in postrevolu-
tionary Ireland. New aspects of life in provincial towns were revealed in the
plays of Lennox Robinson,* George Shiels,* and Brinsley MacNamara.*

By the late 1930s, Dublin had shown that it was sufficiently mature to
accept satire of national institutions in the plays of Paul Vincent Carroll*
and Denis Johnston.* Some critics have contended that O'Casey's early
plays had done much to heal the bitterness of the Civil War. O'Casey, as
well as Carroll and Johnston, seemed to say that patriotism was not enough.
It was a natural reaction to the idealism of the fight for freedom, which was
now somewhat dulled by the stern realities of the everyday struggle for
existence in a new and undeveloped state. A harsh literary censorship,
although it did not apply to the stage, created a climate of repression that
was not conducive to the free expression of ideas. Although playwrights
remained uncommitted to any particular political ideology, the prevailing
note was one of cynicism and disillusion. Yeats, who had been a senator
in the Irish Free State government, remained a father figure. In the early
1930s, he began to flirt with a crypto-fascist movement, the Blueshirts.
When he wanted to stage *Coriolanus* in modern dress as a parable for
the times, his fellow-directors of the Abbey opted for more conventional
costuming.

After Yeats' death, Ireland's neutrality in World War II made Irish drama
of the period not only neutral but indifferent. This same indifference can
be more deadly than the puritanism that usually precedes it. The later plays
of Sean O'Casey, such as *Cock-a-Doodle Dandy* and *The Bishop's Bonfire*,
in which he castigates an Ireland of his own imaginings, were nonchalantly
dismissed as an old man's petulant joke. There were fewer protests and no
riots in Dublin theatres. Apart from the customary internal dissension at
the Abbey, there was no public controversy on the grand scale. It had been
supplanted by a niggling, negative criticism. Overseas, the Irish theatre had
gained status and prestige in the academic world. American tours by the
Abbey in 1931 and 1938 found the children of those who had booed *The
Playboy* highly appreciative and obviously proud of the Irish contributions
to world theatre. But there were ominous signs of a decline of standards
at home. A young poet and a young university lecturer stood up in the
Abbey stalls one night during a production of *The Plough and the Stars* to
protest not against the play, but against the standards of production and
acting. It is noteworthy that the O'Casey play was no longer a political
issue, but an accepted classic in which the performers might expect the
vociferous criticism that Italians direct at opera singers. The idea was prev-

alent in Dublin that the Abbey, like Christmas, was not what it used to be. But, as Lennox Robinson succinctly replied, "It never was!"

During and after World War II, the national theatre produced several distinguished plays by M. J. Molloy,* Bryan MacMahon,* Louis D'Alton,* and Walter Macken.* While no masterpieces emerged, things were going reasonably well for the Abbey until the disastrous fire in 1951. Now the Abbey seemed to have met the fate that the sourest of its critics had foretold for it: it had expired beneath a mountain of rubble and black ashes.

The fifteen years which the company spent at the old Queen's Theatre on the south side of the Liffey were in the nature of a Babylonian Captivity. At times, it seemed that the work of half a century had gone for nothing. Nevertheless, there was some good work done under difficulties. Walter Macken's *Home Is the Hero* fulfilled the promise that he had shown in his earlier play, *Mungo's Mansion.* Louis D'Alton's satirical *This Other Eden* was a clever updating of the Irish question through an Englishman's eyes, which had been the subject of Bernard Shaw's *John Bull's Other Island* nearly half a century earlier. John McCann's* comedies, *Give Me a Bed of Roses* and *I Know Where I'm Going,* although making greater concessions to popular appeal than was customary in the past, helped to lessen the financial burden that had arisen from the transfer to the larger Queen's. M. J. Molloy, a Galway writer, who was closer in spirit to Synge and Colum than were most of his contemporaries, was particularly successful in his dramatic reconstructions of a vanished Ireland in *The King of Friday's Men, The Paddy Pedlar,* and *The Wood of the Whispering.* The dominant lyrical note gives his best work an authenticity ranking with that of the folk dramatists of the earlier period.

Most of the best plays written in Ireland since the 1950s, whether staged at the Abbey or elsewhere, conform to the Abbey pattern. Although not all of the plays of Molloy, Macken, John B. Keane,* Brendan Behan, Brian Friel,* Eugene McCabe,* Thomas Kilroy,* and Thomas Murphy* are set in kitchens, tenements, or prisons, all are written within a naturalistic framework while making use of somewhat non-naturalistic dialogue, often with poetic overtones. Just as O'Casey took the Abbey play into the tenement, Behan took it behind prison walls in *The Quare Fellow* and into the brothel in *The Hostage.* Brian Friel, who is one of the most technically accomplished, living Irish playwrights, shows us the country boy setting off for America in *Philadelphia, Here I Come!,* and the Irish countrywoman coming home from the states in *The Loves of Cass Maguire.*

In 1966, the Irish government gave the Abbey an excellently designed and splendidly equipped modern theatre on the old site. Some critics expressed the opinion that giving such a theatre to the Abbey was akin to putting a Christian Dior creation on a barefooted Connemara colleen. Since 1966, however, the company has visited Florence, Vienna, Brussels, Paris, Edinburgh, Frankfort, London, New York, Boston, Philadelphia, and

Washington. And for the first time ever, the Abbey has brought plays in Irish to the Aran Islands and the Irish-speaking districts in the West.

In the early 1900s, the Abbey Players won rave notices from critics such as Max Beerbohm, C. E. Montague, and A. B. Walkley. The players and plays were a new phenomenon in the theatre. Today, the Abbey Company, no longer a source of novelty, is the inheritor and upholder of a tradition that must be redefined and revivified for each succeeding generation of theatre-goers. The prowess of many of the earlier players has to be taken more or less on trust. Most playgoers of today can only recall the work of Sara Allgood, Arthur Sinclair, Maire O'Neill, and W. G. Fay after each had passed his zenith; what they can and do enjoy is the work of the present company, many of whom have not reached even the meridian of their careers. But they have already proved themselves not only in the native repertoire, but also in their interpretations of Chekhov, Brecht, and Sophocles. This turn in the tide of the Abbey's fortunes, under directors such as Tómas Mac Anna and Hugh Hunt, will come as a surprise to those who have heard allegations that the theatre was dead or dying. But the fabulous invalid has made a remarkable recovery in spite of some of the ailments which might have killed a younger and less hardy patient.

The Abbey's recent dependence on adaptations has been noted as indicative of a dearth of original plays. Although some new plays by Brian Friel, Thomas Murphy, and Thomas Kilroy are at least of the same high standard as many of the plays that kept the theatre going in earlier years, it would be unwise to claim that the last decade has seen a great upsurge of mature Irish playwriting, normally the high watermark of creativity in the theatre. The work produced in the Peacock, the Abbey's smaller experimental theatre, may, however, help shape the drama of the future.

Another ground for criticism has been the preponderance of revivals, but as the Broadway critic Walter Kerr recently asked, "What is a revival?" In the Abbey context, a revival is something brought back from the near-dead, like Boucicault's* *The Shaughraun* or *Arrah na Pogue*. The term should not be applied to plays from the Abbey repertoire that have proved successful decade after decade. These would include not only such unchallenged masterpieces as *The Playboy of the Western World* and *The Plough and the Stars*, but at least a score of other pieces that have earned a permanent place on the playbills of a national theatre.

MICHEÁL Ó hAODHA

WORKS: Some of the early Abbey plays were published in two series by Maunsel in Dublin. The first series of fifteen volumes included: J. M. Synge, *The Well of the Saints* (1905); Lady Gregory, *Kincora* (1905); Padraic Colum *The Land* (1905); W. B. Yeats, *The Hour-Glass, Cathleen Ni Houlihan, The Pot of Broth* (1905); W. B. Yeats, *The King's Threshold* (1905); W. B. Yeats, *On Baile's Strand* (1905); William Boyle, *The Building Fund* (1905); Lady Gregory, *The White Cockade* (1906?); Lady Gregory, *Spreading the News, The Rising of the Moon*, and Lady Gregory and Douglas

Hyde, *The Poorhouse* (1906); J. M. Synge, *The Playboy of the Western World* (1907); Thomas MacDonagh, *When the Dawn Is Come* (1908); Lennox Robinson, *The Cross Roads* (1909); Padraic Colum, *Thomas Muskerry* (1910); St. John G. Ervine, *Mixed Marriage* (1911). The plays in the second series were: Lady Gregory, *The Image* (1911); Lennox Robinson, *Patriots* (1912); Joseph Campbell, *Judgment* (1912); T. C. Murray, *Maurice Harte* (1912); Seumas O'Kelly, *The Bribe* (1912); George Fitzmaurice, *The Country Dressmaker* (1914); Edward McNulty, *The Lord Mayor* (1917); J. Bernard McCarthy, *Crusaders* (1918); Maurice Dalton, *Sable and Gold* (1922). In 1977, a New Abbey Theatre Series of plays began to appear, published by Proscenium Press of Newark, Delaware. Thus far, the New Series includes P. J. O'Connor, *Patrick Kavanagh's Tarry Flynn*; and W. J. White, *The Last Eleven* (1978).   REFERENCES: Blythe, Ernest. *The Abbey Theatre.* Dublin: National Theatre Society, Ltd., 1963; Boyd, Ernest A. *The Contemporary Drama of Ireland.* Dublin: Talbot, 1917/London: T. Fisher Unwin, 1918/Boston: Little Brown, 1928; Ellis-Fermor, Una. *The Irish Dramatic Movement.* London: Methuen, 1939/2d ed., 1954; Fay, Frank J. *Towards a National Theatre.* Robert Hogan, ed. Dublin: Dolmen, 1970; Fay, Gerard. *The Abbey Theatre, Cradle of Genius.* London: Hollis & Carter, 1958; Fay, W. G., & Carswell, Catherine. *The Fays of the Abbey Theatre.* London: Rich & Cowan, 1935/New York: Harcourt Brace, 1935; Flannery, James. *Miss Annie F. Horniman and the Abbey Theatre.* Dublin: Dolmen, 1970; French, Frances-Jane. *The Abbey Theatre Series of Plays.* Dublin: Dolmen, 1969. (Bibliography); Gregory, Lady Augusta. *Our Irish Theatre.* London & New York: Putnam's, 1913/2d ed., with added material, Gerrards Cross: Colin Smythe, 1970; Hogan, Robert. *After the Irish Renaissance.* Minneapolis: University of Minnesota Press, 1967/London: Macmillan, 1968; Hogan, Robert, & Kilroy, James. *The Irish Literary Theatre 1899-1901.* Vol. 1 of *The Modern Irish Drama.* Dublin: Dolmen, 1975; Hogan, Robert, & Kilroy, James. *Laying the Foundations 1902-1904.* Vol. 2 of *The Modern Irish Drama.* Dublin: Dolmen, 1976; Hogan, Robert, & Kilroy, James. *The Abbey Theatre: The Years of Synge 1905-1909.* Vol. 3 of *The Modern Irish Drama.* Dublin: Dolmen, 1978; Holloway, Joseph. *Joseph Holloway's Abbey Theatre.* Robert Hogan & Michael J. O'Neill, eds. Carbondale: Southern Illinois University Press, 1967; Holloway, Joseph. *Joseph Holloway's Irish Theatre.* Robert Hogan & Michael J. O'Neill, eds. 3 vols. Dixon, Calif.: Proscenium, 1968-1970; Kavanagh, Peter. *The Story of the Abbey Theatre.* New York: Devin-Adair, 1950; McCann, Sean, ed. *The Story of the Abbey.* London: New English Library, 1967; Mac Liammóir, Micheál. *Theatre in Ireland.* 2d ed., with added material. Dublin: Cultural Relations Committee of Ireland, 1964; MacNamara, Brinsley. *Abbey Plays, 1899-1948.* Dublin: At the Sign of the Three Candles, 1949; Malone, Andrew E. *The Irish Drama.* London: Constable/New York: Scribner's, 1929/New York: Benjamin Blom, 1974; Nic Shiubhlaigh, Maire, & Kenny, Edward. *The Splendid Years.* Dublin: James Duffy, 1955; O'Connor, Frank. *My Father's Son.* London: Macmillan, 1968; Ó hAodha, Micheál. *Theatre in Ireland.* Totowa, N.J.: Rowman & Littlefield, 1975; Robinson, Lennox. *Ireland's Abbey Theatre.* London: Sidgwick & Jackson, 1951/Port Washington, N.Y.: Kennikat, 1968; Robinson, Lennox, ed. *The Irish Theatre.* London: Macmillan, 1939/New York: Haskell House, 1971; Weygandt, Cornelius. *Irish Plays and Playwrights.* London: Constable/Boston & New York: Houghton Mifflin, 1913/Port Washington, N.Y.: Kennikat, 1966; Yeats, W. B., ed. *Beltaine.* London: Frank Cass, 1970; Yeats, W. B., ed. *Samhain.* London: Frank Cass, 1970.

AE (1867-1935), poet, painter, economist, and editor. AE is the pseudonym of George William Russell, who was a pivotal figure in the Irish Revival. His pen name was adopted from a proofreader's query, "AE—?" about an earlier pseudonym "Aeon," suggesting mankind's age-old, mysterious quest, his constant theme.

Born on April 10, 1867, in Lurgan, County Armagh, Russell moved to Dublin in 1878. At the Metropolitan School of Art, he met W. B. Yeats* and the theosophist Charles Johnston, both of whom confirmed his bent toward mystical speculation and identification with Ireland's spiritual mission. Yeats, a close associate for fifteen years, later became increasingly distant. Dublin's Theosophical Society and the Hermetic Society, however, gave Russell the first forum for his beliefs. From 1891 to 1897, he lived at the Theosophical Household with fellow believers, among them Violet North, whom he married in 1898. The Household's regimen included asceticism, meditation, and study of esoteric philosophy.

Meanwhile, he left a job with a local draper to work for the Irish Agricultural Organization Society, a cooperative sponsored by Sir Horace Plunkett, who also supported two influential journals which AE edited, *The Irish Homestead* (1905-1923) and *The Irish Statesman** (September 15, 1923-April 12, 1930). Journalism and travel through Ireland for the Society did not interfere with AE's steady outpouring of verse, constant activity as a painter, or his role as spokesman for the conscience of Ireland.

With publication of *Homeward: Songs by the Way* in 1894, AE was hailed as a poet equal to Yeats, an opinion soon revised as Yeats continued to develop and AE did not. *The Earth Breath and Other Poems* (1897) and *The Divine Vision and Other Poems* (1904) preceded his *Collected Poems* (1913), which underwent successive editions and enlargements. *Gods of War* (1915) was followed by four volumes published by Macmillan: *Voices of the Stones* (1925), *Vale and Other Poems* (1931), *The House of the Titans and Other Poems* (1934), and *Selected Poems* (1935).

AE's poetry is predominantly visionary. Trusting his intuitions and eschewing the meticulous craftmanship of Yeats, he was too often content with vague symbols, cloudy metaphors, and misty colors. These faults are found also in his painting and sometimes in his prose. *The Candle of Vision* (1918) and *Song and Its Fountains* (1932) present his beliefs.

Welcome exceptions to the prevailing monotony can be found. The metallic clarity of some lines suggests Yeats—for example: "The golden heresy of truth," "We are men by anguish taught," or "The Greece of Pericles is cold." Some poems echo folk themes; the most direct confront the tragedies of war. More surprising is the sly humor, a feature of his famed conversational ability. It emerges in the parodies printed in *Secret Springs of Dublin Song* (1918), written by several unnamed authors. AE's "S. O'. S" (Seumas O'Sullivan*) can be seen as self-mockery in its caricature of the Celtic Twilight. It opens with the line "Child, there are mists in my mind."

AE was active in the Irish Literary Society and in the early stirrings of the theatre. In 1902, his drama on the lengendary Deirdre was acclaimed as an evocation of Irish ideals. His delight in discovering new talent was exemplified by his edition of *New Songs* (1904) with works by Padraic Colum,* Seumas O'Sullivan, Eva Gore-Booth,* Thomas Keohler (1874-1942), Alice Milligan,* Susan Mitchell,* George Roberts (1873-1953), and Ella Young.*

To an unusual degree, Russell was both dreamer and planner, but when he spoke of the political upheavals of the time he was ignored, at great cost to Ireland. Speaking out with surprising force, he attacked "The Masters of Dublin" for their Lockout of 1913, which reduced thousands to abject poverty. In "Salutation," he celebrated the leaders of the 1916 Easter Rising. He scorned Ulster for its intransigence and attempted to conciliate England by serving briefly in the fruitless Convention of 1917-1918. He opposed the anti-Treaty Republicans but retired from politics by refusing in 1922 to become a member of the Irish Free State Senate, in which Yeats and Oliver Gogarty* served.

Much of AE's prose was ephemeral, but *The National Being* (1916) and two prose fantasies, *The Interpreters* (1922) and *The Avatars: A Futurist Fantasy* (1933), represent his thought, as does Monk Gibbon's* selection of prose, *The Living Torch* (1937) and Alan Denson's *Letters from AE* (1961).

Disillusioned by the decline of Irish culture and bereaved by the loss of his wife, AE retired to England in 1933. He had lectured in the United States in 1928 and 1930; a final trip, to advise Roosevelt's secretary of agriculture, Henry A. Wallace, was cut short by fatal illness. He died at Bournemouth, England, on July 17, 1935.

At the zenith of his career, he was widely loved and regarded as a seer. Now he is an almost forgotten figure in the Irish scene, upstaged by Yeats, Joyce,* Synge,* and others. His facile talent achieved versatility at the expense of artistic perfection. Only a handful of poems and a cluster of anecdotes remain, but his historical importance is becoming more widely recognized.

                                        RICHARD M. KAIN

WORKS: *Homeward Songs by the Way*. Dublin: Whaley, 1894; *The Earth Breath and Other Poems*. New York & London: John Lane, 1896; *The Nuts of Knowledge*. Dundrum: Dun Emer, 1903; *The Mask of Apollo and Other Stories*. London & New York: Macmillan, 1903; *The Divine Vision and Other Poems*. London & New York: Macmillan, 1904; *Some Irish Essays*. Dublin: Maunsel, 1906; *By Still Waters*. Dundrum: Dun Emer, 1906; *Deirdre*. Dublin: Maunsel, 1907; *Collected Poems*. London: Macmillan, 1913; *Gods of War, with Other Poems*. Dublin: Privately printed, 1915; *Imaginations and Reveries*. Dublin & London: Maunsel, 1915; *The National Being*. Dublin & London: Maunsel, 1916; *The Candle of Vision*. London: Macmillan, 1918; *The Interpreters*. London: Macmillan, 1922; *Voices of the Stones*. London: Macmillan, 1925; *Midsummer Eve*. New York: Crosby Gaige, 1928; *Enchantment and Other Poems*. New York: Fountain/London: Macmillan, 1930; *Vale and Other Poems*. London: Macmillan, 1931; *Song and Its Fountains*. London: Macmillan, 1932; *The Avatars*. London: Macmillan, 1933; *The House of Titans and Other Poems*. London:

Macmillan, 1934; *Selected Poems.* London: Macmillan, 1935; *Some Passages from the Letters of AE to W. B. Yeats.* Dublin: Cuala, 1936; *The Living Torch.* Monk Gibbon, ed. London: Macmillan, 1937; *Letters from AE.* Alan Denson, ed. London: Abelard-Schuman, 1961. A collected edition is being published jointly by Colin Smythe in England and Humanities Press in the United States. Thus far, the first part has appeared: *Selections from the Contributions to The Irish Homestead,* Henry Summerfield, ed. 2 vols. Gerrard's Cross: Colin Smythe; Atlantic Highlands, N.J.: Humanities Press, 1978. REFERENCES: Davis, Robert B. *George William Russell ("AE").* Boston: Twayne, 1977; Denson, Alan. *Printed Writings of George W. Russell (AE): A Bibliography.* Evanston, Ill.: Northwestern University Press, 1961; Eglinton, John (W. K. Magee). *A Memoir of A. E.* London: Macmillan, 1937; Figgis, Darrell. *AE (George W. Russell): A Study of a Man and a Nation.* Dublin & London: Maunsel, 1916/Port Washington, N.Y.: Kennikat, 1970; Howarth, Herbert. *The Irish Writers 1880-1940.* London: Rockliff, 1958; Kain, Richard M., & O'Brien, James H. *George Russell (A.E.).* Lewisburg, Pa.: Bucknell University Press, 1976; Summerfield, Henry. *That Myriad-Minded Man: A Biography of G. W. Russell—"A. E."* Totowa, N.J.: Rowman & Littlefield, 1975.

ALLEN, ALFRED (1925-), poet and farmer. Allen was born on January 24, 1925, at Clashenure House, Ovens, County Cork, where he still lives and farms. As a farmer, he has been generally outside the literary milieu and so has formed his style largely by his own reading and study. Consequently, among poets writing in Ireland today he probably is most committed to traditional form. He is capable of considerable awkwardness, but his rigid adherence to form gives some of his work strength and memorableness scarcely paralleled in the more sophisticated and much better known work of his contemporaries Thomas Kinsella* and John Montague.* Allen seems a kind of masculine Emily Dickinson. His poetic vision is a direct pondering on the small physical world that immediately surrounds him, or a personal reduction of the larger issues that he has read about in the world outside. The couplets of his first short collection, *Clashenure Skyline,* are a somewhat incongruous form for his subject, but they are a form, and he frequently uses them with considerable effect. His second and longer collection, *Interrogations,* is more miscellaneous than the cohering evocations of his own countryside in *Clashenure Skyline,* but it is also better work. The pieces in *Interrogations* range from those of personal emotion and common sense comment to a series of literary character studies of figures from the Trojan War. In time, Allen could develop into an extraordinary poet; he is already a more individual one than most of those who have appeared in the 1970s.

WORKS: *Clashenure Skyline.* Dublin: Dolmen, 1970; *Interrogations.* Cork: Tower Books, [1975].

ALLINGHAM, WILLIAM (1824-1889), poet. Because his diary and letters are valuable sources of information about Tennyson, Browning, and other English writers of the Victorian period, Allingham is mentioned regularly in English literary history. But as a poet, and specifically as an Irish poet, he deserves recognition on his own.

Allingham was born on March 19, 1824, in Ballyshannon, County Donegal. Although a member of the Ascendancy or Anglo-Irish ruling class, he knew and sympathized with the peasants. He worked as a customs official most of his adult life before turning to a career as a writer and editor. He died in Hampstead, England, on November 18, 1889.

He was a close friend of many literary men, and he dedicated his first book, *Poems* (1850), to Leigh Hunt. Later, as editor of *Fraser's* Magazine, he was in the center of London's most lively literary set; his intimate friends included Tennyson, Browning, Carlyle, and Dante Gabriel Rossetti. Although his diary is most often consulted for information on such celebrities, it has artistic merit of its own, for his perceptions were keen and his accounts reveal a sympathetic nature. Unlike many literary observers of great men, he was always willing to assert his own convictions; and the diaries contain a number of vehement disagreements with such friends, particularly on the matter of English policies toward Ireland. He was consistent and vocal in his anti-imperialist persuasions, although not quite an Irish nationalist. Although Yeats* praised him as "The Poet of Ballyshannon,' he is no spokesman for Irish patriotism, as comparison with his contemporary James Clarence Mangan* would prove.

Nevertheless, Allingham knew the Irish people and wrote accurately about them. It is this sympathy with the lower classes and the precision of his descriptions of village and countryside that give substance to his poetry. He also developed an unusual knowledge of folk literature, including ballads; his collection *The Ballad Book* (1864) reveals both his mastery of the form and his lively humor and imagination.

In the best of his poems, the long narrative entitled *Lawrence Bloomfield in Ireland* (1864), Allingham reveals a depth of understanding of contemporary political issues, along with rare skills of description. Its subject is the conflict between landlords and tenants over control of the land, including specific consideration of the tactic of evictions. It is long, possibly too long, but the scope allows the poet to range widely in his comments. There even are nice bits of satire. His descriptions of landlords and tenants are thorough and fair, and his affection for the land is palpable. This is Allingham's most convincingly Irish poem, in that he shows himself to be clearly allied with the peasants in their struggle for the land.

In later poems, he resembles his friend Tennyson in his attempts at long narratives, domestic romances, and even an historical drama, *Ashby Manor* (1883). However, these efforts are less successful, tending towards prettiness and sentimentality. He was more fanciful, and more sensitive to nature and to subtle human impulses than were his Irish contemporary poets, but in most of his poems he lacked passion or conviction. At his best, in

Lawrence Bloomfield, his political and social sympathies and his keen poetic skills combined to achieve real artistry.

JAMES KILROY

WORKS: *Poems.* London: Chapman & Hall, 1850; *Day and Night Songs.* London: Routledge, 1854; *Peace and War.* London: Routledge, 1854; *The Music Master.* London: Routledge, 1855; *Laurence Bloomfield in Ireland.* London: Macmillan, 1864/ reprint, New York: AMS, 1972; *Fifty Modern Poems.* London: Bell & Daldy, 1865; *In Fairyland. A Series of Pictures by Richard Doyle with a Poem by William Allingham.* London: Longmans, Green, 1870; *Songs, Ballads and Stories.* London: Bell, 1877; *Evil May-Day.* London: Stott, 1882. (Poetry); *Ashby Manor.* Oxford: Stott, 1882. (Drama); *The Fairies.* London: De La Rue, 1883. (Poetry); *Blackberries.* London: Philip, 1884. (Poetry); *Rhymes for the Young Folk.* London: Cassell, 1887; *Irish Songs and Poems.* London: Reeves & Turner, 1887; *Flower Pieces and Other Poems.* London: Reeves & Turner, 1888; *Life and Phantasy.* London: Reeves & Turner, 1889. (Poetry); *Thought and Word, and Ashby Manor.* London: Reeves & Turner, 1890; *Laurence Bloomfield in Ireland.* Revised, London: Reeves & Turner, 1890; *Blackberries.* Revised. London: Reeves & Turner, 1890; *Varieties in Prose.* London: Longmans, Green, 1893. (Collected prose); *Sixteen Poems,* selected by William Butler Yeats. Dundrum: Dun Emer, 1905; *By the Way: Verses, Fragments, and Notes.* Helen Allingham, ed. London: Longmans, Green, 1912; *Poems,* selected & arranged by Helen Allingham. London: Macmillan, 1912; *The Poems of William Allingham.* John Hewitt, ed. Dublin: Dolmen, 1967; *William Allingham: A Diary.* Helen Allingham & Dollie Radford, eds. London: Macmillan, 1907/revised ed. by Geoffrey Grigson, London: Centaur, 1967.   REFERENCES: Allingham, Helen, & Williams, E. Baumer, eds. *Letters to William Allingham.* London: Longmans, 1911; Hill, George Birkbeck, ed. *Letters of Dante Gabriel Rossetti to William Allingham, 1854-1870.* London: Fisher Unwin, 1897; O'Hegarty, Patrick S. *A Bibliography of William Allingham.* Dublin: Privately printed by Thom, 1945. Reprinted from *The Dublin Magazine* of January-March and July-September 1945; Warner, Alan. *William Allingham: An Introduction.* Dublin: Dolmen, 1971; Warner, Alan. *William Allingham.* Lewisburg, Pa.: Bucknell University Press, 1975. Warner, Alan. "William Allingham: Bibliographical Survey." *Irish BookLore* 2 (1976): 303-307.

ARMSTRONG, GEORGE FRANCIS SAVAGE. *See* SAVAGE-ARMSTRONG, GEORGE FRANCIS.

ATKINSON, SARA (1823-1893), writer on religious and historical subjects. Atkinson was born Sara Gaynor in Athlone on October 13, 1823. She married George Atkinson, part-owner of *The Freeman's Journal.* According to such friends as Katharine Tynan* and Rosa Mulholland,* she was a sweet and pious lady much given to charitable good works. She died in Dublin on July 8, 1893.

Atkinson's life of Mary Aikenhead contains much out-of-the-way information about the Penal days and was commended by W.E.H. Lecky.* Her posthumous *Essays* contain lives of O'Curry, John Hogan, and John Henry Foley, as well as of St. Brigid, St. Fursey, and Dervorgilla. Today, however, her works probably are read only for their subject matter.

WORKS: *Mary Aikenhead,* by S. A. Dublin: Gill, 1875/2d ed., revised, 1882; *Essays,* with a memoir by Rosa Mulholland Gilbert. Dublin: Gill, 1895.

BANIM, JOHN (1798-1842) and **BANIM, MICHAEL** (1796-1874),
novelists. Born in Kilkenny on April 3, 1798, John Banim was the guiding
force in shaping the O'Hara stories, a project completed with the close cooperation of his older brother Michael, who was born in Kilkenny on
August 5, 1796. The brothers were given good educations by their father,
a prosperous farmer and merchant, and very early their different temperaments received special training. Michael, the more pragmatic, at first read
for the bar, but later was forced to go into business to cover his father's
losses; John, the more artistic, was sent in 1813 to Dublin, where he studied
drawing at the Academy of the Royal Dublin Society. After returning to
Kilkenny, John taught drawing and fell deeply in love. This brief but romantic attachment, cut short by the girl's death, was the turning point in his
career, for he began to devote himself to literature.

After a long poem, "The Celt's Paradise" (February 1821), in which he
drew upon his early familiarity with Irish mythology, John wrote an unsuccessful drama, *Turgesius,* and the successful *Damon and Pythias.* The
latter was performed at Covent Garden on May 28, 1821, with Charles
Kemble and William Charles Macready in the chief roles. After several
unsuccessful tragedies drawing on non-Irish material, John suggested to his
brother that they collaborate on a series of Irish tales in the style of Sir
Walter Scott.

During the following decade, John and Michael, as the O'Hara Brothers,
created the novels that earned John the title the Scott of Ireland. But success was bittersweet for both brothers. John, who had married in 1822,
suffered from a progressive spinal disease that made him a cripple by 1829
and caused his death on August 13, 1842. Meanwhile, Michael, who had
been a prosperous trader, lost his fortune in 1840-1841 through the failure
of a merchant. Thereafter, he suffered delicate health while acting as post-
master for Kilkenny. He died in Booterstown on August 30, 1874, almost
thirty-five years after his brother.

In their attempt in the 1820s to create a distinctive Anglo-Irish literature
that would find a wide audience in England, John and Michael sought to
make the Irish character sympathetic without falsifying it by excessive
sentimentality. In their twenty-four volumes, they portrayed Irish cabin
life as a mixture of rich humor and lawlessness often verging on violence
and even brutality. Although their writing occasionally is marred by an
attempt to capture Irish speech in outlandishly garbled phonetic transcriptions and by catering to the English audience's desire for supernatural
thrills, they present a portrait of Irish life that is historical in scope and
realistic in depth. The mature works of the O'Hara Brothers readily fall
into three categories. First are novels that deal with life in the cabin supposedly as it was at the time. *The Nowlans* (1826), *The Mayor of Wind-
Gap* (1835), and *Father Connell* (1842) are among the most realistic and
best written of these novels. In each of the novels in this category, the

brothers take pains to place the characters in a world that is carefully and fully (sometimes too fully) detailed. Hence, the stories are sharp vignettes of pre-Famine cabin life merged into the Banims' melodramatic treatment of murder, betrayal, seduction, and the like. Second are a large number of works that attempt to join realism and otherworldliness. These novels— among them *Crohoore of the Billhook* (1825), *The Fetches* (1825), and *The Ghost Hunter and His Family* (1831)—seek to bring what the Banims conceived of as Irish otherworldliness and folklore into the framework of English realism. The resulting hybrid satisfies neither component, though this kind of fusion fascinated many readers. Third, and perhaps most significant, are the Banims' historical novels—*The Boyne Water* (1826), *The Croppy* (1828), and *The Denounced* (1830). In these novels, the brothers analyze the crucial historical events that had shaped Ireland as they understood it—the Williamite Wars, the Penal Age, and the Rebellion of 1798. Seeking in these events the causes for Ireland's problems in the 1820s, they wrote with maturity and insight.

While today largely forgotten, John and Michael Banim share an important niche in the development of the Anglo-Irish novel. Coming between Maria Edgeworth* and William Carleton,* they helped the Irish novel evolve from its focus on the Big House to an emphasis on the "mere Irish." They imitated Scott but had neither his richness of style nor his depth of insight. Nevertheless, in their limited way they helped to prepare the audience for Griffin* and Carleton, and began to give English readers a faithful picture of cabin life.

MARK D. HAWTHORNE

WORKS—by John Banim: "The Celt's Paradise." London: John Warren, 1821. (Poem); *Damon and Pythias*. London: John Warren, 1821. (Tragedy in five acts); *Revelations of the Dead Alive*. London: J. Simpkin & R. Marshall, 1824; *The Sergeant's Wife*. London: T. H. Lacy, [1824]. (Drama in two acts); *The Fetches*. London: Simpkin & Marshall, 1825. Vol. 2 of *Tales by the O'Hara Family; The Nowlans*. London: Colburn: 1826. Vols. 1 & 2 of *Tales by the O'Hara Family*. 2d Series; *The Anglo Irish of the XIXth Century*. 3 vols. London: Colburn, 1828; *The Denounced*. 3 vols. London: Colburn & Bentley, 1830; *The Smuggler*. 3 vols. London: Colburn & Bentley, 1831. by Michael Banim: *Crohoore of the Bill-Hook*. London: Simpkin & Marshall, 1825. Vol. 1 & part of Vol. 2 of *Tales by the O'Hara Family; The Croppy*. London: Colburn, 1828; *The Ghost-Hunter and His Family*. London: Smith, Elder, 1833; *The Mayor of Windgap*. 3 vols. London: Saunders & Otley, 1835; *The Town of the Cascade*. 2 vols. London: Chapman & Hall, 1864. by John and Michael in collaboration: *John Doe*. London: Simpkin & Marshall, 1825. Vol. 3 of *Tales by the O'Hara Family; Peter of the Castle*. London: Colburn, 1826. Vol. 3 of *Tales by the O'Hara Family*. 2d Series; *The Bit o' Writing and Other Tales*. 3 vols. London: Saunders & Otley, 1838; *Father Connell*. 3 vols. London: Newby & Boone, 1842. There is no full or scholarly edition of the Banims' novels, nor is there any definitive study of the attribution. The fullest collection is *The Works of the O'Hara Family*, collected by Michael Banim (New York: D. & J. Sadlier, 1869).   REFERENCES: The most complete biography is Patrick Joseph Murray's *The Life of John Banim* in the tenth and last volume of this collection. Consult also: Flanagan, Thomas. *The Irish Novelists, 1800-1850*.

New York: Columbia University Press, 1959; Hawthorne, Mark D. *John and Michael Banim (the "O'Hara Brothers")*. Salzburg, Austria: Institut für Englishche Sprache und Literatur, 1975.

BANVILLE, JOHN (1945-), novelist. Banville, born in Wexford on December 8, 1945, was educated at the Christian Brothers school and at St. Peter's College in Wexford. He is married and lives in Howth on the north point of Dublin Bay. He works as a copy editor on a daily newspaper, *The Irish Press*, and writes a regular book column for *Hibernia*, the weekly current affairs magazine. He has published a number of short stories in literary magazines as well as four novels.

His first novel was *Long Lankin* (1970). Long Lankin was a murderer in an old song who killed a woman and her child in the belief that a leper could heal himself by spilling innocent blood into a silver cup. Banville relates this theme to modern Ireland. Part one of the book consists of nine brief episodes, each of which might be read as a short story, showing their separate characters caught in the hell of a peculiar guilt. In part two, Mrs. Livia Gold, who punishes herself for the death of her small son, holds a very Irish party. To this party come characters from the previous episodes, including Ben White, a writer, and his sister Flora. White has incestuous feelings for Flora. Their make-believe world has maimed them both, rendering it impossible for them to act without being bruised by reality. White is a catalyst for the other characters, each of whom—in the midst of the drunkenness, the music, the violence, and the vomit—is seeking to be cleansed. Salvation's consolation prize is freedom.

Banville's theme is ambitious, and he handles it well, selecting an unusual form for the novel and an individual tone. The writing is quick, nervous and poetic with a rich and apt vocabulary. The book was praised widely and marked the debut of a major talent.

Banville's second novel, *Birchwood* (1973), concerns the large estate of the Godkin family, in rural Ireland during the middle of the nineteenth century. That period of famine and agrarian unrest witnesses the ruin and decay of the once prosperous property.

The novel takes the form of a first-person narrative. Gabriel Godkin, the last son of the house and the product of a misalliance between brother and sister, tells the story of the Godkins from memory, hindsight, and guesswork. This method allows Banville to tease the diligent reader with hints, clues, and allusions, and to give the work the tension of a good detective story.

The book has many Gothic elements—love, incest, madness, snobbery, pride, and greed; violence and sudden death. But the author suspends the reader's disbelief with writing that is always elegant and exact, and he manages to wring from his material many moments of pain, truth, and beauty. Some minor anachronisms and a certain insecurity of place and period do not mar the novel's considerable achievement. In 1973, *Birchwood* won the prestigious Allied Irish Banks Award, which is administered by the Irish Academy of Letters.

At the end of *Long Lankin*, Ben White says that, maybe, he will go back to Greece: "I have to find somewhere to belong. . . . I think I might write a book . . . tell a story about the stars. . . ." *Nightspawn* (1971) finds him living alone on an Aegean island, wanting to "write a little book" but, in his freedom, suffering from a morbid fear of open spaces and public places. His private world is invaded by a number of comic but sinister and impressive characters, who seem to be refugees from some bad suspense movie. White's aid is enlisted to overthrow the colonels' government; there is a plot concerning a vital hieroglyph.

The book contains a great deal of blood, violence, and vomit, but all the same it aims at profundity. It is narrated by White with strength and beauty. While the novel makes no specific identification of the author with the narrator, there are intriguing parallels. The narrator is "a man who loves words" and enjoys word games. Early in the book, White says: "Look, it was not I who arranged this particular farce, so do not blame me if the leading players are hams, the script unspeakably banal, the whole shebang played out years ago—personally, I despise such trappings." At the book's end, the narrator delivers this testimony: "I love words, and I hate death. Beyond this, nothing." The last words of the book are "Chapter One. My story begins at a—"

Nightspawn earned wide acclaim, especially for its use of language, a quality also apparent in *Doctor Copernicus* (1976). This novel tells the life story of Nicholas Koppernigk, or Copernicus, and is a powerful and compelling book which has been researched with meticulous care. Through its passion and concern, the book manages to make the man Copernicus meaningful for the reader in his time, place, and preoccupations.

Copernicus, a star-gazing priest who succumbed to the flesh, had scruples about publishing his revolutionary theory. He is implicated, for the most part against his will, in wars, plots, and intrigues. He achieves an ordered inner life only at enormous cost to himself.

Unlike most historical novels, *Doctor Copernicus* has no cardboard characters; the people who surround Copernicus, impinging and demanding, are brought to palpable life. Some elements in Banville's imaginative evocation—the priest's mistress Anna and a homosexual relationship—would have given the book greater popular appeal had they been treated more luridly. That Banville eschewed such trappings is admirable. *Doctor Copernicus* demanded much of its writer; it demands much of its readers as well, but the effort is amply repaid. Were Ben White to write his "story about the Stars" he would be lucky, indeed, to manage so fine an achievement as this book.

John Banville is among the most exciting of the younger Irish writers.

In addition to the Allied Irish Banks Prize, he was awarded the Irish-American Foundation Literary Award in 1967 and a Macaulay Fellowship by the Irish Arts Council in 1973.

JAMES DOUGLAS

WORKS: *Long Lankin*. London: Secker & Warburg, 1970; *Nightspawn*. London: Secker & Warburg, 1971; *Birchwood*. London: Secker & Warburg, 1973; *Doctor Copernicus*. London: Secker & Warburg, 1976.

BARDWELL, LELAND (ca. 1930-), poet and novelist. Bardwell was born in India of Irish parents, but grew up in Leixlip, County Kildare, and was educated in Dublin. She has published a volume of verse, *The Mad Cyclist*, and a novel, *Girl on a Bicycle*, and is one of the editors of the literary magazine *Cyphers*. Her poems tend to be flip and formless and sometimes lively. Her novel is sparely written and concretely observed. Its plot—mainly a succession of fornications, drinking bouts, and subsequent vomitings—does not, however, so much conclude as simply stop. Thus far, Bardwell's work, in both verse and prose, exhibits a lively talent, a clear eye, and an untutored judgment.

WORKS: *The Mad Cyclist*. Dublin: New Writers', 1970; *Girl on a Bicycle*. Dublin: Co-op Books, 1977.

BARLOW, JANE (1857-1917), poet and novelist. Barlow was born at Clontarf, County Dublin, in 1857, and lived most of her life at Raheny. Her father was the Reverend J. W. Barlow, later vice-provost of Trinity College. She published much fugitive prose and verse before the appearance of her very popular *Bog-Land Studies* in 1892. This volume contains a series of narrative poems in dialect, often with a strong melodramatic or pathetic story. The meter is obtrusive enough to charm the popular ear, and the dialogue has more "mushas, bedads, begorrahs and whishts" than ever occurred in the speech of even the quaintest peasant. Her prose fiction also deals with peasant life, but the style ranges uneasily from the rather stagey dialect to a stilted formality. She lacked the fine humor or redoubtable talents of Maria Edgeworth* or Somerville and Ross*, and her once popular work is now little read. She died in Bray on April 17, 1917.

WORKS: *History of a World of Immortals without God: Translated from an Unpublished Manuscript in the Library of a Continental University, by Antares Skorpios* [pseud]. Dublin: William McGee; London: Simpkin, Marshall, 1891; *Bog-Land Studies*. London: Unwin, 1892. 2d ed., enlarged, London: Hodder & Stoughton, 1893. (Verse); *Irish Idylls*. London: Hodder & Stoughton, 1892; *The Land of Elfintown*. London: Macmillan, 1894. (Verse); *Kerrigan's Quality*. London: Hodder & Stoughton, New York: Dodd, Mead, 1894; *Maureen's Fairing, and Other Stories*. London: Dent, New York: Macmillan, 1895; *Strangers at Lisconnel, a Second Series of Irish Idylls*. London: Hodder & Stoughton/New York: Dodd, Mead, 1895; *Mrs. Martin's Company, and Other Stories*. London: J. M. Dent, 1896; *A Creel of Irish Stories*. London: Methuen, 1897/New York: Dodd, Mead, 1898; *From the East unto the West*. London:

Methuen, 1898. (Tales); *From the Land of the Shamrock*. New York: Dodd, Mead, 1900/London: Methuen, 1901; *Ghost-Bereft*. [London]: Smith, Elder, 1901. (Stories in verse); *At the Back of Beyond*. New York: Dodd, Mead, 1902; *The Founding of Fortunes*. London: Methuen, 1902; *By Beach and Bog-Land*. London: Unwin, 1905. (Stories); *Irish Neighbours*. London: Hutchinson, 1907; *The Mockers and Other Verses*. London: G. Allen, 1908; *Irish Ways*. London: G. Allen, 1909; *Flaws*. London: Hutchinson, 1911. (Novel); *Mac's Adventures*. London: Hutchinson, 1911. (Stories); *Doings and Dealings*. London: Hutchinson, 1913; *Between Doubting and Daring*. Oxford: B. H. Blackwell, 1916. (Verses); *In Mio's Youth*. London: Hutchinson, 1917.

BARRINGTON, SIR JONAH (ca. 1760-1834), memoirist and politician. Barrington was born at Knapton, near Abbeyleix, Queen's County, probably in 1760. He was educated at Trinity College, Dublin, admitted to the bar in 1788, and served in the Irish Parliament from 1790 until its dissolution by the Act of Union in 1800. Although he voted against the Act of Union, he was by no means a simple nationalist. He was appointed judge of the Admiralty Court in 1798 and knighted in 1807. To escape his creditors, he removed to France in about 1815, although he retained his office and emoluments. However, after it was discovered that he had misappropriated court funds, he was deprived of office in 1830.

Barrington's histories and memoirs are of great value to the political and social historian, and his three-volume *Personal Sketches* are a considerable charm and delight to the general reader. The Ireland he portrays is an intriguing mixture of civilization and barbarism, a world of raucous pranks, heavy drinking, hardy fighting (he had fought his duels, including an amusing one with Leonard McNally*), political intrigue, and tolerance for loutishness as well as appreciation of wit and good address. Barrington has given us some vivid sketches of important personalities of his time, such as John Philpot Curran, Wolfe Tone, and the immortal word-garbler Sir Boyle Roche. Since his complete *Sketches* suffer from excessive length, he is probably best read in the modern abridgment by Hugh B. Staples. He died in Versailles on April 8, 1834.

WORKS: *Personal Sketches of his own Times*. 3 vols. London: Henry Colburn, & H. Colburn & R. Bentley, 1827-1832; *Historic Memoirs of Ireland*. 2 vols. London: R. Bentley for H. Colburn, 1833; *Rise and Fall of the Irish Nation*. Paris: G. G. Bennis, 1833; *The Ireland of Sir Jonah Barrington, Selections from His Personal Sketches*. Hugh B. Staples, ed. Seattle & London: University of Washington Press, 1967.

BARRINGTON, MARGARET (ca. 1895-?), novelist. Barrington was the daughter of Richard Barrington of the Royal Irish Constabulary. She married Edmund Curtis*, the historian, in 1918, but the marriage was dissolved. In 1926, she married Liam O'Flaherty* from whom she separated in 1932, after having one child. Barrington published a number of fugitive sketches and stories as well as a novel, *My Cousin Justin* (1939). Basically about a love triangle, the novel is not particularly successful in its modern scenes, especially those set in London. However, the initial section about a rural childhood is beautifully evoked.

WORK: *My Cousin Justin*. London: Jonathan Cape, 1939.

BECKETT, SAMUEL (1906-), novelist, playwright, and winner of the Nobel Prize for Literature. Beckett is one of today's most influential avant garde writers. After he won the Nobel Prize for Literature in 1969, he also became one of the few extremely well-known experimental writers.

He was born Samuel Barclay Beckett on April 13 or May 13, 1906, in Foxrock, a fashionable southern suburb of Dublin, into a prosperous Protestant family. From 1920 to 1923, he attended Portora Royal School in Enniskillen, County Fermanagh, as had Oscar Wilde* before him. In October 1923, he entered Trinity College, Dublin. After a lackluster beginning, he distinguished himself in modern languages and received his B.A. in 1927. In 1928, he taught French for nine months at Campbell College in Belfast, and then for two years (1929-1930), he served as *lecteur* at the École Normale Supérieure in Paris.

While in Paris, he met his lifelong friend, the poet and art critic Thomas McGreevy,* who introduced him to the English novelist Richard Aldington and, more importantly, to James Joyce.* Joyce's later work was undoubtedly the single greatest literary influence on Beckett. He was not, as has sometimes been said, Joyce's paid secretary, but, as he himself has said, "like all his friends, I helped him. He was greatly handicapped because of his eyes. I did odd jobs for him, marking passages for him or reading to him, but I never wrote any of his letters." For some time, Beckett was closely involved with Joyce and his family, and he contributed the first essay in the collection of Joycean apologetics, *Our Exagmination Round His Factification for Incamination of Work in Progress*. He also published in the magazine *transition*. His first separately printed piece, the poem *Whoroscope*, appeared in 1930 and was followed in 1931 by his short critical book *Proust*.

In the fall of 1930, Beckett returned to Dublin to serve as a lecturer in French at Trinity College. McGreevy introduced him to Jack B. Yeats* whom he came to admire and revere, but in general Beckett's sojourns in Dublin, at this time and later, were such unhappy experiences that they made him acutely, physically ill; his demanding mother was apparently much to blame. In December 1931, he received his M.A., and, after fleeing to the Continent, he resigned his lectureship.

Beckett's next twenty years were years of great difficulty for him. He lived in Paris, intermittently in London, and was often drawn back to Dublin by the demands of his family. He suffered a remarkable variety of physical ailments, many of them apparently psychosomatic and brought on by his having to return to Ireland from time to time.

In 1932, Beckett wrote a still unpublished novel called *Dream of Fair to Middling Women*, and in 1934 he published a collection of stories called *More Pricks than Kicks*. His later novel, *Murphy*, was finally accepted after more than forty publishers had rejected it, and appeared in 1938 to relatively little notice.

During World War II, Beckett was active in the French Resistance in Paris. In the fall of 1942, he was forced to flee from the Germans to Roussillon, a village in southeast France. There he remained until 1945, managing in the interim to write his novel *Watt*. After the war, in 1945, he received the Croix de Guerre for his work in the Resistance.

It is not until after the war that Beckett, now back in Paris, entered upon his most productive period. *Molloy*, which is perhaps his best novel, was begun in September 1947 and was finished in January 1948; like most of his best work, it was written in French. It was followed in 1948 by a kind of sequel, *Malone meurt* or *Malone Dies*, and then by his most famous play *En Attendant Godot* or *Waiting for Godot*, which was written between October 9, 1948, and January 29, 1949. In the fall of 1949 and the winter of 1950, he completed his trilogy of novels with *L'Innommable* or *The Unnamable*.

Early in 1953, *Waiting for Godot* was produced in Paris to immediate wide acclaim and equally wide bafflement. Subsequent productions of *Godot* in London and New York were similarly startling. The play became a topic for excited debate and made its author famous—partly because of the play's undoubted merit and partly because of its novelty. Theatre is a commercial and, therefore, conventional art. Audiences in the early 1950s were used to explicit and rather simple statements in plays. The most admired dramatists were Jean Paul Sartre, Christopher Fry, Arthur Miller, Tennessee Williams, and even T. S. Eliot, none of whom made particularly elusive theatrical statements. Here, however, was a work that offered the tantalizing ambiguity that the well-read had come to expect in the modern poem and novel. Hence, the play was warmly attacked, hotly defended, and feverishly discussed. The vogue of *Godot* not only established its author as important, but also cleared the way for a whole new wave of theatrical experiment—by Ionesco, Adamov, Pinter, and all of those writers who were to be classed as dramatists of the Absurd.

After *Godot*, Beckett's other major works began to be published; much of his subsequent effort would now be taken up in translating his own work from French into English or from English into French. Much of his time in recent years has been devoted to rehearsing various productions of his plays. In 1956, however, he wrote what is probably his second best known play, *Fin de Partie* or *Endgame*. In the years since his Nobel Prize in 1969, Beckett has tended to write more plays than fiction, and his pieces have tended to become increasingly more brief.

Perhaps the greatest influences on Beckett as a writer have been Joyce,

Ireland, and illness. Beckett met Joyce at an early and impressionable age. He was in his early twenties, and Joyce at that time was engaged in writing the most complicated experimental novel in the English or probably any other language. The enormous impact of Joyce and of *Finnegans Wake* made it impossible for Beckett to conceive of rich and meaningful writing as being conventional in form or realistic in view. So appreciative a Joycean could hardly be expected to embrace the methods of a Frank O'Connor* or Sean O'Faolain.*

Beckett's other major influences, Ireland and illness, seem quite interconnected. He has been afflicted with an astonishing array of ailments in his life, and often his worst symptoms seemed brought on by a return to Ireland. His catalogue of ills is so extensive and so painful that it brings to mind Pope's remark about "that long disease, my life." It also does much to explain his gallery of enfeebled, debilitated characters and his constant theme of life as a kind of incurable disease. The Beckett characters do not really exist in an identifiable Irish landscape, but they do seem refugees from that landscape. There are so many Irish overtones, faint Irish allusions, and Irish words and turns of speech, that the bleak Beckett landscape seems to be the Irish landscape after someone has dropped an H-bomb on it.

Beckett's works, then, represent experiments in form, which have been influenced by Joyce, illness, and Ireland; which depict an unrealistic world filled with repugnant and pointless details; and which make the point that the real world is repugnant and pointless. Such characteristics would seem unpromising indeed for the creation of works of art, but Beckett has three extraordinary qualities as an experimental writer. First, there is the ingenious, often comic objectification that he finds for his world-view. The details of *Molloy* and *Godot* and *Endgame* create a world as inimitable as the worlds of Lewis Carroll or William Faulkner. The details of such works are probably so engaging, so dourly droll, that to some extent they defeat the author's purpose. In his later, more austere works, he keeps a much tighter rein upon his comic invention.

Second, there is the quality of his prose which, phrase by phrase and sentence by sentence, has an utterly unJoycean simplicity and clarity. In *Finnegans Wake*, Joyce is the great "accretor," piling nuance upon nuance, until the density of meaning defies conventional reading and demands translation. Beckett goes almost to the other extreme. His prose is always lucid and always fluent and never quirky or idiosyncratic, as the simple styles of Gertrude Stein or Ernest Hemingway sometimes become. Beckett's prose is always a clear mirror of his content.

Third, there is Beckett's attempt to wrench his form into an emphasis of his statement, and this attempt is both his most daring and least successful. One of the not always true "truisms" of aesthetics is that form should emulate, or at least emphasize, content. Certainly, form can sometimes do that, and one can cite innumerable successful examples in modern literature, from Walt Whitman on. However, a rigid form like the Shakespearean sonnet, for instance, suggests nothing except a certain pattern of reasoning; yet, into that form poets have poured a multitude of diverse meanings and emotions.

Beckett, by rigidly molding his form to his content, has at his most Beckettian broken the mold. Someone has said that *Waiting for Godot* is a play in which nothing happens twice. That same point can be made about many of Beckett's other works. The Moran portion of *Molloy* is basically a reprise of the Molloy portion. The second half of the play, entitled *Play*, repeats the first half verbatim, the only difference being that Beckett thinks the second half should be done more hesitantly. The "Dramaticule" *Come and Go* in its scant ten minutes repeats the same action three times. The play *Breath* in its thirty-five or forty seconds repeats its initial action in reverse. The only difference in these works is that Beckett succeeds in being boring in an ever shorter period of time.

"Boring," however, is too innocuous a word. As the Beckett world-view is of an intolerable existence which it is not worthwhile terminating, the appropriate Beckettian form is necessarily a worthless one, an anti-form. Such a form evokes neither emotion nor amusement; it passes the time at worst tediously and at best intolerably. Increasingly over the years, Beckett seems to have refined that form, to have stripped it of details, and to have made it more austere. He has used fewer words and even no words; he has used fewer actors, parts of actors, and even no actors.

There is no question that Beckett's form emulates his meaning; there is the question of how valid the effect of his form is upon an audience. In 1960, when the Irish actor Cyril Cusack consummately played *Krapp's Last Tape* as an afterpiece rather than as a curtain-raiser to Shaw's* *Arms and the Man*, he succeeded in half-emptying his theatre of an up-to-then highly appreciative audience. That may, of course, have been the effect Beckett wanted; the effect was not a dramatic one, but it certainly was memorable. Similarly, one may set off a cannon during a Shakespearean production at the Globe Theatre; and, when the theatre burns down, the effect is certainly memorable, even though the dramatic experiment has destroyed the form of the drama.

To a conventional or traditional view of what literature can do, it would seem that Beckett's most successful works are those in which he has been less Beckettian. In this view, the early novel *Murphy*, *Molloy* and *Endgame*, and to some extent *Malone Dies* and *Godot* would appear to be the works by which Beckett will be remembered. In these works, his subsequently stifled comic imagination is brilliantly apparent. While that comic imagination may work against the author's intention, it triumphantly works for the traditional methods of the artist.

WORKS: *Whoroscope*. Paris: Hours, 1930. (Poem); *More Pricks Than Kicks*. London: Chatto & Windus, 1934. (Stories); *Echo's Bones and Other Precipitates*.

Paris: Europa, 1935. (Poems); *Murphy*. London: Routledge, 1938/translated into French by Beckett & Alfred Péron, Paris: Bordas, 1947. (Novel); *Molloy*. Paris: Editions de Minuit, 1951/translated into English by Beckett & Patrick Bowles, Paris: Merlin/Olympia, 1954/New York: Grove, 1955. (Novel); *Malone Meurt*. Paris: Editions de Minuit, 1951/translated into English as *Malone Dies* by Beckett, New York: Grove, 1956/ London: Calder & Boyars, 1958. (Novel); *En Attendant Godot*. Paris: Editions de Minuit, 1952/translated into English as *Waiting for Godot* by Beckett, New York: Grove, 1954/London: Faber, 1956. (Play); *Watt*. Paris: Merlin/Olympia, 1953/New York: Grove, 1959/London: Calder & Boyars, 1961. (Novel); *L'Innommable*. Paris: Editions de Minuit, 1953/translated into English as *The Unnamable* by Beckett, New York: Grove, 1958. (Novel); *Nouvelles et Textes pour Rien*. Paris: Editions de Minuit, 1955/translated into English as *Stories and Texts for Nothing* by Beckett, New York: Grove, 1967/collected edition under the title of *No's Knife*, London: Calder & Boyars, 1966; *All That Fall*. London: Faber, 1957/New York: Grove, 1960/translated into French by Beckett and Robert Pinget as *Tous ceux qui tombent*, Paris: Editions de Minuit, 1957. (Radio play); *Fin de Partie*. Paris: Editions de Minuit, 1957/translated into English as *Endgame* by Beckett, New York: Grove, 1958/London: Faber, 1958. (Play); *Acte sans Paroles I*. Paris: Editions de Minuit, 1957 (together with *Fin de Partie*)/translated into English as *Act Without Words I* by Beckett, London: Faber, 1958 (together with *Endgame*)/in *Krapp's Last Tape and Other Dramatic Pieces*, New York: Grove, 1960; *From an Abandoned Work*. London: Faber, 1958/in *First Love and Other Stories*, New York: Grove, 1974/*Krapp's Last Tape*. London: Faber, 1959/ New York: Grove, 1960/translated into French as *La dernière bande* by Beckett & Pierre Leyris, Paris: Editions de Minuit, 1959. (Play); *Embers*. London: Faber, 1959/ in *Krapp's Last Tape and Other Dramatic Pieces*, New York: Grove, 1960; *Happy Days*. New York: Grove, 1961/London: Faber, 1962/translated into French as *Oh les beaux jours* by Beckett, Paris: Editions de Minuit, 1963. (Play); *Comment C'est*. Paris: Editions de Minuit, 1961/translated into English as *How It Is* by Beckett, New York: Grove; London: Calder & Boyars, 1966. (Novel); *Words and Music* in *Play and Two Short Pieces for Radio*, London: Faber, 1964/in *Cascando and Other Short Dramatic Pieces*, New York: Grove, 1969/translated into French as *Paroles et Musique* by Beckett, in *Comédie et Actes divers*, Paris: Editions de Minuit, 1966; *Play*. London: Faber, 1964/in *Cascando and Other Short Dramatic Pieces*, New York: Grove, 1967; *Imagination morte imaginez*. Paris: Editions de Minuit, 1965/translated into English as *Imagination Dead Imagine* by Beckett, London: Calder & Boyars, 1966/in *First Love and Other Shorts*, New York: Grove, 1974; *Bing*. Paris: Editions de Minuit, 1966/translated into English as *Ping* by Beckett, London: Calder & Boyars, 1967/in *First Love and Other Shorts*, New York: Grove Press; *Acte sans Paroles II* in *Comédie et Actes divers*. Paris: Editions de Minuit, 1966/translated into English as *Act Without Words II* by Beckett, in *Krapp's Last Tape and Other Dramatic Pieces*, New York: Grove, 1960/in *Eh Joe and Other Writings*, London: Faber, 1967; *Cascando in Comédie et Actes divers*. Paris: Editions de Minuit, 1966/translated into English as *Cascando* by Beckett, in *Cascando and Other Short Dramatic Pieces*, New York: Grove, [1968] in *Play and Two Short Pieces for Radio*, London: Faber, 1964; *Film in Cascando and Other Short Dramatic Pieces*. New York: Grove, [1968] in *Eh Joe*, London: Faber, 1967; *Eh Joe in Cascando and Other Short Dramatic Pieces*. New York: Grove, 1967/ London: Faber, 1967/translated into French as *Dis Joe* by Beckett in *Comédie et Actes divers*, Paris: Editions de Minuit, 1966; *Assez*. Paris: Editions de Minuit, 1967, in *Têtes-Mortes*/translated into English as *Enough* by Beckett in *First Love and Other Shorts*, New York: Grove, 1974; *Mercier et Camier*. Paris: Editions de Minuit, 1970/ translated into English as *Mercier and Camier* by Beckett, New York: Grove, 1974/ London: Calder & Boyars, 1974. (Novel); *Premier Amour*. Paris: Editions de Minuit,

1970/translated into English as *First Love* in *First Love and Other Shorts,* New York: Grove, 1974; *The Collected Works of Samuel Beckett.* 19 vols. New York: Grove, 1970; *Le Depeupleur.* Paris. Editions de Minuit, 1971/translated into English as *The Lost Ones* by Beckett, New York: Grove, 1972/London: Calder & Boyars, 1972; *Not I.* London: Faber, 1973/ in *First Love and Other Shorts,* New York: Grove, 1974; *Fizzles.* New York: Grove, 1976; *Ends and Odds.* New York: Grove, 1976. (Contains *That Time, Not I, Footfalls, Radio I, Radio II, Theatre I, Theatre II,* and *Tryst*); *For to End Yet, and Other Fizzles.* London: Faber, 1977; *Four Novellas.* London: J. Calder, 1977; *Collected Poems in English and French.* London: J. Calder, 1977. REFERENCES: Bair, Deirdre. *Samuel Beckett.* New York: Harcourt Brace Jovanovich, 1978. (Biography); Cohn, Ruby. *Samuel Beckett: The Comic Gamut.* New Brunswick, N.J.: Rutgers University Press, 1962; Federman, Raymond. *Journey to Chaos, Samuel Beckett's Early Fiction.* Berkeley & Los Angeles: University of California Press, 1965; Federman, Raymond, & Fletcher, John. *Samuel Beckett, His Works and His Critics.* Berkeley & Los Angeles: University of California Press, 1970. (Bibliography); Fletcher, John. *Samuel Beckett's Art.* London: Chatto & Windus, 1967; Kenner, Hugh. *Samuel Beckett: A Critical Study.* New York: Grove, 1961/ revised, Berkeley & Los Angeles: University of California Press, 1968; Mercier, Vivian. *Beckett/Beckett.* New York: Oxford University Press, 1977; Worth, Katherine, ed. *Beckett the Shape Changer, a Symposium.* London: Routledge & Kegan Paul, 1975.

BEHAN, BRENDAN [FRANCIS] (1923-1964), playwright and novelist. Behan was born in Dublin on February 9, 1923, while the Irish Civil War was drawing to a close and his father was imprisoned for Republican activities. This conflict was to mold Behan's career: he spent many of his formative years in prison for political offenses, and there he found the raw material for his major works. Though his writings reflected a growing disenchantment with all kinds of violence, he clung to the ideal of a free Ireland, and when he died on March 20, 1964 he was given a military-style funeral by the illegal Irish Republican Army.

From the beginning, Behan's literary activities were a function of his dedication to the creation of an Irish republic. As a member of Fianna Éireann, the junior branch of the IRA, he contributed patriotic prose and verse to the magazine *Fianna: The Voice of Young Ireland* and to other radical organs. Brought up to revere the memory of those who had fought and suffered for Irish freedom, he longed to strike a blow himself. The campaign of bombing which the IRA launched in England in 1939 seemed an ideal opportunity: Behan was trained in the use of explosives but waited in vain for the call to active service. In November 1939, despite the appeals of family and friends, he traveled to Liverpool where he was spotted and soon picked up by detectives. On February 7, 1940, he was tried, convicted of possessing explosives, and sentenced to three years' detention at Borstal—the maximum sentence a frustrated judge could hand down to a juvenile.

Behan enjoyed most of his time in Borstal; he served only two years and was deported to Ireland in November 1941. Shortly afterwards he was in court again, this time for firing several shots at a detective during an IRA ceremony on April 5, 1942. He was considered fortunate to escape a death sentence. Instead, he got fourteen years, of which he served five before being released under a general amnesty at the end of 1946. These were relatively pleasant and fruitful years for him, and he remembered them as a period of higher education. Various classes were organized by Republican prisoners: there was a fairly high standard of instruction, which led to a wide range of debate, reading, and writing. Behan's convivial wit was well known, while his literary ability was noted by Sean O'Faolain,* who published *I Become a Borstal Boy* in *The Bell** in June 1942. With the assistance of Seán Ó Briain, a fellow prisoner who was a native speaker of Irish, Behan studied the language and literature of Gaelic Ireland. With the idea of writing in Irish, he glimpsed the possibility of integrating his literary and political aspirations. He translated his play *The Landlady* into Irish and submitted it to the Abbey Theatre* without success. He also offered the Abbey a play about hanging entitled *Casadh Súgáin Eile* (*The Twisting of Another Rope*), on which he continued to work outside prison.

In December 1946, Behan's first poem in Irish, in honor of an IRA leader who had died on a hunger-strike, was published in *Comhar*, the Irish language magazine. Over the next six years, he wrote some dozen short poems in Irish, two of which were included in *Nuabhéarsaíocht*, an anthology of contemporary verse edited by Seán Ó Tuama in 1950. The quality of Behan's Gaelic verse is uneven. In the more sombre lyrics, he found a medium of self-scrutiny, which often escaped him when writing in English. Such efforts revealed a vulnerable personality, prone to anguish at the frustration of his dreams. More jovial pieces suggested a clash between his own hopes for a revival of Irish culture and his lack of sympathy with those of the revivalist establishment whom he found dull and puritanical. In *Guí an Rannaire* (*The Rimer's Prayer*), he seemed to imply that his poetic gift was insufficient to provide the desired revolution; shortly afterwards he abandoned Irish verse.

By the late 1940s, Behan was beginning to establish himself as a writer in English and as a Dublin "character." After short spells in prison and an effort to settle in Paris, he returned to Dublin in 1950 to make his living as a journalist while working on what would become *The Quare Fellow* and *Borstal Boy*. In the early 1950s, he published three short stories, "A Woman of No Standing" (*Envoy*, Dublin, 1950), "After the Wake" (*Points,* Paris, 1950), and "The Confirmation Suit" (*The Standard,* Dublin, 1953); two short plays for radio, *Moving Out* and *A Garden Party* (1952); and a very entertaining crime story which was serialized in *The Irish Times* in 1953 and published in book form as *The Scarperer* in 1964. The exceptions among these are "A Woman of No Standing" and "After the Wake," one a story of forbidden love, the other of homosexuality, both written in a quiet contemplative style. Almost all the other works depict Behan's particular demimonde of early-opening pubs and extravagant char-

acters, which were realized in what may be termed *Behanese*, a highly cultivated comic language based on the working-class dialect of Dublin and
liberally laced with ballads and historical allusions.

In 1954, the year of his marriage to Beatrice Salkeld, Behan's play about
hanging, *The Quare Fellow*, was accepted by the Pike Theatre in Dublin.
The full story of the production is told by Alan Simpson in *Beckett and
Behan and a Theatre in Dublin* (London, 1962). Two years later, a splendid production of the play by the Theatre Workshop in London earned
Behan critical esteem outside Ireland. He himself won another kind of
fame by appearing drunk on television—then considered an outrage—and
by generally presenting an image of himself as a roaring boy to the gratified
media. *The Quare Fellow* was taken as a protest against capital punishment
but was much more than that and never lapsed into propaganda: with gruesome humor it lacerated the idea of institutionalized violence and celebrated man's efforts to cope with oppression and death. Seen in the context
of Behan's career, it was an attempt to exorcise the nightmare memory of
his own narrow escapes from execution.

Behan was now in great demand. *The Big House*, commissioned by the
BBC and broadcast in 1957, is an exhilarating romp on the fate of the
Anglo-Irish after Irish independence, similar in tone and texture to the
pieces Behan wrote in his *Irish Press* column. *An Giall* (*The Hostage*)
was written for An Halla Damer, a small Irish-language theatre in Dublin.
That Behan, on the crest of an international wave, provided a play for the
Damer showed his deep commitment to the ideal of an Irish Ireland; the
play itself marked his imaginative rejection of political violence and fanaticism and his sympathy for those caught up in ideological conflicts. The
applause which greeted *An Giall* in 1958 was soon drowned in the outbursts
of wild enthusiasm which greeted *The Hostage* and Behan in London, Paris,
and New York. *The Hostage* was by no means a simple translation of *An
Giall*, and Behan's part in the metamorphosis of a naturalistic tragedy into
a music hall *mélange* of song, dance, and knockabout satire is a matter of
dispute. The success of *The Hostage* showed that it was right for the time,
and the script was continually changed to keep it so. It is doubtful if the
play will retain its initial impact.

No such doubts arise in the case of *Borstal Boy*, which also appeared in
1958. This creative autobiography pretended to be a spontaneous account
of Behan's detention in England from 1939 to 1941; in fact, it was a carefully wrought portrait of the artist as a young prisoner. The narrator was
not so much a pioneer of the British as of his own inherited prejudices;
these were severely tested when he came face to face with the old enemy
and found much to love and admire in him. The young Brendan of *Borstal
Boy* remains Behan's finest creation, while some of the episodes—The
Stations of the Cross, for example—are among the best in comic literature.

Towards the end of *Borstal Boy*, there were signs of a slight loss of control. By 1958, Behan was a prisoner of his own success, unable to climb off the international merry-go-round, discard the mask of the roaring boy, and return to the typewriter. He spoke into tape recorders the books he was unable to write; not surprisingly, there was a falling off in quality. *Confessions of an Irish Rebel* takes up the story of *Borstal Boy*, but that is all. Behan made little progress with a novel of Dublin life to be called *The Catacombs*. English and Irish versions of a new play, *Richard's Cork Leg*, were rejected as mere drafts. His efforts to begin again were thwarted by diabetes and alcoholism, and he had abandoned writing when he died in 1964. Many of the thousands who attended his funeral had probably read none of his books, but to working-class Dublin, Behan was much more than a writer: he was a favorite, charming, wayward son.

COLBERT KEARNEY

WORKS: *An Giall*. Dublin: An Chomhairle Naisiunta Dramaiochta, n.d.; *Borstal Boy*. London: Hutchinson, 1958. (Prison autobiography); *Brendan Behan's Island*. London: Hutchinson,1962. (Includes "The Big House," "The Confirmation Suit," and "A Woman of No Standing"); *Hold Your Hour and Have Another*. London: Hutchinson, 1963. (Sketches); *Brendan Behan's New York*. London: Hutchinson, 1964; *The Scarperer*. New York: Doubleday, 1964. (Novel); *Confessions of an Irish Rebel*. London: Hutchinson, [1965]; *The Complete Plays of Brendan Behan*. London: Eyre Methuen, 1978.   REFERENCES: Behan, Beatrice, with Des Hickey & Gus Smith. *My Life with Brendan*. London: Leslie Frewin, 1973; Behan, Dominic. *My Brother Brendan*. London: Leslie Frewin, 1965; de Burca, Seamus. *Brendan Behan, a Memoir*. Newark, Del.: Proscenium, 1971; Jeffs, Rae. *Brendan Behan, Man and Showman*. London: Hutchinson, 1966; Kearney, Colbert. *The Writings of Brendan Behan*. Dublin: Gill & Macmillan, 1977; McCann, Sean, ed. *The World of Brendan Behan*. London: New English Library, 1965; O'Connor, Ulick. *Brendan*. London: Hamish Hamilton/Englewood Cliffs, N.J.: Prentice-Hall, 1970. (Biography).

BELL, THE (1940-1954), literary magazine. *The Bell*, together with Seumas O'Sullivan's* *The Dublin Magazine*,* shares the honor of being the longest lived and most distinguished modern Irish literary magazine. It was founded by Sean O'Faolain* in October 1940, and its distinguished first number included stories, poems, essays, and reviews by O'Faolain, Frank O'Connor,* Elizabeth Bowen,* Patrick Kavanagh,* Brinsley Mac-Namara,* Flann O'Brien,* Peadar O'Donnell,* Lennox Robinson,* Maurice Walsh,* and Jack B. Yeats.* Succeeding numbers continued that high standard. The magazine published items by most of Ireland's established writers and fostered the early work of Bryan MacMahon,* John Montague,* Conor Cruise O'Brien* ("Donat O'Donnell"), James Plunkett,* Anthony Cronin,* and Val Mulkerns,* among others.

Under the wartime editorship of O'Faolain, *The Bell* emerged as a lonely liberal voice evaluating and criticizing establishment standards, such as the government censorship of books. This social orientation was even more emphasized when Peadar O'Donnell, the novelist, succeeded O'Faolain as editor in 1946. Rudi Holzapfel, the magazine's subsequent bibliographer, wrote that *The Bell* under O'Donnell "seemed to lose favour among the Irish people due to its aggressive, punchy left-wingism. However, to be fair, it is precisely this increased interest in Irish social welfare which makes the later issues of *The Bell* such a valuable document for historians of the day."

The magazine ceased publication in its fifteenth year with the December 1954 issue, its one-hundred and thirty-first number.

REFERENCE: Holzapfel, Rudi, comp., *The Bell: An Index of Contributors*. Blackrock: Carraig Books, 1970.

BELL, SAM HANNA (1909-), novelist, short story writer, and broadcaster. Bell was born in Glasgow on October 16, 1909, of Irish emigrant parents. His father worked as a journalist on the *Glasgow Herald*, but when he died, young Bell was sent to live with his mother's people at Raffrey near Strangford Lough. A rather patchy rural education was followed by a brief period in Belfast Art School, and then Bell held a wide variety of jobs, including night watchman, laboratory attendant, salesman, and clerk with the Canadian Steamship and Railway Company. His first writing was for the BBC in Belfast. Since there was little artistic stimulation in Belfast, Bell, like other Northern writers of his generation who were without the fare to London, turned to Dublin for encouragement. He received it from Sean O'Faolain,* who was then editing *The Bell*.* Sam Hanna Bell wrote some short stories for the magazine which were collected in 1943 as *Summer Loanen and Other Stories*.

Bell's major work, the novel called *December Bride* (1951), grew out of a comic short story which O'Faolain stimulated Bell to write about his mother's family. Written in an old-fashioned prose style reminiscent of Hardy, the book marvelously evokes the harshness of rural life in the Ards Peninsula at the turn of the century. The plot centers around a servant girl, Sarah Gomartin, and her affair with two brothers. Her refusal to name the father or to marry either of them leads to ostracism and other savage reprisals from the narrow rural community. Sarah, an interesting study of a strong-willed, manipulating woman who resents the strictures of her time, finally bows to public opinion and marries for the sake of her daughter. The attitudes of Presbyterians toward their Catholic neighbors are skillfully depicted, and there is also one especially funny episode in a Belfast pub when an old drunk, not realizing he is in a Catholic pub, requests an Orange song. The novel was banned in the 1950s in the South, although it is difficult now to see why.

Bell has written two other novels—*The Hollow Ball* (1961) about a footballer and unemployment, and *A Man Flourishing* (1973) about the '98 Rising—but *December Bride* is justly considered his best work. He has also written a folklore volume entitled *Erin's Orange Lily* (1956) and a theatrical history entitled *The Theatre in Ulster* (1972). He continues to work for radio, while running the literary section of the *Ulster Tatler* and writing a novel for Gollancz about plantation times in Ulster.

MARY ROSE CALLAGHAN

WORKS: *Summer Loanen and Other Stories.* Newcastle, County Down: Mourne, 1943; *December Bride.* London: Dobson, [1951]/Belfast: Blackstaff, 1974; *Erin's Orange Lily.* London: Dobson, 1956; *The Hollow Ball.* London: Cassell, 1961; *The Theatre in Ulster.* Dublin: Gill & Macmillan, 1972; *A Man Flourishing.* London: Gollancz, 1973; ed., with Nesca A. Robb & John Hewitt, *The Arts in Ulster.* London: Harrap, [1951].

BERKELEY, GEORGE (1685-1753), philosopher. Berkeley, bishop of Cloyne, Ireland's most eminent philosopher, was born on March 12, 1685, in County Kilkenny. He attended Kilkenny College and then entered Trinity College, Dublin, at the early age of fifteen. He received his B.A. in 1704 and his M.A. in 1707, when he also received a fellowship. As an undergraduate, he became acquainted with John Locke's *Essay Concerning Human Understanding*, in reaction to which he wrote his major works—*Essay Towards a New Theory of Vision* (1709), *The Principles of Human Knowledge* (1710), and *Three Dialogues between Hylas and Philonous* (1713). With these three volumes, Berkeley defined his philosophical position; for the last forty years of his life, his interest was in a variety of concerns other than philosophy.

In 1713, Berkeley went to London and made the acquaintance of the leading literary men of the day: Swift,* Steele,* Addison, Pope, and Arbuthnot. Then for several years he traveled in France and Italy, first as chaplain (on Swift's recommendation) to Lord Peterborough and later as a tutor. He returned to Ireland in 1723 when he received the deanery of Dromore and later the deanery of Derry. In 1725, he received half of the estate of Hester Van Homrigh, Swift's Vanessa, although she had never or, at most, briefly met him.

Much of his energies in the 1720s were taken up with advancing a project to found a college in the Bermudas, and for a time he seemed likely to receive £20,000 from the government to inaugurate the college. He moved to America and lived for nearly three years in Newport, Rhode Island, at the end of which time he despaired of ever receiving aid for the college, and so returned in 1732 to London.

In 1734, Berkeley was consecrated bishop of Cloyne where he spent most of the next eighteen years. In that time, he wrote pacificatory essays on the state of Ireland, and he wrote on economics, somewhat anticipating the theories of Adam Smith. However, he was interested chiefly in promoting a resinous fluid called tarwater as an almost universal panacea. His last major work, *Siris* (1744), was written largely as a result of his interest in tarwater, and its rambling erudition added nothing to his reputation.

He retired in bad health to England in 1752, and he died in Oxford on January 14, 1753.

Berkeley's philosophic position was developed as a refutation of John Locke whose espousal of a material universe seemed to Berkeley to have pernicious implications for religion. Locke accepted a Newtonian universe of real matter which presumably God had set in motion, but which now, like some vast machine, ticked on by its own self-sustaining and inexorable rules. To Berkeley, there was very little need or place for God in such a universe, and very little place either for soul or spirit. Consequently, to put God and soul back into the center of things, Berkeley posited that matter was, in fact, nonexistent. A weakness of Locke's position is that man perceives matter only by an idea of it in his mind, but, to Berkeleyan common sense, there is no way of ascertaining whether any perception is in fact true. Berkeley asserted that all one could be certain of was the idea in one's mind and that there need be no corresponding matter to the idea at all. In Berkeley's view, what exists is not material bodies in a material universe, but only in the mind of God who communicates the ideas of matter to the finite minds of man.

Berkeley systematically elaborated this view in *The Principles of Human Knowledge* and proselytized for it in the quite readable *Three Dialogues*. Despite his pious motivations and his reliance on common sense, Berkeley seemed nonsensical to most of his contemporaries. As one later writer remarked, "In assaulting matter he seemed to destroy reality." The view of the ordinary thinking man was well summed up by Dr. Johnson who kicked a stone and truculently remarked, "Thus I refute Berkeley." However, as G. J. Warnock wrote: "Locke gave the classic exposition of one of the traditional accounts of perception and the material world, Berkeley set out no less ably the classic response; and between them they established a pattern of argument on this subject which has remained central in philosophy right down to the present day." (Introduction to *The Principles of Human Knowledge and Other Writings*. London: Collins/Fontana, 1962.) By his *Principles of Human Knowledge* Berkeley became a central figure in modern philosophy; but in his *Three Dialogues* he wedded, as had Plato before him, philosophy to literature.

WORK: *The Works of George Berkeley, Bishop of Cloyne*. A. A. Luce & T. E. Jessop, eds. 9 vols. London: Nelson, 1948-1957.   REFERENCES: Luce, A. A. *The Life of George Berkeley, Bishop of Cloyne*. London: Nelson, 1949; Tipton, I. C. *Berkeley, the Philosophy of Immaterialism*. London: Methuen, 1974.

BIRMINGHAM, GEORGE A. (1865-1950), novelist, playwright, and humorist. George A. Birmingham was the pseudonym of Canon James Owen Hannay, who is rather unfairly remembered only as a prolific writer of humorous light fiction. Hannay was born in Belfast on July 16, 1865, the son of the Reverend Robert Hannay. He was educated at Haileybury and Trinity College, Dublin, from which he graduated in 1887. He was ordained a deacon of the Church of Ireland in 1888 and served as curate in Delgany, County Wicklow. He was ordained a priest in 1889 and appointed in 1892 to the parish at Westport, County Mayo, where he served until 1913.

Birmingham met and was much influenced by Standish O'Grady,* Horace Plunkett, the agricultural reformer (1854-1932), Arthur Griffith,* and particularly Douglas Hyde*, with whom he was involved in the Gaelic League. He began publishing a series of political novels in 1905 with *The Seething Pot*, but it was not until the great success of *Spanish Gold* in 1908 that he found a wide popular audience. His books appeared regularly at about yearly intervals. He also did some writing for the stage, including *Eleanor's Enterprise* performed by Count Markievicz's Independent Theatre in 1911, and *General John Regan* performed with much success by Charles Hawtrey in London in 1913. When a touring company presented *General John Regan* in Westport in 1914, it occasioned a night of rioting far more violent than the more celebrated frays over *The Playboy of the Western World* and *The Plough and the Stars*. As with *The Playboy*, the audience rioted over a presumed insult to Irish womanhood.

After an extended lecture tour to America before the war, Birmingham served as a chaplain in France in 1916 and 1917. From 1918 to 1920, he was rector of a small parish in County Kildare and chaplain to the lord lieutenant of Ireland. He resigned these posts in 1922 and went to Budapest for two years as chaplain of the British legation. In 1924, he accepted a living in Mells in Somerset. After his wife died, he moved to a small London parish in 1934. He was awarded a D. Litt. from Trinity College, Dublin, in 1946, and he died in London on February 2, 1950. He was a man of immense industry, publishing over eighty books, as well as uncounted fugitive pieces in newspapers and magazines. While he was active in many public capacities, he was even more active in the ministry and always put his priestly functions before his writing.

Despite the extreme popularity of his light fiction, the more patriotic Irish often suspected Birmingham of being Ascendancy and Protestant in his views. D. P. Moran, the editor of the patriotic journal *The Leader*, for instance, usually referred to him as "the bigot of Westport," and the citizens of Westport burned him in effigy during the *General John Regan* riot. Nothing could have been further from the truth than the charge of bigotry or bias, however, and even in his serious novels about the contemporary scene, Birmingham was scrupulously fair in seeing all sides. Indeed, his rather dull *Benedict Kavanagh* fails largely because much of the book is a plea not only for the Gaelic League, but also for mutual religious tolerance. The best of these early serious novels are *The Seething Pot* (1905), *Hyacinth* (1906), and *The Northern Iron* (1907). As R.B.D. French justly remarks of them, "The spirit of comedy in these novels and a new gift for satiric portraiture is revealed, but they are fundamentally serious works, even tragic in their implications, and they are the work of a Christian moralist."

Birmingham followed up the charming *Spanish Gold* of 1908 with several similar volumes, especially *The Search Party* (1909), *Lalage's Lovers* (1911), *The Inviolable Sanctuary* (1912), and *The Adventures of Dr. Whitty* (1913). In such books, he mined a vein of happy-go-lucky adventures involving amiable follies and engaging characters. Like the Irish R. M. stories of Somerville and Ross,* they are full of keen observation, deft phrasing, and, despite some droll comedy about the "mere Irish," utter tolerance. Birmingham's Reverend J. J. Meldon of *Spanish Gold* and some other books is one of the truly endearing comic creations of modern Irish literature. As a comic writer, Birmingham is not quite of the first rank, and his plots tend to fade in the memory. Nevertheless, one may return to the best of these books at intervals with unstinted delight.

The more political books which followed these comedies were increasingly permeated by good spirit and jovial satire, but they were not the kind of books to endear Birmingham to his Irish readers. For instance, the excellent *The Red Hand of Ulster* (1912) appeared in the midst of the Home Rule ferment, and the satiric *reductio ad absurdum* of its plot (in which Ulster is so opposed to Home Rule that it stages its own revolt and sets up its own independent government) was far too close to what might actually happen. *Up the Rebels!*, which appeared in the bad times of 1919, was full of gaiety, tolerance, and lightheartedness, but it could hardly have gone down well with the Irish patriots, for the charmingly foolish rebellion of the book was much too close in time to the ferocities of Easter Week.

Birmingham left Ireland for England in the early 1920s. His books continued to appear with their usual frequency, but there was a slow falling away from the excellence of his first twelve or fifteen years. Birmingham was rarely a hard satirist like Sean O'Casey* or Eimar O'Duffy,* but the times were out of joint for even mild satire. Still and all, he was a congenial, civilized, and humane writer, and, although thus far he rates merely a sentence in the literary histories, he is an immensely better writer than many with much more inflated reputations.

WORKS—as J. O. Hannay: *The Life of Frederick Richards Wynne*. London: Hodder & Stoughton, 1897; *The Spirit and Origin of Christian Monasticism*. London: Methuen, 1903; *The Wisdom of the Desert*. London: Methuen, 1904; *Is the Gaelic League Political?* Dublin: 1906. (Pamphlet); *Can I Be a Christian?* London: Hodder & Stoughton, 1923; *The Consecration of Churches*. London: Humphrey Milford, 1927; *Early Attempts at Christian Reunion*. London: 1929. (Pamphlet); *The Potter's Wheel*. London: Longman's, 1940. as George A. Birmingham: *The Seething Pot*. London: Edward Arnold, 1905; *Hyacinth*. London: Edward Arnold, 1906; *Benedict Kavanagh*. London: Edward Arnold, 1907; *The Northern Iron*. Dublin: Maunsel, 1907; *The Bad Times*. London: Methuen, 1908; *Spanish Gold*. London: Methuen, 1908; *The Search Party*. London: Methuen, 1909; *Lalage's Lovers*. London: Methuen, 1911; *The Lighter Side of Irish Life*. London & Edinburgh: T. N. Foulis, 1911; *The Major's Niece*. London: Smith, Elder, 1911; *The Simpkins Plot*. London: Nelson, 1911; *The Inviolable Sanctuary*. London: Nelson, 1912; *The Red Hand of Ulster*. London: Smith, Elder, 1912; *The Adventures of Dr. Whitty*. London: Methuen, 1913; *Fidgets*. London: Hodder & Stoughton, 1913; *General John Regan*. London: Hodder & Stoughton, 1913. (Novel); *Irishmen All*. London & Edinburgh: T. N. Foulis, 1913; *The Lost Tribes*. London: Smith, Elder, 1914; *Gossamer*. London: Methuen, 1915; *Minnie's Bishop*. London: Hodder & Stoughton, 1915; *The Island Mystery*. London: Methuen, 1918; *A Padre in France*. London: Hodder & Stoughton, 1918; *An Irishman Looks at His World*. London: Hodder & Stoughton, 1919; *Our Casualty*. London: Skeffington, 1919; *Up, the Rebels!* London: Methuen, 1919; *Inisheeny*. London: Methuen, 1920; *Lady Bountiful*. London: Christophers, 1921; *The Lost Lawyer*. London: Methuen, 1921; *The Great-Grandmother*. London: Methuen, 1922; *A Public Scandal*. London: Hutchinson, 1922; *Fed Up*. London: Methuen, 1923; *Found Money*. London: Methuen, 1923; *King Tommy*. London: Hodder & Stoughton, 1923; *Send for Dr. O'Grady*. London: Hodder & Stoughton, 1923; *The Grand Duchess*. London: Hodder & Stoughton, 1924; *Bindon Parva*. London: Mills & Boon, 1925; *The Gun-Runners*. London: Hodder & Stoughton, 1925; *A Wayfarer in Hungary*. London: Methuen, 1925; *Goodly Pearls*. London: Hodder & Stoughton, 1926; *The Smuggler's Cave*. London: Hodder & Stoughton, 1926; *Spillikins*. London: Methuen, 1926. (Essays); *Now You Tell One*. Dundee & London: Valentine, 1927; *Ships and Sealing Wax*. London: Methuen, 1927; *Elizabeth and the Archdeacon*. London: Gollancz, 1928; *The Runaways*. London: Methuen, 1928; *The Major's Candlesticks*. London: Methuen, 1929; *Murder Most Foul!* London: Chatto & Windus, 1929; *The Hymn Tune Mystery*. London: Methuen, 1930; *Wild Justice*. London: Methuen, 1930; *The Silver-Gilt Standard*. London: Methuen, 1932; *Angel's Adventure*. London: Methuen, 1933; *Connaught to Chicago*. London: Methuen, 1933; *General John Regan*. London: G. Allen & Unwin, 1933. (Play); *Pleasant Places*. London: Heinemann, 1934. (Autobiography); *Two Fools*. London: Methuen, 1934; *Love or Money*. London: Methuen, 1935; *Millicent's Corner*. London: Methuen, 1935; *Daphne's Fishing*. London: Methuen, 1937; *Isaiah*. London: Rich & Cowan, 1937; *Mrs. Miller's Aunt*. London: Methuen, 1937; *Magilligan Strand*. London: Methuen, 1938; *Appeasement*. London: Methuen, 1939; *God's Iron*. London: Skeffington, 1939; *Miss Maitland's Spy*. London: Methuen, 1940; *The Search for Susie*. London: Methuen, 1941; *Over the Border*. London: Methuen, 1942; *Poor Sir Edward*. London: Methuen, 1943; *Lieutenant Commander*. London: Methuen, 1944; *Good Intentions*. London: Methuen, 1945; *The Piccadilly Lady*. London: Methuen, 1946; *Golden Apple*. London: Methuen, 1947; *A Sea Battle*. London: Methuen, 1948; *Laura's Bishop*. London: Methuen, 1949; *Two Scamps*. London: Methuen, 1950; *Good Conduct*. London: John Murray, n.d.; *Golden Sayings from George A. Birmingham*. London: L. B. Hill, 1915.

BLACKWOOD, CAROLINE [MAUREEN] (1931-), novelist. Blackwood was born in Ulster on July 16, 1931, the daughter of the fourth marquis of Dufferin and Ava. On her mother's side she is a Guinness, and on her father's side she is a direct descendant of Richard Brinsley Sheridan.* Her first husband was a grandson of Sigmund Freud, and her third husband was the American poet Robert Lowell.

Her first book, *For All That I Found There* (1974), is a collection of short stories, journalism, and memoirs of an Ulster childhood. Although funny, the stories are also sad illustrations of human weakness and vulnerability. They portray an unstable world where the props, such as the kind old priest of "How You Love Our Lady" and the nanny of "Baby Nurse," are only temporary. Among the journalistic articles is an hilarious account of a women's lib meeting, as well as a terrifying report of a visit to a hospital for burns. The memoirs of childhood are perhaps the best parts of the book, especially "Piggy," the account of a prep school bully, and "Never Breathe a Word," the writer's weird experience with her pony's groom.

The Stepdaughter, her first novel, won the David Higham Prize for fiction in 1976. The book is a haunting indictment of the callous treatment of a young girl by her father and stepmother, but is so skillfully done that the reader feels as much for the awful adults as for the unhappy, rejected child.

Great Granny Webster, a best-selling novella published in 1977, traces the influence of a grim, parsimonious old woman on three generations of her family. The novella contains some marvelous characterization and a memorable depiction of life in an Anglo-Irish mansion reeking of damp and madness. Blackwood contrives to treat madness with a witty detachment, and her depictions of the pathetic life in a leaky Anglo-Irish mansion are both sad and funny. Nevertheless, although characters like Lavinia and Granny Webster are most memorably drawn, some of the other characters are elusive. In addition, some questions are raised and never answered. Why, for instance, is the narrator's father so unhappy? What happened to the narrator's mother? One gets the feeling that the book was at one time longer, and one wishes that it still were. There is so much suggestion of undeveloped plot in the present book that one wishes the author had worked it out fully and given us more than brilliant sketches of several characters.

MARY ROSE CALLAGHAN

WORKS: *For All That I Found There*. London: Duckworth, 1974; *The Stepdaughter*. London: Duckworth, 1976; *Great Granny Webster*. London: Duckworth, 1977.

BOLAND, EAVAN [AISLING] (1944-), poet. Boland was born in Dublin on September 24, 1944. Her father was a diplomat in external affairs, and her mother, Frances Kelly, a painter, studied with the post-expressionists in Paris in the 1930s. Eavan was educated in Dublin from 1949 to 1950 and in London from 1950 to 1956. Because of an IRA campaign at that time, London in the early 1950s was strongly anti-Irish. "To this day," writes Boland, "I carry an aversion to the whole of British culture." From 1956 to 1960, she went to school in New York, which remains for her "a beautiful, bizarre city." Returning to Ireland in 1960, she attended the Convent of the Holy Child, Killiney, County Dublin, until 1962: "I was convent-educated entirely. I have no ambivalence about it: I'm certain I lost my faith and kept my virginity there." At Trinity College, Dublin, from 1962 to 1966, she had a brilliant undergraduate career, achieving a first-class moderatorship. She lectured in Trinity College during 1967-1968, after which she resigned to devote her life to writing. She is married to Kevin Casey* the novelist and has a daughter.

Despite the international flavor of her life, Boland's work is strongly rooted in the traditions and life of Ireland of which she has a passionate, precise understanding. Despite her stated "aversion" to English culture, she has learned a great deal from it. (Two of the most accomplished poems in her first book, *New Territory*, are in praise of Shakespeare.) Yet, it is also true that what she has learned from the English tradition has served to confirm and deepen her dedication to her own concept of Irish culture. This concept is the most intriguing single aspect of her work, since it includes the main thematic and structural movements of her poetry as well as her own changing, deepening convictions as a writer.

The most ambitious work in her first book is called "The Winning of Etain." Although the poem understandably shows influences ranging from Spenser to Keats to Francis Ledwidge,* it deserves much more attention than it has received. Not only does it exhibit a controlled sensuality of language and superb narrative style, but also it has a sustained formal beauty, a psychological astuteness, a tone of calm yet intense intelligence, and—for want of a better way of phrasing it—the poem's confidence, at once naive and unshakable, in itself. Very few twentieth-century poets tell a story in verse as well as Eavan Boland; very few poets, one might reply, would be *interested* in telling a story in verse. But it is precisely this spirit of unobtrusive independence, this calm confidence in what she is doing, which distinguishes Boland's poetic career to date. In addition to handling the long narrative form in her first book, she also demonstrated her ability to produce brief, concentrated lyrics, such as "Requiem for a Personal Friend (On a half-eaten blackbird)". Here is the full text of the poem:

> A striped philistine with quick
> Sight, quiet paws, today—
> In gorging on a feathered prey—
> Filleted our garden's music.
>
> Such robbery in such a mouthful!
> Here rests, shovelled under simple
> Vegetables, my good example—
> Singing daily, daily faithful.
>
> No conceit and not contrary—
> My best colleague, worst of all,
> Was half-digested, his sweet whistle
> Swallowed like a dictionary.
>
> Little victim, song for song—
> Who share a trade must share a threat—
> So I write to cheat the cat
> Who got your body, of my tongue.

Like many poets who begin in the mists of mythology (Yeats* and Austin Clarke* are examples), Boland moves implacably towards a confrontation of her own vision of the modern world. Her vision is that of a poet and of a woman. "Nothing has ever been a greater influence on me," she writes, "than to move from the world of urbane learning, speculative possibility, the cherishing of literature, to the quiet barbarities of the suburbs. It's almost as if I had moved from the grandeur of a Van Eyck painting into the interior of a French or Dutch artist; where everything is surreally domestic, oppressive, noticeable. This is the poetry I'll write."

This indeed is the poetry which began to appear in her second book, *The War Horse*, and which she is now deeply involved in as she prepares her third collection. This poetry of quiet domestic barbarity is a far cry from the brilliant colors of "The Winning of Etain," but it is done with greater authority and conviction.

> The wash is done, the kettle boiled, the sheets
> spun and clean, the dryer stops dead.
> The silence is a death, it starts to bury
> the room in white spaces. She turns to spread
> a cloth on the board and irons shirts
> in a room white and quiet as a mortuary.

As a poet, Boland has accepted the challenge implicit in the grind of normality. She is a writer of unspectacular independence; her work will one day, I believe, be of spectacular importance.

BRENDAN KENNELLY

WORKS: *New Territory*. Dublin: Allen Figgis, 1967; *The War Horse*. London: Gollancz, 1975; *W. B. Yeats and His World*, with Micheál Mac Liammóir. London: Thames & Hudson, 1971/New York: Viking, 1972.

BOUCICAULT, DION (1820 or 1822-1890), playwright and actor. Playwright, adapter of plays and novels, actor, director, manager, commentator, and entrepreneur, Boucicault was perhaps the most eminent man in the theatre of England, America, and Ireland in the mid-nineteenth century. His birth and his parentage, like much else in his personal life, are mysterious. He was born Dionysius Lardner Boursiquot in Dublin in 1820 or 1822; he always gave his birthdate as December 26, 1822, thus establishing the record of his precocity in writing the hit *London Assurance* in 1841. No parish records exist. He was named after Dionysius Lardner, who became well known in London as a lecturer and encyclopedist, whom Boucicault much resembled and whose protege he became. Although his formal schooling from age seven on was English, he retained his brogue both on and off stage throughout his life. In his teens, he left his training as an engineer to become a provincial actor and playwright under the name of Lee Moreton. Encouraged by Charles Mathews of Covent Garden to write a modern comedy, he wrote (with some help from John Brougham [1814–1880]) the comedy *London Assurance*, which ran for sixty-nine nights. For the next fifty years, he was so heavily involved in personal and theatrical activities that they can barely be summarized in a short space.

In his twenties, Boucicault wrote and adapted many plays, lived in France for several years, learning the language fluently, and returned to England following the mysterious death of his first wife, Anne Guiot. As a reader for Charles Kean at the Princess, he met Kean's protegee, the actress Agnes Robertson, with whom he moved to America, probably in 1852. While they may not have been legally married, they lived and worked together as a married couple for many years. She achieved instantaneous success in Boston as a matinee idol, and Boucicault wrote five plays for her in the star role, touring widely throughout the United States. Partly as a result of Boucicault's efforts, Congress in 1856 changed the U.S. copyright laws to ensure playwrights a greater reward from their productions. Boucicault's *The Poor of New York* (1857, variously titled according to the city it was playing in) and *The Octoroon* (1859) revealed his enormous skill for seizing a currently popular or inflammatory issue, simplifying it into melodramatic terms, and providing a "sensational" theatrical climax, usually in Act Three of a three-act play. The burning of a tenement, the explosion of the river boat, the climb up and leap from the high tower, the rescue of the heroine from drowning, the enactment on stage of the Oxford-Cambridge boat race, and the heroine tied to the railroad track (a scene which he actually stole from Augustin Daly's *Under the Gaslight*) became the trademark of Boucicault's melodrama.

The success of *The Colleen Bawn* ("the fair-haired girl") in New York and London in 1861 and in Dublin in 1862 led to another Boucicault innovation, the touring company, and another Boucicault advance, his Irish plays. While stars had been touring for decades, generally they used local talent from repertory companies. Boucicault put together the whole show. By acting with Agnes Robertson in his own play and touring with his own company, he earned money as a manager, playwright, and actor. Simultaneously, he benefited by sending out other companies on tour and through the newly increased royalties. With a succession of hit plays, Boucicault was to earn an estimated $5 million in his theatrical lifetime, while at the same time advancing the importance of the playwright in the whole process of theatrical production. He toured throughout the United States and for many years played regularly in Boston, New York, and Philadelphia. He returned to Dublin three times and to London at least three, all but one of these engagements being successful.

With his play *The Colleen Bawn* (1860), he had discovered what was perhaps his most moving theatrical genre, the Irish play. Highly aware of the Stage Irishman as a long-established English stereotype, he reversed the stereotype by taking the same character traits and showing them favorably. His country people were not slovenly and stupid but charming and beguiling, with a native wit and resourcefulness that belied upper-class condescension and occasionally twitted the English. In 1864-1865, he produced *Arrah-na-Pogue* ("Arrah of the Kiss") in Dublin and London, and in 1874 he opened *The Shaughraun* ("The Wanderer") in New York, both of them enormously successful. Their melodrama and their sentimentality account for only part of their appeal. It lies also in the charming dialogue and the creation of vivid characters like Danny Mann and the scampish Myles na Coppaleen. Not all of Boucicault's Irish plays were as good as these two. As in many other of his potboilers, he had a strong tendency towards stage emotion and dialogue rather than real emotion.

Boucicault had a knack as an adapter of plays, usually French, which he produced as his own, and as a dramatizer of fiction, like Dickens' "Cricket on the Hearth" and Scott's *The Heart of Midlothian*. His version of *Rip Van Winkle* in 1865 established Joseph Jefferson as a star and is still the acted version. Boucicault was not as skilled as a theatrical manager because he usually overspent money on elaborate refurbishing of his the- atres and on extravagant productions. At times he managed theatres in New Orleans, Washington, New York, and London. However, he was enormously skilled as a set designer and technician, attentive to the smallest details. His productions were noted for their sets, their special effects, and the well-rehearsed ensemble nature of the acting. Late in his life, Boucicault published papers on acting and for a short while directed an acting school for the entrepreneur A. M. Palmer at Madison Square Garden. His emphasis was on movement and gesture rather than on the elocutionary manner of speech then popular.

Boucicault's personal and financial lives were puzzles to his contemporaries and remain so to the modern student. He made and lost three fortunes, some in gold mine stock, some in bad theatrical management, and some in personal extravagance. Following *London Assurance*, he dressed, dined, and entertained in the highest style. He was devoted to the six children Agnes Robertson bore him, several of whom followed him onto the stage. In the early 1880s, he and Agnes separated. His subsequent marriage to the very young actress Louise Thorndike, while on tour in Australia in 1885, and the public bickerings over the divorce from Agnes caused scandal in New York and London—partly because Boucicault now denied they had ever been married. After his death in New York City on September 18, 1890, there was extended fighting over his estate, which seemed to be almost nonexistent. He was always in the public eye, and he had a wide circle of nontheatrical as well as theatrical friends. Thousands of mourners attended his funeral at the Little Church Around the Corner, and obituaries appeared in the hundreds of cities in the United States and England where he had played on tour. It was an internationally reported event.

Boucicault's theatrical influence was pervasive rather than sharply focused. He could fill the great theatres in the cities and in the remote provinces. With his *London Assurance* and his *Old Heads and Young Hearts* (1844), he helped carry on the English tradition of drawing room comedy. Through numerous comedies and thrillers adapted from the French, he carried on the joint influence of English and French theatre. The organization of the touring company brought New York professional theatre to the provinces—and helped kill local repertory theatre. In the age of the great actor-managers, of which he was one, he led the audiences to expect exciting staging and ensemble acting, and he increased the importance of the playwright. He helped launch the careers of Henry Irving and Joseph Jefferson, and he encouraged the young Oscar Wilde* in the early part of his American tour. To the Irish stage he gave respectability and three notable plays. While Edmund Booth concentrated on Shakespeare and Gilbert and Sullivan on operetta, Boucicault influenced all areas of the theatre. By the time of his death in 1890, his taste was out of touch with the emerging theatre of Wilde, Shaw,* Synge,* Ibsen, and Chekhov, and by an irony of fate, his very great fame was soon forgotten. The Hollywood feature film rather than the theatre continued his tradition of spectacular effects and melodrama. Douglas Fairbanks, Jr., played his *Corsican Brothers* (derived from Dumas) in a film as late as 1941. But both Shaw and O'Casey* acknowledged his early influence, and Chekhov, who surely did not know him but did know his French and German equivalents, strenuously wrote his theatre of real life against the Boucicault traditions, using it in order to change it.

SVEN ERIC MOLIN

WORKS: *London Assurance*. London: Printed for the Author, 1841; *The Irish Heiress* (also called *West End*). London: Andrews, 1842; *Alma Mater; or, A Cure for Coquettes*. London: Webster, [1842?]; *Curiosities of Literature*. London: Webster, [1842?]; *Don Caesar de Bazan; or Love and Honour*. London: Acting National Drama, [1844]; *The Fox and the Goose; or, The Widow's Husband*. London: Acting National Drama, [1844]; *Old Heads and Young Hearts*. New York: French's Standard Drama, No. 62, n.d.; *A Lover by Proxy*. London: Acting National Drama, [1845?]; *The Wonderful Water Cure*. London: Acting National Drama, [1846?]; *The School for Scheming* (later revised and retitled *Love and Money*). London: Acting National Drama, [1847?]; *A Romance in the Life of Sixtus the Fifth, entitled the Broken Vow* (later called *The Pope of Rome*, and often referred to as *Sixtus the Fifth*). London: Hailes Lacy, 1851; *Love in a Maze*. London: Hailes Lacy, 1851; *The Queen of Spades; or, The Gambler's Secret* (also called *The Dame of Spades*). London: Hailes Lacy, 1851; *The Corsican Brothers; or, The Vendetta*. London: Hailes Lacy, [1852]; *The Vampire*. London: French, [1852?]/later shortened and retitled *The Phantom*, New York: French's Standard Drama, 1856; *Faust and Marguerite*. London: French, [1854?]; *The Willow Copse*. Boston: William V. Spencer, [1856?]; *Wanted a Widow, with Immediate Possession*. New York: Samuel French, n.d.; *The Poor of New York* (also produced under many other titles). New York: Samuel French, [1857?]; *Jessie Brown; or, The Relief of Lucknow*. New York: Samuel French, 1858; *Pauvrette* (also called *The Snow Flower*). New York: Samuel French, [1858?]; *The Colleen Bawn; or, The Brides of Garryowen*. [New York]: Printed but not published, [1860?]/also in *Nineteenth Century Plays,* ed. by George Rowell. London: Oxford University Press, 1853, and in *The Dolmen Press Boucicault,* ed. David Krause. Dublin: Dolmen, 1964; *The Lily of Killarney.* Philadelphia, 1867. An operetta based on *The Colleen Bawn,* with words by Boucicault and John Oxenford, and music by Sir Jules Benedict; *How She Loves Him.* London: Chapman & Hall, [1868]; *The Knight of Arva.* New York: French's Standard Drama, [1868?]; with Charles Reade, *Foul Play.* London: Bradbury, Evans, 1868. (Novel); *Arrah-na-Pogue; or, The Wicklow Wedding.* London: French's Acting Edition, [1865], also in *The Dolmen Press Boucicault; The Long Strike.* New York: Samuel French, [1870?]; *Foul Play.* Chicago: Dramatic Publishing Co., n.d.; *After Dark: A Tale of London Life.* New York: De Witt's Acting Plays, n.d.; *The Rapparee; or, The Treaty of Limerick.* Chicago: Dramatic Publishing Co., n.d.; *Jezebel; or, The Dead Reckoning.* Chicago: Dramatic Publishing Co., n.d.; *Elfie; or, The Cherry Tree Inn.* Chicago: Dramatic Publishing Co., n.d.; *Night and Morning* (also called *Kerry; or, Night and Morning*). Chicago: Dramatic Publishing Co., n.d.; reprinted in *Irish University Review* 3 (Spring 1973); *Led Astray.* New York & London: French, [1873?]; *The Shaughraun.* Published in acting editions by French, Dicks, Lacy's, and Webster, and currently available in *The Dolmen Press Boucicault; The Story of Ireland.* Boston: James R. Osgood, 1881. (Short history); *Andy Blake; or, The Irish Diamond* (later called *The Dublin Boy* and *The Irish Boy*). London: Dicks' Standard Plays, [1884]; *A Legend of the Devil's Dyke.* London: Dick's Standard Plays, [1898]; *The Old Guard* (a revision of his first play, *Napoleon's Old Guard*). London: Dick's Standard Plays, [1900?]; *The Jilt.* London & New York: French, [1904]; *Daddy O'Dowd; or, Turn About is Fair Play* (later revised as *The O'Dowd; or, Life in Galway,* and still later revised as *Suil-a-mor; or, Life in Galway*). London & New York: French, [1909]; *Belle Lamar* (revised as *Fin Mac Cool of Skibbereen*), in *Plays for the College Theatre.* Garrett H. Leverton, ed. New York: French, 1932; *Forbidden Fruit and Other Plays.* Princeton, N.J.: Princeton University Press, 1940. (Also contains *Louis XI, Presumptive Evidence, Dot,* and *Robert Emmet*); *Flying Scud; or, A Four Legged Fortune,* in *Favorite American Plays of the Nineteenth Century.* Barrett H. Clark, ed. Princeton, N.J.: Princeton University Press, 1943; *The Octoroon; or, Life in Louisiana* and *Rip Van Winkle,* in *Representative American Plays, from 1767 to the Present Day.* Arthur Hobson Quinn, ed. 7th ed. New York: Appleton-Century-Crofts, 1953; *The Dolmen Press Boucicault.* David Krause, ed. Dublin: Dolmen, 1964. (Contains *The Colleen Bawn, Arrah na Pogue,* and *The Shaughraun*); *Lost at Sea; or, A London Story,* in *The Golden Age of Melodrama.* Michael Kilgarriff, ed. London: Wolfe, 1974. (Abridged version).

The above list is probably a fairly complete compilation of Boucicault's major published works. However, because most of his plays were printed cheaply in ephemeral acting editions, some problems in his bibliography will probably never be solved. Most of his plays were not printed at all. For a listing of their productions, consult the bibliography in Hogan below.   REFERENCES: Hogan, Robert. *Dion Boucicault.* New York: Twayne, 1969; Molin, Sven Eric, and Goodefellowe, Robin. "Dion Boucicault, the Shaughraun, a Documentary Biography. Part One, the Early Years," *George Spelvin's Theatre Book, II,* 1979; Tolson, Julius H. "Dion Boucicault." Philadelphia: University of Pennsylvania, Ph.D. dissertation, 1951; Walsh, Townsend. *The Career of Dion Boucicault.* New York: Dunlop Society, 1915.

BOWEN, ELIZABETH [DOROTHEA COLE] (1899-1973), novelist and short story writer. A line from her best novel, *The Death of the Heart,* reveals the central conviction underlying all of Bowen's fiction: "Illusions are art, for the feeling person, and it is by art that we live, if we do." The human need for personal vision, for support in dealing with an impersonal world, and the identification of that vision with art are elements which determine the shape and content of her stories and novels.

Although she was born in Dublin on June 7, 1899, Elizabeth Bowen was educated and spent most of her life in England. Upon her father's death in 1928, she inherited the family estate, Bowen's Court, in County Cork, but she did not live there until after her husband's death in 1952. She remained at Bowen's Court until 1960 when she returned to England; she died in London on February 22, 1973. Her childhood was unhappy, and the forsaken, lonely children in many of her novels and stories seem to have been based on her own experience. But her adult life was full and satisfying, including her marriage to Alan Charles Cameron and her numerous friendships with Virginia Woolf, E. M. Forster, and other leading writers of the time. She was a prolific but careful writer, the author of ten novels, over seventy short stories, a half dozen works of nonfiction, and over six hundred reviews and essays in the major periodicals of England, Ireland, and America.

Her first publications were short stories, the first collection being entitled *Encounters* (1923). These and later stories, particularly "The Demon Lover," exhibit Bowen's gift for economical description and characterization, and her bold treatment of elemental human feelings. The stories typically center on alienated characters who speak the kind of wisdom which disarms our reasonable but conventional attitudes. She is also skilled at conveying intense emotion, as "The Demon Lover" illustrates; the growing terror of the woman in that story is evoked with surprisingly few words.

Good as her stories are, Bowen's reputation rests on her novels. *The Last September* (1929) is one of her earliest, yet one of her best. It is set in Ireland during the Troubles and deals with the destruction of a Great House. Here, as in most of the novels, Bowen's skill in both presenting and utilizing setting is remarkable. Walter Sullivan, in an essay in *Sewanee Review* (Winter 1976), remarks on this achievement: "it is impossible to read Miss Bowen and not be aware of how architecture and topography give weight to her fiction and contribute actively to the development of plot and theme."

The House in Paris (1935) treats a subject which recurs in many of her novels: adult-child relations. A mother who cannot cope with her own life and her lonely, confused child are the central characters, but the entire cast leads the reader to weigh adult conformity against the child's sensitivity.

Bowen's masterpiece, *The Death of the Heart*, appeared in 1938. Again a child serves as the center of consciousness. Portia, who has lived with her mother traveling throughout Europe, is now orphaned and so enters the sterile world of her brother and his wife in London. They and others seek to control her, for she is spontaneous, natural, and, to them, threatening. In contrast to the old, restricted world of their proper London house, Portia's exposure to the disorderly life of a set of fast young people reveals the crass values of this new generation—a group as deceitful and determined to control her as her brother had been. The title points to the main theme: we must overcome the self and live with others, but not at the cost of sensitivity and necessary, sustaining illusions. The novel ends abruptly, suggesting that Portia has been unable to escape the world which is set against her; but the theme is clearly established and Bowen's sympathies are clear. The novel relies on symbolism, oblique expression, and a complicated juxtaposition of the perceptions of various characters; yet, it clearly conveys a strong and challenging theme.

The Heat of the Day (1949) treats more extreme emotions. Stella Rodney, a divorcee living in wartime London, encounters a world of mistrust and even espionage. Its war-torn setting and complex theme are effectively interwoven.

Bowen's last novel, *Eva Trout* (1969), represents a significant change of direction. The title character, like so many others in Bowen's works, is a misfit in a conventional world. Nonetheless, she tries to enter it, to adapt to social expectations. She acquires a child, perhaps by adoption in the black market, and attempts to build a life for herself like that of her old friend and teacher. Naturally, she upsets the lives of all those she deals with, and, predictably, her attempts fail. Eva's encounters with normal society are often comic, yet essentially painful to behold. The novel's ending is startling, and some critics claim melodramatic: she is accidentally killed by her adopted son just when they are about to set off on a new life together. On the whole, *Eva Trout* is less realistic, less subtle, but more powerful than Bowen's other novels.

In Bowen's novels, the reader is expected to make inferences, read symbols carefully, and evaluate everything that is claimed. Sensitive as they are, hers are not novels of sensibility, for Bowen had a formidable intellect, a deep knowledge of English literature, and a firm commitment to certain standards of behavior. Furthermore, her novels and stories, for all their verbal polish and restraint, reveal intense passions: selfless love, jealousy, hatred, and, most frequently, loneliness.

Bowen's relation to Ireland is undeniable, since she took pride in her possession of Bowen's Court. One of her best novels, *The Last September* (1929), deals with an Irish subject. But her interests transcend national boundaries, just as she defies categorizing as a woman novelist. Above all, she is a writer committed to the development of her art and to revealing the inherent relationship of fact to feeling, actuality to art.

J A M E S   K I L R O Y

WORKS: *Encounters*. London: Sidgwick & Jackson, 1923/New York: Boni &

Liveright, 1925/republished in *Early Stories,* New York: Alfred A. Knopf, 1950; *Ann Lee's and Other Stories.* London: Sidgwick & Jackson, 1926/New York: Boni & Liveright, 1926/republished in *Early Stories,* New York: Alfred A. Knopf, 1950; *The Hotel.* London: Constable, 1927/New York: Dial, 1928; *Joining Charles and Other Stories.* London: Constable/New York: Dial, 1929; *The Last September.* London: Constable/ New York: Dial, 1929; *Friends and Relations.* London: Constable/New York: Dial, 1931; *To the North.* London: Gollancz, 1932/New York: Alfred A. Knopf, 1933; *The Cat Jumps and Other Stories.* London: Gollancz, 1934; *The House in Paris.* London: Gollancz, 1935/New York: Alfred A. Knopf, 1936; *The Death of the Heart.* London: Gollancz, 1935/New York: Alfred A. Knopf, 1936; *Look at All Those Roses.* London: Gollancz/New York: Alfred A. Knopf, 1941; *Bowen's Court.* London: Longmans, Green/New York: Alfred A. Knopf, 1942/2d ed., with Afterword, London: Longmans, Green/New York: Alfred A. Knopf, 1964; *English Novelists.* London: W. Collins, 1942; *Seven Winters: Memories of a Dublin Childhood.* Dublin: Cuala, 1942/ republished as *Seven Winters: Memories of a Dublin Childhood and Afterthoughts: Pieces on Writing,* New York: Alfred A. Knopf, 1962; *The Demon Lover and Other Stories.* London: Jonathan Cape, 1945/published in America as *Ivy Gripped the Steps,* New York: Alfred A. Knopf, 1946; *Anthony Trollope: A New Judgment.* New York & London: Oxford University Press, 1946; *Why Do I Write? An Exchange of Views Between Elizabeth Bowen, Graham Greene, and V. S. Pritchett.* London: Percival Marshall, 1948; *The Heat of the Day.* London: Jonathan Cape/New York: Alfred A. Knopf, 1949; *Collected Impressions.* London: Longmans, Green/New York: Alfred A. Knopf, 1950; *The Shelbourne: A Center in Dublin Life for More Than a Century.* London: George G. Harrap, 1951/published in America as *The Shelbourne Hotel,* New York: Alfred A. Knopf, 1951; *A World of Love.* London: Jonathan Cape/New York: Alfred A. Knopf, 1955; *Stories by Elizabeth Bowen.* New York: Alfred A. Knopf, 1959; *A Time in Rome.* New York: Alfred A. Knopf/London: Longmans, Green, 1960; *Afterthought: Pieces About Writing.* London: Longmans, Green, 1962; *The Little Girls.* London: Jonathan Cape/New York: Alfred A. Knopf, 1964; *A Day in the Dark and Other Stories.* London: Jonathan Cape, 1965; *The Good Tiger.* New York: Alfred A. Knopf, 1965. (Children's book); *Eva Trout or Changing Scenes.* New York: Alfred A. Knopf, 1968/London: Jonathan Cape, 1969.   REFERENCES: Austin, Allen. *Elizabeth Bowen.* New York: Twayne, 1971; Blodgett, Harriet. *Patterns of Reality: Elizabeth Bowen's Novels.* The Hague: Mouton, 1975; Heath, William. *Elizabeth Bowen, an Introduction.* Madison: University of Wisconsin Press, 1961.

BOYD, JOHN (1912-), playwright. Boyd was born on July 19, 1912, in Belfast and was educated at the Royal Belfast Academical Institution, Queen's University Belfast, and Trinity College, Dublin. He married Elizabeth McCune in 1939 and has three children. Before joining the Belfast BBC as a producer in 1947, he taught at grammar schools in Newry, Lisburn, and Belfast. He is at present literary adviser to the Lyric Theatre* and editor, since 1971, of its publication *Threshold.*

Boyd has been active in encouraging Ulster writing, notably through the periodical *Lagan* (1942-1946), of which he was editor. As a BBC producer, he was responsible for a great number of valuable documentaries, interviews, and programs of criticism and reminiscence by such writers as Sean O'Faolain,* Frank O'Connor,* Louis MacNeice,* and, more recently, Brian Friel.*

Boyd now devotes himself to writing and is known primarily as a dramatist, his continuing interest being the heritage of the North and the outcroppings of its violent disunities. He renders the local language common to the adherents of the disunited faiths. Each can understand the idiom, though not sharing the belief, of the other. Boyd's plays draw on this common idiom for his dramatic statement of the origins and the manifestations of factional hatreds.

The Assassin (Gaiety, Dublin, 1969) opens into the frightening landscapes of ostensibly religious paranoia. *The Flats* (Lyric, 1971) places domestic tragedy in the midst of collective violence and the conflict of slogans which brutalize any genuine political critique. These naturalistic plays, together with *The Farm* (Lyric, 1972) and *Guests* (Lyric, 1974), speak to the local immediacies of tribal dispossessions, and to Boyd's sense of the gulf between experience and its factional interpretations.

D. E. S. MAXWELL

WORK: *The Flats*. Belfast: Blackstaff, 1974.

BOYLE, PATRICK (1905-), novelist and short story writer. Boyle was born in Ballymoney, County Antrim, in 1905. He worked for forty-five years for the Ulster bank, spending twenty of those years in Donegal and retiring as manager of the bank's Wexford branch. He did not turn to writing until late in life. In 1965, he submitted the fourteen stories of his first collection pseudonymously to a short story contest held by *The Irish Times* and judged by Terence de Vere White,* Mary Lavin,* and Frank O'Connor.* White later wrote, "When I came to look at the entries I found an extraordinary thing. The first, second, fourth, fifth had all been written by the one man, Patrick Boyle."

At this writing, Boyle has produced three excellent volumes of stories and one strong, if flawed, novel. The general impression left by his work is that it depicts mainly the middle-aged, hard-drinking, and wenching bachelor in the provincial town. Indeed, the main character of Boyle's novel, *Like Any Other Man* (1966), is just such a person. There is much that is excellent about this readable book, particularly the evocation of the pub milieu and of the daily business of a provincial bank. However, the melodramatic climax seems a bit too much, with Boyle punishing his protagonist more than the poor slob's character would warrant.

Boyle's stories have a considerable range of subject and of tone, and are generally much less hardhearted than his novel. Particularly notable are "Interlude," about the snaring of a bachelor into marriage; "Dialogue," a finely comic sketch of an eccentric priest and his dog; "Sally," an appealing tale of adolescent attraction; "A Quiet Respectable Couple," with its effective peasant melodrama; and "Age, I Do Abhor Thee," which must rank with Frank O'Connor's finest stories about small boys and their fathers. Indeed, Boyle has so many successes in his three collections of stories, that one deeply regrets he did not start writing them thirty years earlier.

WORKS: *Like Any Other Man*. London: MacGibbon & Kee, 1966; *At Night All Cats Are Grey*. London: MacGibbon & Kee, 1966; *All Looks Yellow to the Jaundiced Eye*. London: MacGibbon & Kee, 1969; *A View from Calvary*. London: Gollancz, 1976.

BOYLE, WILLIAM (1853-1923), playwright. Boyle, born in Dromiskin, County Louth, in April 1853, was employed as an excise officer until his retirement in 1914. He died in London on March 6, 1923. His writing includes a collection of short stories, *A Kish of Brogues* (1899), and three remarkably popular plays for the Abbey*: *The Building Fund* (1905), *The Eloquent Dempsy* (1906), and *The Mineral Workers* (1906). In protest against the *Playboy*, he severed connections with the Abbey but returned in 1912.

His plays may be divided into two categories. *The Mineral Workers* and *Nic* (1916) examine the impact of modern ideas on traditional Irish life. The others are humorous (in the Jonsonian sense) studies of "deadly" sins: avarice in *The Building Fund*, political duplicity in *Dempsy*, and indolence in *Family Failing* (1912).

Symmetrically structured and broadly characterized, Boyle's plays are entertainments. Only in *Nic* is there a tragic figure—a gentle old farmhand who, urged to improve his economic lot, robs his employer. *The Building Fund* approaches dark comedy in the maneuverings of relatives and church workers for the estate of a dying, avaricious old woman, and *Dempsy* might have been an effective satire on political extremism. Generally, however, Boyle, to paraphrase the other Johnson, pleased his age and did not aim to mend.

WILLIAM J. FEENEY

WORKS: *A Kish of Brogues*. London: Simpkin, Marshall, 1899. (Stories); *The Building Fund*. Dublin: Maunsel, 1905; *The Mineral Workers*. Dublin: M. H. Gill, 1910; *The Eloquent Dempsy*. Dublin: M. H. Gill, 1911; *Family Failing*. Dublin: M. H. Gill, 1912.

BRENNAN, JAMES (1944-), novelist. Brennan was born in Dublin on October 18, 1944. He has published one novel, *Seaman* (1978), which is a study of six people in Dublin in the summer of 1969, most of whom are afflicted with a profound sense of the worthlessness of existence. Although the opening seems to promise little more than another aimless literary pub-crawl around Dublin, the novel settles down to a workmanlike evocation of character. The sketch of a Liam O'Flaherty*-like novelist is particularly well done. Although the prose is much less well considered than Hemingway's, the novel is reminiscent of a more self-indulgent *The Sun Also Rises*.

WORK: *Seaman*. [Dublin: Irish Writers' Co-Operative, 1978].

BRODERICK, JOHN (1927-), novelist. Broderick, born in Athlone on July 30, 1927, has described himself as "self educated, in spite of the efforts of six schools." Since 1961, Broderick has published six novels which are highly critical of life in the Irish Midlands. As Michael Paul Gallagher remarks, "He has stayed with one dominant theme so far, the 'snobberies, hypocrisies and pretensions' of the 'little grocer's republic' that he finds in provincial Ireland. . . . He sees a 'great field for an Irish Balzac,' and in the last three of his books shows an increasing concern to expose the masks of the moneyed bourgeoisie." In perhaps the best of his novels, *The Waking of Willie Ryan* (1965), Broderick is something of an Irish Balzac, but in his later work he increasingly seems a sour, dour, awkward satirist. Many of his characters are not so much psychologically believable, as forced into the molds of Jonsonian humors by the author's themes. His best creations usually are not his main characters, but his peripheral ones, such as his choral gossips, Mrs. Fallon and Mrs. Lagan in *The Fugitives* (1962) and Miss Price and Miss Fall in *An Apology for Roses* (1973). In addition, his main characters seem so manipulated by his condemnatory attitude that they become not merely humors but thoroughly repellent ones placed in a gallery of grotesques. Few figures in Broderick are written with love or sympathy; hence, his books possess a coldness ultimately and even triviality. Two fine exceptions are the decrepit Anglo-Irish ladies, Bessie and Violet, in *The Pride of Summer* (1977). They are treated with a gentle comedy and yet are given a kindness, an indomitability, and a dignity lacking in nearly all of Broderick's other characters. Indeed, most of those other characters are so warped by the theme that they become two-dimensional monsters.

The prime importance of theme to Broderick even harms his work stylistically. Michael Paul Gallagher has noticed the frequency of authorial intrusions, what he calls "essayism," in the stories, especially in *The Waking of Willie Ryan* and *Don Juaneen* (1963). Certainly, there are innumerable turgid generalizations, such as, "Every woman who has been scorched by the fires of sensuality will always choose death rather than the lack of love," or "For a man the passivity of passion is never enough; for a woman it is the essence of love" (both from *The Fugitives*). Gallagher also notes a prolixity of adjectives and adverbs; these, however, are not an unconscious stylistic habit, but a quite deliberate choice dictated by the author's attitude. For instance, in *The Fugitives*, the evocative words of one typical paragraph are these:

> rusty, ancient, rattling, soiled, crouched, resigned, grey, humid, oyster-coloured, livid, unearthly, muffled opaque, glassy, narrow, grey-green, muffled, filmy, putty-coloured, drooping, acid-yellow, black-clothed, grey-capped, heavy, flat, big-tongued, apathetic, grey, langourous, grey, dead, buried, mortified.

The descriptive details in this long paragraph (the second paragraph of Chapter 20) are overwhelmingly and pejoratively slanted. If there is a choice of an epithet, Broderick inevitably opts for the more dismal one. Even his daffodils are "drooping, acid-yellow daffodils." Through thousands of conscious stylistic choices throughout the novel, Broderick consistently stacks his deck to impel the reader towards his own bleakly condemnatory attitude. Fair enough, and any author does something of the same, but Broderick is so thoroughgoing that the final effect is not so much one of authorial control as it is of forcing an exaggeration, a partial truth, and a myopic vision upon the reader. He is so thoroughgoing that finally his stylistic device ceases to be effectively subliminal and becomes obtrusive and unconvincing.

Broderick's vision also determines the development of his plots, but sometimes it deflects those plots from their true and inevitable course. This fact is especially obvious in the one-sentence final chapter of *The Pilgrimage*, which reduces the entire, meticulously built-up realism to a sardonic joke. It is also obvious in *The Pride of Summer*, which contains some of Broderick's very best work side by side with some of his most unconvincing. The characters of the heroine, of the two Anglo-Irish ladies, and perhaps even of the heroine's brother-in-law are excellently drawn. If their stories had been worked out with the appropriate realism in which they had been so lovingly established, Broderick would have drawn a superb and convincing portrayal of provincial life. However, he insists that his village be seen not implicitly, but overtly, as a paradigm of modern Ireland. This insistence makes the other portions of the novel too satirically exaggerated and unbelievably out of tone. Broderick even goes so far as to give some characters names closely resembling those of certain eminent contemporary Irishmen. In one scene, some gigolos are compared to such politicians as Conor Cruise O'Brien,* and the upshot is a lengthy, tasteless, and mirthless satire which nearly swamps the book.

The Pride of Summer may be taken as representative of Broderick's basic problem as a novelist. Yet, he has many talents, even a little-used one for humor. It is unfortunate that thus far his grim morality has flawed his work, and possibly flawed it irretrievably, for he sometimes appears to take a masochistic enjoyment in depicting what he is nominally condemning.

WORKS: *The Pilgrimage*. London: Weidenfeld & Nicholson, 1961/reprinted as *The Chameleons*, London: Panther Books, 1965; *The Fugitives*. London: Weidenfeld & Nicholson, 1962; *Don Juaneen*. London: Weidenfeld & Nicholson, 1963; *The Waking of Willie Ryan*. London: Weidenfeld & Nicholson, 1965; *An Apology for Roses*. London: Calder & Boyars, 1973; *The Pride of Summer*. London: George G. Harrap, 1977.   REFERENCE: Gallagher, Michael Paul. "The Novels of John Broderick." In *The Irish Novel in Our Time*. Patrick Rafroidi & Maurice Harmon, eds. [Lille, France]: Publications de l'Universite de Lille, [1976].

BROPHY, ROBERT. *See* RAY, R. J.

BROWN, CHRISTY (1932-), novelist and poet. Brown is an extra-ordinary writer and personality. His finest book, the eloquent autobio-graphical novel *Down All the Days* (1970), will undoubtedly become a classic of modern Irish writing. The book is not merely a literary triumph, but also a human triumph, testifying to the indomitable courage of the author, his family, and his friends.

Christy Brown was born in Dublin on June 5, 1932. His father was a bricklayer, and his mother bore twenty-one children besides Christy, thir-teen of whom lived into adulthood. He himself was born almost completely paralyzed by cerebral palsy. He could not speak but only grunt, and the only part of his body over which he had any control was his left foot. Many doctors regarded him as imbecilic, but his mother staunchly refused to believe them. Her faith was rewarded when he was five. He was watching his sister write on a slate when his foot almost involuntarily reached out, his toes grasped the chalk, and he attempted to write on the slate. With his mother's patient teaching, he slowly and painfully mastered the alpha-bet and finally put letters together to make words. In his teens he came to the attention of the physician and playwright Robert Collis, who worked with him and slowly improved his coordination and his speech. Collis also encouraged and coached him to write his first book. That book, *My Left Foot*, is a short, factual account of his life, and it was laboriously typed out with the little toe of his left foot. Certainly no other Irish book has been written with such pain and courage and fortitude.

As a writer, Brown is unusually uneven, and the strongest symptom of his varying quality is probably most apprent in his prose style. *My Left Foot* is told in an unadorned, terse prose that does not interfere with the interest and the power of the narrative. *Down All the Days*, which is an emotionally charged fictional recreation of the same events, is told in an elaborate, sometimes florid prose that owes much to the American writer Thomas Wolfe. Occasional passages in the novel are too lush to be effec-tive, but at its overall best the prose lifts the deeply felt events to an emo-tional eloquence of high intensity. Brown's second novel, *A Shadow on Summer*, is a fictional recreation of a trip to America; the prose is elabo-rated to a turgidity that is nearly unreadable. At the same time, the events and preoccupations of the novel—the author's casual personal relations, his casual loves, and his feelings about writing—have little of the felt in-tensity that was so remarkable in *Down All the Days*. Brown's third novel, *Wild Grow the Lilies,* is an attempt to get outside the frame of autobio-graphical fiction, but is little more successful than *A Shadow on Summer*. *Wild Grow the Lilies* depicts the Stage Ireland of Brendan Behan,* full of drinking and sex and utter falseness. While the prose is less self-indulgently florid, it is still overwritten and needs drastic cutting. The book has been charitably described as refreshingly bawdy and hilariously vulgar, but it is tedious, interminable, contrived, and untrue.

Brown has also published three volumes of poems which are more personal statements than works of art. He has not mastered the craft and techniques of poetry, but rich phrases abound, and one or two pieces are unpolished gems.

Christy Brown is a writer of immense ability, and thus far he has produced one good book and one superb one. His talents—as well as his handicaps—are much greater than those of most of his contemporaries. Whether his talents will be disciplined and his handicaps overcome is one of the most interesting questions in contemporary Irish writing.

WORKS: *My Left Foot.* London: Secker & Warburg, 1954/New York: Simon & Schuster, 1955/republished as *The Story of Christy Brown,* New York: Pocket Books, 1971, and as *The Childhood Story of Christy Brown,* London: Pan, 1972; *Down All the Days.* London: Secker & Warburg/New York: Stein & Day, 1970; *Come Softly to My Wake.* London: Secker & Warburg, 1971/published as *The Poems of Christy Brown,* New York: Stein & Day, 1971; *Background Music: Poems.* London: Secker & Warburg/New York: Stein & Day, 1973; *A Shadow on Summer.* London: Book Club Associates, 1974; *Wild Grow the Lilies.* London: Secker & Warburg/New York: Stein & Day, 1976; *Of Snails and Skylarks.* London: Secker & Warburg, 1978. (Poems).

BROWNE, FRANCES (1816-1879), poet, novelist, and writer of children's stories. Browne, "the blind poetess of Donegal," was born in Stranolar, County Donegal, on January 16, 1816. Although blind from infancy, as a result of an attack of smallpox, she grew up with a good grasp of English literature and earned her living by writing. Her first poem was published in *The Irish Penny Journal,* and later she published in *Hood's Magazine, The Keepsake,* and *The Athenaeum*; the editor of the last-named did much to publicize her work. She left Ireland in 1847 and made her home in either Edinburgh or in London. She was granted a small pension from the civil list by Sir Robert Peel and died in London on August 25, 1879.

During her life she published an autobiography, novels, stories for chilren, and many poems. Her poetry was well thought of in its day and is still not to be dismissed, but she is best remembered for *Granny's Wonderful Chair and the Stories It Told,* a collection of fairy stories for children. These delightful fantasies, written in lucid prose, illustrate Christian values without ever descending to smugness. The book was deservedly a worldwide best-seller, but had an unusual publishing history. First published in 1856, it went through two editions which quickly sold out. Then, in 1877, Frances Hodgson Burnett wrote her version of the stories and called them *Stories from the Lost Fairy Book as Retold by the Child Who Read Them.* It was soon discovered that the lost book was Frances Browne's *Granny's Wonderful Chair,* and it was republished in 1880. This edition sold out quickly, as did many others until in 1891 an edition with colored pictures by Mrs. Seymour Lucas had an enormous success. In recent years, the book has again fallen into obscurity, but its merits are so perennially appealing that it may well be discovered again.

MARY ROSE CALLAGHAN

WORKS: *The Star of Atteghei; the Vision of Schwartz; and Other Poems.* London: Moxon, 1844; *Lyrics and Miscellaneous Poems.* Edinburgh: Sutherland & Knox, 1848; *The Ericksons. The Clever Boy; or, Consider Another (Two Stories for my Young Friends).* Edinburgh: Paton & Ritchie, 1852; *Pictures and Songs of Home.* London: Nelson, [1856]; *Granny's Wonderful Chair, and its Tales of Fairy Times.* London: Griffith & Farran, 1857. (Many later editions); *Our Uncle the Traveller's Stories.* London: W. Kent, 1859; *My Share of the World. An Autobiography.* London: Hurst & Blackett, 1861; *The Castleford Case.* 3 vols. London: Hurst & Blackett, 1862; *The Orphans of Elfholm.* London: Groombridge, [1862]; *The Young Foresters.* London: Groombridge, [1864]; *The Hidden Sin.* 3 vols. London: n.p., 1866. (Published anonymously); *The Exile's Trust, a Tale of the French Revolution, and Other Stories.* London: Leisure Hour, [1869]; *The Nearest Neighbours, and Other Stories.* London: R. T. S., [1875]; *The Dangerous Guest. A Story of 1745.* London: R. T. S., [1886]; *The Foundling of the Fens.* London: R. T. S., [1886]; *The First of the African Diamonds.* London: R. T. S., [1887].

BUCHANAN, GEORGE [HENRY PERROTT]

(1904-), journalist and man of letters. Buchanan was born in Kilwaughter, Larne, County Antrim, in 1904. He attended Larne Grammar School with his friend Lyle Donaghy,* the poet, and later attended Campbell College in Belfast. In 1925, he went to London, worked on various newspapers, and contributed many poems to journals and many reviews to the *Times Literary Supplement.* During World War II, he served in the RAF. He has published novels, journals, volumes of autobiography, collections of poems, and some plays. The background of Europe in economic depression and at war is strongly present in his work, which has sometimes been described as journalistic fiction. Thus far, little recognition or discussion has been given to his considerable and individual body of work. The best introduction is the excellent George Buchanan number of *The Honest Ulsterman* (March-June 1978).

WORKS: *Passage Through the Present.* London: Constable, 1932. (Journal); *A London Story.* London: Constable, 1935. (Novel); *Dance Night.* London: [French's Acting Edition, 1935]. (Play); *Words for To-night.* London: Constable, 1936. (Journal); *Rose Forbes,* Part 1. London: Constable, 1937. (Novel); *Entanglement.* London: Constable, 1938. (Novel); *Serious Pleasures, the Intelligent Person's Guide to London.* London: London Transport, 1938/revised, Westminster: London Transport, 1939; *The Soldier and the Girl.* London, Toronto: Heinemann, 1940; *Rose Forbes,* Parts 1 & 2. London: Faber, 1950; *A Place to Live.* London: Faber, 1952. (Novel); *Bodily Responses.* London: Gaberbocchus, 1958. (Poems); *Conversation with Strangers.* London: Gaberbocchus, 1959. (Poems); *Green Seacoast.* London: Gaberbocchus, 1959. (Autobiography); *Morning Papers.* London: Gaberbocchus, 1965. (Autobiography); *Annotations.* Manchester: Carcanet, 1970. (Poems); *Naked Reason.* New

York: Holt, Rinehart & Winston, 1971. (Novel); *Minute-book of a City*. South Hinksey: Carcanet, 1972. (Poems); *Inside Traffic*. Manchester: Carcanet, 1976. (Poems); *The Politics of Culture*. London: Menard, 1977. (Essays).   REFERENCE: Ormsby, Frank, ed. *The Honest Ulsterman* 59 (March-June 1978): 17-87. (The George Buchanan Supplement includes an article on Buchanan's poetry by James Simmons, an article on his fiction by Val Warner, an article on his journals, autobiography, and essays by Arthur McMahon, and an interview by Ormsby.)

BULLOCK, SHAN F. (1865-1935), novelist. Bullock wrote over a score of books, more than a dozen of these being novels and the rest volumes of stories, books of verse, and biographies. His most notable work is *Thomas Andrews, Shipbuilder* (1912), the story of the man who built the *Titanic* and lost his life when it sank. The author was born on May 17, 1865, in Crom, south Fermanagh, where his father was a steward on the Earl of Erne's estate. Soon after leaving Farra School, County Westmeath, Bullock went to London where he spent his working life as a civil servant. He died on February 27, 1935, at Cheam, Surrey.

The two vastly different experiences of Bullock's life, Fermanagh and London, were the biographical impetus behind most of his fiction. Out of voluntary incarceration as a minor official came *Robert Thorne: The Story of a London Clerk* (1907), an interesting sortie into Edwardian realism replete with documentary details of the lives, at desk and hearth, of "pen-drivers," emasculated drudges beset by poverty, duty, and routine. The novel also attempts to write "a page from the awful Day-book of London town," a city paying "the penalty of civilisation"—adulterated food, jerry-built housing, and shoddy clothes. Thorne's deliverance at novel's end is by emigration to New Zealand, but the real answer lies in the "manliness" of life he might have achieved in his native Devon. *By Thrasna River: The Story of a Townland* (1895), a loose-limbed narrative that is one of Bullock's best, shows that whereas manliness is more likely in the countryside, its enemies—in this case poverty, land-hunger, and an adverse climate— can be as fatally powerful as in London. The unassured urban naturalism of *Robert Thorne* succeeded the more mature rural naturalism of this novel, wherein romanticism (represented by the absurd Englishman Harry Thomson driven off by the narrow-minded tenants of an estate for courting one of their daughters) is at once given a larger say and a more definitive routing. Sectarianism is knowingly handled in the novel.

In *After Sixty Years* (1931), an autobiography confined to the Fermanagh years and most of the events that are in *By Thrasna River*, Bullock admitted that he found it easier to portray Catholics than Protestants because, though himself Protestant, he felt drawn towards them. He described himself as a "poor child of a world between two gate-houses" (England and Ireland, Protestant and Catholic). His first and un-Protestant name, Shan, was self-bestowed and is a further indication that of all Ulster writers

Bullock perhaps comes closest to an intimate knowledge of both sects. Yet, Catholic characters also permitted him to exercise that democratic and paradoxically Protestant sympathy for the underdog that runs through his fiction. *After Sixty Years* is low-keyed but occasionally moving. It is of great documentary value in depicting, through his father's recollections, the semi-feudal Ireland of pre-Famine and pre-Land Act days, and, through Bullock's own recollections, the end of the Big House. Benedict Kiely has remarked in *The Irish Times* (December 29, 1972) that Bullock was the last Irish writer to see the Big House functioning efficiently, though the view was that of an outsider, albeit favored.

The odd combination of rural naturalism and mock-romantic melodrama can be found in such attempts at tragedy as *The Squireen* (1903), *Dan the Dollar* (1905), and *The Loughsiders* (1924) in which Bullock tries to capture the hubris of his unprepossessing heroes. These novels exhibit the virtues and failings of all Bullock's fiction. They are enjoyably readable, fair-minded (no petty virtue in Ulster fiction), and valuable as social history, but the author staidly lacks sympathy with his own, often unpleasant, characters, particularly the Protestant characters. This lack drains his fictional world of warmth and life, despite the quirky humor. Moreover, there is no stable point of view, no intelligible signals to the reader that Bullock is or is not employing irony. It is not merely that Bullock's attitude to his chief characters is usually enigmatic, but that motives (for example, those of John Farmer, the narrator of *By Thrasna River*, or of Richard Jebb in *The Loughsiders*) are often damagingly garbled or obscure. This intractability of Bullock's fiction could be taken as an ironic comment on the Ulster border country (as it was later to become) that bred him.

JOHN WILSON FOSTER

WORKS: *The Awkward Squads and Other Stories*. London: Cassell, 1893; *By Thrasna River*. London: Ward, Lock & Bowden, 1895; *Ring o' Rushes*. London: Ward, Lock & Bowden, 1896; *The Charmer*. London: Bowden, 1897; *The Barrys*. London: Harper, 1899; *Irish Pastorals*. London: Grant Richards/New York: McClure, Phillips, 1901; *The Squireen*. London: Methuen, 1903; *The Red Leaguers*. London: Methuen, 1903; *Dan the Dollar*. Dublin: Maunsel, 1905; *The Cubs*. London: Laurie, 1906; *Robert Thorne*. London: Laurie, 1907; *A Laughing Matter*. London: Laurie, 1908; *Master John*. London: Laurie, 1909; *Hetty*. London: Laurie, 1911; *Thomas Andrews, Shipbuilder*. Dublin & London: Maunsel, 1912/published in the United States as *A "Titanic" Hero*. Baltimore: Norman, Remington, 1913; with Emily Lawless, *The Race of Castlebar*. London: John Murray, 1913; *Mr. Ruby Jumps the Traces*. London: Chapman & Hall, 1917; *Mors et Vita*. London: Laurie, 1923. (Poems); *The Loughsiders*. London: Harrap, 1924; *Gleanings*. Sutton, Surrey: William Pile, 1926. (Poems); *After Sixty Years*. London: Sampson Low, 1931.   REFERENCES: Foster, John Wilson. *Forces and Themes in Ulster Fiction*. Dublin: Gill & Macmillan/Totowa, N.J.: Rowman & Littlefield, 1974; Kiely, Benedict. *Modern Irish Fiction—A Critique*. Dublin: Golden Eagle Books, 1950.

BURKE, EDMUND (1729-1797), political philosopher, orator, and aesthetician. Burke, the father of modern conservatism, as some have called him, was born in Dublin on January 12, 1729. His father, an Anglican, was a solicitor of good middle-class standing; his mother was a Catholic, a fact that would later haunt him as he began his political career in the 1760s, only a few years after his marriage (in 1756) to Jane Mary Nugent, also a Catholic. In their public and private attempts to discredit him, Burke's enemies rarely failed to mention his "low" origins and his questionable family connections: his Dublin birthplace and suspected Roman leanings; his inability to claim a distinguished lineage; the large crowd of Irish relatives, some of them quite disreputable, who always hung about him and whom he protected lovingly, passionately, sometimes perhaps unwisely. Occasionally, Burke's friends were chagrined for him, but never Burke himself—at least not seriously. His persistent refusal to find any reason for embarrassment in his background and station provides a clue to some of the abiding preoccupations of his life and career. Always an Anglican, he was nonetheless a staunch defender of Catholic rights in England and Ireland alike. His posture in this matter on behalf of fundamental human rights is consistent with the stance he assumed during two of the momentous episodes of his political career: his lonely and unsuccessful campaign for conciliation with the American colonies in the early 1770s, and the many years (from 1786 to 1795) of equally unsuccessful impeachment proceedings against Warren Hastings for his major part in the corruption of the colonial government in India. Burke's lifelong devotion to a troublesome family suggests that for him, as an Anglican moralist and practical man, the family, though capable of imperfections, was an important personal and social tradition, a force for stability and humanity in the day-to-day business of living. The essence of every civilized tradition, as the inevitably flawed but necessary product of generations of trial and error, needs desperately to be preserved by those who have the capacity for thought and learning and judgment, preserved against the erosions of indifference or ignorance and against the mad zeal of democratic reformers whose impractical, abstract philosophical notions of a perfect human society are the results of but a moment's hysterical folly and can only bring chaos —so Burke said with matchless brilliance and eloquence in his *Reflections on the Revolution in France* (1790).

Paradoxically, one of Burke's last significant pieces of work, the *Letter to a Noble Lord* (1795), castigated the duke of Bedford, one of the truly conspicuous symbols of the aristocratic tradition Burke had so vigorously defended and sought to join. Bedford, he charged, was a weighty baggage who enjoyed his privileges by birth only, and not by merit; while he, Edmund Burke, a man of humble beginnings, had risen to a certain eminence and earned the reward of a government pension by dint of his effort. It is almost the statement of a democratic reformer, dangerously close (as some, including Samuel Taylor Coleridge, have thought) to the ideals of the leveling Jacobins whom Burke despised and wrathfully reviled. And yet what is really meant seems abundantly clear. The rabble is to be distrusted and feared, and even a duke of Bedford must be protected from its menace. But socially unpretentious men of intelligence, learning, industry, honor, and some wisdom possess a kind of natural nobility and surely ought not be denied the benefits of privilege or, more important, the opportunity to participate in carrying out the responsibilities for wise government that tradition, as the cohering force in social and political order, requires.

Burke had no systematic philosophy of government, and he cannot be reduced to a single statemnt. Yet, it is clear that his every action in public life announced his commitment to those virtues which he so justly ascribed to himself, with becoming modesty and with crystalline clarity of under-standing and expression, in the *Letter to a Noble Lord*. Above all things, Burke admired practical wisdom, and it was to the past he looked as its source, though not worshipfully or in mere nostalgia.

Despite the important consistencies in Burke's life and public career, Isaac Kramnick has characterized him astutely in *The Rage of Edmund Burke* (1977) as an ambivalent man, a man of paradoxes. Born and edu-cated (at Trinity College, Dublin) an Irishman, he became an authentic genius of English political and parliamentary history. As a young man, however, he was unable to finish his studies at the Middle Temple in Lon-don, where his father had sent him in 1750—the law did not "open and liberalize the mind," he said. Always suspicious of theory, in his youth he wrote an ingenious satire called *A Vindication of Natural Society* (1756) in which he impersonated Bolingbroke, making a mockery of that noble lord's doctrine of natural theology by translating it into the practical realm of politics. In the very next year, however, he published a profoundly im-portant treatise on aesthetics, his *Philosophical Enquiry into the Origin of Our Ideas of the Sublime and the Beautiful* (1757), which is a brilliant study of the emotional responses called forth by a variety of images and effects. Burke was a deeply skeptical man, but he nevertheless reserved for tradition—tradition as a practical consequence of man's successful living— the kind of reverence by which idealism usually bows before some noble vision of the good. Many have always considered his conservative reaction to the French Revolution as a turnabout from his earlier "liberal" stand on the taxation of the American colonies. He was a Whig turned Tory defender, the same man who, some twenty years earlier, had published his *Thoughts on the Cause of the Present Discontents* (1770), an attack on Toryism and on some of the evils of monarchy embodied in George III and his court circle. And there is, of course, the *Letter to a Noble Lord,* wherein Burke the apologist for inherited privilege almost becomes the prophet of the self-made man, the proponent of merit as the chief measure, whatever one's class, of worth and fitness for position. Though it may seem a con-tradiction to say it, Burke was consistent in his principles but (sometimes) inconsistent in his behavior and public utterances. In other words, he was human. Until very recently, Burke studies have revered him as the almost legendary apostle of straightforward political conservatism—or occasionally of political liberalism. Now scholars are coming round to a new understanding of the kind of depth and complexity of feeling and thought hinted at in the title of Kramnick's book and made rather plain by Burke himself in the *Letter* to Bedford.

Burke's public career was spectacular, but only in the sense that the amazing brilliance of his speeches and essays on the great subjects of his day attracted everyone's attention and have continued to do so. Though he must be called a grand statesman, he never reached the pinnacle of power. He first came to the attention of those in political circles as the editor and chief writer for Robert Dodsley's *Annual Register* of current politics, history, and literature. After beginning this work in 1758, he became known as a young man possessed with immense knowledge of public affairs, and in 1759, he was made private assistant to William Hamilton, secretary to the lord lieutenant of Ireland. Following a short official stay in his native island, Burke returned to London in 1764 and, along with his old friends Samuel Johnson and Joshua Reynolds, was an original member of "The Club." He joined the short administration of the marquis of Rockingham as private secretary to the prime minister in 1765 and was elected (with Rockingham's help) a member of Parliament from the borough of Windover. He enjoyed instant success as an orator in the House of Commons. In 1767, he undertook a venture as grand as any of his speeches when he borrowed a huge sum of money to purchase Gregories, his magnificent country estate at Beaconsfield, which he loved but which remained a crushing financial burden for the rest of his years.

Burke's *Speech on American Taxation* (1774) and his address on *Conciliation with America* (1775) were models of rhetorical eloquence and practical wisdom. Conciliation may not be pleasant, Burke argued, but it is the only expedient. Everyone marveled, even the staunchest exponents of English prerogatives, but Burke's advice was, of course, not followed, though he was proven right by the outcome of the Revolutionary War. His unpopular stand on the American question and his advocacy of religious toleration and of fair trade practices with Ireland cost him the Bristol seat he had won in 1774. In 1780, he was elected member of Parliament from Malton, the seat he held until his retirement to Beaconsfield in 1794.

Burke's next great undertakings included a magnificent *Speech on the Economical Reformation*, which he delivered upon taking his new seat (his economics was hardly distinguishable from Adam Smith's); a campaign for parliamentary reforms begun in his *Speech on the Representation of the Commons in Parliament* (1782); and pursuit of policies of fair treatment for Ireland (*Letter to a Peer of Ireland*, 1782). Burke joined the second Rockingham administration in 1782 and was briefly paymaster-general under the Fox-North coalition in 1783. He began to fade when the younger Pitt and his fresh generation came to power in 1784. He was all but thrown out of the Whig party following a dramatic break with Fox in 1791. He wrote about this event with feeling and characteristic eloquence in *An Appeal from the New to the Old Whigs*, which expressed his reverence for the ideals of the Old Whigs whose origins lay in the Glorious Revolution of 1688.

The last decade of Burke's career was largely consumed by the Hastings affair and the French Revolution, but he continued his abiding interest in the problems of Ireland. In fact, besides the *Reflections* and the *Letter to a Noble Lord,* his most important works during those last years concerned the plight of the Irish. Burke was much distressed by the political and social injustices visited upon the Roman Catholic majority, and he yearned for reforms, as he explained in his powerful *Letter to Sir Hercules Langrishe on the Subject of the Roman Catholics of Ireland* (1792). He dispatched his son Richard there, since he could not go himself, and restated his concerns publicly in *A Letter to Richard Burke* (1793). The subject preoccupied him until his death; the last thing he wrote, before he died at Beaconsfield on July 9, 1797, was a *Letter on the Affairs of Ireland.*

Burke's attitudes towards Ireland were consistent with his political attitudes generally and were a natural outgrowth from them. He was, always, committed to "the principle of *common naturalization* which runs through this whole empire," as he said in a *Letter to Sir Charles Bingham, Bart., on the Irish Absentee Tax* (1773). He exercised this principle in his public statements on Ireland, America, and India, and it was the foundation of his arguments for fair taxation policies, free trade, and religious tolerance. He despised gratuitous injustice and harmful prejudice, and hearkened to what he called the "tolerating maxims of the Gospel." In his *Speech at Bristol Previous to the Election* (1780), he told his listeners that he wished to cultivate "the locality of patriotism," to make the empire "one family, one body, one heart and soul," to follow "the grand social principle, that unites all men, in all descriptions, under the shadow of equal and impartial justice." To achieve this end, it was not necessary to destroy the traditions upon which rested a system that fostered injustice or oppression. However, it *was* necessary for men and their governments to act humanely, wisely, with a sense of their past as guide to their present and their future. Burke repeated this idea over and over again, in many forms and from many forums—indeed, it is the essence of his genius and his greatness. The eloquence with which he always said it, the stunning beauty of his language so rich in images, metaphors, and analogies, gave it form as a strong and enduring idea. Burke may never have reached the highest seat of power, and he may have enjoyed only limited success at the business of parliamentary maneuvering. But this Irishman of modest beginnings, through the sheer force of his mind and his language and his principles, had an enormous impact on political thought in his own day and left a legacy of brilliance which has affected the course of Western political history ever since.

JERRY C. BEASLEY

WORKS: *The Works of Edmund Burke.* 8 vols. Bohn's Standard Library. London: George Bell, 1900; *Burke's Politics: Selected Writings and Speeches of Edmund Burke on Reform, Revolution, and War.* Ross J. S. Hoffman & Paul Levack, eds. New York: Alfred A. Knopf, 1949; *Letters, Speeches, and Tracts on Irish Affairs by Edmund Burke.* Matthew Arnold, ed. London: Macmillan, 1881; *A Note-book of Edmund Burke.* H. V. F. Somerset, ed. Cambridge: Cambridge University Press, 1957; *Selected Writings of Edmund Burke.* W. J. Bate, ed. Modern Library Edition. New York: Random House, 1960; *The Correspondence of Edmund Burke.* Thomas W. Copeland, et al., eds. 9 vols. Chicago: University of Chicago Press & Cambridge: Cambridge University Press, 1958-1971.   REFERENCES—Biographies: Bryant, Donald Cross. *Edmund Burke and His Literary Friends.* St. Louis, Mo.: Washington University Press, 1939; Cone, Carl B. *Burke and the Nature of Politics.* 2 vols. Lexington: University of Kentucky Press, 1957; Magnus, Philip. *Edmund Burke: A Life.* London: John Murray, 1939; Morley, John. *Burke.* English Men of Letters. London: Macmillan, 1874; O'Brien, William. *Edmund Burke As an Irishman.* 2d ed. Dublin: M. H. Gill, 1926; Wector, Dixon. *Edmund Burke and His Kinsmen.* Boulder: University of Colorado Press, 1939. Critical Studies: Boulton, James T. *The Language of Politics in the Age of Wilkes and Burke.* London: Routledge & Kegan Paul, 1963; Cameron, David. *The Social Thought of Rousseau and Burke.* Toronto: University of Toronto Press, 1973; Canavan, Francis P. *The Political Reason of Edmund Burke.* Durham, N.C.: Duke University Press, 1960; Chapman, Gerald W. *Edmund Burke: The Practical Imagination.* Cambridge, Mass.: Harvard University Press, 1967; Cobban, Alfred B. C. *Edmund Burke and the Revolt Against the Eighteenth Century.* London: Allen & Unwin, 1929; Copeland, Thomas W. *Our Eminent Friend Edmund Burke.* New Haven, Conn.: Yale University Press, 1949; Fussell, Paul. *The Rhetorical World of Augustan Humanism. Ethics and Imagery from Swift to Burke.* London: Oxford University Press, 1965; Kramnick, Isaac. *The Rage of Edmund Burke: Portrait of an Ambivalent Conservative.* New York: Basic Books, 1977; Kramnick, Isaac, ed. *Edmund Burke.* Great Lives Observed. Englewood Cliffs, N.J.: Prentice-Hall, 1974; Mahoney, Thomas H. D. *Edmund Burke and Ireland.* Cambridge, Mass.: Harvard University Press, 1960; Parkins, Charles. *The Moral Basis of Burke's Political Thought.* Cambridge: Cambridge University Press, 1956; *Studies in Burke and His Times.* Published three times a year. 1959—.

BYRNE, DONN (1889-1928), novelist and short story writer. Byrne was born in New York City on November 20, 1889, and was christened Brian Oswald Donn-Byrne. His parents were from South Armagh where they returned after a few months in America and where young Donn-Byrne was raised. As a youth, as Brian O'Beirne, he became an enthusiastic Irish speaker, fluent enough to win prizes and to receive the commendation of Douglas Hyde,* one of his teachers in University College, Dublin. He is said to have studied at the Sorbonne and at Leipzig where, according to his biographer, he refused his Ph.D. on the grounds that no Irish gentleman could possibly wear the prescribed evening clothes in the morning. In about 1911, he moved to New York and married Dorothea Cadogan, a girl from the South of Ireland, who, later, as Dolly Donn Byrne, had some success as a playwright, her plays being produced both by the Ulster Theatre and on Broadway.

Under the semi-pseudonym of Donn Byrne, Brian began writing prolifically, first poetry and then short stories, for various New York magazines such as *The Smart Set*, *Red Book*, and *Scribner's*. His first book, a collection entitled *Stories Without Women*, appeared in 1915, and his first novel, *The Stranger's Banquet*, in 1919. Ten more novels, two more volumes of stories, and a short book about Ireland appeared in the 1920s. Byrne gained great popularity and earning power during this period. He lived in Europe during much of the 1920s; he died in a car accident at Courtmacsherry Bay in West Cork on June 18, 1928.

Despite his years in America, many of Byrne's stories and novels are Irish in subject, and the best are compulsively readable and highly entertaining. However, his work has been described as "ersatz," his popularity is long past, and academic critics generally ignore him today. Although his tertainer, his best trembles on the verge of something better. If he has never poorest work has merely the smooth canniness of the slick magazine enquite achieved literary respectability, the reasons are that his romanticism is too rampant and his morality too simplistic. His ability to spin a yarn, however, is so fine that he frequently buries one's critical sensibilities, and it is only after the book is put down that one feels the whole business has been a bit spurious.

If one puts Byrne's pretensions to artistry aside and takes him on his own legitimate ground, Byrne still can evoke pleasure. His short stories are probably his tinniest work, but among the novels, *Messer Marco Polo*, *The Wind Bloweth*, *Hangman's House*, *Brother Saul*, and *The Power of the Dog* all have their persuasive devotees.

WORKS: *Stories Without Women*. New York: Hearst's International Library, 1915; *The Stranger's Banquet*. New York: Harper's, 1919. (Novel); *The Foolish Matrons*. New York, Harper's, 1920/London: Sampson Low, 1923. (Novel); *Messer Marco Polo*. New York: Century/London: Sampson Low, 1922. (Novel); *The Wind Bloweth*. New York: Century/London: Sampson Low, 1922. (Novel); *Changling, and Other Stories*. New York: Century, 1923/London: Sampson Low, 1924; *Blind Raftery*. New York: Century, 1924/London: Sampson Low, 1925. (Novel); *O'Malley of Shanganagh*. New York: Century, 1925/also published as *An Untitled Story*, London: Sampson Low, 1925. (Novel); *Hangman's House*. New York: Century/London: Sampson Low, 1925. (Novel); *Brother Saul*. New York: Century/London: Sampson Low, 1927. (Novel); *Crusade*. Boston: Little, Brown/London: Sampson Low, 1928. (Novel); *Destiny Boy*. Boston: Little, Brown/London: Sampson Low, 1928. (Stories); *Field of Honor*. New York: Century, 1929/also published as *The Power of the Dog*. London: Sampson Low, 1929; *Ireland: The Rock Whence I was Hewn*. Boston: Little, Brown/London: Sampson Low, 1929. (Travel); *The Golden Goat*. London: Sampson Low, 1930. (Novel).   REFERENCE: Macauley, Thurston. *Donn Byrne, Bard of Armagh*. London: Sampson Low, Marston & Co., [1931].

BYRNE, JOHN KEYES. *See* LEONARD, HUGH.

BYRNE, LAURENCE PATRICK. *See* MALONE, ANDREW E.

BYRNE, SEAMUS (1904-1968), playwright. Byrne was born in Dublin on December 27, 1904, and died in Dublin in 1968. He received an LL.B. from the National University and practiced law for nine years in Leitrim. In 1940, he was jailed for his involvement with the IRA, but he was released nine months later after a hunger strike of twenty-one days.

A proposed hunger strike among political prisoners in Mountjoy Jail is the subject of Byrne's finest play, *Design for a Headstone* (Abbey,* 1950). The conflict in the play is basically between the prisoners' political loyalties and their religious ones. On the sixth night of production, some outspoken criticisms of the Catholic Church within the play caused a disturbance in the theatre by a right-wing Catholic organization. Police were brought into the theatre on the following night, and the protest, which had no popular support, died away. The play has occasionally been compared to Brendan Behan's* later and better known prison drama, *The Quare Fellow*, but there is little point to the comparison. Behan is to Byrne rather like O'Casey* is to Denis Johnston*; Behan's theme is a simple emotional statement, but Byrne's is deeper and much more complex. On a merely theatrical level, Behan's play has a freewheeling broadness which Byrne's lacks, but Byrne's has effective comedy as well as more deeply drawn characters and its own quite stark intensity.

Little City (*Theatre Festival*, 1964) is a three-pronged condemnation of the quality of life in modern Dublin. The strongest prong of the attack is directed at the social hypocrisies surrounding abortion, and this topic effectively delayed the play's production for years. There is some lack of proportion between the play's various strands of plots, and recent events have made the play something of a period piece. Nevertheless, Byrne again demonstrates that he was the strongest, if not almost the only, social commentator writing for the Irish stage in the 1950s. To the detriment of the Irish drama, he has had few followers.

WORKS: *Design for a Headstone*. Dublin: Progress House, 1956; *Little City*. Dixon, Calif.: Proscenium, 1970.

CALLANAN, J. J. (1795-1829), poet. J. J. (Jeremiah Joseph, James Joseph, or even Jeremiah John) Callanan was born in Cork in 1795. After attending Maynooth and then Trinity College, Dublin, without graduating, Callanan spent much time collecting Irish legends and ballads. Of his translations, Padraic Colum* remarks, "The poet brought, in one instance, anyway, a recognisable Gaelic cadence into translations from the Irish. That cadence is in 'The Outlaw of Loch Lene.' " Although Callanan's English equivalents of Irish poetry are not particularly accurate, his renderings are fluent, as in these verses from "The Lament of O'Gnive":

> How dimmed is the glory that circled the Gael
> And fall'n the high people of green Innisfail;
> The sword of the Saxon is red with their gore;
> And the mighty of nations is mighty no more! . . .
>
> O'Neil of the Hostages; Con, whose high name
> On a hundred red battles has floated to fame,
> Let the long grass still sigh undisturbed o'er thy sleep;
> Arise not to shame us, awake not to weep.

Sometimes Callanan rises to a strength that quite overcomes the conventions of nineteenth-century poetic diction, as in this stanza from "O Say. My Brown Drimin":

> When the prince, now an exile, shall come for his own,
> The isles of his father, his rights and his throne,
> My people in battle the Saxons will meet,
> And kick them before, like old shoes from their feet.

Or, as in this curse from "Dirge of O'Sullivan Bear":

> Scully! may all kinds
>   Of evil attend thee!
> On thy dark road of life
>   May no kind one befriend thee!
> May fevers long burn thee,
>   And agues long freeze thee!
> May the strong hand of God
>   In His red anger seize thee!

In 1829, Callanan went to Lisbon for his health, but, when his condition rapidly deteriorated, he determined to die in Ireland and boarded a vessel bound for Cork. His tuberculosis was so advanced, however, that he was returned to shore, and he died on September 19.

WORKS: *The Recluse of Inchidony and Other Poems*. London: Hurst, Chance, 1830; *The Poems of J. J. Callanan*. Cork: Bolster, 1847; *The Poems of J. J. Callanan*. Cork: Daniel Mulcahy, 1861; *Gems of the Cork Poets: Comprising the Complete Works of Callanan, Condon, Casey, Fitzgerald, and Cody*. Cork: Barter, 1883. REFERENCE: MacCarthy, Bridget G. "Jeremiah J. Callanan. Part I: His Life. Part II: His Poetry." *Studies* 35 (1946): 215-229, 387-399.

CAMPBELL, JOSEPH (1879-1944), poet. Campbell was born in Belfast, on July 15, 1879. From his father, William Henry, a building contractor, he inherited his strong nationalistic tendencies; from his gentle, cultured mother he received an interest in literature, music, art, folklore, and a love of everything Gaelic.

Literary criticism has generally belittled Campbell, and literary history has undervalued his part in the creative upsurge of the early twentieth century. Apart from his being represented in anthologies by a few of his more popular poems, Campbell's individual contribution to Irish life and literature is ignored.

Poet, patriot, scholar, writer, and a man of vision, culture, and idealism, Campbell was one of the rarest and most Gaelic of minds of our time, as, indeed, Austin Clarke* remarked on Radio Éireann in 1938. Campbell's knowledge of Gaelic life and literature was profound. He was steeped in traditional lore, and he stimulated an interest in Ireland's cultural heritage everywhere he went. His poetry differs in some respects from that of other Irish poets who were writing at the opening of this century. He is essentially a lyric poet inspired directly by Irish folklore and folksong, a poet who expresses in clear, simple English the traditional spirit of Irish life. A little unpublished poem entitled "The Key" (written on June 19, 1939) expresses his own consciousness of his "Irishness":

> Who would unlock me
> Must file for himself a key of three words—
> Vision, Energy, Bleakness.

Campbell considered these three qualities characteristic of Irish poetry, and he strove to maintain them in his poetry. Vision he understood as imagery, energy as avoidance of the commonplace, and bleakness as austerity. The austerity of early Gaelic art and its concentrated brevity inspired him. His power of expressing a memorable simplicity is the result not only of inspiration, but also of subtle art:

> I am the mountainy singer—
> The voice of the peasant's dream,
> The cry of the wind on the wooded hill,
> The leap of the fish in the stream.

The first stirrings of the Irish Literary Revival reached Belfast in the early years of the century, and Campbell, with other young Ulstermen, was attracted to it. Introduced in 1902 by his friend Padraic Colum* to the Dublin literary leaders, Campbell published articles and poems in Arthur Griffith's* *The United Irishman* and Standish O'Grady's* *All Ireland Review*. In 1904, he collaborated with Herbert Hughes, the musician, in the publication of *Songs of Uladh,* a collection of folksongs. Campbell supplied the words for these beautiful, long-forgotten traditional airs which Hughes had collected in Donegal—"My Lagan Love," "The Ninepenny Fidil," and others. These genuine folksongs so capture the artlessness, freshness, and liquid ease of the ballad that they have passed into the anonymous folk tradition of Anglo-Irish ballads whose authorship is forgotten. Friendship with Francis Joseph Bigger, the Ulster politician, brought Campbell into contact with the Ulster Literary Theatre, and he became actor, playwright, and an editor of *Uladh*, its quarterly journal. The reception given his play *The Little Cowherd of Slainge,* produced by the company in May 1905, convinced him that his talent lay elsewhere, but as an actor of fine voice and presence he showed distinct promise.

After a short stay in 1905 in Dublin where, as an Ulsterman, he felt he got scant recognition, Campbell went to London in 1906 in search of a more sympathetic audience. He was employed as a teacher of English in the London County Council Schools. He also acted as secretary of the Irish Literary Society, London, and as assistant to Eleanor Hull of the Irish Texts Society. While in London, he became acquainted with the poetic theories and movements of the twentieth century, especially the Imagist movement, and he developed an interest in contemporary Russian, French, American, and German literature. Having married a London girl, Nancy Maude, who shared his literary interests, he returned to Dublin in 1911 and set up home outside the city on the Dublin-Wicklow border, hoping to settle down seriously to a literary career.

Campbell's early volumes of verse—*The Garden of the Bees* (1905), *The Rushlight* (1906), *The Man-Child* (1907), *The Gilly of Christ* (1907), and *The Mountainy Singer* (1909)—have a certain freshness and a distinct vein of originality. He wrote of the simple things of Irish life in an utterly individual and spontaneous manner reminiscent of Gaelic poetry. The traditions of the Irish people, their religious outlook, and their strong faith permeate these poems. Campbell is very unequal, however. Many of these earlier poems lack ease of utterance and smoothness, and reflect the difficult wrestling of a poet with his material. Many poems have a looseness of style reminiscent of Whitman, and others show the too active influence of English poetry, particularly that of the Romantic school. The best of the early poems have been included by Austin Clarke in *Poems of Joseph Campbell* (1963).

Mearing Stones (1911) revealed Campbell in a new light, that of prose writer and artist. Subtitled *Leaves from My Note-book on Tramp in Donegal* and illustrated with black and white pencil drawings, this unusual collection of prose sketches showed Campbell's capacity for impressionistic portraiture verbally as well as visually. The book is alive with mood and atmosphere. In the following year, 1912, Campbell published a play, *Judgment,* set in the same wild mountain area of Donegal. The play, produced at the Abbey* in April, is one of social realism and recalls Synge* in its grim tragedy and wild beauty, although it was scarcely as effective as Synge in the theatre. A second play, *The Turn Out,* was published in *The Irish*

*Review** in 1912 but was not produced. Campbell lacked a sense of dramatic structure and a sure command of technique.

The later volumes of verse, *Irishry* (1913) and *Earth of Cualann* (1917), marked Campbell's highest achievement as a poet. These show a development of style, a distinct improvement in technique, a tightening of the line, a more marked subtlety in diction, and a more confident use of difficult meters and even of free verse. Austin Clarke claimed that Campbell was the first Irish poet to use free verse effectively and that *Earth of Cualann* was his greatest achievement. This book, inspired by the matchless beauty of the Wicklow countryside of Cualann, is deeply charged with atmosphere. The terse symbolism, the epigrammatic conciseness, the allusions to Gaelic myths, the austerity, and the restraint which Campbell sought lessen its appeal for the average reader. His more popular *Irishry,* with its vivid and realistic character lyrics, forms an interesting study of the people of the Irish countryside. A comparison with Padraic Colum's lyrics is obvious, but the austerity, realism, and absence of sentiment in Campbell's portraits form a vivid contrast with Colum's kindlier, gentler approach. Included in *Irishry* is Campbell's little masterpiece, "The Old Woman":

> As a white candle
> In a holy place,
> So is the beauty
> Of an aged face.
>
> As the spent radiance
> Of the winter sun,
> So is a woman
> With her travail done.
>
> Her brood gone from her,
> And her thoughts as still
> As the waters
> Under a ruined mill.

This sensitive, impressionistic lyric was inspired by his mother. Campbell playfully remarked on Radio Éireann on January 28, 1942, "Poets rarely make money, but I have made some on that. Indeed it has gotten into so many anthologies that I have been accused of living on 'The Old Woman'!"

In 1913, Campbell became involved in the struggle for national freedom. He was one of the promoters of the Irish Volunteers, did rescue work in Dublin during the Easter Rising, acted as chairman of the Wicklow County Council in 1920 and 1921, opposed the setting up of the Irish Free State in December 1921, was arrested early in the Civil War, and was interned in Mountjoy Jail and later in the Curragh internment camp until the general jail delivery of Christmas 1923. A "Jail Journal" which he wrote still remains unpublished. On his release, a broken and dispirited man, disillusioned with life and with Ireland's political leaders, and despairing of ever finding happiness or suitable employment in Ireland, he decided to emigrate to America.

Campbell's life in New York from 1925 to 1939 marked a new beginning. This man, fired with enthusiasm and love for Ireland's cultural inheritance, dreamed of establishing in America a permanent center of Irish culture. It seems incredible that one man, burdened with financial worries and dogged by misfortune, could attempt so much. He founded the School of Irish Studies in New York in 1925, the Irish Foundation in 1931, and *The Irish Review* in 1934; he pioneered cultural travel trips to Ireland in 1933; he lectured on Irish literature at Fordham from 1927 to 1938; and through lectures, plays, recitals, summer schools, and exhibitions of Irish arts and crafts, he sought to bring Ireland to America and America to Ireland.

Financial worries, poor health, and a desire to get down to the publication of his Collected Poems and to complete some unfinished work brought Campbell back to Ireland in 1939, to the security of his mountain farm in Wicklow where he lived an eremitic existence until his death in June 1944.

Campbell slipped away quietly, almost unknown to the general public. The literary world paid a passing tribute and soon forgot him. Not a single one of his books was in print, and so his name became just a name "with a hundred others / In a book in the library." Austin Clarke's* publication in 1963 of *The Poems of Joseph Campbell* suggested some reawakened interest in Campbell's work, but since then no other recognition has come. Campbell remains, unaccountably, a forgotten poet, one of the most neglected and undervalued of our time.

NUALA SAUNDERS

WORKS: *The Little Cowherd of Slainge*, in *Uladh* 1 (November 1904). (Play); *The Garden of the Bees and Other Poems.* [Belfast: W. Erskine Mayne; Dublin: Gill, 1905]; *The Rushlight.* Dublin: Maunsel, 1906; *The Gilly of Christ.* Dublin: Maunsel, 1907; *The Man Child.* [Dublin?]: Loch Press Series, 1907; *The Mountainy Singer.* Dublin: Maunsel, 1909/Boston: Four Seas Co., 1919; *Mearing Stones.* Dublin: Maunsel, 1911; *Judgment.* Dublin & London: Maunsel, 1912. (Play); *Irishry.* Dublin & London: Maunsel, 1913; *Earth of Cualann.* Dublin & London: Maunsel, 1917; *Orange Terror*, by "Ultach." Dublin: Reprinted from *The Capuchin Annual*, 1943; *The Poems of Joseph Campbell*, ed. & with an Introduction by Austin Clarke. Dublin: Allen Figgis, 1963.   REFERENCE: O'Hegarty, P. S. *A Bibliography of Joseph Campbell—Seosamh Mac Cathmaoil.* Dublin: A. Thom, 1940.

CAMPBELL, [HONORABLE] MICHAEL [MUSSEN] (1924-), novelist.

Campbell, the second son of the second Baron Glenavy, was born in Dublin on October 25, 1924. His older brother and the present Baron Glenavy is Patrick Campbell, the well-known journalist. Campbell was educated at the College of St. Columba and at Trinity College, Dublin, where he obtained a B.A. and a B.L. After some practice of law, Campbell was for some years a journalist on the London staff of *The Irish Times*. He has written six novels, of which the first, *Peter Perry,* has the most Irish interest. *Peter Perry* is more a character sketch than a story, but its heroine, the eccentric and bohemian old lady, is memorable, and the cultural milieu of the early 1950s in Dublin is beautifully caught.

WORKS: *Peter Perry*. London: Heinemann, 1956; *Oh, Mary, This London.* London: Heinemann, 1959; *Across the Water*. London: Heinemann, 1961; *The Princess in England*. London: Heinemann, 1964; *Lord Dismiss Us*. London: Heinemann, 1967; *Nothing Doing*. London: Constable, 1970.

CAMPION, JOHN T[HOMAS] (1814-189?), poet and novelist. Campion was born in Kilkenny in 1814, practiced medicine there for most of his life, and died sometime in the 1890s. Both as poet and novelist, he can be taken as typical of dozens of popular nineteenth-century Irish writers whose literary abilities were not commensurate with their patriotism. In subject matter, Campion's works were jingoistically patriotic, but in manner they were conventionally imitative of English modes. Campion differs from many popular writers, however, in that some few works have a vigor that captured the popular imagination, and a vitality that sometimes transcends craftsmanship. For instance, his widely known poem "Emmet's Death," which was originally published in *The Nation** in 1844, is a fair example of the patriotic poetry that was technically proficient enough to be stirring and that also had an honest although quite unsubtle emotionalism. These qualities go far to compensate for its basic badness. Its last stanza reads:

> "He dies to-day," thought a fair, sweet girl—
>   She lacked the life to speak,
> For sorrow had almost frozen her head,
>   And white were her lip and cheek—
> Despair had drank up her last wild tear,
>   And her brow was damp and chill,
> And they often felt at her heart with fear,
>   For its ebb was all but still.

Champion's novels and his novelized history of Michael Dwyer are marred by the faults of his poetry, as well as by the conventional excesses of popular English fiction and theatrical melodrama. For, instance, from *Michael Dwyer:*

> "Your doom is sealed, Williams!"
> "My doom was sealed when my name was first entered on your list. It was at once death or dishonour: I choose death!"

> "And die you shall!"
> "Praise be to God!"
> "You blaspheme, rebel."
> "I am an Irishman, and I die for Ireland!"
> "Faugh! Summon the court-martial."

In their descriptive and narrative sections, Campion's fictions have a literary pretentiousness of style. However, in Campion, as in much better writers like Fenimore Cooper in America or Carleton* in Ireland, the florid writing is not sufficient to deflect the vigorous forward thrust of the narrative. Campion's work is more interesting as evidence of Irish political sentiment than as literature, but the tradition he was working in has been used by a few modern writers to great effect, as in, for instance, Denis Johnston's* *The Old Lady Says "No!"* and portions of Sean O'Casey's* *The Drums of Father Ned.*

WORKS: "Ballads and Poems," *Traces of the Crusaders in Ireland.* Dublin: Hennessy, 1856; *Alice: A Historical Romance of the Crusaders in Ireland.* Kilkenny: Coyle, 1862. (Novel); *The Last Struggles of the Irish Sea Smugglers.* Glasgow: Cameron, Ferguson, 1869. (Novel); *Michael Dwyer; or, The Insurgent Captain of the Wicklow Mountains.* Glasgow: Cameron, Ferguson, [ca. 1869].

CARBERY, ETHNA (1866-1902), poet. Carbery was the pen name of Anna Isabel Johnston who was born in Ballymena on December 3, 1866. She lived most of her life in Belfast where, from 1896 to 1899, she and Alice Milligan* edited the nationalistic literary magazine *The Shan Van Vocht.* She was a prolific contributor of verse and stories to similar Irish periodicals. In 1901, she married Seumas MacManus,* the Donegal story writer, but their marriage was shortlived, for she died on April 21, 1902. Of all the many patriotic lady poets of her day, Ethna Carbery, possibly partly because of her early death, generated the most excitement in patriotic clubs and debating societies. Her poems, collected in the volume *The Four Winds of Eirinn,* were widely read and frequently reprinted, and as late as 1922 Padraic Colum* found them charming. While they are facile, they contain only the conventional sentiments and the usual phrasing of a hundred poets before her. One ballad, "Roddy McCorley," is still sung today.

WORKS: *The Four Winds of Eirinn.* Dublin: Gill, 1902/new edition, with additional poems & memoir by Seumas MacManus (Dublin: Gill, 1918); *The Passionate Hearts.* London: Isbister, 1903; *In the Celtic Past.* Dublin: Gill, 1904. (Stories).

CARLETON, WILLIAM (1794-1869), novelist and short story writer. For most literary historians, Carleton's fame is based more on his peasant background than on his artistic achievements. Indeed, it is remarkable that a simple boy from County Tyrone, trained only in a hedge-school, could rise to popular fame as a writer. And he never forgot that life; in all his writings, he presented a fresh, unsophisticated apprehension of peasant life in the years before and during the Great Famine. However, his critical reputation as a writer should be based on more than claims of his native genius and naivete; he was a superb storyteller, an accurate reporter, and one of the few true spokesmen for the masses of Irish country people in the nineteenth century.

Born on February 20, 1794, one of a large family, Carleton had no access to formal schooling. Yet, under the tutelage of a hedge-schoolmaster, he acquired skill in expression and a curiosity about learning which made him want to succeed. First he pursued the priesthood, but once in Dublin he turned away sharply from that vocation. Under the influence of Caesar Otway,* he began to write sketches of Irish country life for the *Christian Examiner*, a journal designed to expose the malign influence of the Roman Catholic Church on the Irish people. However, Carleton's descriptive gifts exceeded the propagandistic purposes they served, and in 1830, his collection of tales, *Traits and Stories of the Irish Peasantry*, was published. These are his best work and were recognized in his lifetime as such. A second series of tales followed in 1833. Encouraged by their reception, Carleton turned to longer forms and published several novels, the best of which are *Fardorougha the Miser* (1839), *Valentine McClutchy* (1845), and *The Black Prophet* (1847). The last is the best of the novels, a tale set in his contemporary Ireland, describing in painful detail the sufferings of the peasants in the Great Famine. He devoted the last years of his life to writing his autobiography, a task left uncompleted when he died in Dublin on January 30, 1869.

Many critics, from Yeats* on, have praised Carleton for his treatment of authentic Irish subjects. For instance, Stephen Gwynn* remarked in *Irish Literature and Drama in the English Language*, "The most notable thing about Carleton is that one feels him to be writing for Ireland, not for England." His Ireland was neither the green isle populated by poets and dreamers, nor the wild place stocked with buffoons and savages, but a recognizable country where many suffered and a few exhibited humor and even heroism.

But Carleton is most likely to be remembered for his achievement in reproducing Irish native speech. At a time when Irish was fading as the predominant language, the people spoke English in the syntax of their native language. As Thomas Flanagan notes in *The Irish Novelists 1800-1850*, "Half a century before John Synge* put his ear to a Wicklow floor to catch the talk of servant girls, Carleton had caught every turn and nuance of Irish speech." It is the colorful speech, accurately revealing characters and even presenting ironic commentary, which sustains the reader's interest, for the plots of his novels are loose and unconvincing. Several generations later, when the writers of the Irish Renaissance returned to peasant speech, they found William Carleton their mentor.

JAMES KILROY

WORKS: *Father Butler; The Lough Dearg Pilgrim.* Dublin: Wm. Curry, 1829; *Traits and Stories of the Irish Peasantry.* 2 vols. Dublin: Wm. Curry, 1830; *Traits and Stories of the Irish Peastry, 2nd Series.* 3 vols. Dublin: W. F. Wakeman, 1833; *Tales of Ireland.* Dublin: Wm. Curry, 1834; *Fardorougha the Miser.* Dublin: Wm. Curry, 1839; *The Fawn of Springvale.* 3 vols. Dublin: Wm. Curry, 1841; *Art Maguire.* Dublin: J. Duffy, 1845; *Parra Sastha.* Dublin: J. Duffy, 1845; *Rody the Rover.* Dublin: J. Duffy, 1845; *Tales and Sketches.* Dublin: J. Duffy, 1845. Later called *Tales and Stories of the Irish Peasantry; Valentine McClutchy, the Irish Agent.* 3 vols. Dublin: J. Duffy, 1845; *The Emigrants of Ahadarra.* London & Belfast: Simms & McIntyre, 1848; *The Tithe Procter.* London: Simms & McIntyre, 1848; *Red Hall,* 3 vols. London: Saunders & Otley, 1852; *The Squanders of Castle Squander,* 2 vols. London: Illustrated London Library, 1852; *Willy Reilly and His Dear Colleen Bawn.* 3 vols. London: Hope, 1855; *The Black Baronet.* Dublin: J. Duffy, 1857; *The Evil Eye.* Dublin: J. Duffy, 1860; *The Double Prophecy.* Dublin: J. Duffy, 1862; *Redmond, Count O'Hanlon, the Irish Rapparee.* Dublin: J. Duffy, 1862; *The Silver Acre and Other Tales.* London: Ward & Lock, 1862; *The Red-Haired Man's Wife.* Dublin: Sealy/London: Simpkin, 1889; *The Autobiography of William Carleton.* London: MacGibbon & Kee, 1968.   REFERENCES: Flanagan, Thomas. *The Irish Novelists 1800-1850.* New York: Columbia University Press, 1959, pp. 255-330; Kiely, Benedict. *Poor Scholar.* New York: Sheed & Ward, 1948; O'Donoghue, David J. *The Life of William Carleton: Being His Autobiography and Letters; and an Account of His Life and Writings from the Point at Which the Autobiography Breaks Off.* 2 vols. London: Downey, 1896; Shaw, Rose. "Carleton in His Own Country." *Carleton's Country.* Dublin & Cork: Talbot, 1930, pp. 83-111.

CARROLL, PAUL VINCENT (1900-1968), playwright. Carroll was born on July 10, 1900, at Blackrock, near Dundalk in County Louth, migrated to Scotland at the age of twenty-one, and taught school in Glasgow for sixteen years until success as a playwright enabled him to devote full time to writing. Although *Things That Are Caesar's* (1932) won an Abbey Theatre* prize, his first outstanding play was *Shadow and Substance*, produced at the Abbey in 1937. In America, it won the New York Drama Critics Circle Award for the best foreign play of the 1937-1938 season. In 1939, *The White Steed* also won the New York Critics Circle Award. Although Carroll had been active in the Scottish theatre, he settled permanently in England in 1945 and wrote film and television scenarios, as well as plays. The most significant of his later works was the satirical extravaganza *The Devil Came from Dublin* (1951). Carroll died of a heart attack at his home in Bromley, Kent, on October 20, 1968.

Most of Carroll's dramas were strongly influenced by Ibsen, and his most successful work was in the genre of the "well-made play." He evinced a strong didactic strain, attempting to stimulate thought and to reform people through the medium of the stage. *Things That Are Caesar's* sounds a recurring conflict in Carroll's works: the struggle between materialism and man's higher aspirations. Julia and Peter Hardy struggle against each other with their daughter Eilish as prize. Julia hypocritically schemes for a loveless marriage, compromise, and mediocrity, while the scholarly and sensitive Peter wants Eilish to be a free spirit, to obtain vision, to develop her individuality, and illuminate the way for others. Julia wins the battle, and although Carroll later revised the play and allowed Eilish to escape from an uninspiring materialistic life, the revised version lacks verisimilitude.

Shadow and Substance focuses on the conflict between Canon Skerritt and schoolmaster Dermot O'Flingsley. Both are idealistic and talented figures who are scarred by hubris. They are contrasted strikingly with the gentle, innocent, and saintly servant girl Brigid. Her warm humanity and spiritual humility bring the two antagonists to an awareness of their shortcomings, but only after Brigid is accidentally killed. Throughout the play, Carroll insists that goodness, faith, and unselfish love are the redeeming virtues of mankind. He contends that the world can improve only when individual hearts become innocent and pure and allow their love to overflow upon humanity.

In *The White Steed*, Father Shaughnessy violates Carroll's credo of love and generosity. Shaughnessy, a rabid puritan and vigilante, is finally overcome by a gentle and humane Canon Lavelle and by Nora Fintry, a spirited librarian who symbolizes Niam, the beloved of Ossian in the ancient Irish legend. Niam is the past spirit of Ireland that will not accept servitude. Her struggle, like Carroll's, is to attain beauty and joy, tolerance and goodness, as well as a reasonable use of freedom.

After *The White Steed*, Carroll went through a period when he permitted his didactic bent to overwhelm his writing. In plays such as *Kindred* (1939) and *The Old Foolishness* (1940), Carroll turns to murky allegory and symbolism which renders his work excessively sentimental and melodramatic. Carroll became bogged down in "philosophical dustbins" and foggy characterizations. Thus, Carroll was working counter to his strengths as a playwright: stinging, pungent, precise dialogue uttered by well-delineated characters who performed in a realistic milieu impregnated with wit, satire, and irony. Without these qualities his lesser work, although always containing some effective passages, becomes vague, and his call for love and generosity and his emphasis on the artistic spirit and the creative mind become simplistic, maudlin, and farfetched.

Near the end of his active career, Carroll wrote two carefree satiric comedies—*The Devil Came from Dublin* and *The Wayward Saint* (1955). Although *The Devil* is the stronger of the two plays, both are merry and perceptive romps full of rollicking satiric humor and delicious observations of the foibles and contradictions of human nature.

Carroll's reputation as a significant dramatist is assured by *Shadow and Substance* and *The White Steed*. In addition to having created several memorable characters, Carroll has drawn the most varied and convincing portraits of Irish clergymen and clerical life ever presented on the stage. Furthermore, at the top of his form, Carroll was one of the wittiest and talented masters of satiric and ironic dialogue and commentary which the Irish theatre has produced.

PAUL A. DOYLE

WORKS: *Things That Are Caesar's*. London: Rich & Cowan, 1934; *Shadow and Substance*. New York: Random House, 1937/London: Macmillan, 1938; *The White Steed and Coggerers*. New York: Random House, 1939; *Plays for My Children*. New York: Julian Messner, 1939. (Contains "The King Who Could Not Laugh," "His Excellency—the Governor," "St. Francis and the Wolf," "Beauty Is Fled," "Death Closes All," and "Maker of the Roads," each short play published separately by Samuel French in London in 1947); *The Old Foolishness*. London: Samuel French, 1944; *Three Plays: The White Steed, Things That Are Caesar's, The Strings, My Lord, Are False*. London: Macmillan, 1944; *Green Cars Go East*. London: Samuel French, 1947; *Interlude*. London: Samuel French, 1947; *Conspirators*. London: Samuel French, 1947/earlier titled *Coggerers; The Wise Have Not Spoken*. London: Samuel French, 1947/New York: Dramatists Play Service, 1954; *Two Plays: The Wise Have Not Spoken—Shadow and Substance*. London: Macmillan, 1948; *The Wayward Saint*. New York: Dramatists Play Service, 1955; *Irish Stories and Plays*. New York: Devin-Adair, 1958. (Contains a full-length play *The Devil Came from Dublin*, the short plays *The Conspirators, Beauty Is Fled*, and *Interlude*, and eight stories); *Farewell to Greatness*. Dixon, Calif.: Proscenium, 1966; *Goodbye to the Summer*. Newark, Del.: Proscenium, 1970; *The Journal of Irish Literature* (January 1972). (A Paul Vincent Carroll number, containing *We Have Ceased to Live*, a full-length play, as well as some letters and an interview.)   REFERENCE: Doyle, Paul A. *Paul Vincent Carroll*. Lewisburg, Pa.: Bucknell University Press, 1971.

CARSON, CIARON (1948-), poet. Carson was born in Belfast in 1948, and his first language was Irish. He studied at Queens University, Belfast, was a civil servant and teacher, and then became Traditional Arts officer with the Arts Council of Northern Ireland. He has published one volume of poems, *The New Estate* (1976). Much of his language is unadorned to the point of being simply flat, almost monosyllabic prose. His occasional metaphors are really much needed and stand out in bold relief. Usually, as with "the ink-bruise in the pansy's heart," they are vivid, but in general his language is not yet a rich one.

WORK: *The New Estate*. Belfast: Blackstaff, 1976.

CARY, [ARTHUR] JOYCE [LUNEL] (1888-1957), novelist. Cary was born on December 7, 1888, in Londonderry. His family had come to Ireland during Elizabeth's reign, and for generations had been respected landlords on the Inishowen Peninsula in Donegal. By the time of Cary's youth, the family fortunes had disappeared, and he was raised mainly in England, ultimately becoming one of the most admired of modern English novelists. Although Cary's best known works, such as *The Horse's Mouth* and *Mr. Johnson*, are set in England or Africa, he spent much time in his youth in Donegal, and his experiences there are used in two of his minor works,

Castle Corner (1938) and *A House of Children* (1941). While neither book is without interest, neither is among Cary's best work. *Castle Corner,* a sprawling chronicle novel intended as the first of a trilogy, depicts the fortunes of an Anglo-Irish landowning family in the years around the turn of this century. Part of the novel is set in Donegal, part in England, and part in Africa. Although the entire book lacks real form, the Donegal sections are done with considerable intensity. *A House of Children* is not so much a novel as a narrative depicting several years in the childhood and young adulthood of a number of characters connected with the landowning class in Donegal. The book reflects much of Cary's own youth and is often lovingly evocative, but it lacks strong characterization and much narrative thrust. Nevertheless, as a view of the landlord class in a time now irretrievably gone, Cary's two Irish books will always be of significance in the literature of Ireland. *A House of Children* won the James Tait Black Memorial Prize in 1941.

Cary died on March 29, 1957, in Oxford.

WORK: The best edition of Cary's work is the Carfax edition, published by Michael Joseph in London in the 1950s.   REFERENCES: Allen, Walter. *Joyce Cary.* London: Longmans, Green, 1953/revised 1954 & 1956. Writers and Their Work pamphlet, No. 41; Foster, Malcolm. *Joyce Cary, a Biography.* Boston: Houghton Mifflin, 1968; Hoffmann, Charles G. *Joyce Cary: The Comedy of Freedom.* Pittsburgh: University of Pittsburg Press, 1964.

CASEY, JOHN KEEGAN (1846-1870), poet. It is indeed easy to say that John Keegan Casey, the young Fenian, was a perfectly dreadful poet. Nevertheless, anyone capable of such a stirring ballad as "The Rising of the Moon" is worth some scrutiny.

Casey was born, the son of a peasant farmer, at Mount Dalton near Mullingar, on April 22, 1846. Despite poverty and hardship, he applied himself to study, and his first poem appeared in *The Nation** under his pseudonym of "Leo" when he was only sixteen. He became a mercantile clerk, but published enough verse to issue his first collection when he was only twenty. In 1867, he was arrested for his connection with Fenianism and for a time imprisoned. It is said that his sufferings in prison weakened him; he was seized with a hemorrhage of the lungs and died on March 17, 1870. His funeral is said to have been attended by fifty thousand people. This great throng may be attributed not merely to political feeling, but also to the extraordinary popularity of Casey's verses.

He is a popular poet, and his themes are the appealing ones of heroic patriotism and romantic, often blighted love. He has hardly a poem which is not marred by the clichés of popular writing, and even "Mairé My Girl," which Padraic Colum* thought enough of to anthologize, has at least one stanza that lapses into clichéd thinness. Nevertheless, if one looks closely, one can discern lines and stanzas in Casey's work which presaged, with the growth of knowledge and taste, a real poet. One can discern not merely a graceful mellifluousness, as in "Song of the Golden-Headed Niamh," but occasionally an utter tightness, as in this stanza from "Mairé My Girl":

> Down upon Claris heath
>   Shines the soft berry,
> On the brown harvest tree
>   Droops the red cherry;
> Sweeter thy honey lips,
>   Softer the curl
> Straying adown thy cheeks,
>   Mairé my girl.

WORKS: *A Wreath of Shamrocks: Ballads, Songs and Legends.* Dublin: McGee, 1866; *The Rising of the Moon, and Other Ballads,* Songs and Legends. Glasgow: Cameron & Ferguson, 1869; *Reliques of John K. Casey ("Leo"),* Eugene David, ed. Dublin: Pigott, 1878. Davis's biographical and critical introduction on pages 1-54 is the fullest account of Casey's life and work.

CASEY, JUANITA (1925-), short story writer, poetess, and novelist. Casey was born on October 10, 1925, in England. Her mother, Annie Maloney, was an Irish traveler or tinker who died when her daughter was born. Her father was Jobey Smith, an English Romany who disappeared when she was a year old. Her early life was divided between private boarding schools and the circus; her circus background explains her deep affection for animals, particularly horses. She became horse master for Robert Brothers Circus and even succeeded in training that most recalcitrant beast, a zebra. She has been married three times—to an English farmer, a Swedish sculptor, and an Irish journalist—and has had a child from each marriage.

Casey turned to writing late, first publishing and illustrating a book of rather amateurish but highly individual short stories called *Hath the Rain a Father?* in 1966. A slim volume of verse with two more drawings, *Horse by the River*, followed in 1968, and then came a short and highly acclaimed novel, *The Horse of Selene*, in 1971. Her last novel to date is *The Circus* (1974).

Casey's two novels are written with a vibrant feeling for language and achieve extraordinary moments of lyrical beauty. The primacy of words in her fictional technique is suggested by these remarks about *The Circus*:

> You know when you were young—before words really sort of crystallized and formed—you used to listen to grownups talking and the words used to flow over you. You'd get a word like "ambulance." It's a beautiful word, and you can see it in colors. So I tried to write this book where words, really, are meaningless and meaningful at the same time. It's very, very difficult. It's a step forward from the early work, the stories, as different as the later

> James Joyce is from the early Joyce. It's about a kid who wants
> to go to the circus and never gets there. When she finally does, I
> won't say what happens, but it's completely spoiled, utterly spoiled.
> Words are beginning to harden into their real meanings. . . . Words
> are so extraordinary! And yet you have the awful feeling that
> they're not meaning anything at all. They go on and on—words
> being bastardized. They come out of newspapers at you and out
> of loudspeakers, and you suddenly see a swallow overhead not
> saying a fucking thing.

If Casey's novels have a major fault, it is that their plots are rather tenuous
and tend to be overwhelmed by the lushness of the prose.

The evocative prose of her novels is more lyrical than her poetry, which
seems casual and relatively flat; but her real strength in language seems
comic. Her more recent uncollected short stories reveal a quirkiness of
view and a rich whimsicality that have not been seen in Irish fiction since
Flann O'Brien*-Myles na Gopaleen.* For instance, there is the beginning
of her inimitable story, "O Come, O Come, Emmanuel":

> Death! cried Emmanuel McGuirk, gardener.
> He pronounced it debt!
> And two slugs, vertically locked in slimy bliss, were cut off from
> all further enjoyment of one of life's supreme moments, reduced to
> a liquified Romeo and Juliet by the scandalized heel of his boot.
> He had not seen God, Who Had Had a Thought.
> How Very Pleasant, Thought God, To See A Garden Again.
> Not Eden, Of Course. A Bad Business, That. O, A Sad Business.
> A Let-Down. (You will note that God thought in capitals.)

Casey may never become a disciplined writer, but she is an amateur of
genius. She also has a good deal else on her mind. She once described her
idea of bliss as composed of "crystals, minerals, rocks, and fossils," and she
also noted that she was "extremely active in quarries, fields containing
fauna, angels, tramps, and silence."

WORKS: *Hath the Rain a Father?* London: Phoenix House, 1966; *Horse by the
River, and Other Poems.* Dublin: Dolmen, 1968; *The Horse of Selene.* [Dublin]:
Dolmen, 1971; *The Circus.* Dublin: Dolmen, 1974.   REFERENCE: Henderson,
Gordon. "An Interview with Juanita Casey." *Journal of Irish Literature* 1 (September
1972): 41-54.

CASEY, KEVIN (1940-), novelist and playwright. Casey was born in Kells,
County Meath, on December 5, 1940, and was educated at the Christian
Brothers school in Kells and at Blackrock College, County Dublin. He is
married to the poet Eavan Boland.* Two of his plays, *The Living and the
Lost* and *Not with a Bang*, have been produced in Dublin, but he is best
known as an intelligent and increasingly craftsmanlike novelist.

As a novelist, Casey is probably more esteemed than enjoyed, for the attitudes behind his books range only from the greyly bleak to the blackly pessimistic. The blackest in tone is his first novel, *The Sinner's Bell* (1968), which is a study of a young marriage in a small town in Meath. The characters are well drawn, and the writing is crisp, lean, clear, and exact in detail. However, probably not one detail in the entire book is affirmatively described. If it is coffee, the taste is strange; if it is tea, it is lukewarm and the taste is rankly tannic; if it is bread, it is becoming stale and the edges are beginning to curl; if it is weather, it is inevitably raining or about to rain; and if it is people, they are faithless, crude, ugly, blotchy, pimply, and afflicted with boils, drunkenness in its last stages, hatred, guilt, apathy, inadequacy, or despair. Indeed, the one sympathetic character, the young wife, has become so indoctrinated by the author's view by the end of the novel that her last reflection about having a baby is that it "would be years before the baby could learn to hate her." That savage glumness, only slightly tempered by pity, is the impelling view of this well-crafted, card-stacked novel.

Casey's second novel, *A Sense of Survival* (1974), is very much in the sour tradition of what Graham Greene called "an Entertainment." Indeed, the novel is so reminiscent of Greene that it seems almost a pastiche. It is set in a remote and exotic place, Tangier; it has a background of sordid intrigue and violence; and its descriptive details are, once again, inevitably depressing. Flakes of plaster fall from walls, a bicycle rusts in the street, flowers decay, a cat is strangled. Perhaps the chief difference between this novel and a Greene entertainment is that Casey's plot is much more in the background and is almost submerged by the emphasis on the limply developed non-love story. Lacking real narrative tension, the book, then, seems more of an able exercise in illustrating a despairing attitude. One would not readily return to a contemplation of these well-caught, sad, seedy, baffled characters.

Dreams of Revenge (1977) is a much less academic exercise. Basically, the novel seems an exploration of guilt and of mixed motives in personal relations. That sound and perceptive insight comes across with considerable power, and the plot is in bolder relief than the plot of *A Sense of Survival* or the simple accumulating chronology of *The Sinner's Bell*. If the novel has notable faults, they might be these two: one incident, in which the hero is apprehended and beaten by Provos in Belfast, is rather far-fetched; and some passages of the generally excellent dialogue between hero and heroine do seem a bit too clever and overly long. Nevertheless, the descriptive details are not so horrifically stacked in this novel, and the investigation of the very three-dimensional hero is a distinct achievement. It provides a more intelligent, if dour, insight into the way people act than one is accustomed to from novels.

Among the new fiction writers of the 1970s, Kevin Casey seems perhaps the most conscious of his craft. His books are careful, polished, growing in power, and, it is to be hoped, lessening in their overwhelming gloom.

WORKS: *The Sinner's Bell*. London: Faber & Faber, 1968; *A Sense of Survival*. London: Faber & Faber, 1974; *Dreams of Revenge*. London: Faber & Faber, 1977.

CASEY, W[ILLIAM] F[RANCIS] (1884-1957), journalist, novelist, and playwright. Casey was born in Capetown, on May 2, 1884, educated at Trinity College, Dublin, and called to the bar in 1909. In 1908, his plays *The Man Who Missed the Tide* and *The Suburban Groove* were performed at the Abbey Theatre* and remained popular pieces in the repertoire for about ten years. *The Man Who Missed the Tide*, a serious study of failure and drunkenness, introduced a brilliant young actor, Fred O'Donovan. *The Suburban Groove* was a comic and satiric dissection of middle-class society in the then-posh Dublin suburb of Rathmines; it was also one of the first Abbey plays of note to break away from the subject of the Irish peasant.

Casey went to London in about 1910, first as a free-lance journalist, and then during the war as a sporting correspondent for *The Times*. He later became a knowledgeable foreign correspondent for *The Times* in Washington, Paris, and elsewhere, and finally the editor of the paper. "No editor," writes A. P. Robbins, "was better loved." He retired in 1952 and died in London on April 20, 1957.

Neither of Casey's plays has been published, but, despite their popularity, they seem to have had more theatrical than literary merit. He published three novels which were rather promising, but the busy life of a professional journalist kept him away from literature.

WORKS: *Zoe*. London: Herbert & Daniel, 1911; *Haphazard*. London: Constable, 1917; *Private Life of a Successful Man*. London: Dent, 1935.

CELTIC TWILIGHT, THE. This term was used as the title of an early (1893) volume of reminiscence and folklore by W. B. Yeats,* and it became a not entirely appropriate tag to describe the ferment of Irish literary activity in the 1890s and for a few years afterwards. The description called up a vision of the mournful, the moody, and the mystical which was, and perhaps even still is, one romantic way of viewing Ireland. This view had probably been fixed in the public consciousness earlier by Matthew Arnold's essay "On the Study of Celtic Literature," delivered at Oxford in 1867. Certainly the description was apt enough for much of young Yeats' work in the 1890s. But in the early years of this century when Yeats gathered around him such co-workers as George Moore,* Lady Gregory,* and J. M. Synge,* much of the Twilight mist began rapidly to be blown away. Other than Yeats, the true Celtic Twilight poets were probably to be found in the ranks of the imitative minor writers, such as Nora Hopper Chesson* or Ella Young.* With the advent of a new generation of realistic writers,

such as Joyce,* O'Casey,* O'Flaherty,* O'Connor,* and O'Faolain,* the
Celtic Twilight seemed anachronistic indeed. In an amusing couplet, John
Montague* repeats Yeats' famous line about romantic Ireland being dead
and gone, and the reason was that it was laid in its grave by O'Connor
and O'Faolain.

CHERRY, ANDREW (1762-1812), dramatist and song writer. Cherry was
born in Limerick on January 11, 1762. He was a quite successful comic
actor, first in Dublin and then in England. His contemporary reputation as
a wit may, possibly, be borne out by this note which he wrote to a former
manager:

> Sir:—I am not so great a fool as you take me for! I have been
> bitten once by you, and I will never give you an opportunity of
> making two bites of
>
> A. CHERRY

He composed about a dozen popular plays of the day, several of which
included some of his engaging songs. He is remembered today for his song
"The Dear Little Shamrock of Ireland," which sounds a trifle inane even
when sung by John McCormack. One of its three stanzas should be
sufficient:

> There's a dear little plant that grows in our isle,
>   'Twas Saint Patrick himself, sure, that set it;
> And the sun on his labor with pleasure did smile,
>   And with dew from his eye often wet it.
> It thrives through the bog, through the brake, through the mireland;
> And he called it the dear little shamrock of Ireland,
>   The sweet little shamrock, the dear little shamrock,
>   The sweet little, green little, shamrock of Ireland.

His one-act operetta, *Spanish Dollars* (1806), is set on the coast of Ireland
and contains his other well-known song, "The Bay of Biscay." Cherry
died on February 7, 1812, at Montmouth.

WORKS: *The Soldier's Daughter.* 9th ed. London: Printed for Richard Phillips,
1804. (Play in 5 acts); *Spanish Dollars; or, The Priest of the Parish.* London: Barker &
Son, 1806. (One-act operatic sketch with music by J. Davy); *The Travellers; or, Music's
Fascination.* London: Printed for Richard Phillips, 1806. (An operatic drama in 5 acts
with music by Mr. Corri); *Peter the Great; or, The Wooden Walls.* London: R. Phillips,
1807. (An operatic drama in 3 acts).

CHESSON, NORA HOPPER (1871-1906), poet, novelist, and writer of
sketches. Chesson was a Celtic Twilight* poetess who lived all her life in
England. Her father, Captain H. B. Hopper, was Irish, but her mother was
Welsh, and she herself was born at Exeter on January 2, 1871. Her father
died when she was an infant, and she lived thereafter with her mother in

London. In 1894, she published her first volume, *Ballads in Prose*, which was admired by W. B. Yeats,* although he felt that she came very close to plagiarizing both Katharine Tynan* and himself. Also in 1894, she met her future husband, W. H. Chesson, whom she married on March 5, 1901. She wrote the libretto for *The Sea Swan*, an Irish legendary grand opera in three acts which was performed at the Theatre Royal, Dublin, on December 7, 1903. George Moore* helped her with the plot; nevertheless (or, perhaps, therefore), Edward Martyn* disliked the piece. She died on April 14, 1906, in London.

Chesson published prolifically in the popular press and achieved a considerable following. Her verses have many allusions to and verbal touches of Ireland, and are usually graceful and mellifluous, if generally somewhat vague and somewhat thin in content. However, Yeats wrote that her *Ballads in Prose* "haunted me as few books have ever haunted me, for it spoke in strange wayward stories and birdlike little verses of things and persons I remembered or had dreamed of." Yeats was perhaps flattered by Chesson's imitation of his own early manner, and gently remarked that her pastiches were only "plagiarisms of inexperienced enthusiasm. . . . She had taken[n] us as documents, just as if we had written hundreds of years ago." However, Yeats liked her second volume, *Under Quicken Boughs* (1896), less than her first, and finally came to feel that "our Irish fairyland came to spoil her work. . . ." In another gentle summation, Ford Madox Ford found both her and her works abstracted and pleasant, and "If she seldom called a spade a spade it was because that particular tool seldom came into her purview." Her world is of fairies, princes slain by elf-bolts, fog, roses, and gently mournful lovers. She was probably the quintessence of what the public regarded as a Celtic Twilight poet—quietly charming and not unpleasantly vapid.

WORKS: *Ballads in Prose*. London: John Lane, 1894; *Under Quicken Boughs*. London: John Lane, 1896; *Songs of the Morning*. London: Grant Richards, 1900; *Aquamarines*. London: Grant Richards, 1902; *Mildred and Her Mills, and Other Poems*. London: Raphael Tuck, 1903; *Old Fairy Legends in New Colours*, by T. E. Donnison, with verses by N. Chesson. London: Raphael Tuck, 1903; *With Louis Wain to Fairyland*. London: Raphael Tuck, 1904; *The Bell and the Arrow: An English Love Story*. London: T. Werner Laurie, 1905; *Dirge for Aoine and Other Poems*. London: Alston Rivers, 1906; *A Dead Girl to Her Lover and Other Poems*. London: Alston Rivers, 1906; *Jack O'Lanthorn and Other Poems*. London: Alston Rivers, 1906; *The Happy Maid and Other Poems*. London: Alston Rivers, 1906; *The Waiting Widow and Other Poems*. London: Alston Rivers, 1906; *Father Felix's Chronicles*. W. H. Chesson, ed. London: Unwin, 1907. (Novel).   REFERENCE: Marcus, Phillip L. *Yeats and the Beginning of the Irish Renaissance*. Ithaca & London: Cornell University Press, [1970]. Pp. 147-157.

CHILDERS, ERSKINE (1870-1922), politician and novelist. Childers belongs more to history than to literature, but he wrote one perennially delightful thriller, *The Riddle of the Sands* (1910). He was born Robert

Erskine Childers in London on June 25, 1870. He took his B.A. in 1893 from Trinity College, Cambridge, and most of the years from 1895 to 1910 he spent as a clerk in the British House of Commons. He served in the Boer War and wrote several war histories and books of military strategy. He also served as an intelligence officer in the Royal Navy in World War I, was several times mentioned in dispatches, and was awarded the Distinguished Service Cross.

Many of the patriotic Irish regarded Childers as an Englishman, even though much of his youth had been spent in Ireland. He grew increasingly sympathetic to Irish nationalism. It was he on his yacht, the "Asgard," who brought the guns to Howth in the celebrated gun-running incident of 1914. After the war, he became an even more fervent nationalist. He went with Arthur Griffith* to Versailles to present the case of Ireland to the Peace Conference, and he was also the principal secretary of the Irish Treaty delegation to London in 1921. However, he was opposed to the signing of the treaty and joined the Republican side in the Civil War. For the Republicans, he edited and published the paper *Poblacht na h-Éireann*. He was arrested at his home in November 1922, court-martialed, and executed by a Free State firing squad at Beggar's Bush on November 24. (In the 1970s, his son became president of Ireland.)

Shortly after his college years, Childers spent his vacations sailing on his yacht in the Channel, in the North Sea, and off the German, Danish, and Baltic coasts, an experience that served as background in what must be the first successful thriller written by an Irishman. *The Riddle of the Sands* was apparently written with the serious purpose of alerting people to the oncoming German threat. Taken simply as a thriller, the book must rank as one of the classics in its field and can be mentioned with the best of Buchan and Ambler.

WORKS: *The Riddle of the Sands*. London: Smith, Elder & Co., 1903/many reprints, including London: Penguin Books, 1952.   REFERENCES: Wilkinson, Burke. *The Zeal of the Convert*. Washington: Robert B. Luce, 1974. (Biography); O'Hegarty, P. S. *A Bibliography of the Books of Erskine Childers*. Dublin: Printed for the author, 1948/reprinted from *The Dublin Magazine*, Vol. 23, No. 2, N.S.; Boyle, Andrew. *The Riddle of Erskine Childers*. London: Hutchinson, 1977.

CLARKE, AUSTIN [AUGUSTINE JOSEPH] (1896-1974), poet, playwright, and novelist. Clarke was born on May 9, 1896, in Dublin. He was educated at Belvedere College, and University College, Dublin, from which he received a B.A. in 1916 and an M.A. in 1917, and was then appointed assistant lecturer in English to replace Thomas MacDonagh.* His *The Vengeance of Finn*, sponsored by AE,* was published in 1917 and widely noticed and admired. In 1920, he married Geraldine Cummins* in a registry office, but the marriage was unconsummated and lasted only ten days. He lost his appointment at University College, Dublin, in 1921, apparently because he had not been married in a church. In 1927, he wrote his first verse play, *The Son of Learning*. From 1929 to 1937, he worked in England, reviewing and writing poems, plays, and his novels *The Bright Temptation* and *The Singing Men at Cashel*, both of which were banned by the Free State government. In 1940, he and Robert Farren* founded the Dublin Verse-Speaking Society which performed on radio and in the Abbey Theatre.* In 1944, he founded with Farren the Lyric Theatre Company which performed at the Abbey until the 1951 fire. He continued to write prolifically, and his old age became his most accomplished period. In 1962, his first autobiography, *Twice Round the Black Church*, appeared, followed in 1963 by *Collected Plays* and *Flight to Africa*, and in 1968 by another autobiography, *A Penny in the Clouds*. Shortly before his death on March 19, 1974, his *Collected Poems* was published. At his death, he was generally considered the finest Irish poet of the generation after Yeats.*

In those flat years in Ireland at the beginning of the 1950s, depressed so thoroughly that one scarcely noticed it, the uneasy silence of Clarke added a certain emphasis. In the last few lines of *Night and Morning*, which he had published in 1938, he reflected that when he was younger and knew no better "God lay upon this tongue." His pain was for lost faith, but after the passage of more than a decade, it was impossible not to feel a pang of loss for the poetry too.

Clarke's had been a curious career, curiously unfulfilled; now it seemed to have settled into a strange balance, with the poet's purely technical urges finding apparent satisfaction in a series of not very satisfactory verse plays. And as for the criticism, those *Irish Times* book reviews. . . .

Matters changed very quickly after that, of course. Within a few years readers had responded with startled pleasure to Kavanagh's* brief fulfillment in *Come Dance with Kitty Stobling*, and with sheer gratitude to Clarke's swift recovery of poetic strength, from *Ancient Lights* to *Flight to Africa*. Readers continued to respond, with deepening respect, to the achievements of that new strength (off and on), to the accumulating evidence of poetic coherence and integrity, to the revelations in new guises of unlooked-for significant potentials in the earlier poetry.

That earlier poetry, such as *The Sword of the West* (1921), is not very impressive, and as a medium for narrative it soon grows unbearable, but the particularity of observation, especially the direct sensual interest in things, is unusual. Our sense of its precision increases when we compare it to a similar work, say, the poem "Cleopatra" by F. R. Higgins,* with whose name Clarke's used so often to be bracketed. Higgins' interest (and the readers') divides between the thing described and the effect sought. The grasp on reality is loose: the particular details, before they are properly established, are already on the way to poesie.

Clarke's grasp on reality was always closer than this, even in the early narratives, and we can sense the real possibility of poetry. Particularly, minute precision, is an element of artistic strength, and as it developed in Clarke's work it is one of the reasons he has become an important poet. This quality is everywhere, in varying manifestations, in the later poems: it is in the drab and painful Chamber-Gothic of "Martha Blake at Fifty-One"; it is the vehicle of a simple and genial sensuality in "The Healing of Mis" from *Orphide*; it appears in a different mode in "Anacreontic" from *A Sermon on Swift*—less innocent, linguistically more elaborate.

Clarke's career was interrupted seriously for a long time at a crucial period in his development, and partly for that reason his work is idiosyncratic in manner: his poems don't travel. His best poetry, however, is not eccentric in substance: it deals with the world on the world's terms. With the publication of *Flight to Africa* in 1963 we discover that the world it deals with, though miniature, is complete.

Like the early poetry, the later poetry, from *Ancient Lights* to *Tiresias,* is uneven, but it is at a different level of achievement. The best of the later poems—a sustained masterpiece like "Martha Blake at Fifty-One," the tiny "Japanese Print" (which would surely have impressed Williams or Pound), and some of the very latest narrative poems—are significant additions to modern poetry. They do not stand alone, as mere occasional unconnected successes. The body of Clarke's poetry, flawed or not, constitutes one of the distinguished modern poetic careers; any study of modern poetry which does not seriously consider his work is not adequate.

The main features of that career, viewed from the vantage point of the later poetry, are fairly clear. It was Yeats who awoke Clarke's interest in poetry; the first excitement was apparently centered mainly on the Abbey Theatre: "All the dear mummocks out of Tara/That turned my head at seventeen" ("The Abbey Theatre Fire," *Flight to Africa*). The Abbey and verse drama have remained central to Clarke's concerns. Yeats himself has been a lifelong fixation, an object of inspiration and emulation, and a cross—directing Clarke, by his example, toward Irish history, legend, and literature; rejecting him from the *Oxford Book of Modern Verse;* always hypnotizing him, even from the grave.

An interest in Irish history, legend, and literature (which was so enraging to Kavanagh, who witnessed the more ludicrous excesses of "the Irish thing") is neither good nor bad, nor ludicrous, in itself. For Clarke, it provided a large part of the pattern of his life and work. The early narrative poems appear to have been planned largely as a new retelling of early sagas in verse (to what purpose, considering Ferguson's* sad example, is not clear). But at the least they served as a workshop, where eye and speech were sharpened. Most of the poems in *Pilgrimage* (1929) are exhibits from Irish history, apparently in continuation or modification of the plan: the young woman of Beare, hermits and scholars, pilgrims and planters. The effort is distinguished from other planned efforts of the kind, certainly from Ferguson's, in producing good individual poems, with the milieu re-imagined and the feeling and sensual details brought up into particular life.

Clarke wrote the following note for *Pilgrimage,* which introduces us to his infatuation with Gaelic prosody:

> Assonance, more elaborate in Gaelic than in Spanish poetry, takes the clapper from the bell of rhyme. In simple patterns, the tonic word at the end of the line is supported by a vowel-rhyme in the middle of the next line. Unfortunately the internal patterns of assonance and consonance in Gaelic stanzas are so intricate that they can only be suggested in another language.

He was not the only Irish writer of his time who wanted to write intricately in the Gaelic manner. Earlier, Douglas Hyde* and Thomas MacDonagh had managed it well in translations. Francis Ledwidge* wrote unusually well (for him) on this basis in the "Lament for Thomas MacDonagh." But Clarke was far more concerned with the Gaelic than any of these poets ever were, and he was the only poet for whom the Gaelic element became a part of his poetic nature. It long remained an essential vehicle of expression for him, and though it resulted in a number of poems that were little more than exercises, it also helped him to many fine statements, even on fairly urgent contemporary matters, like "Inscription for a Headstone" in *Ancient Lights.* Gaelic prosody is not a very important issue in itself, but it is by means of such devices that a poet seeks, and may find (as here), imaginative freedom and ease.

In *Night and Morning* (1938), the historical concerns of *Pilgrimage* have almost disappeared, and another and more profound theme dominates: a Joycean struggle with issues of conscience and authority, faith and the Church. The tortured darkness of apostasy hangs over the whole book. Faith and thought, intellectual doubt and pride, mutilate each other; the poet is an agonized Luther, as in "Temebrae."

There is a new difficulty in these poems. The diction has compacted and constricted, and is full of puns; the elements of grammar and syntax transfer and contort. The area of reference is also constricted to a claustrophobic world in which the rituals and minutiae of Catholicism are necessary information for survival. These are real difficulties, but they are not in any way a diminishment of the poetry. An energetic and attentive reader who meets this poetry's demands will find it rewarding. In an "ordinary" career, this change in style might indicate a time of transition, a deepening of the poetry, with the poet undergoing some preliminary difficulties.

But it is at this point, as noted earlier, that Clarke the poet turned silent and remained so for seventeen years. (Clarke would probably have disagreed with this way of putting it, perhaps pointing to the continued appearance of his verse dramas. But I think it doubtful that these works will enter quite as seriously into a final estimate of his work.)

In 1955, with *Ancient Lights,* Clarke emerged from silence in sudden,

full-fledged humanitarian rage. The struggles of conscience were over—
sluiced away in "Ancient Lights"—and a fund of energy was released, outward and inward. The poetry, equipped with a new emotional fire and a
new epigrammatic power, was employed with ferocity, as in the three
"Poems About Childhood"; with mildness, as in "The Envy of Poor Lovers";
or with humor, as in "An Early Start." Along with these poems there begins a more dramatic, less occasional, investigation of the significant scene
in poems written in the key of reminiscence or autobiographical summing
up—a developing autobiography of ideas, feelings, significant scraps, the
darts and twists of life. In Clarke's new poetic voice, certainly by the time
he was writing the poems in *Flight to Africa,* nothing was unsayable.

This was not achieved without cost; it was no easy or "natural" voice.
The thickening texture noticed in the "apostate" poems in *Night and Morning* is thicker still in some of these new ones. The diction is ruptured, truncated, displaced; elements are fused—and confused—under the jamming
pressures. In "Ancient Lights," for example, some details and one whole
section remain inscrutable. In the fable of the birds, it is not always possible
to say what happens, even which bird is which, though the obscuring detail
is itself vigorous and clear.

This is a technical obscurity which, as I have suggested earlier, has a lot
to do with Clarke's allowing his language to lie unused for too long over
most of its lyric range. Unfortunately, it affects some of the most important
of his transitional poems, notably "The Loss of Strength." The congestion
is rapidly cleared, however, and by *Flight to Africa* it has yielded to an
easier tone generally. While this poetry was no less completely responsive
or idiosyncratic, it no longer struggled with itself in disproportionate fury.
The rich and supple tone which Clarke achieved enabled him to finish the
extraordinary *Mnemosyne Lay in Dust.* In any event, the congestion had
not marked all the new poetry. "The Flock at Dawn" in *The Horse Eaters,*
for example, is a fine and unflawed poem in the new manner, as are
"Usufruct" and "Miss Marnell' in *Too Great a View.*

In their narrowness of reference, however, most of the poems of this
period raise the whole question of legitimate obscurity in poetry. Some of
them are virtually private, or so particular in their comments that it would
be a help to have the relevant newspaper cutting handy. One of the least
difficult in this way, "Usufruct" (if we are to understand it fully), requires
us to extract the essential facts from it with Holmesian care. But the facts
can be extracted. A reading of "Miss Marnell," two pages later, acts as a
confirming footnote: it gives us much the same basic plot as "Usufruct"
from the other angle. The later poems accumulate in this way: they establish relationships among themselves and help to illuminate each other. With
detail after detail of personal history brooded upon, of local hypocrisy and
meanness cursed or pitied, a microcosm of the whole human scene—with

·Templeogue as center, and very little radius—is described. Raising a fundamental question of obscurity, these poems, by their authority and integrity, lay the question to rest.

It is idle to claim that Clarke's poetry has marched confidently onward since *Flight to Africa* and *Mnemosyne*. It has not; there is always the unevenness. *Old-Fashioned Pilgrimage* is a worrisome book, but in *A Sermon on Swift*, published in the following year, among other things we find a little group of humorous, accomplished, and wise sexual poems—horrifying for a brief moment in "Stopples" but all startling and new.

These poems ushered in his last poetic theme: a cheerful sensuality gathered up from the novels and plays and set glittering wickedly before us in the limpid, classic narratives in *Orphide* and *Tiresias*, poetry as pure entertainment, serene and full of life. In the tortured time of *Night and Morning*, it would have been hard to foresee such a resolution, but looking back over the course that has been travelled, it seems right and humanely inspired.

THOMAS KINSELLA

WORKS: *The Vengeance of Fionn*. Dublin & London: Maunsel, 1918; *The Fires of Baal*. Dublin & London: Maunsel & Roberts, 1921; *The Sword of the West*. London: Maunsel & Roberts, 1921; *The Cattledrive in Connaught*. London: Allen & Unwin, 1925; *The Son of Learning*. London: Allen & Unwin, 1927; *Pilgrimage and Other Poems*. London: Allen & Unwin, 1929; *The Flame*. London: Allen & Unwin, 1930; *The Bright Temptation*. London: Allen & Unwin, 1932; *Collected Poems*. London: Allen & Unwin, 1936; *The Singing Men at Cashel*. London: Allen & Unwin, 1936; *Night and Morning*. Dublin: Orwell, 1938; *Sister Eucharia*. Dublin: Orwell/ London: Williams & Norgate, 1939; *Black Fast*. Dublin: Orwell, 1941; *The Straying Student*. Dublin: Gayfield, 1942; *As the Crow Flies*. Dublin: Bridge, 1943; *The Viscount of Blarney and Other Plays*. Dublin: Bridge/London: Williams & Norgate, 1944; *First Visit to England and Other Memories*. Dublin: Bridge, 1945; *The Second Kiss*. Dublin: Bridge/London: Williams & Norgate, 1946; *The Plot Succeeds*. Dublin: Bridge, 1950; *The Sun Dances at Easter*. London: Andrew Melrose, 1952; *The Moment Next to Nothing*. Dublin: Bridge, 1953; *Ancient Lights*. Dublin: Bridge, 1955; *Too Great a Vine: Poems and Satires*. Dublin: Dolmen, 1957; *The Horse-Eaters*. Dublin: Bridge, 1960; *Later Poems*. Dublin: Dolmen, 1961; *Forget-Me-Not*. Dublin: Dolmen, 1962; *Poetry in Modern Ireland*. Cork: Mercier (for the Cultural Relations Committee of Ireland), 1962; *Twice Round the Black Church*. London: Routledge & Kegan Paul, 1962; *Collected Plays*. Dublin: Dolmen, 1963; *Flight to Africa*. Dublin: Dolmen, 1963; *Mnemosyne Lay in Dust*. Dublin: Dolmen, 1966; *Old-Fashioned Pilgrimage and Other Poems*. Dublin: Dolmen, 1967; *A Penny in the Clouds*. London: Routledge, 1968; *A Sermon on Swift and Other Poems*. Dublin: Bridge, 1968; *The Echo at Coole and Other Poems*. Dublin: Dolmen, 1968; *Two Interludes Adapted from Cervantes*. Dublin: Dolmen, 1968; *The Celtic Twilight and the Nineties*. Dublin: Dolmen, 1969; *Orphide*. Dublin: Bridge, 1970; *Tiresias*. Dublin: Bridge, 1971; *The Impuritans*. Dublin: Dolmen, 1973; *Collected Poems*. Dublin: Dolmen, 1974. REFERENCES: Halpern, Susan. *Austin Clarke, His Life and Works*. Dublin: Dolmen, 1974; *Irish University Review*. Maurice Harmon, ed. Vol. 4 (Spring 1974). (An Austin Clarke number which contains some detailed biographical notes by Maurice Harmon, critical articles on various aspects of Clarke's work, and Gerard Lyne's bibliography which is the most complete thus far. Clarke himself contributed a play, "The Visitation.")

CLARKIN, SEAN (1941-), poet. Clarkin was born in New Ross, County Wexford, in 1941. He was educated at the Gregorian University in Rome, at University College, Cork, and at Trinity College, Dublin. In 1971, he won the first Patrick Kavanagh Poetry Award, and he has published one pamphlet of verse. His work in in short lines of free verse, and his rhythms and sentences are abrupt and often fragmentary. He is capable of sharp images and, occasionally, witty comparisons, as when he describes "A man / as un-Italian / as tinned spaghetti."

WORKS: *Without Frenzy*. Dublin: Gallery, 1974.

CLEEVE, BRIAN (1921-), novelist, journalist, and scriptwriter. Cleeve was born in 1921 in Essex of a Limerick family and traveled all over the world before settling in Dublin where he has lived since the mid-1950s. Many of his novels are insignificant thrillers, although *Death of a Painted Lady* (1962) does manage a glumly effective picture of certain aspects of modern Dublin. His serious work would include a volume of short stories, *The Horse Thieves of Ballysaggert* (1966), which is uneven but contains at least two admirable tales. His most ambitious works of fiction are two long novels, *Cry of Morning* (1971) and *Tread Softly in This Place* (1972). The first deals with the modern Dublin of building developers and television antennas, and the second is a study of the clash between the modern world and provincial Ireland. Both books seem consciously intended for the mass best-seller market. The writing is fluent but unindividual, and the reader is carried along by a large number of simply differentiated characters in rather complex plots. Both novels provide pleasant enough reading, but both fade quickly in the memory as does the work, say, of a Leon Uris or an Arthur Hailey.

Cleeve is also the author of a *Dictionary of Irish Writers* (1969) in three paperback volumes, which offers capsule biographies and often short evaluations of perhaps two thousand Irish writers. Although the work has been criticized for its inaccuracies, it nevertheless is an extraordinary achievement for one man.

WORKS: *The Far Hills*. London: Jarrolds, 1953. (Novel); *Portrait of My City*. London: Jarrolds, 1953. (Novel); *Birth of a Dark Soul*. London: Jarrold's, 1953/published in America as *The Night Winds*, Boston: Houghton Mifflin, 1954. (Novel); *Assignment to Vengeance*. London: Hammond, Hammond, [1961]. (Novel); *Death of a Painted Lady*. London: Hammond, Hammond, [1962]. (Novel); *Death of a Wicked Servant*. London: Hammond, Hammond, [1963]. (Novel); *Vote X for Treason*. London: Collins, 1964. (Novel); *Dark Blood, Dark Terror*. London: Hammond, Hammond, [1966]. (Novel); *The Horse Thieves of Ballysaggert*. Cork: Mercier, 1966. (Stories); *Violent Death of a Bitter Englishman*. New York: Random House, 1967; *Dictionary of Irish Writers*. Vol. 1, Fiction. Cork: Mercier, 1967; *Dictionary of Irish Writers*. Vol. 2, Nonfiction. Cork: Mercier, 1969; *Dictionary of Irish Writers*. Vol. 3, Writers in the Irish Language. Cork: Mercier, 1971; *Cry of Morning*. London: Michael Joseph, 1971. (Novel); *Tread Softly in This Place*. London: Cassell, 1972. (Novel).

COCHRANE, IAN (1942-), novelist. Cochrane was born in Northern Ireland in 1942. He has written three novels, the first of which, *Gone in the Head*, was a runner up for the Guardian Fiction Prize. Possibly his most successful book, however, is *A Streak of Madness,* an exaggerated recreation of family life in the North of Ireland. The book is not so corruscated with verbal high-jinks as is the work of John Morrow,* and so remains a ripely entertaining farcical-comedy with some effective sentimental overtones.

WORKS: *A Streak of Madness.* London: Allen Lane, 1973; *Gone in the Head.* London: Routledge & Kegan Paul, 1974; *Jesus on a Stick.* London: Routledge & Kegan Paul, 1975.

COFFEY, BRIAN (1905-), poet. Coffey, born in County Dublin on June 8, 1905, is the son of the first president of University College, Dublin. Although his academic work began in Ireland, his philosophic bent turned him toward France, where he studied with Jacques Maritain. His interest in European and Catholic culture has continued throughout his life, as shown by his bachelor's degree from Institution St. Vincent in 1924, his study at Institut Catholique in Paris, and the awarding of his doctoral degree there in 1947. Of equal importance is his translation of French poets, mainly the early moderns, and his friendship with Denis Devlin.*

While studying for his B.A., B.Sc., and M.Sc. at University College from 1924 to 1930, Coffey was also publishing poetry. His poems were openly dependent on Paul Claudel, who has proved to be a continuing influence on Coffey. These poems were published with poems by Denis Devlin in 1930, the year they met. He and Devlin soon met Thomas McGreevy.* (These three, together with Samuel Beckett* constitute a formidable tie with the European avant-garde movement.) While a student in Paris, Coffey published *Three Poems.* In 1938, he was married and published *Third Person* in London.

Coffey's doctoral work, begun in Paris in 1937, was interrupted by World War II until 1947. During the intervening years, he worked in London as a teacher. After the awarding of his degree, he taught at St. Louis University in Missouri until he resigned in 1952. In that year, he and his family moved to London, where he taught sixth form mathematics in London schools. His translation of Mallarmé's *Coup de Dés* in 1965 published by Dolmen signals his return to poetry in Ireland and indicates the course he will follow. *Coup de Dés* is a seminal work for contemporary visual poetry, though Claudel remains an important influence. The majority of the poetry Coffey has published in the past ten years has been visual.

Recognition in Ireland has come late for Coffey. After Devlin's death in 1959, Coffey was named his literary executor. He then edited Devlin's *Collected Poems* (1964) and *The Heavenly Foreigner* (1967). His own *Selected Poems* appeared in 1971, and in 1975 a special issue of *The Irish University Review* was devoted to his poetry.

Consistently avant garde in form, Coffey has nevertheless retained distinctly Irish and Catholic concerns in his poetry. The Jansenist probing of the self when turned outward often results in one of his "meaner smiles," as he described *The Big Laugh,* one of his recent visual and narrative volumes.

FRANK KERSNOWSKI

WORKS: With Denis Devlin, *Poems.* Dublin: Printed for the Authors, 1930; *Three Poems.* Paris: Librairie Jeannette Monnier, 1933; *Third Person.* London: George Reavy, 1938; ed., Denis Devlin's *Collected Poems.* Dublin: Dolmen, 1964; *The Heavenly Foreigner.* Dublin: Dolmen, 1967; *Dice Thrown Never Will Annul Chance.* Translation of Mallarmé. Dublin: Dolmen, 1965; *Selected Poems.* Dublin: New Writers, 1971; *The Irish University Review 5* (Autumn 1975). A Brian Coffey Special Issue, with an Introduction by James Mays.

COFFEY, THOMAS (1925-), playwright. Coffey, an extremely popular and promising playwright in the early 1960s, was born on September 3, 1925, in Ennis, County Clare. After graduating from St. Flannan's College in Ennis, he worked at a variety of jobs before qualifying as a teacher of English, Gaelic, and mathematics. In the mid-1950s, he won prizes for short plays in Irish and had several short plays in English broadcast on Irish radio. His first full-length stage play, *Stranger Beware* (Abbey,* 1958), is set in West Kerry; it is more interesting for its realistic observation than for its melodramatic plot. Other plays include *Anyone Could Rob a Bank* (Abbey, 1959), a broad farce and his most popular piece; *The Long Sorrow* (Abbey, 1960), a one-act plea for tolerance between the North and the South; and *Them* (Eblana, 1962), a superb study of how a family copes with an imbecile son. *Gone Tomorrow* (Gate,* 1965), a technically accomplished study of sensitive youth, won the Irish Life Drama Award. *The Call* (Abbey, 1966), a study of religious fanaticism in a small town, is written with little distinction. In the mid-1960s, Coffey gave up teaching, moved to Limerick, and went into business. Since then, he has apparently written little.

WORKS: *The Call.* Dublin: James Duffy, 1967; *Anyone Could Rob a Bank.* Dublin: James Duffy, 1974.   REFERENCE: Hogan, Robert. *After the Irish Renaissance.* Minneapolis: University of Minnesota Press, 1967. Pp. 82-85.

COLUM, MARY [CATHERINE GUNNING MAGUIRE] (1887-1957), critic and autobiographer. Colum was born June 13, 1887 and was educated in convents and at University College, Dublin. She taught at St. Ita's, Padraic Pearse's schools for girls, and in 1912 married Padraic Colum,* the poet. Her *Life and the Dream* (1947) gives a romantic view of the Irish Revival as seen by an impressionable student. Her gift for anecdote is also apparent in passages about Joyce* collected after her death in *Our Friend James Joyce* (1958). Her other book, *From These Roots,* explores the origins of modernism. From 1914 she and her husband resided in the United States and were very active in New York literary circles. Colum became a well-known literary critic, serving as literary editor of the *Forum*, critic for *The New York Times* and *Tribune*, and a frequent contributor to the major literary periodicals in the United States and Ireland. Colum died on October 22, 1957.

RICHARD M. KAIN

WORKS: *From These Roots: The Ideas That Have Made Modern Literature.* New York: Scribner's, 1937; *Life and the Dream.* Garden City, N.Y.: Doubleday/London: Macmillan, 1947; with Padraic Colum, *Our Friend James Joyce.* Garden City, N.Y.: Doubleday, 1958.

COLUM, PADRAIC (1881-1972), poet, playwright, biographer, novelist, short story writer, essayist, folklorist, and writer of children's stories. Colum was a practitioner of so many of the literary arts that he is difficult to label. He wrote sixty-one books and hundreds of essays, articles, introductions, and separately published poetry as well as a number of plays. His career spans nearly a century, beginning with the early days of the Irish Renaissance and extending into the seventh decade of the twentieth century. An intimate friend of the giants of modern literature in America and France, as well as in England and Ireland, Colum had a major part in shaping the direction of the Irish theatre and in bringing classical literature to children in comprehensible, appealing form.

Padraic was born to Patrick and Susan Colum on December 8, 1881, in the workhouse at Longford where Patrick was the master. His early years were spent in Longford and Cavan before the family moved to Sandycove where the elder Colum got a job as railway station master. Colum attended the Glasthule National School in Sandycove and worked for his father delivering packages until he graduated. When he was seventeen, he obtained a position as clerk in the Irish Railway Clearing House; he worked there for five years until he was given a five-year scholarship by a wealthy American to pay for a period of study, development, and writing.

Around 1902, his poems began to appear in Arthur Griffith's* *United Irishman,* and he won a contest of the *Cumann na nGaedeal* with his early play, *The Saxon Shillin'.* Colum became a member of the National Theatre Society, was an original Abbey* charter signer, and wrote three of the Abbey's earliest plays, *The Fiddler's House* (1907), *The Land* (1905), and *Thomas Muskerry* (1910). By this time, his poetry was extremely popular, and he was an intimate of George Russell,* W. B. Yeats,* Lady Gregory,* and James Stephens.*

Colum met Mary Catherine Gunning Maguire while she was a student at University College, Dublin, and married her in 1912. Padraic and Mary both taught at St. Ita's and St. Enda's and began *The Irish Review** with two of their colleagues, David Houston and Thomas MacDonagh.*

The Colums migrated to America in 1914, where Colum began a new career in children's literature by writing a series of stories for the children's column of the *New York Sunday Tribune.* Publication in 1916 of a volume of his poetry, *Wild Earth,* and his first volume of children's stories, *The King of Ireland's Son,* quickly established his reputation in the United States. Colum supported himself throughout his life principally with his popular children's books and his translations of the classics and mythology. Under a commission from the Hawaiian legislature, he recorded in three volumes the lore of the Islands for children in Hawaiian schools.

The Colums lived in Paris and Nice from 1930 to 1933. They finally returned to the United States, first settling in New Canaan, Connecticut, and later in New York City where they both taught part time at Columbia University. After Mary died in 1957, Colum divided his time among New York, Woods Hole, Massachusetts, and Ireland. He never stopped writing poetry; a new poem written in his ninetieth year in a nursing home in Connecticut was subsequently published in *The New York Times,* and *Carricknabauna,* a musical based on his poems and songs, was produced in New York in 1967. He was completing a series of Noh plays at the time of his death on January 11, 1972. He was interred in Ireland.

Colum's poetry, as all his work, is characterized by simplicity and craftsmanship. His character studies in verse, such as "An Old Woman of the Roads," "The Toy-Maker," "The Poor Scholar," and "The Ballad Singer," embody the essence of a nearly forgotten rural picture-book Ireland. His poetry, generally regular in meter and rhyme, captures the rustic peasant speech of the Midlands. Colum had the ability to recreate the past authentically, and for many American Irish as well as modern-day citizens of Ireland, his work is an echo of the idyllic Ireland they had only heard about at their parents' knees.

Colum's early plays appealed to a large popular audience in Ireland and England, and he was hailed as one of the greatest young writers of the Irish theatre. Unfortunately, that early promise as a dramatist never completely materialized. Although he continued to write plays throughout his life and thought of himself as a dramatist, his later works never were as successful as his earliest productions.

Colum's close ties with the great Irishmen of his times led him to write two widely read biographies—one of Arthur Griffith,* *Ourselves Alone* (1959), and the other, *Our Friend James Joyce* (1958). The first was principally a scholarly history of the Sinn Féin party and the second a collection of personal reminiscences, written in collaboration with Mary Colum. The tone of the two books is so different that it is difficult to think they came from the same pen. *Ourselves Alone* is written in stark, matter-of-fact language, well-researched, full of dates, and heavily annotated. *Our Friend James Joyce* is a conversational, largely anecdotal series of personal reminiscences.

Colum's two novels are also widely contrasting. The first, *Castle Conquer* (1923), is an apprentice work, full of nationalistic propaganda, but the second, *The Flying Swans,* written thirty-four years later, is a classic in its own right, though largely ignored by the critics. It captures in realistic but picturesque prose the verisimilitude of life in late nineteenth-century Ireland.

Colum's many volumes of Irish essays and children's stories are written in the same style. Never condescending to children, he writes with the same simplicity in both children's works and in his Irish travel stories for adults. His character studies are largely one-dimensional and easy to understand—often vignettes—but they have a unique archetypal quality. Colum's work often contains the expected, but it is said with such simple eloquence that the experience remains a pleasant memory long after the bizarre and unusual are forgotten. Colum falls easily into the role of storyteller, much like the itinerant poets and raconteurs he knew in his youth. Tales are told for their wonder, humor, and familiarity, their ultimate aim being the delight and enjoyment of the audience.

ZACK BOWEN

WORKS: *The Land.* Dublin: Abbey Theatre, 1905. (Play); *The Fiddler's House.* Dublin: Maunsel, 1907. (Play); *Heather Ale.* 1907. (Poetry pamphlet); *Studies.* Dublin: Maunsel, 1907. (Sketches and a short play); *Wild Earth.* Dublin: Maunsel, 1907. (Poetry); *Thomas Muskerry.* Dublin: Maunsel, 1910. (Play); *The Desert.* Dublin: Devereux, 1912. (Play); *My Irish Year.* London: Mills & Boon, 1912; *A Boy in Eirinn.* New York: E. P. Dutton, 1913/London: Dent, 1915; *The King of Ireland's Son.* New York: Macmillan, 1916/London: Harrap, 1920; *Wild Earth, and Other Poems.* New York: Holt/Dublin: Maunsel, 1916. (A new edition with additional poems); *Mogu the Wanderer.* Boston: Little, Brown, 1917. (New version of *The Desert*); *Three Plays.* Dublin & London: Maunsel, 1917/revised, New York: Macmillan, 1925. (Contains *The Fiddler's House, The Land,* and *Thomas Muskerry*); *The Boy Who Knew What the Birds Said.* New York: Macmillan, 1918; *The Adventures of Odysseus.* New York: Macmillan, 1918/London: Harrap, 1920; *The Girl Who Sat by the Ashes.* New York: Macmillan, 1919; *The Boy Apprenticed to an Enchanter.* New York: Macmillan, 1920; *The Children of Odin.* New York: Macmillan, 1920/London: Harrap, 1922; *The Golden Fleece and the Heroes Who Lived Before Achilles.* New York: Macmillan, 1921; *The Children Who Followed the Piper.* New York: Macmillan, 1922; *Dramatic Legends and Other Poems.* New York: Macmillan, 1922; *Castle Conquer.* New York: Macmillan, 1923. (Novel); *At the Gateways of the Day.* New Haven, Conn.: Yale University Press, 1924; *The Island of the Mighty.* New York: Macmillan, 1924; *The Peep-Show Man.* New York: Macmillan, 1924; *Six Who Were Left in a Shoe.* London: Brentano, 1924; *The Bright Islands.* New Haven, Conn.: Yale University Press, 1925; *The Forge in the Forest.* New York: Macmillan, 1925; *The Voyagers.* New York: Macmillan, 1925; *The Road Round Ireland.* New York: Macmillan, 1926; *Creatures.* New York: Macmillan, 1927. (Poems); *The Fountain of Youth.* New York: Macmillan, 1927; *Balloon.* New York: Macmillan, 1929. (Play); *Cross-Roads in Ireland.* New York & London: Macmillan, 1930; *Old Pastures.* New York: Macmillan, 1930. (Poems); *Orpheus. Myths of the World.* New York & London: Macmillan, 1930; *Three Men.* London: Elkin Mathews & Marrot, 1930. (A story); *A Half-Day's Ride.* New York: Macmillan, 1932. (Essays); *Poems.* New York & London: Macmillan, 1932; *The Big Tree of Bunlahy.* New York: Macmillan, 1933/London: Macmillan, 1934 (Stories); *The White Sparrow.* New York: Macmillan, 1933; *The Legend of Saint Columba.* New York: Macmillan, 1935/London: Sheed & Ward, 1936; *Legends of Hawaii.* New Haven, Conn.: Yale University Press, 1937; *The Story of Lowry Maen.* New York & London: Macmillan, 1937; *Flower Pieces: New Poems.* Dublin: Orwell, 1938; *The Jackdaw.* Dublin: Gayfield, 1939 (Pamphlet poem); *Where the Winds Never Blew and the Cocks Never Crew.* New York: Macmillan, 1940; *The Frenzied Prince, Being Heroic Stories of Ancient Ireland.* Philadelphia: McKay, 1943; *The Collected Poems of Padraic Colum.* New York: Devin-Adair, 1953; *A Treasury of Irish Folklore.* New York: Crown, 1954; *The Vegetable Kingdom.* Bloomington, Ind.: Indiana University Press, 1954. (Poems); *The Flying Swans.* New York: Crown, 1957. (Novel); *Ten Poems.* Dublin: Dolmen, 1957; *Garland Sunday.* Dublin: Dolmen, 1958. (A poem); *Irish Elegies.* Dublin: Dolmen, 1958/augmented, 1961 & 1966. (Poems); with Mary Colum, *Our Friend James Joyce.* Garden City, N.Y.: Doubleday, 1958; *Ourselves Alone.* New York: Crown, 1959/European edition entitled *Arthur Griffith (1872-1922),* Dublin: Browne & Nolan, 1959. (Biography of Griffith); *The Poet's Circuits. Collected Poems of Ireland.* London: Oxford University Press, 1960; *Story Telling, New and Old.* New York: Macmillan, 1961; *Moytura:A Play for Dancers.* Dublin: Dolmen, 1963; *The Stone of Victory and Other Tales of Padraic Colum.* New York: McGraw-Hill, 1966; *The Journal of Irish Literature* 2 (January 1973), a Padraic Colum Number, Zack Bowen & Gordon Henderson, eds.   REFERENCES: Bowen, Zack. *Padraic Colum.* Carbondale, Ill.: Southern Illinois University Press, 1970; Denson, Alan. "Padraic Colum: An Appreciation with a Checklist of His Publications." *The Dublin Magazine* 6 (Spring 1967); 50-67.

CONGREVE, WILLIAM (1670-1729), dramatist. Born at Bardsey, near Leeds, in 1670, his father the son of a Staffordshire squire, young Congreve was taken to Ireland at age four. He was well educated at Kilkenny College, where he became acquainted with Swift,* and at Trinity College, Dublin. He entered the Middle Temple in London in 1691, nominally to study law, but he soon became a friend and protege of Dryden, who published with high praise a portion of his translation of Homer and other poems. In 1692, using the pseudonym Cleophil, he published a novella-length romance, *Incognita,* which follows the conventions of romance so perfectly as to be a parody of them. His first play, *The Old Bachelor*—produced in January 1693 at Covent Garden—ran for fourteen nights; his second, *The Double-Dealer,* produced the same year, was not as successful, even though in some ways it is his strongest, most direct satire. Congreve briefly joined other actors and playwrights at the new theatre at Lincoln's Inn Fields, which successfully produced *Love for Love* in 1695 and his only tragedy, *The Mourning Bride,* in 1697. In "An Essay Concerning Humour in Comedy" (1697), Congreve carefully defined wit and humor in the English theatrical tradition, linking them to character development and to nature rather than to the grotesque of farce. Congreve's last play, *The Way of the World* (1700), has come to be regarded as his finest because of its characters, especially Lady Wishfort, Sir Wilfull Witwoud, and the witty young lovers Mirabell and Millamant; its polished dialogue and pointed scenes; and its multiplicity of action and of social commentary. Nonetheless, as Congreve anticipated, it had only middling success on its first run. As the epitome of the Restoration comedy of witty manners, it was also outdated for an audience that wanted the new comedy of good example and of sentiment. At thirty, Congreve virtually retired from the stage. He wrote the libretto for an opera, published occasional verse, and carefully revised his writings for a three-volume collected *Works* (1710).

Congreve's plays were the main object of attack in Jeremy Collier's *Short View of the Immorality and Profaneness of the English Stage,* published in 1698, to which Congreve (and several others) replied later in the year with his *Amendments of Mr. Collier's False and Imperfect Citations.* In the sense that Collier's *Short View* spoke for the rising taste for reform of the stage in the direction of exemplary sentimental comedy, it and his *Defence of the Short View* (also 1698) were the victors. At times, Collier seems to attack all theatre, or at least all comic theatre. In the sense that Congreve's *Amendments* presented the classic defense of comedy from its beginnings to the present day, he was the victor: the morality of comedy consists not of preaching and of poetic justice, but of holding folly and vice up to ridicule. Nonetheless, Congreve was hurt by the attack, and he left the stage partly because he was aware that his own and his audience's tastes were at odds.

For ten years Congreve was friendly with the famous actress Mrs. Bracegirdle, for whom he wrote the celebrated part of Millamant, and in his later years with Henrietta, second duchess of Marlborough, who erected his monument in Westminister Abbey. He lived his last years as a retired gentleman, suffering from ill health and supported by government sinecures. In a famous meeting, the young Voltaire scorned Congreve's pose as a gentleman rather than a writer. Through the turmoil surrounding the death of Queen Anne and the Hanoverian succession, Congreve stayed aloof from politics. He managed to remain in the Whig Kit-Cat Club and to keep the friendship and respect of his fellow Irishmen Swift and Steele* as well as of Addison and Pope. He was widely mourned at his death in 1729, for what seemed the passing of the earlier generation of wit.

SVEN ERIC MOLIN

WORKS: *The Complete Works of William Congreve.* Montague Summers, ed. London: Nonsuch, 1923; *The Works of Congreve,* F. W. Bateson, ed. London: Peter Davies, 1930.   REFERENCES: Avery, Emmett Langdon. *Congreve's Plays on the Eighteenth-century Stage.* New York: Modern Language Association of America, 1951; Gosse, Edmund. *Life of Congreve.* New York: Scribner's, 1924; Hodges, John C. *William Congreve, the Man.* New York: Modern Language Association of America, 1941; Hodges, John C., ed. *William Congreve: Letters & Documents.* New York: Harcourt, Brace & World, 1964; Holland, Norman. *The First Modern Comedies.* Cambridge, Mass.: Harvard University Press, 1959; Love, Harold. *Congreve.* Totowa, N.J.: Rowman & Littlefield, 1975; Lynch, Kathleen Martha. *A Congreve Gallery.* Cambridge, Mass.: Harvard University Press, 1951; Novak, Maximillian E. *William Congreve.* New York: Twayne, 1971; Van Voris, W. H. *The Cultivated Stance.* [Chester Springs, Pa.]: Dufour Editions, [1967].

CONNELL, VIVIAN (1905-), novelist and playwright. Connell was born in Cork in 1905, and lived there until he was thirty, after which he traveled

on the Continent and lived in Sussex and Sicily. He now lives in the south
of France. His first story was published by AE* in *The Irish Statesman,*
after which he had nothing more published for over a decade. He wrote a
number of plays, the most successful being *The Nineteenth Hole of Europe*
(1943), but his great success was the novel *The Chinese Room* (1943),
which sold over three million copies. On the dust jacket of one of his books,
he is quoted as saying:

> I was taught to read and write by my father. I gathered the rest of
> my education in the Irish pubs, the hurling fields, and on the
> athletic track. I have carried a horn with several packs of hounds.
> And I once ran the half-mile and mile. I consider the habit of
> physical endurance thus gathered, through long days of riding or
> running across the Irish country, an explanation of my ability to
> drive on a play or book to the end without flagging.

Connell gives such a background and such tenacious literary ability to
the obviously autobiographical novelist hero of *The Golden Sleep* (1948),
who finishes his novels in two months flat. Cleeve* calls Connell a distinguished man of letters, but he belongs more in the company of the Donn
Byrnes* and Constantine Fitzgibbons* than of the Shaws* or Joyces,* or
even of the O'Connors* and O'Faolains.* His novels have a portentousness
and yet a spuriousness. They have a sleek craft that makes them easy to
read, while they also have heavy pretensions to meaning. The considerable
popularity of *The Chinese Room* arises partly from its theme, which is an
attack on sexual inhibition and a celebration of sexual openness. The book
owes a heavy debt to the later D. H. Lawrence, but it is a Lawrence
euphemized for the coffee tables of the 1940s. At the same time, the book
has a running mystery story plot (in which the villain turns out to be the
most mechanically sexual character), and finally there is an embroidery of
Sax Rohmer hocus-pocus.

Ultimately, this book and its less popular successors ring tinny. First, the
characters, especially the women, are the stereotypes of racy and romantic
fiction; and second, the writing at the intense and crucial moments sinks into
the most hackneyed banality. In fact, there can be no greater condemnation
of Vivian Connell than to quote him. The following is from *The Golden
Sleep*:

> He stopped and bent down and kissed her and she had the odor
> of the figs in Spain in her mouth and her lips clung in the plasm of
> desire. . . .
> "I . . . I think I've come asunder. . . . I . . . Let me alone for a
> minute."
> He walked onto the quay and knew that everything he had felt
> in his life was only an illusion compared to this surging and genetic

love that left his body now quivering like a seismograph and his soul riding out on midnight air.

WORKS: *The Peacock Is a Gentleman.* New York: Dial, 1941. (Novel); *The Squire of Shaftesbury Avenue.* London: Constable, [1941]. (Play); *Throng o' Scarlet.* London: Constable, [1941]. (Play); *The Chinese Room.* New York: B. C. Hoffman, Dial, 1942. (Novel); *The Nineteenth Hole of Europe.* London: M. Secker & Warburg, 1943. (Play); *The Golden Sleep.* New York: Dial, 1948. (Novel); *A Man of Parts.* New York: Fawcett, 1950. (Novel); *The Hounds of Cloneen.* New York: Dial, 1951 (Novel); *September in Quinze.* London: Hutchinson/New York: Dial, 1952. (Novel).

CONNER, [PATRICK] REARDON (1907-), novelist. Conner was born on February 19, 1907, in Dublin. His father was a head constable in the Royal Irish Constabulary, and he was educated at Presentation College, Cork. He went to England when he was in his teens and worked at a variety of jobs, principally that of gardener. His first published novel, *Shake Hands with the Devil* (1933), has been his most successful; it was a book club choice in America and some twenty-five years later was made into a film. The book still stands up as one of the better novels of Irish political violence and can be ranked with the well-known works of Liam O'Flaherty* and F. L. Green.* Conner's novel depicts the period of the Black and Tan War which he observed as a boy, and he is about equally critical of both sides. The book is not as crudely written as is O'Flaherty's *The Informer,* nor as floridly as is Green's *Odd Man Out.* Unlike those other two volumes, it also contains a good deal of specific detail and realistic observation, but it would finally have to be called powerful rather than deeply realized. Perhaps Conner's other important book is the autobiographical *A Plain Tale from the Bogs* (1937) which describes his life in Ireland from Easter Week through the Black and Tan War, but which is more interesting in its depiction of the life of a manual laborer in London during the Depression.

WORKS: *Shake Hands with the Devil.* London: J. M. Dent, 1933; *Rude Earth.* London: J. M. Dent, 1934/published in America as *Salute to Aphrodite,* New York: Bobbs-Merrill, 1935; *I Am Death.* London: Chapman & Hall, 1936; *Men Must Live.* London: Cassell, 1937; *A Plain Tale from the Bogs.* London: John Miles, 1937. (Autobiography); *The Sword of Love.* London: Cassell, 1938; *Wife of Colum.* London: Michael Joseph, 1939; *The Devil Among the Tailors.* London: MacDonald, 1947; *My Love to the Gallows.* London: MacDonald, 1948; *Hunger of the Heart.* London: MacDonald, 1950; *The Singing Stone.* London: MacDonald, 1951; *The House of Cain.* London: MacDonald, 1952. (as Peter Malin): *To Kill Is My Vocation.* London: Cassell, 1939; *River, Sing Me a Song.* London: Cassell, 1939; *Kobo the Brave.* London: Warne, 1950.

CONNOLLY, JAMES (1868-1916), labor leader, socialist theoretician, and nationalist. Connolly was born on June 5, 1868, in Edinburgh and was executed on May 12, 1916, for his prominent part in the Easter Rising. Much of Connolly's life was spent in Scotland and America, but the most significant part was undoubtedly the years from 1910 when, after Jim Larkin had gone to America, he emerged as the major spokesman for organized labor in Ireland and as a fiery proponent of armed rebellion. Connolly's major works are *Labour in Irish History, The Reconquest of Ireland*, and the long essay *Labour, Nationality and Religion*. He has been called "one of the first great working class intellectuals" and "the only Irish philosopher of consequence since the days of Bishop Berkeley*." Such strong claims for Connolly as a deep or original economic thinker seem extravagant, however, and are based on a general regard for the man's character and accomplishment. Connolly was primarily a political activist, and his prolific writing practically always had an immediate propagandistic function. For Ireland, his significant positions were his Marxian reading of Irish history, his attempt to reconcile Catholicism and socialism, and his assumption that Irish nationalism and Irish socialism were inextricably intertwined. Much of his writing has a fiery, if traditional, vigor, and all of it is permeated by an utter dedication and a burning sincerity. His occasional poems and apparently his two unpublished plays were also motivated more by propaganda than by art. Connolly is important as a social force and a humane conscience more than as an original journalist or artist or economic thinker. However, in modern Ireland his influence has remained more latent and superficial than active and profound.

WORKS: *Labour, Nationality and Religion*. Dublin: Harp Library, 1910; *Labour in Ireland* (containing *Labour in Irish History* and *The Reconquest of Ireland*). Dublin: Maunsel, 1917; *The Best of Connolly*. Proinsias Mac Aonghusa & Liam O Reagain, eds. Cork: Mercier, 1967; *James Connolly: Selected Writings*. P. Berresford Ellis, ed. Harmondsworth, Middlessex: Penguin, 1973.   REFERENCES: Edwards, Owen Dudley. *The Mind of an Activist—James Connolly*. Dublin: Gill & Macmillan, 1971; Greaves, C. Desmond. *The Life and Times of James Connolly*. London: Lawrence & Wishart, 1961; Levenson, Samuel. *James Connolly*. London: Martin Brian & O'Keefe, 1973; Nevin, D. *Connolly Bibliography*. Dublin: Irish T.U.C., 1968.

CORK DRAMATIC SOCIETY (1908-1914), amateur dramatic group. The Cork Dramatic Society was formed by Daniel Corkery* and others in Cork city in 1908. Originally, the group intended to produce new plays by its members as well as translations by its members from various foreign languages. No translations were ever produced, but for a few years the group produced new Cork plays in a Gaelic League hall in Queen Street, and on one occasion even played for several days in the Cork Opera House. The Society brought forth no masterpieces, but it did produce seventeen new plays by new Cork writers—among them Corkery himself, Terence J. MacSwiney,* T. C. Murray,* Lennox Robinson,* Con O'Leary,* and J. Bernard MacCarthy.* A handful of the Cork plays were later produced by the Abbey Theatre,* and about half of them have been published.

WORKS: Hogan, Robert, and Burnham, Richard, eds. *Lost Plays of the Irish Renaissance. Vol. II, The Cork Dramatic Society*. Newark, Del.: Proscenium, 1979.

CORK REALISTS. This term, apparently coined by W. B. Yeats,* was used as a blanket description of several playwrights who were first performed by the Abbey Theatre* in the years immediately following the death of J. M. Synge.* Principally, Yeats was referring to Lennox Robinson,* T. C. Murray,* and R. J. Ray,* and had in mind such plays as Robinson's *The Cross Roads* (1909), Ray's *The White Feather* (1909), and Murray's *Birthright* (1910). Robinson and Murray both had early one-acts performed by the Cork Dramatic Society,* but there was really no school of realistic drama growing up in Cork, and these three men at the time hardly knew each other. They were simply writing "strong" dramas in a language which mirrored life around them, rather than heightened reality as did Synge's dialogue. Yeats' descriptive term was a journalistic label of no more relevance than "The Beat Generation" or "The Angry Young Men." Playwrights such as Padraic Colum,* St. John Ervine,* and W. F. Casey* were writing realistically about other sections of the country at the same time.

CORKERY, DANIEL (1878-1964), man of letters. Corkery, whose life centered in Cork, was born in that city on February 14, 1878, to William and Mary Corkery, and was paternally a descendant of generations of carpenter-craftsmen. Crippled in one leg, supposedly by poliomyelitis, he matured into a puritanical, deeply religious man, very lucky in friends. Unmarried, he was cared for by his sister Mary until the two were persuaded to join a niece (Maureen) in her home on the Lee in County Cork. There he died on December 31, 1964, to be buried in St. Joseph's Cemetery, Cork.

Corkery's life was relatively quiet and his education, very sparse: a period (followed by a monitorship) at the Presentation Brothers Elementary School, Cork; a year at St. Patrick's College, Dublin, 1906-1907; and night study at the Crawford Municipal School of Art, Cork, which eventually led to his sensitive water colors of the Lee Valley. Meanwhile, his violent fanaticism for the Irish language had begun in 1901, though presumably he never became fluent in writing it. In 1908, he helped organize the Cork Dramatic Society and thus got into playwriting. Miscellaneous teaching preceded his M.A. for independent research on Synge* from the National University (1929) and his professorship in English at University College, Cork (1931-1947), which gave him an honorary D.Litt. after retirement. He served in the Seanad Éireann from 1951 to 1954 and on the Arts Council from 1952 to 1956. For the rest, he wrote, reviewed, and painted, sometimes exhibiting.

Corkery's efforts at scholarship—*The Hidden Island* (1925), *Synge and Anglo-Irish Literature* (1931), and *The Fortunes of the Irish Language* (1954)—have stirred much controversial, sometimes acidulous, opinion, and it seems that there is a good basis for the negative assessment. Certainly Corkery's linguistic fanaticism, with extravagant claims of literary significance; inadequate knowledge; chauvinism; religious zealotry; and propagandistic inclination are hardly impressive guarantees of scholarship. One must turn to the creative work, and much of that is unexciting: e.g., the mild verse (cf. *I Brhreasil/A Book of Lyrics*, 1921), the sentimental novel (*The Threshold of Quiet*, 1917), most of the MS plays, and two that got printed (the mawkish "Resurrection": *Theatre Arts Monthly*, April 1924; and the tractarian *The Labour Leader*, 1920). But the best of the creative work is very fine indeed. *The Yellow Bittern and Other Plays* (1920) concentrates in three one-acters the finest of Corkery's dramatic work; they are spiritual, moving, poetic, and compassionate, and its title piece is in the "miracle" tradition, as Frank O'Connor* recognized. The romantic, though imperfect play, *Fohnam the Sculptor* (Newark, Del.: Proscenium, 1973) could be associated with it. The grey-toned short stories (except for *The Hounds of Banba*, 1920, a pathetic and sentimental memorialization of Irish guerrilla activities) are Corkery's prime claim to distinction, established by *A Munster Twilight* (1916). *The Stormy Hills* (1929) and portions of *Earth Out of Earth* (1939) helped to consolidate that claim; the tension of suppressed wildness often underlies these tales.

Corkery's realistic, but never vulgar, handling of Cork and Kerry life; his handling of colloquial speech; his poetic response to the malign and uncontrollable in nature; and his sheer originality in such tales as "The Ploughing of Leacana-Naomh," "The Stones," and "Refuge" place him in the forefront of the short story writers of his day.

GEORGE BRANDON SAUL

WORKS: *A Munster Twilight*. Dublin & Cork: Talbot, 1916/New York: Stokes, 1917; *The Threshold of Quiet*. Dublin & Cork: Talbot/London: Unwin, 1917; *The Hounds of Banba*. Dublin & Cork: Talbot, 1920/New York: Huebsch, 1922; *The Labour Leader*. Dublin: Talbot/London: Unwin, 1920; *The Yellow Bittern and Other Plays*. Dublin: Talbot/London: Unwin, 1920; *I Bhreasail/A Book of Lyrics*. Dublin: Talbot/London: Mathews & Marot, 1921; *Rebel Songs* by "Reithin Siubhalach." [Cork]: Provinces Publishing Co., [1922]; *The Hidden Ireland/A Study of Gaelic Munster in the Eighteenth Century*. Dublin: Gill, 1925; *The Stormy Hills*. Dublin: Talbot/London: Jonathan Cape, 1929; *Synge and Anglo-Irish Literature*. Cork: Cork University Press/London: Longmans, Green, 1931; *Earth Out of Earth*. Dublin & Cork: Talbot, 1939; *Resurrection*. Dublin & Cork: Talbot, n.d.; *What's This About the Gaelic League?* Ath Cliath: Connradh na Gaedhilge, n.d.; *The Philosophy of the Gaelic League*. Dublin, 1948; *The Wager and Other Stories*. New York: Devin-Adair, 1950; *An Doras Dunta*. Baile Atha Cliath, 1953; *The Fortunes of the Irish Language*. Dublin: Fallon, 1954.   REFERENCES: Hutchins, Patricia. "Daniel Corkery, Poet of Weather and Place." *Irish Writing*, 25 (December 1953), 42-49; O'Faolain, Sean. "Daniel Corkery." *Dublin Magazine* 11 (April-June 1936): 49-61; Saul, George Brandon. *Daniel Corkery*. Lewisburg, Pa.: Bucknell University Press, 1973.

COULTER, JOHN (1888-), playwright. Coulter, born in Belfast on February 12, 1888, has divided his lifespan almost evenly between Ireland and Canada. While living in Ireland, he witnessed the rise of the Abbey* and the Ulster Literary Theatre*; moving to Toronto in 1936, he became an important figure in the development of Canadian drama.

Coulter's plays of Ulster life include *The House in the Quiet Glen* (1925), a matchmaking comedy, and *Family Portrait* (1935), a satire on a materialistic Belfast family. *The Drums Are Out*, a drama of divided loyalties, set in Belfast during the Troubles, enjoyed a long run at the Abbey beginning on the anniversary of the Battle of the Boyne, appropriately, on July 12, 1948. A two-part tragedy, *God's Ulsterman* (1974), traces the legacy of sectarian hatred bequeathed to Ireland by Cromwell from the civil war of the 1640s to the era of Ian Paisley. These plays take no dogmatic stance and offer no solution to the torment of the North. If any hope is intimated, it lies in the possibility that the young will ultimately reject the ancient hostilities.

In addition to his plays, Coulter wrote a short novel entitled *Turf Smoke* (1945), adapted from his play *Holy Manhattan* (1941); this is the wistful tale of an elderly emigrant who tries to maintain a rural Ulster life-style in the canyons of New York. Coulter also wrote the libretto for Healey Willan's opera *Deirdre of the Sorrows* (1944).

Coulter's principal contribution to Canadian drama is the *Riel* trilogy (1950, first major production 1975). In 1869 and 1885, Louis Riel, a man of French and Metis Indian parentage, led uprisings in what is now Manitoba to protest wrongs done to the Metis people. There are some similarities between Riel and some Irish revolutionary leaders, between the situation in nineteenth-century Manitoba and in contemporary Quebec and Belfast. While the Ulster plays of John Coulter are a sensitive distillation of first-hand knowledge, *Riel* may be considered his masterwork because of its originality of subject and treatment.

WILLIAM J. FEENEY

WORKS: "The Catholics Walk." *Living Age,* 323 (November 22, 1924): 433-435. (Fiction); *The House in the Quiet Glen* and *Family Portrait.* Toronto: Macmillan, 1937; *Deirdre of the Sorrows:* An Ancient and Noble Tale Retold by John Coulter for Music by Healey Willan. Toronto: Macmillan, 1944. 2d ed., 1965; *Churchill.* Toronto: Ryerson, 1944. (Biography); *Turf Smoke.* Toronto: Ryerson, 1945; *The Blossoming Thorn.* Toronto: Ryerson, 1946. (Poetry); *The Trial of Louis Riel.* Ottawa: Oberon, 1968; *The Drums Are Out.* Irish Drama Series, Vol. 6. Chicago: De Paul University, 1971; *Riel.* Hamilton: Cromlech, 1972. Coulter's plays, stories, articles, radio and television scripts, and other documents are stored in the Coulter Archives, Mills Memorial Library, MacMaster University, Hamilton, Ontario, Canada.   REFERENCES: Anthony, Geraldine. *John Coulter.* Twayne's World Authors Series. Boston: G. K. Hall, 1976; "John Coulter." *Contemporary Authors* 7-8 (1963): 115-116; Dempsey, Marion. "Profile: John Coulter." *Performing Arts* 8 (Spring 1971): 20-21.

COUSINS, JAMES H[ENRY SPROULL] (1873-1956), poet and playwright. Cousins was born in Belfast on July 22, 1873. He was educated at a national school in Belfast and then became an office boy, a clerk, and the private secretary to the lord mayor. In 1897, he moved to Dublin where he was first a clerk in a coal and shipping firm, and where he met AE,* Yeats,* Martyn,* Hyde,* and other writers of the Literary Revival. In

1901, he met Frank and Willie Fay and, learning of their desire to produce Irish plays, introduced them to AE who had written the first act of his *Deirdre*. Cousins acted in small parts for the newly formed Irish National Theatre Society, and he also wrote a number of plays, among them *The Sleep of the King* (1902), *The Racing Lug* (1902), and *The Sword of Dermot* (1903). Some of his short pieces were poetic versions of Irish stories and, except in quality, were not unlike some of the early plays of Yeats. Yeats, however, deplored "too much Cousins," succeeded in squashing a production of Cousins' comedy *Sold*, and firmly detached Cousins from the theatre movement.

In 1905, Cousins became an assistant master of English at the high school in Harcourt Street. In 1908, he joined the Theosophical Society. He was also a prolific poet. It was probably his volume *The Bell-Branch* (1908) which Joyce* had in mind in "Gas from a Burner" when he referred to a "tablebook of Cousins" which would "give you a heartburn in your arse." Cousins also edited a suffragette journal and rode many other hobbyhorses, among them vegetarianism.

In 1913, he and his wife left Dublin for Liverpool and then for India. On this occasion, the Theatre of Ireland gave him a special benefit evening, and Yeats made some amends by contributing £5 and writing a letter mentioning how much he valued Cousins. Cousins spent most of the rest of his life in India as a much admired individual and a highly valued teacher. He continued to write prolifically, and he died in India on February 20, 1956.

As a playwright, Cousins' most successful piece was the short tragedy *The Racing Lug* which predates John Synge's* somewhat similar *Riders to the Sea*. His bibliographer Alan Denson thinks, rather too enthusiastically, that "There are perhaps fifty poems of James Cousins which will endure." However, Denson goes on to note that "Much of his verse is in one key, and palls if read often."

Cousins is more interesting as a personality than as a writer. Although he was a catalyst in the early days of the theatre movement, he is most memorable as an engaging and enthusiastic eccentric. Perhaps the best judgment on him is again Denson's:

> The unflattering (and offensive) gibes levelled at him in the W. B. Yeats and James Joyce canon deserve to be weighed against one important fact. Neither Yeats nor Joyce appears to have had any knowledge of Cousins' books written after 1915. Whilst they lived out their lives in service to their own self-centered ideals James Cousins devoted his best energies and his subtlest intellectual powers to the education of the young and the welfare of the poor and oppressed.

WORKS: *Ben Madighan and Other Poems*. Belfast: Marcus Ward, [1894]; *The*

Voice of One. London: T. Fisher Unwin, 1900. (Poems); *The Quest.* Dublin: Maunsel, 1906. (Poems). *The Awakening and Other Sonnets.* Dublin: Maunsel, [1907]; *The Bell-Branch.* Dublin: Maunsel, 1908. (Poems); *Etain the Beloved and Other Poems.* Dublin: Maunsel, 1912; *The Wisdom of the West.* London: Theosophical Publishing Society, 1912. (Mythological studies); *The Bases of Theosophy.* Madras, Benares & Chicago: Theosophical Publishing House, 1913; *Straight and Crooked.* London: Grant Richards, 1915. (Poems); *The Garland of Life.* Madras: Ganesh, 1917. (Poems); *New Ways in English Literature.* Madras: Ganesh, [1917] revised, 1919; *The Renaissance in India.* Madras: Ganesh, [1918]; *Footsteps of Freedom.* Madras: Ganesh, 1919. (Essays); *The King's Wife.* Madras: Ganesh, 1919. (Play); *Moulted Feathers.* Madras: Ganesh, 1919. (Poetry); *Sea-Change.* Madras: Ganesh, 1920. (Poetry); *Modern English Poetry.* Madras: Ganesh, 1921; *The Cultural Unity of Asia.* Adyar, Madras: Theosophical Publishing House, 1922; *Surya-Gita.* Madras: Ganesh, 1922. (Poetry); *Work and Worship.* Madras: Ganesh, 1922. (Essays); *The New Japan, Impressions and Reflections.* Madras. Ganesh, 1923; *Forest Meditation and Other Poems.* Adyar, Madras: Theosophical Publishing House, 1925; *Heathen Essays.* Madras: Ganesh, 1923; *The Philosophy of Beauty.* Adyar, Madras: Theosophical Publishing House, 1925; *Samadarsana . . . A Study in Indian Psychology.* Madras, Ganesh, 1925; *Above the Rainbow and Other Poems.* Madras: Ganesh, 1926; *The Sword of Dermot.* Madras: Shama's Publishing House, 1927. (Play); *The Girdle.* Madras: Puck/Ganesh, 1929. (Poems); *The Wandering Harp, Selected Poems.* New York: Roerich Museum Press, 1932; *A Bardic Pilgrimage, Second Selection of the Poetry of James H. Cousins.* New York: Roerich Museum Press, 1934; *A Study in Synthesis.* Madras: Ganesh, 1934; *The Oracle and Other Poems.* Madras: Ganesh, 1938; *Collected Poems, 1894-1940.* Adyar, Madras: Kalakshetra, 1940; *The Faith of the Artist.* Adyar, Madras: Kalakshetra, 1941. (Essays); *The Hound of Uladh, Two Plays in Verse.* Adyar, Madras: Kalakshetra, 1942; *The Aesthetical Necessity in Life.* Kitadistan, Allahabad: University of Madras, 1944; *Reflections Before Sunset.* Adyar, Madras: Kalakshetra, 1946. (Poems); *Twenty-Four Sonnets.* Adyar, Madras: Kalakshetra, [1949]; *We Two Together,* with Margaret E. Cousins. Madras: Ganesh, [1950]. (Autobiography). REFERENCE: Denson, Alan. *James H. Cousins and Margaret E. Cousins, a Bio-Bibliographical Survey.* Kendal: Alan Denson, 1967. (An authoritative listing of many minor works not included above.)

COX, WILLIAM TREVOR. *See* TREVOR, WILLIAM.

CRAIG, MAURICE [JAMES] (1919-), poet and social historian. Craig was born on October 25, 1919, in Belfast, and was educated at Magdalene College, Cambridge, and at Trinity College, Dublin, from which he received his Ph.D. In the 1940s, he published some superbly controlled poetry. His understanding of traditional form is finely apparent, for instance, in "Ballad to a Traditional Refrain," where he suffuses the simple public form of the popular ballad with a pervasive irony, and uses a Yeatsian refrain with devastating cumulative effect. His more recent books deal with Irish bookbinding and archaeological subjects. His best known work is *Dublin, 1660-1860,* a companionable social and architectural history of immense information, consummate taste, and engaging charm.

WORKS: *A Poem: Black Swans.* Dublin: Gayfield, 1941; *Twelve Poems.* Dublin: Privately printed, 1942; *Some Way for Reason.* London: Toronto: Heinemann, 1948;

The Volunteer Earl, Being the Life and Times of James Caulfeild, First Earl of Charlemont. London: Cresset, 1948; *Dublin, 1660-1860.* London: Cresset, 1952/Dublin: Figgis, 1969; *Irish Bookbinding, 1600-1800.* London: Cassell, 1954.

CROKER, JOHN WILSON (1780-1857), politician and man of letters. Croker was born in Galway on December 20, 1780, educated at Trinity College, Dublin, and at Lincoln's Inn, and admitted to the Irish bar in 1802. He wrote a few early satires and historical essays about Ireland which are little read today. His real career was in England as a member of Parliament, as secretary to the Admiralty, and as one of the founders (in 1809) of the influential *Quarterly Review* for which he wrote over 250 articles. His literary criticism for the *Review* was not always very perceptive (see his damning notice of Keats' "Endymion" in September 1818); and his edition of Boswell's *Life of Johnson* was savagely attacked by his frequent sparring partner, Thomas Babington Macaulay, in *The Edinburgh Review.* His own ferocious assault on Macaulay's *History of England* was defined by Sydney Smith as an attempt at murder that ended in suicide. He also quarreled with Lady Morgan,* and he was unfairly pilloried as the despicable Rigby in Disraeli's *Coningsby.* He died at Hampton, Middlesex, on August 10, 1857.

WORKS: [*The Opinion of an Impartial Observer Concerning the Late Transactions in Ireland.* Dublin: J. Parry, 1803.]; *An Intercepted Letter, from J— T—, Esq., Writer at Canton, to His Friend in Dublin, Ireland.* Dublin: M. N. Mahon, 1804; *Familiar Epistles to Frederick J. —S, Esq. on the Present State of the Irish Stage.* Dublin: John Barlow, 1804; *The Amazoniad; or, Figure and Fashion.* Dublin: John King, 1806; *A Sketch of the State of Ireland Past and Present.* Dublin: M. N. Mahon, 1808; *The Battles of Talavera.* Dublin: Mahon, 1809. *The Croker Papers.* Louis J. Jennings, ed. 3 vols. London: Murray, 1884; *The Croker Papers 1808-1857.* Bernard Pool, ed. London: Batsford, 1967.

CROKER, T[HOMAS] CROFTON (1798-1854), folklorist. Croker, the pioneering collector of Irish folklore, was born in Buckingham Square, Cork, on January 15, 1798. At the age of fifteen, he was placed as an apprentice in a mercantile firm in Cork, but his main interest was already in old legends and stories. He made several excursions throughout the South of Ireland to sketch and to study the traditions of the countryside. In 1818, after the death of his father, he moved to London. John Wilson Croker,* who was no relation, secured him a clerkship at the Admiralty, where he served until his retirement in 1850.

In 1830, Croker married Marianne Nicholson who published two novels, *The Adventures of Barney Mahoney* and *My Village Versus Our Village* (both 1832), under her husband's name.

Croker's own first book, *Researches in the South of Ireland* (1824), was admired but not greatly successful. However, his *Fairy Legends and Traditions of the South of Ireland* (1825) was an immediate popular success, and also brought the author enthusiastic praise from Wilhelm Grimm,

Maria Edgeworth,* and Sir Walter Scott. (On his first meeting with Croker, Scott described him as "little as a dwarf, keen-eyed as a hawk, and of easy, prepossessing manners, something like Tom Moore.") *Fairy Legends* is a collection of tales about such strange and wondrous beings as Banshees, Merrows, Phookas, and Cluricaunes. The stories are perhaps not as faithfully rendered as modern folklorists would desire, but they are delightful stories. Croker did not merely take them down verbatim, but arranged them into effective narrative structures. "The Haunted Celler" is an obvious example of how successfully Croker rearranged his incidents to lead to an effective climax. However, it was not only the charm of his subjects and the craft of his organization, but also the terse yet rich prose that captivated his readers. As W. B. Yeats* remarked, Croker "caught the very choice of the people, the very pulse of life—giving what was most noticed in his day. Croker, full of the ideas of harum-scarum Irish gentility, saw everything humorized. His work is touched everywhere with beauty—a gentle Arcadian beauty."

Croker's last years were busy ones, and his important publications include *Legends of the Lakes; or Sayings and Doings at Killarney* (1829), *A Memoir of Joseph Holt* (1838), and *Popular Songs of Ireland* (1839). He died on August 8, 1854, at Brompton, leaving behind at least one volume, *Fairy Legends*, which is as fresh and captivating today as it was 150 years ago.

WORKS: *Researches in the South of Ireland*. London: J. Murray, 1824/reprint. Dublin: Irish University Press, 1968, with an introduction by Kevin Danaher; *Fairy Legends and Traditions of the South of Ireland*. London: J. Murray, 1825 & 1828; *Daniel O'Rourke; or, Rhymes of a Pantomime*. London: Ainsworth, 1828; *Legends of the Lakes; or, Sayings and Doings at Killarney*. London: Ebers, 1829; *Landscape Illustrations of Moore's "Irish Melodies"*. London: Power, 1835; *The Tour of the French Traveller M. de la Boullaye le Gouz in Ireland. A. D. 1644*. London: T. & W. Boone, 1837; *Memoirs of Joseph Holt, General of the Irish Rebels in 1798*. London: H. Colburn, 1838; *The Popular Songs of Ireland*. London: H. Colburn, 1839; *The Historical Songs of Ireland*. London: Printed for the Percy Society by G. Richards, 1841; *Narratives Illustrative of the Contests in Ireland in 1641 and 1690*. London: Printed for the Camden Society by J. Bowyer Nichols, 1841; *A Kerry Pastoral*. London: Reprinted for the Percy Society by T. Richards, 1843; *The Keen of the South of Ireland*. London: Printed for the Percy Society by T. Richards, 1844; *Popular Songs, Illustrative of the French Invasions of Ireland*. London: Percy Society, 1845-1847; *A Walk from London to Fulham*. London: W. Tegg, 1860.   REFERENCE: MacCarthy, Bridget G. "Thomas Crofton Croker 1798-1854." *Studies* 32 (1943): 539-556.

CRONE, ANNE (1915-), novelist. Crone was born in Dublin in 1915 and was educated in Belfast and at Oxford.

Crone's novels focus on rural Ulster families whose histories are narrated by young women. Land and love are her main themes. For example, the orphaned Catholic heroine of *Bridie Steen* (1948), her first novel, roams the shores of Lough Erne free of any ties until she falls in love with her cousin who reunites her with her termagant Protestant grandmother. A painful love affair matures her, but when her grandmother, an embittered Protestant, presses her to renounce her religion to inherit family land, the conflict drives her to her death. The novel has other charming characters in addition to Bridie, and it is a passionate, nonpartisan plea for religious tolerance in Ulster.

This Pleasant Lea (1951), like *Bridie Steen*, is set on the windy shores of Lough Erne. Faith, the young heroine, falls in love, suffers the pain of rejection and the dissipation of her family's land by a feckless brother, but finally finds happiness in marriage to a wealthy farmer. Like Bridie, she is an intense, romantic young woman whose fortunes command our interest and sympathy. Not so Grace Maguire, the heroine of *My Heart and I* (1955), whose self-effacing virtue is tedious in the extreme. No doubt hers is a realistic portrait of Irish womanhood, but it is without humor. The novel is thematically sound, however: Grace is finally cared for by her lost love whose life has been ruined by his ties to the land.

Crone's writing, though sensitive and lyrical, is mannered and dated. Nonetheless, she does understand human emotions and does know the foibles of her character. Her characterization of young women is excellent. *Bridie Steen*, for example, has Emily Bronte's depth of feeling and Jane Austen's charm and common sense. *This Pleasant Lea* is almost as good as *Bridie Steen*, but *My Heart and I* is much inferior.

MARY ROSE CALLAGHAN

WORKS: *Bridie Steen*. New York: Scribner's, 1948/London: Heinemann, 1949; *This Pleasant Lea*. New York: Scribner's, 1951/London: Heinemann, 1952; *My Heart and I*. London: Heinemann, 1955.

CRONIN, ANTHONY (1926-), poet, critic, and novelist. Cronin was born in County Wexford in 1926. He was connected with *The Bell** under the editorship of Peadar O'Donnell,* and he also spent some time in London where he was connected with *Time and Tide*. That latter portion of his career is reflected in his memoir of the literary life of the 1950s, *Dead as Doornails* (1976), in which he offers unsentimental and, indeed, somewhat rancid portraits of Kavanagh,* Behan,* Flann O'Brien,* and several English figures. His best work in prose is a novel, *The Life of Riley* (1964), about Dublin Bohemia in the 1950s. The book is something of a *roman à clef* and has its distinctly successful moments of satire, particularly about literary life on *The Bell* and in the corridors of Radio Éireann. It is a cruel, sour, grumpy, and yet often very funny book.

Cronin has also published a small amount of verse and a volume of criticism. The verse is most various in quality. At its worst, it ranges from unprofessional Auden to such splenetic silliness as a poem which repeats the name "Yeats" four times, and then repeats the word "fart" four times. Nevertheless, a handful of his poems, such as "Small Hours," "Song," and

"Anarchist" are extraordinarily good. His "Apology" and his sonnet called "Poem" rise from a smooth competency to conclude with some really striking lines. His long poem "R.M.S. Titanic" has been widely disseminated and generally admired.

Cronin's one volume of criticism, *A Question of Modernity* (1966), suggests that he could have been a significant critic had he worked at it conscientiously. Despite passages in which he belabors a simple point for pages, and despite entirely too many parentheses for forceful writing, he is particularly fine on Joyce,* Beckett,* and the autocratic and influential English critic F. R. Leavis. In the mid-1970s, he has contributed a weekly column to *The Irish Times* on life and letters. Occasionally, as in one vitriolic attack on the poetry of Thomas Kinsella,* the column has some vigor, but it is usually prolix and curiously dull.

WORKS: *Poems*. London: Cresset, 1957; *The Life of Riley*. London: Secker & Warburg. (Novel), *A Question of Modernity*. London: Secker & Warburg, 1966. (Criticism); *Collected Poems, 1950-1973*. Dublin: New Writers', 1973; *Dead as Doornails*. Dublin: Dolmen, 1975, in association with Talbot, Dublin, and with Calder & Boyars, London. (Literary reminiscences).   REFERENCE: Scully, Maurice. "A Chat with Anthony Cronin." *Icarus* (May 1976).

CROSS, ERIC (1903-), writer of sketches and stories. Cross, born in Newry, County Down, in 1903, is a scientist, inventor, chemist, and general philosopher, as well as a writer. He has lived in the west of Ireland for many years. He is the author of the minor Irish classic *The Tailor and Ansty* (1942), an ever-fresh and ripely witty collection of sketches commemorating the talk of his friend, the Tailor of Gougane Barra. In 1943, Cross' book was banned by the Irish Censorship Board; its suppression was one of the most ludicrous instances of holy narrowness in those insular de Valera years. The Tailor's friend, Frank O'Connor,* remarked of the four-day debate in the Irish Senate about the banning, "Reading it is like a long, slow swim through a sewage bed."

In 1978, after a long silence, Cross collected his fugitive pieces under the title *Silence Is Golden*. The book is an uneven but engaging collection of the whimsical, the fey, and the supernatural. Its best pieces are the rural japes and exaggerations, such as "The Powder of Levity," which recall the brilliance of his early masterpiece.

WORKS: *The Tailor and Ansty*. London: Chapman & Hall, 1942/Cork: Mercier, 1970; *Silence Is Golden and Other Stories*. Dublin: Poolbeg, 1978.

CUALA PRESS (formerly the Dun Emer Press) (1902-), publishing house. The Dun Emer Industries were established at Dundrum County Dublin in 1902 by Evelyn Gleeson "to find work for Irish hands in the making of beautiful things." All the workers were Irish girls, and the industries originally comprised embroidery on Irish linen, the weaving of tapestry and carpets, and the printing of books by hand. A bookbinding workshop was added later.

Elizabeth Corbet Yeats and her sister Lily returned to Ireland from London to assist Gleeson in establishing the Industries. Lily Yeats organized the embroidery workshop, and Elizabeth founded the Dun Emer Press as part of the scheme. Their brother W. B. Yeats* acted as editorial adviser to the Press, and Emery Walker, who had worked as adviser to the Kelmscott Press, the Doves Press, and several other notable private presses in England, advised on typography and book production.

The typeface chosen for the Press was Caslon, and all text composition was done in the fourteen point size of that face. The printing was done on an Albion hand press which was built in 1853, and a special paper was made in County Dublin for all the regular books printed at the Press. The format of the books was a small quarto, with a page size of 8¼ x 5¾ inches. The books, with the exception of the first, were issued in colored boards with an Irish linen spine.

Printing of the first book was completed on July 16, 1903. This was *In the Seven Woods,* a collection of new poetry by W. B. Yeats, together with his play *On Baile's Strand.* The edition consisted of 325 copies, priced at 10s 6d. This was the first of many books by living Irish writers to appear from the Press over the next forty three-years, almost thirty of them by Yeats.

Although few of the books were illustrated, most of them had one or more decorative devices, usually on the title page. The first such symbol appeared in the second book, *The Nuts of Knowledge* by AE.* A pressmark, engraved on wood by Elinor Monsell and depicting the Lady Emer, was first used in 1926. Other devices were designed by AE, Robert Gregory, T. Sturge Moore, Edmund Dulac, and E. C. Yeats.

The first series of *A Broadside* was issued from 1908 to 1915. Each number contained ballad poetry, new and traditional, with three drawings by Jack B. Yeats.* Many of the drawings were colored by hand, and the series ran to eighty-four numbers. Two later series were published, in 1935 and 1937, each of twelve parts, and these had illustrations by several other artists as well as the music of the airs for the songs.

In addition to the books and *A Broadside,* the Press also published many hand-colored prints and greeting cards, and undertook commissions to print private editions of some thirty books and booklets. Bookplates were also designed and printed at the Press, including those for John Quinn, Lennox Robinson,* and members of the Yeats family. In 1908, after eleven books had been published and the first series of *A Broadside* commenced, the Yeats sisters left the Dun Emer Industries and, as Cuala Industries, continued the embroidery and hand printing. The first book from the Cuala Press, *Poetry and Ireland* by W. B. Yeats and Lionel Johnston, was finished in October 1908. Sixty-six Cuala Press books were published before publication of books was suspended in 1946. During this period, the Press was first at Churchtown in County Dublin and later at Merrion Square, at Baggot Street, and at Palmerstown Road in Dublin.

In addition to books by W. B. Yeats, his father, and his brother, the Press published books by, among others, AE, Douglas Hyde,* Lady Gregory,* J. M. Synge,* Lord Dunsany,* Rabindranath Tagore, John Masefield, Ezra Pound, Oliver St. John Gogarty,* Frank O'Connor,* F. R. Higgins,* Louis MacNeice,* Donagh MacDonagh,* Elizabeth Bowen,* and Patrick Kavanagh.*

Elizabeth Corbet Yeats died in 1940, and a memorial tribute by her sister Lily was printed at the Press. The work was continued under the management of Mrs. W. B. Yeats. Fifteen additional books were published between 1940 and 1946, when publication was suspended with the seventy-seventh book, *Stranger in Aran,* written and illustrated by Elizabeth Rivers. The Press continued to produce hand-colored prints and greeting cards until the death of Mrs. Yeats in August 1968.

The Cuala Press was reorganized in 1969 to continue the tradition established in 1903 by its founder, Elizabeth Corbet Yeats. Since then, the Press has printed seven other books in the regular series, as well as some booklets. Prints from designs by Jack B. Yeats and illuminated poems by W. B. Yeats are also being printed. The aim of the Press is to include the best new work being written in Ireland, and to print it with the same craftsmanship and care that has distinguished its work since 1903.

LIAM MILLER

REFERENCE: Miller, Liam. *The Dun Emer Press, Later the Cuala Press.* Dublin: Cuala, 1973; also issued in 1973 by Dolmen as No. VII of the *New Yeats Papers.*

CUMMINS, G[ERALDINE] D[OROTHY] (1890-?), woman of letters. Cummins was born in Cork in 1890. She was active in the woman's suffrage movement with her friend Suzanne R. Day, with whom she wrote two comic plays produced by the Abbey Theatre*—*Broken Faith* (1913) and *Fox and Geese* (1917). *Fox and Geese* is a genial matchmaking comedy set among the Cork peasantry. If not brilliant, it was written in short, supple lines and was eminently playable. Cummins has also written two novels, *The Land They Loved* (1919) and *Fires of Beltane* (1936), as well as a volume of short stories entitled *Variety Show* (1959). Her stories are a mixed bag in subject, tone, and quality: some are tragic vignettes of the peasantry, some are comic glimpses of the middle class, and one is a sophisticated account of a dissolving marriage in the upper middle class, Cummins is at her best in "The Tragedy of Eight Pence," with its two misers who are almost Jonsonian humors. Among her other writings are a biography of Edith Somerville* and quite a number of volumes of psychical research. Many of the psychical volumes have been dictated to her by an unseen intelligence while she is in a light trance.

WORKS: *Fox and Geese,* with Suzanne R. Day. Dublin & London: Maunsel, 1917; *The Land They Loved.* London: Macmillan, 1919; *Fires of Beltane.* London: Michael Joseph, [1936]; *Dr. E. OE. Somerville.* London: Dakers, [1952]; *Variety Show.* London: Barrie & Rockliff, 1959.

CURTIS, EDMUND (1881-1943), historian. Curtis was born of a Donegal father and a Belfast mother on March 25, 1881, at Bury, Lancashire. By good luck and his own considerable ability, he succeeded in entering Oxford in 1900, and he graduated with a First in modern history four years later. By 1914, he was appointed professor of modern history at Trinity College, Dublin. He is known for his *History of Medieval Ireland* (1923) and his *History of Ireland* (1936). T. W. Moody has written of his "bold and original scholarship" and has remarked that "he had the merits of a pioneer." His obituary in *The Irish Times* remarks that he brought Irish history to the fore at Trinity College at a time when little provision was made for it. His writing is ever in a terse, fluent style that has as its best a dramatic immediacy about it. He died in Dublin on March 25, 1943.

At one time he was married to Margaret Barrington.*

WORKS: *A History of Mediaeval Ireland.* Dublin: Maunsel & Roberts, 1923; *A History of Ireland.* London: Methuen, 1936/revised 1937, 1943.

D'ALTON, JOHN (1792-1867), poet, historian, and antiquarian. D'Alton was born at Bessville, County Westmeath, on June 20, 1792. He was educated at Trinity College, Dublin, and was called to the bar in 1813. In 1814, he published a now-forgotten romance in twelve cantos called *Dermid, or Erin in the Days of Boroimhe.* He made a good many translations from the Irish for Hardiman's *Irish Minstrelsy* (1831), and, although his translations are seldom reprinted, his "Why, Liquor of Life!" after Carolan and his own "Carroll O'Daly and Echo" are both deft and droll. Indeed, even his conventionally patriotic "Oh! Erin!" has a couple of admirable lines. He died in Dublin on January 20, 1867.

WORKS: *Dermid; or, Erin in the Days of Boroimhe.* London: Longman/Dublin; J. Cumming, 1814; *Essay on the History, Religion, Learning, Arts and Government of Ireland.* Dublin: R. Graisberry, 1830. Vol. 16 of *Transactions of the Royal Irish Academy; The History of Ireland.* 2 vols. Dublin: Published by the author, 1845; (Also some translations in Hardiman's *Irish Minstrelsy.* 2 vols. London: Joseph Robins, 1831).

D'ALTON, LOUIS [LYNCH] (1900-1951), playwright and novelist. D'Alton, son of actor-producer Charles D'Alton, was born in Dublin in 1900. After working as a civil servant and a cartoonist, he joined Victor O'Donovan Power's* traveling drama company, acted briefly at the Queen's, Dublin, and formed his own touring group. Two novels, *Death Is So Fair* (1936) and *Rags and Sticks* (1938), preceded most of his dramatic work. *The Man in the Cloak,* staged in 1937, marked the beginning of his association with the Abbey* as playwright, actor, and producer. He died in London on June 15, 1951.

The Man in the Cloak, based on the life of poet James Clarence Mangan* (1803-1848), effectively combines an impressionistic study of Mangan's chaotic personality and an almost documentary treatment of Dublin slums during a cholera epidemic. Published with the Mangan play is *The Mousetrap,* a pallid offspring of O'Casey's* *Juno* in theme—unwedded pregnancy —and dialogue. *To-morrow Never Comes* (1939) charts the psychological breakdown of a weak-minded, frightened murderer. *The Spanish Soldier* (1940) deals with the troubled return to civilian life of an Irish volunteer in Franco's army.

The Money Doesn't Matter (1941) is the first of a series of thematically related plays. Rags to riches businessman Michael Mannion spends freely to buy or coerce the affection of his children. In every case, through their failure or his, Mannion is disappointed. At the close, a creature of habit, he continues to claw for the money that doesn't matter.

Lovers Meeting (1941) might be called a matchmaking tragedy. Mrs. Jane Sheridan, overcoming the scruples of her husband Tom, matches their daughter Mary to a grizzled boor. Mary's lover, Joe Hession, thinking Mrs. Sheridan has written him off as a poor provider, kills his uncle so that he can inherit land and money. But the money doesn't matter. The buried truth emerges: Joe is Mrs. Sheridan's illegitimate son. The ending resembles Greek tragedy, with the elder Sheridans separated, Joe hanged, and Mary a suicide.

Garrulous, improvident Bartley Murnaghan, in *They Got What They Wanted* (1947), represents another aspect of the money doesn't matter theme. He has none, but by manipulating the nebulous possibility of an inheritance and the greed and gullibility of his neighbors, he becomes a small town financier. It is not the best of D'Alton's plays, but it was made into a movie, *Smiling Irish Eyes,* by an English producer.

Money enters peripherally into *The Devil a Saint Would Be* (1951). Seventy-year-old Stacy, advised by a saint visible only to herself, gives her money to a doubtfully deserving lot of poor folk as a means of attaining sanctity. Everybody but the parish priest consider her "certifiable": he rightly fears that the saint is an evil spirit. The real saint, whom the evil spirit counterfeited, defines saintliness: "There is no virtue without humility, and the temptation of the saints is to think of themselves as saints." Part of the delightful third act is a colloquium at the gate of Heaven between Stacy, a sorely tried Peter, and the saint embarrassed by Stacy's loquacity.

This Other Eden (1953) is the land across the Irish Sea, depending on the direction in which one is facing. An Irish girl escapes from religiosity and parochialism to find freedom—in Birmingham; an Englishman fed up with the welfare state and, ironically, with an influx of "foreigners" buys an estate in Ireland. A woefully confused commemorative service for a clay-footed IRA hero provides the framework for what is basically a discussion drama, in the manner of Bernard Shaw,* of life in Ireland.

Cafflin' Johnny (1958) slightly resembles the comic reprobate sketches of George Shiels.* Johnny Fortune's Excelsior banner is inscribed Do Nothing, and to the end he holds it aloft with eloquence and wistful pride.

D'Alton's novels are overshadowed by his reputation as playwright. *Death Is So Fair* examines differing responses to the Easter Week Rising. Its terrible beauty inspires Manus Considine to become an idealistic revolutionary. Andrew Gilfoyle, seeing it as a fiasco of poets playing soldier, becomes an efficient killer. *Rags and Sticks* relates the decline and fall of the Superlative Dramatic Company, a tattered, anachronistic survival of vagabond tradition. Both novels are masterful in characterization and description, but D'Alton sometimes indulges in speechmaking and intrusive commentary.

As playwright, D'Alton in his mature work updates traditional themes such as made marriages and money-grubbing, bestowing on them a cerebral quality which makes most of the earlier specimens seem gauche by comparison. His finest play, *This Other Eden,* skillfully blends crackling dialogue with a thoughtfully posed question, "how's dear old Ireland and how does she stand three decades after the Treaty?"

                                                        WILLIAM J. FEENEY

WORKS: *Death Is So Fair.* London: Heinemann, 1936; *Rags and Sticks.* London: Heinemann, 1938; *Two Irish Plays (The Man in the Cloak* and *The Mousetrap).* London: Macmillan, 1938; *To-morrow Never Comes: A Play in Three Acts.* Dublin: Duffy, 1945/new edition, Dublin: Bourke, 1968; *The Devil a Saint Would Be: A Morality in Three Acts.* Dublin: Bourke, 1952; *They Got What They Wanted: A Comedy in Three Acts.* Dundalk: Dundalgan, 1953; *This Other Eden: A Play in Three Acts.* Dublin: Bourke, 1954; *The Money Doesn't Matter: A Play in Three Acts.* Dublin: Duffy, 1957; *Lovers Meeting: A Tragedy in Three Acts.* Dublin: Bourke, 1964.   REFERENCES: Hogan, Robert. *After the Irish Renaissance.* Minneapolis: University of Minnesota, 1967; Hogan, Thomas. "Theatre." *Envoy* 2 (May 1950): 80-84. (Review of *They Got What They Wanted*); *The Irish Sunday Independent,* June 17, 1951, 1:3-5. (Obituary).

DALY, PADRAIG J. (1943-), poet. Daly was born in Dungarvan, County Waterford, in 1943. He is an Augustinian priest and thus far has published one volume, *Nowhere But in Praise* (1978). Despite an occasional striking phrase or arresting figure, this collection is basically written in clear, careful, flat prose, which is broken up into arbitrary line lengths. That device does not make these short reflections poems, but does not greatly detract from some frequently solid writing. Among the better pieces is a reflection on Canon Sheehan, called "Summers in Doneraile."

WORK: *Nowhere But in Praise.* [Clondalkin, County Dublin]: Profile, [1978].

DANA. *See* EGLINTON, JOHN.

DARLEY, GEORGE (1795-1846), poet, mathematician, and art and drama critic. Darley was born in Dublin in 1795. His works on mathematics were much respected, but his poetry—although admired by Coleridge, Lamb, Carlyle, and Tennyson—was never popular. In 1950, A. J. Leventhal tried to revive interest in Darley, noting that he was ahead of his time and that some of his poetry seems particularly modern. The truth seems to be that Darley was out of his time; for instance, his most famous lyric, "It is not beautie I demande," was printed as a genuine anonymous Caroline lyric in the 1861 edition of Palgrave's *Golden Treasury*. Also, despite being a drama (and an art) critic for prominent London journals, Darley's dramas were so entirely for the closet that there was never any thought of them being staged. In his public work, there is nothing of Irish inspiration, although his letters reveal some nostalgia for and preoccupation with Ireland. His younger brother Charles (1800-1861) was a clergyman and professor of modern history and English literature at Queen's College, Cork; Charles' play, *Plighted Troth,* was produced with great lack of success by Macready at Drury Lane in 1842. At about the same time, Darley himself was publishing his own virtually ignored closet dramas on English history. This dual failure may have been galling to the Darley brothers particularly because their scapegrace young nephew, Dion Boucicault,* had made the hit of the season in 1841 with his comedy *London Assurance,* which was produced at Covent Garden. The brothers never, in any document so far discovered, mentioned their precocious and vulgar nephew, but Boucicault said in later life that they both regarded him as a schoolboy who ought to be whipped back to his lessons. Darley may have been out of his time partly because of an appalling stutter which was a considerable social embarrassment. In any event, his reclusive life and elegant but disengaged verses largely succeeded in minimizing his quite real wit and warmth.

WORKS: *The Errors of Ecstasie.* London: G & W. B. Whittaker, 1822; *The Labours of Idleness,* under the pseudonym of Guy Penseval. London: J. Taylor, 1826; *Sylvia; or, The May Queen.* London: J. Taylor, 1827; *The New Sketch Book,* under the pseudonym of Geoffrey Crayon, Jr. 2 vols. London: Printed for the Author, 1829; *Nepenthe.* London: ?, 1835/London: E. Matthews, 1897; *Thomas A Beckett.* London: E. Moxon, 1840; *Ethelstan; or, The Battle of Brunanburh.* London: E. Moxon, 1841; *Poems.* Liverpool: Printed for private circulation, 1890; *Selections from the Poems of G. Darley,* with an Introduction and Notes by R. A. Streatfeild. London: Methuen, 1904; *The Complete Poetical Works of George Darley.* Ramsay Colles. ed. London: G. Routledge/New York: E. P. Dutton, 1908.   REFERENCES: Abbot, Claude C. *The Life and Letters of G. Darley, Poet and Critic.* Oxford: University Press/London: Humphrey Milford, 1928; Leventhal, A. J. *George Darley (1795-1846).* [Dublin]: Dublin University Press, 1950.

DAVIS, THOMAS (1814-1845), poet, patriot, and journalist. Davis was born in Mallow on October 14, 1814, the posthumous child of a surgeon in the Royal Artillery, John Thomas Davis. His mother was Mary Atkins, a lady who included the O'Sullivan Beare family among her ancestors. The family removed to Dublin when Thomas was four years old, and he was educated there (showing no particular promise) at the school of a Mr. Mongan and at Trinity College. At Trinity he came under the influence of a group of young Protestant intellectuals who were developing a national consciousness in the wake of the eclipse of the Irish Ascendancy ruling class by the transfer of the center of power to London under the Act of Union 1800. Davis graduated in 1836, kept his law terms in London, and was called to the bar in 1837. Reared as a high Tory Episcopalian, he was at this time a utilitarian. In 1840, he was auditor of the College Historical Society, and his inaugural address included the famous phrase "Gentleman, you have a country."

The dominant figure in the Irish politics of this epoch was, of course, Daniel O'Connell, and in 1841 Davis joined O'Connell's Repeal Association (agitating for repeal of the Act of Union) and was put on the general committee and several subcommittees. In 1842, with Charles Gavan Duffy* and John Blake Dillon, he founded *The Nation** newspaper, a weekly of advanced national views and considerable journalistic merit. *The Nation* reached a circulation of eleven thousand, although newspaper prices were still remarkably high and the paper sold at sixpence.

In 1843, Davis became disenchanted with O'Connell, following O'Connell's cancellation of the proclaimed mass meeting at Clontarf, and adopted a federalist position, which O'Connell regarded as less than the Repeal movement demanded. A final rift with O'Connell came when Davis and his immediate colleagues, known as the Young Ireland group, favored acceptance of a government proposal for the establishment of nondenominational third-level education, while O'Connell and the conservatively minded clergy claimed to regard it as state-sponsored godlessness. The confrontation, at which O'Connell proclaimed his allegiance to Old Ireland, took place at a meeting at which Davis took the chair and was reduced to tears.

Davis died on September 16, 1845 of scarletina, after a brief illness. In his last years, he had a charming relationship with Annie Hutton, to whom he was engaged at the time of his death.

Davis' principal achievements were his enthusiasm in the national cause, which won over many of his associates, and his articulation of a nationalist apparatus of thought in his essays in *The Nation*. He had broad cultural as well as political interests and wrote on Irish music and the Irish language, for example, with intense feeling. His style was that of polished journalism, with rhetorical flourishes typical of his age. His verse is false and bombastic to the modern ear and reveals a racialist preoccupation kept in restraint in the more controlled prose.

Through Fenianism, Sinn Fein, the Rising of 1916, and up to modern times, Davis has been a main inspiration of the nationalist movement. He was canonized, so to speak, when Pearse* included him in his list of the four evangelists of separatism in the pamphlets Pearse published in the last months of preparation for the Easter Rising.

Davis' manner and personality exercised a great influence on his contemporaries, and by their accounts he was a person of immense personal charm. The principal source is Sir Charles Gavan Duffy's *Thomas Davis, the Memoirs of an Irish Patriot* (London, 1890), in which Duffy, an intimate friend and colleague, quotes a large number of letters and other writings by Davis. There is a considerable volume of later scholarship on the politics of the period, though it is to be noted that many later anthologists have failed to give integral texts of what purport to be reprints of Davis' works.

ALF MACLOCHLAINN

WORKS: *The Poems of Thomas Davis.* Dublin: Duffy, 1846; *Literary and Historical Essays.* Dublin: Duffy, 1846; *Letters of a Protestant, on Repeal.* Thomas Meagher, ed. Dublin: Irish Confederation, 1847; *Prose Writings of Thomas Davis.* T. W. Rolleston, ed. London: W. Scott, [1890]; *Essays Literary and Historical,* with notes by D. J. O'Donoghue and an essay by John Mitchel. Dundalk: W. Tempest, 1914; *Thomas Davis, the Thinker and Teacher.* Arthur Griffith, ed. Dublin: Gill, 1914; *Essays and Poems.* Dublin: Gill, 1945.   REFERENCES: Ahern, J. L. *Thomas Davis and His Circle.* Waterford: Carthage, 1945; Duffy, Charles Gavan. *Thomas Davis: The Memoirs of an Irish Patriot, 1840-6.* London: Kegan Paul, Trench & Co., 1892; Hone, J. M. *Thomas Davis.* London: G. Duckworth/Dublin: Talbot, 1934; MacLochlainn, A. "The Racism of Thomas Davis." *Journal of Irish Literature* 5 (May 1976): 112-122; MacManus, M. J., ed. *Thomas Davis and Young Ireland.* Dublin: Stationery Office, 1945; Moody, T. W. *Thomas Davis, 1814-45.* Dublin: University of Dublin Historical Society, 1945; Quigley, Michael, ed. *Pictorial Record: Centenary of Thomas Davis and Young Ireland.* Dublin: Public Sales Office, 1945; Yeats, W. B. *Tribute to Thomas Davis.* Cork: Cork University Press, 1947; Yeats, W. B., & Kinsella, Thomas. *Davis, Mangan, Ferguson?* Dublin: Dolmen, 1971.

DAWE, GERALD (1952-), poet. Dawe was born in Belfast in 1952, and was educated at the New University of Ulster, Coleraine, and at University College, Galway, where he is now a tutor in the Department of English. His poems, collected in the slim volume *Sheltering Places,* are usually written in short, unrhymed, and irregularly stressed lines of about three to six syllables. The shortness of the lines consistently calls attention to the importance of the words; and, although Dawe's words are precisely chosen, generally they are not happily or eloquently enough chosen to bear such emphasis.

WORK: *Sheltering Places.* [Belfast]: Blackstaff, [1978].

DAY-LEWIS, C[ECIL] (1904-1972), poet. Although born in Ballintubber on April 27, 1904, and although related on his mother's side to Goldsmith,* Day-Lewis spent only his early childhood in Ireland and is basically an English poet. Nevertheless, he never forgot his Irish connection, and, when he wrote about Ireland, he wrote knowledgeably and well. The best of such poems are "The House Where I Was Born," "Fishguard to Rosslare," "My

Mother's Sisters," and "Remembering Con Markievicz." *The Private Wound,* one of the better detective novels which he wrote under the pseudonym of Nicholas Blake, is laid in the west of Ireland. His name is frequently connected with W. H. Auden and Stephen Spender as a prominent example of the English social poets of the 1930s. In 1968, he succeeded John Masefield as Poet Laureate of England. He died on May 22, 1972, in London at the home of his friend Kingsley Amis.

WORKS: *Collected Poems, 1954.* London: Jonathan Cape & Hogarth, 1954; *Selected Poems.* New York: Harper & Row, 1967; as Nicholas Blake, *The Private Wound.* London: Collins, 1958.   REFERENCES: Handley-Taylor, Geoffrey, & d'Arch Smith, Timothy. C. Day-Lewis, *The Poet Laureate, A Bibliography.* Chicago & London: St. James, 1968; Riddel, Joseph N. *C. Day Lewis.* New York: Twayne, 1971. Neither of the above volumes contains an adequate bibliography of the Nicholas Blake volumes.

DEANE, JOHN F. (1943-), poet and publisher. Deane was born on Achill, County Mayo, in 1943 and now teaches in Dublin. His first collections of poems, *Stalking After Time* (1977), was extremely uneven. Some of it is simply flat prose cut into arbitrary line lengths, some good prose cut into arbitrary line lengths, and once, in "The Blackbird," heavily but effectively rhythmical. His writing can be sharp and the images vivid, but it also can be flaccid and even banal. The volume and its short successor *Island* are quite a mishmash of the botched and the promising. In 1978, Deane and his wife began publishing poetry in attractive, short paperback pamphlets, under the name of St. Bueno's Hand-printed Limited Editions. Among the first authors were Brendan Kennelly,* Robert Greacen,* and Padraig J. Daly.*

WORKS: *Stalking After Time.* Clondalkin, County Dublin: Profile, 1977; *Island.* [Dublin]: St. Bueno's Hand-printed Limited Editions, [1978].

DEANE, SEAMUS [FRANCIS] (1940-), poet. Deane was born in Derry City, Northern Ireland, on February 9, 1940. He received a B.A. and M.A. from Queen's University, Belfast, and a Ph.D. from Cambridge. He is a lecturer at University College, Dublin, and has taught at Oregon and Berkeley in America. He was one of the editors of the excellent, although short-lived, literary magazine *Atlantis,* and he frequently publishes academic literary criticism.

Deane's first volume of poetry, *Gradual Wars* (1972) is somewhat more satisfying than the work of most other Irish poets of his age, for he has the English teacher's sense of syntax which gives strength to those parts of his pieces that are literal statement. The chief promise of Deane's work is that it implies form, but the chief fault is that it does not possess form—it only implies it. A favorite device, for instance, is to rhyme the last word of the last line of a stanza with the last word of some previous line, any previous line; with such a simple flourish he presents a pseudo-pattern. When he attempts, as in "The Lake," to establish a consistent pattern of meter and rhyme, he cannot hold it, and by the end of the piece, the pattern has simply broken down and been bowled over by the content. Worse than his rhyming are the intermittent attempts at meter, which are never sustained through a whole work and rarely through a whole stanza. Frequently, however, he does pull off the arresting image. Even if there are many other images that are arresting chiefly because they are outré, his pieces may be generally said to be interesting as language, if not yet as poems.

Deane's second volume, *Rumours* (1977), seems to reflect a little less embarrassment about emotion but is otherwise no advance. His work is basically a language of statement, often abstract and sometimes pedantic. The images and metaphors appear sparely and unspectacularly. A flirtation with form is again apparent: a sense of rhythm is weak to nonexistent, but there are frequent abortive attempts at rhyme schemes. These are not really poems but reflections arbitrarily arranged upon the page, with some finicky attention paid to diction. Nonetheless, they do contain some excellent random phrases.

WORKS: *Gradual Wars*. Shannon: Irish University Press, 1972; *Rumours*. Dublin: Dolmen, 1977.

DE BURCA, SEAMUS (1912-), playwright. De Burca was born James Bourke in Dublin on March 16, 1912. His father was P. J. Bourke, the actor, costumier, and author of several neo-Boucicaultian patriotic melodramas; his uncle was Peadar Kearney,* the author of the Irish national anthem "The Soldier's Song"; and his cousin was Brendan Behan.* De Burca's early theatre experience was at the Queen's which his father managed in the 1920s, and the best of his own plays, such as *Limpid River* (1962), reflect the influence of the popular theatre of the past. De Burca is steeped in Dublin's past. That knowledge is shown in his droll and savage *The Howards,* which was given a semi-professional production at the Gate* in 1959, and also in his broadly comic and rambling imitation of Brendan Behan, *The End of Mrs. Oblong* (1968). This preoccupation with the past also seems apparent in two excellent theatrical adaptations—*Knocknagow* (1945) after Charles Kickham*, which has been produced on several occasions by the Dublin comedian Jack Cruise, and *Handy Andy* after Samuel Lover* which remains unproduced. De Burca has also written a biography of Peadar Kearney and a short memoir of Brendan Behan. On paper, much of de Burca's work seems slovenly, long-winded, and even amateurish, but on stage, in a sympathetic production, it can be splendidly theatrical.

WORKS: *Knocknagow, or The Homes of Tipperary*. Dublin: P. J. Bourke, 1945. (Play after Kickham); *Find the Island*. Dublin: P. J. Bourke, [1950?]. (Play); *Family Album*. Dublin: P. J. Bourke, 1952; *The Soldier's Song: The Story of Peadar O Cearnigh*. Dublin: P. J. Bourke, 1957. (Biography); *The Howards*. Dublin: P. J. Bourke, [1960]. (Play); *The Boys and Girls Are Gone*. Dublin: P. J. Bourke, 1961.

(Play); *Thomas Davis*. Dublin: P. J. Bourke, 1962. (Play); *Limpid River*. Dublin: P. J. Bourke, 1962. (Novel); *Limpid River* in *First Stage* (Spring 1966): 30-55. (Play); *The End of Mrs. Oblong*. Dixon, Calif.: Proscenium, 1968. (Play); *Brendan Behan, a Memoir*. Newark, Del.: Proscenium, 1971.

DEEVY, TERESA (?-1963), playwright. Deevy was born in Waterford around the turn of the century, possibly in 1903, and died there on January 19, 1963. Early in life she became deaf, but she overcame her affliction by learning to lip read. Later she wrote plays which showed an extraordinary sensitivity to the nuances of speech.

Her first Abbey* play, *The Reapers* (March 18, 1930), was followed by the one-act comedy *A Disciple* (August 24, 1931). In 1931, she and Paul Vincent Carroll* were the joint winners of an Abbey play competition; her prizewinning play, *Temporal Powers,* was produced on August 24. Her best known one-act play, *The King of Spain's Daughter,* was done on April 29, 1935, and was followed by her memorable *Katie Roche* on March 16, 1936. The Abbey produced her *The Wild Goose* on November 9, 1936, and her one-act *Light Falling* was presented in the Experimental Theatre on October 25, 1948. Her unpublished *Wife to James Whelan,* which has been considered better than *Katie Roche,* was done at Madame Bannard Cogley's Studio Theatre Club on October 4, 1956. Many of her later plays, including *Going Beyond Alma's Glory* (1951), were written for radio.

Despite her broad range, Deevy is remembered most for her brilliant portraits of high-strung, romantic young women caught in rural Ireland. Through remarkable poetic dialogue, she catches them almost in flight at a moment in life when they put aside their youthful illusions and accept a greyer but more plausible adult reality. Her best character in this mold is Annie Kinsella, the heroine of *The King of Spain's Daughter,* a mad, wild young girl who lives completely in her dreams. She is roughly brought down to earth by her brute of a father who forces her to marry Jim Harris, "a sensible boy." She has to agree, but she is determined to make her world what she wants it to be. Her man will be heroic and that is that. Browsing through his notebook, she discovers that he has methodically entered an account of his weekly savings, and suddenly she exults. "He put by two shillings every week for two hundred weeks. I think he is a man that— supposin' he was jealous—might cut your throat."

Katie, the heroine of the play *Katie Roche,* is a more developed version of Annie Kinsella. Katie marries a dull older man, Stanislaus Gregg, but after the marriage she continues to flirt with a local young man. Her husband, exhausted by what he has taken on, disappears to Dublin. When Katie discovers she is the illegitimate daughter of the local Big House, it seems to her a most fitting origin. Reuben, a wandering mystic and her father in disguise, realizes that Katie's wild temperament needs a strong man. He talks to Stanislaus who finally brings Katie firmly off to Dublin where she will be out of temptation. Katie, like Annie, decides there is glamor in facing the future bravely, but her character is more complex than Annie's. Katie's motives in marrying Stanislaus and then in flirting as she does are never clearly understood. For this reason, and because of a looseness in plot, the play is not as successful as *The King of Spain's Daughter*. Here Deevy has tried to do more than the simple art of the drama will allow, but if she has failed she has done so brilliantly.

In Search of Valour and *The King of Spain's Daughter* were performed with considerable success by the BBC in the pioneering days of prewar television. The heroine of *In Search of Valour,* Ellie Irwin, precedes Annie and Katie, but she shares their characteristics. She works as a maid and wants a man like Coriolanus who "done things proper." She is fascinated by the local bandit, Jack the Scalp, and sees a comparison between him and Mr. Glitterton, the local squire who has just divorced his wife. Both are like the heroes of old, unafraid to take action. When Ellie actually meets Mr. Glitterton, she cannot believe that the little old man hobbling about on a stick is her hero. "—An' I thinkin' of him! Dreamin' of him!—"

The play ends on a comic but dismal note. Ellie is trapped in a house with her hero Jack the Scalp. She offers herself to him defiantly, but he refuses her, afraid of losing his soul. When he runs from her arms to the police, she shouts after him, "I hopes they'll get you! I hopes you'll be hanged!" Then she laments to herself, "Them were best off that were born long ago. Wirra—why weren't I born in a brave time?!"

Another romantic character is Martin Shea, the held of *The Wild Goose,* a play set in rural Ireland at the end of the seventeenth century. Usually a dramatic hero has the dilemma of two simple alternatives, but here Teresa Deevy poses a more complex problem. Martin vacillates between the church, the army, and marriage, and while this psychological portrait is recognizable, it is doubtful whether it is successful for the stage. Moreover, Martin is always seen through the eyes of the other characters in the play, and so he never gets an opportunity to explain himself as Katie Roche or Annie Kinsella do. Hence, he is an intangible character, indecisive and never progressing to maturity; correspondingly, the plot seems to wander and appears weak and ill made.

Two small pieces that are generally considered outside Deevy's range are *Strange Birth* and *Going Beyond Alma's Glory. Strange Birth* is a tightly woven one-act play set in a guest house. Sara Meade is a servant girl of about thirty who serves as a link to all the other characters in the play. She is unmarried and the only person in the house who does not feel the stab of love; all the others do and suffer accordingly. Sara has to prop them all up by being constantly cheerful. The postman enters and declares his love and desire to marry Sara. At first she refuses, but realizing what she is missing by not loving anyone she accepts. *Going Beyond Alma Glory,*

Deevy's last play, is a radio piece, but with its simple set it could easily be staged. It concerns the attempt of two middle-aged people to retrieve a lost past. There are two excellent characterizations, Martin Spillane and his wife, Mona Pewitt. Here we get an opportunity to see, not the usual young Deevy romantics, but older and faded members of the same family, for whom romance has failed.

In world terms Deevy's talent might have been small, but in any terms it was definite. Her dialogue is often close to brilliant, and one cannot but regret that she was restricted by the Catholic Ireland of the 1930s and 1940s. If she had found a more accommodating stage than the Abbey Theatre of those years, her talent might have flowered. Her last production in the Abbey was *Light Falling* in October 1948. For ten years previous to that she had no productions, which leaves a gap of twenty-five unfruitful years. For a dramatist of her stature, the first essential is a stage; plays for religious orders or scripts for radio, both of which occupied much of her time, are poor substitutes. Since she was neglected in her lifetime, it is not surprising that today no edition of her best play, *Wife to James Whelan,* is available.

MARY ROSE CALLAGHAN

WORKS: "The Enthusiast," *One Act Play Magazine* 1 (1938); *Three Plays.* London: Macmillan, 1939. (Contains *Katie Roche, The King of Spain's Daughter,* and *The Wild Goose*); *The King of Spain's Daughter and Other One-Act Plays.* Dublin: New Frontiers, 1947. (Also contains *In Search of Valour* and *Strange Birth*); "Going Beyond Alma's Glory." *Irish Writing* 17 (December 1951):21-32.   REFERENCES: Hogan, Robert. *After the Irish Renaissance.* Minneapolis: University of Minnesota Press, 1967; Riley, J. D. "On Teresa Deevy's Plays." *Irish Writing* 32 (Autumn 1955).

DERMODY, THOMAS (1775-1802), poet. Dermody was an astonishing child prodigy whose precocious abilities as a classical scholar and poet were rivaled only by his equally precocious proclivities as a toper. He was born on January 15, 1775, in Ennis, County Clare, the son of a schoolmaster. At the age of four, his father set him to learning Latin and Greek, and by the age of nine he was teaching these subjects in his father's school. When a younger brother died of smallpox in 1785, Thomas produced a commemorative poem entitled "Corydon," which reads in part:

> "Yet cease to weep, ye swains; for if no cloud
>   Of thwarting influence mar my keener sight,
>   I mark'd a stranger-star serenely bright,
> Burst from the dim inclosure of a shrowd.
> 'Twas Corydon! a radiant circlet bound
> His brow of meekness; and the silver sound
> Shook from his lyre, of gratulations loud,
>   Smooth'd the unruffled raven-plum of Night."—
> Thus chanted the rude youth his past'ral strain,

> While the cold earth his playmate's bosom press'd.
> And now the sun, slow westing to the main,
> Panted to give his wearied coursers rest;
> The azure curtains took a crimson stain,
> And Thetis shone, in golden garments drest.
> The shepherd-minstrel bent his homeward way,
> And brush'd the dew-drops from the glitt'ring spray.

Although filled with echoes of Milton and of his classical reading, young Dermody's poem was an extraordinary production for a boy of ten. The influence of his father may undoubtedly be seen in Dermody's early training as may a more baneful paternal influence, his father's habitual drunkenness. By the age of ten, young Dermody was already an experienced drinker and, chafing at the constraints of home life, ran away to Dublin where he arrived penniless. He was shortly discovered reading Anacreon at bookstore stalls and received the protection of various charitable and learned people who were dazzled by his broadness of reading, his ability to translate almost instantly the classics into English poetry, and the facility of his own poetic invention. Dermody was always lucky in his patrons, and some of the early ones were Robert Owenson, Lady Morgan's* father, the dowager countess of Moira, Lord Chief Justice Kilwarden, and Henry Grattan.* Inevitably, however, he disillusioned and rebuffed them all, and refused every opportunity to advance himself, including the opportunity of attending Trinity College. In personality, he seemed to shift from the proud and autocratic to the humble and engaging, but he was always devious, untrustworthy and willing to waste all of his income on conviviality and drink. At one time he is said to have characterized himself by the remark, "I am vicious because I like it."

In his early teens, Lady Moira brought him to the village of Killeigh to continue his studies under the local clergyman, but he found the life of the village tavern morn congenial and celebrated it in a number of rollicking songs reminiscent of Burns. Particularly fluent is "Lory's of the Lane" which begins:

> There never was sa rare a fight
> Described since Kirst-kirk squabble,
> As that which hap'd on Tuesday night
> At Lory's near the stable:
> For all the lads were drunken quite,
> To stand or sit unable;
> Some lay in hole till morning light,
> Some underneath the table,
>   Fu black that night.

"My Own Epitaph" with its deft heroic couplets is also quite remarkable; as is "An Ode to Myself," which begins:

> Thrice hail, thou prince of jovial fellows,
> Turning so blithe thy lyric bellows,
> Of no one's brighter genius jealous;
>   Whose little span
> Is spent 'twixt poetry and alehouse,
>   'Twixt quill and can!

Back in Dublin, Dermody went from bad to worse, often pawning his clothes or appearing in filthily unpresentable fashion. On one occasion he walked into Wicklow from Dublin, borrowed £5 from Grattan, but had drunk and dispersed all of it by the time he got back to the city. He then walked three miles out to Ranelagh and attempted to arouse his future biographer, James Grant Raymond, by heaving stones through the windows. By the time Raymond was aroused, so was the entire neighborhood, and the drunken and disheveled poet had been collared by the watch.

After being saved from having been pressed into the army on two occasions, Dermody finally enlisted as a private, and, with only occasional drunken lapses, served with such distincton in France that he was raised to the rank of second lieutenant. Twice wounded and mustered out on halfpay, he spent the rest of his life in London, writing, alienating his friends and becoming a hopeless alcoholic. He died in utter poverty on July 15, 1802, at Sydenham in Kent. He was only twenty-seven years old.

Dermody wrote a few perceptive critical essays, but his serious work was poetry. His more formal pieces tended to be conventional and imitative, and were permeated with echoes of his voluminous reading. All his works, however, reflect his consummate ease of expression, and often an individual note brilliantly breaks through. That individuality is most apparent in his pieces of invective, satire, or whimsy. His "Battle of the Bards," for instance, is one of the very few productions of its time to beg comparison with Pope's "Rape of the Lock." His "Farewell to Ireland" commences with the marvelously energetic lines

> Rank nurse of nonsense; on whose thankless coast
> The base weed thrives, the nobler bloom is lost:
> Parent of pride and poverty, where dwell
> Dullness and brogue and claumny:—farewel!

Such lines make him a superb antidote to the multitude of patriotic poets discussed elsewhere in this volume, but it might be noted that Dermody's poem also contains the lines

> For spite of anger, spite of satire's thrill
> Nature boils o'er; thou art my country still.

Dermody the man is difficult to sum up, for, as his dozens of begging letters show, he was an accomplished self-dramatizer. In one vein, he may truculently assert:

> 'Fore heav'n! you'll find no saint in me,
>   From passion's furnace glowing hot;
> And as for prim hypocrisy,
>   Hypocrisy! I know her not.

But in a more self-pitying manner, he will advise Ireland to:

> Thy artists cherish; bid the mighty soul
> Of wisdom range beyond cold want's control;
> And haply when some native gem you see
> Unknown, unfriended, lost—oh, think on Me!

Nevertheless, the reader's final judgment might best be based on his lines from his "The Fate of Genius," which are engraved on his tombstone:

> And though fell passion sway'd his soul,
> By Prudence seldom ever won,
> Beyond the bounds of her control,
> He was dear Fancy's favour'd son.

> Now a cold tenant does he lie
> Of this dark cell, all hush'd his song:
> While Friendship bends with streaming eye,
> As by his grave she wends along;

> On his cold clay lets fall a holy tear,
> And cries, "Though mute, there is a poet here."

WORKS: *Poems*. Gilbert Austin, ed. Dublin: Chambers, 1789. *Poems, Consisting of Essays, Lyrics, Elegiac, &c., Written between the 13th and 16th Year of His Age*. Dublin: J. Jones, 1792; *The Rights of Justice; or, Rational Liberty*. Dublin: J. Mehain, 1793. (Essay); *Poems, Moral, and Descriptive*. London: Vernor & Hood/Lockington, Allen, 1800; *The Histrionade*, by Marmaduke Myrtle (pseud). London: R. S. Kirby, 1802; *Poems on Various Subjects*. London: J. Hatcherd, 1802; *The Harp of Erin*. James G. Raymond, ed. 2 vols. London: Richard Phillips, 1807.   REFERENCE: Raymond, James Grant. *The Life of Thomas Dermody: Interspersed with Pieces of Original Poetry . . . and Containing a Series of Correspondence . . .* 2 vols. London: Miller, 1806.

DE VERE, SIR AUBREY (1788-1846), poet and dramatist. De Vere was born Vere Hunt at Curragh Chase, County Limerick, on August 28, 1788, and was educated at Harrow with Byron and Peel. He was an enlightened and responsible landlord and wrote little until he was thirty. His most ambitious works were a number of verse dramas, of which the best is probably the posthumously published *Mary Tudor* (1847). This drama is written in a much more muscular style than some of the more famous closet dramas of the nineteenth century.

Some of de Vere's poems were about Ireland, and the best were in the form of the sonnet which he came to practice and to admire. As a sonneteer, he was a disciple, and also a good friend, of Wordsworth who called de Vere's sonnets "the most perfect of our age." Wordsworth's judgment was much too kind, but it was not ridiculous. De Vere's Irish sonnets are typical of his style. However, they were less successful than his more general work because the English manner, the Wordsworthian romantic diction, just did not graft well onto the Irish subject matter. De Vere is also extremely uneven from line to line in the same poem. He is capable of a line of authentic Wordsworthian simplicity, or even grandeur, as in "Lismore" where he writes of Raleigh:

> . . . now soon his star
> Should set, dishonoured, in a bloody sea!

But in the same poem he has a good deal of soporific and vague romantic imagery such as:

> . . . umbrageous glade;
> Dark, dimpling eddies, 'neath bird-haunted shade. . . .

In "The Sea-Cliffs of Kilkee," he can dust off a line from the lumber-room of poetry, like:

> Ere the poised Osprey stoop in wrath from high.

And in the same poem he is capable of an incredibly flat line like:

> Awfully beautiful art thou, O sea!

Or he can even palm off such a flat line and then redeem it by one which is utterly tight:

> Where all is simply great that meets the eye—
> The precipice, the ocean, and the sky.

Contemporary taste would probably deem no one de Vere poem thoroughly admirable. Yet, he is worth reading, for among the sunbeams and the rills, the bastioned islets and the desecrated fanes, one will constantly meet lines like these from the first poem in "Glengarriff":

> Gazing from each low bulwark of this bridge,
>   How wonderful the contrast! Dark as night,
>   Here, amid cliffs and woods, with headlong might,
> The black stream whirls, through ferns and drooping sedge. . . .

De Vere's second son, Sir Stephen, was a translator of Horace; his third son was Aubrey Thomas de Vere,* a neglected but quite considerable Irish poet. De Vere died at Curragh Chase on July 5, 1846.

WORKS: *Ode to the Duchess of Angoulême.* London: Longman, 1815; *Julian, the Apostate; a Dramatic Poem.* London: Warren, 1822; *The Duke of Mercia; an His-*

torical Drama. The Lamentation of Ireland and Other Poems. London: Hurst, Robinson, 1823; *A Song of Faith, Devout Exercises and Sonnets.* London: Pickering, 1842;
*Inaugural Address . . . At the House of the Limerick Philosophical and Literary So-
ciety.* Dublin: Grant & Bolton, 1842; *Mary Tudor, an Historical Drama, The Lamentation of Ireland and Other Poems.* London: Pickering, 1847; *Dramatic Works.* London:
Pickering, 1858.   REFERENCES: De Vere, Aubrey Thomas. *Recollection of Aubrey De Vere.* New York: Arnold, 1897. (This is an autobiography, but it contains
many recollections of the author's father); Dixon, William Macneile. "The Poetry of
the De Veres." *In the Republic of Letters.* London: Nutt, 1898, pp. 64-118.

DE VERE, AUBREY THOMAS (1814-1902), poet. De Vere, the third
son of Sir Aubrey de Vere,* was born at the family estate, Curragh Chase,
County Limerick, on January 10, 1814. He was educated at Trinity College, Dublin. He then traveled a good deal in Europe and was frequently
in England where he became friends with many of the eminent men of the
day, including Wordsworth, Tennyson, Carlyle, Sir Henry Taylor, and
Cardinal Newman. He was a deeply pious man who never married. After
long consideration, he left the Anglican faith in 1851 and was received into
the Roman Catholic by his friend, the future Cardinal Manning.

De Vere was much concerned with the problems of Ireland, and he and
his family worked diligently to alleviate the sufferings in their neighbourhood during the Famine. In 1848, he published a book on the Irish situation called *English Misrule and Irish Misdeeds.* This was not precisely the
work of an Irish patriot, but of an enlightened Christian gentleman of his
class. Concerning the book, modern sentiment would probably agree with
John Stuart Mill who wrote to de Vere, ". . . I look much more than you
do to reclamation of waste lands and alteration of landed tenures, and less
to emigration as a remedy." However, one of his biographers, Mary Paraclita O'Reilly, notes that, "Throughout his life he worked diligently in
behalf of his countrymen, promoting religious equality, lending his support
to the Irish Land Act of 1881, to the earlier establishment of the Irish
Church, and to the cause of popular education."

De Vere was a cultivated man of leisure who devoted much of his life
to writing. He produced four volumes of essays, two of travel, one of
Recollections, six of poetry and two poetic dramas, in addition to much
fugitive work. He is little read today. One critic in a recent literary history
devotes only two sentences to him, misspelling his name once and remarking that he "produced some superficially 'Irish' poetry, but rarely gives the
impression that he is more than a conventional Victorian who occasionally
successfully exploited material from his Irish homeland" (Richard Fallis,
The Irish Renaissance, 1978). Patrick Rafroidi's view that de Vere is, with
Sir Samuel Ferguson* and Standish O'Grady,* a major link between the
Romanticism of the early nineteenth century and the Celtic Renaissance at
the end is a much sounder position (*L'Irlande et le Romantisme,* 1972).

Perhaps only a third or a fourth of de Vere's poetic production can

strictly be labeled Irish, but much of that is extremely interesting. His retelling of the *Tain* under the title of *The Foray of Queen Maeve* is certainly
spotted with some nineteenth-century poetic diction and some poetic inversions, but mainly it impresses by a terse (sometimes almost too terse)
masculine style that hurtles the story fluently along. Of nearly equal interest
are his retellings of "the Sons of Usnach" and "The Children of Lir." His
best Irish work may be in two shorter pieces, "Oiseen and Saint Patrick"
and "The Bard Ethell." These works reflect his deeply felt Christianity
and yet do not dissipate the un-Christian heroism of an earlier day. In
the metrically jaunty first part of his Oiseen and Patrick colloquy, the
pagan hero loses none of his intractability by his confrontation with the
Christian saint:

> "Old man, thou hearest our Christian hymns;
> Such strains thou hadst never heard—"
> "Thou liest, thou priest! for in Letter Lee wood
> I have listened its famed blackbird!
>
> "I have heard the music of meeting swords,
> And the grating of barks on the strand,
> And the shout from the breasts of the men of help
> That leap from the decks to land!"

The character of the thirteenth-century poet in "The Bard Ethell" is a
beautifully drawn sketch of pagan surliness not yet entirely dimmed by
conversion to Christianity. Ethell can still say:

> Man's deeds! Man's deeds! they are shades that fleet,
> Or ripples like those that break at my feet;
> The deeds of my chief and the deeds of my King
> Grow hazy, far seen, like the hills in spring.
> Nothing is great save the death on the Cross!
> But Pilate and Herod I hate, and know,
> Had Fionn lived then, he had laid them low. . . .

De Vere is not a modern poet, but his handling of Irish themes is no more
superficial than that of Yeats. Neither is he an inconsiderable poet, for he
can handle strong narrative, draw a memorable character, and fashion
fluent verse. He died on January 21, 1902.

WORKS: *English Misrule and Irish Misdeeds*. London: Murray, 1848; *Picturesque
Sketches of Greece and Turkey*. London: Bentley, 1850; *The Sisters and Inisfail*. Lon-
don: Longmans, 1867. (Poems); *Ireland's Church Question*. London: Longmans,
1868; (*Irish Odes and Other Poems*. New York: Catholic Publication Society, 1869);
May Carols. London: Richardson, 1870; London: Burns & Oates, 1881. (Poetry);
Alexander the Great. London: King, 1874. (Poetic drama); *Saint Thomas of Canter-
bury*. London: King, 1876. (Poetic drama); *Antar and Zara: An Eastern Romance*.
London: King, 1877; *Legends of the Saxon Saints*. London: Kegan, Paul, 1879; *Con-

stitutional and Unconstitutional Political Action. Limerick: McKern, 1881; *The Foray of Queen Maeve.* London: Kegan, Paul, Trench, 1882; *The Search after Prosperpine and Other Poems.* London: Kegan, Paul, 1884; *Legends and Records of the Church and Empire.* (Poetry); *Essays, Chiefly on Poetry.* London: Macmillan, 1887; *Legends of St. Patrick.* London: Cassell, 1889; London: Macmillan, 1892. (Poetry); *Mediaeval Records and Sonnets.* London: Macmillan, 1893; *Religious Problems of the Nineteenth Century.* London: St. Anselm's Society, 1893; *Selections from the Poems of Aubrey de Vere,* ed. George Edward Woodberry. New York: Macmillan, 1894; *Recollections.* New York: Arnold, 1897; *Poems from the Works of Aubrey de Vere,* ed. Lady Margaret Domvile. London: Catholic Truth Society, 1904; *The Poetical Works of Aubrey de Vere.* Vols. 1-3. London: Kegan Paul, 1898; Vols. 4-6. London: Macmillan, 1898.   REFERENCES: Gunning, John P. *Aubrey de Vere: A Memoir.* Limerick: Guy/London: Simpkin & Marshall, 1902; Reilly, Mary Paraclita. *Aubrey de Vere, Victorian Observer.* Lincoln: University of Nebraska Press, 1953; Ward, Wilfrid. *Aubrey de Vere: A Memoir.* London: Longmans, Green, 1904; Winckler, Paul A., & Stone, William V. "Aubrey Thomas de Vere 1814-1902: A Bibliography." *Victorian Newsletter,* No. 10, Supplement (1956): 1-4.

DEVLIN, DENIS (1908-1959), poet, translator, and diplomat. Devlin was born in Greenock, Scotland, on April 15, 1908, the son of a prosperous Irish businessman. In 1918, when Devlin was ten, the family returned to Ireland. Devlin was the eldest of nine children, and the interests of his large, hospitable family were lively. There was a formidable library and much stimulating discussion of current affairs, the household being frequented by such political notables as Michael Collins and Éamon de Valera with whom Devlin retained acquaintance throughout his life.

Devlin received his primary education from the Christian Brothers, and his secondary education from the Jesuits at Belvedere College, Dublin, the school attended by James Joyce.* He then spent one year in seminary at All Hallows College, before deciding, despite his religious fervor, not to enter the priesthood. He entered University College, Dublin, and gave himself over with characteristic vitality to pursuits artistic as well as intellectual. He acted in dramatic productions, among them *Twelfth Night*, and was one of the founders of the Dramatic Society. He also began his career as a poet with the publication of a few poems in *The National Student.* In 1930, he and his friend and fellow poet Brian Coffey* had a slim volume of their combined efforts privately printed at their own expense. The collection contained four poems by Devlin and five by Coffey and, as Coffey says, was intended to "show that the pre-treaty tradition of writing from U.C.D. was not dead" (*University Review* 2, No. 10). In *Advent VI*, a publication devoted to Devlin, Mervyn Wall,* the novelist and lifelong friend who had met Devlin at Belvedere, remembers him as "the perfect friend, very well-read, humorous, and always radiating a quiet charm . . . who introduced me to Eliot and Pound." Wall gives this portrait:

> While standing and listening to what others had to say, Denis often
> adopted a slightly comic stance, his arms and hands hanging loosely

by his sides. A College cartoonist once drew him as a penguin with a cherrywood pipe in its mouth, and those who saw the drawing immediately recognized whom the cartoon represented.

After taking a degree in languages at University College, Dublin, Devlin made a brief visit to the Blaskets to improve his knowledge of Gaelic, and then went on scholarship to study at Munich University (1930-1931) and at the Sorbonne (1931-1933). During these years, he and his friend Niall Montgomery took on the unorthodox challenge of translating nineteenth-century French poetry into Gaelic; their manuscript remains unpublished. There was also a short trip to Spain with American journalist Sam Pope Brewer. Devlin was to capture his reactions to that country in the poem "Meditations at Avila." For a short time, he was assistant lecturer in English Literature at University College, Dublin. The salary, however, was quite small, and Mervyn Wall recalls the poet's struggle in deciding to leave teaching for a more lucrative position with the Irish diplomatic service: " 'I know the academic life is the superior,' he said, 'but I admit that the diplomatic life attracts me' " (*Advent VI*).

Devlin left the university in 1935 and entered the Department of External Affairs as a cadet. He was to remain in the Irish diplomatic service until his death in 1959, becoming progressively more proficient in the execution of his duties. But his dedication to poetry remained constant, and the successful pursuit of this avocation runs parallel to his successful pursuit of his vocation. Indeed, poetry was as much his vocation as was diplomacy. All that he encountered in his travels provided his poetry with a world vision that is perhaps unequaled in modern poetry, with the exception of Ezra Pound, with whom he shares many affinities.

Intercessions, a collection of fifteen poems, appeared in 1937. The technical control, rich and complex imagery, broad vocabulary, and themes of love, justice, family, and mystical union that mark the later work abound in these early poems of passionately religious fervor. They reflect his thorough acquaintance with and respect for European literature, and the influence of those French poets he held in highest regard: Gide, Villon, and most particularly Eluard. Coffey tells us that "Devlin used a copy of *Longer Poems of the English Language* until it fell apart" and that he always kept Eluard beside him (*University Review* 2, No. 10). In certain of the poems, the mimicry of the French *symbolistes* is awkward and inhibiting, and echoes of Baudelaire are destructive. In "Est Prodest" and "Argument with Justice," however, Devlin's own unique voice emerges. His poetic development, as Frank Kersnowski says, his "progression . . . from a surrealistic portrayal of disgust to a mythic celebration of love" (*Sewanee Review*, Winter 1973), has only just begun and is only just perceptible. Several of the poems in *Intercessions* reappear in *Selected Poems*

(1963) and one, "The Statue and the Perturbed Burghers," has been anthologized.

In 1938, Devlin went to Rome as first secretary to the Legation to Italy and made a first visit to Greece. In 1939, he left for the United States where he spent one year as consul in New York and six years (1940-1947) as first secretary to the Irish Legation in Washington. It was there, at the home of Katherine Anne Porter, that he met Robert Penn Warren, who two years earlier had read and admired his "Lough Derg" and published it in *The Southern Review*. Many of Devlin's poems appeared in American journals and magazines during this time. One may find them in *Accent, Briarcliff Quarterly, New Republic, Sewanee Review, Poetry*, and *Maryland Quarterly*, among others. America gave Devlin a wife as well as an audience: in 1946, he married Marie Caren Radon, an American of French descent.

A great deal of Devlin's poetic virtuosity may be attributed to his translations, particularly those of French poets. A series of his translations of St. John Perse were published immediately following the war, culminating in the publication of the bilingual edition *Exile and Other Poems* in New York in 1949.

A collection of his own verse, *Lough Derg and Other Poems*, was published in New York in 1946. Included in the collection were many of the best poems previously published in *Intercessions* and in various periodicals. The volume was quite favorably received, despite one critic's reaction that "Devlin is a learned rather than an accomplished craftsman" (Babette Deutsch, *Weekly Book Review*, July 28, 1946). Although there are poems in the book that would create that impression, the title poem is not one of them. "Lough Derg" is of primary importance among Devlin's work. The story centers around an Irish abbey famous for centuries as a place of religious pilgrimage, and the reference to Dante, who centuries before had celebrated the spot, is more than incidental. In "Lough Derg," the poet-pilgrim reaches a celebration of life derived from a Blakean awareness of mystical union and reunion, which may serve as an analogue for Devlin's search for poetic vision in general. Inez Boulton accurately remarks that "the poet gives us a glimpse of that philosophy which recognizes the unity of all consciousness. . . . This thought stream runs through all the poems. Sometimes it is bright with humor, sometimes dim in the tarnishment of life's tragic background, but always an essential part of the pattern" (*Poetry*, December 1946). More than one critic has commented that "Lough Derg" will stand beside Stevens' "Sunday Morning" and Eliot's "Gerontion" as an answer to the modern dilemma. As Mary Salmon puts it, Devlin approaches the theme of modern man's "loss of God and the seeming bankruptcy of efforts at replacement . . . from the standpoints of humanism ancient and modern, the theocratic symbolism of European Christianity and the emotional piety which he found in the Ireland of his time" (*Studies*, Spring 1973).

Returning to Europe in 1947, Devlin was assigned the post of counsellor attached to the Office of the High Commission, London. He returned to headquarters in Dublin in 1949. In 1950, he went to Italy, and most of the ensuing years were spent there, first as minister plenipotentiary and later (1958) as Ireland's first ambassador to Italy. A brief post as minister plenipotentiary to Turkey in 1951 is reflected in the poem "Memoirs of a Turkish Diplomat," first published in *Botteghe Oscure* and later in both *Selected Poems* and *Collected Poems*. This poem is not one of Devlin's best, but it displays the complex patterning of irony that runs through most of his work. Its counterpointing of philosophical argument and evocative imagery, standing out as it does, prepares the reader for that more subtle rhetoric and obscure metaphor that moves the better poems. Not the least of the merits of "Memoirs" is its exploitation of the culturally alien situation for the purpose of contrast which highlights the universal human condition. As always, Devlin's keen sensibilities penetrate the variety of experience and synthesize it to poetic advantage.

Devlin died on August 21, 1959, in Dublin. He was survived by his wife, Caren, and his son, Stephen. During the years following his return from America, a few new poems were published in literary journals, but no books appeared. It is known that he was busy translating, among others, the work of Goethe, Appolinaire, and Quasimodo, and that he was working on an autobiography, unfinished and unpublished.

In 1963, *Selected Poems by Denis Devlin*, edited and prefaced by Robert Penn Warren and Allen Tate, appeared, as well as *Collected Poems*, edited and introduced by Brian Coffey. There are forty-two poems in *Selected Poems*, representing approximately half of those finished by the poet. Among the most notable not heretofore published in book form are the long poems "The Tomb of Michael Collins," "The Passion of Christ" (dedicated to Allen Tate), and "The Colours of Love" (dedicated to Caren). These are beautifully crafted poems, wherein Devlin's celebration of man's divinity, in several ways, is carried off in lyrical and grand style. In these poems, the vision of a fragmented world is unified by a resounding metaphysical awareness of oneness, and in retrospect much of the irony and paradox of the earlier poems is illuminated. Maurice Harmon says of "The Passion of Christ": ". . . the grandeur of theme is matched with suitable elevation of language . . . Devlin seems to have found a mode entirely suitable to his needs as man and poet: the great theme of Christ, son of man and son of God, the act of atonement and the act of redemption, the absolute certainty of the journey towards transfiguration" (*Advent VI*). By *Selected Poems*, the poet has found his vision and his voice. Tate and Warren, whose affectionate preface is primarily biographical, consider "The Passion of Christ," "From Government Buildings," and "Lough Derg" to be Devlin's best poems. They find his work neither Irish nor English (there is little there, they say, of Yeats*), but rather European in the manner of Valery and St. John Perse. However, when they refer to what they consider Devlin's "eccentricity" in punctuation and his deviation from iambic pentameter in parts of "Lough Derg," they evoke a response from Brian Coffey, whose *Collected Poems* appeared almost simultaneously with their edition. In *Poetry Ireland* (Spring 1973), Coffey "vindicates" Devlin's technique—to use a term which Coffey tells us Devlin applied to the responsibility of the poet to his talent (*University Review* 2, No. 10).

In *Collected Poems* (Dublin, 1963 and 1964), Coffey has gathered all of the poems published during the poet's lifetime (with the exception of the translations), all of the poems published posthumously, and some few others not before published. Coffey was named executor of Devlin's manuscripts upon his death. The introduction to *Collected Poems* is valuable for a variety of reasons, particularly for the information drawn from unpublished notes and poems and the autobiography. Coffey has also provided a critical edition of "The Heavenly Foreigner," Devlin's most difficult poem, at least in terms of its obscurity, and perhaps his best work in terms of complexity and completeness of vision. *The Heavenly Foreigner* (Dolmen Press, 1967) is the first edition of the revised edition of the poem; it was completed before the poet's death and contains his worksheets. "The Heavenly Foreigner" was originally published in *Poetry Ireland* in 1950, and Coffey includes in his text Niall Sheridan's* introduction to that version. What Sheridan says of the poem holds true for all of Denis Devlin's verse: that it makes "what may seem unusual demands on the reader," but that "on careful reading, superficial obscurities vanish, new imaginative horizons open," as "complexities of thought and feeling fuse into a glowing lyricism. . . ." In handling the themes of "Time and human destiny" and "the anguished alliance of flesh and spirit," Devlin "shows a rare power of stating abstract ideas and philosophical concepts in terms of poetry."

Devlin brought much to his poetry: excellent education, broad cultural experience, religious training and genuine conviction, native intelligence, and a gift for language and its cadence. In reading his work, one is reminded as much of Blake and his fellows as of Yeats and the moderns of French and English verse, especially of Pound. His bent is surely romantic, and his technique is strikingly modern. An effort must be made to avoid confusing his sophistication with artifice. Critics place him with Austin Clarke* and Patrick Kavanagh*; he ranks with Yeats. It is only exposure that is lacking; wider circulation will surely yield greater critical acclaim.

NORA F. LINDSTROM

WORKS: with Brian Coffey, *Poems*. Dublin, 1930; *Intercessions*. London: Europa, 1937; *Lough Derg and Other Poems*. New York: Reynal & Hitchcock, 1946; trans., *Exile and Other Poems,* by St. John Perse. New York: Pantheon Books, 1949; *Selected Poems*. Robert Penn Warren & Allen Tate, eds. New York: Holt, Rinehart &

Winston, 1963; *Collected Poems*. Brian Coffey, ed. Dublin: Dolmen, 1964. (Previously published as a special number of *University Review*, University College, Dublin, 1963); *The Heavenly Foreigner*. Brian Coffey, ed. Dublin: Dolmen, 1967.   REFERENCES: *Advent VI*. Denis Devlin Special Issue. Southhampton: Advent Books, 1976; Coffey, Brian. "Of Denis Devlin: Vestiges, Sentences, Presages." *University Review* (Dublin), 2, No. 10 (1965): 3-18; Kersnowski, Frank L. "The Fabulous Reality of Denis Devlin." *Sewanee Review* (Winter 1973):113-122; Salmon, Mary. "Modern Pilgrimage: Denis Devlin's 'Lough Derg.' " *Studies: An Irish Quarterly Review* (Spring 1973):75-83.

DILLON, EILIS (1920-), novelist and children's writer. Dillon was born in Galway City on March 7, 1920. Her father was professor of chemistry at University College, Galway, and her mother was the former Geraldine Plunkett. She married Cormac O Cuilleanain, professor of Irish at University College, Cork; their daughter, Eiléan Ní Chuilleánain,* is a well-known poet. After her husband's death, Dillon married Vivian Mercier, the critic. She is a prolific writer in Irish and English, and her many delightful children's books have been much admired by adults and enjoyed by children. *The Singing Cave* (1959) is a particularly fine example of her work in this genre. In 1973, her long, romantic historical novel, *Across the Bitter Sea*, became a best seller. It was followed by a sequel entitled *Blood Relations* (1977).

WORKS: *Midsummer Magic*. London: Macmillan, 1949; *The Lost Island*. London: Faber, 1952; *The San Sebastian*. London: Faber, 1953; *Sent to His Account*. London: Faber, 1954; *Death at Crane's Court*. London: Faber, 1955. *The Wild Little House*. London: Faber, 1955; *Death in the Quadrangle*. London: Faber, 1956; *The Island of Horses*. London: Faber, 1956; *Plover Hill*. London: Hamilton, 1957; *Aunt Bedelia's Cats*. London: Hamilton, 1958; *The Bitter Glass*. London: Faber, 1958; *The Singing Cave*. London: Faber, 1959; *The Head of the Family*. London: Faber, 1960; *The Fort of Gold*. London: Faber, 1961; *King Big-Ears*. London: Faber, 1961; *The Cat's Opera*. London: Faber, 1962; *A Pony and Trap*. London: Hamilton, 1962; *The Coriander*. London: Faber, 1963; *A Family of Foxes*. London: Faber, 1964; *Bold John Henebry*. London: Faber, 1965; *The Sea Wall*. London: Faber, 1965; *The Road to Dunmore*. London: Faber, 1966; *The Lion Cub*. London: Transworld, 1967; *The Five Hundred*. London: Hamilton, 1972; *Across the Bitter Sea*. London: Hodder & Stoughton, 1973; *The Hamish Hamilton Book of Wise Animals*. London: Hamilton, 1975; *Living in Imperial Rome*. London: Faber, 1975; *Blood Relations*. London: Hodder & Stoughton, 1977.

DOLMEN PRESS (1951-), publishing house. The Dolmen Press was founded by Liam* and Josephine Miller in Dublin in 1951 as a small hand-press to publish the works of Irish writers as well as works of Irish interest by writers from other countries. Since then, over 250 books have appeared under the Dolmen imprint, and the list, which has an emphasis on poetry, includes most of the foremost Irish writers of the present day. The scope of the list has broadened over the years so that current titles include fiction, drama, poetry, biography, and bibliography.

Several Dolmen poetry titles have been choices or recommendations of the Poetry Book Society in London. Other awards to authors have included the AE Memorial Award, the Irish Arts Council Poetry Award, the Marten Toonder Award, the Kavanagh Award, the W. H. Smith Award, the Irish-American Cultural Foundation Award, and bursaries from the Arts Council of Great Britain and of Northern Ireland.

The Dolmen Press undertakes almost all of its own printing and, in addition, offers clients the services of its printing house. Although the press is small in size, it carries a distinguished range of typefaces and prints many kinds of letterpress work, especially bookwork, for publishers in Europe and America.

Illustration is often a feature of the Dolmen Press books. Such distinguished graphic artists as Tate Adams, Leonard Baskin, Jack Coughlin, S. W. Hayter, Louis le Brocquy, Elizabeth Rivers, and Anne Yeats are represented by cover design and illustrations. Several of the books have received design awards in Ireland. A comprehensive bibliography appeared in 1976 to mark the first twenty-five years of the Press.

While most of the early editions from the Press were limited, publications now include paperbacks, general books in hard cover, and limited editions. Several continuing series are published; among them are "Dolmen Editions," which are limited editions of the best Irish writings, often with illustrations, and "The Tower Series of Anglo-Irish Studies," which consist of essays published in conjunction with the Anglo-Irish Department in University College Dublin. An Irish Theatre series is devoted to the Irish theatre and includes critical works and a documentary history of modern Irish drama. New Yeats Papers, studies of the poet's life, work, and influences, have been appearing since 1971.

LIAM MILLER

REFERENCE: Miller, Liam, comp. *Dolmen XXV: An Illustrated Bibliography of the Dolmen Press 1951-1976*. Dublin: Dolmen, 1976.

DONAGHY, JOHN LYLE (1902-1947), poet. Donaghy was born in Ulster in 1902 and was educated at Larne Grammar School, where he was a childhood friend of George Buchanan,* and at Trinity College, Dublin. He was a schoolmaster for some years, and he published, both as John Lyle Donaghy and as Lyle Donaghy, much fugitive verse and several slim volumes of poetry. Some critics believe that Donaghy could have developed into a significant talent; whatever the case may be, he was never able to harness an apparently terrific poetic ambition to an effective form. His early book *Primordia Caeca* (1927) is mystical in content, elevated in manner, and written in florid and formless prose poetry. Its most ambitious poem, "The Pit," is a conversation on elemental questions between the author and Virgil, Dante, and Milton. The poems in *The Flute over the Valley* (1931) are much simpler, but they are also slack and metrically muddled, with many flabby lines that exist merely to fill out a stanza scheme or to make a rhyme. The poems in *The Blackbird* (1933) are generally romantic descriptions of nature and apostrophes to love and God. The diction is hardly individual, but the rhyming verses are more controlled, and there is the occasional tight line in such poems as "Dreadnought," "The Falcon," or "The Heron." Even his *Selected Poems* (1939) contains many examples of the poet's inability to control his form. His longest and last book, *Wilderness Sings* (1942), abandons form almost entirely; it is a practically unreadable volume of ecstatic free verse and prose poetry, in which even syntax often disappears. Donaghy's career seemed to move from the immaturely grandiose, through some not completely unsuccessful attempts at form, and then into a final formless personal shout.

WORKS: *At Dawn above Aherlow: Poems*. Dublin: Cuala, 1926; *Primordia Caeca: Poems*. Dublin: Eason, 1927; *Ad Perennis Vitae Fontem*. Dublin: Minerva, 1928; *The Flute Over the Valley: Antrim Song*. Larne: Inver, 1931; *The Blackbird: Songs of Inisfail*. Larne: Inver, 1933; *Into the Light, and Other Poems*. Dublin: Cuala, 1934; *Selected Poems*. Dublin: Orwell, 1939; *Wilderness Sings*. Dublin: Printed for the Author by Wood Printing Works, 1942.

DONLEAVY, J[AMES] P[ATRICK] (1926-), novelist. Donleavy was born in Brooklyn, New York, on April 23, 1926. After World War II, he attended Trinity College, Dublin, and was one of the bohemian group that gathered in the Georgian cellar known as the Catacombs. Other notable habitués were Brendan Behan,* Anthony Cronin,* and a rather legendary American named Gainor Christ who was attending Trinity on the G.I. Bill and who became the inspiration for the protagonist of Donleavy's first and still most famous novel, *The Ginger Man* (1955). The book's hero, Sebastian Dangerfield, has much in common, in both eloquence and fecklessness, with John Osborne's angry young man Jimmy Porter in *Look Back in Anger*. Nevertheless, his story makes one of the most rowdy, raucous, vulgar, funny, and thrillingly written books about Dublin in the last quarter of a century. *The Ginger Man* established its author's international reputation, but a stage version was withdrawn in Dublin in 1959 as a result of clerical pressure.

Of Donleavy's widely read later novels, *The Beastly Beatitudes of Balthazar B* (1968) is largely laid in Ireland, and *The Destinies of Darcy Dancer, Gentleman* (1977) is wholly laid there. These two books may be taken as representative of Donleavy's later work. They are picaresque *Tom Jones*-like novels, but their exuberance, broad satire, and effectively exaggerated comic scenes stamp them as inimitably Donleavy's. Another noticeable characteristic of his work is an overwhelming preoccupation with sex, which is often described in a tongue-in-cheek, apparent parody of the literary soft-core pornography of the Victorian age. Donleavy's finest qualities, however, are an ability to create vivid characters and a racy, eloquent, and highly individual prose. These qualities go far to disguise the fact that his novels are usually not about very much.

Donleavy has become an Irish citizen and lives near Mullingar.

WORKS: *The Ginger Man*. Paris: Olympia Press, [1955], London: Spearman, [1956], revised, New York: McDowell, Obolensky, [1958], complete & unexpurated ed., New York: Delacorte, [1965]; *Fairy Tales of New York*. New York: Random House; Harmondsworth, England: Penguin, [1961]. (Play); *The Ginger Man, a Play*. London: MacGibbon & Kee, [1961], New York: Random House [1961]; *A Singular Man*. Boston: Little, Brown, [1963]; *Meet My Maker the Mod Molecule*. Boston: Little, Brown, [1964]. (Stories); *A Singular Man, a Play*. London: Bodley Head, [ca. 1964]; *The Saddest Summer of Samuel S*. New York: Delacorte, [1966]; *The Beastly Beatitudes of Balthazar B*. New York: Delacorte, [1968]; *The Onion Eaters*. London: Eyre & Spottiswoode; New York: Delacorte, 1971; *The Plays of J. P. Donleavy*. [New York]: Delacorte, [1972]; *A Fairy Tale of New York:* London: Eyre Methuen; [New York]: Delacorte/S. Laurence, [1973]. (Novel); *The Unexpurgated Code: A Complete Manual of Survival & Manners*. London: Wildwood House, 1975; *The Destinies of Darcy Dancer, Gentleman*. New York: Delacorte, [1977]. REFERENCE: Jacobsen, Kurt. "An Interview with J. P. Donleavy." *Journal of Irish Literature* 8 (January 1979).

DONOGHUE, DENIS (1928-), literary critic. Donoghue, professor of modern English and American literature at University College, Dublin, was born in Tullow, County Carlow, on December 1, 1928. He is probably the only modern Irish literary critic of international stature, and his lengthy and thoughtful essays frequently appear in such publications as *The New York Review of Books* and the *New York Times Book Review*. His own principal books have been *The Third Voice, Connoisseurs of Chaos, The Ordinary Universe, Jonathan Swift, Emily Dickinson, Yeats,* and *The Sovereign Ghost*. He was to have written the authorized biography of Yeats* but withdrew after a well-publicized brouhaha over other scholars' access to Yeats' unpublished material. His writing probably appeals more to the academic mind than to the generally cultured one; he is more of an F. R. Leavis than an Edmund Wilson.

WORKS: *The Third Voice: Modern British and American Verse Drama*. Princeton, N.J.: Princeton University Press, 1959; ed., *The Integrity of Yeats*. Cork: Mercier, 1964; *Connosseurs of Chaos: Ideas of Order in American Poetry*. London: Faber, 1966; *The Ordinary Universe: Soundings in Modern Literature*. London: Faber, 1968; *Emily Dickinson*. Minneapolis: University of Minnesota Press, 1969. (Monograph); *Jonathan Swift: A Critical Introduction*. London: Cambridge University Press, 1969; ed., *Jonathan Swift, a Critical Anthology*. Harmondsworth, Middlesex: Penguin, 1971; *Yeats*. London: Fontana, 1971; ed., *Memoirs of W. B. Yeats*. London: Macmillan, 1973; *Thieves of Fire*. London: Faber, 1974; *Imagination, the Twenty-Fifth W. P. Ker Memorial Lecture*. Glasgow: University of Glasgow Press, 1975.

DOUGLAS, JAMES (1929-), playwright and short story writer. Douglas was born in Bray, County Wicklow, on July 4, 1929. After school, he became an apprentice electrician, and he still works as an electrician three or four days a week. His first produced play, *North City Traffic Straight Ahead*, was directed by Alan Simpson for the 1961 Theatre Festival. In the 1963 Theatre Festival, *Carrie* was based on one of his stories. In the 1964 Festival, his *The Ice Goddess* was produced at the Gate,* and in 1970 his *The Savages* was produced at the Eblana. His *Time Out of School* won the O. Z. Whitehead Award for one-act plays; *What Is the Stars?*, written in collaboration with Robert Hogan, won the final Irish Life Award. That last play was a study of a playwright resembling Sean O'Casey,* and its award was rescinded when O'Casey's widow threatened a law suit. Since 1961, Douglas has written frequently for television and radio. He devised and spent twenty-six painful weeks writing the television serial *The Riordans* which, in its continuations by other writers, has remained over the years the most popular and longest running drama on Irish television. Some of his other television plays include *The Bomb*, *The Hollow Field*, *How Long Is Kissing Time?*, and *Babbi Joe* which appeared Off-Off Broadway in a stage adaptation in 1978. His many short stories have appeared in most of the Irish literary periodicals but have not been collected.

Douglas' first two plays, *North City Traffic* and *The Ice Goddess*, have a tersely distinctive style which seems mannered upon the page but can be most effective upon the stage. Beginning with *The Savages*, this almost stylized simplicity begins to change to a fuller, more realistic dialogue. In his most recent and as yet unpublished work, he has allowed his rhetorical range to expand enormously. These late plays have passages of wit and eloquence. Douglas' first long stage plays—*North City*, *The Ice Goddess*, and *The Savages*—are about defeat, disillusionment, weltschmerz, and anguish. Only their solid theatrical sense keeps them from being depressingly bleak. Similarly, his short stories have generally been glumly contemporary and powerfully brackish. In his more recent work, however, welcome indications of geniality and even gaiety have appeared.

WORKS: *The Bomb*. Dixon, Calif.: Proscenium, 1966. (One-act play); *The Ice Goddess*, in *Seven Irish Plays, 1946-1964*, R. Hogan, ed. Minneapolis: University of Minnesota Press, 1967; *North City Traffic Straight Ahead*. Dixon, Calif.: Proscenium, 1968; *The Savages*. Newark, Del.: Proscenium, 1979.

DOWLING, RICHARD (1846-1898), journalist, humorist, and novelist. Dowling was born in Clonmel on June 3, 1846. He wrote for *The Nation*,* edited the comic periodical *Zozimus*, and wrote for *Ireland's Eye*, before going to London and writing for *The Illustrated Sporting and Dramatic News* and editing his own comic paper, *Yorick*. He deserves some contemporary attention, for he had a good comic talent and wrote with fluency. His chief work of fiction is *The Mystery of Killard*, which is in a mordant vein. He died in 1898.

WORKS: *The Mystery of Killard*, 3 vols. London, 1879/London: Tinsley, 1884; *The Sport of Fate*. 3 vols. London: Tinsley, 1880; *Under St. Paul's*. 3 vols. London:

Tinsley, 1880; *The Weird Sisters.* 3 vols. London: Tinsley, 1880; *The Duke's Sweetheart.* 3 vols. London: Tinsley, 1881; *The Husband's Secret.* 3 vols. London: Tinsley, 1881; *A Sapphire Ring, and Other Stories.* 3 vols. London: Tinsley, 1882; *Sweet Inisfail.* 3 vols. London: Tinsley, 1882; *The Last Call.* 3 vols. London: Tinsley, 1884; *On the Embankment.* London: Tinsley, 1884; *The Hidden Flame.* 3 vols. London: Tinsley, 1885; *Fatal Bonds.* 3 vols. London: Ward & Downey, 1886; *The Skeleton Key.* London: Ward & Downey, 1886; *Tempest-Driven.* 3 vols. London: Tinsley, 1886; *With the Unhanged.* London: Swan Sonnenschein, 1887; *Miracle Gold.* 3 vols. London: Ward & Downey, 1888; *Ignorant Essays.* New York: Appleton, 1888; *Indolent Essays.* London: Ward & Downey, 1889; *An Isle of Surrey.* 3 vols. London: Ward & Downey, 1889; *The Crimson Chair, and Other Stories.* London: Ward & Downey, 1891; *Catmur's Caves; or, the Quality of Mercy.* London: A. & C. Black, 1892; *While London Sleeps.* London: Ward & Downey, 1895; *Old Corcoran's Money.* London: Chatto & Windus, 1897; *A Baffling Quest.* 3 vols. London: Ward & Downey, n.d.; *Below Bridge.* London: Ward & Downey, n.d.; "Letters to a Young Writer." *Cornhill Magazine,* NS 15 (1903): 80-86; *Zozimus Papers.* New York: Kennedy, 1909. (as Marcus Fell): *London Town: Sketches of London Life and Character.* 3 vols. London: Tinsley, 1880. (as Emmanuel Kirk): *On Babies and Ladders. Essays on Things in General.* London: Hotten, [1873]; *School Board Essays.* London: Ward & Downey, 1888.

DOYLE, LYNN (1873-1961), humorist. Lynn Doyle was the pseudonym of Leslie Alexander Montgomery, the humorist, who was born at Downpatrick, County Down, on October 5, 1873. Educated in Dundalk, he entered the Northern Banking Company when he was sixteen and remained until his retirement. He is remembered chiefly for several volumes of droll stories about the fictional Northern village of Ballygullion. The stories are broadly comic and are told in dialect. The best of them are as fresh today as when they first began to appear in 1908. Lynn Doyle also wrote a number of plays, mainly for the Ulster Literary Theatre*; one of them, *Love and Land,* was successfully produced in London under the title *Preserving Pat.* Montgomery's pseudonym was originally Lynn C. Doyle, which was suggested by a bottle of linseed oil he saw in a grocer's shop. He was briefly a member of the Irish Censorship Board in 1936 and 1937. He died on August 13, 1961, leaving behind him a long series of entertainments which must certainly rank just below those of Somerville and Ross* and of George A. Birmingham.*

WORKS: *Ballygullion.* Dublin: Maunsel, 1918; *An Ulster Childhood.* Dublin: Maunsel, 1921; *Lobster Salad.* London: Duckworth, 1922; *Dear Ducks and Other "Ballygullion" Stories.* London: Duckworth, 1925; *The Lilac Ribbon.* Dublin: Talbot, [1927]. (One-act play); *Love and Land (Preserving Pat).* Dublin: Talbot, [1927]. (Four-act play); *Turncoats.* Dublin: Talbot, 1928. (One-act play); *Me and Mr. Murphy.* London: Duckworth, [1930]; *Rosabelle and Other Stories.* London: Duckworth, 1933; *Ballygullion Ballads and Other Verses.* London: Duckworth, 1936; *Fiddling Farmer.* London: Duckworth, 1937; *The Shake of the Bag.* London: Duckworth, 1939; *Lilts and Lyrics.* Dublin: Talbot, 1941; *Yesterday Morning.* London: Duckworth, 1943; *Babel Babble,* an extravaganza. Transliterated and translated from the original Assyrian Brickfield by Gil McGamish. Dublin: Talbot, 1945; *A Bowl of Broth.* London: Duckworth, 1945; *Not Too Serious.* London: Duckworth, 1946;

Green Oranges. London: Duckworth, 1947; *Mr. Wildridge of the Bank*. London: Duckworth, 1947; *Love and Roberta*. Belfast: Carter, 1951; *Back to Ballygullion*. London: Duckworth, 1953.

DRENNAN, WILLIAM (1754-1820), nationalist and poet. Drennan was born in Belfast on May 23, 1754; he received an M.A. in 1771, and a doctorate in medicine from Edinburgh in 1778. A founder of the nationalist organization the United Irishmen, he was tried for sedition with Hamilton Rowan for issuing the Address of the United Irishmen to the Volunteers of Ireland. Although he had written the address, he was acquitted, while Rowan was fined and imprisoned. His most notable poems include "The Wake of William Orr" and "When Erin First Rose"; in the latter he coined the phrase "the Emerald Isle." Even in these, the best of his poems, he verges from conventional phrasing to extreme tightness and strength. His sons, William Drennan, Jr. (1802-1873) and John Swanwick Drennan (1809-1895), both contributed work to his best volume, *Glendalloch and Other Poems*. He died in Belfast on February 5, 1820.

WORKS: *Fugitive Pieces in Verse and Prose*. Belfast: Printed by F. D. Finlay, & sold by R. Rees, 1815; *The Electra of Sophocles*. Belfast: Printed by F. D. Finlay, 1817; *Glendalloch and Other Poems*, 2d ed., with additional verses by his sons. Dublin: W. Robertson/London: Simpkin/Edinburgh & Belfast, 1859; *The Drennan Letters*. D. A. Chart, ed. Belfast: His Majesty's Stationery Office, 1931.

DRUMMOND, WILLIAM HAMILTON (1778-1865), poet. Drummond was born in August 1778 at Larne, County Antrim, and was educated at Glasgow University. In 1800, he became pastor of a congregation in Belfast and in 1815, pastor of a congregation in Dublin. Some of his poems are on Irish subjects—*Hibernia, The Giant's Causeway, Clontarf, Bruce's Invasion of Ireland*. In his *Ancient Irish Minstrelsy*, he made some translations from the saga stories of Finn and his companions. Occasionally, he manages a strong eighteenth-century line, as in these couplets from *The Giant's Causeway*:

> The victor here and vanquished side by side
> Sleep ghastly pale, sad wrecks of human pride. . . .

> And cursed Ambition, drunk with folly, plan
> The guilt, the crimes, and miseries of man!

But more often he simply has the eighteenth-century mannerisms, as in his references to "Ye feathered tribes" and "Ye finny nations" in "Benevolence of the Good Man to the Inferior Animals." His versions of the Irish stories, despite an archaic fluency, are finally incongruous in their smooth English meters and diction. Drummond died on October 16, 1865.

WORKS: *Hibernia*. Belfast, 1797; *The Man of Age*. Belfast, 1797; *The Battle of Trafalgar*. Belfast: Archer & Ward, 1806; *The Giant's Causeway*. Belfast: Longman,

1811; *An Elegiac Ballad on the Funeral of Princess Charlotte.* Dublin: Graisberry & Campbell, 1817; *Who Are the Happy?* Dublin: Graisberry & Campbell, 1818; *Clontarf.* Dublin: Archer, Hodges & McArthur, 1822; *Bruce's Invasion of Ireland.* Dublin: Hodges & McArthur, 1826; *The Pleasures of Benevolence.* London: Hunter/Dublin: Wakeman, Hodges & Smith, 1835; *Life of Michael Servetus.* London: Chapman, 1848; *Ancient Irish Minstrelsy.* Dublin: Hodges & Smith, 1852; (Also some translations in Hardiman's *Irish Minstrelsy.* 2 vols. London: Joseph Robins, 1831).

DUBLIN MAGAZINE, THE (1923-1958), literary magazine. *The Dublin Magazine*, founded by the poet and bibliophile Seumas O'Sullivan* (the pen name of James Sullivan Starkey), has been called "the major Irish literary periodical of its day" and "Ireland's greatest literary periodical." In modern times, it was the longest lived literary magazine, and over six hundred writers appeared in its pages. It was founded as a monthly in August 1923, and it ran in that format until the August 1925 issue. Its original cover was a stylish Beardsley-like drawing by Harry Clarke, and its original number contained stories, poems, and articles by, among others, James Stephens,* Brinsley MacNamara,* Donn Byrne,* John Masefield, Ella Young,* and O'Sullivan himself.

After the first two years of publication, as a result of lack of money, insufficient original material, and editorial overwork, the magazine had to appear less frequently. In its new format as a quarterly, the magazine reappeared in January 1926, and it continued until its editor's death, the final issue being that for April-June 1958.

In its long life, the magazine was sometimes uneven, but it published a very large amount of excellent and even extraordinary work. Most of the major figures of the time contributed, and the magazine was particularly strong in its poets; among the most frequently represented were Padraic Colum,* Austin Clarke,* F. R. Higgins,* Patrick Kavanagh,* John Lyle Donaghy,* and Padraic Fallon.* However, among the short story writers were O'Flaherty* and O'Connor,* and also the young Mary Lavin* who received particular encouragement. Rather unusually, the magazine printed quite a few plays, among them those of Rutherford Mayne,* John MacDonagh,* Lennox Robinson,* Seumas O'Kelly,* Padraic Colum, Paul Vincent Carroll,* Austin Clarke, Gerald MacNamara,* and Padraic Fallon. Of special interest was the first printing of the *Diarmuid and Grania* of W. B. Yeats* and George Moore,* as well as (to O'Sullivan's great credit) the printing of no less than eight plays by George Fitzmaurice.*

As an enthusiastic bookman, O'Sullivan included a generous selection of short but interesting reviews, as well as commentaries on book catalogues and highly useful bibliographies by P. S. O'Hegarty and M. J. MacManus. Criticism, and even scholarship, were well represented by many contributors, including W. J. Lawrence* and La Tourette Stockwell. Nor was the magazine provincial in its outlook: it gave much space to translation and to consideration of foreign works.

As O'Sullivan was married to the artist Estella Solomons, the magazine was often and beautifully illustrated by artists such as Nora McGuinness, Harry Kernoff, Sean Keating, Sarah Purser, Jack B. Yeats,* Augustus John, and Solomons herself.

The thirty-five year achievement of *The Dublin Magazine* can hardly be underrated, and Irish letters owes an immense debt to O'Sullivan's brave tenacity. When his magazine ceased publication, it left a gap that has never been filled.

REFERENCES: Holzapfel, Rudi. *An Index of Contributions to the Dublin Magazine.* Dublin: Museum Bookshop, 1966; Holzapfel, Rudi. "A Note on the Dublin Magazine." *The Dublin Magazine*† 4 (Spring 1965): 18-27; Pressley, Stuart. "The Archives of the *Dublin Magazine, 1923-58.*" *The Long Room,* No. 7 (Spring 1973).

†A later literary magazine of the 1960s and 1970s, which grew out of *The Dubliner.*

DUFFERIN, LADY (1807-1867), poet and novelist. Helen Selina Sheridan Blackwood, Lady Dufferin, was the grand-daughter of Richard Brinsley Sheridan* and the elder sister of Caroline Norton.* She was born in England in 1807. Early in her childhood, she accompanied her parents to South Africa, returning to England on her father's death when her mother was given lodgings at Hampton Court. In 1825, at the age of eighteen, she married Captain Price Blackwood, heir to the marquess of Dufferin and Ava. To escape the Dufferins' disapproval, the couple lived at first in Italy, and in 1826 a son was born, later the distinguished British diplomat Lord Dufferin. In 1841, her husband died. She remained a widow for twenty-one years, until 1862 when she married the dying Earl of Gifford. She was widowed again after a few months; she died on June 13, 1867, in London. Caroline Blackwood* is her direct descendant.

Unlike her sister, Caroline Norton, Lady Dufferin never regarded herself as a serious writer. She is remembered today for humorous and sentimental ballads, such as "Terence's Farewell," "Katey's Letter," and particularly "The Lament of the Irish Emigrant," where she partially succeeds in lifting sentiment to a higher level. Her poems were widely anthologized, and some were set to music. A prose work, *The Hon. Impulsia Gushington,* a satire on high life in the nineteenth century written to amuse a sick friend, is forgotten today.

Her son, the Right Honorable Frederick Temple Blackwood, earl of Dufferin, was, among other things, under secretary for India, under secretary for war, governor general of Canada, British ambassador to the Court of St. Petersburg, to Italy, and to France, governor general of India, and lord rector of St. Andrew's. He wrote frequently about the state of Ireland. His main contribution to literature is his *Letters from High Latitudes* which went through several editions. In these reminscences, he evidences much urbanity and humor, and his sketch called "An Icelandic Dinner" is a comic gem worthy of his great-grandfather.

MARY ROSE CALLAGHAN

WORKS: *Lispings from Low Latitudes*. London: J. Murray, 1863; *Songs, Poems, and Verses by Helen, Lady Dufferin (Countess of Gifford)*. Edited with a Memoir and Some Account of the Sheridan Family by her Son the Marquess of Dufferin and Ava. London: J. Murray, 1894; *A Selection of the Songs of Lady Dufferin (Countess of Gifford)*. Marquess of Dufferin and Ava, ed. London: J. Murray, 1895.

DUFFY, BERNARD (?-1952), playwright and novelist. The plays of Duffy prove that modern knockabout comedy is not vastly different from Tudor era interludes. He relies on such time-hallowed devices as the cheater in *The Coiner* and *The Plot*; farcical matchmaking with surprise endings in *The Counter Charm* and *Cupboard Love*; blundering burglars who solve domestic problems in a home they invade in *Special Pleading*; the triumph of the clever little fellow, seasoned with political jokes, in *Fraternity*; the smile and the tear in *The Old Lady*, wherein a sweet Irish mother rescues her son from a predatory chorus girl.

Of his Abbey* plays—*Fraternity*, *The Coiner*, and *The Counter Charm* (all in 1916) and *The Piper of Tavran* (1921)—only the last, adapted from a Douglas Hyde* tale, rises above situation comedy. An old piper, who has converted a wicked woman to the good life, comes to exorcise a devil from an abbey. While the man dreams of a beautiful tune the sainted woman is teaching him, the devil is blasted by lightning. The poor piper wakes, cannot remember the tune, and leaves the abbey unrewarded.

Duffy also wrote two novels. *Oriel* (1918) is another "coming of age in Ireland" story. *The Rocky Road* (1929) has an old flute player and a young girl singer earning their way along country paths and in Dublin slums. His stories, like his plays, are pleasantly subliterary. He died on March 31, 1952.

WILLIAM J. FEENEY

WORKS: *Four Comedies (The Counter Charm, The Coiner, Special Pleading, The Old Lady)*. Dublin: Talbot, 1916; *Oriel*. Dublin: Talbot, 1918. (Novel); *The Rocky Road*. Dublin: Talbot, 1929. (Novel); *Cupboard Love*. Dublin: Duffy, 1930. (Play); *The Plot*. Dublin: Duffy, 1941. (Play).

DUFFY, SIR CHARLES GAVAN (1816-1903), journalist, politician and poet, Duffy was born in Monaghan on April 12, 1816, and became a journalist in Dublin and Belfast. In 1842, with Thomas Davis* and John Blake Dillon (1816-1866), he founded *The Nation*,* the famous nationalist paper which published the fiery young patriots of the Young Ireland group. After the collapse of that group and his own trial for sedition, Duffy entered Parliament in 1852. Then, losing all hope for parliamentary agitation, he emigrated to Australia, where he became prime minister in 1871. In 1873, he was knighted, and in 1880, he retired to Nice where he died on February 8, 1903. He edited *The Ballad Poetry of Ireland*, an anthology which contained pieces by John Banim,* J. J. Callanan,* William Carleton,* Thomas Davis, William Drennan,* Samuel Lover,* James Mangan,*

Thomas Moore,* and many others, and which went through more than fifty editions. His own few poems are spirited and fluent, if conventional.

WORKS: ed., *The Ballad Poetry of Ireland*. Dublin: Duffy, 1845; *Young Ireland: A Fragment of Irish History, 1840-1850*. London & New York: Cassell, Petter, Galpin, 1880; *Four Years of Irish History, 1845-1849*. London & New York: Cassell, Petter, Galpin, 1883. *The League of North and South: An Episode in Irish History, 1850-1854*. London: Chapman & Hall, 1886; *Thomas Davis*. London: Kegan Paul, Trench, 1890; *Conversations with Carlyle*. London: Sampson, Low, 1892; *What Irishmen May Do for Irish Literature*. London, 1892; *The Prospects of Irish Literature for the People*. London: Printed for private circulation, 1893; *The Revival of Irish Literature*. Addresses by Sir Charles Gavan Duffy, Dr. George Sigerson, & Dr. Douglas Hyde. London: Fisher Unwin, 1894; *My Life in Two Hemispheres*. 2 vols. London: Fisher Unwin, 1898.   REFERENCE: O Broin, Leon. *Charles Gavan Duffy: Patriot and Statesman*. Dublin: Duffy, 1967.

DUFFY, JAMES (ca. 1809-1871), publisher. Duffy, the founder of the publishing house which still bears his name, was born in County Monaghan in about 1809 and educated at a hedge-school. He became a small Dublin bookseller, establishing himself by buying up Protestant Bibles which the Bible Society would give to Catholics and which they would pawn. He then took the Bibles to Liverpool and traded them for more salable volumes. Originally in an obscure shop in Anglesea Street, Duffy had been publishing popular thrillers which sold at a mere twopence each, when he was approached by the editors of *The Nation** to print books for them. *The Spirit of the Nation* and the "Library of Ireland" volumes sold hugely, and Duffy was able to move to larger premises on Wellington Quay, where at one time he is said to have employed 120 people. After 1848, his business was in occasional difficulties, but he continued to run it, his patriotic Young Ireland books being the staple of his list. He died on July 4, 1871.

During most of the twentieth century, James Duffy and Company was located at Westmoreland Street and published many plays by new Irish writers, although the Duffy list in no measure rivaled that of Maunsel and Company.* During the great flourishing of the amateur drama that lasted at least until the coming of television in the 1960s, there was a good market for inexpensive acting copies. That market has much diminished, but the firm lingers on, publishing a few volumes each year from obscure premises on Shaw Street.

DUN EMER PRESS. *See* CUALA PRESS.

DUNNE, [CHRISTOPHER] LEE (1934-), novelist and scriptwriter. Dunne was born in Dublin on December 21, 1934. He has followed many professions—sailor, singer, actor, taxi-driver, and scriptwriter for an interminable serial on Radio Éireann. His first and very promising novel, *Goodbye to the Hill* (1965), contains an evocative recreation of a work-

ing-class section of Dublin. Even his poorer second novel, *A Bed in the
Sticks* (1968), contains interesting details about an actor's life in the fit-ups,
or provincial touring companies which played in the smallest towns. His
style is colloquial, simple, and usually told in the first person. It seems to
be modeled on the neo-American style of "tough" writing for popular
magazines. A typical paragraph reads:

> On the way down we went into the convent at Milltown. Ma held
> me with one hand. In the other she carried a half-gallon can. An
> old nun filled the can with soup and bits of meat and potatoes and
> my mother thanked her, and there was a lot of talk about the good
> God in his almighty glory, blessing you and yours. I hated the sight
> of the nun in her long robe or whatever it's called, but I gave her
> a smile that warmed her feet. I liked the look of the soup.

This pared-to-the-bone style, a legacy from Hemingway and his many
imitators, can quickly pall. Dunne's subsequent novels have been simple
and lurid entertainments for the mass paperback market. His stage version
of *Goodbye to the Hill* was produced with some success at the Oscar
Theatre in Dublin in the fall of 1978.

WORKS: *Goodbye to the Hill*. London: Hutchinson, 1965; *A Bed in the Sticks*.
London: Hutchinson, 1968; *Does Your Mother*. London: Arrow, 1970; *Paddy
Maguire Is Dead*. London: Arrow, 1972; *Midnight Cabbie*. London: Coronet, 1974;
The Cabbie Who Came in from the Cold. London: Coronet, 1975; *The Cabfather*.
London: Coronet, 1975; *Maggie's Story*. London: Futura, 1975.

DUNSANY, LORD (1878-1957), fantasist, playwright, and short story
writer. The ancestral home of Edward John Morton Drax Plunkett, the
eighteenth Baron Dunsany, is near Tara in County Meath, but the future
Lord Dunsany was born on July 24, 1878, at 15 Park Square in the Regents
Park Section of London. Dunsany was the chess champion of Ireland, a
great sportsman, a brave soldier, a dedicated family man, and an adventurer,
as well as a man of letters. Unlike other writers of the Irish Renaissance,
such as Yeats,* Synge,* Colum,* and even James Joyce,* Dunsany was
neither of old Celtic stock, Irish Catholic peasantry, or Protestant ascen-
dancy-turned-Irish-nationalist. He was a loyal British subject who fought
for the Crown in Africa, France, and Dublin, and his associations were
with the British aristocracy more than with the Irish serfdom with whom
many of his contemporaries sought so painstakingly to identify themselves.
One of the principal aims of the Irish Literary Revival, the glorification of
Ireland, had no place in the Dunsany canon, although he knew all of the
main figures in the movement and his first play, *The Glittering Gate*
(1909), was written in response to a request from Yeats for a production
for the Abbey.*

The Dunsany family was founded by a Norman, John Plunkett, after the Norman conquest of Ireland in the twelfth century. Dunsany's remarkable life encompassed eighty years and represented the nearly idyllic combination of activities requisite of one of the oldest peerages in the British Empire. His first formal training came from a local school in Kent. He then attended his father's school, Cheam, where he learned the Greek language and the mythology which he emulated in so many of his works. He also became acquainted with Grimm's and Anderson's fairy tales, the works of Edgar Allan Poe, and the strategies of tournament chess.

From Cheam he went to Eton, and then to a crammer in Dublin, later qualifying for Sandhurst, from which he graduated with a military education. He next joined the Coldstream Guards and was soon transferred to Gibraltar. There he developed his fascination for the Near East in the settings that he was to use in his tales *The Fall of Babbulkund* and *A Fortress Unvanquishable Save for Sacnath*. With the beginning of the Boer War, Dunsany transferred to South Africa, where he saw extensive combat and met Rudyard Kipling, who became a lifelong friend.

After the war, he returned to Meath and the duties of his estate. In 1904, he married Lady Beatrice Villiers, who became his most devoted reader, his sometime secretary, and his honest critic. His first book, *The Gods of Pegana*, was published at his own expense in 1905 by Elkin Mathews. The book was successful and was followed quickly by two others, *Time and the Gods* and *The Sword of Welleran*. He began to dictate to Lady Dunsany and wrote with exceptional speed and great productivity. Dictation accounts in part for the enormous quantity of his writing, but even in Lady Dunsany's absence he turned out whole plays in an afternoon with quill and ink. Although the Dunsanys traveled a great deal in Europe, America, North and Central Africa, and India, all the time he was producing short stories, plays, and novels at an exceptionally rapid pace.

During World War I, Dunsany joined the Royal Inniskilling Fusiliers. While at home on a weekend pass for the Easter holiday of 1916, he came to Dublin to see how he might help quell the rebellion. He was shot through the head and taken to a hospital which was under siege for nearly a week. He recovered slowly and then was sent to France, where he again saw front-line combat. Later during the war, he was transferred to British Intelligence, where he wrote propaganda items, articles, stories, and books for the government. The least of his literary accomplishments, *Tales of War* (1918), was a product of his military service. Between the two world wars, Dunsany became an international chess player, a big game hunter, and a celebrated lecturer in the United States and Great Britain. During those years, his literary acquaintanceships included H. G. Wells, Oliver St. John Gogarty,* and Mary Lavin.*

Throughout his career, Dunsany felt the lack of critical scholarly recognition of his work on the one hand and a good deal of popular success, especially with his dramas and fantasies, on the other. He sensed a sort of reverse snobbery in the critical barbs he received, feeling that critics considered him a sort of dilettante, taking bread out of the mouths of honest professional writers. He was often regarded as being in a sort of literary limbo. Perhaps much of this attitude stemmed from the fact that Dunsany did not write for any identifiable literary movement or faction. Although he produced a few plays for Yeats and the Abbey Theatre over the course of years, and though these were popular successes in America as well as in England and Ireland, Dunsany could hardly have received great national accolades in a country in which he was so preeminently for the British Crown and so apolitical in his creative work. His reputation as a playwright equals his fame as a fiction writer. He specialized in one act plays, though his full-length plays were among his best.

His prose works are primarily stories of the fantastic and beautiful. His prose is much like poetry, often nearly metrical and highly stylized, occasionally even Biblical. His stories dealing with the remote and exotic are heavily romantic in character. A forerunner of such writers as Tolkien, Dunsany created his own mythology with people, planets, and lands removed from ours in time and temperament, but redeemed by a pervasive humor which was part of Dunsany's own character both in and out of his literary works. He was unpretentious throughout his life and possessed a sense of the incongruous which was reflected in his stories by a puckish sense of the ludicrous.

Dunsany collaborated with the well-known illustrator S. H. Sime on a large number of his works. Sime's illustrations, uncharitably called by a critic a combination of Blake and Beardsley but without the messages of either, were as fanciful and elaborate as Dunsany's tales. They are neither deep nor difficult to grasp but are filled with the exotic wonder of fantasy and fairy tales. Dunsany eschews the difficult and erudite, claiming such heavy intellectual endeavors are out of place as the matter of serious literature, which he regarded as principally escapist and pleasure producing.

Most of Dunsany's characters, lacking individuality, depth, and verisimilitude, are principally the instruments of plot. His narratives inspire readers with leaps of fantastic imagination, but make little attempt to probe psychological complexities or establish intricacies of theme or symbol. Later Dunsany critics often saw his work as heavily symbolic, but such symbolism was certainly not part of the author's initial intent.

Dunsany, did, however, develop one of the drollest contemporary literary characters in a barfly named Joseph Jorkens, whose fabulations, chiefly in return for drinks at the mythical Billiards Club, encompassed five volumes. Jorkens' character is archetypal, lovable, and often Dickensian. While Jorkens expected to be believed, his tales defy credulity. In a sense, Jorkens and Dunsany are much alike in their narration of the fantastic, in their search for artistic approbation, and in their abundant good humor. Dunsany's prolific career is evidenced by more than fifty-five published volumes and hundreds of plays, articles, and introductions. He died in Dublin on October 25, 1957.

ZACK BOWEN

WORKS: *The Gods of Pegana*. London: Elkin Mathews, 1905; *Time and the Gods*. London: Heinemann, 1906; *The Sword of Welleran*. London: George Allen, 1908; *A Dreamer's Tales*. London: George Allen, 1910; *The Book of Wonder*. London: Heinemann, 1912; *Five Plays*. London: Grant Richards, 1914; *51 Tales*. London: Elkin Mathews, 1915; *Tales of Wonder*. London: Elkin Mathews, 1916; *Plays of Gods and Men*. Dublin: Talbot, 1917; *Tales of War*. London & New York: Putnam, 1918; *Tales of Three Hemispheres*. Boston: Luce, 1919; *Unhappy Far-off Things*. London: Elkin Mathews, 1919; *If*. London & New York: Putnam, 1921; *The Chronicles of Rodrigues*. London & New York: Putnam, 1922; *Plays of Far and Near*. London & New York: Putnam, 1922; *The King of Elfland's Daughter*. London & New York: Putnam, 1924; *Alexander*. London & New York: Putnam, 1925; *The Charwoman's Shadow*. London & New York: Putnam, 1926; *The Blessings of Pan*. London & New York: Putnam, 1927; *Seven Modern Comedies*. London & New York: Putnam, 1928; *50 Poems*. London & New York: Putnam, 1929; *The Old Folk of the Centuries*. London: Elkin Mathews, 1930; *The Travel Tales of Mr. Joseph Jorkens*. London & New York: Putnam, 1931; *Lord Adrian*. Cranberry, N.J.: Golden Cockerel Press, 1933; *If I Were Dictator*. London: Methuen, 1934; *Jorkens Remembers Africa*. London: Heinemann, 1934; *The Curse of the Wise Woman*. London: Heinemann, 1935; *Mr. Faithful*. New York: Samuel French, 1935; *Up in the Hills*. London: Heinemann, 1935; *My Talks with Dean Spanley*. London: Heinemann, 1936; *Rory and Bran*. London: Heinemann, 1936; *My Ireland*. New York: Jarrolds, 1937; *Plays for Earth and Air*. London: Heinemann, 1937; *Mirage Water*. London & New York: Putnam, 1938; *Patches of Sunlight*. London: Heinemann, 1938; *The Story of Mona Sheehy*. London: Heinemann, 1939; *Jorkens Has a Large Whiskey*. London & New York: Putnam, 1940; *War Poems*. London: Hutchinson, 1940; *Wandering Songs*. London: Hutchinson, 1943; *Guerilla*. London: Heinemann, 1944; *The Journey*. London. Macdonald, 1944; *While the Sirens Slept*. London: Hutchinson, 1944; *The Donellan Lecture 1943*. London: Heinemann, 1945; *The Sirens Wake*. London & New York: Jarrolds, 1945; *A Glimpse from a Watchtower*. London & New York: Jarrolds, 1946; *The Year*. London & New York: Jarrolds, 1946; *The Man Who Ate the Phoenix*. London & New York: Jarrolds, 1947; *The Odes of Horace,* translated into English Verse. London: Heinemann, 1947; *The Fourth Book of Jorkens*. London & New York: Jarrolds, 1948; *To Awaken Pegasus*. Oxford: G. Ronald, 1949; *The Strange Journeys of Colonel Polders*. London & New York: Jarrolds, 1950; *His Fellow Men*. London & New York: Jarrolds, 1951; *The Last Revolution*. London & New York: Jarrolds, 1951; *The Little Tales of Smethers*. London & New York: Jarrolds, 1952; *Jorkens Borrows Another Whiskey*. London: Michael Joseph, 1954.   REFERENCES: Amory, Mark. *A Biography of Lord Dunsany*. London: Collins, 1972; Bierstadt, Edward Hale. *Dunsany The Dramatist*. Boston: Little Brown, 1917; Boyd, Ernest A. *Appreciations and Depreciations*. Freeport: Books for Libraries, 1918; Saul, George Brandan. "Strange Gods in Far Places: The Short Stories of Lord Dunsany." *Arizona Quarterly* 19 (Autumn 1963): 197-210.

DURCAN, PAUL (1944-), poet. Durcan was born in Dublin in October 1944 and graduated from University College, Cork, with First Class Honors in archaeology and medieval history. A selection of his poems received the Patrick Kavanagh Award for Poetry in 1974 and was incorporated in the first of his two published volumes. The material in these volumes, as well as his fugitive work, must be described as "writings" rather than as poetry. His work strives toward form—and paradoxically—only in his spasmodic attempts to dispense with conventional punctuation. His strength is in the occasional vividness of his diction, but it is so far an intermittent strength.

WORKS: *O Westport in the Light of Asia Minor*. Dun Laoghaire: Anna Livia Books, Dublin Magazine Press, 1975; *Teresa's Bar*. Dublin: Gallery Books, 1976; *Sam's Cross*. Dublin: Profiler, 1978.

EDGEWORTH, MARIA (1767-1849), novelist. If the term *Anglo-Irish Literature* designates those works written by Irish writers on Irish subjects, Maria Edgeworth's novels have a reasonable claim to be considered the first Anglo-Irish novels. Surely she is the first regional novelist, as Sir Walter Scott recognized. Yet, her place in literary history is not just one of influence, for several of her novels have artistic merit of their own.

Edgeworth was born on January 1, 1767, the third child of Richard Lovell Edgeworth by the first of his four wives. Because he had large families by the later wives, and because Maria exhibited a keen mind and a willing spirit, he enlisted her to help in the task of educating her younger stepbrothers and stepsisters. From 1782 when the family settled in Edgeworthstown, County Longford, Maria worked with her father, formulating an ideal system of education, developing a humane system for treating his tenants, and, of course, teaching the children. Like John Stuart Mill's father, whom he resembled in many ways, Richard Edgeworth was a powerful influence on his children, stressing mature analysis, utility, and equity in all considerations.

It was her father's interest in theories of education which prompted her first attempts at serious writing: children's stories. They reveal her skill even from the start, but they are laden with morals. With her father, Maria wrote various essays on education, collected in *Practical Education* (1798).

In 1800, Edgeworth's major novel, *Castle Rackrent*, was published. Its subject and its artistry qualify it as the first Anglo-Irish novel. It is a tale of the decline of the Rackrent family over several generations, as told by the family steward, Thady Quirk. Although the novel is short and the plot uncomplicated, Edgeworth's skill at characterization is remarkable. Each of the characters is portrayed with economy and deft skill. The moral is clear but not ponderous: the family's irresponsibility as landlords leads to destruction. But the author's greatest achievement lies in the creation of the narrator. It is Thady who inherits it all at the end, and so he has a special interest in telling the tale throughout—a certain ironic view which is both credible and appealing. His speech seems right, although the dialect seems stylized to modern readers. Thady is unreliable, of course, for he had a vested interest in what happened; and the tale is told in retrospect, after Thady has become respectable. The very use of such an involved narrator advanced the novel in important ways, and the novel realized one of its objectives: to make the English reading public aware of the island which they either misunderstood or disregarded. It gave rise to a taste for fiction about Ireland and other regions of Britain outside of fashionable London. Edgeworth's reminder was deliberately timed, for the Act of Union, by the time the novel was composed, was recognized as inevitable.

Edgeworth continued to treat Irish subjects in her later fiction: in *Ennui* (1809) and *The Absentee* (1812). Like her father, she continued to attack the neglect of landlords and the irresponsibility of the landed gentry. But these novels rely on comic characters and plots more extensively than did *Castle Rackrent*.

Ormond, which appeared in 1817, resembles Fielding's *Tom Jones* in its humor, fast-paced plot, and, most of all, in its depiction of the education of a lively young man. It is a novel of education, like most of Edgeworth's stories, but again it serves as a reminder to the English of how little they knew of Ireland in the previous century.

After her father's death in 1817, Edgeworth wrote less. She finished his memoirs, which he had left uncompleted at his death, and supervised the edition of her Collected Works, which ran to eighteen volumes. Her last novel, *Helen*, appeared in 1834; it shows how firm her control of characterization remained, and it contains some exceptionally strong women characters.

During the Great Famine, Edgeworth acted on her principles by working tirelessly to help the tenants and peasants of the area; she died shortly thereafter, on May 22, 1849.

Sometimes cited as an influence on her friend Sir Walter Scott, on Thackeray, and even on Turgenev, Maria Edgeworth achieved much in her literary career. She was a skillful social critic who could pinpoint the pretenses and misunderstandings of the English when viewing their Irish neighbors without venom or exaggeration. She had a lively, inquisitive mind which proceeded beyond social manners to intellectual analysis. In this regard, the often-raised comparison with Jane Austen is justified. She was an effective theorist on education; her essays on the subject are consistent and reasonable. She even had an attractive sense of humor. The moral points of most of her stories and novels do not seem overbearing, largely because they are mixed with such comic scenes. In her children's stories and her essays on education, she portrayed children more convincingly than did her predecessors. If she was unable to present the Irish peasant in the detail which Carleton* did, she nevertheless recognized his presence and asserted his humanity. She was a spokesman for the landed class in Ireland, but a most humane one, convinced that the major responsibility for improving life for the Irish people rested with her own class.

More lasting than any of these qualities is Edgeworth's achievement as a literary craftsman. Her perfect choice of incident and telling detail make her novels short but satisfying. Through the use of an involved narrator, she succeeded in conveying ironic effects with relevant points. Regarding her major novel, Thomas Flanagan, in *The Irish Novelists 1800-1850*, notes that it is Thady who creates the myth of the nobility of the Rackrent family, and it is finally a fiction which serves his own gratification. In all her works a moral intention is prominent; yet, it is conveyed with such a light touch that an ideal kind of fiction is achieved.

JAMES KILROY

WORKS: *Letters for Literary Ladies*. London: J. Johnson, 1795; *The Parent's Assistant; or Stories for Children*. 2 vols. London: J. Johnson, 1796. (An expanded edition in 6 vols. appeared in 1800); *Practical Education*. 2 vols. London: J. Johnson, 1798; *A Rational Primer*. London: J. Johnson, 1799; *Castle Rackrent*. London: J. Johnson, 1800; *Early Lessons*. London: J. Johnson, 1801; *Belinda*. 3 vols. London: J. Johnson, 1801; *Moral Tales for Young People*. 5 vols. London: J. Johnson, 1801; *Essay on Irish Bulls*, with Richard Lovell Edgeworth. London: J. Johnson, 1802; *Popular Tales*. London: J. Johnson, 1805; *Leonora*. 2 vols. London: J. Johnson, 1806. *Essays on Professional Education*. London: J. Johnson, 1809. (This volume was published solely under her father's name, but Maria collaborated on it); *Tales of Fashionable Life*. 3 vols. London: J. Johnson, 1809; *Tales of Fashionable Life*. 3 vols. London: J. Johnson, 1812; *Continuation of Early Lessons*. 2 vols. London: J. Johnson, 1814; *Patronage*. 4 vols. London: J. Johnson, 1814; *Readings on Poetry*, with Richard Lovell Edgeworth. London: R. Hunter, 1816; *Harrington, a Tale; and Ormond, a Tale*. 3 vols. London: R. Hunter, Baldwin, Cradock & Joy, 1817; *Comic Dramas in 3 Acts*. London: R. Hunter, etc., 1817. (Contains *Love and Law, The Two Guardians*, and *The Rose, Thistle and Shamrock*); *Memoirs of Richard Lovell Edgeworth, Esq.*, begun by himself and concluded by Maria. 2 vols. London: R. Hunter, etc., 1820; *Rosamund*. 2 vols. London: R. Hunter, etc., 1821; *Frank*. 3 vols. London: R. Hunter, etc., 1822; *Harry and Lucy*. 4 vols. London: R. Hunter, etc., 1825; *Tales and Miscellaneous Pieces*. 14 vols. London: R. Hunter, etc., 1825; *Little Plays for Children*. London: R. Hunter, etc., 1827; *Garry Owen; or, The Snow-Woman: and Poor Bob, the Chimney-Sweeper*. London: J. Murray, 1832; *Tales and Novels*. 18 vols. London: Baldwin, etc., 1832-1833; *Helen*. 3 vols. London: R. Bentley, 1834. *Orlandino*. Edinburgh: W. & R. Chambers, 1848; *The Novels of M. Edgeworth*. 12 vols. London: J. M. Dent/New York: Dodd, Mead, 1893. REFERENCES: Butler, H. J., & Butler, H. E. *The Black Book of Edgeworthstown and Other Memories*. London: Faber & Gwyer, 1927; Butler, Marilyn. *Maria Edgeworth: A Literary Biography*. Oxford: Clarendon Press, 1972; Clarke, Isabel C. *Maria Edgeworth, Her Family and Friends*. London: Hutchinson, 1949; Edgeworth, Mrs. F. A. *A Memoir of M. Edgeworth with Selections from Her Letters*. 3 vols. London: Privately printed, 1867; Flanagan, Thomas. *The Irish Novelists 1800-1850*. New York: Columbia University Press, 1959, pp. 53-106; Harden, O. Elizabeth McWhorter. *Maria Edgeworth's Art of Prose Fiction*. The Hague: Mouton, 1971; Hare, Augustus. *The Life and Letters of Maria Edgeworth*. 2 vols. London: Arnold, 1894; Hausermann, H. W. *The Genevese Background*. London: Routledge & Kegan Paul, 1952; Hawthorne, Mark D. *Doubt and Dogma in Maria Edgeworth*. Gainesville: University of Florida Press, 1967; Hill, Constance. *Maria Edgeworth and Her Circle in the Days of Buonaparte and Bourbon*. London & New York: John Lane, 1910; Hurst, Michael. *Maria Edgeworth and the Public Scene*. London: Macmillan, 1969; Inglis-Jones, Elisabeth. *The Great Maria*. London: Faber, 1959; Lawless, Emily. *Maria Edgeworth*. London: Macmillan, 1904; Newby, Percy H. *Maria Edgeworth*. London: A. Barker, 1950. Newcomer, James. *Maria Edgeworth the Novelist, 1768-1849*. Forth Worth: Texas Christian University Press, 1967; Zimmern, Helen. *Maria Edgeworth*. London: Allen, 1883.

EGAN, DESMOND (ca. 1940-), poet and publisher. Egan was born in Athlone and was educated at Mullingar and at University College, Dublin, where he received an M.A. in 1965. He founded the Goldsmith Press in 1972 and the occasional literary magazine *Era* in 1974. Physically, the Goldsmith books are both striking and amateurish. Some of Egan's notable authors have been Michael Hartnett*, Eugene Watters, Kevin Faller, and Desmond O'Grady.* He has also published a posthumous novel, *By Night Unstarred*, by Patrick Kavanagh.*

Egan's own early poetry is a language of words and phrases rather than of sentences. His free verse is usually made up of short, even one-word lines. Despite the occasional dramatic image, the effect is usually more erratic than poetic. His best, and at this date most recent, volume is *Woodcutters* (1978), in which he uses various devices of punctuation to attain intensity. However, there is only so much that italics and capitalization can do for limp diction. Some few poems, such as "when DNNNNNNNNNN" and "The Old Question: *What Next?*", have details that are so well and forcefully chosen that a language of ebullient assertion partially compensates for the lack of technique.

WORKS: *Midland*. Dublin: Goldsmith, 1973; ed., with Michael Hartnett, *Choice*. Dublin: Goldsmith, 1973. (Poetry anthology); *Leaves*. Castleknock, County Dublin: Goldsmith, 1974; *Siege*. The Curragh, County Kildare: Goldsmith, 1976; *Woodcutter*. Dublin: Goldsmith, 1978.

EGLINTON, JOHN (1868-1961), essayist. John Eglinton was the pseudonym of William Kirkpatrick Magee, who was born in Dublin in 1868, the second son of a Presbyterian clergyman. Magee and W. B. Yeats* were classmates at the High School. Magee then went on to be a classical honorsman at Trinity College and four times won the Vice-Chancellor's Prize for the best composition in English, Greek, or Latin verse, the examiners being the redoubtable trio of Mahaffy,* Tyrrell, and Dowden. After his graduation, he went to work at the National Library, much against his will, and remained there from 1895 to 1921. He appears in the Scylla and Charibdys chapter of Joyce's* *Ulysses*, which is set in the library, and is treated with more respect than Joyce usually accorded his real-life subjects. Magee was an early member of the theosophical movement in Dublin, and his many friends included AE,* Stephen MacKenna,* and George Moore* who describes him in *Hail and Farewell* as "a sort of lonely thorn tree." Magee, who for a time acted more or less as Moore's secretary, said that Moore was "almost intolerably tedious about literary trifles."

Although somewhat austere and aloof, Magee's John Eglinton essays were highly regarded. His two early volumes, *Two Essays on the Remnant* and *Pebbles from a Brook*, are full of transcendental generalization. He later wrote of them, "There was a young man in the nineties into whom the very breath of Emerson and Thoreau had entered, with those tongue he spoke (or at least in their tone of voice). Now there is a battered and somewhat incredulous person who blushes when he runs across some quotation from either book." Nevertheless, W. B. Yeats, who crossed swords with Magee in the press, called him "our one Irish critic," but one who was "in permanent friendly opposition to our national literary movement." "Opposition" was too strong a word, for Magee and Fred Ryan* did launch one of the important, if too shortlived, magazines of the literary movement. This was *Dana*, which appeared twelve times from May 1904 through April 1905. Among the contributors were AE, Colum,* Gogarty,* Joyce (whose *Portrait of the Artist* was rejected as a serial), George Moore, Seumas O'Sullivan,* and W. B. Yeats. In 1920, Magee married M. L. O'Leary who worked with him at the National Library. After the formation of the Free State, Magee found himself out of sympathy with the new Ireland and moved to England where he died in Bournemouth on May 9, 1961. His important later books were his *Irish Literary Portraits* (1935) and *Memoir of A.E.* (1937).

WORKS: *Two Essays on the Remnant*. Dublin: Whaley, 1894; *Bards and Saints*. Dublin: Maunsel, 1899; *Pebbles from a Brook*. Kilkenny & Dublin: Standish O'Grady, 1901; *Some Essays and Passages by John Eglinton*, selected by W. B. Yeats. Dublin: Dun Emer, 1905; *Anglo-Irish Essays*. Dublin: Talbot/London: T. Fisher Unwin, 1917; ed. and trans., G. Moore, *Letters to Edouard Dujardin*. New York: Crosby Gaige, 1929; *Irish Literary Portraits*. London: Macmillan, 1935/reprint, Freeport, N.Y.: Books for Libraries, 1967; *A Memoir of A.E.* London: Macmillan, 1937; ed., *Letters of George Moore, with an Introduction by John Eglinton, to Whom They Were Written*. Bournemouth: Sydenham, [1942]; *Confidential; or, Take It or Leave It*. London: Fortune, 1951. (Poems).

ELLMANN, RICHARD (1918-), American biographer and critic. Although he is an American, Ellmann has made a major contribution to Irish letters by his superbly thorough literary biography of James Joyce.* He has also edited a two-volume addition to Stuart Gilbert's collection of Joyce's letters and written some subtle academic criticism of W. B. Yeats* and Wilde.* He was born on March 15, 1918, in Highland Park, Michigan, and was educated at Yale and at Trinity College, Dublin. He has taught at Harvard, Northwestern, Indiana, Chicago, and Oxford.

WORKS: *Yeats, the Man and the Masks*. New York: Macmillan, 1948/London: Macmillan, 1949; *The Identity of Yeats*. London: Macmillan/New York: Oxford University Press, 1954; *James Joyce*. New York: Oxford University Press, 1959; ed., *Letters of James Joyce*. Vols. 2 & 3. New York: Viking, 1966; *Eminent Domain: Yeats among Wilde, Joyce, Pound, Eliot, and Auden*. New York: Oxford University Press, 1967; *Ulysses on the Liffey*. New York: Oxford University Press, 1972; *Golden Codgers*. New York: Oxford University Press, 1973; ed., *Selected Letters of James Joyce*. London: Faber, 1975. (Contains several significant and elsewhere unpublished letters from Joyce to his wife.)

EMMET, ROBERT (1778-1803), nationalist. Emmet was born in Cork on March 4, 1778, and was executed in Dublin on September 20, 1803. The abortive rising which he led had enormous impractical influence in Irish history. His noble speech from the dock and his appealing love affair with Sarah Curran have captured the imagination of succeeding generations. The tale of Bold Robert Emmet, the Darlin' of Erin, has been celebrated by dozens of writers, among them his friend Thomas Moore,* and by the playwrights Lennox Robinson,* Denis Johnston,* Paul Vincent Carroll,* John O'Donovan,* and Conor Farrington.* His speech from the dock concludes with these famous lines:

> I have but one request to make at my departure from this world, it is—the charity of its silence. Let no man write my epitaph; for as no man, who knows my motives, dare now vindicate them, let not prejudice or ignorance asperse them. Let them rest in obscurity and peace! Let my memory be left in oblivion, and my tomb remain uninscribed, until other times and other men can do justice to my character. When my country takes her place among the nations of the earth, *then*, and *not till then*, let my epitaph be written. I have done.

By his great speech, Emmet made a small eloquent addition to Irish literature; by his death, he had an incalculable emotional effect on Irish history.

ENNIS, JOHN (1944-), poet. Ennis, born in Westmeath in 1944, was educated at University College, Cork, and at University College, Dublin. He lives and teaches in Waterford. He won the Patrick Kavanagh* Award in 1975; published his first volume, *Night on Hibernia*, in 1976; and won the Open Poetry Competition at Listowel Writers' Week in 1976 and 1977. His "Orpheus," which won at Listowel in 1977, forms the bulk of his book published later in the year, *Dolmen Hill*.

Night on Hibernia is rather foppishly full of unusual words, such as lixiviate, helices, guillemot, filbert, haulms, glaubed, grume, waifed, berried, undine, lactic, staggy, glaur, condescent, britchen, cutis, smalt, prepuce, amnion, nard, pelagic. It is also full of many faintly awkward coined words, such as hiss-lipped, haw-warm, grassovered, dew-greasy, thunder-tiered, starling-crowned, defunct-winged, truthhoods. And many of the sentences are rather scrunched up, as if written by an enormously literate Tarzan. For instance, "Son, father wake, exit greyly once-trodden familiar haunts/ Kitchen, sheds, fields." Nevertheless, the volume reeks with talent.

Dolmen Hill is even more interesting. In this work, Ennis writes in extremely long lines; therefore, his occasional rhyming is usually ineffective. Still, as symptoms of growth, it might be noted that the erratic punctuation of the first volume is less in evidence, and the language is fascinating. Many tersely jammed-up short sentences still occur without that usual grease of discourse, the article "the"; and so the poet still sometimes sounds like a lobotomized German in a basic English language course. But his "Orpheus," for all of its cluttering obfuscation and silly eclecticism of diction, must still be considered the most amazing long poem any Irish poet has written since Kavanagh's* *The Great Hunger*.

WORKS: *Night on Hibernia*. Dublin: Gallery Books, 1976; *Dolmen Hill*. Dublin: Gallery Books, 1977.

ENVOY (1949-1951), literary magazine. *Envoy* was the lively but short-lived literary magazine whose editor was John Ryan*and whose poetry editor was Valentin Iremonger.* The magazine first appeared in December 1949, and in all, it published twenty monthly numbers. It is important chiefly for the forum it gave to Patrick Kavanagh,* but Brendan Behan,* Brian O'Nolan,* Sean O'Faolain,* Francis Stuart,* and many other important writers also appeared in its pages.

ERVINE, ST. JOHN GREER (1883-1971), playwright. John Greer Ervine (the "St." was added when he began to write) was born in Ballymacarrett, in suburban Belfast, on December 28, 1883. Moving to London at the age of seventeen, he became acquainted with Bernard Shaw* and the Fabian Society, and developed an interest in repertory theatre. Between 1911 and 1915, Ervine contributed to the Abbey* four plays of Ulster life: *Mixed Marriage*, *The Magnanimous Lover*, *The Orangeman*, and *John Ferguson*.

Ervine was appointed manager of the Abbey in the autumn of 1915. Rejecting all that was distinctive in the theatre, he sought to convert it into a typical repertory theatre. By the end of the season, all of the actors had resigned or were dismissed by the contentious, outspoken manager. The Abbey directors had to replace Ervine and rebuild a company. He then went into military service and in 1918 suffered a wound which necessitated the amputation of one leg.

In the 1920s, Ervine wrote drawing room comedies for London theatres. His only work for the Abbey was the sarcastically titled *The Isle of Saints*. In 1924, the Gaiety, Dublin, staged Ervine's *The Ship*, a father-son conflict spoiled by an operatic ending. In 1936, he returned to the Abbey stage and an Ulster locale with *Boyd's Shop*, followed by *William John Mawhinney* (1940) and *Friends and Relations* (1941). The Ulster Drama Group in Belfast performed three of his less important plays—*My Brother Tom*, *Ballyfarland's Festival*, and *Martha*—in the 1950s.

His formidable productivity included several novels, abrasive commentary on the theatre of his time (the Abbey did not appear to advantage), and biographies of such personalities as Shaw, Parnell, and Wilde,* which, like Johnson's *Lives*, were more notable for the opinions than for the scholarship.

As drama critic for the *New York World* in 1929, he predictably was at odds with other critics. Ervine married Leonora May Davis in 1911; they had no children. He died in London on January 24, 1971.

Like Lennox Robinson,* Ervine began with localized realism, turned to Londonized sophistication, and then came back to Erin. But whereas Robinson's earliest dramas were apprentice work, Ervine's first creations were successful.

In Ervine's 1911-1915 Ulster dramas, the dominant figure is the fundamentalist patriarch, dogmatic in all things religious and political. Into the seemingly rigid format implied by such characterization Ervine introduced variety. For John McClurg, in *The Orangeman* (1914), July 12 is a chamber of horrors; rheumatism keeps him out of The Parade, and a rebellious son breaks John's drum. John Rainey, in *Mixed Marriage* (1911), is an extremely unwilling party to two "mixed marriages," one between his son and a Catholic girl, and another between Catholic and Protestant workers on strike. Bigotry, in the latter instance, cannily augmented by management, shatters both alliances. At the catastrophic close, with religious warfare churning in the streets and his sons estranged from him, Rainey mutters his apologia, "A wus right." The strength of otherwise melodramatic *John Ferguson* (1915) is molded in the title character, whose Old Testament concepts of right and wrong are shaken when his daughter is raped and his son carries out violent reprisal.

Ulster phariseeism is the topic of *The Magnanimous Lover* (1912). Henry Hinde, "born again" years after fathering an illegitimate child, offers marriage to the mother, whom he admittedly does not love. She turns him down. Replying to journalists who found the subject matter offensive, Ervine wrote *The Critics* (1913), in which reviewers sit in the vestibule of the Abbey and condemn an anti-Irish play by one of the Cork realists, entitled *Hamlet*.

Ervine's work for British theatres has not aged well. The best of the lot, *Mary Mary Quite Contrary* (1923), lightheartedly examines show business personalities. *Anthony and Anna* (1926) is the old formula of the brash, penniless man and the spoiled rich girl. *The First Mrs. Fraser* (1929), a box office triumph, tells of a middle-aged man who wants to end his marriage to a trashy young thing and remarry his first wife. *The Christies* (Glasgow, 1947; Belfast, 1948) is a semi-serious treatment of the rehabilitation of an unrepentant financier who was imprisoned for fraud.

In *Boyd's Shop* (Liverpool, 1936; Abbey, 1936) one sees a changed Ulster, or a changed Ervine. It is no longer the greybeards but the young who are dogmatic and intolerant. The peaceful realm of Andrew Boyd, a grocer descended from grocers, and a superannuated Presbyterian minister, the Reverend Arthur Patterson, is invaded by John Haslett, a rival grocer with modern ideas, and the Reverend Ernest Dunwoody, an ordained social climber. Boyd, too, can say in effect at the close, "A wus right," but his rightness comes from a shrewd, yet kindly, understanding of his fellow men. *Friends and Relations* is set in suburban Belfast, but only the servants are stock Ulster types. Crusty old Sir Samuel Lepper wills his estate to his second cousin, Adam Bothwell, an unread novelist who does not want the money but whose friends and relations do.

Ervine's main contribution to Irish literature is a realism diverging from that of the Cork writers. They see men coarsened by bleak environment; the hardness of Ervine's Ulstermen is a projection of their stony creed. The mothers in Lennox Robinson's and T. C. Murray's* early plays are aggressive and manipulative. The mothers in Ervine's Ulster plays, Martha Martin in his novel *Mrs. Martin's Man* (1914), and the heroine of his play *Jane Clegg* (Manchester, 1913) all have an infinite capacity for endurance and self-denial.

Life in the North is judiciously examined in Ervine's writing. One finds characters narrow in bigotry and supple in hypocrisy, along with those who possess the traits Ervine commends—integrity, patience, and industry. Throughout his biography of Bernard Shaw, he praises the upright workingman and worries about the erosion of character which a welfare state might cause. Ervine also brought the agonies of divided Belfast onto the stage several years before Scan O'Casey* did as much for Dublin.

Compared to the coarse texture of his serious work, Ervine's comedies may have a satiny feel, but ideas sometimes lurk behind the sheen. *Anthony and Anna*, *Friends and Relations*, *The Christies*, and, to some extent, *Boyd's Shop* bear the common theme of what Alexander Pope called the Use of Riches.

Whatever his truculent personality, whatever temporary harm he wrought as manager of the Abbey, St. John Ervine was a conscientious craftsman, artistically at home in a "smart set" drawing room or in an Ulster cottage.

W I L L I A M   J.   F E E N E Y

WORKS: *Four Irish Plays (Mixed Marriage, The Magnanimous Lover, The Critics, The Orangeman)*. Dublin: Maunsel, 1914; *Jane Clegg*. London: Sidgwick & Jackson, 1914; *Mrs. Martin's Man*. Dublin: Maunsel, 1914. (Novel); *Alice and a Family*. Dublin: Maunsel, 1915. (Novel); *John Ferguson: A Play in Four Acts*. Dublin: Maunsel, 1915; *Sir Edward Carson and the Ulster Movement*. Dublin: Maunsel, 1915; "The Case For Conscription." *New Ireland* 2 (July 3, 1915): 118-120; "After the Abbey." *New Ireland* 2 (March 4, 1916): 277-278; *The Ship: A Play in Three Acts*. New York: Macmillan, 1922; *Mary Mary Quite Contrary: A Light Comedy in Four Acts*. London: Allen & Unwin, 1923; *The Organized Theatre: A Plea in Civics*. New York: Macmillan, 1924; *Anthony and Anna: A Comedy in Three Acts*. New York: Macmillan, 1925; *Parnell*. Boston: Little, Brown, 1927; *How to Write a Play*. London: Allen & Unwin, 1928; *The First Mrs. Fraser: A Comedy in Three Acts*. New York: Macmillan, 1930; *The Theatre of My Time*. London: Rich & Cowan, 1933; *God's Soldier: General William Booth*. London: Macmillan, 1935; *Boyd's Shop: A Comedy in Four Acts*. London: Allen & Unwin, 1936; *Friends and Relations: A Comedy in Three Acts*. London: Allen & Unwin, 1947; *The Christies: A Play in Three Acts*. London: Allen & Unwin, 1948; *Oscar Wilde: A Present Time Appraisal*. London: Allen & Unwin, 1951; *My Brother Tom: A Country Comedy in Three Acts*. London: Allen & Unwin, 1952; *Bernard Shaw, His Life, Work, and Friends*. New York:

William Morrow, 1956.   REFERENCES: Bell, Sam Hanna. *Theatre in Ulster.* London & Dublin: Gill & Macmillan, 1972; Boyd, John. "St. John Ervine, a Biographical Note." *Threshold* 25 (Summer 1974): 101-115; Ireland, Denis. "Red Brick City and Its Dramatist: A Note on St. John Ervine." *Envoy* 1 (March 1950): 59-67.

EVANS, PAMELA. *See* WYKHAM, HELEN.

FALLON, PADRAIC (1905-1974), poet and playwright. Fallon is one of the most accomplished but neglected of modern Irish writers. He was born in Athenry, County Galway, on January 3, 1905, and he worked as a customs official for forty years, mainly in Wexford. He contributed widely to periodicals, particularly poetry, but no collection of his work appeared during his lifetime. That fact certainly contributed to his being much less well-known than Austin Clarke* and Patrick Kavanagh* with whom he can be ranked. He died on October 9, 1974, in Kent, England.

A selection of Fallon's poetry was in the press at his death in 1974, and its posthumous appearance collected some of the most controlled and craftsmanlike poems to appear in many years. In his poem "Fin de Siecle," Fallon wrote "Who makes the rhyme/Will have the resonance." However, his own poems do not resonate merely with rhyme, but also with unexpected patterns of rhyme and, more usually, off-rhyme which is used most subtly and satisfyingly. No particular manner or tone of voice or subject is discernible from poem to poem, for the poet plays eclectically with line and stanza length, and his subjects are most various. Those subjects range from local descriptions, dialogues of the blind nineteenth-century Irish poet Anthony Raftery, love poems with a Yeatsian bite, and indeed some of the best poems about Yeats,* as well as some religious poems which are probably his weakest, and some poems of personal reminiscence, such as "Poem for My Mother," "Painting of My Father," and "March Twentysix," which are among his strongest. If any qualities are constant in Fallon's poetry, they would be the richness of his imagery and the power of his rhetoric. His diction ranges from the casual to the eloquently formal, and he is such a phrasemaker that one cannot begin to quote with fairness. His sentences can be a terse five words or lengthy in the Faulknerian mode. Not all of Fallon's fugitive verse has been collected in *Poems*, and there has been some criticism that even better work has been left out. Obviously, he is a major poetic voice, demanding study and assimilation and, quite as much as Clarke or Kavanagh, a Collected Poems.

Fallon also wrote two plays for the stage, *The Seventh Step* (1954) and *Sweet Love Till Morn* (Abbey, 1971), as well as several plays which were broadcast over Radio Éireann. His radio plays included his finest dramatic work, his *Diarmuid and Grainne* (Radio Éireann, 1950) and his masterly *The Vision of Mac Conglinne* (Radio Éireann, 1953). Micheál Ó hAodha, who produced his radio plays, has written that "In many respects, these two plays are the most successful modernizations of old Irish Literature"

(*Theatre in Ireland*, 1974). That seems a highly extravagant statement when one considers that Yeats, Synge,* Stephens,* and so many other remarkable writers have turned their hands to modern versions of classic Irish material. Nevertheless, to anyone who has read the unpublished pieces, the wit, the gusto, and the riot of rhetorical exuberance seem rarely paralleled and hardly excelled in modern Irish dramatic writing. If any modern Irish drama begs for publication, it is surely *The Vision of Mac Conglinne*, and if any modern Irish writer cries out for proper attention and evaluation, it is certainly Padraic Fallon.

WORKS: *Lighting-up Time*. Dublin: Orwell, 1938. (Story); *Poems*. [Dublin]: Dolmen, [1974].

FALLON, PETER (1951-), poet and publisher. Fallon was born on February 26, 1951, in Germany of Irish parents. Except for some teaching and reading tours in America, he has lived in County Meath and in Dublin since 1957. He founded the Gallery Press in February 1970 and as of 1978 the press has published about fifty volumes. His press specializes in new Irish poetry and has published, among others, Eiléan Ní Chuilleanáin,* Desmond O'Grady,* Michael Hartnet,* and MacDara Woods.* Although the typography is open to some criticism, the bindings, end-papers, and jackets of these small volumes are distinctive and handsome. In 1979, the press began publication of a new series of Irish plays, including works by Thomas Murphy,* Eugene McCabe,* and Heno Magee.*

Fallon's own poems have appeared in several small collections. His work is generally in free verse, in which the syntax often tends to get a bit jumbled (as in "She for a Moment Sings") or even ambiguous (as in "A Single Babe").

WORKS: *Among the Walls*. Dublin: Tara Telephone Publications, 1971; *Coincidence of Flesh*. Dublin: Gallery, 1973; *The First Affair*. Dublin: Gallery, 1974; *A Gentler Birth*. Deerfield, Mass.: Deerfield, 1976; *Victims*. Deerfield, Mass.: Deerfield, 1977; *Finding the Dead*. Deerfield Mass.: Deerfield, 1978; *The Speaking Stones*. Dublin: Gallery, 1978.

FARQUHAR, GEORGE (1677-1707), playwright. Biographical information on dramatist George Farquhar is sketchy. The son of an Anglican clergyman, he was born in 1677 in Londonderry, lived through the siege of that city, and may have been with the Williamite army at the Boyne in 1690. After mediocre performances as a student at Trinity and as an actor in Dublin's Smock Alley Theatre, he went to London in 1697 with the script of a comedy, *Love and a Bottle*, which was staged in 1698. His second play, *The Constant Couple* (1699), was a major triumph, but his next three works, *Sir Harry Wildair* (1701), *The Inconstant* (1702), and *The Twin-Rivals* (1702), were failures. Farquhar was chronically impecunious during his short life, and marriage in 1703 brought him a meager dowry. His last two plays are his masterpieces. *The Recruiting Officer* (1706) was based on Farquhar's experience as a recruiter in Shrewsbury in 1704. *The Beaux Stratagem*, written during a fatal illness, was brought on stage shortly before the author's death on about May 23, 1707.

Of the Irish characters in his plays, the most important is Roebuck, "an Irish gentleman of a wild, roving temper, newly come to London," in *Love and a Bottle*. He is a gauche precursor to the urbane rakes of the later comedies. Teague, the loyal comic servant in *The Twin-Rivals*, and Macahone, the booby squire from Tipperary in *The Stage Coach* (1704), differ only in name. Foigard, chaplain to French prisoners-of-war in *The Beaux Stratagem*, in spite of his atrocious pidgin-Irish dialect, pretends to be a native of Brussels. His Jesuitical role in the attempted seduction of an English lady makes Foigard a more complex and less likable figure than Farquhar's other "Teagues" who are cut from the regular Stage Irish pattern. Anti-Catholicism, probably heightened by the religious warfare in Ireland, surfaces often, as in the character of Foigard and in *The Constant Couple*, which ridicules the pomp and commercialism of papal authority.

When Farquhar arrived in London, Restoration drama was coming under attack by moralists, and sentimental comedy was in its formative state. He worked in both genres. His early and middle period plays, in the Restoration mode, were inferior to the verbal rocketry of Congreve* and the tormented intensity of Wycherley. In *The Recruiting Officer* and *The Beaux Stratagem*, he grafts leering Restoration dialogue and the sexual poaching plot onto a quasi-sentimental attitude from which the wits and scintillating ladies of good King Charles' golden days would have recoiled in horror: there is life, pleasant life, in the outer space beyond London; small-town girls have their own sweet style—they are neither apple-cheeked hoydens nor easy conquests for smugly confident city rakes; and elderly persons are capable of wisdom and simple dignity.

Full-blown sentimental comedy, with its thick-ankled altruism and weepy distresses, as in Richard Steele's* *The Conscious Lovers*, seems to a modern reader as unintentionally campy as *Ten Nights in a Bar-room*. Farquhar's variations, as their long stage history will attest, have passed through the wild vicissitudes of taste and have kept most of their bounce.

WILLIAM J. FEENEY

WORKS: *The Complete Works of George Farquhar*. George Stonehill, ed. 2 vols. New York: Gordian, 1930/reprint 1967.   REFERENCES: Burke, John D. "The Stage History of the London Productions of George Farquhar's 'The Recruiting Officer,' 1706-1964." Ohio State University, 1971. *Dissertations Abstracts International*, 32A: 6596; Connely, Willard. *Young George Farquhar: The Restoration Drama at Twilight*. London: Cassel, 1949; Farmer, Albert. *George Farquhar*. London: Longman's, 1966; Jeffares, A. Norman. "George Farquhar." *Times Literary Supplement*, July 23, 1971: 861. (On dating of Farquhar's plays); Jordan, Robert J. "George Farquhar's Military Career." *Huntington Library Quarterly* 37 (1973-1974): 251-264; Kenny, Shirley S. "George Farquhar." *Times Literary Supplement*, September 17, 1971: 1119. (On dating of Farquhar's plays); Roper, Alan. "The Beaux Stratagem,

Image and Action." In Earl Miner, ed., *Seventeenth Century Imagery: Essays on Uses of Figurative Language from Donne to Farquhar*. Berkeley: University of California, 1971; Rothstein, Eric. *George Farquhar*. New York: Twayne, 1967.

FARRELL, J[AMES] G[ORDON] (1935-), English novelist. Farrell was born on January 23, 1935, in Lancashire. The only one of his five novels about Ireland is *Troubles* (1970), which is set in 1919 in a decaying Big House now converted into an unsuccessful hotel inhabited by old ladies and cats. Farrell spent much of his childhood in Ireland, and his recreation of the strife-torn times after World War I seems as utterly authentic as his loving portrayal of down-at-the-heels Anglo-Irish. The volume is unquestionably one of the most realized and satisfying novels written about Ireland by anyone since World War II.

WORK: *Troubles*. London: Jonathan Cape, 1970/New York: Alfred A. Knopf, 1971.

FARRELL, MICHAEL (1899-1962), novelist. Farrell was born in 1899 in Carlow where his parents were prominent in business. He studied medicine at the National University. During the Troubles, with which he was only peripherally involved, he was imprisoned in Mountjoy Jail for six months. On his release, he went on a walking tour of France before taking a job as marine superintendant in the Belgian Congo. After a few years he returned to Ireland, and in 1930 he married Frances Cahill who ran "The Crock of Gold," a handweaving business in Dublin. He resumed his medical studies at Trinity College, Dublin, but made little headway and so finally stopped. For the next seven or eight years, he worked on a draft of his novel *Thy Tears Might Cease*, before plunging full time into journalism. He was compere, scriptwriter, and producer for Radio Éireann, and for several years he ran the program "Radio Digest." During the war he was "Gulliver" for Sean O'Faolain's* *Bell*.* He finally abandoned journalism altogether and took over the management of his wife's handweaving business. He died in June 1962.

His life's work, the novel *Thy Tears Might Cease*, has an unusual publishing history. It originally ran to five unwieldy volumes, and in 1937 Sean O'Faolain brought these to London in a suitcase. The publisher agreed to accept them when complete, but, O'Faolain, writes "the author viewed this encouraging news with the sort of haughty smile proper to an aristocrat who has just heard he is for the guillotine in the morning. It was his constant attitude toward his MS.: avid to see it printed, terrified to let it go." The book was finally published posthumously in 1963 through the efforts of Monk Gibbon* who cut it by a hundred thousand words. In that form, it became something of a best-seller.

In the novel, orphan Martin Matthew Reilly grows to manhood during ten vital years of Ireland's history. The halcyon days of Redmond's Home Rule party are reflected in his early life. He moves from his prosperous

Catholic merchant uncle's home to a pleasant boarding school, from which he spends holidays with his dead mother's landed Protestant friends. In this way, Catholic Martin sees the Irish question from both sides. In spite of bereavements he is happy. He makes idyllic childhood friendships, and there is cosy nursery tea, order, harmony. With the coming of World War I, this peace begins to crack. Martin's painful adolescence is not helped by the death of his guardians. He changes school, loses his religion, and falls in love. The 1916 Rising, which changed Ireland, effects a similar drastic change in him. Once unsympathetic to the Irish cause, he now throws himself into Ireland's fight for freedom.

The novel gives a clear feeling of what life before World War I must have been like, both in the prosperous country towns and in the homes of the landed gentry. There are many memorable minor characters and much exciting action, but the book is marred by patches of lush writing and hazy romanticism. Up to the Rising, it reads almost like a boy's book, and after that, the change in Martin seems too drastic. Even though it is marvelously readable and accurate social history, the book owes nothing to modern fiction and could almost have been published not in 1963, but in 1863 by a second cousin of the Brontes.

M A R Y   R O S E   C A L L A G H A N

WORK: *Thy Tears Might Cease.* London: Jonathan Cape, 1963.   REFER-ENCE: Costello, Peter. *The Heart Grown Brutal.* Dublin: Gill & Macmillan/Totowa, N.J.: Rowman & Littlefield, 1977.

FARREN, ROBERT. *See* Ó FARACHÁIN, ROIBEÁRD.

FARRINGTON, CONOR (1928-), playwright. Farrington was born on June 17, 1928, in Dublin. After graduating from Trinity College, he acted with an English touring company in Malta and India, and from 1955 he has been a member of the repertory company of Radio Éireann. He has written many radio plays and seven stage plays, the most successful of which have been *The Last P. M., or Stella and the Big Bang* and *Aaron Thy Brother. The Last P.M.*, which was performed by the Gate Theatre* for the 1964 Theatre Festival, is a satirical fantasy which was highly re-garded by Frank O'Connor* and Micheál Mac Liammóir.* *Aaron Thy Brother*, performed by the Abbey* in the Peacock in 1969, is an historical play about John Philpot Curran but has a modern chorus of Irish soldiers serving in the Congo. The play is in loose verse, and Farrington is one of the few modern Irish dramatists who consistently write in verse.

WORKS: "Playwrights and the Stationary Carrot." *Theatre Arts* 46 (February 1962): 21-22. (Article); "The Ghostly Garden." *Prizewinning Plays of 1964*. Dublin: Progress House, 1965. (One-act play); *Aaron Thy Brother*. Newark, Del.: Proscenium, 1975.

FEENEY, JOHN (1948-), journalist, novelist, and publisher. Feeney was born in Dublin in 1948 and graduated from University College, Dublin. He is an able journalist, writing largely on religious matters, and has been editor of *The Standard*. He has published a gentle monograph on Archbishop McQuaid, a somewhat crude and awkward novel about television journalism, and a volume of short stories entitled *Mao Dies* (1977). One story in that collection, "The Exorcism," is gratuitously horrendous but, nevertheless, memorable and his best work. He has also been involved in several publishing ventures, chiefly the Irish Writers' Co-operative and his own the Egotist Press.

WORKS: *John Charles McQuaid*. Dublin: Mercier, 1974; *Worm Friday*. Dun Laoghaire: Anna Livia, 1974. (Novel); *Mao Dies and Other Stories*. Dublin: Egotist, 1977.

FERGUSON, SIR SAMUEL (1810-1886), poet. For his work in putting Irish legends into verse, Ferguson has an assured place in literary history as an influence on succeeding writers.

He was born in Belfast on March 10, 1810, and at an early age embarked on a career as a writer. His early efforts received the kind of attention which encouraged him to go on. "The Forging of the Anchor," a poem in praise of industrial progress written when he was twenty-one, was cited by Christopher North as preferable to the pieces contained in Alfred Tennyson's 1830 volume of poems. Modern civic progress and allegiance to the Orange cause were the dominant subjects of his early verses. His most virulent attack on Irish nationalism is contained in "An Irish Garland," which appeared in *Blackwoods* in 1833.

Despite Ferguson's abhorrence of the nationalist cause, his best work resulted from his investigations of the native Irish heritage. He began to look back at the Gaelic originals of the Irish sagas and legends and wrote new versions of them which were more accurate than previous translations and were better verse as well. Interest in the native Irish culture dominated the rest of his life. He continued to write poems based on the Irish heroic tales, versions of the bardic poems, and translations of a variety of Irish poems. It should be added that he neglected the most insistent patriotic verse, unlike his contemporary James Clarence Mangan,* who emphasized precisely those poems in his translations.

Ferguson's efforts were rewarded in his lifetime. He became president of the Royal Irish Academy and enjoyed a successful career as a lawyer. He died on August 9, 1886, in Howth, near Dublin.

W. B. Yeats* was generous in his praise of Ferguson. In an 1886 essay in *The Dublin University Review*, Yeats claimed that while almost all poetry of that time was academic and bookish, Ferguson's was "truly bardic, appealing to all natures alike, to the great concourse of the people." But today it is difficult to claim popular appeal for the long heroic tales which con-stitute Ferguson's major work. Even *Congal* (1872), his best work, is unnecessarily long, and the plot shows strain and contrivance. The poet embroiders his descriptions, and the prosodic ingenuity further distracts from the plot. His version of the most famous love tale in Celtic mythol-ogy, *Deirdre* (1880), is also flawed by pretty diction and rhetorical ex-cesses. He domesticates Irish legend, subjecting some of the most sensual and violent tales to decoration and sentimentalizing so that they become harmless parlor tales. Certainly there is something familiar in that, and he finds a place with scores of mid-Victorian popular poets, particularly English ones. But he has little of the vigor and passion of the best of the Irish poets of his time, Mangan in particular.

Yet, in his attempt to treat Irish myth and legend in verse, Ferguson made a genuine contribution. Like Yeats, he aspired to writing the Irish epic. If he did not succeed in producing a work of genuine art, he brought attention to the indigenous culture of the Irish and may have helped counter the English caricature of the Irish as savages or apes. Finally, he treated the supernatural elements—ghosts, fairies, and magic—with unusual seri-ousness, an approach which appealed to Yeats and some later writers. As an influence on later writers and on popular attitudes, his contributions to Irish literature are substantial.

JAMES KILROY

WORKS: *Cromlech on Howth.* . . . London: Day, 1841. (Poetry); *On the Ex-pediency of Taking Stock: A Letter to James Pim, Jun., Esq.* Dublin: McGlashan, 1847; *Dublin, a Satire.* Dublin, 1849. (Poetry); *Inheritor and Economist.* Dublin: McGlashan, 1849. (Poetry); *Father Tom and the Pope; or, a Night at the Vatican.* . . . Baltimore: Robinson, 1858. (Prose); *Lays of the Western Gael, and Other Poems.* London: Bell & Daldy, 1865; *Congal; a Poem in Five Books.* Dublin: E. Ponsonby/London: Bell & Daldy, 1872; *Deirdre: A One-Act Drama of Old Irish Story.* Dublin: Roe, 1880; *Poems.* Dublin: W. McGee/London: G. Bell, 1880; *The Forging of the Anchor.* London, Paris, New York: Cassell, 1883. (Poetry); *Hibernian Nights' Entertainments.* Dublin: Sealy, Bryers & Walker/London: G. Bell, 1887. (Prose); *Ogham Inscriptions in Ireland, Wales, and Scotland.* Edinburgh: Douglas, 1887; *The Remains of St. Patrick.* . . . Dublin: Sealy, Bryers & Walker/London: G. Bell, 1888. (Translation from Latin into English blank verse); *Lays of the Red Branch,* with an introduction by Lady Ferguson. London: T. Fisher Unwin/Dublin: Sealy, Bryers & Walker, 1897; *Poems of Sir Samuel Ferguson,* with an Introduction by Alfred Perceval Graves. Dublin: Talbot/London: T. Fisher Unwin, [1918]; *Poems.* Padraic Colum, ed. Dublin: A. Figgis, 1963. REFERENCES: Brown, Malcolm. *Sir Samuel Ferguson.* Lewisburg, Pa.: Bucknell University Press, 1973; Ferguson, Lady Mary C. *Sir Samuel Ferguson in the Ireland of His Day.* 2 vols. London: W. Blackwood, 1896; O'Driscoll, Robert. *An Ascendancy of the Heart: Ferguson and the Beginnings of Modern Irish Literature in English.* Dublin: Dolmen, 1976.

FIACC, PADRAIC (1924-), poet. Padraic Fiacc is the pseudonym of Patrick Joseph O'Connor, who was born in the Lower Falls Road, Belfast, in 1924. He spent his childhood in the "Markets" area and then emigrated with his family to New York City where he was educated at Commerce and Haaren High Schools and then at St. Joseph's Seminary in Calicoon. He returned to Belfast in 1946.

Fiacc is perhaps the most considerable poet emerging from the Ulster disturbances and is more committed to enduring the terror and the blood letting than any other Northern Irish writer. Fiacc's early poems are pleasantly low-keyed and sometimes suggest translation from early Irish nature poetry. This bright visual quality is present in his later work, but lyric absorption reaches for social absorption. As Terence Brown has written, Fiacc's Gaelic vision of purity is "tested against brutally explicit images of sectarian warfare and guerilla activity."

With the publication of *Odour of Blood* (1973) and *Nights in the Bad Place* (1977), Fiacc becomes the first of a European species to appear in Irish writing: a Holocaust child, whose mental cast is formed by a milieu of violence. In "Son of a Gun," the poet is more involved than Yeats* was in "Easter 1916." He feels guilt because he is unable to fulfill his parents' role; he cannot carry a gun. The surface of the poem is dismembered like a dream. Fiacc's lyricism reads like a Rimbaudian enactment of Hell. His poems jerk, grimace, and end quickly to convey the idea that there is no way out of the pain. In "The British Connection," he senses racial calamity for the minority: a British-unionist nexus that is itself hopelessly involved. In another fine poem, "Glass Grass," he walks through scorched and burnt Catholic Belfast to give a reading in Ballymurphy. "The Black" is in him, the poison born of violence. The poem attacks all those who can take it less easily than himself. Belfast is quiet, "a beaten sexless dog," waiting for the next outrage. In his controversy with James Simmons in *The Honest Ulsterman* (November 1974-February 1975), Fiacc defends his seminal anthology *The Wearing of the Black*: "The bad odour surrounding *The Wearing of the Black* is the bad odour of blood and it stinks of a society that has hopelessly degraded itself and consequently degraded those of us who have to exist in it."

A tragedy in Fiacc's life was the murder of a young poet, Gerry McLaughlin, whom he commemorates in a lovely elegy in *Nights in the Bad Place*.

A major figure in Fiacc is Padraic Pearse*; the landscape of young men caught up, dying in terrible actions, reflects Pearse's ideals and poetry. The sensual theme connects Fiacc and Pearse to Whitman. Fiacc typically is not Anglo-Irish in his verse methods. He organizes a free verse technique, and he is influenced by William Carlos Williams and the Black Mountain School of poets in America.

JAMES LIDDY

WORKS: *By the Black Stream*. Dublin: Dolmen, 1969; *Odour of Blood*. Dublin: Goldsmith, 1973; *Nights in the Bad Place*. Belfast: Blackstaff, 1977; ed., *The Wearing of the Black*. Belfast: Blackstaff, 1974. REFERENCE: Brown, Terence. *Northern Voices: Poets from Ulster*. Dublin: Gill & Macmillan, 1975.

FIGGIS, DARRELL [**EDMUND**] (1882-1925), politician and man of letters. Figgis was born in Rathmines, a suburb of Dublin, in 1882 of an Anglo-Irish family. As a child he lived in India, and as a young man he worked in London for a firm of tea merchants. He then turned to journalism and to more ambitious writing, and also became deeply involved in the Irish nationalist movement. It was he, for instance, who negotiated the purchase of arms that were landed in Howth in the famous gun-running incident of 1914. Immediately after the Rising, in which he did not take part, he was interned in England for several months as a prominent member of the Volunteers. He was again interned for a longer period in 1919. He drew up the Constitution for the Irish Free State, and he was a member of Dail Éireann for County Dublin. His wife shot herself in 1923, and in 1925 Figgis himself committed suicide.

Both his life and his writing were active and so curiously various that he really seems several different individuals. When his best known novel, *The Return of the Hero*, was published under the pseudonym of Michael Ireland in 1923, it was generally thought to be the work of James Stephens,* because of its subject, its style, and its whimsical tone. Indeed, the book so little resembles anything else by Figgis that James Stephens remarked in his introduction to the American edition: ". . . if Darrell Figgis wrote *The Return of the Hero*, then literary criticism stands baffled, and we must admit that occasions can arise in which the impossible becomes possible, and the unbelievable is to be credited."

As a writer, Figgis' work falls into the broad categories of historical and political journalism, of poetry and of verse drama, of literary criticism, and of the novel. As an historian and political journalist, his work was mainly for the moment and need not concern us here, although his two short "Jail Chronicles" do possess an eloquent simplicity. As a poet, Figgis seems a talentless AE* (to whom, indeed, he dedicated his volume *The Mount of Transfiguration*). His subjects are cosmic emotions and vaguely perceived nature. His higgledypiggledy rhyming only faintly suggests some sort of form and does not disguise a surprisingly faulty control of meter. This lack of control is noticeable also in the frequent and awkward syntactical inversions. He is much given to poetic spelling and archaic words, such as, for instance, the verb "to high-trape." His favorite adjective seems to be "dewy," and a typical line is, "Visions of light that fill the air with brightness like a floating mist." G. K. Chesterton thought him, with Francis Thompson, one of a poetic breed of new Elizabethans, an opinion which must rank in the vanguard of G.K.C.'s most misguided. Figgis' play, *Queen Tara* (1913), was produced by F. R. Benson. Despite its title, it is not Irish in subject matter but takes place in a Maeterlinckean Ruritania. Although the piece received long and respectful reviews on its Dublin appearance, it is distinctly closet drama. As a literary critic, Figgis is more various. Most of his essays are simply long pieces culled from his journalism, but he is interesting on the subject of J. M. Synge* and well worth attention on the subject of his friend AE, about whom he wrote a short book. Figgis' best and most extended piece of criticism is his *Shakespeare, a Study* (1911). This volume is neither modern nor scholarly criticism, but on a continuum of Shakespearean criticism ranging from the lively unprofessionalism of a Frank Harris to the magisterial analyses of an A. C. Bradley, Figgis would be fairly close to the middle. He is extremely knowledgeable and full of plausible ideas always delivered gracefully, if sometimes upon insufficient evidence. He makes some provocative comparisons to the practices of playwrights in other eras, particularly to Ibsen, and he is extremely interesting on Shakespeare's plot structure. This remains a book worthy of some attention.

Nevertheless, Figgis is most important for his five unread and out-of-print novels, of which the most significant are the last three: *Children of Earth* (1918), *The House of Success* (1921), and *The Return of the Hero* (1923). These books are so different in both subject and style that their author seems a literary chameleon. *Children of Earth* is probably his finest novel, and it is an extraordinary one—visually evocative, structurally powerful, and rhetorically eloquent. It takes place on an island, like Achill where Figgis lived for several years, off the West Coast, and it is a study of the elemental life and peasant character formed there. Much of the book seems an emulation of Thomas Hardy with the Wessex dialect replaced by the dialect of the Synge of *In the Shadow of the Glen* or *The Well of the Saints*. However, Figgis' attempt in the last fifty pages to portray a state of mind in a sort of mystical communion with the earth is eerily reminiscent of a book written at almost the same time by Thomas Hardy's most distinctive pupil—that is, *The Rainbow* by D. H. Lawrence. There are some lengthy descriptive passages in Figgis' novel, particularly at the beginning of sections, that do not work because he is waxing too poetic. That flaw apart, this novel grows in beauty and power. It has been long out of print and is unmentioned by critics or historians, who have called lesser books masterly.

If *Children of Earth* is redolent of Hardy, *The House of Success* is permeated by the spirit of Henry James. There is a quintessentially Jamesian narrator, and there is the prudish avoidance of the specific that lifts the whole story out of the real world into the ambiguities of Jamesian psychology. The book is mainly a leisurely contrast between a successful, self-made entrepreneur of a father and a son eventually hardened by patriotic idealism. The major events lead up to the 1916 Rising and its aftermath, but are related mainly in terms of the emotional struggle between father and son, which takes place within the confines of their own sitting room. The novel is basically about two views of what is good for Ireland; although in the novel the palm is given to the son, the father's personal qualities are more dynamic and perhaps more admired. Figgis' diagnosis was, of course, correct, for the somewhat unscrupulous gombeen (or business) man and the sometimes fanatical patriot have been the major figures in Irish political life until today. The book is not entirely a success because of its technique and its style, but it does have two strongly developed characters and some intense moments.

The subject of *The Return of the Hero* is the famous Oisin-St. Patrick colloquy after the hero has returned from the Land of Youth. This clash between the Irish legendary past and the beginnings of modern Irish Christianity is developed with a simple charm and a mild humor. Nevertheless, it implies a genial criticism of contemporary established religion and its inability, even at its best intentioned, to deal with the unfamiliar. Although the book is little read today, it is not in the least dated and deserves the small but irreducible stature of a minor classic. That small but irreducible stature is also the least that Darrell Figgis himself deserves.

WORKS: *A Vision of Life,* Introduction by G. K. Chesterton. London & New York: J. Lane, 1909. (Poems); *Broken Arcs.* London: Dent, 1911/New York & London: M. Kennerley, 1912. (Novel); *The Crucibles of Time and Other Poems.* London: Dent, 1911; *Shakespeare, a Study.* London: Dent, 1911/New York & London: M. Kennerley, 1912; *Studies and Appreciations.* London: Dent, 1912. (Essays); *Queen Tara.* London: Dent, 1913. (Play); *Jacob Elthorne.* London & Toronto: Dent, 1914. (Novel); *The Mount of Transfiguration.* Dublin: Maunsel, 1915. (Poems); *AE (George W. Russell), a Study of a Man and a Nation.* Dublin & London: Maunsel, 1916; *A Chronicle of Jails.* Dublin: Talbot, 1917; *The Gaelic State in the Past and Future.* Dublin & London: Maunsel, 1917; *Bye-Ways of Study.* Dublin: Talbot/London: Urwin, 1918. (Essays); *Children of Earth.* Dublin: Maunsel, 1918. (Novel); *A Second Chronicle of Jails.* Dublin: Talbot, 1919; *The Economic Case for Irish Independence.* Dublin & London: Maunsel, 1920; *The Historic Case for Irish Independence.* Dublin & London: Maunsel, 1920; *The House of Success.* Dublin: Gael Co-operative Society, 1921. (Novel); *The Irish Constitution.* Dublin: Mellifont, [1922]; *The Return of the Hero.* London & Sydney: Chapman & Dodd, 1923, published under the pseudonym of Michael Ireland/New York: C. Boni, 1930, published under his own name, with an Introduction by James Stephens and a second unsigned Introduction probably by Padraic Colum; *The Paintings of William Blake.* London: E. Benn/New York: Scribner's, 1925; *Recollections of the Irish War.* London: E. Benn, 1927. REFERENCE: Costello, Peter. *The Heart Grown Brutal.* Dublin: Gill & Macmillan/Totowa, N.J.: Rowman & Littlefield, 1977.

FINNEY, PATRICIA (1958-) novelist. Nearly the most precocious writer included in this dictionary is Patricia Finney, who was born on May 12, 1958, in London, and who published two novels before she was twenty. Although she is English by birth and upbringing and of Hungarian extraction on her mother's side, her father's people came from Cork, and her great-uncle is Frank Gallagher,* the short story writer and journalist.

Finney's two books, *A Shadow of Gulls* (1977) and *The Crow Goddess* (1978), actually form one long narrative. Her story takes place early in the second century A.D. and is set in Ireland and Britain. It is the story of an Irish harper named Lugh Mac Romain, whose life is closely bound up with the events recounted in the Ulster Cycle of hero tales. The chief events of the Ulster Cycle—the stories of Deirdre of the Sorrows, the Cattle Raid of Cooley, and the life and death of Cuchulain—are all woven into the story of Lugh, as are various historical personages such as the Roman Emperor Hadarin. The author cites Lady Gregory's* *Cuchulain of Muir-themne* as her main source of Irish legend, but she seems as much indebted to Sir James Frazer and Robert Graves for her treatment of myth and ancient religion. Her story has considerable narrative skill and emotional power. Even more remarkable is her convincing recreation of a far-distant time and realistic humanizing of the legend, thereby making it both plausible and modern.

WORKS: *A Shadow of Gulls.* London: Collins, 1977; *The Crow Goddess.* London: Collins, 1978.

FITZGIBBON, [ROBERT LOUIS] CONSTANTINE [LEE-DILLON] (1919-), novelist, journalist, and translator. Fitzgibbon was born on June 8, 1919, in Lenox, Massachussetts, of an American mother and a Northern Irish father. He was educated at Munich University, the Sorbonne, and Exeter College, Oxford. During World War II, he served first in the British and then in the American Army. Then, after a short period of school-mastering in Bermuda, he turned full time to writing. He lived for about ten years in England and for the last ten years in Ireland, of which he is now a citizen. He is also a member of the Irish Academy of Letters.

Fitzgibbon has been a prolific translator from the French and German, often of war memoirs. He himself has written about thirty volumes of fiction and nonfiction, including the life of Dylan Thomas and an effective thriller-fantasy in the 1984 vein called *When the Kissing Had to Stop*. His Irish writing consists of a biography of de Valera, some short popular histories, and a novel about Michael Collins entitled *High Heroic*. That novel, like all of his work, has a journalist's fluency and craft, but treats its subject with little more than a plausible superficiality.

WORKS: *Miss Finnigan's Fault.* London: Cassell, 1953. (Travel in Ireland); *High Heroic.* London: Dent, 1969. (Novel); *Out of the Lion's Paw.* London: Macdonald, 1969. (History); *Red Hand: The Ulster Colony.* London: Joseph, 1971. (History); *The Life and Times of Eamon de Valera.* Dublin: Gill & Macmillan, 1973.

FITZMAURICE, GEORGE (1877-1963), playwright. Fitzmaurice was first a writer of broad, conventional peasant comedy in his short stories and in his most popular play, *The Country Dressmaker*. Then, partly impressed by Synge* and partly motivated by his own eccentric individuality, he wrote a number of short, grotesque tragicomedies, such as *The Pie-dish* and *The Magic Glasses*. Withdrawing ever more into his own rich imagination and from the theatre—and, indeed, from the ordinary concourse of life—he followed his fantastic fairy tale *The Dandy Dolls* with increasingly fanciful and sardonic plays. In posthumously produced works such as *The Enchanted Land* and *The King of the Barna Men*, he has created an Irish never-never land rivaled only by that of James Stephens.*

Fitzmaurice was born on January 28, 1877, in Bedford House, near Listowel, County Kerry. His father was a Church of Ireland minister and his mother a Catholic, and he was the tenth of twelve children. After working briefly in a bank in Cork, he moved to Dublin where he was a clerk in the civil service for most of the rest of his life. He was out of Dublin only for a period of service in the British Army in World War I and for occasional visits back to Kerry.

Although Yeats* had predicted that Fitzmaurice's first produced play, *The Country Dressmaker*, would be even more inflammatory than Synge's *The Playboy of the Western World*, the *Dressmaker*, after its initial production in October 1907, became one of the most popular of all Abbey* plays. In 1908, the Abbey produced *The Pie-dish* and in 1913 *The Magic Glasses*, but these rich one-act tragicomedies were before their time, and Abbey audiences did not quite know how to react to them. Yeats himself did not rank Fitzmaurice highly. A number of other Fitzmaurice plays were rejected, among them his strong peasant tragedy *The Moonlighter* and a peasant comedy which Fitzmaurice wrote with John Guinan.*

After the war, Fitzmaurice returned to Dublin to work with the Land Commission, and in 1919 he wrote *'Twixt the Giltinans and the Carmodys*. This rather conventional peasant farce was staged at the Abbey in March 1923, about a month before the first production of O'Casey's* *The Shadow of a Gunman*. This was the last Fitzmaurice play to be staged by the Abbey in his lifetime. Acutely sensitive to criticism, Fitzmaurice withdrew his plays from the Abbey. He lived for forty years more, and he continued to write new work and to revise old work, but during that time he received only the slimmest handful of productions. His name was kept before the public at all only by his friend Seumas O'Sullivan,* who occasionally persuaded him to allow a play to appear in *The Dublin Magazine*.*

There is the tendency to see Fitzmaurice simply as the product of a rich folk culture, but, because his father was an Anglo-Irish minister, Fitzmaurice had only one foot in the door of the whitewashed cabin. Even his early popular stories, informed as they are, tend to see the peasant from the outside. Fitzmaurice was no rural realist like T. C. Murray*; he was more like Lady Gregory,* presenting and exaggerating the foibles of the peasant for the purpose of often quite broad comedy. And so Fitzmaurice's best folk plays present a galaxy of the quaint, the eccentric, and the mad. We are presented with Jaymoney Shanahan who hides in his loft seeing visions in his magic glasses; with Morgan Quille the quack doctor; with Leum Donoghue the fanatical creator of the pie dish, and with Lena Hanrahan the beauty who wears false teeth, a wig, and a wooden leg.

From the exaggerations of the comic vision, it is not far to the exaggerations of satire and fantasy. As Fitzmaurice grew older and further removed from a past that he was not even originally firmly rooted in, satire and fantasy began to take over. We see this particularly in *The Waves of the Sea*, *The Linnaun Shee*, and *The Green Stone*, and triumphantly in *The Enchanted Land* and *The Ointment Blue*. Fitzmaurice did make a couple of attempts to write about the city. One, *The Coming of Ewn Andzale*, is his only really tedious play, but the other, *One Evening Gleam*, is a little *tour de force*. However, Fitzmaurice was such a recluse that he was never really of the city, and his most characteristic and finest work came out of memory and a most extraordinary imagination.

If this isolation gave Fitzmaurice his strength as a writer, it also gave him two weaknesses. His language is generally as Synge would have wanted it: as ripe as a berry. It is rare, rich, hypnotically fluent, and as playfully inventive as the Synge of *The Playboy* or the O'Casey of *Purple Dust*. In the hands of a memorable Kerry actor, such as Eamon Kelly or Eamon Keane, Fitzmaurice's long fancies are often a memorable joy. But the long speeches are also a problem in many of the later plays. Despite engaging experiments with sound, repetition, malapropisms, and different levels of language, many of these speeches are more literary than dramatic. If the speeches are read as portions of a novel in dialogue, they are delightful. If they are read with a theatrical ear, as scripts to be spoken in plays to be staged, they are a bit of a problem. Engaging, charming, even marvelous, but a bit of a problem.

A second symptom of Fitzmaurice's isolation is the frequent laziness of his plot construction. A prime example is the published version of his brilliant *The Enchanted Land*. The first and second acts are loaded down with exposition which could profitably and excellently have been dramatized. Indeed, they cry out to be dramatized. The result is that much of the chat in Act One simply tells us what should have been the dramatized story of Act One. Fitzmaurice has attacked his story at the wrong place and has caused his director a quite unnecessary problem of dullness.

Nevertheless, in these brilliant fantasies, Fitzmaurice has truly created his own worlds, just as did Lewis Carroll or James Stephens or Kenneth Grahame. The use of fantasy was the making of Fitzmaurice as an artist. Fantasy allowed him free play for gaiety and wit, and was a liberating influence. Poorer writers have usually but one tone, one emotional slant, one angle of vision on the world. Fitzmaurice seems to have had three: the grotesque in such early work as *The Magic Glasses* and *The Pie-dish*; the bleakly glum, in which so many of his plays are concluded with a stoical acceptance of failure or, at best, second-best; and the fantastic which allowed him to palliate the grotesquerie and to alleviate the glumness.

Fitzmaurice died on May 12, 1963, in his room at 3 Harcourt Street in Dublin. After his death, all of his available printed plays and manuscripts were collected and published in three volumes. Several of them have been either revived or produced for the first time at the Abbey Theatre. Among the early Abbey playwrights, his reputation today is probably second only to that of Synge. He probably would have found some dour solace in that.

WORKS: *Five Plays.* London & Dublin: Maunsel, 1914/Boston: Little, Brown, 1917. (Includes *The Country Dressmaker, The Moonlighter, The Pie-Dish, The Magic Glasses,* and *The Dandy Dolls*); *The Plays of George Fitzmaurice.* Vol. 1, *Dramatic Fantasies,* with an Introduction by Austin Clarke. Dublin: Dolmen, 1967. (Includes *The Magic Glasses, The Dandy Dolls, The Linaun Shee, The Green Stone, The Enchanted Land,* and *The Waves of the Sea*); *The Plays of George Fitzmaurice.* Vol. 2, *Folk Plays,* with an Introduction by Howard K. Slaughter. Dublin: Dolmen, 1970. (Includes *The Ointment Blue or The King of the Barna Men, The Pie-Dish, The Terrible Baisht, There Are Tragedies and Tragedies,* and *The Moonlighter*); *The Plays of George Fitzmaurice.* Vol. 3, *Realistic Plays,* with an Introduction by Howard K. Slaughter. Dublin: Dolmen, 1970. (Includes *The Toothache, The Country Dressmaker, One Evening Gleam, 'Twixt the Giltinans and the Carmodys, The Simple Hanrahans,* and *The Coming of Ewn Andzale*); *The Crows of Mephistopheles,* ed. and with an Introduction by Robert Hogan. Dublin: Dolmen, 1970; "Chasing a Ghoul." *The Irish Emerald* (June 24, 1905)/reprint, *Journal of Irish Literature* 6 (September 1977): 57-63. (Story); with Guinan, John, *The Wonderful Wedding. Journal of Irish Literature* 6 (September 1978): 3-36.   REFERENCES: Gelderman, Carol W. *George Fitzmaurice.* Boston: Twayne, 1979; Henderson, Joanne L. "Checklist of Four Kerry Writers." *Journal of Irish Literature* 1 (May 1972): 101-119; McGuinness, Arthur E. *George Fitzmaurice.* Lewisburg, Pa.: Bucknell University Press, 1975.

FITZPATRICK, WILLIAM J[OHN] (1830-1895), historian. FitzPatrick was born in Dublin in 1830 and died there in 1895. He was a prosperous tallow merchant who spent part of his profits on acquiring Secret Service records and other useful historical documents from government archives. Such materials were supposed to be in safe keeping at Dublin Castle, but unaccountably kept turning up in the private market. With these sources of inside information, supplemented by *viva voce* inquiries throughout a city whose remarkable acoustics were so admired by George Moore,* FitzPatrick uncovered many deplorable governmental activities and practices. He then published his findings in a series of books which caused virtuous indignation or hilarity among readers according to their temperament. The best of these books are *The Life, Times and Contemporaries of Lord Cloncurry* (1855), *Ireland Before the Union* (1867), and *"The Sham Squire"* (1866).

ANDREW MARSH

WORKS: *The Life, Times and Contemporaries of Lord Cloncurry.* Dublin, 1855; *Who Wrote the Waverly Novels?* London: Effingham Wilson, 1856; *A Note to the Cornwallis Papers.* Dublin, 1859; *Lady Morgan.* London, 1860; *The Life, Times, and Correspondence of Dr. Doyle, Bishop of Kildare and Leighlin.* Dublin, 1861/new ed., greatly enlarged, Dublin: Duffy, 1880; *Memoirs of R. Whatley, Archbishop of Dublin.* London, 1864; *"The Sham Squire" and the Informers of 1798.* London, 1866; *Curious Family History; or, Ireland Before the Union. . . .* Dublin, 1867; *Irish Wits and Worthies; Including Dr. Lanigan. . . .* Dublin, 1873; *The Life of Charles Lever.* London, 1879/new ed., revised, London: Ward, Lock [1884]; *The Life of . . . Thomas N.*

Burke. London: Kegan Paul, 1885/new ed., revised, 1894; *Secret Service Under Pitt.* London: Longmans, 1892/2d ed., enlarged, 1892; *History of the Dublin Catholic Cemetaries,* continued & edited by Gerald P. FitzPatrick. Dublin: [Catholic Cemetaries Offices], 1900.

FITZSIMON, ELLEN O'CONNELL (1805-1883), poet. Fitzsimon, the eldest daughter of Daniel O'Connell, was born in Dublin on November 12, 1805. She is remembered for her poem "The Song of the Irish Emigrant in America," which is not only the prototypical nostalgic song, but also contains the immortal line "my ears are full of tears." She died in 1883.

WORK: *Darrynane in Eighteen Hundred and Thirty-two, and Other Poems.* Dublin: W. B. Kelly, 1863.

FLOWER, ROBIN [ERNEST WILLIAM] (1881-1946), Celtic scholar, translator, and poet. Flower, one of the most erudite of Celtic scholars and graceful of translators, was born in England on October 16, 1881. He was educated at Leeds Grammar School and Pembroke, College Oxford; from 1929 to 1944, he was deputy keeper of manuscripts at the British Museum. Flower did not live to complete a history of Irish literature which he had been preparing for years, but his many translations and scholarly works (particularly *The Irish Tradition*), are an admirable body of work. His reminiscences of life on the Great Blasket Island, *The Western Island,* is a loving recreation of a vanished way of life, written with an appreciative poet's eye. He died in Southgate, London, on January 16, 1946.

WORKS: *Eire, and Other Poems.* London: Locke Ellis, 1910; *Hymenaea, and Other Poems.* London: Selwyn & Blount, 1918; *The Leelong Flower.* [London]: 1923. (Poems); with Ida M. Flower, *The Great Blasket.* London, 1924. (Poems); *Love's Bitter-Sweet: Translations from the Irish Poets of the Sixteenth and Seventeenth Centuries.* Dublin: Cuala, 1925; *Monkey Music.* London, 1925. (Poems); *Trirech inna n-en, From the Irish.* London: David Macbeth, 1926. (Poems); *The Pilgrim's Way.* London, 1927. (Poems); *Fuit Ilium.* London, 1928. (Translations of Irish poems); *Ireland and Medieval Europe.* London, [1928]. (Lecture); *Poems and Translations.* London: Constable, 1931; *The Western Island; or, the Great Blasket.* Oxford: Clarendon, 1944; *The Irish Tradition.* Oxford: Clarendon, 1947.   REFERENCE: Bell, Sir Harold Idris. *Robin Ernest William Flower, 1881-1946.* London: Geoffrey Cumberlege, [1948]. (Pamphlet).

FORRISTAL, DESMOND [TIMOTHY] (1930-), playwright. Forristal was born in Dublin on September 25, 1930. He was educated at the O'Connell School, at Belvedere College, and at University College, Dublin, where he received a Ph.D. in philosophy in 1956. He was ordained a Roman Catholic priest in 1955 and has worked for many years in the field of communications. He has written books on communications and on religious subjects, but is best known as a playwright. His plays include *The True Story of the Horrid Popish Plot* (Gate,* 1972), *Black Man's Country* (Gate, 1974), and *The Seventh Sin* (Gate, 1976). *Black Man's Country,* probably his most moving piece, is about Catholic missionaries in Nigeria. The often breezy fluency of the dialogue sets a tone that is impressively counterpointed to the sombre political action and the moving personal one. Like all of Forristal's works, *Black Man's Country* views a complex problem with a wry clarity. If he has a special lack as a playwright, it would seem to be the quality of his writing in the serious scenes. There, the prose is straightforward and adequate enough, but hardly of the excellence of his lighter moments. Those moments are so good that one wishes he would essay a pure comedy. In any event, he is one of the most intelligent of contemporary Irish playwrights, and one can look forward to his new work with a certainty of its solid merit.

WORKS: *Black Man's Country*. Newark, Del.: Proscenium, 1975; *The True Story of the Horrid Popish Plot*. Dublin: Veritas, 1976.

FOLKLORE, IRISH. The oral tales, beliefs, and traditions of the Irish peasantry attracted little attention or admiration prior to the nineteenth century. Collectors of Irish folklore were inspired by the enormous popularity of Jacob and Wilhelm Grimm's early nineteenth-century folktale collections and of Sir Walter Scott's *Minstrelsy of the Scottish Border* (1803) and Waverley novels, which Scott claimed in the Postscript to *Waverley* had been inspired by Maria Edgeworth's* portraits of the Irish peasant. The anthologies of Thomas Crofton Croker* (1798-1854) encouraged the collection of Irish folklore both by demonstrating the continued existence of what many had believed to be forgotten superstitions and by proving how much the beliefs and legends of the Irish countryside appealed to the curiosity of the reading public. Croker's most well-known collection, *Fairy Legends and Traditions of the South of Ireland* (1825), became so popular that a second series dedicated to Walter Scott and a third series dedicated to Wilhelm Grimm were published in 1828; the entire work was reissued throughout the century. Croker patronizingly presented his materials as antiquarian curiosities and transformed them into fiction. Croker's collections reflected a dichotomy between folklore and fiction reminiscent of Scott: while the tales themselves were highly fictionalized narratives, Croker's "Notes" after each story offered a wealth of unadorned information about local legends, customs, and beliefs. Croker attempted to expand the significance of Irish folklore with numerous references to English literary parallels and international analogues.

The popularity of Croker's collections encouraged Irish novelists to write about the peasantry. William Carleton,* John and Michael Banim,* Samuel Lover,* and Gerald Griffin* recorded many of the tales, beliefs, and customs of rural Ireland in their novels. William Carleton (1794-1869), whose mother and father were both Gaelic-speaking peasants noted for their knowledge of traditional songs and stories, presented the most complete and authentic picture of pre-Famine peasant life in nineteenth-century Irish fiction, especially in the two series of *Traits and Stories of the Irish Peasantry* (1830, 1833) and in *Tales and Sketches Illustrating the Character of the Irish Peasantry* (1845). John and Michael Banim's *Tales of the O'Hara Family* (1825, 1827), Samuel Lover's *Legends and Stories of Ireland* (1831, 1834), and Gerald Griffin's *Holland-Tide* (1827), *Tales of the Munster Festivals* (1827), *The Collegians* (1829), and *Talis Qualis; or Tales of the Jury Room* (1842) also include a great deal of Irish folklore. However, the folklore depicted in these works, as in Carleton's, inevitably was colored by the propaganda, sentimentality, and comic caricature which pervade much of nineteenth-century Irish fiction. The popularity and literary possibilities of materials from Irish folklore were also demonstrated by Thomas Moore's* *Irish Melodies.*

Literary periodicals like the *Dublin University Magazine* and the *Dublin and London Magazine* were the major publishers of Irish folklore during the forty years after Croker's collections of the 1820s. Their anonymous contributors made no effort to preserve the oral tales and traditions of the country people in their original form. Usually what was presented as folklore in such periodicals kept to the tradition of "literary folklore" begun by Croker. Supposedly authentic peasant legends were rewritten to conform to nineteenth-century standards of fiction. The introductions to such "legends" contained other, unelaborated examples of the beliefs and tales of the peasantry plus skeptical, patronizing comments by the "enlightened" narrator. However, the folklore in such articles was generally less adulterated than in Croker's collections and in Irish novels. The least adulterated Irish folklore was contained in some of the many county histories published throughout the century.

Patrick Kennedy (1801-1873), who had contributed folklore to the *Dublin University Magazine,* published several important collections of the tales and traditions of his native County Wexford. Kennedy's *Legends of Mount Leinster* (1855), *The Banks of the Boro* (1876), and *Evenings in the Duffrey* (1869) present Irish folklore against a fictional background. Kennedy had read Croker, Carleton, and Griffin, but his work represents significant advances in the collection of Irish folklore. His collections contain relatively few literary mannerisms and are much closer to the original idiom and structure of oral traditions. Kennedy was motivated by an antiquarian zeal similar to Croker's, but whereas Croker had presented only legends, Kennedy's collections of tales, *Legendary Fictions of the Irish Celts* (1866), *The Fireside Stories of Ireland* (1870), and *The Bardic Stories of Ireland* (1871), included the entire spectrum of oral prose traditions in Ireland. The Ossianic tales which Kennedy recorded in *Legendary Fictions* demonstrated that the native heroic and mythological cycles found in medieval manuscripts in Dublin libraries also existed in oral form among the peasantry. Later in the century the noted Celtic folklorist, Alfred Nutt (1856-1912), would claim that the medieval Irish manuscripts themselves were derived from a worthy and poetic oral folk tradition still current among the nineteenth-century Irish peasantry. The great popularity of Kennedy's collections and the revelation that the peasantry of predominantly English-speaking County Wexford had preserved an exclusively Gaelic tradition for over one thousand years encouraged further collecting, especially in the Irish-speaking districts in the west of Ireland, by literary nationalists in the last quarter of the century.

Ancient Irish myths and hero tales were given a new scholarly significance by nineteenth-century developments in philology, anthropology, and comparative mythology. Ireland's ancient literature underwent the same process of popularization and literary transformation in the last quarter of the century that the more contemporary tales, beliefs, and traditions of the peasantry underwent throughout the century. Standish J. O'Grady* freely rewrote ancient Irish myths and legends in the guise of a nineteenth-century novel in his immensely popular and influential *History of Ireland: Heroic Period* (1878) and its sequel, *Cuchulain and His Contemporaries* (1880). As with the Irish folklore published throughout the century, the intrinsic quality and importance of O'Grady's materials transcended the limitations of his style and inspired Irish literature and politics for years to come.

The nationalism implicit in earlier anthologies of Irish folklore and mythology became obvious propaganda in Lady Wilde's* collections *Ancient Legends, Mystic Charms, and Superstitions of Ireland* (1887) and *Ancient Cures, Charms, and Usages of Ireland* (1890). Lady Wilde (1826-1896), who had contributed to *The Nation** under the pseudonym "Speranza," filled her anthologies with materials which her husband, Sir William Wilde* (1815-1876), an eye surgeon, occultist, and antiquarian, had collected after he published *Irish Popular Superstitions* (1853). The folklore in Lady Wilde's collections is colored by her political and ethnological nationalism and her occult theories rather than by literary elaboration.

In the last quarter of the century, the study of Irish folklore fostered some of the worst and some of the best literature ever written in Ireland. Literary popularizations of Irish folklore such as David Rice McAnally's *Irish Wonders, The Ghosts, Giants, Pookas, Demons, Leprechawns, Banshees, Fairies, Witches, Widows, Old Maids and Other Marvels of the Emerald Isle* (1888) reduced the Irish peasantry to humorous, sentimental buffoons who spoke a ridiculous dialect. On the other hand, the early energies of the Irish Renaissance were generated in large part by the study of Ireland's ancient and contemporary traditional literature. William Butler Yeats,* John M. Synge,* and Lady Gregory* all collected Irish folklore and transformed it into great literature. As Yeats remarked in *The Celtic Twilight*, "Folk art is . . . the soil where all great art is rooted."

William Butler Yeats (1865-1939) devoted much time and effort in the 1880s and 1890s to collecting Irish folklore from printed and oral sources while preparing his three anthologies of Irish folklore. In *Fairy and Folk Tales of the Irish Peasantry* (1888) and *Irish Fairy Tales* (1892), Yeats surveyed, organized, and, in some cases, freely rewrote the available corpus of Irish folklore. Yeats' appreciation of Irish folklore as a serious subject matter and the quality of his introductions and notes in these anthologies represent important advances in the study of Irish folklore. In 1893, Yeats published the folklore he had collected from oral sources in *The Celtic Twilight, Men and Women, Dhouls and Faeries*, which he revised and enlarged in 1902. The fairy beliefs and visionary traditions of Irish folklore provided Yeats with a perfect link between his literary nationalism and his occult interests. He also selected materials from novels about the Irish peasantry for his two anthologies of nineteenth-century Irish fiction, *Stories from Carleton* (1889) and *Representative Irish Tales* (1891). Irish folklore offered Yeats a link with Ireland's heroic past, a living mythological tradition, a folk speech which invigorated his poetic vocabulary, and a subject matter and symbolism at once ancient and novel for his poetry and plays.

The writings of John Millington Synge (1871-1909) are even more markedly focused on subjects from Irish peasant life and traditions. The plots and the dialect of all his plays are derived from Irish folklore and folklife. Synge recorded his first-hand observations of the Irish peasantry and their lore in *The Aran Islands* (1906) and *In Wicklow, West Kerry, and Connemara* (1912). Like Yeats, Synge found in Irish folklore a joyous energy and a simplicity of life and language next to which modern life and literature seemed pallid and sterile indeed.

Lady Gregory (1859-1932) shared Yeats' view that Irish folklore was a living link with Ireland's heroic past and that a great literature could be re-created for modern Ireland from contemporary folklore and ancient legends. With Yeats' encouragement, she retold the two major legend cycles of ancient Ireland in *Cuchulain of Muirthemne: The Story of the Men of the Red Branch of Ulster* (1902) and *Gods and Fighting Men: The Story of the Tuatha de Danaan and of the Fianna of Ireland* (1904). During the 1890s, she had taught herself Irish and, inspired by Yeats' *The Celtic Twilight* and Douglas Hyde's* *The Love Songs of Connacht*, avidly collected folklore in her native County Galway. She published several rich collections of this folklore: *Poets and Dreamers* (1903), *The Kiltartan History Book* (1909), *The Kiltartan Wonder Book* (1910), *The Kiltartan Poetry Book* (1918), and *Visions and Beliefs in the West of Ireland* (1920). Her collections represented a significant development in the study of Irish folklore because she presented literal, objective accounts of her materials without the literary elaboration, sentimentality, comedy, nationalistic propaganda, or patronizing commentary which had marred so many of the earlier collections. Nor did she use folklore as a vehicle for personal reverie as Yeats and Synge had done in *The Celtic Twilight* and *The Aran Islands*. Her collections were a scholarly achievement, just as her folk-history plays and her comedies of peasant life were an artistic achievement.

The nationalistic, literary, and scholarly significance of Irish folklore culminated in the work of Douglas Hyde (1860-1949), a preeminent folklorist who was also a nationalist, poet, and scholar. Hyde, the founder of the Gaelic League, devoted his life to the preservation of the Irish language and culture. Hyde's literary genius is apparent in his prose and verse translations from the Irish in *Beside the Fire: A Collection of Irish Gaelic Folk Stories* (1890) and in *The Love Songs of Connacht* (1893) which capture the beauty and vigor of the Irish originals and demonstrate the poetic richness of the English spoken by the Irish peasantry. A scholar as well as a poet and nationalist, Hyde accurately recorded and carefully annotated the folklore he collected and published. Hyde's collections inspired Yeats, Synge, and Lady Gregory in their collection and literary adaptation of Irish folklore. Hyde himself wrote many poems and plays based on Irish folklore. In addition, his scholarship elevated Irish folklore into a respected field of knowledge. Under his influence, William Larminie* and Jeremiah Curtin (1835-1906) published important collections during the 1890s. Like Hyde, Larminie and Curtin collected their materials in Irish, published literal translations and some annotation, and valued the scholarly as well as the imaginative significance of Irish folklore. Hyde's preeminence as a nationalist poet and playwright, as the first president of the Republic of Ireland, and as an outstanding collector and scholar of Irish folklore exemplifies the closely related literary, political, and scholarly dimensions of Irish folklore.

Hyde's accomplishments were largely responsible for the founding in 1926 of the Folklore of Ireland Society, the first organized effort to collect and to study the entire spectrum of Irish oral tradition. In 1935, the Irish government created the Irish Folklore Commission for the purpose of collecting, cataloguing, and publishing Irish folklore. A rich tradition remained to be explored—in 1935, the parish of Carna in West Galway had more unrecorded folktales than the whole of Europe. By 1964, manuscript collections in the commission's archives totaled more than 1.5 million pages. Today the Irish Folklore Commission (now the Department of Folklore at University College, Dublin) is renowned for the abundance and quality of its folklore research. Sean O'Sullivan's *A Handbook of Irish Folklore* (1942) is the foremost such guide in the world. With Reidar Christiansen, O'Sullivan published *The Types of the Irish Folktale* (1963), an index to the forty-three thousand versions of popular tales collected during the commission's first twenty-one years. Kevin Danaher's massive bibliography of Irish folklore studies, published in 1978, attests to the magnitude of Irish folklore research. Once the hobby of amateur collectors in search of antiquarian curiosities, Irish folklore was a crucial influence in the literary and political history of late nineteenth-century and early twentieth-century Ireland, and today is in the forefront of international folklore studies.

MARY HELEN THUENTE

REFERENCES. The following works provide a good introductory survey of the materials and the historical developments involved in the study of Irish folklore: Evans, E. Estyn. *Irish Folk Ways*. London: Routledge & Kegan Paul, 1957; *Fairy and Folk Tales of Ireland*. W. B. Yeats, ed. 2d ed. Gerrards Cross: Colin Smythe, 1977; O'Sullivan, Sean. *Folktales of Ireland*. Chicago: University of Chicago Press, 1966; O'Sullivan, Sean. *A Handbook of Irish Folklore*. Detroit: Singing Tree, 1970.

FRAZER, JOHN D[E JEAN] (ca. 1810-ca. 1850), poet. Frazer (or Fraser) was a cabinet maker by trade and hence sometimes known as the "Poet of the Workshop." He was born in Birr, King's County (now County Offaly). The date of his birth is variously given as 1804, 1809, and 1813, and the date of his death as 1849 and 1852. He contributed much verse about the beauties of nature and the ills of Ireland to *The Nation** and *The Irish Felon*. Despite his fluency, he lacks judgment, and both his meter and his diction sometimes become amusingly incongruous. For instance, his "Lament for Thomas Davis" bears some resemblance metrically to W. S. Gilbert's "The Flowers that Bloom in the Spring," with the "tra-la" being replaced by such lines as "Woe, woe" or "Gloom, gloom." Similarly, despite some sincerity and real feeling that manages to break through his conventional poetic diction, the effect is often silly. For example, in his description of "The Holy Wells," he writes:

How sweet of old the bubbling gush—no less to antlered race
Than to the hunter and the hound that smote them in the chase.

In his patriotic moments, he is extremely jingoistic. In "The Holy Wells" again, Ireland is "The Emerald garden, set apart for Irishmen by God." At the same time, his martial poetry is full of tyrants and cowards, gauntlets and swords. Probably his most anthologized piece is "Song for July 12th, 1843," four lines of which O'Casey* quotes for comic effect in *The Drums of Father Ned*.

WORKS: *Eva O'Connor, a Poem in Three Cantos by an Author Yet Unknown*. Dublin: Milliken, 1826; *Poems for the People*. By J. De Jean. Dublin: J. Browne, 1845; *Poems*. By J. De Jean. Dublin: J. McGlashan, 1851; *Poems*. By J. De Jean. With a Memoir by James Burke. Dublin: Mullany, 1853.

FRENCH [WILLIAM] PERCY (1854-1920), humorist and entertainer. French was born in Cloonyquin, County Roscommon, on May 1, 1854. He was educated at Trinity College, Dublin, and became a civil engineer, but his great talent was as a humorist in prose and in verse. Many of his pieces appeared in his comic paper *The Jarvey*. Their delightful quality may be suggested by the beginning of his sketch "The First Lord Liftinant":

"Essex," said Queen Elizabeth, as the two of them sat at break-whisht in the back parlor of Buckingham Palace, "Essex, me haro, I've got a job that I think would suit you. Do you know where Ireland is?"

"I'm no great fist at jografy," says his lordship, "but I know the place you name. Population, three millions; exports, emigrants."

French was best known as a public entertainer, playing the banjo, making lightning sketches, and singing his own songs. Many of those songs—such as "Come Back, Paddy Reilly," "The Mountains of Mourne," "Phil the Fluter's Ball," and "Are Ye Right There, Michael?"—have never lost their popularity. Indeed, a popular musical of the 1950s, *The Golden Years*, was based on French's life and songs. He died at Formby, Lancashire, in 1920.

WORKS: *The First Lord Liftinant and Other Tales*. Dublin: Mecredy & Kyle, 1890; *The Irish Girl, Comedy Opera*. Book & lyrics by Percy French, assisted by Brendan Stewart. London: Boosey, 1918; *Chronicles and Poems of Percy French*. Mrs. de Burgh Daly, ed. Dublin: Talbot, 1922; *Our House-Warming*. London & New York: Samuel French, 1925. (Eight-page monologue); *Prose, Poems and Parodies*. Mrs. de Burgh Daly, ed. Dublin: Talbot/London: Simpkin, Marshall, 1925.   REFERENCE: Healy, James N. *Percy French and his Songs*. Cork: Mercier/London: Herbert Jenkins, 1966.

FRIEL, BRIAN (1929-), playwright and short story writer. Friel was born in Omagh, County Tyrone, on January 5, 1929. He was educated in Derry at Long Tower School, where his father taught; at St. Columb's College; and at Maynooth College, County Kildare. He left Maynooth in 1948, after two years, for St. Joseph's Teacher Training College, Belfast. In 1954, he married Anne Morrison. With their five children they live in County Donegal.

Teaching in Derry (1950-1960), Friel began writing short stories, mainly for the *New Yorker*, and radio plays for the BBC. The earliest play he regards with any approval is *The Enemy Within* (Abbey Theatre,* 1962), suggested by the exiles of St. Columba. The play which brought Friel fully to public notice was *Philadelphia, Here I Come!*, written after five months (Friel's words) "hanging around" the Tyrone Guthrie Theatre in Minneapolis observing Guthrie at work. It played at the Dublin Theatre Festival in 1965, continuing to a long Broadway run.

The territory of Friel's short stories, where real and imaginary coalesce, stretches from County Tyrone to the west of Donegal. Their characters are mostly rural and poor. For all their inventive humor and their often devastating satire of Irish cant, the stories are essentially elegiac. They celebrate the small gains of loss endured, the solace of illusions that do not wholly deceive, the transience of moments that might harbor a whole relationship. "Foundry House," "The Flower of Kiltymore," and "The Gold in the Sea" speak to what "Among the Ruins" calls "continuance, life repeating itself and surviving."

Friel's drama inhabits the same regions. In *Philadelphia*, Gar O'Donnell addresses the past which has brought him to the eve of exile. His "Public" and "Private" voices are complementary, not antithetical. Now they reinforce each other's mood, now correct, now evade. Gar's relationships— with his father, his dead mother, his lost sweetheart, his wishful friends— are bleakly and tenderly regarded, giving rise to questions which may shadow answers.

In *The Loves of Cass McGuire*, Cass, hopefully returning to her family from squalid exile in America, surrenders to the illusions of an Old People's Home. *Lovers* suggests a continuing theme: the fallible hopes and disenchantments of the varieties of love. Fox Melarkey, of *Crystal and Fox*, in a series of bitter rejections, destroys the present of his pitiful traveling show for a past which, if it ever existed, is irrecoverable.

The Freedom of the City appears to take up the subject matter of contemporary Northern violence, but the setting and events compose a metaphor of individuals glimpsing private recognitions clouded by myths and institutions. In *Volunteers*, a Viking "dig" worked by volunteer "political prisoners" sets historical against immediate modes of sacrifice. Like Friel's two most recent plays, *Living Quarters* and *Faith Healer* (the latter, four related monologues), it accommodates speech to a world of intolerable isolations. Country, family, and faiths offer easy solace which the individual, to find a self independent of their molding, must resist. The comic spirit, especially that of parody, remains, but more and more is colored by a compassion tested to its limit.

In ten major plays, Brian Friel has developed a register of dramatic voices, coherent within their evolving modulations. He is unique among contemporary Irish dramatists, and his craft constantly engrosses new perceptions.

D.E.S. MAXWELL

WORKS: *The Saucer of Larks*. London: Gollancz, 1962. (Stories); *Philadelphia, Here I Come!* London: Faber, 1965. (Play); *The Gold in the Sea*. London: Gollancz, 1966. (Stories); *The Loves of Cass McGuire*. London: Faber, 1967. (Play); *Lovers*. New York: Farrar, Straus, Giroux, 1968/London: Faber, 1969. *Crystal and Fox*. London: Faber, 1970. (Play); *Two Plays*. New York: Farrar, Straus & Giroux, 1970. (Contains *Crystal and Fox* and *The Mundy Scheme*); *The Gentle Island* [London]: Davis-Poynter, [1973]. (Play); *The Freedom of the City*. London: Faber, 1974. (Play); *The Enemy Within*. Newark, Del.: Proscenium, 1975. (Play); *Living Quarters*. London & Boston: Faber, 1978. (Play);   REFERENCE: Maxwell, D.E.S. *Brian Friel*. Lewisburg, Pa.: Bucknell University Press, 1973.

FURLONG, ALICE (ca. 1875-?), poet. Furlong was born in Tallaght, County Dublin, in about 1875. Her older sister Mary (ca. 1868- September 22, 1898) was a frequent contributor of romantic verse to the popular press; her ability may be judged by the first stanza from "An Irish Love Song":

> I love you, and I love you, and I love you, O my honey!
> It isn't for your goodly lands, it isn't for your money;
> It isn't for your father's cows, your mother's yellow butter.
> The love that's in my heart for you no words of mine may utter!

Apparently inspired by both the quality and content of her sister's verse, Furlong became a prolific writer of poems for the nationalist press and of stories for the popular press. Her subjects are Ireland—its romance, its whimsy, its weather, and its landscape. She is a better poet than Mary and has had a few successes, as in "The Warning" and "The Betrayal."

WORKS: *Roses and Rue*. London: E. Mathews, 1899; *Tales of Fairy Folks, Queens and Heroes*. Dublin: Browne & Nolan, [1907].

FURLONG, THOMAS (1794-1827), poet. Furlong, although a poet of great skill, is unfortunately neglected today. At his best, as in his long poem "The Doom of Derenzie," he tells a powerful, Wordsworthian story movingly, and his handling of the blank verse is exceptionally fluent. He was born at Scarawalsh, County Wexford, in 1794, the son of a small farmer. With little education, he was apprenticed to a Dublin grocer. An elegy which he wrote on the death of his master came to the notice of Jameson the whiskey distiller, who encouraged him in his writing efforts. His poem "The Misanthrope" gained him the friendship of Thomas Moore* and Lady Morgan.* He became a regular contributor to Dublin journals and helped found *The New Irish Magazine* in 1821. His political satire "The Plagues of Ireland" appeared in 1824, and he became a friend and confidant of O'Connell. He produced a graceful translation of "The Remains of Carolan" and other poems from the Irish, about which he also wrote:

> Fling, fling the forms of art aside—
>   Dull is the ear that these forms enthrall;
> Let the simple songs of our sires be tried—
>   They go to the heart, and the heart is all.

Nevertheless, his own supple translations did not fling the forms of art aside.

Furlong died of consumption on July 25, 1827, and is buried in Drumcondra.

WORKS: *The Misanthrope, and Other Poems*. London: H. Colburn, 1819/Dublin: Underwood, 1821; *The Plagues of Ireland*. Dublin: Printed for the Author, 1824; *The Doom of Derenzie*. London: J. Robins, 1829. (Furlong also has some translations from the Irish in Hardiman's *Irish Ministrelsy*.) 2 vols. London: Robins, 1831. Indeed, Brian McKenna attributes nearly all the translations in Vol. I to Furlong.

REFERENCES: De Blacam, Aodh. "Two Poets Who Discovered Their Country." *Irish Monthly* 74 (1946): 357-365; Hardiman, James. "Memoir of Thomas Furlong." In *Irish Ministrelsy* (London: Robins, 1831. Vol. I, pp. lxix-lxxx; Russell, Matthew. "Our Poets, No. 17: Thomas Furlong." *Irish Monthly* 18 (1888): 421-426.

GALLAGHER, FRANK (1893-1962), journalist, historian, and short story writer. Gallagher was born in Cork in 1893. He became a member of the Irish Volunteers and later worked closely with Erskine Childers* on the publicity staff of the Republican government and as editor of the clandestine *The Irish Bulletin*. He was several times in prison and was once involved in a long hunger strike which he described in one of his short stories and in *Four Glorious Years*. He was editor of the *Cork Free Press* and of *The Irish Press* from 1931; deputy director of Radio Éireann; head of the Government Information Bureau; and from 1954, a member of the National Library.

As an historian, Gallagher was diligent and as accurate as partisanship would allow. His best book is a collection of journalistic pieces, *Four Glorious Years* (1953). This is a totally slanted, occasionally overwritten, often tedious, and yet intermittently fascinating personal reminiscence of the years leading up to the signing of the Anglo-Irish Treaty. His *The Indivisible Island* (1957) is a well-researched, book-length tract against partition. *The Anglo-Irish Treaty,* posthumously published in 1965, was part of an uncompleted biography of de Valera. Its separate publication was scarcely warranted, for the fragment adds little or nothing to Frank Pakenham's previously published study of the Treaty negotiations, *Peace by Ordeal*. Under one of his pseudonyms, David Hogan, Gallagher published some short stories dealing with the Troubles. These stories are leanly written and technically craftsmanlike, but with their patriotic simplicity, melodrama, and romance, they cannot be considered seriously as literature. Gallagher died in Dublin in July 1962.

WORKS: (as Frank Gallagher) *Days of Fear*. London: John Murray, 1928; *The Indivisible Island*. London: Gollancz, 1957; *The Anglo-Irish Treaty,* ed. with an Introduction by Thomas P. O'Neill. London: Hutchinson, 1965. (as David Hogan): *The Challenge of the Sentry and Other Stories of the Irish War*. Dublin: Talbot, 1928; *Dark Mountain and Other Stories*. Dublin & Cork: Talbot, 1931; *The Four Glorious Years*. Dublin: Irish Press, 1953.

GALLAHER, LEE (ca. 1935-), playwright. Gallaher was born in Bray, County Wicklow, in the mid-1930s, and since 1969 his plays have been produced at Trinity College, and at the Focus, Lantern, and Project Theatres. He was awarded the Abbey Theatre* Playwright's Bursary for 1973 and 1974. Probably his most talked-about work thus far is *The Velvet Abbatoir* (Project, 1976), which was a mixed media show that also featured Gallaher's collages. To date, he has published two one-act plays, *Kiss Me, Mister Bogart* (Lantern, 1970) and *All the Candles in*

Your Head (Lantern, 1974). The more effective of the two, the *Mister Bogart* play, is a Pinter-like exercise in what used to be called the Theatre of Menace.

WORK: *Two Plays*. Dublin: Lantern Writers Workshop, 1974.

GALLIVAN, G[ERALD] P. (1920-), playwright. Gallivan was born on July 29, 1920, in Limerick. Upon graduating from Crescent College at eighteen, he wrote a book which he could not get published. In 1940 he emigrated to England where he worked for five years. Returning to Ireland in 1946, he found a job in business. His first six plays were produced in Limerick by the College Players when he was working for T.W.A. at Shannon. His first Dublin production was *Decision at Easter* (Globe, 1959) about the 1916 Rising. This play was followed by *Mourn the Ivy Leaf* (Globe, 1960) about Parnell, and by *The Stepping Stone,* which was produced in Cork, Belfast, and Dublin in 1963, and which was about Michael Collins. His plays *Campobasso* (Theatre Festival, 1965) and *A Beginning of Truth* (Lantern, 1968) are about modern politics. *Campobasso* is set in some unspecified European country, but has distinct parallels to the career of de Valera; *A Beginning of Truth* is set in present-day Ireland and is probably his best play. His more recent work includes *The Dáil Debate* (Peacock, 1971) and *Dev* (Project, 1977), both concerned with modern Irish history. *The Dáil Debate* was largely an arrangement of actual quotations from the participants in the argument about whether to accept the Anglo-Irish Treaty which Griffith and Collins had signed in December 1921. However, the undigested speeches proved less theatrical than the real-life events had been. *Dev* is, of course, a consideration of the commanding figure in modern Irish politics, but the play did not probe very deeply into de Valera's complex and enigmatic character.

Obviously, Gallivan's main preoccupation in the theatre has been the subject of Irish politics, but, with an exception or two, his work has been worthy but somewhat lacking in bite. Still, more than any other contemporary Irish playwright he has addressed himself constantly to a significant topic. In his never less than competent plays, he has worked quietly for an adult and untrivial theatre.

WORKS: *Decision at Easter*. Dublin: Progress House, 1960; *Mourn the Ivy Leaf*. Dublin: Progress House, 1965; *Dev*. Dublin: Co-op Books, 1978.

GALVIN, PATRICK (ca. 1927-), playwright, poet, and ballad singer. Galvin was born in Cork City, on April 15 or possibly August 15, 1927, although it could have been 1929 or even later. He is uncertain about his birthdate because his mother forged different dates on his birth certificate so that he might appear older than he was and more easily get jobs. He was one of seven children in a poor famliy, and his father was illiterate.

He was scantily educated by the Christian Brothers, and when he left school at about eleven could barely read or write. He has spent some time working in London and in a kibbutz in Israel. He has cut several records of Irish ballads and lectured in East Germany on Irish folksongs. He has also published several volumes of verse and has had about a half a dozen plays produced.

Typical of his verse are the pieces in *The Wood-burners* (1973), which might better be described as written in vigorous slabs of language rather than in poetry. As a poet he has little conception of form, but his best pieces, such as "Statement on the Burning of Cork," have freshness and a sense of the individuality of the man who wrote them. For instance, he is quite effectively able to conclude an adaptation from the Irish with the line " 'Tis bloody fabulous!" His worst pieces are trivial, but what personality can accomplish in lieu of technique he does accomplish.

His plays *Cry the Believers* and *And Him Stretched* were produced in Dublin in the early 1960s. In the early 1970s, three more plays were produced by the Lyric Theatre* in Belfast when he was attached to the theatre on a Leverhulme Fellowship in Drama. His Belfast plays, which are his only plays yet to be published, are rather thin stuff. With excellent productions, they could work in the theatre as immediately meaningful entertainments, but the simplicity of their themes, the flatness of their characterization, and the pedestrian quality of their language work against them. Even the ballad opera *We Do It for Love,* which focuses on the Northern troubles of the 1970s, does not get enough theatrical life from its tunes, which is strange considering Galvin's wide knowledge of Irish folk music. In sum, Galvin has remained an amateur writer; his best work is the product of his strength of personality rather than judgment or craftsmanship.

WORKS: *The Wood-Burners*. Dublin: New Writers', 1973; *Three Plays*. Belfast: Threshold, 1976.   REFERENCE: Kiely, Niall. "The Saturday Interview." *The Irish Times* (July 24, 1976).

GATE THEATRE, THE (1928-) The Gate Theatre has been a complement to rather than a rival of the Abbey Theatre.* At times in their histories, especially when the Gate productions have been particularly scintillating and the Abbey productions dully pedestrian, the Gate has seemed the more important theatre. Any such comparison of relative importance is irrelevant, however, for the aims of the two organizations have always been different. The Abbey has been engaged primarily in producing new Irish plays, and even at the dreariest periods in its long history, it has never wavered from that intention. In contrast, the younger Gate, from its founding in 1928, has concentrated on producing an eclectic selection from world drama in nearly every period. While the Gate has sporadically produced new Irish plays, some of which have been extremely distinguished, its founders have never viewed their primary function as the encouragement of native Irish drama.

The Gate was founded by a young English actor, Hilton Edwards, and a young Irish actor and painter, Micheál Mac Liammóir.* They were inaugurating nothing new in the Irish theatre but were continuing an impulse that had been present from the beginning. In the early years of the dramatic movement, three strands of future development may be distinguished: the poetic drama of W. B. Yeats,* the realistic native drama of Padraic Colum,* and the interest in the continental drama of Ibsen and Strindberg. This interest in continental drama was most evident in the plays of Edward Martyn.* Although Martyn's own dramatic talent was small, he continued to be involved in and even to launch small theatres, such as the Irish Theatre in Hardwicke Street, that produced some of the more interesting and depressing contemporary European plays. However, two of Martyn's key people, Thomas MacDonagh* and Joseph Mary Plunkett,* were executed after the 1916 Rising. Hence, the Dublin Drama League was initiated in 1918 by Yeats,* Robinson,* James Stephens,* and others, to continue the production of foreign masterpieces that would not otherwise be seen in Dublin. The League existed for ten years, staging intermittent productions of one or two performances and using actors recruited from the Abbey and from the amateur movement. In 1928, Edwards and Mac Liammóir, who had met while touring in Anew McMaster's company, joined forces to produce a season of plays at the Abbey's little experimental theatre, the Peacock. The season began with a noteworthy performance of *Peer Gynt* and continued with two plays by O'Neill and others by Wilde,* Evreinov, Mac Liammóir, and Elmer Greensfelder. Its second season, also in the Peacock, saw works by Tolstoy, Rice, Capek, Galsworthy, Evreinov, and Paul Raynal, as well as three new Irish plays, the finest being Denis Johnston's* now-famous *The Old Lady Says "No!"* With these exciting productions, the new theatre was obviously the heir of Edward Martyn's tradition.

After this second season, Edwards and Mac Liammóir moved their operations to the Rotunda where a second-storey ballroom was converted into a theatre. There the Gate has maintained its permanent home ever since. From that third season in 1930, the Gate has produced well over three hundred plays from world drama, ranging from the high tragedy of Aeschylus, Sophocles, and Shakespeare, to the high comedy of Shaw,* Wilde, and Sheridan,* to broad farce, airy romance, poetic drama, expressionism, and the Broadway and West End success. The company is not associated with any individual style. Rather, the productions have been noted for an eclecticism of approach, as well as consummate taste in staging and a meticulous professionalism. In the thirty years after 1930 until the advent of television, there was no more potent force than the Gate in educating Ireland in the drama.

The interest of the Gate for literature lies in the new Irish plays and playwrights that it has fostered. The most significant new Irish plays produced by the Gate were those by Denis Johnston, Lord Longford,* Lady Longford,* and Mary Manning,* but it also presented plays by such interesting dramatists as Padraic Colum,* T. C. Murray,* Lennox Robinson, Austin Clarke,* St. John Ervine,* Andrew Ganly, Maura Laverty,* Donagh MacDonagh,* and others. In the 1960s, the theatre attained international success with plays by the Northern writer Brian Friel* and attracted considerable local admiration with the plays of Desmond Forristal.*

Of these writers, the most eminent theatrically is Johnston, whose reputation finally, in its different way, is beginning to rival that of O'Casey.* Some of Johnston's plays were produced by the Abbey, but his most experimental were done by the Gate, including *The Old Lady* and *A Bride for the Unicorn*. In the 1930s, the Gate had an aura of clever sophistication that did not at all attach to the Abbey, which at that time was largely producing "kitchen comedies" (and indeed one wit compared the differences between the Gate and the Abbey as the differences between Sodom and Begorrah). If there was a kind of Gate play, it was a clever, witty satire or satirical comedy. The most brilliant writers of this genre were Mary Manning, Lady Longford, and Mac Liammóir himself. In such pieces as *Youth's the Season—?*, *Mr. Jiggins of Jigginstown*, and *Ill Met by Moonlight*, the Gate managed enormously stylish productions.

In 1936, Lord Longford, who had been a major financial supporter of the theatre, formed his own company, Longford Productions. For many years, Longford shared the building on a half-yearly basis with the original company. In the 1970s, after more than forty years of financial struggle, the Gate received a subsidy from the Irish government. Today, despite Edwards' age and Mac Liammóir's death in 1978, the theatre still mounts a season for several months each year and rents the stage out to visiting companies for the rest of the time.

If the Gate is not as prominent as the Abbey in either literary or theatrical history, the reason may be that its main interest was never the production of new Irish plays. However, what the theatre has produced— including, of course, more than fifty new Irish plays—it has done brilliantly.

REFERENCES: Hobson, Bulmer, ed. *The Gate Theatre, Dublin*. Dublin: Gate Theatre, 1934. (Contains articles, list of productions, sketches, and many photographs); Edwards, Hilton. *The Mantle of Harlequin*. Dublin: Progress House, 1958; Mac Liammóir, Micheál. *All for Hecuba*. Dublin: Progress House, 1961; Mac Liammóir, Micheál. *Each Actor on His Ass*. London: Routledge & Kegan Paul, 1961; Mac Liammóir, Micheál. *Theatre in Ireland*. 2d ed. Dublin: Cultural Relations Committee of Ireland, 1964. Luke Peter ed. *Enter Certain Players, Edwards-Mac Liammóir and the Gate*. [Dublin]: Dolmen, [1978].

GEOGHEGAN, ARTHUR GERALD (ca. 1810-1889), poet. Geoghegan was born in 1809 or 1810, worked in the civil service, and was a collector of Irish antiquities. His long narrative poem, *The Monks of Kilcrea*, appeared anonymously, but went into two editions and was translated into French. He wrote for *The Dublin Penny Journal, The Dublin University Magazine, The Nation,** and many other magazines. His work is consistently euphonious, and his deft little "After Aughrim" is sometimes reprinted. He died in London in November 1889.

WORKS: *The Monks of Kilcrea, a Ballad Poem.* Dublin: McGlashan, 1853; *The Monks of Kilcrea, and Other Ballads and Poems.* London, 1861.

GIBBON, [WILLIAM] MONK (1896-), poet and man of letters. Gibbon was born in Dublin on December 15, 1896, and was educated at St. Columba's College, Rathfarnham, and at Keble College, Oxford. He served in World War I from 1914 until he was invalided out in 1918. After the war he taught at Oldfield School, Swanage, Wales, for twelve years. He is a member of the Irish Academy of Letters and a Fellow of the Royal Society of Literature.

As a poet, Gibbon is conventional and even old-fashioned. He is capable of poetic spellings such as "o'er," of poetic inversions such as "chestnuts young" or "they turned from him away," of personifications of Love and Truth and "blind greed," "deaf pride," and "purse-proud Time," and his work is full of poetic diction such as O, Ah, Aye, Nay, oft, spake, alas, thou and thy, art, wilt, lest, twixt, pelf, and so on. All of these archaic qualities notwithstanding, Gibbon is, at his best, graceful, terse, immediate, and strong. What, for instance, could be tighter or defter than his excellent poem "Microcosm," which begins:

> What if all that surely is
> Shadow also surely be,
> And the finite fountain jets
> Waters of infinity?

He handles conventional quatrains and couplets and sonnets with ease and fluency, and can even manage effective pastiches of Gerard Manley Hopkins, who is rather far from his own style. He is not a highly individual poet, but he has had so many successes that a Selected Poems would well be in order.

Gibbon has done a good deal of miscellaneous writing, including prose poems, travel books, some criticism, a novel, a biography, a refractory critical memoir of Yeats* (who found him argumentative), and some autobiographical volumes, of which the best are probably *The Seals* (1935) and *Mount Ida* (1948). *The Seals* is a reflective narrative of a seal hunt in Donegal, and is incongruously reminiscent of (and superior to) Hemingway's *Green Hills of Africa. Mount Ida* is a self-indulgent, lengthy account of three romances at various times in the author's life and in various places —Wales, Italy, and Austria. Although much too long for the strength of emotion involved, the book has charm; at half its length it could have been a minor classic.

WORKS: *The Tremulous String*. Fair Oak: A. W. Mathews, 1926. (Prose poems); *The Branch of Hawthorn Tree*. London: Grayhound, 1927. (Poems); *For Daws to Peck at*. London: Gollancz/New York: Dodd, Mead, 1929. (Poems); *A Ballad*. Winchester: Grayhound, 1930; *Seventeen Sonnets*. London: Joiner & Steele, 1932; *The Seals*. London: Jonathan Cape, 1935; ed and with an introductory essay, *The Living Torch* by AE. London: Macmillan, 1937; *Mount Ida*. London: Jonathan Cape, 1948; *The Red Shoes Ballet*. [London]: Saturn, [1948]. (Criticism); *Swiss Enchantment*. London: Evans, 1950. (Travel); *This Insubstantial Pageant*. London: Phoenix House, 1951. (Prose poems); *The Tales of Hoffmann: A Study of the Film*. London: Saturn, 1951; *An Intruder at the Ballet*. London: Phoenix House, 1952. (Criticism); *Austria*. London: Batsford, 1953. (Travel); *In Search of Winter Sport*. London: Evans, 1953. (Travel); *Western Germany*. London: Batsford, 1955; *The Rhine and its Castles*. London: Putnam, 1957. (Travel); *The Masterpiece and the Man: Yeats as I knew Him*. London: Hart-Davis, 1959; *Netta*. London: Routledge & Kegan Paul, 1960. (Biography); *The Climate of Love*. London: Gollancz, 1961. (Novel); ed. with an Introduction, *Poems from the Irish* by Douglas Hyde. Dublin: Figgis, 1963; ed. with an Introduction, *The Poems of Katharine Tynan*. Dublin: Figgis, 1963; *The Brahms Waltz*. London: Hutchinson, 1970. (Autobiographical); *The Velvet Bow and Other Poems*. London: Hutchinson, 1972.

GILBERT, LADY (1841-1921), novelist, short story writer, and poet. Lady Gilbert was born Rosa Mulholland in Belfast in 1841. She married John T. Gilbert,* the historian, in 1891, and she became a prolific writer for the popular press. Her fiction is informed by some real knowledge of the peasantry of the West but is overly romantic and heavily religious. Like the hero of one of her books, Lady Gilbert wrote for "the nobler and purer-minded section of the reading public." The intellectual level of that public may perhaps be demonstrated by the conclusion of her novel, *The Wild Birds of Killeevy* (1883):

> We will now take leave of our hero and heroine on a summer evening after sunset as they sit in their own little territory—a garden of roses extending down to the cliffs, with the crimsoned ocean at their feet and all the hundred isles they know so well burning on it like so many jewels, set with amethyst and amber and gold.
>
> Kevin has just finished reading his new poem to Fanchea. Her hand is in his; her eyes are full of tears. She is not thinking of the applause of the world which may follow this work, but of the higher audience that have been present at the reading, the choirs of angels that have witnessed this new utterance of a strong man's soul. "Let them be the judges," is the thought of her heart; and she smiles, feeling conscious of their approval.
>
> A cloud of sea-birds rises from their favourite island; they circle and wheel, and fly off in a trail towards the glory of the sun.
>
> So wing all white souls to a happy eternity.

After penning hundreds of such sweet and innocuous fiction, she died in Dublin in 1921.

WORKS: *Hester's History,* published anonymously. 2 vols. London, 1869; *The Wicked Woods of Tobereevil.* London, 1872/London: Burns & Oates, [1897]; *The Little Flower Seekers.* London, [1873]; *Eldergowan . . . and Other Tales.* London, 1874; *Five Little Farmers.* London, 1876; *Four Little Mischiefs.* London: Blackie, 1883; *The Wild Birds of Killeevy.* London: Burns & Oates, [1883]; ed., *Gems for the Young from Favourite Poets.* Dublin: Gill, 1884; *Hetty Gray, or Nobody's Bairn.* London: Blackie, 1884; *The Walking Trees, and Other Tales.* Dublin: Gill, 1885; *The Late Mrs. Hollingford.* London: Blackie, [1886]; *Marcella Grace, an Irish Novel.* London: Kegan Paul, 1886; *Vagrant Verses.* London: Kegan Paul, 1886/London: E. Mathews, [1889]; *A Fair Emigrant.* London: Kegan Paul, 1888; *Gianetta.* London: Blackie, 1889; *The Mystery of Hall-in-the-Wood.* London: Sunday School Union, [1893]; *Marigold and Other Stories.* Dublin: Eason, 1894; *Banshee Castle.* London: Blackie, 1895; *Our Own Story and Other Tales.* London: Catholic Truth Society, [1896]; *Nanno.* London: Grant Richards, 1899; *Onora.* London: Grant Richards, 1900/later published as *Norah of Waterford,* London & Edinburgh: Sands, 1915; *Terry; or, She Ought to Have Been a Boy.* London: Blackie, [1900]; *Cynthia's Bonnet Shop.* London: Blackie, 1901; *The Squire's Grand-Daughters.* London: Burns & Oates/New York: Benziger, 1903; *The Tragedy of Chris.* London, Edinburgh: Sands, 1903; *A Girl's Ideal.* London: Blackie, 1905; *Life of Sir John T. Gilbert.* London: Longman's, 1905; *Our Boycotting.* Dublin: Gill, 1907. (Play); *Our Sister Maisie.* London: Blackie, 1907; *The Story of Ellen.* London: Burns & Oates/New York: Benziger, 1907; *The Return of Mary O'Murrough.* Edinburgh & London: Sands, 1908; *Spirit and Dust.* London: Elkin Mathews, 1908; *Cousin Sara.* London: Blackie, 1909; *Father Tim.* London & Edinburgh: Sands, 1910; *The O'Shaughnessy Girls.* London: Blackie, 1911; *Fair Noreen.* London: Blackie, 1912; *Twin Sisters, an Irish Tale.* London: Blackie, 1913; *Old School Friends.* London: Blackie, 1914; *The Daughter in Possession.* London: Blackie, 1915; *Dreams and Realities.* London & Edinburgh: Sands, 1916. (Poems); *Narcissa's Ring.* London: Blackie, 1916; *O'Loughlin of Clare.* London & Edinburgh: Sands, 1916; *The Cranberry Claimants.* London: Sands, [1932].

GILBERT, SIR JOHN T[HOMAS] (1829-1898), historian. Gilbert was born in Dublin in 1829. He wrote the first real history of that city, a book which is still most readable and full of excellent anecdote. He was the secretary of the Public Record Office, published also a *History of the Viceroys of Ireland,* and retrieved and published many valuable historical documents. He married Rosa Mulholland* in 1891, was knighted in 1897, and died on May 23, 1898.

WORKS: *A History of the City of Dublin.* 3 vols. Dublin: James McGlushan, 1854-1859/Dublin: James Duffy, 1861. Gilbert wrote a good deal of other scholarly historical work, but probably nothing else of great literary interest.   REFERENCE: Gilbert, Lady. *Life of Sir John T. Gilbert.* London: Longmans, 1905.

GILBERT, STEPHEN (1912-), novelist. Gilbert, born in July 1912, at Newcastle, County Down, was the elder son of William Gilbert, a wholesale seed and tea merchant of Belfast. He was a reporter on *The Northern Whig* from 1931 until 1933 when he joined his father at Samuel McCaus-

land, Limited. On the death of his father, he was appointed a director. At the outbreak of World War II, Gilbert joined the 3rd Ulster Searchlight Regiment as a gunner. He was awarded the Military Medal in 1940, and later in that year he was commissioned. In 1941, he was released from service to return to business. He was actively associated with the Campaign for Nuclear Disarmament in Northern Ireland, acting as secretary for two years.

Gilbert's latest novel, *Ratman's Notebooks*, was published in 1968 and was made into the very successful film *Willard*. The book was subsequently reissued in paperback with the latter title and has also been translated into Italian, German, Portuguese, Dutch, and Japanese. His previous publications are *The Landslide* (1943), *Bombadier* (1944), *Monkeyface* (1948), and *The Burnaby Experiments* (1952).

Gilbert stands apart from other Irish writers both in subject matter and style. Although his fantasies are influenced by the work of his friend Forrest Reid,* Gilbert broke free of that influence with the publication of *Bombadier,* one of the best written novels of World War II. His highly imaginative prose is marked by its extreme lucidity and simplicity. Though *Ratman's Notebooks* is his most popular novel, *The Landslide* is perhaps his outstanding achievement, formally and stylistically.

Gilbert is married and has four children. He is director or chairman of a number of companies operating in Ireland, Scotland, and England. He lives about twelve miles from Belfast in County Antrim, where his wife farms seventy-five acres of land and breeds Shetland ponies.

JOHN BOYD

WORKS: *The Landslide*. London: Faber, 1943; *Bombadier*. London: Faber, 1944; *Monkeyface*. London: Faber, 1948; *The Burnaby Experiments*. London: Faber, 1952; *Ratman's Notebooks*. London: Michael Joseph, 1968.

GOGARTY, OLIVER ST. JOHN (1878-1957), poet. Gogarty was born in 5, Rutland (now Parnell) Square, Dublin on August 17, 1878. He attended the local Christian Brothers school and, after his father's early and unexpected death from appendicitis, was a boarder at Mungret, Stonyhurst, and Clongowes. Following a period at the Royal University, he entered the medical school of Trinity College.

Gogarty's amusing personality and athletic prowess ensured his popularity with fellow students. For a time he and James Joyce* were close friends, a relationship discussed in J. B. Lyons, *James Joyce and Medicine* (1973). The dons, too, were impressed by his knowledge of literature and his flair for parody. He formed lasting friendships with the Trinity College classical scholar, Robert Yelverton Tyrrell (1844-1914) and John Pentland Mahaffy,* and won the Vice-Chancellor's Prize for English Verse in 1902, 1903, and 1905. Hoping for similar success with the Newdigate Prize, he spent a term at Worcester College, Oxford, in 1904 but placed

second to G.K.C. Bell, a future bishop of Chichester. His letters to Bell
(*Many Lines to Thee*, 1971) display a sensitivity concealed in his correspondence with Joyce where a cynical bawdiness predominates.

While at Oxford, he became friendly with R. S. Chenevix Trench who
stayed with him in a Martello Tower in Sandycove which he rented in the
autumn of 1904. James Joyce was the third member of the party. The
young men are featured in *Ulysses* as Buck Mulligan, Haines, and Stephen
Dedalus, respectively.

Gogarty's multifarious interests (he was a strong swimmer and a champion cyclist) conflicted with professional studies and delayed graduation
until 1907. Meanwhile, he had married Martha Duane of Moyard, Connemara. (They were to have three children.) A period of postgraduate study
in Vienna equipped him to practice ear-nose-and-throat surgery. He purchased a house in Ely Place, Dublin, where his neighbors included George
Moore* and Sir Thornley Stoker whose brother Bram Stoker* was the
author of *Dracula*.

As an undergraduate, Gogarty published signed and unsigned poems and
articles in *Dana* and other periodicals, but the conservative traditions of
the medical profession obliged him to delay a public appearance as a poet.
He used a pseudonym when his plays *Blight* (1917), *A Serious Thing*
(1919), and *The Enchanted Trousers* (1919) were staged in the Abbey
Theatre.* His personality was too strong, however, to be fettered, and
through politics he became a national figure when appointed to the Irish
Free State Senate in 1922. Unfortunate consequences in those troubled
times were an attempt on Senator Gogarty's life and the burning of his
country property, Renvyle House, where his guests had included W. B.
Yeats* and Augustus John.

The Senate provided Gogarty a forum for advising on how the building
of the new state should proceed and for castigating political opponents.
On the whole, his advice was sound, and peppered with wit. His castiga-
tions, though not undeserved, were almost indecently vehement, his special
target being Eamon de Valera. The remark that "Dev" looked like "a cross
between a corpse and a cormorant" was made in private, but in the Senate
he referred to "our Celtic Calvin" and on another occasion said, "Instead
of seizing the opportunity of Plenty, like a fanatical edition of St. Francis
he is to wed his Lady Poverty . . ." Giving tit for tat, Sean MacEntee said
that Gogarty reminded him "of a surgeon operating with a pickaxe."

When Gogarty's patients in the Meath Hospital overflowed into the beds
of his colleague Sir Lambert Ormsby, a general surgeon, Ormsby's assistant
remonstrated, saying that Ormsby needed the beds. "Beds!" exclaimed
Gogarty, "he needs slabs." The remark is characteristic of his mordant wit.
The publication of *As I Was Going Down Sackville Street* (1937) led to
a libel suit which Gogarty lost. This is his best known book, an interesting
memoir of his times, but inferior in comic individuality to *Tumbling in the*

Hay (1939). The latter work, incidentally, describes an evening in Holles Street Hospital which may have been Joyce's inspiration for the Oxen of the Sun episode of *Ulysses*. The third major prose work is *I Follow Saint Patrick* (1938).

Gogarty left Ireland in 1939 and, apart from occasional visits home, spent the remainder of his life in America. He died in New York City on September 22, 1957. During his years abroad, the novels *Going Native* (1940), *Mad Grandeur* (1941), and *Mr. Petunia* (1945) were published, as well as an autobiography *It Isn't that Time of Year at All* (1954) and books of essays and reminiscence. Some of these, deriving from repetitive homeward glances, lack freshness, but in any case Gogarty's principal claim on our attention is through his poetry. He had emerged from the cloak of anonymity with *An Offering of Swans* (1923), *Wild Apples* (1928), and a larger volume, *Selected Poems* (1933). His *Collected Poems* was published in 1950.

Envious contemporaries thought W. B. Yeats* overvalued Gogarty in the Preface to the *Oxford Book of Modern Verse* (1936) when he called him "one of the great lyric poets of our age." Today, Gogarty is *under*valued except by eclectics who are still receptive to themes, moods, and measures influenced by antiquity and the Elizabethans and owing nothing to Pound and Eliot. The future will surely bring redress, with adequate appreciation of Gogarty's exquisite lyrics and of epigrams worthy of the *Greek Anthology*.

A. N. Jeffares remarks in "Oliver St. John Gogarty, Irishman" (*The Circus Animals*, 1970) that the volume *Collected Poems* contains what "would be considered a dangerous spread of subject by some of our contemporary critics who confuse solemnity with seriousness." Vivian Mercier has written perceptively of Gogarty in *Poetry* (1958, 93, 35); he regards "Leda and the Swan" as a masterpiece of great originality. David R. Clark contributes an analysis of "The Crab Tree" in *Lyric Resonance* (1972); he selects "Ringsend" as deserving of Yeats' high praise and disagrees with both Mercier's and Jeffares' assessment of this poem, which may indicate that a fuller critical evaluation is merited.

The infinite range of personal tastes helps to explain the irreconcilable judgments on Gogarty. One should perhaps turn to a nonacademic opinion. The late William Doolin, an erudite medical editor, made the enthusiastic affirmation (*The Lancet*, October 5, 1957) that Gogarty's lyrics will be remembered "so long as there are men to quote them."

J. B. LYONS

WORKS: *Hyperthuleana*. Dublin: Printed by F. J. Walker, at the Gaelic Press, 1916. (Poems); *Blight, the Tragedy of Dublin*, with Joseph O'Connor, under the pseudonyms of Alpha and Omega. Dublin: Talbot, 1917; *The Ship and Other Poems*. Dublin: Talbot, 1918; *An Offering of Swans*. Dublin: Cuala, 1923; London: Eyre & Spottiswoode, [1934?]. (Poems); *To My Mother . . . 1924*. Prize ode, written by Gogarty, with music by Louis O'Brien. Dublin: Pigott, [1924]; *Wild Apples*. Dublin:

Cuala, 1928, 1930; New York: J. Cape & H. Smith, [ca. 1929]. (Poems); *Selected Poems*. New York: Macmillan, 1933, published in U.K. as *Others to Adorn*. London: Rich & Cowan, 1938; *As I Was Going Down Sackville Street*. London: Rich & Cowan; New York: Reynal & Hitchcock, 1937. (Reminiscences); *I Follow Saint Patrick*. London: Rich & Cowan; New York: Reynal & Hitchcock, 1938; London: Constable, 1950; *Elbow Room*. Dublin: Cuala, 1929; New York: Duell, Sloan & Pearce, 1940. (Poems); *Tumbling in the Hay*. London: Constable; New York: Reynal & Hitchcock, 1939. (Novel); *Going Native*. New York: Duell, Sloan & Pearce, 1940; London: Constable, 1941. (Novel); *Mad Grandeur*. Philadelphia & New York: J. B. Lippincott, [1941]; London: Constable, 1943. (Novel); *Mr. Petunia*. New York: Creative Age, [1945]; London: Constable, 1946. (Novel); *Perennial*. London: Constable, 1946. (Poetry); *Mourning Becomes Mrs. Spendlove, and Other Portraits Grave and Gay*. New York: Creative Age, [1948]. (Stories and essays); *Rolling Down the Lea*. London: Constable, 1950; *Intimations*. New York: Abelard, [1950]. (Essays); *The Collected Poems of Oliver St. John Gogarty*. London: Constable, 1951; New York: Devin-Adair, [1954]; *It Isn't This Time of Year at All!* London: MacGibbon & Kee; Garden City, N.Y.: Doubleday, 1954. (Autobiographical); *Unselected Poems*. Baltimore: Contemporary, 1954; *Start from Somewhere Else; An Exposition of Wit and Humour, Polite and Perilous*. Garden City, N.Y.: Doubleday, 1955; *The Plays of Oliver St. John Gogarty*, James F. Carens, ed. Newark, Del.: Proscenium, 1971; *Many Lines to Thee*, James F. Carens, ed. Dublin: Dolmen, 1971. (Letters).   REFERENCES: Carens, James F. "Four Revival Figures: Lady Gregory, A.E. (George W. Russell), Oliver St. John Gogarty, and James Stephens." In *Anglo-Irish Literature, a Review of Research,* Richard J. Finneran, ed. New York: Modern Language Association of America, 1976; Lyons, J. B. *Oliver St. John Gogarty*. Lewisburg, Pa.: Bucknell University Press, 1976; O'Connor, Ulick. *Oliver St. John Gogarty: A Poet and His Times*. London: Cape, 1964.

GOLDSMITH, OLIVER (1728-1774), man of letters. Goldsmith is one of Ireland's greatest contributions to English literature. He was the second son and fifth child of a clergyman, and was born at Pallas, near Ballymahon, County Longford, on November 10, 1728. He entered Trinity College, Dublin, on June 11, 1744, and was a contemporary though probably not an acquaintance of Edmund Burke* at that time. (Statues of the two eminent alumni now stand flanking the entrance gates to Trinity in College Green.) After a rackety and impoverished college career, Goldsmith received his B.A. on February 27, 1749. He then began his travels, studied medicine at Edinburgh, and wandered around the Continent, picking up a living as best he could. In 1756, he reached London and embarked upon a literary career which involved him in much hack writing as well as in the production of several minor but enduring masterpieces in several genres. His poems "The Traveller" and "The Deserted Village," his essays in *The Bee* and *The Citizen of the World*, his novel *The Vicar of Wakefield*, and his comedy *She Stoops to Conquer* were among the happiest productions of their day and have continued to charm and delight readers and audiences ever since.

The clearest picture of Goldsmith is probably in Boswell's *Life of Johnson*. Boswell can hardly be exempted from the charge of painting Goldsmith's foibles in bold strokes, but undoubtedly Goldsmith was one of the most feckless, if lovable, of men.

The Irish influence in Goldsmith is small, although it has been justly pointed out that the description of Sweet Auburn in "The Deserted Village" owes much to Goldsmith's memories of his native Lissoy.

He died in London on April 4, 1774, much mourned by his friends. As a counter to Boswell's picture of Goldsmith as the consummate booby, it might be noted that his intimate friends included the most eminent men of the day—Burke, Reynolds, and Dr. Johnson.

WORKS: *New Essays by Oliver Goldsmith*. R. S. Crane, ed. Chicago: University of Chicago Press, 1927; *The Collected Letters of Oliver Goldsmith*. Katherine Balderston, ed. Cambridge. Cambridge University Press, 1928; *Collected Works of Oliver Goldsmith*. Arthur Friedman, ed. 5 vols. Oxford: Clarendon, 1966.   REFERENCES: Boswell, James. *The Life of Samuel Johnson*. G. B. Hill, ed. Revised, L. C. Powell. 6 vols. Oxford: Oxford University Press, 1939-1950; Ginger, John. *The Notable Man*. London: Hamish Hamilton, 1977; Hopkins, Robert. *The True Genius of Oliver Goldsmith*. Baltimore: Johns Hopkins University Press 1969; Rousseau, G. S., ed. *Goldsmith, the Critical Heritage*. London & Boston: Routledge & Kegan Paul, 1974; Scott, Temple (pseud. of J. H. Isaac). *Oliver Goldsmith Bibliographically and Biographically Considered*. New York: Bowling Green Press, 1928; Sells, A. Lytton. *Oliver Goldsmith, His Life and Works*. London: Allen & Unwin/New York: Barnes & Noble, 1974.

GORE-BOOTH, EVA [SELENA] (1870-1926), poet and verse dramatist. Gore-Booth was born at Lissadell, County Sligo, on May 22, 1870, the third child of a prominent Anglo-Irish landlord and the younger sister of Countess Constance Markievicz (1868-1927), the nationalist. Of the sisters, W. B. Yeats* wrote one of his finest poems, "In Memory of Eva Gore-Booth and Con Markievicz" (1927).

While her older sister Constance was most dramatically engaged in the major Irish social and political questions of the day, Eva spent her life much less flamboyantly as a social worker in Manchester. In her quiet but useful and busy life, she found time to write enough poems and verse dramas to fill nearly 650 pages when they were posthumously collected. She was not actively engaged in the Irish Literary Revival, but she was certainly much influenced by it. One of her verse dramas, *Unseen Kings*, about Cuchullain, was considered for production by the Irish National Theatre Society but was finally rejected because it was technically impossible to manage certain of the play's requirements, such as birds flying across the stage. Gore-Booth's poetic plays were really closet dramas, but both they and many of her poems were impelled by a strong feeling for her country. Unfortunately, she was influenced most by the Celtic Twilight* school of Irish writing. Hence, although she is always graceful, she is always conventional and vague in diction. She is a more considerable poet than many of her female contemporaries in Ireland, but she never managed to break out of the poetic conventions of her youth. If she seldom was inept, she really never was memorable. She died in Manchester on June 30, 1926.

WORKS: *Poems of Eva Gore-Booth,* with a biographical introduction by Esther Roper. London: Longmans, Green, 1929.

GRATTAN, HENRY (1746-1820), orator, politician, and lawyer. Grattan was born in Dublin on July 3, 1746. He was the moving spirit of the Irish Parliament from 1782 until it dissolved itself by the Act of Union in 1800. He was also one of the most eloquent orators of his day. Lecky* the historian has probably given the last word on Grattan's language:

> The eloquence of Grattan in his best days was in some respects perhaps the finest that has been heard in either country since the time of Chatham. Considered simply as a debater he was certainly inferior to Fox and Pitt, and perhaps to Sheridan; but he combined two of the very highest qualities of a great orator to a degree that was almost unexampled. No British orator except Chatham had an equal power of firing an educated audience with an intense enthusiasm, or of animating and inspiring a nation. No British orator except Burke had an equal power of sowing his speeches with profound aphorisms, and associating transient questions with eternal truths. His thoughts naturally crystallized into epigrams; his arguments were condensed with such admirable force and clearness that they assumed almost the appearance of axioms; and they were often interspersed with sentences of concentrated poetic beauty, which flashed upon the audience with all the force of sudden inspiration, and which were long remembered and repeated.

Grattan died in London on June 4, 1820, and was buried against his wishes in Westminster Abbey. His flamboyant statue, however, stands in College Green opposite the old House of Parliament.

WORKS: *The Speeches of the Rt. Hon. Henry Grattan.* D. O. Madden, ed. Dublin: James Duffy, 1853.   REFERENCE: McHugh, Roger. *Henry Grattan.* Dublin: Talbot/London: Duckworth, 1936.

GRAVES, ALFRED PERCEVAL (1846-1931), poet. Graves, the son of the Protestant bishop of Limerick, was born in Dublin on July 22, 1846. He was educated in England and at Trinity College, Dublin, but he lived most of his life in London and was an official of the Board of Education. He was a frequent and fluent author of sentimental and humorous verse, much of it set to Irish airs. His most famous piece is the rollicking "Father O'Flynn." Graves also wrote the libretto of a one-act opera, *The Post Bag,* which was subtitled "A Lesson in Irish." The music was composed and arranged from old Irish airs by Michele Esposito, and was presented at the Gaiety Theatre, Dublin, in March 1902. Although received with little enthusiasm, the piece was one of the earliest of the very few attempts at an Irish opera.

Graves was a member of a talented writing family, the most notable of which is his son, the English poet and novelist Robert Graves. (Incidentally, Robert Graves once remarked, "Yeats'* father once confided to my father: 'Willie has found a very profitable little by-path in poetry'. . . .") Alfred Perceval Graves died in Harlech, North Wales, on December 27, 1931.

WORKS: *Songs of Killarney*. London, 1873; *Irish Songs and Ballads*. Manchester: A. Ireland, 1880; ed., *Songs of Irish Wit and Humour*. London: Chatto & Windus, 1884; *Father O'Flynn and Other Irish Lyrics*. London: Swan Sonnenschein, 1889; ed., *The Irish Song Book*. London: Unwin, 1894; *The Postbag: A Lesson in Irish*. Libretto by Graves, music by M. Esposito. London: Boosey, [1902]; *The Irish Poems of Alfred Perceval Graves*. Dublin: Maunsel/London: Unwin, 1908; with W. W. Keene, *Lyrics from "The Absentee,"* an Irish Play in Two Acts. London: Women's Printing Society, [1908]; *An Irish Fairy Book*. London: Unwin, [1909]/London: A. & C. Black, 1938; *Poems for Infants and Juniors*. London: Sir Isaac Pitman, [1910]; ed., *The Poetry Readers*. London: Horace Marshall, [1911]; ed., *The Golden Dawn Reader*. London: James Nisbet, [1911-1917]; *Irish Literary and Musical Studies*. London: Elkin Mathews, 1913; ed., *The Book of Irish Poetry*. London: Unwin, [1914]; with Guy Pertwee, *The Reciter's Treasury of Irish Verse and Prose*. London: Routledge, [1915]; *A Celtic Psaltery*. London: S. P. C. K., 1917. (Translations from the Irish and Welsh; *Songs of the Gael*. Dublin: Talbot, [1925]; *Irish Doric in Song and Story*. London: Unwin, 1926; ed., *The Celtic Song Book*. London: E. Benn, 1928. (Folk songs); *To Return to All That*. London, Toronto: Jonathan Cape, 1930. (Autobiography); *Lives of the British and Irish Saints*. London & Glasgow: Collins' Clear-Type Press, [1934].

GREACEN, ROBERT (1920-), poet. Greacen was born in Derry on October 24, 1920, and was educated at the Methodist College, Belfast, and at Trinity College, Dublin. In the 1940s, he published two volumes of poetry, but no further volumes appeared until 1975. His 1940 poems are extremely various in style, ranging from the tightly formal to the loosely casual. Such poems as "Written on the Sense of Isolation in War-time Ireland" are almost Yeatsian; others, such as "Chorus of Irresponsibles," "The Kingdom Shall Come," and "On My Arm Your Drowsy Head," are quite reminiscent of Auden. These tightly controlled pieces strike one as much better work than the freer "The Poet Answers" or "Lament for France." At his best, Greacen writes in sharply etched images and strong phrasing that make many of his short pieces, such as "Through the Red Canyon" or "The Hopeless Man," cling in the memory. His 1975 volume, *A Garland for Captain Fox*, is a sequence of poems that characterize a shady but civilized wheeler-dealer. The book is even more notable than the early books for its colloquial ease and freshness of diction.

Since 1948, Greacen has lived in London where he works as an editor and teacher.

WORKS: ed., with Alex Comfort. *Lyra: An Anthology of New Lyric.* Billerlcay: Grey Walls Press, 1942; ed., *Northern Harvest.* Belfast: Derrick MacCord, [1944]. (Anthology of Ulster writing); *One Recent Evening.* London: Favil, 1944 (Poems); ed., *Irish Harvest.* Dublin: New Frontiers, 1946; *The Undying Day.* [London]: Falcon, [1948]. (Poems); ed., with Valentin Iremonger.* *Contemporary Irish Poetry.* London: Faber, [1949]; *The World of C. P. Snow.* London: Scorpion, 1952; *The Art of Noel Coward.* Aldington, Kent: Hand & Flower, [1953]; *Even Without Irene.* Dublin: Dolmen, 1969. (Autobiographical); *A Garland for Captain Fox.* Dublin: Gallery Books, 1975. (Poems); *I, Brother Stephen.* Dublin: St. Bueno's hand-printed Limited Editions, [1978].

GREEN, F[REDERICK] L[AURENCE] (1902-1953), English novelist. Green was born in Portsmouth in 1902 and died in Bristol on April 14, 1953. In 1932, he settled in Belfast and spent much of the rest of his life there. His most valuable contribution to Irish literature is his 1945 novel *Odd Man Out*, which is something of a Graham Greene-like entertainment or thriller with distinctly serious overtones. The story tells of the aftermath of an IRA raid, in which the leader is gravely wounded and wanders, dying, around the city as both the police and his friends attempt to find him. Green's primary interest is not the recreation of an historical situation but rather a probing into more elemental questions of how men should regard each other. Although the narrative interest of the book is considerable and the characterization is at least adequate, *Odd Man Out* is not up to the standards of a Graham Greene, for it is consistently flawed by florid and pretentious writing, such as: "Whereas it was an immortal soul in its raiment of flesh and bone. This was a curious phenomenon which has emerged from aeons of life on the world. The body was sustained by certain known processes. But the forces which supported the soul were secret and unfathomable." The quite faithful film of the book, for which Green and R. C. Sherriff wrote the script, is considered one of the finest cinematic treatments of an Irish subject, and probably ranks with the films *Man of Aran* and *The Informer*. It contains some excellent performances by Irish actors, among whom are W. G. Fay, Maureen Delany, Denis O'Dea, Cyril Cusack, and a rare and superb film appearance by F. J. McCormick.

WORKS: *Julius Penton.* London: John Murray, 1934; *The Sound of Winter.* London: Michael Joseph, 1940; *Give Us the World.* London: Michael Joseph, 1941; *Music in the Park.* London: Michael Joseph, 1942; *On the Night of the Fire.* London: Michael Joseph, 1942; *A Song for the Angels.* London: Michael Joseph, 1943; *On the Edge of the Sea.* London: Michael Joseph, 1944; *Odd Man Out.* London: Michael Joseph, 1945; *A Flask for the Journey.* London: Michael Joseph, 1946; *A Fragment of Glass.* London: Michael Joseph, 1947; *Mist on the Waters.* London: Michael Joseph, 1948; *Clouds in the Wind.* London: Michael Joseph, 1950; with R. C. Sheriff, *Odd Man Out* in *Three British Screenplays.* Roger Manvell, ed. London: Methuen in association with the British Film Academy, 1950, pp. 83-202. *The Magician.* London: Michael Joseph, 1951; *Ambush for the Hunter.* London: Michael Joseph, 1952.

GREGORY, DAME ISABELLA AUGUSTA (1852-1932), playwright and folklorist. Lady Gregory was hailed by Bernard Shaw* as "the greatest living Irishwoman." She was born Isabella Augusta Persse at Roxborough, County Galway, on March 15, 1852. As a playwright, essayist, poet, translator, and editor, she could not have differed more from her proselytizing, unionist, nonliterary, gentleman-farming family. Even in childhood she showed her sympathy for the rebel stories and folktales told by her Irish-speaking nurse by collecting Fenian pamphlets and ballad poetry. Later, she established a solid grounding in agrarian economy, forcing the local shopkeepers to cut their prices by setting up in competition on her brother's estate. With her marriage to Sir William Gregory of neighboring Coole on March 4, 1880, she gained access to the political, artistic and social life of Europe. Sir William, thirty-five years her senior, had recently retired as governor of Ceylon but continued to maintain his trusteeship of the National Gallery, his keen interest in the tenant rights for which he had campaigned as member of Parliament for Galway City, and the knowledge of classical literature and antiquities which he shared with his close friend Sir Henry Layard. Married life alternated between London for the season, Coole for the shooting, and travel to India, Ceylon, Egypt, Spain, and Italy. Their only son, William Robert, was born in London in May 1881; Sir William died in March 1892.

By this time, Lady Gregory had already begun her literary career, drawing on her experiences both at home and abroad. Encouraged by Sir William and the poet W. S. Blunt who became a lifelong friend, in 1882 she published a pamphlet defending the Egyptian officer Arabi Bey's revolt against Turkish rule. During the following decades, she campaigned in similar manner for funds for a parish in south London (*Over the River*, 1888 and 1893), support of cottage industries in the west of Ireland (*Gort Industries*, 1896), Irish tax rebates (*A Short Catechism on the Financial Claims of Ireland*, 1898), and against Gladstone's Home Rule bill (*A Phantom's Pilgrimage*, 1893). Although she was constant in her concern that Ireland be sufficiently prepared for the responsibilities of independence, her political beliefs altered radically during the 1890s. In editing her husband's autobiography (1894) and selections from the correspondence of Sir William's grandfather during his years as undersecretary of state for Ireland (*Mr. Gregory's Letter Box 1813-1830*), she laid the foundation both for her own easy, graceful prose style and her determination to rescue Ireland from the English "overgovernment." By 1898, she had become a sufficiently strong nationalist to be involved in the celebrating of the centenary of the 1798 Fenian uprising; three years later, she edited a collection of essays debating literary nationalism (*Ideals in Ireland*, 1901). A combination of social tact and disinterested service enabled her to retain the friendship and active support of such unionist and conservative friends of her late husband as the historian W.E.H. Lecky* and the English diplomat Sir Henry and his wife Enid Layard.

By the 1890s, too, she had begun the collection of folktales and legends of Galway which was to absorb her for the rest of her life, leading to the publication of five volumes of folktales and folk history (*A Book of Saints and Wonders*, 1906; *The Kiltartan History Book*, 1909; *The Kiltartan Wonder Book*, 1910; and the two-volume *Visions and Beliefs in the West of Ireland*, 1920). Although the original impetus for these collections came from her jealousy of W. B. Yeats'* collection of tales for Sligo, *The Celtic Twilight* (1893), it was not until 1896 that she met the poet, who was visiting her neighbor Edward Martyn.* An invitation to Coole led to the lifelong relationship of which Yeats was later to write in his *Memoirs* (1972): "She has been to me mother, friend, sister and brother. I cannot realize the world without her—she brought to my wavering thoughts steadfast nobility." Shortly after her meeting with Yeats, she assisted Douglas Hyde* in founding a Kiltartan branch of the Gaelic League, revived her own earlier desire to learn Irish, and embarked on the ambitious task of translating the epics *Cuchulain of Muirthemne* (1902) and *Gods and Fighting Men* (1904), followed by *The Kiltartan Poetry Book, Translations from the Irish* (1919).

Meanwhile, collaboration with Yeats, Hyde, and Martyn led to the work which was to become Lady Gregory's chief concern: the establishment of an Irish literary theatre. At first considered primarily a fundraiser, she was soon suggesting scenarios for little plays in Irish to Hyde and, while taking dictation, recommending phrases to Yeats. She discovered to her great surprise that the years of listening to good talk, directing affairs in London, Roxborough, and Coole, and researching historical manuscripts in the Royal Irish Academy and the British Museum had sharpened her ear for dialogue, developed clarity of argument, and provided keen insight into character and action. So, at the age of fifty she saw produced the first of her forty plays, most of them written in the Kiltartan dialect which, along with the language of Hyde's *Love Songs of Connacht* (1893), was to offer John Millington Synge* the key he, too, was seeking. From now on her interests—restoring the language and literature of Ireland to its rightful esteem, preparing the country for political independence, and freeing art from the bondage of patriotism and propaganda—merged and led to the foundation, first with Yeats, Martyn, and George Moore,* and later with Yeats, Synge, and the Fay brothers, of the Abbey Theatre* movement.

From the beginning, Lady Gregory had hoped for a touring company which would carry plays based on Irish history and legend to all parts of the country. Her two volumes of folk-history plays, even her later children's wonder plays, were written with that goal in mind. But the plays most frequently associated with her name, the one-act comedies, provided what she was later to refer to in *Our Irish Theatre* (1913) as "the base of realism" balancing the apex of her colleagues' poetic dramas. In these plays, she developed a genius for comedy which is almost eighteenth century in the balanced precision and deliberate avoidance of sentiment. Set in the mythical township of Cloon, yet readily identifiable as the west of Ireland, her characters thrive and act upon "the talk." *Spreading the News*, the title of one of her most delightful comedies, is also an apt description of the life force pervading the "Gregorian universe." Like Don Quixote, one of her favorite literary models (and the subject of her last play, *Sancho's Master*, 1927), her characters assert, believe, and thereupon act, frequently leading to a conundrum of argument and activity which involves the entire community. When still more comedy was required, not surprisingly she turned to Molière. Her adaptation into Kiltartan of *The Doctor in Spite of Himself* (1906), *The Rogueries of Scapin* (1908), *The Miser* (1909), and *The Would-Be Gentleman* (1926) were spirited successes on the Abbey stage.

To one intensely devoted to preserving the history and folklore of her country, the temptation to mythologize which she observed in her countrymen did not always lead to lighthearted comedy. One of her earliest plays, *The Rising of the Moon* (1904), combined the surprised self-commentary of her comic characterizations with the revolutionary spirit of the folk ballad. Her own favorite three-act play, *The Image* (1909), celebrates the leader who follows his heart-secret to tribulation and certain defeat. *The Deliverer* (1911) looks back not only to Moses, but also to the defeat and rejection of Charles Stewart Parnell; *The Story Brought by Brigit* (1924) is a sombre reinterpretation of the passion play as seen through the eyes of one of Ireland's saintly "traveling women." Her strangely powerful but unsuccessful mystery play *Dave* (1927) explores the dark side of the dreamer without the sentiment clinging to *The Travelling Man* (begun with Yeats as early as 1902). Yet, although many of her folk-history plays are aptly labeled "tragic comedies," she wrote few tragedies, the most successful being the one-act threnody *The Gaol Gate* (1906), rising simply, like the keen, to a passionate outburst of heroic grief. Of *Dervorgilla* (1907) Frank O'Connor* wrote in *The Saturday Review* (December 10, 1966): "Her last great speech is as noble as anything in Irish literature." Yeats commented in his journal of her first, much revised history play, *Kincora* (1909): "This play gives me the greatest joy—colour, speech, all has music, and the scenes with the servants make one feel curiously intimate and friendly with those great people who otherwise would be far off—mere figures of speech." More frequently, the mixture of mythmaking and mischief is introduced under the guise of laughter. Her fondness for the cracked idealist and personal idiosyncrasy led to the harmless worlds of *The Jester* (1923, a graceful tribute to her good friend Bernard Shaw), *Hyacinth Halvey* (1906, her version of the paradox of Synge's *Playboy*), and *The Full Moon* (1910, drawing on the character Yeats would later mythologize as Crazy Jane).

In her seventy-fifth year, Lady Gregory decided to stop writing plays,

but she remained a staunch help to the Abbey Theatre as director, administrator, fundraiser, teacher, and critic. She was chiefly responsible for the
discovery of Sean O'Casey* and defender of the rights, both at home and
on tours to Britain and America, of many another playwright whose work
she may have personally disliked. But more and more of her energy, especially after the death of her son during World War I, was taken up with
unsuccessfully persuading the British government to honor the unwit-
nessed codicil to his will prepared by her nephew Hugh Lane, leaving his
collection of Impressionist paintings to Ireland. One of her last stage
pieces was the monlogue "The Old Woman Remembers," recited on the
Abbey stage on December 31, 1923, by her favorite performer Sara Allgood. Her final publication during her lifetime, in 1931, was a return to
her starting place, a spare and powerful evocation of the house, library,
and lands of Coole. A selection from her journals edited by Lennox Robinson* was published in 1946. Forty years after her death, the typescript of
Seventy Years, the autobiography she worked on with the help of Yeats,
was discovered and subsequently published by Colin Smythe in his Coole
series of her collected works.

The complexity of Lady Gregory's activities and interests over an energetic lifetime makes it difficult to define her clearly. Having begun her
writing career as a strong unionist, she then courageously defended Synge's
Playboy of the Western World against overzealous patriots and Shaw's
Shewing-up of Blanco Posnet against the Castle. Later, she published outspoken articles on the Black and Tan atrocities. A romantic idealist who
delighted in her countrymen's "incorrigible genius for myth-making," she
continually fought against any trace of sentimentality in her life and her
work. She never allowed delicacy of feeling to dull truth in her history
plays, yet she did not hesitate to refine and simplify the ancient sagas for
drawing room and cabin. An unflinching realist with a keen sense of the
practical, she nevertheless wrote what Shaw called one of the best ghost
plays he had ever seen (*Shanwalla,* 1915) and with Yeats consulted
mediums in an effort to make contact with the spirit of Hugh Lane. Although she was a natural moralist and believed in rigid standards of behavior, she wrote comedies in which a strain of daftness is revealed through
horseplay, harmless magic, and innocent shape-changing, as well as near-
tragedies based on the themes of conflicting loyalties and the need to follow
one's dream despite the consequences. The most flexible and experimental
of the early Abbey dramatists, she possessed a strong sense of what was
possible on stage and in dialogue, reveling in clarity of action, motive, setting, and characterization. At the same time, she pushed her creations—and
frequently her audiences—through the door of wonder into a world ruled
by beggar, ballad-maker, and weird messenger. Unless one attempts to
reconcile these apparent contradictions, it is dangerously easy to over-
simplify both her character and her contribution.

Perhaps the most damaging misconception of all has to do with what George Moore described in *Hail and Farewell* as "the interdependence of these two minds," Lady Gregory's and Yeats'. Beginning with *Cathleen ni Houlihan* (1902) and *The Stories of Red Hanrahan* (1904) until as late as *King Oedipus* (1928), she helped Yeats with dialogue and sometimes plot. At times the debt is obvious, as in *The Pot of Broth* (1902) and *The Unicorn from the Stars* (1907), but at other times the collaboration extended over so many revisions and such a length of time that identification of contribution becomes impossible. Throughout his lifetime, Yeats never hesitated to acknowledge gracefully the great debt he owed his closest friend and helper. A scribbled note of thanks written on her deathbed movingly records her own tribute to that unique and unbroken partnership. As image-maker herself and helper of countless other workers for Ireland, like her hero Patrick Sarsfield of *The White Cockade* (1905), her name too should be "set in clean letters in the book of the people." She died at Coole Park on May 22, 1932.

ANN SADDLEMYER

WORKS: *Arabi and His Household*. London: Privately printed, 1882; *Over the River*. London: Privately published, 1888/revised 1893; *A Phantom's Pilgrimage; or, Home Ruin*, published anonymously. London: Ridgway, 1893; ed., *The Autobiography of Sir William Gregory*. London: John Murray, 1894; "Ireland, Real and Ideal," *The Nineteenth Century* (November 1898): 770-774; ed., *Mr. Gregory's Letter Box, 1813-1830*. London: Smith, Elder, 1898; ed., *Ideals in Ireland*. London: Unicorn, 1901; *Cuchulain of Muirthemne*. London: John Murray, 1902; *Gods and Fighting Men*. London: John Murray, 1904; *A Book of Saints and Wonders*. Dundrum: Dun Emer, 1906; *The Kiltartan History Book*. Dublin: Maunsel, 1909; *Seven Short Plays*. Dublin: Maunsel, 1909. (Contains *The Rising of the Moon, Spreading the News, Hyacinth Halvey, The Gaol Gate, The Jackdaw, The Travelling Man*, and *The Workhouse Ward*); *The Kiltartan Molière*. Dublin: Maunsel, 1910. (Contains *The Doctor in Spite of Himself, The Rogueries of Scapin*, and *The Miser*); *The Kiltartan Wonder Book*. Dublin: Maunsel, 1910; *Irish Folk History Plays, First Series*. London: Putnam, 1912. (Contains *Kincora, Dervorgilla*, and *Grania*); *Irish Folk History Plays, Second Series*. London: Putnam, 1912. (Contains *The White Cockade, The Canavans*, and *The Deliverer*); *New Comedies*. New York & London: Putnam, 1913. (Contains *The Full Moon, McDonagh's Wife, The Bogie Men, Damer's Gold*, and *Coats*); *Our Irish Theatre*. London: Putnam, 1913; *The Golden Apple*. London: John Murray, 1916; *The Kiltartan Poetry Book: Translations from the Irish*. London: Putnam, 1919; *Visions and Beliefs in the West of Ireland*. With two essays and notes by W. B. Yeats. 2 vols. London: Putnam, 1920; "A Week in Ireland," *The Nation* (October 16, October 23, November 13, December 4, December 18, 1920); *Hugh Lane's Life and Achievement*. London: John Murray, 1921; *The Image and Other Plays*. London: Putnam, 1922. (Contains also *The Wrens, Shanwalla*, and *Hanrahan's Oath*); *Three Wonder Plays*. London: Putnam, 1923. (Contains *The Dragon, The Jester*, and *Aristotle's Bellows*); *Mirandolina*. London: Putnam, 1924, (After Goldoni); "The Old Woman Remembers," *The Irish Statesman* (March 22, 1924): 40-41; *The Story Brought by Brigit*. London: Putnam, 1924; *A Case for the Return of Sir Hugh Lane's Pictures to Dublin*. Dublin: Talbot, 1926; *On the Racecourse*. London: Putnam, 1926; *Three Last Plays*. London: Putnam, 1928. (Contains *The Would-Be Gentleman, Sancho's Master* and *Dave*); *My First Play: Colman and Guaire*. London: Elkin Mathews & Marot,

1930; *Coole*. Dublin: Cuala, 1931; *Lady Gregory's Journals, 1916-1930*. Lennox Robinson, ed. London: Putnam, 1946; "The Lady Gregory Letters to Sean O'Casey." A. C. Edwards, ed. *Modern Drama* 8 (May 1965): 95-111; "Lady Gregory's Letters to G. B. Shaw." Daniel Murphy, ed. *Modern Drama* 10 (February 1968): 331-345. The Complete writings of Lady Gregory, including much formerly unpublished material, can be found in *The Coole Edition of Lady Gregory's Writings*. Colin Smythe & T. R. Henn, general eds. Gerrards Cross: Colin Smythe/New York: Oxford University Press, 1970- . Of particular interest among the volumes published thus far is Lady Gregory's autobiography, *Seventy Years* (1974).   REFERENCES: Adams, Hazard. *Lady Gregory*. Lewisburg, Pa.: Bucknell University Press, 1973; Coxhead, Elizabeth. *Lady Gregory: A Literary Portrait*. Revised ed., Gerrards Cross: Colin Smythe, 1966; Gregory, Anne. *Me and Nu: Childhood at Coole*. Gerrards Cross: Colin Smythe, 1966; Saddlemyer, Ann. "Augusta Gregory, Irish Nationalist." In *Myth and Reality in Irish Literature*. Joseph Ronsley, ed. Waterloo, Ontario: Wilfred Laurier University Press, 1977, pp. 29-40. Saddlemyer, Ann. *In Defence of Lady Gregory, Playwright*. Dublin: Dolmen, 1966; Yeats, William Butler. *Memoirs*. Denis Donoghue, ed. London: Macmillan, 1972.

GRIFFIN, GERALD (1803-1840), novelist and man of letters. Griffin, born on December 12, 1803, at Limerick, was the ninth child (and seventh son) of an Irish family with the ancestral name O'Griobhth. The family moved to Fairy Lawn (1810) on the Shannon; then the parents emigrated to Pennsylvania (1820), and the remaining children moved to Adare and then to Pallas Kenry, which remained Griffin's home in Ireland.

In autumn 1823, Griffin went to London where John Banim* encouraged his writing. He lived in extreme poverty while working as anonymous hack, translator, book reviewer, and parliamentary reporter until 1827 when he became famous for *Holland Tide*. An attack of rheumatism in 1825 left him with recurrent illness the rest of his life.

The year 1829 marked three events: the publication of *The Collegians;* his term as London law student as an alternative to the "fickleness of public literary taste"; and a meeting in Limerick with a Quaker, Mrs. Lydia Fisher, who became "the secret patron of his minstrelsy." Around 1830, his religious habits gained ascendancy over his literary aspirations, and at Pallas Kenry he even began catechizing neighborhood children.

In 1836, he spent some time at Taunton and in Paris. In 1835, Griffin went to Scotland, and on his return he burned his manuscripts preparatory to joining, in September, the Christian Brothers at Dublin. From there he moved to the monastery in Cork, where he died of typhus on June 12, 1840.

Griffin was a romanticist who drew on history for examples of devoted and virtuous women and for heroes who strove for loyalty and honor in the face of conflicting values. His subjects ranged from lycanthropy and self-combustion, to magical folklore and supernatural tales, including a vampire story.

His best remembered works are the song "Aileen Aroon" and the novel *The Collegians* (1829), based on a true account of an Irish colleen who was drowned by her husband so that he might marry a woman of wealth.

Now judged by some as the best nineteenth-century Irish novel, it became the play *Colleen Bawn* by Dion Boucicault* and the opera *Lily of Killarney* by Jules Benedict. Its plot reappears in Theodore Dreiser's *American Tragedy*.

Much folklore may be found in *Tales of the Munster Festivals,* which appeared in three volumes under the titles *Holland-Tide* (1827); *Card Drawing, The Half-Sir,* and *Suil Dhuv the Coiner* (1829); and *The Rivals* and *Tracy's Ambition* (1830). He also wrote *The Christian Physiologist* (1830), *Tales of My Neighbourhood* (1835) in three volumes, and *Tales of the Jury Room* (1842). His historical novels are *The Invasion* (1832), set in the eighth century, and *The Duke of Monmouth* (1836), set in 1685. His tragedy *Gisippus* was performed at Drury Lane in 1842. Griffin's *Life and Letters* (1843) was written by his brother Daniel. His known letters and manuscripts are held by the Christian Brothers—"Commonplace Book A" in Dublin and letters in the archives in Rome.

Throughout his fifteen years of writing poems, plays, operas, essays, juvenile tales, stories, and novels, Griffin was caught between the restrictions of religion and the expanse of knowledge that he admitted contradicted many of his tales, while he lamented the failure of literature as adequate moral instruction. Amid many reversals in his attitudes and subjects, he compromised his excellent folklore with apologies and explanations.

Many of the virtues and sentiments Griffin extolled have passed out of style. William Butler Yeats* praised Griffin's work as an authentic source for Irish folklore; this fact, plus his rich dramatic qualities and scenes of stark realism, constitute his strongest attractions.

GRACE ECKLEY

WORKS: *Holland-Tide; or, Munster Popular Tales.* London: W. Simpkin & R. Marshall, 1827; *Tales of the Munster Festivals.* 3 vols. London: Saunders & Otley, 1826-1827; *The Collegians.* 3 vols. London: Saunders & Otley, 1829; *The Christian Physiologist.* London: E. Bull, 1830. (Stories); *The Invasion.* 4 vols. London: Saunders & Otley, 1832; *Tales of My Neighbourhood.* 3 vols. London: Saunders & Otley, 1835; *The Duke of Monmouth.* 3 vols. London: Bentley, 1836; *Gisippus.* London: Maxwell, 1842. (Play in 5 acts); *Talis Qualis; or, Tales of the Jury Room.* 3 vols. London: Maxwell, 1842; *The Works of G. Griffin.* 8 vols. London: Various publishers, 1842-1843; *The Works of Gerald Griffin.* 10 vols. New York: D. & J. Sadlier, 1857; *The Poetical and Dramatic Works.* Dublin: J. Duffy, 1877.   REFERENCES: Cronin, John. *Gerald Griffin.* London: Cambridge University Press, 1978; Flanagan, Thomas. *The Irish Novelists, 1800-1850.* New York: Columbia University Press, 1958; MacLysaght, William. *Death Sails the Shannon: The Tragic Story of the Colleen Bawn.* Tralee: Anvil Books, 1953; Mannin, Ethel. *Two Studies in Integrity.* New York: G. P. Putnam's, 1954.

GRIFFITH, ARTHUR (1872-1922), journalist and politician. Griffith is important to Irish literature for his brilliant editing of *The United Irishman* (1889-1906) and *Sinn Fein* (1906-1914). He was born in Dublin on March 31, 1872, the son of a printer. From 1896 to 1899, Griffith was in the Transvaal, editing a small paper. When he returned to Dublin, his new paper, *The United Irishman,* quickly became the most important organ of the Irish national movement. In 1904, he published his influential pamphlet, *The Resurrection of Hungary, a Parallel for Ireland.* He was the initiator of the Sinn Fein movement, and, although he did not take part in the 1916 Rising, he was interned after it. With Michael Collins, he headed the Treaty delegation to London in 1921 and was the head of government in the new Free State after the de Valera split. He died of overwork on August 12, 1922, in Dublin.

Although the purpose of Griffith's journals was primarily political, they were cordially receptive to new Irish writing and encouraged such major new talents as Padraic Colum* and James Stephens.* However, Yeats,* Martyn,* Gogarty,* Alice Milligan,* Seumas O'Sullivan,* James Cousins,* and many others (including the awful poet Lizzie Twigg, who is mentioned in Joyce's *Ulysses*) often appeared in their pages. As James Stephens wrote, "the best poetry and literary criticism in the English language was written weekly by us in The United Irishman." The intimate connection between politics and the literary movement received an early partial rupture, however, over the plays of John Synge.* Griffith is remembered by literary historians for his vehement criticism of Synge and his growing antipathy to Yeats and to the Abbey Theatre.* Nevertheless, that fact does not obscure the immense early service of Griffith to Irish letters.

Of Griffith's own writing, Stephens remarked:

> His was one of the easiest pens that ever took naturally to ink, and at its best his prose was actually masterly. He was, in my opinion, the greatest journalist working in the English tongue, with an astonishing lucidity of expression, and with a command of all the modes of tender, or sarcastic or epigrammatic expression, and always that ample, untroubled simplicity of utterance which ranks him among the modern masters of the English language.

REFERENCES: Colum, Padraic. *Arthur Griffith.* Dublin: Browne & Nolan, 1959; Davis, Richard P. *Arthur Griffith and Non-Violent Sinn Fein.* Dublin: Anvil Books, 1974; Kenny, H. E. (Sean-Ghall). *Arthur Griffith.* Dublin, 1922; Lyons, G. A. *Some Recollections of Griffith and his Times.* Dublin: Talbot, 1923; Ó Luing, Seán. *Art Ó Griofa.* Dublin: Sairseal agus Dill, 1953; Stephens, James. *Arthur Griffith, Journalist and Statesman.* Dublin: Wilson, Hartnell, [1922]; Younger, Carleton. *A State of Disunion.* London: Fontana, 1972.

GUINAN, JOHN (1874-1945), playwright. Guinan was born in Ballindown, Birr, Offaly, in 1874. A civil servant, he spent much of his working life in the offices of the Congested Districts Board and of the Land Commission. He was a frequent writer of short stories for the popular press and had four plays produced at the Abbey Theatre*: *The Cuckoo's Nest* (1913), *The Plough Lifters* (1916), *Black Oliver* (1927), and *The Rune of Healing* (1931). His plays tend to be rather overelaborated in dialogue and over-convoluted in plot. He collaborated on a play, probably called *The Wonderful Wedding,* with George Fitzmaurice* with whom he worked in the Land Commission. A conventional matchmaking comedy, the piece was hardly the best work of either Fitzmaurice or Guinan; it was rejected by the Abbey but was finally published in 1978. Guinan died in Sutton on March 7, 1945.

WORKS: *Black Oliver* in *One-Act Plays for Stage and Study: Fifth Series.* New York: 1929; *The Cuckoo's Nest.* Dublin: Gill, [1933]; with George Fitzmaurice, "The Wonderful Wedding" in *The Journal of Irish Literature* 7 (September 1978):3-36.

GUINNESS, BRYAN [WALTER] (1905-), man of letters. Guinness, the second Baron Moyne, was born on October 27, 1905. A member of the famous brewing family, he was educated at Eton and at Christ Church, Oxford, where he received a B.A. in 1928 and an M.A. in 1931. He was called to the English bar in 1930. In Ireland, he has been something of a patron of the arts, and he has received honorary degrees from Trinity College and the National University. He has written novels, short stories, poems, plays, and children's books. Most of his work has an English background and is informed by charm, delicacy, and wit. A good introduction to his work, showing both his excellences and limitations, would be the volume of short stories entitled *The Girl with the Flower* (1966). Guinness is a member of the Irish Academy of Letters.

WORKS: *Twenty-three Poems.* London: Duckworth, 1931; *Singing Out of Tune.* London: Putnam, 1933. (Novel); *Landscape with Figures.* London: Putnam, 1934. (Novel); *Under the Eyelid.* London: Heinemann, [1935]. (Poems); *The Story of Johnny and Jemima.* London: Heinemann, 1936. (Children's story); *A Week by the Sea.* London: Putnam, 1936. (Novel); *Lady Crushwell's Companion.* London: Putnam, 1938. (Novel); *The Children in the Desert.* London: Heinemann, 1947. (Children's story); *Reflexions.* London: Heinemann, 1947. (Poems); *The Animals' Breakfast.* London: Heinemann, 1950. (Children's story); *Collected Poems, 1927-1955.* London: Heinemann, 1956; *A Fugue of Cinderellas.* London: Heinemann, 1956. (Novel); *The Story of Catriona and the Grasshopper.* London: Heinemann, 1958. (Children's story); *The Story of Priscilla and the Prawn.* London: Heinemann, 1960. (Children's story); *Leo and Rosabelle.* London: Heinemann, 1961. (Novel); *The Giant's Eye.* London: Heinemann, 1964. (Novel); *The Rose in the Tree.* London: Heinemann, 1964. *Diary Not Kept: Essays in Recollection.* Salisbury, Wilts: Compton, 1975.

GWYNN, STEPHEN [LUCIUS] (1864-1950), politician and man of letters. Gwynn was born on February 13, 1864, at St. Columba's College near Dublin. His father, John Gwynn, was the warden of the college and became Regius professor of divinity at Trinity College. His mother was the daughter of William Smith O'Brien, the patriot, while one of his brothers became provost of Trinity and another brother vice-provost.

Gwynn attended Brasenose College, Oxford, graduated with distinction in 1896, and then turned to journalism in London. He returned to Ireland to live in 1904, and from 1906 to 1918 he was a nationalist member of

Parliament for Galway City. Despite his age, he entered World War I as a private. He was promoted to captain, served in France until 1917, and was made a chevalier of the Legion of Honor. In late life, he was honored by the Irish Academy of Letters and awarded a D.Litt. both from the National University and Trinity. He died in Dublin on June 11, 1950.

Gwynn led an intensely active public life, and yet his literary output was immense. He attempted with distinction practically every literary form except the drama. He wrote poems, novels, sketches, stories, essays, books on fishing, guidebooks to Ireland, works on politics, biographies of Thomas Moore,* Scott, Swift,* Goldsmith,* Robert Louis Stevenson, and others, and he was a prolific editor and a particular authority on the eighteenth century.

The extraordinary fact about Gwynn's work is that, despite its great bulk, it is unvaryingly competent. He has no lost masterpieces, but he is a supple and vigorous writer of prose and the best of genial companions. While he sometimes repeats his best stories in different works, he always has ideas, his literary taste is excellent, and his political remarks are full of humane good sense. For instance, there could be few more succinct and more telling characterizations of the nineteenth-century Irish novel than his seventeen-page essay in *Irish Books and Irish People* (except perhaps the next essay in the book on Irish humor which covers the same ground). One may dip into Gwynn almost at random—say, in his autobiography, *Experiences of a Literary Man,* or in his discursive books on fishing, or in a loving recreation of Dublin and its characters like his *Dublin Old and New*—and find interest, information, and charm.

Oliver Gogarty* thought Gwynn "a considerable poet," and he has indeed a fine command of technique. He is at his best as a poet in the old-fashioned, but stirring, "A Lay of Ossian and Patrick." Gogarty also summed him up well:

> Gwynn's long life witnessed many changes both slow and abrupt: three major wars, a rebellion, and a civil war. None of these affected his imperturbability. He was stationary but not a recluse. Unobtrusively he lived and died, but for patriotism, scholarship, and integrity he was the greatest figure in the Ireland of his time.

WORKS: *Memorials of an Eighteenth Century Painter: James Northcote.* London: Unwin, 1898; *The Repentance of a Private Secretary.* London: John Lane, 1898. (Novel); *The Decay of Sensibility.* London: J. Lane, 1899. (Sketches, essays); *Highways and Byways in Donegal and Antrim.* London: Macmillan, 1899; *The Old Knowledge.* London: Macmillan, 1901; *The Queen's Chronicler.* London & New York: J. Lane, 1901. (Poems); *John Maxwell's Marriages.* London: Macmillan, 1903. (Novel); *To-Day and To-Morrow in Ireland.* Dublin: Hodges, Figgis, 1903. (Essays); *A Lay of Ossian and Patrick.* Dublin: Hodges, Figgis, 1904. (Poems); *Fishing Holidays.* London: Macmillan, 1904; *The Masters of English Literature.* London: Macmillan, 1904/rev. ed., 1925/2d ed., 1938; *Thomas Moore.* London: Macmillan, 1904; *The Fair Hills of Ireland.* Dublin: Maunsel, 1906. (Guidebook); *The Glade in the Forest.*

Dublin: Maunsel, 1907. (Stories); *A Holiday in Connemara*. London: Methuen, 1909; *Robert Emmet*. London: Macmillan, 1909. (Novel); *Beautiful Ireland*. London: Blackie, 1911. (Guidebook); *The Case for Home Rule*. Dublin: Maunsel, 1911; *The Famous Cities of Ireland*. Dublin & London: Maunsel, 1915; *For Second Reading*. Dublin & London: Maunsel, 1918. (Essays); *John Redmond's Last Years*. London: Edward Arnold, 1919. (Biography); *Irish Books and Irish People*. Dublin: Talbot/ London: Unwin, 1920; *Irish Literature and Drama in the English Language*. London: Nelson, 1920; *Garden Wisdom*. Dublin: Talbot/London: Unwin, 1921; *The Irish Situation*. London: Jonathan Cape, 1921; *Collected Poems*. Edinburgh & London: Blackwood, 1923; *The History of Ireland*. London: Macmillan/Dublin: Talbot, 1923; *Duffer's Luck*. Edinburgh & London: Blackwood, 1924. (Fishing); *The Student's History of Ireland*. London: Longman's, 1925; *Experiences of a Literary Man*. London: Thornton Butterworth, 1926. (Autobiography); *In Praise of France*. London: Nisbet, 1927; *Ireland*. London: Harrap, 1927; *Captain Scott*. London: J. Lane, 1929. (Biography); *Saints and Scholars*. London: Thornton Butterworth, 1929; *Burgundy*. London: Harrap, 1930; *The Life of Horace Walpole*. London: Thornton Butterworth, 1932; *The Life of Mary Kingsley*. London: Macmillan, 1932; 2d ed., 1933; *The Life of Sir Walter Scott*. London: Thornton Butterworth, 1932; *The Life and Friendships of Dean Swift*. London: Thornton Butterworth, 1933; *Claude Monet and his Garden*. London: Country Life, 1934; *Mungo Park and the Quest of the Niger*. London: J. Lane, 1934; *Ireland in Ten Days*. London: Harrap, 1935; *Oliver Goldsmith*. London: Thornton Butterworth, 1935; *The Happy Fisherman*. London: Country Life, 1936; *River to River*. London: Country Life, 1937; *Dublin, Old and New*. Dublin: Browne & Nolan/London: Harrap, [1938]; *Fond Opinions*. London: Frederick Muller, 1938. (Essays); *Munster*. London & Glasgow: Blackie, [1938]; *Two in a Valley*. London: Rich & Cowan, [1938]. (Travel); *Henry Grattan and His Times*. Dublin: Browne & Nolan, 1939; *Robert Louis Stevenson*. London: Macmillan, 1939; *Salute to Valour*. London: Constable, 1941. (Poems); *Aftermath*. Dundalk: W. Tempest, 1946. (Poems); *Memories of Enjoyment*. Tralee: Kerryman, 1946. (Selections from his writing).

HACKETT, FRANCIS (1883-1962), novelist, historian, and critic. "A myopic, astygmatic, fatty, apprenhensive bundle of human expectancy," Hackett was born on January 21, 1883, in Kilkenny. After completing his only formal education in Clongowes Wood College, he emigrated to the United States at eighteen. An editorial writer for the *Chicago Evening Post,* he graduated to editor of its weekly literary review, from which he moved to the position of literary critic for the just-established *New Republic* in 1912. By 1922, he had married Danish-born Signe Toksvig and published his first six books: three books on Ireland—*Ireland, A Study in Nationalism* (1918), *The Irish Republic* (1920), and *The Story of the Irish Nation* (1922); two collections of his essays and reviews—*Horizons* (1919) and *The Invisible Censor* (1921); and one book of impressions, *The American Rainbow* (1922).

In 1923, Hackett left the *New Republic* in order to pursue a more creative literary career and moved to southern France where he wrote a first novel, *That Nice Young Couple* (1924). Free-lance political reporting for the *Survey Graphic* financed the five-year research resulting in his first historical work, *Henry the Eighth,* which was completed at Kiladreenan House, a cottage in County Wicklow. Its American publication in 1929 and immediate choice as a Book-of-the-Month Club "first" was a personal and financial triumph after seven years of penury. Another five years brought *Francis the First, Gentleman Of France* (1935), followed by a second novel, *The Green Lion* (1936). When the Irish Censorship Board simultaneously banned this novel and his wife's first novel, *Eve's Doctor* (1937), the Hacketts left Ireland on the anniversary of Parnell's death for Signe Toksvig's native Denmark. They settled in Copenhagen.

In December 1939, the novel *Queen Anne Boleyn,* considered for dramatic adaptation, brought the Hacketts to New York. The German Occupation of Denmark prevented their return to Denmark, and the adaptation was canceled. They then rented a house on Martha's Vineyard where Hackett wrote a biweekly literary review for *The New York Times* and completed his semi-autobiographical . . . *I Chose Denmark*, for which he was later awarded the King Christian Liberty Medal. This work was followed by his Washington novel *The Senator's Last Night* (1943).

After the war, Hackett returned to Copenhagen, edited a collection of reviews, *On Judging Books* (1947), and pursued an independent and chosen life. He died on April 25, 1962, at the age of seventy-nine.

Politics, history, and literary criticism were Hackett's keenest interests. Consequently, with the singular exception of *Queen Anne Boleyn*, which is a novel only in the fact that Hackett invents dialogue for his historical characters, his novels, spaced between other works requiring a greater exactitude, are often simply entertainments. *The Green Lion* and *The Senator's Last Night,* however, reveal his egalitarian political principles. *The Green Lion,* banned because its Irish hero is the bastard child of a passionate mountain girl and a neophyte in the Church, is the story of a young boy's hero-worship of Parnell and of a half-understood but wholly felt love of liberty. The political liberalism of *The Green Lion* found more mature expression in *The Senator's Last Night,* in which the senior senator from Nebraska suffers a living death on the night he is later to die. The senator represents all that is reprehensible to Hackett: an isolationist in time of war; a power-mogul whose rise from penury to wealth and power makes him a secret admirer of Hitler; a husband whose sexual loyalties lie elsewhere; a father without a shred of paternal feeling. Hackett's obvious delight in doing him in is a fine example of his assurance that in politics as in all things, there is progress.

Somewhat dampened political optimism emanates from his expository works on Ireland. *Ireland, A Study in Nationalism* (a separately published "Preface," *The Irish Republic,* accompanied the printing of the third edition in 1920) fully blames British insensitivity for the Easter Rising but conservatively pleads for Dominion Home Rule to save Ulster from the exclusion of Republicanism. Hackett recants in the "Preface" of 1920 in which he argues complete separatism. *The Story of the Irish Nation,* written in response to Herbert Bayard Swope's challenge that Hackett could write a history of Ireland in three days, took three months, with the obvious result that Ireland from the Firbolgs to the Treaty of 1922 skims glibly along the surfaces of time.

Hackett's excellence lies in his focused histories (with which must be included the novel *Queen Anne Boleyn*) and in part, too, in his detailed and dramatic evocation, and in his finding of an "objective correlative" he did not have when writing about Ireland directly. The two histories, *Henry the Eighth* and *Francis the First,* discuss the birth and tenure of nationalism. Henry VIII's harsh and uncompromising consolidation of England under Crown authority (an authority which was nearly undermined by the commoner's daughter, Anne Boleyn, whose gift it was to foment power struggles which a country just emerging from feudalism was only too ready to engage in) is contrasted to the rule of Francis I. Youthful and extravagant, militarist and gangster, friend of Rabelais and patron of Cellini, a king who made mistakes, Francis I ushered his country into the glories of the Renaissance. These two men together form Hackett's symbol of leadership: authority for the child in man; pride, for his self-respect; a common humanity, in which he hopes to see himself; a paternalism to which he clings; and a flamboyance, for his aspirations, his entertainment, and just for the fun of it. If everyman sees enough of himself in his nation's leader, enough of himself will become his country.

Perhaps it was such thinking which led Hackett to "choose" Denmark, a country which having achieved nationhood, allowed its symbols of nationality to recede. Denmark's symbolic monarchy and social progressiveness was a twentieth-century ideal of authority and democracy functioning in accord. In . . . *I Chose Denmark,* Hackett (indirectly saying a great many things about his native Ireland) praises a nation not only for its cleanliness, honesty, and independence, but also for the fact that its premier rides a streetcar, its farming cooperatives work, and only ten taxpayers earn more than $100,000 in a single year. Its citizens, freed from social, political and economic harassment, express themselves without fear. In *On Judging Books,* Hackett wrote: "The might of judgment adheres in a free man. . . . Religious have wiped out books. States have burned them. The right of private judgment is obviously the passkey out of prison. Without it men are dependents, whether happy or unhappy, and dependents end as slaves." To this ideal Francis Hackett adhered and towards its realization he wrote.

M. KELLY LYNCH

WORKS: *Ireland, a Study in Nationalism.* New York: B. W. Huebsch, 1918; *Horizons.* New York: B. W. Huebsch, 1919. (Literary criticism); *The Irish Republic.* New York: B. W. Huebsch, 1920; ed., *On American Books.* New York: B. W. Huebsch, 1920; *The Invisible Censor.* New York: B. W. Huebsch, 1921. (Sketches and reviews); *American Rainbow.* New York: Liveright, 1922. (Reminiscences); *The Story of the Irish Nation.* New York: Appleton-Century, 1922; *That Nice Young Couple.* London: Jonathan Cape, 1925. (Novel); *Henry the Eighth.* London: Jonathan Cape, 1929.

(History); *Francis the First, Gentleman of France.* London: Heinemann, 1934. (History); *The Green Lion.* London: I. Nicholson & Watson, 1936. (Novel); *Queen Anne Boleyn.* New York: Doubleday, Doran, 1939. (Novel); *The Senator's Last Night.* New York: Doubleday, Doran, 1939. (Novel); . . . *I Chose Denmark.* New York: Doubleday, Doran, 1940. (Autobiography and political and social commentary); *On Judging Books in General and in Particular.* New York: J. Day, 1947. (Essays and reviews).

HALL, MRS. S. C. (1800-1881), novelist and short story writer. Mrs. Hall was born Anna Maria Fielding in Dublin on January 6, 1800, but she lived most of her first fifteen years at Bannow in County Wexford. She was taken to London where she met and, in 1824, married Samuel Carter Hall. Her husband was born on May 9, 1800, near Waterford where his father, an army officer, was stationed. After a few years in Cork, Hall moved to London and founded a number of journals, such as *The Amulet* and *The Art Journal,* in which much of his wife's work appeared. She was vastly productive of sketches, stories, and novels of Irish peasant life, and it has been estimated that she published over five hundred books, some of which she wrote in collaboration with her husband. Like Maria Edgeworth,* Somerville and Ross,* and Lady Gregory,* Mrs. Hall was observing the peasant from the outside. Unfortunately, she had little of the comic genius of these writers, and, while some of her work is pleasant enough, little of it is memorable. Her rather awesome energies were also utilized in a good deal of philanthropic work, as well as in antialcoholic campaigns, proselytization for women's rights, and spiritualism. She died in East Mousley on January 30, 1881. Her husband died in Kensington on March 16, 1889.

The bibliography below is highly selective, but contains her best known and probably most representative work.

WORKS: *Sketches of Irish Character.* London: F. Westley & A. H. Davis, 1829; *Sketches of Irish Character, Second Series.* London: F. Westley & A. H. Davis, 1831; *The Buccaneer.* London: R. Bentley, 1832; *The Outlaw.* London: R. Bentley, 1835; *Tales of Woman's Trials.* London: Houlston, 1835; *Uncle Horace.* London: H. Colburn, 1837; *The Groves of Blarney.* London: Chapman & Hall, ca. 1838. (Three-act play); *Lights and Shadows of Irish Life.* London: H. Colburn, 1838; *Marian.* London: H. Colburn, 1840; with S. C. Hall, *Ireland.* London: How & Parsons, 1841; with S. C. Hall, *A Week at Killarney.* London: J. How, 1843; *The Whiteboy.* London: Chapman & Hall, 1845; *A Midsummer Eve.* London: Longman, 1848; *Stories of the Irish Peasantry.* Edinburgh: W. & R. Chambers, 1850; *The Fight of Faith.* London: Chapman & Hall, 1869.   REFERENCES: Anon. "The Didactic Irish Novelists: Carleton, Mrs. Hall." *Dublin University Magazine* 26 (1845): 737-752; Hall, S. C. *Retrospect of a Long Life.* New York: Appleton, 1883; Mayo, Isabella Fyvie. "A Recollection of Two Old Friends: Mr. and Mrs. S. C. Hall." *Leisure Hour,* 38 (1889): 303-307.

HALPINE, CHARLES GRAHAM (1829-1868), journalist and popular writer. Halpine was born in Oldcastle, County Meath, on November 20, 1829. His father, Nicholas John Halpine, after a brilliant career at Trinity College, was editor for many years of *The Dublin Evening Mail.* Halpine himself graduated from Trinity and then turned to journalism, first in Dublin and then in London. In 1851, he emigrated to America where he became for a while the private secretary to P. T. Barnum. His journalistic career flourished, and he distinguished himself in the American Civil War and retired a brigadier general. He was a prominent member of the Democratic party of his day and an outspoken critic of municipal corruption. He died on August 3, 1868, from an accidental overdose of chloroform.

Halpine's verses, written under the pseudonym of Private Miles O'Reilly, are comic, patriotic, and sentimental. The worst of them are rather dreadful, but a few, such as "Irish Astronomy," are somewhat clever. In that poem we learn how St. Patrick placed O'Ryan [sic] in the firmament as thanks for the following occasion:

> St. Pathrick wanst was passin' by
>   O'Ryan's little houldin',
> And, as the saint felt wake and dhry,
>   He thought he'd enther bould in.
> "O'Ryan," says the saint, "avick!
>   To praich at Thurles I'm goin',
> So let me have a rasher quick,
>   And a dhrop of Innishowen."

> "No rasher will I cook for you
>   While betther is to spare, sir,
> But here's a jug of mountain dew,
>   And there's a rattlin' hare, sir." . . .

Halpine also write two Irish historical novels which are justifiably neglected.

WORKS: *Lyrics by the Letter H* (published anonymously). New York: J. C. Derby/Cincinnati: H. W. Derby, 1854; *The Poetical Works of Charles Graham Halpine (Miles O'Reilly)*, R. B. Roosevelt, ed. New York: Harper, 1869; *The Patriot Brothers; or, the Willows of the Golden Vale.* Dublin: A. M. Sullivan, [1869]; *Mountcashel's Brigade; or, the Rescue of Cremona: an Historical Romance.* 5th ed. Dublin: T. D. Sullivan, 1882. As Miles O'Reilly: *Baked Meats of the Funeral. A Collection of Essays, Poems, Speeches, Histories and Banquets.* New York: Carleton, 1886; *The Life and Adventures, Songs, Services . . . of Private Miles O'Reilly.* New York: Carleton, 1864/Tarrytown, N.Y.: W. Abbatt, 1926.

HANNAY, CANON JAMES OWEN. *See* BIRMINGHAM, GEORGE A.

HARTNETT, MICHAEL (1941-), poet. Hartnett was born in 1941 in Newcastle West, County Limerick. His first small collection of verse, *Anatomy of a Cliché*, was published when he was twenty-seven. It is a talented, if overwrought and pretentious, collection of love poems, in which the author eschews capital letters, consistent punctuation, conventional syntax, and discernible rhythm, although he rhymes when convenient. The diction ranges from the banal to the florid; that is, from "delicate footsteps of spring" and "love is . . . wonderful!" to remarks about "conceptual orgasms" and a personification of Ireland as a multi-breasted female who invites her children to suckle her many breasts, after which she promises to make them love her by devouring them and then vomiting them all up.

In *Selected Poems* (1970), Hartnett is more concerned with form, but in such pieces as "I Have Exhausted the Delighted Range," "I Have Managed," "Fairview Park: 6 A. M.," "The Lord Taketh Away," and "For My Grandmother, Bridget Halpin," the form is uncontrolled and disintegrates before the close of the poem. "The Poet as Black Sheep" and "The Poet as Woman of Ireland" are somewhat better, despite a couple of metrical breakdowns. Hartnett's best collection to date is *A Farewell to English* (1975) in which he fashions some strong images in "The Oat Woman" and "Death by the Santry River." The longish title poem, however, veers between limp eloquence and lame satire, with detours into rather frantic imagery. There is, for instance, one extraordinary and extended image about deformed dwarfs riding other deformed dwarfs around a race track while jabbing them with electric prods and while being covered with excrement and mucous. The purpose of this activity is to win "a glass and concrete anus."

The sentiment of the title poem received considerable publicity at the time, but most of Hartnett's next two volumes have nevertheless been written in English. Hartnett's Irish reputation may perhaps be inferred from his *Collected Poems* issued in 1977 by the country's most prestigious publisher of poetry. Certainly he is an improving poet, but hardly the acknowledged master which his book blurbs and his reviewers proclaim.

WORKS: *Anatomy of a Cliché*. Dublin: Dolmen, 1968; *The Hag of Beare, a Rendition of the Old Irish*. Dublin: New Writers', 1969; *Selected Poems*. Dublin: New Writers', 1970; *Tao: A Version of a Chinese Classic of the Sixth Century, B.C.* Dublin: New Writers', 1971; *Gipsy Ballads: A Version of the Romancero Gitano (1924-27) of Federico Lorca*. Dublin: Goldsmith, 1973; ed., with Desmond Egan. *Choice*. Dublin: Goldsmith, 1973. (Poetry anthology); *A Farewell to English*. Dublin: Gallery Books, 1975; *The Retreat of Ita Cagney/Cúlú Íde*. Dublin: Goldsmith, 1975; *Collected Poems*. Dublin: Dolmen, 1977.

HAYES, DAVID (1919-), playwright. Hayes was born in Dublin on June 7, 1919, and graduated from University College, Dublin. He worked for industry for many years, before turning to writing full time. Much of his work has been done for radio and television. His *Gift of Tears* won the play competition which marked the Twenty-First Anniversary of the Irish Broadcasting Authority's radio repertory company. His stage play, *Sorry! No Hard Feelings?*, is thus far his only published drama. It is a strong but rather sadistic black comedy about government's inhumanity to man.

WORK: *Sorry! No Hard Feelings?* Newark, Del.: Proscenium, 1978.

HAYWARD, N. RICHARD (1892-1964), travel writer. Hayward was born in Larne in 1892 and died in an auto crash on October 13, 1964, in Belfast. His career was enormously busy and varied. He published a novel and many travel books about Ireland. He wrote two curtain-raisers for the Ulster Players; he was a prominent actor with the group and managed it for some years. He was later the founder of the Belfast Repertory Theatre and, with Tyrone Guthrie, of the Belfast Radio Players. As a ballad singer, he cut over a hundred records, and he directed the first sound motion picture made in Ireland. His travel books are informal and minutely knowledgeable, but finally a bit irksome to read because of his obtrusive stage-Ulster jocularity. More dated but charming companions for travelers are Colum's* *The Road Round Ireland,* Harold Speakman's *Here's Ireland,* or even Thackeray's *Irish Sketch Book.*

WORKS: *Sugarhouse Entry.* London: Barker, 1936. (Novel); *In Praise of Ulster.* London: Barker, 1938/revised, Belfast: William Mullan, 1946; *Where the River Shannon Flows.* London: Harrap, 1940; *The Corrib Country.* Dundalk: W. Tempest, 1943; *In the Kingdom of Kerry.* Dundalk: W. Tempest, 1946; *This Is Ireland. Leinster and the City of Dublin.* London: Barker, 1949; *This Is Ireland. Ulster and the City of Belfast.* London: Barker, 1950; *Belfast Through the Ages.* Dundalk: Dundalgan, 1952; *This Is Ireland. Connacht and the City of Galway.* London: Barker, 1952; *This Is Ireland. Mayo, Sligo, Leitrim and Roscommon.* London: 1953; *The Story of the Irish Harp.* Dublin: Arthur Guinness, 1954. (Pamphlet); *Border Foray.* London: Barker, 1957; *Munster and the City of Cork.* London: Phoenix House, 1964.

HEALY, GERARD (1918-1963), playwright and actor. Healy was born in Dublin in 1918, and was educated at the Synge Street Christian Brothers School. After working in a Dublin drapery store, he joined the Gate Theatre* as assistant stage manager and toured with the company to the Balkans and to Egypt. He married one of the company's actresses, Eithne Dunne, and played himself in a number of Gate productions. In 1939, he and his wife moved to the Abbey* and played there for five years. In 1943, the Abbey produced his first play, *Thy Dear Father.* In 1945, he helped to form the short-lived Players' Theatre, which staged in that year his second play *The Black Stranger.* Illness forced him temporarily from the stage, and he wrote radio notes for *The Irish Times* before joining the Radio Éireann Repertory Company. He wrote many scripts and documentaries for radio, and also became a member of Austin Clarke's* verse-speaking team on Radio Éireann. When asked why he did not write more plays, he replied, "I cannot satisfy myself. . . . Playwriting is an art. I'm afraid my work is purely ephemeral."

While *Thy Dear Father* would probably not bear revival, as a study of fanatic religiosity it was an outspoken piece for the 1940s. A stronger work is *The Black Stranger,* which is set during the Potato Famines of the 1840s and sees this overwhelming national trauma through the microcosm of two families. The play is a leanly written, understated, tightly structured piece of realism that remains persuasive, powerful, and moving.

Healy wrote his two plays in his middle twenties. Although he lived about twenty years longer, he regrettably wrote no more for the stage. He died in London on March 9, 1963, while playing the role of the Jesuit in Hugh Leonard's* *Stephen D.*

WORKS: *The Black Stranger.* Dublin: James Duffy, 1950; *Thy Dear Father.* Dublin: P. J. Bourke, 1957.

HEANEY, SEAMUS (1939-), poet. Seamus Heaney, one of the two or three most important Irish poets writing today, was born in County Derry on April 13, 1939. Before the appearance of his widely acclaimed *Death of a Naturalist* in 1966, he had attended St. Columb's College and later Queen's University, Belfast, where he earned First Class Honors in English. After a year teaching in a secondary school, he lectured at St. Joseph's College of Education and finally returned to Queen's as a lecturer. Among his many awards and prizes are the E. C. Gregory Award, the Somerset Maugham Award, the Geoffrey Faber Prize, and the Denis Devlin Award. He has been a contributor to the BBC and has guest lectured at the University of California.

Like Robert Frost, with whom he is often compared, Heaney established himself with his first three volumes of verse as a regional poet of the North of Ireland. "I was thought of as a Northern Writer," he confessed to Monie Begley. "I was trying to clear my head to become a *writer.*" His roots indeed go deep in the very dirt of Ulster—its bogs, its peat, its turf, its rural processes, and even, as one perceptive reviewer notes, its "felt philology." For some readers, however, almost universal admiration for Heaney's concrete physicality has been mixed with a sense that finally his idiom comes out as "too many details failing to add up to enough," or that his verse ultimately comes to "magazine poems in the sense that the thinking doesn't go very deep," even though "the peat does, squishy as a leaky boat."

Death of a Naturalist introduces Heaney's reliably consistent modus operandi with its opening poem "Digging": "Between my finger and my thumb / The Squat pen rests. / I'll dig with it." And dig he does in this volume, and throughout his career, into personal reminiscences of a rural childhood in Ulster couched in language as wet, clammy, fibrous, and vitally real as the Mossbawn turf he spades on almost every page. Here we are shown frogs as "mud grenades," "great slime kings" whose "slap and plop were obscene threats." Along with them comes a sense of the menace and fear lying in wait behind nature, so characteristically Frostian, blended with a blunt straightforwardness of perhaps the poet Ted Hughes, with whom he is also often compared.

Door into the Dark (1969) clearly shows the effort Heaney was expending to "clear his head and become a *writer*," for it marks a movement beyond the regional self-consciousness of *Death of a Naturalist* into primitive collective truths of all men. The closing poem, "Bogland," gives a sense of that direction, as Heaney himself has pointed out:

> The allusion was that the bog was a kind of Jungian ground or landscape in that it preserved traces of everything that had occurred before. It had layers of memory. The objects, the material culture by which the nation identifies itself, were mostly found in the bogs and are now in museums. I remember when we were children, they used to tell us not to go near the bog because there was no bottom to it.

For Heaney, digging into personal recollection clearly had expanded into an archeological quest for the cultural heart of Ireland itself. "Under the humus and roots / This smooth weight. I labour towards it still. It holds and gluts," he writes in "Bann Clay."

Heaney's third and most perplexing collection, *Wintering Out* (1972), may for some substantiate the charge that he is still groping about for a theme in the midst of all his furious digging. Having unearthed the "hidden" self (and in some cases the "hidden" artist) he now seems more resolute than ever to bring to light a "hidden" Ireland. To be sure, this means conscientious spadework into politics, but even more consciously into language itself. Both language and politics, Heaney feels, have been buried beneath an imposed, alien culture. However technically remote Heaney is to Yeats,* he shares the older poet's commitment to the resuscitation of the cultural integrity of Ireland.

Poems such as "The Tollund Man" and "Nerthus" reveal the potency of Heaney's anthropological quest for Irish origins and identities literally buried in the bogs whose "dark juices" work the Tollund Man "to a saint's kept body." Heany avers that the "cauldron bog" becomes "Our holy ground," and something of the Tollund Man's "sad freedom / As he rode the tumbril / Should come to me, driving, / Saying the names / Tollund, Grabaulle, Nebelgard, / Watching the pointing hands / Of country people, / Not knowing their tongue." Lost traditions, the relation of individuals to the land, the connection of the land and language, the contrasting heritages in the two Ulsters, all demonstrate a movement away from the easy earthy accessibility of the earlier volumes, but the cleanly delineated physical objects, crisp as spadecuts in the turf, remain his exclusive medium.

Heaney's latest volume, *North* (1976), resolutely continues the familiar digs, as a random list of poem titles quickly shows: "Funeral Rites," "The Digging Skeleton," "Bone Dreams," "Bog Queen," and "The Grauballe Man." But a bit of Irish social concern, so obviously expected of a contemporary Ulster poet, begins to find forceful articulation. The autobiographical section called "Singing School," for example, opens with "The Ministry of Fear" which evokes the psychological and cultural toll of domination from without:

> Ulster was British, but with no rights on
> The English lyric: all around us, though
> We hadn't named it, the ministry of fear.

"The Constable Calls" and "Orange Drums, Tyrone, 1966" continue the sad chronicles of the strife-torn North of Ireland, but perhaps the final poem, "Exposure," gives the best, although enigmatic, insight into Heaney's complicated relationship with his battered homeland:

> I am neither internee nor informer;
> An inner emigre, grown long-haired
> And thoughtful; a wood-kerne
>
> Escaped from the massacre,
> Taking protective colouring
> From bole and bark, feeling
> Every wind that blows . . .

THOMAS MERRILL

WORKS: *Death of a Naturalist*. London: Faber, 1966; *Door Into the Dark*. London: Faber, 1969; *Wintering Out*. London: Faber, 1972; *North*. New York: Oxford University Press, 1976; *After Summer*. Old Deerfield, Mass.: Deerfield/Dublin: Gallery, 1978.   REFERENCES: Beer, Patricia. "Seamus Heaney's Third Book of Poems." *The Listener* (December 7, 1972):795; Begley, Monie. "The North: Silent Awarenesses with Seamus Heaney." *Rambles in Ireland*. Old Greenwich, Conn.: Devin-Adair, 1977; Buttel, Robert. *Seamus Heaney*. Lewisburg, Pa.: Bucknell University Press, 1975; Kiely, Benedict. "A Raid into Dark Corners: the Poems of Seamus Heaney." *The Hollins Critic* 7 (October 4, 1970):1-12; Longley, Michael. "Poetry." *Causeway: the Arts in Ulster*. Belfast: Arts Council of Northern Ireland, 1971, pp. 106-107; McGuinness, Arthur E. "Hoarder of the Common Ground": Tradition and Ritual in Seamus Heaney's Poetry." *Éire-Ireland* 13 (Summer 1978):71-92; Montague, John. "Order in Donnybrook Fair." *Times Literary Supplement* (March 17, 1972): 313; Silken, Jon. "Bedding the Locale." *New Blackfriars* 54 (March 1973):130-33.

HENRY, DR. JAMES (1798-1876), classical scholar. Henry, sometime vice-president of the King and Queen's College of Physicians of Ireland, reflected not only an acquaintance with "the Two Cultures" but in the liberal arts was a profound scholar of both English literature and ancient classics. His eccentricity must have made him endearing as well as infuriating, and his decision to avoid commercial booksellers (his privately published books were presented to friends and scholars) may explain his present neglect. His pamphlets, verse collections, and exegetical works are now collectors' items. His major contribution was to Virgilian studies. His own creative efforts are uneven, descending at times to doggerel. He was an instinctive satirist, however, and many passages in his longer poems show a remarkable ability to interweave his lines with detailed botanical knowledge.

Born in Dublin in 1798, the son of Robert Henry, a woolen draper, and his wife, Katharine Olivia Elder, he took a degree in classics in Trinity College before studying medicine. He practiced his profession in York Street and Fitzwilliam Square and to the irritation of his colleagues declared the usual guinea fee excessive. He charged five shillings, to be paid in silver. He married Anne Patton of County Donegal; of their three daughters, only the youngest, named Katharine Olivia after her grandmother, survived to adult life.

During his years in practice, James Henry wrote a number of pamphlets, of which *A Dialogue Between a Bilious Patient and a Physician* (1838) and *An Account of the Drunken Sea* (1840) deal with constipation and alcoholism, respectively. Ireland's domination by her neighbor is the theme of *Little Island and Big Island* (1841), and *An Account of the Police in the City of Canton* (1840) tilts at the newly established Dublin Metropolitan Police.

A legacy Henry received in the mid-1840s enabled him to devote himself wholly to classical study. He spent almost the remainder of his life traveling on foot from one great European library to another collating Virgilian manuscripts. This labour resulted in *Notes of a Twelve Years Voyage of Discovery in the First Six Books of the Eneis* (1853) and the five-volume *Aeneidea*, most of which was published posthumously. Robert Yelverton Tyrrell in *Latin Poetry* (1894) described this monumental work as "perhaps the most valuable body of original comment and subtle analysis which has ever been brought together for the illustration of a Latin poet." R. D. Williams, in an appraisal in *Hermathena* (1973, pp. 27-43), states that more than a thousand authors are cited. Indeed, it is remarkable with what ease Henry, in order to emphasize a point, can supply an apt quotation from, say, Milton or Scott.

In *Poematia* (1866), he admitted that "To bid me write's to bid the drunkard drink / The miser hoard, the dice player play on." The verses included in *My Book* (1853), *A Half Year's Poems* (1854), and *Poems Chiefly Philosophical* (1856) are for the greater part the art of the rhymer, but he has a flair for epigrams: "All the whole world loves twaddle—'How do you know?' / All the whole world reads Harriet Beecher Stowe."

One suspects that when versifying, Henry was filling in time as another might have occupied himself with crossword puzzles, but he is a master of rhetorical prose with a taste for polemics. No respector of persons, he dismisses Dryden's translation of the *Aeneid* contemptuously: "—that translation which, up to the present day, is the only recognised representative at the court of English literature, of the sweet, modest, elegant, and generally correct muse of Virgil. Blush, England! For shame, English criticism! English poets, what or where are ye?" Wordsworth fares worse.

Having quoted a passage from the Second Book of the *Aeneid,* Henry remarks: "It is one of the finest passages which ever issued from the hand of man which is thus—shall I say travestied? or shall I say degraded?"

Librarians overzealous in the guardianship of their treasures, especially those of the Vatican and the British Museum, he regarded as his natural enemies. *The Dictionary of National Biography* credits him with a combination of kindness and rudeness, of softness and severity: "His long white locks and somewhat fantastic dress were combined with great beauty and vivacity of countenance..."

Henry's wife died in 1849 in Arco, but Katharine Olivia remained his companion in travels during which they crossed the Alps at least seventeen times. One such journey from Dresden to Venice is described in *Thalia Petasata Iterum* (1877). Here, Henry displays a detailed knowledge of natural history, indulges his agnosticism and anticlericalism, and composes a palinode inspired by the vines, before reaching their destination and the lodgings on the Ripa dei Schiaveni which had once been Petrarch's.

Eventually, "the wandering Irish Gleeman and his daughter" returned to Ireland and lived for some years in Dalkey Lodge, Dalkey, County Dublin, where she died on December 11, 1872. Henry himself died on July 14, 1876. The neglected genius is paid a fitting tribute by W. B. Stanford, who in *Ireland and the Classical Tradition* (1976) ranks him with other scholar-physicians—Linacre, Campion, and Sir Thomas Browne.

J. B. LYONS

WORKS: *My Book.* Dresden, 1853; *Notes of a Twelve Years Voyage of Discovery in the First Six Books of the Eneis.* Dresden, 1853; *A Half-Year's Poems.* Dresden: Meinhold, 1854; *Poematia.* Dresden: Meinhold; 1866; *Aeneidea: or, Critical, Exegetical, and Aesthetical Remarks on the Aeneis.* Vol. 1, London, 1872; Vol. 2, London, 1878; Vol. 3, Dublin, 1881; Vol. 4, Dublin, 1889; *Thalia Petasata Iterum.* Leipsig: Gieseche & Devrient, 1877.   REFERENCES: Lyons, J. B. "Doctors and Literature." *Conjoint Annual General and Scientific Meeting Proceedings, 1976.* Dublin: Irish Medical Association, 1976, pp. 164-173; Richmond, John. *James Henry of Dublin.* Dublin: Published by the Author, 1976.

HEWITT, JOHN (1907-), poet. Hewitt was born of nonconformist parents in Belfast in 1907. He was educated at Queen's University in Belfast, and from 1930 to 1957 he was on the staff of the Belfast Museum and Art Gallery. From 1957 to 1972, he was director of the Herbert Art Gallery and Museum, Coventry. In 1972, he returned to Ireland to spend his retirement in his native city. His volumes of poetry include *Conacre* (1943), *Compass* (1944), *Those Swans Remember* (1956), and *No Rebel Word* (1948). His *Collected Poems,* which contains works written over a period of thirty years, appeared in 1968. Since then, Hewitt has published two other collections of poetry. *Out of My Time* (1974) and *Time Enough* (1976), as well as a number of small pamphlets including *The Day of The Corncrake* (1969).

The recurrent poetic concerns in Hewitt's measured cumulative output have been an involvement in modes owing something to eighteenth-century English landscape poetry and something to Wordsworth. He has drawn the Ulster countryside and attempted to define the nature of Ulster Protestant identity and the relation of the planter stock in the province with the Irish past and present. Poems like "A Country Walk in March" are notable for topographical accuracy; "First Snow in the Glens," "Colour," and "The Ram's Horn" for a Wordsworthian joy in the landscape; while "Once Alien Here," "Ireland," and "The Colony" are analyses of the planter in the Irish context which do not hesitate to confront political and social issues. (Hewitt has always declared himself to be a member of the left.)

During the 1840s, Hewitt was involved in an Ulster regionalist movement in the arts and a revival of poetry in Belfast. At that time, he hoped a cultivation of local traditions and pieties might help solve the political and national conflicts experienced in his province. His M.A. thesis was on the forgotten minor poets of early nineteenth-century Ulster, and his *Rhyming Weavers and Other Country Poets of Antrim and Down* was published in 1974. He was associate editor of *Lagan* (1945-1946), the Belfast literary periodical edited with regionalist intentions, and of the volume *The Arts in Ulster* (1951). From 1957 to 1962, he was poetry editor of the literary periodical associated with Belfast's Lyric Theatre,* *Threshold*. He also edited the poems of the nineteenth-century Donegal poet, William Allingham* (with whose poetry his own has affinities); in 1967 and 1975, his monograph on the Ulster painter, Colin Middleton, appeared. In the 1960s, Hewitt's work influenced the young poets writing in Belfast at that time. Since his return to Belfast in 1972, he has given generously of his time and energy in furthering the arts under the most difficult of circumstances.

Hewitt's poetry has a strength and integrity of purpose that can occasionally suggest limitations of range and depth but that remind us of human continuities and moral courage in the midst of historical flux and the permanencies of nature. His lifelong attachment to the local has been a strong-minded celebration of man the maker in his society, family, and tribe. The scrupulous care of his art is a reflection of his faith in human making, while its moments of calm lyricism are his testimony to the fundamentally benign realities of man's life.

                                                     TERENCE BROWN

    WORK: *Collected Poems 1932-67*. London: MacGibbon & Kee, 1968; *The Rain Dance*. Belfast: Blackstaff, 1978.   REFERENCES: Brown, Terence. *Northern Voices: Poets from Ulster*. Dublin: Gill & Macmillan, 1976, pp. 86-97; Heaney, Seamus. "The Poetry of John Hewitt." *Threshold* 22 (Summer 1969):73-77.

HIGGINS, AIDAN (1927-), novelist and short story writer. Higgins was born on March 3, 1927, in Celbridge, County Kildare, in a Georgian house on a seventy-two-acre farm. He had a happy childhood and was educated at Clongowes Wood College. There he had a few "disciplinary problems" and rejected the "Republican bigotry" of his Jesuit Irish teacher. As their fortunes declined, his family moved to Greystones, Dalkey, and Dun Laoire. Higgins, after leaving Clongowes, wandered through the country and from job to job in England, reading Joyce,* spending time in the company of Patrick Collins, the painter, and in Clonskea Fever Hospital recovering from scarlet fever brought on by malnourishment. He met his wife, Jill Damaris Anders, in London, and with her and John Wright's Marionette Company toured much of Europe, Rhodesia, and South Africa. He lived in South Africa for two years, subsequently in Spain, Germany, London, and most recently in Connemara. His fiction has won him numerous prizes and distinctions, including the James Tait Black Memorial Award, an Irish Academy of Letters Award, the Daad Scholarship of Berlin, and, in 1977, the American Irish Foundation Literary Award. His works have been translated into a dozen languages.

His first work, *Felo de Se* (1960), consists of six stories (one a novella) dealing with man's drift towards self-destruction. Set in Ireland, England, Germany, and South Africa, they are told in a rich, dark, grotesque, painterly prose that ushers their scarcely realized or realizing characters to their respective dooms. Here are examples of savagely comic virtuosity juxtaposed with others of melancholia and violence. The promise in this book is handsomely fulfilled in the novel *Langrishe, Go Down* (1966), which developed from "Killachter Meadow," one of the pieces in *Felo de Se.* This account of an affair between Imogen Langrishe, the last flower of a decaying Anglo-Irish family, and Otto Beck, an aging (thirty-five year old) German student of bohemian tastes, is set in north Kildare in the 1930s. In a delicately evocative style, and with unflagging attention to detail, Higgins manages an acute, poignant rendition of the time, the place, and the sensibilities of his characters. In many ways a return to the late Victorian novel, it contrasts the ambiance of a leisured, feckless Big House gentility with the intellectualism, brutality, and self-centerdness of the new rulers of Europe. The seduction and abandonment of Imogen focuses a field of images from the landscape, its birds and animals, local history, the nooks and shadows of Springfield House, juxtaposing them with fragments of philosophical German and glimpses of contemporary newspaper headlines as war approaches. The method and theme set Higgins apart from the more parochial realists writing in Ireland, but at the same time his rather belated subscription to the Yeatsian version of Irish history. Despite some structural flaws and occasional shreds of self-consciousness, this study of entropy is a marvel of linguistic virtuosity, which rightly gained its author several prizes and accolades. An adaptation for BBC-TV (screenplay by Harold Pinter; director, David Jones) has been made.

In 1971 appeared *Images of Africa (1956-60),* a vivid diary of the author's voyage to Rhodesia, his life in Johannesburg, and his return to England. It contains a minutely observed account of South Africa before the Sharpville massacre and exemplifies Higgins' search for the telling image.

His second novel, *Balcony of Europe* (1972), takes place in Nerja, Andalusia, in 1962-1963, and centers on the clandestine love affair between a middle-aged Irish painter and a complacent young American Jewish wife. The background to this encounter is richly textured with exotica, recherché allusions, and semantic jokes. The main characters lack sufficient weight to counterbalance all of these impedimenta, so that we are left with mere portentousness. Higgins' return home in his next work, *Scenes from a Receding Past* (1977), promised a more passionate concern. But this attempt to rediscover an Irish childhood and adolescence as unbiased impressions, and the extension of that into adult life as an ironic self-examination, is another misjudged effort. A brave experiment in style and form, it falsifies the consciousness of the child and betrays the effects of much literary labor. Higgins' works-in-progress include "a Boyes Buke" (illustrated), a travel book on Ireland, and a novel, *Schoenberg's Last Pupil*. Always brilliant, more often pedantic than not, Higgins has yet to supersede the humane balance of *Langrishe, Go Down*. Literary reputations have been built on considerably less.

COILIN OWENS

WORKS: *Felo de Se*. London: John Calder, 1960/reissued 1978/As *Killachter Meadow*, New York: Grove, 1961; *Langrishe, Go Down*. London: Calder & Boyars, 1966/New York: Grove, 1967; *Images of Africa, 1956-60*. London: Calder & Boyars, 1971; *Balcony of Europe*. London: Calder & Boyars, 1972/New York: Delacorte, 1973; *Scenes from a Receding Past*. London: John Calder, 1977. REFERENCES: Beja, Morris. "Felons of Our Selves: The Fiction of Aidan Higgins." *Irish University Review* 3 (Autumn 1973):163-78; Garfitt, Roger. "Constants in Contemporary Irish Fiction." *Two Decades of Irish Writing*. Douglas Dunn, ed. Chester Springs, Pa.: Dufour, 1975; Hall, John. Interview. *The Manchester Guardian* (October 11, 1971): 8. Skelton, Robin. "Aidan Higgins and the Total Book." *Mosaic* 10 (Fall 1976): 27-37; Walsh, Caroline. Interview. *The Irish Times* (October 15, 1977):12.

HIGGINS, FREDERICK ROBERT (1896-1941), poet. Born in Foxford, County Mayo, on April 24, 1896, in the Catholic and Gaelic-speaking West, Higgins grew up in the English Pale. His father, a County Meath engineer, was a strict unionist of the Protestant Ascendancy tradition. Fred Higgins was, among other things, a pioneer of the labor movement. He founded a Clerical Workers Union, started a little paper called *The Irish Clerk,* edited several trade journals with titles such as *Oil and Colour Paint Review* and *The Furniture Man's Gazetter,* and was the first to establish a woman's magazine in Ireland. This magazine ran for two issues; the first issue was called *Welfare* and the second *Farewell*. Higgins was also a contributing editor to several shortlived literary papers such as *The Klaxon* (1923-1924) and *To-Morrow* (1924). However, it is as a poet passionately interested in Irish folk tradition that Higgins will probably be remembered.

In 1923, the Irish Bookshop published six of his poems in an eight-page pamphlet called *The Salt Air*. The edition was limited to five hundred copies and, although the poems in it were melodic and delicately wrought, they suffered because they were too wistful and overembroidered. Higgins' second book of poetry, *Island Blood* (1925), established a distinctly Irish note. Its poems were full of phrases that breathed Connemara. However, it was in his third book of poetry, *The Dark Breed* (1927), that Higgins began to publish appealing and sophisticated folk poems like "The Island Dead of Inchagoill." In this poem, he lamented the death of an island through the use of contrasting sounds, both past and present. Higgins' poem, like much of Austin Clarke's* historical and mythic poetry, reflected a richness of life and the intensity of a dark people. It evoked the spirit of a particular time and place, and restated Higgins' belief that Irish poets "must work more and more out of that realistic beauty found only in the folk, fusing nature with a personal emotion that incidently revealed the all important quality of a racial memory."

In 1933, Higgins published his fourth volume of poetry, *Arable Holdings*. One of the best poems in this volume was "The Woman of the Red-Haired Man," which discussed the plight of one man in love with another man's wife. In this poem, Higgins appeared to be concerned more with imagery, melody, and the texture of language than with theme. He believed that poetry should aspire to the condition of music and produce an effect so absolutely aesthetic that understanding would be held in abeyance. He frequently tried to make sounds and associations do all the work so that meaning would almost not matter. Echoes of sweet harmony and the assonance found in many a Connacht song were present in the first two stanzas of "The Woman of the Red-Haired Man."

After the publication of *Arable Holdings,* Higgins' approach to the writing of poetry changed. He discarded the image of himself as a folk poet, and the lyricism which had been present in so much of his early verse vanished. The first stanza of the poem "The Past Generation," first published in the October 1936 *Dublin Magazine,** indicated this change. Once Higgins lost his lyrical touch, symbolism became too overt, and in his search for passion and quick emotional effects he created clichés.

By 1935, Higgins had become an intimate friend of W. B. Yeats* and a director of the Abbey Theatre* for which he wrote a remarkably unsuccessful Dublin verse play, *The Deuce of Jacks*. Higgins' late writing, like Yeats', coarsened. Although Higgins claimed that Yeats never tried to shape and form his writing, no young writer as susceptible to the heroic as Higgins could live long in the company of the master of Byzantium and remain indifferent. Higgins only published one more book of poetry, *The Gap of Brightness*, before his death on January 8, 1941.

RICHARD BURNHAM

WORKS: *Island Blood*. London: J. Lane, 1925; *The Dark Breed*. London: Macmillan, 1927; *Arable Holdings*. Dublin: Cula, 1933; *The Gap of Brightness*. London: Macmillan, 1940.   REFERENCE: MacManus, M. J. "A Bibliography of F. R. Higgins," *Dublin Magazine*, new series, 12 (1937), 61-67.

HOEY, MRS. CASHEL (1830-1908), novelist and journalist. Hoey was born Frances Sarah Johnston at Bushy Park, County Dublin, on Febraury 14, 1830, and was largely self-educated. She was married at sixteen and widowed at twenty-five. In 1853, she had begun contributing to *The Freeman's Journal* and to *The Nation*,* and after her husband's death she went to London with a letter of introduction from Carleton* to Thackeray. There she married John Cashel Hoey, who had been editor of the revived *Nation*. She became a Roman Catholic like her second husband and launched into a prolific career as journalist, translator from the French, and novelist. Although admired by such an astute critic as Mary Manning,* Mrs. Hoey's usual quality may be seen in this typical extract from one of her romantic and melodramatic productions about fashionable life:

> She drew a little nearer; a wild light came into her eyes, her white cheeks were streaked with crimson. Her hands fluttered like leaves, and her gown stirred with the trembling of her knees.
>
> "I will repent, I will repent, if the chances are for you; and, if you will give me a chance then, Dominick, my darling, my lover—I love you—how shall it be, since you have beaten me, and I cannot die for you, if the chances are for you?"
>
> She clasped her hands, and stretched them towards him. A terrible yearning, half madness, half memory, all anguish, was in her beautiful, dreadful face. He recoiled still farther, and answered her thus:
>
> "Woman, if the chances were for me, I would rather be hanged twice over than see your face again."

Elizabeth Lee in *The Dictionary of National Biography* says that Mrs. Hoey collaborated on the following novels which appeared under the name of Edmund Yates: *Land at Last* (1866), *Black Sheep* (1867), *Forlorn Hope*, and *Rock Ahead* (1868). Lee also states that *A Righted Wrong* (1870), published under Yates' name, was entirely written by Mrs. Hoey. In 1892, she was awarded a Civil Pension List of £50, and she died on July 8, 1908, at Beccles, Suffolk.

WORKS: *A House of Cards*. 3 vols. London: Tinsley, 1868; *Falsely True*. 3 vols. London: Tinsley, 1870/revised, London: Ward & Downey, 1890; *A Golden Sorrow*. 3 vols. London: Hurst & Blackett/New York: Harper, 1872; *Nazareth*. London: Burns & Oates, 1873. (Nonfiction); *Out of Court*. 3 vols. London, 1874; *The Blossoming of an Aloe, and the Queen's Token*. 3 vols. London: 1875/New York: Harper, 1975; *Griffith's Double*. 3 vols. London, 1876; *Kate Cronin's Dowry*. New York: Harper, 1877; *Ralph Craven's Silver Whistle*. London, 1877; *All or Nothing*. 3 vols. London, 1879; *The Question of Cain*. 3 vols. New York: Harper, 1881/London: Hurst & Blackett, 1882/revised, London: Ward & Downey, 1890; *The Lover's Creed.* 3 vols. London: Chatto & Windus/New York: G. Munro, 1884; *A Stern Chase.* 3 vols. London: Sampson Low/New York: Harper, 1886; *The Queen's Token.* London, 1888.

HOGAN, DAVID. *See* GALLAGHER, FRANK.

HOGAN, DESMOND (1951-), novelist and short story writer. Hogan was born in Ballinasloe, County Galway, in 1951. Since the age of seventeen, he has published prolifically. His many stories, as well as a few plays produced at the Peacock and the Project, have been the subject of much attention. His main themes have been the traumas of early adolescence and a somewhat ambiguous preoccupation with homosexuality. Both themes are prominent in his short novel, *The Ikon Maker* (1976), whose main characters, a mother and her son, appear more manipulated than real. The son is misty, romantic, Byronic; the mother suffers, suffers, suffers. Indeed, there is a good deal of crying in the story's wandering plot. To take a random sample of consecutive pages, we find that the girl friend cries on page 114, the mother cries on page 115 and again on pages 116 and 117, and again on page 119 ("She stood weeping. Tears flowed. Her whole being became like a tidal wave"), a baby cries on page 122, the mother cries on page 123, and so on. Much of the novel is written in sentence fragments and in one-line paragraphs, but the style is clear and in places vivid. On the basis of several of his fugitive short stories, Hogan must be considered a promising, if yet too narcissistic, young talent.

WORK: *The Ikon Maker.* Dublin: Co-op Books, 1976.

HOGAN, MICHAEL (1832-1899), poet. Hogan, "the Bard of Thomond," was born at Thomond Gate, County Limerick, in 1832 and published much abominable verse in *The Nation** and lesser known periodicals of the day. His patriotic, satiric, and humorous squibs are indeed fluent but could have been written by dozens of other public poets of the day. A few commentators, including Críostóir Ó Floinn,* have claimed that Hogan was a genius. Ó Floinn, for instance, makes the extraordinary claim that *Drunken Thady and the Bishop's Lady* is a masterpiece, "much more masterly," in fact, than Burns' "Tam o Shanter." The Bard Hogan, a nominal employee of the Limerick Corporation, died in 1899. He produced many poetry pamphlets in small editions, and most of them are quite rare. The following list of his works, then, is undoubtedly incomplete.

WORKS: *The Light of Munster.* Limerick: Goggin, 1852; *Anthems to Mary; For the Month of May.* Dublin: Mullany/London: Catholic Publishing & Bookselling Co., 1859; *Songs and Legends of Thomond.* Dublin: Mullany/London: Catholic Publishing & Bookselling Co., 1860; *Lays and Legends of Thomond.* Limerick: Munster News Office, 1865-1869; Dublin: Gill, 1808; *The Story of Shawn-a-Scoop, Mayor of*

Limerick. . . . , Nos. 1-4. Dublin: The Author, 1868-1870; Nos. 5-8, Limerick: The Author, 1871-1876; *The Limerick Election 1880.* . . . Limerick, 1880; *The Pictorial Gallery of the Limerick Election.* . . . Limerick: The Author, 1880; *Newest Romance of Love.* Limerick, 1883; *Drunken Thady and the Bishop's Lady.* C. Ó Floinn, ed. [Dun Laoghaire?: O'Floinn?, ca. 1976].

HOLLOWAY, JOSEPH (1861-1944), diarist. Holloway, one of the notable Dublin characters of his day, was an unacademic student of the Irish stage, an unsystematic collector of theatrical memorabilia, and the author of a unique theatrical diary. He was born on March 21, 1861, in Dublin, attended the School of Art in Kildare Street, then studied architecture, and finally set up as a practicing architect in 1896. Architecture, however, did not deeply or long engage his attention. Possessed of a small private income, he was able to devote most of his life to his great love, the theatre. Over the course of about sixty years he attended practically every first night in the Dublin theatre. He was an enthusiastic supporter of the Irish Literary Theatre* and attended so many rehearsals of its successor, the Irish National Theatre Society, that he was considered something of an unofficial adviser or mascot. When A.E.F. Horniman was planning a permanent home for the Society, she hired Holloway to renovate the old Mechanics' Theatre which became, of course, the Abbey.*

Deeply religious and thoroughly conservative, Holloway early fell out of total sympathy with the Abbey Theatre. He incurred the suspicion and dislike of Yeats* and Lady Gregory* for his violent objections to Synge's* *The Playboy of the Western World* and later, to some extent, to Sean O'Casey's* *The Plough and the Stars.* Nevertheless, his theatrical knowledge was so extensive and his theatrical taste so generally sound that many playwrights and actors continued to value his opinions and to seek out his advice. Mary Walker, one of the early actresses, remarked that Holloway was the finger which the players kept upon the public pulse.

Every day of his adult life, Holloway wrote about two thousand words in his diary, describing what he had seen and whom he had talked to that day. The basic diary, housed in the National Library of Ireland, consists of 221 manuscript volumes and totals approximately 25 million words. Written in a semi-legible scrawl and with scant attention to style, spelling, or punctuation, the diary is an immense desert of aridity which is dotted with innumerable oases of fascination. It has long served as a mine of information and gossip for scholars, and four volumes of selections have been quarried from it. In addition to his diary, which he called *Impressions of a Dublin Playgoer,* Holloway edited a shortlived Irish theatrical journal, *The Irish Playgoer,* in the 1890s; he published a slovenly but still unsuperseded bibliography of the Irish drama in Stephen J. Brown's *A Guide to Books on Ireland* (1912); and he wrote innumerable, if mainly inconsequential, pieces on the theatre for the Dublin press.

As a person, he was both crusty and kind; as a scholar, he was amateurish but encyclopedic; as a critic, he was often predictably narrow but basically surprisingly broad. He died in Dublin on March 13, 1944.

WORKS: *Joseph Holloway's Abbey Theatre.* Robert Hogan & M. J. O'Neill, eds. Carbondale & Edwardsville: Southern Illinois University Press, 1967; *Joseph Holloway's Irish Theatre, Vol. One—1926-1931.* Robert Hogan & M. J. O'Neill, eds. Dixon, Calif.: Proscenium, 1968; *Joseph Holloway's Irish Theatre, Vol. Two—1932-1937.* Robert Hogan & M. J. O'Neill, eds. Dixon, Calif.: Proscenium, 1969; *Joseph Holloway's Irish Theatre, Vol. Three—1938-1944.* Robert Hogan & M. J. O'Neill, eds. Dixon, Calif.: Proscenium, 1970.

HONE, JOSEPH [MAUNSEL] (1882-1959), biographer. Hone was probably the foremost Irish literary biographer. He was born on February 8, 1882 in Killiney, County Dublin, and was educated at Cheam School, Wellington College, and Jesus College, Cambridge. He was one of the founders of the distinguished publishing house of Maunsel and Company.* His own most notable works were well researched and quite readable lives of Berkeley,* George Moore,* and W. B. Yeats.* In 1957, he was elected president of the Irish Academy of Letters. He died on March 26, 1959.

WORKS: *Bishop Berkeley.* London: Faber, 1931. (Introduction by W. B. Yeats); *Ireland Since 1922.* London: Faber, 1932. (Pamphlet); *Thomas Davis.* London: G. Duckworth, 1934; with M. M. Rossi, *Swift; or, the Egoist.* London: Gollancz, 1934; *The Life of George Moore.* London: Gollancz, 1936; *The Life of Henry Tonks.* London, Toronto: Heinemann, 1939; *The Moores of Moore Hall.* London: Jonathan Cape, 1939; *W. B. Yeats, 1865-1939.* London: Macmillan, 1942. ed., *J. B. Yeats, Letters to His Son W. B. Yeats and Others, 1869-1922.* London: Faber, 1944. (as Nathaniel Marlowe): with Warre Bradley Wells, *History of the Irish Rebellion of 1916.* Dublin & London: Maunsel, 1916; with Warre Bradley Wells, *The Irish Convention and Sinn Fein.* Dublin & London: Maunsel, 1918. Hone also did many translations, including Halévy's life of Nietzsche, Montegut's life of Mitchell, and Rossi's *Viaggio in Irlanda.*

HOPPER, NORA. *See* CHESSON, NORA HOPPER.

HOULT, NORAH (1898-), novelist and short story writer. Hoult was born in Dublin on September 20, 1898, of Anglo-Irish parents who died in her early childhood. She was educated in England, but returned to Ireland to collect material for her writing from 1931 to 1937. Just prior to World War II, she spent two years in America. She now lives in Greystones, County Wicklow.

Her first book, *Poor Women,* appeared in 1928. This collection of short stories was a critical success and has been reprinted several times, both individually and in selected editions. The stories explore the consciousness of women in different walks of life; the best of them is "Bridget Kiernan," a study of a young domestic servant in prewar Britain. The other stories, especially "Violet Ryder," are interesting psychological studies, but Hoult tends to overburden them with dull realistic details and thus to impede the action. This unselectivity was to become a marked feature of her later style.

Since 1928, Hoult has published a formidable list of titles, but only two books, *Holy Ireland* (1935) and its sequel *Coming from the Fair*, (1937), are concerned with Irish life. They depict Irish family life from the end of the nineteenth century up to 1916 and particularly explore religious prejudice. In *Time Gentlemen! Time!* (1930), we see the horror of marriage to an alcoholic waster and the grimness of middle-class poverty. Here the drab realism is probably accurate enough but grows depressingly soporific in its accumulation. *Only Fools and Horses Work,* a later novel, is a more cheerful study of widowhood.

MARY ROSE CALLAGHAN

WORKS: *Poor Women!* London: Scholartis, 1928. (Stories); *Time Gentlemen! Time!* London: Heinemann, 1930; *Violet Ryder.* London: E.Mathews & Marot, 1930. (Novelette); *Apartment to Let.* London: Heinemann, 1931; *Ethel.* London: Peppercorn, 1931. (Story, first published in *Poor Women*); *Youth Can't Be Served.* London: Heinemann, 1933; *Holy Ireland.* London: Heinemann, 1935; *Coming from the Fair.* London: Heinemann, 1937; *Nine Years Is a Long Time.* London: Heinemann, 1938. (Stories); *Four Women Grow Up.* London: Heinemann, 1940; *Smilin' on the Vine.* London: Heinemann, 1941; *Augusta Steps Out.* London: Heinemann, 1942; *Scene for Death.* London: Heinemann, 1943; *There Were No Windows.* London: Heinemann, 1944; *House Under Mars.* London: Heinemann, 1946; *Selected Stories.* London, Dublin: Maurice Fridberg, 1946; *Farewell Happy Fields.* London: Heinemann, 1948; *Cocktail Bar.* London: Heinemann, 1950. (Stories); *Frozen Ground.* London: Heinemann: 1952; *Sister Mavis.* London: Heinemann, 1953; *A Death Occurred.* London: Hutchinson, 1954; *Journey into Print.* London: Hutchinson, 1954; *Father Hone and the Television Set.* London: Hutchinson, 1956; *Father and Daughter.* London: Hutchinson, 1957; *Husband and Wife.* London: Hutchinson, 1959; *The Last Days of Miss Jenkinson.* London: Hutchinson, 1962; *A Poet's Pilgrimage.* London: Hutchinson, 1966; *Not for our Sins Alone.* London: Hutchinson, 1972.

HUTCHINSON, PEARSE (1927-), poet. Hutchinson was born in Glasgow in 1927 of Irish parents. He was the last pupil to be enrolled in St. Enda's school, and was also educated at the Christian Brothers school in Synge Street and at University College, Dublin. His first English poem was published in 1945 in *The Bell*,* and his first poem in Irish appeared in 1954 in *Comhar*. He has worked as a journalist in Dublin and lived for long periods in Spain and elsewhere in Europe. From 1971 to 1973, he was Gregory Fellow in poetry at the University of Leeds. He has published a volume of poems in Irish, two volumes of Spanish and Portuguese translations, and four volumes in English.

Hutchinson's work is sparing of simile and metaphor and even, relatively, of imagery. His earlier poems tended toward some formality, but his recent work has become much looser, conversational, even colloquial. However, even when the early work resorts to meter, the meter does not merely loosen before the poem concludes; it disintegrates. Hutchinson is seen at his best in such early pieces as "Petition to Release" and "Málaga," and at his worst in such late pieces as "All the Old Gems." His early work is superior to his later because the early poems usually preserved a certain authorial detachment, and many of the later ones are directly, even baldly personal. Moreover, his work in the 1970s, no matter in what line lengths it is arbitrarily chopped, has diverged more and more into prose and sometimes rather flat prose.

WORKS: *Tongue Without Hands*. Dublin: [Dolmen], 1963; *Faoistin bhacach*. Baile Atha Cliath: An Clóchomar, 1968; *Expansions*. Dublin: Dolmen, 1969; *Watching the Morning Grow*. Dublin: Gallery Books, [1973]; *The Frost Is All Over*. Dublin: Gallery Books, 1975.

HYDE, DOUGLAS (1860-1949), scholar, poet, translator, founder of the Gaelic League, and first president of the Republic. Hyde was born on January 17, 1860. He was the third son of the Reverend Arthur Hyde, Protestant rector of Tibohine, Frenchpark, County Roscommon, and his wife Elizabeth, daughter of the Reverend John Oldfield, Protestant rector at Castlerea, County Roscommon. In 1873, Hyde was sent to a boarding school in Dublin, but after a few weeks he returned home to convalesce from the measles and did not return to school. He received a good education at home, especially in languages, but, more importantly, he developed an avid interest in Irish during these years which proved to be the determining force in his life. In 1874, Hyde began a series of diaries, composed in both Irish and English (and now at the National Library of Ireland), which record how eagerly he began learning Irish and collecting the oral songs and tales of the local country people. Hyde took the entrance examination for Trinity College, Dublin, in June 1880 and placed seventh out of a hundred candidates. His personal library at the time included over one hundred books written in Irish, twenty-four books mainly in English but on Irish subjects, and eighteen Irish manuscripts—an extraordinary collection for a young man of twenty who had never had a formal lesson in Irish languages or literature and who was about to enter a university which was a bastion of prejudice against Irish language and culture. Hyde perfunctorily fulfilled his formal studies at Trinity, first in divinity and then in law. He reserved his real enthusiasm for his ongoing efforts to teach himself Irish and to learn as much as possible about Irish culture. His early booklists indicate that by 1888 he had read almost all Gaelic poetry in print and a considerable amount in manuscript. Hyde received an LL.D. in 1888, but the prizes he won while at Trinity—the Vice-Chancellor's Prize for English Verse in 1885, for prose in 1886, and both prizes in 1887—demonstrate that his genius and enthusiasm were for language and literature rather than for law.

Hyde had begun writing poetry in Irish and English in 1877. Between 1879 and 1883, he published original poems in Irish in *The Irishman* and *The Shamrock* under the pseudonym "An Craoibhin Aoibhinn" (the Pleasant Little Branch). The Fenianism he had absorbed in Roscommon and expressed in his early poetry and diaries was transformed into a cultural nationalism in Dublin during the 1880s. He was an active member of the Contemporary Club which Charles Oldham had founded in 1885. Its weekly meetings were a lively forum of debate about politics and literature among John O'Leary,* W. B. Yeats,* George Sigerson,* T. W. Rolleston,* and others who became the leaders of the Literary Revival. John O'Leary inspired Yeats to devote himself to producing a distinctively Irish literature written in English. But Hyde's devotion to the preservation of Irish language and culture made it inevitable that his nationalism would be modeled on that of George Sigerson who had succeeded James Clarence Mangan* as translator of the Irish poems in John O'Daly's *Poets and Poetry of Munster* (Second Series, 1860). Hyde devoted his life and his considerable talents as a poet, folklorist, and scholar to the restoration of Irish which he considered to be above and more important than divisive revolutionary nationalism. Nevertheless, his collection and translation of Irish oral traditions had a profound effect on Yeats and his literary movement, and Hyde's avowedly unpolitical propagandizing on behalf of Irish inevitably influenced Irish political events.

Hyde proclaimed his linguistic nationalism in an essay entitled "A plea for the Irish Language" in Charles Oldham's *Dublin University Review* in August 1885. Hyde's own immense knowledge of Irish oral tradition is apparent in the notes and three stories translated from the Irish which he contributed to W. B. Yeats' *Fairy and Folk Tales of the Irish Peasantry* (1888). In the same year, Hyde contributed six poems in English to the anthology of the emerging literary revival, *Poems and Ballads of Young Ireland*. His main interest, however, continued to be Irish, and his first book, *Leabhar Sgéulaigheachta* (1889), a collection of folk stories, rhymes, and riddles, was the first of its kind ever to be published in Irish. In *Beside the Fire: A Collection of Irish Gaelic Folk Stories* (1890), Hyde presented English translations of about half the stories in his first book, together with six other traditional tales in the original Irish with English translations. *Beside the Fire* is a landmark both in Irish folklore studies and in Irish literary history. Numerous collections of Irish folktales in English had been published throughout the nineteenth century, but Hyde was the first to present the exact language, names, and various localities of his informants. The "Index of Incidents" which he included at the end anticipated the use of motifs by twentieth-century folklorists. Hyde's forty-page preface reviewed the entire tradition of Irish folklore, presenting a scholarly evaluation of its significance and evaluating earlier collectors who had tampered with the substance and idiom of their originals. Hyde's own translations represented the first attempt to render Irish folklore in a true Anglo-Irish idiom. Hyde's prose bore little resemblance to the imaginary and ludicrous English of the Stage Irishman or the artificial literary style of his predecessors in the publication of Irish folklore. The poetic possibilities of this Anglo-Irish idiom were even more apparent in Hyde's translations of folk poetry, the "Songs of Connacht," which began to appear in serial form in *The Nation** in 1890. The fourth chapter of these songs, published in *The Weekly Freeman* in 1892 and early 1893 and in book form as the *Love Songs of Connacht* (1893), was a poetic and scholarly achievement and had immense literary significance. Hyde published the originals with translations to preserve them from oblivion and to aid students of Irish. He translated most of the poems twice. The first version, a free translation, reproduced the rhythm of the Irish verse; the second version, given as a footnote, was a literal translation. W. B. Yeats wrote that "the prose parts of that book were to me, as they were to many others, the coming of a new power into literature." Ironically, Hyde's achievement as a translator and a poet in the *Love Songs of Connacht* frustrated his own goal, for it furnished Yeats, Synge,* and Lady Gregory* with Irish themes in a beautiful idiom which made an Irish literature in English seem all the more possible.

The year 1893 also marked what Hyde considered to be the most important event in his life—his marriage to Lucy Kurtz, the daughter of a German research chemist who had left Russia to settle in England. The Hydes had two daughters, Nuala, who died of consumption in 1916, and Una, who married James Sealy, a Dublin judge.

On his return from a one-year interim professorship at the University of New Brunswick in 1891, Hyde had assumed the presidency of the new National Literary Society. His inaugural address, "The Necessity for De-Anglicising Ireland," given in November 1892, is his most famous and influential lecture. This lecture marked the beginning of an organized effort not only to preserve but to revive Irish language and culture. In 1893, largely as a result of Hyde's energetic propaganda on behalf of the language, the Gaelic League was founded with Hyde as its president. The two aims of the Gaelic League, which was founded as a cultural rather than as a political organization, were to revive Irish as the national language and to create a modern Irish literature. The Gaelic League was an immensely popular movement which attracted and inspired many literary as well as revolutionary nationalists. Hyde managed to keep the League from becoming politicized until 1915 when its constitution was amended to declare that its aim would be the realization of "a free, Gaelic-speaking Ireland." Hyde resigned immediately from the presidency and from the Gaelic League. In *The Young Douglas Hyde* (1974), Dominic Daly summed up the political implications of Hyde's movement as "immense and profound":

> Although the actual course of events was not what he would have chosen, his ideology was the mainspring that set these events in motion. It was he who created the ground-swell on which the Volunteer movement was launched; his students and disciples were the officers and men of the insurrection. With the zeal of a convert he opened the eyes of Irish men and women to the source of their identity as a nation.

Hyde continued his work as a poet, folklorist, and scholar of Irish literature during and after the twenty-two years he was a very active president of the Gaelic League. He wrote *The Story of Early Gaelic Literature* (1895) as an answer to those who still repeated the popular fallacy that there was no literature in Irish. His *A Literary History of Ireland* (1899) surveyed the diversity and importance of Irish literature written in Irish. Hyde's achievements as a scholar were recognized when he was appointed to the chair of modern Irish at University College, Dublin, in 1905. His genius as a poet-translator produced three more chapters of the "Songs of Connacht": *Songs Ascribed to Raftery* (1903), which saved the oral poems of the blind poet Anthony Raftery (ca. 1784-ca. 1835) from oblivion, and two volumes of *Religious Songs of Connacht* (1906), which had been serialized in the *New Ireland Review* from June 1895 to June 1905.

Hyde was also a playwright and an amateur actor. He is credited with writing the first play in Irish produced at a professional theater. *Casadh an tSugáin* was performed by members of the Gaelic League Amateur Dramatic Society at the Gaiety Theatre, Dublin, on October 21, 1901, and translated by Lady Gregory as "The Twisting of the Rope." The play, with Hyde playing the principal part, was an immense success and both Synge and Padraic Colum* wrote of the audience's emotional and enthusiastic response at its first performance. From 1902 until 1904 Hyde wrote several more plays in Irish, often from scenarios by Yeats and Lady Gregory, to help the language movement: *The Tinker and the Fairy, The Marriage, The Nativity, The Lost Saint, The Bursting of the Bubble, King James, The Schoolmaster, and The Poorhouse. (The Poorhouse* was rewritten by Lady Gregory as "The Workhouse Ward." Hyde's literary publications also include two additional collections of Irish folklore: *Legends of Saints and Sinners* (1916) and *Mayo Stories Told by Thomas Casey* (1939).

Hyde retired from University College in 1932 and went to live near Frenchpark at Ratra, the house purchased and given to him by the Gaelic League. When the new Irish Constitution was adopted in 1938, Douglas Hyde was elected unopposed as the first president of the Republic of Ireland, an office he held until 1944. In 1940, he suffered a stroke which left him a semi-invalid. He died in Dublin on July 13, 1949, and is buried in the graveyard of the Protestant Church, Portahard, near Frenchpark.

Hyde's significance to the preservation of Irish and to the establishment of a free Ireland has been generally acknowledged, but his literary genius as a poet and translator and his influential pioneer work with the Anglo-Irish idiom have, until recently been unjustly overshadowed by the literary accomplishments of his more well-known contemporaries. Yet, Yeats, Synge, and Lady Gregory all acknowledged their immense debt to Douglas Hyde. Susan Mitchell's tribute to Hyde, written thirty-three years before his death in her book on George Moore,* was even more appropriate when Hyde died in 1949 because it recognized that Douglas Hyde's legacy to Ireland encompassed much more than language, poetry, folklore, and scholarship: "We who remember those days know what Ireland owes to Hyde's fiery spirit, his immense courage, his scholarship, his genius for organization, his sincerity, his eloquence, and the kindness of his heart."

MARY HELEN THUENTE

WORKS: *Beside the Fire: A Collection of Irish Gaelic Folk Stories*. London: David Nutt, 1890/facsimile edition, New York: Lemma, 1973; *Love Songs of Connacht*. Dublin: Gill, 1893/facsimile edition, Shannon: Irish University Press, 1969; *A Literary History of Ireland from the Earliest Times to the Present Day*. London: Unwin, 1899/revised & edited by Brian Ó Cuív, London: Ernest Benn/New York: Barnes & Noble, 1967; "The Necessity for De-Anglicising Ireland." In *The Revival of Irish Literature*. London: Unwin, 1901; *The Religious Songs of Connacht*. Dublin: Gill, 1906/facsimile edition, Shannon: Irish University Press, 1972.   REFERENCES: Coffey, Diarmid. *Douglas Hyde: President of Ireland*. Dublin: Talbot, 1938; Conner, Lester. "The Importance of Douglas Hyde to the Irish Literary Renaissance." *Modern Irish Literature*. R. J. Porter and J. D. Brophy, eds. New York: Twayne, 1972, vol 1, pp. 95-114; Daly, Dominic. *The Young Douglas Hyde: The Dawn of the Irish Revolution and Renaissance 1874-1893*. Totowa, N.J.: Rowman & Littlefield, 1974.

INGRAM, JOHN KELLS (1823-1907), scholar and poet. Ingram was born at the rectory at Temple Crane, County Donegal, on July 7, 1823. He was educated at Trinity College, Dublin, received a B.A. in 1843, was elected a fellow in 1846, and continued his connection with the university for fifty-three years. In 1852, he was made Erasmus Smith professor of oratory and was thus the first to give formal instruction in English literature at the university; in 1866, he became Regius professor of Greek, in 1879 librarian, in 1884 senior fellow, in 1887 senior lecturer, in 1891 was awarded a D. Litt., and in 1898 became vice provost. He was also on the Board of the National Library and was involved in the founding of Alexandra College for Women in 1866. He wrote much on the history of religion and on political economy, and he translated Comte. As a literary man, he is remembered only for his poem "The Memory of the Dead" which he published anonymously as a young man. The first famous stanza reads:

> Who fears to speak of Ninety-Eight?
>   Who blushes at the name?
> When cowards mock the patriot's fate,
>   Who hangs his head for shame?
> He's all a knave or half a slave
>   Who slights his country thus:
> But a true man like you, man,
>   Will fill your glass with us.

Ingram did not formally acknowledge his authorship of the poem until 1900, and, in fact, became somewhat embarrassed by its fiery sentiments. He died in Dublin on May 1, 1907.

WORKS: *Sonnets, and Other Poems*. London: A. & C. Black, 1900.   REFER-

ENCE: T. W. Lyster, *Bibliography of the Writings of J. K. Ingram, 1823-1907*. Dublin: Browne & Nolan, 1909.

IREMONGER, VALENTIN (1918-), poet and diplomat. Iremonger was born in Dublin on February 14, 1918, and was educated at the Synge Street Christian Brothers school and at Colaiste Mhuire. In 1945, he won the AE Memorial Prize for a manuscript collection of poems, some of which were printed in his first volume, *Reservations* (1950). In November 1947, supported by Roger McHugh,* he protested from the audience of the Abbey Theatre* that an inadequate production of O'Casey's* *The Plough and the Stars* was a debasement of the theatre's ideals. From 1949 to 1951, he was poetry editor of *Envoy,*＊ which published his *Reservations*. He has spent most of his life in Ireland's foreign service—in London as first secretary and then counsellor, as ambassador to Sweden, Norway, and Finland, and as ambassador to India. He has made translations from the Irish of two modern prose narratives, and his collected poems appeared in 1972 under the title *Horan's Field*.

Iremonger is a thoroughly glum poet, full of nostalgia, regret, remorse, and the consciousness of growing old. He speaks constantly of "the debris of years"; winter is always coming and threatens to "pay us back for spring, blow by blow." But actually "Spring and winter are the same," for his "life's short roots / Snap and break off in Society's tough earth," and he only knows "the pity and the pain," etc.

Iremonger's work is in free verse at best and prose at worst, although sometimes the prose is decorated with rhyme. His sentence structure is generally straightforward, and his diction restrained, except for some awkwardly used colloquialisms. When he attempts to set up a rhyme scheme, as in "By the Dodder in Flood at Herbert Bridge" or in "Time, the Faithless," he cannot hold to it, and either abandons it or settles for vague similarities of sound. Fairly often, however, he does manage a strong image or metaphor, even an extended one. One of his most effective pieces is the concluding poem in *Horan's Field*, a translation from Catullus in which the language is both modern and racy.

WORKS: *Reservations*. Dublin: Envoy, 1950; *Horan's Field and Other Reservations*. Dublin: Dolmen, 1972. (Contains his poetry since 1950, with those poems from his first book which he wishes to retain); Trans., *The Hard Road to Klondike* by Michael MacGowan. London: Routledge & Kegan Paul, 1962; Trans., *An Irish Navvy, the Diary of an Exile* by Donall MacAmhlaigh. London: Routledge & Kegan Paul, 1964; ed., with Robert Greacen, *Contemporary Irish Poetry*. London: Faber, 1949; ed., *Irish Short Stories*. London: Faber, 1960.

IRISH LITERARY THEATRE, THE. *See* ABBEY THEATRE.

IRISH REVIEW, THE (1911-1915), literary magazine. *The Irish Review* was founded by three young people who worked at Padraic Pearse's* St.

Enda's School, by a friend who lived down the road from the school, and
by James Stephens. The three young people were Thomas MacDonagh*,
Padraic Colum*, and his future wife, Mary Maguire*; the friend was David
Houston, a North of Ireland man who worked at the College of Science
and published a magazine called *Irish Gardening*. As Padraic Colum wrote:

> David Houston was an outgoing, enthusiastic, hospitable man, with
> a tinge of Orangism that was provocative. Now his house open on
> Sunday afternoons was crammed with Irish Revivalists. Thomas
> MacDonagh from the school down the road appeared amongst
> them. So did James Stephens, who was now a cherished guest at
> every reception in Dublin. I would come with M.C.M. [Mary Ma-
> guire], who was a favourite in the Houston household.
>
> One evening the sanguine householder announced to the four
> of us that he had the establishment of an Irish monthly in mind. It
> is a measure of the faith that obtained in those days that this dis-
> closure was discussed, not merely seriously, but eagerly. Houston,
> MacDonagh, Stephens and myself were to conduct it. We named
> the future publication—at my suggestion, I think—*The Irish Re-
> view*. M.C.M. was to have the office of critic-in-chief. And the
> Review, mind you, was not to be quarterly, but monthly, with the
> same number of pages as a quarterly of today, and to be sold for
> sixpence. [*The Dublin Magazine* 5 (Spring 1966): 42-43.]

From 1911 to 1912, the main editor was Houston; from 1912 to 1913,
Colum, and from 1913 to 1914, Joseph Mary Plunkett.* Like most fine
literary magazines, *The Irish Review* finally expired not because of lack
of interest, but because of lack of funds. Nevertheless, in its short life, it
published poems, stories, plays, criticism, and reviews by and about the
best writers of the day—among them Yeats,* Pearse,* AE,* Corkery,*
Dunsany,* Birmingham,* Gogarty,* Forrest Reid,* Eimar O'Duffy,* Douglas Hyde,* and Seumas O'Sullivan.*

IRISH STATESMAN, THE (1919-1930), magazine of contemporary comment. *The Irish Statesman* was edited by AE* (George W. Russell) and is
quite indispensable for the study of modern Irish letters. It grew out of
The Irish Homestead, the journal founded in 1895 by Sir Horace Plunkett
(1854-1932) as the organ for his Irish Agricultural Organisation Society,
and edited from 1905 by AE. The *Homestead* was interested mainly in
agricultural matters, but did, especially in its Celtic Christmas numbers,
publish works of literary interest. James Joyce* referred to it scathingly as
"the pigs' paper," but that "bullock-befriending bard" was willing to publish some early stories from *Dubliners* in it.

The Irish Statesman, also supported by Plunkett, was much broader in
its interests than the *Homestead*; it gave a lively and intelligent survey of

Irish, and of foreign politics and art. Because of limited funds, AE had to write much of the journal himself, but most of the important Irish writers of the day appeared in it. Of AE's abilities as its editor, Monk Gibbon* wrote:

> The most gentle and good-natured of editors, his good-nature never betrayed him into publishing work which was shoddy. If there are any who doubt this they need only consult the files. Apart from his more illustrious contributors like Yeats,* Bernard Shaw* and others, he discovered and encouraged a great deal of new talent. And though his own note might tend sometimes to echo itself he took care to introduce variety into what he accepted from others. He had no prejudices. His journal was open to contributors of any nationality, of any point of view, from any school, provided only their work was good. Nor were any allowed to dominate the paper or monopolise it to the point of wearying the reader. No hobby-horses were allowed to be ridden too long—unless perhaps those wonderful courses, the winged hobby-horses of A.E. himself.

REFERENCES: A. E. *The Living Torch*. Monk Gibbon, ed. New York: Macmillan, 1938. (A collection of AE's writings from *The Irish Statesman*, with a long introduction by Gibbon); Smith, Edward Doyle. "A Survey and Index of *The Irish Statesman*." Ph.D. dissertation, University of Washington, 1966.

IRISH THEATRE, THE (1914-1920). Founded in 1914 by Edward Martyn,* Thomas MacDonagh,* and Joseph Plunkett,* the Irish Theatre was conceived as an alternative to the commercial playhouses in Dublin and to the "peasant drama" of the Abbey.* The directors announced that they would offer Irish language plays, contemporary continental masterpieces, and works by Irish writers who dealt with urban and upper middle-class life. Only a few Irish language plays were staged because few were being written; otherwise, the actual programming conformed to the original intent.

The theatre was located in an eighteenth century building in Hardwicke Street, in a North Dublin neighborhood sliding into shabby gentility. It had served as a convent for Poor Clare nuns, a Jesuit chapel and day school, and a Methodist normal school. In 1910, the derelict structure was purchased by the Plunkett family as a workshop for the Dun Emer Guild of female artisans who worked with textiles and precious metals, and as a place in which the family could put on private dramatic entertainments. From 1911 to 1912, the small auditorium was used by the Theatre of Ireland. It seated, with minimal comfort, about 120 patrons. While it was being renovated, the first Irish Theatre production, Edward Martyn's *The Dream Physician*, a satire aimed at Yeats,* Joyce,* and George Moore,* was presented in the Little Theatre, 40 Upper O'Connell Street, on November 2-7, 1914. Thereafter, all the plays were staged in the Hardwicke Street hall.

Most of the actors were professional persons for whom theatre was an avocation: J. B. Magennis, for instance, was a doctor, Norman Reddin a lawyer, and Katherine MacCormack a textile designer. Occasionally, an Abbey player, welcoming an opportunity to move outside his customary repertoire, moonlighted in Hardwicke Street, contributing his services because no salaries were paid. A few amateurs with professional aspirations had a chance to display their acting ability. Among those who appeared on the little stage were Frank Fay, Una O'Connor, Maire nic Shiubhlaigh (Mary Walker), F. J. McCormick, Paul Farrell, Noel Purcell, Patrick Hayden, Jimmy O'Dea (as old Firs in *The Cherry Orchard*, a part far removed from his later stage work), Nell Byrne (Blanaid Salkeld), and, diffidently under the stage name "Richard Sheridan," Thomas MacDonagh.* Young Micheál Mac Liammóir* created the mountaintop set for the final act of Martyn's *Regina Eyre*, a spectacular set by Irish Theatre standards. It had a more favorable reception than the play.

Between 1914 and 1920, the Irish Theatre developed an able corps of actors, brought to Ireland for the first time a number of major continental dramas (no work by English playwrights was offered), and introduced some original Irish plays. It also sponsored the appearance of the young men of St. Enda's School in plays by Padraic Pearse* and a lecture by Pearse on May 20-22, 1915. John MacDonagh,* sometimes working with materials furnished by the ladies of Dun Emer Guild, achieved striking stage effects. On the negative side, the theatre was physically inadequate, dismal in atmosphere, and inconveniently located. If a play ran late, patrons had to scurry through dark streets to catch the last tram leaving Nelson's Pillar. Too, the subtleties of Maeterlinck, Strindberg, and Chekhov generally proved unpalatable to audiences habituated to Queen's Theatre melodrama or the sledgehammer comedy sometimes dispensed by the Abbey.

The Easter Week Rising crippled the Irish Theatre. Thomas MacDonagh, Joseph Plunkett, and William Pearse, Padraic's brother and an able actor, were shot. John MacDonagh, who doubled as actor and stage manager, and several other actors were interned. But by November 1916, Martyn, the only remaining director, John MacDonagh, and a sufficient number of players were able to regroup.

Martyn had hoped to develop a school of dramatists who, while writing of Irish life, would be open to the best continental influences. Only a few playwrights came forward. Eimar O'Duffy* contributed two thoughtful comedies, *The Phoenix on the Roof* and *The Walls of Athens* in 1915. Henry B. O'Hanlon,* like Martyn a dedicated Ibsenite, created *To-morrow* (1916), *Speculations* (1917), and *The All-Alone* (1918). John MacDonagh* wrote incisive topical comedies, *Author! Author!* (1915) and *Just Like Shaw* (1916), and a serious Chekovian play, *Weeds* (1919). It was one of the few Irish Theatre presentations from which patrons had to be turned away for lack of room; not uncommonly, there would be only a score of persons in the house. *Weeds* dramatized the transition, delayed by mutual hostility and suspicion, from the old Clanricardian concept of landownership (the tenants were weeds to be rooted out) to a more enlightened system. Martyn primed the pump with his own original plays and revivals: *The Dream Physician* (1914, 1915), *The Privilege of Place* (1915), *The Heather Field* (1916, 1918), *Romulus and Remus* (1916), *Grangecolman* (1917), and *Regina Eyre* (1919). But on the whole the response to his appeal for non-peasant drama was disappointing.

While it lasted, the theatre steadfastly refused to lower its standards and remained deaf to the taunts of Dubliners that it was a zoo populated by highbrows and freakish aesthetes. Late in 1919 began a series of unfortunate circumstances. Martyn's health and financial condition both took a sharp turn for the worse. John MacDonagh left to work in the developing Irish motion picture industry. Robert Herdman Pender, chosen by Martyn to replace MacDonagh as stage manager, had served in the British Army. The actors, most of them ardent nationalists, greeted the new manager with open hostility. He produced only one play, Chekhov's *The Cherry Orchard*, which closed on the evening of January 31, 1920, after the usual week's run. Soon afterward, the Plunkett family canceled the theatre's lease to the Hardwicke Street building; it was a coup de grace.

A few years later, another attempt was made to establish a sophisticated, unparochial playhouse in Dublin. This time, with a better company, somewhat better facilities, and certainly better fortune, the Gate Theatre* accomplished what the men and women of the Irish Theatre valiantly but unsuccessfully tried to bring about.

WILLIAM J. FEENEY

IRISH WRITING (1946-1957), literary magazine. *Irish Writing* was a quarterly edited from 1946 to 1954 by David Marcus* and Terence Smith, and from December 1954 to its demise in 1957 by Sean J. White. Thirty-seven issues in all appeared, and its list of contributors was extraordinarily distinguished. Its first issue alone contained work by O'Flaherty,* O'Connor,* O'Faolain,* James Stephens,* Louis MacNeice,* Lord Dunsany,* Teresa Deevy,* Patrick Kavanagh,* Somerville and Ross,* L.A.G. Strong,* and Myles na gCopaleen.* Its second issue contained O'Casey,* Colum,* Mary Lavin,* Jim Phelan,* Ewart Milne,* Oliver Gogarty,* Seamus Byrne,* and others.

REFERENCE: *Irish Writing.* Nos. 1-28. Nendeln/Liechtenstein: Kraus Reprint, 1970.

IRVINE, JOHN (1903-1964), poet. The Ulster poet John Irvine was born in County Antrim in 1903 and died in 1964. None of his work is known outside of Ireland. He is not without merit, and a small judicious selection of his poems, or at least a reissue of the 1948 volume, would be in order.

WORKS: *A Voice in the Dark.* Belfast: Quota, 1932; *Wind from the South.* Belfast: Mullan, 1936; *Willow Leaves, Lyrics in the Manner of the Early Chinese Poets.* Dublin: Talbot/Belfast: Mullan, 1941; *Nocturne.* Dublin: Orwell, 1941; *Two Poems.* Dublin: Gayfield, 1942; *The Fountain of Hellas, Poems from the Greek Anthology attempted in English Verse.* Belfast: MacCord, 1943; *Sic Transit Gloria Mundi.* [Dublin: Sign of the Three Candles, 1943?]; *The Quiet Stream.* Belfast: MacCord, 1944; ed., *The Flowering Branch, an Anthology of Irish Poetry Past and Present.* Belfast: MacCord, 1945; *With No Changed Voice.* Belfast: Mullan/Dublin: Talbot, 1946; *Selected Poems.* [Belfast]: Arden, 1948; *By Winding Roads.* Belfast: Carter, 1950; *Green Altars.* [Belfast]: Owenvarra, 1951; *Lost Sanctuary and Other Poems.* Belfast: Quota, 1954; *A Treasury of Irish Saints.* Dublin: Dolmen, 1964.

IRWIN, THOMAS CAULFIELD (1823-1892), poet and fiction writer. Irwin was born on May 4, 1823, at Warren Point, County Down. His family was wealthy, and he was privately educated; however, the wealth had disappeared by 1848. Irwin then became a prolific writer for *The Nation,** *The Dublin University Magazine*, and other Irish journals. His fiction and verse are now little remembered, but he was highly skilled in both. Only one collection has been made of his stories and sketches, *Winter and Summer Stories* (1879), but they bear rereading especially for their gentle humor, and it might be a profitable task for a scholar to glean the best of his fugitive prose. Lorna Reynolds, in a perceptive couple of pages on Irwin's poetry, makes two sound points about it: that it is overly generalized and not sufficiently tied down to a specific place; and that it seems strongly influenced by the major nineteenth-century English poets. Certainly, one can see the influence of Keats and Shelley in "Hymn to Eurydice," of Keats in "An Urn," and of Tennyson in "England." If Irwin never attained the individual voice of his masters, he did, at any rate, have an uncommon fluency and control of his medium. If he spoke in no inimitable voice, he did have many minor successes. His short poem "A Character" is much more specific than is his wont and is perfectly charming. His "Hearth Song" is excellently musical, and his "L'Angelo" has some effectively understated lines.

In old age, Irwin became increasingly eccentric, "a weird and uncouth but venerable figure." John O'Donovan,* the great Celtic scholar, wrote of him to Sir Samuel Ferguson*:

> I understand that the mad poet who is my next-door neighbor claims acquaintance with you. He says I am his enemy, and watch him through the thickness of the wall which divides our house. He threatens in consequence to shoot me. One of us must leave. I have a houseful of books and children; he has an umbrella and a revolver. If, under the circumstances, you could influence and per-

suade *him* to remove to other quarters, you would convey a great favour on yours sincerely.

Irwin died in Rathmines on February 20, 1892.

WORKS: *Versicles.* Dublin: W. M. Hennessy, 1856; *Poems.* Dublin: McGlashan & Gill, 1866; *Irish Poems and Legends.* Glasgow: Cameron & Ferguson, [1869]; *Songs and Romances.* Dublin: Gill, 1878; *Winter and Summer Stories, and Slides of Fancy's Lantern.* Dublin: Gill, 1879; *Pictures and Songs.* Dublin: Gill, 1880; *Sonnets on the Poetry and Problems of Life.* Dublin: Gill, 1881; *Poems, Sketches, and Songs.* Dublin: Gill, 1889. REFERENCES: Rooney, William. "Thomas Caulfield Irwin." *New Ireland Review* 7 (1897): 86-100; Taylor, Geoffrey. "A Neglected Irish Poet." *The Bell* 3 (1942): 308-312; Victory, Louis H. "Thomas Caulfield Irwin." *The United Irishman* (November 30, 1901): 6.

JOHNSTON, ANNA. *See* CARBERY, ETHNA.

JOHNSTON, [WILLIAM] DENIS (1901-), playwright. Johnston is primarily a playwright, and a very distinguished one, but he has been a multitude of other things: lawyer, actor, play director, war correspondent, teacher, scholar, literary critic, and mystical philosopher. He was born in Dublin on June 18, 1901, and was educated at St. Andrew's in Stephen's Green, at Merchiston in Edinburgh, at Cambridge, and at Harvard Law School. While still in his twenties, he wrote the brilliant *The Old Lady Says "No!"* and directed *King Lear* for the Abbey.* In 1931, he became a director of the Gate.* The Gate produced some of his plays, as did Longford Productions; he did some producing and acting for both groups. In the late 1930s, he was a writer and director for the BBC, first in radio and then in the prewar days for television. He is one of the very first writers to do original scripts for television and radio. During the war, he was a correspondent in the Middle East, Africa, Italy, and Germany; later, he wrote *Nine Rivers to Jordan,* a disconcerting, not entirely realistic book about his experiences. After the war, he was for two years or so a program director for BBC television. In his early fifties, he began teaching in American colleges, first at Amherst, then at Mount Holyoke, and then at Smith. In 1955, on a Guggenheim Fellowship, he wrote a book called *In Search of Swift* which has proved more disconcerting to scholars than his plays have to drama critics. To that account, one might add that Johnston, after his retirement from Smith, was a visiting professor at various American universities and published *The Brazen Horn,* an extraordinary mélange of personal mysticism and philosophic speculation about science. A child of his first marriage is Jennifer Johnston,* one of the finest Irish novelists to emerge in the 1970s.

It is only in the 1970s that Johnston himself has begun to emerge as an Irish playwright to be reckoned with on the same level as Synge,* Yeats,* and O'Casey.* The reason for his late recognition is probably that his plays are so eclectic in technique, so dense in texture, and so relatively complex in theme that they have resisted easy pigeon-holing. His first produced play, *The Old Lady Says "No!"*, produced by the Gate in 1928, was avant-garde both in its allusions to and borrowings from popular Irish literature, and in its dream technique which owed something to expressionism and something to the fluidity of the cinema. However, the broadness of its jokes and the trenchancy of its satire assured its popularity for years. Only in 1977, in a bland Abbey revival, did the play show signs of thinness and datedness; this fact in itself is a symptom of how long it took the bourgeois theatre to assimilate Johnston's technique.

Johnston's second play, *The Moon in the Yellow River*, was produced by the Abbey and is one of his enduring works. Although set in a particular historical milieu, the aftermath of the Civil War, the questions it poses about human sympathy and public loyalty are ever-relevant. The close interweaving of complicated content with broad theatrical techniques makes this play rather more than a Shavian sugarcoated pill.

A Bride for the Unicorn, staged by the Gate in 1933, is Johnston's most thematically opaque play and a more thoroughgoing advance into expressionistic allegory than his *Old Lady*. Never adequately staged and seldom revived, the piece remains to be theatrically tested, but it is Johnston's favorite play. *Storm Song*, produced by the Gate in 1934, is his least favorite, for as he has explained, it was written as a conscious attempt to achieve a hit. The play is about the shooting of a film very like *Man of Aran* and poses some noncommercial thoughts about art and commercialism. *Blind Man's Buff* (Abbey, 1936) and *Strange Occurrence on Ireland's Eye* (Abbey, 1956) are variations on a theme; the second is sometimes a close paraphrase of the dialogue of the first. Perhaps both may also be seen as attempts, by use of the evergreen stock situation of a murder trial, to capture a popular audience. Nevertheless, neither is merely a "whodunnit" or even a "whydunnit," but a thoughtful meditation on the nature of justice. *The Dreaming Dust* (Gate, 1940) is a technically facile attempt to make sense of the enigmatic character of Swift* and is quite successful in its unusually complex presentation of the main character. *The Golden Cuckoo* (Gate, 1939) is a somewhat talky attempt to wed farce to substantial content; even though principal character is given less space than his noble madness demands, the piece is an engaging, individual attempt.

The Scythe and the Sunset (Abbey, 1958) must rank with Johnston's best work. A study of the Easter Rising, it is, as its parodic title suggests, a companion piece—if not, indeed, something of an antidote—to O'Casey's *The Plough and the Stars*. However, where O'Casey's play is a simple emotional indictment of war (although, of course, its technique is far from simple), Johnston's play is an intellectual assessment of the personal and public issues. The *Scythe* is more complicated in its statement, but it is not the least untheatrical in its technique, even though it is considerably more demanding upon an audience.

Johnston's other dramatic work has been chiefly for radio and television, and is of much less interest. However, he has been the most intelligent and, with Samuel Beckett,* the most daring Irish playwright of his time. Unlike O'Casey, his work has rarely fallen much below a high level of excellence, and his finest plays are among the best the modern Irish theatre has to offer.

WORKS: *Nine Rivers from Jordan.* London: Derek Verschoyle, 1953; *In Search of Swift.* Dublin: Allen Figgis, 1959; *The Brazen Horn.* Dublin: Dolmen, 1977. *Collected Plays,* Vol. 1. Gerrards Cross, Buckinghamshire: Colin Smythe, 1977; *Collected Plays,* Vol. 2. Gerrards Cross, Buckinghamshire: Colin Smythe, 1979.   REFERENCES: Barnett, Gene A. *Denis Johnston.* New York: Twayne, 1978; Ferrar, Harold. *Denis Johnston's Irish Theatre.* Dublin: Dolmen, 1973; Hogan, Robert. "The Adult Theatre of Denis Johnston," *After the Irish Renaissance.* Minneapolis: University of Minnesota Press, 1967: 133-146.

JOHNSTON, JENNIFER [PRUDENCE] (1930-), novelist Johnston was born in Dublin on January 12, 1930, the first child of Denis Johnston* the playwright, and of Shelagh Richards the actress and producer. She was educated at Park House School and Trinity College, Dublin. In 1951, she married Ian Smyth, and they have four children. She now lives in Northern Ireland.

Since 1972, she has published four compact and highly praised novels. Each centers on an individual who loves someone of a different age or class; this love is usually betrayed. In *The Gates* (1973), her first written but second published novel, Minnie McMahon returns from England to live with her Uncle Prionnsias in their decaying Irish ancestral home. Her uncle mutters about renovating the house, but does nothing except rub his chilblains and drink in the boot room. He represents the declining Anglo-Irish tradition, while Minnie, the orphaned daughter of his republican brother and a shopgirl, bridges the two classes, the Irish and the Anglo-Irish. Minnie falls in love with Kevin, a local boy, and they decide to restore the vegetable garden. To raise money, they secretly sell the demesne gates to rich Americans. But Kevin, desperate to escape his unhappy background, pockets the money and leaves Minnie to face her uncle. That confrontation, however, unites the girl and her uncle, and the novel ends on a hopeful note. This is a skilled first novel with well-realized characters and some delightful comic touches.

The Captains and the Kings (1972), Johnston's first published novel, is a brilliant portrait of old age. Charles Prendergast, a scion of the Big House and the last of his family, awaits death as dispassionately as he has lived. His experiences in the trenches, where his gifted elder brother was killed, and his rejection by his mother have left him with a despair which no other relationship could eradicate. His isolation is disturbed by a local boy whose trust gradually transmutes the old man's exasperation into affection. Their relationship is most touching, but to the boy's loutish Irish Catholic parents it is homosexual and to be snuffed out. Although betrayed, the old man's love for the boy somehow redeems his life, and he dies happy.

In *How Many Miles to Babylon?* (1974), two young men do manage to defy class barriers and the even more rigid barriers of army rank to maintain a friendship, but in doing so they both die. The novel is the testimony of one of them, Alexander Moore, who is awaiting death for the mercy killing of the other, Gerry. Alexander is the only child of wealthy and estranged parents, and his friendship with a working-class boy, captured in delightfully comic flashbacks, has been his happiest experience. Parallels with *The Captains and the Kings* are obvious, and it is probably no accident that the author calls her hero Alexander, the name of Charles Prendergast's dead brother. This novel, however, catches the Big House in its heyday, before the final collapse brought about by the Great War and the 1916 Rising.

Johnston's fourth novel, *Shadows on Our Skin* (1977), departs from the great rooms of the Anglo-Irish to the mean streets of present-day Derry. Joe Logan, who lives with his parents in a Catholic working-class district, is a teenage boy who falls in love with a young woman teacher. When jealousy of his older brother, an IRA member, makes him reveal that the teacher is engaged to a British soldier, the retaliation is swift and the relationship is destroyed. The author is at her best in portraying adolescence. Joe is a beautifully realized character, and the intensity of his emotion is psychologically apt. The young woman's feelings and actions are not so easily understood, and Johnston descends, for the first time, into woolly romanticism. However, Joe's relationship with his mother who, like the women in O'Casey,* works to keep the home together, is touchingly rendered. The dialogue, although not quite working class, does not usually grate.

Only in this fourth novel does Johnston not portray the native Irish as mean, grasping, and boorish, but she is hardly the first writer, whether of Anglo-Irish stock or not, to have taken that view. Certainly, her view of the Anglo-Irish as a dispossessed class, neither thoroughly English nor comfortably Irish, is not unjustified. If Yeats* romanticized the Anglo-Irish, it was that he rightly saw hope for Ireland in the tradition that produced such patriots as Swift,* Wolfe Tone, Lord Edward, Thomas Davis,* Parnell, and so many others. Yeats knew, however, that the Great Houses would soon be silent and their gardens overgrown; Johnston's novels are a brilliant insight into that fast-disappearing and increasingly silent world. Her own distinct prose style, with its extraordinary terseness and its civilized accuracy of diction, would seem to evoke that silence. Perhaps the justest assessment of her highly realized world comes from Anthony Burgess: "This is a unique and perfect art, born of a time and place and temperament, not contrived against their grain. It represents no movement, and one can learn nothing from it except the ancient virtues of human concern and verbal economy."

MARY ROSE CALLAGHAN

WORKS: *The Captains and the Kings*. London: Hamish Hamilton, 1972; *The Gates*. London: Hamish Hamilton, 1973; *How Many Miles to Babylon?* London: Hamish Hamilton, 1974; *Shadows on our Skin*. London: Hamish Hamilton, 1977.

JORDAN, JOHN (1930-), literary critic, novelist, and poet. Jordan was born in Dublin on April 8, 1930, and was educated by the Christian Brothers of Synge Street. Information on his childhood can be found in his letters to the critic James Agate in the latter's *Ego 8* and *Ego 9*: "There is nothing as boring as a conventional childhood for one who knows that there is such a thing as an unconventional childhood. People in my circle don't read anything worthwhile, don't say anything witty, and for a young prig like me that's unbearable." He obtained a First Class Honors B.A. in English and French at University College, Dublin, an M.A. in 1954, and a B.Litt from Oxford where he worked on the verse letters of John Donne. In 1959, he became assistant lecturer to the professor of English at University College, college lecturer in 1965, and resigned in 1969.

Jordan involved himself in the theatre, working with Micheál Mac Liammóir* and Hilton Edwards and with Edward* and Christine Longford* at the Gate.* In the 1950s, he started to gain a reputation as a critic in many departments of letters. His most innovative criticism was the championship of the later O'Casey* as in his essay, "Illusion and Actuality," in *Sean O'Casey*, edited by Ronald Ayling (1969). He also did pioneer work on other dramatists such as Teresa Deevy* (*University Review*, Spring 1956). (Jordan has an extensive memory of Dublin theatre productions; his stage knowledge has become an archive.)

A friend of writers such as Patrick Kavanagh* and Kate O'Brien,* Jordan has lavished the intelligent heart well on both of them. He has written the most seminal post-Yeatsian criticism of Irish poetry. He wore the novel reviewer's laurels with grace for *The Irish Times*; his main form as a commentator on cultural affairs remains his column in *Hibernia*. Jordan's mind is Alexandrian and nostalgic, with acerbic moods. As a writer of poetry and fiction, Jordan developed slowly, well behind his criticism. He published fugitive pieces in both genres under the name Stephen Renehen, in magazines such as *Irish Writing*.* and *Arena*. His collection of stories, *Yarns*, appeared only in 1977. The book at its best captures the seedy student Dublin of the late 1940s and 1950s; in this work, he exhibits a fine ear for the sentiments of fading middle-aged ladies and unfading (as yet) young men. Where the stories are weak as in "Miss Scott" and "Misadventure," either the character or the scene is miscast.

The later prose in *Blood and Stations* (1976) is private and hermetic. His poetry seems charming and febrile. In *A Raft from Flotsam* (1975), a minimal elegance mocks itself, and confession arises from repression. The volume contains too much juvenilia, but the expanded and revised "Patrician Stations" in *Blood and Stations* reads better. Thematically and linguistically a meditation on Austin Clarke* under the eye of eternity, it combines tenderness and vituperation, particularly the latter in a splendid polemic against Robert Graves. Jordan's mannered life becomes cathartic material as he explores his chlorotic Catholic humanism. Self-heroism expiates, and absolute self-heroism expiates absolutely.

JAMES LIDDY

WORKS: "Off the Barricades: Notes on Three Poets." *The Dolmen Miscellany of Irish Writing* (1962), pp. 107-116; "Writer at Work," *St. Stephen's* (Michaelmas Term, 1962), pp. 17-20; *Patrician Stations.* Dublin: New Writers', 1971; *A Raft from Flotsam.* Dublin: Gallery Books, 1975; *Blood and Stations.* Dublin: Gallery Books, 1976; *Yarns.* Dublin: Poolbeg, 1977. ed., *The Pleasures of Gaelic Literature.* Dublin & Cork: Mercier & RTE, 1977.

JORDAN, NEIL (1951-), short story writer. Jordan was born in Sligo in 1951. He has published a slim volume of short stories, of which the title story, "Night in Tunisia," is an excellent recreation of youth. He was awarded an Arts Council bursary in 1976.

WORK: *Night in Tunisia and Other Stories.* Dublin: Co-op Books, 1976.

JOYCE, JAMES [**AUGUSTINE**] (1882-1941), novelist and short story writer. Joyce was born in Dublin on February 2, 1882, the oldest of ten children born to John Stanislaus and Mary Jane Murray Joyce. His father, an extroverted, witty man never able to live within his means, is accurately described in the autobiographical *A Portrait of the Artist as a Young Man*:

> A medical student, an oarsman, a tenor, an amateur actor, a shouting politician, a small landlord, a small investor, a drinker, a good fellow, a storyteller, somebody's secretary, something in a distillery, a taxgatherer, a bankrupt and at present a praiser of his own past.

Having inherited some property in Cork, the elder Joyce did not see himself as poor, but rather as a man who suffered reverses. His days as a tax collector ended when he was forty-two, and he was pensioned off at a modest sum during a reorganization of the Rates Office. This small pension, his principal source of income, was not enough to sustain both his family and his intemperate habits. During James' childhood and youth, the monetary restraints caused the family to move constantly from one rented house to another. Such moves were accomplished by obtaining recommendations from landlords who wanted to get the family out of the house. The Cork properties eventually were sold along with all their furnishings.

John Joyce also was an ardent nationalist and had a great deal to say about the fall from power of Charles Stewart Parnell. Nine-year-old James, caught up in his father's fervor, wrote a poem entitled *"Et Tu,* Healy," which his father had published. Indeed, the Parnell episode sparked a deep distrust of the Roman Catholic Church in the elder Joyce, which left its mark on James as well. Joyce's mother, on the other hand, was as devout as John was anticlerical. Thus, their family life, particularly as James grew into puberty, was difficult in both religious and monetary matters.

James began his schooling at Clongowes Wood College in 1888 and went quickly to the head of his class. He was unable to return in 1891, however, and was forced to spend some time in a Christian Brothers school before enrolling in Belvedere, a Jesuit secondary school in Dublin, in 1893. This placement was made possible because Father John Conmee, formerly rector at Clongowes, had assumed the position of prefect of studies at Belvedere and, remembering James, arranged for him to study at Belvedere without fees. In Belvedere, James experienced violent changes in attitude and a new sense of isolation from parents, teachers, and religion. He began to write a series of prose sketches and a volume of verse.

Throughout his pubescence and early manhood, as the eldest child, Joyce was increasingly expected to assume the responsibility for his brothers and sisters. His decision to follow his art instead of being the family provider is outlined in *Portrait*.

Turning down an offer to study for the Holy Orders, Joyce was admitted to University College, Dublin, in 1898. By the time he graduated four years later, he already had a substantial local reputation as an eccentric intellectual and writer. Earlier he had become devoted to the works of Henrik Ibsen and was a staunch advocate of the playwright in a period in which Ibsen was condemned for immorality by many of Joyce's contemporaries and teachers. Joyce's essay "Ibsen's New Drama," published when he was just eighteen years old in no less prestigious a journal than *The Fortnightly Review*, drew considerable notice from his colleagues, especially when it was learned that Joyce had received payment of twelve guineas for his contribution. When Ibsen wrote a note of thanks, young Joyce was overwhelmed. After receiving it, he began the systematic study of foreign languages and literature, seeking to become European rather than merely Irish. "The Day of the Rabblement," an attack on what he saw to be the parochialism of the Irish theatre, was published at his own expense after it had been rejected by the school magazine, *St. Stephen's*. By now, Joyce's circle of literary acquaintances had expanded to include George Russell,* W. B. Yeats,* and Lady Gregory.*

On his graduation from University College, Joyce emigrated in December 1902 to Paris, where he was to undertake the study of medicine while supporting himself with some reviewing that Yeats and Lady Gregory had arranged. However, the nearly starved Joyce spent his days in arguments with John Synge* and in the literary section of the library, rather than the medical section, until his mother's failing health prompted his return to Ireland.

Once back in Dublin, he lived in the now famous Martello Tower in Sandycove with Oliver St. John Gogarty,* whose urbanity and wit grace the character of Buck Mulligan in *Ulysses*. Joyce took a job as teacher at the Clifton School in Dalkey, and on June 16, 1904, the date on which *Ulysses* occurs, he had his first date with Nora Barnacle, a Dublin boarding house employee. In October the couple left Ireland permanently, first traveling to Paris and then to Zurich and Trieste.

Joyce lived all his life with Nora, and though it was 1931 before they were formally married, it was a remarkably monogamous relationship—despite doubts about Nora's fidelity and occasional indiscretions of his own. The Joyces had two children, Giorgio and Lucia. Giorgio died in 1976, and Lucia, at the time of this writing, is committed to a sanatorium in England.

Joyce was befriended by Ezra Pound, who was then the most influential literary figure in Europe. Pound first published serially Joyce's *Dubliners* and *Portrait* in the *Egoist*, which he edited. He also introduced Joyce to Harriet Shaw Weaver, who took over the editorship of the *Egoist* and who supported Joyce for the rest of his life. Although Joyce had a great deal of difficulty with the publication of his stories and the *Portrait*, he had many friends and devoted followers who always regarded him as the genius the world was later to accept. Joyce knew all the major figures of the literary renaissance that occurred between the wars. He was a frequenter of the Shakespeare Bookshop in Paris, and it was under the auspices of Shakespeare and Company that *Ulysses* was first published in its entirety in 1922.

Joyce's life in Paris was interrupted by World War II; he fled the city ahead of the Germans to settle finally in Zurich (where he died on January 13, 1941). Always in need of money and continually fighting with editors and critics, Joyce nevertheless was surrounded by a host of friends and was supported by his family, especially his brother, Stanislaus, who criticized, edited, provided funds, and devotedly carped his way through decades of attempts to improve his brother's intemperate drinking and fiscal habits.

Joyce's eyes were never good, and they deteriorated over the years until he approached total blindness. He had a number of amanuenses, particularly as his last work progressed. The most well known of these was Samuel Beckett,* whose refusal of Lucia's affections may have been a major cause of her mental problems. Never a great family man, Joyce was a full-time artist, formal and reserved, distant from his children, living for his work, never doubting his own genius.

The fifteen years spent in the composition of his longest work, known for the major portion of its time in composition as "Work in Progress," were spent in the company of great modern writers, and readings of the work were often given. Even before *Finnegans Wake* was formally published as a book, a number of essays on it were published and a full-length books of essays, *Our Exagmination Round His Factification for Incamination of Work in Progress*, was published in 1929, with studies by twelve outstanding men of letters of their day: Samuel Beckett, Marcel Brion, Frank Budgen, Stuart Gilbert, Eugene Jolas, Victor Llona, Robert McAlmon, Thomas

McGreevy,* Elliot Paul, John Rodker, Robert Sage, and William Carlos Williams.

Joyce was almost exclusively devoted to literary pursuits, but there was time to champion several artists. The first cause was that of the Irish poet James Clarence Mangan* (1803-1849), who Joyce claimed never achieved the fame he deserved because of the narrow attitudes of the Irish nationalists. The second and more prolonged *cause célèbre* was that of John Sullivan, whom Joyce thought the leading tenor of Europe, though one who had never received his just fame or rewards. Joyce was a tenor himself, who might have won the Feis Ceoil had he been able to sight read. When he was asked to read a piece, he strode indignantly from the stage and the gold medal was given to another. Although Joyce gave up the idea of a professional singing career, his works were to be sprinkled liberally with musical allusions, and his last work, *Finnegans Wake*, drew its name and theme from a ballad.

The influences on Joyce were as catholic as his reading. Besides his preoccupation with Ibsen, Joyce was undoubtedly influenced by his reading of W. B. Yeats. Many of Joyce's ideas came from the nineteenth-century aesthetes' movement, but his sources cover the whole range of European and classical literature. The theory of aesthetics advanced by Stephen Dedalus in *Portrait* has its origins in Plato and Aristotle. The influence of Joyce's heavily theological indoctrination also plays a paramount role in his literature, as do the realistic-naturalistic strains of Flaubert, Maupassant, Balzac, Ibsen, and Zola and the surrealism of Strindberg and others.

To begin to enumerate Joyce's sources is as frustrating as to attempt to identify all of the authors whose works in whole or part bear heavy strains of his influence. While writers like Woolf and Dos Passos are obviously indebted to Joyce, and most other major writers since have paid him homage, there is little in modern literature which does not reflect either directly or indirectly his innovation or stamp, from the surrealism of his literary nightmares to his refinements of the stream-of-consciousness technique.

Although all of Joyce's works were derived in large measure from his personal experience and so are heavily autobiographical, they have the distance and integrity of art. Readers must be wary of trying to extrapolate anything of Joyce's own life or his own philosophy from his fiction. Above all, Joyce was the consummate artist, creating distanced works of art with their own individual integrity.

INTRODUCTION TO THE WORKS

The measure of Joyce's literary achievement is reflected in his stature as one of the greatest writers of Western civilization. His major published works became increasingly complex and erudite as his career progressed, while his experimentation with the possibilities of the written word became more profound and at the same time more fundamental.

In his earlier works, Joyce's characters operate on the naturalistic level but do not always function symbolically. By the Circe episode of *Ulysses*, however, character and symbol have merged, and in his last work, *Finnegans Wake*, verisimilitude in language, plot, and action has been abandoned and replaced by archetype, innuendo, and impression. His erudition is evidenced in the abundance of allusions to untold numbers of literary works both classical and contemporary, Eastern and Western. In *Finnegans Wake* in particular, his handling of language reflects an acquaintance with scores of foreign tongues, and his parodies of previous literary styles, particularly in the Oxen of the Sun episode of *Ulysses*, suggest an intimacy with the major prose stylists of the English language from its beginnings through the nineteenth century. His use of contemporary dialects in the same episode also reveals a linguistic preciosity with the contemporary idiom, while his whole canon contains a broad sampling of common speech and a variety of language which has yet to be equaled by any other modern author.

Joyce's themes are at the same time as simple and as complex as life itself. *A Portrait of the Artist* is on one level a straightforward *bildungsroman*, but one which investigates, in both traditional and innovative ways, the relationship of life to art and the nature of truth. In *Ulysses*, Joyce sets up, through the contrast between the archetypal figure of Odysseus and the contemporary man, Leopold Bloom, the fundamental similarities to be found in people and situations of all ages. In his last work, *Finnegans Wake*, Joyce attempts a unique task in literature—the depiction of the macrocosm —all of everything—which is then related to the microcosm of H. C. Earwicker and his family. The universality of *Finnegans Wake* is reflected in the plethora of languages in the text which act with their English counterpart to produce multiple layers of meaning.

Joyce's works grew increasingly comic in both tone and language. In addition, throughout his work he retained aspects of pure realism even as his style of writing became more ingenious and difficult to comprehend. While he steadfastly denied any indebtedness to Freud or Jung, their influence is especially evident in his later works. Thus, Joyce is a symbolist, mythmaker, comic writer, naturalistic writer, satirist, linguistic innovator, and psychoanalytic novelist.

Chamber Music

Chamber Music, his slightest and simplest work, consists of thirty-six lyric poems about love and its failure. The original sequence of the poems differed from the final printed arrangement, which Joyce's brother Stanislaus ordered in such a way to comprise a story in which the persona of the poems meets a girl, falls in love, enjoys a period of relative bliss, but later experiences the dissolution of the relationship. The last poems recall the relationship, now passed, and the final poem, perhaps the best of the lot, is emotionally charged and yet poetically distant. Other structural progressions in the poetry are the evolution of the seasons and the light/darkness motif.

One interesting aspect of the poems is their lyrical quality. Joyce himself provided music for several of them, and most of the thirty-six have been set to music by various composers.

The poems most resemble Elizabethan, principally Jonsonian, lyrics, but they are heavily indebted to the lyrics of Yeats. Joyce also drew heavily upon the "Song of Solomon" for theme, diction, and symbol. Thus, the woman of the poems is a universal figure, representing multiple aspects of the female archetype, the Great Mother, the temptress, and the Church, as well as the aspects of the Virgin and Beatrice. Many of the themes that Joyce was to use prominently in later works can be seen first in *Chamber Music*, especially the motifs of betrayal, jealousy, and masochism.

The best critical treatment of the poems is by William York Tindall in his introduction to the 1954 edition. Tindall's splendid explication is marred only by an occasional overinsistence on Freudian and Jungian interpretation, chamberpots, and carthy allusion. Such ingredients were cornerstones of Joyce's later work but are more difficult to see in *Chamber Music*.

In summary, the poetry of *Chamber Music* is imitative, often naive, but occasionally striking. It is a product of youth, most of it written when Joyce was eighteen or nineteen. All poems were composed by the time he was twenty-one. Doubtless, it would never have received notice at all if it had to stand alone.

Pomes Pennyeach

The eleven poems contained in *Pomes Pennyeach* are mostly reflections of a much maturer man. They are less lyrical than *Chamber Music*, though still heavily metered. The themes are diverse. Some, like "Bahnhofstrasse," deal with age, while others, like "A Flower Given to My Daughter," are concerned with family. Many themes reappear in later works: the situation and the cadences of "She Weeps Over Rahoon" can be found again in the conclusion of "The Dead," and the lost love motif of "Tutto È Sciolto" is seen later in the Sirens chapter of *Ulysses*.

A final poem "Ecce Puer," published separately, is of special interest because it treats the theme of the relationship among the generations and life cycles—a concern that grew more important in Joyce's later work, until in *Finnegans Wake* it became paramount.

The poetry, then, taken in its entirety, is a very small segment of the Joyce canon, in both volume and importance. While it has its enthusiasts among Joyce critics, it is so far overshadowed by the major prose works that it becomes ancillary in any overview of Joyce.

Exiles

Joyce's single play, *Exiles*, likewise contains a number of flaws, especially when it is considered beside his novels and short stories. The structure of the work is laid out in a series of confessions in which the four principal characters, all overburdened with guilt, admit their relations with each other. The principal character, Richard Rowan, like the later heroes Stephen

Dedalus and Shem the Penman, bears a striking resemblance to Joyce himself, in terms of both personal history and temperament. However, readers can make a serious mistake by identifying his protagonists wholly with Joyce.

Part of the problem of *Exiles* is that the domestic situation is too close to Joyce's own. Joyce's notes on the play, provided at the end of the Viking edition, indicate the heavy emotional involvement Joyce had in the action. Consequently, the artistic potentialities are not completely realized. Nevertheless, the play deals interestingly with the freedom and restraints of the marital situation. Richard, the protagonist, and Bertha have tried to live a monogamous life unfettered by the formal ceremonies of marriage. Then, in an effort to attain an idealized kind of freedom, Richard places his mate in circumstances which could compromise her fidelity.

The play, like Joyce's later work, operates on an archetypal and symbolic level as well as a realistic one. The characters are classic representations of the major figures that dominate all of Joyce's work. Beatrice is the frail, intelligent, inspirational figure with intellectual pretensions; Bertha is the earth mother, a fertility-temptress figure who takes on characteristics of Ireland itself; Robert Hand is the classic antithesis of the artist, the succcessful public man who is extroverted, occasionally hypocritical, opportunistic, and charming, a figure later represented in *Ulysses* as Buck Mulligan and in *Finnegans Wake* as Shaun. His counterpart, Richard Rowan, is an artist in the mold of Stephen Dedalus and Shem, an introverted, egotistical, self-sacrificing pursuer of art and truth. At the same time he is self-centered, giving no quarter in the battle for artistic integrity and freedom.

All of the characters revolve around Richard and are in various states of emotional crisis in inverse proportion to their distance from him and in direct proportion to their commitment to and love for him. He is in effect the artist trying to manipulate those about him as if he were manipulating characters in fictive events. In a way, the complexities of Richard's mind and his motivation form the essence of the play's meaning. First, his feelings are much like that of a cuckold pretending he will overcome his wife's infidelity and his concurrent feelings of inadequacy by precipitating her liaison with Robert. His action strongly suggests masochism. But Richard is also sadistic when he insists upon telling his wife all the details of his own infidelities. At least part of Richard's action is motivated by love and a genuine concern for his wife's happiness with another man, but he is also motivated in part by pride and abhors the righteousness of her fidelity in the face of his own indiscretion. However, he gets an emotional kick out of thinking his wife desirable to other men, and the affair enhances his own Byronic self-image. Whether or not he does this remains ambiguous, as does the question of whether Bertha actually commits adultery with Robert Hand. In the end, the characters are at least as miserable as they were in the beginning, and the problem has been merely stated rather than resolved.

A final ambiguity is the character of Archie, the son of Richard and

Bertha. Obviously some projection of the future, Archie is last seen being led off by Robert to hear a fairy story. The ultimate meaning of his role remains obscure, however, since he is both the product of the bond between Richard and Bertha, and the embodiment of the sort of faultless freedom Richard so desires.

While the tone of the play is almost unrelieved seriousness, there are classically comic situations—almost burlesque—such as Robert's preparations of the room for his prospective liaison and Richard's standing in the rain spying on the amorous couple. There is also some funny *double entendre* dialogue about where Robert will kiss Bertha.

The panorama of emotions from guilt to uncertainty to anguish, and the complicated responses of four intelligent and introspective characters, are simply too great for resolution or even complete development in the fairly brief confines of a three act play.

The range of complexities and the dilemmas represented in *Exiles* come into full flower in the larger forum of Joyce's novels, but encapsulated in this drama they lack the room to develop and thus form an artifice. The work is tantalizing and thought-provoking, but still not up to the high artistry of Joyce's fiction.

Dubliners

The first of Joyce's major works and his only volume of short stories, *Dubliners*, revealed for the first time the complexity of Joyce's artistic vision. The fifteen stories comprising the volume appear to be completely realistic and composed of commonplace situations of Dublin life. Many of the early reviewers and critics, in fact, saw little of great significance in them, and they were often characterized as plotless and trivial. Often one or another of the stories is anthologized, but at the expense of the meaning it draws from the others in overall tone and specific image. For instance, the reference to the former tenant of the boy's house in "Araby" as a priest, and the yellowing photograph of a priest in Eveline's room are both linked to the image of the priest in "The Sisters." The escape role of the opera *The Bohemian Girl* in "Eveline" is reinforced in "Clay," where Maria closes the story with a rendition of a song from the opera, leading us to assume that Maria is a sort of older Eveline, who, unable to escape, still cherishes the romantic notions of her younger counterpart from the earlier story. The coin extracted from the slavey in "Two Gallants" is returned to the servant Lily by Gabriel in "The Dead" as the stories merge in theme and symbol.

The structure of *Dubliners* follows a basic life-cycle pattern, with the first three stories covering early life; the next four, young adulthood; the following four, mature life from middle to advanced age; the next three, public life in Dublin politics, arts, and religion; and finally a summary story, "The Dead," with its sisters who bring us back full circle to the first story. "The Dead" also incorporates and summarizes most of the major themes and formulas in this collection of entrapment narratives.

The first three stories are all narrated by their youthful protagonists. These stories are in the *bildungsroman* tradition, with the first, "The Sisters," serving as introduction to the entire collection in its emphasis on paralysis, entrapment, and death. The lesson of "The Sisters" is a good deal more ambiguous to the boy than the revelations of the second and third stories, each of which reveals to the protagonists some sort of inadequacy about his own self-image.

These moments of enlightenment assert themselves in a form later formularized in *Stephen Hero* as the epiphany. The nature and meaning of epiphanies has been a central point in critical debate over Joyce through five decades of criticism. Briefly, in the broadest and most popular definition, the term *epiphany* refers to moments of self-revelation or illumination of truth in events. These enlightenments may be acquired by the protagonist, the readers, or both. It must be stressed here that epiphanies, with all their aura of unassailable veracity, are often really only what appear at the time to be truth to the protagonists who experience them. While epiphanies are experienced by many of the protagonists of *Dubliners*, the lessons are frozen with the end of each story, so that there is no opportunity to analyze them in the light of subsequent events, such as there is in *A Portrait of the Artist*.

The second group of stories, the young adulthood section, further develops actions and metaphors of entrapment, as the protagonists at this stage of life have the maturity to realize that they are locked into life patterns. Some of the characters such as Corley and Mrs. Mooney realize and exploit the entrapment, while others, like Eveline and Bob Doran, struggle against it. Marriage, fleeing Ireland, and remaining single are all offered as alternative means of liberation in "Eveline" and "The Boarding House," while business success in "After the Race" and sexual exploitation in "Two Gallants" are other escape routes which fail.

In the third group of stories, the more mature characters are locked in so completely that the possibility of ultimate freedom exists only in fantasy. Again the alternatives of escape from place, from occupation, from marriage, and from the single life are explored, but the increasingly unavoidable answers are only frustration, violence, self-deception, resignation and death.

Stories in the middle sections are often paired in different ways, exploring alternative responses to entrapment and alternative modes of living, such as the married state in "A Little Cloud" and spinsterhood and bachelorhood in "Clay" and "A Painful Case"; the violent and the passive responses in "Counterparts" and "A Little Cloud"; and exploring and being exploited in "Two Gallants" and "After the Race."

The fourth group of stories explores the institutions themselves. In his accounts of political, artistic, and social life in Dublin, Joyce turns for the first time to satire and the deep vein of humor which would become increasingly apparent in his later works. At the same time the greed, pettiness, meanness, and outright stupidity which for Joyce characterize the practice of those institutions in Dublin are uncompromisingly portrayed.

"The Dead," one of the great short story masterpieces in any language, proceeds from a specific set of circumstances to an all-encompassing metaphor of universality. The large cast of characters at the Morkan sisters' dinner party discusses such immediate topics as the newspapers for which Gabriel writes or the sleeping habits of monks. However, these are topics which lead naturally into the underlying universals: escape and, more importantly, life and death. The scope of the account broadens as the implications of the action assume for Gabriel more and more universality until he reformulates them into his final powerful metaphor of the ultimate connection between all the living and the dead.

In *Dubliners*, Joyce begins with a first person narrative in the first three stories and then proceeds to a third person narrator who closely approximates the mind of each protagonist. The realistic tenor and style of the description stem from these individualized perspectives, which provide corresponding changes in dominant tone and metaphoric pattern for each story. The range is enormous, from the fury in "Counterparts" to the saccharine in "Clay"; from the subjectivity of "A Little Cloud" to the stentorian sermon-like tones of "Grace"; and from the tentativeness and ambiguity of "The Sisters" to the finality of "The Dead." The collection subtly shifts focus and style through a range of individual problems, moods, and solutions, finally combining in an artistic vision of communality across time, sex, class, and occupation.

Joyce had no easy time finding a publisher for his collection. Refused by publisher after publisher, with unhonored agreements from Grant Richards and later George Roberts, the book was finally published nine years after Joyce's first attempt. Objections were made about the language (words like "bloody" were anathema); about its disrespect for God, the Crown, and local politicians; and about libel. The publication squabbles produced a broadside poem from Joyce, "Gas from a Burner," printed at the author's expense in 1912. In a letter, Joyce recounts the publication history of the collection:

> The type of the abortive first English edition (1906) was broken up. The second edition (Dublin 1910) was burnt entire almost in my presence. The third edition (London 1914) is the text as I wrote it and as I obliged my publisher to publish it after 9 years. . . . *Dubliners* was refused by *forty* publishers in the intervals of the events recorded above. [Ellmann, p. 429]

No other book except *Ulysses* was beset by such publication difficulties. Early reviews were decidedly mixed but not vociferously unfavorable, with many of the stories classified as "cynical, pointless or both." Among the early critics, only Ezra Pound saw the genius of the collection and sensed its real significance.

A Portrait of the Artist as a Young Man

Many of the critical problems of *A Portrait of the Artist as a Young Man* grow out of the critics equating the protagonist, Stephen Dedalus, with Joyce himself. In writing this *bildungsroman*, Joyce while using the events of his own life as a basic design, nevertheless succeeded in distancing himself from his novel. Readers are often duped into equating Stephen's hopes, ideas, and experiences with Joyce's own in part because the narrative perspective of the novel is essentially that of Stephen, though it is related in the third person omniscient voice. The central conscience of the novel is, however, greatly distanced from Joyce's own, and the author, to repeat Stephen's words, "remains within or beyond or above his handiwork, invisible, refined out of existence, indifferent, paring his fingernails." When the reader acknowledges that this distancing is also one of the hallmarks of Stephen's own aesthetic theory, he begins to grasp the complexities of this book, which is as much about composing a work of art as it is a novel of youthful experience or ritual passage.

Since the book begins with a protagonist of about the age of three and takes him through his graduation from University College, Dublin, the narrative line paralleling his thoughts undergoes a continual and dramatic shift in style, tone, and concerns. Yet, at the same time the opening pages encompass all of the major themes which will occupy the book and the mind of its hero. These will be restructured, refined, reshaped, and remolded by Stephen Dedalus time and time again into new revelations of himself and his role in life. Each of the five chapters encompasses a phase of Stephen's development and produces a new revelation, plateau, or stage of increasing awareness of his own position in the world. Concurrent with this is the developing motif of art and what it means in terms of the truths of existence. The novel is not only about how a boy grows up, but also about how the very process is in itself transformed into a work of art. Part of this process is a rationalization on Stephen's part for his own feelings of inadequacy, a means of protecting himself from the harsh derisions of childhood comrades, of coping with inconsistencies of fact and ideal in his early training, and of separating himself from other youngsters against whom he might be judged. Another aspect of artistic creation stems from Stephen's natural verbal inclination and his enormous talent and intellect. The developing consciousness of the young man is reflected in his initial linguistic preoccupation with sounds, words, and meaning.

The development of Stephen's intellect is partly revealed through a gradual evolution of the narrative line from the childish language of the first pages to an abstruse and often tortured and analogical prose heavily sprinkled with Latin and St. Thomas in Chapter Five. The implications of identifying the narrative perspective as Stephen's are enormous for the reader. First of all, symbols do not exist outside of Stephen's awareness of them, for he makes and later evolves the symbolic patterns of the book. Beginning, for instance, with his mother as the foundation of his eventually complex female principle, he adds the Blessed Virgin and later, as he reads more courtly love and romance, the figure of Mercedes from *The Count of Monte Cristo,* finally adding the temptress figure as he reaches pubescence. His earlier association with Eileen merges with his infatuation for E.C., and subsequently they both blend with their archetypal literary and religious counterparts, until at the end of the fourth chapter an inspiration figure emerges in the all-encompassing vision of the girl on the beach, both a herald and a symbol of Stephen's art. His final villanelle in Chapter Five extols and abstracts his relationship with this composite symbol-reality, turning his experiences into art at the same time he makes an art work out of his description of the process.

Stephen's evolving self-image also encompasses the political and religious influences upon him. Coupling his early fever-ridden reception of the news of Charles Stewart Parnell's death with the religious conflict of the subsequent Christmas dinner scene, Stephen begins to conceive of himself as a sort of Parnell figure, a savior for Ireland, who, like Christ, must bear the interrogations of youth and manhood, suffer, and from the body of his own experience mold the uncreated conscience of his race. His difficulties with the boys first at Clongowes, later at Belvedere, and finally at University College lead to a series of confrontations or "admit" scenes in which Stephen increasingly assumes the role of Christ-like savior, derided by those he would save by transforming his life into an art of salvation as the priest transforms the wine and wafer into the body and blood of Christ. Not being content to provide merely the sacrifice, Stephen will also assume the role of priest or agent of transformation. Invited by the director of studies to join the Jesuit Order, Stephen rejects the formal boundaries of Holy Orders but accepts the principle of himself in a priestly role, transubstantiating life into art instead of wine and wafer into the Holy Eucharist. As a defense against the Philistine demands and derision of Irish society and his peers, Stephen will lead them out of their bondage with his own sacrifice and the truth which evolves from its transformation into art.

Each chapter builds on Stephen's initial realistic external surroundings, while also elaborating the images and resolution of preceding chapters. By the end of the chapter, the result is a new mental stance for Stephen, a new epiphany or revelation of his position. With the exception of Chapter Two, the moment of enlightenment or structural climax of the episode is followed by a denouement or period of reflection in which Stephen glories in the certainty of his newly established image. With the beginning of the next chapter, however, he is returned into the mundane world of his external surroundings and forced once again to take stock, to reevaluate and reform his image.

In the final chapter, Stephen refines and divides into two parts his process of self-definition. He provides the theoretical background in his aesthetic theory, and his artistic expression of himself as sacrifice and priest in his poem, the villanelle. Having decided what he wants to do, he must detach himself from everything which inhibits the development of his art: his family, his home, his religion, and his country. The book closes with his decision to leave, carrying with him the raw materials of his experience to form into the artifacts of art.

Like *Dubliners*, *A Portrait* is an extremely compact book, with nothing in it extraneous or tangential to Stephen's development. *Portrait* is a much abridged version of a longer and earlier manuscript, a part of which was preserved and later provided enough material for a fair-sized book in its own right. *Stephen Hero*, the earlier work, is worth mentioning here because of the contrast between its technique and that of *Portrait*. Because the central narrative consciousness is not as close to Stephen's, *Stephen Hero* is a less impressionistic, more naturalistic book, with long dialogues and a good deal of description omitted from its successor. Scenes, thoughts, and ideas which are developed in explicit detail in *Stephen Hero* are hinted at, reduced, or merely suggested without editorial comment by the narrator in *Portrait*. The reader of *Stephen Hero* is told the significance of actions by the narrator, while readers are led to extrapolate from the action often just what is taking place in Stephen's mind. In *Portrait* the technique results in a closely crammed text which can be read over and over with new insights each time. The result is perhaps the greatest *bildungsroman* ever written.

ULYSSES

The greatest work in the Joycean canon of classics, *Ulysses*, operates simultaneously on many levels of realism, symbolism, comedy, tragedy, and satire. At once a great comic satire and a serious in-depth psychological novel, *Ulysses* casts the least of all men, a humble and largely unsuccessful advertising salesman, Leopold Bloom, as the modern day Odysseus, the primary heroic figure of Western civilization. His wife, a sensual adulteress, becomes the faithful Penelope, and the intellectually snobbish and disdainful Stephen Dedalus, who apparently has nothing at all in common with his surrogate father, and who before the end of the day rejects any offer of a permanent or even semi-permanent association, becomes his devoted and searching son, Telemachus.

Rather than an epic journey of ten years' duration, however, the action of the novel is contained in a span of less than twenty-four hours, and the scene, instead of the entire Hellenic world, is the city of Dublin. Operating through paradox and understatement on the parody level, through the direct literalness of Bloom's perspective, and through historical, literary, and theological analogy in the symbolic frame of reference of Stephen Dedalus, Joyce weaves his way through a complex pattern of relationships, finally culminating in a unity of thought, method, and plot which universalize the situations of the several principal characters into a mélange of themes often mind-boggling in their complexity, and at the same time unified in a synonymy of events and situations.

Seen in its broadest and simplest context, *The Odyssey* is a homecoming story, a tale of a man returning and reestablishing his rights and sovereignty in his home. He is aided in his struggle by his son, who has carried on his father's image and sense of values, even in the face of usurping suitors, and by his wife's faithfulness despite her husband's long wanderings. In a sense she is the sanction of his behavior; hers is the home and the establishment for which the suitors vie, and hers is the approbation which must be given for the recalcitrant wanderer to regain his place as head of his life and home.

Leopold Bloom's lost key renders him the momentarily homeless wanderer. The suitors in the present form of Blazes Boylan also threaten his position. Like Bloom, Stephen Dedalus also is keyless, having surrendered his to his fellow tenant, Buck Mulligan. Bloom and Stephen begin parallel odysseys, ending for Bloom back at Seven Eccles Street, his home. Bloom's day is filled with seeming trivia, as he tries to obtain an ad for his paper (from a firm by the name of Keyes), attends a funeral, has lunch, stops to inquire about a friend in the maternity hospital, goes to several pubs and a brothel, and has a late night cup of coffee with his new acquaintance, Stephen. Each one of the scenes is mirrored in the epic journey of Odysseus, and the commonality of their lives gives both characters greater stature because of the universality of the episodes and events. For instance, Bloom's altercation with the Citizen in Barney Kiernan's pub is a comic version of Ulysses' encounter with the Cyclops. The seeming disparity of the two heroes provides some of the incongruity and comedy of Joyce's novel, and at the same time much of its significance in identity.

The themes of the novel are themselves universal. Communality among all people is not only a part of the structure of the novel, but is also a theme with a number of apparently disparate but essentially similar variations. Stephen considers several ecclesiastical models, such as consubstantiality (when father and son or wine and wafer are at the same time separate entities and both the same) and transubstantiation (the metamorphosis of one substance into another); while Bloom ponders such physical phenomena as parallax (when one thing appears as two from different vantage points) and metempsychosis and reincarnation (the return of one thing as another). All are manifestations of the identity motif.

The father and son theme, on the other hand, blends with the *Hamlet*, Shakespeare, and artistry metaphors in both Bloom's and Stephen's thoughts. Bloom and Stephen both quote lines from *Hamlet*, and the essential link between Hamlet senior and junior becomes a potential source of atonement. Stephen in the Scylla and Charybdis episode develops the theory that Shakespeare, in creating both Hamlets, senior and junior, was in a sense writing out his own sense of identity. Like Leopold, Shakespeare has had difficulties with an unfaithful wife and seeks identification with his son. The fictive reality of the play *Hamlet* encompasses not only Shakespeare's own domestic difficulties but also the story of Bloom and Stephen and their own identity crises and betrayal motifs. All of the father and son couples in the novel play variations on the father-son motif: God and Christ, Hamlet senior and junior, Patty Dignam and son, Reuban J. Dodd and son, Stephen and Simon Dedalus, Bloom and Rudy, and Bloom and Stephen, as well as other less prominently mentioned pairs.

The Odyssey and *Hamlet* are not Joyce's only structural metaphors of the novel. The Mass plays a role in the beginning with Mulligan's opening incantation and with Stephen's chanting of the Introit at the beginning of Circe. Like the Mass, which ritually celebrates episodes in the life of Christ and is about transubstantiation, *Ulysses* celebrates episodes in the lives of the modern-day Christ figures, Bloom and Stephen. Bloom is, of course, a surrogate not only for Christ but also for Elijah, Moses, Parnell, and other political-historical-theological figures. All of this becomes objectified in the *walpurgis nacht* of the Circe episode, when the subconscious minds of the two protagonists are objectified in drama form.

The novel is divided into eighteen episodes, each with a parody of some action, character, or scene from *The Odyssey* and named in Joyce's early drafts according to their appropriate Odyssean counterparts. The book is further divided into three sections, the first consisting of three episodes and 51 pages of the Random House edition; and the last, of 45 pages, comprising one episode. The great bulk of the book, the middle section of some 687 pages, deals principally with the major character, Leopold Bloom, while the introductory section, the Telemachea, concentrates on Stephen Dedalus, and the last episode, the Penelope chapter, is wholly a stream-of-consciousness monologue by Molly Bloom. The first section sets a theoretical framework for the novel and the last acts as a recapitulation, throwing the events into the relief of Molly Bloom's value system. The main section deals with the mind and life of Leopold Bloom on June 16, 1904, affectionately known to Joyce enthusiasts as Bloom's Day.

Stylistically, *Ulysses* is a *tour de force* with multiple shifts in narrative point of view, emphasis, and tone. The narrative is shared for much of the book among a third person omniscient narrator, dialogue, and stream-of-conscious thought. The character of Bloom is developed through other people's perceptions of him, through his own conscious thought processes, and eventually through the representation of his subconscious thoughts in the Circe episode. Throughout this vital episode, the day's events are filtered through a Freudian perspective and appear in dramatic form as the dialogue and stage directions of a play. Incidents reappear in grotesque pantomime and caricature, as manifestations of the id.

The narrative point of view remains consistent throughout the first ten chapters with the exceptions of the intrusion of newspaper headlines in the

Aeolus episode and a brief dramatic presentation in Scylla and Charybdis. But there are major changes in tone and character in each succeeding episode beginning with Sirens, which makes heavy use of musical devices in the narration. One episode contains more than a score of shifts in narrative style, paralleling the evolution of the English language from medieval Latin tracts to contemporary dialects. Altogether the novel represents an ingeniously comic assortment of narrative parodies.

Nonetheless, the story remains basically realistic in presentation, with a plethora of mundane details of varying significance. *Ulysses* requires an attention to minutiae which is unequaled in any lengthy work of contemporary prose. On the one hand, the streets of Dublin are represented with amazing verisimilitude; the businesses, characters, addresses, and activities of the day are nearly exactly what they were on June 16, 1904. At the same time, this layer of realism on the parody of Odysseus creates a belief in the theme of history repeating itself and a background of contemporary realism against which the book displays its sometimes grotesque and surrealistic scenes. Antiquity and analogy give an archetypal sanctity to the contemporary Dublin scene at the same time that they provide a basis of incongruity for the comedy of the novel.

Through it all, the gigantic figure of ineffectuality, Leopold Bloom, emerges as one of the most sympathetic, heroic, and understandable literary characters of Western literature. This microcosm of all men is married to the sensual embodiment of all womanhood, Molly Bloom. An infertile fertility figure, a stultifying inspirational figure, faithful temptress, and adulteress, she emerges as the measure of all things, the final judge and commentator, the eternal affirmation and concomitant denial. The ambiguities of the novel are as large as the history of man and as small as a day in the life of a nobody. There is in the book the spirit of eternal affirmation for some and existential denial for others. The conclusions of *Ulysses* are as complex and varied as life itself.

The publication history of *Ulysses* is as tangled as that of *Dubliners* and a good deal more famous. After Sylvia Beach published the first edition under the imprint of Shakespeare and Company in 1922, thousands of copies were smuggled into the United States by tourists, and it achieved an early reputation as a modern classic. When in 1933 Bennet Cerf decided to attempt to break the United States Post Office's censorship stranglehold over literature, he arranged publication terms with Joyce, and a Random House representative dutifully asked a customs official to confiscate his copy so a court case could be initiated. The result was the epic decision of United States District Court Judge John M. Woolsey lifting the ban on *Ulysses* and setting the standards for defining pornography.

FINNEGANS WAKE

Finnegans Wake, Joyce's last great work, had fewer publication difficulties than its predecessors. Joyce began serious work on the *Wake* in

1922, and, although it was not to be finished completely until 1939 and was known only as "Work in Progress" throughout most of the intervening seventeen years, much of it was published serially and in separate volumes such as *Anna Livia Plurabelle, Tales Told of Shem and Shaun,* and *Haveth Childers Everywhere.*

Finnegans Wake took the author a third of his life to compose. It was intended as the culmination of his work, the ultimate answer to the multitude of themes in his other works and a panorama of human existence both present and past. In short, it is about all of everything. It is an allegory of the fall and resurrection of mankind. Campbell and Robinson summarize its complexity:

> It is a strange book, a compound of fable, symphony, and nightmare—a monstrous enigma beckoning imperiously from the shadowy pits of sleep. Its mechanics resemble those of a dream, a dream which has freed the author from the necessities of common logic and has enabled him to compress all periods of history, all phases of individual and racial development, into a circular design, of which every part is beginning, middle, and end. [*Skeleton Key,* p. 3]

Its hero, HCE, lives his own life as a pubkeeper in Chapelizod and at the same time lives through the lives of scores of other heroes of antiquity and literature. In *The Second Census of Finnegans Wake*, Adaline Glasheen deals entirely with identifying and cross-referencing the characters and their historical counterparts.

The universalization process exists also on the level of style and language. There are phrases, words, and expressions in scores of foreign languages interwoven with Joyce's pseudo-English double, triple, quadruple, and even quintuple entendres to produce paradoxes in meaning, and association of events and times which seem to be wholly incongruous, and at the same time fraught with meaning beyond the wildest imagination of the reader. The book thus produces a feeling of frustration, of impenetrability, which caused early and casual readers, and even many serious scholars, to shrug it off as not being worth the effort to attain even a rudimentary understanding of what it was all about.

Serious readers now have several first-rate guides and critical crutches upon which to lean as they try to make their way through the literary brambles of the *Wake*. One of the first and still the most useful is *A Skeleton Key to Finnegans Wake* by Joseph Campbell and Henry M. Robinson. William York Tindall's later *Reader's Guide to Finnegans Wake* also deals with line-by-line allusion and explication. While Campbell and Robinson's work contains a heavy accent on mythopoeic elements, Tindall's is often Freudian in its bias.

The novel is based in part upon the song that provides its title, "The Ballad of Finnegan's Wake." Tim Finnegan is a hod carrier who falls from a ladder to his death only to be revived again at his wake when some whiskey, the Irish "water of life," is spilled on his lips. From this action the whole death and resurrection motif stems, becoming universalized in ever-broadening historical cycles until everything is included. Finnegan's fall is, of course, symbolic as well as literal, the symbolic fall encompassing Adam and Lucifer on one level and Humpty Dumpty and Newton's apple on another. So the world goes through a four-phase cycle analogous to Giambattista Vico's cycles in *La Scienza Nuova*.

At the wake, the mourners tell Finnegan that his replacement is Humphrey Chimpden Earwicker, whose initials provide a clue to his counterparts in the novel, particularly Here Comes Everybody and Haveth Childers Everywhere. Dublin, again utilized as the locale of the novel, becomes a universal scene. The sleeping giant of Irish legend, Finn MaCool, is the counterpart of Tim Finnegan, with his body the whole landscape of greater Dublin, "Howth Castle and Environs." The giant Finn, like his namesake in the ballad, also represents the great heroes of the past. HCE commits some nameless sin in Phoenix Park (which itself literally as well as figuratively fits the resurrection theme). We are led to suspect that he indecently exhibits himself to two girls in the park, but he is observed also by three drunken soldiers, who are really not quite sure of what they have seen. The vagueness of the sin allows its universal connotation, as it becomes a species of Original Sin from which springs the guilt and punishment theme motivating much of the action throughout the novel and providing the basis of the nightmare which forms the substance of the book. One ramification of the Sin is a host of old man-young girl situations and cuckoldry references which permeate the text.

Earwicker is both original hero and usurper to the populace and to his family. He becomes the brunt of a rumor which runs through the city and throughout history. There is a letter which would either convict or vindicate him, found on a dung heap by a hen. There are slogans, advertisements, and speeches ostensibly dealing with the subject. There are twelve drunken jurymen and four judges who hear various aspects of HCE's case. They have counterparts in practically everything with which the numbers twelve and four are historically associated, as well as with the mourners at Finnegan's funeral and the patrons of HCE's pub.

HCE's wife, Anna Livia Plurabelle, is the symbolic center of the book, assuming all the attributes of the women of Joyce's earlier works, in addition to other historical roles women have traditionally assumed. She is also a personification of the River Liffey, always changing and always the same. Her identification with the Liffey further expands to include other rivers from the Nile to the Mississippi. Their sons, Shem and Shaun, represent the dichotomies of ego and super ego, of introvert and extrovert, of artist and public man discussed earlier (as well as all pairs of opposites). In fact, the entire book can be seen as a manifestation of Bruno's theory that each thing contains its opposite. Characters frequently change identities in *Finnegans Wake*, and both character and objects continually merge into their opposites. In *Finnegans Wake*, however, Shem the Penman is ostensibly the author of the Book, *Finnegans Wake*. The boys represent extensions of their father just as Issy, their sister, is a manifestation of her mother.

The novel follows its course through letters and lectures which purport to explain; through trials, denials, accusations, vindications, and convictions; through rumor and evidence; through incest and reproduction; through the old and the new; through the cataclysms of history and the closing of the pub; through the observations of the washerwomen and the end of the world to rebirth and a new beginning for the novel until the last sentence of the book becomes the beginning of the first.

The book is a series of paradoxes, with the most incredible complexities evolving into mundane simplicities, and the whole panorama of man reduced to its simplest comic form. Above all, *Finnegans Wake*, like the ballad from which it draws its name, is funny. The final line of the song, "lots of fun at Finnegans Wake," is the only way in which an intelligent reader can approach the novel. Its puns and situations, universal though they may be, are more ludicrous and comic than pathetic or tragic, and its pages riotously joyful even in their pain.

The magnitude of the book, while initially baffling all but the most avid Joyceans, has over the years spawned a library of critical and scholarly commentary, and every year the pages of *PMLA Bibliography* reveal still more studies of one aspect or the other of *Wake* criticism. An entire periodical devoted to *Wake* explication and commentary, *A Wake Newsletter*, is published quarterly. This augments the *James Joyce Quarterly* which also carries longer articles on the *Wake* as well as general Joycean articles, notes, and reviews.

The entire catalogue of Joyce criticism encompasses too great a list even to begin to enumerate here.

ZACK BOWEN

WORKS: *Chamber Music*. London: Elkin Mathews, 1907; *Dubliners*. London: Grant Richards, 1914; *A Portrait of the Artist as a Young Man*. New York: W. B. Huebsch, 1916; *Exiles*. London: Grant Richards, 1918; *Ulysses*. Paris: Shakespeare & Co., 1922; *Pomes Penyeach*. Paris: Shakespeare & Co., 1927; *Collected Poems*. New York: Black Sun, 1936; *Finnegans Wake*. London: Faber/New York: Viking, 1939; *Stephen Hero*. Theodore Spencer, ed. London: Jonathan Cape/New York: New Directions, 1944; *The Portable James Joyce*. New York: Viking, 1947. (Contains *Dubliners, A Portrait of the Artist as a Young Man, Exiles, Collected Poems,* and selections from *Ulysses* and *Finnegans Wake*); *Letters of James Joyce*. Stuart Gilbert, ed. New York: Viking, 1957; *The Critical Writings of James Joyce*. Ellsworth Mason & Richard Ellmann, eds. New York: Viking, 1959; *Letters of James Joyce*. Richard Ellmann, ed. Vols. 2 & 3. New York: Viking, 1966; *Giacomo Joyce*. New York: Viking, 1968; *Selected Letters*. Richard Ellmann, ed. New York: Viking, 1976. (Contains several previously unpublished letters from Joyce to his wife). REFERENCES: Bibliographies—Beebe, Maurice, Phillip F. Herring, & Walton Litz. "Criticism of James Joyce: A Selected Checklist." *Modern Fiction Studies* 15 (Spring 1969): 105-

182; Deming, Robert. *A Bibliography of James Joyce Studies. Second Edition, Revised and Enlarged.* Boston: G. K. Hall, 1977; Slocum, John J., & Herbert Cahoon. *A Bibliography of James Joyce.* New Haven: Conn.: Yale University Press, 1953. Each year Alan Cohen updates the checklist in the *James Joyce Quarterly.* Biography—Ellmann, Richard. *James Joyce.* New York & London: Oxford University Press, 1959. Criticism—Adams, Robert Martin, *James Joyce: Common Sense and Beyond.* New York: Random House, 1966; Adams, Robert Martin. *Surface and Symbol: The Consistency of James Joyce's Ulysses.* New York: Oxford University Press, 1962; Anderson, Chester. *James Joyce and His World.* New York: Viking, 1968; Begnal, Michael H. & Fritz Senn, eds. *A Conceptual Guide to Finnegans Wake.* University Park, Pa.: Pennsylvania State University Press, 1974; Benstock, Bernard. *Joyce-Again's Wake: An Analysis of Finnegans Wake.* Seattle: University of Washington Press, 1965; Blamires, Harry. *The Bloomsday Book: A Guide Through Joyce's Ulysses.* London: Methuen, 1966; Bowen, Zack. *Musical Allusions in the Works of James Joyce: Early Poetry Through Ulysses.* Albany: State University of New York Press, 1974; Budgen, Frank, S.C. *James Joyce and the Making of Ulysses and Other Writings.* Introduction, Clive Hart. London: Oxford University Press, 1972; Campbell, Joseph, & Henry Morton Robinson. *A Skeleton Key to Finnegans Wake.* New York: Harcourt, Brace, 1944; Connolly, Thomas E. *Joyce's Portrait: Criticisms and Critiques.* New York: Appleton-Century-Crofts, 1962; Ellmann, Richard. *Ulysses on the Liffey.* New York: Oxford University Press, 1972; French, Marilyn. *The Book as World: James Joyce's Ulysses.* Cambridge: Harvard University Press, 1976; Gifford, Don, & Robert J. Seidman. *Notes for Joyce: An Annotation of James Joyce's Ulysses.* New York: E. P. Dutton, 1974; Gifford, Don, with Robert J. Seidman. *Notes for Joyce: Dubliners and Portrait of the Artist as a Young Man.* London: Faber & Faber, 1959/New York: E. P. Dutton, 1967; Gilbert, Stuart. *James Joyce's Ulysses: A Study.* London: Faber & Faber, 1930; Glasheen, Adaline. *A Third Census of Finnegans Wake: An Index of Characters and Their Roles.* Berkeley: University of California Press, 1977; Hart, Clive, ed. *James Joyce's Dubliners: Critical Essays.* New York: Viking, 1969; Hart, Clive, *Structure and Motif in Finnegans Wake.* Evanston, Ill.: Northwestern University Press, 1962; Hayman, David. *Ulysses: The Mechanics of Meaning.* Englewood Cliffs, N.J.: Prentice-Hall, 1970; Kain, Richard M. *Fabulous Voyager: James Joyce's Ulysses.* Chicago, Ill.: University of Chicago Press, 1947; Kenner, Hugh. *Dublin's Joyce.* London: Chatto & Windus, 1955/Bloomington: Indiana University Press, 1956; Levin, Harry. *James Joyce: A Critical Introduction.* Norfolk: New Directions, 1941; Litz, Walton A. *The Art of James Joyce: Method and Design in Ulysses and Finnegans Wake.* London: Oxford University Press, 1961; Magalaner, Marvin, & Richard Kain. *Joyce: The Man, The Work, The Reputation.* New York: New York University Press, 1956; Morse, J. Mitchel. *The Sympathetic Alien.* New York: New York University Press, 1959; Noon, William T., S.J. *Joyce and Aquinas.* New Haven, Conn.: Yale University Press, 1957; Prescott, Joseph. *Exploring James Joyce.* Carbondale, Ill.: Southern Illinois University Press, 196; Shechner, Mark. *Joyce in Nighttown.* Berkeley: University of California Press, 1974; Scholes, Robert E., & Richard M. Kain. *The Workshop of Daedalus: James Joyce and the Materials for A Portrait of the Artist as a Young Man.* Evanston, Ill.: Northwestern University Press, 1965; Shutte, William M. *Joyce and Shakespeare: A Study in the Meaning of Ulysses.* New Haven: Yale University Press, 1957; Steinberg, Erwin. *The Stream of Consciousness and Beyond in Ulysses.* Pittsburgh: University of Pittsburgh Press, 1973; Strong, L.A.G. *The Sacred River: An Approach to James Joyce.* London: Methuen, 1949; Sullivan, Kevin. *Joyce Among the Jesuits.* New York: Columbia University Press, 1958; Sultan, Stanley. *The Argument of Ulysses.* Columbus: Ohio State University Press, 1965; Thornton, Weldon. *Allusions in Ulysses.* Chapel Hill, N.C.: University of North Carolina Press, 1961; Tindall, William York. *A Reader's Guide to Finnegans Wake.* New York: Farrar, Straus & Giroux, 1969.

JOYCE, P. W. (1827-1914), scholar. Joyce, one of the most extraordinary Irish scholars, was born in Ballyorgan, County Limerick, in 1827. He was educated at private schools and then at Trinity College, Dublin, where he received a B.A. in 1861, an M.A. in 1864, and an LL.D. in 1870. He entered the service of the Commissioners of National Education in 1845 and held successive posts until 1874, when he was appointed professor and later principal of the Commissioners' Training College in Dublin, a position he held until his retirement in 1893. Joyce is noted particularly for his work on Irish place names, for his anthology of airs entitled *Ancient Irish Music* (1873), and for his excellent translations of the ancient Bardic tales entitled *Old Celtic Romances* (1879), which was used by Tennyson for his "The Voyage of Maledune." However, the breadth and the extent of Joyce's learning may be better measured by a glance at the only partial bibliography below. Joyce died in Rathmines on January 7, 1914. He was the brother of R. D. Joyce, the poet.

WORKS: *A Handbook of School Management and Methods of Teaching.* Dublin: McGlashan & Gill, 1863; *The Origin and History of Irish Names of Places.* 3 vols. Dublin: McGlashan & Gill, 1869-1870/Dublin: Gill, 1913; *Irish Local Names Explained.* Dublin: McGlashan & Gill, [1870]; *Ancient Irish Music.* Dublin: McGlashan & Gill, 1873; *A Grammar of the Irish Language.* Dublin: Gill, [1878]; *Old Celtic Romances.* London: C. Kegan Paul, 1879; *The Geography of the Counties of Ireland.* London: Philip, 1883; *A Concise History of Ireland from the Earliest Times to 1837.* Dublin: Gill, 1893; *A Child's History of Ireland.* London: Longmans, Green, 1897; *Atlas and Cyclopedia of Ireland.* New York: Murphy & McCarthy, ca. 1900. Part I by Joyce and Part II, the General History, by A. M. Sullivan and P. D. Nunan; *Ireland.* Philadelphia: J. D. Morris, ca. 1900; *A Reading Book in Irish History.* London: Longmans, Green, 1900; *A Social History of Ancient Ireland.* 2 vols. London: Longmans, Dublin: Gill, 1907; *English as We Speak It in Ireland.* London: Longmans/Dublin: Gill, 1910; *The Wonders of Ireland, and Other Papers on Irish Subjects.* London: Longmans/Dublin: Gill, 1911. Most of these books went through many editions.

JOYCE, ROBERT DWYER (1830-1883), poet. Joyce was born in Glenosheen, County Limerick, the younger brother of P. W. Joyce.* Primarily a poet, his *Deirdre* (1876) sold ten thousand copies on its first publication in Boston, and his *Blanid* (1879) was almost equally successful. Nevertheless, these works are rather uninteresting today, and Joyce's poorer, more public poetry is a good deal more fun. For instance, his swashbuckling "The Blacksmith of Limerick," which reads in part:

> The blacksmith raised his hammer, and rushed into the street,
> His 'prentice boys behind him, the ruthless foe to meet—
> High on the breach of Limerick, with dauntless hearts they stood
> Where the bombshells burst and shot fell thick, and redly ran the
>   blood....
> The first that gained the rampart, he was a captain brave!
> A captain of the Grenadiers, with blood-stained dirk and glaive;

He pointed and he parried, but it was all in vain,
For fast through skull and helmet the hammer found his brain!

The next that topped the rampart, he was a colonel bold,
Bright through the murk of battle his helmet flashed with gold.
"Gold is no match for iron!" the doughty blacksmith said,
As with that ponderous hammer he cracked his foeman's head!

Joyce's song "The Wind That Shakes the Barley" is still heard today. After some years in America, Joyce returned to Ireland where he died in Dublin on October 24, 1883.

WORKS: *Ballads, Romances and Songs.* Dublin: Duffy, 1861; *Legends of the Wars in Ireland.* Boston: J. Campbell, 1868; *Irish Fireside Tales.* Boston: P. Donahoe, 1871; *Ballads of Irish Chivalry.* Dublin: Talbot, n.d./Boston: P. Donahoe, 1872/ London: Longmans, Green, 1908/Dublin: Gill, 1908; *Deirdre.* Boston: Roberts Brothers, 1876; *Blanid.* Boston: Roberts Brothers, 1879.   REFERENCE: Taylor, Geoffrey. "A Neglected Irish Poet." *The Bell* 3 (1942): 308-312.

JOYCE, TREVOR (1947-), poet. Joyce was born in Dublin and was educated at Blackrock College. In his three volumes of verse, he appears utterly enchanted with language, and so quite frequently he writes the memorably, but unintentionally, funny line. He is also given to the strong and squalid image, and his work abounds in descriptions of mucous, swill, worms, dung, and rat-droppings. His third volume, *Pentahedron* (1972), seems a little less frenetic, but is described with rather too much portentousness as "an essay towards the description of an epistemology of poetic apprehension." It hardly seems that, but it does have some better lines in it than do the first two volumes.

WORKS: *Sole Glum Trek.* Dublin: New Writers', 1967; *Watches.* Dublin: New Writers', 1969; *Pentahedron.* Dublin: New Writers', 1972.

JUDGE, MICHAEL (1921-), playwright. Judge is a Dublin teacher who during the 1960s and 1970s, has been an effective and prolific writer for Irish television, radio, and the stage. He was born in Dublin on July 26, 1921, and was educated at Colaiste Mhuire and University College, Dublin. His first stage work was an adaptation of his television play, *The Chair.* He has since written *Death Is for Heroes* (Abbey,* 1966), *Please Smash the Glass Gently* (Eblana, 1967), *Saturday Night Women* (Eblana, 1971), *There's an Octopus in the Gentlemen* (Peacock, 1972), *A Matter of Grave Importance* (Project, 1973), and *Someone to Talk to* (Project, 1973). *Saturday Night Women*, his only published play, is a black, woman's liberation comedy with songs. Its long prologue is in his wittiest, most effectively satiric style. The body of the play, despite the clever songs, is less trenchant, but the ending is startling and theatrical.

WORK: *Saturday Night Women.* Newark, Del.: Proscenium, 1978.

KAVANAGH, PATRICK (1904-1967), poet and novelist. Kavanagh may well be the most controversial writer of the post-Celtic Revival period. He has been dead for over ten years, but his presence is still very much alive in Irish literary circles. His followers, a varied but vocal group, speak of him admiringly as an important force in Irish letters, second only to Yeats.* His detractors, fewer in number but every bit as vocal, dismiss him as a loud-mouthed, ill-mannered peasant who disrupted rather than advanced the development of modern literature. While there is no denying that Kavanagh had his eccentricities, a number of his poems, particularly "The Great Hunger," his novel *Tarry Flynn*, and his autobiography *The Green Fool*, rank among the finest portrayals of peasant life in Ireland.

Born October 21, 1904, Patrick Joseph Kavanagh was the fourth child (and first son) of James and Bridget (Quinn) Kavanagh. Like his father, Kavanagh worked as a part-time cobbler and small farmer in the townland of Mucker, Inniskeen Parish, County Monaghan. The most complete account of his early years is contained in *The Green Fool* (1938). Flowers, stones, ditches, and trees, as well as such social commonplaces as cattle and hiring fairs, drew his attention and served as agencies for insight into the glories and complexities of rural life. Like most boys, Kavanagh was led to believe it was not manly to feel poetic emotion, let alone express it. Nonetheless, he began to write juvenile verses in his school notebook sometime after his twelfth birthday.

During the years when he wrote his notebook verse, Kavanagh's relationship with his family and his growing interest in literature combined to make him feel an outsider in his native community. This predilection for seeing himself apart from his family and, later in his life, society as a whole, was constant from his childhood to his last days in Dublin, and is reflected in much of his writing, from his sense of personal fault in the early poetry to his declaration of failure in *Self Portrait* (1964). While he treats this aspect of his personality with humor in *The Green Fool*—the very title of the book suggests his concern, however—*Tarry Flynn* (1948) is the most sustained, and perhaps the most serious, attempt to explain this facet of his personality.

Kavanagh discovered modern literature as a result of his trips to Dundalk in the late 1920s. Here he purchased a variety of magazines, ranging from popular periodicals like *John O' London's Weekly* to literary journals such as *Poetry* and *The Irish Statesman*.* In every sense of the phrase Kavanagh was a self-made man. He left school after his twelfth birthday and was forced to educate himself. This lack of formal education occasionally was an embarrassment to Kavanagh, particularly during his early years in Dublin in the late 1930s, and may account in part for his pose as the blustery peasant poet.

The period 1928-1939 served as Kavanagh's apprenticeship to literature. It was during these years that he wrote many of his finest lyric poems, such as "Ploughman," "To a Blackbird," and "Inniskeen Road: July Evening." These and other verses were published in his first book, *Ploughman and Other Poems*, in 1936. Along with the autobiography *The Green Fool*, *Ploughman* is important because it contains many of the ideas Kavanagh would pursue throughout his career as a writer. His concern with the meaning and function of poetry, for example, which is common to so much of his creative and critical writing, is one of the themes that dominates his early period. Perhaps the most significant theme present in both of these books is the urge to speak about the nature of the poet and the meaning of art.

In 1939, Kavanagh moved from his small farm in Inniskeen to Dublin on a more-or-less permanent basis. He managed to scrape a living out of various journalistic pursuits while he made himself into a professional writer. He wrote a column, "City Commentary," for *The Irish Press* from late 1942 to early 1944; a film review for *The Standard* from February 1946 to July 1949; and a lively, thought-provoking monthly diary in *Envoy** from December 1949 to July 1951. These writings were in addition to dozens of signed and unsigned book reviews, human interest stories, and critical pieces. By the early 1940s and well into the 1950s, Kavanagh was a popular fellow on the literary scene. The publication of *The Great Hunger* (1942), *A Soul for Sale* (1947), and *Tarry Flynn* (1948) signaled his arrival as a major force in the development of Irish letters.

Kavanagh's most interesting venture during this period was his newspaper, *Kavanagh's Weekly*, which appeared from April 12 to July 5, 1952. Stating that his purpose "was to introduce the critical-constructive note into Irish thought," Kavanagh spared no one from his bombastic indictments. His investigations ranged from questioning the need for Irish embassies around the world to revealing the pathetic state to which gossip had sunk on Grafton Street. Church, government, films, drama, poetry, painting, and other topics relevant and irrelevant to Irish life came under Kavanagh's scrutiny. However, for all its bluster and dogmatism, *Kavanagh's Weekly* had a certain freshness and sense of wit that made it popular with some and abhorrent to others. The enterprise finally closed from lack of funds rather than lack of interest.

In October 1952, an unsigned "Profile" of Kavanagh was published in *The Leader*, a popular weekly of the period. It contained bittersweet (with the emphasis on bitter) appraisal of Kavanagh, his journalism, and his creative work; the appearance of this article brought Kavanagh back to Dublin from London, where he had gone after the close of *Kavanagh's Weekly*. What followed was the darkest period of Kavanagh's life. He sued *The Leader* for libel, spent thirteen hours in the witness box defending his ideas before a hostile jury, fell ill, lost his case, and was ordered to pay costs, appealed, had the case continued, was granted a new trial, and, before he could get *The Leader* back in court, entered the Rialto Hospital in Dublin suffering from cancer of the lung. Against great odds and to the surprise of nearly everyone, including himself, he made a heroic recovery and spent the summer of 1955 regaining his strength on the banks of the Grand Canal in Dublin. This period, from summer 1955 to late 1956, Kavanagh referred to as his "rebirth."

The poetry Kavanagh wrote after 1955 is marked by a return to his early lyric voice. These poems differ from his earlier works, however: they are characterized by a depth of wisdom and a sense of understanding not found in his previous writing. Kavanagh's health began to decline again in the late 1950s, and by the early 1960s he was often too ill to write. His last years were once again given over to journalism. When he did attempt to write poetry, his efforts frequently fell artistically short of his earlier work. On April 19, 1967, Kavanagh married Katherine Moloney, whom he had known for a number of years. In the autumn, Kavanagh's health declined rapidly, and he died on November 30 at the age of sixty-three.

While he wrote fiction, journalism, autobiography, and literary criticism, Kavanagh is best known for his poetry. The best of his early poems are featured in *Ploughman and Other Poems*, a collection of thirty-one poems written between 1930 and 1935. This book demonstrates Kavanagh's growth from a schoolboy poet of the late 1920s to an accomplished literary artist. One of the central themes which unifies the collection is the vision of nature as explicator. Here the poet sees various truths revealed through such natural phenomena as the twisted furrows of fields, birds in song, or late blooming trees. Most of the poems are short. Many, such as "The Intangible," "The Chase," and "After May," give in to sentiment too easily or suffer from clumsy rhymes. Yet, the bulk of these lyrics demonstrate a real talent, a talent that in six years was to produce one of the best long poems in modern literature.

Various commentators on Irish poetry have called *The Great Hunger* Kavanagh's best creative effort. Some of these critics, such as Liam Miller* ("The Future of Irish Poetry," *The Irish Times*, February 5, 1970), have hailed the poem as a watershed for future Irish poets. The poem is fashioned from Kavanagh's own personal observations of how life on the land could restrict and demean human development. Paddy Maguire, the poem's central figure, is sensitive to the possibilities of life, perceiving the powerful beauty and mystery of nature. He lacks the poet's insight, however, and fails to learn the lessons nature teaches until it is too late. Maguire's world is a web of personal and social entanglements where a man can easily become caught between social custom and personal desire. The Church, his mother, and the land itself combine to seal his fate, proving to be paralyzing forces against which he has no defense. The details of Maguire's slow discernment of his predicament, as well as the circumstances and nature of his paralysis, are presented through a series of descriptive and reflective passages that are among the best in Irish poetry. Though Kavanagh rejected this poem late in his life (see *Self Portrait*), it stands as one of his most significant achievements.

Kavanagh's other realistic portrait of rural life written during the 1940s is his novel, *Tarry Flynn*, which he liked to call "not only the best but the only authentic account of life as it was lived in Ireland in this century"(*Self Portrait*). Lighter in tone and atmosphere than *The Great Hunger*, and more accurate in its presentation of literal detail than *The Green Fool*, this novel lacks the vitality, verve, and power of the two earlier works. For all of its authenticity, and despite the fact that it illuminates Kavanagh's youthful struggle with his talent and his environment, *Tarry Flynn* is flawed by a lapse into artificial romanticism in its conclusion. Pressured between a need for security and the reassurance familiarity provides on the one hand, and a desire to escape the confines of rural Ireland to pursue adventure and a literary career on the other, the hero Tarry Flynn (whom Kavanagh would have us believe is himself at age twenty-eight) flees the townland of Drumnay with a vagabond uncle, produced out of nowhere, to find fortune and fame in the world beyond. Whatever shortcomings the novel may have, it is a valuable portrait of rural Ireland and, with *The Green Fool* and *The Great Hunger*, demonstrates the skillful use Kavanagh could make of his country background.

Kavanagh was less successful in writing about Dublin. During the period 1944-1952, he wrote a number of verse satires about the Dublin literary scene. Perhaps the most successful piece among such works as "Bardic Dust," "The Wake of the Books," "The Paddiad," and "Who Killed James Joyce?" is "A Wreath for Tom Moore's Statue." Here Kavanagh attacks the attitudes and intentions of the insensitive and artless souls who wreathe statues rather than honor living poets. From the poem's opening lines, Kavanagh establishes and then sustains the attack without wandering into side issues or sinking into an emotional harangue against the philistines, his term for those Irishmen who valued artifice over art. The poem also attacks those writers who waste their energies treating mere appearances instead of the realities of life. In other poems, such as "Adventures in the Bohemian Jungle" and "House Party to Celebrate the Destruction of the Roman Catholic Church in Ireland," Kavanagh's satiric thrusts were less successful because of lapses in craft or a tendency to preach instead of parody.

Most of the poetry Kavanagh wrote during the 1940s and 1950s was neither satiric nor about Dublin. In *A Soul for Sale* (1947), for example, the majority of the poems deal with private rather than public themes. These poems continue his investigation of the self that began in *Ploughman and Other Poems*. The central subject of the book is failure. While it may be incorrect to say that Kavanagh was suffering a loss of confidence in his talent during the mid- and late 1940s, he was very conscious of not achieving the success he had hoped his move to Dublin would bring him. The title of his second book thus seems to underscore the degree to which failure was involved in his self-examination. It is one of the ironies of Kavanagh's literary development that while the public, satiric voice was so strong and confident in its outcries against the philistines, the private, lyric voice was often subdued in its utterances about the state of Kavanagh's own poetic soul.

Kavanagh seemed to be aware of this distinction when he noted in "The Gallivanting Poet" (*Irish Writing,** November, 1947) that the essential difference between a public and a private speaker is that the former merely reports circumstances while the latter lives them. The extent of Kavanagh's creative failure is clearly revealed in "Pegasus," where the reader is told that the poet's soul "was an old horse/Offered for sale in twenty fairs." Finding no takers among the Church, the state, or business, the soul grows "wings/Upon his back" and the poet rides off to visit "Every land my imagination knew." Wallowing in sentimentality, the poem accurately summarizes the sources of Kavanagh's frustration and documents his overly romantic response to failure.

Perhaps to compensate for his failure to achieve a greater degree of financial and literary success, Kavanagh struck out at many of his contemporaries through his journalism and his critical articles. In addition to many of his *Envoy* "Diary" pieces and the bulk of *Kavanagh's Weekly*, he delivered his attacks upon friends, foes, and bystanders through such essays as "The Gallivanting Poet" (*Irish Writing,** November 1947) and "Coloured Balloons" (*The Bell,** December 1947). While these pieces often contained interesting insights and apt judgments, they suffered on the whole from an inconsistent critical approach.

Kavanagh's final three books of poems were *Recent Poems* (1958), *Come Dance with Kitty Stobling and Other Poems* (1960), and *Collected Poems* (1964). The best of his later poems were the sonnets he wrote during his "rebirth" during the mid-1950s. In "Canal Bank Walk," "Lines Written on a Seat on the Grand Canal," "Dear Folks," "The Hospital," "Yellow Vestment," and others, Kavanagh emphasized the visible rather than the ideological. By depicting the excitement of the habitual, the ordinary, Kavanagh vitalized the self and articulated his doctrine of "not caring." The basis of this doctrine was a belief in the comic muse. To Kavanagh, comedy was the natural outgrowth of detachment—of not caring—while tragedy was occasioned by involvement. The ultimate truth of art, of life, Kavanagh preached in his last prose pieces (see *Self Portrait* in particular) was not to take the self too seriously. This same message was at the heart of his best poetry.

By the early 1960s, with his health in decline, Kavanagh's creative output declined in both quantity and quality. His literary energy was used up to fuel columns in *The Irish Farmers' Journal* (from June 1958 to March

1963) and in the *RTV Guide* (from January 1964 to October 1966). On the whole, his most successful poems include a half dozen lyrics from *Ploughman and Other Poems*, the sonnets from *Come Dance with Kitty Stobling and Other Poems*, and *The Great Hunger*. However, one chooses to view him, the vitality that he brought to Irish literature, his lyrically articulated vision of rural Ireland, and his final affirmation of life combine to ensure his continued reputation as one of Ireland's great literary artists. He died in Dublin on November 30, 1967.

JOHN NEMO

WORKS: *The Green Fool*. London: Michael Joseph, 1938; *Tarry Flynn*. London: Pilot, 1948; *Collected Poems*. London: MacGibbon & Kee, 1964; *Collected Pruse*. London: MacGibbon & Kee, 1967; *Lapped Furrows*. New York: Peter Kavanagh Hand Press, 1969; *The Complete Poems*. New York: Peter Kavanagh Hand Press, 1972; *By Night Unstarred*, Peter Kavanagh, ed. The Curragh, Co. Kildare; Goldsmith, 1978. REFERENCES: Kennelly, Brendan. "Patrick Kavanagh." *Ariel* 1 (July 1970): 7-28; Nemo, John. "A Bibliography of Materials By and About Patrick Kavanagh." *Irish University Review* 3 (Spring 1973): 80-106; Nemo, John. "The Green Knight: Patrick Kavanagh's Venture into Criticism." *Studies* 63 (Autumn 1974): 282-294; O'Brien, Darcy. *Patrick Kavanagh*. Lewisburg, Pa.; Bucknell University Press, 1975; Sealy, Douglas. "The Writings of Patrick Kavanagh." *The Dublin Magazine* 3 (Winter 1965): 5-23; Warner, Alan. *Clay Is the Word*. Dublin: Dolmen, 1973.

KEANE, JOHN B. (1928-), playwright and fiction writer. John B[rendan] Keane was born on July 21, 1928, in Listowel, County Kerry. Save for two years as a laborer in England, he has stayed close to Listowel where he owns a much-frequented public house. Keane's first play, *Sive*, presented by the Listowel Drama Group, won the All-Ireland Amateur Drama Festival in 1959, and its enormous impact immediately made Keane's reputation. *Sive*, as well as Keane's 1960 plays, *The Highest House on the Moutain* and *Sharon's Grave*, seemed to give a vital new impetus to the presumably worn-out genre of the peasant play. However, Keane's fidelity to life in Kerry as well as his strong eye for the theatrical made these plays intensely gripping theatre. *Sive*, for instance, treats the extremely traditional theme of the made marriage and does not differ in content from many other Irish plays on the same subject, particularly Louis D'Alton's* *Lovers Meeting*. However, a rousing song done by a chorus of two wandering tinkers lifts the play with a startling theatricality.

Nevertheless, the rich rural life that Keane wrote about in these plays, and which is reflected in the plays of Listowel's other notable dramatists George Fitzmaurice* and Bryan MacMahon,* was even in Keane's own youth something of an anachronism. His next plays turned away somewhat from the folk past of North Kerry and attempted, with varying success, to depict some of the elements of change in modern rural Ireland. *Many Young Men of Twenty* (1961), presented by Southern Theatre Group of Cork, is a musical about emigration. Its milieu did reflect the fading past, but the lack of jobs in the present was forcing the people of Keane's small

Irish town to leave for the modern world of England. Nearly as rich as *Sive* or *Sharon's Grave*, the play was enlivened by the haunting title tune which memorably underscored the play's blend of jaunty comedy and mournful nostalgia.

Keane's subsequent plays dealt more overtly, but rather less success-fully, with the modern world. The unpublished *No More in Dust* (1961) relates the misfortunes of two country girls forced to make a living in the city. *The Man from Clare* (1962) is about the Irishman's childish obses-sion with sport, which for many years was a kind of national sublimation. Quiet and well-drawn, the play is probably too specifically Irish to work well outside of the country. Most of Keane's plays at this time were pre-sented by the Southern Theatre Group, but *Hut 42* (1962) was originally done by the Abbey.* It is a melancholy play about the longing of Irish workers in England to return to Ireland. Better than these plays is *The Year of the Hiker* (1963), an understated but moving study of a modern farm family whose father had taken to the roads and now, years later, re-turns. As traditional in subject as Colum's* *The Fiddler's House,* the play is probably one of Keane's more underrated works; it is a successful con-trast of the values of the old and the modern generations.

A similar theme, but stronger plot and characterization, make *The Field* (1965) one of Keane's best plays. In it the leasing of a field to an outsider results in murder, and the local inhabitants conspire to shield the culprit, despite pleas from both priest and police. In this powerful fable, Keane shows how deeply ingrained values, even pernicious ones, linger on.

The Rain at the End of Summer (1967) is an ineffectual attempt to deal with the urban middle class, but *Big Maggie* (1969) is more success-ful, treating a familiar Irish phenomenon, the domineering mother. Although somewhat arbitrary in the arrangement of its plot, the play creates a strong central character and a superb role for an actress. The main character in *The Change in Mame Fadden* (1971) is also a woman, and certainly this marks the first Irish play which attempts to treat deeply the psychological problems of menopause. Mame Fadden is not as con-vincing a character as Big Maggie, however, and the play remains more well-intentioned than successful. *Moll* (1971) is another woman's play, the main character being a canny and domineering housekeeper of the local parish priest. A pleasantly sardonic comedy, the play attempts less than the previous two, but more successfully achieves its goal.

Keane's 1973 plays represent his weakest work to date. *The Crazy Wall* has an engaging first act and then simply goes off the tracks of its plot. Of the three one-act plays in *Values,* two are so trivial that they should never have been published. *The Good Thing* (1978) is considerably better. Al-though some of its dialogue is unpolished and one character is a too easy theatrical joke, the play seriously addresses itself to the problem of sexu-ality after ten years of marriage, a topic not often investigated in Irish drama.

Keane is a quick and prolific writer, and has also published much fugitive journalism, some of which has been collected in volumes of short, chatty essays. He has published a short, straightforward autobiography, a volume of rather traditional verse, and a slim volume of rather old-fashioned short stories.

In 1967, with *Letters of a Successful T. D.,* Keane began a series of epistolary novellas. The other titles now include *Letters of an Irish Parish Priest, Letters of a Love-Hungry Farmer, Letters of a Matchmaker, Letters of a Civic Guard, Letters of a Country Postman,* and *Letters of an Irish Minister of State.* The most successful was the first volume in which his Tull MacAdoo is an eminently droll and only faintly satiric portrait of a highly usual character in Irish politics. The later volumes are uneven, as Keane seems increasingly to play for the easy laugh and the broad caricature. However, *Letters of an Irish Minister of State* returns most delightfully to the career of Tull MacAdoo.

The cliché about Keane is that he produces too much too quickly and with too little consideration and revision. The charge is not entirely true. James N. Healy, of the Theatre of the South, has been associated with many Keane plays and testifies that in rehearsals he is always receptive to suggestions for improvements. Nevertheless, Keane has produced an extremely uneven body of work. The poorest of it gives evidence of such hasty plotting and such trite dialogue that it seems written by quite another writer than the eloquent author of *Sive.* Even the best of Keane has a tendency to rely on melodrama rather than drama, and on caricature rather than character. But the best also has such warm feeling, gentle melancholy, pervasive sympathy, and tough determination to investigate the New Ireland, rather than merely to apostrophize the old, that it tends to sweep away minor criticisms as insignificant. Keane's problem would seem to be his failure to consolidate his great strengths into a few slowly germinated and deeply considered serious works.

WORKS: *Sive.* Dublin: Progress House, 1959. (Play); *Sharon's Grave.* Dublin: Progress House, 1960. (Play); *The Highest House on the Mountain.* Dublin: Progress House, 1961. (Play); *Many Young Men of Twenty.* Dublin: Progress House, 1961 reprinted in *Seven Irish Plays.* Robert Hogan, ed. Minneapolis: University of Minnesota Press, 1967. (Play); *The Street and Other Poems.* Dublin: Progress House, 1961. *The Man from Clare.* Cork: Mercier, 1962. (Play); *Strong Tea.* Cork: Mercier, 1963. (Essays); *The Year of the Hiker.* Cork: Mercier, 1963. (Play); *Self-Portrait.* Cork: Mercier, 1964. (Autobiography); *The Field.* Cork: Mercier, 1966. (Play); *Hut 42.* Dixon, Calif.: Proscenium, 1968. (Play); *Letters of a Successful T. D.* Cork: Mercier, 1968. (Fiction); *The Rain at the End of Summer.* Dublin: Progress House, 1968. (Play); *Big Maggie.* Cork: Mercier, 1970. (Play); *The Change in Mame Fadden.* Cork: Mercier, 1972. (Play); *Letters of an Irish Parish Priest.* Cork: Mercier, 1972. (Fiction); *Moll.* Cork: Mercier, 1972. (Play); *The One-Way Ticket.* Barrington, Ill.: Performance Publishing, 1972. (One-act play); *The Crazy Wall.* Cork: Mercier, 1973. (Play); *The Gentle Art of Matchmaking and Other Important Things.* Cork: Mercier, 1973. (Essays); *Values.* Cork: Mercier, 1973. (One-act plays); *Letters of an Irish Publican.* Cork: Mercier, 1974. (Fiction); *Letters of a Love-Hungry Farmer.* Cork: Mercier, 1974. (Fiction); *Letters of a Matchmaker.* Cork: Mercier, 1975. (Fiction); *Death Be Not Proud.* Cork: Mercier, 1976. (Fiction); *Letters of a Civic Guard.* Cork: Mercier, 1976. (Fiction); *Is the Holy Ghost Really a Kerryman? and Other Items of Interest.* Cork: Mercier, 19   (Fiction); *Dan Pheaidí Aindí.* Baile Átha Cliath & Corcaigh: Cló Mercier, 1977; *Letters of a Country Postman.* Dublin & Cork: Mercier, 1977. (Fiction); *Unlawful Sex and Other Testy Matters.* Dublin & Cork: Mercier, 1978. (Essays); *Letters of an Irish Minister of State.* Dublin & Cork: Mercier, [1978]; *The Good Thing.* Newark, Del.: Proscenium, 1978.

KEARNEY, PEADAR (1883-1942), song writer. Kearney, author of the Irish national anthem "The Soldier's Song," was born on December 12, 1883, and was educated by the Christian Brothers, the Capel Street Library, the theatre, and the music hall. After his father died (when Peadar was just thirteen), he went to work at various blind-alley jobs to help his mother, sisters, and brothers. He joined the Irish Republican Brotherhood, the revolutionary organization, when he was twenty and began writing patriotic songs. In 1907, he wrote "The Soldier's Song," set to music by his friend Patrick Heeney. The first man to sing the song was P. J. Bourke (1883-1932), the playwright, who was married to his sister Margaret; the song was first printed by Bulmer Hobson in 1912 in *Irish Freedom.* On the formation of the Irish Volunteers in 1914, it became their marching song. It was sung by the Republican soldiers in the Rebellion of 1916, and it became the official national anthem of the Irish Free State in 1926. Kearney was associated with the Abbey Theatre* from its first performance on December 27, 1904, first as property man and later as stage manager; he toured with the company in England in 1911 and 1916. Kearney was arrested in 1920 and interned in Ballykinlar Internment Camp, County Down, for more than a year. After the Civil War, he returned to civilian life. He had been a close friend of many of the national leaders, such as Tom Clarke and Sean McDermott who were executed in 1916, and Liam Mellowes and Michael Collins who died in the Civil War. He died on November 24, 1942, in Dublin, in comparative poverty. Apart from "The Soldier's Song," he is remembered for such songs as "The Three-Coloured Ribbon O!", "Down by the Glenside," and "Down by the Liffey Side." He was the uncle of Brendan Behan.*

SEAMUS DE BURCA

REFERENCE: De Burca, Seamus. *The Soldier's Song: The Story of Peadar O Cearnaigh.* Dublin: P. J. Bourke, 1957.

KEEGAN, JOHN (1809-1849), poet. Keegan was born at Laois in 1809 and was educated at a hedge-school. He wrote a great many poems for Irish periodicals such as *The Nation** and *Dolman's Magazine*, but his work was not collected until 1907. It is extremely simple public poetry, often written in the voice of a peasant speaker, but some few pieces—such as "Caoch the Piper" and "Bouchalleen Bawn"—are so simple that they escape many defects. He died of cholera in 1849 and was buried as a pauper in Glasnevin.

WORK: *Legends and Poems*. Canon O'Hanlon, ed. With a memoir by D. J. O'Donoghue. Dublin: Sealy, Bryers, & Walker, 1907.

KELLY, HUGH (1739-1778), playwright and journalist. Born in Killarney in 1739, Hugh Kelly was raised and educated in Dublin, where his father became a publican following the loss of his estate. Kelly had no higher education, but, during his apprenticeship as a staymaker, he frequented the theatre and became friendly with actors. He moved to London when he was twenty-one, at first working as a staymaker and then as a scrivener to a lawyer. He soon became an industrious hack writer, editing in succession three magazines, *The Court Magazine, The Ladies' Museum*, and *The Public Ledger*. He contributed a regular column to *Owen's Weekly Chronicle* which he published anonymously as *The Dabler* in 1767. In 1766 and 1767, he established himself as a theatrical commentator with two long works, written in heroic couplets, called *Thespis: or, A Critical Examination into the Merits of All the Principal Performers Belonging to Drury Lane Theatre* and *Covent Garden Theatre*. In the first, he praised Garrick but attacked the other actors "with a ruffian cruelty," which he subsequently toned down. Neither of these forestalled the performers of both theatres from acting in his plays, and Kelly in several prefaces was effusive over the acting his plays received in what was evidently a series of well-mounted productions. In 1767, he also published a novel, *Memoirs of a Magdalen*, which is sentimental and reformist in tone.

In 1768, encouraged by Garrick, Kelly wrote *False Delicacy*, which Garrick wrote the prologue for and produced at Drury Lane in September. It was presented as competition to Goldsmith's* *The Good Natured Man*, which opened six nights later at Covent Garden. While everyone now prefers the Goldsmith play, *False Delicacy* ran for eight nights, was acted often throughout the season, became a standard in provincial repertories, and earned Kelly £700 from its first two editions. A comedy of intrigue and sentiment, it revolves around lovers who are too refined to express themselves directly and are thus trapped into arranged courtships. As Dr. Johnson said, it is "totally devoid of character." Kelly was a sentimentalist and a moralist. The denouement depends on the unlikely reformation of the rake and on the candor of characters not too falsely delicate but not involved in the plot either. The success of the play led to an incident in which Kelly insulted Goldsmith; although the two never spoke again, Kelly was seen crying openly at Goldsmith's funeral.

Kelly's second play, *A Word to the Wise*, caused a theatrical furor at its production at Drury Lane on March 3, 1770. Kelly, a supporter of Lord North's ministry and a suspected hireling, attracted the scorn of the followers of John Wilkes. They catcalled and shouted loudly enough for two nights to prevent its performance, while Garrick tried vainly to quiet the house. Kelly defended his politics in a long preface to the printed version of *A Word to the Wise*, in which he bitterly described the fate of playwrights of his time, dependent on audience approval but condemned without a hearing. *A Word for the Wise* was produced after Kelly's death on a benefit night for his widow. For this production Dr. Johnson wrote a prologue that begins:

> This night presents a play, which public rage
> Or right or wrong, once hooted from the stage:
> From zeal or malice, now no more we dread,
> For English vengeance wars not with the dead.

The play itself is stronger in plot and comic situations than *False Delicacy*, although its besetting weaknesses, as in all of Kelly's plays, are sentimentality in language and an unlikely plot resolution.

Inspired by his friends' notion "that his genius excelled in the sentimental and pathetic," Kelly next wrote a blank verse tragedy, *Clemantina* (produced at Covent Garden, 1771), that has all the earmarks of the sterile tragedy of the time: artificial situations and an implausible resolution of the plot, caused by adherence to the three unities, and operatically rhetorical language. He deals with two of his favorite themes: the tyrannical father who blindly misarranges a marriage for his daughter, and true lovers blighted by society from admitting their love. Kelly returned to comedy with *The School for Wives* in 1773, a play not derived from Molière. It is his most complicated play in its diversity of characters and situations, which take a very long fifth act to unravel.

Kelly wrote two more plays, the two-act farce *The Romance of an Hour* (1774) and *The Man of Reason* (1776). The last failed at Covent Garden, was never printed, and ended his theatrical career. He was called to the bar in 1774—with what success is disputed. He died on February 2, 1778, at the age of thirty-eight, as the result of excessive drinking (according to the *Dictionary of National Biography*) or an abcess (according to his anonymous biographer).

While Kelly, like Arthur Murphy,* immersed himself in English life, he openly defended the Irish, especially by attacking the Stage Irishman. He created the sympathetic, peacemaking character of Connolly, complete with a brogue, in *A School for Wives* "to remove the imputation for barberous ferocity" which the Irish had gained. In his epilogue, which was intended to have been spoken by the character of Sir Callaghan O'Brallaghan in Macklin's farce *Love a la Mode*, he lectures the English audience for scorning the Irish, celebrates Irish accomplishments, and compares the Irish and the English as "the equal heirs of liberty and fame."

SVEN ERIC MOLIN

WORKS: No modern life or editions of any of Kelly's works exist. Following his death, his plays, verse, and a short essay on metrics were published as *The Works of Hugh Kelly, to which is prefixed the Life of the Author* . . . Printed for the Author's Widow, 1778. The biographer is unidentified.   REFERENCES: Short critical assessments may be found in: Bernbaum, Ernest. *The Drama of Sensibility*. Gloucester, Mass.: Peter Smith, 1958; Boas, Frederick S. *An Introduction to Eighteenth-Century Drama*. Oxford: At the Clarendon Press, 1953.

KELLY, JAMES PLUNKETT. *See* PLUNKETT, JAMES.

KELLY, MAEVE (1930-), short story writer. Kelly was born in Dundalk in 1930 and now lives in Limerick with her husband and two children. One of her stories won a Hennessy Award in 1972, and she has published one collection of stories, *A Life of Her Own* (1976). Her work is conventional in form, and the slighter stories fade quickly from the memory. She is at her best in stories about women and farmers. In "The Sentimentalist" and "The False God" she can be wry, as in "Lovers" and "A Life of her Own" she can be moving.

WORK: *A Life of Her Own and Other Stories*. Dublin: Poolbeg, 1976.

KENNELLY, BRENDAN (1936-), poet. Kennelly, professor of modern literature at Trinity College, Dublin, was born in Ballylongford, County Kerry, on April 17, 1936. He was educated at Trinity College, Dublin, and at Leeds from which he received a Ph.D. In 1967, he was awarded the AE Memorial Prize for Poetry. He is one of the most prolific of contemporary poets and regards his calling with a high and enthusiastic seriousness. In 1969, he wrote that he saw poetry "basically as a celebration of human inadequacy and failure. . . . It leads . . . into severe definitions. It outlaws vagueness." His work is not in the least vague, but it does suffer from a usualness of diction that spreads over much of it a rather soporific effect. His work is full of phrases like: "flood-tide of grief, waves' delicate fingers, God's gold burning eye [the sun], the meadows of the sky, cold and grey as a stone, a frenzy of excitement, more wonderful than April skies, more lightly than gossamer, sheer delight, dumb fear, still as a sleeping child, true destiny, evil power, natural grace, the wind's fist, gasping maw, suffocating darkness, music in his heart, eyes bright with menace, cringed with fear, blind with joy, sigh with relief."

And yet, in Kennelly's best work, this flatness is transmuted into a sometimes even noble austerity. His "My Dark Fathers" contains a few phrases that border on the cliché, but most of the poem has a pared-down and memorable eloquence. His recent poem cycle, *Islandman* (1977), contains several individual poems and many individual lines of a stark and brilliant clarity.

> Those who live alone
> Should die alone.

Every wave that breaks on the gravelled shore
Is a lonely man.

Practically all of Kennelly's best work seems in this vein. His occasional forays into a more florid diction usually lead him into romantic murkiness—phrases such as "the crowded clay of doom, the red wine's glittering infinities, the tightening fist of time, the white eye of eternity [a star], the measureless squalor of man, the sea's insatiate lust," or:

A decimation and scattering of herself
To the four winds of the insatiate future.

Occasionally, he will push his style even further into a—what should one call it?—charismatic language. Then, as in these lines from "The Pig," he simply falls into embarrassing excess:

What thighs opened wide
To let out that snout
Rammed on a carcase of timeless slime?

Or, from the same poem:

What breasts
Gave it suck?
Suck, suck.

There seems no more dedicated poet writing in Ireland today, and he has written a handful of poems that will be in future anthologies, but he has not yet battered out a voice. In his poem "Milk," he wrote, "Language had fought a pitched battle and lost." In Kennelly's large output, language has won some skirmishes and taken more than a few beatings, but the issue is still in abeyance.

Early in his career, Kennelly wrote two novels, one of university life and one quite well-realized study of life in rural Kerry.

WORKS: *Cast a Cold Eye*, with Rudi Holzapfel. [Dublin]: Dolmen, [1959]; *The Rain, the Moon*, with Rudi Holzapfel. [Dublin]: Dolmen, 1961; *The Dark about Our Loves*. Dublin: Printed by John Augustine, [1962]; *The Crooked Cross*. Dublin: Figgis, 1963. (Novel); *Green Townlands*. Leeds: University Bibliographical Press, 1963; *My Dark Fathers*. Dublin: New Square Publications, 1965; *Up and At It*. Dublin: New Square Publications, 1965; *Collection One: Getting Up Early*. Dublin: Figgis, 1966; *The Florentines*. Dublin: Figgis, 1967. (Novel); *Good Souls to Survive*. Dublin: Figgis, 1967; *Selected Poems*. Dublin: Figgis, 1969; *A Drinking Cup: Poems from the Irish*. Dublin: Figgis, 1970; ed., *The Penguin Book of Irish Verse*. Harmondsworth: Penguin Books, 1970; *Bread*. Dublin: Tara Telephone Books, 1971; *Love Cry*. Dublin: Figgis, 1972; *Salvation, the Stranger*. Dublin: Tara Telephone Publications, 1972; *The Voices, A Sequence of Poems*. Dublin: Gallery Books, 1973; *Shelley in Dublin*. Dun Laoire: Anna Livia Books, 1974; *A Kind of Trust*. Dublin: Gallery Books, 1975; *New and Selected Poems*. Peter Fallon, ed. Dublin: Gallery Books, 1976; *Islandman*. Clondalkin: Profile, 1977. *The Visitor*. [Dublin]: St. Bueno's Hand-printed Limited Editions, [1978].

KETTLE, THOMAS (1880-1916), economist, politician, and man of letters. Born in Artane, County Dublin, Kettle was the son of the Land League advocate Andrew Kettle. He was educated at the Christian Brothers school in Richmond Street, Dublin, at Clongowes Wood College, and at University College, where he was auditor of the Literary and Historical Society and editor of *St. Stephen's*. After graduation, he had an active life in nationalist politics, often using his oratory to reconcile disagreeing factions. He became the first president of the Young Ireland Branch of the United Irish League in 1904, edited the shortlived *The Nationalist* in 1905, and received his little-used law degree in that same year. Kettle held the East Tyrone seat in Parliament from 1906 until he resigned in 1910. He was appointed the first professor of national economics in the National University in 1909. Kettle was chairman of the Peace Committee for the Dublin Strike of 1913, served on the Education Commission, and helped found the National Volunteers. The Easter Rebellion of 1916 was not in accord with his vision of "a free united Ireland in a free Europe," and Kettle was killed in the Battle of Somme, while serving in the British Army. The essays in *The Ways of War* (1917) describe the ideals that sent Kettle to Belgium and report his early experiences there.

Kettle was well grounded in economic literature and the philosophies of Aquinas, Schopenhauer, Guyau, Nietzsche, Heine, and Hegel. His political and economic writing is strongly humanistic and enlivened with witty images and aphorisms. Important works in the group are *Home Rule Finance: An Experiment in Justice* (1911), "The Economics of Nationalism," contained in *The Day's Burden* (1918, reprint 1968), and his "Introduction" to his translation of Louis Paul-Dubois' *Contemporary Ireland*. His poetry contained in *Poems and Parodies* (1912) is an interesting footnote to his oratory and prose. The subject is usually patriotic or martial, and the imagery often resembles the Celtic Twilight school of AE.* Occasionally there is a memorable metaphysical conceit, but his appealing philosophical side is under-represented.

Kettle was a critic of Irish literature throughout his life. He was among the protestors who disrupted Yeats'* *The Countess Cathleen*, and in an essay which appeared in the *United Irishman* he argued that Yeats had reversed the true image of the Irish Catholic's faith and "historical definiteness" in order to make the countess' white soul shine forth. Kettle had a sustained literary friendship with James Joyce.* Together in University College papers, they defended the literature of the 1890s and criticized the emphasis on folklore in the literature of the Celtic Revival. In the essays "On Saying Goodbye" and "Crossing the Irish Sea," both in *The Day's Burden*, Kettle detects the paralysis and tendency toward betrayal that Joyce ascribes to his *Dubliners*. Often a pessimist, Kettle used his natural curiosity to reinvigorate himself and his writing. Other works are *The Open Secret of Ireland* (1912), his editions *Battle Songs for the Irish Brigades*

(1915) and *Irish Orators and Oratory* (1916), and his translation of Kneller's *Christianity and the Leaders of Modern Science.*

BONNIE KIME SCOTT

WORKS: *The Day's Burden.* Dublin: Maunsel, 1910; *Home Rule Finance.* Dublin: Maunsel, 1911; *The Open Secret of Ireland.* London: W. J. Ham-Smith, 1912; ed., *Irish Orators and Oratory.* London: Unwin, [1916]; *Poems and Parodies.* London: Duckworth, 1916; *The Ways of War.* London: Constable, 1917; *An Irishman's Calendar. A Quotation from the Works of T. M. Kettle for Every Day in the Year,* Compiled by Mary S. Kettle. Dublin: Browne & Nolan, [1938].

KICKHAM, CHARLES J. (1828-1882), novelist and Fenian. Charles Joseph Kickham was born on May 9, 1828, at Cnoceenagow near Mullinahone, County Tipperary, the son of a prosperous shopkeeper and farmer. Kickham became deaf after an accident with gunpowder when he was thirteen. As a young man he took part in the Young Ireland movement, and he became a Fenian in about 1860. In 1865, James Stephens, the Fenian leader, appointed Kickham to the supreme executive of his Irish Republic, and Kickham became one of the editors of the Fenian newspaper *The Irish People.* When the Fenian insurrection was suppressed, Kickham was arrested on November 11, 1865, and sentenced to fourteen years' penal servitude. He served four years of the sentence at Woking and at Portland prisons before he was released, broken in health. In prison, however, he did manage to write his novel *Sally Kavanagh.* He died in Blackrock, a suburb of Dublin, on August 22, 1882.

One or two of Kickham's poems, such as "Rory of the Hill," have retained some popularity, but today he is remembered mainly for his long novel *Knocknagow; or, The Homes of Tipperary* (1879), which has gone through many editions and is still in print. By purely literary standards, *Knocknagow* is inconsequential. It is overly sentimental and overly farcical, its characters are caught in unchanging Dickensian molds, and it is not very well written. Nevertheless, the book still has considerable appeal. Its complicated plot is engrossing. Its large cast contains some character types, such as Barney Broderick, Phil Lahy the tailor and, the stalwart Mat the Thresher, that cling in the memory. The death scene of Nora Lahy is reminiscent of some of the death scenes in Dickens or even in Mrs. Henry Wood, but is moving for all that. Its emotions, although simple, are never mawkish; and its deeply felt nostalgia still has charm. It has been effectively adapted for the stage by Seamus de Burca.*

WORKS: *Sally Kavanagh; or, The Untenanted Graves.* Dublin: W. B. Kelly/ London: Simpkin, Marshal, 1869; *Knocknagow; or, The House of Tipperary.* Dublin: Duffy, [1879]; *For the Old Land; a Tale of Twenty Years Ago.* Dublin: Gill, 1886; *The Eagle of Garryroe.* Dublin: Martin Lester, [1920]; Dublin: Talbot, 1963; *Tales of Tipperary.* Dublin: Talbot, [1926]; *Poems of Charles Joseph Kickham.* Dublin: Educational Co., [1931]; *The Valley near Slievenamon, a Kickham Anthology.* James Maher, ed. [Kilkenny: Kilkenny People, 1942]. (Contains poems, memoirs, dairy excerpts, letters, essays, etc.); *Sing a Song of Kickham: Songs of Charles J. Kickham.*

With Gaelic Versions and Musical Notation. James Maher, ed. Dublin: Duffy, 1965. (Includes essays by Maher, Benedict Kiely, Katharine Tynan, & W. B. Yeats). REFERENCES: Healy, James J. *Life and Times of Charles J. Kickham.* Dublin: Duffy, 1915; Kelly, Richard J. *Charles Joseph Kickham: Patriot and Poet.* Dublin: Duffy, 1914.

KIELY, BENEDICT (1919-), novelist, short story writer, and critic. Like James Joyce* and Flann O'Brien,* Benedict Kiely is heir to the archaic Irish comic tradition characterized by linguistic verve, inventiveness of plot (to the extent of fantasy on occasions), and a satiric impulse. Like them, too, he is learnedly aware of his forebears, proven in Kiely's case by the range of reading demonstrated in his pioneering critical survey *Modern Irish Fiction—A Critique* (1950). One predecessor who has influenced Kiely's fiction is William Carleton,* of whom Kiely wrote a critical biography entitled *Poor Scholar* (1947). In the manner of his fellow Tyrone-man, Kiely has written short stories, novelle, and novels that seem to bridle in their narrative and anecdotal energies against the constraints and shapeliness of form. In both writers, the speaking voice of the storyteller is paramount, which perhaps is why Frank O'Connor,* who sought to preserve that voice in his own fiction, highly praised the stories of Kiely.

Benedict Kiely was born near Dromore on August 15, 1919, and was educated by the Christian Brothers in Omagh. In 1937, he entered the Jesuit novitiate in County Laois, but during a lengthy convalescence from a tubercular spinal ailment the following year, he decided not to answer the call to clerical life. Instead, he enrolled at the National University in Dublin from which he graduated with a B.A. in 1943. The abortive religious vocation and the severe illness and long convalescence have provided Kiely with material for several otherwise dissimilar novels, including *Honey Seems Bitter* (1952), *There Was an Ancient House* (1955), and *Dogs Enjoy the Morning* (1968). From 1945 until 1964, Kiely was a Dublin journalist with, successively, *The Standard, The Irish Independent,* and *The Irish Press,* following which he became a professor of creative writing at universities in Virginia, Oregon, and Georgia. Kiely returned to Dublin in 1968 and has since lectured at University College, written newspaper features and reviews, and made radio and television broadcasts.

Between 1946 and 1955, Kiely published six novels, ranging in subject matter and style from a psychological murder mystery, *Honey Seems Bitter,* to a modernized folktale, *The Cards of the Gambler* (1953). Three themes recur: crime or sin, clericalism, and initiation into manhood. These novels are eminently readable, but rarely are the central characters conveyed with sufficient penetration to ensure artistic triumph. As if in realization that his true strength lay with the short story, with which he has had successs in *The New Yorker, The Kenyon Review,* and other American magazines, Kiely published only three novels between 1955 and 1977, including *Proxopera* (1977), which is really a novella. But *The Captain with the*

Whiskers (1960), a brooding mock-romance, and *Dogs Enjoy the Morning,* a comic extravaganza drawing on Celtic mythology, are in fact more richly textured than the earlier novels and are in every way larger books.

It is as a short story writer that Kiely is likely to be remembered, for the form allows him to turn his archaic storytelling ability to artistic advantage. He is at his best when his plots, comedy, and pathos must be honed to fulfill the formal demands of the short story. The stories in his two volumes to date, *A Journey to the Seven Streams* (1963) and *A Ball of Malt and Madame Butterfly* (1973), are packed with memorable Irish figures, comic anecdotes, and blunt ironies. These weave a kind of tapestry around a scarcely satiric love of humanity and its foibles, a humanity whose symbolic residence is for Kiely the Ireland of living memory in which, despite their wide range of historical and geographic reference and allusion, all his stories are set. Few writers have known Ireland better than Kiely. Although he is most familiar with Ulster, especially the country west of the Bann, the settings of his stories and novels range freely throughout the thirty-two counties. In their artistic achievement, the stories prove that as a short story writer, he is within hailing distance of O'Connor* and Sean O'Faolain.*

Proxopera (1977) is a fictional departure for Kiely insofar as this attack on Republican terrorism in Northern Ireland is unwontedly bitter and outspoken. The irony of this work coming from the pen of the man who thirty-two years earlier had attacked partition in *Counties of Contention* (1945) is a capsulized object-lesson in Irish history during the 1970s. Formally, however, *Proxopera* exhibits the author's increasing fondness for the longer than conventional short story which he clearly feels can more satisfactorily accommodate his ample talent.

JOHN WILSON FOSTER

WORKS: *Counties of Contention: A Study of the Origins and Implications of the Partition of Ireland.* Cork: Mercier, 1945; *Land Without Stars.* London: Christopher Johnson, 1946; *Poor Scholar: A Study of the Works and Days of William Carleton.* London & New York: Sheed & Ward, 1947; *In a Harbour Green.* London: Jonathan Cape, 1949; *Call for a Miracle.* London: Jonathan Cape, 1950; *Modern Irish Fiction —A Critique.* Dublin: Golden Eagle Books, 1950; *Honey Seems Bitter.* New York: E. P. Dutton, 1952 / London: Methuen, 1954 / reprinted as *The Evil Men Do,* New York: Dell, 1954; *The Cards of the Gambler.* London: Methuen, 1953; *There Was an Ancient House.* London: Methuen, 1955; *The Captain with the Whiskers.* London: Methuen, 1960; *A Journey to the Seven Streams: Seventeen Stories.* London: Methuen, 1963; *Dogs Enjoy the Morning.* London: Gollancz, 1968; *A Ball of Malt and Madame Butterfly: A Dozen Stories.* London: Gollancz, 1973; *Proxopera.* London: Gollancz, 1977; *All the Way to Bantry Bay—and Other Irish Journeys.* London: Gollancz, 1978. (Travel); *A Cow in the House.* London: Gollancz, 1978 (stories).   REFERENCES: Casey, Daniel J. *Benedict Kiely.* Lewisburg, Pa.: Bucknell University Press, 1974; Eckley, Grace. *Benedict Kiely.* New York: Twayne, 1975; Foster, John William. *Forces and Themes in Ulster Fiction.* Dublin: Gill & Macmillan / Totowa, N.J.: Rowman & Littlefield, 1974, pp. 72-81, 91-100.

KILROY, THOMAS (1934-), playwright and novelist. Kilroy was born in Callan, County Kilkenny, on September 23, 1934. He received a B.A. and an M.A. from University College, Dublin, and has lectured there in English; he has also been a visiting professor at various American universities, including Notre Dame and Vanderbilt. From his academic background, he has published a deal of fugitive criticism of fiction and drama, and has also edited a selection of critical essays about O'Casey.* In 1971, he published one of the most admired of recent Irish novels, *The Big Chapel,* which won the *Guardian* Fiction Prize, the Royal Irish Academy of Letters-Allied Banks Prize, and the Royal Society for Literature Heinemann Award. The book is a recreation of some anticlerical riots that occurred in County Kilkenny in the last quarter of the nineteenth century. Without being really powerful or remaining vividly in the memory, *The Big Chapel* is a satisfying book, smoothly written, low-keyed but absorbing. Kilroy's stage plays include *The Death and Resurrection of Mr. Roche* (1969), *The O'Neill* (Peacock, 1969), *Tea and Sex and Shakespeare* (Abbey, 1976), and *Talbot's Box* (Abbey, 1977). His *Mr. Roche* is a strong and effective tragicomic study of middle-aged bachelors in Dublin, and undoubtedly one of the more distinguished Irish plays of the 1960s. *The O'Neill* is a competent but rather pedestrian historical play which would probably have benefited from brilliant verse rather than merely adequate prose. *Tea and Sex and Shakespeare* is an intermittently absorbing story of a writer, but its plot is too skimpy and its daydreaming too uninventive to carry the weight of a full-length play. However, *Talbot's Box,* on the subject of Matt Talbot, the Dublin laborer and mystic, was greeted with admiration and was transferred to London for a short run. At the end of 1977, Kilroy was appointed play editor for the Abbey Theatre,* succeeding Hugh Leonard* and Denis Johnston.* In 1978, he accepted a professorship of English at University College, Galway. He has as yet created no single overpowering work of either fiction or drama, but he is generally considered one of the few contemporary Irish writers capable of that accomplishment.

WORKS: *The Death and Resurrection of Mr. Roche.* London: Faber, 1969; *The Big Chapel.* London: Faber, 1971.

KINSELLA, THOMAS (1928-), poet. Born on May 4, 1928, in Dublin, Thomas Kinsella emerged in the 1950s as one of Ireland's most original and stimulating poets. Although his well-received translations from the early Irish, particularly the translation of the eighth-century prose epic *The Táin* (1969), might type him as an obvious Irish poet, the real matrix of his poetic creativity is not the Irish experience but the more profound human experience which Kinsella manages to examine with all the emotional and intellectual scrupulosity that that most intricate interior terrain requires.

Kinsella abandoned a science scholarship while he was attending University College, Dublin, in order to enter the Irish civil service. In the civil service he eventually rose to the post of assistant principal officer in the Department of Finance. In 1965, after his election to the Irish Academy of Letters, he left the Department of Finance to accept an artist-in-residency at Southern Illinois University. In 1970, he joined the English Department at Temple University in Philadelphia as a professor. During his civil and academic career, he also served as a director of the Dolmen and Cuala Presses and founded Peppercanister, a small publishing company in Dublin.

Almost from the very beginning, Kinsella's poetry won public honor and acclaim. *Another September* (1958) was the Poetry Book Society choice, an award received also by *Downstream* (1962). "Thinking of Mr. D," a haunting, meditative poem in *Another September,* was the winner of the Guinness Poetry Award in 1958, and *Poems and Translations* (1961) was selected for the Irish Arts Council Triennial Book Award. Two volumes of poetry, *Wormwood* (1966) and *Nightwalker and Other Poems* (1968), were selected for the Denis Devlin Memorial Award. Kinsella himself was awarded Guggenheim fellowships in 1968-1969 and 1971-1972.

Kinsella's versatility might be accounted for by the fact that prose, not poetry, dominated the Irish literary scene when he began writing, encouraging a tendency, as Maurice Harmon points out in *The Poetry of Thomas Kinsella* (1974), "to search for models outside Ireland." Indeed, Kinsella's early poems are not obviously Irish nor do they particularly reflect his Catholic upbringing. They do, however, reveal a variety of debts to Auden, Pound, Eliot, and other American influences. The driving force of his themes, however—love, marriage, risk, the view of life as "ordeal," the necessity to strive for order, the threat of time and extinction—fashions a densely thicketed, deeply subjective style that is, finally, derivative of Kinsella's anguished experience alone. Typical of the subjectively directed, yet objectively controlled, poem is "First Light," where the minute details of a landscape, illuminated by the rising sun, provide the setting for an upstairs "whimper or sigh" which "lengthens to an ugly wail. . . ." Kinsella describes the poems up to *Nightwalker and Other Poems* (1968) as "almost entirely lyrical," dealing with "love, death and the artistic act; with persons and relationships, places and objects seen against the world's processes of growth, maturing and extinction." The love poems in *Another September,* for example, are suffused with a sense of threat, as in "In the Ringwood," where "Dread, a grey devourer,/Stalks in the shade of love." The organic development of this theme can be seen in the intensely subjective *Wormwood* (1966), a series of eight poems dealing with the risks and ordeals of marriage in which lovers "renew each other" but with a "savage smile."

Kinsella becomes more concerned with "questions of value and order" in *Nightwalker and Other Poems,* "seeing the human function . . . as the eliciting of order from experience." Many of the poems in this collection show a conscious social revulsion to the mediocrity and materialism of modern Ireland, but even here the brave celebration of marriage in "Phoenix Park" and the touching farewell to Dublin it accomplishes show the deeper organic growth of Kinsella still in process: the enduring quality of life and marriage "ordered" by "ordeal" and healthy against extinction.

After 1968, according to Kinsella, his poetry "turned downward into the psyche toward origin and myth, and is set toward some kind of individuation." *Notes from the Land of the Dead and Other Poems* (1972), for example, demonstrates this direction and has caused some Kinsella admirers to suppose with Calvin Bedient in *The New York Times Book Review* that "Ireland's best living poet has brooded himself to pieces." That "brooding" could, of course, be seen as merely another form of "eliciting order from experience"—here, the experience enlarging into a mythically accessible order embedded perhaps in some sense of the collective unconscious. At any rate, Kinsella's myth-employing and mythmaking talents transform the commonplaces of experience into vivid, sometimes hair-raising spectaculars: a newly laid egg slips from an old lady's hand and is reconstituted into sheer Being which falls through "vast indifferent spaces" only to smash (having become a real egg again) into a suddenly appearing iron grating. What saves such mythic acrobatics from surrealistic excess, and even sentimentality, is the objective control that Kinsella always manages to sustain—not only the clear, precise language he uses, but the objectivist's eye for the telling image. The deeply psychological thrust of the poetry's intent in *Notes from the Land of the Dead,* ballasted by objective precision, conspires to produce reasonably authentic myth.

Some of the power of Kinsella's public poetry can be seen in works such as "Butcher's Dozen," a poignant longer poem which responds movingly to the Widgery tribunals into the British Army's fatal shooting of thirteen civil rights demonstrators in January 1972, and *The Good Fight* (1973), a poem commemorating the tenth anniversary of the death of John F. Kennedy. In the latter, Kinsella achieves historical and philosophical scope through extensive quotations from Plato, selected for their ironic pertinence, but it is the evocation of the memorable moment at the Kennedy Inauguration when Robert Frost stood blinded by the sun and snow which validates the effort here—an objective image enlivened and ordered by a vibrant contextual, even mythic, past.

THOMAS MERRILL

WORKS: *The Starlit Eye.* Dublin: Dolmen, 1952; *Three Legendary Sonnets.* Dublin: Dolmen, 1952; trans., *The Breastplate of St. Patrick.* Dublin: Dolmen, 1954/ as *Faeth Fiadha: The Breastplate of St. Patrick,* 1957; trans., *The Exile and Death of the Sons of Usnech,* by Longes Mac n-Usnig. Dublin: Dolmen, 1954; trans., *Thirty Three Triads, Translated from the XII Century Irish.* Dublin: Dolmen, 1955; *The Death of a Queen.* Dublin: Dolmen, 1956; *Poems.* Dublin: Dolmen, 1956; *Another September.* Dublin: Dolmen/Philadelphia: Dufour, 1958/revised Dublin: Dolmen, and London: Oxford University Press, 1962; *Moralities.* Dublin: Dolmen, 1960;

Poems and Translations. New York: Atheneum, 1961; *Downstream.* Dublin: Dolmen, 1962; *Six Irish Poets,* with others. Robin Skelton, ed. London & New York: Oxford University Press, 1962; *Nightwalker.* Dublin: Dolmen, 1966; *Wormwood.* Dublin: Dolmen, 1967; *Nightwalker and Other Poems.* Dublin: Dolmen/London: Oxford University Press/New York: Alfred A. Knopf, 1968; *Poems,* with David Livingstone & Anne Sexton. London & New York: Oxford University Press, 1968; *Tear.* Cambridge, Mass.: Pym Randall, 1969; trans., *The Tain.* Dublin: Dolmen, 1969/London & New York: Oxford University Press, 1970; *Butcher's Dozen.* Dublin: Peppercanister, 1972; *Finistere.* Dublin: Dolmen, 1972; *Notes from the Land of the Dead and Other Poems.* Dublin: Cuala, 1972/New York: Alfred A. Knopf, 1973; *A Selected Life.* Dublin: Peppercanister, 1972; *The Good Fight.* Dublin: Peppercanister, 1973; *New Poems, 1973.* Dublin: Dolmen, 1973; *Selected Poems, 1956-1968.* Dublin: Dolmen/London: Oxford University Press, 1973; *Vertical Man.* Dublin: Peppercanister, 1973; *One.* Dublin: Peppercanister, 1974.   REFERENCE: Harmon, Maurice. *The Poetry of Thomas Kinsella.* Dublin: Wolfhound, 1974.

KNOWLES, JAMES SHERIDAN (1784-1862), playwright and actor. Knowles was born in Cork city on May 12, 1784, and was the second cousin of Richard Brinsley Sheridan.* His only really Irish piece is *Brian Boroihme* (1812); his great successes were *Virginius* (1820), *William Tell* (1825), and *The Hunchback* (1832). He was a friend of Hazlitt, Lamb, Coleridge, Kean, and Macready. An early editor, R. Shelton MacKenzie, remarked of him, "The public had to learn that a genius like that of Knowles, soars, as on eagle pinions, taking a higher flight at each effort it makes. . . . His body may be resolved to dust, but his name will be immortal. He is inferior only to Shakespeare." The modern reader, however, would have to agree with Allardyce Nicoll's opinion: "If only Knowles could have escaped from melodrama on the one hand and from Elizabethanism on the other, he might have done something notable on the stage. As it is, many of his plays are but glorified tales of black evil and white innoncence." He died in Torquay on December 1, 1862.

   WORK: *Selected Dramatic Works of James Sheridan Knowles.* Baltimore: Edward J. Coale, 1835.   REFERENCE: Meeks, Leslie H. *Sheridan Knowles and the Theatre of His Time.* Bloomington, Ind.: Principia, 1933.

LANE, TEMPLE (1899-?), novelist and poet. Temple Lane was the pseudonym of Mary Isabel Leslie, novelist, poet, and doctor of philosophy, who was born in Dublin in 1899 and spent most of her childhood in Tipperary. She was educated in England and later in Trinity College, Dublin, where she won the Large Gold Medal in 1922.

   She was a prolific and popular writer of what could be termed "female fiction before the Liberation." Her *Watch the Wall* (1927) is a formula romantic novel set in England during the Napoleonic Wars, and it uses the old trick of disguised identity rather unbelievably. Did the spirited young heroine really not recognize that her idle, laconic suitor and the heroic, daring smuggler were one and the same? A reader who was only half asleep would spot it on page two, but, if he continued ploughing through the turgid and stilted prose, he would find the whole effort a rather bad mixture of Georgette Heyer and Baroness Orczy, with neither the charm of the former nor the excitement of the latter.

Full Tide (1923) deals with the complex subject of snobbery and the breakdown of class barriers between the wars in England. Although lucidly written and well observed and plotted, the novel is imbued with an irritating simplicity and nursery morality. A young widow whose husband was afflicted with "the vice of Drink" turns her hand to running a boarding house and manages a public school education and Cambridge for her son. But she neglects to spank him, so he turns out a snob and ashamed of her. All is forgiven when he acts the honorable gentleman in accordance with his education. After a spell in South America, no doubt he will come back and be the pillar of the family. This novel unwittingly upholds the system it aims to condemn. Virtue equals money: if you are brilliant and work hard to make enough, it does not matter if your father was only a chauffeur or your mother runs a boarding house. Money is honorable, or at least it covers a multitude of sins.

Friday's Well (1943), set in Ireland during World War II, suggests the danger of falling for the first good-looking American airman who drops from the sky. This is the fate of two sisters on a rural farm, but the airman is not what he seems, and they pay dearly. One sister is accidentally killed, but the other, after suffering, learns the true nature of love and marries the local bank manager. While the novel would be much better if edited to half its length, it does reflect the author's authentic knowledge of rural life and her ability to create fairly believable characters.

On the whole, however, Temple Lane writes to formula. There is little individuality in her novels and much simplicity and humorless earnestness. Her poetry is not much better. It draws heavily on nature and expresses a sentimental hankering for the simple peasant life. Although she is sometimes remembered for "The Fairy Tree," set to music by Dr. Vincent O'Brien, her verses are little more than skillful rhyming and merry tinkles.

MARY ROSE CALLAGHAN

WORKS: *Burnt Bridges.* London: John Long, 1925; *No Just Cause.* London: John Long, 1925; *Defiance.* London: John Long, 1926; *Second Sight.* London: John Long, 1926; *Watch the Wall.* London: John Long, 1927; *The Bands of Orion.* London: Jarrolds, [1928]; *The Little Wood.* London: Jarrolds, [1930]; *Blind Wedding.* London: Jarrolds, [1931]; *Sinner Anthony.* London: Jarrolds, 1933; *The Trains Go South.* London: Jarrolds, [1938]; *Battle of the Warrior.* London: Jarrolds, [1940]; *Fisherman's Wake.* London: Longmans, [1940]; *House of My Pilgrimage.* Dublin: Talbot, 1941/London: Frederick Muller, 1941; *Friday's Well.* Dublin: Talbot, 1943; *Come Back!* Dublin: Talbot, 1945; *Curlews.* Dublin: Talbot, 1946. (Poems); *My Bonny's Away.* Dublin: Talbot, 1947.

LARMINIE, WILLIAM (1849?-1900), folklorist, poet, and critic. Larminie was born in Castlebar, County Mayo, in 1849 or 1850 and graduated from

Trinity College. Toward the end of his life, he published some carefully collected and charmingly told folktales as well as two volumes of verse. He is
critically interesting because he advocated the use of the assonance of
Gaelic poetry in English verse. His influence was not immediately apparent,
perhaps partly because he was not as able a practitioner of poetry as he was
a critic. It remained for Austin Clarke* several decades later to adapt
assonance into English poetry in a more thoroughgoing and satisfying manner. AE* remarked of Larminie's poetry that "he is much more concerned
with the subject of his thought than with the expression. . . . I might describe
him as a poet by saying that the spirit is indeed kingly, but without the
purple robe which would be the outer token of his lofty rank." Phillip L.
Marcus justly points to his poem "Consolation" as his finest achievement.
Larminie also made an unpublished translation of Johannes Scotus
Eriugena which has been described as superb. He died in Bray on January
19, 1900.

WORKS: *Fand and Other Poems.* Dublin: Hodges, Figgis, 1892; *West Irish Folk-
Tales and Romances.* London: Elliot Stock, 1893; "The Development of English
Metres." *Contemporary Review* 66 (November 1894): 717-736; "Joannes Scotus
Eriugena." *Contemporary Review* 71 (April 1897): 557-572; *Glanlua and Other
Poems.* London: Kegan Paul, 1899.   REFERENCES: Eglinton, John. "William
Larminie." *Dublin Magazine,* New Series XIX (April-June 1944): 12-16; Marcus,
Phillip L. *Yeats and the Beginning of the Irish Renaissance.* Ithaca & London: Cor-
nell University Press, [1970], pp. 207-221.

LAVERTY, MAURA [KELLY] (1907-1966), novelist, playwright, and
author of cookbooks. Laverty was born and raised in Rathangan, a small
village in County Kildare, a milieu which she vividly describes in her first
novel, *Never No More* (1942). Following the death of the beloved grandmother who had provided her a home at "Derrymore House," she studied
school teaching at the Brigadine Convent in County Carlow. In 1925, she
went to Madrid as a governess. The need for a young girl to set her own
values in a foreign culture is described in a second autobiographical novel,
No More than Human (1944). In Spain, she became a secretary to Princess
Bibesco, a foreign correspondent in the Banco Calamarte, and finally a
journalist for the paper *El Debate*. She returned to Ireland as a journalist
and broadcaster in 1928 and resided in Dublin.

Laverty's most noteworthy work is *Lift Up Your Gates* (1946; also published under the title, *Liffey Lane,* 1947). This well-structured, naturalistic
novel follows Chrissie Doyle, a fourteen-year-old, fatherless girl of the
Dublin slums, through her evening paper route. As she visits at the shops
and mews-flats on the better side of Liffey Lane, we experience the backgrounds and present concerns of each of her customers. With all but one,
there is an exchange of feeling and an attempt at mutual understanding.
Chrissie's love of her small cousin, Kevin, and her need to make reparation
to Sister Martha, a nun who believes in and fosters Chrissie, provide con-

tinuity and direction. Telefis Éireann's popular serial "Tolka Row" was based on this novel.

Sean O'Faolain* wrote an enthusiastic preface for *Never No More,* finding its innocent heroine, its garrulous, meandering narrative, and its mixture of village hyperbole and candor irresistible. Memories of her grandmother's cookery prompted Laverty to compose this first novel, and she tends to include recipes in all her rural books. She has written several cookbooks as well: *Flour Economy* (1941), *Kind Cooking* (1946), and *Full and Plenty* (1960).

Touched by Thorn (1943; also published as *Alone We Embark*) received an Irish Women Writers' Award and was banned in Ireland, probably because one of its heroines was guilty of marital infidelity. The novel has several memorable village characters and a typically strong, mature woman who provides guidance and culinary delicacies for village young people. The work is seriously marred, however, by a melodramatic conclusion that solves everyone's problems.

Laverty has also published several children's works, including *Gold of Glanaree* (1945), which combines a charming depiction of the daily lives of village children with an intriguing treasure hunt.

Laverty focuses on the sensitive, innocent point of view of girls and women. She represents Irish hospitality and rural life with spirit, feeling and candor, but sometimes has difficulty resolving plots and holding sentimentality in check.

BONNIE KIME SCOTT

WORKS: *Flour Economy.* Dublin: Browne & Nolan, [1941]; *Never No More.* London & New York: Longmans, 1942; *Alone We Embark.* London: Longmans, 1943/ in the United States as *Touched by the Thorn.* New York: Longmans, Green, 1943; *No More Than Human.* London: Longmans, 1944; *Gold of Glanaree.* New York: Longmans, Green, 1945; *The Cottage in the Bog.* Dublin: Browne & Nolan, 1946; *Lift Up Your Gates.* London: Longmans, Green, 1946/in the United States as *Liffey Lane,* New York: Longmans, Green, 1947; *Maura Laverty's Cook Book.* London: Longmans, Green, 1946/New York & Toronto: Longmans, Green, 1947; *The Green Orchard.* London: Longmans, Green, [1949]; *Kind Cooking.* Dublin: Electricity Supply Board, [1955].

LAVIN, MARY (1912-), short story writer and novelist. Lavin was born on June 11, 1912, in Walpole, Massachusetts, the only child of Thomas and Nora Lavin. Nora, dissatisfied with life in the United States, returned with her eleven-year-old daughter Mary to the family home in Athenry where they lived for the better part of a year before purchasing a house in Dublin. Mary attended the Loreto Convent and University College, where she won First Honors in English and stayed to write an M.A. thesis on Jane Austen. Abandoning a dissertation on Virginia Woolf, she taught French for two years at the Loreto Convent before marrying a Dublin lawyer, William Walsh. With money inherited from Tom Lavin's estate, the Walshes bought the Abbey Farm next to Bective Abbey. Lavin still divides her time between the Abbey and a small mews-home in Dublin. She had two daughters by Walsh, Valentine and Caroline, born in 1943 and 1953, respectively. After Walsh's death in 1954 she married a former Jesuit priest, Michael MacDonald Scott, presently dean of the School of Irish Studies. Her first short story, "Miss Holland," was published in 1938. Currently, there are eighteen volumes in her canon, including two novels and one novelette, as well as a number of separately published stories and a handful of poems.

Lavin is foremost a realistic writer who often writes with a lively sense of humor, but whose vision of the world is essentially tragic rather than comic. Her stories are generally of domestic situations and deal with mundane but universal aspects of everyday life: marriages good and bad, the struggles of children, loneliness, poverty, and the all-pervasive topic of social caste and order. These situations, particularly the last, lead to the theme of freedom and escape which runs through the greatest part of her work. The social mores of the small villages which her characters inhabit are stern and unforgiving, so that illicit passion often leads to pregnancy and finally death. Working within the Victorian social structure, her characters struggle against their passions, seek solitude in nature, and eventually liberation in death. Suicide in these Roman Catholic stories never presents a legitimate alternative, but most of Lavin's characters expect to achieve some sort of heavenly reward after life's struggle. While few of her characters do escape their difficult existences, the rest generally manage to cope, to rationalize, and to make the best of their lot. The measures Lavin's characters adapt to cope with present vicissitudes are effective and quietly heroic as well as interesting. Her best stories are frequently little more than vignettes, gracefully, realistically, and artfully done. Because so many of her stories are really character studies, she has often been unfairly accused of writing pieces without resolutions or discernible plots.

The death of Lavin's first husband and her subsequent monetary struggle in trying to raise a family under reduced circumstances have manifested themselves in a remarkable series of later stories on widowhood. Among these are some of Lavin's finest. Although she has written two long novels, she prefers to write short fiction because of the fairly brief periods in which she has to work and because she finds this medium congenial for distillation of character, plot, and theme. Recognized with various prizes such as the Katherine Mansfield Award, the Ella Lynam Cabot Award, and two Guggenheim fellowships, Lavin's work is only now acquiring serious scholarly and critical notice. Her clarity of prose and its absence of idiosyncrasies make her work difficult to describe and leave literary scholars little to say, but her stature as a major literary figure in contemporary Irish letters is now established.

ZACK BOWEN

WORKS: *Tales from Bective Bridge*. Boston: Little, Brown, 1942/London: Michael

Joseph, 1943; *The Long Ago and Other Stories*. London: Michael Joseph, 1944; *The House in Clewe Street*. Boston: Little, Brown/London: Michael Joseph, 1945; *The Becker Wives and Other Stories*. London: Michael Joseph, 1946; *At Sallygap and Other Stories*. Boston: Little, Brown, 1947; *Mary O'Grady*. Boston: Little, Brown/ London: Michael Joseph, 1950; *A Single Lady and Other Stories*. London: Michael Joseph, 1951; *The Patriot Son and Other Stories*. London: Michael Joseph, 1956; *A Likely Story*. New York: Macmillan, 1957/Dublin: Dolmen, 1957; *Selected Stories*. New York: Macmillan, 1959; *The Great Wave and Other Stories*. London & New York: Macmillan, 1961; *Stories of Mary Lavin*. London: Constable, 1964; *In the Middle of the Fields*. London: Constable, 1967/New York: Macmillan, 1969; *Happiness and Other Stories*. London: Constable, 1969; *The Becker Wives*. New York: New American Library, 1971; *Collected Stories*. Boston: Houghton Mifflin, 1971; *The Second Best Children in the World*. Boston: Houghton Mifflin, 1972; *A Memory and Other Stories*. Boston: Houghton Mifflin, 1973.   REFERENCES: Bowen, Zack. *Mary Lavin*. Lewisburg, Pa.: Bucknell University Press, 1975; Peterson, Richard. *Mary Lavin*. New York: Twayne, 1978.

LAWLESS, EMILY (1845-1913), novelist and poet. Lawless, known in her day as the Honorable Emily Lawless, was born on June 17, 1845, the daughter of the third Baron Cloncurry, a wealthy Anglo-Irish nobleman whose family rose to prominence in the late eighteenth century. The family was star-crossed, however, and Emily's father and two of her sisters committed suicide. She herself was noted for eccentricity and led a somewhat unhappy, if full, life. During her final years she retreated into seclusion. In her heyday, she was one of the foremost Irish writers in the genres of both poetry and fiction. Her second novel, *Hurrish* (1886), appeared at a time when the question of Home Rule dominated politics in Ireland and England; the book examines the relationship of the Irish tenant farmer to the English law. Although it is sentimental and melodramatic, it won the praise of Gladstone who felt that it shed much light on the Irish problem. Subsequently, Gladstone became Lawless' friend and occasional correspondent. Indeed, her ties with important figures in the political world, especially Sir Horace Plunkett, played a large part in her emotional and intellectual life until the very end of her life. Always, however, she remained a loyalist. Although she spent her final years in Surrey for reasons of health, her disenchantment with the turn that she discerned in Ireland was equally important in her decision to leave Ireland.

Lawless wrote ten novels, four books of verse, and numerous short stories and historical essays. The best of her works are *Grania* (1892), *Maelcho* (1894), and *With the Wild Geese* (1902). *Grania* is a romantic depiction of life on the Aran Islands; the heroine dies tragically, her fiancé failing to come to her aid when she attempts to cross the rough seas in search of a priest for her dying sister. Sentimentality predominates, but the evocation of the landscape and day-to-day life of the Aran peasants is detailed and realistic. Emily Lawless preceded Synge* in realizing the artistic possibilities of the barren islands. *Maelcho* is a historical novel set in the Desmond Rebellion; it is panoramic, overlong, and sometimes disjointed in plot. The author's grasp of the political and economic causes of the war as well as her recreation of the suffering and persecution endured by the Gaels give the work enduring value. In general, Lawless' historical fiction is superior to her other work. Mention should also be made of *With Essex in Ireland* (1890), which was originally published as an authentic sixteenth-century document but which Lawless later admitted having written herself. The work is noteworthy for its poetic rendering of a war-torn land and the antique richness of its language. *With the Wild Geese* contains the best of the author's verse. These are ballads and lyrics, many based upon historical themes. Early in the century, this verse was highly praised in Ireland by both sides in the Home Rule controversy.

Rather than a member of the literary renaissance per se, Emily Lawless shrould be regarded as one of its forerunners. Her best work, verse or prose, is that with a historical dimension. Some correspondence is contained in Marsh's Library in Dublin. She died in Surrey on October 19, 1913.

WILLIAM J. LINN

WORKS: *A Chelsea Householder.* 3 vols. London: Sampson Low, 1882; *Ireland,* with additions by Mrs. A. Bronson. London: Unwin, 1885/revised, with two new chapters, London: Unwin, 1912; *A Millionaire's Cousin.* London: Macmillan, 1885; *Hurrish.* Edinburgh: Blackwood, 1886; *Major Lawrence, F.L.S.* 3 vols. London: J. Murray, 1887; *Plain Frances Mowbray and Other Tales.* London: J. Murray, 1889; *With Essex in Ireland.* London: Smith, Elder, 1890; *Grania: The Story of an Island.* 2 vols. London: Smith, Elder, 1892; *Maelcho.* 2 vols. London: Smith, Elder, 1894; *Traits and Confidences.* London: Methuen, 1898; *A Garden Diary, September 1899— September 1900.* London: Methuen, 1901; *With the Wild Geese.* London: Isbister, 1902; *Maria Edgeworth.* London: Macmillan, 1904; *The Book of Gilly: Four Months Out of a Life.* London: Smith, Elder, 1906; with Shan F. Bullock, *The Race of Castlebar.* London: J. Murray, 1913.

LAWRENCE, W[ILLIAM] J. (1862-1940), historian and critic of the drama. Lawrence was born in Belfast on October 29, 1862. His formal academic training ended in his middle teens, and his formidable learning and scholarship are owing only to his own prodigious industry and capacity for grubbing through innumerable dusty manuscripts and journals. He became best known as an historian of the Elizabethan stage. Critics as prestigious as T. S. Eliot admired such books as *Pre-Restoration Stage Studies* (1927), *The Physical Conditions of the Elizabethan Public Playhouse* (1927), *Shakespeare's Workshop* (1928), *Those Nut-Cracking Elizabethans* (1935), *Old Theatre Days and Ways* (1935), and *Speeding up Shakespeare* (1937). Lawrence's fascination with the stage led him into almost equally significant work on the eighteenth- and nineteenth-century theatre.

Lawrence's importance for Irish literature lies in his influence as a drama critic, largely for the London journal *The Stage.* From the time of Synge* to the time of O'Casey,* he wrote the most thoughtful, knowledgeable

critiques of Irish plays and productions. His strength as a critic was, nevertheless, diminished by a strong Ulster puritanism and by a violent dislike of
W. B. Yeats.* Thus, Lawrence often found himself in untenable but never
relinquished critical positions, such as his vitriolic condemnations of Synge's
Playboy of the Western World. Despite his deficiencies, Lawrence was the
most engaged Irish theatre critic of the first quarter of this century. Even his
most arrant prejudices brought to the drama an embattled and probably
healthy vigor. He died in August 1940.

WORK: *The Irish Theatre of W. J. Lawrence,* Robert Hogan, ed. Newark, Del.:
Proscenium, 1979.

LEADBEATER, MARY (1758-1826), writer of sketches. Leadbeater née
Shackleton was born of a Quaker family in Ballitore, County Kildare, in
December 1758. She became a friend of Maria Edgeworth* who helped her
circulate her *Cottage Dialogues.* Her *Annals of Ballitore* and her posthumous *Leadbeater Papers* retell with clarity and energy anecdotes of life
in her Irish Quaker village. In her account of the effect of the Insurrection
of 1798 on her village, her direct style well captures the confusion and
terror. She died in Ballitore on June 27, 1826. Her daughter, Mrs. Lydia
Fisher, was the friend and inspiration of Gerald Griffin* and preserved
many of his poems.

WORKS: *Extracts and Original Anecdotes for the Improvement of Youth.* Dub-
lin: Jackson, 1794; *Poems.* . . . Dublin: Keene, 1808; *Cottage Dialogues among the
Irish Peasantry.* London: Johnson, 1811; *The Landlord's Friend.* Dublin: Cumming,
1813; with Elizabeth Shackleton, *Tales for Cottagers, Accomodated to the Present
Condition of the Irish Peasantry.* Dublin: Cumming, 1814; *Cottage Biography.*
Dublin: C. Bentham, 1822; *Memoirs and Letters of Richard and Elizabeth Shackleton.* . . . London: Harvey & Darton, 1822; *Biographical Notices of Members of the
Society of Friends, Who Were Resident in Ireland.* London: Harvey & Darton, 1823;
The Pedlars. Dublin: Bentham & Harvey, 1826; *The Leadbeater Papers.* 2 vols. London: Bell & Daldy, 1862.   REFERENCE: Young, Margaret Ferrier. "Ballitore
and Its Institutions." *Journal of the County Kildare Archaeological Society* 8 (1916):
167-179. Contains some Leadbeater letters.

LECKY, W[ILLIAM] E[DWARD] H[ARTPOLE] (1838-1903), historian. Lecky was born on March 26, 1838, at Newtown Park, County
Dublin. He attended Trinity College where he also taught and which he
represented in the Westminister Parliament from 1895 to 1903. His formidable learning is apparent in his *Leaders of Public Opinion in Ireland*
(1861), his two-volume *History of the Rise and Influence of Rationalism
in Europe* (1865), and his two-volume *History of European Morals from
Augustus to Charlemagne* (1869). His magnum opus is the twelve-volume
History of England in the Eighteenth Century (1892). Five of the twelve
volumes are devoted to a history of Ireland. This imbalance occurred because Lecky wanted to refute what he considered the calumnies of the

historian Froude against the Irish people. Nevertheless, although a fair historian, Lecky was not a conventional nationalist; as a member of Parliament he opposed Home Rule. He died on October 22, 1903, in Dublin.

WORK: *A History of England in the Eighteenth Century.* London: Longmans, Green, 1918-1925.   REFERENCES: Auchmuty, James Johnston. *Lecky.* Dublin: Hodges, Figgis/London: Longmans, Green, 1945; Lecky, Mrs. Elisabeth. *A Memoir of the Right Hon. William Edward Hartpole Lecky.* London: Longmans, 1909.

LEDWIDGE, FRANCIS (1887-1917), poet. Born on August 19, 1887, in Slane, County Meath, and largely self-educated, Francis Ledwidge became a grocer's assistant, a miner, laborer, and foreman with the County Council. His first poems, in *Songs of the Fields* (1915), published with an introduction by his patron Lord Dunsany,* betray many unassimilated influences of Gray, Goldsmith,* and Keats. Edward Marsh's *Georgian Poetry II* (1913-1915) fairly accommodated some of Ledwidge's conventional, decorative, vapid escapism. But with access to Dunsany's advice and castle library, he began to overcome his weaknesses for trite allusion, archaism, and insincere posing, and to develop his genuine sympathies for landscape and local history. After his introduction to Yeats'* Dublin circle, a number of poems with mythological themes appeared. These are set in the Boyne Valley and reflect fresh rural scenes, discriminating changes of light and season, rain showers, birdsongs, fox-hunts, and folk customs. He began to write in the Irish mode: after Douglas Hyde's* *Love Songs of Connacht* and Thomas MacDonagh's* translations, dialect poems following Lady Gregory's* example, and many showing the influences of AE* and Yeats (*Songs of Peace,* 1917).

Like thousands of nationalists of his generation, Ledwidge joined the British Army in World War I and served with the Royal Inniskilling Fusiliers at Gallipoli, in Serbia, and on the Western Front. This was a cruelly ironic predicament for one who had been a founding member of the labor movement in Meath, an organizer of the Irish Volunteers in Slane, and the lone defender of the Sinn Fein party against the predominantly Redmondite elected offialdom. His decision to join the Royal Inniskilling Fusiliers was not primarily political, however. A love affair with a landowner's daughter —Ellie Vaughey—had ended abruptly in the summer of 1913, and as a large proportion of his work over the subsequent two years shows, he brooded long over this rejection. The protracted horrors of the Gallipoli episode, the shock at the news of Ellie's sudden death in 1915, and, some months later, the news of the execution of Thomas MacDonagh and Joseph Plunkett,* produced in Ledwidge deeper moods of doubt and despair, leading to recurring premonitions of his own imminent death. His gentle nature seems to have responded to the events of Easter Week principally because of the participation of other poets. And unlike the war poets, he wrote nothing—jingoist or pacifist—that springs directly from the experience of that conflict. Francis Ledwidge remained a regional and pastoral poet, whose single source of constant wonder is the local landmarks and vistas "where even the fields have their names and traditions." His work in some ways foreshadows that of Patrick Kavanagh* and Seamus Hearney.*

The news of Easter Week affected Ledwidge deeply. His elegies for the poets of the Rising grieve for personal and racial losses: the leaders, Ledwidge's flock of blackbirds, were reincarnations of "The Dead Kings" of Tara. The natural aristocracy of Ireland had revealed itself in his generation. The figure of Cathleen Ni Houlihan superseded that of Ellie Vaughey in his poems, and in the apparent futility of the deaths of MacDonagh and Plunkett he saw images of his own fate. The poetry of his last year turns to religious meditations and combines a sparer use of nature imagery, a wider range of Irish literary and historical allusion, a less artificial invocation of Celtic myth, and more experimentation in the Irish mode. This work contains most of his best achievements, though no poem in the collection is wholly successful. On July 31, 1917, at Boesinghe, near Ypres, Belgium, a bomb put an end to his growing. Ledwidge's lament for Thomas MacDonagh, recorded on Slane Bridge, is appropriately his own:

> He shall not hear the bittern cry
> In the wild sky where he is lain,
> Nor voices of the sweeter birds
> Above the wailing of the rain.

COILIN OWENS

WORK: *The Complete Poems of Francis Ledwidge.* Alice Curtayne, ed. London: Martin Brian & O'Keefe, 1974.   REFERENCE: Curtayne, Alice. *Francis Ledwidge: A Life of the Poet.* London: Martin Brian & O'Keefe, 1972.

Le FANU, JOSEPH SHERIDAN (1814-1873), novelist and short story writer. A generation younger than C. R. Maturin,* whom he resembles in various ways, Le Fanu conveys less of the melodramatic effects of Gothic fiction and more of psychological investigation. As a novelist, he exhibits some of the faults of the Gothic writers: he relies on plot contrivances, exaggerates emotional responses, and plays with serious intellectual themes. However, in his presentation of historical settings, his analysis of subconscious motives, and even in narrative techniques, his works represent an advance on those of his predecessors.

Born in Dublin on August 28, 1814, Le Fanu was related on his mother's side to the playwright Richard Brinsley Sheridan.* He was educated at Trinity College and was called to the bar in 1839 before turning to a career as a journalist. Many of his stories were contributions to the *Dublin University Magazine,* of which he was editor from 1861 to 1869. He was prolific in his writing, publishing fourteen novels and a great number of tales and stories. After his wife's death in 1858, he withdrew from polite society and remained a recluse until his death on February 7, 1873, in Dublin.

As a short story writer, he developed from the author of short, facile tales to a craftsman skilled in narrative techniques. *Ghost Stories and Tales of Mystery* (1851), his first collection, presents a good deal of suspense and shocks, but the plots are strained and the characters wooden. The five long stories which make up *In a Glass Darkly* (1871) reveal unusual skill in portraying subtle subconscious conflicts, including sexual frustration and self-destructiveness. Human wickedness rather than supernatural forces motivates the character in the best of the late stories, and the narrative techniques employed are suitably complex. A. P. Graves'* edition of *The Purcell Papers* (1880) consists of three volumes of the supernatural tales and poems.

Three of his novels deserve special attention. *The Cock and Anchor* (1845) shows skill at presenting eighteenth-century Dublin and contains incisive commentary on moral corruption. *The House by the Churchyard* (1863), set in Chapelizod, features a number of realistic characters involved in a convincing mystery plot. *Uncle Silas* (1864), his highest achievement, is narrated by a young girl who became the victim of the title character. Her growing horror as she discovers the plot to control and destroy her is not exaggerated, but vivid and moving. By the end, it is so highly charged with emotion that unusual degrees of suspense are achieved. Yet here, as in his best short stories, subtle shadings of fear and frustration are conveyed by narrative techniques which expose the suffering of the victims while revealing the subconscious motives of cruelty of the villains as well. Both Elizabeth Bowen,* in her introduction to *Uncle Silas* (1947), and V. S. Pritchett, in his essay in *The Living Novel* (1964), cite his manner of telling stories as more important than the plots themselves; through the use of a convincing narrator, the most vivid experiences of terror are conveyed.

JAMES KILROY

WORKS: *The Cock and Anchor, Being a Chronicle of Old Dublin City.* Dublin: W. Curry, 1845; *The Fortunes of Colonel Torlogh O'Brien.* Dublin: J. McGlashan, 1847; *Ghost Stories and Tales of Mystery.* Dublin: J. McGlashan, 1851; *The House by the Church-yard.* 3 vols. London: Tinsley, 1863; *Uncle Silas.* 3 vols. London: R. Bentley, 1864; *Wylder's Hand.* 3 vols. London: R. Bentley, 1864; *Guy Deverell.* 3 vols. London: Downey, 1865; *The Prelude: Being a Contribution Towards a History of the Election for the University* [of Dublin] by John Figwood, Esq. [Pseud.] Dublin: G. Herbert, 1865 (Pamphlet); *All in the Dark.* 2 vols. London: Guildford, 1866; *The Tenants of Malory.* 3 vols. London: Tinsley/New York: Harpers, 1867; *Haunted Lives.* 3 vols. London: Tinsley, 1868; *A Lost Name.* 3 vols. London: R. Bentley, 1868; *The Wyvern Mystery.* 3 vols. London: Tinsley, 1869; *Checkmate.* London: Hurst & Blackett, 1871; *The Rose and the Key.* 3 vols. London: Chapman & Hall, 1871; *In a Glass Darkly.* 3 vols. London: R. Bentley, 1872; *Morley Court.* London: Chapman & Hall, 1873; *Willing to Die.* London: Downey, [1873?]; London: Hurst & Blackett, 1873; *The Bird of Passage.* New York: D. Appleton, 1878; *The Purcell Papers.* London: R. Bentley, 1880; *The Evil Guest.* London: Ward & Downey, [1894]; *The Watcher and Other Weird Stories.* London: Downey, [1894]; *A Chronicle of Golden Friars and Other Stories.* London: Downey, 1896; *Shamus O'Brien,* Comic Opera founded on a Poem by Le Fanu, Book by G. H. Jessop. London: Boosey, 1896; *Madam Crowl's Ghost, and Other Tales of Mystery.* Collected & edited by M. R. James. London: G. Bell, 1923. REFERENCES: Begnal, Michael. *Joseph Sheridan Le Fanu.* Lewisburg, Pa.: Bucknell University Press, 1971; Browne, Nelson. *Sheridan Le Fanu.* London: Arthur Barker, 1951; Penzoldt, Peter. *The Supernatural in Fiction.* London: Peter Nevil, 1952, pp. 67-91.

LEITCH, MAURICE (1933-), novelist. Leitch was born in Muckamore, County Antrim, on July 5, 1933. He was educated in Belfast and was a schoolteacher before becoming a features producer for the BBC in Northern Ireland. He now works for the BBC in England.

The most striking feature of Leitch's novels is their dark and angry vision of Ulster, be it the Belfast of *The Liberty Lad* (1965), the County Antrim of that same novel and of *Stamping Ground* (1975), or the south Armagh of *Poor Lazarus* (1969), which won the *Guardian* annual fiction prize. His characters are held in the stranglehold of an inhibitive environment, a post-World War II Ulster that is shabby and unpleasant and whose beauties are largely unsung by the author. In part, this is because his Ulster is mainly planter Protestant, cut off (as Leitch is himself) from any nationalist dream of a beautiful past or beautiful future, but in part because his Ulster is a portion of twentieth-century Ireland, pseudo-Americanized and myopically expedient. The one leader in the novels, Bradley the Unionist member of Parliament in *The Liberty Lad* (the author's *bildungsroman*), is a corrupt homosexual. Uneasy bonds between men underlie, in varying degrees of explicitness, the male camaraderie of Leitch's "hell-raisers" whose desperate antics conceal their loneliness and misogyny. When "hell-raising" becomes violent, as in *Poor Lazarus* and *Stamping Ground,* Leitch's fiction approaches the grotesquerie and even diabolism of the Irish comic tradition. Sectarianism is, of course, a constant source of violence and hatred. Leitch courageously explores the uneasy, peacetime concealment of sectarianism in *Poor Lazarus,* a fine and troubling story of a brief relationship between a local Protestant and a Catholic Irish-Canadian.

Leitch creates his world through his story lines but also through his prose style, the appropriateness of which is a two-edged sword, since he has cultivated a rather costive and flairless way of writing in order to create a social world equally devoid of flair and fluency. *Stamping Ground* is his densest work to date. It supports more characters than his two earlier novels (including Minnie Maitland, the spinster inhabitant of the local Protestant "Big House" and an almost Faulkerian creation), and it consists entirely of foreground, the characters' thoughts and musings, which are sometimes trivial. For density of texture, Leitch pays the price of a certain narrative and perspective and interest.

Northern Ireland did not maintain an unbreakable grip on Leitch, except perhaps in that psychic way familiar to exiled Irish authors. After some years as a schoolteacher—an experience he exploits in *The Liberty Lad*—he joined BBC Northern Ireland, and soon after that left for London where he is the Head of BBC Radio's drama features.

JOHN WILSON FOSTER

WORKS: *The Liberty Lad.* London: MacGibbon & Kee, 1965; *Poor Lazarus.* London: MacGibbon & Kee, 1969; *Stamping Ground.* London: Secker & Warburg, 1975.

LEONARD, HUGH (1926-), playwright. Hugh Leonard is the pseudonym of John Keyes Byrne, who was born in Dalkey, County Dublin, on November 9, 1926. Leonard is one of the cleverest and most amusing stylists among contemporary Irish writers. With Brian Friel,* is probably the best known and the most commercially successful Irish playwright outside of Ireland to emerge since Brendan Behan.*

Leonard was originally a civil servant. His first long play, *The Big Birthday,* was produced by the Abbey* in January 1956. A year later, the Abbey produced his second play, *A Leap in the Dark,* and in March 1958 the Globe Theatre produced his charming farce *Madigan's Lock.* In 1959, Leonard left the civil service and moved to England where he was a contract writer for Granada television. For television, he has written many original plays, as well as a broadly farcical series called *Me Mammy* and numerous adaptations from writers as various as Dickens and Frank O'Connor.*

Many of the stage plays that Leonard wrote in the 1960s were also adaptations. Particularly notable were his *Stephen D* (1962), an extraordinarily theatrical version of Joyce's* *Portrait of the Artist;* his *Dublin One* (1963), taken from some of the stories in Joyce's *Dubliners;* and *When the Saints Go Cycling In* (1965), a droll reworking of the seemingly intractable dramatic material of Flann O'Brien's* *The Dalkey Archive.* Leonard's fascination with the technique of nineteenth-century French farce is apparent in *The Family Way* (194), an adaptation of Labiche's *Célimare.* In his own original Irish farce, *The Patrick Pearse Motel* (1971), Leonard's mastery of this tightly difficult form rivals that of his masters. Tending more to comedy than to farce was an Irish version of *Billy Liar,* under the title of *Liam Liar* (1976); and tending more to fantasy than to farce was the rather tedious *Time Was* (1976).

Leonard's serious original work includes *The Poker Session* (1963); *The Au Pair Man* (1966), a thoughtful allegory of England and Ireland; *Mick and Mick* (1966); and probably his best work, *Da* (1973), in which a successful writer confronts his dramatized memory of his dead and maddeningly selfless foster father. In many of Leonard's plays, one finds little emotional strength, but the character of Da is a well-rounded, compassionately observed, and warmly human creation.

In the early 1970s, Leonard returned to Ireland, partly to take advantage of the new tax laws for creative writers. Since then, he has written a humor colume, first for *Hibernia* and then for the *Irish Sunday Independent*. Originally somewhat adolescent in its preoccupations, the column is redeemed by its clever quips, barbed insults, and occasional genuine wit.

Undoubtedly, Leonard's prolific television writing has been an invaluable discipline in honing his craft; in technical expertise he is scarcely rivaled by any of his contemporaries. Indeed, in cleverness, facility in dialogue, and plot construction, Leonard is perhaps better equipped to create great plays than any present writer in Ireland. His prolific production over a twenty-year period has given the Irish stage a long succession of genuine entertainments, but it is perhaps this facile ability to be entertaining that has kept him from writing much of enduring substance. Of the works written during his first twenty years of constant work, only two or three plays would strongly warrant revival.

In the summer of 1978, *Da* was produced on Broadway, winning the Tony Award and the Drama Critics Circle Award as the best play of the year.

WORKS: *Stephen D*. London: Evans, 1963; *The Poker Session*. London: Evans, 1964; *Mick and Mick,* in *Plays and Players* 14 (December 1966): 31-46; *The Patrick Pearse Motel*. London: Samuel French, 1971; *The Au Pair Man*. New York: Samuel French, [1974]; *Da*. Newark, Del.: Proscenium, 1975; New York: Atheneum, 1978; *Leonard's Last Book*. Dublin: Egotist, 1978. (Essays); *Home Before Night*. London: Andre Deutsch, 1979. (Novel).

LESLIE, MARY ISABEL. *See* LANE, TEMPLE.

LESLIE, SIR SHANE (1885-1971), man of letters. Sir Shane Leslie, third baronet of Glaslough, was born John Randolph Leslie on September 24, 1885, at Castle Leslie in County Monaghan. He was educated at Eton and at King's College, Cambridge, where he became a Roman Catholic and assumed the name of Shane, an Irish version of John. After graduating in 1907, he journed to Russia where he met Tolstoy and became influenced by his social theories. In 1910, he stood as nationalist candidate for Derry, an incident portrayed in his autobiographical novel *Doomsland* (1923). In the remainder of his long and busy life, he published some forty volumes which included poetry, novels, short stories, memoirs, biographies, and nonfiction of various kinds. He was an extremely fluent writer and a member of the Irish Academy of Letters, but his major contribution to Irish literature is *Doomsland,* a *bildungsroman* of exceptional interest which has been most unfairly neglected. Much of his life was spent in England where he died on August 31, 1971, at Hove.

WORKS: *The Landlords of Ireland at the Cross-Roads*. Dublin: Duffy, 1908. (Pamphlet); *Songs of Oriel*. Dublin: Maunsel, 1908. (Poems); *Isle of Columbcille*. Dublin: Catholic Truth Society of Ireland, 1909; *Lough Derg in Ulster*. Dublin:

Maunsel, 1909; *A Sketch of the Oxford Movement.* Dublin: Catholic Truth Society
of Ireland, 1909; *The End of a Chapter.* London: Constable, 1916/revised, London:
Constable, 1917/revised & rewritten, London: Heinemann, 1929. (Autobiography);
Verses in Peace and War. London: Burns & Oates, 1916; *The Irish Issue in Its
American Aspect.* New York: Scribner's, 1917/London: T. Fisher Unwin, 1918;
The Story of St. Patrick's Purgatory. St. Louis, Mo., & London: B. Herder, 1917;
Henry Edward Manning, His Life and Labours. . . . London: Burns, Oates, 1921;
The Oppidan. London: Chatto & Windus, 1922. (Novel); *Doomsland.* London:
Chatto & Windus, 1923. (Novel); *Mary Sykes: His Life and Letters.* London: Cas-
sell, 1923; *Masquerades.* London: John Long, 1924; ed., *An Anthology of Catholic
Poetry.* London: Burns, Oates, 1925/revised, London: Burns, Oates, 1952; *The
Cantab.* 2d ed., revised, London: Chatto & Windus, 1926; *George the Fourth.* Lon-
don: Ernest Benn, 1926; *The Delightful, Diverting, and Devotional Play of Mrs.
Fitzherbert.* London: Ernest Benn, 1928; *The Poems of Shane Leslie.* London: Cayme,
1928; *The Skull of Swift.* Indianapolis: Bobbs-Merrill/London: Chatto & Windus,
1928; *The Anglo-Catholic.* London: Chatto & Windus, 1929. (Novel); *A Ghost in
the Isle of Wight.* London: E. Mathews & Marot, 1929. (Short story); *Lines Written
in the Month's Mind of Mona Dunn. Dec. 19, 1928—Jan. 19, 1929.* [London: C. H.
St. J. Hornby at the Ashendene Press, 1929]; *The Hyde Park Pageant.* [London]:
Fortune, 1930. (Verse pamphlet); *Jutland, a Fragment of Epic.* London: Ernest
Benn, 1930. (Poem); *Memoirs of John Edward Courtenay Bodley.* London, Toronto:
Jonathan Cape, 1930; ed., *St. Patrick's Purgatory, a Record from History and Literature.* London: Burns, Oates, 1932; *Studies in Sublime Failure.* London: Ernest Benn,
1932. (Biographies); *The Oxford Movement, 1833 to 1933.* London: Burns, Oates,
1933; *Poems and Ballads.* London: Ernest Benn, 1933; *The Passing Chapter.* London:
Cassell, 1934. (Autobiography); *Fifteen Odd Stories.* London: Hutchinson, [1935];
The Script of Jonathan Swift, and Other Essays. Philadelphia: University of Pennsyl-
vania Press, 1935; *American Wonderland.* London: Michael Joseph, 1936. (Travel);
Men Were Different . . . *Five Studies in Victorian Biography.* London: Michael
Joseph, 1937; *The Film of Memory.* London: Michael Joseph, 1938; *Sir Evelyn
Ruggles-Brise.* London: John Murray, 1938. (Biography); *Mrs. Fitzherbert.* London:
Burns, Oates, 1939. (Biography); *Poems from the North.* Dublin, 1945. (Pamphlet);
The Irish Tangle for English Readers. London: MacDonald, [1946]; *Salutation to
Five.* London: Hollis & Carter, 1951. (Biographies); *Cardinal Gasquet, a Memoir.*
London: Burns Oates, 1953; *Lord Mulroy's Ghost.* Dublin: At the Sign of the Three
Candles, [1954]. (Play); *Shane Leslie's Ghost Book.* London: Hollis & Carter,
1955; ed., *Edward Tennyson Reed, 1860-1933.* London: Heinemann, 1957. (Biog-
raphy); *Long Shadows.* London: Murray, 1966. (Autobiographical).

LETTS, WINIFRED M. (1882-?), poet, playwright, and fiction writer. Letts
was born in 1882 and was educated at St. Anne's Abbots, Bromley, and
at Alexandra College, Dublin. She was a masseuse, and she married W. H. F.
Verschoyle. In her later years, she lived in Faversham, Kent, and she may
have died in about 1950.

Letts wrote mostly of rural Leinster and, with less devotion, of its urban
center, Dublin. Occasionally sentimental but never stridently political, she
created poetry, fiction, stories for children, hagiography, a book of reminiscences titled *Knockmaroon* (1933), two one-act plays for the Abbey,*
and a three-act play, *Hamilton and Jones* (1941), for the Gate.* In her
Abbey play *The Eyes of the Blind* (1907), a murderer gives himself up

when a blind man claims knowledge of the covert crime. *The Challenge* (1909) tells of a duel between elderly men over a long-remembered insult. Her plays are of interest as artifacts of Abbey history. If she is remembered, it will be for her poetry and the wistful charm of *Knockmaroon*. It would be unrealistic to make any great claims for her poetry, although many of her pieces are rather better than the usual dialect poems about the peasant. Her ear seems more authentic; there are fewer clichés; there are touches of humor in her slum poems; and there are occasional touches of individuality, as in "For Sixpence" where she expresses her delight in the productions of the early Abbey Theatre.

WILLIAM J. FEENEY

WORKS: *The Mighty Army*. New York: F. A. Stokes, 1912. (Lives of Saints); "The Company of Saints and Angels." *Irish Review* 1 (January 1912): 537-544. (Short story); "The Challenge." *Irish Review* 2 (April 1912): 87-96. (Short story adaptation of her play of the same title); *Songs from Leinster*. London: J. Murray, 1913. (Poems); "The Man Who Burnt His Crucifix." *Irish Review* 4 (May 1914): 143-167. (Reprinted in *Knockmaroon*); *Halloween and Poems of the War*. London: Smith, Elder, 1916; *The Spires of Oxford and Other Poems*. New York: E. P. Dutton, 1917; *More Songs from Leinster*. London: J. Murray/New York: E. P. Dutton, 1926; *St. Patrick the Travelling Man*. London: J. Nicholson & Watson ,1932; *Knockmaroon*. London: J. Murray, 1933.

LEVER, CHARLES JAMES (1806-1872), novelist. Lever was born in Dublin on August 31, 1806, the son of an English architect and builder. He studied medicine at Trinity College and practiced that profession. He lived most of his life on the Continent and died in Trieste on June 1, 1872.

The popularity of the novel in the mid-nineteenth century brought fame to a number of writers who could accurately gauge popular tastes and produce what the public wanted on schedule. Such a writer was Charles Lever who was better than a hack, but because of his personal extravagance and lack of discipline, he only rarely reached his potential level of artistry.

Lever's first novel, *The Confessions of Harry Lorrequer* (1839), was a popular success on its first appearance in the *Dublin University Magazine*. That very immediate success probably harmed his literary career, for he never acquired the discipline required for greater art. He wrote too much, and too quickly, usually prompted to do so by financial debts resulting from gambling and extravagance. We must grant him candor for admitting as much, however. Late in life he described his work: "You ask me how I write. My reply is, just as I live—from hand to mouth."

As a result, although his collected works run to thirty-seven volumes, only a few of his novels are worth reading a century later. In addition to *Harry Lorrequer,* only *Charles O'Malley* (1841) and *The Martins of Cro-Martin* (1856) reveal his talents. His gift for comedy, his good ear for dialogue, and his sense of incongruities make those novels lively and amusing. He did not overwrite, but told stories directly and with some economy of style. As a result, the novels make their comic points easily. Lever was also skilled in the analysis of contemporary political situations. *The Martins* investigates the social consequences of the Emancipation Bill and reveals his ability to deal with the complexities of politics. Like his friend Trollope, he was interested in everyday politics and was a keen observer of manners. Furthermore, he was one of the first to treat the most important recent historical events in his novels; *Charles O'Malley* is set during the Napoleonic Wars. Having lived much of his life in Brussels and elsewhere on the continent, he had accurate knowledge of such events.

Lever was an appealing man, a friend of the leading novelists of the day —Dickens, Thackeray, and Trollope. But the chaos of his life, the fact that he seemed constantly to be seeking preferment in order to pay off his debts, is reflected in his works as well. They seem facile, in need of rewriting and close to the surface. Only occasionally does he attempt more than the mere amusement of his readers. In those few works, however, he reveals the wit, style, broad knowledge, and awareness of human personality which could have made him a greater writer. The comparison with Trollope reveals his gifts as well as his failings. Trollope analyzes familiar, even universal conflicts after parading his caricatures and showing his wit; Lever rarely gets beyond artifice.

JAMES KILROY

WORKS: *The Confessions of Harry Lorrequer.* Dublin: W. Curry, June & Co./ Edinburgh: Fraser & Crawford, 1839; *Charles O'Malley, the Irish Dragoon.* 2 vols. Dublin: W. Curry, 1841; *Our Mess; Jack Hinton, the Guardsman.* Dublin: W. Curry, 1843; *Arthur O'Leary.* 2 vols. London: Colburn, 1844; *Tom Burke of "Ours."* 2 vols. Dublin: W. Curry, 1844; *Nuts and Nutcrackers.* London: Orr/Dublin: Curry, 1845, *The O'Donoghue.* Dublin: W. Curry, 1845; *St. Patrick's Eve.* London: Chapman & Hall, 1845; *Tales of the Trains.* London: W. S. Orr/Dublin: W. Curry, 1845; *The Knight of Gwynne.* London: Chapman & Hall, 1847; *Diary and Notes of Horace Templeton, Esq.* 2 vols. London: Chapman & Hall, 1848; *Confessions of Con Cregan, the Irish Gil Blas.* London: W. S. Orr, ca. 1850; *Maurice Tiernay, the Soldier of Fortune.* London: Hodgson, ca. 1850; *Roland Cashel.* London: Chapman & Hall, 1850; *The Daltons.* 2 vols. London: Chapman & Hall, 1852; *The Dodd Family Abroad.* London: Chapman & Hall, 1854; *Sir Jasper Carew.* London: T. Hodgson, ca. 1854; *The Martins of Cro' Martin.* London: Chapman & Hall, 1856; *The Fortunes of Glencore.* 3 vols. London: Chapman & Hall, 1857; *Davenport Dunn.* London: Chapman & Hall, 1859; *Gerald Fitzgerald.* New York: Harper, ca. 1859; *One of Them.* London: Chapman & Hall, 1861; *A Day's Ride.* London: Chapman & Hall, 1862; *Barrington.* London: Chapman & Hall, 1863; *Luttrell of Aran.* London: Chapman & Hall, 1865; *Tony Butler.* London & Edinburgh: Blackwood, 1865; *Cornelius O'Dowd.* 3 vols. Edinburgh & London: Blackwood, 1864-1865; *Sir Brook Fossbrooke.* 3 vols. Edinburgh & London: Blackwood, 1866; *The Bramleighs of Bishop's Folly.* 3 vols. London: Smith, Elder, 1868; *Paul Goslett's Confessions.* London: Virtue, 1868; *A Rent in a Cloud.* London: Chapman & Hall, 1869; *That Boy of Norcott's.* London: Smith, Elder, 1869; *Lord Kilgoblin.* 3 vols. London: Smith, Elder, 1872; *The Novels of Charles Lever,* ed. by his daughter, Julia Kate Neville. 37 vols. London: Downey, 1897-1899.   REFERENCES: Downey Edmund. *Charles Lever: His Life in His*

Letters. 2 vols. London: Blackwood, 1906; Stevenson, Lionel. *Dr. Quicksilver: The Life of Charles Lever.* London: Chapman & Hall/New York: Russell & Russell, 1939.

LIDDY, JAMES (1934-), poet. Liddy's grandfather, Daniel Reeves, immigrated to America where he started the first chain of grocery stores in New York before dying at age thirty-six in 1910. Liddy's mother was born in New York but returned to Ireland where James was born on July 1, 1934. He was raised in County Clare. Liddy was trained as a barrister and practiced law in Ireland until the mid-1960s when he decided to devote himself to writing.

At the heart of Liddy's poetry is an uncompromising commitment to love, but it is love in opposition to traditional attitudes. The kind of love Liddy acknowledges in his work is paradoxical and contradictory. It includes a recognition of anguish, pain, and evil, as well as an unapologetic delight in sexual pleasure. The work of William Blake, particularly *The Marriage of Heaven and Hell* (which Liddy parodies in *Corca Bascinn,* 1977), seems to have had a real impact on Liddy's imagination. Throughout *Baudelaire's Bar Flowers* (a book of translations and reworkings of Baudelaire), Liddy associates love and sex with Hell and Satan. He writes that "evil redeems good" (p. 17), echoing Blake's beliefs that "Evil is the active springing from Energy" and the "true Poet" is "of the Devil's party."

With Blake, and with his friend and mentor Patrick Kavanagh,* Liddy also shares an unswerving hostility to bourgeois values. From his earliest publication, *Esau, My Kingdom for a Drink* (1962), Liddy began attacking the "phoneyness and lies" (p. 10) around him. The world is ". . . a prison / Run by elderly bores . . ." (*Blue Mountain,* 1968, p. 9) and bureaucrats who stand in the way of "the revolution we imagine / in which each of us will love / the other . . ." (*In a Blue Smoke,* 1964, p. 13).

Liddy's relationship with Kavanagh illustrates his attraction to an intensified kind of friendship in which his taste for "Conversation, unusual people, a casual life" (*Blue Mountain,* p. 23) is honored. In his later poetry, he increasingly rejects the standards of "straight" society in favor of homosexuality. In *A Munster Song of Love and War,* his "gay" sensibility starts to emerge more openly in the poems. By *Corca Bascinn* he calls himself a "wandering pervert" (p. 45).

In *A Life of Stephen Dedalus,* Liddy bids "Irish poets" to leave "the paraphernalia" of "literature" out of their work. He is not comfortable with what he calls elsewhere the "beautiful and decorative" language of Yeats* ("Open Letter to the Young about Patrick Kavanagh," *The Lace Curtain,* p. 55, Dublin, No. 1, n.d.). In Yeats' work, "There are flourishes brilliantly rhymed and stanza'd . . .", but Liddy finds the work impersonal and "evasive" (ibid.). He is drawn to poems of "emotional intelligence" in which the "language and imagery are clear and evocative yet mysterious . . ."

(ibid., p. 56). Liddy's poems are written in a language of heightened conversation. They are often flat, stark poems. He rejects the idea of "the poem waiting there to be put together by the Department of English grammatical kit" in favor of "responsibility to the poem," in which the poem is founded on its allegiance to the imagination (*Baudelaire's Bar Flowers,* p. 23).

                                                              TERENCE WINCH

WORKS: *Esau, My Kingdom for a Drink.* Dublin: Dolmen, [1962]; *In a Blue Smoke.* Dublin: Dolmen, Philadelphia: Dufour, [1964]; *Blue Mountain.* Dublin: Dolmen, Chester Springs, Pa.: Dufour, 1968; with Jim Chapson & Thomas Hill, *Blue House: Poems in the Chinese Manner.* Honolulu: Nine Beasts Press, [ca. 1968]; *A Life of Stephen Dedalus.* San Francisco: White Rabbit Press, 1969; *A Munster Song of Love and War.* San Francisco: White Rabbit Press, 1971; *Homage to Patrick Kavanagh.* Dublin: New Writers', 1971. (Poetry pamphlet); *Corca Bascinn.* Dublin: Dolmen, 1977.

LONGFORD, LADY (1900-), playwright and woman of letters. Lady Longford's reputation has never been great outside of her adopted Ireland, but she is a sophisticated and accomplished novelist, as well as an able and prolific playwright.

She was born Christine Patti Trew in 1900 in Chedder, Somerset. She attended Somerset College, Oxford, and received an M.A. She married Edward Pakenham,* the sixth earl of Longford, and has subsequently resided in Ireland. Her husband became one of the backers of the Gate Theatre* and then in 1936 founded his own company which lasted until his death in 1961. For the Gate Theatre, and then for her husband's company, Lady Longford wrote many plays, including translations of the Greek classics, adaptations of English and Irish novels, original Irish historical plays, and contemporary comedies of Irish life. Of these more than twenty plays, only some of the histories and comedies have been published. The histories are generally less interesting. *Lord Edward* (Longford Productions, 1941) is merely competent, but *The United Brothers* (Longford Productions, 1944) has been called "as vivid and accomplished a historical play as any dramatist has written in modern Ireland."

Lady Longford's dramatic forte, however, is in genially satiric comedies of contemporary life, of which the best may be *Mr. Jiggins of Jigginstown* (Gate, 1933), a witty fantasy adapted from her own novel, and *The Hill of Quirke* (Longford Productions, 1953), which is about the efforts to plan for a civic festival in a small town.

Of her novels, which appear to be more substantial and lasting work, two might be singled out as indicating her range. *Making Conversation* (1931) is a sensitive and subtle exercise in the vein of Virginia Woolf, and *Country Places* (1932) seems almost an Irish version of Evelyn Waugh. Her close involvement with the running of a theatre may have prevented her from developing her bent toward fiction as well as a more individual voice, but her intelligence and craft are deserving of a much wider audience.

WORKS: *Vespasian and Some of His Contemporaries*. Dublin: Hodges, Figgis, 1928. (Nonfiction); *Making Conversation*. London: Stein & Gollancz, 1931. (Novel); *Country Places*. London: Gollancz, 1932. (Novel); *Mr. Jiggins of Jigginstown*. London: V. Gollancz, 1933. (Novel); *Printed Cotton*. London: Methuen, 1935. (Novel); *A Biography of Dublin*. London: Methuen, 1936. (Nonfiction); *Mr. Jiggins of Jigginstown* in *Plays of Changing Ireland*. Curtins Canfield, ed. New York Macmillan, 1936. (Play); *Lord Edward*. Dublin: Hodges, Figgis, 1941. (Play); *The United Brothers*. Dublin: Hodges, Figgis, 1942. (Play); *Patrick Sarsfield*. Dublin: Hodges, Figgis, 1943. (Play); *The Earl of Straw*. Dublin: Hodges, Figgis, 1945. (Play); *The Hill of Quirke*. Dublin: P. J. Bourke, 1958. (Play); *Mr. Supple, or Time Will Tell*. Dublin: P. J. Bourke, n.d. (Play); *Tankardstown*. Dublin: P. J. Bourke, n.d. (Play).   REFERENCE: Hogan, Robert. *After the Irish Renaissance*. Minneapolis: University of Minnesota Press, 1967. 126-132.

LONGFORD, LORD (1902-1961), playwright and translator. The sixth Earl of Longford was a theatrical producer, a playwright, and a translator from the Irish. He was born Edward Arthur Henry Pakenham on December 29, 1902, into a family which had been in Ireland from the middle of the seventeenth century. He was educated at Eton and then at Christ Church, Oxford, where he received an M.A. in 1925. In 1931, he became closely involved with the Gate Theatre* which produced a number of his original plays and translations. In 1936, he formed his own independent production company, Longford Productions, whose repertoire for many years consisted primarily of classic plays staged at the Gate Theatre. He served in the Irish Senate from 1946 to 1948; he was a member of the Irish Academy of Letters; and he received a D. Litt. from Dublin University in 1954. He died on February 4, 1961, in Dublin.

Longford translated a good deal from the Irish, including a version of Brian Merriman's *The Midnight Court*. His work for the theatre included *The Melians* (1931), *Yahoo* (1933), *Ascendancy* (1935), *The Armlet of Jade* (1936), *Carmilla*, after Le Fanu* (1937), and *The Vineyard* (1943). With Lady Longford* he translated *The Oresteia*; alone he translated Sophocles, Euripides, Calderon, Molière, and Beaumarchais. Longford's great contribution to the theatre was his own worthy production which existed until his death. His own work for the stage will not for the most part bear revival. One possible exception is his version of the Swift* story, *Yahoo*, which has an effective expressionistic conclusion.

WORKS: *A Book of Poems*. London: Privately printed by Bumpus, 1920; *The Oresteia of Aischylos*, with Christine Longford. Dublin: Hodges, Figgis, 1933; *Yahoo*. Dublin: Hodges, Figgis, 1934/reprinted in Curtis Canfield's *Plays of Changing Ireland*, New York: Macmillan, 1936; *Armlet of Jade*. Dublin: Hodges, Figgis, 1935. (Play); *Ascendancy*. Dublin: Hodges, Figgis, 1935. (Play); *The Vineyard*. Dublin: Hodges, Figgis, 1943. (Play); *Poems from the Irish*. Dublin: Hodges, Figgis, 1944; *More Poems from the Irish*. Dublin: Hodges, Figgis, 1945; *The Dove in the Castle*. Dublin: Hodges, Figgis, 1946. (Translations from the Irish); *The School for Wives*, by Molière. Dublin: Hodges, Figgis, 1948; *The Midnight Court*, by Brian Merriman in *Poetry Ireland*, No. 6 (July 1949).   REFERENCES: *Longford Productions: Dublin Gate Souvenir, 1949*. Dublin: Corrigan & Wilson, 1949.

LONGLEY, MICHAEL (1939-), poet. Longley was born in Belfast in 1939 and was educated at the Royal Belfast Academical Institution and Trinity College, Dublin, where he studied classics. He has published three collections of poetry—*No Continuing City* (1969), *An Exploded View* (1973), and *Man Lying on a Wall* (1976); his hope was to complete his next book, *The Linen Industry*, in 1978. He is also one of the three poets featured in *Penguin Modern Poets 26* (1975). The editor of that collection, Anthony Thwaite, has written that Longley is "the most promising new voice in the province." Longley is presently literature director of the Arts Council of Northern Ireland, for whom he edited *Under the Moon*: *Over the Stars* (1971), an anthology of children's verse, and *Causeway* (1971), a survey of the arts in Ulster. He and his wife Edna Longley, the literary critic, are working on the official biography of Louis MacNeice.*

Though Longley is not as well known as some of his contemporaries, his poetry has received the serious consideration of reviewers and critics. D.E.S. Maxwell, in *Two Decades of Irish Writing* (Douglas Dunn, ed., 1975), praises Longley's "technical command" of language, and Terence Brown in *Northern Voices* (1975) expresses particular admiration for the "economy of statement" and the "hard-edged clarity of image and diction" in *An Exploded View*. The *Times Literary Supplement* praised Longley's first book for its "tight formal discipline," and when his second book appeared, it referred to Longley as a "distinctive and accomplished poet."

Most critics applaud Longley's technical accomplishments, but occasionally they are less satisfied with his subject matter. Some claim he focuses too much on the objective, giving insufficient attention to his subjective experiences. But Longley does express significant relationships between subjective and objective matters. In "The Ornithological Section," for example, he begins with a fine and exact description of stuffed birds, and then captures the relation between those birds and ourselves. Poems combining skillful description and insight are easily found in Longley's collections.

Sometimes critics demand more than skill and insight, however; they like to prescribe subject matter as well. For example, Tom McGurk in *Hibernia* says: "Exceptionally, Longley produced some of the few memorable poems about the situation in Ulster, and this new collection *Man Lying on a Wall* seems all the weaker for lack of a follow-up." One of these memorable poems concerns the death of a bus-conductor:

> He collapsed beside his carpet-slippers
> Without a murmur, shot through the head
> By a shivering boy who wandered in
> Before they could turn the television down
> Or tidy away the supper dishes.
> To the children, to a bewildered wife,
> I think "Sorry Missus" was what he said.

What else can be said either by a shivering boy or by a poet? We can't expect either to delineate plans for politicial action. Once a poet portrays the futility of a situation, why should we expect continued variations on a theme? A poet's subject is basically his own affair. And critics are best when they speak of skill more than subject, as Peter Porter does in reference to Longley's last volume. "It is a pleasure to read a poet who bends words to his will and does so without sweating blood or syntax" (*Observer*).

KATHLEEN DANAHER PARKS

WORKS: *No Continuing City*. London: Macmillan, 1969; ed., *Causeway*. Belfast: Arts Council of Northern Ireland, 1971; ed., *Under the Moon: Over the Stars*. Belfast: Arts Council of Northern Ireland, 1971; *An Exploded View*. London: Gollancz, 1973; *Man Lying on a Wall*. London: Gollancz, 1976.   REFERENCE: Allen, Michael. "Options: The Poetry of Michael Longley." *Éire-Ireland* 10 (Winter 1975): 129-136.

LOVER, SAMUEL (1797-1868), novelist, dramatist, song-writer, and painter. Lover was born on February 24, 1797, in Dublin, the eldest son of a Dublin stockbroker. He was a precocious child who was educated privately and who quite early demonstrated considerable talent both in music and in art. At the age of seventeen, he began to earn his living as a painter and was extremely successful, particularly as a miniaturist. The third string to his bow was literature, and he was equally at ease in several genres. For instance, he transformed his popular ballad "Rory O'More" (1826) into a popular novel and then into an equally popular play.

He was one of the founders of *The Dublin University Magazine* in 1833. After he removed to London in 1835, he became well known in literary and artistic circles, and with Dickens and others he founded *Bentley's Miscellany*.

His plays, especially *Rory O'More* (1837), *The White Horse of the Peppers* (1838), *The Happy Man* (1839) as well as his musical dramas and burlesque operas were popular fare in their day but have not held the stage.

After 1844, failing eyesight caused him to abandon painting, and he took to public recitals of his work in the manner of Dickens. His "Irish Evenings," as he called them, were as successful in the United States and Canada as they were in England.

Despite his fluency in all he attempted, Lover is most remembered for his fiction. His *Legends and Stories of Ireland* (1831), *Rory O'More* (1837), and, above all, *Handy Andy* (1842) are his most enduring productions. His Handy Andy is the great, amiable, awkward, moronic lout of Irish literature. But if he is exaggerated beyond the probabilities of reality, so it might also be said are Mr. Micawber and Mrs. Gamp. Despite its broadness, the book is genial, unforced good fun.

He died at St. Heliers, Jersey, on July 6, 1868.

WORKS: *Legends and Stories of Ireland*. 1st Series. Dublin: Wakeman, 1831; *The Parson's Horn Book*. Dublin: Printed & sold at the office of *The Comet*, 1831. (Illustrations & probably some of the satiric poems were by Lover); *Legends and*

Stories of Ireland. 2d Series. London: Baldwin, 1834; *Popular Tales and Legends of the Irish Peasantry.* Dublin: Wakeman, 1834; *Rory O'More, a National Romance.* 3 vols. London: Bentley & Sons, 1837; *Rory O'More.* London: Dick's Standard Plays, 1837. (Adaptation in three acts of the novel); *The White Horse of the Peppers.* London: Acting National Drama, 1838. (Comic drama in 2 acts); *The Hall Porter.* London: Acting National Drama, 1839. (Comic drama in 2 acts); *The Happy Man.* London: Acting National Drama, 1839. (Extravaganza in 1 act); *Songs and Ballads.* London: Chapman & Hall, 1839; *English Bijou Almanack for 1840.* London: A. Schloss, 1840; *The Greek Boy.* London: Acting National Drama, 1840. (Musical drama in 2 acts); *Il Paddy Whack in Italia.* London: Duncombe's British Theatre, 1841. (Operetta in 1 act); *Handy Andy.* London: F. Lover, 1842/London: Dent, 1954; *Mr. Lover's Irish Evenings: The Irish Brigade.* London: Johnson, 1844. (Poem); *Treasure Trove.* London: F. Lover, 1844; *Characteristic Sketches of Ireland and the Irish.* Dublin: P. D. Hardy, 1845; *Barney the Baron.* London: Dick's Standard Plays, 1850. (Farce in 1 act); ed., *The Lyrics of Ireland.* London: Houlston & Wright, 1858; *Metrical Tales and Other Poems.* London: Houlston & Wright, 1860; *Mac Carthy More.* London: Lacy, 1861. (Comic drama in 2 acts); with Charles Mackay & Thomas Miller, *Original Songs for the Rifle Volunteers.* London: C. H. Clarke, 1861. REFERENCES: Bernard, W. B. *The Life of S. Lover, R. H. A., Artistic, Literary and Musical.* 2 vols. London: H. S. King, 1874; Symington, A. J. *Samuel Lover.* London: Blackie, 1880.

LYNCH, PATRICIA [NORA] (1900-1972), writer of children's books. Lynch was born in Cork on June 7, 1900, and was educated in convent schools in Ireland, England, and Belgium. On October 31, 1922, she married R[ichard] M[ichael] Fox, the journalist and historian. Her first book for children, *The Cobbler's Apprentice*, was published in 1932, and she was to publish about fifty more similar volumes. Her books have been greatly popular, translated into many languages, and won a number of awards. The pleasantest among them, perhaps, are the Turf-Cutter's Donkey series of books, the Brogeen the leprechaun series, *Orla of Burren*, and *The Bookshop on the Quay*. However, Lynch preserved such a constant standard of quality, that any such listing is bound to seem arbitrary and personal. She possessed such a supple and lucid prose style, such a keen ability to tell a swiftly moving story, and such a cosy and delightful sense of the pleasures of the home, the hearth, and the table that many of her books have given as much pleasure to adults as they have to children. Her *Storyteller's Holiday* (1947), a somewhat fictionalized recreation of her own girlhood, is perhaps an adult's best general introduction to her work. The first hundred pages before Patricia Nora leaves Ireland are a droll, vivid, almost enchanting recollection of childhood. If one has any reservation about Lynch's underplayed, minor, but genuine talent, it would only be the mild surprise about the extraordinary amount of eating in her books. With Maura Laverty,* she must be one of the most food-obsessed writers in all of Irish literature. She died on September 1, 1972, in Dublin.

JANE HEALY

WORKS: *The Green Dragon.* London: Harrap, [1925]; *The Turf-cutter's Donkey.*

London & Toronto: Dent/New York: E. P. Dutton, 1935; *The Turf-cutter's Donkey Goes Visiting*. London: Dent, 1935/published in the United States as *The Donkey Goes Visiting*. New York: E. P. Dutton, [1936]. *King of the Tinkers*. London: Dent, 1938; *The Grey Goose of Kilnevin*. London: Dent, [1939]; *Fiddler's Quest*. London: Dent, 1941; *Long Ears*. London: Dent, 1943; *Strangers at the Fair, and Other Stories*. Dublin: Browne & Nolan, [1945]; *Knights of God*. London: Hollis & Carter, [1946]/ Chicago: H. Regnery, 1955/London & Sudney: Bodley Head, 1967/New York: Holt, Rinehart & Winston, [1969]; *The Turf-cutter's Donkey Kicks Up His Heels*. Dublin: Browne & Nolan, 1946; *Brogeen of the Stepping Stones*. London: Kerr-Cross, 1947; *The Cobbler's Apprentice*. London: Hollis & Carter, 1947; *A Storyteller's Childhood*. London: Dent, [1947]. (Autobiography); *The Mad O'Haras*. London: Dent, [1948]; *Lisheen at the Valley Farm, and Other Stories*. [Dublin: Gayfield, 1949]; *The Seventh Pig, and Other Irish Fairy Tales*. London: Dent, [1950]. *The Dark Sailor of Youghal*. London: Dent, [1951]; *The Boy at the Swinging Lantern*. London: Dent, [1952]; *Brogeen Follows the Magic Tune*. London: Burke, [1952]; *Grania of Castle O'Hara*. Boston: L. C. Page, [1952]; *Tales of Irish Enchantment*. Dublin: Clonmore & Reynolds, [1952]; *Brogeen and the Green Shoes*. London: Burke, [1953]; *Delia Daly of Galloping Green*. London: Dent, [1953]; *Brogeen and the Bronze Lizard*. London: Burke, [1954]/New York: Macmillan, [1970]; *Orla of Burren*. London: Dent, [1954]; *Brogeen and the Princess of Sheen*. London: Burke, [1955]; *Tinker Boy*. London: Dent, [1955]; *The Bookshop on the Quay*. London: Dent, [1956]; *Brogeen and the Lost Castle*. [London]: Burke, [1956]; *Cobbler's Luck*. London: Burke, [1957]; *Fiona Leaps the Bonfire*. London: Dent, [1957]; *Brogeen and the Black Enchanter*. London: Burke, [1958]; *The Old Black Sea Chest*. London: Dent, [1958]; *Shane Comes to Dublin*. New York: Criterion Books, [1958]; *The Black Goat of Slievemore, and Other Irish Fairy Tales*. London: Dent, [1959]; *Jimmy and the Changeling*. London: Dent, [1959]; *The Runaways*. Oxford: Blackwell, 1959; *The Stone House at Kilgobbin*. [London]: Burke, [1959]; *The Lost Fisherman of Carrigmore*. London: Burke, 1960; *Sally from Cork*. London: Dent. [1960]; *The Longest Way Round*. London: Burke ,1961; *Ryan's Fort*. London: Dent, 1961; *The Golden Caddy*. London: Dent, [1962]; *Brogeen and the Little Wind*. New York: Roy Publishers, [1963]; *Brogeen and the Red Fez*. London: Burke, 1963; *The House by Lough Neugh*. London: Dent, 1963; *Guests at the Beach Tree*. London: Burke, 1964; *Holiday at Rosquin*. London: Dent, [1964]; *The Twisted Key, and Other Stories*. London: Harrap, 1964; *Mona of the Isle*. London: Dant, 1965; *The Kerry Caravan*. London: Dent. 1967.

LYND, ROBERT [WILSON] (1879-1949), essayist and journalist. Lynd, born in Belfast on April 20, 1879, was the son of a Presbyterian minister. He graduated from Queen's College in 1899 (and also received a D.Litt. from there in 1946). In 1901, he went to England and worked on *The Daily Dispatch* in Manchester. Then as a free-lance journalist in London, he shared a studio for a while in Kensington with Paul Henry, the artist. In 1908, he joined the *London Daily News*, became literary editor in 1912, and remained in that position until near the end of his life. His best work was done under the pseudonym of "Y. Y." which he used in *The New Statesman* for a long series of light essays. His popularity in this decreasingly popular genre was immense, and, although he lacked Chesterton's wit and individuality, he wrote with charm, urbanity, and good sense. He was a fervent Irish nationalist and a sound, if unacademic, guide to literature. He published about thirty-five books and collections of his fugitive material, and he died in Hampstead on October 6, 1949.

WORKS: *Irish and English*. London: Francis Griffiths, 1908; *Home Life in Ireland*. London: Mills & Boon, 1909; *Rambles in Ireland*. London: Mills & Boon, 1912; *The Book of This and That*. London: Mills & Boon, 1915; *If the Germans Conquered England*. Dublin & London: Maunsel, 1917; *Ireland a Nation*. London: Grant Richards, 1919; *The Art of Letters*. London: Unwin, 1920; *The Passion of Labour*. London: G. Bell, 1920; *Books and Authors*. London: Richard Dobden-Sanderson, [1922]/London: Jonathan Cape, 1929; *Solomon in All His Glory*. London: Grant Richards, 1922; *The Sporting Life and Other Trifles*. London: Grant Richards, 1922; *The Blue Lion, and Other Essays*. London: Methuen, 1923; *The Peal of Bells*. London: Methuen, 1924; *The Pleasures of Ignorance*. London: Methuen, 1924; *The Money Box*. London: Methuen, 1925; *The Little Angel*. London: Methuen, 1926; *The Orange Tree*. London: Methuen, 1926; *The Goldfish*. London: Methuen, 1927; *The Green Man*. London: Methuen, 1928; *It's a Fine World*. London: Methuen, 1930; *Rain, Rain, Go to Spain*. London: Methuen, 1931; *An Anthology of Essays*, under the pseudonym of "Y. Y." London: Methuen, 1933; *The Cockleshell*. London: Methuen, 1933; *Both Sides of the Road*. London: Methuen, 1934; *I Tremble to Think*. London: Dent, 1936; *Searchlights and Nightingales*. London: Dent, 1939; *Life's Little Oddities*. London: Dent, 1941; *Things One Hears*. London: Dent, 1945; *Essays on Life and Literature*. London: Dent/New York: E. P. Dutton, 1951; *Books and Writers*. London: Dent, 1952.

LYRIC PLAYERS THEATRE, THE (1951-). Belfast's Lyric Players Theatre was inaugurated in 1951 in the drawing room of Mary O'Malley and her husband Dr. Pearse O'Malley in Lisburn Road. The initial productions were three poetic plays by Yeats,* Robert Farren,* and Austin Clarke.* For the first sixteen years or so of its existence, the theatre produced mainly plays which were either in verse or at least rich in language. In 1952, the O'Malleys moved to Derryvolgie Avenue and erected a tiny stage at the back of their house. There, for the next sixteen years, were presented an astonishing repertoire of about 180 plays, including all of Yeats' plays, as well as Irish work by Synge,* Shaw,* O'Casey,* Lady Gregory,* Denis Johnston,* Donagh MacDonagh,* Valentin Iremonger,* Samuel Beckett,* Brian Friel,* Eugene McCabe,* and others. These Irish pieces were intermingled with plays from world drama by Aristophanes, Euripides, Shakespeare, Schiller, Ibsen, Chekhov, Lorca, O'Neill, Eliot, Fry, Brecht, and others. Meticulous attention was paid to staging; Yeats himself would have approved of Mrs. O'Malley's principle that "Scenery and costumes are simple and nonrealistic, and each play is designed to a narrow colour-scheme . . . expressive of its particular atmosphere." At the same time, the theatre branched out into other areas of the arts: it held art exhibitions and sponsored lectures, recitals, and even a drama school.

One of the finest byproducts of the theatre was its literary magazine, *Threshold*, which began as a quarterly on February 1957 and was edited by Mrs. O'Malley until 1961. Thereafter, it has appeared much more intermittently under the changing editorship of various writers such as Roy

McFadden,* Seamus Heaney,* John Montague,* John Boyd,* and Patrick Galvin.* The magazine has published many of the significant contemporary Irish writers, both North and South, and is particularly notable for its twenty-first number, which was a fine collection of Ulster writing. Also of special interest were its twenty-seventh number, which was devoted to three new plays by Patrick Galvin, and its twenty-eighth number, which focused on Forrest Reid.*

In 1960, the group became a nonprofit association and opened a drive for funds to build a real theatre. The cornerstone was laid for that theatre in 1965, and the theatre, seating three hundred, opened on October 26, 1968. Despite the Northern Troubles and Mrs. O'Malley's withdrawal in the 1970s, the theatre has continued to function and now receives a substantial subsidy from the Northern Arts Council. Nevertheless, any theatre, no matter how well subsidized, must fill seats; and some recent productions have had more popular appeal than poetic merit.

REFERENCE: Bell, Sam Hanna. *The Theatre in Ulster*. Dublin: Gill & Macmillan, 1972, 114-124, 140-147.

LYSAGHT, EDWARD (1763-ca. 1810), poet. Lysaght was born at Brickhill, County Clare, on December 21, 1763, and was educated at Trinity College, Dublin, and at Oxford. He practiced law without much success in London, but then returned to Dublin where he was for a while quite successful at law and where he spent the last thirteen years of his life. He was engaged in Irish politics and strongly opposed the Act of Union, but was even better known as a wit and *bon vivant* than as a barrister and politician. He died impoverished, but was so popular that a subscription of more than £2000 was collected for his wife and family. In 1909, a Dublin newspaper gave the date of his death as February 28, 1809, but it seems more likely that he died in 1810 or even 1811.

Lysaght was a rhymster rather than a poet, and much of his work seems dashed off to delight a drawing room rather than to impress posterity. As such, his poor work is always better than vile, and his good work is so extremely deft that he was credited with writing a number of popular pieces that he probably did not—such as "The Rakes of Mallow," "Donnybrook Fair," and "Kitty of Coleraine." The last stanza of his "My Ambition" is nicely droll; his satiric "A Prospect" on the Act of Union contains one verse worthy of Swift*; and his poem on Grattan,* "The Man Who Lead the Van of Irish Volunteers," is a rousing good public piece with a rattling meter and a complex and charming pattern of internal rhyme and rhyme. Perhaps the first stanza of his "Sweet Chloe" might stands as an example of how deft a technician he was:

> Sweet Chloe advised me, in accents divine,
>   The joys of the bowl to surrender;
> Nor lose, in the turbid excesses of wine,

> Delights more exstatic and tender;
> She bade me no longer in vineyards to bask,
> Or stagger, at orgies, the dupe of a flask,
> For the sigh of a sot's but the scent of the cask,
> And a bubble the bliss of the bottle.

He was the godfather of Sydney Owenson, Lady Morgan.*

WORK: *Poems.* Dublin: Gilbert & Hodges, 1811.

LYSAGHT, S[IDNEY] R[OYSE] (ca. 1860-1941), novelist and man of letters. Lysaght was born near Mallow, County Cork, probably in the early 1860s. A good deal of his early life can be inferred from his autobiographical novel, *My Tower in Desmond* (1925). Like the novel's hero, Lysaght went into business and devoted the greater part of his life to the South Wales iron firm of John Lysaght, Ltd. Despite his apparent success in business, Lysaght's real interest was letters, and he managed to write a good deal, most of it with considerable fluency. His finest work is *My Tower in Desmond*, which has some effective evocation of place, particularly in the early sections. A somewhat romantic novel, nevertheless it is absorbing for its story and interesting for its rather dissociated view of the Irish Troubles. Lysaght's poetry is conventional and Edwardian without being memorable or striking, and his sympathies were thoroughly antimodern. In one uncharacteristically irascible passage in his poetic testament, "A Reading of Poetry," he roasts Pound, Eliot, the Sitwells, and Gertrude Stein ("a pure humbug"), and then concludes, "God help those who mistake the eruptive cacophony of Mr. James Joyce* for poetry." That essay appears in a collection called *A Reading of Life* (1936), in which much gracefully expressed love of beauty and faith in God walk hand in hand with the most appallingly reactionary remarks about racial inequality. Lysaght's other interesting volume is an unstageable 320-page play, entitled *The Immortal Jew* (1931). The interior monologues are written in bland verse, but the prose dialogues rise to some passages of real power. Lysaght died at Hazlewood, Mallow, County Cork, on August 20, 1941.

WORKS: *A Modern Ideal, a Dramatic Poem.* London: Kegan Paul, Trench, 1886; *The Marplot.* New York & London: Macmillan, 1893. (Novel); *One of the Grenvilles.* London: Macmillan, 1899. (Novel); *Poems of the Unknown Way.* London: Macmillan, 1901. *Her Majesty's Rebels.* London & New York: Macmillan, 1907. (Novel); *Horizons and Landmarks.* London: Macmillan, 1911. (Poems); *My Tower in Desmond.* New York: Macmillan, 1925. *The Immortal Jew.* London: Macmillan, 1931. (Closet drama); *A Reading of Poetry; an Essay.* London: Macmillan, 1934. *A Reading of Life.* London & New York: Macmillan, 1936.

MACARDLE, DOROTHY [MARGARET CALLAN] (1899-1958), historian, novelist, and playwright. Macardle was born in 1899 to Anglo-Irish parents. Nevertheless, she became an avid Republican and a close acquaintance of Éamon de Valera. She was educated at University College, Dublin, and taught at Alexandra College, where she is said to have been arrested by the British. Between the wars, she served as a journalist at the League of Nations in Geneva. Following World War II, she worked for the cause of displaced and refugee children, producing the documentary *Children of Europe: A Study of Liberated Countries, Their War-time Experiences, Their Reactions and Their Needs* (1949).

Macardle's most important historical work is *The Irish Republic* (1937), a carefully documented, massive account of the political aspects of the Revolution, concentrating on the 1912-1923 era. While admitting that the narrative is written from the viewpoint of an Irish Republican, Macardle has consulted non-Republican and British authorities in an attempt at fairness and accuracy. In his preface to the work, de Valera heralds it as a "complete and authoritative record." He notes further that Macardle's "interpretations and conclusions are her own" and are sometimes at variance with his. A related political work is *Without Fanfares: Some Reflections on the Republic of Éire* (1946).

The human impact of the revolutionary period is studied by Macardle in several short stories written in Mountjoy and Kilmainham prisons and later collected in *Earth-Bound: Nine Stories of Ireland* (1924). The realistically portrayed situations include the midwinter cross-country evasion of the Black and Tans by two escaped prisoners, a young rebel's sacrifice of his life to prevent the capture of his "Chief," the hallucinatory experiences of a hunger-striking prisoner, and the troubling premonitions of a revolutionary's wife. Frequently, the ghosts of recent companions or heroes from former Irish uprisings make mystical interventions, saving the day. Supernatural visions also intrude into Macardle's nonpolitical stories about rural parish priests, a child nearly lost to the fairies, and a selfish, eccentric painter—a character type that reappears in Macardle's novels.

Macardle's plays include *Atonement* (1918), *The Old Man* (1925), *Witch's Brew* (1931), *The Loving Cup* (1943), and *Ann Kavanagh* (1937). The last-named drama, about the Rising of 1798 was first produced at the Abbey Theatre* on April 6, 1922. Like several of her stories, this play demonstrates the psychological stresses that revolutions impose on women. In this case, the heroine's compassion for the fugitive—be it her rebel husband or the spy he hunts—is stronger than political allegiances.

In her novels *The Uninvited* (1942; also filmed), *The Unforeseen* (1946; also published under the title *Fantastic Summer*), and *Dark Enchantment* (1953), Macardle places her characters in lonely situations, indulges extensively in the supernatural, an interest already detected in her stories, and manages to quiet the haunting forces and unite young couples in matrimony by the conclusion. An uninitiated heroine and a young hero concerned for her safety are usually featured characters. *The Uninvited* is a rather strung-out tale of double exorcism set in a haunted house on the North Devon cliffs. In *The Unforeseen*, the author explores a woman's gift of "precognition"—the power to have visions of future events—and the effects of this power on her own psyche and the lives of her daughter and their acquaintances. Macardle, aware of American research into ESP, hinges her plot on the difficulty of interpreting and acting on premonitions. This novel is set mostly in the Dublin hills near Glencree, near where Macardle spent much of her life. One of its strengths is the author's apparent interest in the Irish countryside, including the stone thrones of the Sugar Loafs, the churches of Glendalough, the woodland birds, and the itinerant tinkers. In *Dark Enchantment,* a busy novel set in the fictional village of St. Jacques in the Maritime Alps, Macardle studies the effects of a supposed sorceress on a superstitious village that seems at first to offer only relaxation and charm to a visiting Irish girl, her father, and a young student of forestry. All of Macardle's mystical mysteries are entertaining, but need not be taken as weighty fiction. Seemingly supernatural events often evoke very melodramatic reactions.

She died on December 23, 1958, in Drogheda.

BONNIE KIME SCOTT

WORKS: *Earth-bound: Nine Stories of Ireland.* Worcester, Mass.: Harrigan, 1924. (Short stories); *Tragedies of Kerry, 1922-23.* Dublin: Emton, [1924]; *Witch's Brew.* London: H. F. W. Deane, [1931]. (One-act play); *Ann Kavanagh.* New York: Samuel French, [1937]. (Play); *The Irish Republic.* London: Gollancz, 1937. (History); *The Children's Guest.* London: Oxford University Press, 1940. (One-act children's play); *Uneasy Freehold.* London: Peter Davies, [1942]/as *The Uninvited* in the United States, Garden City, N.Y.: Doubleday, Doran, 1942. (Novel); *The Loving-Cup.* London: Nelson, 1943. (One-act children's play); *The Seed Was Kind.* London: Peter Davies, 1944. (Novel); *Fantastic Summer.* London: Peter Davies, [1946]/as *The Unforeseen* in the United States, Garden City, N.Y.: Doubleday, 1946. (Novel); *Without Fanfares, Some Reflections on the Republic of Eire.* Dublin: Gill, 1946. (Pamphlet); *Children of Europe, A Study of the Children of Liberated Countries* . . . London: Gollancz, 1949/Boston: Beacon, 1951; *Shakespeare, Man and Boy.* George Bott, ed. London: Faber, 1961.

McCABE, EUGENE (1930-), playwright and fiction writer. McCabe was born in Glasgow on July 7, 1930, and was educated at Castleknock College in Dublin and at University College, Cork, where he took an arts degree. After graduation, McCabe dairy-farmed for ten years and did not turn to writing until 1962. In 1964, his *King of the Castle* won the first Irish Life Drama Award and was produced, with much acclaim, at the Theatre Festival. The play is a strong, realistic rural drama with a plot resembling that of Sidney Howard's *They Knew What They Wanted.* His later plays, *Breakdown* (1966) and a rather rambling *Swift* (1969), made less of an impact. In 1976, a trilogy of plays for television, dealing with the problems of the North, was extremely well received. McCabe published one section of the trilogy as a novelette entitled *Victims.* None of his plays has thus far been published, but he is generally regarded as one of the outstanding dramatic talents to emerge in the 1960s.

WORKS: *Victims*. London: Gollancz, 1977; *Heritage and Other Stories*. London: Gollancz, 1978.

McCALL, P[ATRICK] J[OSEPH] (1861-1919), poet and humorist. McCall was born in Dublin on March 6, 1861, and was educated at the Catholic University. He contributed both fictional sketches and poetry to the popular press around the turn of the century. As a popular writer, McCall was hardly considered a member of the Literary Revival, and some of his humorous retellings of the heroic stories were utterly opposed to its spirit. Nothing could be further from the manner and tone and spirit of Yeats'* misty and beautiful "The Wanderings of Oisin" (1889) than McCall's retelling of the stories in contemporary low dialect in *The Fenian Nights' Entertainment* (1897):

> "Well, me lad," says Fan, stoopin' for another [stone] as big as a hill, "I'm sorry I have to bate you; but I can't help it," sez he, lookin' over at the Prencess Maynish, an' she as mute as a mouse watchin' the two big men, an' the ould king showin' fair play, as delighted as a child. "Watch this," sez he, whirlin' his arm like a windmill, and away he sends the stone, buzzin' through the air like a peggin'-top, over the other three clochauns, and then across Dublin Bay, an' scrapin' the nose off ov Howth, it landed with a swish in the say beyant it. That's the rock they calls Ireland's Eye now!

McCall's verses are smoother than much popular verse, but that is about all that can be claimed for them. He wrote the song "Herself and Myself," which O'Casey* used in "Nannie's Night Out." His most popular song is "Boulavogue." He died in 1919.

WORKS: *In the Shadow of St. Patrick's* Dublin: Sealy, Bryers & Walker, 1894; *Irish Noinins (Daisies)*. Dublin: Sealy & Bryers, 1894; *The Fenian Nights' Entertainments*. Dublin: T. G. O'Donoghue, 1897; *Songs of Erin*. London: Simpkin, Marshall, 1899; *Pulse of the Bards*. Dublin: Gill, 1904; *Irish Fireside Songs*. Dublin: Gill, 1911.

McCANN, JOHN (1905-), playwright and politician. McCann was born in Dublin in 1905 and was educated by the Christian Brothers of Synge Street. He became a journalist and also wrote plays for Radio Éireann. In 1939, he was elected to the Dail, and in 1946-1947, he served as lord mayor of Dublin. In 1954, he lost his seat in the Dail, but by then his plays were being produced by the Abbey Theatre*. Such pieces as *Twenty Years A-Wooing* (1954), *Blood Is Thicker than Water* (1955), *Early and Often* (1956), and *Give Me a Bed of Roses* (1957) probably became the Abbey's biggest box-office draws during its long exile in the Queen's Theatre. The plays have been described as being all cut from the same cloth and as presenting a genial picture of lower-middle-class Dublin families, with stock comic characterization, topical allusions, a plot usually revolving around money, and a platitudinous theme. While the plays are much akin to today's rather broader television situation comedies, they do show a command of conventional stagecraft. The best of them, *Early and Often*, a well-observed study of Irish political machinations, may take an honorable place beside such worthy previous studies as William Boyle's* *The Eloquent Dempsy*, Edward McNulty's* *The Lord Mayor,* and John MacDonagh's* *The Irish Jew*.

WORKS: *War by the Irish*. Tralee: The Kerryman, [1946]. (Historical memoir); *Twenty Years A-Wooing*. Dublin: James Duffy, 1954; *Early and Often*. Dublin: P. J. Bourke, 1956; *I Know Where I'm Going*. Naas: Printed for the Author by the Leinster Leader, 1965.

MacCARTHY, DENIS FLORENCE (1817-1882), poet and translator. MacCarthy, the translator of Calderón, was born in Dublin in 1817 and died in Blackrock, County Dublin, on April 7, 1882. Today unread and unreadable, he was saluted by his contemporaries as Ireland's own Poet Laureate, the only true successor of Thomas Moore.* He contributed to Irish magazines with the copiousness that one would expect from a breadwinner for a wife and nine children. This burden can be regarded as an extenuating circumstance for his acceptance of the professorship of English literature in the local Catholic university and for his more frequent verse:

> An uncountable assemblage
> All recumbent in the fire:
> Through their bodies and their members
> Burning spikes and nails were driven . . .
> Vipers of red fire the entrails
> Gnawed of some; while others lying,
> With their teenth in maniac frenzy
> Bit the earth.

(From MacCarthy's translation of Calderón's *The Purgatory of Patrick*.)

ANDREW MARSH

WORKS: ed., *The Book of Irish Ballads*. Dublin: Duffy, 1846; *The Poets and Dramatists of Ireland*. Dublin: Duffy, 1846; trans., *Justina, a Play by Calderón de la Barca*. London: J. Burns, 1848; *Ballads, Poems and Lyrics, Original and Translated*. Dublin: J. McGlashan, 1850; trans., *Dramas of Calderón, Tragic, Comic, and Legendary*. London: C. Dolman, 1853; *The Bell-Founder, and Other Poems*. London: D. Bogue, 1857; *Underglimpses and Other Poems*. London: D. Bogue, 1857; *Irish Legends and Lyrics*. Dublin: McGlashan & Gill, 1858; trans., *Mysteries of Corpus Christi by Calderón de la Barca*. London: Duffy, 1867; trans., *The Two Lovers of Heaven*, by Calderón de la Barca. Dublin: John F. Fowler, 1870; *Shelley's Early Life from Original Sources*. London: J. C. Holten, [1872]; *The Centenary of Moore. May 28th, 1879. An Ode*. London: Privately printed, 1880; *Poems*. Dublin: Gill, 1882.

MacCARTHY, J[OHN] BERNARD (1888-1979), playwright and short story writer. A Cork realist,* MacCarthy (sometimes McCarthy) was born in Crosshaven, County Cork, on June 24, 1888. He worked most of his life as a postman in Crosshaven and was active in amateur theatrics there.

Although MacCarthy wrote of land-hunger and concern for reputation, the staples of Cory realism, he expanded its range to include seafaring life in plays such as *Wrecked* (1922), *The Sea-Call* (1917), and *The Long Road to Garranbraher* (1928). His fundamental tragic situation is a family caught in an ethical dilemma, a theme typified by the powerful *Crusaders* (1918): Father Tom Moran must choose between abandoning his success- ful temperance campaign and running his father's tavern business.

With one exception MacCarthy's best drama was produced by the Abbey*: *Kinship* (1914), *The Supplanter* (1914), *Crusaders* (1918), and *Garranbraher* (1923). The exception is *The Sea-Call*, a poignant tragedy of a man in love with the sea, and his childless wife who left the green quiet of inland Cork for the endless tumult of the Atlantic Coast.

Of MacCarthy's numerous farces written for amateur companies, *Dead Men's Shoes* (1919) is representative. Friends and relatives of Timothy Conroy, hearing a false report of his death, are squabbling over his posses- sions when he returns.

MacCarthy's poetry and fiction are more significant in quantity than in artistic merit. His legacy to Irish literature is a few strong, tightly wound tragedies. He died on January 18, 1979.

WILLIAM J. FEENEY

WORKS: *Wrecked.* Dublin: Gill, 1912. (Tragedy in one act); *The Sea-Call.* Dub- lin: Talbot, [1916]. (Tragedy in one act); *Crusaders.* Dublin: Maunsel, 1918. (Play in two acts); *The Shadow of the Rose.* Dublin: Talbot, 1919. (Poems); *The Romantic Lover.* Dublin: Gill, 1922. (Comedy in one act); *Cough Water.* Dublin: Gill, 1922. (Farce in one act); *The Men in Possession.* Dublin: Gill, 1922. (Farce in three acts); *The Rising Generation.* Dublin: Duffy, [1922?]. (Comedy in three acts); *Covert.* London: Hutchinson, [1925]. (Novel); *Possessions.* London: Hutchinson, [1926]. (Novel); *Exile's Bread.* London: Hutchinson, [1927]. (Novel); *The Able Dealer.* Dublin: Gill, 1928. (Farcical comedy in three acts); *The Down Express.* Dublin: Gill, 1928. (Farcical comedy in three acts); *Fine Feathers.* Dublin: Gill, 1928. (Farcical sketch); *The Long Road to Garranbraher.* Dublin: Gill, 1928. (Play in one act); *Old Acquaintance.* Dublin: Gill, 1928. (Farcical comedy in one act); *Poachers.* Dublin: Gill, 1928. (Comedy in one act); *All on One Summer Day and Julia Josephine Goes First.* Dublin: Catholic Truth Society of Ireland, [1928]. (Stories); *Heirs at Law and Donny Takes a Wife.* Dublin: Catholic Truth Society of Ireland, [1928]. (Stories); *The Magic Sign and Allotments.* Dublin: Catholic Truth Society of Ireland, [1928]. (Stories); *The Crossing and The Six Months' Corner.* Dublin: Catholic Truth Society of Ireland, [1929]. (Stories); *The Life of Trade and At the Show.* Dublin: Catholic Truth Society of Ireland, [1929]. (Stories); *A Marriage of Convenience and The Betrayal.* Dublin: Catholic Truth Society of Ireland, [1929]. (Stories); *Rope Enough and Julia Maud Goes to the Races and The Passing of the Torch.* Dublin: Catholic Truth Society of Ireland, [1929]. (Stories); *The Valuation and A Musical Interlude.*

Dublin: Catholic Truth Society of Ireland, [1929]. (Stories); *Verbatim and The End of a Holiday*. Dublin: Catholic Truth Society of Ireland, [1929]. (Stories); *Wheels o' Fortune and Those Who Smile before Dawn*. Dublin: Catholic Truth Society of Ireland, [1929]. (Stories); *The Wooing of Michael and His Royal Highness*. Dublin: Catholic Truth Society of Ireland, [1929]. (Stories); *Who Will Kiss Cinderella?* [London]: George Roberts, 1929. (Romantic comedy in three acts); *Andy Takes an Outing*. Dublin: Catholic Truth Society of Ireland, [1930]. (Story); *Annie All-Alone*. Dublin: Catholic Truth Society of Ireland, [1931]. (Story); *Easy Money*. Dublin: Catholic Truth Society of Ireland, [1931]. (Story); *The Fiddle Men*. Dublin: Catholic Truth Society of Ireland, [1931]. (Story); *The Grain of the Wood*. Dublin: Gill, [1931]. (Comedy in three acts); *The Partition*. Dublin: Catholic Truth Society of Ireland, [1931]. (Story); *A Test of Intelligence*. Dublin: Catholic Truth Society of Ireland, [1931]. (Story); *Until Dawn*. Dublin: Catholic Truth Society of Ireland, [1931]. (Story); *The Valley Farm*. Dublin: Gill, [1931]. (Drama in three acts); *Bridget's Biddy*. Dublin: Gill, [1932]. (Play in one act); *Dead Men's Shoes*. Dublin: Duffy, [1932]. (Comedy in one act); *Over Cassidy's Counter*. Dublin: Catholic Truth Society of Ireland, [1932]. (Story); *Wheel of Fortune*. Dublin: Gill, [1932]. (Comedy in one act); *When a Man Marries*. Dublin: Gill, [1932]. (Comedy in two acts); *The Missing Prince*. Dublin: Gill, [1934]. (Fairy play in four scenes); *A Change in Partners and A Midsummer Knight's Dream*. Dublin: Catholic Truth Society of Ireland, 1935. (Stories); *The White Souls and A St. Patrick's Day Presentation and The Sweeterie*. Dublin: Catholic Truth Society of Ireland, 1935. (Stories); *Murtagh's Monument and The Skipper Strikes his Flag*. Dublin: Catholic Truth Society of Ireland, [1936]. (Stories); *Plays*. Dublin: Gill, [1936]. (Includes "Watchers for the Dawn," "Kinship," "Green Leaves," "Rolling Stones," "Widows are So Fascinating," "The Ugly Duckling," and "The Man for Mannarue"); *Green Leaves*. Dublin: Gill, [1936]. (Farce in one act); *The Man from Mannarue*. Dublin: Gill, [1936]. (Comedy in three acts); *Rolling Stone*. Dublin: Gill, [1936]. (Comedy in one act); *A Disgrace to the Parish and A Quiet One*. Dublin: Catholic Truth Society of Ireland, [1937]. (Stories); *Old Times and Toys*. Dublin: Catholic Truth Society of Ireland, [1937]. (Stories); *The Playboy of the Seven Worlds*. Dublin: Gill, 1944. (Comedy in four acts); *The Duplicity of David*. Dublin: Duffy, 1945. (Farce in one act); *The Gold Train*. Dublin: Gill, [1947]. (Farcical thriller in three acts); *Crime Comes to Ballyconeen*. Dublin: Gill, [1947]. (Drama in four acts); *You Might Call It a Day*. Dublin: Catholic Truth Society of Ireland, 1948. (Story); *Master of the House*. Dublin: Gill, [1950?]. (Play in three acts); *The Wide Open Spaces*. Dublin: Duffy, [ca. 1950]. (Comedy in one act); *The Town Museum*. Dublin: Duffy, [ca. 1950]. (Farce in one act); *Fair Play's Bonnie Play*. Belfast: Carter, 1951. (Comedy in one act); *The Land Where Dreams Come True*, with music and lyrics by B. Walsh MacCarthy. Dublin: Gill, 1952. (Comedy in one act); *One Day You'll Find It*. Dublin: Gill, 1953. (Comedy in three acts); *Marriage Is a Lottery*. Dublin (Farcical comedy in one act); *Ladies, Take Your Partners*, with music and lyrics by B. Walsh MacCarthy. Belfast: Carter, 1953. (Light comedy in two acts); *Mister Storm Along*. Dublin: Gill, 1960. (Drama in one act); *The White Jackdaw*. Dublin: Gill, [1960?]. (Comedy in one act).

McCARTHY, JUSTIN (1830-1912), journalist, historian, and novelist. McCarthy was born in Cork on November 22, 1830, and became an incredibly prolific writer whose many books are now quite forgotten. Perhaps the most popular was his four-volume *A History of Our Own Times* (1879), which went into many editions. McCarthy was not an original writer, but a fluent and pleasant popularizer. He was a member of Parliament in the Irish party during the Parnell divorce case, and it was through him that Gladstone put pressure on Parnell to retire from the leadership. After the famous debate on the subject in Committee Room 15, McCarthy led the majority of the members out. Nevertheless, through all of the acrimony, McCarthy is said to have retained Parnell's friendship and, indeed, to have made no enemies at all. In 1904, he published a ten-volume anthology, *Irish Literature*, for which he enlisted the aid of Standish O'Grady,* W. B. Yeats,* Douglas Hyde,* AE,* Lady Gregory,* and others. Despite a preponderance of dross in its many pages, the work is still of interest and utility. McCarthy left public life in 1900 but continued to write by dictation up to 1911. He died at Folkestone on April 24, 1912.

WORKS: *A History of Our Own Times*. 4 vols. London: Chatto & Windus, 1879; *Reminiscences*. London: Chatto & Windus, 1899; *An Irishman's Story*. New York & London: Macmillan, 1904.

McCARTHY, THOMAS (1954-), poet. McCarthy was born in Cappoquin, County Waterford, in 1954 and attended University College, Cork. The poems in his first collection, *The First Convention*, won the 1977 Patrick Kavanagh Award. At his best, McCarthy uses words with realistic precision; at his worst, in pieces like "Marie, Marie" or "The Word 'Silk'," his phrasing verges on the trite.

WORK: *The First Convention*. [Dublin]: Dolmen, [1978].

McCORMACK, WILLIAM JOHN. *See* MAXTON, HUGH.

MacDONAGH, DONAGH (1912-1968), poet and playwright. MacDonagh was born on November 22, 1912, the son of Thomas MacDonagh,* one of the executed leaders of the 1916 Rising. About a year after his father's death, his mother drowned in a swimming accident. He received his early education at Belvedere College and then went to University College, Dublin, where he and his contemporaries—Niall Sheridan,* Denis Devlin,* Cyril Cusack the actor, Brian O'Nolan,* Charlie Donnelly the young poet, and Mervyn Wall*—made up one of the liveliest student generations since the time of James Joyce.* Already in college, his main literary preoccupations were emerging. He and Sheridan published a joint volume, *Twenty Poems*, and with Liam Redmond, who was to become his brother-in-law, he staged the first Irish production of Eliot's *Murder in the Cathedral*.

He practiced at the bar from 1935 until 1941 when he was appointed a district justice, a position he retained until his death. He became a popular broadcaster on Radio Éireann which provided him a platform for his lifelong interest in folk ballads. His own plays are either poetic dramas or ballad operas in which, like John Gay, he wrote new words to traditional tunes. His most successful play was *Happy as Larry* (1946) which in a good production is an enchanting piece of theatre. It received a highly successful production in London, and an elaborate and extremely unsuccessful production by Burgess Meredith in New York. His ballad opera *God's Gentry* (Belfast Arts, 1951) about tinkers remains unpublished, as does his excellent verse treatment of the Deirdre story, *Lady Spider*. His *Step-in-the-Hollow* (Gaiety, 1957) is a broad comedy of intrigue and mistaken identity with a Falstaffian main character. However, this work (and really all of MacDonagh's plays) are essentially theatrical rather than literary. Their language requires the immediacy of spoken speech or the extra dimension of song to lift them into a transient wit and eloquence. His words per se are too often flat and pedestrian, and even trembling on the verge of doggerel. In *Happy as Larry*, he will sometimes in the same passage use exact rhyme in a definite pattern and then suddenly shift into irregularity for no apparent reason. That is, he will rhyme exactly, then give an off-rhyme or an assonance, and then drop any similarity of sound entirely.

A similar thinness is noticeable in MacDonagh's small output of verse, though a few lyrics such as "The Hungry Grass" and "Dublin Made Me" will always find their places in anthologies. He was personally a quick and witty man; he died in Dublin on January 1, 1968.

WORKS: *Veterans and Other Poems*. Dublin: Cuala, 1941; *Happy as Larry*. Dublin: Maurice Fridberg, 1946/Dublin: Fridberg & Dolmen, 1967/included in *Modern Verse Plays*, E. Martin Browne, ed. Harmondsworth, Middlesex: Penguin, 1958. (Play); *The Hungry Grass*. London: Faber & Faber, 1947. (Poems); *The Oxford Book of Irish Verse*, ed. with Lennox Robinson. Oxford: Clarendon, 1958; *Step-in-the-Hollow* in *Three Irish Plays*. Harmondsworth, Middlesex: Penguin, 1959. (Play).   REFERENCE: Hogan, Robert. *After the Irish Renaissance*. London: Macmillan, 1968, pp. 154-158.

MacDONAGH, JOHN (?-1961), playwright and play director. MacDonagh was a versatile man of the theatre—producer, actor, author of plays and revues, a pioneer in the Irish motion picture industry, and productions director for Radio Éireann.

Because of his experience in English and American theatre he was appointed producer of the Irish Theatre in 1914. During the 1916 Rising he was with his brother Thomas* in the Jacob's Biscuit Factory garrison; afterwards he was interned for a few months in England. In addition to taking roles in most of the Irish Theatre plays, MacDonagh wrote two one-act comedies, *Author! Author!* (1915), a satire on peasant drama, and *Just Like Shaw* (1916), a mocking commentary on British officialdom in Ireland. *Weeds* (1919) was a serious three-act study of Irish landlordism.

Leaving the Irish Theatre in 1919, he worked with the Film Company of Ireland and later with Irish Photoplays. Among the pictures he directed were *Willie Reilly and his Colleen Bawn*, *Cruiskeen Lawn*, *The O'Casey Millions*, and *Wicklow Gold*.

MacDonagh's four-act comedy *The Irish Jew* was first performed at the

Empire Theatre, Dublin, on December 13, 1921, and frequently revived. Its hero, Abraham Golden, Lord Mayor of Dublin, prevents an attempted swindle by members of the Corporation. For the commercial theatre Mac-Donagh wrote several revues, among them *Dublin To-night* (1924), *All Aboard for Dublin* (1931), and *Dublin on Parade* (1932), which offered home-grown talent and topicality as an alternative to the material presented by British touring companies.

As productions director of Radio Éireann from 1938 to his retirement in 1947, he created the popular quiz game "Question Time," wrote a satirical play *Attempted Murder* (the victim is the Stage Irishman), and on January 16, 1947, gave a short talk on his remembrances of Edward Martyn* and the Irish Theatre, as a prelude to a radio adaptation of Martyn's *The Heather Field* on January 19.

Born in Cloughjordan, County Tipperary, MacDonagh died in Dublin on July 1, 1961.

WILLIAM J. FEENEY

WORKS: "Enterprise at the Irish Theatre." *New Ireland,* III (March 10, 1917), 293-295; *Just Like Shaw: A Play in One Act. The Dublin Magazine,* I (January 1924), 141-148; "Edward Martyn." *The Dublin Magazine,* I (January 1924), 465-467; *Author! Author! The Dublin Magazine,* I (February 1924), 621-628; "Film Production in Ireland in the Early Days." *Cinema Ireland 1895-1976.* Dublin Arts Festival, 1976. REFERENCE: Boyd, Ernest. "The Work of the Irish Theatre." *The Irish Monthly,* XLVIII (February 1919), 71-76.

MacDONAGH, PATRICK (1902-1961), poet. MacDonagh was born in the North of Ireland in 1902. From the middle 1920s to the late 1950s, he published many poems in periodicals and in a few short volumes. The best of his work is gathered in the 1958 volume *One Landscape Still.* A comparison of that book with a collection of nearly thirty years earlier, *A Leaf in the Wind,* is rather instructive. The poems in *A Leaf in the Wind* seem for their day anachronistically conventional, and, if any poetic presence broods over the book, it is the spirit of Wordsworth (although John Hewitt* discerns Yeats,* AE,* and Richard Rowley*). Romantic in diction, conventional in technique, and full of nostalgic yearning for lost love, the book nevertheless manages a number of lines of compressed strength. *One Landscape Still* of thirty years later is discernibly by the same poet. The rue, the nostalgia, and the romance are still present, but so also are some satire and some bitterness. More impressive is the improvement in technique. There are still gaffes and failures, but in nearly half of the poems MacDonagh moves easily and impressively from the tight three-stressed line to the usually cumbersome six-stressed, from deft couplets and quatrains to fluent blank verse and even free verse. In any good subsequent anthology of modern Irish poetry, MacDonagh must be represented; the anthologist might do well to consider "One Landscape Still" or "Feltrim Hill" or the very impressive "The Bone-Bright Tree."

WORKS: *Flirtation, Some Occasional Verses.* Dublin: G. F. Healy, 1927; *A Leaf in the Wind.* Belfast: Quota, [1929]; *The Vestal Fire, a Poem.* Dublin: Orwell, 1941; *Over the Water and Other Poems.* Dublin: Orwell, 1943; *One Landscape Still.* London: Secker & Warburg, 1958.

MacDONAGH, THOMAS (1878-1916), patriot, poet, and man of letters. MacDonagh was born in Cloughjordan, County Tipperary, on February 1, 1878. Educated at Rockwell College, Cashel, he decided at an early age to enter the Holy Ghost Order, but gave up his vocation after a personal religious crisis, which is the subject of his first book of poems, *Through the Ivory Gate* (1902), an otherwise unremarkable volume. Like many of his generation, he joined the Gaelic League and held offices in league branches in Kilkenny and Fermoy, where he taught, respectively, at St. Kieran's and St. Colman's Colleges. Continuing to write poetry, he published *April and May* (1903), which in part echoes his first book and also Gaelic League nationalism, and *The Golden Joy* (1906), a volume influenced by his readings in Plotinus and Walt Whitman.

The year 1908 marked a turning point in his life. He came to Dublin and joined Patrick Pearse*at St. Enda's, a school founded on Gaelic League principles. St. Enda's introduced him to an expanding circle of acquaintances—Martyn,* Hyde,* and Yeats,* among many others—and the production of his first play, *When the Dawn Is Come*, by the Abbey* in October 1908 established him as a minor literary figure. In its earliest drafts, *Dawn* was a play about a poet/patriot who, by means of his poetry, inspires the Irish to rebellion and freedom from a foreign power. Much revised on guidelines suggested by Yeats and Synge,* the play in its final form has stilted dialogue, a lopsided construction, and, ironically, a purely nationalist message. The Abbey production left MacDonagh embittered. More disappointment followed, in the form of a frustrated love affair with Mary Maguire* (later Mrs. Padraic Colum*), and in the late spring of 1910, he left Dublin for a summer of isolation in Paris.

MacDonagh returned from Paris in September 1910 and moved to Grange House Lodge, determined to live a hermit-like existence in the foothills of the Dublin mountains. But, as James Stephens* has said in his introduction to *The Poetical Works of Thomas MacDonagh* (1916), "he fled into and out of solitude with equal precipitancy." Rejoining Pearse at nearby St. Enda's, he commenced studies toward the M.A. at University College, Dublin. His Master's thesis, *Thomas Campion and the Art of English Poetry* (published in 1913), contains a fairly unoriginal study of Campion's life and work, and then, by MacDonagh's own admission, it digresses into a treatise on English prosody, dividing poetry into "speech verse" and "song verse." During this period he also wrote a play, *Metempsychosis* (produced by the Theatre of Ireland in April 1912), in which Yeats is satirized as Earl Winton-Winton de Winton, a visionary type who believes in the transmigration of souls. *Metempsychosis* shows considerably more talent than

Dawn in that it is an amusing, and very actable, drawing room comedy. Poems of this period, *Songs of Myself* (1910), also show signs of advance in MacDonagh's literary capabilities. "John-John" is straightforward and colloquial in language, a rejection of the stilted, conventional manner of his earlier work.

The happiest period of MacDonagh's adult life began with his marriage to Muriel Gifford on January 3, 1912. Now steadily employed at University College and working with Stephens and Colum (and, later, Joseph Plunkett*) in editing *The Irish Review*,* he seemed destined for the life of an academic, and one with literary aspirations. *Lyrical Poems* (1913) contained healthy revisions of earlier work and some new pieces—"The Yellow Bittern," "The Man Upright," and "The Night Hunt"—which indicate, as did "John-John," that he had found an original poetic voice. He also began a study of Anglo-Irish literature, the result of which was *Literature in Ireland*, published posthumously in 1916. A very uneven book, *Literature in Ireland* is nonetheless significant because it is the acknowledgment of an Irish Catholic nationalist that Anglo-Irish literature, and language, had arrived as the literature and speech of the Irish people. MacDonagh concluded that the Irish language had caused a "prose intonation" and " conversational tone" in the poetry written in English, i.e., Anglo-Irish, in modern Ireland. He called this influence "the Irish Mode."

All the manuscript evidence suggests that MacDonagh never had enough time, or scholarly discipline, to devote to the book: as much as a third of the material had been published previously as book reviews or articles. With the formation of the Irish Volunteers in November 1913, he entered the last, fateful phase of his life. Ever a joiner of idealistic causes, he embraced Volunteer activities to such an extent that literature became a minor part of his life. The years 1914 and 1915 saw piecemeal work on *Literature in Ireland*, some poetry (including some very jingoistic marching songs), a realistic play, *Pagans*, done as part of Edward Martyn's ill-fated Irish Theatre* venture, and a great deal of organizing, speaking, and parading for the Volunteer movement. Despite these latter activities, there is no evidence to prove that he was a confidant in the planning of the Easter Rising. As Marcus Bourke has suggested (*Irish Sword*, summer 1968), he probably became involved at the last moment as an intermediary between Pearse and Eoin MacNeill, when MacNeill attempted to abort the Rising.

MacDonagh commanded the garrison at Jacob's Biscuit Factory—a post which saw little action—during the Rising itself, and for his part was executed on May 3, 1916. His participation in the Rising has, over the years, distorted the meaning of his literary work. It is doubtful that he was, as Loftus has suggested in *Nationalism and Modern Anglo-Irish Poetry* (1964), a Messianic idealist, or that the Easter Rising was, for him, a "blood sacrifice." Rather, he was a fairly ordinary man, one who could never give to any single aspect of his life the concentration it deserved. He

loved literature and life, but was, finally, a victim of his enthusiastic nature.
JOHANN A. NORSTEDT

WORKS: *April and May, with Other Verses.* Dublin: Sealy, Bryers, [1903]; *Through the Ivory Gate.* Dublin: Sealy, [1903]. (Poems); *When the Dawn Is Come.* Dublin: Maunsel, 1908. (Play); *Songs of Myself.* Dublin: Hodges, Figgis, 1910; *Lyrical Poems.* Dublin: Irish Review, 1913; *Thomas Campion and the Art of English Poetry.* Dublin: Hodges, Figgis, 1913; *Literature in Ireland: Studies Irish and Anglo-Irish.* Dublin: Talbot, 1916; *The Poetical Works of Thomas MacDonagh.* James Stephens, ed. Dublin: Talbot/London: Unwin, 1916; *Pagans.* Dublin: Talbot/London: Unwin, 1920. (Play); *Poems,* selected by his sister. Dublin: Talbot, [1925].   REFER- ENCES: MacDonagh, Donagh. "Plunkett and MacDonagh." In *Leaders and Men of the Easter Rising: Dublin 1916.* F. X. Martin, ed. London: Methuen, 1967; Norstedt, Johann A. "Thomas MacDonagh: A Biography." Ph.D. dissertation, University Col- lege, Dublin, 1972; Parks, Edd Winfield, & Aileen Wells Parks. *Thomas MacDonagh: The Man, the Patriot, the Writer.* Athens: University of Georgia Press, 1967.

McFADDEN, ROY (1921-), poet. McFadden was born on November 14, 1921, in Belfast, where he is a solicitor. He is also one of the group of Northern Irish writers, including Robert Greacen,* who began to come to prominence in the mid- and late 1940s. The group talked about a Northern literary renaissance and published much of their work in *Rann,* a periodical edited (1948-1953) by McFadden and Barbara Edwards. The twenty-fifth number of the periodical contains a useful bibliography of work by Ulster authors from 1900 to 1953, but in the middle of the century there was no consequential Northern literature there to be reborn. The movement also had its internal contradictions. Although the members wanted a distinc- tively Ulster voice, they were at the same time solicitous of a British audi- ence and British approval, and they seemed to emulate fashionable British models.

McFadden's early poetry emerges from these irresolutions with some confidence. There are apocalyptic rumbles here and there, but not sufficiently to impair scenes deployed in crisp particulars and with bare evocations of sectarian menace. In this early work, McFadden is speaking from and to the inviting and forbidding ghosts and presences of his region. His more recent poetry undertakes even more acute and less distracted views of his "clabbered clout of ground," which is now peopled by real or real-imagined characters, such as his Jackie Dugan. In *The Garryowen* (1971) and *Veri- fications* (1977), deeply personal poems like "Portrush" and "Family Al- bum" consort with more public poems celebrating Synge* and Behan,* and there is an awareness of the presence of public terror in literary and domestic orders. In these books, McFadden has achieved a remarkable late realization of his powers.

D.E.S. MAXWELL

WORKS: *A Poem: Russian Summer.* Dublin: Gayfield, 1942. (Pamphlet poem); *Swords and Ploughshares.* London: Routledge, 1943; *Flowers for a Lady.* London: Routledge, 1945; *The Heart's Townland.* London. Routledge, 1947; *Elegy for the*

Dead of the Princess Victoria. Belfast: Lisnagarvey, 1953. (Pamphlet poem); *The Garryowen.* London: Chatto & Windus, 1971; *Verifications.* Belfast: Blackstaff, 1977; *A Watching Brief.* Belfast: Blackstaff, 1978.

McGAHERN, JOHN (1934-), novelist and short story writer. Born on November 12, 1934, in Dublin, the son of a police officer, John McGahern was raised in Coothall, County Roscommon. He was educated at Presentation College, Carrick-on-Shannon, St. Patrick's College, Drumcondra, and University College, Dublin. He taught at St. John the Baptist's Boys National School in Clontarf for seven years until he won a Macauley fellowship in 1964 for his novel *The Barracks* (1963), the early chapters of which had won him the first AE Memorial Award in 1962. His second novel, *The Dark*, appeared in 1965, and that same year he married the Finnish theatrical producer Annikki Laaksi.

The Dark was banned by the Irish Censorship Board in June 1965, and its author dismissed, without explanation, from his teaching post that autumn. When his dismissal became publicly known the following spring, there was a furious controversy and futile attempts were made to have McGahern reinstated (see Skeffington in "References" below). He moved to London, and since then has lived in Spain, the United States, England, and, more recently, County Leitrim. He has lectured at various British and American universities (among them Durham, Newcastle, and Colgate), and has received several Arts Council and other awards and fellowships. *Nightlines*, a collection of short stories, appeared in 1970, and *The Leavetaking*, a novel, in 1974. Short stories continue to appear (especially in *The Irish Press*), and a new work is expected in 1979.

In *The Barracks* Elizabeth Reegan has returned to a small Irish village to marry the local police sergeant, a widower with a young family. Already oppressed by the monotonous provinciality and her husband's incoherent struggles with his servile rounds, she discovers that she is dying of cancer. Against a background of the indifferent sounds of the countryside, the church rituals, the comings and goings at the barracks, punctuated by ritual dark humor and occasional fumbling affection, she does quiet, heroic battle with death and despair. McGahern's portrait of Elizabeth is a triumph: she is marvelously observed, thoughtful, sympathetic, and entirely credible. Her relationship with Reegan, however, lacks the same clarity. However, the domestic interiors, dialogue, and local color of this dull Shannon backwater are unerringly rendered. The major achievement of the novel is its technical control: the spare, cool, narrative style; the disciplined, unsentimental management of descriptive detail; and the assured handling of interior monologue and flashback. The tension between the desire for security and the fear of petrifaction is a major theme, but, more profoundly, *The Barracks* redefines the impact of a not quite articulate agnosticism on an imagination shaped by the canons of Irish Catholicism.

In the story of a tortured adolescent, *The Dark* commits to confessional form essentially the same vision, yet without the flashes of mystical joy of *The Barracks*. The anonymous protagonist is emotionally thwarted by the loss of his mother, an ambiguous relationship with his father, repressive religious training, poverty, and an examination-ridden school. The conflicts between his emotional needs, ambitions, and these constrictions make for a bleak and desperate farce. The banning of this novel—no doubt because of its frank depiction of masturbation and suggestions of homosexuality in father and priest—may have dramatized its relevancy in Ireland, but it also deflected attention from McGahern's achievement: the grim, humorless, spartan narrative, and the depiction of the hero, caught between hopelessly irreconcilable needs, as depersonalized. This effect, however, tends to undermine the reader's belief in the hero's final realization of his personal independence despite the encircling futility.

Some of the dozen stories in *Nightlines* extend beyond McGahern's familiar Roscommon-Leitrim landscapes to Dublin, London, and Spain. But he is most persuasive in his steely keen sketches of rural Ireland. Speech rhythms are always true; symbols are cunningly chosen; and the prose oscillates between unflinching objectivity and guarded lyricism. These devices reveal the void beneath much of Irish life: in the words of one of his characters, he "refines our ignorance."

The "leave" in the title of McGahern's third novel is taken from the guilt and repression of Ireland to the commitment of adult human love. Much of this work is a review of the road traveled in the first two, resolved by Patrick's idyllic love affair with and marriage to an American (who is escaping her debilitating past). Although the first half contains some of McGahern's most lyrical prose to date, the rest—depicting the American businessman, his daughter, the tryst—is singularly mawkish. The novel is not an advance over the earlier works, where the sense of loss is modulated by a poised phrase or a measured silence. Here the commitment takes shape in a language that, for all its passionate overtones, springs from relative emotional shallows.

McGahern's reputation as the leading Irish novelist of his generation is sure. He has assimilated Joyce* and Mauriac, and has been characterized by Roger Garfitt as "perhaps the most truly Existentialist writer working in English today." His courage and integrity, dark but humane vision, and passionate intelligence have advanced Irish realistic fiction in new directions of poetry and intellect.

                                                                    COILIN OWENS

WORKS: *The Barracks*. London: Faber, 1963/New York: Macmillan, 1964; *The Dark*. London: Faber, 1965/New York: Alfred A. Knopf, 1966; *Nightlines*. London: Faber, 1970/Boston, Toronto: Little, Brown, 1971; *The Leavetaking*. London: Faber, 1974/Boston, Toronto: Little, Brown, 1975; *Getting Through*. London: Faber, 1978. REFERENCES: Garfitt, Roger. "Constants in Contemporary Irish Fiction." *Two Decades of Irish Writing*. Douglas Dunn, ed. Chester Springs, Pa.: Dufour, 1975, pp.

207-211, 221-224; Sheehy Skeffington, Owen. "The McGahern Affair." *Censorship* 2 (Spring 1966): 27-30.

McGEE, THOMAS D'ARCY (1825-1868), politician, journalist, and poet. McGee was born in Carlingford, County Louth, on April 13, 1825. He emigrated to America when he was seventeen and made such a reputation as a dynamic and forceful speaker that he was made editor of *The* [Boston] *Pilot* when only nineteen. He returned to Ireland, became strongly involved in Nationalist activities, and worked on *The Nation** under Gavan Duffy.* After the 1848 Rising, he escaped to America where he edited journals, and in 1858 he moved to Canada, quickly becoming prominent in Canadian politics. His own Irish revolutionary fervor had by then died down, and on visits to Ireland he was highly critical of the young Fenian movement. He was assassinated, possibly by an Irish revolutionary, on the streets of Ottawa on April 7, 1868. His poems are thoroughly fluent and show an easy control of form. However, they are unoriginal popular poems, lacking individuality or real literary taste. They are full of shamrocks, tears, patriotism, death, and the other preoccupations of the sea-divided Gael. McGee is probably seen at his conventional best in a sentimental but still somewhat effective poem like "Death of the Homeward Bound." Despite some fluency and vigor, he was always liable to slip into lines like:

> A cypress wreath darkles now, I ween,
> Upon the brow of my love in green.

WORKS: *Historical Sketches of O'Connell and his Friends.* Boston: Donahoe & Rohan, 1844; *Gallery of Irish Writers: The Irish Writers of the XVIIth Century.* Dublin: Duffy, 1846; *A Memoir of the Life and Conquest of Art McMurrough.* Dublin: Duffy, 1847; *Memoir of Charles Gavan Duffy.* Dublin: W. Hogan, 1849. (Pamphlet); *Poems.* Dublin: reprinted for *The Nation*, 1852; *Canadian Ballads and Occasional Verses.* Montreal: Lovel, 1858; *A Popular History of Ireland.* Glasgow: Cameron & Ferguson, 1862; *The Poems of Thomas D'Arcy McGee.* London, New York, Montreal: Sadlier, 1869.   REFERENCES: Brady, A. *Thomas D'Arcy McGee.* Toronto: Macmillan, 1925; Phelan, J. *The Ardent Exile: The Life and Times of Thomas D'Arcy McGee.* Toronto: Macmillan, 1951; Skelton, I. M. *The Life of Thomas D'Arcy McGee.* Gardenvale, Canada: Garden City Press, 1925.

MacGILL, PATRICK (1891-1963), novelist and poet. MacGill was born in 1891 in the Glen of Glenties, County Donegal. The eldest of eleven children of a small farmer, he received his only formal education at the National School of Mullanmore. He left school at twelve and hired out for six months at a time as a farm laborer for a fee of £5. When he was fourteen, he emigrated to Scotland to work in the potato fields and then as an itinerant navvy. In 1911, while working on the Glasgow-Greenock Railway Line, he published at his own expense a volume of verse entitled *Gleanings from a Navvy's Scrapbook*. He sold the book from door to door in Greenock, and, incredible as it may seem, it reportedly sold eight thousand copies.

Gleanings was followed quickly by *Songs of a Navvy* and *Songs of the Dead End*, and his work came to the attention of London critics who were both amused and impressed. Some of the verses in these books were conventionally romantic, but the more characteristic were bitter and realistic portrayals of the navvy's life. The books achieved considerable popularity for several reasons—the novel and appalling picture of the laborer's life; the utter, burning sincerity of the social indictment; and, among working people, the simple attraction of the writing. The long and heavily rhythmic lines and the emphatic end and internal rhymes had a particular charm for the untutored ear. To the well-read, the verses were simply reminiscent of the jingles of Robert W. Service, although their actual literary provenance owes much to folk poetry.

MacGill was a skilled versifier in this popular poetry and was occasionally strong in his diction and imagery, but it is as a novelist that he compels serious attention. In 1914 and 1915, respectively, he published his two interlocking novels *Children of the Dead End* and *The Rat Pit*. These books caused a literary sensation, and the first sold ten thousand copies within fifteen days of publication. With these books, MacGill became the spokesman for a mute and ignored section of society. As a self-taught writer, the author was lionized much as Sean O'Casey* was in the 1920s. However, World War I intervened, and MacGill served throughout as a private with the London Irish Rifles. His experiences were the basis for the account of his personal experiences in *The Amateur Army* (1915) and in some blistering fictional accounts of life in the ranks. MacGill continued to write into the 1930s, drawing on his memories of Ireland and of his laboring days, and always as the voice of the forgotten people at the bottom of society. He was little, if at all, influenced by the writers of the Irish literary renaissance. What literary influence he had came from the social realism of Emile Zola in novels such as *Germinal*. Nor was he interested in Irish nationalism; for him the one burning social issue was the plight of the underprivileged who scrambled for existence at the bottom of society.

MacGill's fiction is much of a piece then, but time seems to have winnowed out his first two novels as his best. These books are parallel accounts of a boy and a girl from a Donegal village who, like thousands of others in real life, made the long journey to Scotland's potato fields. The lives of the two diverge and then coalesce, and MacGill makes effective use of some nearly identical scenes in both novels. *Children of the Dead End* follows Dermod in his harrowing experiences as an itinerant navvy to his first steps in journalism, while *The Rat Pit* charts the ever-downward path of Norah through seduction, abandonment, prostitution, and death. *Children of the Dead End* is the better book because it depicts the immense vigor and even humor of life in the work camps, and because of the memorable portrait of Moleskin Joe. The book contains a few romantic flights and some savage moralizing, but the point of view and the power of the narrative sustain these merely literary flaws, if indeed they be flaws at all. The books have their crudities, but their power and compassion have little dissipated over the years. It would be a mistake to ignore MacGill and to let his now nearly forgotten novels remain in obscurity. His poems may be the lowbrow stuff of popular literature, but his novels at their best have much of the strength of Zola, as well as MacGill's own horrific eloquence. He died in 1963, almost totally forgotten.

WORKS: *Gleanings from a Navvy's Scrapbook*. Derry: Printed by the Derry Journal, 1911; *Songs of a Navvy*. Windsor: P. MacGill, [1911]; *Songs of the Dead End*. London: Year Book Press, 1912; *Children of the Dead End*. London: Herbert Jenkins, 1914; *The Amateur Army*. London: Herbert Jenkins, 1915; *The Ratpit*. London: Herbert Jenkins, 1915; *The Great Push, an Episode of the Great War*. London: Herbert Jenkins, 1916; *The Red Horizon*. London: Herbert Jenkins, 1916; *The Brown Brethren*. London: Herbert Jenkins, 1917; *Soldier Songs*. London: Herbert Jenkins, 1917; *The Diggers: the Australians in France*. London: Herbert Jenkins, 1919; *The Dough-boys*, by John O'Gorman, Pseud. London: Herbert Jenkins, 1919; *Glenmornan*. London: Herbert Jenkins, 1919; *Maureen*. London: Herbert Jenkins, 1920; *Songs of Donegal*. London: Herbert Jenkins, 1921; *Lanty Hanlon: a Comedy of Irish Life*. London: Herbert Jenkins, 1922; *Moleskin Joe*. London: Herbert Jenkins, 1923; *The Carpenter of Orra*. London: Herbert Jenkins, 1924; *Sid Puddiefoot*. London: Herbert Jenkins, 1926; *Black Bonar*. London: Herbert Jenkins, 1928; *Suspense: a Play in Three Acts*. London: Herbert Jenkins, [1930]; *The Glen of Carra*. London: Herbert Jenkins, 1934; *Tulliver's Mill*. London: Herbert Jenkins, 1934; *The House at the World's End*. London: Herbert Jenkins, 1935; *Helen Spenser*. London: Herbert Jenkins, [1937].

MacGREEVY, THOMAS (1893-1967), critic and poet. MacGreevy is of most interest, from a literary standpoint, for his intimate relationships with many of the most interesting Irish writers of his day, among them Samuel Beckett,* James Stephens,* Stephen MacKenna,* Denis Devlin,* and Brian Coffey,* as well as James Joyce* and Jack B. Yeats* of whose wills he was the executor. In the late 1920s and early 1930s, he lived in Paris and wrote his two books of literary criticism (on T. S. Eliot and Richard Aldington), as well as much fugitive work for *The Dial, The Criterion* and *Transition*. The close of that period of his life also saw the publication of his one volume of poems, the best of which faithfully, if not always excellently, reflect the avant-garde poetry of that eminently exciting time.

MacGreevy was born at Tarbert, County Kerry. He fought in World War I, was twice wounded, and after being demobilized was educated at Trinity College, Dublin. Following his years as art critic and lecturer in Paris and London, he returned to Dublin in 1941 and in 1950 was appointed director of the National Gallery, a post that he held until his retirement in 1964. He died in Dublin on March 16, 1967.

WORK: *Collected Poems*, edited by Thomas Dillon Redshaw, with a Foreword by Samuel Beckett. Dublin: New Writers', 1971.

McHUGH, MARTIN J. (?-1951), playwright and short story writer. McHugh wrote short stories for the popular press and several short plays, three of which were performed by the Abbey Theatre* in the second decade of the twentieth century. His many unpublished letters to Joseph Holloway*are incredibly garrulous and so mind-bogglingly boring that, if printed (which they should not be), they would prove something of an antiliterary comic masterpiece. He was for a while employed by *The Irish Times*, but later moved to England. The best-known of his daughters is Mary Frances McHugh.* His multitudinous comic stories in the popular press in the first decade of the century are no better than those of George Fitzmaurice* or Maurice Walsh,* who at that time were also writing Stage Irish stories of little merit. Of his several broad farces, however, *A Minute's Walk* (Abbey, 1914) is a small, sweetly silly theatrical gem. It was one segment of John Ford's film *The Rising of the Moon* and featured the eminent Irish comedian Jimmy O'Dea. Sean O'Casey* utilized precisely the same situation for his late one-act *The Moon Shines on Kylenamoe*. McHugh died on November 11, 1951.

WORKS: *Straws in the Wind*. Aberdeen: Moran, 1896; with Henry T. Hunt Grubb, *A Modern Mage*. London: Simpkin, Marshall, 1904; *A Minute's Wait*. Dublin: Duffy, [1922]; *The Philosopher*. Dublin: Duffy, [1922?]; *Tommy Tom-Tom*. Dublin: Duffy, [1922?]; *A Girl Like Mary*. Dublin: Duffy, [1935]; *The Trifler*. Dublin: Duffy, [1946].

McHUGH, MARY FRANCES (fl. first half of the twentieth century), woman of letters. McHugh was the daughter of the playwright and popular short story writer Martin J. McHugh.* A typical work is her *Thalassa* (1931), which is subtitled "A Story of Childhood by the Western Wave" and which is a memoir of her childhood in the west of Ireland. The book is written in stiff, English-composition-prizewinning prose. Clouds are "Small, tossed, white"; hills are "limpid"; cottages "nestle"; and the sea is "murmuring and melancholic." In sum, "every moment changed to something more indescribable and entrancing, until it seemed one's heart would break with beauty." McHugh's evocation of the scenery is a barrier to enjoyment, but when she forgets about beauty and simply describes the people who lived around her, the little book becomes an engrossing and valuable social record of life in the west of Ireland at the beginning of the century.

Her poems are as literary as her prose, and quite conventional.

MARY ROSE CALLAGHAN

WORKS: *Poems*. Dublin: Martin Lester, [1919]; *Thalassa*. London: Macmillan, 1931/Dublin: Parkside, 1945; *The Bud of Spring*. London: Macmillan, 1932.

McHUGH, ROGER [JOSEPH] (1908-), critic and playwright. McHugh, born in Dublin on July 14, 1908, was professor of Anglo-Irish literature and drama at University College, Dublin. He has edited several useful books on Anglo-Irish literature and has written a short life of Henry Grattan.* Two of his plays were performed by the Abbey Theatre:* *Trial at Green Street Courthouse* (1941) and *Rossa* (1945), which won the Abbey Theatre Prize for that year. Neither was memorable, but both were worthy. A third play, in collaboration with Alfred Noyes, about Roger Casement, has not been published.

WORKS: *Henry Grattan.* Dublin: Talbot/London: Duckworth, 1936; *Trial at Green Street Courthouse.* Dublin: Browne & Nolan, [1945]; *Rossa.* Tralee: Kerryman, [1946?]; ed., *Letters to Katharine Tynan.* New York: McMullen, [1953]; ed., *Dublin, 1916.* New York: Hawthorn Books, [1966]; ed., *Jonathan Swift 1667-1967.* [Dublin]: Dolmen, 1967; ed., *Ah, Sweet Dancer: W. B. Yeats, Margot Ruddick, a Correspondence.* London: Macmillan, 1970.

MacINTYRE, TOM (1933-), man of letters. MacIntyre has developed into one of the most promising and provocative writers of the 1970s. He has written in a wide variety of forms—the novel, the short story, the drama, the political documentary, and free verse translations of Gaelic poetry. His novel, *The Charollais* (1969), a short, fantastic story reminiscent of Joyce,* Beckett,* and Flann O'Brien,* is told in a highly individual, free-wheeling style. For instance:

> In short, Drumgoon was over the barrel—they knew it, and so, by the cut of him, did he. A pimpled, pock-marked, pre-pubescent omadhaun could tell him that he might as well accept a situation he couldn't alter, nor would it alter, not—C lammed the table—not if he went down on his knees and washed that floor with a mixture of his own anointed spittle, oil, chrism, and/or diced carrots to the full-dress accompaniment of the *Diocesan Chapter* chanting [sic] *Ecce Sacerdos Magnus* in catatonic thirds, diatonic fifths, galvanic sevenths, macaronic—. . . .

This excerpt is typical of the style and, indeed, the quality of imagination in the book, and predictably the book begins to pall after about fifty pages. Character is sacrificed to fantasy, fantasy is camouflaged by style, and the style finally becomes more clever than funny, as the author more often than not opts for the easy gag, the half pun, and the quip. MacIntyre's first collection of stories, *Dance the Dance* (1969), however, was conventional in style and form, but somewhat uneven in quality. If there is a common situation in the stories, it might be that of fate or of people playing bad jokes on other people. The collection's best piece is an excellently realized long story entitled "Epithalamion." MacIntyre's short plays are so far unpublished, but his *Jack Be Nimble* (Peacock, 1976) and his *Eye Winker Tom Tinker* (Peacock, 1972) were certainly among the better productions of their years.

WORKS: *The Charollais.* London: Faber & Faber, 1969; *Dance the Dance.* London: Faber & Faber, 1969; *Through the Bridewell Gate.* London: Faber & Faber, 1971. (Reportage); *Blood Relations.* Dublin: New Writers', 1972.

MACKEN, WALTER (1915-1967), playwright, novelist, and actor. Macken was born on May 3, 1915, in the city of Galway. He wrote his first story at the age of twelve, and when he was seventeen he joined the Taibhdhearc, the Irish language theatre in Galway. For the Taibhdhearc he not only acted and directed, but also wrote several plays in Irish. In the 1940s and 1950s, he was a prominent Abbey* actor, and he also played leading roles on Broadway in Michael J. Molloy's* *The King of Friday's Men* and in his own *Home Is the Hero* in 1954. He also played leading roles in the film versions of *Home Is the Hero* and of Brendan Behan's* *The Quare Fellow*. Early in 1966, he became artistic director and manager of the Abbey Theatre in its last days at the Queen's, but he gave up the job after a few months to devote full time to writing. He died on April 22, 1967, in Galway.

Macken's four published plays are *Mungo's Mansion* (Abbey, 1946), *Vacant Possession* (produced only by amateurs), *Home Is the Hero* (Abbey, 1952), and *Twilight of a Warrior* (Abbey, 1955). The first two plays are somewhat larger-than-life attempts at doing for Galway City what O'Casey* had done in his first plays for Dublin. Macken's plays, however, hang between O'Caseyan tragicomedy and a broader farcical-melodrama, but they do have considerable theatrical vitality. *Home Is the Hero* is probably Macken's best, and certainly most produced, play. Its central character is a figure of the father as outcast, as in John B. Keane's* later *The Year of the Hiker*; the play somewhat suffers for insufficient sympathy with this simple, though brutal, man. *Twilight of a Warrior* is an intriguing character study of the type of man who created de Valera's new Ireland—a hero of the Troubles grown into a successful businessman. Macken's Dacey Adam is not quite arresting enough to hold the play together, but, like Macken's later study of alcoholism, *The Voices of Doolin* (Dublin Theatre Festival, 1960), the play shows a lessening concern with easy theatricality and an increasing interest in character drawing.

Macken's greater growth as a dramatist was limited mainly by his considerable success as a novelist and his increasing fascination with fiction. Some of his books found a wide audience in America, and many of them are kept in print by an English popular market paperback firm. Macken's fiction, like his plays, hangs between entertainment and art—say, between the excellent popular novels of a Maurice Walsh* and the serious work of a Liam O'Flaherty.* Macken's books are what is sometimes called a good read; they have usually well-drawn, if somewhat simple, characters, strong plotting, and an easy and often evocative style. At his best, as in his study of Claddagh fishermen, *Rain on the Wind*, Macken is not only powerful but memorable. His most ambitious work is an historical trilogy comprising *Seek the Fair Land* about Cromwellian Ireland, *The Silent People* about the Famine years of the nineteenth century, and *The Scorching Wind* about the Troubles of the twentieth century. The first novels are effective recreations of their time, but the last seems hurried and thin. Macken's work in both fiction and drama has force, energy, and a confident craftsmanship. At its best, it only narrowly misses lasting excellence.

WORKS: *Mungo's Mansion*. London: Macmillan, 1946. (Play); *Quench the Moon*. London: Macmillan, 1948/New York: Viking, 1948. (Novel); *Vacant Possession*. London: Macmillan, 1948. (Play); *I Am Alone*. London: Macmillan, 1949. (Novel); *Rain on the Wind*. London: Macmillan, 1950. (Novel); *The Bogman*. London: Macmillan, 1952. (Novel); *Home Is the Hero*. London: Macmillan, 1953. (Play); *Sunset on the Window-Panes*. London: Macmillan, 1954. (Novel); *The Green Hills and Other Stories*. London: Macmillan, 1956; *Twilight of a Warrior*. London: Macmillan, 1956. (Play); *Sullivan*. London: Macmillan, 1957. (Novel); *Seek the Fair Land*. London: Macmillan, 1959. (Novel); *God Made Sunday and Other Stories*. London: Macmillan, 1962; *The Silent People*. London: Macmillan, 1962. (Novel); *The Scorching Wind*. London: Macmillan, 1964; *Island of the Great Yellow Ox*. London. Macmillan, 1966; *Brown Lord of the Mountain*. London: Macmillan, 1967; *The Coll Doll and Other Stories*. Dublin: Gill & Macmillan, 1969; *The Flight of the Doves*. London: Pan, 1971.   REFERENCE: Hogan, Robert. *After the Irish Renaissance*. Minneapolls: University of Minnesota Press, 1967, pp. 65-70.

McKENNA, JAMES (1933-), playwright and sculptor. McKenna was born in Dublin in June 1933. He spent five years studying at the College of Art, after which he received a Macaulay fellowship in sculpture in 1960. In the same year, his Dublin "Teddy-Boy" musical, *The Scatterin'*, was presented at the Theatre Festival in a lively production by Alan Simpson; it eventually moved to London's Theatre Royal, Stratford East. The play is in the vein of Behan's* *The Hostage*, except that it is less comic than romantic-realistic. The piece has a strong plot line, but the writing and characterization are thin; hence, *The Scatterin'* remains "theatre" rather than literature. However, given the necessary lift by its music and by an able producer, it is most effective theatre. A second play, *At Bantry,* won a prize in the 1916 Commemoration Competition and was produced at the Peacock in 1967. The play is a stylized treatment of the attempted landing of the French at Bantry Bay. It is written in unmemorable verse and was originally played in masks designed by the author. McKenna has also published a volume of verse and has written perhaps a dozen other plays, none of them a great advance over his first.

WORKS: *At Bantry*. Dublin: Sceptre Books, 1968; *Poems*. The Curragh, County Kildare: Goldsmith, 1973; *The Scatterin'*. The Curragh, County Kildare: Goldsmith, 1977.

MacKENNA, STEPHEN (1872-1934), translator. MacKenna is known for his eloquent translation of Plotinus, a labor which occupied him for many difficult years. His importance for Irish literature lies in his personality and his friendships. Among the writers who esteemed his vivid conversation and qualities of mind were AE,* J. M. Synge,* and James Stephens.* MacKenna was born on January 15, 1872, but did not attend university. In the late 1890s, he led a penurious bohemian life in Paris, during which he was

Synge's best friend. "How do those two young men live?" said an inquisitive person. "Oh, Synge lives on what MacKenna lends him, and MacKenna lives on what Synge pays him back." MacKenna joined the Greek side in the war between Greece and Turkey in 1897, later apparently visited New York, and then became the continental representative of *The New York World*. For a time he was a prosperous journalist, covering, for instance, the 1904-1905 Russian revolution and visiting Tolstoy. However, thoroughly disenchanted with journalism and refusing to act as personal valet to the visiting Joseph Pulitzer, who owned the paper, he resigned in 1907. He then returned to Dublin, becoming a leader writer for *The Freeman's Journal*, commencing his Plotinus, and gathering around him a group of interesting young men such as J. M. Hone,* Edmund Curtis,* the Celtic scholar Osborn Bergin, Padraic Colum,* Thomas MacDonagh,* Seumas O'Sullivan,* and James Stephens. His translating was hampered by his own ill health, and the long and lingering illness of his wife. After her death and after his disillusionment about the Anglo-Irish Treaty, he lived in England, working intermittently and living in some poverty. He died on March 8, 1934. His letters, particularly the whimsical and loosely written later ones, are still a delight to read, but, as he once wrote to AE: "I am not a man of the pen. I can say more in five minutes with my little tongue than with the longest fountain-pen in the world."

(He is not to be confused with the English novelist Stephen McKenna.)

WORK: *Journal and Letters,* ed. with a Memoir by E. R. Dodds and a Preface by Padraic Colum. New York: William Morrow, [1936].

MACKLIN, CHARLES (1699?-1797), playwright and actor. With the exception of David Garrick, Charles Macklin was possibly the most considerable actor on the English stage during the eighteenth century. As a playwright, some critics claim that he is excelled only by his countrymen Sheridan,* Goldsmith,* and Farquhar.*

Macklin is sometimes said to have been born in 1690, and there is a story that his mother spirited him away from the Battle of the Boyne where his father was fighting for King James. However, the most reliable commentators, as well as Macklin himself, assert that he was born in 1699. His family name was probably originally Melaghlin or MacLoughlin, and most scholars believe that he was born at Culdaff on the Inishowen peninsula, County Donegal. Very little is known about him until he made his way upon the English stage in 1733. There, he had a long and distinguished career, playing over two hundred roles and being particularly admired in such forceful characters as Macbeth, Shylock, and Sir Pertinax Macsychophant in his own best play, *The Man of the World*. Of his realistic performance as Shylock, Pope, according to legend, said, "This is the Jew that Shakespeare drew."

Macklin seems to have been Irish enough in his temper, and in 1735 in a quarrel over a wig in the greenroom of Drury Lane, he plunged the tip of his cane into another actor's eye. When the actor died, Macklin was arraigned, ably conducted his own defense, and was sentenced to be branded —but only with a cold iron. He seems to have been a blunt, outspoken, honest man, somewhat given to litigation to protect his rights. He was an advocate of a more realistic style of acting, as opposed to the somewhat artificial declamatory style of James Quinn and others, and he was an effective teacher of actors. In 1789, his memory finally failing, he broke down in his old part of Shylock and thereafter appeared no more on the stage. In his last years he was somewhat senile; he died on July 11, 1797, and was buried in St. Paul's, Covent Garden.

As a playwright, Macklin does not rank with Goldsmith or Sheridan, but his character drawing is usually strong, and his best work would bear revival today. His most famous characters were not Irishmen but Scotsmen, such as the superb Sir Pertinax and Sir Archy Macsarcasm in *Love à La Mode*. That quite funny play has a querulous and family-proud Scotsman, a booby of a fox-hunting English squire, a Jewish dandy named Beau Mordecai, and a warlike Irishman named Sir Callaghan O'Brallaghan, all contesting for the hand of the heroine. The Irishman being naturally the noblest wins. Sir Callaghan is something of a Stage Irishman, but Macklin's other Irish hero, Murrough O'Dogherty, is quite solidly drawn. In *The True-born Irishman*, O'Dogherty is realistically cynical about politicians, but he avoids misanthropy and is firmly level-headed and concerned for the welfare of his country. His opinions are grafted onto a conventional, yet effective, plot in which a good deal of fun is poked at the foppish Englishman and at the Irish foolishly aping English customs. At its most recently known revival, by the Theatre of Ireland in Dublin in 1910, the play was very successful.

WORKS: *King Henry VII, or, The Popish Imposter*. London: Dodsley, 1746. (Play); *The Fortune Hunters*. London: McCulloh/Dublin: Powell, 1750. (Play); *The Man of the World and Love à la Mode*. London: Bell, 1793. (Play); *The True-born Irishman*. Dublin: Jones, 1793; *Four Comedies*. J. O. Bartley, ed. London: Sidgwick & Jackson, 1968. (Contains *Love à la Mode, The True-born Irishman, The School for Husbands,* and *The Man of the World*).   REFERENCE: Appleton, William W. *Charles Macklin, an Actor's Life*. Cambridge, Mass.: Harvard University Press, 1960.

MacLAVERTY, BERNARD (ca. 1945-), short story writer. MacLaverty, a Belfast writer, worked for ten years as a medical technician before entering Queen's University where he took a degree in English in 1974. In 1975, the Northern Arts Council awarded him a bursary for his stories which had appeared in various magazines and anthologies. A first collection, *Secrets*, was published in 1977, and was the winner of a book award from the Scottish Arts Council. Most of the stories are about the loneliness of youth and middle age, but a couple of them are also extremely funny. His work is conventional in technique but careful in craftsmanship. He has also written and illustrated two children's stories.

WORKS: *Secrets*. [Belfast]: Blackstaff, [1977]; *A Man in Search of a Pet*. Belfast: Blackstaff, 1978; *Mochua the Monk*. Belfast: Blackstaff, 1978.

McLAVERTY, MICHAEL (1907-), novelist and short story writer. McLaverty was born in Carrickmacross, County Monaghan, on July 6, 1907, but lived part of his childhood on Rathlin Island off the northern coast of County Antrim. Later, he lived and was educated in Belfast, first at St. Malachy's College and then at Queen's University where he read science and was awarded his M.Sc. in 1933. Until his retirement, he was a teacher of mathematics and later headmaster in the northern capital, during which time he maintained a steady output of novels and stories.

A great deal of McLaverty's fiction depicts the North of Ireland during the years between the two world wars when the decline of the small farmer, rural depopulation, and the accompanying growth of the industrial working class of Belfast began to accelerate. In such novels as *Call My Brother Back* (1939), *Lost Fields* (1941), and *In This Thy Day* (1945), he shuns direct treatment of public and political issues for the more local and urgent concerns of his characters: the conflicts between an individual and the rural community, within families and between generations, and, of course, poverty. Although one senses that they belong to a social and religious minority, rarely do McLaverty's people question either their Catholic faith or the larger social system that is the essential backdrop to their conflicts. Their vague dissatisfaction with their lot, not in society or in Northern Ireland, but in the world at large lends them an innocence that reminds one of Hardy's peasants.

His chief characters' broken relationship with the ancestral fields is the upshot of most of these conflicts and might be said to be McLaverty's principal theme in whichever of his favorite locales—Rathlin Island, the shores of Strangford Lough, the damp country rimming Lough Neagh, or the back streets of Belfast—a particular work may be set. In *Call My Brother Back*, his first and perhaps finest novel, McLaverty couples this theme with a blurred account of the sectarian outrages in Belfast during the creation of Northern Ireland. In addition, since both themes are presented in the strange and dreamlike currency of boyhood (a thirteen-year-old Rathlin islander is the central character), it is a troubled and poetic song of the awakening adolescent heart. McLaverty returned to Rathlin Island for his fictional setting in a later novel, *Truth in the Night* (1952).

The writing in *Call My Brother Back* represents McLaverty at his best. The limpness of style is at first glance almost childlike: large brushstrokes and broad, primary effects. But the untutored appearance of McLaverty's prose, as well as suiting the novel's point of view, barely disguises the author's deliberate attempt to isolate the subject matter by draining the style of affectation. At its worst, McLaverty's prose sinks with a leaden pathos; at its best, it is as single-minded and elemental as a mountain stream.

At the expense of a certain vigor, McLaverty has continued to cultivate quiet, even delicate powers of observation whose results are recorded on a restricted canvas. The short story, of which he is close to being a master, is probably his true *métier*, though he has not been prolific in the form. Whether he is writing about country people, as in "The Wild Duck's Nest," or of first-generation Belfast people, as in "The Game Cock," McLaverty tends to achieve a poignant and meditative quality that is hardly threatened by subdued irony or rueful humor. "The Game Cock," "Pigeons," and "Six Weeks On and Two Ashore" are among the best of his very fine stories.

JOHN WILSON FOSTER

WORKS: *Call My Brother Back*. London & New York: Longmans, Green, 1939/ reissued Dublin: Allen Figgis, 1970; *Lost Fields*. New York & Toronto: Longmans, Green, 1941; *The White Mare and Other Stories*. Newcastle, County Down: Mourne, 1943; *In This Thy Day*. London: Jonathan Cape, 1945; *The Game Cock and Other Stories*. New York: Devin-Adair, 1947; *The Three Brothers*. London. Jonathan Cape, 1948; *Truth in the Night*. New York: Macmillan, 1951; *School for Hope*. London: Jonathan Cape, 1954; *The Choice*. London: Jonathan Cape, 1958; *The Brightening Day*. New York: Macmillan, 1965; *The Road to the Shore and other Stories*. Dublin: Poolbeg, 1976; *Collected Short Stories*. Dublin: Poolbeg, 1978. REFERENCE: Foster, John Wilson. *Forces and Themes in Ulster Fiction*. Dublin: Gill & Macmillan/ Totowa, N.J.: Rowman & Littlefield, 1974, pp. 36-47, 59-63.

Mac LIAMMOIR, MICHEAL (1899-1978), playwright, actor, and man of letters. Micheál Mac Liammóir was born Alfred Willmore in Cork on October 25, 1899. As a child actor, he played in London in *Peter Pan* and with Beerbohm Tree. For sixty years Mac Liammóir was one of the sights and delights of Dublin. He was one of the ablest modern Irish actors, with a range from light romantic comedy to darkest tragedy. His Robert Emmet in Denis Johnston's* *The Old Lady Says "No!"* is considered an Irish classic; he has been a preeminent interpretor of Oscar Wilde* and has toured his one-man show, *The Importance of Being Oscar*, all over the world; and he has played with much success roles as disparate as Hamlet and Liam O'Flaherty's* Gypo Nolan. In 1928, he and his English partner, Hilton Edwards, founded the Dublin Gate Theatre.* He had been involved as actor, director, author, set designer and costume designer in over three hundred productions. Few of his many plays have been published, but his several volumes of theatrical reminiscences are, in their graceful and witty mandarin style, a delightful recreation of theatrical history. In 1977, he published a thinly disguised autobiographical novel, *Enter a Goldfish*. His panache and brio, his sweetness and urbanity, were notable in a city so seldom associated with such qualities. His literary taste was perhaps bounded by the English *fin de siècle,* and, consequently, much of his writing seems only charmingly lightweight. His theatrical taste, however, was healthily eclectic, and the Gate Theatre, although hardly in the vanguard of theatrical experiment, has been healthily various and long vigorous. Mac Liammóir died on March 6, 1978.

WORKS: *Diarmuid agus Grainne*. Baile Atha Cliath: Oifig Dialta Foillseachain Rialtais, 1935. (Play); *All for Hecuba*. London: Methuen, 1946/revised, Dublin: Progress House, 1961. (Memoir); *Each Actor on his Ass*. London: Routledge & Kegan Paul, 1961. (Memoir); *Where Stars Walk*. Dublin: Progress House, 1962. (Play); *The Importance of Being Oscar*. Dublin: Dolmen/London: Oxford, 1963; *Ill Met by Moonlight*. Dublin: Duffy, 1964. (Play); *Theatre in Ireland*. 2d ed., with sequel. Dublin: Three Candles, 1964; *An Oscar of No Importance*. London: Heinemann, 1968; with Eavan Boland, *W. B. Yeats*. London: Thames & Hudson, 1971/New York: Viking, 1972; *Enter a Goldfish*. London: Thames & Hudson, 1977. (Autobiographical novel).   REFERENCE: Luke Peter, ed. *Enter Certain Players*; *Edwards, Mac Liammóir and the Gate*. [Dublin]: Dolmen, [1978].

MacLOCHLAINN, ALF (1926-), novelist and librarian. MacLochlainn was born in Dublin in 1926. He joined the staff of the National Library of Ireland in 1949 and has been director of the library since 1976. In addition to many scholarly papers, he has published *Out of Focus* which is described as a novella, but which would appear to be four short reflections of Flann O'Brien's* de Selby as dictated to Samuel Beckett.*

WORK: *Out of Focus*. Dublin: O'Brien, 1977.

MacMAHON, BRYAN (1909-), novelist, short story writer, dramatist, translator, ballad-maker, and author of children's books. MacMahon was born on September 29, 1909, in Listowel, County Kerry, in a rich, rural environment that also produced George Fitzmaurice,* Maurice Walsh,* and John B. Keane.* MacMahon attended St. Michael's College in Listowel, and one of his early teachers was the writer Seamus Wilmot (1902-1977). Later, he attended St. Patrick's College in Drumcondra and qualified as a national teacher. For more than forty years he taught in the National Parochial School in Listowel. He also ran a bookstore and was a moving spirit in the town's amateur dramatic society.

MacMahon's first poems and plays were published in *The Bell** and were much admired by Frank O'Connor* and Sean O'Faolain.* His first collection of stories, *The Lion-Tamer* (1948), immediately established his reputation as a fresh and vital new voice in Irish fiction. If there is any serious fault in this excellent collection, it probably stems from MacMahon's own personality. He is a man of great enthusiasms and boundless energy, and his early prose sometimes becomes romantically florid. His later collections indicate a growing craft, and he is generally conceded to be one of the few masters of the Irish short story to appear after O'Connor and O'Faolain.

MacMahon is steeped in rural tradition. This knowledge pervades his work and is particularly evident in *The Honey Spike* (1967), which is probably both his finest play and his finest novel. This picaresque tale of a young tinker couple traveling through Ireland is much enriched by MacMahon's intimate knowledge of the tinkers or Travelling People, including an acquaintance with their secret language, Shelta. The story is by turns humorous, melodramatic, and full of local color, and at the end it is movingly eloquent. The fictional version perhaps loses something of the dramatic intensity of the play, but the play is probably one of the half dozen best pieces to appear on the Irish stage since World War II. Its closest rival among MacMahon's own work is *The Song of the Anvil*, a blend of folklore, fantasy, and romance that, nevertheless, retains a firm grip on reality.

MacMahon is a member of the Irish Academy of Letters and a chief organizer of the Writers' Week in Listowel. In 1972, he was awarded an LL.D. from the National University of Ireland for his services to Irish writing.

WORKS: *The Lion-Tamer and Other Stories*. Toronto: Macmillan, 1948/New York: E. P. Dutton, 1949, 1958/London: Dent, 1958; *Jack O'Moora, and the King of Ireland's Son*. New York: E. P. Dutton, 1950. (Children's book); *Children of the Rainbow*. New York: E. P. Dutton/London & Toronto: Macmillan, 1952. (Novel); *The Red Petticoat and Other Stories*. New York: E. P. Dutton/London: Macmillan, 1955; *Brendan of Ireland*. London: Methuen, 1965/New York: Hastings House, 1967. (Children's book); *The Honey Spike*. New York: E. P. Dutton/London: Bodley Head/ Toronto: Clarke, Irwin, 1967. (Novel); *The Song of the Anvil*, in *Seven Irish Plays, 1946-1964*. R. Hogan, ed. Minneapolis: University of Minnesota Press, 1967; *Patsy-O and His Wonderful Pets*. New York: E. P. Dutton, 1970. (Children's book); *Here's Ireland*. New York: E. P. Dutton/London: Batsford, 1971. (Travel book); trans., *Peig: The Autobiography of Peig Sayers of the Great Blasket Island*. Dublin: Talbot, 1974; *The End of the World and Other Stories*. Dublin: Poolbeg, 1976. REFERENCES: Henderson, Gordon. "An Interview with Bryan MacMahon." *Journal of Irish Literature* 3 (September 1974): 3-23. Henderson, Joanne L. "Four Kerry Writers: Fitzmaurice, Walsh, MacMahon, Keane, a Checklist." *Journal of Irish Literature* 1 (May 1972): 112-118.

MacMANUS, FRANCIS (1909-1965), novelist. MacManus was born in Kilkenny on March 8, 1909. He was educated at the local Christian Brothers school, at St. Patrick's Teacher Training College in Dublin, and at University College, Dublin. He taught for eighteen years in the Synge Street Christian Brothers school in Dublin before joining Radio Éireann in 1948 as general features editor. He traveled widely in Europe, was a member of the Irish Academy of Letters, and was a moving force in introducing the Thomas Davis lecture series on Radio Éireann. His genial and helpful disposition endeared him to many writers. He died suddenly of a heart attack in Dublin on November 27, 1965.

MacManus wrote eleven novels and two interesting biographies, *Boccaccio* (1947) and *St. Columban* (1963). The novels begin with an historical trilogy based on peasant life in eighteenth-century Ireland: *Stand and Give*

Challenge (1934), *Candle for the Proud* (1936), and *Men Withering* (1939). Unity is given to the trilogy by the central character, Donnacha Ruadh Mac Conmara, a hedge-schoolmaster and Gaelic poet.

From imaginative recreation of his racial past, "the hidden Ireland" of Daniel Corkery,* MacManus turned to depiction of the contemporary rural scene. The Drombridge trilogy, comprising *This House Was Mine* (1937), *Flow On, Lovely River* (1941), and *Watergate* (1942), is the first result. Dombridge is the fictional town in MacManus' native County Kilkenny. *This House Was Mine* concerns the self-destructive effects of land greed. *Flow On, Lovely River* is the diary of a schoolmaster thwarted by circumstances from marrying the girl he loves. Its title, a snatch from a popular song, is given Dantesque overtones; for the river is human life and unhappy human willing which flow to the sea of eternity and to God. *Watergate* (which has absolutely no connection with Richard M. Nixon) is the tale of a woman who returns to Ireland from the states and gradually finds her native rural Kilkenny not quite "the land of heart's desire."

MacManus was most prolific in the early 1940s, when he also composed *The Wild Garden* (1940), *The Greatest of These* (1943), and *Statue for a Square* (1945). The last-mentioned is MacManus' only true failure. Its parody of the small-town bumptiousness involved in erecting a public memorial is quite boring. Perhaps lighthearted satire was not an appropriate genre for so morally serious a writer. *The Wild Garden*, on the other hand, evokes brilliantly the fears and joys of childhood, and *The Greatest of These* is a fine delineation of a pre-Vatican II Irish bishop grappling with the psychological problems involved in practicing the highest theological virtue. Like Thomas Kilroy's* novel *The Big Chapel* (1971), *The Greatest of These* is based on the ecclesiastical conflicts in the town of Callan, County Kilkenny, during the 1870s.

The Fire in the Dust, MacManus' chief novel, appeared in 1950. The "fire" is the fire of normal sexual appetite, wrongly identified by the novel's puritans as the fire of lust. The "dust" is human mortality, especially the adolescents of Kilkenny City. Strongly autobiographical in flavor, the novel courageously attacked the Jansenistic tendencies of Irish Catholicism through affirming the sane humanistic values of the *philosophia perennis*. *American Son* (1959), the last MacManus novel, explores these values in the dramatic conflicts between New Mexican Indian Catholic religiosity, American capitalism, beatnik Franciscanism, and middle-class Irish Catholicism.

MacManus' *oeuvre* is best viewed, like Paul Claudel's, as the fruit of a mind which accepted willingly and liberatingly the dogmas of orthodox Catholic scholasticism. In this religious acceptance, as in his benign acceptance of the Irish race and language (as witness his U.S. travel book, *Seal Ag Rodaiocht/On the Road for a Time* of 1955), MacManus is the diametric opposite of James Joyce* and is also estranged from his acerbic contemporaries—O'Flaherty,* O'Faolain,* and O'Connor.* An absence of overt sexual detail, dictated only by artistic preference, ensured that, unlike those contemporaries, none of his works was banned by the Irish Censorship Board. His literary achievement, however, is often quite as high as theirs, and certainly needs reevaluation.

DENIS COTTER, JR.

WORKS: *Stand and Give Challenge.* Dublin: Talbot, 1934; *Candle for the Proud.* Dublin: Talbot, 1936; *This House Was Mine.* Dublin: Talbot, 1937; *Men Withering.* Dublin: Talbot, 1939; *The Wild Garden.* Dublin: Talbot, 1940; *Flow On, Lovely River.* Dublin: Talbot, 1941; *Watergate.* Dublin: Talbot, 1942; *The Greatest of These.* Dublin: Talbot, 1943; *Statue for a Square.* Dublin: Talbot, 1945; *Boccaccio.* London: Sheed and Ward, 1947; *The Fire in the Dust.* London: Jonathan Cape, 1950; *Seal Ag Rodaiocht/On the Road for a Time.* Baile Atha Cliath: Sairseal agus Dill, 1955; *American Son.* London: Jonathan Cape, 1959; *St. Columban.* Dublin: Clonmore & Reynolds, 1963. REFERENCES: Kiely, Benedict. "Praise God for Ireland." *The Irish Monthly* 76 (September 1948): 402-406. An extended version of this article appears in *The Kilkenny Magazine,* No. 14 (Spring-Summer 1966): 121-136; MacMahon, Sean. "Francis MacManus's Novels of Modern Ireland." *Eire-Ireland* 5 (1970): 116-130.

MacMANUS, SEUMAS (ca. 1868-1960), man of letters. MacManus, a prolific writer of popular stories, verse, and plays, was born James MacManus in County Donegal and was the son of a poor farmer. Joseph Holloway* and other early commentators give his birthdate as December 31, 1868, although other authorities have cited 1869, 1870, and even 1860. At eighteen years of age, he became a National School teacher in the school where he himself had been taught. He soon began contributing pieces to many Irish papers, and he published his first book, *Shuilers from Healthy Hills,* in 1893. He was a contributor to the Belfast Nationalist magazine *The Shan Van Vocht,* and in 1901 he married one of its editors, the poet Anna Johnston who wrote under the name of Ethna Carbery* (died 1902). One of MacManus' early plays, *The Townland of Tamney,* was presented by the Irish National Theatre Society in January 1904. When the Abbey* first toured America in 1911, MacManus was one of the most virulent detractors of Synge's* *Playboy of the Western World*; Lady Gregory* referred to MacManus as "Shame-Us MacManus." For more than fifty years after his first wife's death, MacManus divided his time between America and Donegal. He continued to write prolifically, his most popular work possibly being his autobiography *The Rocky Road to Dublin* (1938) and a very long history of Ireland.

MacManus' conventional, sentimental, and patriotic verse has its banalities (see, for instance, the second saccharine stanza of "Lullaby," which Padraic Colum* anthologized), but has occasional small excellences (see, for instance, the fourth tight stanza of the otherwise piffling "A Stor, Gra Geal Mochree"). His plays are usually too simple and too broad, but one drama, *The Townland of Tamney,* might work if played with restraint in-

stead of gagged as it was by the pre-Abbey players. His stories and retellings of folktales are often, despite his patriotism, an exaggeration for a
foreign audience. Nevertheless, despite their Mr. Dooleyish broguing, they
do contain many authentic and racy turns of phrase and even some eloquent
writing. For instance, this passage from *The Humours of Donegal*:

> He was as merry as a mouse in a cornstack, but as roguish as a rat
> that grew gray in mischief and morodin'. The lark herself didn't sing
> sweeter, nor rise earlier, nor think less of the troubles of the morra.
> The hare hadn't a lighter foot scuddin' from the corn, the throstle
> of Murvagh Wood a lighter heart, nor the *Bacach Beag* [little beg-
> garman] a lighter purse. Barney wrought to any man in the parish
> —or the next to it—by day, and he attended every spree in the
> parish—or the next to it—by night. No wake missed Barney; no
> weddin' missed Barney; no berral missed Barney; no christenin'
> missed him. If there was a fair, Barney was the second man at it;
> if there was a raffle, Barney was the first; if there was a dance,
> Barney was there; if there was a scuffle, me brave Barney was
> everywhere. He owned as much clothes as was on his back, as much
> land as stuck to the soles of his brogues, and as much motherwit as
> would dower a townland. As for the amount of thickery in his head,
> there's no tellin' of it. Och, it's Barney was the boy out an' out!

MacManus died at about age ninety in New York City on October 23, 1960,
as a result of a fall out of the seventh-story window of his nursing home.

WORKS: *Shuilers from Healthy Hills,* by "Mac." Donegal: G. Kirke, 1893; *The
Leadin' Road to Donegal, and Other Stories,* by "Mac." London: Digby, Long, ca.
1895; *'Twas in Dhroll Donegal,* by "Mac." 2d ed. London: Downey, 1897; *The Bend
of the Road,* by James MacManus ("Mac"). London: Downey, 1898; *The Humours
of Donegal,* by James MacManus ("Mac"). London: Unwin, 1898; *In Chimney
Corners, Merry Tales of Irish Folk-lore.* New York: Doubleday & McClure, 1899/
many other editions, the latest, Garden City, N.Y.: Doubleday, Doran, 1935; *Through
the Turf Smoke,* by "Mac." New York: Doubleday & McClure, 1899/London: Unwin,
1901; *The Bewitched Fiddle and Other Irish Tales.* New York: Doubleday & McClure,
1900; *Donegal Fairy Stories.* New York: McClure, Phillips, 1900/London: Isbistor,
1902/Garden City, N.Y.: Doubleday & Page, 1910/New York: Doubleday, 1912/
Garden City, N.Y.: Doubleday, 1943; *A Lad of the O'Friels.* New York: McClure,
Phillips, 1903/various other editions, the latest, New York: Devin-Adair, 1947; *The
Red Poacher.* New York: Funk & Wagnalls, 1903; *Ballads of a Country Boy.* Dublin:
Gill, 1905; *The Hard-Hearted Man.* Dublin: Gill, 1905. (Play); *Doctor Kilgannan.*
Dublin: Gill, 1907; *Yourself and the Neighbours.* New York: Devin-Adair, [1914],
1944; *Ireland's Curse.* New York: Irish Publishing Co., ca. 1917; *Lo, and Behold Ye!*
New York: Frederick A. Stokes, [1919]; *Tales That Were Told.* Dublin: Talbot/Lon-
don: Unwin, 1920; *Top o' the Mornin'.* New York: Frederick A. Stokes, [1920]; *The
Story of the Irish Race.* New York: Irish Publishing Co., 1921/New York: Devin-
Adair, 1945, 1955; *The Donegal Wonder Book.* New York: Frederick A. Stokes, 1926;
O, Do You Remember. . . . Dublin: Duffy, 1926; ed., *The Four Winds of Eirinn,*
Poems of Ethna Carbery, 25th Anniversary edition. Dublin: Gill, 1927; *A Short Story
of the Irish Race.* Dublin: Browne & Nolan, [1928]; *Bold Blades of Donegal.* New

York: Frederick A. Stokes, 1935/London: Marston, [1937]; *The Rocky Road to Dublin*. New York: Macmillan, 1938/New York: Devin-Adair, 1947; *Dark Patrick*. New York: Macmillan, 1939; *The Well o' the World's End*. New York: Macmillan, 1939/New York: Devin-Adair, 1949, 1954; *Woman of Seven Sorrows*. Dublin: Gill, 1945. (Play); *Tales from Ireland*. London: Evans [1949]; *We Sang for Ireland, Poems of Ethna Carbery, Seumas MacManus, Alice Milligan*. New York: Devin-Adair, 1950; *Heavy Hangs the Golden Grain*. New York: Macmillan, 1950/Dublin: Talbot, [1951]; *The Bold Heroes of Hungry Hill, and Other Irish Folk Tales*. New York: Ariel Books, [1951]/New York: Pellegrini & Cudahy, 1951/London: Dent, [1952]; *The Little Mistress of the Eskar Mór*. Dublin: Gill, 1960; *Hibernian Nights*. New York: Macmillan, 1963. (There is also an early volume, apparently from the 1890s: *Barney Brean and Other Boys*. Dublin: "Irish Nights" Office, n.d.) Most of MacManus' plays were issued from about 1905 by D. O'Molloy of Mount Charles, County Donegal. These were paperback editions for amateur actors, and included: 1. *The Leadin' Road to Donegal;* 2. *The Resurrection of Dinny O'Dowd;* 3. *The Lad from Largymore;* 6. *The Townland of Tamney*, reprint, Chicago: De Paul University, 1972; 7. *Orange and Green*; 8. *Nabby Heron's Matching*; *Bong Tong Comes to Balruddery*; 10. *Rory Wins;* 11. *Mrs. Connolly's Cashmere;* 12. *The Miracle of Father Peter;* 13. *The Rale True Doctor;* 14. *The Bachelors of Braggy*.

McNALLY, LEONARD (1752-1820), playwright. The infamous, though fascinating, Leonard McNally was born in Dublin in 1752, and was admitted to the Irish bar in 1776 and to the English bar in 1783. He edited *The Public Ledger*, and several of his plays were successfully performed at Covent Garden. He was counsel for Napper Tandy in 1792 and was one of the original members of the United Irishmen. Indeed, he even fought a duel with Sir Jonah Barrington* to defend the honor of the United Irishmen. However, from at least 1794, he was in the pay of Dublin Castle from which he received a substantial yearly stipend of £300 until his death. Thoroughly trusted by the United Irishmen, he was in the habit of entertaining them and then reporting their conversations to the authorities. He put the finger on Lord Edward Fitzgerald in 1797, and he sold Emmet* in 1803 for £200. However, he was the defense counsel for the most prominent men of '98 and his defense of Emmet in 1803 was thought brilliantly eloquent. He is also said to have consoled Emmet in his death cell by pointing out that the young patriot would soon be united with his mother in Heaven. He died in Harcourt Street, Dublin, on February 13, 1820, and was buried in Donnybrook church, his villainies still undetected.

McNally was a personally brave man who fought several duels, and he was the most engaging company. His plays and comic operas have not held up and were not Irish in subject, but they were droll and entertaining in their day. Several are available on microprint from the Larpent collection, and his five-act comedy *Fashionable Levities* (1785) is available in the reprint of Mrs. Inchbald's *Modern Theatre*. The popular song "The Lass of Richmond Hill" is his. He adapted *Tristram Shandy* to the stage (1783), and he also wrote a fictional parody of Sterne* in his *Sentimental Excursions to Windsor* (1781). As a writer, he would repay examination.

WORKS: *The Apotheosis of Punch*. London: J. Wenman, 1779. (Satirical masque);
Sentimental Excursions to Windsor and Other Places. London: J. Walker, 1781;
Retaliation. London: F. Blythe, 1782. 2d ed./Dublin: Printed by R. Marchbank, for
the Company of Booksellers, 1782. (Farce in two acts); *Tristram Shandy*, a senti-
mental, Shandean bagatelle in two acts. London: S. Bladon, 1783; *Fashionable
Levities*. London: G.G.J. & J. Robinson, 1785/also in Mrs. Inchbald's *The Modern
Theatre*, Vol. 10; *Critic upon Critic*, a dramatic medley in three acts. London: G.
Brand, 1788.

MacNAMARA, BRINSLEY (1890-1963), novelist, short story writer, and
playwright. MacNamara was born John Weldon on September 6, 1890, in
Ballinacor, Hiskinstown, Delvin, County Westmeath, one of the seven children of the local schoolmaster, James Weldon. In 1910, while in Dublin
ostensibly to study for a career in the Excise, MacNamara joined the Abbey
Theatre Company* as an actor, eventually going with the company in 1911
on the first Abbey tour of America. He remained in America until 1913
attempting to make a career in New York, but he failed and returned to
Ireland. From 1913 until 1918, he retired to the relative obscurity of Delvin
from whence he published numerous derivative poems and stories in Dublin
newspapers and magazines. His burgeoning talent gradually evidenced a
peculiar turn, a whimsical, ironic, curious eye for reality as he perceived it—
a multivision towards experience.

This period of apprentice work and obscurity ended with the 1918 publication of his novel *The Valley of the Squinting Windows*, a young man's
scathing but humorous demythologizing of Irish village life. This was the
first of seven novels he was to write and, though not his finest work, the
book with which he has unfortunately been associated ever since. The notoriety which the novel brought him had several disastrous effects: the book
was publicly burned in the best medieval fashion in Delvin; his father's
school was boycotted (James Weldon eventually unsuccessfully sued the
parish priest and several parishioners, citing a conspiracy which affected his
pension); he was driven from Delvin in fear of his life, ever after to consider himself an outsider, an exiled man of the country forced to live in
Dublin; and, most unfortunately, Andrew E. Malone described MacNamara
as the originator of the "squinting windows" school of Irish realistic fiction,
which depicts provincial narrowness.

MacNamara's life became a continuous growing away, an alienation,
from that area he most loved and hated, for what Dublin had to be for
James Joyce,* the Midlands had to be for MacNamara. They were the true
center of his Ireland, and no Irish novelist ever so painstakingly delineated
a rural Irish mentality. His novels and stories describe a people whose only
traditions were the traditions of orthodoxy, greed, and ignorance—and
always the antagonist is the Church and its clergy. MacNamara had determined, at excessive personal sacrifice and with the heroism essential to the
truly dedicated artist, not to succumb to the bleak anomaly of this life, but

to become its master, its historian, and its savior. Always, though, there is a sense of the tragicomic, the presence of what he called "the long, low chuckle of the mind."

In the summer of 1920, he married Ellen Degidon in Quin, County Clare. An only child, Oliver Weldon, was born in Quin on May 16, 1921. Ellen remained in Quin to raise the child when MacNamara took up permanent residence in Dublin in 1922. That year, he assumed the post of registrar in the National Gallery. By this time, he had published three additional novels: *The Clanking of Chains* (1919), in which he pursued his relentless, idealistic indictment of the Irish village (this time in political terms) while accepting the inevitable death of his own idealism; *The Irishman* (1920), using the pseudonym "Oliver Blyth," wherein he clearly works out his literary aesthetic, explains how *The Valley of the Squinting Windows* came to be written, and broadly satirizes aspects of the Irish Literary Renaissance; and the hauntingly beautiful and tragic *The Mirror in the Dusk* (1921), in which MacNamara appears to have finally become convinced of the ultimate failure of his role as savior.

MacNamara was never again to experience years of such generally consistent quality in his work (including a series of twenty-three highly informed articles entitled "Books and Their Writers" for *The Gael*) as he did in the war-torn period between 1916 and 1922. During this period of rampant Irish nationalism he struggled heroically and alone to tell the truths others would tell in retrospect. The struggle proved too much for one man. The dedicated novelist who worked arduously to produce four novels of high merit in less than six years was to produce only three more novels in the remaining forty years of his life—two of which, *The Various Lives of Marcus Igoe* (1929) and *Return to Ebontheever* (1930), were partially completed during this same six-year period.

Between 1919 and 1945, MacNamara had nine plays produced at the Abbey, the most memorable and powerful of which is *Margaret Gillan* (1933), a stark, remorseless, Ibsen-like study of a woman's frustrated love, repressed passions, and revenge. It was awarded the Casement Prize as the best Irish play of the year, as well as the Harmsworth Literary Award. MacNamara's comedies, the best of which were *The Glorious Uncertainty* (1923) and *Look at the Heffernans* (1926), show that he compromised himself as an artist to produce commercially successful Abbey formula plays. MacNamara was never truly a man of the theatre, however, despite a lifelong association with the Abbey, for which he served briefly in 1935 on the Board of Directors. That same year he resigned in protest over the production of Sean O'Casey's* *The Silver Tassie*. He was later the drama critic for *The Irish Times*, but his reviews reveal a man who did not consider drama a serious form of literature. After *The Glorious Uncertainty*'s financial success, his future life was to be far more given to the life of literary raconteur and popular, fashionable dramatist than to the personally more demanding and less visible life of *enfant terrible* of Irish fiction. Still, he was a founding member of the Irish Academy of Letters in 1932, and his peers always acknowledged him to be a most knowledgeable literary man.

In 1929, MacNamara produced his finest novel, *The Various Lives of Marcus Igoe*, an intensely personal, self-evaluative, tragicomic fantasy. In the multiplicity of its concerns and its undeniably existential musings, it emerges as MacNamara's masterpiece, a most profound and challenging work, a too long neglected gem worthy of a Flann O'Brien.* His primary concerns here are the immortality of the artist, existence, nonbeing, and reality. MacNamara vigorously asserts the supremacy, reliability, and immortality of the reality of characters in literature over the inconstancy, mutability, and unreliability of characters in reality.

The year 1929 also saw the publication of his book of stories *The Smiling Faces*, which were mostly reworked material from an earlier period. In 1930, he published *Return to Ebontheever*, a mirthless but beautifully written novel based on Shakespeare's *Othello* and committed to an enthusiastic denunciation of a too strict adherence to any orthodoxy.

A long fictional silence (*The Grand House in the City* [1936] and *The Three Thimbles* [1941] had been produced at the Abbey) was broken in 1945 with the publication of a book of stories entitled *Some Curious People*. The stories are uniquely his: unhurried, ironic, poetically idiomatic, sad, often brilliantly humorous, sensitively remembered, and compelling.

His final novel, *Michael Caravan* (1946), is in a lighter, forgiving, more sentimental vein than his other novels. This is a novelized comedy of rural manners and affectations, by turns touchingly naive and nostalgic, set in a remote time far more innocent than post-World War II Ireland.

The Whole Story of the X.Y.Z. (1951), a novella, deals with a man's absorption in his life-giving fantasies. MacNamara did not appear in print again, with the exception of a single story, until the posthumous reminiscence "Growing Up in the Midlands" (1964). Crippled by arthritis and old age, he resigned from the National Gallery only a few years before his death in 1963.

MacNamara may have been driven to the whimsy of his Abbey comedies for relief from the financial burden of his marriage, from the bitter disappointment of being a prophet in his own country, from the pressure to succeed, or merely from his sure sense of the ultimate sadness of human destiny. Whatever the reasons, in thus retreating into himself and away from reality in his work, he discovered the milieu which best suited his peculiar talents, and in *The Various Lives of Marcus Igoe* he produced what must eventually be his most acclaimed work and the assurance of his real place in twentieth-century Irish literature.

MICHAEL McDONNELL

WORKS: *The Valley of the Squinting Windows*. London: Sampson Low, Marston,

1918; as "Oliver Blyth," *The Irishman.* London: Everleigh Nash, 1920; *The Clanking of Chains.* Dublin: Maunsel, 1920; *The Mirror in the Dusk.* Dublin & London: Maunsel & Roberts, 1921; *Look at the Heffernans!* Dublin & Cork: Talbot, n.d. (Play); *The Smiling Faces.* London: Mandrake, 1929. (Short stories); *The Various Lives of Marcus Igoe.* London: Sampson Low, Marston, 1929; *Return to Ebontheever.* London: Jonathan Cape, 1930/reissued in 1942 as *Othello's Daughter; Margaret Gillan.* London: George Allen & Unwin, 1934. (Play); *Marks and Mabel.* Dublin: Duffy, 1945. (Play); *Some Curious People.* Dublin: Talbot, 1945. (Short stories); *Michael Caravan.* Dublin: Talbot, 1946; *Abbey Plays, 1899-1948.* Dublin: At the Sign of the Three Candles, 1949. (Pamphlet listing Abbey plays, with an Introduction); *The Whole Story of the X.Y.Z.* Belfast: H. R. Carter, 1951. (Novella); *The Glorious Uncertainty.* Dublin: P. J. Bourke, 1957. (Play).   REFERENCES: Flanagan, Thomas. "The Night the Book Was Burned." *Irish Evening Press* (July 18, 1964); Hogan, Robert. *After the Irish Renaissance.* Minneapolis: University of Minnesota Press, 1967; Kiely, Benedict. *Modern Irish Fiction.* Dublin: Golden Eagle Books, 1950; McDonnell, Michael. "Brinsley MacNamara: A Checklist." *Journal of Irish Literature* 4 (May 1975): 79-88. Malone, Andrew E. "Brinsley MacNamara: An Appreciation." *The Dublin Magazine* (July 1929); Meehan, Donnchadh A. "Of Four Fantasies." *The Bookman* (December 1948).

MacNAMARA, GERALD (1866-1938), playwright and actor. Gerald MacNamara was the pen and stage name of Harry C. Morrow, who was born in 1866 and died in Belfast on November 1, 1938. One of four talented brothers, he became one of the most important actors and writers for the Ulster Literary Theatre.* Like his colleague Rutherford Mayne,* he was a brilliant amateur actor, and he excelled in comic character parts. As a writer, he contributed a long succession of slight but quirky comedies to the Ulster Theatre. His plays tended to be burlesques, satires, or fantasies, and his one separately published play, *Thompson in Tir na nOg* (1918), was constantly revived and was rivaled in popularity only by Mayne's *The Drone.* MacNamara's *Thompson* is an Irish equivalent of *A Connecticut Yankee in King Arthur's Court,* and in it a rather dense Orangeman is transported, with incongruous results, back into the Land of Youth. Among MacNamara's most popular other plays were *The Mist That Does Be on the Bog* (1909), an unpublished satire of the Abbey Theatre* peasant play, and *Suzanne and the Sovereigns* (1907), written with Lewis Purcell, an unpublished burlesque about Orangemen and Catholics. Toward the end of his life, a few short pieces and closet dramas appeared in *The Dublin Magazine,* but MacNamara's dozen or so plays have never been collected, and more than half have never been published. To judge by contemporary reactions and by what few manuscripts have come to light, one would have to conclude that MacNamara was a minor but most individual talent. His colleague Rutherford Mayne called him "one of the finest comic geniuses that the Irish dramatic revival has produced."

WORKS: *Thompson in Tir na nOg.* Dublin: Talbot, 1918. "Stage Directions for a Play Called *William John Jamieson.*" *The Dublin Magazine,* 1 (1923-1924); "trans. from the Norwegian of Gibson's *Babes in the Wood.*" *The Dublin Magazine* 1 (1924);

Tcinderella." *The Dublin Magazine* 2 (1924); "Little Devil Dought." *The Dublin Magazine* 2 (1925); "Who Fears to Speak of '98." *The Dublin Magazine* 4, New Series (1929).   REFERENCE: Mayne, Rutherford. "Gerald MacNamara." *The Dublin Magazine* 12, New Series (1938): 53-56.

MacNEICE, LOUIS (1907-1963), poet. MacNeice was born in Belfast on September 12, 1907, the third child of the Reverend John Frederick Mac- Neice who was to become Church of Ireland bishop of Down and Connor and Dromore. MacNeice was educated at Sherbourne, Marlborough, and at Merton College, Oxford, where he read classics and philosophy. From 1930 to 1939, he lectured in classics in Birmingham and London.

MacNeice's name was linked in the 1930s with those of W. H. Auden, Stephen Spender, and C. Day-Lewis.* It was assumed that he shared the ideological commitment of those left-wing poets, but in fact his work at that period, while conscious of contradictions in the social order, lacked any distinctive political faith, expressing rather melancholy, fear of the future, and a heightened apprehension of transience. At this point in his career, his work focused on exploitation of cliché or rhythms drawn from popular songs and was remarkably sensitive to sensory experience. *Autumn Journal* (1939) is both representative of this work and a culmination of his art to that date. A long journalistic poem, it records the impressions, fears, and hopes of a young intellectual in London in the months surrounding the Munich crisis, assessing a middle-class education, a childhood and past in Ireland, and an adult experience of sexual relations, political and social realities, and human values tested in the crucible of civil war in Spain. The poem is a *tour de force*, brilliantly evoking the life of a city and the par- ticulars of a period. It manages readability and seriousness of purpose, combining a journalistic ease of metaphor and simile with structural com- pleteness.

In 1940, MacNeice returned to England from the United States where he was lecturing, so that he could be part of the war effort. He entered the BBC features department in May 1941 where he revealed a considerable talent for radio drama. His play *The Dark Tower* (first broadcast in Jan- uary 1946) is an acknowledged classic of the genre.

In the 1940s, MacNeice's poetic ambitions deepened. His effort to com- prehend the work of the Irish poet W. B. Yeats* (his book *W. B. Yeats* appeared in 1941) allowed his own interest in folklore, myth, and dreams to break through the superficial colors and sequinned elegance of his style to suggest depths and heights of experience that he had hitherto ignored. The poet's temperamental melancholy deepened during the war and its anti- climactic aftermath, becoming something altogether more metaphysically troubled. "Brother Fire," written around 1943 about the German blitz on London, is representative of these sombre poems which, while maintaining a realistic grasp on external events, reach down into folk memory and dream.

The 1950s were a difficult time for MacNeice. His most ambitious work to date, *Ten Burnt Offerings* (1952), was received without much enthusiasm by the critics, while his long journalistic poem *Autumn Sequel* (1954) did not, in the main, achieve the same level as his earlier journal poem. The writing in *Autumn Sequel* is slack, often superficially attractive but without the sense of real personal involvement in the contemporary scene that made *Autumn Journal* so readable a work.

MacNeice's last three volumes, *Visitations* (1957), *Solstices* (1961), and *The Burning Perch* (published shortly after his death in 1963), reflected a resurgence of poetic energy. The earlier lyrical zest and panache are present but are now directed to the treatment of bleak truths. The passage of time, the imminence of death, the loss of love and ambition, and the degradation of the spirit in a mean-spirited time are treated with a ghoulish glee and a laconic, slangy offhanded wit, which suggest emotional and metaphysical despair acknowledged but not yet allowed final victory.

MacNeice's poetic involvement with Ireland is an important aspect of his work. In the 1930s, his poems impatiently dismissed a country he felt had little to offer the modern world. In the 1939-1944 war years, his distaste for Ireland's neutrality was expressed in "Neutrality." As he grew older, however, and as the contemporary city world in which he had early found excitement and inspiration began to pall in postwar enervation, the Irish countryside came increasingly to occupy an area in his imagination related to his developing interest in myth and folktale. MacNeice began to consider his own identity in terms of his Irish background, seeking some adequate means of relating to the country despite his alienation from the actual political and social facts of North and South. Ireland became for him an image of human imaginative possibilities remote from the squalor and compromises of modern social experience, a world of ultimate belonging.

MacNeice was an extraordinarily prolific writer. His *Collected Poems* runs to six hundred pages; his output of literary journalism was prodigious; he wrote plays, radio dramas, features, film scripts, and three full-length critical works; he did translations of Aeschylus and Goethe; and he was a competent travel writer. His final claim to remembrance must be as a poet, however, and it is as a poet whose work captures the tang and texture of living while suggesting depths as yet unplumbed by human consciousness, that he commends himself to our attention. The zest and energy of life, the fear of death and loss, are the poles of his imagination. It is in his very fine love poems ("The Sunlight On The Garden," "Meeting Point") that we encounter the essential MacNeice—elegant, controlled, formally accomplished to an admirable degree, attentive to surfaces, to the passing moment, but conscious of significances beyond the moment, celebratory, with a

Horatian grasp of sufficiencies, of the gifts of life, which are all life has to offer.

TERENCE BROWN

WORKS: *Blind Fireworks*. London: Gollancz, 1929; *Roundabout Way* by Louis Malone (pseudonym). London & New York: Putnam, [1932]. (Novel); *Poems*. London: Faber, [1935]; *The Agamemnon of Aeschylus*. London: Faber, [1936]. (Translation); with W. H. Auden, *Letters from Iceland*. London: Faber, [1937]; *Out of the Picture*. London: Faber, [1937]. (Verse play); *Poems*. New York: Random House, [1937]; *The Earth Compels*. London: Faber, [1938]; *I Crossed the Minch*. London, New York, Toronto: Longmans, Green, [1938]. (Prose); *Modern Poetry*. Oxford: Oxford University Press, [1938]. (Criticism); *Zoo*. London: Michael Joseph, [1938]. (Prose); *Autumn Journal*. London: Faber, [1939]/New York: Random House, 1940; *The Last Ditch*. Dublin: Cuala, 1940/Shannon: Irish University Press, 1971; *Selected Poems*. London: Faber [1940]; *Plant and Phantom*. London: Faber, [1941]; *Poems 1925-1940*. New York: Random House, [1941]; *The Poetry of W. B. Yeats*. London, New York, Toronto: Oxford University Press, 1941; *Meet the U.S. Army*. London: His Majesty's Stationery Office, [1943]. (Prose pamphlet); *Christopher Columbus*. London: Faber, [1944]. (Radio play); *Springboard. Poems 1941-1944*. London: Faber, 1944/ New York: Random House, [1945]; *The Dark Tower and Other Radio Scripts*. London: Faber, [1947]; *Holes in the Sky. Poems 1944-1947*. London: Faber, [1948]/New York: Random House, [1949]; *Collected Poems 1925-1948*. London: Faber, 1949/New York: Oxford University Press, [1963]; *Goethe's Faust, Parts I and II*, with E. L. Stahl. London: Faber, [1951]/New York: Oxford University Press, 1952; *Ten Burnt Offerings*. London: Faber, [1952]/New York: Oxford University Press, 1953; *Autumn Sequel*. London: Faber, [1954]; *The Other Wing*. London: Faber, [1954]. (Four-page poem); *The Penny That Rolled Away*. New York: Putnam's 1954/as *The Sixpence That Rolled Away*, London: Faber, [1956]. (Children's story); *Visitations*. London: Faber, [1957]/New York: Oxford University Press, 1958; *Eighty-Five Poems*. London: Faber, 1959/New York: Oxford University Press, [1961]; *Solstices*. London: Faber/New York: Oxford University Press, 1961; *The Burning Perch*. London: Faber/New York: Oxford University Press, 1963; *Astrology*. London: Aldus Books in association with W. H. Allen/New York: Doubleday, 1964. (Prose); *The Mad Islands and The Administrator*. London: Faber, [1964]. (Radio plays); *Selected Poems of Louis MacNeice*, selected and introduced by W. H. Auden. London: Faber, [1964]; *The Strings Are False*. E. R. Dodds, ed. London: Faber, [1965]/New York: Oxford University Press, 1966. (Autobiography); *Varieties of Parable*. Cambridge: Cambridge University Press, 1965. (Criticism); *The Collected Poems of Louis MacNeice*. E. R. Dodds, ed. London: Faber, [1966]/New York: Oxford University Press, 1967; *One For the Grave*. London: Faber/New York: Oxford University Press, 1968. (Play); *Persons from Porlock*. London: British Broadcasting Corp., [1969]. (Radio plays); *The Revenant: A Song Cycle for Hedli Anderson*. Dublin: Cuala, 1975. REFERENCES: Armitage, Christopher. *A Bibliography of the Works of Louis MacNeice*. London: Kaye & Ward, 1973; Brown, Terence. *Louis MacNeice: Sceptical Vision*. Dublin: Gill & Macmillan/New York: Barnes & Noble, 1975; Brown, Terence, & Alec Reid, eds. *Time Was Away: The World of Louis MacNeice*. Dublin: Dolmen, 1974.

McNEILL, JANET (1907-), novelist. McNeill was born in Dublin on September 14, 1907, the daughter of a minister, and was educated in England and later in St. Andrew's University, from which she received an M.A. in

1929. She worked as a journalist on the *Belfast Telegraph* from 1929 to 1933, before marrying Robert Alexander and becoming the mother of four children. From 1956 to 1957, she was chairman of the Belfast Centre of Irish Pen and from 1959 to 1964, she served on the Advisory Council of the BBC. She has written novels, a great number of children's books, and two stage plays, one of which, *Signs and Wonders*, was produced in Belfast in 1951. She is now living in Bristol.

McNeill's novels mainly examine the disillusions and compromises of middle age. In *A Child in the House* (1955), her first novel, Maud and Henry's dead and barren marriage is interrupted by a visit from Maud's niece Elizabeth. With this child comes the past. The one redeeming feature of Henry's life has been his love for Grace, the child's mother, who is now dying. But Henry's failure is one of action. Even now he cannot shake off conventional notions of propriety and visit the dying woman. When the child makes the painful choices necessary for a moral life, Henry feels for her and so becomes involved in humanity. But Maud, whose love preys on Henry and who believed the child's presence would heal their marriage, is isolated further through her irrational jealousy.

Aubrey and Alice, the married couple in *Talk to Me* (1965), are bound together through pity as well as convention. Alice is blind and sits in the dark imagining a golden past, while Aubrey has imaginary talks with the TV announcer. Their lives run on parallel lines which seldom touch. Aubrey flirts ineffectually with the girls in his chemist shop and runs from any real encounters. From behind his counter, he has a goldfish's view of the world:

> For all their blatancy, he believed that most of the young girls who came into the shop were looking for a defence against sex, preferring the ideal to the reality; they took their mirrors to bed with them and laid them down at the last possible moment, replacing the dream lover reluctantly with flesh and blood and sharing as little as they were able. He had sympathy with them. When he made love to Alice he had sometimes, just before the final anonymous moment, resented the fact that she was there.

This unwillingness to face reality plagues most of the characters in the novel, except Aubrey and Alice's practical, phlegmatic daughter. For the others, real encounters are too threatening, and Aubrey even finally upholds Alice in her refusal to believe that her cat has been killed.

Middle age is still the subject of *The Maiden Dinosaur* (1964). Sarah is a spinster school mistress who has been frightened into frigidity and tentative lesbianism by a sexual shock in childhood. She is the center of a group of friends whose middle-aged marriages are in various stages of collapse. When Helen, the object of Sarah's devotion, deserts her for her ex-husband, Sarah is bereft and has to face life on her own. She is at first miserable, but before the novel ends, she feels the first stirrings of adult sexuality. Contrasted to Sarah is Sally, a schoolgirl who has a painful infatuation for Sarah. When Sarah unwittingly repulses the child's affections, Sally goes out with a boy who sexually molests her. But it is with Sally that Janet McNeill sees hope for the future, as well as with a girl idly playing with her baby whom Sarah observes from her window. These young people will not be prisoners of their milieu as their middle-aged elders have been.

The Small Widow (1967) examines the complexity of character as well as the incompatability of fantasy with reality. The novel opens with Julia widowed and lost without the physical presence of her husband Harold. All her life she had wanted passion from him, but believing the marriage happy because she satisfied him, she settled for children and security. She is shocked and outraged when she learns that Madge, Harold's dotty naive cousin, has been his lifelong passionate love. Unable to live without Harold, Madge commits suicide. Julia finally comes to accept the idea that she supplied something Harold needed, as he did her. The novel ends with Julia looking for a stamp and reflecting that "Harold had been unfailingly good at stamps."

McNeill has much to say about human loneliness, the generation gap, the roles society imposes on men and women, and their methods of coping with those roles. She is a tough, adult novelist who charts the complex, mundane territory of middle age with perception and intelligence. For Protestant Belfast, she is the counterpart and often the equal of Brian Moore.* Over the years, her style has tightened into the excellence of *The Maiden Dinosaur*, which is her best novel and deserves to be much better known.

MARY ROSE CALLAGHAN

WORKS: *Gospel Truth*. Belfast: H. R. Carter, [1951]. (Play); *A Child in the House*. London: Hodder & Stoughton, 1955; *My Friend Specs McCann*. London: Faber, 1955; *The Other Side of the Wall*. London: Hodder & Stoughton, 1956; *A Pinch of Salt*. London: Faber, 1956; *Tea at Four O'Clock*. London: Hodder & Stoughton, 1956; *A Light Dozen*. London: Faber, 1957. (Stories); *A Finished Room*. London: Hodder & Stoughton, 1958; *Specs Fortissimo*. London: Faber, 1958; *Search Party*. London: Hodder & Stoughton, [1959]; *This Happy Morning*. London: Faber, 1959; *As Strangers Here*. London: Hodder & Stoughton, 1960; *Special Occasions*. London: Faber, 1960. (Stories); *Various Specs*. London: Faber, 1961; *The Early Harvest*. London: Geoffrey Bles, 1962; *Finn and the Black Hag*, libretto by McNeill, music by Raymond Warren, children's opera in two acts. London: Novello, [1962]; *Try These for Size*. London: Faber, 1963; *The Maiden Dinosaur*. London: Geoffrey Bles, 1964; *Talk to Me*. London: Geoffrey Bles, 1965; *Tom's Tower*. London: Faber, 1965; *I Didn't Invite You to My Party*. London: Hamish Hamilton, 1967; *The Small Widow*. London: Geoffrey Bles, 1967/New York: Atheneum, 1968; *Switch-On, Switch-Off, and Other Plays*. London: Faber, 1968; *A Helping Hand*. London: Hamilton, 1971; *Much Too Much Magic*. London: Hamilton, 1971; *The Prisoner in the Park*. London: Faber, 1971; *The Nest Spotters*. London: Macmillan, 1972; *Wait for It, and Other Stories*. London: Faber, 1972; *A Fairy Called Andy Perks*. London: Hamilton, 1973; *The Other People*. London: Chatto & Windus, 1973; *The Snow-*

Clean Pinny. London: Hamilton, 1973; *Umbrella Thursday and a Helping Hand*. Harmondsworth, Middlesex: Puffin, 1973; *The Family Upstairs*. London: Macmillan, 1974; *The Magic Lollipop*. London: Knight Books, Brockhampton Press, 1974; *We Three Kings*. London: Faber, 1974; *Ever After*. London: Chatto & Windus, 1975; *Go On, Then*. London: Macmillan, 1975; *Growlings*. London: Macmillan, 1975; *My Auntie*. London: Macmillan, 1975; *Just Turn the Key, and Other Stories*. London: Hamilton, 1976; *Billy Brewer Goes on Tour*. London: Macmillan, 1977; *The Day Mum Came Home*. London: Macmillan, 1977; *The Hermit's Purple Shirts*. London: Macmillan, 1977; *Look Who's Here*. London: Macmillan, 1977; *The Three Crowns of King Hullaballoo*. London: Knight Books, Brockhampton Press, 1977.

McNULTY, [MATTHEW] EDWARD (1856-1943), playwright and novelist. McNulty, born in Antrim in 1856, was a classmate of Bernard Shaw* at a day school in Dublin and a friend of Shaw's sister Lucy. The young men shared an interest in music and writing. In John O'Donovan's* biographical play *The Shaws of Synge Street*, staged at the Abbey* in 1960, naive, goodhearted McNulty is one of the characters. A bank manager, novelist, and playwright, McNulty died on May 12, 1943. His remembrances of Shaw, in manuscript at the time of McNulty's death, are a warm, if not entirely accurate, account of their friendship.

Two McNulty plays were performed at the Abbey. *The Courting of Mary Doyle* (1921) is a broad comedy in which a domestic servant is wooed because of her supposedly large bank account. *The Lord Mayor* (1914) is somewhat more substantial theatre. Jimmy O'Brien is forced into politics by his wife, manipulated into office by a self-serving faction with its eye on lucrative municipal contracts, and is offered a baronetcy by the Castle if he formally welcomes a visiting monarch. His sudden change from puppet to leader is unconvincing, but the play uproariously uncovers the hinder parts of Irish political and social life.

WILLIAM J. FEENEY

WORKS: *Misther O'Ryan*. London: Edward Arnold, 1894. (Novel); *The Son of a Peasant*. London: Edward Arnold, 1897. (Novel); "George Bernard Shaw as a Boy." *The Candid Friend* (July 6, 1901); *Maureen*. London: Edward Arnold, 1904. (Novel); *Mrs. Mulligan's Millions*. London: Hurst & Blackett, 1908. (Novel); *The Lord Mayor*. Dublin: Talbot, 1914. (Play); *Mrs. Mulligan's Millions*. Dublin: Maunsel, 1918. (Play); *The Courting of Mary Doyle*. Dublin: Gill, 1944. (Play). REFERENCES: Coolidge, Olivia. *George Bernard Shaw*. Boston: Houghton Mifflin, 1968; Ervine, St. John. *Bernard Shaw, His Life, Work, and Friends*. New York: William Morrow, 1956; O'Donovan, John. *The Shaws of Synge Street*. Dixon, Calif.: Proscenium, 1966. (Play).

MacSWINEY, TERENCE (1879-1920), patriot and playwright. MacSwiney was a nationalist leader who, while lord mayor of Cork, underwent a lengthy seventy-four day hunger strike when he was interned in Brixton Prison. As a result of it, he died on October 25, 1920. His suffering and death received widespread sympathetic attention throughout the world.

MacSwiney was born in Cork on March 28, 1879. He received the B.A.

from the Royal University there in 1907, and he subsequently became a fervent nationalist, taught himself Irish, and was interned in 1916. While MacSwiney is more significant to the history than the literature of Ireland, he has some importance as a playwright and polemicist.

At the end of 1908, with Daniel Corkery,* he founded the Cork Dramatic Society, and produced a number of his plays. None has been published, and the only manuscript known is *The Last Warriors of Coole* (1910), a "hero play in one act." The piece takes place, of course, in the Irish heroic period, but it is extremely static and is written in correct but quite undistinguished blank verse. His other early plays include *The Holocaust* (1910), a one-act patriotic tragedy, and *The Wooing of Emer* (1911), a three-act heroic play. A political play, *The Revolutionist*, was produced posthumously at the Abbey* in 1921; it is long, vague, high-minded, and dull. Also published posthumously was a collection of fugitive pieces, *Principles of Freedom* (1921)—patriotic exhortations and theorizing which are lucidly written but of only historical interest.

Although MacSwiney was not a good writer, he was an intensely earnest, utterly idealistic, and personally brave and noble man. The dramatic society which he helped to found gave first productions to such notable writers as Danie Corkery, Lennox Robinson,* T. C. Murray,* Con O'Leary,* and J. Bernard MacCarthy.* That in itself was an achievement.

WORKS: *The Revolutionist*. Dublin & London: Maunsel, 1914. (Play); *Principles of Freedom*. Dublin: Talbot, 1921. (Essays); *Despite Fools' Laughter*. B. G. MacCarthy, ed. Dublin: Gill, 1944. (Poems).   REFERENCES: Chavasse, M. *Terence MacSwiney*. Dublin: Clonmore & Reynolds, 1961; O'Hegarty, P. S. *A Short Memoir of Terence MacSwiney*. Dublin: Talbot, 1922.

MAGEE, HENO (1939), playwright. Magee was born into a typical Dublin working-class background. At fourteen, he quit primary school to take a job as a messenger boy. For five years, he served abroad in the British Royal Air Force; drawn back to Dublin, he found work in a tobacco factory.

Always a "voracious but indiscriminate reader," Magee started writing on impulse one rainy Sunday afternoon, sitting at a tenement window. The first words he wrote were: "I'm getting out of this kip"; these words formed the title of his first play in 1968. Since then, he has written several more plays, poetry, and character sketches, and for some years, he was drama critic on the Dublin weekly newspaper, *The Catholic Standard*.

His plays explore with bawdy humor, poetic insight, and deep compassion the manners, mores, and morals of Dublin's working-class ghettos. If one treats Behan's* theatrical cartoons as a case apart, not since O'Casey* have the denizens of the backstreets been put on the stage with such truth and accuracy. Magee's characters speak a rich, low-life vernacular which has been sieved through a shrewd intelligence.

Magee's is a shabby, sedimentary world which festers with an ingrowing energy and frustration: a world which the city's affluent middle class, secure and complacent in the fat of contentment, is happy to ignore. There are no evil men or women in Magee's plays, but there are blighted and befuddled victims of birth and circumstances. These characters articulate their condition through sex, booze, and violence, for no other antidotes are available to them against the sameness, sullenness, and lethargy of life and against the poverty and its pains. Each of the plays enshrines an eloquent, anguished plea to understand—and to be understood. Blind force leads to blinder futility.

If Magee's people are maimed and marred by original sin, they are also blessed with a sanctifying grace. To power his dramatic motor, Magee allows them to carry within themselves the seeds of their own salvation. He provides flickering visions of other attainable worlds and says that to acquiesce is to go down in leaden defeat. His common theme is the struggle to survive with dignity.

To date, one of his plays has been published, and three have been produced: *I'm Getting Out of This Kip* (1972), *Hatchet* (Abbey, 1972), and *Red Biddy* (Abbey, 1974). In 1976, Magee won the Rooney Prize in Irish Literature and was awarded the Abbey Theatre bursary.

JAMES DOUGLAS

WORK: *Hatchet.* [Dublin]: Gallery/[Newark, Del.]: Proscenium, 1978.

MAGEE, WILLIAM KIRKPATRICK. *See* EGLINTON, JOHN.

MAGINN, WILLIAM (1794-1842), journalist and man of letters. Maginn, that prodigy of wit, erudition, humor, energy, and genial dissipation, was born in Cork on July 10, 1794. At the early age of twelve, he entered Trinity College. On graduating, he assisted at his father's private school in Cork and then ran the school for several years after his father's death. At the same time, he was making a reputation for his humorous Irish sketches; in 1823, he went to London and continued his prolific writing for journals such as *Blackwood's*. In 1830, he was involved in the founding of *Fraser's Magazine*, for which Carlyle and Maginn's friend Thackeray wrote. His *Noctes Ambrosianae* and *Homeric Ballads* won vast audiences, and his clever Irish sketches and adroit verses are well worth a modern edition. His startling fluency may be seen in the following stanza from "The Wine-Bibber's Glory," which is quite as amusing in his Latin version "Toporis Gloria."

> Fair Sherry, Port's sister, for years they dismissed her
>   To the kitchen to flavour the jellies—
> There long she was banish'd, and well nigh had vanished
>   To comfort the kitchen maids' bellies;
> Till his Majesty fixt, he thought Sherry when sixty
>   Years old like himself quite the thing;

So I think it but proper, to fill a tip-topper
Of Sherry to drink to the king.

Huic quamvis cognatum, Xerense damnatum,
  Gelatâ culinâ tingebat,
Vinum exul ibique dum coquo cuique
  Generosum liquorem praebebat.
Sed a rege probatum est valdè pergatum
  Cum (ut ipse) sexagenarium—
Largè ergo implendum, regique bibendum
  Opinor est nunc necessarium.

Maginn was imprisoned for debt in 1840. When finally released in 1842, he
was broken in health and died on August 21.

WORKS: *Miscellaneous Writings of the Late Dr. Maginn.* R. Skelton Mackenzie,
ed. 5 vols. New York: Redfield, 1855-1857; *Noctes Ambrosianae,* by Maginn, Lock-
hart, Hogg and others, ed., with memoirs and notes by R. Skelton Mackenzie. 5 vols.
New York: W. J. Middleton, 1863-1865; *Miscellanies: Prose and Verse.* R. W.
Montagu, ed. 2 vols. London: Sampson, Low, 1885; *Ten Tales.* London: Partridge,
1933.   REFERENCE: Kenealy, Edward Vaughan Hyde. "Our Portrait Gallery,
no. 34: William Maginn L.L.D." *Dublin University Magazine* 23 (1844): 72-101.

MAGLONE, BARNEY. *See* WILSON, ROBERT A.

MAHAFFY, JOHN PENTLAND (1839-1919), scholar and wit. Even at
this late date, one hesitates to call Mahaffy a Dublin character; let us rather
call that formidable individual a figure on the Dublin scene. He was born
at Chapponnaire, near Vevey in Switzerland, on February 26, 1839. He
was educated at Trinity College, Dublin, where he remained as tutor, professor, vice-provost, and provost for fifty-five years. As a major scholar of
his day, he published books on Kant and Descartes, and on Greek and
Egyptian history, and he was knighted in 1918. As a prominent feature of
the life of Dublin, he founded the Georgian Society and was a president of
the Royal Irish Academy, but, more memorably, he was an inveterate diner-
out and a conversationalist with something of the force of a Dr. Johnson.
Despite an overwhelming snobbery, he was a famous wit and raconteur, who
wrote a monograph, *The Art of Conversation,* and whose most successful
pupils were Oscar Wilde* and Oliver Gogarty.* He is credited with the
classic definition of an Irish Bull ("An Irish Bull, Madam, is always pregnant"), as well as such memorable epigrams as, "Ireland is a place where
the inevitable never happens, and the unexpected often occurs." When
asked the difference between a man and a woman, he is said to have replied,
"I can't conceive." Shane Leslie* remarked of his conversation:

Until you heard Mahaffy talk, you hadn't realised how language could be used to charm and hypnotise. With this gift, there were no doors which could not be opened, no Society which was proof against its astonishing effect. Kings and Queens, famous men and beautiful women, all must come under its powerful and compelling spell.

Mahaffy was most contemptuous of Celtic studies and once proscribed a meeting at Trinity College at which "a man called Pearse*" was scheduled to speak. Although he ably directed the defense of Trinity College against the rebels in 1916, he did propose in 1917 that Ireland should have a federal constitution with Ulster as an autonomous province—a solution which still seems the only workable one. Mahaffy was something of a throwback to, not so much the nineteenth century, as the eighteenth. He died on April 30, 1919, thereby making Dublin considerably less habitable by civilized man.

WORKS: *The Decay of Modern Preaching*. London: Macmillan, 1882; *A History of Classical Greek Literature*. 2d ed. revised. 2 vols. London: Longmans, Green, 1883; *The Principles of the Art of Conversation*. London: Macmillan, 1887/2d ed., enlarged. London: Macmillan, 1896; *An Epoch in Irish History*. T.C.D. Its Founda-larged. London: Macmillan, 1887; *Greek Life and Thought*. 2d ed., corrected and enlarged. London: Macmillan, 1896; *An Epoch in Irish History, T.C.D. Its Foundation and Early Fortunes, 1591-1660*. London: Unwin, 1903; *The Plate in Trinity College, Dublin: A History*. London: Macmillan, 1918.   REFERENCE: Stanford, William Bedell. *Mahaffy*. London: Routledge & Kegan Paul, 1971.

MAHON, DEREK (1941-), poet. Mahon was born in Belfast on November 23, 1941, and grew up in Glengormley. He was educated at Belfast Institute and at Trinity College, Dublin, where he received a B.A. in 1965. Since then he has taught English at Belfast High School in Newtownabbey, County Antrim, at the Language Centre in Dublin, and since 1977 at the New University of Ulster in Coleraine.

Of the poets who began to make their reputations after Kinsella,* Montague,* and Heaney* had established themselves, probably Mahon and Desmond O'Grady* appear to be the most impressive. Mahon has a tight, precise style which is frequently enhanced by the memorable phrase. He has an accurate eye and a deft satiric sense, and as language the best of his work is as interesting as any poetry written in Ireland today. Like O'Grady, he appears to have the most awareness of form of his contemporaries; but like them, he appears to have little understanding of it.

Perhaps his most significant and controlled long piece is "Beyond Howth Head," a sombre light-verse jeremiad which owes something, both good and bad, to W. H. Auden. Yet Auden, whatever his occasional thematic triviality, was a poet's poet who never abandoned form. In "Beyond Howth Head," the form consists of rhymed or off-rhymed couplets. The couplets appear meterless, but some of the rhymes are clever and effective. In Mahon's later work, he has not usually pursued form much further. For instance, the poems in *The Snow Party* (1975) are formally a highly diverse mélange, ranging from a puerile shaped verse called "The Window"—a shaped verse is a poem like George Herbert's "Easter Wings" or "The Altar," in which the typographical arrangement of the words visually resembles the subject—to a couple of finely written examples of poetic prose ("A Hermit" and "The Apotheosis of Tins"), to various examples of free verse, to various faulty examples of meter and rhyme, and finally, to one almost total formal achievement in "September in Great Yarmouth."

What is one to make of such diversity? The obvious alternatives are that Mahon does not fully understand or that he does not care for what he is doing. The sober themes of many of the pieces make it clear that he does indeed care, and so it would seem that, like his Coleraine colleague James Simmons,* he is still conducting his prosodic education in public. However, his diction is so frequently memorable that, if his technique ever catches up with it, Ulster will have produced an important poet. At present, Mahon seems as untutored as are many of his generation, if more talented than most.

WORKS: *Twelve Poems.* Belfast: Festival Publications, 1965; *Night-Crossing.* London: Oxford University Press, 1968; *Ecclesiastes.* Manchester: Phoenix Pamphlet Poets, 1970; *Beyond Howth Head.* Dublin: Dolmen, 1970; *Lives.* London: Oxford University Press, 1972; *The Man Who Built His City in Snow.* London: Poem-of-the-Month Club, 1972; ed., *Modern Irish Poetry.* London: Sphere, 1972; *The Snow Party.* London: Oxford University Press, 1975; *Light Music.* Belfast: Ulsterman Publications, 1977; *The Sea in Winter.* Dublin: Gallery Books, 1979.

MAHONY, FRANCIS SYLVESTER. *See* PROUT, FATHER.

MALONE, ANDREW E. (1888-1939), drama critic and journalist. Andrew E. Malone was the pen name of Laurence Patrick Byrne who was born in Dublin in 1888 and died there on April 13, 1939. He was a journalist, author, and probably the best Dublin drama critic of the twentieth century to date. While he was an honest and conscientious writer who had fortified himself with uncommonly wide reading in world drama, he was unable to shake off entirely the bonds of the ultra-conservative and narrow cultural attitudes in the Dublin of his time. His criticisms contain a few odd judgments, and his praises of the newly arrived Sean O'Casey* are niggardly, a consequence of his fastidious tastes in humor and of his tendency to view every work of man *sub specie aeternitatis.* But his book *The Irish Drama* (1929) is authoritative, invaluable, and still highly readable. His forecast in this book about the Abbey Theatre* was devastatingly accurate:

> The pioneer directors of the Abbey have grown weary of pioneering, and it seems that the Abbey Theatre is to settle down to the

repertory work of a State Theatre, where the "great plays" of the Masters will be presented at suitable intervals, and the works of expatriate Irishmen, from Farquhar to Shaw, O'Neill and Munro, will be claimed for the greater glory of Ireland . . . very useful and necessary work, but it is not quite the work for which the Irish National Theatre was founded: it is the work of the Irish Literary Theatre revived after thirty years, and a triumph for Edward Martyn* long after his death.

ANDREW MARSH

WORK: *The Irish Drama.* London: Constable, 1929.

MANGAN, JAMES CLARENCE (1803-1849), poet. No writer of the nineteenth century was more intensely Irish in his sympathies, more committed to experimentation in literary technique, or more inspiring to both later writers and the broad public than James Clarence Mangan. It is no wonder that James Joyce* and W. B. Yeats* were inspired by him as young men and attempted critical accounts of his achievement.

Mangan's life was one of almost unrelieved misery. He was born on May 1, 1803, into a life of unrest, poverty, and physical illnesses. His adult life was no less tortured, and he was addicted either to alcohol or to opium for most of its duration. He was an eccentric character who dressed in the bizarre style of his idol Maturin;* he had very few friends or confidants. The most important event of his adult career was his association with Petrie,* O'Donovan,* and O'Curry* in the work of the Ordnance Topographical Survey. It was that affiliation which inspired him to work on the rich lore of early Irish poetry and folklore. Although he contributed a poem to the first edition of *The Nation*★ in 1842, most of his poems and prose pieces appeared in the leading Dublin literary journals, chiefly in *The Dublin University Magazine.* He died of cholera in Dublin on June 20, 1849.

Mangan is frequently compared with his American contemporary Edgar Allan Poe, not only on the basis of their lives and personalities, but also their art. The comparison is instructive, for both experimented with verse techniques, investigating the various effects to be achieved by multiple rhymes, refrains, and elaborate prosodic schemes. Both were fascinated by extreme states of psychological distress. Even their stories are similar, and we would conclude that Mangan would even have agreed with Poe's literary theories.

But Mangan's fame rests on his poems on his native country, and there the resemblances to Poe stop. He wrote a number of poems based on others' translations which approximate the Old Irish originals in their complicated rhyme schemes and long lines. "Dark Rosaleen" is the best known of these, a stirring poem on its own merits, and "O'Hussey's Ode to the Maguire" is as fine. In these and in many of his original poems on Ireland, Mangan reveals a commitment to Ireland which inspired the following generations.

Yet, it is not only fervor which distinguishes his poetry. A glance at *The Spirit of the Nation*, the immensely popular collection of nationalist verses, reveals the superior artistry of Mangan. He was a consummate craftsman; beneath the strong patriotic proclamations is an attention to sound effects and a sophisticated handling of a variety of verse techniques.

Mangan's verse translations are skillful. The best are his translations from nineteenth-century German poets, which are both accurate and musical. In addition, he published translations or "versions" of Spanish and Islamic poems, based on translations by others. Some, such as the Oriental fantasies, are probably not authentic, but many reveal ingenuity and poetic force.

His prose tales reflect the taste of the times: Gothic stories, humorous observations, and fantasies. The best of his prose writings is his partial *Autobiography*, which reveals his narrative skill and, it must be added, his powers of fiction.

Mangan was a singular character, probably a genius, who lived a brief but tormented life. He is the one Irish poet of the nineteenth century who cannot be overlooked, for he treated the subject of Ireland with a fervor that none has matched, and he was a consummate craftsman of poetic technique.

JAMES KILROY

WORKS: *Poems*. D. J. O'Donoghue, ed. Dublin: M. H. Gill & Son, Ltd., 1903; *Prose Writings*. D. J. O'Donoghue, ed. Dublin: M. H. Gill & Son, Ltd., 1904; *Autobiography*. James Kilroy, ed. Dublin: Dolmen, 1968.   REFERENCES: Donaghy, Henry J. *James Clarence Mangan*. New York: Twayne, 1974; Kilroy, James. *James Clarence Mangan*. Lewisburg, Pa.: Bucknell University Press, 1970; O'Donoghue, D. J. *The Life & Writings of J. C. Mangan*. Edinburgh: P. Geddes, 1897.

MANNIN, ETHEL (1900-), novelist. Although born in London on October 6, 1900, of British parents, the prolific Ethel Mannin can be called an Irish writer by virtue of her Connemara residence as well as her best selling novel *Late Have I Loved Thee*, her *Connemara Journal*, and her *Two Studies in Integrity* which is about Gerald Griffin* and Father Prout.*

Late Have I Loved Thee (1948), a study of a late vocation to the priesthood, for years held an exalted position in Irish convent libraries, and thus in the mind of every Irish Catholic schoolgirl of a certain generation. The aristocratic and cynical Francis Sable is brought to his knees by God in a manner predictable from page two. In spite of a rather good evocation of Paris and of the west of Ireland, the novel is superficial and plastic and often sinks into the appalling sentimentality that Mannin mistakes for feeling. Although the novel sentimentalizes religion, it was responsible for many vocations to the Catholic Church. In her autobiographical journals, however, the author states that the book was written without any belief in that church.

In her journals, Mannin goes on about (at considerable length) her cat, vegetarianism, and the Arab Cause. (She also wrote a novel about the last-named subject.) Apparently, she can turn her hand to anything. *Two Studies in Integrity* (1954) compares the depressing Gerald Griffin, who somehow contrived to write the admired novel *The Collegians*, with the waggish and scholarly Francis Mahoney who created Father Prout. The book is interesting for the specialist, but not sufficiently well written to retain the interest of the average reader.

MARY ROSE CALLAGHAN

WORKS: *Martha.* London: Leonard Parsons, 1923/revised, London: Jarrolds, 1929; *Hunger of the Sea.* London: Jarrolds, 1924; *Pilgrims.* London: Jarrolds, [1927]; *Green Willow.* London: Jarrolds, [1928]; *Crescendo.* London: Jarrolds, [1929]; *Forbidden Music,* with *Martyrdom* by Warwick Deeping and *The House Behind the Judas Tree* by Gilbert Frankau. London: Readers Library, [1929]; *Children of the Earth.* London: Jarrolds, [1930]; *Confessions and Impressions.* London: Jarrolds, [1930]. (Autobiographical); *Bruised Wings and Other Stories.* London: Wright & Brown, [1931]; *Commonsense and the Child.* London: Jarrolds, [1931]; *Green Figs.* London: Jarrolds, [1931]. (Stories); *Ragged Banners.* London: Jarrolds, [1931]; *The Tinsel Eden, and Other Stories.* London: Wright & Brown, [1931]; *All Experience.* London: Jarrolds, 1932; *Linda Shawn.* London: Jarrolds, [1932]; *Love's Winnowing.* London: Wright & Brown, [1932]; *Dryad.* London: Jarrolds, 1933. (Stories); *Venetian Blinds.* London: Jarrolds, 1933; *Forever Wandering.* London: Jarrolds, 1934. (Travel); *Men Are Unwise.* London: Jarrolds, 1934; *Cactus.* London: Jarrolds, 1935/revised, London: Jarrolds, [1944]; *The Falconer's Voice.* London: Jarrolds, 1935. (Stories); *The Pure Flame.* London: Jarrolds, 1936; *South to Samarkand.* London: Jarrolds, 1936. (Travel); *Commonsense and the Adolescent.* London: Jarrolds, [1937]; *Women Also Dream.* London: Jarrolds, 1937; *Darkness my Bride.* London: Jarrolds, [1938]; *Rose and Sylvie.* London: Jarrolds, [1938]; *Women and the Revolution.* London: Secker & Warburg, 1938; *Privileged Spectator.* London: Jarrolds, 1939/revised, London: Jarrolds, [1948]. (Autobiographical); *Julie.* London: Jarrolds, [1940]; *Rolling in the Dew.* London: Jarrolds, [1940]; *Christianity—or Chaos?* London: Jarrolds, [1941]; *Red Rose.* London: Jarrolds, [1941]; *Captain Moonlight.* London: Jarrolds, [1942]; *Castles in the Street.* London: Letchworth, [1942]; *Commonsense and Morality.* London: Jarrolds, [1942]; *The Blooming Bough.* London: Jarrolds, [1943]; *No More Mimosa.* London: Jarrolds, [1943]; *Bread and Roses.* London: Macdonald, [1944]; *Proud Heaven.* London: Jarrolds, [1944]; *Lucifer and the Child.* London: Jarrolds, 1945; *The Dark Forest.* London: Jarrolds, 1946; *Selected Stories.* Dublin, London: Maurice Fridberg, 1946; *Comrade, O Comrade; or, Low-Down on the Left.* London: Jarrolds, [1947]; *Connemara Journal.* London: Westhouse, 1947; *Sounding Brass.* London: Jarrolds, [1947]; *German Journey.* London: Jarrolds, [1948]. (Travel); *Late Have I Loved Thee.* London: Jarrolds, [1948]; *Every Man a Stranger.* London: Jarrolds, [1949]; *Jungle Journey.* London: Jarrolds, [1950]. (Travel); *Moroccan Music.* London: Jarrolds, 1951. (Travel); *At Sundown, the Tiger.* London: Jarrolds, 1951; *The Fields at Evening.* London: Jarrolds, 1952; *This Was a Man. Some Memories of Robert Mannin, by His Daughter.* London: Jarrolds, 1952; *The Wild Swans, and Other Tales Based on the Ancient Irish.* London: Jarrolds, 1952; *Love under Another Name.* London: Jarrolds, 1953; *So Tiberius. . . .* London: Jarrolds, 1954; *Two Studies in Integrity: Gerald Griffin and the Rev. Francis Mahony.* London: Jarrolds, 1954; *Land of the Crested Lion.* London: Jarrolds, 1955. (Travel); *The Living Lotus.* London: Jarrolds, 1956; *The Country of the Sea.* London: Jarrolds, 1957. (Travel); *Pity the Innocent.* London: Jarrolds, 1957; *Fragrance of Hyacinths.* London: Jarrolds, 1958; *Ann and Peter in Sweden*. London: Frederick Muller, [1959]; *The Blue Eyed Bay*. London: Jarrolds, 1959; *Brief Voices*. London: Hutchinson, 1959. (Autobiographical); *Ann and Peter in Japan*. London: Frederick Muller, 1960; *The Flowery Sword*. London: Hutchinson, 1960. (Travel); *Sabishisa*. London: Hutchinson, 1961; *Ann and Peter in Austria*. London: Frederick Muller, 1962; *Curfew at Dawn*. London: Hutchinson, 1962; *With Will Adams through Japan*. London: Frederick Muller, 1962; *A Lance for the Arabs*. London: Hutchinson, 1963. (Travel); *The Road to Beersheba*. London: Hutchinson, 1963. (Travel); *Aspects of Egypt*. London: Hutchinson, 1964. (Travel); *Bavarian Story*. London: Arrow Books, 1964; *Rebel's Ride*. London: Hutchinson, 1964; *The Burning Bush*. London: Hutchinson, 1965; *The Lovely Land*. London: Hutchinson, 1965. (Travel); *Loneliness: a Study of the Human Condition*. London: Hutchinson, 1966; *An American Journey*. London: Hutchinson, 1967. (Travel); *Bitter Babylon*. London: Hutchinson, 1968; *The Midnight Street*. London: Hutchinson, 1969; *Practitioners of Love*. London: Hutchinson, 1969; *The Saga of Sammycat*. Oxford: Pergamon, 1969; *England at Large*. London: Hutchinson, 1970; *My Cat Sammy*. London: Joseph, 1971; *Young in the Twenties*. London: Hutchinson, 1971. (Autobiographical); *The Curious Adventures of Major Fosdick*. London: Hutchinson, 1972; *England My Adventure*. London: Hutchinson, 1972; *Sounding Brass*. London: Hutchinson, 1972; *Mission to Beirut*. London: Hutchinson, 1973; *Stories from My Life*. London: Hutchinson, 1973; *Kildoon*. London: Hutchinson, 1974; *An Italian Journey*. London: Hutchinson, 1975; *Pity the Innocent*. London: Hutchinson, 1975; *The Late Miss Guthrie*. London: Hutchinson, 1976; *Sunset over Dartmoor*. London: Hutchinson, 1977.

MANNING, MARY (1906-), playwright and novelist. Manning was born in Dublin on June 30, 1906. She was educated at Morehampton House School and Alexandra College in Dublin, and later studied art in London and Boston. She studied acting at the Abbey school and played with the Irish Players in England and with the Abbey* in Dublin before joining the Gate,* where she was publicity manager and editor of *Motley*, the theatre's amusing, shortlived magazine. Micheál Mac Liammóir* has written that during this period Manning's "brain, nimble and observant as it was, could not yet keep pace with a tongue so caustic that even her native city . . . was a little in awe of her." That satiric wit was beautifully displayed in the finest of her three Gate plays, *Youth's the Season—?* (1931). This is a sardonic, yet moving and thoroughly well-written, study of a group of young middle-class Dubliners caught just at that moment before their lives are set in a permanent pattern. It was undoubtedly one of the most accomplished first plays ever to be seen in Dublin. Her two other Gate plays, *Storm over Wicklow* (1933) and *Happy Family* (1934), were less successful and have not been published.

In the mid-1930s, Manning married Mark De Wolfe Howe, Jr., the authority on Justice Holmes, and left Dublin for Boston. She wrote no more plays for several years, but in the interval of raising a family she published two novels in America, *Mount Venus* (1938) and *Lovely People* (1953). The better of the two, *Lovely People*, is a stylish and witty entertainment about the upper middle class of Boston and Cambridge. She was one of the founders of the Cambridge Poets' Theatre, which gave the first production of her adaptation of *Finnegans Wake* in April 1955. This play, called vari-ously *Passages from Finnegans Wake* and *The Voices of Shem*, is a suc-cessfully theatrical adaptation of enormously recalcitrant material. After her husband's death, she returned to Ireland. In the 1970s, she was a per-ceptive, if astringent, theatre critic for *Hibernia*. She also returned to play-writing, her most successful piece being a comic but moving adaptation of Frank O'Connor's* novel *The Saint and Mary Kate*, performed at the Abbey in 1968. In 1978, there appeared *The Last Chronicles of Bally-fungus*, which is a volume of short stories so nicely interconnected that they grow into a novel. The book is a droll and accurate satiric caricature of quickly changing modern Ireland, but the satire is leavened by sympathy, and the glum conclusion is unfortunately appropriate.

One of her daughters is Fanny Howe, the American novelist and poet.

WORKS: *Youth's the Season—?* in *Plays of Changing Ireland*. Curtis Canfield, ed. New York: Macmillan, 1936; *Mount Venus*. Boston: Houghton Mifflin, 1938. (Novel); *Lovely People*. Boston: Houghton Mifflin, 1953. (Novel); *Passages from Finnegans Wake by James Joyce*. Cambridge, Mass.: Harvard University Press, 1957. Also published as *The Voices of Shem; Frank O'Connor's The Saint and Mary Kate*. [Newark, Del.]: Proscenium, [1970]; *The Last Chronicles of Ballyfungus*. Boston: Houghton Mifflin, 1978.

MARCUS, DAVID (1924-), editor. Marcus was born in Cork City on August 21, 1924. He was educated by the Presentation Brothers, at Uni-versity College, Cork, and at King's Inns, Dublin. He was a founder-editor of the important literary magazine *Irish Writing** from 1946 to 1954, and from 1948 to 1954 he was editor of *Poetry Ireland*. In 1968, he became literary editor of the Dublin newspaper *The Irish Press*, for which he in-augurated a New Irish Writing page that continues to appear once a week and publishes new poetry and short stories. The New Irish Writing page has given great impetus to the short story and has fostered many new tal-ents. Marcus has collected many of these stories in various anthologies. In 1976, he formed Poolbeg Press which has published distinguished volumes by such established writers as Michael McLaverty,* Bryan MacMahon,* Benedict Kiely,* and James Plunkett,* and promising collections by such new writers as Maeve Kelly* and Gillman Noonan.* As a writer himself, Marcus is perhaps best known for his translation of Brian Merriman's *The Midnight Court*.

WORKS: *Six Poems*. Dublin: Dolmen, 1952; trans., *The Midnight Court* by Brian Merriman. Dublin: Dolmen, 1953; *To Next Year in Jerusalem*. London: Macmillan, 1954. (Novel).

MARTIN, [WILLIAM] DAVID (1937-), novelist. Martin was born in July 1937 in Belfast and was educated locally. From 1951 to 1952, he worked at such odd jobs as apprentice electrician, and from 1955 to 1962 he served in the Royal Navy. From 1967 to 1971, he attended the University of Keele and received a B.A. in English and philosophy. After lecturing in English from 1971 to 1975 at the Northern Ireland Polytechnic in County Antrim, he attended the University of Warwick and received an M.A. in English literature. Since 1976, he has been senior lecturer at Northern Ireland Polytechnic. He has published two novels, *The Task* (1975) and *The Ceremony of Innocence* (1977), both of which are set in contemporary Belfast amidst the current troubles. Their realism, authenticity, and strength have been much admired. *The Task* is technically interesting for its attempt to tell the story from a number of different points of view, but that technique does seem to clog the progress of the narrative considerably.

WORKS: *The Task*. London: Secker & Warburg, 1975; *The Ceremony of Innocence*. London: Secker & Warburg, 1977.

MARTIN, VIOLET. *See* SOMERVILLE and ROSS.

MARTYN, EDWARD (1859-1923), playwright. Martyn was born in Tulira, Ardrahan, County Galway, on January 30, 1859. After studying without distinction at preparatory schools and at Oxford, he returned to his ancestral home. His first writing, *Morgante the Lesser*, published pseudonymously in 1890, was a mixture of Rabelaisian satire and utopianism. With his neighbor Lady Gregory* and W. B. Yeats,* he became in 1899 a co-founder of the Irish Literary Theatre, to which he contributed *The Heather Field* and *Maeve* and paid whatever financial deficits were incurred during the group's three-year existence.

Partly because of personality conflicts with Yeats and George Moore,* and partly because of his dislike of "peasant" plays and Celtic Twilight romanticism, Martyn broke away from the main movement of Irish drama which evolved into the Abbey.* In 1906, he helped to organize the Theatre of Ireland, and in 1914, he, Thomas MacDonagh,* and Joseph Plunkett* founded the Irish Theatre.* At a small building in Hardwicke Street, Dublin, they presented continental masterpieces in translation, nonpeasant plays by Irish authors, and a few works in Irish. Despite limited facilities and the death or imprisonment of several members of the company after the 1916 Rising, the theatre remained in operation until early 1920.

Martyn's interests were not confined to literature. Initially a conservative landowner, he swerved into ardent, though not revolutionary, nationalism. From 1904 to 1908, he was president of Sinn Fein. His devout Catholicism was manifested in the endowment of a choir in the Dublin Pro-Cathedral and in his crusade to improve the quality of ecclesiastical art in Ireland.

In his final years, failing health and disturbances in rural Galway during the Troubles forced his retirement from active life. He died at Tulira on

December 5, 1923, the last of a family that had resided in Ireland since the twelfth century.

The major influences on Martyn were continental writers, particularly Ibsen. As a straight-line moralist, Martyn did not subscribe to the specific ideas of the Norwegian master, but he did admire the craftsmanship and intellectual fiber of Ibsen's plays.

The influence of Ibsen's dramas of municipal corruption is apparent in Martyn's comic satires, although much of the humor lies in the topical allusions and the flimsy concealment of actual persons as characters. Political patronage and the servility of "West Briton" Irishmen are ridiculed in *The Tale of a Town* (1905), *The Place-Hunters* (printed in 1902, not staged), and the unpublished *The Privilege of Place*, performed in 1915. The comic history of *The Tale of a Town*, and its revision by George Moore as *The Bending of the Bough*, is told with malicious glee in Moore's *Hail and Farewell*. *The Dream Physician* (1914) and *Romulus and Remus* (1916) are allegories of the activities and personalities of the Irish Literary Theatre. Yeats is portrayed as an extravagant poseur, Moore as an egotistical hack writer, and Lady Gregory as a sensible person mesmerized into silliness by Yeats. Martyn casts himself as a slightly bemused gentleman remaining calm in the midst of chaos and lunacy.

The standard plot of Martyn's serious drama is a conflict between an idealistic, reclusive man (not unlike Martyn himself) and an aggressive, unscrupulous woman. Typical is his best and earliest play, *The Heather Field*, performed by the Irish Literary Theatre in 1899. Carden Tyrrell and his wife Grace both violate laws of nature—he by cultivating a heather field, she by demanding that her dreamy husband become a socialite and a prudent manager. Nature retaliates. The field reverts to its wild state, and the bankrupt, insane Tyrrell reverts to living in the happy days of his youth.

Realistic-idealistic roles are reversed in *Maeve* (1900). The O'Heynes, an impoverished Irish chief, expediently offers his daughter Maeve in marriage to a wealthy Englishman. The play is an allegory of the Norman invasion of Ireland, but it is also a variation on *The Heather Field*. Maeve finds in death what Tyrrell found in madness: retreat from a world too full of weeping into one of unfading beauty.

In *An Enchanted Sea* (1904), which owes much to Ibsen's *The Lady from the Sea*, Guy Font's mother is arranging the marriage of Lord Mask to her daughter Agnes. Her opposition is young Guy, who has infected Mask with his mystical obsession with the sea. Like Martyn's other tough-minded women, Mrs. Font lets nothing stand in her way. She murders Guy, Mask drowns himself, and as the law closes in, Mrs. Font commits suicide by hanging.

Michael Colman, a melancholy widower in *Grangecolman* (1912), falls in love with his young secretary. His daughter Catharine, embittered by her failure as a wife and as a physician, destroys the match with a vindictive, suicidal gesture. She disguises herself as the family ghost, a figure in white, knowing that the secretary, an expert marksman, will show her scorn for the ghost by firing a pistol at it.

The unpublished *Regina Eyre* (1919) was hooted even by critics friendly to the Irish Theatre. Only a mountaintop set designed by young Micheál Mac Liammóir* was applauded. In this play, Martyn reverses the gender of the *Hamlet* characters, changes the scene from Elsinore to Kerry, and superimposes on Shakespeare an Ibsenite ending: a symbolic mountain-climb in which pure-souled Regina attains the summit and her vicious step-mother (like Claudius she poisons people) plunges to her death.

Martyn was a loser in everything he attempted. His taste in liturgical music drove the gross-eared faithful away from the Pro-Cathedral. The violence engendered by Ireland's struggle for independence greatly distressed him. The Theatre of Ireland and the Irish Theatre failed, although their concepts were embodied successfully in the Gate Theatre.* He never again matched the high level of craftsmanship and intellectual control displayed in *The Heather Field*, nor did he ever learn to write believable, free-flowing dialogue.

To his credit, this high-minded, pleasantly eccentric gentleman chose not to take the easy road to popularity. He was ever ready to advance his artistic, political, and social beliefs, whatever the cost, with all his resources and full-spirited dedication.

WILLIAM J. FEENEY

WORKS: *Morgante the Lesser, His Notorious Life and Wonderful Deeds*, under the pseudonym of Sirius. London: Swan Sonnenschein, 1890; *The Heather Field: A Play in Three Acts and Maeve: A Psychological Drama in Two Acts*. Introduction by George Moore. London: Duckworth, 1899. (*The Heather Field* was reprinted in Vol. 1, Irish Drama Series, Chicago: De Paul University, 1966. *Maeve* was reprinted in Vol. 2, 1967.); "A Plea for a National Theatre in Ireland." *Samhain*, No. 1 (October 1901): 14-15; *The Place-Hunters: A Political Comedy in One Act. The Leader*, July 26, 1902; *The Tale of a Town: A Comedy of Affairs in Five Acts and An Enchanted Sea: A Play in Four Acts*. Kilkenny: Standish O'Grady/London: Fisher Unwin, 1902; *Romulus and Remus, or The Makers of Delights: A Symbolist Extravaganza in One Act*. Christmas supplement to *The Irish People*, December 21, 1907, 1-2; *Grangecolman: A Domestic Drama in Three Acts*. Dublin: Maunsel, 1912; *The Dream Physician: A Play in Five Acts*. Dublin: Talbot, 1914/reprinted in Vol. 7, Irish Drama Series, 1972; "A Plea for the Revival of the Irish Literary Theatre." *The Irish Review* 4 (April 1914):79-84; "*The Cherry Orchard* of Tchekoff." *New Ireland* 8 (June 21, 1919):108-109.   REFERENCES: Courtney, Sr. Marie-Therese. *Edward Martyn and the Irish Theatre*. New York: Vantage, 1956; Gwynn, Denis. *Edward Martyn and the Irish Revival*. London: Jonathan Cape, 1930; MacDonagh, John. "Edward Martyn." *The Dublin Magazine* 1 (February 1924):465-467; McFate, Patricia. "*The Bending of the Bough* and *The Heather Field*." *Éire-Ireland* 8 (Spring 1973):52-61; Moore, George. *Hail and Farewell*. 3 vols. London: Heinemann, 1937; Setterquist, Jan. *Ibsen and the Beginnings of Anglo-Irish Drama. II: Edward Martyn*. Upsala: Lundquist, 1960.

MATHEWS, AIDAN CARL (1956-), poet. Mathews was born in Dublin in 1956. A collection of his poems, *Windfalls*, won the Patrick Kavanagh Poetry Award in 1976. For so young a poet, the collection is a remarkably controlled statement. Some of the sentences are a little syntactically squashed, and no lyric leaps are taken whatsoever, but there are no gauche or slovenly moments.

WORK: *Windfalls*. Dublin: Dolmen, 1977.

MATURIN, CHARLES ROBERT (1780-1824), novelist. The best example of the Gothic novel, in its excesses as well as its strengths, is *Melmoth the Wanderer*. Its author, Charles Robert Maturin, was as strange as his title character. He was born in Dublin on September 25, 1780, and spent most of his life there. He graduated from Trinity College and was ordained a minister. He was eccentric in dress and manner, and in later years he became a strange, brooding man whose life seems to have been miserable. He died in October 1824 in Dublin.

His first novel, *Fatal Revenge* (1807), imitates Radcliffe and others in its contorted revenge plot and reliance on horrible details. It is a representative Gothic novel, including instances of unmotivated cruelty and anti-Catholic bias. The next two novels, *The Wild Irish Boy* (1808) and *The Milesian Chief* (1811), were no more accomplished, although their subjects are Irish. Maturin's drama *Bertram*, produced in 1816, brought him attention, particularly since Edmund Kean played the title role with great success.

Maturin's masterpiece is undoubtedly *Melmoth the Wanderer* (1820). It is a long novel, containing numerous digressions and a confusing narrative line, but it centers on a clear moral theme, one stated by the author: a man would not willingly sell his soul for any price. Despite that didactic theme, the book abounds with instances of extreme cruelty, masochism, even satanism. These diabolical elements appealed to some writers later in the century; Baudelaire once proposed translating it, and the English writers of the decadence praised it. The obsession with suffering seems truly sadistic, but the novel's analysis of self-destructive impulses is, finally, perceptive. As Robert D. Hume notes in his essay in *PMLA* (1969), ". . . Melmoth, like Marlowe's Faustus, is damned not by what he does, but by his own proud despair of forgiveness and salvation." Such rejection of help also has political and religious implications in the novel. Like many of the Gothic novels, the spirit of republicanism is a motivating force; rejection of civil authority and exposure of the aristocracy's decadence are conveyed by serious subplots. Likewise, the subject of religious belief is treated seriously; Calvinism is weighed against Catholicism, and the author reveals a depth of concern for the nature of faith. The novel's structure is confusing and possibly unnecessarily complicated, but it may reflect the inner state of the human mind or at least of a neurotic mind. From every plot the same conclusions are drawn: man cannot escape death, and life is on the whole sheer misery. Some have claimed that the novel excels in its investigation of human psychology, but the cases are so abnormal, so extreme, that few general insights can be derived. It is rather in the intensity of feeling, the unbridled indulgence in terror and horror, that the book makes its strongest impression. There is no work quite like it: a highly colored, sprawling account of perverse experience. It relies on theatrical effects, coincidence, unmotivated action, and stock villains, but it does it so deliberately that the critic is disarmed. The author's hopeless view of human existence is conveyed by sheer overstatement, and that seems a viable manner of presentation for the subjects at hand.

Although Maturin wrote another novel, *The Albigenses* (1824), he never again achieved the vivid effects of Melmoth. He died in October 1824 in his native city.

JAMES KILROY

WORKS: *The Family of Montorio; or the Fatal Revenge.* 3 vols. London: Longmans, Hurst, Rees, & Orme, 1807; *The Wild Irish Boy.* 3 vols. London: Longmans, Hurst, Rees, & Orme, 1808; *The Milesian Chief.* 4 vols. London: Henry Colburn, 1812; *Bertram; or the Castle of St. Aldobrand.* London: John Murray, 1816. (Play); *Manuel.* London: John Murray, 1817. (Play); *Women; or Pour et Contre.* 3 vols. Edinburgh: Constable, 1818; *Fredolfo.* London: Constable, 1819. (Play); *Melmoth the Wanderer.* 4 vols. Edinburgh: Constable, 1820/Douglas Grant, ed. London: Oxford University Press, 1968; *The Albigenses.* 4 vols. London: Hurst, Robinson, 1824. REFERENCES: Idman, Nilo. *Charles Robert Maturin: His Life and Works.* London: Constable, 1923; Kiely, Robert. *The Romantic Novel in England.* Cambridge: Harvard University Press, 1972, pp. 189-207; Kramer, Dale. *Charles Robert Maturin.* New York: Twayne, 1973; Lougy, Robert E. *Charles Robert Maturin.* Lewisburg, Pa.: Bucknell University Press, 1975; Scholten, Willem. *Charles Robert Maturin: The Terror-Novelist.* Amsterdam: H. J. Paris, 1933.

MAUNSEL AND COMPANY (later MAUNSEL AND ROBERTS) (1905-1925), publishing house. Maunsel and Company Limited was founded in 1905 by Joseph Maunsel Hone,* George Roberts, and Stephen Gwynn.* Roberts was interested in all aspects of book production and design, and from 1910 he printed over one hundred books for the firm—between 1910 and 1916 under the imprint of "Maunsel and Co. Ltd."; between 1917 and 1920 under the imprint of "George Roberts"; and between 1920 and 1925 under the imprint of "Maunsel and Roberts, Ltd." Several of the books which Roberts designed and printed, such as the 1910 de luxe edition of Synge's* Collected Works, are highly regarded even today as examples of good book design.

By the autumn of 1906, Maunsel and Company's publications were already being extensively distributed by several London booksellers. One of the firm's most successful and widely known publications, *The Shanachie*, a quarterly literary magazine edited by Hone, appeared in 1906. This magazine counted Yeats,* Shaw,* Synge, and Lady Gregory* among its contributors, although it only lasted for six issues. In its early years, Maunsel concentrated on publishing literary works, especially poetry and drama, although it also published some novels and volumes of essays. It gradually broadened its publishing ventures to include books in Irish and school editions.

In 1906 and 1907, Maunsel and Company published two books by Yeats in conjunction with A. H. Bullen—*Poems 1899-1905* and *Deirdre*. In 1908, Bullen arranged for special title pages to be printed for fifty sets of the Collected Edition of Yeats' Works, with Maunsel's name on the title pages. Synge, however, was Maunsel's most important author and the firm is remembered by many as Synge's publisher. Several different editions of Synge's works were published by Maunsel; his plays under the title *Dramatic Works* were also published for the first time by Maunsel in December 1914.

In the years after 1910, Maunsel and Company, having already established itself as the most important publishing firm in Ireland, went on to consolidate that position and to acquire a reputation outside Ireland. In the spring of 1912, it opened a London office, and henceforth the firm began to publish a number of books about non-Irish subjects and by non-Irish authors. Morever, around 1912 Maunsel and Company made arrangements for distributing its most important books in America through the Boston publishing house of John W. Luce.

In July 1915, Maunsel made an arrangement with George Allen and Unwin, Ltd., a London publishing house, whereby Maunsel undertook to stock George Allen and Unwin's publications on a sale or return basis. It is probable that some kind of reciprocal arrangement was made whereby George Allen and Unwin undertook to stock Maunsel's publications on a similar basis. For about this time Maunsel closed its own London office at Oakley House, Bloomsbury, and from then until the firm closed in 1925, Maunsel's London address was 40 Museum Street, which was and still is George Unwin's office. This would indicate that George Unwin was acting as Maunsel's London representative in some capacity. In fact, George Allen and Unwin benefited much more from the arrangement than did Maunsel. In time they managed to persuade several of Maunsel's established authors, such as St. John Ervine* and the trustees of the Synge estate, to transfer their publishing rights from Maunsel to themselves, whereas many of the George Allen and Unwin books stocked by Maunsel were, in the words of George Allen and Unwin's managing director, "only fit for waste paper!"

In January 1916, Dr. Edward MacLysaght joined Maunsel as a junior director. Shortly thereafter, the firm was destroyed in the Easter Week Rising. Maunsel was fortunate for once because it had done much to foster the climate which produced the events of Easter Week 1916. In fact, much material on the premises at the time was semi-treasonable, including the manuscript of the first volume of Pearse's* Collected Works, which had been entrusted by Pearse, shortly before Easter Week, to George Roberts for safekeeping and subsequent publication.

By 1920, Maunsel and Company was in financial difficulty. Roberts, never a good businessman, had lost all sense of proportion when the firm received its vastly overassessed compensation from the British government for the destruction of its Dublin premises. Roberts used Maunsel's sudden affluence to overproduce and publish books and pamphlets. From May 1916 to December 1919, in two and one-half years, the firm published 117 new books and pamphlets, of which Roberts printed 66 himself. Another 30 books and pamphlets were set up and reached page proof stage, before coming to grief at the hands of the press censor. Unfortunately, the financial difficulties of 1920 continued for Roberts until his firm's demise in 1925. Toward the end of its existence, Maunsel and Roberts published very few books, and those often by little known authors of small merit.

RICHARD BURNHAM

MAXTON, HUGH (1947-), poet. Hugh Maxton is the pseudonym of William John McCormack, who was born in County Wicklow in 1947 and was educated at Trinity College. He has lived in Derry and in Yorkshire, and his collection *The Noise of the Fields* was a Poetry Book Society choice in the summer of 1976. His first short collection, *Stones* (1970), was severely abstract in its language and glum in its themes, while its chief obeisance to form was a rather sybylline terseness. *The Noise of the Fields* (1976) was more concrete and fleshed out in its language, but form was still an unsolved problem. When, for instance, Maxton essayed a conventional form like the sonnet, as in his "De Profundis," he could handle neither the rhyming nor the meter, and even a poem composed of simple four-stress couplets falls into lame lines. Nevertheless, pieces like "A Blank Map" and "Elegies" contain many effective single lines.

WORKS: *Stones*. Dublin: Allen Figgis, 1970; *The Noise of the Fields, Poems 1970-1975*. Dublin: Dolmen, 1976.

MAXWELL, WILLIAM HAMILTON (1792-1850), novelist and writer of sketches. Maxwell was born in 1792 at Newry, County Down, and was educated at Trinity College, Dublin. Apparently as "Hamilton Maxwell," he obtained a captaincy of foot in 1812 and served in the Peninsular campaigns and at Waterloo. He later took Holy Orders somewhat against his inclinations and in 1820 was presented a living at Ballagh in Connemara. His duties were light in that little-tenanted district, and he was able freely to indulge his taste for hunting and to write his popular fictions on sporting and military subjects. His more serious pieces have a quaint nineteenth-century stiffness, but his comic sketches are well done, particularly in the easy dialogue. He is credited with popularizing the rollicking Harry Lorrequer kind of hero, and, although he is not quite of Lever's* calibre, he is nonetheless a pleasant read. He died at Musselburgh, near Edinburgh, on December 29, 1850.

WORKS: *O'Hara; or 1798.* 2 vols. London: J. Andrews, 1825; *Stories of Waterloo, and Other Tales.* 3 vols. London: H. Colburn, 1829; *Wild Sports of the West.* 2 vols. London: R. Bentley, 1832; *The Field Book; or, Sports and Pastimes of the United Kingdom.* London: Effingham Wilson, 1833; *The Dark Lady of Doona.* London: Smith, Elder, 1834; *My Life.* 3 vols. London: R. Bentley, 1835; *The Bivouac; or, Stories of the Peninsular War.* 3 vols. London: R. Bentley, 1837; *The Victories of the British Armies.* 2 vols. London: R. Bentley, 1839; *Life of Field-Marshall His Grace the Duke of Wellington.* 3 vols. London: A. K. Baily, 1841; *Rambling Recollections of a Soldier of Fortune.* Dublin: W. Curry, 1842; *The Fortunes of Hector O'Halloran and His Man Mark Antony O'Toole.* London: R. Bentley, n.d.; *Wanderings in the Highlands and Islands.* 2 vols. London: A. H. Baily, 1844; *Hints to a Soldier on Service.* 2 vols. London: T. C. Newby, 1845; *History of the Irish Rebellion in 1798.* London: Baily Brothers, Cornhill, 1845; *Peninsular Sketches by Actors on the Scene.* 2 vols. London: H. Colburn, 1845; *Captain O'Sullivan; or, Adventures, Civil, Military, and Matrimonial of a Gentleman on Half-Pay.* 3 vols. London: H. Colburn, 1846; *Hill-Side and Border Sketches.* 2 vols. London: R. Bentley, 1847; *Brian O'Linn; or, Luck Is Everything.* 3 vols. London: R. Bentley, 1848; *The Irish Movements: Their Rise, Progress and Certain Termination.* London: Baily Brothers, 1848; *Erin Go Bragh; or, Irish Life Pictures,* with a biographical sketch by Dr. Maginn. 2 vols. London: R. Bentley, 1859.

MAYNE, RUTHERFORD (1878-1967), playwright and actor. Rutherford Mayne, born Samuel Waddell in Japan in 1878, was to Ulster theatre what Yeats,* Robinson,* and Lady Gregory* were to the Abbey,* a person of many parts. Between 1906 and 1923, he contributed nine plays to the Ulster Literary Theatre,* Belfast, including *The Turn of the Road* (1906), *The Drone* (1908), and *The Troth* (1909). An amateur actor, Mayne performed in Belfast, Dublin, and English cities, sometimes in his own plays. Withdrawing from his long association with the Literary Theatre in 1930, he wrote *Peter* (1930) and *Bridgehead* (1934) for the Abbey. His study of engineering and his employment with the Irish Land Commission before and after the Treaty are reflected in his writing. In 1960, at age eighty-two, he was appointed a trustee of the Lyric Players Theatre* of Belfast. He died in Dublin on February 25, 1967. His sister was Helen Waddell,* the scholar.

Mayne's early plays examine the life of rural County Down. The Ulster work ethic enters seriously into *The Turn of the Road* and humorously into the kitchen comedy *The Drone.* In the former, Robbie John Granahan leaves home rather than yield to the stern demand of his parents that he throw away his violin and dedicate himself to farming. Easygoing Daniel Murray, the drone, forced by Northern mores to do something, spends his time puttering at a worthless mechanical invention. *The Troth* is a harrowing account of an agreement between a Catholic and a Protestant farmer, fellow sufferers at the hands of an unfeeling landlord, to murder their oppressor. If either is killed or apprehended, the other will care for both families. Implicit in *The Troth* is a call for unity and social justice.

Mayne shifts the locale to Galway for his one-act agrarian tragedy *Red Turf* (1911). Martin Burke, goaded by his termagant wife, kills a neighbor in a dispute over a tiny patch of land.

Peter, dedicated in part to Lennox Robinson,* may have been influenced by Robinson's dramatic experiments. The prologue and epilogue take place while Peter Grahame is awake. The rest is a dream in which he fails in his engineering studies and goes to work as an entertainer-gigolo in a hotel patronized by eccentrics and owned by boorish Sam Partridge. Mayne subtly disciplines the comedy by his understanding of the insecurity of a young man preparing for entry into the real, competitive world.

Distilled from Mayne's experience with the Land Commission, *Bridgehead* is a triumph of dramatic art over material better suited to a novel or a documentary movie. It is essentially a character study of plain, dogged Stephen Moore, who must plan for Ireland's future even as he is adjudicating the conflicting land and money claims of the old Ascendancy, hungry have-nots, and ruthless grabbers.

For many years, Mayne's cottage dramas were sentimental favorites, especially in Belfast. Today they suffer from association with an overworked and confined genre, although their muffled lyricism and a sympathy for the characters not always evident in the Cork realists* or St. John Ervine* gain for them a measure of distinctiveness. Modern audiences are more likely to respond to the skillful unconventionality of *Peter* or *Bridgehead*.

WILLIAM J. FEENEY

WORKS: *The Turn of the Road: A Play in Two Scenes and an Epilogue*. Dublin: Maunsel, 1907/reprinted, Dublin: Duffy, 1950; *The Drone: A Play in Three Acts*. Dublin: Maunsel, 1909; *The Troth: A Play in One Act*. Dublin: Maunsel, 1909; "The Freeholder." *The Irish Review* 1 (November 1911):432-434. (Short story); "A Prologue." *The Dublin Magazine* 2 (June 1925):723-725. (A play in one act); *Bridgehead: A Play in Three Acts*. London: Constable, 1939. Also in *Plays of Changing Ireland*. Curtis Canfield, ed. New York: Macmillan, 1936; *Peter: A Comedy in Three Acts and a Prologue and Epilogue*. Dublin: Duffy, 1964.   REFERENCES: Bell, Sam Hanna. *The Theatre in Ulster*. Dublin: Gill & Macmillan, 1972; Kane, Whitford. *Are We All Met?* London: Elkins, Mathews & Marrot, 1931; McHenry, Margaret. *The Ulster Theatre in Ireland*. Philadelphia: University of Pennsylvania, 1931.

MELDON, MAURICE (1926-1958), playwright. Meldon was born in Dublin in 1926, became a civil servant, and died most prematurely in a traffic accident on November 12, 1958. His best work seems reminiscent of an expressionistic Gerald MacNamara,* satiric and relying strongly on Irish history and myth. The best of his three published plays is *Aisling* (37 Theatre Club, 1953). An Aisling is a dream-vision, and the play is a freewheeling social and political satire set during a highly stylized time of the Troubles but with much obvious contemporary relevance. Meldon's use of allusion to, as well as parody and pastiche of, various styles of Irish writing, make this a trenchant, eminently witty, and unfortunately neglected play. Indeed, Hugh Leonard* referred to Meldon as "probably our most neglected author."

WORKS: "Purple Path to the Poppy Field," in *New World Writing, Fifth Mentor Selection.* New York: New American Library, 1954; *Aisling.* Dublin: Progress House, 1959; *House under Green Shadows.* Dublin: Progress House, 1962.

MILLIGAN, ALICE (1866-1953), poet, novelist, and dramatist. Milligan was born in Omagh, County Tyrone, on September 14, 1866. She studied history at King's College, London, and afterward traveled through Ireland, under the auspices of the Gaelic League, lecturing on Irish history. From 1896 to 1899, she and Ethna Carbery* edited the nationalist and literary magazine *The Shan Van Vocht* in Belfast. In 1898, she was involved in what was apparently the first production of a play in Irish, in the town of Letterkenny.

Milligan's early verse dealt with scenery and legend. *Hero Lays* (1908) and most of her subsequent poems were historical and nationalistic, ranging in subject from pre-Christian figures to the heroes of the 1916 Rising.

A Royal Democrat, a novel written in 1892, begins with an unusual plot line: a shipwrecked English prince lands in Ireland and becomes, incognito, an Irish patriot. But the story dwindles into stock love-and-honor romanticism.

Milligan's one-act play, *The Last Feast of the Fianna,* the beginning of a trilogy on the adventures of Oisin, was the earliest specimen of Celtic Twilight drama to emerge from the Irish theatre movement. The slender, graceful work was staged in 1900 by the Irish Literary Theatre. *The Daughter of Donagh,* a stilted historical melodrama set in Cromwellian Ireland, was published serially in *United Irishman* in 1909.

Most of Milligan's work, impressive in volume if not always in quality, was done before 1922. Saddened by the division of her native Ulster and the Free State, she wrote little after the Treaty. She died at Omagh on April 13, 1953.

                                                        WILLIAM J. FEENEY

WORKS: *A Royal Democrat.* London: Simpkin, Marshall/Dublin: Gill, 1892; *The Life of Theobald Wolfe Tone.* Belfast: J. W. Boyd, 1898; *The Last Feast of the Fianna.* London: David Nutt, 1900/reprinted, Chicago: De Paul University, 1967; *The Daughter of Donagh, a Cromwellian Drama in Four Acts,* in *United Irishman* (December 5, 12, 19, 26, 1903)/reprinted, Dublin: Lester, 1920; *Hero Lays.* Dublin: Maunsel, 1908; "Oisin in Tir nan Og," *Sinn Fein* (January 23, 1909). (One-act play); "Oisin and Padraic," *Sinn Fein* (February 20, 1909). (One-act play); with W. H. Milligan. *Sons of the Sea Kings.* Dublin: Gill, 1914; with Ethna Carbery & Seumas MacManus. *We Sang for Ireland.* Dublin: Gill, 1950; *Poems by Alice Milligan,* edited with an Introduction by Henry Mangan. Dublin: Gill, 1954. (Mangan's introduction is the best source of biographical information.)   REFERENCE: MacDonagh, Thomas. "The Best Living Irish Poet." *The Irish Review* 4 (September-November 1914): 287-293.

MILLIGAN, SPIKE (1918-), humorist and actor. Milligan was born of Irish parentage in 1918 at Admednagar in India. He first attended school in a tent in the Hyderabad Sindh desert. From there he went to various Roman Catholic schools in India and England, and then on to Lewisham Polytechnic. After starting his career as a band musician, he explored other fields and is now a well-known author, actor, humanist, composer, painter, and conservationist. He was one of the founding members of the Goon Show, and his *The Goon Show Script Book* has become a best seller. His other best seller is a novel, *Adolf Hitler—My Part in His Downfall*. Milligan's contribution to Irish literature is his first novel *Puckoon* (1963) which "bursts at the seams with superb comic characters involved in unbelievably likely troubles on the Irish border" (*Observer*). In addition to his novels, Milligan has written poetry, drama, and children's books, as well as film, television, and radio scripts, and other miscellaneous works. He adapted and narrated Paul Gallico's *The Snow Goose* for an L.P. recording, and he has acted and starred in theatre, film, and television productions. His current commitments are writing and acting for the BBC television series *Melting Pot* and *Q.7*.

Milligan's *Puckoon* is brilliantly comic. Though the hero, Dan Milligan, is forced to live "off his pension and his wits, both hopelessly inadequate," he seems to accept those deficiencies. But what he doesn't like are his legs. As a newly created character, he has never seen his legs before. (They are really only "two thin white hairy affairs of the leg variety.") So, when he does see them, his first response is "Holy God! Wot are dese den? Eh?" He looks around for an answer, then repeats the question angrily, "Wot are dey?" The reader expects the question, which can only be rhetorical, to disappear into the Irish mist. But instead, an answer comes: "Legs." Without thinking who the speaker might be, Milligan instantly cries out, "Legs? LEGS? Whose legs?" And the conversation continues:

> "Yours,"
> "Mine? And who are you?"
> "The Author."
> "Author? Author? Did you write these legs?"
> "Yes."
> "Well, I don't like dem. I don't like 'em at all at all. I could ha' writted better legs meself. Did you write your legs?"
> "No."
> "Ahhh. *Sooo*! You got some one else to write your legs, some one who's a good leg writer and den you write dis pair of crappy old legs fer me, well mister, it's not good enough."
> "I'll try and develop them with the plot."
> "It's a dia-bo-likal liberty lettin' an untrained leg writer loose on an unsuspectin' human bean like me."

The comedy is not limited to the author's unconventional conversations with his main character. There is a wake scene that is more fully orchestrated than the most elaborate version of Finnegan's wake. Another scene is so packed with marvelous slapstick that it is reminiscent of the hot chestnut fiasco of *Tristram Shandy*. The final scene brings all elements crashing together and leaves Dan Milligan hanging from a tree with a rusty organ pipe lodged over his head, crying "You can't leave me like this!" to which the author replies, "Oh, can't I?" And the book ends.

Between the major scenes, the author continually provides the reader with descriptions that guarantee hearty and audible laughter. For example, "The pub door opened, and in bore a podgy police uniform carrying the body of Sgt. MacGillikudie," or "Peering intently from behind a wall was something that Milligan could only hope was a face. The fact that it was hanging from a hat gave credulity to his belief." Spike Milligan is such a gifted comedian that he even sees comic potential in a single moment: "There was a short pause, then a longer one, but so close were they together, you couldn't tell the difference."

KATHLEEN DANAHER PARKS

WORK: *Puckoon*. London: Anthony Blond, 1963.

MILLIKEN, RICHARD ALFRED (1767-1815), poet. Milliken was born at Castlemartyr, County Cork, on September 8, 1767. He was an attorney, painter, and musician, though not very successful in any of these areas. With his sister, who was a very minor novelist indeed, he founded *The Casket, or Hesperian Magazine* in 1797. *The Casket* lasted only a year, until the Rebellion of 1798, which Milliken helped to put down. He wrote poems and plays, but is remembered only for his poem "The Groves of Blarney," a pastiche of a popular ballad which has been widely reprinted. Geoffrey Taylor in *Irish Poets of the Nineteenth Century* notes that the meter is derived from the Gaelic and that "The parade of learning, the inconsequence, and the decorative use of words not fully understood, hark back to the proverbial grandiloquence of the hedge-schoolmasters." The popularity of the poem undoubtedly derives from its ear-arresting meter and its charmingly inane rhyming, but its imagery is sometimes scarcely less remarkable, and the description of "comely eels in the verdant mud" deserves some sort of immortality. The poem was attractive enough for Father Prout* to add a stanza. Milliken, although no patriot, was a convivial and lovable man who earned the sobriquet "Honest Dick." He died on December 16, 1815.

WORKS: *The River-Side, a Poem, in Three Books*. Cork: Connor, 1807; *The Slave of Surinam, or Innocent Victim of Cruelty*. Cork: Mathews, 1810. (Novel); *Poetical Fragments of the late Richard Alfred Milliken*. London: Longman, 1823.

MILNE, EWART (1903-), poet.

> (Charles) Eward Milne: Born Dublin 1903. Student-teacher; sea-
> man; works-clerk; journalist; estate manager. Poet and writer of
> letters and essays. Published 14 volumes of poetry, four in Dublin,
> the rest in England, the last being *Drift of Pinions* and *Cantata
> Under Orion*. Contributor to Irish and British national press, and
> to leading Irish, British, and American literary magazines over
> forty years. Mem. Society of Authors and British Interplanetary
> Society. Recreations: reading science fiction and watching tele-
> vision.

This is Milne's summary of himself, characteristically wry about the self
and studied about the poetry. Born in Dublin of an Anglo-Irish family, he
grew into leftist politics as the political split in his family and his nation
became more pronounced. Perhaps the early rejection of his father fostered
his marriage to an Irish girl, as it did his years of wandering rather than
accept his father's pro-British politics.

After the death of their first-born, the Milnes returned to Dublin, though
Ewart intended to go to sea. He published poems in *Comment* and wrote
letters to the newspapers about the problems in Spain. At the same time,
his developing antipathy to "Gaelicism" kept him from supporting de Valera. He drifted back to London to work for the Spanish Medical Aid; in
1937, he followed his friend Charles Donnelly to Madrid, only to find
Donnelly had been killed.

Milne's pro-Republican affiliation cooled, and he returned to London
in 1941 to work for Edward Sheehy's *Ireland Today* before again moving
to Ireland. By the time he moved to England, he had published three volumes of poetry. Curiously, even these early volumes have a post-Yeatsian
ring and an Anglo-Irish hauteur, though no single style then or later characterizes Milne's poetry. During the war, he worked on a farm, continued
his publishing, and met Thelma Dobson, whom he married in 1948. During the war years and through the 1950s, he was very pro-Irish and published *Galion*, a mock epic at Liam Miller's* Dolmen Press* in 1953. By
1962, the Milnes were living in Dublin, and he published his nationalistic
A Garland for the Green (1962), which found no favor with the new circle
of poets and critics who formed literary Dublin.

Milne's wife died in 1964. In going through her papers, he discovered
her involvement with (or victimization by, as Milne sees it) a close friend
of theirs. He then began a period of withdrawal and self-examination that
resulted in *Time Stopped* (1967), a book-length study in poetry and prose
in which he presented his love and accepted his Anglo-Irish background.
That he would continue to write after such a strong statement seemed unlikely, but he has since published two volumes of poetry.

The writing of poetry has been the major force in Milne's life. Always poetry led him to consider his relationship with Ireland, which has changed with the circumstances of his life. Perhaps that is why he has restlessly changed styles.

FRANK KERSNOWSKI

WORKS: *Forty North Fifty West*. Dublin: Gayfield, 1938; *Letter from Ireland: Verses*. Dublin: Gayfield, 1940; *Listen Mangan: Poems*. Dublin: Sign of the Three Candles, 1941; *Jubilo: Poems*. London: Muller, 1944; *Boding Day*. London: Muller, 1947; *Elegy for a Lost Submarine*. Burnham-on-Couch: Plow Poems, 1951; *Diamond Cut Diamon: Selected Poems*. London: Bodley Head, 1953; *Galion: A Poem*. Dublin: Dolmen, 1953; *Life Arboreal: Poems*. Tunbridge Wells: Pound, 1953; *Once More to Tourney: A Book of Ballads and Light Verse, Serious, Gay, and Grisly*. Introduction by J. M. Cohen. London: Linden, 1958; *A Garland for the Green: Poems*. London: Hutchinson, 1962; *Time Stopped: A Poem-Sequence with Prose Intermissions*. London: Plow Poems, 1967; *Cantata Under Orion*. Isle of Sky: Aquila Poetry, 1976; *Drift of Pinions*. Isle of Sky: Aquila Poetry, 1976.   REFERENCE: Kersnowski, Frank. *The Outsiders*. Fort Worth, Tex.: Texas Christian University Press, 1975.

MITCHEL, JOHN (1815-1875), journalist and historian. Mitchel, the Irish patriot, was born on November 3, 1815, at Camnish, near Dungiven, County Londonderry, the third son of a Presbyterian minister. He matriculated at Trinity College, Dublin, in 1830, and according to one biographer took his degree in 1834, although his name does not appear in the Catalogue of Graduates. He was intended by his father for the ministry but began life as a bank clerk in Londonderry before entering a solicitor's office at Newry. When he was nineteen, he eloped with Jane Verner, a school girl of sixteen, but they were caught at Chester, and Mitchel was taken back to Ireland in custody. A year later they eloped again, and this time got married.

In 1842, Mitchel met Thomas Davis* who "filled his soul with the passion of a great ambition and a lofty purpose." In 1843, he qualified as a lawyer and joined the Repeal Association, and in 1845, he began writing for *The Nation*.* He soon emerged as one of the most effective Irish journalists of the century, but, as *The Nation* was not radical enough for Mitchel in its political stand, he founded *The United Irishman* in 1848. In this paper, he advocated armed insurrection to achieve an Irish republic which would secure "the land for the people." In May 1848, he was arrested, convicted of treason by a packed jury, and sentenced to fourteen years' transportation. He was first shipped to Bermuda where he spent ten awful, asthmatic months and nearly died in close confinement. From there he sailed to South Africa, but an uprising of the colonists prevented the convicts from landing, so the ship sailed on to Tasmania. There Mitchel sent for his wife and children and lived happily as a farmer until 1853 when he escaped to America. He worked as a journalist in America for twenty years and gained notoriety during the Civil War for his defense of slavery. His bad eyesight prevented him from fighting, but he accepted the editorship of *The Enquirer*, a semi-official organ of President Jefferson Davis. Two of his sons were killed fighting for the Confederate side, and the third lost an arm.

After the war, Mitchel went to New York where he became editor of *The Daily News*. He was arrested by the military authorities and imprisoned for nearly five months because of his articles defending the South. He retained an interest in Irish politics of the more extreme variety, and in February 1875 he was elected to a Tipperary seat after he indicated he would not go to Westminster. He was unseated as a convicted felon but returned again in March. He traveled to Ireland for the election but died at Newry within a few days of his success on March 20, 1875.

Mitchel was a prolific journalist and historian, but today is remembered mainly for the *Jail Journal*, a record of his time in captivity. Although a sacred cow of Irish literature, this book makes fairly dull reading. Occasionally, however, a striking phrase does break through the Carlylean prose: "Dublin city, with its bay and pleasant villas—city of bellowing slaves, villas of genteel dastards—lies now behind us." The journal's chief interest is political rather than literary. Mitchel's hatred of England spilled out in bloodletting prose which influenced Pearse,* and his ideas for a complete restructure of society filtered through to Connolly.*

Nevertheless, the patriot's concern for social justice did not quite extend to criminals or to blacks:

> Not that I think it wrong to flog convicted felons for preservation of discipline . . . but I had rather as a matter of personal taste be out of hearing.

Or:

> What to do with all our robbers, burglars and forgers? Why hang them, hang them.

Or:

> Jails ought to be places of discomfort; the sanitary condition of miscreants ought not to be cared for more than the health of honest industrious people, and for "ventilation" I would ventilate the rascals in front of the country jails at the end of a rope.

Or, as he remarked about Tasmania:

> Here a freeman is a king; and the convict class is regarded just as the negroes must be in South Carolina; which indeed is perfectly right.

In domestic life he is said to have been the gentlest of men, but one shudders to think of the social consequences had this champion of liberty ever come to power in Ireland.

MARY ROSE CALLAGHAN

WORKS: *The Life and Times of Aodh O'Neill, Prince of Ulster*. Dublin: Duffy, 1846; *Jail Journal; or, Five Years in British Prisons*. [New York: *The Citizen*, 1854]/

New York: P. M. Haverty, 1868/Dublin: Gill, 1913; *The Last Conquest of Ireland (Perhaps)*. Dublin: *The Irishman* Office, 1861.   REFERENCES: Dillon, W. *Life of J. Mitchel.* 2 vols. London: Kegan Paul, Trench & Co., 1888; MacCall, S. *Irish Mitchel: A Bibliography*. London: T. Nelson, 1938; O'Hegarty, P. S. *J. Mitchel: An Appreciation, with some account of Young Ireland*. Dublin & London: Maunsel, 1917.

MITCHELL, SUSAN [LANGSTAFF] (1866-1926), poet and editor. Mitchell was born at Carrick-on-Shannon on December 5, 1866. She stayed with relatives in Ireland and with the Yeats* family in London, before becoming, in 1901, assistant editor for George William Russell (AE)* on *The Irish Homestead* and its successor, *The Irish Statesman.* Unmarried, she lived quietly with a sister. Despite frail health, she was noted for her wit and charm, as J. B. Yeats,* AE, and Seumas O'Sullivan* testify. Nostalgia, sentiment, and mystical feeling pervade *The Living Chalice* (1908). Her religious poetry, muted in tone, is slightly reminiscent of Emily Dickinson. Her humor appears in her contributions to the parody on the *Playboy* riots, *The Abbey Row, Not Edited by W. B. Yeats* (1907), and to *Secret Springs of Dublin Song* (1918). Her satires were appropriately entitled *Aids to the Immortality of Certain Persons in Dublin: Charitably Administered* (1908). The cover of the first edition of *Aids* has a delightful caricature of Dublin celebrities. Though dated by topicality, these poems evoke the issues of the time, viewed with gaiety. George Moore's* pretensions were also a favorite target, both in verse and in her mocking study *George Moore* (1916). She died in Dublin on March 4, 1926.

                                                RICHARD M. KAIN
     WORKS: *Aids to the Immortality of Certain Persons in Ireland: Charitably Administered*. Dublin: The New Nation, 1908/enlarged, Dublin: Maunsel, 1913; *The Living Chalice*. Dublin: Maunsel, 1908/enlarged, 1913; *George Moore*. Dublin: Maunsel, 1916; *Secret Springs of Dublin Song*. Dublin: Talbot, 1918. Contributed to *The Abbey Row, Not Edited by W. B. Yeats*. Dublin: Maunsel, 1907.   REFERENCE: Kain, Richard M. *Susan L. Mitchell*. Lewisburg, Pa.: Bucknell University Press, 1972.

MOLLOY, M[ICHAEL] J[OSEPH] (1917-), playwright. Molloy was born on March 3, 1917, in Milltown, County Galway. He trained for the priesthood until illness forced him to discontinue his studies, and most of his adult life he has worked a small farm outside of Milltown. Molloy's plays, whether historical or modern, are steeped in the tradition, customs, folklore, and language of the west of Ireland. The modern plays show characters fighting to stave off the death of a culture, and the historical plays show characters fighting to stave off the literal and metaphorical deaths that the culture caused. There are triumphs in a Molloy play, but muted ones, temporary and transient. The rich texture of the best Molloy plays has sometimes caused him to be compared to J. M. Synge,* but, because Molloy has a more mournful note than Synge in such plays as *Old Road* or *The Wood of the Whispering* or the conclusion of *The King of Friday's Men*, there may be a tendency to forget that he is as capable as Synge of grotesque comedy and sudden violence. His best characters are often mournful eccentrics, droll, fatalistic, and ultimately just a bit too resilient to be quite totally defeated. The thick Western texture of his plays and his overelaborate plots have probably militated against any great popularity of the plays outside of Ireland, but, with Synge and Fitzmaurice,* he must be accounted the most individual of modern Irish dramatists.

His first play, *The Old Road* (Abbey, 1943), is about emigration and the depopulation of the West, and shows many of Molloy's continuing characteristics: barmy character parts, young lovers, a complicated plot, a fight scene, and rich dialogue. *The Visiting House* (Abbey, 1946) combines these qualities with the elaborate playmaking of an old-time Visiting House. In the Merryman or Master of the Visiting House and in his two ancient cronies, the Man of Learning and the Man of Education, Molloy has created a rare trio of eccentrics to stand for the values of the traditional past. The plot of the play is one of the most snarled of any Irish play, but some of the long speeches contain passages of great eloquence.

Molloy's masterpiece, *The King of Friday's Men* (Abbey, 1948), is an historical play set in the late eighteenth century; it contains both his faults and his virtues in abundance. Indeed, a rich abundance is the best way to describe this play that in its many well-drawn and memorable characters, in its tangled plot, in its grotesquerie and violence, and, especially, in its noble melancholy, must rank among the most densely textured, difficult to produce, and potentially rewarding pieces of folk drama since García Lorca.

The Wood of the Whispering (Abbey, 1953) has none of the violence of *The King of Friday's Men*, but its genial comedy and quaint ruefulness give it a pervasive and attractive charm. It is set in modern times and is a reprise of the themes of *Old Road*, romantic love and emigration. It must be taken at its own pace to work, and its pace is meandering and leisurely. A venue, such as it received in its English production at Joan Littlewood's Stratford East, is utterly wrong. This is one of the most appealing of Molloy's plays, but it is in a muted minor key and all the richer for it.

Although *The Paddy Pedlar* (Abbey, 1953) is a one-act play, it must stand with Molloy's best work. Like much of his work, it is based on a story that he has heard, and tells of how a ne'er-do-well attempts to rob a pedlar of the contents of his sack, only to discover therein the corpse of the pedlar's mother. The play is a unique blend of the macabre and, amazingly, the sweet. It must rank with the best half-dozen one-act plays of the Irish drama.

Molloy's later work, such as *The Will and the Way* (1955) and *Daughter from Over the Water* (1962) and the professionally unproduced *Tess Leitrim, Knight Errant*, have more of Molloy's characteristic faults than his qualities, but they are so individual that they could have been written by no other Irish dramatist. After fifty years, the Irish theatrical movement has finally produced an authentic folk dramatist.

WORKS: *The King of Friday's Men*. Dublin: James Duffy, 1953; *The Paddy Pedlar*. Dublin: James Duffy, 1954; *The Will and the Way*. Dublin: P. J. Bourke, n.d.; *Old Road*. Dublin: Progress House, 1961; *The Wood of the Whispering*. Dublin: Progress House, 1961; *Daughter from over the Water*. Dublin: Progress House, 1963; *The Bitter Pill* in *Prizewinning Plays of 1964*. Dublin: Progress House, 1965; *The Visiting House* in *Seven Irish Plays, 1946-1964*. Minneapolis: University of Minnesota Press, 1967; *Three Plays by M. J. Molloy (The King of Friday's Men, The Paddy Pedlar,* and *The Wood of the Whispering)*. Newark, Del.: Proscenium, 1975; "The Making of Folk Plays." In *Literature and Folk Culture: Ireland and Folk Culture*. Alison Feder & Bernice Schrank, eds. St. John's, Newfoundland: Memorial University of Newfoundland, 1977, pp. 58-80.

MONTAGUE, JOHN (1929-), poet and short story writer. Montague was born in Brooklyn, New York, on February 28, 1929. His childhood was spent in County Tyrone. He was educated at University College, Dublin, lived in Paris, and now teaches in the English department of University College, Cork.

Montague began as a Southern writer, a young man in Dublin's difficult literary circles of the 1950s. He made his debut in its magazines. His early poems were published in 1958 by Dolmen Press*; MacGibbon & Kee published a second, more ambitious collection in 1961. Here the poet is beginning to take a long look at his Northern background. Village and townland experiences are already being assessed and assorted into folk imagery that wears a Jungian aspect. Montague has always been serious about his work; he has none of the casualness of Patrick Kavanagh* or the devil-may-care subversion of Austin Clarke.* *Tides* (1970), a mixture of lapidary styles and short-lined poetry exploring a moon landscape of love, serves as an overture to Montague's gradual return to Ulster themes. He planned a book that would take in the Northern conflict in its parameters of consciousness, in *The Rough Field* (1972). The work, elaborate in its sectioning and epic in its attempted range, includes poems written during a ten-year period. Montague retells the history of the truncated province, edging back to its roots in the Plantation. The least successful section is "Hymn to the New Omagh Road," where a confused medley of comment, quotation, and halfhearted real lines obscures every facet of the poem except its intent. The use of marginalia gives an artificial ambiance to parts of the book. What remains brilliant about it is the series of family vignettes and anecdotes; memories of a divided, and in many ways betrayed, family haunt Montague. His father and uncle appear as Virgilian characters in Hades: his exorcisms of them evoke the wonder of art.

The steel of the political temper in Montague shines in an ideological poem like "Penal Rock/Altamuskin." At least to Irish readers, Montague's tribalism must be fascinating. In his more recent book, *A Slow Dance* (1975), Montague has his eyes wide open, especially in the pieces dealing with the North. "Falls Funeral" reports with deadly accuracy the burial of a murdered Catholic child, while "Northern Express" hits at the center of the terrorism that involves the most average citizen. In his later poems Montague grips the fear of Ulster. There are no panaceas, no ways to accept or sublimate what is occurring. In this atmosphere, Montague represses what had been a feature of his early work, especially in his love poems: coy gestures. He begins to make good on Hugh MacDiarmaid's encouragement in *Agenda* (Spring-Summer 1973), "How far we are here from anything savouring of the Celtic Twilight!"

J A M E S   L I D D Y

WORKS: *Forms of Exile*. Dublin: Dolmen, 1958; *Poisoned Lands and Other Poems*. London: MacGibbon & Kee, 1961/Chester Springs, Pa.: Dufour, 1963/Dublin: Dolmen, 1977; *Death of a Chieftain*. London: MacGibbon & Kee, 1964. (Stories); *Home Again*. Belfast: Festival Publications, 1966; *Patriotic Suite*. Dublin: Dolmen, 1966; *A Chosen Light*. London: MacGibbon & Kee, 1967; *Tides*. Dublin: Dolmen, 1970; *The Wild Dog Rose*. London: MacGibbon & Kee, 1970; *The Rough Field*. Dublin: Dolmen, 1972; *A Slow Dance*. Dublin: Dolmen, 1975; *The Great Cloak*. Dublin: Dolmen, 1978.   REFERENCES: Brown, Terence. *Northern Voices*. Totowa, N.J.: Rowman & Littlefield, 1975; Dunn, Douglass, ed. *Two Decades of Irish Writing*. Cheadle: Carcanet, 1975; Kersnowski, Frank. *John Montague*. Lewisburg, Pa.: Bucknell University Press, 1975; Kinsella, Thomas. "Note on John Montague." *Contemporary Poets of the English Language*, 1970.

MONTGOMERY, LESLIE ALEXANDER. *See* DOYLE, LYNN.

MOORE, BRIAN (1921-), novelist. Moore, by using his successive countries of residence as settings for his novels, has set critics the problem of assigning him a literary nationality. Despite this difficulty, he can perhaps be claimed with least argument as one of the best novelists Ulster has produced. His first novel, *Judith Hearne* (1955), has been hailed as a minor masterpiece in its incisive portrayal of a pathetic Belfast spinster. *The Feast of Lupercal* (1957) attempts less successfully the similar theme of a social failure ironically regarded by the community as a threat to its puritanical, Irish-Catholic virtues. Moore's partly comic *bildungsroman*, *The Emperor of Ice-Cream* (1965), recreates Belfast during the World War II German "Blitz," whose effects precipitate the hero into manhood. *An Answer from Limbo* (1962) is the author's very fine *künstlerroman*, whose central figure has been strong enough to escape Ulster's provincialism, philistinism, and sectarianism only to discover in America the perplexing moral problems of his craft. In these four novels the city of Belfast is evocatively drawn.

Since *The Luck of Ginger Coffey* (1960), his third novel and a work of comic pathos that follows the harrowing adventures in Canada of an Irish immigrant, Moore's fiction has become more cosmopolitan. Subsequent novels have mirrored, with the expected refractions and reversions, the author's own movements. Born in Belfast on August 25, 1921, into a Catholic family that had recently converted from Protestantism, Moore left Northern Ireland twenty-two years later when he joined the British Ministry of War Transport during World War II and was stationed briefly in North Africa, Italy, and France. In 1948, he emigrated to Canada and there took out citizenship. He spent several years as a journalist and struggling fiction writer in Montreal, the setting for *Ginger Coffey*. Following the publication of this novel, the Canadian writer and critic Jack Ludwig wrote an article entitled "Brian Moore: Ireland's Loss, Canada's Novelist." Moore was regarded for a few years as Canada's most promising writer and in 1960 received the Governor General of Canada's Award for Fiction. In 1959, the author moved to the United States, first to Long Island and then to New York City, the setting for *An Answer from Limbo*, which is in part an energetic, bitter portrait of that city's literary and bohemian scene. Later he moved to Malibu, California, which provided him with the motive and material for *Fergus* (1970), a novel that is an equally bitter portrait of Hollywood's literary side-industry in which Moore has been involved, writing motion picture scripts. On the strength of such novels, Moore has been acclaimed a prominent United States writer.

Through a tyrannizing memory stirred by guilt, remorse, or depression, Moore's Irish-born Americans vainly try to exorcise the Ireland they thought they had left behind. Moreover, their solution to an Irish problem itself becomes merely a new American problem and a new theme: thus, the escape from provincialism leads to the dreadful freedom of the cosmopolis, and the escape from religion becomes the new problem of faithlessness. For Moore America is Ireland's probable future, but in the provocative and fable-like *Catholics* (1972), a late twentieth-century Ireland becomes the hideously bureaucratic and faithless future of both. And when there is no continuity of theme and crisis between Ireland and America, Moore senses analogies. The sectarianism of Ulster, no doubt, as well as his knowledge of Quebec, supply him with the idea and necessary insights for a book on the Quebec separatist kidnapping and murder of a cabinet minister. This work, *The Revolution Script* (1972), has been called documentary fiction in the manner of Norman Mailer.

The realistic surfaces of Moore's novels derive as much from English and American as from Irish models, but there is a preoccupation with ritual in the novels that may be attuned to the primitive echoes of Irish society. From his fellow-countryman James Joyce* (also an uncompromisingly urban writer), Moore has learned the technique of internalizing at length his characters' thoughts and feelings. His most psychologically revealing successes with it are his vivid portraits of women under sexual stress: the titular heroines of *Judith Hearne*, *I Am Mary Dunne* (1968), and *The Doctor's Wife* (1976). Moore has a seductive storytelling ability, great honesty, and a profound sympathetic identification with his heroes. He is unwilling, however, to explore the complexity of ethical and theological issues in addition to dramatizing their psychological causes and effects. A certain flatness of diction and a marked thinning of fictional texture developed after *I Am Mary Dunne*. That novel, alongside *Judith Hearne* and *An Answer from Limbo*, represents Moore's finest writing.

JOHN WILSON FOSTER

WORKS: *Judith Hearne*. London: Andre Deutsch, 1955/reprinted as *The Lonely Passion of Judith Hearne*. Boston & Toronto: Little, Brown, 1956/reprinted as *The Lonely Passion of Miss Judith Hearne*. Harmondsworth: Penguin, 1959; *The Feast of Lupercal*. Boston & Toronto: Little, Brown, 1957/reprinted as *A Moment of Love*. London: Panther Books, 1965; *The Luck of Ginger Coffey*. Boston & Toronto: Little, Brown, 1960; *An Answer from Limbo*. Boston & Toronto: Little, Brown, 1962; *The Emperor of Ice-Cream*. New York: Viking, 1965; *I Am Mary Dunne*. New York: Viking, 1968; *Fergus*. New York: Holt, Rinehart & Winston, 1970; *Catholics*. London: Jonathan Cape, 1972; *The Revolution Script*. London: Jonathan Cape, 1972; *The Great Victorian Collection*. New York: Farrar, Straus & Giroux, 1975; *The Doctor's Wife*. New York: Farrar, Straus & Giroux, 1976.   REFERENCES: Dahlie, Hallvard. *Brian Moore*. Toronto: Copp Clark, 1969; Flood, Jeanne. *Brian Moore*. Lewisburg, Pa.: Bucknell University Press, 1974; Foster, John Wilson. *Forces and Themes in Ulster Fiction*. Dublin: Gill & Macmillan/Totowa, N.J.: Rowman & Littlefield, 1974, pp. 122-130, 151-185; Ludwig, Jack. "Brian Moore: Ireland's Loss, Canada's Novelist." *Critique: Studies in Modern Fiction* 5 (Spring-Summer 1962): 5-13.

MOORE, GEORGE (1852-1933), novelist and man of letters. For all practical purposes, the Moore family had its vague beginnings as English Protestants who settled in County Mayo in the seventeenth century, asserted an unproved claim of descent from Sir Thomas More, made a fortune in the wine trade in Spain during the period of Catholic disabilities in Ireland, and married into a Spanish Catholic family for political and commercial advantage. In about 1790, George Moore, the merchant, returned to Ireland, acquired some twelve thousand acres of land, and built Moore Hall. One of the merchant's three sons, a studious man with a taste for literature and history, married into a Protestant family, let his strong-willed wife manage practical affairs, and retired to his library to read and write. His eldest son, the novelist's father, distinguished himself at the Roman Catholic college of Oscott, went to Cambridge, turned his interests to racing, hunting, and women, traveled in the East, including Palestine, and kept the notebooks which his son, Colonel Maurice Moore, incorporated into a biography (*An Irish Gentleman: George Henry Moore*, 1913). George Henry successfully bred and raced horses, saw his estate threatened by economic disasters, became concerned about the political and economic welfare of Ireland, entered politics, and married a lady from the Catholic gentry.

By this point in the family's history, all the diverse interests and temperaments that seem to have been absorbed by the novelist had been established: the Catholic and Protestant lines, the shrewd landlord-businessman and the contemplative writer, the man of action and the dreamer, the sensualist and the austere moralist, the indecisive and the strong-willed mentality.

George Augustus Moore was born on February 24, 1852, at Moore

Hall, County Mayo. He was tutored locally, and as a child he heard romantic tales of adventures in the East, his mother's redactions of episodes from the novels of Walter Scott, and the tales the servants and the local storytellers told. He also spent much of his time around his father's racing stables. In the winter of 1861, he was sent to Oscott, an experience he later recalled with much bitterness (*Salve*, 1912). At Oscott, George was regarded as a dunce, at least in the conventional studies, and later wrote of himself as the "boy that no schoolmaster wants" (*Confessions of a Young Man*, 1888). However, he developed an instinct for literature, read ardently whatever happened to attract him, and determined only to "know what he wanted to know" (Hone, *Life*, p. 25). He read some history, Miss Braddon's *Lady Audley's Secret*, and *The Doctor's Wife*, which in turn led him to his obsession with Shelley. Without the aid of Shelleyan ideas, however, George had already openly expressed his doubts about supernatural religion. In about 1867, George was permitted, probably even urged, to withdraw from Oscott. His father sided with the land reformers against the landlords and won election to Parliament in 1868; in 1869, he moved his family to London. During this period, young George was interested primarily in horse racing and betting, reading Dickens fairly systematically, and learning about art from the painter Jim Browne.

This first phase of Moore's life ended with the death of his father in April 1870. Although grief-stricken, Moore also saw his father's death as liberation from the threat of continued formal cramming for a career in one of the gentlemanly professions. He painted, visited art galleries, spent too much money on scent and clothes, and generally imitated the life of a sophisticated young man about town. However, he also read or at least sampled Godwin, Buckle, Mill, Lecky,* George Eliot, Berkeley,* and Plato. The early years in Ireland and in London always remained vivid in his memory; hence, their importance should not be overshadowed by the much-discussed French period and the influence of French artists and writers.

The second phase of Moore's development began in 1873 when his attaining legal maturity freed him to go to Paris. In Paris, Moore studied at the Beaux Arts and at Jullian's Academy. In 1874, he briefly took a studio in London, where he was visited by Millais, painted, came to know Whistler, overspent on amusements, and again returned to Paris. In 1875, he saw his first major Impressionist exhibition and, like others at the time, disliked their work. Although he had some ability as a painter, Moore himself decided his talent was not great enough. In 1876, he connived to get introductions to influential hostesses, which eventually led to his meeting Degas, Ludovic Halévy, Fromentin, and others.

In the mid-1870s, Moore had met Bernard Lopez, the dramatist; had probably written *Worldliness* (1874?), a comedy of which no copies have survived; began *Martin Luther* (1879), a tragedy in collaboration with Lopez; and moved to the apartment in Montmarte which he describes in

Confessions. He read Baudelaire, Gautier, probably Poe, and others, and began to write poems. He frequented the Nouvelle Athènes, a café where most of the avant-garde painters and writers of the time gathered. The café became, as he was to say, his university. Here he met Villiers de l'Isle Adam, Mallarmé, Manet, Monet, Degas, Pissarro, Renoir, Sisley, and perhaps Zola. "With the patience of a cat before a mouse-hole," he later wrote in *Confessions*, "I watched and listened." The watching and listening soon bore fruit. He published his first slim volume of poems, *Flowers of Passion* (1878 [1877]), which was viciously reviewed by Edmund Yates under the heading "A Bestial Bard," and his play, *Martin Luther*. Around this time, he reversed his earlier attitude toward the Impressionists, capitulating to the art and personalities of Manet and Degas. He acclaimed Zola, whom he knew only slightly, and Paul Alexis, whom he knew much better.

Moore's residency in Paris ended abruptly and unexpectedly early in 1880. The Moore estates in Ireland were in a disastrous state. Rents were uncollectable, Michael Davitt's Land League was becoming a threat to the landlords, and Moore's credit was overextended. He recorded his first supposed reaction in his usual *épater-les-bourgeois* manner in *Confessions*. "That some wretched farmers and miners should refuse to starve, that I may not be deprived of my *demi-tasse* at Tortoni's, that I may not be forced to leave this beautiful retreat, my cat and my python—monstrous!" However, this moment may have been one of the most crucial in the record it left on his waxplate. He did return to England, he did, if impatiently, put his affairs in order, he did begin to inform himself about legal, political, and economic conditions in Ireland, and he did commit himself to becoming a professional writer. In fact, he became a highly self-disciplined person, a shrewd businessman, perhaps discovering in himself some of the qualities of that forebear, the wine merchant, who founded the Moore fortune. Moore patched up his financial condition and probably worked briefly on the *Examiner*.

Within the next few years, Moore published work reflecting both the Irish and the French experiences: *Pagan Poems* (1881), a total critical failure in its barely being noticed at all; *A Modern Lover* (1883), a three-volume novel indebted to Henry James, Balzac, the Goncourts, and Zola, respected for its candor and realism but suppressed by Mudie's, the ubiquitous lending library; *A Mummer's Wife* (1885 [1884]), a one-volume novel intended to circumvent the lending libraries and undoubtedly his best work in the Zolaesque vein; *Literature at Nurse; or Circulating Morals* (1885), his polemic against the lending libraries; *A Drama in Muslin* (1886), a satirical treatment of Irish society and politics and like most of his work pervaded with autobiographical allusions; *A Mere Accident* (1887), a novel in which Zolaesque naturalism gives way to French symbolism and the influence of J.-K. Huysmans; and *Parnell and His Island* (1887), a collection of satirical essays on Irish society. From the mid-1880s on, Moore had as much difficulty keeping Ireland and boyhood experience out of his work as Dick Babley in Dickens' *David Copperfield* had in keeping King Charles I out of his Memorial.

The major landmark between Moore's return from France in 1880 and the publication of *Esther Waters* in 1894 is undoubtedly *Confessions*. Year by year until 1888, Moore published on a wide range of subjects in various newspapers and periodicals, including portions of his *Confessions*. It is a delightful record of what Walter Pater had called "mind-building," the progress of an artist's soul, a mixture of penetrating self-analysis, outrageous effrontery to "good taste," flamboyant but highly quotable phrasemaking, comic and pathetic self-portraiture, and shrewd observations on art and life. The book contains beautifully controlled passages of reverie as well as clumsy rhetoric.

Spring Days (1888) and *Mike Fletcher* (1889), in various ways related to *A Mere Accident* and *A Drama in Muslin*, were in nearly every way critical failures. In 1891, however, Moore brought together a large body of essays, reviews, and sketches in *Impressions and Opinions*. The essays, however inaccurate in details or wrong-headed in critical stances, are, like *Confessions*, remarkable revelations of a vigorous, curious, sensitive, and highly independent mind. As a result of this book, Moore became a regular art critic for the *Speaker*.

Vain Fortune (1891), although certainly not among Moore's better performances, is markedly superior to *A Mere Accident*, *Spring Days*, and *Mike Fletcher*. As his three failures in a decadent or aesthetic mode suggest a partial rejection of the naturalist mode, so *Vain Fortune* suggests a partial rejection of the decadent mode and prepares the way for *Esther Waters*. Hubert Price, the hero of *Vain Fortune*, voices Moore's own indecisiveness about artistic means and goals as well as Moore's fear of waning artistic energy, and his concern about his economic circumstances. Moore's participation in founding the Independent Theatre in 1890-1891 and his efforts to write an Ibsenian play, which became *The Strike at Arlingford* (1893), are also reflected in the greater emphasis on dialogue and scenic development and the diminished character analysis and authorial intrusion of various kinds.

Moore's reputation as an art critic advanced rapidly between 1888 and 1893, when he was publishing essays on drama and art and reviews of exhibitions and the like in the *Speaker*. This activity was capped by *Modern Painting* (1893), a volume which introduced to many generations of readers the innovative work of the French Impressionists and the New English Art Club. Although this book will not satisfy the modern scholarly art historian, it is a highly readable, often perceptive, and imaginative personal view of one of the most important and exciting movements in the pictorial arts. (For the family background and Moore's life and career to about 1895, see Joseph Hone's *The Life of George Moore* [1936] and *The Moores of*

Moore Hall [1939]; Malcolm Brown's *George Moore: A Reconsideration* [1955]; E. Jay Jernigan's dissertation, "George Moore's 'Re-tying of Bows': A Critical Study of the Eight Early Novels and Their Revisions" [1966]; and Milton Chaikin's dissertation, "The Influence of French Realism and Naturalism on George Moore's Early Fiction" [1954].)

Esther Waters is a brilliant climax to Moore's productive career to 1894. In this novel, he brought together in a coherently structured form and with a masterfully restrained style nearly everything he had learned. What he had learned from the pictorial arts, Flaubert, and Zola, is remarkably demonstrated in the Derby Day chapters, a brilliant verbalization of W. P. Frith's painting, "Derby Day"; his memories of the racing stables and betting are assimilated in his depiction of Woodview; his fondness for Dickens is reflected in such caricatures as Swindles, the Demon, Ginger, and others, though these figures are functionally integrated into the novel; his now more calculated watching and listening are reflected in his use of visits to pubs, his interview with a wet-nurse, and his reading of contemporary journalism (Bartlett and Sporn, in *English Literature in Transition*, 1966 and 1968, respectively). The novel is also especially interesting insofar as it brings to a head Moore's lifelong distaste for Hardy's novels. *Esther Waters* is an anti-*Tess* novel and makes for fruitful comparison with *Tess of the d'Ubervilles* and George Eliot's *Adam Bede* (Gregor and Nicholas, *The Moral and the Story* [1962]).

In *Celibates* (1895), Moore's first collection of short stories, some of his developing artistic interests were sharpened and new directions tentatively indicated. Moore had dealt with celibacy in *A Drama in Muslin* and in *A Mere Accident*. In *Celibates*, however, the psychological studies are far more penetrating and probably influenced by his study of Dostoevski and Turgenev.

With the success of *Esther Waters*, Moore apparently felt he had exhausted what he could do in the realist vein. At this point in his career, he seems to have been particularly concerned about the possibility of declining talent, and he began to flounder in search of new subject matter and new techniques. Clearly, a break in his artistic stride had occurred. His involvement in censorship controversies, his anger over the British prosecution of the Boer War, and, in the late 1890s, Edward Martyn's,* Arthur Symons', and Yeats'* appeals that he help them launch an Irish drama movement— all combined to develop in Moore considerable hostility to the British cultural scene.

That Ireland was on his mind between 1895 and 1901 is at least covertly evident in *Evelyn Innes* (1898) and *Sister Teresa* (1901). It is evidenced by the dedication of *Evelyn Innes* to Yeats and Symons, by the likelihood that AE* and Yeats were partly models for the character of Ulick, by his advising Yeats in 1898 on the structure of *The Countess Cathleen*, by references in letters to Yeats and in *Evelyn Innes* to the Irish heroine Grania, and by his writing a preface to two of Edward Martyn's plays. In addition, Maud Burke, the one woman whom Moore seems genuinely to have loved, married; he quarreled with Pearl Craigie, a collaborator with whom Moore also seems to have had a more personal relationship; and his relationship with his publisher, T. Fisher Unwin, became increasingly more strained toward the turn of the century. Further, *Evelyn Innes* and *Sister Teresa* had been particularly difficult to write, and he was fearful that his creative energies had dried up. By 1901, therefore, circumstances compounded to make the move to Ireland, his "messianic mission," as he called it, very attractive.

The next phase of Moore's career (1901-1910) was undoubtedly one of the richest and most invigorating periods for his artistic renewal and development. In Ireland, Moore took charge: he organized play productions, wrote plays, gave speeches, and defended and propagandized on behalf of the theatre movement. By about 1904, he appears to have quarreled with nearly everyone and to have given up much hope for an effective cultural revival anywhere in the Western world—a melancholy view that was to deepen during the rest of his life. The Irish landscape, the old ruins, the myths, even the Irish language, however, revitalized his imagination, markedly influenced the development of what he came to call his "melodic line," and gradually turned his attention away from contemporary life to explorations of the past.

Out of his "messianic mission" came the stories of *The Untilled Field* (1903); *The Lake* (1905), his symbolic novel of the "swimming priest"; his remarkable imaginative autobiography, *Hail and Farewell* (1911, 1912, 1914); the stories of *A Story-Teller's Holiday* (1918); and the short novel *Ulick and Soracha* (1926). Although he left Ireland in 1911, Ireland and Irish speech rhythms colored much of his work thereafter. (For Moore's career from about 1894 to about 1911, see H. E. Gerber's *George Moore in Transition* [1968] and Jack Wayne Weaver's dissertation, "A Story-Teller's Holiday: George Moore's Irish Renaissance, 1897 to 1911" [1966].)

In 1911, Moore set up residence in a modest house in London; kept in touch with Irish, French, and English friends; visited France frequently; and traveled to Palestine in preparation for the writing of *The Brook Kerith* (1916). On the whole, however, he devoted most of his energies to his art, to publication of new works for "subscribers only," and to the preparation of collected editions and revisions of his works. Although this last phase of Moore's career has received much less attention than the period of the naturalist-realist novels (1880-1895) or the Irish period (1901-1911), it was a time of rich productivity. He developed a finely honed style at this time and amalgamated much that he had learned from extraordinarily diverse authors and from several arts and genres: Pater, Zola, Turgenev, Dostoevski, Dickens, Wagner, the Dolmetsch circle, D'Annunzio, even Schopenhauer and Nietzsche, Yeats and Edward Martyn, Dujardin, the

Impressionist painters, authorities on history, myth, and Biblical exegesis. In 1912, in a statement that has an unexpectedly modest ring, he said with both conviction and a touch of wonder, "I am a little nearer the summit of Parnassus" (letter to Dujardin, February 12, 1912). His perhaps premature self-assessment was to be justified by his recreation of Biblical history in *The Brook Kerith*, biography in *Héloise and Abélard* (1921), myth in *Daphnis and Chloe* (1924), and Irish history in *Ulick and Soracha*. Despite declining creative energies and frequent illness between 1927 and 1933, he wrote short stories, wrote and had two plays produced, recreated the Greece of the fifth century B.C. in *Aphrodite in Aulis* (1930), and worked on *Madeline de Lisle*, the novel about convent life and the religious temperament which he left unfinished upon his death on January 21, 1933. (For Moore's career from about 1910 to 1933, see H. E. Gerber's forthcoming *George Moore on Parnassus* and Hone's *Life*.)

Moore will be acclaimed in cultural history for his contributions to the naturalist-realist movement in English fiction; his lifelong attacks on censorship; his contributions, as writer, critic, and apologist, to candor in realistic drama and to the beginnings of the Irish dramatic movement; his contributions to the development of the modern short story, with emphasis on symbolism, penetrating psychological character studies, and the revival of the oral narrator; his brilliant models for modern imaginative autobiography; his introduction of the French Impressionist painters and Symbolist poets to the English-speaking world; his amalgamation of pictorial arts, music, history, myth, and autobiography in imaginative fiction; and his contributions to the structure and style, to the painstaking artistry, of the modern novel. He is not only a writer's writer, but a reader's writer.

Moore could undoubtedly be difficult in personal relationships. He could be arrogant, he could be foolish, he could be troublesome to his publishers and agents, but to the last day of his life he remained profoundly devoted to his one enduring mistress—his art. Many left their marks on his imagination, but he, too, left his mark on cultural history.

HELMUT E. GERBER

WORKS: Collected Editions—There is no complete collected edition, but the first two items, below, are generally regarded as the best. Moore's multiple revisions of nearly every major title should make one wary of any title in one of the collected editions (see Gilcher's bibliography for notes on variant editions). Carra Edition. 21 vols. New York: Boni & Liveright, 1922-1924. Plus 2 supplementary vols., 1925, 1926; Uniform Edition. 20 vols. London: Heinemann, 1924-1933. (Reissued as the Ebury Edition.) Poetry—*Flowers of Passion* (1878), *Pagan Poems* (1881). Plays—*Worldliness* (1874?), *Martin Luther* (1879, with Bernard Lopez), *The Strike at Arlingford* (1893), *The Bending of the Bough* (1900, a rewriting of Edward Martyn's *The Tale of the Town*), *The Apostle* (1911; rewritten, 1923; revised as *The Passing of the Essenes*, 1930), *Esther Waters* (1913), *Elizabeth Cooper* (1913; rewritten as *The Coming of Gabrielle*, 1920), *The Making of an Immortal* (1927), and *Diarmuid and Grania* (produced, 1901; published, 1951; with W. B. Yeats). Critical Essays, Reviews, and Polemics (some with autobiographical significance)—*Literature at*

Nurse; or Circulating Morals (1885), *Parnell and His Ireland* (1887; in French, 1886), *Impressions and Opinions* (1891), *Modern Painting* (1893), *Reminiscences of the Impressionist Painters* (1906, a pamphlet), *Memoirs of My Dead Life* (1906), *Avowals* (1919), and *Conversations in Ebury Street* (1924). Imaginative Autobiographies—*Confessions of a Young Man* (1888), *Hail and Farewell* (*Ave.*, 1911; *Salve*, 1912; *Vale*, 1914), *A Communication to My Friends* (1933). Short Stories—*Celibates* (1895; includes revision of *A Mere Accident* as "John Norton"; rewritten and rearranged with varying contents as *In Single Strictness* [1922] and *Celibate Lives* [1927]), *The Untilled Field* (1903; in Gaelic, 1902), *A Story-Teller's Holiday* (1918). Novels—*A Modern Lover* (1883; rewritten as *Lewis Seymour and Some Women*, 1917), *A Mummer's Wife* (1885), *A Drama in Muslin* (1887; rewritten as *Muslin*, 1915), *A Mere Accident* (1887; rewritten and condensed as "John Norton" for *Celibates*, 1895), *Spring Days* (1888), *Mike Fletcher* (1889), *Vain Fortune* (1891), *Esther Waters* (1894), *Evelyn Innes* (1898), *Sister Teresa* (1901), *The Lake* (1905), *The Brook Kerith* (1916), *Héloïse and Abélard* (1921), *The Pastoral Loves of Daphnis and Chloë* (1924), *Ulick and Soracha* (1926), *Aphrodite in Aulis* (1930). Miscellaneous—*Pure Poetry* (1924, an anthology). Collections of Letters—Additional letters and excerpts have been published in various books and articles (see Gilcher's bibliography and Gerber's chapter in *Anglo-Irish Literature: A Review of Research*). *Letters from George Moore to Ed. Dujardin, 1886-1922*, selected, edited and translated by John Eglinton. New York: Crosby Gaige, 1929. (124 letters); *Letters of George Moore*, "with an introduction by John Eglinton, to whom they were written." Bournemouth: Sydenham & Co., 1942. (119 letters); *George Moore: Letters to Lady Cunard, 1895-1933*. Rupert Hart-Davis, ed. London: Hart-Davis, 1957. (247 letters); "The Letters of George Moore to Edmund Gosse, W. B. Yeats, R. I. Best, Miss Nancy Cunard, and Mrs. Mary Hutchinson." Ph.D. thesis, University of Maryland, 1958. (302 letters); *George Moore in Transition: Letters to T. Fisher Unwin and Lena Milman, 1894-1910*, ed., with a commentary, by Helmut E. Gerber. Detroit: Wayne State University Press, 1968. (298 letters), "Letters of George Moore (1852-1933) to His Brother, Colonel Maurice Moore, C. B. (1857-1939)." Seamus mac Donncha, ed., National University of Ireland (Galway) thesis, 1972-1973. (94 letters). *George Moore on Parnassus: Letters (1900-1933) to Secretaries, Publishers, Printers, Agents, Literati, Friends and Acquaintances*, ed., with notes and critical-biographical essays, by Helmut E. Gerber. Forthcoming. (1,214 letters).   REFERENCES: Cunard, Nancy. *GM: Memories of George Moore*. London: Hart-Davis, 1956; Gerber, Helmut E., ed. *George Moore in Transition* (see Collections of Letters); Gerber, Helmut E., ed. *George Moore on Parnassus* (see Collections of Letters). Hone, Joseph. *The Life of George Moore*. New York: Macmillan, 1936. The standard life; supplemented by Hone's *The Moores of Moore Hall*. London: Jonathan Cape, 1939; Noel, Jean C. *George Moore: L'Homme et l'oeuvre* (1852-1933). Paris: Didier, 1966. (A critical biography, the fullest and most scholarly to date); Criticism—Blissett, William F. "George Moore and Literary Wagnerism." *Comparative Literature* 13 (Winter 1961): 52-71; Brown, Malcolm. *George Moore: A Reconsideration*. Seattle: University of Washington Press, 1955; Firth, John. "George Moore and Modern Irish Autobiography." *Wisconsin Studies in Literature*, No. 5 (1968): 64-72; Gerber, Helmut E. "From Pure Poetry to Pure Criticism." *Journal of Aesthetics and Art Criticism* 25 (Spring 1967): 281-291; Gerber, Helmut E., ed. *George Moore in Transition. . . .* Detroit: Wayne State University Press, 1968. (Inter alia critical commentary. To be supplemented by *George Moore on Parnassus. . . .*); Gettmann, Royal A. "George Moore's Revisions of *The Lake*, 'The Wilde Goose,' and *Esther Waters*." *PMLA* 69 (June 1944): 540-555; Hough, Graham. *Image and Experience*. Lincoln: University of Nebraska Press, 1960, pp. 177-199, 200-210. Jeffares, A. Norman. *George*

Moore. London: Longmans, Green [Writers and Their Work]. 1965. (Good introduction for the nonspecialist); Kennedy, Eileen. "Turgenev and George Moore's *The
Untilled Field." English Literature in Transition* 18, No. 3 (1975): 145-159. Noel,
Jean C. *George Moore: L'Homme et l'oeuvre* (1852-1933). Paris: Didier, 1966; Nye,
Francis L. "George Moore's Use of Sources in *Héloise and Abélard." English Literature in Transition* 18, No. 3 (1975): 161-180; Shumaker, Wayne. *English Autobiography: Its Emergence, Materials, and Form.* Berkeley & Los Angeles: University
of California Press, 1954, pp. 185-213; Stevenson, Lionel. "Introduction." *Esther
Waters.* Boston: Houghton Mifflin, 1963; Temple, Ruth Z. *The Critic's Alchemy.* New
York: Twayne, 1953. Part V, pp. 231-271; Uslenghi, Rafaella M. "Una prospettiva di
unita nell'arte di George Moore." *English Miscellany* 15 (1964): 213-258. Collections
of Critical Essays—Hughes, Douglas, ed. *The Man of Wax: Critical Essays on George
Moore.* New York: New York University Press, 1971. (Includes Hughes' introductory
appreciation, seventeen essays and selections from essays and books, a chronology, a
selected bibliography, and an index); Owens, Graham, comp. & ed. *George Moore's
Mind and Art.* London: Oliver & Boyd, 1968/New York: Barnes & Noble, 1970. (Includes nine critical essays, four reprinted and five commissioned for this volume).
Bibliographies— Gerber, Helmut E. "George Moore." In *Anglo-Irish Literature: A
Review of Research.* Richard J. Finneran, ed. New York: MLA, 1976, pp. 138-166. (A
critical survey to about 1975, noting bibliographies and manuscript locations; editions
and textual studies; autobiographies, letters, and biographies; and criticism. To be
updated periodically); Gerber, Helmut E., comp. & ed. "George Moore: An Annotated
Bibliography of Writings About Him." *English Fiction* [now *Literature*] *in Transition,* II: 2, pts. i and ii (1959), 1-91, and supplements in various issues thereafter. A
book-length, thorough revision and updating, to include well over 3,000 entries, is in
progress for the Annotated Secondary Bibliography Series being published by Northern
Illinois University Press; Gilcher, Edwin. *A Bibliography of George Moore.* Dekalb,
Ill.: Northern Illinois University Press, 1970. (Definitive); Harris, Wendell V. "The
Critics [VI. George Moore (1852-1933)]." In *Victorian Prose: A Guide to Research.*
David J. DeLaura, ed. New York: MLA, 1973, pp. 451-454.

MOORE, THOMAS (1779-1852), poet. In his lifetime, Thomas Moore
was probably better known as a writer than any of his contemporaries whom
we now regard as his masters. That enormous popularity has now passed
and he is remembered chiefly as the friend and biographer of Byron. Yet if
the public does not remember the man, many of his poems have entered
popular culture to such an extent that some measure of fame is guaranteed.
Many of the songs contained in his *Irish Melodies* are classics, including
"Believe Me, If All Those Endearing Young Charms" and "The Last
Rose of Summer."

Moore's life consisted of extremes of good fortune and misery, although
the cheerful personality which made him so popular to both upper and
lower classes concealed the depths of his suffering. He was born in Dublin
on May 28, 1779, and lived his early years above his father's grocery shop.
Well loved by his family, he was given a solid education in the classics. He
attended Trinity College, which only recently has begun admitting Catholics, and there he began the long project of translating poems attributed to

Anacreon. In 1800, a year after he received his B.A. degree, *The Odes of Anacreon* appeared.

The next year a collection of his own verse, *The Poetical Works of Thomas Little, Esq.*, was published. The pseudonym was transparent, and the public received this set of light verses with such enthusiasm that he achieved popular fame.

Because he had no independent income, Moore required employment; therefore, he secured a post as registrar of the Admiralty Prize Court in Bermuda. However, he spent only a few months there in 1804 before returning to England.

His next collection, *Epistles, Odes and Other Poems* (1806), added to his popularity, partly because some of its contents were considered *risqué*. His satiric skills were beginning to emerge, and he became identified with a political position which opposed those in power.

Moore next started work on his most ambitious project, the *Irish Melodies*, a series of volumes in which his own verse compositions were set to Irish folk airs. Ten volumes were published in all, beginning in 1808 and concluding in 1834. The fame he derived from the series was immediate and lasting. The melodies are still his best known work, and some of the songs are his best lyrics. Moore had a strong musical sense, and the fact that he himself sang some of his pieces in various London salons surely helped win him admirers.

At the height of his fame, everything went well. Moore married an actress, Elizabeth Dyke, to whom he was devoted for the rest of his life. He soon published one of the most popular works of the century, *Lalla Rookh* (1817). It consists of four verse narratives sung in honor of the title character, an Indian princess, by her lover, an Indian prince disguised as a court minstrel. The exotic setting and the elaborate decorations, of course, appealed to Moore's audience, which was developing a peculiar taste for oriental decorations. But like the Royal Pavilion at Brighton, where cast iron is painted to look like bamboo and where Chinese decoration is mixed with Indian, the details of the mysterious East in *Lalla Rookh* are more profuse than authentic. The atmosphere is lush and the music intoxicating, but it little resembles the Near or Far East. The poem's exoticism is somewhat counterbalanced by its satire. One of the tales, "The Veiled Prophet of Khorassan," attacks the demagoguery of actual contemporaries such as Daniel O'Connell, for whom Moore had a long-standing contempt. The theme of patriotism is also prominent in several of the tales, indicating Moore's awareness of his Irish heritage.

The satiric impulse predominates in the best of Moore's later poems. *Intercepted Letters, or the Two-Penny Post Bag* (1813) contains satiric poems on various Tory leaders. *The Fudge Family in Paris* (1818) consists of lighter satire and is directed at English tourists abroad. That combination proved most pleasing, for Moore's mastery of intoxicating musical effects needed leavening with the more acerbic content of satire. He took up various political and social causes, including a defense of Catholicism in *Travels of an Irish Gentleman in Search of a Religion* (1834).

Moore was a close friend of Lord Byron, who before his death gave Moore his memoirs with the permission to publish them. Moore, often in need of money, lent the memoirs to the publisher, John Murray, in return for a loan. Upon Byron's death, he found himself in a law suit over possession of those papers, with Lady Byron and the poet's half-sister Augusta Leigh claiming he could not publish the memoirs. As a result, the memoirs were burned, for fear they might reveal anything incriminating. He did proceed to complete *The Letters and Journals of Lord Byron, with Notices of His Life*, which appeared in 1830. As the title indicates, it relies on available materials, but Moore's commentary on Byron's writings is so perceptive that the whole is still a useful, judicious work.

The deaths of each of his children came as profound blows in Moore's later life, and his attempts at prose writing during this period reflect the strain he was experiencing. His most ambitious effort was the four-volume *History of Ireland* (1835-1846), a project for which he was temperamentally unsuited; as a result, it is superficial and dull. He died on February 25, 1852.

As sources of literary history, Moore's letters and journals are important documents, and the author's engaging personality makes them lively reading as well. He was an exceptionally influential writer. The *Melodies*, for instance, created a taste for songs of a certain kind, and they remain popular. Although scholarly analysis demonstrated that *Lalla Rookh* was not an authentic version of oriental romance, it was much more popular than works based on more careful research. For the modern reader, Moore's fame rests with his satiric verse, in which his comic and musical skills are engaged in more assertive efforts. Yet even there he is rarely partisan and not firmly committed to any course, even that of his own native country. His personal magnetism, wit, and musical abilities made him a revered personality in his own time and an enduring minor poet in ours.

JAMES KILROY

WORKS: *Odes of Anacreon*. London: John Stockdale, 1800; *Poetical Works of Thomas Little Esq*. London: J. & T. Carpenter, 1801; *Epistles, Odes, and Other Poems*. London: Carpenter, 1806; *Corruption and Intolerance*. London: Carpenter, 1808; *Irish Melodies*. 2 vols. London: James Power/Dublin: William Power, 1808; *The Sceptic: A Philosophical Satire*. London: Carpenter, 1809; *Irish Melodies*. Vol. 3. London & Dublin: J. & W. Power, 1810; *A Letter to the Roman Catholics of Dublin*. London: Carpenter, 1810; *Irish Melodies*. Vol. 4. London & Dublin: J. & W. Power, 1811; *M.P., or The Blue-Stocking*. London: J. Power, 1811; *Intercepted Letters, or the Two-Penny Post-Bag*, by "Thomas Brown the Younger." London: J. Carr, 1813; *Irish Melodies*. Vol. 5. London & Dublin: J. & W. Power, 1813; *Irish Melodies*. Vol. 6. London & Dublin: J. & W. Power, 1815; *Sacred Songs*. Vol. 1. London & Dublin: J. &

W. Power, 1816; *Lalla Rookh, An Oriental Romance.* London: Longman, Hurst, Orme & Browne, 1817; *The Fudge Family in Paris,* by "Thomas Brown the Younger." London: Longmans, 1818; *Irish Melodies.* Vol. 7. London: J. Power, 1818; *National Airs.* Vol. 1. London & Dublin: J. & W. Power, 1818; *The Works of Thomas Moore.* 7 vols. Paris: Galignani et Cie, 1819; *Irish Melodies.* Dublin: W. Power, 1820. (First collection); *National Airs.* Vol. 2. London & Dublin: J. & W. Power, 1820; *Irish Melodies.* Revised ed. with Prefatory Letter on Music. London: J. Power, 1821; *Irish Melodies.* Vol. 8. London: J. Power, 1821; *National Airs.* Vol. 3. London: J. Power, 1822; *National Airs.* Vol. 4. London: J. Power, 1822; *Fables for the Holy Alliance,* by "Thomas Brown the Younger." London: Longmans, 1823; *The Loves of the Angels.* London: Longmans, 1823; *Irish Melodies.* Vol. 9. London: J. Power, 1824; *Memoirs of Captain Rock, the Celebrated Irish Chieftain, with Some Account of his Ancestors.* London: Longmans, 1824; *Sacred Songs.* Vol. 2. London: J. Power, 1824; *Memoirs of the Life of the Right Honourable Richard Brinsley Sheridan.* London: Longmans, 1825; *Evenings in Greece.* London: J. Power, 1826; *National Airs.* Vol. 5. London: J. Power, 1826; *The Epicurean. A Tale.* London: Longmans, 1827; *National Airs.* Vol. 6. London: J. Power, 1827; *Legendary Ballads.* London: J. Power, 1828; *Odes upon Cash, Corn, Catholics, and Other Matters.* London: Longmans, 1828; *Letters and Journals of Lord Byron: with Notices of His Life.* London: John Murray, 1830; *Evenings in Greece: The Second Evening.* London: J. Power, 1831; *The Life and Death of Lord Edward Fitzgerald.* London: Longmans, 1831; *The Summer Fête.* London: J. Power, 1831; *Travels of an Irish Gentleman in Search of Religion.* London: Longmans, 1833; *Irish Melodies.* Vol. 10. London: J. Power, 1834; *The Fudge Family in England.* London: Longmans, 1835; *The History of Ireland.* Vol. 1. London: published jointly by Longman, Rees, Brown, Green & Longman of Paternoster Row, & John Taylor, 1835; *Alciphron: A Poem.* London: John Macrone, 1839; *The History of Ireland.* Vol. 2. London: Longmans, & Taylor, 1840; *The History of Ireland.* Vol. 3. London: Longmans, & Taylor, 1840; *The Poetical Works of Thomas Moore,* Collected by Himself. 10 vols. London: Longmans, 1841; *The History of Ireland.* Vol. 4. London: Longmans, & Taylor, 1846; *The Memoirs, Journal and Correspondence of Thomas Moore.* Lord John Russell, ed. 8 vols. London: Longmans, 1853-1856; *Poems and Verse, Humourous, Satirical and Sentimental, with Suppressed Passages from the Memoirs of Lord Byron, and Including Contributions to the Edinburgh Review between 1814 and 1834.* London: Chatto & Windus, 1878; *The Poetical Works of Thomas Moore.* A. D. Godley, ed. London: Henry Frowde, 1910; *The Letters of Thomas Moore.* Wilfred S. Dowden, ed. 2 vols. Oxford: Clarendon, 1964.   REFERENCES: deFord, Miriam Allen. *Thomas Moore.* New York: Twayne, 1967; Gwynn, Stephen L. *Thomas Moore.* London: Macmillan, 1905; Jones, Howard Mumford. *The Harp That Once.* New York: Henry Holt, 1937; Strong, L.A.G. *The Minstrel Boy, A Portrait of Tom Moore.* New York: Alfred A. Knopf, 1937; White, Terence deVere. *Tom Moore: The Irish Poet.* London: Hamilton, 1977.

MORAN, MICHAEL. *See* Zozimus.

MORGAN, LADY (1776?-1859), novelist and woman of letters. The birthdate of Sydney Owenson, Lady Morgan, must be an assumption, for she carefully kept it a secret. However, she was probably born in 1775 or 1776. Her father, Robert Owenson (born MacOwen), was an Irishman and a Protestant derived from a line of Catholics. He was an actor—a Stage Irishman—and a failed producer. Her mother was an English Methodist. Sydney Owenson herself personified everything that was essentially Irish in her time; in her were met all the contradictions that identified Irish conflicts and troubles.

The future Lady Morgan received a sound education, relieved the family penury by serving as a governess, began her writing career with a volume of poetry in 1801, published two probationary novels, and became famous with *The Wild Irish Girl* in 1806. Other works, such as *O'Donnell, Florence Macarthy, The O'Briens and the O'Flahertys*, and *Dramatic Scenes from Real Life*, were extremely popular in their day and made her a good deal of money.

She married Sir Charles Morgan in 1812. Until 1837 she lived in Dublin, and then removed to London. She steeped herself in Irish life by moving about the country in childhood and youth, knew English and aristocratic life well, and traveled in France, Italy, and Belgium in order to write books about them.

Lady Morgan fought all her life for two goals: liberty for all and the emancipation of Ireland. The Emancipation of Catholics Act of 1829 was in no small part the result of her persistent, strident, and energetic work, chiefly by means of her novels. In her four national tales, she depicted Irish struggles and troubles in realistic detail. Her solution was to bring Catholic and Protestant together in amity, submerge the romantic past in the realistic present, give the Irishman opportunity for labor and reward for his work, and free Ireland from English domination. Her goals were generous, but her style was often flamboyant and careless. She died in London on April 13, 1859.

J A M E S   N E W C O M E R

WORKS: *Poems*. Dublin: Printed by Alex. Stewart . . . , 1801. *St. Clair; or, The Heiress of Desmond*. London: Harding/Dublin: J. Archer, 1803. (Novel); *A Few Reflections*. Dublin: Printed by J. Parry, 1804; *The Novice of St. Dominick*. 4 vols. London: R. Phillips, 1805. (Novel); *Twelve Original Hibernian Melodies*. London: Preston, [1805]; *The Wild Irish Girl*. 4 vols. London: Phillips, 1806. (Novel); *The Lay of an Irish Harp; or, Metrical Fragments*. London: R. Phillips, 1807; *Woman, or, Ida of Athens*. 4 vols. London: Longman, 1809. (Novel); *The Missionary, an Indian Tale*. 3 vols. London: J. J. Stockdale, 1811. (Novel); *O'Donnell, a National Tale*. 3 vols. London: H. Colburn, 1814. (Novel); *France*. 2 vols. London: Colburn, 1817; *Florence Macarthy, an Irish Tale*. 4 vols. London: H. Colburn, 1818. (Novel); *Italy*. 2 vols. London: H. Colburn, 1821; *The Life and Times of Salvator Rosa*. 2 vols. London: H. Colburn, 1824; *Absenteeism*. London: H. Colburn, 1825; *The O'Briens and the O'Flahertys, a National Tale*. 4 vols. London: H. Colburn, 1827. (Novel); *The Book of the Boudoir*. 2 vols. London: H. Colburn, 1829; *France in 1829-30*. 2 vols. London: Saunders & Otley, 1830; *Dramatic Scenes of Real Life*. 2 vols. London: Saunders & Otley, 1833; *The Princess; or, the Beguine*. 3 vols. London: R. Bentley, 1835. (Novel); *Woman and her Master*. 2 vols. London: H. Colburn, 1840. (A study of woman through the ages); with Sir Charles Morgan, *The Book Without a Name*. 2 vols. London: H. Colburn, 1841; *Letter to Cardinal Wiseman*. London: Westerton, 1851; *Passages in My Autobiography*. London: R. Bentley, 1859; *Lady Morgan's Memoirs. Autobiography, Diaries and Correspondence*. W. Hepworth Dixon, ed. 2 vols. London: W. H. Allen, 1862.   REFERENCES: Fitzpatrick, William John. *The Friends,*

Foes, and Adventures of Lady Morgan. Dublin: W. B. Kelly, 1859; Fitzpatrick, William John. Lady Morgan, Her Career, Literary and Personal. London: Charles J. Skeet, 1860; Flanagan, Thomas. The Irish Novelists 1800-1850. New York: Columbia University Press, 1959; Stevenson, Lionel. The Wild Irish Girl. New York: Russell & Russell, 1936.

MORROW, HARRY C. See MacNAMARA, GERALD.

MORROW, JOHN (1930-), novelist and short story writer. Morrow, the only comic writer to emerge from the Northern Ireland Troubles of the 1970s, was born in Belfast. He left school at age fourteen to work in the shipyards; he has since served an apprenticeship in the linen trade, and has worked as a navvy, furniture salesman, and insurance agent. He has contributed short stories to The Honest Ulsterman and the New Irish Writing page of The Irish Press; he has done considerable writing and broadcasting for radio; and he has published a novel entitled The Confessions of Proinsias O'Toole (1977). In 1975, he was awarded a bursary by the Arts Council of Northern Ireland.

Morrow's fiction deals with the disrupted contemporary North, but treats the subject in a manner quite his own: by means of comic exaggeration. His best quality is a cynical eye which lights gleefully on venality, opportunism, self-serving attitudes, and corruption among the combatants, and this attitude is a refreshing antidote to the bloated idealism of public rhetoric. He has also been admired for his prose style which is reminiscent of the American humorist S. J. Perelman, being characterized by quips, gags, and satiric exaggerations. The witticisms are most various in quality, however, ranging from the highly imaginative to the simply puerile. Moreover, there are so many witticisms that they clog virtually every sentence, considerably impeding the narrative. Morrow's greatest fault is that his characters are constantly engaged in heroic bouts of drink and sex. His humor then seems less out of Rabelais than out of Playboy magazine, and quickly becomes adolescent and tedious. Nevertheless, the ability to make jokes is rare, and Morrow could develop into an excellent writer. He is already a distinctive one.

WORK: The Confessions of Proinsias O'Toole. [Belfast]: Blackstaff, [1977].

MULDOON, PAUL (1951-), poet. Muldoon was born in County Armagh in 1951. He was educated at Armagh College and Queen's University, Belfast, and is Talks Producer for the BBC in Belfast. He has published several slim volumes of verse, which have received considerable acclaim. Seamus Heaney,* for instance, has remarked, "Muldoon seems to me unusually gifted, endowed with an individual sense of rhythm, a natural and copious vocabulary, a technical accomplishment and an intellectual boldness that mark him as the most promising poet to appear in Ireland for years." Upon

close scrutiny, however, the more specific and verifiable qualities which
Heaney mentions do not seem that apparent. For instance, if one marks the
stresses in the typical poem entitled "Blemish," one hardly finds "an individual sense of rhythm":

> Was it indeed an accident of birth
> That she looks on the gentle earth
> And the seemingly gentle sky
> Through one brown and one blue eye.

The first line is such regular iambic pentameter that it imposes a definite
pattern. The second line can, without great violence, be pushed into a four-
stress iambic pattern, although the normal speech rhythms would put the
stress on "looks" and "gen" and "earth." The third line, however, makes
the reader in effect go back to the second line and revise his estimate. The
third line can only be forced into iambics by two terrifically disruptive inversions in the first two feet and must really be read with the stresses on
"seem" and "gen" and "sky." This reading makes the second and third lines
identical in pattern, but only at the expense of making the reader stop reading the poem, in order to study it. The fourth line, with its stresses on
"brown" and "one" and "blue" and "eye," completes the chaos by resisting
any kind of pattern.

Heaney's claim for "a natural and copious vocabulary" seems refuted by
the first two typical stanzas from Muldoon's "How to Play Championship
Tennis":

> That winter of my third-form year,
> While the other boys played penny poker
> Or listened to the latest Hendrix,
> Or simply taunted Joe and Cyril,
>
> I fell in with the school caretaker.
> He was like me, from the country,
> We seemed to speak the same language.
> He knew the names of all the trees, ...

Here the language is natural enough but hardly copious, while the metrical
pattern seems nonexistent.

Heaney's claim of "technical accomplishment" does not seem to be borne
out either by any syntactical strength or by any control of sound in Muldoon's work. Muldoon's attention to sound appears almost entirely in the
end words of his lines. For instance, the final words of the poem "Epona"
are these:

> madder, grass, meadow, jackass
> blade, over, rid, slither
> back, snaffle, back, life

Or, worse, the final words of the poem "The Mixed Marriage" are these:

> boy, nine, loy, own
> mistress, Pollux, class, which
> Proust, farcy, hedge, Quarter
> table, Apostles, Travels, upstairs
> light, ferrets, fights, Caravets

Here, the author seems not to be in command of rhyme, alliteration, or assonance, but to be settling for any vague similarity.

Heaney also cites Muldoon's "intellectual boldness," but the themes of the poems seem conventional enough; a line like "Alleluia on my prick!" is, fortunately, so rare as to be quite uncharacteristic.

Muldoon is not as bad a writer as these, nevertheless typical, examples suggest, but thus far he is not at all "a wholly distinctive sensibility" (*The Irish Times*) or "a distinctive voice" (*Times Literary Supplement*).

WORKS: *Knowing My Place.* [Belfast]: Honest Ulsterman, 1971; *New Weather.* London: Faber, 1973; *Spirit of Dawn.* Belfast: Ulsterman Publications, 1975; *Mules.* London: Faber, 1977.

MULHOLLAND, ROSA. *See* GILBERT, LADY.

MULKERNS, VAL (1925-), novelist and short story writer. Mulkerns was born on February 14, 1925, in Dublin. She was an assistant editor of *The Bell** from 1952 to 1954. Her first novel, *A Time Outworn*, is a rather romanticized story of a young love affair but contains many nice bits of observation about young girls. A second novel, *A Peacock Cry* (1954), was no great advance, but her volume called *Antiquities*, published almost a quarter of a century later (1978), shows the author quite in control of her material. *Antiquities* is a volume of connected short stories dealing with several generations of a single family. Although the endings of several of the stories are somewhat contrived, this work is quite satisfying and even distinguished.

WORKS: *A Time Outworn.* London: Chatto & Windus, 1951/New York: Devin-Adair, 1952; *A Peacock Cry.* London: Hodder & Stoughton, [1954]; *Antiquities.* London: Andre Deutsch, 1978.

MURPHY, ARTHUR (1727-1805), playwright. Murphy was born at Cloonyquin, County Roscommon, on December 27, 1727. Because his father died when Murphy was but two, he was educated principally in France at the English Jesuit school at St. Omar, where he was an outstanding student of the classics. His maternal uncle intended him for a career in business and sent him to Cork for a two-year apprenticeship. He disliked the work but enjoyed the hospitality. When he returned to London against his uncle's will, he was disinherited. Soon after, Murphy originated a newspaper column and then a separate weekly paper called *The Gray's Inn*

Journal (1752-1754), modeled on *The Spectator*. Under the name of Charles Ranger, he commented frequently on theatrical matters. To earn money, at the suggestion of his friend the mimic Foote, he became an actor for two seasons, one at Covent Garden and the second at Drury Lane under David Garrick, who produced his first play, the longlived farce *The Apprentice*, in 1756. He left acting for a spate of political journalism and then studied law, which he practiced successfully for most of his life, carrying on a double career as a playwright. *The Apprentice, The Way to Keep Him* (1761), *Three Weeks After Marriage* (1776), and *Know Your Own Mind* (1777), all comedies or farces, were produced well into the nineteenth century. *The Orphan of China* (1759) and *Zenobia* (1768) established him as a writer of tragedy as well. He favored laughing rather than sentimental comedy, and *The Way to Keep Him* holds up favorably to the best of Goldsmith* and Sheridan.* He published translations of Sallust and of Tacitus; his translation of Tacitus, with notes, was long the standard version. He wrote brief, rather informal, but well-informed biographies of his close friends Dr. Johnson (whom he was responsible for introducing to the Thrales) and of David Garrick, with whom his personal and professional relationship was long and sometimes explosive. He was noted for his informed and amiable conversation. He died in London on June 18, 1805.

SVEN ERIC MOLIN

WORKS: *The Works of Arthur Murphy, esq.* 7 vols. London: T. Cadell. (There are many editions of his most famous plays: *All in the Wrong, The Apprentice, The Citizen, The Grecian Daughter, Know Your Own Mind, The Old Maid, The Orphan of China, Three Weeks After Marriage,* and *The Way to Keep Him*); *New Essays.* Arthur Sherbo, ed. [Ann Arbor]: Michigan State University Press, 1963.   REFERENCES: Dunbar, Howard Hunter. *The Dramatic Career of Arthur Murphy.* New York: Modern Language Association/London: Oxford University Press, 1946; Emery, John Pike. *Arthur Murphy.* Philadelphia: University Press for Temple University Publications, 1946.

MURPHY, RICHARD (1927-), poet. Murphy was born at Milford House, County Galway, on August 6, 1927, and spent some of his early life in Ceylon. He was educated at Magdalen College, Oxford, and received a B.A. in 1948. He later studied at the Sorbonne and did some teaching. He first gained wide recognition with *Sailing to an Island* (1963); his subsequent publications have been *The Battle of Aughrim* (1968), *The God Who Eats Corn* (1968), and *High Island* (1974). He has lived much in the west of Ireland and in 1959 bought the "Ave Maria," a fishing boat about which he wrote his poem "The Last Galway Hooker." He has taught frequently at universities in England and America; he won the AE Memorial Prize in 1951, the Guinness Poetry Prize in 1962, and British Arts Council awards in 1967 and 1976. Much of his poetry deals with the sea; his longest poem, "The Battle of Aughrim," places that historical event of 1691 effectively in a context of the present.

Murphy's poetry is overwhelmingly straightforward and literal, and presents a clear, plain surface which poses few puzzles. While his language is not precisely flat, it does not rise memorably either. For instance, several critics have called the storm at sea depicted in "The Cleggan Disaster" "Conradian." If one bears in mind the unforgettable storms of *Typhoon* and *The Nigger of the Narcissus*, however, it is apparent that Murphy's writing is far from attaining Conrad's eloquence. Similarly, if one compares the battle of "The Battle of Aughrim" with any of half a dozen great battle scenes in literature, one sees that Murphy has severely limited his scope and effects. Given the theme and the strategy of the poem, the limitation is appropriate, but it is a limitation.

If in "The Battle of Aughrim," Murphy invites us to look not on a panorama but on successive facets of historical fact and significant corners of a battlefield, his poetic technique analogously invites attention to the detail rather than to the overall form. Seamus Heaney* makes the point that Murphy's "objective and concrete" language is "closer to the staccato and stress of Anglo-Saxon poetry than to the melody and syntactical complexity of the Spenserean tradition." There are perhaps a few affinities with Anglo-Saxon poetry, such as occasional heavy alliteration in odd lines, but Murphy's technique seems a simpler, thinner, and more arbitrary version of Austin Clarke's* adaptation to English of various devices from poetry in Irish. Murphy makes frequent use of various cousins to rhyme, especially assonance and consonance, and of some more tenuous relatives of rhyme also. However, he rarely sustains a pattern even in a short poem, and one often feels that a Clarke would have considered much of this work an imperfect minor draft. For instance, one of Murphy's favorite forms is the three-line stanza with, not a rhyme scheme, but a sound scheme of ABA, BCB, CDC, and so on. Thus, the first three stanzas of "The Sheepfold" section of "The Battle of Aughrim" end with these words: some, be, him; tree, pox, melody; meadowstalks, cuirass, tucks. But a later trio of three-line stanzas ends like this: then, camp, run; Suck, camp, luck; tramp, shot, limp. Many other passages in Murphy break down much more drastically. There is a good deal of specific pleasure in certain individual correspondences of sound in many of his poems, but it is rare to find any tightly thoroughgoing form.

The same point might be made of his meter, particularly in the section called "New Poems" of *High Island*. He does get some marvelous effects in many individual lines of "Sailing to an Island," but the general effect is so patternless that the main difference between his language and prose is the cut-off lines. They, however, do insist at least that we attend to the varying rhythm of each particular line.

Murphy aims high, and he does not entirely fail. Because of his technical casualness, he seldom entirely succeeds either. All the same, he is generally considered to be one of the better poetic talents of the post-Clarke and

Kavanagh* generation, and a worthy colleague of Kinsella,* Montague,* and Heaney.

WORKS: *The Archaeology of Love: Poems.* Glenageary: Dolmen, 1955; *Sailing to an Island: A Poem.* Dublin: Privately printed at Dolmen, 1955; *The Woman of the House: An Elegy.* Dublin: Dolmen, 1959; *The Last Galway Hooker.* Dublin: Dolmen, 1961; *Sailing to an Island.* London: Faber & Faber, 1963/New York: Chilmark, 1964; *The Battle of Aughrim & The God Who Eats Corn.* London: Faber & Faber/New York: Alfred A. Knopf, 1968; *High Island.* London: Faber & Faber, 1974; *High Island. New and Selected Poems.* New York & London: Harper & Row, 1974. (This edition includes parts of *Sailing to an Island* and the full texts of *The Battle of Aughrim* and London *High Island* volumes); *Irish University Review.* Maurice Harmon, ed. Vol. 7, No. 1 (Spring 1977). (A most useful compilation, containing a biographical note by Harmon, seven new poems by Murphy, a glossary to *The Battle of Aughrim* and *The God Who Eats Corn* by Jonathan Williams, an excellently full biography by Mary FitzGerald, a not-too-impressive critical assessment by Seamus Heaney, and several moderately germane background pieces.)

MURPHY, THOMAS [BERNARD] (1935-), playwright. Murphy was born in Tuam, County Galway, on February 23, 1935. While he taught metalwork, math, and religion at Mountbellew Vocational School from 1957 to 1962, he was involved in amateur drama. From 1962 until 1970, he lived in London as a full-time writer for stage, television, and films. Then he returned to Dublin with his wife, Mary Hippisley, and his two children. From 1971 to 1973, he worked on the International Committee for English in the liturgy. In 1972, he received the Irish Academy of Letters Award for distinction in literature, and in 1973 he became a director on the board of the Abbey Theatre.*

Kenneth Tynan anticipated the reaction in Dublin and New York when he called Joan Littlewood's production of Murphy's *A Whistle in the Dark* "the most uninhibited display of brutality that the London theatre has ever witnessed" (*The Observer*, September 17, 1961). In *Famine* (1968), Murphy managed a stage full of over thirty characters to depict the issues and the consequences of the great national nineteenth-century trauma. *The Orphans* (1968) portrays a group of "limbo" people who, at a time when men can reach the moon, still cannot reach one another. *A Crucial Week in the Life of a Grocer's Assistant* (1969) is the best of Murphy's provincial plays in which he shows the poverty of small-town, dead-end lives. What for Murphy was "the liberating influence of Tennessee Williams" can be seen in the flexible use of dream sequences, unusual lighting, stylized movement, and exuberant language. *The Morning After Optimism* (1971) uses a form of fairytale to show the results of feeding the heart on fantasies. In a surrealistic forest, a soiled couple meet and kill their ideal counterparts. *The White House* (1972) and *On the Outside/On the Inside* (1975) each comprise two plays written some years apart. Both enact the wasted lives of young provincials, "chattering away irredeemable time." *The Sanctuary Lamp* (1975), like many of Murphy's plays, was premiered at the

Dublin Theatre Festival by the Abbey Theatre. It is one of the most bitter attacks against the Catholic Church ever presented on an Irish stage. In this mood piece without much plot or spectacle, three misfits look for a glimmer of salvation in a dark church, and perhaps find it in the sharing of their solitude. *The J. Arthur Maginnis Story* (1977) is a broad, perhaps satirical, comedy.

CHRISTOPHER GRIFFIN

WORKS: *The Fooleen.* Dixon, Calif.: Proscenium, 1968. (An early version of *A Crucial Week in the Life of a Grocer's Assistant*); *A Whistle in the Dark.* New York: Samuel French, 1970; *The Morning after Optimism.* Dublin & Cork: Mercier, 1973; *The Orphans.* Newark, Del.: Proscenium, 1974; *On the Outside/On the Inside.* Dublin: Gallery, 1976; *The Sanctuary Lamp.* Dublin: Poolbeg, 1976; *Famine.* Dublin: Gallery, 1977; *A Crucial Week in the Life of a Grocer's Assistant.* [Dublin]: Gallery 1 [Newark, Del.]: Proscenium, 1978.

MURRAY, PAUL (1947-), poet. Murray was born in 1947 in Newcastle, County Down. He was educated at St. Malachy's College, Belfast, and entered the Dominican Order in 1966. He has published one small collection of poetry entitled *Ritual Poems.* The poems are short, simple, pithy, and sometimes moving, but, despite various typographic arrangements on the page, they remain quite stubbornly prose. One partial exception is the short piece called "Statements."

WORK: *Ritual Poems.* Dublin: New Writers', 1971.

MURRAY, T[HOMAS] C[ORNELIUS] (1873-1959), playwright. Murray was born in Macroom, County Cork, on January 17, 1873. In addition to writing plays, he taught at St. Patrick's College, Dublin, and was headmaster of the model school at Inchicore, County Dublin, from 1915 until his retirement in 1932. He served as director of the Authors' Guild of Ireland and was a member of the Irish Academy of Letters. He died on March 7, 1959, at Ballsbridge, Dublin.

Murray's plays of life in rural Cork reflect the countryman's acquisitive hunger and his fear of poverty and disgrace. *Birthright* (1910), his first Abbey* play, ends with brothers fighting to the death over a patch of farmland. The title character of *Maurice Harte* (1912) continues to study for the priesthood, and suffers a mental breakdown, because his family has gone into debt for his schooling and will be humiliated if he leaves the seminary. In *The Briery Gap* (1917), a man delays marriage to a pregnant girl until he can obtain a farm; she counters by appealing to the ultimate voice of public opinion, the priest. *Spring* (1918) depicts a woman embittered by penury trying to force her aged father-in-law into the workhouse. Even a matchmaking comedy, *Sovereign Love* (Cork, 1909, titled *The Wheel of Fortune*; Abbey, 1913), darkens when a girl is virtually auctioned to the highest bidder.

Incompatible marriage is a recurring theme in Murray's middle period.

In *Aftermath* (1922) and *Michaelmas Eve* (1932), a man, prompted by his mother, forsakes the woman he loves and marries the woman with land. *Autumn Fire* (1924) deals with the May-December union of widower Owen Keegan and young Nance Desmond. As gossipers predict, Owen's son Michael is drawn into a love rivalry with his father. *Autumn Fire* is strikingly similar to Eugene O'Neill's tragedy *Desire Under the Elms* (which opened two months after *Autumn Fire*) and does not emerge badly when compared with O'Neill's better known play.

Most of Murray's late efforts were devoted to reworking earlier material. Although he sets *The Blind Wolf* (1928) (afterward titled *The Karavoes*) in Hungary and *A Stag at Bay* in England, he does not expand his dramatic range. *Illumination* (1939) is the *Maurice Harte* theme with a happy ending. Only *The Pipe in the Fields* (1927) is a departure from Murray's basic realism: Peter Keville creates beautiful music and experiences visions when he plays a "magic" fife. But this play, too, contains a veteran Murray character, the well-intentioned, domineering mother. *Spring Horizon* (1937) is a gently paced autobiographical novel of growing up in a Cork village. A planned sequel never materialized.

Although Murray worked with combustible material—murder, insanity, families in conflict (how often the old disable the young), clerical influence, incest—he was not a controversialist. Primeval passions are disciplined by his intense Catholicism, and the result is a darkly brooding view of life. It is enhanced by lyrical passages influenced by Synge,* sad as Synge's can be but never joyfully surging. The comic muse was not his friend; his comedy *A Flutter of Wings* (1929, Gate) was rejected by the Abbey. Of his tragic plays, *Autumn Fire* and *Maurice Harte* have an enduring place in Irish dramatic literature.

WILLIAM J. FEENEY

WORKS: *Birthright*. Dublin: Maunsel, 1911; *Maurice Harte*. Dublin: Maunsel, 1912/reprinted with *A Stag at Bay*, London: Allen & Unwin, 1934; *Spring and Other Plays* (*Sovereign Love* and *The Briery Gap*). Dublin: Talbot, 1917; *Aftermath: A Play in Three Acts*. Dublin: Talbot, 1922; *Autumn Fire: A Play in Three Acts*. London: G. Allen & Unwin, 1925; *The Pipe in the Fields: A Play in One Act*, in *The Dublin Magazine* 2 (April-June 1927):7-30. Reprinted with *Birthright*. London: G. Allen & Unwin, 1928; *Michaelmas Eve: A Play in Three Acts*. London: G. Allen & Unwin, 1932; *Spring Horizon*. London: T. Nelson & Sons, 1937. A typescript of *Illumination* is in the Boston College Library.   REFERENCES: Connolly, Terence L. "T. C. Murray, The Quiet Man." *The Catholic World* 190 (March 1960): 364-369; Fitzgibbon, T. Gerald. "The Elements of Conflict in the Plays of T. C. Murray." *Studies* 64 (Spring 1975):59-65. Hogan, Thomas. "T. C. Murray." *Envoy* 3 (November 1950):138-148; Macardle, Dorothy. "The Dramatic Art of T. C. Murray." *The Dublin Magazine* 2 (January 1925):393-398; Ó hAodha, Micheál. "T. C. Murray and Some Critics." *Studies* 47 (Summer 1958):185-191.

na GOPALEEN, MYLES. *See* O'NOLAN, BRIAN.

NALLY, T[HOMAS] H[ENRY] (ca. 1869-1932), playwright. Nally was born in County Mayo around 1869. He is known (though probably only to historians) for his play *The Spancel of Death* which was to have been produced at the Abbey Theatre* during Easter Week 1916. After the Rising, no attempt was made to produce the play, which was thought to be too gloomy for the times. It was never produced or published. In 1917, Nally's Irish fairy pantomime, *Finn Varra Maa*, was produced for matinees at the Theatre Royal and was rather successful. During the war years, he also wrote the books for a few Irish musical revues, such as *The King of Dublin*.

WORK: *Finn Varra Maa*. Dublin: Talbot, 1917.

NATION, THE (1842-1892), periodical. *The Nation*, probably the most famous Irish periodical, was founded by Sir Charles Gavan Duffy,* Thomas Davis,* and John Blake Dillon (1816-1866) in 1842. It was initially the mouthpiece of the Young Ireland movement, and its policy of idealistic and vehement nationalism quickly made itself felt. After the collapse of Daniel O'Connell's proscribed mass meeting at Clontarf in 1843, the fervently patriotic spirit of the paper grew ever more inflammatory, and it aroused the enthusiasm of thousands. When Lord Plunket was asked to describe the tone of the paper, he simply and aptly replied "Wolfe Tone." However, the reclamation of the patriotic past was done to inflame a revolutionary future and to ensure complete separation from England.

The Nation was primarily political, but it also attempted to raise the national consciousness of the country by fostering a cultural awareness as well as an historical pride. Through the publisher James Duffy,* the paper disseminated over twenty volumes of its "Library of Ireland." These books, issued cheaply at a shilling in paper wrappers, were widely circulated. They contained collections of ballad poetry and songs, novels by Carleton,* essays by Davis, biographical sketches of earlier Irish writers, as well as lives of great Irishmen such as Aodh O'Neill and Curran and several works of history.

The writers for the journal itself constitute a Who's-Who of Irish literary talent at midcentury—Davis, Mitchel,* Mangan,* Lalor,* and a huge group of new ballad writers and poets, the most famous of whose work was published in *The Spirit of the Nation* and *The New Spirit of the Nation*. However, apart from a handful of poems mainly by Davis and Mangan, the poetry of *The Nation* is conventional, imitative popular poetry in which much more emotion than ability is apparent. Still, many of the pieces by John de Jean Frazer,* Denis Florence MacCarthy,* John Kells Ingram,* and Richard D'Alton Williams* have remained in the consciousness of several generations of readers. Many of the poets were women who wrote under pseudonyms, the most famous being Speranza, Mary, Eva, Thoma-

sine, and Finola. Speranza was Jane Francesca Elgee, later Lady Wilde*;
Mary was Ellen Mary Patrick Downing (1828-1869); Eva was Mary Anne
Kelly (ca. 1825-1910); Thomasine was Olivia Knight, later Mrs. Hope
Connolly (ca. 1830-1909); and Finola was Elizabeth Willoughby Treacy
who married the Cork poet Ralph Varian. Both Mary and Eva were in love
with Young Irelanders who were exiled. Eva was in love with Kevin Izod
O'Doherty who could have been pardoned had he admitted his guilt. When
he asked Eva's advice, she said, "Be a man and face the worst. I'll wait for
you however long the sentence may be." The sentence was ten years; two
days after his return they were married. Mary was in love with another
Nation poet, Joseph Brenan (1828-1857), but, as A. M. Sullivan* writes,
"Less happy was the romance of Mary's fate. . . . Alas! in foreign climes
he learned to forget home vows. 'Mary' sank under the blow. She put by
the lyre, and in utter seclusion from the world lingered for a while; but ere
long the spring flowers blossomed on her grave." Actually, Mary entered
the North Presentation Convent in Cork in 1849, taking the name of Sister
Mary Alphonsus, and she did not die until twenty years later.

In 1848, the Young Irelanders had an ineffective Rising, the only military engagement being, as Conor Cruise O'Brien* puts it, "under the chiv-
alrous and incompetent leadership of William Smith O'Brien." The Rising
was swiftly put down, *The Nation* was quashed, and the principal leaders
transported to Australia. A new series of *The Nation* was begun in 1849,
and, under one editor or another, the journal continued until 1896. It was
the initial volumes, however, which fomented, as Edmund Curtis* put it,
"a revival of the Gaelic, militant, and aristocratic spirit, and the cult of
'the Dark Rosaleen', formerly expressed in the native tongue but now
poured into the new mould of the English language which was steadily
spreading among the common people." It was also the initial volumes and
the writings of Davis, Mitchel, Lalor, and the rest that kept alive for succeeding generations the spirit of revolt and of national pride in the country's
history and culture. What is called the Literary Renaissance, that astonishing movement which began at the end of the century and that fostered
Yeats,* Hyde,* Synge,* and Stephens,* most assuredly had its seeds in
the simple verses of the poets of *The Nation*.

WORKS: *The Spirit of the Nation*. Dublin: J. Duffy, 1843; *The Spirit of the Nation,
Part II*. Dublin: J. Duffy, 1843; *A Voice from the Prison, or, The Voice of the Nation*.
Dublin: J. Duffy, 1844. (Prose); *The New Spirit of the Nation*, ed. with an Introduc-
tion by Martin Mac Dermott. London: T. Fisher Unwin/Dublin: Sealy/New York:
Kenedy, 1894.

NI CHUILLEANAIN, EILEAN (1942-), poet. Ní Chuilleánain was born
in 1942 in Cork City. Her father was professor of Irish at the university
there, and her mother, Eilis Dillon,* is a prolific writer in both Irish and
English. Eiléan herself was educated at University College, Cork, and be-

came a lecturer in English at Trinity College, Dublin. She has published *Acts and Monuments* (1972) which won the Patrick Kavanagh Award for Poetry, *Site of Ambush* (1975) which won the Books Ireland Publishers' Award, and *The Second Voyage* (1977) which is largely a collection of the best work from the first two volumes. Her poetry is usually in free verse, and its strengths lie in the quality of imagination, the clarity of particular images, and a frequent ability to spin the memorable phrase. Her weakness is chiefly syntactical, a failure to realize the relative importance of clauses and sentences which are often strung together with little rhetorical strength. A symptom of this weakness is a punctuation often so erratic as to be confusing and to appear simply unconsidered. She may be seen at her best in her poem about Odysseus, "The Second Voyage."

WORKS: *Acts and Monuments.* Dublin: Gallery Books, 1972; *Site of Ambush.* Dublin: Gallery Books, 1975; *The Second Voyage.* Dublin: Gallery Books, 1977.

NOONAN, GILLMAN (1937-), short story writer. Noonan was born in Kanturk, County Cork, in 1937. He graduated from University College, Cork, and then spent several years working on a German newspaper in Hamburg. He has published one collection of short stories entitled *A Sexual Relationship* (1976). His stories range from simple and static character sketches to rather complicated studies such as the excellent title story. Despite some tendency to the essay rather than the dramatic style, several of Noonan's stories are quite accomplished and evince a fine humorous observation as well as some technical inventiveness, and even a pleasantly whimsical imagination.

WORK: *A Sexual Relationship and Other Stories.* Dublin: Poolbeg, 1976.

NORTON, CAROLINE ELIZABETH SARAH (1808-1877), poet and novelist. Norton was one of several talented members of the astonishing Sheridan family. The granddaughter of Richard Brinsley Sheridan* and the younger sister of Lady Dufferin,* she was born in London in 1808. After her father died in 1816, she moved with her mother and six brothers and sisters into Hampton Court, an accommodation arranged by the Duke of York, a friend of her grandfather. Although her two sisters made brilliant marriages, Caroline was not so fortunate. Her husband, George Chapple Norton, was a worse cad than Victorian fiction could dream up, and the couple separated in 1836. That year Norton cited Lord Melbourne as corespondent in a divorce suit, although Norton had encouraged Melbourne's friendship with Norton to secure his own advancement. The suit was defeated, but the scandal caused Caroline to be hounded all her life by scandal-mongering journalists. For the next six years, Norton refused to let her see her children and only relented after the youngest died. Her sufferings led her to write pamphlets which helped to change the law about custody of infants.

Despite a hasty temper, Caroline was a loving and witty woman who inspired the lifelong friendships of many brilliant men. Melbourne died protesting her innocence, but the stuffy Victorians always suspected her. Even George Meredith in his novel *Diana of the Crossways*, for which she was the inspiration, implied that she had betrayed government secrets. Her husband mercifully died in 1869, and in June 1877 Caroline married an old friend, Sir W. Stirling-Maxwell. She died only a few months later.

The publication when she was eleven of *The Dandies Rout*, a pastiche of a famous series called *The Dandy Books*, began a prolific writing career. Her poetry, which often touched on the condition of women, children, and factory workers, was as highly regarded as Elizabeth Barrett Browning's, and Hartley Coleridge referred to her as "The Byron of Modern Poetesses." Some of her poetry is remembered today, and, although hardly literature, it is always fluent and sometimes fun. For instance, "The Arab's Farewell to his Steed" or "Bingen on the Rhine" which begins with marvellous panache and triteness:

> A soldier of the Legion lay dying in Algiers,
> There was lack of woman's nursing, there was dearth of
>   woman's tears. . . .

Her novels—*The Wife and Woman's Reward* (1836), *Stuart of Dunleath* (1851), *Lost and Saved* (1865), and *Old Sir Douglas* (1867)—are much alike and forgotten today. The plots are melodramatic, and the protagonists all sensitive, intelligent women persecuted by brutal men, scheming relatives, or callous public opinion. Influenced by her own unhappy life, they lack the wit and humor for which she was renowned.

WORKS: Selected Poems in *The Poets and the Poetry of the Century*. A. H. Miles, ed. Vol. 7. London: Hutchinson, 1892.   REFERENCE: Acland, Alice. *Caroline Norton*. London: Constable, 1948.

O'BRIEN, CONOR CRUISE (1917-), politician, historian, and man of letters. O'Brien was born on November 3, 1917. His father was a well-known journalist, and his mother was Kathleen Sheehy who appears as Miss Ivors in Joyce's* story, "The Dead." O'Brien received a Ph.D. from Trinity College and then entered the Department of External Affairs. In 1945, he began contributing articles to literary magazines under the pseudonym of Donat O'Donnell. Some of these pieces were gathered into his first book, *Maria Cross* (1952). Subtitled "Imaginative Patterns in a Group of Modern Catholic Writers," the book is a highly regarded, if unnecessarily abstruse, discussion of Mauriac, Bernanos, Claudel, Waugh, O'Faolain,* Leon Bloy, and Graham Greene. O'Brien's second book, *Parnell and His Party* (1957), was a version of his doctoral dissertation and an excellently thorough conventional history. However, certain events in

O'Brien's life were to push him to the writing of much more personal criticism and history.

In 1956, O'Brien became a member of the first Irish delegation to the United Nations, and he held that post until 1961 when he was appointed by Dag Hammarskjold as U.N. Representative in Katanga. There he quickly launched, more or less on his own authority, a military operation to end Katanganese secession from the Congo. This action, as well as his publicized resignation from the United Nations, for a short time made him a minor actor on the world stage. O'Brien's feelings about his involvement in Katanga are explained in *To Katanga and Back* (1962), and his feelings about the United Nations are explored in *The United Nations: Sacred Drama* (1968).

After his resignation, from 1962 to 1965, O'Brien served as vice-chancellor of the University of Ghana, and from 1965 to 1969, he taught at New York University. His casual writing in these years continued to embrace both literature and politics, and the best of his fugitive pieces were collected in *Writers and Politics* (1965). His time in Katanga was also reflected in *Murderous Angels* (1968), a play about Hammarskjold and the African leader Patrice Lumumba. Although it received considerable exposure, the play is probably too thoughtful for great theatrical success.

In 1969, O'Brien returned to Ireland to enter politics as a member of the Labour party, and in the general election of 1969 he secured a seat in the Irish Parliament. In the general election of 1973, Labor joined with the Fine Gael party in a coalition to form a government, and in the coalition O'Brien became the Minister for Posts and Telegraphs. His best writing during these years was *States of Ireland* (1972), which was a personal investigation of the now-inflamed North-South conflict, and a refreshing attempt to assess the situation in terms of contemporary actualities rather than of traditional rhetoric.

O'Brien's years as a member of the government were highly visible ones, and he received a press coverage rather out of proportion to his influence—partly because of his world eminence and partly because of his trenchant and articulate opinions. His initial popularity soon waned, and the reasons may be that he made little improvement in the wretched Irish telephone service, that he was an intellectual, and that he seemed to grow more intractable in 1976 and 1977. For a liberal, his public remarks became increasingly authoritarian, a result, perhaps, of an understandable exasperation at the futility of power when faced with irresolvable questions. In the general election of 1977, the National Coalition lost to Fianna Fail, and O'Brien lost his own seat. Shortly afterward, he secured election to the Senate as a representative of Dublin University. Later in the year, he accepted the editorship of the London Sunday paper *The Observer*.

His *Herod, Reflections on Political Violence* appeared in 1978. The first

two-thirds of the book is the most interesting; this part collects some fugitive essays, addresses, and reviews which collectively present his views about
the violence in Ulster. He is particularly sound on the relation of the Catholic Church to the revolutionary movement and in his historical analysis
of the Fianna Fail party. He also makes a much better case than one would
have thought possible for censorship of television news broadcasting. The
last third of the book is composed of three short plays which are more
thoughtful than dramatic.

It is difficult to regard O'Brien with the simple admiration that bookish
people are usually too willing to extend to the writer-politician who is an
intellectual and a liberal. Nevertheless, to the liberal mind, his views on
contemporary Irish politics remain among the most plausible and persuasive in the country. His lasting impact will undoubtedly be as a commentator rather than as a doer.

WORKS: *Maria Cross*. New York & Toronto: Oxford University Press, 1952;
Parnell and His Party, 1880-1890. Oxford: Clarendon, 1957; *To Katanga and Back:
A U. N. Case History*. London: Hutchinson, 1962; *Writers and Politics*. London:
Chatto & Windus, 1965; *Murderous Angels*. Boston: Little, Brown, 1968/London:
Hutchinson, 1969. (Play); *The United Nations: Sacred Drama*. London: Hutchinson,
1968; *Camus*. London: Fontana, Collins, 1970; with Marie Cruise O'Brien, *A Concise
History of Ireland*. London: Thames & Hudson, 1972/published in America as *The
Story of Ireland*, New York: Viking, 1972; *States of Ireland*. London: Hutchinson,
1972; *The Suspecting Glance*. London: Faber, 1972; *Herod, Reflections on Political
Violence*. London: Hutchinson, [1978].   REFERENCES: Lysaght, D.R. O'Connor.
End of a Liberal: The Literary Politics of Conor Cruise O'Brien. [Dublin: Plough
Books, 1976]; Young-Bruehl, Elisabeth, & Hogan, Robert. *Conor Cruise O'Brien, an
Appraisal*. Newark, Del.: Proscenium, 1974. (Contains a Conor Cruise O'Brien Check-
list by Joanne L. Henderson).

O'BRIEN, EDNA (1930-), novelist and short story writer. O'Brien was born
on December 15, 1930, in Tuamgraney, County Clare, Ireland, and was
educated at the National School in Scarriff, the Convent of Mercy at Loughrea, and the Pharmaceutical College in Dublin. She married Ernest Gebler
in 1951, but the marriage was dissolved in 1964. She has two sons, Carlos
and Sasha.

County Clare remains so much in O'Brien's veins that the people there
continue to find themselves in her works; of these a dominant figure has
been a mother, or several mothers (Mrs. O'Brien died in spring 1977).
The content of her work has also been colored by Irish lore and history
and by distinctive geographic features such as Druids' circles and the Holy
Island (Inis Cealtra) in Lough Derg.

In 1959, O'Brien moved to London, where she maintains residence, but
she often returns to Ireland. During her first month of residence in London, she wrote her first novel, *The Country Girls*. With *The Lonely Girl*
(1962) and *Girls in Their Married Bliss* (1964), it comprises a trilogy of
a country girl's maturation and disappointment in love.

Love in many variations continues to be a dominant theme of O'Brien's writing, through succeeding novels set mainly in both London and County Clare: *August Is a Wicked Month* (1965), *Casualties of Peace* (1967), *A Pagan Place* (1970), *Night* (1972), and *Johnny I Hardly Knew You* (1977).

Collections of short stories are *The Love Object* (1968) and *A Scandalous Woman and Other Stories* (1974). Her stage plays are *A Cheap Bunch of Nice Flowers* (1963), *A Pagan Place* (1972), and *The Gathering* (1974). She has written for television and has adapted *The Lonely Girl* for the film *Girl with Green Eyes* (1964), a short story for the film *Time Lost and Time Remembered* (1966), and Andrea Newman's novel for the film *Three into Two Won't Go* (1968). Her screenplay *Zee and Co,* published as a book (1971), was filmed as *X, Y and Zee* (1972), starring Elizabeth Taylor. Her major nonfiction works are *Mother Ireland* (1976), a personalized history of the country from its founding to the present, and *Arabian Days* (1978).

More so than with many other writers, an assessment of O'Brien's art is intricately interwoven with an assessment of her person. Known as an Irish beauty, much photographed and much interviewed, she is often required to explain why she writes—as if any number of other choices were available to her.

Her work has been consistently scrutinized by academics and avidly pored over by the populace, as if she has two faces: one which gains her publication in respectable magazines such as *The New Yorker* and the *Atlantic Monthly*, and one which slightly titillates and scandalizes. The latter face deserves less attention than it gets, but it has been promoted by her deliberately artistic creation of a "true confession" atmosphere, which encourages readers to believe the experiences are her own (they are not, any more than many other writers are somewhat autobiographical). This atmosphere has also been encouraged by publishers' gimmicks such as the British Penguin's distribution of paper covers with photos of a nude woman, which some people naively believed was Edna O'Brien herself (it was not). Such a public buys many copies while it privately denounces the content. Much of the public regrets that the naive enchantment of *Country Girls*, which they call "Edna's best novel," was not faithfully repeated in all subsequent stories.

O'Brien's practice of naivete as an art continues, however, and explains much of the fetching, perhaps mesmeric, quality of her work. Innocence is so closely allied to naivete that the public typically expresses outrage at the choices which her characters inevitably make and the fate (likewise inevitable) that befalls them. However, in a male-dominant society, women have always been more used than adored. The naive means by which they attempt compromises and seek sexual love—temporary at best—leaves both male and female readers feeling guilty and vociferously protesting.

In O'Brien's works, men are often active enemies of women, and women, while combating pregnancy, loss, loneliness, and economics, try to overcome their desires for vengeance against men.

In spite of innocence and naivete, then, some of the women characters— Mary Holligan of *Night* and Zee of *Zee and Co*—endure and triumph through adversity. These two characters exhibit a central core of independence and fitness which the other characters in O'Brien bare only when misfortune (most frequently misuse by men) requires the most courageous of survival tactics. This often means survival without love when love has been regarded as necessity. Edna O'Brien's exposure of this passion has ranged through a child's love of mother (*A Pagan Place*) to a young woman's love for an older man (the trilogy) or another man (*Casualties of Peace* and *August*), to a mother's love for her son (*Night*), to an older woman's love for a younger man (*Johnny I Hardly Knew You*).

Believing in the necessity for "truth and authenticity" in literature, O'Brien often chooses a simple, convincing, and carefully pared style, with a very accurate and startling single word—often with a rural flavor—in a strategic place. While the point of view has been largely first person, her concern with the development of her craft has led to experimentation in form, including the unusual use of the second person in *A Pagan Place*, in which the child-heroine is known only as "you," and the modified stream of consciousness in *Night*, which is possibly her best novel.

The limitations of the love theme should be the greatest fault of O'Brien's art, but she proves it to be an inexhaustible theme, and explores it with a frankness heretofore afforded only male writers.

GRACE ECKLEY

WORKS: *The Country Girls*. London: Hutchinson, 1960; *The Lonely Girl*. London: Jonathan Cape/New York: Random House, 1962. Reprinted as *Girl with the Green Eyes*, London: Penguin, 1964; *Girls in Their Married Bliss*. London: Jonathan Cape, 1964/New York: Simon & Schuster, 1968; *August Is a Wicked Month*. London: Jonathan Cape/New York: Simon & Schuster, 1965; *Casualties of Peace*. London: Jonathan Cape, 1966/New York: Simon & Schuster, 1967; *The Love Object*. London: Jonathan Cape, 1968/New York: Alfred A. Knopf, 1969. (Stories); *A Pagan Place*. New York: Alfred A. Knopf, 1970; *Zee & Co*. London: Weidenfeld & Nicolson, 1971; *Night*. London: Weidenfeld & Nicolson, 1972/New York: Alfred A. Knopf, 1973; *A Pagan Place*. London: Faber, 1973. (Play); *A Scandalous Woman*. London: Weidenfeld & Nicolson/New York: Harcourt, Brace, Jovanovich, 1974; *Mother Ireland*. London: Weidenfeld & Nicolson, 1976. (On Ireland); *Johnny I Hardly Knew You*. London: Weidenfeld & Nicolson, 1977. (Novel); *The Collected Edna O'Brien*. London: Collins, 1978.   REFERENCES: "Dialogue with Edna O'Brian." *Under Bow Bells: Dialogues with Joseph McCulloch*. London: Sheldon Press, 1974; Dunn, Nell, ed. "Edna." *Talking to Women*. London: MacGibbon & Kee, 1965; Eckley, Grace. *Edna O'Brien*. Lewisburg, Pa.: Bucknell University Press, 1974.

O'BRIEN, FLANN. *See* O'NOLAN, BRIAN.

O'BRIEN, KATE (1897-1974), novelist, playwright, journalist, critic, and travel writer. O'Brien was born in Limerick on December 3, 1897. She was educated by French nuns at Laurel Hill Convent, Limerick, and in the autumn of 1916, she went to Dublin to continue her education at University College. The height of the Irish Renaissance was an exciting time to be in school in Dublin, but O'Brien maintained a detachment from it.

While a governess in Bilboa, Spain, in the early 1920s, she began to write and continued to do so when she returned. She took up residence in England and began to work for the *Manchester Guardian*. Her first efforts were plays; *A Distinguished Villa*, produced in 1926, won critical acclaim. However, she soon turned to novels, which, she said, you could "carry on your back" (*New York Times*, December 4, 1949, p. 22), avoiding the extensive collaboration involved in producing a play.

Her first novel, *Without My Cloak* (1931), a chronicle of an Irish family through three generations, won two of the leading British literary prizes: the Hawthornden Prize and the James Tait Black Prize. The theme of family, societal, and religious solidarity and restraint versus individual freedom, which had already been manifested in her plays and is central here, continues throughout all of her work. Her characters struggle against consuming parental love, the constraints of society, and the dictates of the Church. Their bids for freedom often fail, but the failure is not always seen as totally negative. For, although her novels are profoundly Catholic, her characters often make decisions based on responsibility toward and love of others as much as on the regulations of society and the Church. However, there are exceptions to this failure. In *Mary Lavelle*, a book which was banned in Ireland in 1936 under the Censorship Act, the heroine learns to be an individual and in the process abandons the moral strictures of her youth. In *As Music and Splendour* (1958), the two heroines also break with their Irish Catholic backgrounds, but here the results are not as positive. Some of O'Brien's novels narrow the conflict with society, focusing on the battle between the individualism and imagination of the artist and the restraining religious and societal codes.

Except for *Pray for the Wanderer* (1938), the major protagonists of all of O'Brien's novels are women, and the stories often deal with their attempts to overcome the rigid roles defined for them by society. In *Mary Lavelle*, *The Land of Spices*, and *The Flower of May*, women have to fight for the opportunities of travel and education which act as catalysts for the development of the individual.

O'Brien's greatest popular success was a sixteenth-century Spanish historical romance, *That Lady* (1946; published in the United States as *For One Sweet Grape*). She adapted it for the stage for Katharine Cornell, who starred in the 1949 Broadway production.

Besides plays and novels, O'Brien wrote two travel books, *Farewell, Spain* (1937) and *My Ireland* (1962). Both are personal, idiosyncratic views which nevertheless capture the essence of those two countries. *Teresa of Avila* (1951) is a portrait of St. Teresa as a "women of genius" rather than as a canonized saint, again reflecting the interests of the author.

O'Brien's work is occasionally marred by overanalysis of her characters' emotions and motives. Such lapses lead to an unnecessary obscurity. For the most part, however, hers is a fluid style which is not obtrusive. This is mirrored by the contrast in many of her works between the internal world of the emotions and the external world of appearances. The surface smoothness of the lives of her characters is set off against the passion, tension, and conflict of their inner lives. She shows a deep understanding of her characterization, and an ability to create atmosphere by her acute observation of detail. She deserves to be ranked with the important novelists of the twentieth century.

After her return from Spain, O'Brien lived in England for twenty years. Then, after a long interim in Ireland, she returned to Britain in 1965. She died in Faversham, Kent, August 13, 1974.

BARBARA DiBERNARD

WORKS: *Distinguished Villa*. London: E. Benn, 1926. (Play in three acts); *Without My Cloak*. London: Heinemann/Garden City, N.Y.: Doubleday, Doran, 1931; *The Anteroom*. London: Heinemann/Garden City, N.Y.: Doubleday, Doran, 1934; *Mary Lavelle*. London: Heinemann/Garden City, N.Y.: Doubleday, Doran, 1936; *Farewell, Spain*. London: Heinemann/Garden City, N.Y.: Doubleday, Doran, 1937; *Pray for the Wanderer*. London: Heinemann/Garden City, N.Y.: Doubleday, Doran, 1938; *The Land of Spices*. London: Heinemann, 1941; *English Diaries and Journals*. London: Collins, 1943; *The Last of Summer*. London: Heinemann/Garden City, N.Y.: Doubleday, Doran, 1943; *That Lady*. London: Heinemann, 1946/published in the United States as *For One Sweet Grape*, Garden City, N.Y.: Doubleday, 1946; *That Lady*. New York: Harper, 1949. (Play); *Teresa of Avila*. London: Max Parrish/New York: Sheed & Ward, 1951; *The Flower of May*. London: Heinemann/New York: Harper, 1953; *As Music and Splendour*. New York: Harper, 1958; *My Ireland*. New York: Hastings House, 1962.

O'BRIEN, KATE CRUISE (1948-), short story writer. O'Brien was born in Dublin in 1948, the daughter of Conor Cruise O'Brien.* Several of her stories have appeared in the New Irish Writing page of *The Irish Press*, and in 1971 she won a Hennessy Literary Award for short fiction. Her only collection thus far, *A Gift Horse and Other Stories* (1978), is largely about girls and young married women, but is remarkably free from the sensibilities and hysterias of much current fiction about women. Except for her short and powerful story, "Ashes," many of her pieces are probably too short, but they are all carefully written and keenly observed. Her better work is in the one or two longer pieces, such as "Henry Died" and "A Matter of Principle."

WORK: *A Gift Horse and Other Stories*. Dublin: Poolbeg, 1978.

O'CASEY, SEAN (1880-1964), playwright. Sean O'Casey was born John Casey in Dublin on March 30, 1880, into a poor Protestant family. He was the last of thirteen children, only five of whom reached adulthood. With the early death of his father, Michael Casey, the fortunes of the family declined further. O'Casey's lifelong eye trouble may probably be traced to early poverty. This enduring affliction began in early youth and made his attendance at school sporadic. Indeed, he only learned to read in his early teens. His first autobiographies, *I Knock at the Door* (1939) and *Pictures in the Hallway* (1942), recreate his early life with Dickensian gusto and poignance.

O'Casey spent his young manhood as an ordinary laborer, but the evenings were, as Lady Gregory* said of her own life, "a succession of enthusiasms." He entered with great fervor into the life of his church, St. Barnabas; into the Orange Lodge, the Gaelic League, and the Irish Republican Brotherhood; and, most importantly, into the labor movement as embodied in Jim Larkin's recently formed Irish Transport and General Workers' Union, and into its political arm, the Irish Citizen Army of which he was the first secretary. His initial idealistic enthusiasms were often dampened by disillusionment, and he so often truculently withdrew from active participation in causes he had once espoused that the patriot Tom Clarke dismissed him as simply "a disgruntled fellow."

At the same time, he was with wonder and delight discovering the world of books. His reading was excited, diverse, and unmethodical, but he was particularly enchanted by Shakespeare and the Elizabethan dramatists, by Shelley, Ruskin, and Shaw.* Their influence may be seen in his early prose and verse, and in the later self-portraits of Donal Davoren in *The Shadow of a Gunman* (1923) and of Ayamonn Breydon in *Red Roses for Me* (1943). In his Citizen Army days, he had written much rather florid journalism for the labor paper, *The Irish Worker*; then, although somewhat estranged from his former associates, he wrote a short history of the Citizen Army (1919) as well as an unpublished Ruskinian treatise, *Three Shouts from a Hill*. He had also been writing poems and greeting card verse for a small Dublin publisher, as well as dramatic sketches for his branch of the Gaelic League. As his interest in the theatre grew, he took part in an amateur production at the Empire Theatre, and he attempted several short plays which he submitted to the Abbey Theatre.* Finally, in 1923, his two-act play *On the Run* was accepted by the Abbey and was produced at the end of the season under the title *The Shadow of a Gunman*. This play was the first effective representation of Dublin slum life on the Irish stage, although, earlier, A. Patrick Wilson* and Oliver St. John Gogarty* had also written slum plays. However, it was probably the genial satiric comedy of the piece and the brilliant acting of the Abbey players, as well as the novelty of the subject, that gave the play its immediate popularity.

In the next year, 1924, the Abbey produced O'Casey's three-act play, *Juno and the Paycock*, which treated the Civil War and which was a considerable extension of the techniques of the *Gunman*. The major male roles of *Juno* were brilliantly created by Barry Fitzgerald and F. J. McCormick. To this day the play remains one of the most revived and popular of all Abbey plays.

O'Casey's next major production was *The Plough and the Stars* (1926). Although as great an artistic advance over *Juno* as *Juno* had been over the *Gunman*, the *Plough* at first shared none of their popularity, but instead caused a week of riotous disturbances in the theatre, as had John Synge's* *The Playboy of the Western World* nearly twenty years before. The motives of the rioters were precisely those of twenty years before. The national self-esteem had once again been insulted, and an Irish writer had once again held up to ridicule Irish patriotism, Irish chastity, and indeed the whole Irish character. O'Casey's view, of course, was that the play was a fair and just representation which cut through much cant and humbug. If it laughed at fustian and hypocrisy, it was also profoundly sympathetic to suffering and sacrifice. This is the view that later audiences, in Ireland and elsewhere, have come to take. W. B. Yeats* delivered his view from the stage to the 1926 audience in a superb short tirade:

> You have disgraced yourselves again. Is this to be an ever-recurring celebration of the arrival of Irish genius? Synge first and then O'Casey. The news of the happenings of the past few minutes will go from country to country. Dublin has once more rocked the cradle of genius. From such a scene in this theatre went forth the fame of Synge. Equally the fame of O'Casey is born here tonight. This is his apotheosis.

Bewildered, angered, and hurt at the denunciations in the theatre and in the press, O'Casey went to London shortly after the production, to receive the Hawthornden Prize for *Juno* and to look over that play's West End production. Except for a few brief visits, he never returned to Ireland.

In London, he was immediately recognized as an original personality, a rough genius from the working class, and he was feted and acclaimed. His first years in London were heady and exciting times. He was encountering an entirely new world. He was making friends with brilliant personalities, such as Bernard Shaw and Augustus John. His plays were produced in the West End to great acclaim and were published by the distinguished firm of Macmillan's, and in 1927, he married a young Irish actress who had played in them.

In the meantime, he was working on a new play, *The Silver Tassie*. This time, the subject was not merely Irish but international—the trauma of World War I—and the technique was in part (particularly in the lyricism and satire of the expressionistic second act) an unexpected divergence from that of the slum plays. The play was submitted first to the Abbey, and O'Casey confidently expected its acceptance, but in an often recounted literary brouhaha, it was rejected by Yeats, Lennox Robinson,* and Lady

Gregory. Angered and chagrined, O'Casey sent the correspondence to the press, and for a while the matter was a cause célèbre. A London production was arranged by the unlikely person of C. B. Cochran, an English Ziegfeld who specialized in musical comedies. With Charles Laughton somewhat miscast in the leading role, but supported by a number of distinguished Irish players, and also with a striking second act set by Augustus John, the play was a critical but not quite a popular success. The play's high production costs also made a fairly early demise inevitable. With this commercial failure and with O'Casey's slow gestation of a new play, his reputation as genius and money-spinner was somewhat deflated. O'Casey tended to think that it was the Abbey rejection which harmed him commercially. If anything, however, the publicity given the Abbey rejection simply whetted interest in the Cochran production. The real reasons for the decline in O'Casey's fortunes on the commercial stage were the tenor of the times and the expense involved in producing large, complicated, and somewhat experimental plays with rather unpalatable themes. The three early plays had certainly been ferocious enough in their statement, but they also had more memorable comic characterizations that evoked a lot of laughter. If it looked profitable, a commercial management might take a chance on art once, but, as a character in a later O'Casey play remarked, "Business is business."

In the next several years, O'Casey wrote a good deal of casual journalism and worked on *Within the Gates*; in 1928, he saw the birth of his first son. Despite a film of *Juno*, his income was declining, and so the production of *Gates* in 1934 was most welcome. The unsuccessful London production further harmed his commercial reputation, but another production, initiated by the enthusiasm of the influential American critic George Jean Nathan, opened in New York in the fall. With help from rich friends, O'Casey was able to travel to New York for rehearsals. Rather predictably, as with the *Tassie*, the play was not a commercial success, although the mixed notices contained much laudatory comment.

O'Casey now found it difficult to get important commercial productions, and the next years saw a good deal of miscellaneous writing. His frustrations with the commercial theatre were reflected in his lively, funny, and acid collection of theatrical comment, *The Flying Wasp*, of 1937. Then, in 1939, the first volume of his lengthy autobiography appeared, and five more volumes followed at intervals until 1954.

In 1935, his second son was born, and in 1938, at Shaw's suggestion, he moved to Devon to be near the experimental school, Dartington Hall, which all of his children subsequently attended. His last child, a daughter, was born in 1939.

In 1940, his communist extravaganza *The Star Turns Red* was given an amateur production in London by the Unity Theatre, and in 1943, Shelagh Richards presented his *Red Roses for Me*, a partial return to his first dramatic manner, in Dublin. Productions of later plays—*Purple Dust* in Liverpool in 1945, *Oak Leaves and Lavender* in Hammersmith in 1947, and *Cock-a-Doodle Dandy* in Newcastle-upon-Tyne in 1949—only showed that for the moment he was a back number in the commercial theatre.

His next important production, and one which heralded an upswing in his fortunes, was that of *The Bishop's Bonfire* in Dublin in 1955. Produced by Cyril Cusack and directed by Tyrone Guthrie at the Gaiety Theatre, it was the first new O'Casey play in Dublin in years and occasioned a good deal of interest in Ireland and abroad. Ireland in the middle 1950s, before the advent of television, was still in the grip of the provincial insularity, bourgeois stuffiness, and clerical puritanism that O'Faolain* had railed at a decade before in *The Bell*.* O'Casey, because of his communism and his occasional combatively critical letters to the Irish press, had become anathema to the more hidebound sections of the community. Consequently, there was a mild pother about the production, and the Irish critics reviewed it with a more strident denunciation than either the play or the production warranted. Nevertheless, O'Casey's fortunes were finally on the mend. The English notices of the *Bonfire* were rather favorable, and then in 1956 there began a long-running off-Broadway production of *Purple Dust*. However, 1956 was not a happy year: O'Casey's second son, Niall, died of leukemia.

O'Casey's deteriorating relations with Ireland received wide publicity in 1958 over his new play, *The Drums of Father Ned*. O'Casey had been begged to allow a production of the play for the Dublin Theatre Festival. However, when John Charles McQuaid, the archbishop of Dublin, refused to say an inaugural Mass for a festival containing works by O'Casey, Beckett,* and Joyce,* the Festival director hastily canceled the production of *Bloomsday*, an adaptation of *Ulysses*. O'Casey and Beckett then withdrew their works, and the Festival for that year was abandoned. *Drums* received its first production by amateurs in Lafayette, Indiana, in 1959.

In 1960, a couple of academic books appeared on O'Casey, heralding a new critical attention that was to burgeon, particularly after the playwright's death, into a spate of books, articles, and even a *Sean O'Casey Review*. In 1962, his last long play received its initial production at an American university, and in the same year an American university press published a collection of his early fugitive material, *Feathers from the Green Crow*. Whether this academic acceptance spurred any of the increasing interest in his plays by the commercial theatre is debatable, but at least it belatedly confirmed his acceptance into the hierarchy of modern letters.

In 1963, O'Casey issued a collection of essays, *Under a Coloured Cap*. After the *Father Ned* affair, he had banned professional productions of his plays in Ireland, but he rescinded the ban for the Abbey productions of *Juno* and *The Plough* at the World Theatre Festival in London in 1964. He was now all but nearly blind, and on September 18, 1964, after a second heart attack, he died in Devon.

Despite his long and extraordinary autobiography and a mass of miscellaneous writing, O'Casey will be remembered primarily as a playwright. For many years, critical opinion about his plays asserted that the three early slum plays were lasting achievements of rough genius, but that, after his departure from the Abbey Theatre and Dublin, his work deteriorated. There was little consensus about the value of individual late plays, but they were generally regarded as flawed experiments. A demurrer to this view was taken by the Irish critics who almost unanimously denounced all of the late plays as hopeless failures. However, elements other than a calmly critical judiciousness impelled their strident comment. If the condemnation of Ireland may be explained by religiosity and rancor, the apathy of England and America may be explained by a basic law of the modern theatre, which is that critical adulation almost invariably follows rather than precedes successful commercial production. Conversely, when O'Casey failed commercially, he had, therefore, failed artistically.

In the dismissal of the late plays, it was customary to look back to the slum plays as unqualified masterpieces; even the recent academic discussion of O'Casey has accepted this view. Still, even in the initial praise for the earliest productions, there were dissenting voices from several notable Irish men of letters. Indeed, to this day some members of the Dublin intelligentsia speak disparagingly of the early work. The reason usually given is poor construction. There is some accuracy in this stricture, although recent academic apologists persist in thinking that everything in a masterpiece must be masterly. A more judicious view would probably be that O'Casey's first long plays are flawed, but contain such striking virtues that the flaws, particularly in a good production, are overwhelmed. This seems a sounder conclusion than simply viewing the Dublin "trilogy" as ever more skillful versions of Chekhovian tragicomedy. By such a standard, the *Gunman* and *Juno* are saved from structural catastrophe only by arbitrary and illogical surprises of genius.

Both the *Gunman* and *Juno* illustrate O'Casey's great strengths: his brilliantly comic observation, his rich dialogue, and his striking and mordant technique of shifting abruptly from the comic to the tragic. In both plays, however, the comic is the more pervasive and powerful element. The *Gunman* is mainly a succession of illustrative comic dialogues, in which examples of cowardice are sometimes subtly and sometimes broadly exposed. These illustrations are threaded together by a thin strand of plot. Indeed, the plot is so tenuous that two major characters of the action, the gunman and the girl, are only sketchily indicated, while the comic characters of the illustrations are much more fully developed. Then, after the illustrative characters have been developed, the plot is arbitrarily, swiftly, and shockingly concluded.

The comedy of *Juno* is more brilliant, and the tragedy is more developed. When they are merged in the extraordinarily ironic final scene, we have a memorable rather than a momentary eloquence. However, the vividness of the dialogue, the strikingness of the characterization, and the intensity of the ending are so remarkable that the play's intrinsic conventionality is forgiven or forgotten. The main strand of plot is a variation on the legacy or Cinderella theme, and one minor plot, that of the daughter, is even more well-worn in its depiction of the seduced and abandoned heroine. In addition, Mary's reading of such "advanced" writers as Ibsen must make her the very last of the nineteenth century's new women. It has been noted that Captain Boyle and Joxer Daly are but new representations of the braggart soldier and the parasite, whose provenance stretches back through the Elizabethans to the Romans and even the Greeks. However, such loving detail has been expended on these two cronies that their individuality is etched in the memory. The daughter, the son, and even, despite her eloquent third act speech, the mother are not developed far beyond stage types.

If Elizabethan tragedies are often punctuated with short scenes of comic relief, O'Casey's first two tragedies are overwhelmingly scenes of comedy, interrupted by short, shocking fragments of tragic relief. The most extended scene in *Juno* is the second act party which does not advance the plot, but which is so superbly comic that it creates its own necessity. The death of Tancred which arbitrarily concludes this hooley is a theatrical shock, but no less arbitrary than the conclusion of the *Gunman*. In the unforgettable conclusion of the third act, however, O'Casey has moved from the arbitrary to the inevitable, and the extent of our surprise at the inevitable is what makes the conclusion of *Juno* literature as well as drama. Also in this third act, the characters of Boyle and Joxer are both darkened, and O'Casey has begun to move from the static illustration of his first plays toward the fluid development of *The Plough and the Stars*.

The *Plough* has no comic characters as memorable as Boyle and Joxer, but in every other way it represents such an advance in technique, and therefore in power, that it is regarded as O'Casey's early, and possibly his only thoroughgoing, masterpiece. The significant technical achievement is the mastery of a large cast in a much more complex plot than O'Casey had previously attempted. At the same time, the terms of the statement are broader, and the particularizing texture of the dialogue is rarely sacrificed to the theme.

As in Chekhov's major plays, the story is told by means of a broad plot and many individual illustrative plots. The broad plot charts the 1916 Rising—its gestation, its gathering momentum, its actuality, and its defeat. Simultaneously, the individual stories of the Clitheroes, of Bessie, Fluther, Mollser, and the other tenement dwellers, are worked out in reaction to the broad social drama. And, at the end of the play, as in Chekhov, the small strands and the large one are knitted together in a tragicomic irony of devastating power.

The play has flaws. The most brilliant comic scene, that in the pub of the second act, has a static and illustrative quality about it; indeed, the scene was originally the basis for a one-act play. However, like the hooley scene in *Juno*, the pub scene does not depend merely on its comic verve to sustain it, but it has emphatically underlined counterpoints to the ongoing broad plot. It has a thematic relevance and is therefore a part of the plot, as the joyous *Juno* scene is not.

There are a few minor blemishes. The young married couple tends to be a trifle mawkish, while the tubercular girl is too sketchily developed to be more than simply a stark illustration, and the Lady from Rathmines needs more development if she is not to be merely a satiric joke. Even some major characters, such as Bessie and Fluther, could stand further development, so that their nobility under stress could be dramatized rather than merely asserted. And certainly the madness of Nora in the last act needs more preparation to keep it from merely arbitrary shock and melodramatic coloring.

Despite these flaws, many of which can be minimized in production, the play has a development of plot and a darkening of tone that sweeps it towards a conclusion blackly comic, tragically ironic, and ferociously harrowing.

The plays of O'Casey's middle period have been lumped together as experiments in expressionism, but it would be more apt to call them mod ern versions of the Morality and Miracle plays. Expressionism emphasizes technique, but the medieval plays emphasized statement. In the last act of *Juno* and in most of the *Plough*, O'Casey had already tended to stress state- ment more than characterization or comedy. For the most part, the middle plays are yet more emphatic attempts to underline some general statement about society rather than to illustrate some aspects of human nature.

The mingling of styles in *The Silver Tassie* has occasioned some casu- istical defenses from O'Casey's purely aesthetic apologists. Probably the fact is simply that O'Casey thought it much more urgent to indict mankind for the mad masochism of creating its own agonies than to create a tidily unified work of art. To him, the unity of the play lay in its statement rather than in its mode of statement, or even the coherence of its plot.

Nevertheless, the expressionistic second act, startling though it was in context, was less of a novelty for O'Casey than was immediately apparent. In 1923, the Abbey had produced a minor one-act play of his, *Kathleen Listens In*, in which he attempted broad statement by type characters. Of course, in both *Juno* and the *Plough* he had already utilized a basically illustrative act which nearly halts the progress of the plot. The great differ- ence of Act II of the *Tassie* is that its language strikingly differs from the rest of the play. *The Wasteland* of Eliot and the *Ulysses* of Joyce set a precedent for startling variations in levels of language, but the theatre as the most public of literary arts is also the most conventional and the slowest to change its conventions. Readers of O'Casey's neo-Biblical chants have trouble accepting the repetitive simplicities. Yet, in a well-produced staging the language does not only hold, but even rivets, the attention with much of the sardonic eloquence which O'Casey desired. The value of *Juno* and the *Plough* can be easily appreciated on the page, but the value of the *Tassie* and the other middle plays can most fully be appreciated on the stage. The paradox of these plays is that, in trying to stress statement, O'Casey was pushed deeper into technique and the technique was often more theatrical than literary. Whether the technique was always successful is another question and one to be answered by production. Recent revivals of the *Tassie* by the Royal Court and the Abbey suggest that, in this instance, the strength of the play's theme and the savagery of its tone are cohesive enough to draw the play's disparate elements together into a moving theatrical experience.

Unlike the *Tassie, Within the Gates* (1934) was in one style, and its theatricality was, if anything, more inventive. Moreover, its statement and scope were as ambitious as those of the *Tassie*. Nevertheless, *Gates* has not been commercially revived and is generally much less highly regarded. The reason is probably that for three acts of the *Tassie* O'Casey held to a semi-realism which worked more or less conventionally. In *Gates*, he opts entirely for a stylized plot and type characters in order, of course, to emphasize his statement. However, on the page the morality play baldness of plot, language, characterization, and, finally, statement is particularly daunting, and a reader is tempted to dismiss the play as an experiment which missed fire. While the inventiveness of the play is of a high order, it resides less in the literary elements than in the theatrical ones. This is an aural and visual play which is couched in demanding theatrical terms. Even more than the *Tassie*, the question about this modern morality for the urban world is how fully in production do the theatrical virtues compensate for the lack of literary ones. To judge by reports of the play's only notable production, the theatricality in that instance did not altogether overcome the simplicity. Like other so-called flawed O'Casey plays, *Gates* probably remains a score which has never found its conductor.

The Star Turns Red (1940) is generally considered O'Casey's weakest long play. It has the morality play simplicity of *Gates*, although there are a couple of scenes of mere funning and a symbolic theatrical use of costume and decor. Its strength of statement, coupled with its weakness of invention, make it seem more propaganda than art.

Red Roses for Me (1943) is regarded with some nostalgic benevolence by many critics but has never proved itself upon the stage. The critics' gentle treatment of the play may stem from the first two acts which resemble, albeit palely, the early manner of the Dublin trilogy. But although somewhat realistic, these first two acts are little more inventive than the stylized *Stars Turns Red*. The hero, Ayamonn Breydon, is, like Donal Davoren of the *Gunman*, largely autobiographical. However, where Davoren was admired for his lyricism but condemned for his cravenness, Breydon is presented as so thoroughly admirable that he seems no more individual than the type characters of *Gates* or the *Star*. The play has a lyric third act of much theatrical potential, but its illustrative power is somewhat lessened by the first two acts, which in their own way have also been little more than illustration. In these acts of static exposition, O'Casey's most intrusive characteristic is his language which here has become gaudy and bloated and tends toward self-parody. Most of the plot is huddled up unsatisfactorily in the first scene of the last act. The lyric coda of the last scene is more theatrical and has a haunting final song. If this last scene does save the play from disaster, it probably does not compensate for the lack of drama.

The self-indulgent lyricism of *Red Roses* is less evident in *Purple Dust* (1945). In it, O'Casey is making a less broad, less urgent, and less personal statement. Primarily, he is contrasting old rural Irish virtues practiced mainly by the young to modern urban decadence which belongs mainly to the old. He is no less involved with his opinions, which indeed will become the major themes of his last work, but his tone is less frantic. This ease seems to allow his fancy a freer play, and this relaxed geniality makes even his villains more absurd than evil. *Purple Dust* is aimed with a smaller, less taut bow and so does not travel as far or hit as hard as the other middle plays, but it is much closer to the center of its target.

Oak Leaves and Lavender, its successor, is no major work but is probably one of the more undervalued of O'Casey's plays. Taking for its subject the British war effort, it was produced in 1947 when the issue was dead. To war-weary Britons, it must have seemed rather like yesterday's newspaper. Now, when the subject has receded, like World War I of *The Silver Tassie* into history, this play might well repay revival. It has the thematic urgency and strong simplicities of the middle plays before *Purple Dust*, some of *Purple Dust*'s warmth, as well as a provocative theatrically in its set and sound effects.

The last group of long plays, of which *Purple Dust* seems a harbinger, consists of *Cock-a-Doodle Dandy* (first produced in 1949), *The Bishop's Bonfire* (1955), *The Drums of Father Ned* (1959), and *Behind the Green Curtains* (1962). These last plays are closely connected in both theme and technique. All of them have at their center the opposition of youth and age. If the plays of the middle period can be regarded as patterns of the medieval Morality play, the plays of the last period can be seen as versions of the Pastoral. In them, O'Casey posits a symbolic Golden Age which is either defeating the materialistic world of the present or being defeated by it. Yet, unlike the middle plays, these are less didactic than opinionated. The difference between the Morality and the Pastoral is not that the Pastoral is divorced from opinion, but that its opinions are less overtly expressed and more fancifully embroidered.

There is a contrast in tone among the last four plays. The first and the third, *Cock* and *Father Ned,* are gay; the second and the fourth, *Bonfire* and *Green Curtains*, are glum. The gay and optimistic plays, in which the Golden Age triumphs, are much the more successful—richer in situation, dialogue, whimsical invention, and comic theatricality. The glum plays, in which the Golden Age is defeated, have moments of inspired feeling, but definite arid passages where O'Casey's pessimistic feelings pull him back to the didactic exhortation of the middle plays. It is in these moments also that, perhaps in compensation, his theatricality becomes emphatic and exaggerated rather than effective.

The conclusion of *The Bishop's Bonfire* and the whole last two acts of *Behind the Green Curtains* are cases in point. Both passages seem rather frantically bolstered by an almost operatic melodrama which is extraordinarily difficult to rise to. With inspired direction, these passages might be made to work, but in the original productions they appeared as major flaws in the plays.

Such dead passages hardly exist in *Cock* and *Father Ned*, which have a comic exuberance and facility of invention rare outside of the most inspired musical comedy. Indeed, in technique both plays seem trembling on the verge of that form. Music pervades the background while characters in gaudy costumes repeatedly burst into song, lyric declamation, or dramatic dance. With these two plays, O'Casey concluded his career with a flamboyant originality as fine as the best of his early work.

O'Casey's one-act plays have received little critical attention, but quite a few productions. In all, they form a body of work much less flawed and quite as various in form as his full-length work. They range from the tragicomedy of his first manner in *Nannie's Night Out*, to the farcical music hall sketch of *A Pound on Demand*, and even to the dancing pastoral of *Time to Go*. Like Strindberg, Shaw, and Tennessee Williams, O'Casey has worked consistently in the short form, and like them he is a master of it.

O'Casey's dramatic criticism has been collected mainly in *The Flying Wasp* (1937), *The Green Crow* (1956), *Under a Coloured Cap* (1963), and in the posthumous *Blasts and Benedictions* (1967). Like D. H. Lawrence's *Studies in Classic American Literature,* O'Casey's criticism is slapdash but vital. The best of it has an infectious verve and a pervasive sense of the author's character. Occasionally, it sinks into a repetitive thinness and stridency, but its freshness is a welcoming antidote to a multitude of dry commentaries.

The six volumes of autobiography were published over a long period, from 1939 to 1954, and then collectively in America in 1954 under the title of *Mirror in My House*, and again in England in 1963 under the simple title of *Autobiographies*. They form a massive and characteristic work. The many facets of O'Casey's personality are luminously apparent, and the chapters vary eclectically in tone, style, and technique. The books do not form a precise and factual account, but an impressionistic, and even sometimes a fantastic one. The best volumes are the first three or four which treat of O'Casey's youth and manhood in Dublin. The last two volumes, *Rose and Crown* (1952) and *Sunset and Evening Star* (1954), are more diffuse and garrulous, and occasionally are shrilly combative. All of the books range fascinatingly in tone from the noble to the whining, from the satiric to the lyric. They range in style from passages of inordinate eloquence to ones of bad semi-puns, gushy fervor, and what Orwell called "basic Joyce." They might, however, stand as a full testament of the faults and qualities of one of the most individual and brilliant figures of contemporary Irish writing.

O'Casey's reputation, which had begun to rise again in the last five or ten years of his life, has since continued to grow. Many of his neglected plays have now received belated attention. For instance, in recent years the Abbey Theatre has done interesting revivals of the *Tassie, Red Roses, Purple Dust,* and *Cock-a-Doodle Dandy.* A great spate of critical attention has continued. Ten or twelve full-length biographical or critical studies have appeared; there have been several collections of criticism; a full-scale bibliography has appeared; and part of a projected three-volume edition of his letters. The current O'Casey boom is probably an overreaction to the years in which he was neglected, and some final reassessment and deevaluation may be looked for in the years ahead. Whatever that reassessment may determine, he will remain at the very least one of Ireland's major dramatists and most vivid individuals.

WORKS: *Windfalls.* London: Macmillan, 1934; *The Flying Wasp.* London: Macmillan, 1937; *Collected Plays.* 4 vols. London: Macmillan/New York: St. Martin's, 1949-1951; *The Green Crow.* New York: George Braziller, 1956; *Mirror in My House: The Autobiographies of Sean O'Casey.* 2 vols. New York: Macmillan, 1956. Reprinted as *Autobiographies.* 2 vols. London: Macmillan, 1963; *The Bishop's Bonfire,* London & New York: Macmillan, 1957; *The Drums of Father Ned.* London: Macmillan/New York: St. Martin's, 1960; *Behind the Green Curtains and Other Plays.* London: Macmillan/New York: St. Martin's, 1961; *Feathers from the Green Crow.* Robert Hogan, ed. Columbia: University of Missouri Press, 1962/London: Macmillan, 1963; *Under a Colored Cap.* London: Macmillan/New York: St. Martin's, 1963; *Blasts and Benedictions.* Ronald Ayling, ed. London: Macmillan/New York: St. Martin's, 1967; *The Letters of Sean O'Casey.* Vol. 1, 1910-1941, David Krause, ed. New York: Macmillan, 1975. REFERENCES: Ayling, Ronald, ed. *Sean O'Casey.* London: Macmillan, 1968; Hogan, Robert. *The Experiments of Sean O'Casey.* New York: St. Martin's, 1960; Kilroy, Thomas, ed. *Sean O'Casey.* Englewood Cliffs, N.J.: Prentice-Hall, 1975; Krause, David. *Sean O'Casey, The Man and his Work.* London: MacGibbon & Kee/New York: Macmillan, 1960; Margulies, Martin B. *The Early Life of Sean O'Casey.* Dublin: Dolmen, 1970; Mikhail, E. H., & O'Riordan, John. *The Sting & the Twinkle: Conversations with Sean O'Casey.* London: Macmillan, 1974; O'Casey, Eileen. *Sean.* J. C. Trewin, ed. London: Macmillan, 1971; Krause, David. *Sean O'Casey and His World.* London: Thames and Hudson, [1976]; Ayling, Ronald, and Durkin, Michael J. *Sean O'Casey, a Bibliography.* [London & Basingstoke]: Macmillan, [1978].

O'CONNOR, CONLETH (1947-), poet. O'Connor was born in Newbridge, County Kildare in 1947 and lives in Dun Laoghaire. He has published a thin volume of verse and poetic prose entitled *Trinities* (1976), and he has written some fugitive stories and unpublished plays. His work in *Trinities* is interesting in language, but it seldom, even on its own terms, approaches effective poetic form.

WORK: *Trinities*. Clondalkin, County Dublin: Profile, 1976.

O'CONNOR, FRANK (1903-1966), short story writer and man of letters. Frank O'Connor, a pseudonym for Michael O'Donovan, is known primarily for his short stories but claims an equally high place in Anglo-Irish literature for his translations from Irish verse. He also wrote novels, biography, criticism, poetry, and autobiography. Michael O'Donovan was a person of fierce sympathies; his idealism was often too buoyant, his bitterness too heavy; his personal affairs swirled in a maze of conflicting impulses. But in his writing Frank O'Connor was a model of discipline and self-control. Everything he wrote displays his contending spirit, but his stories and translations in particular reveal his struggle for artistic integrity and personal freedom.

Michael O'Donovan was born on September 17, 1903, in Cork, where he was raised in impoverished conditions. These early years are brilliantly drawn by O'Connor in *An Only Child* (1964). Being frail and sensitive as well as poor, Michael found escape in his books and his dreams. Formal schooling ended when he was twelve, though not before he had come under the tutelage of Daniel Corkery,* who introduced him to the Irish language and the richness of his native past and showed him the breadth of European culture. Corkery's nationalistic fervor led Michael to enlist with the Volunteers and eventually to stand adamant with the Republicans in the Civil War. For this activity he was imprisoned at Gormanstown. Much of his early writing emanates from the unrestrained idealism of those troubled times; his first volume of stories, *Guests of the Nation* (1931), indulges the romanticism of ambushes, guns, and flying-columns. The brilliance and appeal of the title story are beyond question. Abstract "duty" forces three Irish rebels to execute their two English hostages after a long night of cards, drink, and talk. The narrator's response to what he had done sounds that note of tragic disaffection which O'Connor himself carried away from prison; the same lonely voice is heard again in story after story. It is heard, too, in his biography of Michael Collins, *The Big Fellow* (1937), a strident and uncompromising book which says as much about Michael O'Donovan as Michael Collins. It represents O'Connor's most extreme attitude toward the Revolution; disillusioned by the Catholic-nationalist establishment of de Valera, he asserted that the heat of genius had been replaced by the chill of normality.

After his release from prison, O'Connor taught Irish, started a theatre group in Cork, and earned his living as a librarian in Sligo, Wicklow, and Cork. While serving in Wicklow he met AE* and began publishing in *The Irish Statesman** under the name "Frank O'Connor" (his middle name and his mother's maiden name). During the short life of that influential magazine, O'Connor contributed over seventy-five pieces (poems, articles, reviews, and stories) and became a prominent figure in Dublin literary circles. He sketched these productive years in *My Father's Son* (1967), including his friendship with AE and Yeats* and his tumultuous tenure on the Board of Directors of the Abbey Theatre.* During that decade in Dublin, he published two volumes of stories, *Guests of the Nation* (1931) and *Bones of Contention* (1936); a novel, *The Saint and Mary Kate* (1932); the biography of Collins; a volume of poetry, *Three Old Brothers* (1936); three volumes of verse translations from the Irish; and even a few plays. By his own admission he was "fumbling for a style" during these years. In the two novels *The Saint and Mary Kate* and *Dutch Interior* (1940), he not only experimented with an unfamiliar form but also explored his past. The young people in both novels seek escape from the provincial narrowness of Cork—from poverty or boredom or loneliness. Like the poems he had been writing for over ten years, the novels were improvisational and imbalanced. But where the poems of *Three Old Brothers* present a detached and mannered voice, the novels are serious and personal. Still, the poetry is as direct and unpretentious as his finest prose; the novels are as dramatic and intense as his stories. Which is to say, these early improvisations on the theme of the writer creating himself help to explain why O'Connor inevitably stayed with the short story. He was a lyric poet ill at ease with the formal limitations of poetry. He was a storyteller interested more in the flash points of human experience than in sustained artifice. As flawed as they are, the novels and poems deal with most of the issues which dominate O'Connor's stories, particularly the burden of loneliness.

By 1939, O'Connor had resigned from the Abbey Theatre after a bitter feud, resigned his library post, married a young Welsh actress, and moved to Wicklow to write. By any reckoning, 1940 marks a dividing line for all Irish writers: Yeats was dead and Joyce* soon would be; a new international war had broken out, testing Ireland's political strength, to say nothing of its intellectual integrity. Censorship and shrinking markets in Britain and America closed the usual publishing channels to writers of O'Connor's generation. Some followed Joyce into exile; O'Connor stayed. In 1940, a new magazine, *The Bell,** appeared in Dublin, edited by O'Connor's old Cork friend Sean O'Faolain.* For the first few years O'Connor was the poetry editor. O'Connor and O'Faolain and the other "strayed revellers" of the Literary Revival sought to clear the air of "convention, imitation, traditionalism, wishful thinking." They also needed an outlet for their work. *The Bell*, literally and figuratively, kept writers and their work alive during those lean years; it stimulated the second wave of significant literary activity in Ireland in this century. O'Connor's role was substantial. In addition to his essays, reviews, and stinging letters to the editor, he contributed some of his best stories ("Bridal Night," "Long Road to Ummera," and "Uprooted") and translations, including "The Midnight Court."

Both O'Faolain and O'Connor believed that the esoteric and elitist forms used by Yeats and Joyce failed to touch the majority of Irishmen. Thus, they took their concerns directly to the "common reader." O'Connor's struggle with Irish provincialism during these years took the form of a campaign to preserve that heritage held in the monasteries, castles, and megalithic sites scattered about the country. The first skirmishes appeared in *The Bell*; more articles appeared in *The Irish Times* and *The Sunday Independent*. *Irish Miles* (1947) was the culmination of this campaign, which established O'Connor as one of the abrasive voices of conscience in Ireland. It is a travel book only to the extent that *The Big Fellow* is biography; as with everything else he wrote it is more like autobiography, for O'Connor believed that a writer's works are an allegory of his life. In the account of the cycling trips he and his wife had been taking around the Irish countryside in search of ruins and other antiquities, *Irish Miles* is vintage O'Connor. It is also Michael O'Donovan playing himself—effusive and restless, lyrical and irascible. Above all, it reveals a storyteller in hot pursuit of stories. These cycling trips kept his curious and contentious spirit alive, but his writing was insufficient to support his growing family. He therefore resorted to broadcasting readings of his stories and of Irish poetry, personal reminiscences, and literary opinions for the BBC. What is striking about his broadcasting and journalistic endeavors is that he did not see them as alien to his artistic commitment. To him a story required the voice of a man speaking. Literature—fiction, poetry, or drama—he considered to be nothing less than the art of collaboration.

By the time he published his third volume of stories, O'Connor had not only explored the limits of the story but had begun to expand them. Consequently, *Crab Apple Jelly* (1944) is at once the most varied and disciplined collection he was to produce. As the title implies, its voice is both sweet and tart, entertaining and serious. O'Connor was at a sufficient distance from his subjects to observe and accept without casting blame or becoming involved. Such stories as "Bridal Night," "Michael's Wife," and "Uprooted" leave little doubt about the power of his prose to evoke highly poetic visual images. Like his translations from the Irish, however, these stories are "lyrical" not because of static description but because the sound of the voice is heard within a supremely resonant environment. The stories of *Crab Apple Jelly* represent the refinement of his technique of exploiting the speaking voice, the voice of the broadcaster or the *shanachie*. Nowhere is this oral quality more evident than in "The Long Road to Ummera," a simple tale about an old woman's wish to be buried in the mountain home of her people. In the same volume were O'Connor's first stories about sexual repression within Irish life; "The Mad Lomasneys," however, was really more subtle than shocking. Still, O'Connor's name gradually became associated with sexual impiety and unpatriotic complaint. *Dutch Interior* (1940) was officially banned as were his translations of "The Midnight Court" and, later, *The Common Chord* (1948) and *Traveller's Samples* (1951).

Thus, by 1950, O'Connor had created a vacuum for himself in Ireland. The pressures of war and his extended absences had complicated his personal life. It was probably inevitable that in 1951, unable to support himself in Dublin or to cope with the turmoil of censorship and his own divorce, O'Connor accepted invitations to teach in the United States. This "exile" was both a personal and a professional necessity; he was able to heal his personal life and to plunge into his writing again. His stories and autobiographical sketches drew great acclaim as they appeared with increasing frequency in American magazines. Readers were more than likely charmed by the deceptively simple manner of his writing, particularly those stories of childhood and adolescence for which he is best known ("My Oedipus Complex," "The Drunkard," "My First Confession"). As his writing became more personal, O'Connor attained a kind of detachment by way of technique. Emotion and lyrical expressiveness were dropped in favor of formal control. A strategy of containment (scaling down of issue, situations, and language) had always been the mark of an O'Connor story. But the stories of the 1950s, particularly those in *Domestic Relations* (1956), are rather too simple, too balanced, too smooth. It is not without significance that O'Connor was also writing his most extensive literary criticism at this time.

O'Connor had always seen life through a veil of literature, and from his first reviews in *The Irish Statesman* to his last articles in *The New York Times Review of Books*, O'Connor's literary opinions were assumptive and flamboyant, revealing as much about him as what he happened to be writing about. *The Mirror in the Roadway* (1956) and *The Lonely Voice* (1962) both grew out of his American teaching experiences. O'Connor took literature seriously, and these books stand not only as explorations of the novel and the short story but also as a defense of literature. In the one, he is an audacious amateur, reading such giants as Dickens, Flaubert, and Tolstoy. What one hears in *The Lonely Voice* is one great writer of short stories collaborating with other great writers of short stories. It is a defense of the writer himself. Shortly after that book, O'Connor turned his hand to the book suggested thirty years before by Yeats—a history of Irish literature. *The Backward Look* (1967) is actually a criticism of a larger life, a synthesis of a culture; it is a personal statement because O'Connor was strictly an Irish writer and Irish culture was his only battleground. In the first half of the book, O'Connor the translator is seen at work, talking about Irish literature in Irish. In the second half, the Anglo-Irish short story writer holds forth on Irish literature in English. The backward look is a forward impulse: coming to terms with what you are, you confront what you are becoming. O'Connor's collaboration with Merriman and Swift,* Ferguson* and Yeats, is a magical and improvisational process.

O'Connor married again in 1953 and frequently visited Ireland with his young American wife after 1956. He had kept tenaciously to his writing during the years of separation and exile. Actually, during the last ten years of his life he published more than in any comparable period in his career. Ireland had remained his primary source of imaginative energy and though his return (finally, in 1961 after a stroke) was not accompanied by an infusion of magic, his writing appeared to regain something of its old vigor and audacity. *Kings, Lords, and Commons* (1959) is the culmination of almost forty years of devotion to the translation of Irish poetry into English. *The Backward Look* is an equally mature and considered affirmation of Ireland's rich heritage. *A Set of Variations* (published posthumously), a collection of stories written mainly in the 1960s, shows flashes of the rough intensity found in his early stories. As a whole, the volume displays a range of themes, characters, and styles as extensive as *Crab Apple Jelly*. O'Connor had moved closer to himself while assuming once again the detached narrative voice. The stories about priests at the end of the volume carry a distinct emotional power. Like the title story, they represent O'Connor's last affirmations of the imaginative way of life, or what he called his "lyric cry in the face of destiny."

O'Connor died in Dublin on March 10, 1966. James Plunkett* in *The Gems She Wore* describes O'Connor at the end of his life as having "the air of someone who had found where he belonged, not an easy thing for a writer to achieve in the Ireland of his time." At the graveside oration, Brendan Kennelly* suggested for an epitaph the lines of Yeats about the "life like a gambler's throw." With all the arrogance of the self-taught, Michael O'Donovan/Frank O'Connor had improvised his way to greatness in a "lonely, personal art," producing simple stories of impeccable design carrying sparse revelations about common folks in language direct and alive. He once said that where Yeats, Synge,* and the rest have their "presences" to offer eternity, "I have only my voices." The voice of such books as *Kings, Lords, and Commons*, *Irish Miles*, and *The Backward Look* will persist, but his stories will inevitably stand as his most enduring contribution to modern literature and to Irish life.

JAMES H. MATTHEWS

WORKS: *Guests of the Nation*. London: Macmillan, 1931. (Stories); *The Saint and Mary Kate*. London: Macmillan, 1932. (Novel); *The Wild Bird's Nest*. Dublin: Cuala, 1932. (Translations from the Irish); *Bones of Contention and Other Stories*. London: Macmillan, 1936; *Three Old Brothers and Other Poems*. London: Nelson, 1936; *The Big Fellow*. London: Nelson, 1937. (Biography of Michael Collins); *The Fountain of Magic*. London: Macmillan, 1939. (Translations from the Irish); *Dutch Interior*. London: Macmillan, 1940. (Novel); *Three Tales*. Dublin: Cuala, 1941; *Crab*

Apple Jelly. London: Macmillan, 1944. (Stories); *Towards an Appreciation of Literature*. Dublin: Metropolitan Publishing Co., 1945. (Criticism); *Selected Stories*. Dublin: Maurice Fridberg, 1946; *The Art of the Theatre*. Dublin & London: Maurice Fridberg, 1947. (Criticism); *The Common Chord*. London: Macmillan, 1947. (Stories). *Irish Miles*. London: Macmillan, 1947. (Travel/architecture); *The Road to Stratford*. London: Methuen, 1948. (Criticism); *Traveller's Samples*. London: Macmillan, 1951. (Stories); *The Stories of Frank O'Connor*. New York: Alfred A. Knopf, 1952/London: Hamish Hamilton, 1953; *More Stories by Frank O'Connor*. New York: Alfred A. Knopf, 1954, 1967; *The Mirror in the Roadway*. New York: Alfred A. Knopf, 1956. (Criticism); *Domestic Relations*. New York: Alfred A. Knopf/London: Hamish Hamilton, 1957; *Kings, Lords, & Commons*. New York: Alfred A. Knopf, 1959. (Translations from the Irish); *Shakespeare's Progress*. Cleveland: World, 1960. (Revised & enlarged version of *The Road to Stratford*); *An Only Child*. New York: Alfred A. Knopf, 1961/London: Macmillan, 1962. (Autobiography); *The Lonely Voice*. Cleveland: World, 1962/London: Macmillan, 1963. (Criticism); *Collection Two*. London: Macmillan, 1964. (Stories); *The Backward Look*. London: Macmillan, 1967/published in the United States as *A Short History of Irish Literature*, New York: Putnam, 1967; *My Father's Son*. London: Macmillan, 1968/New York: Alfred A. Knopf, 1969. (Autobiography); *Collection Three*. London: Macmillan, 1969/published in the United States as *A Set of Variations*, New York: Alfred A. Knopf, 1969; *The Journal of Irish Literature* 4 (January 1975), a Frank O'Connor Number. James H. Matthews, ed.   REFERENCES. Matthews, James H. *Frank O'Connor*. Lewisburg, Pa.: Bucknell University Press, 1976; Sheehy, Maurice, ed. *Michael/Frank: Studies on Frank O'Connor*. Dublin: Gill & Macmillan, 1969. (Includes the most extensive bibliography of O'Connor's work, as well as essays on most aspects of his work by eminent scholars); Wohlgelernter, Maurice. *Frank O'Connor: An Introduction*. New York: Columbia University Press, 1977.

O'CONNOR, PATRICK JOSEPH. *See* FIACC, PADRAIC.

O'CURRY, EUGENE (1796-1862), scholar. O'Curry was born in Dunaha, County Clare, in 1796. He was self-educated, and in 1834 was employed in the topographical and historical section of the Ordnance Survey. This employment brought him into contact with such learned contemporaries as George Petrie* and John O'Donovan* and made him aware of the rich collections of Irish manuscript material in Dublin, London, and Oxford. With Petrie and O'Donovan, O'Curry laid the foundations of modern scholarship in Irish, by his prodigious cataloguing and voluminous transcribing of Irish manuscripts, as well as his translations of a number of them. On the foundation of the new Catholic University, O'Curry became professor of Irish History and Archaeology and gave his first lectures in 1855. These lectures, published in 1861, ran to over seven hundred pages and gave a full account of the chief Irish medieval manuscripts and their contents. He died in Dublin on July 30, 1862.

WORKS: *The Sick Bed of Cuchulainn and The Only Jealousy of Emer. The "Tri Thruaighe na Scéalaigheachta": The Three Most Sorrowful Tales of Erinn*. Dublin: J. F. Fowles, 1858; *Lectures on the Manuscript Materials of Ancient Irish History*. Dublin: J. Duffy, 1861; *On the Manners and Customs of the Ancient Irish*. 3 vols. London: Williams & Norgate / Dublin: W. B. Kelly / New York: Scribner's, 1873.

O'DONNELL, DONAT. *See* O'BRIEN, CONOR CRUISE.

O'DONNELL, PEADAR (1893-), novelist, editor, and social reformer. O'Donnell was born on February 22, 1893, on a farm at Meenmore, County Donegal, obtained his teaching credentials at St. Patrick's College, Dublin, and taught for several years before espousing socialist views and becoming an organizer for the Transport and General Workers' Union in 1918.

In 1919, he joined the Volunteers and participated in the IRA's guerrilla warfare against the British. He sided with the anti-Treaty forces against the Free Staters. When the Civil War broke out, he was seized in July 1922 and imprisoned for almost two years. His first novel, *Storm*, appeared in 1926, and his second, *Islanders* (1927), attracted considerable literary attention. For several years, he edited both *An t'Oglach* and *An Phoblacht*, and in 1932 he published *The Gates Flew Open*, the first of three perceptive autobiographical commentaries. He continued to combine political and literary concerns, breaking away from the IRA in 1934 to help form the Republican Congress, and in 1936 he began organizing support against Franco. From 1946 until it finally ceased publication in 1954, *The Bell** was edited by O'Donnell. He then campaigned to improve economic conditions in western Ireland, worked to ban the atomic bomb, and served as a delegate to the World Peace Congress. In 1965, he joined the republican Dan Breen in forming a group called the "Irish Voice on Vietnam."

O'Donnell's most persistent theme is his concern for the poor farmers and fisherfolk who live in the west of Ireland, where hunger is omnipresent. Mary Doogan in *Islanders* must starve herself so that her children will have enough to eat. *Adrigoole* is based on a true tragedy involving the death by starvation of a mother and child while the husband is imprisoned. The family had been shunned by its neighbors because of the support it had given to the anti-Treaty group in the Civil War.

In Ireland, even hard work does not bring security because of the rocky, nonfertile soil, the uncertainty of fishing catches, and the storms which oppress the fishermen. To endure, the peasants must hire out their children or take seasonal employment in Scotland. The emigrant laborers then force down the wages and amount of work for the Scottish poor. When Brigid Gallagher in *The Knife* remarks to a Scotswoman working beside her: "Over at home we blame the Scotch for takin' the land we should be on," her co-worker responds: "It's a pickle, an' it's naw you an me can put it right, lassie."

O'Donnell's lifelong goal was to "put it right"—to improve economic conditions for the poor by freeing the land from British domination and from the avarice of the shopkeepers. Idealistically, he advocated the creation of worker-oriented cooperatives, socialist trade unions, and a government controlled by the working class.

As a novelist, O'Donnell's strongest qualities are his exceedingly realistic descriptions, his mastery of dialogue (which is enhanced by his first-hand command of Gaelic speech rhythms and phraseology), and his penetrating character portrayals. On the negative side, his novels are frequently too slow paced, often overly detailed, and sometimes tinged with propaganda. Nevertheless, in his narratives, journalism, and autobiographical studies, O'Donnell has presented a painfully comprehensive picture of Ireland in one of its most turbulent periods.

PAUL A. DOYLE

WORKS: *Storm*. Dublin: Talbot, [1925]; *Islanders*. London: Jonathan Cape, 1928/ published in the United States as *The Way It Was with Them*, New York: Putnam's, 1928; *Adrigoole*. London: Jonathan Cape/New York: Putnams, 1929; *The Knife*. London: Jonathan Cape, 1930/published in the United States as *There Will Be Fighting*, New York: Putnams, 1931; *The Gates Flew Open*. London: Jonathan Cape, 1932. (Autobiography); *Wrack*. London: Jonathan Cape, 1933. (Play); *On the Edge of the Stream*. London: Jonathan Cape, 1934; *Salud! An Irishman in Spain*. London: Methuen, 1937. (Autobiography); *The Big Windows*. London: Jonathan Cape, 1955; *There Will Be Another Day*. Dublin: Dolmen, 1963. (Autobiography); *Proud Island*. Dublin: O'Brien, 1975. REFERENCES: Doyle, Paul A. "Peadar O'Donnell: A Checklist." *Bulletin of Bibliography* 28 (January-March 1971): 3-4; Freyer, Grattan. *Peadar O'Donnell*. Lewisburg, Pa.: Bucknell University Press, 1973; McInerney, Michael. *Peadar O'Donnell: Irish Social Rebel*. Dublin: O'Brien Press, 1976.

O'DONOGHUE, D[AVID] J[AMES] (1866-1917), scholar and editor. O'Donoghue was born in London on July 22, 1866, of Cork parents. In 1896, he came to Dublin and became a bookseller and then, in 1909, librarian to University College, Dublin. Like his friends W. J. Lawrence and Joseph Holloway,* he was a self-taught scholar of prodigious industry and incredible learning. He did much valuable editing, including a Life and Writings of Mangan* and a six-volume edition of Lover.* He also wrote the first biography of William Carleton,* and his *The Poets of Ireland: A Biographical Dictionary* is still an impressive compilation, to which "this Dictionary owes much." He died in Dublin in 1917.

WORKS: ed., *The Humour of Ireland*. London: Walter Scott, 1894; *The Life of William Carleton*. 2 vols. London: Downey, 1896; *The Life and Writings of James Clarence Mangan*. Edinburgh: P. Geddes, 1897; *Life of Robert Emmet*. Dublin: Duffy, 1902; *The Geographical Distribution of Irish Ability*. Dublin: O'Donoghue, 1906; *The Poets of Ireland. A Biographical Dictionary*. Dublin: Hodges, Figgis/London: Henry Frowde, Oxford University Press, 1912.

O'DONOGHUE, JOHN (1900-1964), novelist. O'Donoghue was born in Kerry in 1900, the son of a small farmer. From 1924 to 1931, he served in the Irish police force, the Garda Siochana. Later he joined a monastery, and then he emigrated to England where he worked as a common laborer. His three published volumes are highly autobiographical, and the first and most successful, *In a Quiet Land* (1957), is perhaps the most typical. Nominally a novel, the book is really a simple, straightforward, and vivid evocation of a primitive society that in the author's youth was already dying but that had its roots in centuries past. Perhaps much more than the literary embroideries of Synge,* O'Donoghue's simple, naive, and eloquent books bring alive the rural Ireland of yesterday. He died in London in 1964, while he was working on his fourth book.

WORKS: *In Kerry Long Ago*. London: B. T. Batsford, 1950; *In a Quiet Land*. London: B. T. Batsford, 1957; *In a Strange Land*. London: B. T. Batsford, 1958.

O'DONOVAN, GERALD (1871-1942), novelist. O'Donovan, the intimate friend of Rose Macauley, the English novelist, was born Jeremiah O'Donovan on July 15, 1871, in County Down, far from his family's native Cork. His father was a builder who moved from place to place erecting piers. As a child, O'Donovan attended schools in Cork, Galway, and Sligo. He obtained a poor education, as he later recalled that he even obtained a pass in agriculture—a subject about which he knew nothing.

He entered a seminary to study for the priesthood and then Maynooth College in September 1889. His academic career was unremarkable, though his Irish teacher was Father Eugene O'Growney, a pioneer of the Gaelic League.

In June 1895, O'Donovan was ordained a priest for the diocese of Clonfert. His first appointment was as a curate for Kilmalinoge and Lickmassy, and he lived in Portumna in Galway. In 1896, he was moved to Loughrea as a curate. In that year Dr. Healy, who had been co-adjutor since 1884, became bishop of Clonfert. Under his administration, O'Donovan flourished as an active, socially minded priest of a type unusual in Ireland at that date. His sympathies were liberal, and his theology veered towards the ideas of modernism; reform, improvement, and progress were his watchwords. During these years, he published articles on progressive themes, such as workhouse reform, practical education for girls, village libraries, and the Celtic Revival.

In about 1897, he joined the Irish Agricultural Organisation Society (IAOS), which was spreading the ideas of cooperation in rural Ireland, under the leadership of Sir Horace Plunkett and George Russell.* In June 1901, O'Donovan was elected along with Edward Martyn* as representatives of Connaught on the IAOS committee.

By now he had become administrator in Loughrea and was deeply involved in the building and decorating of the new cathedral of St. Brendan. Jack B. Yeats* and Sarah Purser were among the artists who worked on this church, the one great architectural achievement of the Revival.

O'Donovan invited the theatrical company which was soon to become the Abbey* down to Loughrea in 1901, their one and only provincial visit at this time. Years later, Maire Walker recalled his excited enthusiasm over the visit. O'Donovan also brought John McCormack, then only a schoolboy, down from Sligo to sing in the cathedral. In Dublin, O'Donovan was on friendly terms with writers and artists. George Moore* based the priest in "Fugitives" in *The Untilled Field* on O'Donovan.

During these years, O'Donovan was also active in the Gaelic League, and in 1902, after a visit to America, he gave for the Gaelic League the O'Growney Memorial lecture in Dublin.

In 1903, the bishop of Tuam died, and Dr. Healy was appointed to the post. Thomas O'Dea became the new bishop of Clonfert and chose to live in Loughrea rather than in Ballinasloe as Healy had. Very quickly relations between O'Dea and O'Donovan became difficult. The reasons have never been fully elucidated, but it seems quite certain that O'Donovan had been the diocesan clergy's choice for the new bishop, but that the Vatican passed over him either because he was too young or for political reasons.

O'Donovan went to America again in November 1903 with some members of the IAOS, where he lectured on the artistic side of the Irish Revival and on the cooperative movement. However, on his return to Loughrea his relations with Dr. O'Dea reached a crisis. In about September 1904, O'Donovan left both Loughrea and the priesthood.

He went first to Dublin, and then to London, taking with him a letter of introduction to various publishers from George Moore. Moore was curious about his character, and O'Donovan's departure from Loughrea was the initial inspiration for Moore's writing of *The Lake*.

At this time, he began to sign himself Gerald O'Donovan, marking a complete break with his past. From London, where he was grubbing for work on the fringes of publishing, he tried to keep up his interest in the IAOS. But this interest lapsed about 1909. In the spring of 1910, he was appointed subwarden of Toynbee Hall in the east end of London.

In October 1910, he married Beryl Verschoyle, the daughter of an Irish Protestant colonel, who had been brought up in Italy. In the years to come, his wife's family was to provide much support for O'Donovan and his family. Three children were born, a boy and two girls, one of whom died tragically young.

In July 1911, O'Donovan left Toynbee Hall, which his wife was beginning to find something of a strain. He now began writing seriously. In the spring of 1913, Macmillan (then publishers in ordinary to the Irish Literary Revival) brought out *Father Ralph*, the first and most effective of his six novels. It was largely autobiographical, drawing on his own experiences as a priest. The crisis in the novel is brought about by the young priest's refusal to submit to the terms of the papal encyclical on modernism (*Paschendi Gregis*), which destroyed the liberal movement within the Church. Deeply felt and vivid in its sketches of rural Ireland, the novel made a sensation and is the work by which O'Donovan will be remembered.

Father Ralph was followed in 1914 by *Waiting*, which deals with the difficulties for a young liberal-minded couple made by the papal decree

Ne Temere concerning the intermarriage of Catholics and non-Catholics. Again O'Donovan was writing about an area of Irish life which many writers neglected (or knew nothing about), and once again one of his books made a distinct impact. Frank O'Connor* recalls being given a copy of the novel in his teens by a workmate who told him it would show him what Ireland "was really like."

During the Great War, O'Donovan worked in the Italian section of the British Department of Propaganda, where his wife's family connections were of use to him. In 1918, he became head of the section, and it was at this period that he first met Rose Macauley.

After the war, he was involved with the establishment of the London office of the publishers William Collins, for whom he worked as a reader. He himself brought out four more novels, two of which had been written during the war. One was *Conquest*, which deals with events in Ireland down to 1919. This interesting book is marred by the many earnest debates which dominate it, but it gives the modern reader a liberal view of the divided nation during that heady period.

Also published in 1920 was *How They Did It*, which focuses on the "Home Front" in Britain during the war. In his last two novels, *Vocations* (1921) and *The Holy Tree* (1922), O'Donovan returned to his earlier material and to the one theme which asserts itself in all of his work, the search for real love. Grace in his last novel was based on Rose Macauley, with whom he had established a special friendship. In her short story "Miss Anstruther's Letters" written after bombs had destroyed her flat and all his letters to her, Rose Macauley gives an idea of what O'Donovan meant to her. Her precise relationship to him is less clear; for he stayed with his wife and children, but Rose was a frequent visitor, godmother to his son's child, and a traveling companion of his daughter.

O'Donovan exerted great influence over Macauley and her literary work, but after he met her, his own creative urge declined. Indeed, what O'Donovan actually did for a living between the wars is not clear even to his children. His daughter Brigid recalls him lying on the sofa all afternoon reading his way through the *Cambridge Ancient History* and endless detective stories, one a day. He rarely mentioned Ireland, and one senses a loss of real purpose in his life.

In 1938, the O'Donovans became involved with helping Czech refugees. On June 26, 1939, while on a holiday in the Lake District with Rose Macauley, he and Macauley were involved in an accident in which he fractured his skull. His already failing health was further weakened. A long illness set in, during which O'Donovan consoled himself by reading Somerville and Ross,* and his old friend George Moore.

On July 26, 1942, O'Donovan died of cancer and was buried in Albury, Surrey, where he had lived for some years. A fortnight later, Rose Macauley writing as "A friend" published a short obituary notice in *The Times*. She concluded the polite formalities with a sudden personal note: "To know him was to love him."

Though now almost forgotten, O'Donovan's novels give a good picture of the progressive and liberal movements in Ireland before 1916, which were to be swamped by the rising nationalism of the new state. They portray a forgotten Ireland which is becoming of increasing interest to readers tired of the cliches that often pass for Irish history.

PETER COSTELLO

WORKS: *Father Ralph*. London: Macmillan, 1913; *Waiting*. London: Macmillan, 1914; *Conquest*. London: Constable, 1920; *How They Did It*. London: Methuen, 1920; *Vocations*. London: Martin Secker, 1921; *The Holy Tree*. London: Heinemann, 1922. REFERENCES: Costello, Peter, *The Heart Grown Brutal*. Dublin: Gill & Macmillan/ Totowa, N.J.: Rowman & Littlefield, 1978; O'Connor, Norrys. "The Irish Uncle Tom's Cabin." In *Changing Ireland*. Cambridge, Mass.: Harvard University Press, 1924.

O'DONOVAN, JOHN (1809-1861), scholar. O'Donovan, the great topographer and Celtic scholar, was born in Attateemore, County Kilkenny, on July 9, 1809. In 1829, he was appointed to a post in the historical department of the Ordnance Survey, where he worked under Petrie* and later with O'Curry* (whose sister he married). O'Donovan's task was to examine old Irish records and manuscripts, in order to decide the nomenclature for maps. As part of his work, he visited every part of Ireland, taking profuse notes. Many of his findings originally appeared in essays on topography and history written for *The Dublin Penny Journal* and *The Irish Penny Journal*. Like O'Curry, he was a diligent transcriber and translator of manuscripts, and he also published *A Grammar of the Irish Language* (1845). Of his many works, his masterpiece is *The Annals of the Four Masters,* which he edited and translated. For his enormous contributions to Irish scholarship, he was awarded an Ll.D. by the University of Dublin. He died on December 9, 1861, in Dublin.

WORK: *Annala Rioghacta Éireann, Annals of the Kingdom of Ireland by the Four Masters*. 7 vols. Dublin: Hodges, Smith, 1848-1851.

O'DONOVAN, JOHN [PURCELL] (1921-), playwright, journalist, raconteur, and wit. O'Donovan was born on January 29, 1921, in Dublin. He grew up to be the despair of his enemies, the delight of his friends, and sometimes vice versa. His plays were done by the Abbey* mainly between 1957 and 1963 when the theatre was in residence at the Queen's, a period usually conceded to be one of the low points of its long history. Nevertheless, O'Donovan's five Abbey plays include three of lasting significance: *The Less We Are Together* (1957), *The Shaws of Synge Street* (1960), and *Copperfaced Jack* (1963). *The Less We Are Together* is a satirical cartoon about Partition; *The Shaws* is a superbly evocative portrait of the eccentric family background of Bernard Shaw;* and *Copperfaced Jack* is an historical play about John Scott, the first earl of Clonmell. The last-named character is portrayed with a richly Rabelaisian gusto, and the play is a splendid antidote to the plethora of popular patriotic melodramas about the '98 period.

O'Donovan has also written *Shaw and the Charlatan Genius* (1965), an account of Shaw's curious mentor Vandaleur Lee. This short book is a happy blend of O'Donovan's interests in Shaw, music, and the by-ways of Irish history.

Since 1960, O'Donovan's abounding energies have been diverted to radio, television, and newspaper journalism, and to establishing the Society of Irish Playwrights, of which he is the chairman and which has done much to raise fees for Irish dramatic authors. There has been no greater loss to the Irish stage since his long vacation from it.

WORKS: *Shaw and the Charlatan Genius*. Dublin: Dolmen, 1965. (Biography); *The Shaws of Synge Street*. Dixon, Calif.: Proscenium, 1966; *Copperfaced Jack*, in *Seven Irish Plays, 1946-1964*. Robert Hogan, ed. Minneapolis: University of Minnesota Press, 1967.

O'DONOVAN, MICHAEL. *See* O'CONNOR, FRANK.

O'DUFFY, EIMAR [ULTAN] (1893-1935), novelist and satirist. O'Duffy, who has been called "modern Ireland's only prose satirist," was born on September 29, 1893, in Dublin. The son of a well-to-do dentist, he attended Stonyhurst in England and then University College, Dublin, where he wrote light verse and facetious stories, and edited the student magazine. After graduating with a Bachelor of Dental Surgery degree, he became increasingly involved in the Irish nationalist and cultural movement. He had some plays produced at Edward Martyn's* Irish Theatre* in Hardwicke Street, and he joined the Irish Republican Brotherhood, became a captain in the Irish Volunteers, and wrote frequently on military tactics for the group's newspaper. It was O'Duffy and J. J. O'Connell who alerted Bulmer Hobson and then Eoin MacNeill on Holy Thursday, 1916, that a Rising was imminent. O'Duffy was then sent by MacNeill to Belfast to quash any insurgency there. O'Duffy's deep disillusionment with the Rising was reflected in his novel *The Wasted Island* (1919), which was more bitterly critical than even O'Casey's* later *The Plough and the Stars*. Naturally, there was little place in the new Free State for a man with such opinions. Even so, O'Duffy worked in Ireland as a teacher and at the Department of External Affairs until 1925. During these years, he published several novels and other books under Bulmer Hobson's "Martin Lester" imprint but made little money by them. Losing his post in External Affairs, O'Duffy moved his family to England in 1925 and spent some of that year free-lancing and working for an American newspaper in Paris. In 1926, the first novel of his Cuandine trilogy, *King Goshawk and the Birds,* was published and was a critical, if not a financial, success. In 1928, the second volume, *The Spacious Adventures of the Man in the Street,* appeared. In the following year, he published a revised version of *The Wasted Island.* In his last years, O'Duffy was much attracted to the social credit theories of Major Douglas and others, and wrote *Life and Money,* a book on economics which went through three editions. He also wrote three potboiling novels, but he managed to complete, albeit faultily, his Cuandine trilogy with *Asses in Clover* (1933). He died in Surrey in 1935 of duodenal ulcers.

Plagued by ill health and little money, O'Duffy nevertheless produced a substantial body of work that ranges in quality from the trivial to the masterly. His many early verses are local and facetious, and yet show a playful facility with words. His early plays—*The Walls of Athens, The Phoenix on the Roof,* and particularly *Bricriu's Feast*—indicate a strong talent for satiric comedy. His major early work, however, was the novel *The Wasted Island* (1919, revised 1929), which is both *bildungsroman* and intellectual history of the years leading up to the Rising. Despite some awkwardness of style, it is one of the best fictional introductions to its era.

In the decade after the Rising, O'Duffy published several minor works of considerable charm and excellence. The most important is an historical novel of the Munster Confederation, *The Lion and the Fox* (1922), which in sweep and power recalls Dumas and which must be accounted one of the finest examples of the genre in modern Irish writing. Two other volumes, *Printer's Errors* (1922) and *Miss Rudd and Some Lovers* (1923), have a lightheartedness which O'Duffy was never to recapture. *Printer's Errors* is a genial satire about Irish cultural life before the Rising, and *Miss Rudd* is a disarming comic love story set incongruously during the Black and Tan War.

O'Duffy's major accomplishment is the Cuandine trilogy composed of *King Goshawk and the Birds, The Spacious Adventures of the Man in the Street,* and *Asses in Clover.* These books are a scathing, funny, and highly inventive satire of modern life, half Erewhonian adventure and half science fiction. The first two volumes range from the mordant to the frivolous in their criticism and embody a flamboyant range of ironic and rhetorical techniques that bear comparison to James Stephens* or Flann O'Brien* or, indeed, to James Joyce* himself. The second volume, *The Spacious Adventures,* is perhaps the most integrated of the trilogy, and the final volume, *Asses in Clover,* composed while gravely ill, is the least successful. However, even this work has superb moments, as in the muted, bleakly savage ending.

In the 1930s, O'Duffy wrote three unimportant detective stories, evidently to make money, and was much impressed by theories of social credit as remedies for the worldwide Depression. This extreme commitment, plus undoubtedly an increasingly sardonic view, erased from his work the lightness, fancy, frivolity, and satiric detachment that were its great strengths. Despite his failures, his false starts, and his potboilers, he is a unique and extraordinary figure in modern Irish literature.

WORKS: *The Walls of Athens*. Dublin: Irish Review, 1914. (Play); *A Lay of the Liffey, and Other Verses*. Dublin: Candle, 1918; *Bricriu's Feast*. Dublin: Martin Lester, [1919?]. (Play); *The Wasted Island*. Dublin: Martin Lester, 1919/revised ed., London: Macmillan, 1929. (Novel); *The Lion and the Fox*. Dublin: Martin Lester, [1922]. (Novel); *Printer's Errors*. Dublin: Martin Lester, 1922/London: Leonard Parsons, [1922]. (Novel); *Miss Rudd and Some Lovers*. Dublin: Talbot, 1923. (Novel); "The Phoenix on the Roof" in *The Irish Review* 1 (1923): 75-82. (One-act play); *King Goshawk and the Birds*. London: Macmillan, 1926. (Novel); *The Spacious Adventures of the Man in the Street*. London: Macmillan, 1928. (Novel); *The Bird Cage*. London: Geoffrey Bles, 1932. (Mystery novel); *Life and Money*. London & New York: Putnam's, 1932/2d ed., revised & enlarged, 1933/3d ed., revised, 1935; *The Secret Enemy*. London: Geoffrey Bles, 1932. (Mystery novel); *Asses in Clover*. London: Putnam's, 1933. (Novel); *Heart of a Girl*. London: Geoffrey Bles, [1935]. (Mystery novel); *The Journal of Irish Literature* 7 (1978), reprints *Printer's Errors, Bricriu's Feast*, and some fugitive material.   REFERENCE: Hogan, Robert. *Eimar O'Duffy*. Lewisburg, Pa.: Bucknell University Press, 1972.

O'FAOLAIN, JULIA (1932-), novelist and short story writer. O'Faolain, daughter of Sean* and Eileen O'Faolain, was born in Dublin in 1932 and was educated there by Sacred Heart nuns. After taking a degree at University College, Dublin, she continued her education in Rome and Paris. In Florence she met and married Lauro Martines, an American historian, and they have one son. They now commute between Los Angeles and London. Julia O'Faolain has worked as a teacher of languages, an interpreter, and a translator.

Her first collection of stories, *We Might See Sights* (1968), has various international backgrounds. The biting, sardonic tone of the Irish stories hits hard at sexual hypocrisies and repressions. Still, one shudders to think there are really children like Madge, the heroine of the title story, who believes sex is the crime of the dirty English, and who satisfies her own sexual curiosity and boredom by trying to stimulate and then by beating a retarded child. "First Conjugation" is an excellent study of teenage infatuation in which an introverted adolescent, in love with her female Italian teacher, gets a coldblooded revenge for wounds inflicted in the classroom. Aunt Adie of "Melancholy Baby" is even more unpleasant. Frantically jealous of her orphan niece's love affair, she is consoled only when the girl contracts a fatal disease. "A Pot of Soothing Herbs" catches bohemian Dublin life in the 1950s. A romantic and reluctant virgin after a night on the town ends up sleeping in a bed with two men. Sadly, a bolster divides them, and she survives unravished to return to screaming, puritanical parents. The captain of "Her Trademark" is a departure into uncharacteristic compassion, and a delight. A lonely little man, probably homosexual and bereft by his mother's death, escorts three sisters to Lourdes in search of husbands and ends up marrying one himself, although the marriage will remain unconsummated. P. J. Phennessy, the medical student of "The Chronic," is a brilliantly funny and realistic study also of the Irish mother-obsessed male. The Italian stories are milder and less concerned with sexual attitudes. Perhaps the best, "That Bastard Berto," illustrates that the things which intimidated us as children continue to do so, and the revengeful hero can finally only offer money to the nun who tormented him as a child. "Dies Irae" points sadly and comically to old age and the way of all flesh, while "Mrs. Rossi" portrays a lonely Italian immigrant woman who is finally hardened by life.

Godded and Codded (in America *Three Lovers*) of 1970 is a novel about a young girl loose in Paris and determined on sexual adventures. Indeed, almost the entire action is boringly spent in various beds, and the main character, Sally, is rather shallowly portrayed. When, for instance, her affair ends in a gruesome abortion, she has no guilt, which does not ring true considering she is fresh from Catholic Ireland. Her appalling parents are dismissed with the same callousness, but they, at least, have asked for it. Characters like Sally's "Hail Mary" ranting father undoubtedly still exist, but he is portrayed very broadly. The other characters, with the possible exception of one aging mistress, are not particularly memorable. In short, this first novel is not on the level of her other work.

Except for two stories, *Man in the Cellar* (1974) tackles the problems which come after sexual initiation. Una, the brutalized wife of the title story, locks her husband in the cellar to get revenge for beatings, but also to demonstrate that she is a person. This story, which inquiries into the unequal battle of the sexes and the nature of marriage, is basically serious, but it is also humorous. "I Want Us to Be in Love" is a comic account of an old man's attempt to seduce a young woman. He dies in the attempt, but the unmolested girl now has some sobering realization about imperfect love. The tender and funny "A Travelled Man" shows an Italian academic in America becoming embroiled in the marital squabbles of his benefactors. In "The Knight," a celibate layman member of an Irish religious society runs down an Englishman who is having an affair with his wife. The story depicts the chauvinism of a smug race and, although described as "gloriously funny" on the book blurb, is decidedly sour and gruesome. "It's a Long Way to Tipperary" is another Irish story, full of rain and madness, in which the wife of a displaced Roman Catholic in the British Army is converted and goes mad.

Woman in the Wall (1975) differs considerably from O'Faolain's previous work: it is a brilliant evocation of sixth-century Gaul, reconstructed from original manuscripts. Radegunda, the child bride of Clotair, experiences sexual passion but runs away from her husband to found a convent. Agnes, a child of twelve and no mystic like Radegunda, goes with her and becomes the abbess. Agnes later has a child by Fortunatus, a poet who eventually becomes a priest. The child, Ingunda, walls herself in to atone for her parents' sin, and her voice acts as a chorus throughout the novel. Radegunda experiences Christ in her visions as a lover, while Agnes comes to a kind of mysticism through love of her child. Radegunda, wanting to establish the Kingdom of God on earth, embroils the convent in the chaos of the outside world, but only leaves the way open for Chrodechild, an inhuman religious, to become abbess. Agnes and even Fortunatus, the fat and greedy cleric, act humanely in trying to save their child, while Radegunda dies and is presumably borne aloft. The novel is not so much a study of mysticism as a study of its failure to help humanity. O'Faolain is saying that we are human and that love can only be expressed in the language humans know. Structurally and thematically, it is her most accomplished book.

O'Faolain is a worthy bearer of her father's name. Even if some of her Irish stories hit too hard in depicting a cruel, grubbing, nasty, and sexually repressed race, there is a growing compassion and a mature humor in her later stories and in her best novel.

                                                    MARY ROSE CALLAGHAN

WORKS: *We Might See Sights and Other Stories*. London: Faber, 1968; *Godded and Codded*. London: Faber, 1970. (In America called *Three Lovers*); ed., with Laure Martines, *Not in God's Image*. London: Temple Smith, 1973; *Man in the Cellar*. London: Faber, 1974; *Women in the Wall*. London: Faber, 1975; *Melancholy Baby and Other Stories*. Dublin: Poolbeg, 1978. (A selection from her first two collections.)

O'FAOLAIN, SEAN (1900-), short story writer and man of letters. In the twentieth century, Ireland has produced a greater number of major short story writers than the much larger English-speaking nations. Beginning with Joyce,* continuing through Frank O'Connor* and including Elizabeth Bowen* and Mary Lavin,* Irish writers have advanced the form of the short story to an extent that even comparison with their great Russian predecessors is justified. Of these stort story writers, Sean O'Faolain is undoubtedly one of the most accomplished.

O'Faolain was born John Whelan in Cork on February 22, 1900, and received his early education there. While a student at University College, Cork, he became involved in Irish Republican activities, and, in accord with his political beliefs, changed his name to its Irish equivalent: Sean O'Faolain. After service with the Irish Republican Army, he continued his education, receiving M.A. degrees in Irish and in English, and later an M.A. from Harvard. After teaching in Boston and in England, he decided to return to Ireland, where he still lives, and to pursue writing as a full-time profession. He has been energetic in that vocation, publishing ten volumes of short stories to date, three novels, a play, numerous prose works, including literary criticism such as *The Vanishing Hero* (1956), biographies of Eamon de Valera (1933 and 1939), Constance Markievicz (1934), Daniel O'Connell (1938), Hugh O'Neill (1942), and Cardinal Newman (1952), as well as travel essays, an autobiographical memoir called *Vive Moi!* (1964), and several editions of the works of Irish authors. Not only has he earned a high reputation among modern Irish writers, but he has, through his editorship of *The Bell*,* promoted modern Irish writing and insisted always on standards of the highest order.

His first collection of stories, *Midsummer Night Madness and Other Stories* (1932), set high standards indeed. The stories present vivid Irish settings, often places where the author himself had served in the Republican Army. Yet, they are essentially lyrical, relying on dreams and symbols, poetic language and reiteration. Like the work of many beginning writers, they are at times too obviously experimental in technique. But many of the stories are superb in their analysis of young men under stress during a war, yet reaching to universal human impulses. "Fugue" represents the collection well; it is a story of a young rebel being pursued by the Blacks and Tans. In his flight to escape, he meets a young girl for whom he feels immediate love, but he is forced to continue to run from his pursuers and can love her only in memory and fantasy. The plot is simple, but the balance between opposed forces is handled expertly, so much so that the story's musical title is appropriate.

O'Faolain's three novels constitute one stage in his development as a writer. *A Nest of Simple Folk* (1933) centers on a character driven alternately by idealism and self-destruction. A parallel to the Irish cause is clear, for although Leo Donnel finds a motivating cause in the Republican effort, he loses his life in the Easter Rising. *Bird Alone* (1936) deals with a similar central subject but emphasizes the destructive force of sectarian conformity in Ireland. O'Faolain called it a novel of "sin and salvation," but the characters never achieve the heroic status needed to sustain such a strong theme. *Come Back to Erin* (1940) treats a subject O'Faolain also knew well: the romantic attitudes of the Irish in America, who forget the political struggle and promote a myth of holy Ireland. The main character experiences the death of idealism and fervor, which parallels, O'Faolain implies, what is happening in contemporary Ireland. As even brief summaries indicate, each of the novels centers on a single character who revolts against the orthodox attitudes of his milieu, and each suffers some painful disillusionment in the process. The novel's form allows O'Faolain to explore the more remote effects of individual revolt, the inheritance from the past, and a complex web of political and social attitudes in which the modern Irishman is caught. What the novels achieve in scope, however, they lose in force and focus; the concentrated form of the short story better suits O'Faolain's incisive talent.

His second collection of short stories, *A Purse of Coppers* (1937), shows an advance in his control of technique but less power. His best collection may well be *The Man Who Invented Sin and Other Stories* (1948). The title story is especially effective. A pair of monks and a pair of nuns, spending the summer in the Gaeltacht to perfect their Irish, are accused by the local curate of immorality over what was only an innocent bit of fun— taking part in singing on a boat trip. But sexual repression and social conformity are such strong forces in Ireland that the parties are driven to fear and deceit in order to escape. The curate is both the instrument of those negative forces and, as the title indicates, the responsible party, working against innocence and pleasure.

I Remember! I Remember!, O'Faolain's 1961 collection, represents his most mature, balanced views. The title story presents a peasant woman who has nearly total recall of past events and reports; by those powers, she becomes a threat to the happiness of her sister, who lives a comfortable life in illusion. Actuality is thus set against a highly colored version of past events so that the self-sustaining beliefs of the sister are threatened. There is clear conflict of those opposed forces, an interesting theme, convincing characters, but no castigation of either party. Even more representative of O'Faolain's approach at this time is "Two of a Kind," in which two misfits, a young Irish sailor and his aunt, abandoned by her husband and now by her son, meet and console each other on Christmas Eve in Manhattan. Their common need for a family, for support and love, is built easily, so that by the story's end each has found in the other what he needs. The tone is gentle but not nostalgic; the analysis of characters incisive but understanding.

The most recent collection, *Foreign Affairs and Other Stories* (1976), focuses on more sophisticated characters and modern concerns, but the thematic concerns are the familiar ones: the complex nature of love, the personal need for illusion, the restrictive forces of sectarian and social conformity, and the difficulties resulting from modernization. "The Faithful Wife" describes the affair between a French diplomat and a Dublin woman who is willing to have a sexual relationship but is finally more committed to upholding her earlier social and religious attitudes. Like the best of his stories, it is told with sympathy and even humor, so that the characters are realized as sympathetic: flawed yet appealing.

In *The Vanishing Hero* (1956), O'Faolain links faith and affirmation with the notion of a hero, which he finds to have passed from the books of novelists of this century. The chapters on Elizabeth Bowen* and Graham Greene reveal his insistence on clarity and commitment and his keen perception of the techniques of fiction. Equally impressive are the comments on writing contained in various periodical essays, especially in *The Bell*, which reveal an exceptional combination of critical acumen with common sense. The best of his stories reveal O'Faolain's adherence to the literary theories set forth in the critical works. Plot is deemphasized, and effects are achieved in a remarkably direct and economical manner. The aura of taletelling is not attempted, resulting in less personal warmth and mystery but greater realism. Striving for a balance between accurate description of reality and the pursuit of essential values and interior questions, O'Faolain finds Stendhal to be a model. In short story technique another model is Chekhov, whose finely honed stories contain only the essential details and incidents, but who views all with both irony and sympathy.

Even in viewing O'Faolain's own early life, that Chekhovian ideal is evident. *Vive Moi!*, his autobiography, is not nostalgic, but it is so accurate in evocation that a clear concept of his character and the importance of recalling the past are established. It is only through unceasing dialogue with the child within himself, remembrance of youthful ideals and goals, that the writer can achieve worthwhile art. Not only in recalling the facts of his own life and literary associations, but in all his fiction O'Faolain has recognized the importance of "ancestral memory," the cultural as well as personal inheritance. Yet, he does not look backwards only. As editor of *The Bell*, he encouraged young writers such as Brendan Behan* and James Plunkett,* while publishing the best Irish writers of the time: Flann O'Brien,* Frank O'Connor, Peadar O'Donnell,* and Austin Clarke.* His intentions there were extensions of his own goals as a writer: to raise standards of taste in his native land, to oppose those forces of restriction such as censorship and social conformity which denied life, and to establish Ireland as part of the modern world, not just as a colorful relic of simpler times. In his work and in his stories, he achieved those goals.

His wife Eileen (née Gould) is a successful writer of children's stories, and his daughter Julia* is an admired novelist and short story writer.

                                                                JAMES KILROY

WORKS: *Midsummer Night Madness and Other Stories*. London: Jonathan Cape, 1932; *The Life Story of Eamon de Valera*. Dublin: Talbot, 1933; *Constance Markievicz, or The Average Revolutionary, A Biography*. London: Jonathan Cape, 1934; *A Nest of Simple Folk*. New York: Viking, 1934; *There's a Birdie in the Cage*. London: Grayson & Grayson, 1935; *Bird Alone*. London: Jonathan Cape, 1936; *The Autobiography of Theobald Wolfe Tone*. London: Thomas Nelson, 1937; *A Purse of Coppers: Short Stories*. London: Jonathan Cape, 1937; *King of the Beggars, A Life of Daniel O'Connell*. New York: Viking, 1938; *She Had to Do Something: A Comedy in Three Acts*. London: Jonathan Cape, 1938; *De Valera*. Harmondsworth, Middlesex: Penguin, 1939; *Come Back to Erin*. New York: Viking, 1940; *An Irish Journey*. London: Longmans, Green, 1940; *The Great O'Neill, A Biography of Hugh O'Neill, Earl of Tyrone*. New York: Duell, Sloan & Pearce, 1942; *The Story of Ireland*. London: William Collins, 1943; *Teresa, and Other Stories*. London: Jonathan Cape, 1947; *The Irish*. West Drayton, Middlesex, 1947/New York: Devin-Adair, 1948; *The Short Story*. London: William Collins, 1948; *The Man Who Invented Sin, and Other Stories*. New York: Devin-Adair, 1949; *A Summer in Italy*. London: Eyre & Spottiswoode, 1949; *Newman's Way, The Odyssey of John Henry Newman*. London: Longmans, Green, 1952; *South to Sicily*. London: William Collins, 1953/ published in America as *An Autumn in Italy*, New York: Devin-Adair, 1953; *With the Gaels of Wexford*. Introduction & compiled by Sean O'Faolain. Enniscorthy, 1955; *The Vanishing Hero, Studies in Novelists of the Twenties*. London: Eyre & Spottiswoode, 1956; *The Finest Stories of Sean O'Faolain*. Boston: Little, Brown, 1958; *I Remember! I Remember!* Boston: Little, Brown, 1961; *Short Stories, A Study in Pleasure*. Sean O'Faolain, ed.

Boston: Little, Brown, 1961; *Vive Moi!* Boston: Little, Brown, 1964; *The Heat of the Sun, Stories and Tales.* Boston: Little, Brown, 1966; *The Talking Trees and Other Stories.* London: Jonathan Cape, 1971; *Foreign Affairs, and Other Stories.* London: Constable, 1976.   REFERENCES: Doyle, Paul A. *Sean O'Faolain.* New York: Twayne, 1968; Harmon, Maurice. *Sean O'Faolain: A Critical Introduction.* South Bend, Ind.: University of Notre Dame Press, 1966; Harmon, Maurice, ed. *Irish University Review* 6 (Spring 1976), Sean O'Faolain Special Issue; O'Donnell, Donat (pseudonym of Conor Cruise O'Brien). *Maria Cross.* Oxford: Oxford University Press, 1952.

O FARACHAIN, ROIBEARD (1909-), poet and critic. Roibeárd Ó Faracháin was born Robert Farren in Dublin in 1909. He is very much a product of de Valera's Ireland, and from that mileu of the 1930s, 1940s, and 1950s, he derives his strengths and his considerable weaknesses. He was trained as a teacher at St. Patrick's College, Drumcondra, and later took an M.A. at the National University. He was a teacher for ten years and then became associated with Radio Éireann. In 1940, he became a member of the Board of the Abbey Theatre,* and in 1943, the theatre presented his verse plays *Assembly at Drium Ceat* and *Lost Light.* His thirty years with the theatre did little to mitigate the somewhat stultifying influence of the Gaelophile ex-politician Ernest Blythe who was the theatre's managing director for most of that time. However, also in 1940, Austin Clarke* and Ó'Faracháin formed the Dublin Verse-Speaking Society, which grew into the Lyric Theatre.*

Ó Faracháin's preoccupation with poetic technique is apparent in his book *How to Enjoy Poetry* (1948). This is an adequate explanatory introduction as well as a small anthology, but the author seems to assume that he is not writing for, but talking to, an audience of bored morons. In addition, many readers will find his chatty jocularity irritating, if not painful. His *The Course of Irish Verse* (1947) is a short introduction for the interested and intelligent reader, and so much of the grating bonhommie is absent. At times, a rather narrow Catholicism and jingoistic patriotism are evident, but Ó Faracháin never becomes as rabid as Daniel Corkery,* and he does have some appreciative remarks about writers with whom he is not thoroughly in sympathy. The later pages on the moderns (up to F. R. Higgins* and Austin Clarke) have enough analyses to be of some persuasiveness, but the earlier pages on the nineteenth-century poets are general, skimpy, and journalistic. Like the slightly older Clarke, he mounts the hobby horse of assonance, but unlike the mature Clarke, he feels that assonance may be sprayed over a poem more or less like salt—and the saltier the better.

Ó Faracháin's own poems are a mixed bag of curate's eggs; they range from damp light-verse squibs to a book-length poetic life of Colmcille. At his most serious, he is a religious poet, but at his most serious he is also a dull poet. His language is usually neither particularly visual nor figurative, and he seems mainly interested in sound and form. His Colmcille poem (or series of poems in a variety of forms and nonforms) lacks drama or any urgent narrative thrust or strong imagery or even much distinction of language. Among his shorter poems, the religious pieces are rather innocuous, as if emotion or piety were being substituted for technique. However, if one rummages through any of his books of lyrics, one may find four or five tight, strong, and controlled pieces. For instance, from *Time's Wall Asunder* (1939), one must single out "Where is an Eye, is Beauty," "After the Fianna," and "Yeats." The pity is that there is not enough of such excellent work for him to rank with Clarke or even with Patrick Kavanagh* or Fred Higgins.

WORKS: *Thronging Feet*. London: Sheed & Ward, 1936; *Time's Wall Asunder*. London: Sheed & Ward, 1939; *The First Exile*. London: Sheed & Ward, 1944; *Rime, Gentlemen, Please*. London: Sheed & Ward, 1945; *The Course of Irish Verse*. New York: Sheed & Ward, 1947/London: Sheed & Ward, 1948. (Critical history); *Towards an Appreciation of Poetry*. Dublin: Metropolitan, 1947. (Essay); *How to Enjoy Poetry*. New York: Sheed & Ward, 1948; *Selected Poems*. London & New York: Sheed & Ward, 1951.

O'FLAHERTY, LIAM (1896-), novelist and short story writer. O'Flaherty was born on August 28, 1896, at Gort na gCapall, Inishmore, the largest Aran island. He was the ninth child and second son of Michael O'Flaherty who worked fifteen acres of barren land. The family cottage stands within sound of the sea, the ruined fort of Dun Aengus rising on the high cliffs beyond. The islanders speak Irish, but young William (or Billy) was educated in English until the age of eleven at Oatquarter School, across the fields. A visiting priest from the Holy Ghost Order offered him a place at the Order's junior seminary at Rockwell College, County Tipperary. At the age of sixteen he moved on to Blackrock College, County Dublin. With a scholarship he completed one year at University College, Dublin, for the first two months of which he was enrolled as a Dublin diocesan seminarian. His vocation to the priesthood evaporated, and claiming he was "tired of waiting for the Irish revolution," he volunteered for the Irish Guards in 1915 under his mother's maiden name of Ganly.

All of his life, O'Flaherty was aware of his twofold temperamental heritage. He was proud of his fierce O'Flaherty blood—"the only princely thing I possess"—but he also inherited a gentler side from his mother Margaret Ganly, descended from Plymouth Brethren from County Antrim, who had settled on Aran two generations before to build lighthouses. His mother was forty when Liam was born, and his second autobiographical volume, *Shame the Devil*, shows how close to her in spirit he remained. From her he learned his love of nature, and from his father came a restless independence and a hatred of restriction and repression. The beauty and the hardship of his childhood both bit deep.

O'Flaherty's service in the Irish Guards also left its lifelong mark. First, he received the intensive initial training which the Guards recruits traditionally receive as an elite corps; then he experienced the mud and blood of the Somme; and finally, in 1917, he was shellshocked and discharged after a year's medical treatment. O'Flaherty's war experience, overlaying his physically tough childhood and religiously disciplined education, left him, at age twenty-one, psychologically disoriented.

Then, still as Bill Ganly, he set off for a period of odd jobs and wandering which was eventually recorded in his first autobiographical volume *Two Years* (1930). During this period, he worked at almost every kind of unskilled job on three continents and claimed he had "developed contempt for dirt, and ceased to think or to be sensitive about myself." In fact, all his life he was to remain hypersensitive about himself, intuitively aware of the feelings of others.

While wandering he visited his elder brother Tom, who had emigrated to Boston years before. Tom urged him to write, and Liam, who had already started writing stories during his convalescence on Aran, wrote more in Boston but after reading Maupassant burned his work in disgust. During this period, he became a communist and stopped using the name of Ganly.

In 1921, O'Flaherty, styling himself "Chairman of the Council of the Unemployed," led a group of unemployed dockers, seized the Rotunda in Dublin, hoisted the red flag, and held the building for several days. On the outbreak of the Civil War, he joined the Republicans against the Free Staters and wrote for Republican papers such as *The Plain People*. He then returned to London and in September 1922 started to write "definitively." In a few weeks he produced a novel and several stories, all of which have been lost. His first published short story was "The Sniper," which appeared on January 12, 1923, in the British socialist weekly *The New Leader*. It was noticed by the critic Edward Garnett (1868-1937). At Garnett's recommendation, O'Flaherty's next attempted novel, *Thy Neighbour's Wife* (1923) was accepted by Jonathan Cape. This flawed book contains O'Flaherty's most detailed description of peasant life on Aran.

O'Flaherty's next novel, *The Black Soul* (1924), was written under Garnett's tutelage. At the same time Garnett, whose wife Constance was a well-known Russian translator, directed O'Flaherty's attention to writers such as Gogol and Dostoyevsky. The correspondence between Garnett and O'Flaherty during this period reveals how close their relationship had become.

Throughout the later 1920s and early 1930s, O'Flaherty continued to form his basic values. During this period his literary output was high. He married Margaret Barrington* and became a father. He was restless, moving to Dublin, to rural isolation in Wicklow, to London, and France, and visiting Russia. In spite of his success, he had financial difficulties, recurring fears of insanity, and two nervous breakdowns, caused perhaps by the aftermath of shellshock and by conflicts within and around him, some of which emerge as satire in works such as *A Tourist's Guide to Ireland* (1929).

In 1932, now separated from his wife and disillusioned with communism, O'Flaherty became one of the founding members of the Irish Academy of Letters. During the 1930s, though much of his work was banned in Ireland, three of his novels were filmed—two in the United States and one in France. He continued to travel and write. During World War II, he moved to the Caribbean and South America and settled temporarily in Connecticut where he wrote more stories. When the war ended he returned to Europe. Between 1946 and 1957, he broadcast several stories in Irish and English over Radio Éireann. He was finally persuaded to record some of his work in 1976 to celebrate his eightieth birthday. O'Flaherty avoids publicity, refusing television and press interviews. The latter part of his life has been spent mostly in Dublin, with frequent periods in France. He rarely visits Aran. His work has been widely translated, but he has kept no consistent record of his publications. His most recently written stories date from the early 1960s.

O'Flaherty's work is variable in tone, style, and quality. He is not an easy writer to pigeonhole by exterior criteria, and it would be entirely false to do so. He had difficulty maintaining consistency in his novels, which tend to become episodic; his best work is to be found in his short stories. He is very Irish in temperament, especially in his use of what Yeats* called "tragic-farce," and as a result, has been accused of being melodramatic. His abrasive sense of humor stems from disappointed idealism. He said: "No ideal is practical, but all ideals are the mothers of great poetry, and it is only from the womb of an ideal that a great race, or a great literature, or a great art can spring."

O'Flaherty formulated his ideal in *The Ecstasy of Angus* (1931), an allegory in which Angus, the Celtic god of love, mates with Fand the earth fairy. Awakening, Angus finds he has lost his youth and beauty, killed the gods, and sown enmity in nature. Behind him has risen the Tree of Knowledge guarded by the warlike Genius of Unrest. The offspring of his union is Man with divine capacity but whose love will always be as unstable as nature herself. O'Flaherty's man, unlike Adam, is not given domination over nature but is part of it. His capacity for thought is both curse and blessing. By this mating of the ideal and the physical, O'Flaherty proclaims the inescapable tension within man's nature.

The allegory was written after a series of novels in all of which the central male character is persecuted by circumstances or by his own neuroticism. *The Black Soul* and *Thy Neighbour's Wife* are both set on Aran; Fergus, the hero of *The Black Soul*, is a projection of the author himself. O'Flaherty said that Dostoyevsky, as well as Gogol and James Joyce,* affected him deeply. The influence of the first can be detected in *Mr. Gilhooley* (1926), *The Assassin* (1928), and *The Puritan* (1931), all three of which are about lost urbanized man. His most acclaimed early novel,

The Informer (1925), he called "a sort of high-blown detective story and its style based on the technique of the cinema." In spite of its plot and setting, this novel is not a serious attempt to write about Irish politics or the secret Irish revolutionary organization. It is about Gypo Nolan's struggle as "a human soul, weak and helpless in suffering, shivering in the toils of the eternal struggle of the human soul with pain."

By the end of the 1920s, O'Flaherty's work shows that he had started to pass beyond his own sufferings, projected into one central character and into the sufferings of others. *The House of God* (1929) has four main characters and a complex plot. As suggested by the title, which is culled from the litany to the Blessed Virgin Mary but also stands for gold as an image of cupidity, the work contains a good deal of symbolism, and the weight of social criticism overpowers the characters.

Didactic idealism also manipulates artistic expression in *The Wilderness* (1927). Here O'Flaherty illustrates that, though man is incapable of rising above his human limitations, there is necessity and even beauty in his struggle for integration. Lawless, Macanasa, and Stevens, the three principal characters, imperfectly represent man's will to immortality, beauty, and power which O'Flaherty was to introduce as a ground-theme in two later novels, *Land* (1946) and *Insurrection* (1954). In all three books, the artistic impact is marred by a too-explicit message. In *Insurrection*, the three characters of *The Wilderness* are redefined: the mystical Lawless becomes the poet Stapleton; the peasant Macanasa becomes the soldier Madden; and the scientific freethinker Stevens becomes the monklike but pragmatic Kinsella who once dreamed of becoming a famous chemist. The thesis also involves social criticism of the specifically Irish situation.

Though novels such as *The Informer, The Assassin, The Martyr, Land, Insurrection*, and *Famine* are related to crucial events in Irish history, the basic human reactions of the characters predominate over the historic setting. *The Martyr* satirizes all civil wars; *The Return of the Brute*, calling on O'Flaherty's experience in the Irish Guards, describes war's bestial effects; the quasi-historic situation of *The Assassin* lends the plot authenticity, but the human reactions described are timeless; *Insurrection* is about the Irish struggle but also suggests that the contradictory forces within man should not weaken themselves in strife but should unite in the face of moral defeat—that common enemy.

O'Flaherty gave his best answer to his question "What is man for?" not in those novels in which he makes the most explicit attempt to do so, but in *Skerrett* (1932) and *Famine* (1937), in both of which the theme grows out of the action rather than the other way around. Skerrett, the Aran schoolmaster, and the Kilmartin family in the 1845-1847 famine fight against outward circumstances, but their true enemy is within themselves. Skerrett and the Kilmartins die undaunted as they had lived; both novels are paeans of praise to endurance. That Skerrett ends in the padded cell of a lunatic asylum and that Thomsy Kilmartin's dead body is savaged by dogs is of lesser importance. In *Famine*, O'Flaherty also created his only full-blown female character, Mary Kilmartin.

O'Flaherty experimented unsuccessfully with drama in *Darkness* (1926) and wrote two good Irish poems, two amusing autobiographical volumes which reveal his volatile temperament, and a good deal of satire in which must be included the novel *Hollywood Cemetery* (1935) and the travelogue *I Went to Russia* (1931). As a writer he will ultimately be remembered, however, for his work in the short story. He is at his best when his gifts as a raconteur are disciplined, when he forgets his sense of frustration or his concern for man at large, and keeps within the limits of either a concentric moment or a dramatic situation. Without the expansiveness of the novel form, however, into which he put his main effort, the artistic economy of his best short stories might never have been achieved.

His best stories tell of Aran, peasants and fishermen, the sea and wildlife. They are based on observation and the memories nearest his heart. He wrote over one hundred and fifty short stories. As in any artist's output, their subject matter, quality, and style vary considerably. Some were written as potboilers, some to a tailored length to suit a specific market; in others, he is careless or allows his subjective feelings to intervene inappropriately. His best stories are based on transposed, well-objectivized, personal experience, such as "The Cow's Death," a story about twelve hundred words long, in which a frenzied cow, after giving birth to a stillborn calf whose body has been thrown over the cliffs, flings herself after it. Other stories as varied as "The Sniper," "The Child of God," and "The Fairy Goose" fall into this category. He writes best when he does not attempt to preach but instead creates a faithful picture of life as he sees it, of human feelings which are universal, of an Aran life-style which has disappeared with the advent of tourism, electricity, and the mass media.

In spite of his vivid visual imagination, illustrated, for example, in "The Mountain Tavern" or "The Touch," there remains something of the oral "seanchai," or Gaelic storyteller, in O'Flaherty. To flavor his entirely, one should read those stories originally written in Irish or later translated by him. His English is often subconsciously affected by Gaelic speech patterns and by the patterns of storytelling he heard as a child when groups used to gather round the O'Flaherty hearth. These influences emerge most strongly in works such as "The Black Mare" and "The Mermaid"—both of which contain formulaic repeated phrases, proverbs, hyperbole, anticipation, and a typical Christian/pagan mixture of imagery.

The O'Flaherty praise of courage which emerged so clearly in *Skerrett* and *Famine* is repeated in short stories such as "The Hawk," "The Landing," and "Red Barbara." For O'Flaherty life is no pastel-colored affair but rather a joyful acceptance of struggle, without which the lyrical aspect of nature, of life, has no meaning.

For O'Flaherty, immortality or godliness consists of an indomitable spirit rather than the perpetuation of an individual soul after death. The defeat or sickness of the spirit during life which he finds so prevalent in modern society he reveals in stories such as "Unclean," "The Tramp," or "Mackerel for Sale." As struggle against defeat is so important, so is the overcoming of fear by love, for the two cannot coexist.

In later stories such as "The Post Office," which is a dramatic mixture of irony and comedy, the world comes to a remote western Ireland village; the rapidly shifting and subtle dialogue represents the juxtaposed trains of thought which these two worlds embody. In this story, the foretaste of the physical disintegration of the old society, shown earlier in "Going into Exile," becomes a cultural certainty.

Apart from their literary pleasure and value, therefore, O'Flaherty's peasant stories also form a valuable record of Irish social change.

A. A. KELLY

WORKS: *Thy Neighbour's Wife*. London: Jonathan Cape, 1923/New York: Boni & Liveright, 1924. (Novel); *The Black Soul*. London: Jonathan Cape, 1924/New York: Boni & Liveright, 1925/Bath: Lythway, 1972. (Novel); *The Informer*. London: Jonathan Cape/New York: Alfred A. Knopf, 1925. (Novel); *Darkness*. London: E. Archer, 1926. (Tragedy in three acts); *Mr. Gilhooley*. London: Jonathan Cape, 1926/ New York: Harcourt, Brace, 1927. (Novel); *The Wilderness*. London: *The Humanist*, 1927 (serialized in six parts)/Dublin: Wolfhound, 1978. (Novel); *The Assassin*. London: Jonathan Cape/New York: Harcourt, Brace, 1928. (Novel); *The House of Gold*. London: Jonathan Cape, 1929/New York: Harcourt, Brace, 1930. (Novel); *The Return of the Brute*. London: Mandrake, 1929/New York: Harcourt, Brace, 1930. (Novel); *A Tourist's Guide to Ireland*. London: Mandrake, 1929; *Two Years*. London: Jonathan Cape/New York: Harcourt, Brace, 1930. (Autobiography); *The Ecstasy of Angus*. London: Joiner & Steele, 1931/Dublin: Wolfhound, 1978; *I Went to Russia*. London: Jonathan Cape/New York: Harcourt, Brace, 1931. (Autobiography cum travel book); *The Puritan*. London: Jonathan Cape, 1931/New York: Harcourt, Brace, 1932/Bath: Lythway, 1973. (Novel); *Skerrett*. London: Gollancz/New York: Long & Smith, 1932/Dublin: Wolfhound, 1977. (Novel); *The Martyr*. New York: Macmillan, 1933/London: Gollancz, 1935. (Novel); *Shame the Devil*. London: Grayson & Grayson, 1934. (Autobiography); *Hollywood Cemetery*. London: Gollancz, 1935. (Novel); *Famine*. London: Gollancz/New York: Random House, 1937. (Novel); *The Short Stories of Liam O'Flaherty*. London: Jonathan Cape, 1937; *Land*. London: Gollancz/New York: Random House, 1946. (Novel); *Two Lovely Beasts*. London: Gollancz, 1948/New York: Devin-Adair, 1950. (Short stories); *Insurrection*. London: Gollancz, 1950/Boston: Little, Brown, 1951. (Novel); *Duil*. (Desire). Dublin: Sairseal agus Dill, 1953. (A collection of stories in Irish); *The Stories of Liam O'Flaherty*. New York: Devin-Adair, 1956; *The Pedlar's Revenge*. Dublin: Wolfhound, 1976. (Stories).   REFERENCES: Doyle, Paul A. *Liam O'Flaherty: An Annotated Bibliography*. New York: Whitston Publishing, 1972; Kelly, A. A. *Liam O'Flaherty, the Storyteller*. London: Macmillan, 1976; Sheeran, Patrick F. *The Novels of Liam O'Flaherty*. Dublin: Wolfhound, 1976; Zneimer, John N. *The Literary Vision of Liam O'Flaherty*. Syracuse, N.Y.: Syracuse University Press, 1970.

O'FLYNN, CRIOSTOIR (1927-), playwright and short story writer. O'Flynn (Ó Floinn in Irish) was born in Limerick on December 18, 1927, and was educated there and at the National University and Trinity College, Dublin. He worked in Ireland and England as teacher, broadcaster, journalist, publicity writer, and lecturer, and is a noted and formidable controversialist. He married in 1952 and now lives in Glenageary with his wife and seven children.

O'Flynn's home language was English, but he writes in both English and Irish. He began to learn Irish in school at the age of four, and his knowledge of it is now both fluent and scholarly. Certain themes and materials are common to his main work in both languages. They turn most notably upon a coalescence of realism and fantasy, and a highly independent reading of the Irish scene, rural and urban.

To English-speaking audiences, O'Flynn is best known for his collection of short stories *Sanctuary Island* (1971) and his two plays *Land of the Living* and *The Order of Melchizedek*. *Land of the Living* modulates between two styles, a naturalistic and a poetic speech. The present of a marriage of convenience between two old people intermingles with the past of a legendary, magical love, mysteriously reenacted. *The Order of Melchizedek* confronts a priest with a young girl who persuades him to believe her a reincarnation of the Virgin Mary. The play ends in a tragic resolution with her and her infant's death, by her own hand, in exile. The priest, by these strange paths, remains in his priesthood.

Sanctuary Island surveys contemporary Ireland with a largely satirical, at times affectionately humorous, regard. It emerges as a land of victims, buffoons, poseurs; capable of a savagery which does not exclude moments of communion between people or between people and their land; moments, too, of richly comic extravagance. *Sanctuary Island*, by its diversity of subject, mood, and manner, sets out prospects inviting O'Flynn's continued exploration. Whatever the form of exploration, its character is essentially dramatic and sustained by a lively sense of the absurdity of the received facts of life.

D.E.S. MAXWELL

WORKS: *Lá Dá bhFaca Thú*. Dublin: Cló Morainn, 1955. (Novel); *Éirí Amach na Cásca*. Dublin: Sáirséal agus Dill, 1966. (Poems); *Learairí Lios an Phúca*. Dublin: F.N.T., 1968. (Novel); *Oineachlann*. Dublin: An Gúm, 1968. (Stories); *Ó Fhás go hAois*. Dublin: Sáirséal agus Dill, 1969. (Poems); *Sanctuary Island*. Dublin: Gill & Macmillan, 1971. (Stories); *Aisling Dhá Abhainn*. Dublin: F.N.T., 1977. (Poems); *Banana*. Dublin: Obelisk, 1977. (Poems). *At Dun Laoghaire Lighthouse*. [Dun Laoghaire: C. O. Floinn, 1978]. (Poem).

O'GRADY, DESMOND [JAMES BERNARD] (1935-), poet. O'Grady was born in Limerick on August 27, 1935, and spent most of his childhood in West Clare and in the Irish-speaking districts of Kerry. He was educated by Jesuits and Cistercians. In the mid-1950s, he lived in Dublin and then in Paris, and published a small collection of poems called *Chords and Orchestrations* (1956). After a brief stay on Caldey Island off the Welsh coast, he moved to Rome, and in 1961, a long collection of poems, *Reilly*, appeared. In the early 1960s, he did postgraduate work at Harvard and received an M.A. in Celtic Studies. He also became the friend and secretary of Ezra Pound in the American poet's last years. O'Grady's own finest collection, *The Dark Edge of Europe*, appeared in 1967. Since then, he has published several other collections and completed a free verse version of the Middle Welsh heroic poem *The Gododdin*. He now lives in a fishing village on a Greek island. (He is not to be confused with the Australian fiction writer and journalist of the same name, who has also lived in Rome.)

O'Grady's *The Dark Edge of Europe* displays great technical proficiency. The rhythms often have a base of anapests and dactyls, varied felicitously by iambs, trochees, and even spondees; as a result, even in long lines the artificial "rocking chair" motion of mere mechanical expertise is avoided. For instance, this stanza from "His Bath" indicates these qualities, as well as an effective use of alliteration:

> He slept through the rest of the morning and rose for lunch.
> Outside, in the first fold of the afternoon,
> The day downed by the dare of the sun and the doped town
> Thumped dull by the heat's punch.

The most technically complex poem in the book is the remarkable "Land," which concludes:

> Hunter and hunted he runs through the world's mad wood
> with his need on his shoulder like blood, to the wanting
>   and wanted
> until, like an ambusher should, she finishes him off for good
> with her love and her hatred.
>
> O husbandman, husbandman, lord of the nail and the hammer,
> open your eyes to the grammar of lies a woman
> will wrap round your finger in the most aphrodital manner
> to bed you, and then
>
> in the digging disguise of the copulate dash, be the fake
> butt of your fury and shake the wool on your thighs.
> O bury your love for your own sake in the chances love cannot
>   take
> and button your eyes.

The poem entitled "Years Ending," the sequence entitled "Sea," and perhaps half a dozen other pieces in this volume show an impressive formal control, some rhetorically effective long sentences, and some occasional echoes of Hopkins and Dylan Thomas. In his later volumes, such as *The Dying Gaul* (1968) and particularly in *Separations* (1973), O'Grady loosens his form and becomes merely fluently chatty or sometimes even phlegmatic, as in "Back to Our Mountains," which starts:

> This evening I returned to the mountain.
> And with you. Though your suggestion,
> the hour was high. We agreed to meet
> at six on the harbour, find
> the old boatman would ferry us
> over the bay before sunset.

O'Grady's later collections are much more relaxed but immeasurably much less accomplished than *The Dark Edge of Europe*.

WORKS: *Chords and Orchestrations*. Limerick: Echo, 1956; *Reilly*. London; Phoenix, 1961; *Professor Kelleher and the Charles River*. Cambridge, Mass.: Carthage, 1964. (Short poem); *Separazioni*. Rome: Edizioni Europei, 1965. (Poems with Italian translations facing); *The Dark Edge of Europe*. London: MacGibbon & Kee, 1967; *The Dying Gaul*. London: MacGibbon & Kee, 1968; *Off Licence*. Dublin: Dolmen, 1968. (Translations from the Italian & Armenian); *Hellas*. Dublin: New Writers', 1971; *Separations*. Dublin: Goldsmith, 1973. *Stations*. Cairo: American University in Cairo, 1976; *The Gododdin*. Dublin: Dolmen, 1977. (Translations from the Welsh); *Sing Me Creation*. Dublin: Gallery Books, 1977; *The Headgear of the Tribe*. London: Martin Brian & O'Keefe, 1978.

O'GRADY, STANDISH (1846-1928), novelist. Although the revival of interest in Irish legend and the development of a new national literature early in the twentieth century resulted ultimately from the linguistic, historical and literary research of Petrie,* O'Donovan,* O'Curry,* and other scholars, credit for directly stimulating the effort is given to Standish O'Grady. Yeats* and AE* considered him to have initiated the Literary Revival, and numerous writers of their generation testify to his influence as being so strong as to make him "the father of the Irish Renaissance."

O'Grady was born on September 18, 1846, in Castletown Berehaven, County Cork. After graduation from Trinity College, Dublin, he practiced law in that city before pursuing an interest in Irish history and mythology which were to dominate the rest of his life. His discovery of the rich store of ancient Irish history and the intriguing tales of early Irish legends and sagas stimulated him to undertake his two-volume *History of Ireland* which he published in 1878 and 1880. Included in this work are versions of the mythological tales and the heroic cycle centering on Cú Cuchulainn, which attempt to be both faithful to the original texts and yet readable and exciting. Predictably, they fail in that intention, for the sources from which O'Grady derived his material are often fragmentary and the tales themselves so foreign to cultured tastes that he felt they required major additions and revisions. Some of these changes converted the vigorous, pagan tone of the original tales to one of proper late-Victorian gentility. To correct what he considered his own inaccuracies in those volumes in the presentation of factual, purely historic information, O'Grady followed them with his *History of Ireland: Critical and Philosophical* (1881), a genuine contribution to public knowledge about Ireland's past.

O'Grady's deepest interest was in the literary artifacts, the heroic tales and legends, and he devoted his energy in the years following to a revival of interest in them. Presupposing his readers' lack of knowledge of the original tales, O'Grady proceeded to rewrite them as adventure novels. Cú Cuchulainn was the hero of a trilogy: *The Coming of Cuculain* (1894), *In the Gates of the North* (1901), and *The Triumph and Passing of Cuculain* (1920). However, he does not emerge as anything more than a wooden, unconvincing character, a strong contrast to the powerful and complicated hero presented by Yeats or Lady Gregory.* O'Grady's treatment of Fionn macCumhaill in *Finn and His Companions* (1892) is more vivid, but less faithful to the originals, for O'Grady imposes a strong moral tone on tales which were often amoral. In all his fiction, the prose is so ornate as to distract from the tales, or at least to contrast to the vigor of the actions described.

O'Grady wrote several other historical novels on Ireland's past, particularly on the Tudor period. As always, the description of historical background is clear and interesting, but in these works the characterization is more sound. Red Hugh O'Donnell, the hero of *The Flight of the Eagle* (1897), is more vivid and forceful than his prototype Cú Cuchulainn. But the novels are rarely more than children's adventure stories, lacking in complexity or analysis of character.

Dedicated to the unionist cause, O'Grady worked hard to remind the landlords of their responsibility to Ireland. In *Toryism and the Tory Democracy* (1886), he proposed a coalition of peasant and landlord classes to revive Ireland's economy and culture. He was frustrated in these efforts, and after the demise of his journal, the *All-Ireland Review*, he withdrew from active involvement in political affairs. He left Ireland in 1918 and died on the Isle of Wight on May 18, 1928.

Whatever his limitations as a writer or political force, Standish O'Grady's influence on later writers is indisputable. His novels and stories inspired Yeats, AE, and others to use Irish legends and tales as literary subjects. His historical works drew attention to the wealth of Ireland's heritage at a time when assertion of identity served the political cause. "The last champion of the Irish aristocracy," AE called him; and as an outspoken advocate of the responsibilities of his own class, the Ascendancy, in Ireland's affairs, his influence on Yeats' thinking is evident in several poems. Finally, as editor of the weekly *All-Ireland Review* from 1900 to 1907, he advanced both the formulation of political theory and the development of indigenous Irish art through his encouragement of a host of young writers. His personality and dedication were so powerful that through his influence, more than through his own writings, he has attained an important place in Ireland's recent history.

JAMES KILROY

WORKS: *History of Ireland: The Heroic Period.* London: Sampson Low, Searle, Marston, & Rivington/Dublin: E. Ponsonby, 1878; *Early Bardic Literature, Ireland.* London: Sampson Low, Searle, Marston, & Rivington/Dublin: E. Ponsonby, 1879; *History of Ireland: Cuculain and His Contemporaries.* London: Sampson Low, Searle, Marston, & Rivington/Dublin: E. Ponsonby, 1880; *History of Ireland: Critical and Philosophical.* London: Sampson Low/Dublin: E. Ponsonby, 1881; *The Crisis in Ireland.* Dublin: E. Ponsonby/London: Simpkin & Marshall, 1882; *Cuculain: An Epic.* London: Sampson Low, Searle, Marston, & Rivington/Dublin: E. Ponsonby, 1882; *Toryism and the Tory Democracy.* London: Chapman & Hall, 1886; *Red Hugh's Captivity.* London: Ward & Downey, 1889; *Finn and His Companions.* London: T. Fisher Unwin, 1892; *The Bog of Stars.* London: T. Fisher Unwin/Dublin: Sealy, Bryers & Walker/New York: P. J. Kennedy, 1893; *The Coming of Cuculain.* London: Methuen, 1894; *Lost on Du-Corrig.* London, Paris, & Melbourne: Cassell, 1894; *The Story of Ireland.* London: Methuen, 1894; *The Chain of Gold.* London: T. Fisher Unwin, 1895; *Ulrick the Ready.* London: Downey, 1896; *In the Wake of King James.* London: J. M. Dent, 1896; *The Flight of the Eagle.* London: Lawrence & Bullen, 1897; *All Ireland.* Dublin: Sealy, Bryers, & Walker/London: T. Fisher Unwin, 1898; *The Queen of the World.* London: Lawrence & Bullen, 1900; *In the Gates of the North.* Kilkenny: Standish O'Grady, 1901; *Hugh Roe O'Donnell.* Belfast: Nelson & Knox, 1902; *The Masque of Finn.* Dublin: Sealy, Bryers & Walker, 1907; *The Triumph and Passing of Cuculain.* Dublin: Talbot/London: T. Fisher Unwin, 1920; *Standish O'Grady: Selected Essays and Passages.* Ernest A. Boyd, ed. Dublin: Talbot, n.d. REFERENCES: Marcus, Phillip. *Standish O'Grady.* Lewisburg, Pa.: Bucknell University Press, 1970; O'Grady, Hugh Art. *Standish James O'Grady: The Man and the Work.* Dublin: Talbot, 1929.

O'HAGAN, JOHN (1822-1890), poet and translator. O'Hagan was born in Newry on March 19, 1822. He was educated at Trinity College, Dublin, and contributed much verse to *The Nation** under the pseudonym mainly of Sliabh Cuilinn. His most popular pieces were "Ourselves Alone" and "Dear Land." After having been active in the Young Ireland movement, he later had a successful career at the bar. He also published a translation of *Le Chanson de Roland* before his death on November 12 or 13, 1890. His best known Irish songs are reprinted in *The Spirit of the Nation*.

WORKS: *Afternoon Lectures on English Literature: Chaucer.* Dublin: Hodges, 1864; *The Song of Roland.* Translated into English Verse. London: Kegan, Paul, 1880; *The Poetry of Sir Samuel Ferguson.* Dublin: Gill, 1887; *The Children's Ballad-Rosary.* London, 1890; *Joan of Arc.* London: Kegan, Paul, 1893. (Biography).

O'HANLON, HENRY B. (fl. early twentieth century), playwright. Edward Martyn* considered playwright-solicitor Henry B. O'Hanlon the most important of the Irish dramatists who wrote for the Irish Theatre,* Hardwicke Street, in its 1914-1920 life span. His opinion is difficult to evaluate, since only two O'Hanlon plays are extant.

To-morrow, a Maeterlinckish "nightmare in one act," performed at the Irish Theatre on December 18-23, 1916, is set in a morgue. The drunken caretaker, who hears or thinks he hears the corpses talking of what their lives had been and of what their eternity will be, suffers a fatal heart attack.

Martyn's favorite, *The All-Alone*, a four-act tragedy, was presented at the Irish Theatre* on June 17-22, 1918. It markedly resembles Ibsen's *The Lady from the Sea*. Esmond Everard, son of a seafaring man whose ship was named "The All-Alone," must choose between sweet, sensible Sheila Cleary and the "spirit of the sea" embodied in the mysterious, alluring Syra. He and Syra are last seen in a tiny boat headed into the open sea.

The unpublished *Her Second Chance* was staged at the Abbey* on May 19, 1914, by the Dramatic Society of St. Mary's College, Rathmines, O'Hanlon's alma mater. In this social melodrama, a repentant wastrel commits suicide so that his wife may have a second chance. Knowledge of *Speculations*, a three-act tragedy offered by the Irish Theatre on November 19-24, 1917, must be pieced together from reviews. Lucien Westray, blinded by congenital disease, is dependent on his sister Mary. When she dies, doctors persuade Mary's friend Constance Beaumont to impersonate the dead woman. To the supposed sister, Westray confides his love for Constance just before he too dies. Of the three-act comedy *Norah's Birthday*, only the title survives. This play was taken on a tour of the west of Ireland in August 1915 as a benefit for Red Cross hospitals.

Like Martyn, O'Hanlon was interested in transplanting Ibsenite themes to Irish soil. Possibly at the time there was a surfeit of discussion drama; at least reviewers complained that O'Hanlon's plays were garrulous to the point of fogging over the plot line. Read today, *The All-Alone* and *To-morrow* seem worthwhile experiments, marked by a competent, if not triumphant, blending of the mundane and the eerie, and a refreshing departure from standard cottage drama.

WILLIAM J. FEENEY

WORKS: "To-morrow." *Studies* 6 (March 1917): 48-57; *The All-Alone*. Preface by Edward Martyn. Dublin: Thomas Kiersey, 1919.

O'KEEFFE, JOHN (1747-1833), playwright and actor. O'Keeffe was born in Abbey Street, Dublin, on June 24, 1747. He acted at the Smock Alley Theatre for twelve years, and there began writing his many farces and comic operas, such as *Tony Lumpkin in Town* (Haymarket, 1778), which was a sequel to Goldsmith's* *She Stoops to Conquer,* and *The Agreeable Surprise* (Haymarket, 1781), which Hazlitt much admired. Indeed, Hazlitt called O'Keeffe "the English Molière. . . . In light, careless laughter, and pleasant exaggerations of the humorous, we have no one to equal him." There is little of Irish interest in O'Keeffe, and nothing that has held the stage. However, one might cite *The Wicklow Gold Mine*, an opera of 1796 (later revised as *The Wicklow Mountains*), and the unpublished *The Sham-*

rock; or, St. Patrick's Day of 1777. In the mid-1970s, one of his last popular plays, *Wild Oats* (1791), was revived with much success in London. A lame production, somewhat Irished by Tom MacIntyre,* was then done at the Abbey* in 1977; much more stylish acting is needed to raise the convoluted plot to success. O'Keeffe retired early from the stage because of blindness, but he continued to write prolifically. His *Recollections*, first published in 1826, are well worth perusal. He died in Southampton on February 4, 1833.

WORKS: *The Dramatic Works of John O'Keeffe, Esq.* 4 vols. London: Printed by T. Woodfall, 1798; *Recollections of the Life of John O'Keeffe.* 2 vols. London: H. Colbourn, 1826.

O'KELLY, SEUMAS (ca. 1875-1918), playwright, novelist, short story writer, and journalist. O'Kelly, once called "Ireland's most neglected genius," was the son of Michael and Catherine Kelly. He was born on an unestablished date (?1875-?1878) at Mobhill, Loughrea, whose lake and "Meadow of the Dead" were to enter his fiction. Scantily educated, he began his main editorial and journalistic career in 1903 on the Skibbereen *Southern Star*. He ended it on *Nationality*, in whose office he died of a cerebral hemorrhage on November 14, 1918, during a rowdy incursion of the premises by anti-Sinn Féin celebrators of the World War I armistice. A huge procession attended his body to its grave in Glasnevin.

Though never robust in health, especially after the rheumatic fever which struck about seven years before his death, O'Kelly managed to produce an amazing amount of journalism, drama, prose fiction, and verse, contributing widely to such journals as *The Irish Rosary*, the *Irish Weekly Independent*, the *Weekly Freeman, Sinn Féin*, and the *Manchester Guardian*, and leaving much for posthumous issue. All this creative work is richly reflective of his Galway youth and often based on literal experience, firsthand or reported. The verse (*Ranns & Ballads*, 1918), however, is unimpressive, being technically defective and rarely evocative or exciting; its finest exemplar is an untitled piece embedded in "The Gray Lake."

The short fiction, though highly variable in quality, is O'Kelly's soundest claim to distinction. The apprentice work of the parochially overpraised first collection, *By the Stream of Killmeen* (1906), published while O'Kelly was editor of the *Leinster Leader*, was no prophecy of the remarkable work to come. That later work is concentrated mainly in *Waysiders, The Golden Barque and The Weaver's Grave*, and *Hillsiders. The Leprechaun of Killmeen* (n.d.; ?1918) and the uncollected tales are negligible.

As Forrest Reid* remarks in *Retrospective Adventures* (1942), "the effect of his [O'Kelly's] finest stories is infinitely richer than the sum of their recorded happenings." This is achieved through a warm handling of country (especially Galway) people, a pastoral-dramatic tone, a realistic approach (sometimes weakened by sentimentality or melodrama), and a frequently poetic concept, though O'Kelly could never rise to a great love story. From his best collections emerge preeminently "The Can with the Diamond Notch," a delightful account of tinker trickery; "The Gray Lake," a memorable tale of the faery drowning of a town; and "The Weaver's Grave," in which a young widow warms to incipient love while it is argued where her late husband should properly be buried. The last-named is a novella that can stand with the finest in English.

Of the novels, *The Lady of Deerpark* is a melodramatic tale of a "Big House" with a grotesquely contrived ending. Nevertheless, as Seumas O'Sullivan* maintains (*Essays and Recollections*, 1944), it has "elements of greatness in it." In contrast, *Wet Clay* (1922) is almost incredibly bad, with its melodramatic sentimentality, clichés, and perverse character manipulations.

The published plays (sometimes transformed short stories) are a mixed lot: nine one-acters (counting a collaboration); one two-acter, *The Shuiler's Child*; and two three-acters, *The Bribe* and *The Parnellite* (n.d.; 1919), the last being basically propaganda. Of these, *The Shuiler's Child* and *The Bribe* (not alone in being well received in production) are enough to give O'Kelly an important place among Irish Renaissance dramatists. *The Shuiler's Child*, involving child desertion followed by a pathetic effort at reclamation, is a moving piece of character presentation, as is *The Bribe*, with its sad complications centering in a retiring dispensary doctor's snaring his job for his incompetent son.

GEORGE BRANDON SAUL

WORKS: *The Shuiler's Child*. Dublin: Maunsel, 1909/Chicago: De Paul University, 1971. (Play); *The Bribe*. London: Maunsel, 1914/Dublin: James Duffy, 1952. (Play); *The Lady of Deerpark*. London: Methuen, 1917. (Novel); *Waysiders*. Dublin: Talbot/London: Unwin, [1917]/New York: Stokes, 1919. (Stories); *Ranns and Ballads*. Dublin: Candle, 1918; *The Golden Barque and the Weaver's Grave*. Dublin: Talbot/London: Unwin, 1919. (Stories); *The Leprechaun of Kilmeen*. Dublin: Martin Lester, 1920; *Hillsiders*. Dublin: Talbot/London: Unwin, 1921. (Stories); *Wet Clay*. Dublin: Talbot/London: Unwin, 1922. (Novel); *The Matchmakers*. Dublin: Talbot, 1925. (One-act play); *Meadowsweet*. Dublin: Talbot, 1925. (One-act play); *The Weaver's Grave*. Dublin: Talbot, 1925. REFERENCE: Saul, George Brandon. *Seumas O'Kelly*. Lewisburgh, Pa.: Bucknell University Press, 1971.

O'LEARY, CON (1887-1958), journalist and novelist. O'Leary was a well known journalist on London's Fleet Street. He was described by *The Times* as "a warm and lovable personality" with a "mercurial temperament . . . a craftsman with style and, at his best, an individual artist." He was born in Cork in 1887. He attended University College, Cork, and while a student there became involved with the Cork Dramatic Society whose leading spirits were Daniel Corkery* and Terence J. MacSwiney.* He acted for the society, and two of his own plays were produced. One of these, *The Crossing*, was later produced by the Abbey* in 1914, as was his one-act *Queer Ones* in 1919. His plays were not too well received and have not been published, but he was described as much influenced by Synge.*

O'Leary worked on *The Freeman's Journal* in Dublin, and then under C. P. Scott on *The Manchester Guardian* and edited its weekly edition. He was brought to London by T. P. O'Connor, and was an assistant editor of *T. P.'s Weekly*. At his death on November 11, 1958, he was working in the London office of *The Irish Press*. He published a charming volume of Irish sketches, *An Exile's Bundle*, in 1923 and probably his best novel, *Break o' Day*, in 1926. His other novels include *This Delicate Creature* (1928) and *Passage West* (1946). He wrote a history of the Grand National and one of the more engaging of the multitudinous travel books on Ireland. He was probably always too much engaged in daily journalism ever to develop fully his undeniable creative talents.

WORKS: *An Exile's Bundles*. London: Andrew Melrose, 1923; *Break o' Day*. London: Cassell & Co., 1926; *This Delicate Creature*. London: Constable, 1928; *A Hillside Man*. London: Lovat Dickson, 1933; *A Wayfarer in Ireland*. London: Methuen, 1935. (Travel); *Grand National*. London: Rockliff, 1945/revised ed., London: Rockliff, 1947; *Passage West*. London: Rockliff, 1945.

O'LEARY, JOHN (1830-1907), Fenian and journalist. O'Leary was born in Tipperary on July 23, 1830. He joined the Young Ireland movement, and later was a prominent Fenian and edited the Fenian journal *The Irish People*. Arrested after the Fenian uprising, he was imprisoned for five years and exiled from Ireland for a further fifteen. When he returned, he became the friend and mentor of the young W. B. Yeats,* who wrote of "O'Leary's noble head." Indeed, everyone who knew O'Leary in his old age was impressed by his lofty character. His chief work is a memoir, *Recollections of Fenians and Fenianism* (1896), which is now little read but which is written with an urbane lucidity and a calm good sense. O'Leary's account of how he was awakened to a national consciousness by reading Thomas Davis* might be taken as a paradigm of how several generations of young men were affected by Davis. His account of his fellow Fenians is refreshingly lacking in hero worship, and he is worth consulting on C. J. Kickham.* He died in Dublin on March 16, 1907.

His sister Ellen (1831-1889) was also active in the Fenian conspiracy, and a posthumous volume of her patriotic and sentimental verse, *Lays of Country, Home, and Friends* (Dublin: Sealy, Bryers & Walker, 1891), was edited by T. W. Rolleston.*

WORK: *Recollections of Fenians and Fenianism*. London: Downey, 1896.

O'NEILL, JOSEPH [JAMES] (1878-1952), novelist. O'Neill was born in Tuam, County Galway, on December 18, 1878, but spent much of his boyhood on the Aran Islands where his father, a member of the Royal Irish Constabulary, had been stationed. He returned to the mainland in 1893 to attend St. Jarlath's College in Tuam, and later, from 1898 to 1901, Queen's

College, Galway, from which he received his B.A. and M.A. in modern literature. O'Neill's years on Aran, and his upbringing in a household where Irish
was the language spoken, contributed to his interest in the revival of Irish
language and literature. In 1903, he left a teaching position at Queen's College to enroll in Kuno Meyer's School of Irish Learning. His first scholarly
work, a translation of "*Cath Boinde*" published in *Eriu*, secured him a
scholarship to Victoria College in Manchester where he studied under John
Strachan, the classical and Celtic scholar (1862-1907). In 1907, he studied
comparative philology at the University of Freiburg where he formed a close
friendship with his fellow-student Osborn Bergin (1872-1950).

Although O'Neill was considered a promising scholar, he abandoned
Irish studies for civil service when, in 1908, his former teacher, William
Starkey, then resident commissioner of education, offered him a job as
second class inspector of primary schools. After his marriage to Mary Devenport,* a student at the National College of Art, on June 29, 1908, O'Neill
rose quickly in the Department of Secondary Education and was appointed
its permanent secretary in 1923, a post he held until his retirement in 1944.

O'Neill always had literary interests. He had published poetry regularly
in *The Freeman's Journal* under the pseudonym "Oisin" and some articles
on cultural and philological subjects for the *Irish Statesman*. His first book-
length work, however, was *The Kingdom-Maker* (1917), a verse play set
at the beginning of the Christian Era in Ireland; the wars between the Firbolgs and the Gaels provided him with a metaphor through which to comment on both World War I and Ireland's suit for independence. By the
1920s, the O'Neills had bought their house at 2 Kenilworth Square, Rathgar, and established a Thursday evening salon, which AE,* Bergin, Yeats,*
Lennox Robinson,* and Austin Clarke,* among many other distinguished
writers, attended.

The company he kept encouraged O'Neill to begin writing in earnest,
although his first novel, *Wind from the North*, took ten years to complete
and was not published until 1934. The novel is a historical romance that
often achieves a chilling epic quality through the conflict that rages within
its protagonist. The protagonist, a nameless Dublin clerk, is hit by a tram-
car and wakes as one of the principal participants in the turmoil that has
beset the eleventh-century Norse town of Dyflin in the weeks preceding
Brian Boru's invasion. The theme of the novel is based on Karl Jung's doctrine of man's search for his Ancestral Self and on AE's belief that every
man lives through repeated reincarnations. In O'Neill's protagonist, the
world of twentieth-century Dublin and eleventh-century Dyflin vie for possession of his soul, and the novel ends with this conflict unresolved. *Wind
from the North* won the Harmsworth Award of the Irish Academy of Letters in 1934.

How man thinking and man acting can function in accord became
O'Neill's persistent theme. The two novels that followed, *Land Under*

England (1935) and *Day of Wrath* (1936), develop this theme in the tradition of the counter-utopian novels of Huxley and the later H. G. Wells. The first is a political and psychological allegory of a young Englishman trapped in a horrifying world beneath the Yorkshire countryside. The area is inhabited by dehumanized automatons, the descendants of the last Roman legionnaires to occupy England, and the hero attempts to fathom the source of man's Oedipal drives and fears of miscegenation. The second, a futuristic political polemic responding to the European political situation of 1936, shows how man will behave when the thin crust of civilization that separates him from his primitive self is broken by a worldwide war. Both novels are structurally and stylistically flawed, *Land Under England* being an exciting but unimpressive work of the imagination, and *Day of Wrath* a total failure in style and conception.

Philip (1940), a return to historical fiction, is the story of a physician, half-Greek, half-Jew, who returns to Israel to seek his Ancestral Past. Set in the teeming, brawling, politically and religiously chaotic streets of Jerusalem in the few months preceding Christ's Crucifixion, the novel is remarkably evocative and structurally flawless and marks the high point in O'Neill's literary achievement. Short historical sketches for *The Dublin Magazine** followed; two in particular, "An Evening with Ben Jonson" and "Audience with Gloriana," served as preparation for his final full-length work, *Chosen By the Queen* (1947). The historical information O'Neill amassed for this study of Robert Devereaux, second earl of Essex, his ignominious fall from Elizabeth's favor, and his execution in the Tower, is not as well controlled as that of *Philip*. Still, the novel projects much of the bustle, intrigue, and grandeur of Elizabeth's court and of an England just emerging into nationhood.

Beset with financial difficulties and having lived long enough to survive most of his friends, O'Neill sold the Kenilworth Square residence and all its furnishings in August 1949 and, with his wife, moved to Nice. The move was disastrous. Not only was living in southern France far more expensive than he had anticipated, but also in a fall, he broke his kneecap which would not knit properly. Fearing that he would become an invalid in a foreign and, for him, uncongenial country, O'Neill returned to Ireland in April 1950. They rented a house in Wicklow where O'Neill began to recover and work on his final project, "Pages from the Journal of Edmund Shakespeare," published serially in *The Dublin Magazine* between 1951 and 1952. Whether this series of journal entries made between 1596 and 1598 by the sixteen-year-old brother of William Shakespeare was another work in progress is uncertain. Walking in the Wicklow Hills in the early spring of 1952, O'Neill suffered a cerebral hemorrhage and was brought to St. John of God's Nursing Home in Stillorgan where he died on May 6.

M. KELLY LYNCH

WORKS: *The Kingdom-Maker: A Verse Play in Five Acts*. Dublin: Talbot, 1917;

Wind from the North. London: Jonathan Cape, 1934. (Novel); *Land Under England.* London: Gollancz/New York: Simon & Schuster, 1935. (Novel); *Day of Wrath.* London: Gollancz, 1936; *Philip.* London: Gollancz, 1940. (Novel); *Chosen by the Queen.* London: Gollancz, 1947. (Novel).

O'NEILL, MARY DEVENPORT (1879-1967), poet. O'Neill was born on August 3, 1879, in Loughrea, County Galway, the daughter of a subconstable. After convent school, she attended the National College of Art in Dublin and, while a student there, began a correspondence with Joseph O'Neill* whose poetry she had read in *The Freeman's Journal* and admired. They eventually married on June 29, 1908.

She kept a respected salon in Rathgar, a "Thursday at Home" attended by many famous writers of the day. She was particularly intimate with W. B. Yeats* and became his consultant while he was writing *A Vision.* Yeats recorded in a notebook the specific literary problems he and Mary O'Neill discussed (National Library of Ireland, Ms. 13576).

In 1917, O'Neill wrote the occasional lyrics for her husband's verse play *The Kingdom-Maker,* which was followed by her only published book *Prometheus and Other Poems,* a collection of lyrics, the single long title poem, and a one-act verse play, *Bluebeard.* Influenced profoundly by Pound, Peguy, and Proust, the shorter poems of this collection show a writer with a keen lyric gift, a sensitivity to tone, and a sharp eye for color, image, and detail. "Prometheus," however, a longer and more ambitious poem which poses the conflict of reality and imagination in the creative spirit, is not as successful as the shorter pieces and tends to lapse into occasional tedium.

Although Mary O'Neill published only this one collection, she remained active in Dublin's literary world. *Bluebeard* was performed by Austin Clarke's* Lyric Theatre Company in 1933 and *Cain,* another verse play, in 1945. Single poems appeared regularly in *The Irish Times, The Bell,* * and *The Dublin Magazine,* * which also published several of her plays and verse plays. These are very much in the tradition of the Celtic Twilight and draw their subject matter principally from Irish and German myth and legend.

After her husband's death in 1952, when her own health began to fail, she lived with relatives in Dublin until her death in 1967.

                                                                    M. KELLY LYNCH

WORKS: "Three Poems." *The Irish Statesman* 4 (August 1, 1926):650; *Prometheus and Other Poems.* London: Jonathan Cape, 1929; "Cain." *The Dublin Magazine* 13 (Spring 1938):30-48. (Verse play); "Dead in Wars and in Revolutions." *The Dublin Magazine* 16 (Winter 1941):7. (Poem); "Scene-Shifter Death." *The Dublin Magazine* 19 (Spring 1944):40. (Poem); "Valhalla." *The Dublin Magazine* 19 (Winter 1944):3. (Poem); "Out of Darkness." *The Dublin Magazine* 22 (Summer 1947):20-39. (Play); "The Visiting Moon." *The Dublin Magazine* 23 (Spring 1948):35-46. (Verse play); "Lost Legions." *The Dublin Magazine* 24 (Spring 1949):16. (Poem).

O'NEILL, MOIRA (ca. 1870-?), poet. Moira O'Neill was the pen name of Agnes Nesta Shakespeare Higginson, who married Walter Clarmont Skrine and lived for a while in Canada and also in Rockport, County Antrim. Her *Songs of the Glens of Antrim* (1901) was extremely popular, and she might be considered a pale Irish version of Burns. She wrote in dialect and in a variety of heavily stressed rhythms and complicated rhyme patterns. Her subjects were the usual ones of the popular poet: nostalgia, patriotism, and occasional mild comedy. Nevertheless, for a popular poet, she was not without quality, and sometimes, as in the refrain to "Corrymella," she uses euphony and rhythm with considerable effect. Sometimes she also manages characterization as well as the young Padraic Colum* did. For instance, this stanza from "Marriage":

> "As sure as ye're young an' fair," says she, "one day ye'll be
>   ugly an' ould.
> If ye haven't a husband, who'll care," says she, "to call ye in
>   out o' the could?
>   Left to yourself,
>   Laid on the shelf,—
>   Now is your time to marry.
> Musha! don't tell *me* ye'll be married to-morrow,
> Wi' the man to find an' the money to borrow."

Her daughter, Mary Nesta Skrine (Mrs. Robert Keane), was born on July 20, 1905, and under the pen name of M. J. Farrell has written a number of light novels and some successful farcical comedies. The most popular of M. J. Farrell's plays are *Spring Meeting* (1938) and *Treasure Hunt* (1950).

WORKS: *An Easter Vacation*. London: Lawrence & Bullen, 1893/New York: E. P. Dutton, 1894; *The Elf-Errant*. London: Lawrence & Bullen, 1893/New York: E. P. Dutton, 1894; *Songs of the Glens of Antrim*. Edinburgh & London: Blackwood, 1901; *More Songs of the Glens of Antrim*. Edinburgh & London: Blackwood, 1921; *From Two Points of View*. Edinburgh & London: Blackwood, 1924; *Collected Poems of Moira O'Neill*. Edinburgh & London: Blackwood, 1933.

O'NOLAN, BRIAN (1911-1966), novelist, journalist, and humorist. Brian O'Nolan (or Ó Nuallain), author of novels, plays, and short stories, was much better known as Flann O'Brien or Myles na gCopaleen, but he had other pseudonymic incarnations: Brother Barnabas, George Knowall, Count O'Blather, and John James Doe. An intensely private man in many ways, he seems to have felt the need to disguise his personality behind a series of "elaborate façades" and once described as "horrible" the type of biography that lifts the veil on the true man. The real Brian O'Nolan was born on October 5, 1911, in Strabane, County Tyrone, the third of twelve children. His father, an Irish speaker, was an officer in the Customs and Excise Service and was moved so often around the country (from Strabane to Dublin to Tullamore) that it was not until the family settled in Dublin again, in 1923, that he went to school. He attended first the Christian Brothers school in Synge Street, which he didn't like, and then Blackrock College. In 1929, he entered University College, Dublin, where he took a B.A. degree in English, Irish, and German, followed by an M.A. with a thesis on Irish poetry. During his years at University College, O'Nolan was renowned as a debater, winning a gold medal for impromptu debate in the 1932-1933 session and challenging, albeit unsuccessfully, Vivian de Valera, for the auditorship of the College's Literary and Historical Society. In the college magazine *Comhthrom Féinne* and in his own magazine *Blather*, he began to write articles in Irish and English which clearly indicated his tendency towards parody, satire, and fantasy.

In 1935, O'Nolan entered the local government section of the Irish civil service where he was to remain for eighteen years until his retirement in 1953. His first novel, *At Swim-Two-Birds*, published in 1939, was not a success, and *The Third Policeman*, completed in 1940, was refused by the publishers and remained unpublished until after his death. His disappointment was slightly alleviated by an invitation to write a column for *The Irish Times*. *Cruiskeen Lawn* by Myles na gCopaleen became famous (or infamous) and remained so for its more than twenty-five years' duration. The next few years saw O'Nolan at a peak of creativity. In 1941, *An Béal Bocht* (trans. *The Poor Mouth*) appeared and was an instant success among the Irish-speaking "establishment" which it mercilessly parodied. In 1943, three plays, *Faustus Kelly, The Insect Play*, and *Thirst*, were produced. Thereafter there was a decline, and until the reissue of *At Swim-Two-Birds* in 1960, there were many years of frustration, poverty, and hack journalism. The success of the reissue led to a period of renewed activity. *The Hard Life* appeared in 1961, and *The Dalkey Archive* in 1964. There were many television scripts, plays, and short stories, and seven chapters of a new novel *Slattery's Sago Saga* had been completed by the time of his death, after a painful illness, on April 1, 1966.

O'Nolan's output, then, was varied and plentiful. There was a slow deterioration in standards over the years, and certainly the best work was produced before 1945. The two novels written after 1960 were, respectively, a rehash of much of the material which had proved so successful in *Cruiskeen Lawn*, and a rewrite of *The Third Policeman*, sunnier in vision but less structurally coherent. His best works are *At Swim-Two-Birds, The Third Policeman, An Béal Bocht,* and *Cruiskeen Lawn*. To a great extent, the characteristics of the *Cruiskeen Lawn* newspaper column are those of the novels as well: distilled and compressed.

O'Nolan's column appeared approximately triweekly from 1940 to 1966. It was written in Irish and English and occasionally in hybrid languages of O'Nolan's own invention. It was full of elaborate puns, linguistic jokes, nonsense, satire, fantastic inventions, unforgettable characters (the Brother and Myles), verbatim reports of the deliberations of local councils and courts of law (often more fantastic than his own wildest imagination!), and analyses of the debasement of language and the clichéd jargon of the various professions. O'Nolan was bilingual and had a more than competent knowledge of several other languages; in a manner characteristic of many Irish writers, he was in love with words. One of his greatest talents was an ear for dialogue, especially for the Dubliners' conversations—repetitive, opinionated, boring, misinformed, and brilliant. He loved the weight and color of words, and linguistic games of all kinds. He was acutely aware of the way different grammatical forms could affect the perception of the people who used them. Many of his statements about languages are serious and penetrating, though he had, of course, an incurable habit of immediately undercutting any even semiserious thought by inventing or exaggerating it until it became nonsense.

The obsession with words is one of the notable features of the novels. Both *At Swim-Two-Birds*, and *An Béal Bocht* can be said to be "about" style. In many ways, O'Nolan's work is typical of the twentieth-century Irish writer, but whereas many of his contemporaries were poised uneasily between the two cultures, the two literary and linguistic traditions, O'Nolan was able to move with confidence within each tradition and to create, from parodied versions of both, his own strange fantastic world. At once conservative and ultramodern, his first three novels are based in part on versions of medieval Irish tales but have recognizable affinities with the world of Joyce* and Beckett* as well as Sartre, the Theatre of the Absurd, and the *nouveau-roman*. In his best work, O'Nolan emerges as a writer of real originality, a satirist, parodist, and fantasist whose main creative impulse arose from the desire to deflate the pretensions of intellectuals and fanatics of all kinds. The forms he chose to embody this deflation led to the creation of fantasy worlds, of situations which had an often disturbing, sideways relationship to reality but in which everything was possible. O'Nolan delighted in the creation of such worlds where the imagination could roam at will. He exulted in the boundless creativity of the human mind, where there were no limits to supposition, where all combinations of experience were equally valid. He had little patience with the demands of realism, though he could be as formally realistic as anyone else. In pursuing the world of imagination and eschewing the realistic, mundane, and moralistic tradition of English novelists, O'Nolan was returning to the Celtic models he admired and, at the same time, fitting very well into some of the main patterns of contemporary European writing.

ANNE CLISSMANN

WORKS: *At Swim-Two-Birds*. London: MacGibbon & Kee, 1960; *The Hard Life*. London: MacGibbon & Kee, 1961; *The Dalkey Archive*. London: MacGibbon & Kee, 1964; *The Third Policeman*. London: MacGibbon & Kee, 1967; *The Best of Myles*.

London: MacGibbon & Kee, 1968; *An Béal Bocht*. Dublin: Dolmen, 1964. Translated by Patrick Power as *The Poor Mouth*, London: Hart-Davis, MacGibbon, 1973; *Stories and Plays*. London: Hart-Davis, MacGibbon, 1973; *The Journal of Irish Literature* 3 (January 1974), a Flann O'Brien number edited by Anne Clissman & David Powell; *The Various Lives of Keats and Chapman and The Brother*. London: Hart-Davis, MacGibbon, 1976.   REFERENCES: Clissmann, Anne. *Flann O'Brien: A Critical Introduction to His Writing*. Dublin: Gill & Macmillan, 1975; O'Keeffe, T., ed. *Myles*. London: Martin, Brian & O'Keeffe, 1973.

O'REILLY, JOHN BOYLE (1844-1890), Fenian, journalist, poet, and novelist. O'Reilly was born at Dowth Castle, County Meath, on June 28, 1844. A soldier in the British Army, he was transported to Australia for disseminating Fenianism but escaped to America where he edited *The* [Boston] *Pilot*. He published a novel, *Moondyne* (1879), about the Australian convict settlements, as well as several volumes of polished popular verse of the usual sentimental and patriotic kind. He died in Boston on August 10, 1890.

WORKS: *Songs from the Southern Seas, and Other Poems*. Boston: Roberts, 1873; *Songs, Legends, and Ballads*. Boston: Pilot Publishing Co., 1878; *Moondyne*. Boston: Pilot Publishing Co., 1879. (Novel); *The Statues in the Block, and Other Poems*. Boston: Roberts, 1881; *The King's Men*. New York: Scribner, 1884. Written in collaboration with several friends. (Novel); *In Bohemia*. Boston: Pilot Publishing Co., 1886. (Poems); *Watchwords from John Boyle O'Reilly*. Katherine E. Conway, ed. Boston: Cupples, 1892; *Selected Poems of John Boyle O'Reilly*. New York & Boston: Caldwell, 1904; *Selected Poems by John Boyle O'Reilly*. Mary J. A. O'Reilly, ed. New York: Kenedy, 1913.   REFERENCE: Roche, James Jeffrey. *Life of John Boyle O'Reilly Together with his Complete Poems and Speeches*. Mrs. John Boyle O'Reilly, ed. New York: Mershon, 1891.

O'RIORDAN, CONAL (1874-1948), novelist and playwright. O'Riordan, one of the most extraordinary modern Irish writers, is also one of the most neglected. In his own day, his work was compared to that of Balzac and Dickens, but today every one of his twenty-seven volumes is out of print.

He was born Conal Holmes O'Connell O'Riordan on April 29, 1874, in Dublin, the younger son of Daniel O'Connell O'Riordan, Q.C. Like James Joyce,* he was educated at Belvedere College, but he left school early to prepare for a military career. This hope was dashed when a fall from a horse caused a permanent spinal ailment. He then went on the stage and was involved in London with J. T. Grein's Independent Theatre, playing Engstrand in the first English production of Ibsen's *Ghosts*. He also began to write plays with some success and to publish novels under the pseudonym of F. Norreys Connell. Yeats* and Lady Gregory* chose him to replace J. M. Synge* on the board of the Abbey Theatre* after Synge's death. Among the plays he produced at the Abbey was the first revival of *The Playboy of the Western World*, a production that occasioned some protests. His own Abbey plays were short curtain-raisers, but one of them, *The*

Piper (1908), seemed about to cause another *Playboy*-like riot until Yeats placated the audience by the explanation that the play was a patriotic political allegory. After a few months, O'Riordan resigned from the Abbey, impatient with the constant interference of Miss Horniman, the theatre's financial backer. Because of his small stature and physical disabilities, O'Riordan was rejected by the British Army in 1914, but he made his way to the front as head of a YMCA rest hut.

After the war, O'Riordan wrote under his own name. He had some success again with plays which were mainly breezy light comedies, especially *Napoleon's Josephine* produced at the Fortune Theatre, London, in 1928. However, his major achievement was a series of twelve novels which traced the fortunes of several connected Irish families from the Napoleonic wars to about 1920. O'Riordan lived the rest of his life in London and among his friends were many of the important writers of the day—Dowson, Yeats, Conrad, Galsworthy, Wilfrid Owen, and a multitude of others. He was small, frail, seemingly crippled, and yet a convivial and witty conversationalist. In an obituary in *The London Times,* John Brophy remarked that courage was one of his lifelong characteristics: "He needed it to overcome his physical disabilities and to endure professional disappointments without rancor or self-pity." Most of his last years were spent in seclusion, and he died at his home in Ealing on June 18, 1948.

O'Riordan's prewar writing was less than successful. His first book, *In the Green Park* (1894), is a group of fancifully connected short stories. Although the book went into a second edition, it is a sophomoric bit of facetiousness by a clever young man facile with words but possessing little taste or judgment. *The House of the Strange Woman* (1895), a novel about love and marriage, is romantic, sardonic, and jejune. The book's main strength is the terse and dramatic fluency of the dialogue, a quality that grows increasingly evident in all of O'Riordan's later work. The descriptive and narrative passages are much stiffer, and the baby-talk of the opening chapter is deplorable. The pervasive disillusionment is both more realistic and less mature than what would be found in conventional books of the day. *The Fool and His Heart* (1896), a sweeter version of *The House of the Strange Woman,* is rather autobiographical and contains some ineffective satire of the bohemian life in *fin de siècle* London. O'Riordan's later prewar work has considerably more technical facility. While none of it is superb, the callowness of the early books has disappeared. For instance, most of the stories in *The Pity of War* (1906) are rather Kiplingesque and suggest a soldier morality of bravery which is often nobler than the cause in which it is engaged. The style is simple and lucid. Some of the stories are too pat, but the book is a creditable advance over *In the Green Park*.

O'Riordan's major work was produced after the war—a twelve-volume cycle which began to appear in 1920 and which was concluded in 1940. The cycle was not written in chronological order but commenced with the

"Adam" novels that conclude the story. The chronological beginning is with the four "Soldier" novels: *Soldier Born* (1927), *Soldier of Waterloo* (1928), *Soldier's Wife* (1935), and *Soldier's End* (1938). It is difficult to find an exact literary parallel to this tetrology. In one sense, in its hero's picaresque wanderings over Europe and America, it is an unfacetious relative of the recent Flashman novels. Or perhaps a better comparison would be to Thackeray's *Henry Esmond*, whose hero O'Riordan's David Quinn in many ways resembles. David Quinn becomes involved with many historical personages and events, such as Princess Charlotte and the battle of Waterloo, Daniel O'Connell and the Irish Potato Famine, Lincoln and the American Civil War, and he finally dies in the Franco-Prussian War. Both the public and personal stories of the tetrology—and, indeed, of the whole cycle—are extraordinarily complex, and the relations of the characters are occasionally an inextricable tangle. *Soldier of Waterloo,* perhaps the best of the David Quinn stories, has been ranked by some critics with *Adam of Dublin* (1920) as O'Riordan's best work. Its tone, however, is typically uneven: it is in part conventional and somewhat stilted romance, in part a vivid depiction of Dublin and London, and in one chapter a brilliantly impressionistic and hideous view of the battle of Waterloo from the vantage point of one individual soldier.

The entire cycle is at its weakest in depicting the relations between men and women. The poorest volumes—*The Age of Miracles* (1925) and its sequel *Young Lady Dazincourt* (1926), and *Judith Quinn* (1939) and its sequel *Judith's Love* (1940)—are, in a pejorative sense, little better than woman's fiction. Indeed, one of the novels is subtitled "A Novel for Women." The conversations are often witty, but the analysis of motives goes on interminably; as a result, the novels seem to be written by a jocular Henry James in collaboration with Mrs. Henry Wood. The characters in these volumes also exhibit a priggish diffidence about sexual love. Judith Quinn, for instance, is so foggy about the two sexual encounters she has over a period of some thirteen years that she does not really know what happened. More importantly, neither does the reader; for one of the most peculiar aspects of the entire cycle is that in several crucial instances it is difficult to know who is whose parent. Indeed, the genealogy of the dozens of important characters in the cycle is almost hopelessly confused.

The Adam novels which conclude the series chronologically are enormously better than the female fiction of the central books. The initial volume, *Adam of Dublin,* is one of the finest evocations of the city ever written by anyone, including Joyce. The portrait of the Jesuit school, Belvedere College, deserves to be set beside the Joyce passages in *Portrait of the Artist*, and the hilarious scene at the Abbey Theatre during the first revival of Synge's *Playboy* is memorable. The comparison to *Portrait of the Artist* is particularly apt, except that the Adam volumes carry O'Riordan's young artist into exile, marriage, and maturity. If the Adam books do not satisfactorily resolve the tangled threads of this 120-year cycle, they are more controlled than the Soldier books and as consummate a recreation of the past. The entire cycle is flawed, wavering in intention and varying in execution from the bathetic to the eloquent. Nevertheless, its scope is so vast and its virtues so many that its rediscovery must establish O'Riordan as one of the major Irish writers of his day.

WORKS: *In the Green Park; or, Half-Pay Deities.* London: Henry, 1894. (Stories); *The House of the Strange Woman.* London: Henry, 1895. (Novel); *The Fool and His Heart.* London: Leonard Smithers, 1896. (Novel); *How Soldiers Fight.* London: James Bowden, 1899; *The Nigger Knights.* London: Methuen, 1900; *The Follies of Captain Daly.* London: Grant Richards, 1901. (Novel); *The Pity of War.* London: Henry J. Glaisher, 1906. (Stories); *The Young Days of Admiral Quilliam.* Edinburgh & London: William Blackwood, 1906; *Shakespeare's End, and Other Irish Plays.* London: Stephen Swift, 1912; *Rope Enough.* Dublin & London: Maunsel, 1914. (Play); *Adam of Dublin.* London: Collins, [1920]. (Novel); *Adam and Caroline.* London: Collins, [1921]. (Novel); *In London: The Story of Adam and Marriage.* London: Collins, [1922]; *Rowena Barnes.* London: Collins, [1923]. (Novel); *Married Life.* London: Collins, [1924]. (Novel); *The Age of Miracles.* London: Collins, [1925]. (Novel); *His Majesty's Pleasure.* London: Ernest Benn, 1925. (Play); *Young Lady Dazincourt.* London: Collins, [1925]. (Novel); *Soldier Born.* London: Collins, [1927]. (Novel); *Soldier of Waterloo.* London: Collins, [1928]. (Novel); *The King's Wooing.* London & Glasgow: Gowans & Gray, 1929. (One-act play); *Napoleon Passes.* London: Arrowsmith, 1933. (History); *Captain Falstaff and Other Plays.* London: Arrowsmith, 1935; *Soldier's Wife.* London: Arrowsmith, 1935. (Novel); *Soldier's End.* [London]: Arrowsmith, 1938. (Novel); *Judith Quinn: A Novel for Women.* Bristol: Arrowsmith, 1939; *Judith's Love.* Bristol: Arrowsmith, 1940. (Novel).

ORMSBY, FRANK (1947-), poet and editor. Ormsby was born in 1947 in County Fermanagh, and was educated at St. Michael's College, Enniskillen, and Queen's University, Belfast. He succeeded James Simmons* as editor of *The Honest Ulsterman,* and that organization published two of his early poetry pamphlets. From those pamphlets, he salvaged a few poems for his first collection, *A Store of Candles* (1977), which was a Poetry Book Society choice. His early work was characterized by clarity of statement and some sporadic attempts toward form. For instance, his "Poem for Paula" was meterless and rhymed ABABCC in its first stanza; its second stanza of five lines was also meterless but did not attempt to rhyme. However, he was capable of an effective image, as in one of his surviving early poems "McQuade," in which cancer is pictured as a football match. *A Store of Candles* represents an advance in Ormsby's style, at least to the extent that he has purged some faults. The poems are still factual, small in scope, and take few chances of either language or emotion, but their lack of poetic skill is somewhat disguised by their adequacy as rhetoric. Ormsby's strivings toward poetic form are rather tentative, but two pieces, "At the Reception" and "Aftermath," are very good.

The Honest Ulsterman, which Ormsby has edited for several years, has at this writing produced more than sixty numbers since its first appearance in 1968, and that is a remarkable longevity for an Irish literary magazine. The *Ulsterman,* except for some imaginative covers, is cheaply produced and physically unprepossessing, but it has a splapdash liveliness unique in Irish literary periodicals. It also provides a forum for the Northern writer and is particularly receptive to new poets. Its many poetry pamphlets have included work by Seamus Heaney,* Derek Mahon,* Paul Muldoon,* Tom Paulin,* Geoffrey Squires,* and many lesser known writers. Indeed, the efforts of the Ulsterman publications have fostered the feeling that there is something of a vital, if slovenly, poetic renaissance going on in the North.

WORKS: *Knowing My Place.* Belfast: Ulsterman, 1971. (Pamphlet); *Spirit of Dawn.* Belfast: Ulsterman, 1973. (Pamphlet); *A Store of Candles.* Oxford, London, New York: Oxford University Press, 1977.

ORR, JAMES (1770-1816), poet. Orr was born at Broad Island, County Antrim, in 1770. He was the only son of a weaver with a few acres of land, and he followed his father's profession. In his teens, he became a United Irishman and contributed verse to the movement's periodical, *The Northern Star.* After fighting heroically in the battle of Antrim, on June 7, 1798, he was jailed and then sent to America. When he returned to his native village of Ballycarry in the early 1800s, he continued to write verse, and a collection of his work appeared in 1804. After this, however, he took to drink, and he died in Ballycarry on April 24, 1816.

Orr's poem "The Irishman" was his most popular, but its undoubted sincerity is defeated by its utterly conventional phrasing. Orr has no totally admirable poems, but portions of certain poems are quite striking. For instance, the early stanzas of "Song of an Exile" are reminiscent of Goldsmith's* "The Deserted Village," and do not quite wither by the comparison. More interesting, because it is more authentic, is "Death and Burial of an Irish Cotter," with its realistic observation and its effective if not thoroughgoing use of dialect. A handful of critics, from D. J. O'Donoghue* to John Hewitt,* have found much to admire in Orr. Perhaps the most judicious view is that Orr had few opportunities for education, and so never developed a discriminating literary judgment commensurate with his considerable native abilities.

WORKS: *Poems on Various Subjects.* Belfast: Smyth & Lyons, 1804; *The Posthumous Works of James Orr, of Ballycarry with a Sketch of his Life.* Belfast: Finlay, 1817; *Poems on Various Subjects.* Belfast: Mullan, 1935. (A new edition of the two previous volumes).

O'SULLIVAN, SEUMAS (1879-1958), poet and editor. Seumas O'Sullivan was born James Sullivan Starkey in Dublin on July 17, 1879. His literary career did not begin until 1902 with the publication of a few poems in *The Irish Homestead, The United Irishman,* and *Celtic Christmas.* With the 1904 publications of *New Songs* edited by George Russell,* five of O'Sullivan's poems were for the first time included in a book. In 1904, O'Sullivan also helped to reestablish the publishing firm Whaley and Company with fellow poet and actor George Roberts (1873-1953), and one year later, in 1905, Whaley and Company published O'Sullivan's first book of poetry, *The Twilight People*. Encouraged by the reception of his verse in *New Songs,* O'Sullivan had decided to put three dozen of his poems into a book. They made delicate use of melody and were concerned more with the establishment of atmosphere than with themes. O'Sullivan's poetry drew the reader into an elemental world populated by waning moons, pale stars, and wandering shades. Many of the moods that infused the early work of W. B. Yeats* and George Russell were resurrected in O'Sullivan: the yearning for the infinite, the turmoil of the soul, the silence and magic of twilight.

Between 1906 and 1908, O'Sullivan co-edited the Tower Press Booklets with James Connolly (not the labor leader). The Tower Press intended to issue monthly booklets of unpublished verse, sketches, and essays by living Irish writers, some established and others less well known—many of whom were personal friends of Seumas O'Sullivan. The first series of booklets originally sold for one shilling, and, with the exception of George Russell's *Some Irish Essays* and George Moore's* *Reminiscences of the Impressionist Painters*, the little booklets were slow to sell. O'Sullivan's own booklets, *Verses: Sacred and Profane,* appeared in 1908. In this poetry, the mood of subjective and tender melancholy, which was so prevalent in *The Twilight People,* was even more prevalent. Here, he was absorbed with the beauty of decay and was immured in sadness. It was only proper for O'Sullivan, the archetypal Celtic poet and incurable idealist, to be depressed since the best that life and nature showed him was meager compared with that unrealized perfection he sought.

In 1909, O'Sullivan's New Nation Press published his third volume of poetry, *The Earth-Lover and Other Verses,* which, like other true lyric verse, expressed a personal mood and not the war-cry of a group. Its delicately wrought verse echoed a mood of calm prevalent in Celtic Twilight poetry. O'Sullivan renounced the energy of sunlight for evening time, which offered the tenderness of the stars and the nirvana of sleep for company. In *The Earth-Lover,* O'Sullivan once again showed an ability to deal simply and directly with life. For the first time, he took impressions of Dublin street life as material for several of his poems: the waif's fondness for the rags and bones man, and the regularity of the organ grinder who came to the street each Monday.

With the 1917 publication of *Requiem and Other Poems,* O'Sullivan's nationalism was apparent for the first time. In the elegy "In Memoriam— T. MacD.," O'Sullivan praised the poet, playwright, and nationalist Thomas MacDonagh* for his ability to learn from the past as well as for his skill to stimulate song in others. In another poem, "Requiem," O'Sullivan exhorted his readers not to greet those who died in the Easter Rebellion with tears; he believed they deserved a more vigorous and noble tribute. Because much of the poetry in this volume was concerned with the feverish period in which it was published, it was not surprising that O'Sullivan's contributions to another 1917 publication, *Aftermath of Easter Week,* edited by Padraic Browne, were also deeply nationalistic and at times almost reverential. O'Sullivan's involvement with Irish nationalism began before and extended beyond the publication of *Requiem* and *Aftermath.* When he first met Arthur Griffith,* O'Sullivan established a friendship that was to continue for many years. His rooms became a favorite place of call for Griffith and for some of those who associated with him in the early days of Sinn Féin. When Griffith went on his weekend tramps in the Dublin mountains or occasional excursions to the Continent, he was often accompanied by O'Sullivan.

When O'Sullivan began to edit *The Dublin Magazine** in 1923, a task that was to occupy him until his death in 1958, he subordinated his nationalism to this work, and the magazine assumed an apolitical and eclectic point of view. O'Sullivan encouraged young writers, and the advent of *The Dublin Magazine* coincided with the rise of a new generation of Irish writers such as Austin Clarke,* F. R. Higgins,* and Liam O'Flaherty.* In an awkward period of transition when the so-called Irish Renaissance had already reached its zenith, O'Sullivan rallied many young Irish writers around himself and *The Dublin Magazine.* Writers like Samuel Beckett,* Patrick Kavanagh,* Padraic Fallon,* and Mary Lavin* started their literary careers in the pages of *The Dublin Magazine.* O'Sullivan was unique as an editor because he combined an ability to attract established writers like W. B. Yeats and George Russell with instant and repeated generosity to the young and unknown. The pages of *The Dublin Magazine* were not limited to Irish writers: the poetry of R. S. Thomas and Alun Lewis first appeared there and writers like Paul Valery, Francis Viele-Griffin, S. S. Koteliansky, and Gordon Bottomley were also given space.

While O'Sullivan edited *The Dublin Magazine* (1923 through 1958), he published few new poems and sketches of his own. He appeared to be more concerned with the careers of those whom he published than with his own creative talent. Realizing that several of his contributors had more talent and greater capacity for creative growth than he possessed, he selflessly devoted his life to the publication and promotion of their work. For this reason, O'Sullivan's contributors developed a strong loyalty toward *The Dublin Magazine.* Padraic Fallon's remark that he would rather see a poem of his in *The Dublin Magazine* than in any other literary journal was not an uncommon attitude among the magazine's contributors.

O'Sullivan died in Dublin on March 24, 1958.

RICHARD BURNHAM

WORKS: *The Twilight People*. Dublin: Whaley/London: A. H. Bullen, 1905; *Verses: Sacred and Profane*. Dublin: Maunsel, 1908; *The Earth-Lover and Other Verses*. Dublin: New Nation, 1909; under the pseudonym of J. H. Orwell, *Impressions*. Dublin: New Nation, 1910; *Poems*. Dublin: Maunsel, 1912; *An Epilogue to the Praise of Angus, and Other Poems*. Dublin: Maunsel, 1914; *Mud and Purple*. Dublin: Talbot, 1917. (Essays); *Requiem and Other Poems*. Dublin: Privately printed, 1917. (Poetry pamphlet); *The Rosses and Other Poems*. Dublin: Maunsel, 1918; *The Poems of Seumas O'Sullivan*. Boston: B. J. Brimmer, 1923; *Common Adventures: A Book of Prose and Verse*. Dublin: Orwell, 1926; *The Lamplighter, and Other Poems*. Dublin: Orwell, 1929. (Poetry pamphlet); *Twenty-Five Lyrics*. Bognor Regis, Sussex: Pear Tree Press, 1933. (Poetry pamphlet); *Personal Talk*. Dublin: Privately printed, 1936; *Poems . . . 1930-1938*. Dublin: Orwell, 1938. (Poetry pamphlet); *Collected Poems*. Dublin: Orwell, 1940; *This Is the House, and Other Verses*. Dublin: Privately printed, 1942. (Poetry pamphlet); *Essays and Recollections*. Dublin: Talbot, 1944; *The Rose and Bottle*. Dublin: Talbot, 1946. (Essays); *Dublin Poems*. New York: Creative Age, [1946]; *Translations and Transcriptions*. Belfast: H. R. Carter, 1950. (Poetry pamphlet).   REFERENCE: Miller, Liam, ed. *Retrospect: The Work of Seumas O'Sullivan and Estella F. Solomons*. Dublin: Dolmen, 1973.

OWENSON, SYDNEY. *See* MORGAN, LADY.

PARKER, STEWART (1941-), playwright and poet. Parker was born in Belfast in 1941 and was educated at Queen's University. A collection of verse, *The Casualty's Meditation*, was published in 1966, but most of his recent work has been in drama. For his play *Spokesong*, he received a prestigious award as one of the most promising new dramatists to be staged in London in 1976. *Spokesong* is a play with music about a bicycle shop in Belfast. Although light and amusing, it affords opportunity for many reflections on the sectarian struggles of the North throughout this century. In a poor production, such as that by the Irish Theatre Company* in 1978, the thinness of the script is very apparent, but in a good production the play can have an engaging charm.

WORKS: *The Casualty's Meditation*. Belfast: Festival Publications, 1966. (Poetry pamphlet); *Maw*. Belfast: Festival Publications, 1968. (Poetry pamphlet); "The Iceberg." *The Honest Ulsterman* 50 (Winter 1975):4-64. (Radio play).

PARNELL, [FRANCES ISABEL] "FANNY" (1854-1882), poet. Parnell was born at Avondale in County Wicklow on September 3, 1854, and was the sister of Charles Stewart Parnell. She was much involved in Land League agitation and in Irish politics generally. In 1864 and 1865, when she was only ten and eleven years old, she published poems in *The Irish People*. Of her later verse, John Boyle O'Reilly* wrote, "Crushed out, like the sweet life of a bruised flower, they are the very soul cry of a race." A less enthusiastically patriotic view would find them rather conventional and poor, although her vigorous individuality does sometimes break through the poetic conventions, as for instance, in the second stanza of "Hold the Harvest," a poem addressed to farmers in 1880:

> The serpent's curse upon you lies—ye writhe within the dust,
> Ye fill your mouths with beggar's swill, ye grovel for a crust:
> Your lords have set their blood-stained heels upon your shame-
>   ful heads,
> Yet they are kind—they leave you still their ditches for your
>   beds!

She died in Bordentown, New York, on July 20, 1882.

WORKS: *The Hovels of Ireland*. New York: T. Kelly, [1879]; *Land League Songs*. Boston, 1882.

PAULIN, TOM (1949-), poet. Paulin was born in Leeds in 1949 and grew up in Belfast. He was educated there and at the Universities of Hull and Oxford. He has lectured in English at the University of Nottingham and has written a critical book on Thomas Hardy's poetry. His own poems have appeared in two small collections, *Theoretical Locations* (1975) and *A State of Justice* (1977). Much of the writing in both is clear and exact but rather flat, as is this stanza from "Near the Christadelphians":

> In a house by the sea, in a bare front room,
> A man saws through a plank watched by his dog.
> He makes a table and chair, the sun comes out
> And cold light catches the most solitary things.
> Man and dog look at the newest table, the starkest chair.

A few of his pieces utilize rhyme or off-rhyme, but there is little sense of rhythm; much of Paulin's work reads like clear, if too often dull, prose.

WORKS: *Theoretical Locations*. Belfast: Ulsterman Publications, 1975; *A Sense of Justice*. London: Faber & Faber, 1977.

PAYNE, BASIL (1928-), poet. Payne was born in Dublin on July 22, 1928. He was educated at the Christian Brothers school in Synge Street and at University College, Dublin. He has lectured at various universities and colleges on the Continent, in Canada, and in the United States, and he received the Guinness Poetry Award at the Cheltenham Festival in 1964 and 1966. He has published three volumes of original verse and a couple of translations from the French and German. He is an easily understood and undemanding writer whose work seems to have moved from conventional form and somewhat pedestrian statement to what is not so much poetry as language to be recited. The work in his most recent volume, *Another Kind of Optimism* (1974), sometimes resorts to the primary devices of poetry, rhyme and meter, but the pieces are basically inflated epigrams or squashed essays. If his longer pieces are difficult to defend and tend to sink into the banal, his shorter ones are sometimes arresting, and practically all of them have a conversational fluency. Thus far, his work does not have enough form or wit to be important light verse, but it is not unpleasant entertainment.

WORKS: *Sunlight on a Square*. Dublin: Augustine, 1961; *Love in the Afternoon*. Dublin: Gill & Macmillan, 1971; *Another Kind of Optimism*. Dublin: Gill & Macmillan, 1974.

PEARSE, PATRICK [HENRY] (1879-1916), patriot, teacher, and man of letters. Pearse is best known for his involvement in the Easter Rising of 1916 and his subsequent execution by a British firing squad on May 3, 1916. During the two years preceding the Rising, he was the leading public spokesman for Ireland's separatism by physical force. When he read the Proclamation of the Irish Republic on the steps of Dublin's General Post Office, he was the president of the shortlived Republic's provisional government and commander-in-chief of its military forces. Yet, Pearse was not a politician or a military man, nor, looking at his private life and public deeds up to 1912, would one have expected him to have become an adherent of armed rebellion. He was a shy, gentle, and pious man whose main interests were language, literature, and education. These interests were channeled into Ireland's cultural revival; cultural nationalism led Pearse to political nationalism and, ultimately, to the belief that only through the use of arms could his nation wrest independence from England.

Born in Dublin on November 10, 1879, Pearse received his schooling from the Christian Brothers at Westland Row and then went on to earn a B.A. at University College, Dublin (then affiliated with the Royal University), and a B.L. at King's Inns, both in 1901. In 1903, he became the editor of the Gaelic League's weekly newspaper, *An Claidheamh Soluis* (*The Sword of Light*), continuing in that position until late 1909, when the school he had founded in 1908, St. Enda's, began to make heavy demands upon his time.

Pearse's interests in education, the Gaelic language, and literature are evident in his journalism for *An Claidheamh*. The newspaper played a leading role in the campaign to get Irish spoken in the schools, pulpits, and homes of Ireland, and Pearse argued for the improvement of teaching methods in the schools. In numberless editorials, articles, and book reviews, he discussed literary theory and practice in relation to what had been done by the Gaelic writers of the past and what should be tried by those attempting to build a new literature in the present.

Despite his many activities connected with St. Enda's and the Gaelic League, Pearse found time to write some plays, short stories, and poems. Between 1909 and 1916, he wrote eight dramatic works, six of them in Gaelic, expressly for production at St. Enda's: they include two outdoor pageants based on the *Táin Bó Cualigne*, a passion play, and four one-act plays. All these works had religious or heroic themes, and sometimes both.

Although Pearse was not a good dramatist and further limited himself by writing for his students, he did produce playable pieces with moments of dramatic intensity. They have interest as products of the Irish Revival and as revelations of the ideas that motivated their author. *The Singer,* composed in English late in 1915 and dealing openly with rebellion and the theme of blood-sacrificing, is the best known. Despite stilted dialogue, the play contains passages of poetic beauty and rhetorical power. Proclaiming the messianic message that heroic self-sacrificing can free Ireland, *The Singer* is a literary analogue for the event of Easter 1916.

The ten short stories in Irish, published in *Iosagan and Other Stories* (1907) and *The Mother and Other Stories* (1916), are important in the history of the Gaelic language and literature revival. They helped to establish a prose style based on spoken Gaelic rather than the archaic, literary Gaelic of previous centuries, and they provided examples of the modern short story, as opposed to the folktale, in Irish. The first collection, *Iosagan,* is marred by sentimentality and idealization of the Irish-speaking inhabitants of Connemara, particularly the children. In addition, the stories are imperfectly shaped and structured, and the narrative method is often unpolished and lacks sophistication. In four of the stories of the second collection, Pearse moved from the child's world, which had dominated *Iosagan,* to that of the adult, exhibiting improved technique, increased control of structure and form, and a deeper awareness of life's struggles. "The Dearg Daol," with its restrained and reticent narration and open ending, and its view of lives of quiet desperation, is a successful story. With "Brigid of the Songs" and "The Keening Woman," "The Dearg Daol" indicates its author had a developing, though modest, talent for prose narrative.

Pearse's poetry represents his best creative achievement. Between 1905 and 1916, he fashioned ten poems in English and eighteen in Gaelic. "The Fool," "The Rebel," and "The Mother," because of their relevance to the Rising of 1916, are the best known. Composed in late 1915, when *The Singer* was written, these poems convey the idealism, dedication, and determination that characterized Ireland's struggle for freedom. First-person dramatic lyrics in free verse, they derive their rhetorical power from direct statement, sincerity of tone, effective employment of Biblical allusion, and repetitive diction and syntax. The twelve Gaelic lyrics of *Suantraidhe agus Goltraidhe (Songs of Sleep and Sorrow)* (1914) are far superior to the poems in English. Using elements of both the syllabic and accentual systems of Gaelic prosody, Pearse wrote lyrics characterized by simplicity and economy of diction, directness of statement, and careful structuring based on skillfully arranged patterns of word, phrase, sound, and image. The general tone of the collection is quiet, serious, and sad; the themes include the transitory nature of earthly pleasure and beauty, the joy and innocence of youth, the sorrow and experience of adulthood, and the inevitable coming of death. With poems such as "A Woman of the Mountain

Keens Her Son," "Why Do Ye Torture Me?" and "Naked I Saw Thee" (sometimes titled "Renunciation" in English translation), Pearse brought Gaelic poetry into the twentieth century and carved a recognized place for himself in the Irish poetic tradition.

With his work in the Irish Volunteers and the Irish Republican Brotherhood, his active involvement in the Gaelic League, his educational experiment at St. Enda's, and his creative efforts in the Irish language, Patrick Pearse made a significant contribution to Ireland's political and cultural life.

RAYMOND J. PORTER

WORKS: *Political Writing and Speeches*. Dublin: Talbot, 1952; *Plays, Stories, Poems*. Dublin: Talbot, 1958.   REFERENCES: Edwards, Ruth Dudley. *Patrick Pearse: The Triumph of Failure*. London: Gollancz, 1977; Porter, Raymond J. *P. H. Pearse*. New York: Twayne, 1973.

PETRIE, GEORGE (1790-1866), antiquarian, artist, musician, and scholar. Petrie, one of the most distinguished Irishmen of the nineteenth century, was born in Dublin in 1790. Much of his work of reclaiming the Irish past is not overtly concerned with literature, although *The Petrie Collection of the Ancient Music of Ireland* (1852) is most significant. With Caesar Otway, Petrie edited *The Dublin Penny Journal*, and he later edited *The Irish Penny Journal* (1840-1841), to which Carleton,* Mangan,* and Ferguson,* as well as his brilliant assistants on the Ordnance Topographical Survey, O'Curry* and O'Donovan,* contributed. He died in Rathmines on January 17, 1866.

WORKS: *On the History & Antiquities of Tara Hill*. Dublin: Printed by R. Graisberry, 1839; *The Ecclesiastical Architecture of Ireland*. Dublin: Hodges & Smith, 1845. (Contains his 1833 essay "The Round Towers of Ireland"); *The Petrie Collection of the Ancient Music of Ireland*. 2 vols. Dublin: University Press, 1855-1882; *Christian Inscriptions in the Irish Language*. 2 vols. Dublin: Royal Historical & Archeological Association of Ireland, 1872-1878.   REFERENCE: Dillon, Myles. "George Petrie (1789-1866)." *Studies* (Autumn 1967): 266-276.

PHELAN, [JAMES LEO] "JIM" (1895-ca. 1960), novelist and short story writer. Phelan was born in Dublin in 1895 into a poor family. Although brilliant in school, he preferred the life of the streets and had little formal education. He held many jobs in a long, wandering career. As a young man, he became an actor in such fit-up companies as Roberto Lena's. He was also a blacksmith, bank clerk, journalist, film technician and script writer, novelist, and tramp. He is said to have been twice sentenced to death and to have spent fourteen years in prison, in Dartmoor and in Parkhurst. He wrote many short stories and some novels as well as factual studies of criminals, gypsies, and tramps. Like Patrick MacGill,* Sean O'Casey,* and Liam O'Flaherty,* he was somewhat outside the literary tradition and his work is permeated by his strong, forceful personality. At his frequent less than best, however, he degenerates into the shortcuts of poor slick writing, his themes become simplistic, and his characters the stereotypes of brutal machismo. Cleeve* suggests that Phelan died in about 1960. However, since his new books appeared frequently throughout the decade, it is possible that he died later, perhaps in 1968 or 1969. Obviously, his vigorous talent deserves attention, and his adventurous and obscure life investigation.

WORKS: . . . *Museum*. New York: W. Morrow, 1937; *Green Volcano*. London: P. Davies, [1938]; *Lifer*. London: P. Davies, 1938; *Ten-a-Penny People*. London: Gollancz, 1938; . . . *In the Can*. London: M. Joseph, 1939; . . . *Churchill Can Unite Ireland*. London: Gollancz, 1940; *Jail Journey*. London: Secker & Warburg, 1940; *Ireland—Atlantic Gateway*. London: John Lane, [1941]; *Letters from the Big House*. London: Cresset, 1943; . . . *And Blackthorns*. London: Nicholson & Watson, [1944]/ published in America as *Banshee Harvest*, New York: Viking, 1945; *Moon in the River*. New York: A. A. Wyn, [1946]; *Turf-Fire Tales*. London: Heinemann, [1947]; *Bog Blossom Stories*. London: Sidgwick & Jackson, [1948]; *The Name's Phelan*. London: Sidgwick & Jackson, [1948]. (Autobiography); *We Follow the Roads*. London: Phoenix House, [1949]/Longcraft: Country Book Club, 1950; *Vagabond Cavalry*. London & New York: T. U. Boardman, [1951]; *Wagon-Wheels*. London: Harrap, [1951]; *The Underworld*. London: Harrap, [1953]/London: Tandem, 1967; *Tramp at Anchor*. London: Harrap, [1954]; *Tramping the Toby*. London: Burke, [1955]; *Criminals in Real Life*. London: Burke, [1956]; *Fetters for Twenty*. London: Burke, [1957]; *Nine Murderers and Me*. London: Phoenix House, 1967; *Meet the Criminal Class*. London: Tallis, 1969.

PLUNKETT, JAMES (1920-), novelist, short story writer, and playwright. James Plunkett is the pseudonym of James Plunkett Kelly, who was born on May 21, 1920, in the Sandymount area of Dublin. When he was four, his family moved to a small flat in Upper Pembroke Street, where he grew up "in the shadow of those tall houses." Dublin was to permeate nearly everything he was to write. Unlike Joyce,* however, Plunkett did not feel compelled to escape Dublin in order to write about it. "Despite its tensions and its tragedies, Dublin was a good city to grow up in. The sea was at its feet, its Georgian buildings gave it nobility, its squares and its expanses of water made it a place of openness and light and air" (*Gems*, p. 37).

Young Jim Kelly soon developed an interest in literature, music, and trade unionism. He attended the Christian Brothers school in Synge Street, where he began writing stories and little satirical verses, and he also studied violin and viola at the College of Music from age eight to age twenty-three. His father, whom he greatly admired, was in the Great War and joined the Transport Union. The world of Plunkett's youth is captured compellingly in *Farewell Companions* (1977), his second novel, just as his first novel, *Strumpet City* (1969), encapsulates his father's world. This youthful milieu is important in view of Plunkett's belief that "it is a truth of literature that nothing much happens to a writer after the age of twenty or so that will affect his work; the small store of material which informs the imagination for the rest of life is made up of the remembered experiences of childhood and youth" (*Gems*, pp. 112-13).

Plunkett left school at the age of seventeen to begin a clerkship in the Gas Company, a position he held for seven years, during which time he became increasingly active in the affairs of the Workers' Union of Ireland. In April 1946, he became a branch and staff secretary, and worked under Jim Larkin until Larkin's death in 1947. Rather than curbing his writing efforts, Plunkett's increasing absorption in the union movement provided him with subjects for "deplorable little verses" (such as the ones which appeared in the Dublin satirical magazine *Passing Variety* from 1942 to 1952) and for his early short story "Working Class." Later, it was to become a focal point for *Strumpet City* and the short story "The Plain People."

Plunkett began to send stories to Seán O'Faoláin* at *The Bell** as soon as the periodical began to appear in 1940. His approach to the short story was influenced in a major way by the early editorial role of O'Faoláin, as it was later by the friendship of Frank O'Connor.* O'Faoláin, Plunkett has noted, "would write back and say not to call a 'meal' a 'repast' and to cut it down and speak plainly and if you didn't have anything to say not to say it." The early stories "The Mother" and "Working Class" appeared under O'Faoláin's editorship in *The Bell* in November 1942 and October 1943, respectively. They were followed by "The Mad Barber" and "The Parrot of Digges Street" in *The Irish Bookman* in February and December 1947, respectively. Plunkett was later to dismiss these stories and left them out of his collections *The Trusting and the Maimed* (1955) and *Collected Short Stories* (1977). The first two stories, which are marred by an overly melodramatic tone, point to the subject matter of later, greatly superior work, while the latter two are somewhat disjointed efforts, yet no less legitimate in their own way than many of O'Connor's comic romps.

The Trusting and the Maimed, a collection of a dozen stories written in the late 1940s and early 1950s (all of which reappear in the *Collected Stories*), is one of the best volumes to have come out of Ireland. Here we see Plunkett finding his true voice, that which Frank O'Connor described as "the lonely voice, the lyric cry in the face of human destiny." Following the publication of this first collection, O'Connor praised Plunkett as "a storyteller of high seriousness." There is a phenomenal range and depth to the volume, moving from the slapstick comedy of "The Scoop" to the political broadside of "The Wearin' of the Green," to the pathos of "Janey Mary," "Mercy," and "Weep for Our Pride," to the penetrating lyricism of "The Trusting and the Maimed" and "The Eagles and the Trumpets." The balance and range of the collection are demonstrated by the fact that four of the stories deal with childhood and adolescence, four with young adulthood, and four with old age. In the course of the volume, interestingly enough, Plunkett comes to grips with his own harrowing visions of death from the perspective of each age group—from that of the child ("The Damned"), the young man ("The Trusting and the Maimed"), and the old man ("Mercy"). This sort of progression will be familiar to students of Joyce's

Dubliners—which is not entirely a coincidence, since *The Trusting and the Maimed* is in many ways an update and extension of Joyce's seedy, decadent Dublin, that "centre of paralysis." Joyce's rhetorical influence can be seen in Marty's stream of consciousness in "Dublin Fusilier," as well as in a double entendre voiced by a musician in the same story who comments that, after rehearsing *Faust* for three hours, he has "a thirst that a parish priest would sell his soul for" (which is reinforced by the barman's subsequent comment that Marty, by joining the army, had "sold his soul for a shillin' ").

"A Walk Through the Summer," "The Trusting and the Maimed," and "The Eagles and the Trumpets" are in many ways Plunkett's most interesting and his most lyrical stories. Here he found a complete individuality as a story writer. While reading these stories, one forgets all about the Joyces, the O'Connors, and the O'Faoláins because these are quite unlike anything they wrote. The principal influence here is not one of Plunkett's prose-writing elders, but rather a poet, T. S. Eliot, whose *Waste Land* seemed to Plunkett to be "a series of impressions, coming from this side and that which finally focused in one intense impression" (reminiscent of O'Connor's "unearthly glow" as well as Joyce's "epiphany"). Eliot's influence casts a most interesting light on the structure and the ambitious nature of these three relatively long stories, whose episodic structure foreshadows the approach at work in *Strumpet City* and *Farewell Companions*. This episodic approach becomes panoramic and almost cinematic. Plunkett goes beyond O'Connor's single "lonely voice" toward the use of multiple voices, achieving a film-like effect as he cuts from one character, situation, and time to another. The main characters of these stories are presented in isolation from each other in time and space. Nonetheless, they are fictively intertwined and are powerfully fused together at the end of each story, whether lying half asleep in a car, resting under the flight of a maimed pigeon, or staring up at the moon as if it were "a big bloody aspirin." The ending of "The Trusting and the Maimed," which sets forth an injured pigeon unwittingly about to die as a symbol for the whole story, is typical of Plunkett's technique:

> "By God," the boy's father said, "That's a night and a half."
>
> Ellis, making his way home along the wall of the river, turned up his collar and said the same thing. It startled Florrie, who was assessing for her mother the value of what was left in the tenantless room with its set of soiled underwear and its bottle of sticky hair dressing. Rain covered mountain and moor and city in an unremitting downpour. It made a torrent of the little stream, nearer which Casey now lay, his shoulders hunched, his arms across his breast, summoning his yielding and outnumbered garrison to stand desperately against this latest assault. It battered the soft earth of the garden and beat to

pulp the piece of paper which the pigeon had dislodged from its ring in its first frantic efforts to find balance. It drummed loudly on the corrugated roof of the pigeon hutch. But the pigeon was undisturbed. Surrounded by familiar odours it dozed comfortably and warmly after the painful length of the day. It was fed and at ease now, and confident once more of love.

Of the half dozen stories in the *Collected Short Stories* which were written and published after *The Trusting and the Maimed,* the two most important are "Ferris Moore and the Earwig" and "The Plain People." "Ferris Moore," according to Plunkett, may well be indicative of his future direction as a writer. A man rests on a river bank, watching an earwig crawl up a twig and eventually drop into the river: this is the entire plot, on the surface, of the story; the real story is built around Ferris Moore's seriocomic, neo-Joycean stream of consciousness. "The Plain People" is like a sequel to *Strumpet City.* It deals with the labor union world of the late 1940s and early 1950s in which the adherents to the old school of hard knocks and direct action must deal with the new pencil-pushing, convention-attending, skyscraper crowd.

"The Plain People" was originally published in 1960, early in Plunkett's period of absorption in the writing of historical fiction and drama. In January 1955, he had visited the Soviet Union as part of a delegation invited by the Soviet secretary of arts. Upon his return he was attacked in print by Irish McCarthyites like the editor of the *Catholic Standard,* who urged that Plunkett be forced to resign his position in the Workers' Union. The union, however, refused to bow to pressure. When Plunkett left his post in August 1955, he did so voluntarily, in response to an offer to take on the job of drama assistant in Radio Éireann.

An important direction in Plunkett's work became focused around this time, and the concrete realities of his situation can be seen to have been crucial in this respect. His entrance into the world of radio and, later, television (where he would become one of Telefís Éireann's first two producers, in 1960), provided him with new outlets for his creative abilities. His contact with the world of radio had been established well before he actually went to work in it himself. His radio plays "Dublin Fusilier," "Mercy," and "Homecoming" had been produced and broadcast by Radio Éireann in March 1952, June 1953, and April 1954, respectively. The radio play "Big Jim" was broadcast in October 1954. Thus, Radio Éireann provided Plunkett with a new market for his talents. At the same time, the success of "Big Jim" and, at least as importantly, Plunkett's own involvement with and absorption in the events of his time caused him to turn more and more to history as a panorama for his drama and his fiction. "Big Jim" was subsequently rewritten, expanded, and adapted for the stage in the shape of *The Risen People,* which was produced successfully at the Abbey Theatre* in 1958. Not long afterward, Hutchinson, the London publisher, suggested to Plunkett that he write a novel of similar historical interest, and so his work for the next decade was cut out for him. ("Farewell Harper" [1956], a radio play which penetrates the Irish 1940s in powerful and subtle ways, and "When Do You Die, Friend?" [1966], a television play which recreates 1798, can only be mentioned here.)

In his historical novel *Strumpet City* (1969), Plunkett made a conscious attempt to present a broad cross-section of the Dublin society of the time, from the working class to the upper classes. He has commented that the novel

> is a picture of Dublin in the seven years, 1907 to 1914. Against the blackcloth of social agitation, it is about the attitudes of various strata of society—from Dublin Castle and people of property down to the destitute poor and the outcasts. Joyce wrote about the moderately middle class, and O'Casey about the slums of the period. I was concerned with finding a form in which all the elements could fit.

Many aspects of the working-class world presented in *Strumpet City* are drawn directly from Plunkett's own experiences. He gives us an entire cast of working-class characters: Fitz, the striking foreman with leadership abilities; his wife Mary, concerned for home and family; Pat, Fitz's mate, an amateur socialist philosopher reminiscent of O'Casey's* "Young Covey"; Hennessy, a scrounging, displaced gentleman, plagued by poverty and his wife; Mulhall, one of the Larkinite faithful, a hard man with his fists; Keever, who becomes a stool-pigeon for the employers; and Rashers Tierney, folk hero and the poorest of the poor. Rashers was based on a fellow Plunkett knew about called "Johnny Forty Coats," and Mulhall on the figure of Barney Conway, a hard-fisted, highly respected right-hand man to Jim Larkin.

Strumpet City captures the world of the upper classes as well, in characters as diverse as Yearling, Father O'Connor, and the Bradshaws. Plunkett may not share the thinking of these upper classes, but he is able to represent it accurately. This ability is explained partly by his reliance upon Arnold Wright's book *Disturbed Dublin: The Story of the Great Strike of 1913,* which was published in 1914, having been commissioned by William Martin Murphy's Dublin Chamber of Commerce as the employers' defense of the stance they had taken. It is a book, as Plunkett has noted, in which "the social thinking of the period is typified."

The contrasts outlined in *Strumpet City* move gradually toward an artistic unity, as individual stories blend and characters collide. Father Giffley leaves the reader with a last lyrical message, scrawled on a piece of paper and then "committed to the sea" in a whiskey bottle: "Time takes all away. This was written by a madman on the shores of a mad island." The conclusion of the novel presents a bleak visage, but the book is informed throughout with a humane and generous spirit.

Farewell Companions (1977), a semi-autobiographical novel which moves from the 1920s up into the mid-1940s, continues the episodic, tapestry-like style of *Strumpet City,* with five parts or "movements" (a term which has been used by Plunkett himself) in comparison to *Strumpet City*'s three (although it is not quite as long altogether). The sweeping, panoramic vision of both novels demonstrates Plunkett's self-confessed tendency to "bring in everything but the kitchen sink."

Farewell Companions takes up where *Strumpet City* leaves off; there is a continuous and contiguous relationship between the two novels. The Dublin of *Strumpet City,* considerably changed but recognizable, is preserved in *Farewell Companions,* along with characters like Bob Fitzpatrick and Aloysius Hennessy. For example, Plunkett returns to the final visage from *Strumpet City* of Fitz fading off in a troop ship to fight in World War I, and this time the anonymous fellow recruit who befriends Fitz turns out to be Plunkett's father (alias Paddy McDonagh). The world of the author's father fades away as the younger generation takes charge, but this happens only very gradually. The child of Part I grows up still beneath the shadows of his elders, shadows which the author, invoking the poetry of John Montague,* has felt to have passed "into that dark permanence of ancient forms." Significantly, the novel is dedicated "to the memory of my father," whose death, for the young Tim McDonagh, has "left a great hole in the world."

Tim McDonagh and the coterie of friends and lovers who populate *Farewell Companions* are clearly transposed from the author's own youthful milieu, but any description of the book as an autobiographical novel must be a qualified one. There is much of Jim Plunkett Kelly in Tim McDonagh, yet nothing of the young Plunkett's lengthy involvement in the Workers' Union, and Tim's final decision to enter the religious life was obviously not shared by the author. This ending, which might prove disappointing to many readers, may perhaps be taken as indicative of the direction that Plunkett's own life might have taken had things gone differently, or it may be symbolic of his real-life retreat into the Joycean priesthood of art.

The final pages of *Farewell Companions* capture overwhelmingly a sense of the loss of companionship through departure and dispersal. Once again, Plunkett puts his last lyrical stream of consciousness into the head of an apparent madman removed from the main course of action—in this case, the seriocomic O'Sheehan, who believes himself to be the mythical Oisín. There is much more than monasteries and mythologies to be found in this book; there is politics as well. Plunkett records much of the spirit of Irish party politics during the 1930s and 1940s, sharply portraying the recurring tug-of-war of the time between the conservative, super-nationalist Fianna

Fáilers and the younger pseudo-socialist crowd. *Farewell Companions,* however, is in general less political and more a personal and introverted work than *Strumpet City.* There is much of fantasy and speculation here, found not only in the person of O'Sheehan, but also in the recurring and central question prompted by the memory of a photograph album: "Have you ever looked at a photograph of yourself as a baby, let's say. And then at the age of seven or thereabouts. Then at fourteen perhaps. Which of them is you? They can't all be."

The novel begins and ends with a picturebook and the mood of reminiscence customarily attendant to such a keepsake. In between, we see numerous individual, episodic "photographs" of Tim at various stages of youth. He is not defined definitively for us, nor is he meant to be. This idea of multi-individuality also turns up comically in "Ferris Moore and the Earwig."

The Gems She Wore (1972), Plunkett's "book of Irish places," is in the tradition of O'Connor's *Irish Miles* and other reflective, nonfictional travel books. It can be mentioned here only as an essential guidebook, not only to Ireland but also to Plunkett's views of Ireland and Irish society. At this writing, James Plunkett still has many productive, creative years ahead of him. Having started out in the O'Connor-O'Faoláin-O'Flaherty school of the short story, he equaled their best with *The Trusting and the Maimed,* although he cannot yet claim the prolific output of his elders in that genre. *Strumpet City* and *Farewell Companions,* however, are deeper, more balanced, and simply better novels than any of those produced by those elder statesmen of the shorter form. They should guarantee a very high reputation to the not-so-elder Mr. Plunkett.

JAMES M. CAHALAN

WORKS: *The Eagles and the Trumpets, and Other Stories.* Dublin: The Bell, 1954. (Published in August 1954 in lieu of Vol. 20, No. 9, of *The Bell*); *Big Jim.* Dublin: Martin O'Donnell, 1955. (A play for radio); *The Trusting and the Maimed, and Other Irish Stories.* New York: Devin-Adair, 1955/London: Hutchinson, 1959; *Strumpet City.* London: Hutchinson, 1969; *The Gems She Wore: A Book of Irish Places.* London: Hutchinson, 1972; *Collected Short Stories.* Dublin: Poolbeg, 1977; *Farewell Companions.* London: Hutchinson, 1977.

PLUNKETT, JOSEPH MARY (1887-1916), patriot and poet. Plunkett, one of the executed leaders of the Easter Rising, was born in Dublin in November 1887. He was the son of George Noble Plunkett, a poet and a papal count. For much of his life, Joseph Plunkett was in ill health, and for this reason he traveled a good deal in Europe and North Africa. He became a close friend of Thomas MacDonagh* with whom he studied Irish; they also exchanged poems and criticisms of each other's work. Plunkett was one of the founders of the Irish Volunteers and a member of the first Executive. He was also a member of the Irish Republican Brotherhood, which sent him on missions to Germany and to America. In 1916, he was director of military operations and drew up the detailed plans for the Rising. On Good Friday of 1916, he was in a nursing home recuperating from an operation, but he still took part in the fighting in the General Post Office. On the eve of his execution, he married Grace Gifford, the artist, and he was executed on May 4, 1916.

In 1911, Plunkett was associated with David Houston, James Stephens,* Padraic Colum,* and MacDonagh in the founding of the distinguished magazine *The Irish Review.** In 1913, he became its editor until its demise in 1914. Also in 1914 he was engaged with Edward Martyn* and Mac-Donagh in the formation of the Irish Theatre* in Hardwicke Street. He later disassociated himself from the theatre because he disapproved of the group producing Strindberg's *Easter*.

Plunkett published only one volume of poems during his lifetime: *The Circle and the Sword* (1911). A posthumous volume of the best of those poems and his later work was edited by his sister Grace, also a poet, in 1916. Plunkett is a difficult poet to assess. William Irwin Thompson wrote, "The poems show talent, but it is anybody's guess if their baroque and chryselephantine lusciousness could ever be brought under control, and once under control, directed toward greatness." It is easy to see why a critic would veer away from Plunkett's romanticism of love and even of God, and from a diction that is sometimes both conventional and florid. However, Plunkett did have a consciousness, albeit intermittent, of form. And, too, he did have some partial successes. To argue analogously, the firmly architectured sentences of his prose might be cited, as in the essay "Obscurity and Poetry" reprinted in his posthumous poems. He also is aware of the Gaelic use of assonance in poetry, as in the pieces printed on pages xiii-xv of his *Poems* (1916). Sometimes, too, he works in an interesting stanza form (in basically iambic trimeter and rhymed ABAAB), which he uses to good effect as in "The Spark." But more important than his awareness of technique is the number of startlingly effective, if romantic, lines in his work. To be sure, they are often buried in language like "Your innocence has stabbed my heart" or "the secrets of your eyes," from "The White Feather," but that poem also has some remarkable lines. So also does "Your Fear" in which he works interestingly with varied line lengths and internal rhyming. He is not even always florid; in a poem like "1841-1891" he is utterly simple. In sum, there is much of interest in Plunkett, so much so that one suspects he might have become a more considerable poet than either Pearse* or MacDonagh.

WORK: *Poems*. Dublin: Talbot, 1916.   REFERENCE: Thompson, William Irwin. *The Imagination of an Insurrection: Dublin, Easter 1916*. New York: Oxford University Press, 1961, 131-139.

POWER, BRIAN (1930-), short story writer. Power was born in 1930, holds an M.A. in sociology from Boston University, and is a Roman

Catholic priest who has been chaplain to University College, Dublin, and curate in various parishes in and around Dublin. He won a Hennessy Award for his short story "Requiem," and in 1977, he published a collection of stories entitled *A Land Not Sown*. The collection is extremely readable, alternately moving and funny, and is written in several styles and techniques. Perhaps the most successful stories are a novella, "Two Hundred Greeners," told from the viewpoint of an ignorant fifteen-year-old slum boy; "The Godmother," told from the viewpoint of a clever middle-class boy of about the same age; and "Games Children Play," told from the viewpoint of a stuffy academic researcher.

WORK: *A Land Not Sown*. Dublin: Egotist, 1977.

POWER, RICHARD (1928-1970), novelist. Richard Power (Risteard De Paor in Irish) was born in Dublin in 1928. In 1945, he entered the Irish civil service in Dublin, where he lived (apart from periods on the Aran Islands and in the United States) until his early death in 1970. On leave from the civil service, he took a degree in English and Irish at Trinity College, Dublin, in 1952, and he also studied Gaelic on the Aran Islands. His book about his experiences on the islands, *Úll i mBarr an Ghéagáin*, was awarded the Gaelic Book Club Award in 1959. He spent 1958-1960 teaching and studying at the Writers' Workshop at the State University of Iowa. His one-act plays in Gaelic were presented at the Abbey Theatre,* Dublin, in 1955 (*Saoirse*) and 1958 (*An Oidhreacht*). He also wrote scripts for Radio Éireann for documentary films.

Power is best remembered for his two completed novels in English. *The Land of Youth* (1964, 1966) is an extended saga of frustrated sexuality and enmity set, in the main, on the Aran island of Inishheever before and after the War of Independence. The central character is Barbara Nora whose failed relationship with a young man destined for the priesthood is the source of a protracted series of emotional savageries played out against the background of wild natural scenery and physical privation. The novel, traditional in narrative form and uncomplicated in structure, has been admired for its sombre reflective sense of emotional currents running, inevitably, deep in the psyche. Power's second novel, *The Hungry Grass* (1969), is structurally much more compact. The last year of a country priest in the post-revolutionary period is treated with a gravely compassionate sense of idealism perverted and family life and affections contaminated by vulgar material and social opportunism. The novel, a haunting study in loneliness, suggests how much Irish writing lost in the early death of its author.

He died in Bray on February 12, 1970.

TERENCE BROWN

WORKS: *The Land of Youth*. New York: Dial, 1964/London: Secker & Warburg, 1966; *The Hungry Grass*. London: Bodley Head, 1969.   REFERENCE: Brown, Terence. "Family Lives: The Fiction of Richard Power." In *The Irish Novel in Our*

Time. Patrick Rafroidi & Maurice Harmon, eds. Villeneuve-d'Ascq: Publications de l'Universite de Lille III, 1975-1976.

POWER, VICTOR O'D[ONOVAN] (fl. late nineteenth and early twentieth centuries), short story writer and playwright. Power, a native of County Wexford, was a vastly prolific writer of popular fiction for the young and also of broadly comic and melodramatic plays. His stories appeared in all of the popular family journals in the first quarter of this century, but were staples of *Ireland's Own* and *Our Boys* in which they continue to be constantly reprinted up to the present day. Power's plays were produced mainly in the provinces by fit-up companies, such as the O'Brien and Ireland Company and, in the 1920s, by Power's own company. One of his plays, *David Mahony*, was presented by the Abbey* with mild success in 1914. Little of Power's enormous output has appeared in book form.

WORKS: *A Secret of the Past*. London: Ward & Downey, 1893. (Novel); *Flurry to the Rescue*. Dublin: James Duffy, 1918. (One-act play); *The Footsteps of Fate*. Dublin: Ireland's Own, [1930]. (Novel).

PROUT, FATHER (1804-1866), humorist and journalist. Although few historians would remember him by his Christian name of Frances Sylvester Mahony, they readily recognize Father Prout, his alter ego, for his wit, genius, and sheer mischief. He was born in Cork on December 31, 1804, the county with which he is associated, despite the fact that he lived most of his life on the Continent. After receiving his training from the Jesuits at Clongowes Wood, he decided to become one himself. His native intelligence surely qualified him for the priesthood, although there was always a question of whether his temperament was suitable. Nevertheless, he entered the seminary in France and later studied in Rome. By all accounts he was brilliant, especially in the study of classical languages. But his superiors discouraged him from pursuing ordination. It is not clear what their grounds were, but we do know that after serving as prefect of studies at Clongowes, he was dismissed and sent back to Rome. The most widespread story is that he led a group of seminarians on a drunken school outing. He was expelled from the Society of Jesus, but nevertheless was ordained in Italy in 1832. However, after years of determined, even stubborn effort to become a priest, he practiced as such for only a short time. He reputedly served in Cork during a cholera epidemic, but by 1834 he was living in London and working as a journalist. He was known to his friends as a priest, but he seems to have been relieved of most of his duties.

The periodical to which he began to contribute was *Fraser's*, at that time the most lively journal on the scene, the one to which Thackeray and Carlyle were regular contributors and to which Southey and Coleridge had turned. For the occasion, Father Prout was introduced. Mahony described him as the child of Dean Swift* and Stella, a humble, learned parish priest in

County Cork only recently deceased. To add credibility, or to compound the humor, Mahony also invented Prout's editor, Oliver Yorke, to comment on the venerable priest's writings. Father Prout's essays on serious matter became regular features of *Fraser's* and were eventually collected as *The Reliques of Father Prout* in 1859, with illustrations by Daniel Maclise. The contributions are varied, but the best reveal his learning and humor. The most outrageous piece is that which attempts to prove that Thomas Moore* was a plagiarist; Mahony went to the trouble of translating some of Moore's *Melodies* into Greek, Latin, and Old French to prove they were stolen by the Irish poet. It is in this essay, "The Rogueries of Tom Moore," that Prout's own poem first appeared, "The Shandon Bells." It is one of the most popular of Irish songs, clearly a comic piece in its context. Yet, some of the most sober literary critics have attacked it on grounds of excessive rhyme and sentimentality. In other essays in the collection, his target was Daniel O'Connell, for whom he sustained antagonism for years, here satirized as Dandeleon. The *Reliques* are all we remember Mahony for, and they show his versatility and skills. His parodies of scholarly criticism are still not far off the mark, and many of the numerous translations from the classics are lyrical. In some respects, the humor now seems academic: showing off his exceptional learning for a classically trained audience which no longer exists. But when we recall that Mahony was a contemporary and close friend of the author of *Sartor Resartus*, the intention is more understandable, and his achievement more substantial. That Dickens, Thackeray, and Browning were his close friends and supporters testifies to his personal charm. Yet, his talents were never fully utilized. He never attempted as much as those friends did, and he seems to have been satisfied to serve as the gadfly or court wit rather than to attempt more serious works.

The facts of Mahony's later life are clouded, but there are indications that he suffered considerably. He died in Paris on May 18, 1866.

JAMES KILROY

WORKS: *The Reliques of Father Prout*. London: Fraser, 1836; *The Tour of the French Traveller M. de la Boullaye le Gouz in Ireland A. D. 1644*. T. Crofton, Croker, ed. with Notes and Illustrative Extracts Contributed by James Roche, the Rev. F. Mahony, T. Wright and the Editor. London: Boone, 1837; *Facts and Figures from Italy*. By Don Jeremy Savanarola, Benedictine Monk (pseud. for Mahony). London: Bentley, 1847; *The Final Reliques of Father Prout*. London: Chatto & Windus, 1876; *The Works of Father Prout*. Charles Kent, ed. London & New York: Routledge, 1881.   REFERENCE: Mannin, Ethel. *Two Studies in Integrity*. London: Jarrolds, 1954.

RAY, R. J. (fl. first quarter of the twentieth century), playwright. R. J. Ray was the pseudonym of Robert Brophy, who worked on newspapers in Kilkenny, Cork, and Dublin. Between 1909 and 1922, he wrote five unpublished plays for the Abbey.* In *The Story of the Abbey Theatre*, Peter Kavanagh surmises that the plays were not printed because Yeats* did not like them. However, this theory ignores several long and helpful letters from

Yeats to Ray, as well as evidence in one of them that Yeats arranged for a revival of Ray's work.

The Casting-Out of Martin Whelan, a three-act play (1910), may be derived from Canon P. A. Sheehan's* novel *Glenanaar*. In both works, a decent person is ostracized because a long-departed relative (Whelan's grandfather in the play) was an informer. *The Gombeen Man*, a play in three acts (1913), deals with a type once common in rural Ireland—a man who acquired wealth and power by lending money to ignorant farmers at exorbitant interest. *The Strong Hand*, a tragedy in two acts (1917), is a reworking of Ray's first Abbey drama, the three-act *The White Feather* (1919). Michael John Dillon, the strong hand seemingly capable of every form of violence, is actually a coward. He shrinks from clearing a man he knows to be innocent of a murder charge, and he must prime himself with drink before killing an unpopular landlord, after which he dies of a heart attack. Ray's final work, *The Moral Law*, a play in one act (1922), is a melodrama of divided loyalties. A retired policeman is certain that his son has killed a district inspector and is ready to turn him in, but at the last moment paternal feeling prevails over duty.

Lennox Robinson,* who like Ray was a Cork realist, comments in *Ireland's Abbey Theatre* (1951) that Ray's works are "undeservedly overlooked." Newspaper reviews are less favorable: they concede his raw power but complain of faulty construction, outworn themes, and straining for picturesque dialogue. Andrew Malone, in *The Irish Drama* (1929), writes that Ray's characters are "almost incredibly brutal types of humanity." One may conclude that Ray's shortcoming is not his preoccupation with violence, which was far from common in early Abbey drama, but a failure to go beyond it and offer insight into his characters and their environment.

WILLIAM J. FEENEY

READ, CHARLES ANDERSON (1841-1878), editor and novelist. Read was born on November 10, 1841, at Kilsella House, near Sligo. After failing in business through an excess of kindness, he moved to London where he wrote many forgotten poems and nine hack novels on Irish themes. The novels were first serialized, but at least two of them, *Savourneen Dheelish* (1869) and *Aileen Aroon* (1870), were published in book form. He began the compilation of *The Cabinet of Irish Literature*, which was a large anthology of Irish writing in English with some biographical and critical commentary. Although Read's taste is—to put it mildly—democratic, this is still an eminently useful compilation. Justin McCarthy's* anthology, *Irish Literature*, leans heavily on Read's work, and much of the criticism is simply quoted from Read. Read died in Surrey on January 23, 1878, and the last volume of his work was completed by T. P. O'Connor.

WORK: *The Cabinet of Irish Literature,* ed. with T. P. O'Connor. 4 vols. London:

Blackie, 1879-1884/new ed., revised and greatly extended, ed. by Katherine Tynan Hinkson. London: Gresham Publishing, 1902-1903.

REDDIN, KENNETH. *See* SARR, KENNETH.

REID, FORREST (1875-1947), novelist. Few Irish writers have written as lucidly or stylishly as Forrest Reid, author of some sixteen novels, several critical studies, and two volumes of autobiography. He was born on June 24, 1875, in Belfast of Presbyterian stock and, except for an education at Cambridge, lived there inconspicuously until his death on January 4, 1947. His father was a firm's manager who had had to begin again after bankrupting himself as a mercantile shipowner; from this side of the family, Reid may have inherited a Protestant liking for self-reliant democracy but also, in reaction, a loathing of middle-class, commercial values. His mother was a last survivor of the Shropshire Parr family that appeared in *Burke's Peerage* and traced itself back to the last wife of Henry VIII. The declining fortunes of this side of the family may have reinforced Reid's fear of social descent and promoted the faint snobbery of decayed gentility that lightly taints the sensibilities of his boy-heroes.

"The primary impulse of the artist springs, I fancy, from discontent, and his art is a kind of crying for Elysium," wrote Reid in the first paragraph of his excellent first autobiography, *Apostate* (1926). This notion of art as inspired nostalgia may have had family origins, or it may have originated in part with the disappearance of the semi-rustic nineteenth-century Belfast in which Reid grew up and which he mourned beautifully, after the inexorable urban sprawl, in *Apostate*. That book breaks off with Reid's apprenticeship to the tea-trade which he later abandoned in favor of Cambridge. He described his time at the university as a "rather blank interlude." Yet, his life and art can be fully understood only if they are set at least partly within the context of the liberal, humane, Hellenistic Cambridge of Lowes Dickinson, who admired Reid's work, and E. M. Forster, who became a lifelong friend and supporter. Stylistically, too, Reid belongs to no peculiarly Irish tradition, even though he influenced a few younger Ulster writers. During his productive but quiet years in Belfast, after having come down from Cambridge, Reid enjoyed the friendship of Forster, Edwin Muir, and Walter de la Mare who all thought highly of his fiction.

Reid, with a deceptive modesty that resembled that of his friend E. M. Forster, was aware of his limitations as a novelist. "I alone knew, how much, as an author, I resembled Mr. Dick," he noted in his second autobiography, *Private Road* (1940). "I could get on swimmingly until I reached my King Charles's head—the point where a boy becomes a man. Then something seemed to happen, my inspiration was cut off, my interest flagged, so that all became a labour, and not a labour of love." Mediocre at portraying adults and heterosexual relationships, Reid cultivated instead his own strength—the depiction of friendship between older children, especially boys. Though he dared not, or did not wish to, go farther in his novels than a Greek conception of friendship between males as a platonic love or tutelage, he incurred the displeasure of Henry James, to whom he had dedicated his second novel, *The Garden God* (1905), the story of a love affair between two boys. Reid furnishes an account of his rift with the revered master in *Private Road*.

AE* and Edmund Gosse considered Reid a realist, and certainly there are flashes of harsh realism in *The Kingdom of Twilight* (1904), Reid's first novel, and *At the Door of the Gate* (1915), his sixth, especially forthcoming when Reid wishes to portray the squalor of working-class Belfast. But one could with more justification call Reid a gentle fantasist—"he who dreamed," as Forster remarked, "and was partly a dream." Much of Reid's best fiction can be found in the Tom Barber trilogy: *Uncle Stephen* (1931), *The Retreat* (1936), and *Young Tom* (1944), the last volume of which won Reid the James Tait Black Memorial Prize. The trilogy is an exploration, without benefit of Jung or Freud, of the relationship between myth and dream, but it can also be read simply as a work that gives voice to the simple joys of discovery that animate boyhood. *Peter Waring* (1937), however, may be Reid's best novel, free as it is from the narcissism and preciosity that occasionally mar the trilogy and beautifully combining as it does realism and dream. This novel, a deft recreation of a sensitive Protestant adolescence in the North of Ireland in the 1890s, follows its young hero through the confusions of art, sexuality, and religion in a style that is rich, fluent, and assured.

Though primarily a novelist, Reid wrote nonfiction that must not be overlooked. Especially important are *W. B. Yeats: A Critical Study* (1915), *Illustrators of the Sixties* (1928), and *Walter de la Mare: A Critical Study* (1929).

JOHN WILSON FOSTER

WORKS: *The Kingdom of Twilight*. London: Unwin, 1904; *The Garden God*. London: David Nutt, 1905; *The Bracknels*. London: Edward Arnold, 1911/rewritten as *Denis Bracknel*, London: Faber, 1947; *Following Darkness*. London: Edward Arnold, 1912/rewritten as *Peter Waring*, London: Faber, 1937/Belfast: Blackstaff, 1976; *The Gentle Lover*. London: Edward Arnold, 1913; *At the Door of the Gate*. London: Edward Arnold, 1915; *W. B. Yeats, a Critical Study*. London: Martin Secker, 1915; *The Spring Song*. London: Edward Arnold, 1916; *A Garden by the Sea*. Dublin: Talbot/London: Unwin, 1918. (Stories and sketches); *Pirates of the Spring*. Dublin: Talbot/London: Unwin, 1919; *Pender among the Residents*. London: Collins, 1922; *Apostate*. London: Constable, 1926/London: Faber, 1947. (Reminiscences); *Demophon*. London: Collins, 1927; *Illustrators of the Sixties*. London: Faber & Gwyer, 1928; *Walter de la Mare: A Critical Study*. London: Faber, 1929; *Uncle Stephen*. London: Faber, 1931; *Brian Westby*. London: Faber, 1934; *The Retreat; or, the Machinations of Henry*. London: Faber, 1936; *Private Road*. London: Faber, 1940. (Autobiography); *Retrospective Adventures*. London: Faber, 1941. (Articles); *Notes and Impressions*. Newcastle, County Down: Mourne, 1942. (Essays); *Young Tom; or,*

Very Mixed Company. London: Faber, 1944; *The Milk of Paradise, Some Thoughts on Poetry.* London: Faber, 1946.   REFERENCES: Bryan, Mary. *Forrest Reid.* Boston: Twayne, 1976; Burlingham, Russell. *Forrest Reid: A Portrait and a Study.* London: Faber, 1953; Forster, E. M. *Abinger Harvest.* London: Arnold, 1936; Forster, E.M. *Two Cheers for Democracy.* London: Arnold, 1951; Foster, John Wilson. *Forces and Themes in Ulster Fiction.* Dublin: Gill & Macmillan/Totowa, N.J.: Rowman & Littlefield, 1974.

REID, CAPTAIN [THOMAS] MAYNE (1818-1883), writer of boys' adventure stories. Reid, the writer of many adventure stories for boys, was born in County Down, possibly on April 4, 1818. In 1838, he ran away to America and led an adventurous and wandering life that culminated in his experiences in the war between Mexico and the United States. Resigning his commission, he turned to writing his enormously popular books such as *The Rifle Rangers, The Boy Hunters, The Scalp Hunter,* and *The Quadroon,* the last of which Boucicault* used as the basis for his play *The Octoroon.* His work has nothing Irish about it and is without literary value, but he does remain one of the many phenomena of popular literature. He died in London on October 22, 1883.

REFERENCES: Reid, Elizabeth, with Coe, C. H. *Captain Mayne Reid, His Life and Adventures.* London: Greening & Co., 1900; Steele, Joan. "Mayne Reid, a Revised Bibliography." *Bulletin of Bibliography* 29 (July-September 1972): 95-100; Steele, Joan. *Captain Mayne Reid.* New York: Twayne, 1977.

ROBERTSON, OLIVIA (1917-), novelist and writer of stories and sketches. Robertson was born in London on Friday, April 13, 1917. She was educated at Heathfield School in Ascot and Alexandra College in Dublin, and then at the Grosvenor School of Modern Art in London and the Royal Hibernian Academy in Dublin. From 1941 to 1945, she worked as a slum playground leader for Dublin Corporation, an experience that was the basis for her first book, *St. Malachy's Court* (1946). This collection of sketches, basically of slum life, is told from the view of an accepted outsider. The book is funny, macabre, poignant, and a good deal more convincing than the steamy glamorizations done by an insider like Paul Smith.* Robertson's writing career lasted a scant ten years, but she is firmly in the tradition of Maria Edgeworth* and Somerville and Ross,* and anyone who reads one of her books will probably search all of the others out and regret there are no more. Among the best of the others is a whimsical and satirical novel, *Miranda Speaks* (1950), but even a simple collection of essays like *It's an Old Irish Custom* (1953) is pervaded by her engaging individuality. For some years, she has lived in a castle near Enniscorthy as a priestess in the Fellowship of Isis, which she and her brother, Lawrence Durdin-Robertson, Baron Strathloch, founded on March 21, 1976. This transformation of a gently humorous writer into a devoted priestess of Isis is perhaps an unusual development, but as she writes:

> So you see the transformation of a modest, intellectual(?) tweed-suited Anglo-Irish woman, very factual, possibly a little politically to the left, a Liberal, and not interested in religion into . . . I'm not really sure what, but something more like a Harry Clarke or AE Painting. . . . It would be meaningless, this Pre-Raphaelite Art Nouveau revival, this sudden change to crowns and robes like a Waite Tarot pack, unless we were totally committed and we are. Luckily we are so sure of the reality of the psychic world that we can actually have a sense of humour.

WORKS: *St. Malachy's Court*. London: Peter Davies, 1946/New York: Odyssey, 1947; *Field of the Stranger*. London: Peter Davies, 1948/New York: Random House, [1948]; *The Golden Eye*. London: Peter Davies, 1949; *Miranda Speaks*. London: Peter Davies, 1950; *It's an Old Irish Custom*. London: Denis Dobson, 1953; *Dublin Phoenix*. London: Jonathan Cape, 1957; *The Call of Isis*. Enniscorthy: Cesara, 1975; *The Isis Wedding Rite*. Enniscorthy: Cesara, 1976. (Pamphlet); *Ordination of a Priestess*. Enniscorthy: Cesara, 1977. (Pamphlet); *Rite of Rebirth*. Enniscorthy: Cesara, 1977. (Pamphlet).

ROBINSON, LENNOX (1886-1958), playwright. From the staging of his first play in 1908 until his death in 1958, Lennox Robinson was associated with the Abbey* as writer, producer, and director. This service, interrupted only from 1914 to 1919, exceeds in length the time devoted to the theatre by Yeats* or Lady Gregory.*

Esme Stuart Lennox Robinson was born in Douglas, County Cork, on October 4, 1886, the son of a Church of Ireland clergyman. Because of poor health he had little formal schooling. An interest in drama developed when he saw the Abbey players on tour in Cork in 1907. His literary career was oriented mostly to playwriting, although he also wrote fiction, biography, autobiography, essays, and a history of the Abbey.

In 1909, Robinson accepted an offer from Yeats and Lady Gregory to work as play director and manager of the theatre. Bernard Shaw* invited him to London to gain theatrical experience. Robinson's decision not to close the Abbey in mourning for the death of Edward VII in 1910 caused a dispute between the directors and their English benefactress Miss A.E.F. Horniman. Following an unsuccessful Abbey tour of the United States in 1914, Robinson resigned from the company but came back in 1919. He was appointed to the Board of Directors in 1923, a post he held until his death, and he doubled as director-producer until 1935. On September 8, 1931, he married Dorothy Travers Smith. They had no children. Robinson frequently traveled to the United States with the Abbey company or as a guest lecturer. In 1956, he went to China to take part in a commemoration of the centenary of Shaw. He died in Dublin on October 14, 1958.

As playwright, Robinson made no territorial conquest as O'Casey* did in tenement drama or Lady Gregory in Kiltartan farce. Instead, he ranged widely, from realism to expressionism, from problems of Irish life before and after the Treaty to easy social comedy.

Robinson's early Abbey plays, set in rural Cork—*The Clancy Name* (1908), *The Cross Roads* (1909), and *Harvest* (1910)—were blemished by unpersuasive didacticism and contrived endings, but they were typical of the shift from the romantic realism of Synge* toward a realism strongly critical of Irish life. The best of his early work is *Patriots* (1912), in which a revolutionary comes home from prison to continue his activity, only to find that negotiation and business as usual are the order of the new day.

Robinson's first important comedy was *The Whiteheaded Boy* (1916). The older Geoghegan children grudgingly sacrifice their futures to provide Denis Geoghegan with a medical education for which he has neither the aptitude nor the desire. Yet, when he sets off on his own as a common laborer, the grumblers unite to prevent him from disgracing the family. The play can be read as an allegory of England's unwillingness to do everything for Ireland but set it free: however, this family format of workers and drones appears in other of Robinson's plays without apparent political ramifications. *The Round Table* (1922) and *The White Blackbird* (1925) involve a family member exerting himself to support his feckless relatives. *The Far-Off Hills* (1928) inverts the plot of *The Whiteheaded Boy*. Marian Clancy delays entrance into the religious life so that she can care for her father and younger sisters, who only want to escape her well-meaning tyranny. And the father in *Bird's Nest* (1938) slaves to educate children who prefer to live according to their own wishes.

In the 1920s and early 1930s, Robinson sometimes moved the locale from Cork to English, or at least not definitely Irish, settings. It was not, on the whole, a fruitful change. Among the plays of this period are *Portrait* (1925), a study of a loser in the rat race; *Ever the Twain* (1929), on the difference between Englishmen and Yanks; *Give a Dog* (1929), a muddled confrontation of creativity and orthodoxy; and *All's Over, Then?* (1932), a melodrama of mother-daughter rivalry.

Robinson's plays with Irish locales and themes are more deeply rooted. *The Big House* (1926), something of a chronicle play, forcefully asserts the right of the Protestant Ascendancy to a proper place in post-Treaty Ireland. *Killycregs in Twilight* (1937) continues the theme of keeping alive Ascendancy tradition. *Church Street* (1934), technically perhaps the most interesting Robinson play, is influenced by Pirandello; at the same time, it is an admission that Ireland is Robinson's ultimate source of strength. A writer of superficial comedies in London pays a duty visit to his Irish home and discovers vital raw material in his seemingly drab townsfellows. *Drama at Inish* (1934) makes another kind of confession. Its plot is the visit of a highbrow drama company to a seaside village for a summer of Serious

Theatre; too serious, it fills the residents with all manner of guilt complexes. This play may be self-mockery of Robinson's own efforts, first at the Abbey, then beginning in 1918 with the forming of the Dublin Drama League, to perform exotic foreign masterpieces for Dubliners who preferred the comedies of William Boyle* or Martin J. McHugh.*

Robinson's late work—*Forget Me Not* (1941), *The Lucky Finger* (1948), *The Demon Lover* (1954)—adds nothing to his stature as a dramatist.

Of his nondramatic writing, a history of the Abbey and its predecessors from 1899 to 1951 is pleasantly reminiscent but useful mostly as a catalogue of plays and players. His other work is characteristically graceful, craftsmanlike, candid, and unpretentious when he is the subject, but it is largely overshadowed by his contributions to Irish drama.

In comedy and tragedy alike, Robinson was an intellectual playwright. Even Robert Emmet,* so often turned into a caricature of romantic patriotism, was portrayed as a thinking man in *The Dreamers* (1915). There is, however, no consistent philosophical motif in the plays, and sometimes after delineating a problem Robinson would not stay for an answer. In *The Lost Leader* (1918), this indecisiveness is effective. One cannot be sure that the seemingly demented Lucius Lenihan is not a resurrected Parnell. Generally, however, the uncertainty is a flaw.

Robinson's chief merits are a penetrating wit edged with enough malice to nick the unwary, a sureness of dialogue, and a gift for characterization. His best works are among the Abbey's best works. His failures are evidence that the law of averages lies in wait for any prolific, boldly experimenting writer.

WILLIAM J. FEENEY

WORKS: *The Cross-Roads: A Play in a Prologue and Two Acts.* Dublin: Maunsel, 1909. (Prologue subsequently deleted); *Two Plays: Harvest: A Play in Three Acts* and *The Clancy Name: A Tragedy in One Act.* Dublin: Maunsel, 1911; *Patriots: A Play in Three Acts.* Dublin: Maunsel, 1912; *The Dreamers: A Play in Three Acts.* Dublin: Maunsel, 1915; *A Young Man from the South.* Dublin: Maunsel, 1917. (Autobiographical novel); *Dark Days.* Dublin: Talbot, 1918. (Political sketches); *The Lost Leader: A Play in Three Acts.* Dublin: Kiersey, 1918; *Eight Short Stories.* Dublin: Talbot, 1919; *The Whiteheaded Boy: A Comedy in Three Acts.* London: Putnam's, 1921; *Crabbed Youth and Age: A Little Comedy.* London: Putnam's, 1924; *The Round Table: A Comic Tragedy in Three Acts.* London: Putnam's, 1924; *Never the Time and the Place: A Little Comedy in One Act,* in *The Dublin Magazine* 1 (May 1924): 856-867/reprinted in Belfast: Carter, 1953; *The White Blackbird: A Play in Three Acts* and *Portrait: A Play in Two Sittings.* Dublin: Talbot, 1926; *The Big House: Four Scenes in Its Life.* London: Macmillan, 1928; *Give a Dog—: A Play in Three Acts.* London: Macmillan, 1928; *Plays.* London: Macmillan, 1928; *Ever the Twain: A Comedy in Three Acts.* London: Macmillan, 1930; *Bryan Cooper.* London: Constable, 1931. (Biography); *The Far-Off Hills: A Comedy in Three Acts.* London: Chatto & Windus, 1931; *Drama at Inish: An Exaggeration in Three Acts* (retitled *Is Life Worth Living?*). London: Macmillan, 1933; *More Plays: All's Over, Then?: A Play in Three Acts* and *Church Street: A Play in One Act.* London: Macmillan, 1935; *Killycreggs in*

Twilight and Other Plays (*Is Life Worth Living?* and *Bird's Nest: A Play in Three Acts*). London: Macmillan, 1939; *Towards an Appreciation of the Theatre*. Dublin: Metropolitan Publishing Co., 1945; ed., *Lady Gregory's Journals*. New York: Macmillan, 1947; *Palette and Plough*. Dublin: Brown & Nolan, 1948. (Biography of Desmond O'Brien); *Ireland's Abbey Theatre: A History, 1899-1951*. London: Sidgwick & Jackson, 1951; co-ed. with Donagh MacDonagh. *Oxford Book of Irish Verse*. Oxford University Press, 1958; *Lennox Robinson Presents William Butler Yeats, Plays and Memories* and *Poems and Memories*. Spoken Arts Recordings.   REFERENCES: Everson, Ida G. "Young Lennox Robinson and the Abbey Theatre's First American Tour, 1911-1912." *Modern Drama* 9 (1966): 74-89; Everson, Ida G. "Lennox Robinson and Synge's Playboy, 1911-1930: Two Decades of American Cultural Growth." *New England Quarterly* 44 (March 1971):3-21; O'Neill, Michael J. *Lennox Robinson*. New York: Twayne, 1964; Spinner, Kaspar. *Die Alte Dame Sagt Nein! Drei Irische Dramatiker, Lennox Robinson, Sean O'Casey, Denis Johnston*. Bern: Franche Verlag, 1961.

RODGERS, W[ILLIAM] R[OBERT] (1909-1969), poet. Rodgers was born on August 1, 1909, in Belfast, where he was educated at the Queens University and at the Presbyterian Theological College. There he prepared for his ordination as a Presbyterian minister which took place in 1935. He served as minister at Loughgall, County Antrim, from 1935 to 1946. In 1941, his first collection of poems appeared. Entitled *Awake! And Other Poems*, the volume collected most of the poems he had written while ministering to his congregation in Loughgall. It was widely praised; critics responded to its exurberant relishing of verbal sound patterns. It was assumed that Rodgers' verbal practices owed something to Gerard Manly Hopkins' example. It is clear, however, that, while other English poets of the 1930s unsuccessfully attempted to emulate Hopkins' experiments, Rodgers managed to endow his diction with an energy and bravura reminiscent of Hopkins without having in fact read that poet's work. The verbal effects of Rodgers' poetry are more properly to be related to his perennial zest for word play, pun, and alliteration, to his almost Joycean awareness of linguistic possibilities. The themes of his early poetry, however, do suggest that he experienced a tension between the priestly role and poetic ambition much as Hopkins did. *Awake! And Other Poems* was also notable for an exact scrupulous intensity in rendering Rodgers' awareness of the physical world—its motions, its comings and goings, its explosions of energy and its moments of stillness. A heightened moral awareness of clash and conflict in the social and political world was expressed in a tendency to employ parable and homiletic rhetoric in a distinctly 1930s English mode.

In 1946, Rodgers resigned from the ministry and settled in London where he made many contributions to the BBC features department. Among his excellent radio programs were "The Return Room" broadcast in 1955, an evocation of life in East Belfast, and his collections of spoken reminiscence on the major figures of the Irish Literary Revival (posthumously published in 1972 as *Irish Literary Portraits*).

In 1952, Rodgers published *Europa and the Bull,* his second collection of poems. This volume reflects a considerable development in thematic range. Myth, religion, sexual relations, as well as landscape and social issues, are treated with a new capacity for fulfilled as well as tense celebration. Poems like "The Net" and "Europa and the Bull" are frank, delightfully cavalier celebrations of sexual experience, while "Lent" is one of the most remarkable poems on a Biblical/Christian theme by an Irish poet in this century.

In 1966, Rodgers accepted a post as writer in residence at Pitzer College, in Claremont, California. None of the poems he wrote in this later period maintained the standard achieved in *Europa and the Bull,* though the verbal dexterity and wit, as in *"Home Thoughts From Abroad,"* occasionally flair into moments of characteristic life.

Rodgers died in Los Angeles on February 1, 1969, and he was buried in Loughgall, County Armagh, in March of that year.

Rodgers' contribution to Irish letters was marked by his election to the Irish Academy of Letters in 1951 and by an Irish Arts Council annuity in 1968. As a whole, his work, through its use of baroque verbal effects and of alliterative and assonantal textures, is memorable chiefly as a revelation of exciting, if not always revelatory, linguistic possibilities.

TERENCE BROWN

WORKS: *Collected Poems.* London: Oxford University Press, 1971.   REFERENCE: O'Brien, Darcy. *W. R. Rodgers.* Lewisburg, Pa.: Bucknell University Press, 1970.

ROLLESTON, T[HOMAS] W[ILLIAM HAZEN] (1857-1920), poet and translator. Rolleston was born in 1857 near Shinrone. He was educated at St. Columba's College, Rathfarnham, and at Trinity College, Dublin. He was a prolific and erudite writer who published *The Teachings of Epictetus* (1886) and *A Life of Lessing* (1899); translated Whitman's *Leaves of Grass* into German; and made some loose translations into English of Wagner. He was much involved in the Irish literary movement and was first honorary secretary of the London Irish Literary Society. Padraic Colum* thought highly of his translations from the Irish; indeed, Rolleston does make some attempt to find equivalents for Irish verse techniques in English. Nevertheless, in both his translations and original verse, he still appears to have been a captive of outmoded English poetic conventions. He died in Hampstead on December 5, 1920.

WORKS: *Sea Spray, Verses and Translations.* Dublin: Maunsel, 1909; *The High Deeds of Finn.* London: Harrap, 1910; *Myths and Legends of the Celtic Race.* London: Harrap, 1911; ed. with S. A. Brooke, *A Treasury of Irish Poetry in the English Tongue.* Revised ed., New York: Macmillan, 1932.   REFERENCE: Rolleston, Charles Henry. *Portrait of an Irishman.* London: Methuen, 1939.

ROONEY, PHILIP (1907-1962), novelist and radio playwright. Rooney was born at Collooney, County Sligo, in 1907. He worked as bank clerk in the Midlands for fifteen years, writing short stories in his spare time. He published his first novel, *All Out to Win*, in 1935 and subsequently published several others. In 1953, he became head of the script writing department for Radio Éireann and wrote or adapted many radio plays. In 1961, he transferred to Irish television but died shortly after in Dublin in 1962.

Rooney's forte is the Irish historical novel with a good deal of action and a dash of romance. Perhaps his best books are *Captain Boycott* (1946), which was made into a film, and *The Golden Coast* (1947). There is a level of competent professionalism in his work, but it is the professionalism of the purveyor of popular entertainment. Even his best work is full of stock characters and tired, slick writing.

WORKS: *All Out to Win*. Dublin & Cork: Talbot, 1935; *Overnight Entry,* under the pseudonym of Frank Phillips. London: Mellifont, [1938]; *Red Sky at Dawn*. Dublin: Gill, 1938/New York: P. J. Kenedy, 1939; *North Road*. Dublin: Talbot, [1943]; *Singing River*. Dublin & Cork: Talbot, [1944]; *Captain Boycott*. Dublin: Talbot/New York & London: Appleton-Century, 1946; *The Golden Coast*. Dublin: Talbot, [1947]; *The Quest for Matt Talbot*. Dublin: Talbot, [1949]. (Radio play); *The Long Day*. Dublin: Talbot, [1951]; (There is said to be another published novel, *Dark Road*.)

ROS, AMANDA M'KITTRICK (1860-1939), novelist and poet. Ros was born Anna Margaret M'Kittrick on December 8, 1860, near Ballynahinch, County Down. She claimed that her mother had named her after the heroine of *Children of the Abbey*, a novel by Regina Maria Roche, and that her full name was Amanda Malvina Fitzalan Anna Margaret McLelland M'Kittrick. This claim was to be typical of the extravagance which characterized much of Amanda M'Kittrick Ros's life and work.

Her father, Edward Amlane M'Kittrick, was head teacher of Drumaness High School near Ballynahinch. Anna Margaret was also a teacher, receiving her training at Marlborough Training College in Dublin in 1884-1886 and afterwards obtaining a post at Larne. There she met Andrew Ross, the stationmaster; they were married on August 30, 1887. Although she told friends that she had been writing since the age of four and that her first novel had been completed before she was sixteen and then locked away until 1897, when it was revised and printed, her biographer, Jack Loudan, believes that she wrote *Irene Iddesleigh* between 1892 and 1896. In any case, as a tenth anniversary present her husband gave her enough money to pay the cost of printing her first novel. In it the author was given as Amanda M'Kittrick Ros, the name by which she was to be known from that time on. She built a house in Larne with the proceeds of the novel and named it "Iddesleigh." Her second novel, *Delina Delaney*, was published in 1898.

In 1908, Amanda M'Kittrick Ros inherited a lime kiln from a friend. This embroiled her in a legal battle which lasted for more than five years. She was finally forced to sell the kiln because of legal costs, and the experience permanently embittered her toward lawyers and the legal profession.

The added responsibilities of the stationmaster during World War I destroyed Andrew Ross's health, and in 1915 he was forced to retire. He never fully recovered and died in August 1917. Ros married a well-to-do farmer, Thomas Rodgers, on June 12, 1922, and she began to write again. A volume of poems, *Fumes of Formation*, was published in 1933. Soon after its publication, her second husband died, and she herself died on February 3, 1939. *Helen Huddleson*, her last novel, was never finished, but it was published in 1969, edited and revised by Jack Loudan, who also added a final chapter.

The works of Amanda M'Kittrick Ros are uniquely dreadful. The style is florid, artificial, and overdone. For instance, eyes are described as "orbs of blinded brilliancy," and passion for one of an inferior class is called a "deceptive demon of deluded mockery." Her titles give some indication of her love of alliteration. Meaning is often lost in a torrent of descriptive phrases. This style has been viewed both positively and negatively by critics. According to her biographer, "She writes with a burning imagination that will disregard sense should it hinder the intensity of her invention" (Loudan, *O Rare Amanda*, p. 28). Mark Twain welcomed one of her books as an addition to his collection of "hogwash literature."

The events in a Ros novel complement the style. Noble gentlemen fall in love with peasant girls at first sight, and people often drop dead of shock upon hearing bad news. Coincidence is carried to the point of absurdity, and time and possibility are ignored.

Ros's writing is also the vehicle of revenge. "All the rancour in her writing is strictly personal" (Loudan, *O Rare Amanda*, p. 46). The lawyers whom she felt wronged her appear in her works as Mickey Monkeyface McBlear and Barney Bloater, and her works include tirades against the profession. *Helen Huddleson* contains a completely extraneous digression on a lawyer who is convicted of forgery and kills a servant rather than pay her wages. *Poems of Puncture* (1913), written during the lime kiln controversy, contains many poems which are fierce in their denunciation of lawyers.

Ros is not a satirist; her attacks are direct and unsubtle. There is no desire to improve or instruct. An attack on *Irene Iddesleigh* by Barry Pain on February 19, 1898, in *Black and White* hurt Ros deeply and created her lasting enmity towards critics. She could not be charitable even at Pain's death; in a poem entitled "The End of 'Pain' " in *Fumes of Formation*, she calls him a "rodent of State." In fact, many of the poems in this collection are vicious attacks on the critics. She ridiculed W.B. Wyndham

Lewis in a ten thousand word essay, *St. Scandalbags* (1954); and *Donald Dudley: Bastard Critic* (1954) is the first episode of a long unfinished work, tentatively entitled *Six Months in Hell*, in which she made sketches of all the people she felt had wronged her.

Despite ridicule and derision, Amanda M'Kittrick Ros took her writing seriously. She has some staunch defenders, and since her death, several of her works have been printed for the first time, including extracts from her letters (*Bayonets of Bastard Sheen*). While there is much—if not everything—that is ludicrous in her writing, there is also a sense of life, a Rabelaisian vigor, that cannot be suppressed.

BARBARA DiBERNARD

WORKS: *Irene Iddesleigh*. Belfast: W. & G. Baird, 1897/London: Nonesuch, 1926/ New York: Boni & Liveright, 1927. (Novel); *Delina Delaney*. Belfast: R. Aickin, 1898/London: Chatto & Windus, 1935. (Novel); *Poems of Puncture*. London: Arthur H. Stockwell, 1913; *Fumes of Formation*. Belfast: R. Carswell, 1933. (Poems); *Bayonets of Bastard Sheen*. East Sheen: Privately printed, 1949; *Donald Dudley: The Bastard Critic*. Thames Ditton, Surrey: Merle, 1954; *St. Scandalbags*. T. Stanley Mercer, ed. Thames Ditton, Surrey: Merle, 1954; *Helen Huddleson*, ed. & with a final chapter by Jack Loudan. London: Chatto & Windus, 1969. (Novel).   REFERENCE: Loudan, Jack. *O Rare Amanda!* London: Chatto & Windus, 1954. (Biography, with a bibliography by T. Stanley Mercer).

ROSS, MARTIN. *See* SOMERVILLE AND ROSS.

ROWLEY, RICHARD (1877-1947), poet and playwright. Richard Rowley was the pseudonym of Richard Valentine Williams, who was born in Belfast on April 2, 1877. Williams went into the family firm, McBride and Williams, which made cotton handkerchiefs, and became its managing director. His first book of poems, *The City of Refuge* (1917), attracted critical attention largely for the wrong reasons. As *The Times Literary Supplement* wrote, "The sound of a great Northern manufacturing city . . . vibrates through these poems." Today we look rather to the dialect poems which Rowley put in the mouths of working-class Belfast people and of country men and women from Mourne, who appeared in this and later collections.

Rowley's firm collapsed in the crisis of 1931. From 1934 to 1943, he was chairman of the Northern Ireland Unemployment Assistance Board. During World War II, he ran the Mourne Press from his Newcastle home. The Press brought out six titles, including work by Forrest Reid* and himself, before going under in 1942 from lack of support. Rowley died at Drumilly, Loughgall, County Armagh, on April 25, 1947.

Ironically, the best poems about ordinary Ulster people are by the industrialist Richard Rowley. Ironically too, he needed the mask of dialect to speak clearly; his work in standard English, in his own voice, is rhetorical and derivative. His dialect work comprises Mourne poems and Belfast poems. The Mourne poems tend to be light and humorous, with considerably folksy charm, but they can show tragic awareness, as in "Thinkin' Long." The Belfast poems are long, free monologues put into the mouths of working people, like "The Stitcher" or "Oul Jane."

Rowley also wrote stories (*Tales of Mourne*, 1937) and plays (including the popular *Apollo in Mourne*, 1926). The latter is a kind of wistful *Playboy* in which the god Apollo, banished from Olympus and coming to earth in Mourne, plays the role of Christy. He wins and renounces the love of Mary Blane, who is left contemplating her earthly lover Paddy Soye, whose mind is taken up with "a rare jewel o' a wee pig." *Apollo* reconciles Rowley's grandiloquent manner, put into the mouths of gods, and his dialect realism. He regarded it as his best work, but the working-class monologues are superior in one respect. As AE* wrote in his review of *Workers* (*The Irish Homestead*, May 12, 1923), "there are no illusions about the life he depicts."

VICTOR PRICE

WORKS: *The City of Refuge*. Dublin: Maunsel, 1917; *City Songs, and Others*. Dublin: Maunsel, 1918; *Workers*. London: Duckworth, 1923; *The Old Gods*. London: Duckworth, 1925; *Apollo in Mourne*. London: Duckworth, 1926; *Selected Poems*. London: Duckworth, 1931; *Tales of Mourne*. London: Duckworth, 1937; *Ballads of Mourne*. Dundalk: Dundalgan, 1940; *One Cure for Sorrow, and Other One-Act Plays*. Newcastle, County Down: Mourne, 1942; *Sonnets for Felicity*. Newcastle, County Down: Mourne, 1942; *The Piper of Mourne*. Belfast: Derrick MacCord, 1944; *Final Harvest*. Belfast: Carter Publications, 1951; *Apollo in Mourne*, ed. and with an Introduction by Victor Price. Belfast: Blackstaff, 1977. (A selection of the poems, plays, and stories).   REFERENCE: Price, Victor. "Richard Rowley—100." *The Honest Ulsterman*, No. 53 (November-December 1976).

RUSSELL, GEORGE W. *See* AE.

RYAN, FREDERICK (1876-1913), journalist and editor. Ryan was secretary of the Irish National Theatre Society, wrote for several journals (sometimes under the pen names of "Irial" and "Finian"), formed the Dublin Philosophical Society in 1906, and founded two monthly journals, *Dana* with John Eglinton* and the *National Democrat* with Francis Sheehy-Skeffington.* He spent some time in Egypt and edited Mustapha Kemel's *Egypt*, and he was also a secretary to Wilfrid Scawen Blunt. His only play, a two-act comedy *The Laying of the Foundations*, was performed by the Irish National Drama Company on October 29, 1902. Its theme is the conflict between labor and the corrupt alliance of business and municipal government, and it was the first realistic social drama of the modern Irish stage. Curiously, W. B. Yeats* thought highly of the play, calling it "excellent" and "a really astonishing piece of satire." That is far too much praise for this rather bald and stiff piece, and Ryan was more interested in fostering liberal opinions than in writing great drama. Socialist, humanist, internationalist (*Sinn Féin* wrote of him, "The suffering Egyptian had no less claim on him than his own countrymen"), he was widely respected as an honest voice of social conscience, despite his unorthodox opinions. He died in England on April 7, 1913, at the age of thirty-nine.

WILLIAM J. FEENEY

WORKS: *Criticism and Courage.* Vol. 6 of the Tower Press Booklets. Dublin: Maunsel, 1906; "The Laying of the Foundations." In *Lost Plays of the Irish Renaissance.* Robert Hogan and James Kilroy, eds. Newark, Del.: Proscenium, 1970. (Act II only; Act I has been lost).   REFERENCE: Sheehy-Skeffington, F. "Frederick Ryan, an Appreciation." *The Irish Review* 3 (May 1913): 113-119.

RYAN, JOHN (1925-), editor. Ryan was born on February 19, 1925, in Dublin, and was educated at Clongowes Wood College and the National College of Art. He has often been involved in the production of plays and was also the proprietor for some years of the popular restaurant The Bailey, but he is most likely to be remembered as the founder-editor of the literary magazine *Envoy** (1949-1951). In the early 1970s, he was editor of the new *Dublin Magazine.* He also edited a collection of essays on Joyce,* *A Bash in the Tunnel* (1970). His memoir, *Remembering How We Stood,* is a lively recreation of Patrick Kavanagh,* Myles na gCopaleen,* Brendan Behan,* Eoin "the Pope" O'Mahony, and other important Dublin figures of the midcentury.

WORK: *Remembering How We Stood.* Dublin: Gill & Macmillan, 1975.

RYAN, RICHARD (1946-), poet. Ryan was born in Dublin in 1946 and was educated at University College, Dublin. He has published two slim collections of verse, *Ledges* (1970) and *Ravenswood* (1973). The pieces in both volumes are straightforward in statement but technically rather formless. Many of them are written in stanzas of two, three, or four very short lines with no recognizable rhythmical pattern. However, the very shortness of the lines does act to emphasize the importance of individual words. The imagery in the first volume ranges from the commonplace to, once or twice, the extraordinarily striking. In the second volume, the remarkable quality of imagery is even more pervasive, and the images have become surrealistic or even science fictional. Whatever its technical deficiencies, Ryan's writing in this second volume is terse, vivid, and frequently quotable.

WORKS: *Ledges.* Dublin: Dolmen, 1970; *Ravenswood.* Dublin: Dolmen, 1973.

SADLIER, MARY ANNE (1820-1903), novelist and journalist. Mary Anne Madden was born in Cootehill, County Cavan, on December 31, 1820. She emigrated to Montreal in August 1844, and there she married a Catholic publisher, James Sadlier. In Canada and after 1860 in New York, she pursued her own career as a Catholic journalist and author of patriotic and romantic historical fiction, such as *The Confederate Chieftains* (1859), *Old House by the Boyne* (1865), *The Heiress of Kilorgan* (1867), and about thirty others. Although her fiction is meant to be uplifting, it is mainly innocuous and full of alternate flushes and blushes on the heroines' cheeks. She also wrote plays and religious tracts, and translated prolifically from the French. Her work is of some interest as an indicator of what the unlearned, homesick Irishman was reading during the latter half of the nineteenth century. She died in Montreal on April 5, 1903.

WORKS: *The Red Hand of Ulster.* Boston: P. Donahoe, 1850; *The Blakes and the Flanagans.* Dublin: Duffy, [1855]; *Elinor Preston.* New York: D. & J. Sadlier, [ca. 1861]; *Old and New; or, Taste Versus Fashion.* New York & Boston: D. & J. Sadlier, 1862; *The Hermit of the Rock.* New York, Boston & Montreal: D. & J. Sadlier, 1863; *The Daughter of Tyrconnell.* New York: D. & J. Sadlier, [1863]; *Bessy Conway; or, The Irish Girl in America.* New York: D. & J. Sadlier, 1863; *The Fate of Father Sheehy.* New York & Boston: D. & J. Sadlier, [ca. 1863]; *Confessions of an Apostate.* New York: Sadlier, [1864]; *Con O'Regan, or, Emigrant Life in the New World.* New York: Sadlier, [1864]; *The Old House by the Boyne.* New York: Sadlier, [1865]; *Aunt Honor's Keepsake.* New York & Boston: D. & J. Sadlier, 1866; *The Heiress of Kilorgan.* New York: D. & J. Sadlier, [1867?]; *MacCarthy More!* New York: D. & J. Sadlier, 1868; *Maureen Dhu, the Admiral's Daughter.* New York: Sadlier, 1870, *The Invisible Hand.* New York: Sadlier, [ca. 1873]. (Two-act play); *The Secret.* London: R. Washbourne, 1880. (Play); *Alice Riordan, the Blind Man's Daughter.* Dublin: Gill, 1884. (Children's story); *The Minister's Wife, and Other Stories.* New York: C. Wildermann, 1898; *O'Byrne; or The Expatriated.* New York: C. Wildermann, 1898; *Short Stories.* New York: C. Wildermann, [1900]. This is a very partial list of Mrs. Sadlier's work, but, with the exception of *The Confederate Chieftains* (1859) which we have been unable to trace, it probably contains everything of hers with any claim to literary merit.

SALKELD, BLANAID (1880-1959), poet. Salkeld was born in Chittagong (now Pakistan) on August 10, 1880. Her father was in the Indian medical service and was a friend of Tagore. Most of her own childhood was spent in Dublin, but when she was twenty-two she married an Englishman in the Indian civil service in Bombay. (Her older son, Cecil ffrench Salkeld, became a prominent Irish artist.) When she was twenty-eight, Mrs. Salkeld returned to Ireland and joined the second company of Abbey Theatre* players, using the stage name of Nell Byrne. On one occasion, she played the title role of Fitzmaurice's* *The Country Dressmaker* with the first company in London. She wrote many verse plays, but none has been published and only one, *Scarecrow over the Corn*, reached the stage; it was done at the Gate* in the 1930s. Her poems appeared in several small volumes, from the 1930s to the 1950s, and might be described as the sensitive attempts of a highly intelligent amateur. She is usually committed to rhyme, but her sense of rhythm is erratic. Even in a traditional and highly restricting form like the sonnet, she seems to think that any ten higgledy-piggledy syllables compose an acceptable line. In fact, her rhythm, much broken up by dashes, parentheses, and three dots (used not for elision but for some manner of pause), is finally chaotic. In other poems, she utilizes spacing within a line rather than conventional punctuation, and it is difficult to determine what rhythm, if any, she had in mind, without knowing the length of pauses and the strength of emphases. Moreover, her capitalization—or, in some cases, the lack of it—usually seems affected. If Mrs. Salkeld relied more on sensitivity than on technique, she did have her occasional successes, as particularly in the tight and accomplished poems vii, xv, and xvii of . . . *the engine is left running* (1937). Her grand-daughter Beatrice married Brendan Behan,* and, to judge by her grand-daughter's memoir, *My Life with Brendan*, Mrs. Salkeld and her very different grandson-in-law seem to have gotten on just famously. She died in Dublin in 1959.

WORKS: *Hello, Eternity!* London: Elkin Mathews & Marot, 1933; *The Fox's Covert.* London: Dent, [1935]; . . . *the engine is still running.* Dublin: Gayfield, [1937]; *A Dubliner.* Dublin: Gayfield, 1943. (Pamphlet); *Experiment in Error.* Aldington, Kent: Hand & Flower, [1955].

SARR, KENNETH (1895-1967), novelist and playwright. Kenneth Sarr is the occasional pen name of Kenneth Shiels Reddin, who wrote two short plays produced by the Abbey Theatre* and who published three readable novels. He was born in Dublin in 1895 and was educated at Belvedere, Clongowes Wood, St. Enda's, and then at University College, Dublin, where his education was interrupted by a prison sentence for his Sinn Féin activities. He was accustomed to a literary milieu from youth, for his mother kept a literary salon in the early years of the century, and he and his brother were involved in the activities of the Irish Theatre* in Hardwicke Street. His occupation, however, was the law. After being admitted to the bar, he became a District Justice in 1922, serving in that capacity for forty-two years. He died in Dublin on August 17, 1967.

Sarr's two one-act plays, which were produced at the Abbey in December 1924, are both very brief, each playing only about twelve minutes. *The Passing* won the Dramatic Award at the Tailteann Games earlier in 1924. Although this slum tragedy offers an excellent opportunity for a brilliant actress, the play is theatre rather than literature and assuredly is not as fine as the second prize winner, *Autumn Fire* of T. C. Murray.* *Old Mag* is a portrait of an old Waterford street vendor and her finding most coincidentally her long-lost son. W. J. Lawrence,* the critic, was apparently baffled by the play's lack of a recognition scene; nevertheless, the little piece has some extremely effective dialogue.

Sarr's novels are substantial and quite excellent recreations of Dublin. The best is *Somewhere to the Sea*, which is set at the end of the Black and Tan War and in the early days of the Treaty negotiations. There is a deal of unnecessary recapitulation of the plot, but the real-life characters, such as AE,* James Stephens,* Susan Mitchell,* and the actress Maire nic

Shiubhlaigh, who wander around the periphery of the story, do much to create a real and persuasive atmosphere. The passing satire of the Dublin intellectual scene in the early 1920s is also excellent. It is definitively a minor work, but like his slighter *Another Shore* (1945) it is a rewarding one.

WORKS: as Kenneth Reddin—*Another Shore*. London: Cresset, 1945. (Novel); *Young Man with a Dream*. New York: Current Books, A. A. Winn, [1946]. (Novel). as Kenneth Sarr—*Old Mag*. Dublin & Cork: Talbot, 1924. (Play); *The Passing*. Dublin & Cork; Talbot, 1924. (Play); *The White Bolle-Trie, a Wonder Story*. Dublin & Cork: Talbot, 1927; *Somewhere to the Sea*. London: T. Nelson, [1936]. (Novel).

SAVAGE-ARMSTRONG, G[EORGE] F[RANCIS] (1845-1906), poet.

Savage-Armstrong was born in County Dublin on May 5, 1845, and was the brother of the promising young poet Edmund J. Armstrong (1841-1865). He was educated at Trinity College, Dublin, and in 1871 was appointed professor of English at Queen's College, Cork. He wrote a number of lengthy closet dramas on Biblical subjects and much generally undistinguished verse. His career is a curious contrast in some respects to that of J. M. Synge,* for both did much tramping in Wicklow and on the Continent, and Savage-Armstrong's great poetic inspiration was landscape. Unlike Synge, however, his descriptions even of Wicklow are the most usual of neo-Wordsworthian effusions. His poem "The Scalp," for instance, begins:

> Stern granite Gate of Wicklow, with what awe,
> What triumph, oft (glad children strayed from home)
> We passed into thy shadows cool, to roam. . . .

It is seldom indeed that he can rise to a line of clear and simple description, such as "Old peasants deep-wrinkled, sat clustered and talked/In their gutteral Gaelic. . . ." He died on July 24, 1906, in Strangford, County Down.

WORKS: *Poems*. London: E. Moxon, 1869; *Ugone. A Tragedy*. London: E. Moxon, 1870; *The Tragedy of Israel*. 3 Parts. London: Longmans, 1872-1876; *A Garland from Greece*. London: Longmans, 1882; *Stories of Wicklow*. London: Longmans, 1886; *Mephistopheles in Broadcloth*. London: Longmans, 1888; *One in the Infinite*. London: Longmans, 1891; *Queen-Empress and the Empire. 1837-1897*. Belfast: M. Ward, 1897; *Ballads of Down*. London: Longmans, 1901; *Poems: National and International*. Dublin: E. Ponsonby, 1917.

SHAW, [GEORGE] BERNARD (1856-1950), probably the preeminent

dramatist in the English language since Shakespeare. There were few indications during the first three decades of the long life of George Bernard Shaw that he would take a place beside Shakespeare as England's most widely recognized man of letters. He was born at 3 Upper Synge Street (now 33 Synge Street) on July 26, 1856, the third child and only son of George Carr Shaw and Elizabeth Gurly Shaw. His father, a wholesale grain merchant, was possibly an alcoholic and certainly a failure as head of his family, being

far less an influence on his son than was the strong, dispassionate mother.
The nominally Protestant Shaws held to the values of the Irish Ascendancy
without enjoying any of its perquisites. Shaw's schooling, wasted on a boy
who could not afford to go on to Trinity, left him unprepared for art, trade,
or profession. He left school at fifteen to serve as a clerk in a land agency
at 15 Molesworth Street.

The only common interest in the Shaw home was music. Mrs. Shaw, a
mezzo-soprano, received lessons from a teacher and impressario, George
John Vandeleur Lee. Following the death of his brother, Lee and the Shaw
family shared a four-story house at No. 1 Hatch Street. This led to perhaps
groundless speculation on an affair between Lee and Mrs. Shaw. G.B.S.'s
portrait of Lee as a genius is unconvincing, but Lee directed ambitious
musical programs in Dublin; his single-minded devotion to music and his
brisk self-confidence left a mark on Shaw's personality.

In 1873, Lee moved to London. The departure of Mrs. Shaw and her
daughters followed too closely to be coincidental. Her marriage had become meaningless. With Lee's help she could obtain teaching work in London, and her daughter Lucy might be able to advance her singing career.
(The other daughter, Elinor Agnes, died of tuberculosis in 1876.) Father
and son moved into lodgings at 61 Harcourt Street.

Shaw joined his mother and sister in London in 1876. He left Dublin
without a sentimental tremor and did not return to Ireland, even when his
father died in 1885, for thirty years. During his first three years in London,
Shaw did nothing in pursuit of his dimly defined goal of success in the
arts. For a few months he was a ghost-writer for Lee, contributing articles
on music to a shortlived weekly, *The Hornet*. They remained in casual
contact until Lee's death on November 28, 1886, at his residence in the
unfashionable end of Park Lane. Much earlier, Mrs. Shaw had broken off
her unromantic connection with the music teacher; no Shaw attended his
funeral.

In 1879, Shaw began to write novels in outmoded early Victorian style:
Immaturity (1879), *The Irrational Knot* (1880), *Love Among the Artists*
(1881), *Cashel Byron's Profession* (1882), *An Unsocial Socialist* (1883),
and a fragment later titled *An Unfinished Novel*. All but *Immaturity* and
the fragment were printed serially in the socialist periodicals *To-Day* and
Our Corner after publishing houses rejected them. Shaw's fame in other
areas eventually led to the publication of the novels in book format. A few
other prose works of this period were accepted by various journals and
later issued as part of a collected edition. They are of negligible merit.

The novels are of interest mostly for the autobiographical elements and
the early intimations of Shaw's hero type. Robert Smith, the young clerk
in *Immaturity*; Ned Connolly, the stolid inventive genius in *The Irrational
Knot*; Owen Jack, the musician rampant in *Love Among the Artists*; and
Sidney Trefusis, doctrinaire socialist and cool philanderer in *An Unsocial*

Socialist, all are adumbrations of what Shaw was or wanted to be. Presumably he had no desire to become a prizefighter like Cashel Byron, though he boxed for exercise. Characterization and dialogue were done with care; plotting he regarded as an irksome necessity.

London in the 1880s was bustling with debating clubs and radical societies. In 1879, Shaw joined the philosophical Zetetical Society. Stimulated by his first taste of intellectual life, he responded, at first haltingly because of innate shyness, then, flitting from one society to another, with growing assurance. He was attracted to socialism in 1882 on hearing a lecture by the American economist Henry George. Soon after the Fabian Society was founded in 1884, Shaw became a member. The Fabians differed from other socialist bodies and splinter groups in repudiating violence and in directing their appeals to intelligent, respectable citizens. Few in number but significant in influence, they operated by infiltrating committees of other organizations, lecturing, debating, and issuing a flood of articulate pamphlets. With them Shaw gained direction, friendships, and an outlet for his burgeoning talent. If he lacked the economic background of many Fabians, such as Sidney Webb, he could hold an audience by his audacity and wit, and the content and style of many Fabian pamphlets bore the stamp of G.B.S.

While he was working for the socialist cause, Shaw became a reviewer. From 1885, when William Archer obtained a position for him as art critic, until 1898, when poor health and mental fatigue forced him to stop, he wrote voluminously: art reviews for Edmund Yates' *The World*, 1885 to 1888; music criticism, 1888 to 1890; signed Corno di Bassetto, for T. P. O'Connor's *The Star* (O'Connor was an Irish nationalist member of Parliament); back to *The World* as music reviewer in 1890; and drama criticism, signed G.B.S., for Frank Harris' *Saturday Review*, 1895 to 1898. Shaw also wrote occasionally for other journals such as the *Pall Mall Gazette* and *Our Corner*. (Collections of his reviews have been published.)

Shaw's articles were candid revelations of his personality and opinions on almost everything. Michelangelo, Beethoven, Wagner, Ibsen, the iconoclasts, the earth-shakers, were the creators against whom other artists were weighed and found wanting. What Shaw observed on the stage infuriated him: mutilated Shakespeare, mechanistic well-made plays, melodrama which bolstered hypocritical conventionality, sham-Ibsen plays which labored the supposed naughtiness and ignored the social criticism.

There was more to his critical writing than freedom of the press bravado and overstated favoritism or dislike. Afternoons in the National Gallery of Ireland had given him some visual appreciation of painting, though it was not his strongest area. Music he knew intimately; he had grown up with it and was a self-taught pianist. Furthermore, he noted affinities between the composition of a symphony and a drama, between song and speech—an awareness he put to practical use. The coruscating wit and combativeness of the play reviews have tended to obscure his perceptive commentary not only on the art of playwriting but also on costumes, staging, lighting, and other aspects of theatre craft.

As a Dubliner, Shaw had elbowed his way into the Theatre Royal or the Gaiety to watch English actors on tour. In London, his knowledge of theatre was greatly expanded. Nevertheless, he became a playwright almost by chance. In 1885, William Archer suggested that they collaborate on an Ibsenite play; Archer would write the plot and Shaw will fill in dialogue. The collaboration lasted for one act. Seven years later the Independent Theatre founded by J. T. Grein was soliciting plays. Shaw dug out the abandoned manuscript. Reworked and entitled *Widowers' Houses* (Mark 12: 38-40), it was staged at the Royalty Theatre on December 9, 1892. This was the first of three dramas published in 1898 under Shaw's designation Unpleasant Plays.

Widowers' Houses and *Mrs. Warren's Profession* dramatize exploitation, not by heartless monsters but by cheerful, pragmatic, well-spoken, otherwise decent and respectable individuals. Responsibility for the evil is not confined to Sartorius, the slumlord in *Widowers' Houses*, and Mrs. Warren, manager of a chain of brothels. It must be shared equally by respectable persons who by acquiescence become a party to the wrong and by a social order which makes exploitation possible. *The Philanderer* (1893) satirizes ladies who emancipate themselves in the fashion of Ibsen's heroines and at the same time insist on being treated as the weaker sex. Awkwardly attached to this plot line is the ridiculing of medical experimenters engaging in vivisection.

Shaw's first plays did not take the theatre by storm. *Widowers' Houses* had a single performance; Grein wisely turned down *The Philanderer*—it was not staged until 1905; and the lord chamberlain unwisely refused to license *Mrs. Warren's Profession*, the best of the lot, for public presentation. A private performance was given by the Stage Society in London on January 15, 1902. A company staging the play in New York on October 30, 1905, was tried for offending public decency and acquitted. Punitive action was threatened, though not carried out, when the Dublin Repertory Company played it at the Little Theatre, 40 Upper O'Connell Street, on November 16, 1914. Not until July 27, 1925, was there a public showing in England, at the Prince of Wales Theatre, Birmingham.

The Unpleasant Plays were followed by a group of Pleasant Plays, also published in 1898: *Arms and the Man, Candida, The Man of Destiny, You Never Can Tell*. They were pleasant in that they dealt with romantic follies.

Arms and the Man, set in Bulgaria during its war with Serbia in 1885, contrasts saber-flailing panache and romantic sensibility to the plain practicality of the Swiss mercenary Bluntschli. On April 21, 1894, it appeared at the Avenue Theatre, London. The curtain-raiser, W. B. Yeats'* *The Land of Heart's Desire*, by chance or intent provided another comparison of sense and sensibility. Both writers looked on a world too full of weeping; Yeats' solution was to escape from it, and Shaw's was to reform the actual world into a land of heart's desire. *Arms and the Man* was the first Shaw play performed in America, at the Herald Square Theatre, New York, on September 17, 1894.

In *Candida*, eighteen-year-old poet Eugene Marchbanks tries to persuade the wife of a robust Christian socialist, the Reverend James Morell, to leave her unappreciative husband and fly with him to a Yeatsian dreamworld. Candida's decision to stay with Morell is founded neither on the sacred marriage contract nor on Victorian right-thinking; in spite of his charisma, he is the weaker man and needs her. Eugene goes off alone, self-assured, to meet his destiny. The play did well on English provincial tours in 1897–1898 and was the hit of the season after its opening at the Princess Theatre, New York, on December 8, 1903.

A one-act comedy, *The Man of Destiny*, is witty triviality about compromising letters in a stolen dispatch case belonging to Napoleon Bonaparte, on the verge of greatness in 1796. It contains an analytical passage in which, except for a few details, the description of Napoleon fits George Bernard Shaw. The play was produced at the Grand Theatre, Croydon, on July 1, 1897.

You Never Can Tell involves the comic reunion of a husband and his family after an eighteen-year separation and points out the folly of preparing for married life by indulging in romantic courtship. This popular farce premiered at the Strand Theatre, London, on May 2, 1900.

Shaw's friendship with Charlotte Payne-Townsend, an Irish heiress, began in 1896. When he became seriously ill in 1898, she was willing to give him better care than he would receive in the indifferent bosom of his family. But where? Though Shaw was a veteran of a few fleshly and several platonic affairs, he would have no part of a live-in with a gracious lady. Royalties from his plays were starting to accumulate, so there could be no whispers of fortune-hunting. On June 1, 1898, they were married in a civil ceremony. A few years later, they moved into an architecturally undistinguished house in Ayot St. Lawrence, a quiet village close to London. Their childless union ended with her death on September 12, 1943. (Shaw's mother died in 1913, and his sister Lucy in 1920.)

G.B.S. turned aside importunities to stand for Parliament, believing that he could accomplish more on the local level. In 1897, running unopposed, he was elected vestryman, and later borough councillor, of the St. Pancras district of London. For six years he worked diligently on its affairs. Speeches in his 1904 campaign to represent St. Pancras on the London County Council offended most of the electorate, and he lost badly.

Recuperating from illness in 1898, Shaw worked on *Caesar and Cleopatra*, the first of a three-play group he called Plays for Puritans. Shaw's own puritanism consisted of abstinence from tobacco, liquor, and meat. Sex

he deemed a groveling sort of pleasure. He dressed with simplicity bordering on shabbiness. The title, however, signified his intent to purge that secular temple, the theatre, of hypocrisy and bad art.

Caesar is a good representative of Shaw's hero. He is not a lover but a
headmaster who chastises Cleopatra whenever she takes her royalty too
seriously; he is tolerant of the shortcomings and inanities of lesser men; he
is calmly ruthless if the occasion demands; and he foresees, unemotionally,
the Ides of March, as Napoleon foresees Waterloo. Shaw considered
Caesar, as did the "revisionist" historians of the nineteenth century, a reformer tilting at the aristocratic Senate; hence, the difference between his
character and Shakespeare's marmoreal pontificator. After performances at
the University of Chicago in 1901 and Berlin in 1907, *Caesar* reached the
London stage on November 25, 1907.

Dick Dudgeon, in revolt against his mother's hate-filled perversion of
puritanism, preaches "diabolonian ethics" in *The Devil's Disciple*. There
is another revolt in progress, that of Americans against British rule. Soldiers come to arrest the Reverend Anthony Anderson, who is to be hanged
as an example to the disloyal, and Dick, visiting the Anderson home, assumes the identity of the absent clergyman. No Sidney Carton doing the
far better thing, Dick cannot explain his conduct to others or to himself;
he is responding to some incomprehensible urge. A last-minute stroke of
fortune saves him from the gallows, and he and the minister reverse roles,
Dick to become a preacher, Anderson a freedom fighter. General John
Burgoyne, one of the most engaging characters in the play, performs with
taste and urbanity what he recognizes as a disagreeable duty to the Empire.
The American presentation at the Fifth Avenue Theatre, premiering at the
Fifth Avenue Theatre, New York, on October 4, 1897, brought Shaw his
first sizable income from writing and gave him artistic heartburn. Actors
read a love affair into the relationship between Dudgeon and the minister's
wife, an interpretation which Shaw categorically did not intend. This interpretation was beyond his corrective reach, but when his plays were
staged in England he meticulously supervised rehearsals.

The philosophical burden of *Captain Brassbound's Conversion*, the last
of the Plays for Puritans, is the difference between justice and revenge.
More intriguing than the ideas is Cicely Waynflete, who without apparent
effort handles an English judge, American naval officers, the English expatriate Brassbound and his rascal gang, and Moroccan sheiks. If this seems
an unlikely dramatis personae, Shaw is parodying melodramas in which
British soldiers rescue a white lady from primitive tribesmen. Cicely converts Brassbound from his monomaniacal revenge for an injustice done him
long ago and sends him off, as Eugene Marchbanks departed, with confidence and a stronger sense of self-identity. The play did not succeed until
Ellen Terry, for whom it was written, assumed the role of Cicely in 1906,
six years after the first production.

On April 26, 1904, at the urging of actor-director Harley Granville-Barker, *Candida* was revived at the Royal Court Theatre, a 614-seat house (about the size of the Abbey*) remote from the fashionable West End. From the autumn of 1904 to June 29, 1907, this little hall sustained one of the most incandescent periods of English theatrical history. Of the 938 performances, 701 were of eleven plays by Shaw; other writers included Euripides, Maeterlinck, Schnitzler, and Hauptmann. It was a fusion of talents: business manager John Vedrenne, the versatile Barker, a strong company, and the creativity of G.B.S.

John Bull's Other Island, staged on November 1, 1904, was written for the emerging Irish theatre, but, proving unsuited to the dramatic ideas prevailing there, it was given to the Court. Shaw inverts, though not completely, the old Stage Irish formula. Irishman Larry Doyle is the realist, scornful of his dreaming countrymen; Englishman Tom Broadbent is a sentimentalist about round towers and colleens and all that, but businessman enough to see opportunities in Ireland. In this symposium on Anglo-Irish matters, Shaw's spokesman is the unfrocked priest Peter Keegan, who outlines in mystic terms the ideal state, a socialist commonwealth. During a command performance on March 11, 1905, Edward VII laughed so heartily he broke his chair. At the Abbey in September 1916, audiences laughed just as vigorously, though no doubt for different reasons.

Coming almost at midpoint in Shaw's life span, *Man and Superman*, staged on May 23, 1905, explicated his concept of creative evolution. He shared with Samuel Butler the belief that evolution by adjustment to environment "banished mind from the universe." Instead, Shaw reasoned, man rises to higher levels of consciousness, eventually to pure intellect, by assertion of his will. The impetus for this conscious effort is the Life Force, a power man senses but does not understand. A woman, impelled by the Life Force, singles out a man with the right characteristics for the breeding of superior children. This creates a battle of the sexes: philosopher man must avoid fleshly entanglements to fulfill his purpose, and woman must entangle him to fulfill hers.

The idea is dramatized on two levels. John Tanner, a bull-in-china-shop socialist reformer, is efficiently captured by Ann Whitefield, and the two aspects of the Life Force merge—the drive toward betterment and the improvement of the species. On the other level, the third act, occasionally performed as a reading or a play in itself, opens on a barren Spanish plain which is transformed into Shaw's vision of Hell. Tanner, Ann, and the other characters are metamorphosed temporarily into the figures in the Don Juan story. (Shaw's mother sang Donna Anna in Lee's Dublin production of Mozart's *Don Giovanni*.) Satan is a glib hedonist. The occupants of Hell choose to stay there because they are self-indulgent and intellectually lazy. In terms of orthodox morality Don Juan should be in Hell because of his earthly philandering, but he dismisses his escapades as an experiment which he outgrew; he scorns an eternity of lowbrow pleasures and opts for a heaven of philosophical contemplation. Donna Anna, in mortal life the epitome of stony, negative virtue, calls out at the end of the Hell sequence, "A father! A father for the Superman!"

As in *Man and Superman*, the events in *Major Barbara*, first performed on November 28, 1905, build to a discussion scene. The main event is a contest between Andrew Undershaft, a munitions manufacturer, and his daughter Barbara, an officer in the Salvation Army. Undershaft wins by proving that the charity is funded by the very exploiters who create poverty. In his utopian factory-community he has abolished poverty, the deadliest sin. Herein lies a paradox, posed by Barbara's fiancé, classical scholar Adolphus Cusins: "Then the way to life lies through the factory of death?" Undershaft, who may be modeled on the Swedish inventor-philanthropist Alfred Nobel, resembles Caesar in his heroic stance. He ruthlessly scraps the obsolete (weapons in his case) for the new. A leader must be willing to destroy to make his ideas prevail—thus, he resolves Cusins' paradox; killing "is the final test of conviction . . . the only way of saying must." Shaw's socialist order cannot begin in an industrially primitive nation; capitalism develops the resources of the good life, as Undershaft has done, and then socialism commandeers the machinery. This evidently is the function assigned to Cusins when Undershaft hands the factory over to him. In the control of armaments, Cusins recognizes "a power simple enough for common men to use, yet strong enough to force the intellectual oligarchy to use its genius for the common good."

In 1882, Shaw contracted smallpox in spite of inoculation. In 1898, an infection was aggravated by improper medication. He retaliated in *The Doctor's Dilemma*, produced on November 20, 1906, by characterizing doctors as narrow dogmatists, each asserting a single cause, hence a single cure, for every illness. (Shaw had his own dogmatic explanation: unsanitary slum living and malnutrition.) The dilemma for Dr. Colenso Ridgeon is whether to devote his limited time to treating a decent, mediocre fellow practitioner or a tubercular young painter, Louis Dubedat, a man faithful to nothing but his art. Ridgeon's choice is complicated by his infatuation with Dubedat's blindly loyal wife Jennifer. In considering the larger issues related to Dubedat's amorality, Shaw appears to equate leaders and artists. The leader's goal is to create a better society; the artist's is, so John Tanner puts it, "to shew us ourselves as we really are." To achieve these desirable ends, artists and leaders must not be hemmed in by the restraints and responsibilities imposed on lesser men. This interpretation of *The Doctor's Dilemma* would be more persuasive if Dubedat were not, away from his easel, such a grubby little confidence man.

The success of the Court venture led to the leasing of the Savoy Theatre in the West End for the 1907-1908 season. A few Shaw plays were revived, but he had nothing new to offer, and production costs were high. The season ended with a considerable deficit; at its conclusion, Barker and Vedrenne went their separate ways.

Between *The Doctor's Dilemma* and *Pygmalion* (Vienna, 1913; London, April 11, 1914), most of Shaw's plays were lighthearted comedies on the nature of marriage and parent-child relationships: *Getting Married* (1908), *Misalliance* (1910), and *Fanny's First Play* (1912). *Fanny*, a potboiler done for Barker and his actress wife Lillah McCarthy at their 278-seat Little Theatre on January 1, 1912, enjoyed the longest run of Shaw's early plays. Generation gap humor is mixed with an essay on criticism. The wealthy father of Fanny O'Dowda invites four prominent critics to a private performance of an anonymous play (written by Fanny). Much of the fun is in their effort to identify the author. One critic thinks it is Shaw, another says it is too good to be his work. Shaw himself did not admit authorship until *Fanny* was published in 1914. It was not a well-guarded secret.

Only two plays of this relatively fallow period are worth much attention: *The Shewing-up of Blanco Posnet* and *Androcles and the Lion*.

Myopic English censorship of *Posnet* on grounds of blasphemy (it is no more blasphemous than "The Hound of Heaven") gave the play notoriety beyond its merits. It is *The Devil's Disciple* reset in the American West. Like Dick Dudgeon, Blanco Posnet is a pariah who barely escapes hanging. He sees more clearly than Dudgeon the hand of God moving him to do the right thing, helping a mother with a sick child, almost in spite of himself: "He made me because he had a job for me. He let me run loose till the job was ready." Yeats and Lady Gregory,* defying threatened revocation of the Abbey patent, staged this very un-Irish play on August 25, 1909. As a result of the controversy, English censorship regulations were amended and the ban against *Posnet* was lifted.

Shaw called *Androcles* an entertainment for children. Except for Androcles' romping with the lion, the play is unintelligible to all but frighteningly precocious youngsters. The familiar story is raw material for Shaw's thesis that there always will be Establishment persecutors (here the pagan Romans) and dissenting martyrs (in this case Christians). Shaw is not writing a brief for Christianity. In another historical context, Establishment Christians will persecute the disturbers of their peace. *Androcles* was first performed in Berlin on November 25, 1912, and in London at the St. James Theatre on September 1, 1913.

The play *Pygmalion* has had to compete for attention with movie and musical comedy variations, and with the snickering over Shaw's temporary infatuation with Mrs. Patrick Campbell, for whom the part of Liza Doolittle was written. She played it in the first English production at His Majesty's Theatre on April 11, 1914.

Shaw had an enduring interest in phonetics, but if *Pygmalion* was written only to promote that science, or to demonstrate the superficiality of polite society, it should have ended with Liza's triumph at the ball. What follows is her greater triumph in declaring independence from her domineering teacher, though it is, all told, a modest rise from guttersnipe to shopkeeper and wife of poor Freddy Eynsford-Hill. Shaw's patience again was sorely tried by those who were determined to see a love affair between Liza and Henry Higgins.

The first run of *Pygmalion* was ended by the outbreak of war. During the years immediately preceding, good repertory theatre flourished, but in wartime England, theatre dwindled into easy entertainment for servicemen and production costs soared. Under these conditions, Shaw wrote only a few inconsequential one-act comedies.

As a humanist, he deplored the slaughter; as a socialist, he anticipated no social betterment in the victory of one set of capitalist powers over another. Shaw likened the war to a battle between pirate ships, in which one's allegiance perforce was with the ship he was on board. His writings and other utterances on the conflict seem, in retrospect, sensible and consistent with his overall thinking, but they deeply offended Englishmen who thought even a licensed jester should become a straight man for the duration.

In wartime Dublin, there was almost a Shaw Festival. Between September 25, 1916, and May 26, 1917, six of his plays were staged by Abbey producer J. Augustus Keogh. This was nothing political. Keogh, like his predecessor St. John Ervine,* sought to expand the Abbey repertoire beyond the "peasant play," and he greatly admired Shaw.

Since the time of Parnell, Shaw had written of Irish affairs. He considered himself Irish or English depending on the point he was making. Parnell's tragedy he attributed to inhumane divorce laws. On the broader political issue, Shaw argued that England would have to come to terms: for three decades, Parliament had been tied up in Home Rule debate, and English rule in Ireland had degenerated into armed occupation. However, in a world of superpowers a wholly independent Ireland could not defend itself from invasion or economic competition. Shaw proposed instead an Irish parliament for national affairs, and Irish membership in a federal parliament to deal with mutual interests of the British Isles. Ulster could not survive as a British enclave with its own version of Home Rule, or as an impotent minority in the British parliament. The North was better off by entering the Irish parliament in which it could exert a strong influence. The Ulsterman's fear of Home Rule was unfounded. The Catholic Church in Ireland had been as conservative and autocratic as English authority. Liberated Ireland, taking a page from the history of Catholic France and Catholic Italy, would curtail the power of the Church.

Shaw's observation that more of Dublin should have been destroyed during Easter Week seems another instance of tactless flippancy. Yet, Shaw knew the squalor of Dublin slums, and unless the change of Ireland's political center from Westminster to Dublin was accompanied by social reforms, the slums would remain. Rejecting the impossiblist stance of the Easter Week rebels, he nonetheless protested the British reprisal, particularly the trial of Roger Casement, who as an Irishman would not be guilty of treason against England.

While Europe was blundering into war, Shaw was working on *Heartbreak House*. He would not permit it to be staged until November 10, 1920, by the New York Theatre Guild, which produced a number of his plays in the 1920s and 1930s. The London premiere was at the Court Theatre on October 18, 1921. Shaw called the play "A Fantasia in the Russian Manner on English Themes." Chekovian influence is present in the country house setting and the futile characters, but Shaw's people are more coherent and less wistful. The English themes actually were the themes of any spiritually exhausted people rushing to war for lack of other stimulation.

In *Major Barbara*, Adolphus Cusins united power and culture. Between it and *Heartbreak House* Shaw's vision darkened. Power lacked direction, culture lacked virility. Heartbreak House is a gathering place of defeated and important hopes: Victorian idealism, colonialism, big business, bohemian revelry, youthful romance. Young Ellie Dunn is disillusioned first by a romantic dreamer who is already married; then by Boss Mangan, who for all his seeming strength is only a manager of enterprises owned by bigger bosses; and finally by Captain Shotover, retired seafarer, whose sham senility masks resolute character and deep-probing philosophy. Yet, even his flights to higher levels of consciousness are sustained by rum. At the close, warplanes are showering destruction, and Hector Hushabye, the suicidal romantic, turns on the lights of Heartbreak House as a beacon to the bombers. It is he who speaks most eloquently of the fatigue and despair of mankind: "Out of that darkness some new creation will come to supplant us as we have supplanted the animals, or the heavens will fall in thunder and destroy us."

The pessimism of *Heartbreak House*, induced by war and the doldrums of the theatre, quickly was superseded by the fantastic optimism of Shaw's most ambitious work, *Back to Methuselah*. If *Man and Superman* was the Genesis of Shaw's own Bible, the five-play sequence of *Methuselah* was the Pentateuch. It begins in the Garden and ends in 31,920 A.D. Eve responds to the Life Force by mothering Cain, the first fascist, but she also bears the artists, philosophers, and scientists who will inherit the earth. The guiding principle is that the post-Methuselah life span of three score and ten is insufficient for full development of man's capacities. He must, by conscious exertion of will, break through nature's dominion over him. By 31,920, he is hatched from an egg fully grown, beyond the folly and confusion of childhood. His ecstasies are intellectual rather than sensual. As in Plato's Republic, the arts are toys to be discarded when one attains the mature level of pure intellect. Death comes only from accident. The obsolete shortlived creature of 1920 A.D. has perished like the dinosaur.

Back to Methuselah was commercially risky theatre. So it proved when the New York Theatre Guild produced the series beginning February 27, 1922. The Birmingham Repertory Theatre, founded by Barry Jackson, was more successful in 1923, with a good company and better spacing of performances.

In 1920, Joan of Arc was canonized, and at the prompting of his wife, Shaw wrote a play on her. His Joan, incidentally, is a soldier and visionary, primarily the first Protestant in her assertion of the right of private judgment. As in many other Shaw plays, the climax is a trial scene in which the defendant tries the accusers. Members of the ecclesiastical court are on the whole astute and gentle, honestly concerned with the ramifications of Joan's individualism. Joan is simply too far ahead of her times, and her fellow men kill her because they do not know what else to do. The epilogue shows that though the Maid of Orleans has been declared a saint, the world still is frightened by her free spirit. She asks rhetorically, "How long, O Lord, how long?" The first production of *Saint Joan* was at the Garrick Theatre, New York, on December 28, 1923, and in England at the New Theatre, London, on March 26, 1924. Among distinguished actresses who have played Joan are Sybil Thorndyke, Elizabeth Bergner, Katherine Cornell, Celia Johnson, Siobhan McKenna, and Barbara Jefford.

At the age of seventy, Shaw was awarded the Nobel Prize in 1926 for the writing of *Saint Joan*. He consistently declined honors and degrees, but he accepted the Nobel Prize in order to establish a foundation for promoting knowledge of Swedish literature in England. The next few years he devoted to the tedious work of writing *The Intelligent Woman's Guide to Socialism and Capitalism*, published in 1928. In this stout volume, he sums up his economic philosophy in simple, though not patronizing, language.

If what Shaw wrote between *Saint Joan* and his death was largely reiterative, it remained witty and provocative. *The Apple Cart* (1929) sports with constitutional monarchy by portraying an independent-minded king matching strategies with a government of Laborite hacks. King Magnus terrifies them into submission by threatening to abdicate and stand for election as a commoner, a move which would replace nominal hereditary status with popular support.

Too True to Be Good (1931) is a postwar *Heartbreak House*. In an exotic outpost of the Empire, an incongruous assortment of equally feckless civilians and soldiers ponder the question raised in *Pilgrim's Progress*, "What shall we do to be saved?" The answer seems to be provided by Private Meek (modeled on Lawrence of Arabia), a Shaw type of doer. While the others are talking and blundering, Meek takes care of their problems, except those problems caused by lack of will and conviction. Shaw had much better control of his material in *Heartbreak House*. *Too True*, despite imaginative staging and a few delightfully weird characters, failed to impress audiences in New York, Warsaw, or London.

Sir Barry Jackson began the yearly Malvern Festival in 1929, principally to stage plays by Shaw. A younger G.B.S. might have done for the festival what he had done for the Court Theatre, but on the whole his autumnal work was not very good. The best of it was *In Good King Charles's Golden Days*, presented on August 11, 1939, a sparkling disquisition on religion, government, man and woman, science and art, by the leading intellectuals and nonintellectuals (e.g., Nell Gwynn) of Restoration England. *Geneva*, produced on August 1, 1938, is another trial play. Bombardone (Mussolini), Battler (Hitler), and Flanco de Fortinbras (Franco) voluntarily appear before a world court with no jurisdiction and no authority to answer their accusers. No verdict is given. Dictators, British and Russian observers, a dotty fundamentalist, and a parochial-minded female member of Parliament all depart convinced of their rightness. The judge, echoing Hector Hushabye, sums up: "Man is a failure as a political animal, the creative forces which produce him must produce something better."

While the Shaws toured South Africa in 1932, Mrs. Shaw was injured in an auto accident. Waiting there for her to recover, Shaw wrote *The Adventures of the Black Girl in Her Search for God*. The girl examines all religions and the irreligion of science, intuitively recognizing their falsities. At last she meets Voltaire and his Irish gardener (G.B.S.), who like John Tanner is caught in the grip of the Life Force. He goes on digging; she raises the children.

In 1933, Shaw made his only visit to the United States, spending one day in San Francisco and one day in New York. On April 11, he spoke in the Metropolitan Opera House on the nationalizing of American resources. Evidently expecting a comic monologue, listeners generally were displeased. A similar lecture by Shaw at the Abbey on October 20, 1918, was accepted by Dubliners as a pleasant way to pass a Sunday afternoon.

Shaw quickly recognized the potential of the motion picture. The development of sound track was, of course, essential to the adaptation of his discussion dramas. He was adamant on what he wanted, the filming of an actual stage production, until Gabriel Pascal persuaded him to revise the texts to take advantage of the flexibility of the camera. Pascal produced in England a romanticized *Pygmalion* (1938), a simplified *Major Barbara* (1941), and a catastrophically expensive and savagely reviewed *Caesar and Cleopatra* (1945). There were sixteen filmings of Shaw plays, including these three, a Czechoslovakian adaptation of *Cashel Byron* (1921), and a British production of *The Millionairess*, a mediocre late Shaw play, in 1961. *Pygmalion* was filmed in German, Dutch, and English. (For this and other useful information, see Donald Costello, *The Serpent's Eye, Shaw and the Cinema*.) Mercifully, the Hollywood vulgarizations of *Androcles*

(1953, by Pascal), *Saint Joan* (1957), and *The Devil's Disciple* (a grin-
ning contest held in 1959) were committed after Shaw's death.

The closing years of Shaw's life could not have been very satisfying. His
health slowly deteriorated. Like other thoughtful persons who lived through
two world wars, he had reason to wonder "when will they ever learn." The
postwar Labor government imposed burdensome taxes without solving
problems. What could Shaw say that he had not already said? The ancients
of his circle were dropping off: Mrs. Shaw and Beatrice Webb in 1943, his
old adversary H. G. Wells in 1946, Sidney Webb in 1947. Of the honors
extended to him in his advanced age, he accepted only a few, including the
Freedom of Dublin (he still disliked the city) on August 28, 1946.

Shaw was not the man for retired ease. He worked constantly, even
during the trips he endured because Mrs. Shaw enjoyed traveling. Always
accident prone, on foot or in vehicles, Shaw broke his leg in September
1950, when he fell while working in his garden. The injury was complicated by a kidney infection. After a short stay in the hospital, he insisted
on going home to die. Among his last visitors was Mrs. Sean O'Casey.
When the Abbey directors refused O'Casey's* *The Silver Tassie* in 1928,
Shaw sided with O'Casey in the paper war that followed. Early on the
morning of November 2, 1950, G.B.S. slipped easily away in his ninety-
fourth year. His ashes, mixed with those of his wife, were scattered in the
garden of the house called Shaw's Corner. It was turned over to the National
Trust. A small portion of his estate was used to encourage the development
of a new phonetic alphabet. The rest was distributed equally to the British
Museum, which also received a mass of his personal documents, to the
Royal Academy of Dramatic Art, and to the National Gallery of Ireland.

Between 1879 and 1950 (compare Shakespeare's productive years, which
at most were twenty-five), G.B.S. wrote more than fifty plays, five completed
novels, a mountain of critical studies, reviews, letters public and private,
Fabian pamphlets, and various expansive statements of opinion. A summary and evaluation of his work in the short space available here must
undergo agonies of compression. Here Shaw will be considered, briefly,
as religious philosopher, political economist, and man of the theatre. The
bibliography will direct readers to more ample studies.

Shaw regards Christ as a good man deluded by his followers into thinking himself the Living God. Shaw flatly rejects the concept of vicarious
atonement. In his socialist utopia he permits ethical but not religious instruction. Yet, there are numerous references to God in his plays. St. Joan's
curtain lines are addressed to Him. In the final stage directions for *Too
True to Be Good*, Shaw writes of the Pentecostal flame. The Black Girl's
search for God does not end in negation. Major Barbara cries out near
the close of the play, "Let God's work be done for its own sake; the work
he had to create us to do because it cannot be done except by living men

and women." This is close to what Blanco Posnet says. The Life Force, which Shaw equates with Providence in the preface to *Farfetched Fables*, sees to it that leaders, great thinkers, and great men are on hand when they are needed. But it "proceeds experimentally by Trial-and-Error, and never achieves 100 per cent success"; it can be "defeated by the imperfection of its mortal instruments." If man is fallible, God is not omnipotent. Through the instrumentality of the Life Force, man strives for the ultimate triumph of what is highest in him, his intellect. Perhaps Shaw's best statement on man's destiny is made in the preface to *Misalliance*, in answer to his own question, What is a child: "A fresh attempt to produce the just man made perfect; that is, to make humanity divine."

Shaw's thinking on socialism was affected by experience and the sweeping historical developments of his time. Basically, he advocated the nationalization of essential production and services, equality of income, and compulsory employment—no idle rich, no welfare handouts. He opposed revolutionary socialism, more vigorously perhaps in his early Fabian days, because even if it succeeded, the proletariat stood in the rubble wondering what to do next. Fascism only transferred power from the capitalists to the state. Labor unions took from management and gave to themselves. Not until poverty and degradation could be abolished by equalization of income could mankind achieve any meaningful betterment.

The harsher side of Shaw's program is inherent in his position that higher and lower forms cannot exist peacefully. Man supplants beast, Superman supplants common man. Even in the arts, new creators war on their predecessors. Shaw supported England in the Boxer Rebellion and the Boer War because the British would bring a higher civilization to China and South Africa. His Caesar shrugs off the burning of the library at Alexandria, for it was a repository of old knowledge; the future will be built on its ruins. Shaw plays which are blueprints of the coming times are characterized by the unfeeling liquidation of anyone who does not fit into the new order. In *The Tragedy of an Elderly Gentleman*, Part IV of *Back to Methuselah*, the Oracle kills the Elderly Gentleman as an act of kindness to an obsolete life-form: "Poor short-lived thing! What else could I do for you?" The worthless are disposed of en masse in *The Simpleton of the Unexpected Isles*. An angel of judgment announces to decadent Europe: "The lives which have no use, no meaning, no purpose will fade out. You will have to justify your existence or perish." To this Prolla, priestess of the Unexpected Isles, adds: "If the angels fail us we shall set up tribunals of our own from which worthless people will not come out alive." And in Part V of *Back to Methuselah* the She-Ancient matter of factly says, "Children with anything wrong do not live here."

Shaw's vision of the future bore a painful resemblance to the Europe of his own age. In Russia and Germany, there were tribunals for dealing with the worthless, as the state defined the term. Mussolini was bringing a higher civilization to primitive Ethiopia, and Spain was a testing ground for conflicting totalitarian ideologies.

An admirer of the unsentimental doer ever since he created Ned Connolly in *The Irrational Knot*, Shaw observed the apparent failure of parliamentary government in postwar Europe and the fact that in Mussolini's Italy the trains were running on time. About the best that can be said, in retrospect, is that Shaw was not the only intellectual who feared the center could not hold and so turned to get-it-done ideologies of the left or right.

However one may be outraged, bewildered, or stimulated by Shaw as philosopher, his place as a consummate man of the theatre is assured. He mastered every phase of dramatic art from writing to the subtleties of the live stage to carefully supervised texts with stage directions as beneficial to readers as to performers. (Bernard F. Dukore, *Bernard Shaw, Director*, is particularly valuable on Shaw's understanding of the techniques of the stage.)

The triumph of the Don Juan in Hell scene as readers' theatre possibly has created the impression that all one needs for an evening of Shaw is reading desks or stools, the requisite number of mellow speakers, and an audience austerely content with highbrow talk. Actually, Shaw makes imaginative use of the stage. His sets range from the left flank of the Sphinx to a dentist's office, a frontier saloon, Eden, the world of 31,920 A.D.—as far as thought can reach. *Major Barbara* is made visually as well as thematically effective by stark contrasts in sets—genteel drawing room, drab Salvation Army shelter, ominous gun emplacement. Shaw was not alone among his contemporaries in achieving emphasis by contrast: Galsworthy did as much in *The Silver Box*, so did J. M. Barrie in the shift from the elegant in Act I to the primitive in Act II of *The Admirable Crichton*. But Shaw also can make small details meaningful. The sets for the first two acts of *The Devil's Disciple*, the Dudgeon and the Anderson homes, respectively, are plain New England colonial. The difference lies in the slight decorative touches attempted by Mrs. Anderson, trinkets perhaps, but indicative of a sense of beauty alien to the life-denying spirit of Mrs. Dudgeon. This is not a case of an academician imposing his own significance on the raw material of the play. Shaw himself makes the point in the stage directions.

The discussion scenes necessarily are static; vigorous movement or intrusive stage business could impede communication of ideas in, for example, the final scene of *Major Barbara*. But before the characters settle down for discussion, Shaw sets the hook of empathy. The colloquium which opens *The Doctor's Dilemma* is an exception. Generally, the plays commence with a brisk confrontation of egos—Joan and the bawling soldier Baudricourt, Tanner and the self-styled progressive Roebuck Ramsden, Dudgeon and his mother. Thus, his characters are established as personalities and are not permitted to dwindle into sound-boxes for projecting ideas.

It would be difficult to write fifty-plus plays without some duplication of characterizations. These are recurring types—the strong woman, the iconoclast, the affable, pragmatic moneymaker, and so on. Yet, within a type one finds recognizable distinctions. Candida Morell displays a touch of the feline in amusing herself with young Marchbanks, a quality absent from the makeup of Cicely Waynflete. Sartorius, Undershaft, and Broadbent have certain general similarities, yet each man is tailored to the context of a particular play. The commanding, faintly boorish, personality of Sartorius would be ill suited to the texture of *John Bull*. One does have the impression that Shaw played favorites with his characters, cutting and polishing all the facets in some cases, tossing in the rough stones in other cases, such as the idle young men and, especially, the ingenues. He preferred mature women (Candida is thirty-three, Cicely between thirty and forty, the glamorous Strange Lady in *The Man of Destiny* is thirty) on and off stage.

Shaw could make good theatre from dramatic forms he candidly regarded as trashy. What could be more blatantly melodramatic in plot outline than *Brassbound* or *The Devil's Disciple*? Would Boucicault* himself take a pig for an auto ride, as Shaw does in *John Bull*? His intent, of course, was to kill theatrical enemies with their own weapons.

The most substantive criticisms of Shaw, aside from fundamental disagreements with his philosophy, are aimed at needlessly intrusive comic turns and indecisive or ambiguous endings.

The first objection is made not to Shaw's blending of comedy and Roman history or religion and farcicality, but rather to comic bit parts which, however amusing, are of doubtful relevance—for example, the microbe made ill by contact with a human in *Too True to Be Good*, the band of squabbling radicals in *Man and Superman*, the inept avenging gunman in *Misalliance*. Shaw conceded that the jesting spirit occasionally descended at inopportune times.

The unwrapped endings are inherent in Shaw's philosophy and dramatic technique. Romance asumes a happy finality, tragedy closes with all passion spent, melodrama justifies the ways of right-thinking men to God. Shaw wrote none of the above. His plots are not built from floor plans, though he could be a craftsman when he chose to be. His plots are, to use his term, organic, shaping themselves as they grow, continuing to grow even after the curtain descends. This approach to play construction is congruent to Shaw's overview of man's lot. As Lilith says at the end of *Back to Methuselah*, life is endlessly expanding and evolving, there is always something beyond. One may agree that real life is a continuum and still ask that an artistic approximation of reality be symmetrical rather than open-ended.

On a less metaphysical level, Shaw gives all the contending forces such articulate spokesmen—even dictators and transparent rascals of the un-

deserving poor class can make an eloquent shyster case for themselves—
that sometimes Shaw appears to be asking "What is truth?" and not staying
for an answer. Anyone who has read enough of Shaw's prefaces, essays, and
treatises might be able to work out by projection the meaning of a play.
Whether he should have to is another matter.

Shaw's ongoing comparative evaluation of himself and Shakespeare began during his tour of duty as drama critic and ended with one of his last
plays, a ten-minute Punch and Judy type of puppet show at Malvern on
August 9, 1949, *Shakes versus Shav*. The essence of Shaw's judgment is
that the true Shakespeare, removed from the blindness of bardolatry and
the perversions of his plays by actor-managers like Henry Irving, was an
incomparable poet and a second-rate mentality whose high-sounding plati-
tudes masqueraded as wisdom. Shaw rested his claim to superiority on his
confrontation with the vital issues of his day and on his advanced, positive thinking.

It is as vain to compare the Globe and the Court Theatres, or prose and
blank verse, as it is to fault Elizabethans for not anticipating Darwin and
Marx. One really is left with a subjective choice of world-views. Shakespeare's vision is of man's finitude: "Men must endure their going hence,
even as their coming hither; ripeness is all." Shaw's vision is, in the universal
sense, comic, as it declares the ultimate victory of man, or some species
better than man, over finitude. Who is right? In the words of Mr. Doolittle,
"I put it to you; I leave it to you."

A comparison of Ibsen and Shaw is somewhat more productive. In the
beginning, Shaw preached the gospel according to Ibsen, took lessons from
the master, and then outgrew him. Ibsen slowly, inexorably peels away
until his characters and their society are fully revealed. His humor is sardonic. Shaw accelerates quickly and keeps moving, not necessarily in a
straight line, until everybody is ready to sit down and discuss. His humor is
wide-ranging, sophisticated, broadly vulgar, expansive, intrusive, whatever
the situation calls for.

When Shaw identified Ibsen as a socialist during a Fabian meeting on
July 18, 1890, Ibsen promptly denied any sort of party line. Though he
recognizes, as Shaw does, the meanness behind the façade of social respectability, Ibsen proposes no broadly dogmatic solutions. For Nora Hel-
mer, the answer is to close the door as she leaves; for the weakling Hialmar
Ekdal, taking refuge in the life-lie is the only way; for Dr. Stockmann, there
is whatever satisfaction comes from being right when everybody else is
wrong. The showing-up of Pastor Manders may be read as an attack on
orthodox Christianity. If it is, Ibsen offers no alternative, unless it is the
bellicose honesty of Pastor Brand, and he winds up with a very small congregation. In sum, Ibsen points to the ring around the collar, while Shaw
prescribes detergents—socialism, creative evolution. One may or may not
want to wear the shirt after Shaw has laundered it.

Samuel Johnson, in the preface to his edition of Shakespeare, wrote that in judging works "of which the excellence is not absolute and definitive, but gradual and comparative . . . no other test can be applied than length of duration and continuance of esteem." So tested, seventy years after *Man and Superman,* fifty years after *Saint Joan,* how will G.B.S. fare?

Social reforms have reduced his more specific problem plays to historical artifacts. Changing mores have blunted what used to be daring. *Mrs. Warren* would not make the front page of *The New York Times* as it did in 1905, no more than a performance of *Ghosts* would shock London critics into writing of an "open sewer" as they did in 1891. On the other hand, Shaw came to grips with problems beyond the reach of legislators, too deeply rooted to be swayed by the light and variable winds of "in" and "out." The link, or confrontation if you will, between man and woman is more than chic contemporary issues of equitable divorce settlements and who gets the credit cards. The most abiding question of all is, who and what is man? To these universal concerns Shaw vigorously addressed himself. The head count of converts to his ideas is not important. What matters is that after one sorts out the potboilers, the plays tossed off as a *jeu d'esprit,* the more grandiose efforts that did not quite come off, a substantial body of master works—live, exciting theatre—remains. Shaw, young man of Dublin, senior citizen of the world, continues to stand before us on his soapbox, Mephistophelian, nimble, provocative, outrageous, teasing, or browbeating us to hear him out.   W I L L I A M J . F E E N E Y

WORKS: *Plays Pleasant and Unpleasant.* 2 vols. London: Grant Richards, 1898; *The Fabian Society, Its Early History.* London: Fabian Society, 1899; *Three Plays for Puritans.* London: Grant Richards, 1901; *How to Settle the Irish Question.* Dublin: Talbot, 1917; *The Intelligent Woman's Guide to Socialism and Capitalism.* New York: Brentano's, 1928; *Immaturity.* London: Constable, 1931; *The Irrational Knot.* London: Constable, 1931; *What I Really Wrote About the War.* London: Constable, 1931; *Cashel Byron's Profession.* London: Constable, 1932; *Essays in Fabian Socialism.* London: Constable, 1932; *Love Among the Artists.* London: Constable, 1932; *Major Critical Essays: The Quintessence of Ibsenism, The Perfect Wagnerite, The Sanity of Art.* London: Constable, 1932; *Music in London, 1890-1894.* London: Constable, 1932; *Our Theatres in the Nineties.* 3 vols. London: Constable, 1932; *An Unsocial Socialist.* London: Constable, 1932; *The Political Madhouse in America and Nearer Home.* London: Constable, 1933/printed in America as *American Boobs,* Hollywood: E. O. Jones, 1933; *Short Stories, Scraps, and Shavings.* New York: Dodd, Mead, 1934; *London Music, 1888-1889, as Heard by Corno di Bassetto.* London: Constable, 1937; *Sixteen Self Sketches.* London: Constable, 1949; *An Unfinished Novel,* ed. Stanley Weintraub. London: Constable/New York: Dodd, Mead, 1958; *Shaw on Shakespeare.* Edwin Wilson, ed. New York: E. P. Dutton, 1961; *The Matter with Ireland.* Dan H. Laurence & David H. Greene, eds. New York: Hill & Wang, 1962; *The Shaw Alphabet Edition of Androcles.* Harmondsworth: Penguin, 1962. *Complete Plays with Prefaces.* 6 vols. New York: Dodd, Mead, 1963; *Religious Speeches of Bernard Shaw.* Warren S. Smith, ed. University Park, Pa.: Pennsylvania State University, 1963. *Collected Letters, 1874-1897.* Dan H. Laurence, ed. New York: Dodd, Mead, 1965; *An Autobiography, 1856-1898,* selected by Stanley Weintraub. New York: Weybright & Talley,

1969; *An Autobiography, 1898-1950,* selected by Stanley Weintraub. New York: Weybright & Talley, 1970; *The Bodley Head Bernard Shaw, Collected Plays with Their Prefaces.* 7 vols. London: Max Reinhardt, 1970-1974. (Probably the definitive collection); *Collected Letters, 1898-1910.* Dan H. Laurence, ed. New York: Dodd, Mead, 1972.   REFERENCES: Adams, Elsie B. "Bernard Shaw's Pre-Raphaelite Drama." *PMLA* 81 (October 1966): 428-438; Bentley, Eric. *Bernard Shaw.* New York: New Directions, 1957; "Bernard Shaw Comforts the *Gaelic Press.*" *Honesty* 2 (April 15, 1916): 3-4. (Amusing correspondence between J. M. Stanley, editor of the *Gaelic Press,* and Shaw on whether *Three Plays for Puritans* violated the Defence of the Realm Act); Berst, Charles R. "The Devil and Major Barbara." *PMLA* 83 (March 1968): 71-79; Bissell, C. T. "The Novels of Bernard Shaw." *University of Toronto Quarterly* 17 (October 1947): 38-51; Brown, John Mason. "G.B.S., Headmaster to the Universe." *Saturday Review of Literature* 33 (November 18, 1950): 11-13, 31; Chesterton, Gilbert K. *George Bernard Shaw.* New York: John Lane, 1909; Coolidge, Olivia. *George Bernard Shaw.* Boston: Houghton Mifflin, 1968; Costello, Donald P. *The Serpent's Eye, Shaw and the Cinema.* Notre Dame, Ind.: Notre Dame University, 1965; Crompton, Louis. *Shaw the Dramatist.* Lincoln: University of Nebraska, 1969; Dietrich, R. F. *Portrait of the Artist as a Young Superman, A Study of Shaw's Novels.* Gainesville: University of Florida Press, 1969; Dukore, Bernard F. *Bernard Shaw, Director.* Seattle: University of Washington, 1971; "An English Master and His Irish Disciple." *The Irishman* 1 (July 15, 1916): 11-12; Ervine, St. John. *Bernard Shaw, His Life, Work, and Friends.* New York: William Morrow, 1956; Harris, Frank. *Bernard Shaw.* London: Gollancz, 1931; Fromm, Harold. *Bernard Shaw and the Theatre in the Nineties.* Lawrence: University of Kansas, 1967; "G.B.S. on Equality." *New Ireland* 6 (October 26, 1918): 393-394; Gerould, Daniel C. "George Bernard Shaw's Criticism of Ibsen." *Comparative Literature* 15 (Spring 1963): 130-145; Gribben, John L. "Shaw's Saint Joan: A Tragic Heroine." *Thought* 40 (December 1965): 549-566; Harvey, Robert C. "How Shavian Is the *Pygmalion* We Teach?" *The English Journal* 59 (December 1970): 1234-1238; Henderson, Archibald. *George Bernard Shaw, His Life and Works.* Cincinnati: Stewart & Kidd, 1911; Henderson, Archibald. *George Bernard Shaw: Man of the Century.* New York: Appleton-Century-Crofts, 1956; Hogan, Robert. "The Novels of Bernard Shaw." *English Literature in Transition* 8 (1965): 63-114; Irvine, William. *The Universe of G.B.S.* New York: Whittlesey House, 1949; Joad, C.E.M. *Shaw.* London: Gollancz, 1949; Jenckes, Norma. "The Rejection of Shaw's Irish Play, *John Bull's Other Island.*" *Eire-Ireland* 10 (Spring 1975): 38-53; Kauffman, R. J., ed. *Twentieth Century Views of Shaw.* Englewood Cliffs, N.J.: Prentice-Hall, 1965; Kaye, Julian B. *Bernard Shaw and the Nineteenth Century Tradition.* Norman: University of Oklahoma, 1958; Kempstor, Ernest. "An Irish Protestant, Bernard Shaw." *New Ireland* 2 (January 29, 1916): 192-193. Part 2 (February 5, 1916): 208-210; Kilty, Jerome. *Dear Liar, A Biography in Two Acts.* London, New York: Samuel French, 1960. (Play based on correspondence between Shaw and Mrs. Patrick Campbell); Lawrence, Kenneth. "Bernard Shaw, the Career of the Life Force." *Modern Drama* 15 (September 1972): 130-146; Levin, Gerald. "Shaw, Butler and Kant." *Philological Quarterly* 52 (January 1973): 142-156; Lowenstein, F. E. *The Rehearsal Copies of Bernard Shaw's Plays.* London: Reinhardt & Evans, 1950; MacCarthy, Desmond. *The Court Theatre, 1904-1907.* London: A. H. Bullen, 1907; MacCarthy, Desmond. *Shaw: The Plays.* London: MacGibbon & Kee, 1951; McDowell, Frederick P. W. "Spiritual and Political Reality: *The Simpleton of the Unexpected Isles.*" *Modern Drama* 3 (September 1960): 196-210; Morgan, Margery M. *The Shavian Playground.* London: Methuen, 1972; "A Mother of Genius." *The Irish Citizen* 1 (March 1, 1913): 322; Nethercott, Arthur. "Bernard Shaw and Psychoanalysis." *Modern Drama* 11 (February 1969): 356-375; Newman, A. (Herbert

George Pim). "Supper and Bernard Shaw." *Nationality* 1 (November 6, 1915): 3; *The New York Times,* November 2, 1950, p. 28. (Obituary); O'Casey, Sean. *Sunset and Evening Star.* New York: Macmillan, 1955; O'Donovan, John. *Shaw and the Charlatan Genius.* Dublin: Dolmen/Chester Springs, Pa.: Dufour Editions, 1966; Ohmann, Richard. *Shaw, The Style and the Man.* Middletown, Conn.: Wesleyan University, 1962; O'Leary, D. J. "Shaw's Blakean Vision: A Dialectic Approach to *Heartbreak House.*" *Modern Drama* 15 (May 1972): 89-103; Pearson, Hesketh. *G.B.S., A Full Length Portrait.* Garden City, N.Y.: Garden City Publishing Co., 1942; Pearson, Hesketh. *G.B.S., a Postscript.* London: Collins, 1951; Purdom, C. B. *A Guide to the Plays of Bernard Shaw.* New York: Crowell, 1963; Rosset, B. C. *Shaw of Dublin: The Formative Years.* University Park: Pennsylvania State University, 1964; Simon, Louis. *Shaw on Education.* New York: Columbia University, 1958; Smith, J. Percy. *The Unrepentant Pilgrim, a Study of the Development of Bernard Shaw.* Boston: Houghton Mifflin, 1965; Ussher, Arland. *Three Great Irishmen.* New York: Devin-Adair, 1953; Wall, Vincent. *Bernard Shaw, Pygmalion to Many Players.* Ann Arbor: University of Michigan, 1973; Weintraub, Stanley. *Journey to Heartbreak.* New York: Weybright & Talley, 1971; Wilson, Colin. *Bernard Shaw, a Reassessment.* New York: Atheneum, 1969.

SHEEHAN, CANON (1852-1913), novelist. Canon Sheehan was born Patrick Augustine Sheehan in Mallow on March 17, 1852. He received his higher education at Maynooth Seminary, and he was ordained a Roman Catholic priest in 1875. He worked for a while in Plymouth and in Exeter before returning to Ireland to work in Mallow and Cobh. In 1895, he was appointed pastor in Doneraile, and he served there until his death on October 5, 1913.

Canon Sheehan was a born novelist, but he had the conventional opinions that one might expect in a Roman Catholic cleric of his day. If that fact is the source of all of the weaknesses in his fiction, it is also the source of many of its strengths. For instance, he was such a well-read, learned, and cultivated man that he startles one by speaking of Du Maurier's *Trilby* as an "abomination," and he saddens one by being able only to deplore Yeats,* Synge,* and George Moore* as "Neo-Pagans and Aesthetes." Similarly, although his comedy is often too broad, his humor is usually so warmly genial that one is shocked by the cold austerity that frequently manipulates his characters into implausible and inhuman stances. In short, there are more contradictions in Canon Sheehan than appear in the hagiographical accounts of him.

As a novelist, Sheehan wavered between saintly austerity and tolerant humanity; certain of his characteristics and opinions do war most engagingly with his sternly regarded priestly functions. He was a thoughtful Irishman, but he was sometimes a fervent patriot; his heart sometimes beat and his pen sometimes wrote with a most unclerical and martial ardor. Indeed, there is a spiritually autobiographical moment in *The Queen's Fillet* (1911), when the once young and dashing hero, now a pious abbot, is sorely tempted to buckle on his sword again and win the day. In Dumas, that is precisely what the abbot would have done. Like Aramis, he would have done it and repented later, and Canon Sheehan would have had a better novel than the merely quite good novel that he does have.

Still, character was one of Canon Sheehan's real strengths, and the intellectual priest Luke Delmege and the old priest in *My New Curate* (1900) are triumphs. But when Canon Sheehan the priest takes away the pen from Canon Sheehan the novelist, characterization begins to ring false. Then we get tintype villains, purer-than-the-driven-snow heroines, and a gallery of saintly clerical simpletons that would give even a Paul Vincent Carroll* pause. Canon Sheehan is thought to be best on peasants and priests, but he is rather better on intellectuals and on the middle or the upper classes. His peasants tend to be seen from the presbytery window, and, even though he had as much sympathy for them as Edgeworth* or Somerville and Ross,* Canon Sheehan, like Lady Gregory* sometimes, seems to be merely putting the quaint peasantry on exhibition.

His long novels are structured with a firm nineteenth-century control. When he fails, the reason is often a blend of the theme manipulating the plot and of the author unsophisticatedly accepting the clichés of melodrama. A prime case in point would be the subplot of *Lisheen* (1907), with its hanky-panky about a talisman ring, Indian magic, and leprosy. And sometimes he fails, as in the subplot of *Luke Delmege* (1901), when prostitution is regarded with a horror that is more bourgeois than Christlike. Yet, even here the conventional novelist and the conventional saint are contradicted (in one of the essays) by the practical, commonsensical, and unpuritanical commentator on the education of children.

Canon Sheehan is so good that one yearns for him to have been better, and, if his literary excellence had not sometimes been in opposition to his clerical goodness, he might have been. Nevertheless, he has been read and enjoyed by many thousands who do not like books, and, despite all, he can be read profitably by hundreds who do like them.

WORKS: *The Triumph of a Failure.* London: Burns & Oates, 1899; *Cithara Mea.* Boston: Marlier, Callanan, 1900. (Poems); *My New Curate.* Boston: Marlier, 1900; *Luke Delmege.* London: Longmans, 1901; *Geoffrey Austin: Student.* Dublin: M. H. Gill, 1902; *Under the Cedars and the Stars.* Dublin: Browne & Nolan, 1903. (Essays); *Lost Angel of a Ruined Paradise.* London: Longmans, 1904; *Glenanaar.* London: Longmans, 1905; *A Spoiled Priest, and Other Stories.* London: Unwin, 1905; *Early Essays and Lectures.* London: Longmans, 1906; *Lisheen.* London: Longmans, 1907; *Canon Sheehan's Short Stories.* London: Burns & Oates, 1908; *Parerga.* London: Longmans, 1908. (Essays); *The Blindness of Dr. Gray.* London: Longmans, 1909; *The Intellectuals.* London: Longmans, 1911; *The Queen's Fillet.* London: Longmans, 1911; *Miriam Lucas.* London: Longmans, 1912; *The Graves at Kilmorna.* London: Longmans, 1915; *Sermons,* ed. M. J. Phelan. Dublin & London: Maunsel, 1920; *The Literary Life, and Other Essays.* Dublin & London: Maunsel & Roberts, 1921; *Poems.* Dublin & London: Maunsel & Roberts, 1921; *Tristram Lloyd,* completed by Rev. Henry Gaffney. Dublin & Cork: Talbot, 1929.   REFERENCES: Boyle, Francis. *Canon Sheehan, A Sketch of His Life and Works.* Dublin: Gill, 1927; Coussens, Arthur. *P. A.*

Sheehan, zijn leven en zijn werken. Brugge, 1923; Heuser, H. J. *Canon Sheehan of Doneraile.* New York: Longmans, 1917; Kiely, Benedict. "Canon Sheehan: The Reluctant Novelist." *Irish Writing* 37 (Autumn 1957):35-45; MacManus, Francis. "The Fate of Canon Sheehan." *The Bell* 15 (November 1947):16-27.

SHEEHAN, RONAN (1953-), novelist. Sheehan was born in Dublin in 1953 and was educated at Gonzaga College and University College, Dublin. In 1974, he won a Hennessy Literary Award for a short story, and in 1977 he published a novel. That novel, *Tennis Players*, uses three junior tennis tournaments as occasions to contrast the direct amoralities of the young with the more devious hypocrisies of the middle-aged. Despite a few tedious passages, the novel is quite successful, sometimes funny and often excellently ironic.

WORK: *Tennis Players.* Dublin: Co-op Books, 1977.

SHEEHY-SKEFFINGTON, FRANCIS (1878-1916), journalist. Francis Sheehy-Skeffington was born Francis Skeffington on December 23, 1878, at Bailieboro, County Cavan. Like many other Irishmen of his time, he combined literary interests with participation in progressive causes, among them women's suffrage, pacifism, and the integrity of small nations.

Primarily a journalist, Skeffington co-edited *The Nationalist* with T. M. Kettle, *The National Democrat* with Frederick Ryan, and in 1913 succeeded James H. Cousins as editor of the feminist weekly *The Irish Citizen*. In June 1915, he was imprisoned for a seditious speech against the conscription and recruiting of Irishmen. Released after a hunger strike, he carried his anti-militarist appeal to America. His wife, née Hanna Sheehy (hence Sheehy-Skeffington), edited *The Irish Citizen* during his absence.

Skeffington went into the streets to prevent looting when the Easter Week Rising began. On the evening of Tuesday, April 25, he was arrested. The next morning, without trial or notice, he was shot on the order of Captain Bowen-Colthurst. The murder of this high-minded pacifist and the subsequent court martial in which the officer was declared insane aroused widespread indignation.

"A Forgotten Aspect of the University Question," Skeffington's essay demanding equal rights for female students, was printed in 1901 together with "The Day of the Rabblement," by a fellow student at University College, James Joyce.* A biography of Michael Davitt (1908) is an idealist's apologia for another idealist. The heroine of Skeffington's one-act play *The Prodigal Daughter* (1914), feminist Lily Considine, is, like the author, undaunted by imprisonment for breaking windows. His novel *In Dark and Evil Days* (1916, posthumously) is a quasi-historical tale of the rebellion of 1798.

Characteristic of his writing is a black-white contrast: Davitt versus opportunistic Parnell and bullying clergymen, Lily Considine versus small-town reactionaries, United Irishmen versus slinking informers. It is an approach better suited to persuasion than to literary art.

WILLIAM J. FEENEY

WORKS: "A Forgotten Aspect of the University Question," with "The Day of the Rabblement" by James Joyce. Dublin: Gerrard Brothers, 1901; *Michael Davitt: Revolutionary, Agitator, and Labour Leader.* London: Unwin, 1908/Boston: Dana Estes, 1909; "More Shavian Prefaces." *The Irish Review* 1 (May 1911): 152-155. (Review of *The Doctor's Dilemma, Getting Married,* and *The Shewing-up of Blanco Posnet*); "Frederick Ryan, An Appreciation." *The Irish Review* 3 (May 1913): 113-119; *The Prodigal Daughter: A Comedy in One Act.* Dublin, 1915. (First performed April 24-25, 1914, in Molesworth Hall, Dublin, as a benefit for the Irish Women's Franchise League); *In Dark and Evil Days.* Dublin: Duffy, 1916/reprinted 1919, with introduction by Hanna Sheehy-Skeffington; "A Forgotten Small Nationality." *Century* 91 (February 1916): 561-569.   REFERENCES: Curran, C. P. *Under the Receding Wave.* Dublin: Gill & Macmillan, 1970, pp. 111-118; Feeney, William J. "The Informers of '98 as Characters in Irish Literature." *Eire 19* (August 1977): 1-16. Shaw, George Bernard. "In Behalf of an Irish Pacifist." *The Matter with Ireland.* Dan H. Lawrence & David H. Greene, eds. New York: Hill & Wang, 1962, pp. 90-92.

SHEIL, RICHARD LALOR (1791-1851), politician, orator, and playwright. Sheil was born on August 16, 1791, near Waterford. He was educated at the English Jesuit college at Stonyhurst, at Trinity College, Dublin, and at Lincoln's Inn where he completed his studies for the bar. He wrote a few plays which were produced in Dublin and London with considerable monetary success, but none of them is of either Irish or permanent interest. Sheil's speeches, which grew out of his involvement in Irish and English politics, have some literary merit and are even today dramatic and eloquent. That their effect was largely from Sheil's rhetorical powers seems also evident by Gladstone's remark that Sheil's voice sounded like "a tin kettle battered about." Sheil's reminiscences of his contemporaries are worth remark, particularly his bustling and vivid picture of Daniel O'Connell in *Sketches of the Irish Bar* (1854). He died in Florence, where he was serving as English ambassador to the court of Tuscany, on May 28, 1851.

WORKS: *Adelaide; or, The Emigrants.* Dublin: Coyne, 1814. (Verse tragedy in five acts); *The Apostate.* 3rd ed. London: J. Murray, 1817. (Verse tragedy in five acts); *Bellamira; or, The Fall of Tunis.* London: J. Murray, 1818. (Verse tragedy in five acts); *Evadne; or, the Statue.* London: J. Murray, 1819. (Verse tragedy in five acts); with John Banim, *Damon and Pythias.* London: J. Warren, 1821. (Tragedy in five acts); *The Speeches of the Rt. Hon. R. L. Sheil, M.P.* Thomas Mac Nevin, ed. Dublin: Duffy, 1845; *Sketches of the Irish Bar.* R. S. Mackenzie, ed. New York: W. J. Middleton, 1854.   REFERENCE: McCullagh, W. T. *Memoirs of the Rt. Hon. R. L. Sheil.* 2 vols. London: H. Colburn, 1855.

SHERIDAN, FRANCES (1724-1766), novelist and dramatist. The wife of Thomas Sheridan the Younger* and the mother of Richard Brinsley Sheridan* was born in Dublin in 1724, the daughter of Reverend Philip Chamberlaine, an Anglo-Irish clergyman. Her father disapproved of schooling for women, believing it led to sentimental scribbling, but her eldest brother taught her secretly. By the age of fifteen, she was writing a two-volume novel, *Eugenia and Adelaide*, years later adapted as a comic opera for the Dublin stage by her daughter Alicia. About 1743, she wrote a poem, "The Owls: a Fable," defending the querulous young Thomas Sheridan for his part in the *Cato* riots at the Smock Alley Theatre. He was touched and asked to meet her; they fell in love, married about 1747, and lived for several years at 12 Dorset Street, Dublin, where five of their children were born. During these years, Mrs. Sheridan was too busy with her children and with buoying up the constantly collapsing hopes of her husband to write. However, in 1861 when the family was living at Windsor, she published a novel, *The Memoirs of Miss Sidney Bidulph*, and the next year her successful play *The Discovery* was produced at Drury Lane by David Garrick. With her husband in a leading role, it ran to full houses for seventeen nights, which in those days was a considerable success. Another play, *The Dupe*, was produced in the same year and failed. In 1764, the Sheridans moved to Blois, France, to escape creditors, and there Mrs. Sheridan wrote the second part of *Miss Sidney Bidulph* and also *A Journey to Bath*, a comic play which was rejected by Garrick but which may well have influenced her son's brilliant comedy *The Rivals*. On September 26, 1766, she died in Blois, to the great grief of her husband and children.

"A most agreeable companion to an intellectual man" was Boswell's comment on Frances Sheridan, but she was much more. A gifted writer, she wrote two hugely successful works while all of her husband's floundered. Her novel, influenced by Richardson, and published anonymously with a dedication to him, was unexpectedly well received. Even the stern Dr. Johnson praised it, and it was translated into French and German. Garrick thought *The Discovery* the best comedy he had ever read, and it was revived twice in the century, in 1775 and again in 1777. In no sense Irish, the play is a typical eighteenth-century sentimental comedy with some stock characters and a predictable plot. However, it is saved by flashes of comic brilliance and characters like Lord Medway, Sir Anthony Branville, and Lord and Lady Flutter, which anticipated the creations of her son and lead one to think that he inherited much from his mother. In 1924, Aldous Huxley adapted it for the modern stage.

MARY ROSE CALLAGHAN

WORKS: *The Discovery*. London, 1763/adapted for the modern stage by Aldous Huxley. London: Chatto & Windus, 1924; *The Dupe*. London, 1764; *Memoirs of Miss Sidney Bidulph*. 2 vols. Dublin: G. Faulkner, 1761; *The History of Nourjahad*. London: J. Dodsley, 1767.

SHERIDAN, JIM (1949-), playwright and director. Sheridan was born in Dublin in 1949. He worked with the Lyric Theatre* in Belfast, the Abbey* in Dublin, and the English 7:84 Company before becoming director of the

Project Arts Center in Dublin. Since 1977, Sheridan and his brother Peter* have given lively productions of several plays for the Project's theatre company, including Sheridan's own *Mobile Homes*. This is a realistic social play about the problems of several young families living on a mobile home site in Dublin. The characters are hardly more than sketches, and the social problem is so specific that the piece is little more than theatrical journalism. Nevertheless, the dialogue is authentic and lively, and the terse and compact scenes are nicely theatrical.

WORK: *Mobile Homes*. [Dublin]: Co-Op Books, [1978].

SHERIDAN, JOHN D[ESMOND] (1903-), novelist and humorist. Sheridan, the humorous essayist, novelist, and light versifier, has published many widely read volumes. Cleeve* calls him "one of the most popular and best loved contemporary Irish writers." That probably is true, but a good deal of Sheridan's popularity may stem from his having been insular, inoffensive, lowbrow, and Catholic at a time when Ireland was even more than usual noted for those qualities. If compared to his contemporary, the comic genius Flann O'Brien,* Sheridan appears bland, innocuous, and of negligible literary worth. Nevertheless, the judicious reader should not pass over his quiet and sincere novel, *The Rest Is Silence* (1953).

WORKS: *Vanishing Spring*. Dublin: Talbot/London: Rich & Cowan, 1934. (Novel); *James Clarence Mangan*. Dublin: Talbot/London: G. Duckworth, 1937; *Here's Their Memory*. Dublin: Talbot, 1941; *I Can't Help Laughing*. Dublin: Talbot, 1944. (Sketches); *Paradise Alley*. Dublin: Talbot, 1945. (Novel); *I Laugh to Think*. Dublin: Talbot, 1946. (Essays); *It Stance to Reason: The Intelligent Rabbit's Guide to Golf*. Dublin: Talbot Press, 1947/enlarged, Dublin: Talbot, 1963; *Half in Earnest*. Dublin: Talbot, 1948. (Essays); *Joe's No Saint, and Other Poems*. Dublin: Gill, 1949; *The Magnificent MacDarney*. Dublin: Talbot, 1949; *My Hat Blew Off*. Dublin: Talbot/London: Dent, 1950; *The Right Time*. Dublin: Talbot, 1951/London: Dent, 1952. (Stories); *The Rest Is Silence*. London: Dent, 1953; *While the Humour is On Me*. Dublin: Talbot, 1954. (Essays); *Stirabout Lane*. Dublin: Talbot/London: Dent, 1955. (Children's verse); *Funnily Enough*. Dublin: Talbot/London: Dent, 1956. (Essays); *Bright Intervals*. Dublin: Talbot/London: Dent, 1958. (Essays); *God Made Little Apples*. Dublin: Talbot/London: Dent, 1964. (Essays); *Joking Apart*. Dublin: Talbot/London: Dent, 1964; *Include Me Out*. Dublin: Talbot, 1967.

SHERIDAN, PETER (1952-), playwright. Sheridan was born in Dublin in 1952. He has directed several plays and had several of his own plays presented at Dublin's Project Arts Center. His only published piece thus far is *The Liberty Suit* (Project, 1978), an effective realistic play about juvenile prison life. Both he and his brother Jim* are committed to the idea of drama as a weapon for bettering social conditions, but so far neither has written anything that transcends its immediate Dublin target.

WORK: *The Liberty Suit*. [Dublin]: Co-op Books, [1978].

SHERIDAN, RICHARD BRINSLEY (1751-1816), playwright and politician. Born at 12 Dorset Street, Dublin, and christened Richard Brinsley
Butler at St. Mary's, on November 4, 1751, Sheridan came from a well-
known family. His grandfather, Thomas Sheridan,* was a friend of Swift.*
His father, also Thomas,* was at the time the successful, controversial manager of the Smock Alley Theatre; later, in England, he was actor, pedagogue,
teacher of elocution, and friend of Dr. Johnson. His mother, Frances
Chamberlaine Sheridan, was a novelist and playwright. He was educated at
Whyte's School in Grafton Street and at Harrow, where he was an indifferent student. He was often separated from his parents and for some time
lived in France to avoid debts. His charm and wit first flourished at Bath in
the 1770s, where he courted and then married the famous singer Elizabeth
Linley, "the Maid of Bath." The courtship involved a rejected suitor, duels,
and an elopement, elements which he later used in *The Rivals* and *The
Duenna*. After their marriage, he refused to allow her to sing in public.

Sheridan's career as a playwright was spectacular and brief. After an
unsuccessful first night (January 17, 1775), his revised and recast *The
Rivals* ran for fourteen nights at Drury Lane and established his reputation.
In the same year, he wrote a farce, *St. Patrick's Day*, for the actor Clinch
who had saved the production of *The Rivals*. In collaboration with his
father-in-law, the musician Thomas Linley, he also wrote the comic opera
The Duenna, which ran for seventy-five nights and became more successful
than *The Beggar's Opera*. In 1777, he revised VanBrugh's *The Relapse* as
The Trip to Scarborough, and on May 8, *The School for Scandal* opened
with a brilliant cast, establishing Sheridan as "the Congreve* of his day."
Like Goldsmith* and Arthur Murphy,* he favored the "laughing comedy"
of the Restoration, although all three of them were also influenced by the
currently popular sentimental comedy. In Sheridan's plays, the sentimental
hero is a hypocrite; the true hero is roguish but decent. Like all Irish writers
of English comedy of manners from Congreve to Wilde* and Shaw,* Sheridan's dialogue sparkles with witty repartee. His last original play was *The
Critic*, a play about the theatre, produced in 1779, when he was twenty-
eight.

In 1776, after long and complicated financial negotiations, Sheridan
purchased the principal ownership of the Drury Lane Theatre from David
Garrick, who was retiring from the stage. From this point on, the theatre's
and Sheridan's own financial situations become a maze. He used his income
from the theatre to finance his profligate private life and his political career.
Using the theatre as a source of income, he was only sporadically attentive
to details of management or artistry. Garrick's theatre seated 2,362 people;
Sheridan remodeled and enlarged it in 1794 to seat 3,611. He thus helped
create the perpetual problem of the theatre in the nineteenth century: both
how to fill such a large house and produce plays of dramatic merit. Sheridan

followed popular vogues—such as Carlo, the dog who rescued the baby; the false "new" play by Shakespeare, *Vortigern*; and the boy-actor, Master Betty. When the theatre burned down in a spectacular fire in 1809, the new manager, Samuel Whitbread, for financial reasons froze Sheridan out of any participation in the rebuilding, although Sheridan still held the royal patent.

In 1780, Sheridan became a member of Parliament for Stafford and served in Parliament until 1812. A faithful Whig when they were out of power, he was only scantly rewarded when they gained it and, unlike Edmund Burke,* was not rewarded with a pension. He was steadfastly pro-Irish on the question of land reform, Catholic Emancipation, and Home Rule. He was reknowned for his wit and his oratory, especially for his speech against Warren Hastings during the extended impeachment trial of Hastings for his governorship of India.

Sheridan's first wife died in 1792. His second, much younger wife, Hester Jane Ogle, lived with him through his final illness when he was beset by creditors. The funeral following his death on July 7, 1816, was spectacular, attended by the highest nobility, and he was buried in the Poets' Corner of Westminster Abbey.

Like Swift and Congreve before him, and like Wilde and Shaw after him, Sheridan gave his best efforts to the literature of England and is only tangentially an Irish writer. There is the fine but broadly comic caricature of Sir Lucius O'Trigger of Blunderbuss Hall in *The Rivals*, and there is the not particularly Irish Lieutenant O'Connor in the short farce *St. Patrick's Day*, which, save for an allusion to shamrocks and another to St. Stephen's Green, has nothing Irish about it.

SVEN ERIC MOLIN

WORKS: *The Plays and Poems of Richard Brinsley Sheridan*. R. Crompton Rhodes, ed. Oxford: Blackwell, 1928; *The Letters of Richard Brinsley Sheridan*. Cecil J.B. Price, ed. 2 vols. Oxford: Clarendon, 1966; *The Speeches of the Right Honourable Richard Brinsley Sheridan*. 3 vols. New York: Russell & Russell, 1969; *The Dramatic Works of Richard Brinsley Sheridan*. Cecil J.B. Price, ed. 2 vols. Oxford: Clarendon, 1973. REFERENCES: Bingham, Madeleine. *Sheridan*. London: Allen & Unwin, 1972; Gibbs, Lewis. *Sheridan, His Life and His Theatre*. New York: Morrow, 1948; Moore, Thomas. *Memoirs of the Life of the Right Honourable Richard Brinsley Sheridan*. London: [Longman], 1825; Rae, W. Fraser. *Sheridan*. 2 vols. New York: Holt, 1896; Rhodes, R. Compton. *Harlequin Sheridan*. Oxford: Blackwell, 1933; Sadlier, Michael T.H. *The Political Career of Richard Brinsley Sheridan*. Oxford: Blackwell, 1912; Sichell, Walter. *Sheridan from New and Original Sources*. 2 vols. London: Constable, 1909.

SHERIDAN, THOMAS (THE ELDER) (1687-1738), schoolmaster, translator, and friend of Swift.* Sheridan was born at Cavan in 1687, the youngest son of Reverend Dennis Sheridan who assisted Bishop Bedell in translating the Bible into Gaelic. He entered Trinity College, Dublin, on October 18, 1707, received a B.A. in 1711 and an M.A. in 1714, and then received a B.D. in 1724 and a D.D. in 1726. Sheridan opened a flourishing school in Capel Street, Dublin. When Jonathan Swift returned to Dublin to take up the deanery of St. Patrick's, he and Sheridan became constant companions. Sheridan often stayed at the deanery, and Swift sometimes taught in the Capel Street school when Sheridan was ill.

According to Swift, Sheridan was a superb schoolmaster. He was also a witty but frivolous fellow who justly wrote of himself, "I am famous for giving the best advice and following the worst." On one occasion Swift persuaded Carteret, the lord lieutenant of Ireland, to give Sheridan a living in Cork. However, Sheridan, not noticing that his first sermon was preached on the day of Queen Anne's death, used the text of "Sufficient unto the day was the evil thereof"—and consequently lost his appointment.

Toward the end of his life, after a long illness in the deanery, Sheridan became alienated from Swift. He died at Rathfarnham on October 10, 1738, while at dinner at the house of a former pupil.

Although Sheridan published little, he translated Persius, Juvenal, Sophocles' *Philoctetes*, and Guarini's *Il Pastor Fido*. Among his many important descendants were his son Thomas* and his grandson Richard Brinsley.*

WORKS: *An Easy Introduction of Grammar in English for the Understanding of the Latin Tongue.* Dublin: Printed for the Author, 1714; with Jonathan Swift, *The Intelligencer,* Nos. 1-19. Dublin, London, reprinted 1729/2d ed., Nos. 1-20. London, 1730; *The Satyrs of Persius.* Dublin: G. Gierson, 1728/London: D. Browne, 1739/ London: A. Millar, 1739. (Translated into English prose); *The Satires of Juvenal.* London, 1739/Dublin, 1769/Cambridge: J. Nicholson, 1777. (Translated into English prose).

SHERIDAN, THOMAS (THE YOUNGER) (1719-1788), actor, elocutionist, lexicographer, and writer on education. The third son of Thomas Sheridan,* the younger Sheridan was born in 1719 either in Capel Street, Dublin, or at Quilca House, County Cavan. He had Swift* for his godfather. He entered Trinity College, Dublin, on May 26, 1735, and received his B.A. in 1739. Sheridan early became entranced by the stage and wrote a farce called *Captain O'Blunder, or the Brave Irishman.* He appeared as Richard III at the Theatre Royal in Smock Alley, Dublin, in January 1743, to considerable acclaim. That year he also gained notoriety in the so-called *Cato* affair. When his gown for the evening's performance of Addison's play was mislaid, Sheridan rushed out of the theatre refusing to act. His part was read by Theophilus Cibber, and a riot and a ridiculous public quarrel ensued. However, through this affair he met his wife Frances Chamberlaine (Sheridan)* who wrote verses in his defense.

In 1744, Sheridan appeared both at Drury Lane and at Covent Garden where he rivalled David Garrick. The next year he returned to Dublin and managed the Smock Alley Theatre. He initiated needed theatrical reforms to restrain the rowdiness of the audience, but he engaged such brilliant actors—such as Garrick, Spranger Barry, and Mrs. Bellamy—that the

1745-1746 season has been described as unequalled in Dublin until the twentieth century. His reforms, however, made him the butt of several outbreaks of public fury. The first was the Kelly riots of 1747, when a drunken young man named Kelly misbehaved all during the play and finally threw an orange at Sheridan. Sheridan stepped out of his part, and said, "I am as good a gentleman as you are." After the play Kelly persisted, and Sheridan gave him a trouncing. Two nights later Kelly's friends broke up the theatre in protest against an actor calling himself a gentleman. Kelly was jailed, but was released at Sheridan's request. The second outbreak in 1754 was politically motivated. The audience tore up the theatre because Sheridan would not face them after refusing to allow West Digges to repeat some politically interpreted lines from the tragedy of *Mahomet the Imposter*.

Finally, Sheridan permanently removed with his family to England in 1758, and set up as a teacher of elocution. He became a voluminous writer on elocution and on educational theory. When, however, he produced a dictionary, his one-time good friend the great lexicographer Samuel Johnson became irritated and remarked to Boswell, "Why, sir, Sherry is dull, naturally dull; but it must have taken him a great deal of pains to become what we now see him. Such an excess of stupidity is not in nature." Nevertheless, Sheridan went on to edit Swift's works in eighteen volumes and to receive many honors. In the meantime, his wife Frances distinguished herself as both novelist and playwright. He died at Margate on August 14, 1788, the expenses of his illness and funeral being defrayed by his famous son Richard Brinsley,* the dramatist.

MARY ROSE CALLAGHAN

WORKS: *The Buskin and Sock; Being Controversial Letters between Mr. T. Sheridan, Tragedian, and Mr. T. Cibber, Comedian*. London, 1743; *A Full Vindication of the Conduct of the Manager of the Theatre Royal*. Dublin, 1747; *The Case of T. Sheridan, Lessee and Manager of the United Theatres of Aungier-Street and Smock-Alley*. [Dublin?: 1750?]; *The Brave Irishman*. [Dublin, 1754]. One-act farce in prose, adapted from Molière's *M. de Pourceaugnac*. Various later printings, including in *Bell's British Theatre* (1784) and *The British Stage* (1786); *Lectures on the Art of Reading*. London, 1755; *British Education*. London, 1756; *An Humble Appeal to the Public, Together with some Considerations on the Present Critical and Dangerous State of the Stage in Ireland*. Dublin, 1758; *A Course of Lectures on Elocution*. London, 1762; *A Plan of Education for the Young Nobility and Gentry of Great Britain*. London, 1769; *The Life of the Rev. Dr. Jonathan Swift*. Dublin, 1784; ed., *The Works of the Rev. Dr. Jonathan Swift*. 17 vols. London: C. Bathurst, W. Strahan, B. Collins, etc., 1784; *A Complete Dictionary of the English Language*. London, 1789.   REFERENCE: Sheldon, Esther K. *Thomas Sheridan of Smock-Alley*. Princeton, N.J.: Princeton University Press, 1967.

SHIELS, GEORGE (1886-1949), playwright. Born in Ballymoney, County Antrim, in 1886, George Shiels emigrated to Canada as a young man. Permanently crippled in a railway accident in 1913, he went back to Ireland, wrote short stories based on his life in Canada, and then turned to drama. His earliest plays, bearing the pen name George Morshiel, were produced by the Ulster Literary Theatre.* In 1921, the Abbey* accepted his one act comedy *Bedmates*. From that time until 1948, it staged one or more of his plays almost every year. He died at Ballymoney on September 19, 1949.

Bedmates and the one-act comedy *First Aid* (1923) are allegories of Ulster-Free State relations. In *Bedmates,* a Catholic and an Ulsterman peacefully share a doss-house bed until a Cockney sharpster creates religious dissension and almost persuades them to saw the bed in half. The "first aid" is administered, by men from the North and the South, to a Little Old Woman who falls into a well.

Paul Twyning (1922) typifies a more familiar Shiels play built on a picaresque character, in this case an itinerant plasterer, who by wit and guile solves a complex of domestic, romantic, and economic problems. In this class are *Professor Tim* (1925), whose title character, a wealthy professor of geology, comes back to Ireland masquerading as a drunken failure; *The Jailbird* (1936), perhaps the weakest of Shiels' plays; and such comedies as *Cartney and Kevney* (1927) and *Grogan and the Ferret* (1933).

Less engaging rascals are key figures in his later plays, such as *The Passing Day* (1936), *Quin's Secret* (1937), *Give Him a House* (1939), *The Old Broom* (Belfast, 1944), and *The Caretakers* (1948). Their common denominator is wholehearted avarice. The most interesting of these plays, in terms of technique, is *The Passing Day*. It opens with John Fibbs stricken by a heart attack and the usual speculations on who will get his money. The next four scenes flash back to the morning of the same day, tracing Fibbs' loveless, grasping relationships with other characters, most of whom deserve no better than they receive. In one poignant moment, Fibbs talks to the ghosts of his avaricious father and tigress mother, and his warped character becomes understandable.

Shiels' most thoughtful plays deal with the clash of modern and traditional values. Characters in *The New Gossoon* (1930) are divided into "oldsters" who subscribe to the work ethic; the young, who have been exposed to motorcycles and the cinema; and the poacher, Rabit Hamil, whose "I'm all right" ethic defies social change. *The Rugged Path* (1940) and *The Summit* (1941) constitute a two-part unit. The progressive farmers of the valley are pitted against the mountainy Dolis family trying to preserve an outmoded clan society. Another cultural anachronism considered in the play is the hatred of informers. When Irish law was superimposed over English law, the informer was a collaborator. However, Shiels argues, Ireland has its own legal machinery, and blind hostility to informers serves only to protect thugs and bullies. *The Fort Field* (1942) touches on a millennium rather than a generation gap. Work on a World War II airbase is delayed because of superstitious fear of disturbing a circular earthen mound, supposedly the dwelling place of the little people. The bulldozers finally win, abetted by prospects of money coming into the village from the airbase. *The New Regime* (1944) is a battle of wills between an arch-conservative Northern mill owner and a lorry driver who decorates his vehicle with a Russian flag.

Some historians of the Irish theatre dismiss Shiels as an entertainer. Within limits the criticism is valid. He shuttles stock characters from play to play, changing little more than the name. To reconcile differences, he sometimes abruptly stiffens mild persons and softens aggressors, at the expense of psychological credibility. Several plays are vulnerable to overly broad treatment by permissive directors or self-indulgent actors. At his best, however, Shiels is no mere purveyor of cotton candy. His comics rarely descend to the Handy Andy level; generally, they are resourceful, pragmatic, and a bit unscrupulous. Contending forces are not always careful of the niceties of statute law or fair play. In his later plays, there is an almost disturbing absence of poetic justice, and the tone is sardonic enough to satisfy the most acidulous taste.

WILLIAM J. FEENEY

WORKS: *Bedmates: A Play in One Act.* Dublin: The Gael Cooperative Society, 1922; *Two Irish Plays: Mountain Dew, a Play in Three Acts* and *Cartney and Kevney, a Comedy in Three Acts.* London: Macmillan, 1930; *The Passing Day: A Play in Six Scenes* and *The Jailbird: A Comedy in Three Acts.* London: Macmillan, 1937; *The Rugged Path: A Play in Three Acts* and *The Summit: A Play in Three Acts.* London: Macmillan, 1942; *Three Plays* (*Professor Tim, Paul Twyning, The New Gossoon*). London: Macmillan, 1945; *The Fort Field: A Play in Three Acts.* Dublin: Golden Eagle Books, 1947; *Give Him a House: A Comedy in Three Acts.* Dublin: Golden Eagle Books, 1947; *Grogan and the Ferret: A Comedy in Three Acts.* Dublin: Golden Eagle Books, 1947; *Quin's Secret: A Comedy in Three Acts.* Dublin: Golden Eagle Books, 1947; *Tenants at Will: A Play of Rural Ireland in the Young Ireland Period.* Dublin: Golden Eagle Books, 1947; *The Caretakers: A Play in Three Acts.* Dublin: Golden Eagle Books, 1948; *The Old Broom: A Comedy in Three Acts.* Dublin: Golden Eagle Books, 1948.   REFERENCES: Feeney, William J. "The Rugged Path: A Modern View of Informers." *Eire-Ireland* 2 (Spring 1967): 41-47; Hogan, Robert. *After the Irish Renaissance.* Minneapolis: University of Minnesota Press, 1967; Kennedy, David. "George Shiels: A Playwright at Work." *Threshold* 25 (Summer 1974): 50-58; Malone, Andrew E. *The Irish Drama.* New York: Benjamin Blom, 1965; Murray, T. C. "George Shiels, Brinsley MacNamara, etc." In *The Irish Theatre.* Lennox Robinson, ed., London: Macmillan, 1939.

SHORTER, DORA [MARY] SIGERSON (1866-1918), poet. Shorter was born Dora Mary Sigerson in Dublin in 1866, the eldest daughter of George Sigerson* and of Hester Varian (who wrote one novel called *A Ruined Place* in 1889 as well as much fugitive verse and fiction). With her friends Katherine Tynan* and Alice Furlong,* she was one of the better of the many women writers who turned to Irish themes for their verse during the

Literary Renaissance. She married the English critic Clement Shorter in 1895 and thereafter lived in London. Douglas Hyde* wrote that "Her very absence from Ireland has made her—a phenomenon which we may often witness—more Irish than if she had never left it. . . ." Her earlier work was suffused with the traditional poet's ubiquitous melancholy, but some of her work after leaving Ireland became more outward-looking. Always a skilled versifier, she frequently managed the deftly phrased fragment to enliven her generally unexciting work. However, a few of her folk poems and simple ballads are quite striking, especially "A Ballad of Marjorie," "The Wind on the Hills," and "The Banshee." She died on January 6, 1918.

WORKS: *Verses*. London: E. Stock, 1893; *The Fairy Changeling and Other Poems*. London & New York: J. Lane, 1898; *Ballads and Poems*. London: J. Bowden, 1899; *The Father Confessor, Stories of Danger and Death*. London: Ward, Lock, 1900; *The Woman Who Went to Hell, and Other Ballads and Lyrics*. London: De La Mare, [1902]; *As the Sparks Fly Upward*. London: Alexander Moring, [1904]; *The Country-House Party*. London: Hodder & Stoughton, 1905; *The Story and Song of Black Roderick*. London: Alexander Moring, 1906; *The Collected Poems of Dora Sigerson Shorter*. London: Hodder & Stoughton, 1907; *Through Wintry Terrors*. London: Cassell, 1907; *The Troubadour and Other Poems*. London: Hodder & Stoughton, 1910; *New Poems*. Dublin & London: Maunsel, 1912; *Do Well and Do Little*. London: Cassell, [1913]; *Love of Ireland, Poems and Ballads*. Dublin & London: Maunsel, 1916; *Madge Linsey and Other Poems*. Dublin & London: Maunsel, 1916; *Sad Years and Other Poems*. London: Constable, 1918; *A Legend of Glendalough and Other Ballads*. Dublin & London: Maunsel, 1919; *A Dull Day in London, and Other Sketches*. London: Eveleigh Nash, 1920; *The Tricolour*. Dublin: Maunsel & Roberts, 1922; *Twenty-one Poems*. London: Ernest Benn, [1926].

SIGERSON, GEORGE (1836-1925), historian and translator. Thomas MacDonagh's* *Literature in Ireland* is dedicated to George Sigerson, "Patriot and sage, Bard of the Gael and Gall, Teacher and Healer, Ollamh of subtle lore." The tribute is not an exaggeration. Thoroughly Irish, he claimed descent from Sigurd the Norseman who was defeated at the battle of Clontarf; a medical practitioner and neurologist, he had been Charcot's pupil and translated his *Lectures* from the French; the doyen of the Royal University, he was appointed to the chair of zoology in Newman's Catholic University and still held it when the National University was well established. His physical appearance was no less striking than his intellectual versatility. Terence O'Hanlon recalled him as "Big and broad-shouldered and straight as a lance, with forked beard and a wealth of snowy locks . . ." (*Capuchin Annual*, 95-97, 1954-1955).

Sigerson was born at Holy Hill near Strabane on January 11, 1836, the son of William Sigerson of Derry and his wife Nancy Neilson, a relative of the United Irishman Samuel Neilson. He was educated at the Letterkenny Academy and in France, and studied medicine at Queen's College, Cork, graduating in 1859. His career in medicine, though successful, does not concern us. His role in zoology was pedagogic. In the early 1900s, James Joyce* attended his class; Sigerson gained brief mention in both *Ulysses* and *Finnegans Wake*.

During his own student days in Cork, Sigerson's friends included Ralph and Isaac Varian. Ten of his poems were published in Ralph Varian's *The Harp of Erin* (1869) including the still popular "On the Mountains of Pomeroy." He married the Varians' sister, Hester; they lived first in Synge Street and later at 3, Clare Street. They had four children, of whom the elder daughter, Dora,* married Clement Shorter and published several books of verse.

Modern Ireland (1868) is a representative collection of Sigerson's political articles, some of which, dealing with the Orange Order, remain apposite today. His chapter in *Two Centuries of Irish History*, edited by R. B. O'Brien, was later published as *The Last Independent Parliament of Ireland* (1919). His *History of the Land Tenures and Land Classes of Ireland* (1871) influenced Gladstone, and he carried on an extensive correspondence regarding education with Lord Acton.

Sigerson's first book, *The Poets and Poetry of Munster* (1860), contains Irish songs collected by John O'Daly and translated by "Erionnach" (i.e., Sigerson). The more easily obtainable *Bards of the Gael and Gall* was published in 1897. Patrick C. Power in *The Story of Anglo Irish Poetry* (1967) credits this work with a far-reaching effect on Anglo-Irish poetry and suggests that "his translation methods call for careful examination."

Sigerson's books may lack general appeal today, but they have considerable historical interest. A child when the first number of *The Nation** appeared, he lived through many phases of Irish political life to become a senator of the Irish Free State Senate. He died after a few days' illness on February 17, 1925.

J. B. LYONS

WORKS: *The Poets and Poetry of Munster*. 2d series. Dublin: John O'Daly, 1860; *Modern Ireland*. 2d ed. London: Longmans, 1869; *Political Prisoners*. London: Kegan Paul, 1890; *Bards of the Gael and Gall*. 2d ed. London: T. Fisher Unwin, 1907. (The Phoenix Press edition [Dublin, n.d.] contains Douglas Hyde's Memorial Preface.); *The Last Independent Parliament of Ireland*. Dublin: Gill, 1919; *The Easter-Song of Sedulius*. Dublin: Talbot, 1922; *Songs and Poems*. Introduction by Padraic Colum. Dublin: Duffy, 1927.   REFERENCE: Lyons, J. B. "Medicine and Literature in Ireland." *Journal of the Irish Colleges of Physicians and Surgeons* 3, No. 1 (1973): 3-9.

SIMMONS, JAMES [STEWART ALEXANDER] (1933-), poet. Simmons was born in Londonderry on February 14, 1933. He was educated at Campbell College, Belfast, and at Leeds University. He taught at the Friends School in Lisburn for five years, during which time he sang songs on radio and television and won the Gregory Award for Poetry. In 1964, he went to Nigeria where he taught for several years, and in 1968, he returned to

Ulster, to the New University in Coleraine, where he still lectures in drama and Anglo-Irish literature. In 1968, he also founded the literary magazine *The Honest Ulsterman*. In the 1970s, he has been one of the most prolific Northern poets and, until his 1976 collection, one of the worst. Perhaps because of his interest in composing popular ballads and song lyrics, the form of most of his poetry has remained so casual as to be simply slovenly. In poem after poem, Simmons sets up some form, such as the loosely rhythmical rhymed couplets of "The First Morning," which he cannot maintain and which, before the end of the poem, he abandons. His images are frequently incongruous, as in "Diary Note," where he compares a woman's breasts to brussell sprouts. Many poems, such as "The End of the Affair" and "Bigger Than Both of Us," are mawkishly personal; many, like "September of My Years," are pedestrian. In his 1973 collection, *The Long Summer Still to Come*, he is still erratic and ragged, but a few pieces like "Uncle Jack" and the ballad "When Did You Last Write to Mother?" have such flashes of merit that one yearns for them to be revised and honed and polished into poetry. Unfortunately, this volume degenerates into several concluding pages of squibs, evidently the detritus of the author's notebooks.

A quatrain such as "I love little Polly," which is mildly obscene but not even mildly witty, might be taken as symptomatic of the early Simmons. Although passable as a quip at the end of a boozy evening with the boys, its inclusion in a volume of poetry suggests that the author's lack of formal authority is paralleled by the anachronistic personal immaturity that was rather usual in many Irishmen of his generation. Simmons was old enough to be influenced and yet too old to be *that* influenced by the mild Irish version of the Swinging Sixties. Consequently, much of his early work has an undergraduate's delight in free expression, a fascination with the details of his own life, and an utterly slovenly care for words and how they are used. Two-thirds of his 1974 collection, *West Strand Visions*, seems impelled by this self-vision of the bourgeois as hipster. Many of the pieces are cabaret songs, some three or four of which are good of their kind. Most of them, however, exist only as doggerel, and the first, serious portion of the book still flounders between form and colloquialism.

However, with his 1976 collection, *Judy Garland and the Cold War*, Simmons makes a startling advance, and begins to be not merely a poet, but an accomplished one. His subject matter, except for a couple of appalling pieces about Judy Garland, is suddenly very literary; there are poems on Tom Moore,* Synge,* Yeats,* D. H. Lawrence, Bertrand Russell, Walter Allen, John Clare, John Donne, Ulster poets, Faber and Faber, Emily Dickinson, Marvell, and Conrad, as well as a parody of Keats' "Ode to a Grecian Urn" called "Ode to Fanny Hill," and a long autobiographical piece which owes something—although hardly enough—to Eliot's *Wasteland*. Literary subjects do not make better subjects than autobiographical reflections necessarily, but in Simmons' case the change in subject matter seemed to impell him into a more serious concern with poetic form. The best of these poems are tightly controlled, memorable, and, once or twice, eloquent. Portions of his "For Tom Moore" will stand up to any anthology piece of his contemporaries. Not every poem in the book is up to that standard. There are still some adolescent jokes, and the Audenish/Mac-Neice*-ish "The Dawning of the Day," fine as it is, needs more work, as do most of the satiric pieces on the literary establishment. Nevertheless, even these are better than Kavanagh's* admired sloppinesses in a similar vein. One symptom of the terrific improvement of this volume is that the faults are smaller in scope. Simmons will use a word like "muddled" or "mean" without realizing that his readers will initially read them as verbs rather than as the adjectives he wants. Small criticisms aside, though, the *Judy Garland* book is the first strong evidence that Simmons is coming of age and is going to be a poet rather than a personality.

WORKS: *The Long Summer Still to Come*. Belfast: Blackstaff, 1973; ed., *Ten Irish Poets*. Cheadle: Carcenet, 1974; *West Strand Visions*. Belfast: Blackstaff, 1974; *Judy Garland and the Cold War*. Belfast: Blackstaff, 1976; *The Selected James Simmons*. Edna Longley, ed. Belfast: Blackstaff, 1978.

SMITH, MICHAEL (1942-), poet and publisher. Smith was born in Dublin. In the late 1960s, he founded the New Writers' Press which specializes in Irish poetry. He has published such writers of an older generation as Thomas MacGreevy* and Brian Coffey,* and such new writers as Michael Hartnett,* Augustus Young,* Trevor Joyce,* and Tom MacIntyre.* He has also published and edited the much too occasional literary periodical entitled *The Lace Curtain*. His own poems are written in regular stanzaic forms but unmetrically. His work has a fine clarity, although it is not deeply musical or technically interesting. Nevertheless, he does rise to the occasional arresting metaphor.

WORKS: *Dedications*. Dublin: New Writers', 1968; *With the Woodnymphs*. Dublin: New Writers', 1968; *Times and Locations*. Dublin: Dolmen, 1972; transl., *Del Camino* by Antonio Machado. Dublin: Gallery, 1974; ed., *Selected Poems* by James Clarence Mangan. Dublin: Gallery Books, 1974.

SMITH, PAUL (ca. 1920-), novelist. Smith was born in Dublin in about 1920, "in a house near a bridge spanning a canal. My education has been rather do-it-yourself. To this day I cannot recite the alphabet or the multiplication tables. . . . I learned to read at pre-school age. I began writing in my twenties." He left school at the age of eight and has followed many jobs in Europe, Australia, and North America. His first novel, *Esther's Altar*, was published in 1959 to enthusiastic critical acclaim in the United States and to widespread moral disapproval in Ireland. His most characteristic work has been in depicting life in the Dublin slums in the 1910s, 1920s, and 1930s. This subject, as well as a frequent boisterousness of style, has often caused him to be compared to Sean O'Casey.* However, Smith is one of the most uneven writers: his books vary in quality from one near-master-piece to a couple of shoddy imitations of Irishness.

Nearly twenty years after its first publication, *Esther's Altar* was revised and retitled *Come Trailing Blood*. The story is nominally set in a south Dublin slum during Easter Week 1916. However, the historical background is skimpy, false, unconvincing, and quite tangential to the novel's main preoccupations, which would seem to be a catalogue of unconvincing brutalities: lust, rape, incest, betrayal, beatings, murder, transvestism, mutilation, and suicide. Presumably all of this is meant to evoke the earthy vigor of slum life, but it almost totally fails. The characters are either vague or simplified, and the style is deeply influenced by the more excessive portions of William Faulkner and Thomas Wolfe (of Wolfe particularly, there are close verbal echoes). Indeed, the style is so florid that it sometimes becomes incoherent and takes on the overripe exaggerations of soft-core pornography. For instance, one of the many rhapsodic descriptions of sex reads in part: "Around the man's furnace-heated unmerciful thrust her arms and legs wrapped loose for what she knew would be a prolonged siege. Until the loaded dewy richness of the man's thick white wax soaked the parched earth like rain falling." In short, the novel vies with Christy Brown's* *A Shadow on Summer* for being the worst, most pretentiously written modern Irish novel.

Incredibly, the author of *Come Trailing Blood* also wrote *The Countrywoman*. That novel, published in 1962, depicts Dublin slum life in the time of the Black and Tan War and of the Civil War. Its heroine is a Juno-like mother, Molly Baines, who is trying to raise her family despite poverty, disease, illness, civil turbulence, and a brutal drunkard of a husband. Although some of the many minor characters are but thinly depicted, the general portrait of swarming life in the tenement is vividly and, this time honestly, caught. Smith's impressive accumulation of details leads to an ending which is profoundly poignant, and the novel seems a collaboration between a Liam O'Flaherty* and a Sean O'Casey, except that it has little of O'Flaherty's stylistic awkwardness and much more space than an O'Casey play in which to detail its richly abominable milieu and its intensity of suffering. It is unquestionably one of the strongest modern Irish novels and deserves the high praise that Anthony Burgess, Kate O'Brien,* W. J. Rodgers,* and others have heaped upon it.

'*Stravaganza!* (1963) is a departure in both setting and tone, for it is a semi-satiric novel set in a remote village of the West. Much of the book contrasts the simple warm humanity of the locals with the silly fecklessness of the arty visitors. The satiric portraits are clever but thin, perhaps the best being a flamboyant actress who seems a faintly disguised portrait of a prominent Dublin actor. Actually, the satire is more clever than amusing, and the best parts of the book are its feeling for landscape and the good-heartedness of its closing. As an entertainment, it is passable but not up to the best of Honor Tracy.*

Smith's latest novel was published as *Annie* in the United States in 1972 and as *Summer Sang in Me* in England in 1975. A return to the Dublin slums, the book contains some of the faults of *Come Trailing Blood* and some of the strengths of *The Countrywoman*. The story is a picaresque series of adventures of a young girl and of a younger boy who helps her try to raise money to buy her a huckster's cart, so that she may avoid being put to work in a biscuit factory. The book has some of the steamy floridness of *Come Trailing Blood* and seems in parts a Stage Irish exaggeration for the American market. Nevertheless, Annie is Smith's best drawn character since Molly Baines, and the latter parts of the book markedly demonstrate the talents of this considerable but erratic writer.

WORKS: *Esther's Altar*. London, New York: Abelard-Schumann, [1960]/revised as *Come Trailing Blood*, London: Quartet Books, 1977; *The Countrywoman*. New York: Scribner's, [1961]/London: Heinemann, [1962]; *The Stubborn Season*. London: Heinemann, [1962]; *'Stravaganza!* London: Heinemann, [1963]; *Annie*. New York: Dial, 1972/retitled *Summer Sang in Me*. London: Quartet Books, 1975.

SMITH, SYDNEY BERNARD (1936-), poet and playwright. Smith lives on the island of Inishbofin, County Galway, a fact which makes him the "Westernmost Man of Letters in Europe." He was born in Glasgow on August 4, 1936, and was brought up in Portstewart, County Derry. He attended Clongowes Wood College and Queen's College, Oxford. He has taught at Clongowes Wood and at the University of Iowa, but he has resided on Inishbofin since 1971. To date, he has published only fugitive pieces and one small pamphlet of poems, *Girl with Violin* (1968). However, his *Priorities*, a work containing his poems from 1968 to 1977, is at this writing awaiting publication. The more serious poems in *Girl with Violin* are rather formless and romantic in diction, but they are balanced by some less serious, but tight, short, and witty pieces. Smith has written several plays which thus far have been performed only by amateurs. Of them, the best is probably *Sherca*, an effective modern embodiment of the Philoctetes story.

WORKS: *Girl with Violin*. Dublin: Dolmen, 1968; *Sherca* in *The Journal of Irish Literature* 8 (January 1979).

SMITHSON, ANNIE M[ARY] P[ATRICIA] (1883-1948), novelist. Smithson was born in Sandymount, Dublin, in 1883. She was a nurse and midwife who became a fervent convert to both Catholicism and nationalism, and who fought in the Civil War on the Republican side. Her more than twenty novels were extremely popular among the poorly educated; they are thickly sweet, wildly patriotic, and romantically melodramatic. Cleeve* finds in them "freshness and innocence," but Eimar O'Duffy* more accurately remarks that her "naive pages are thronged with people who live in a state of chronic patriotic hysteria and cannot open their mouths without telling us about their 'faith' and 'ideals.' " Although Smithson is very bad indeed, she is not quite of the classic badness of Amanda M'Kittrick Ros.* She died in Dublin in 1948.

WORKS: *Her Irish Heritage*. Dublin: Talbot, 1917; *By Strange Paths*. Dublin: Talbot/London: Unwin, 1919; *The Walk of a Queen*. Dublin: Talbot, 1922; *Carmen Cavanagh*. Dublin: Talbot, [1925]. *The Laughter of Sorrow*. Dublin: Talbot/London: Simpkins, Marshall, 1925; *Norah Connor, a Romance of Yesterday*. Dublin: Talbot, [1925]; *These Things, the Romance of a Dancer*. London: Unwin, 1927; *Sheila of the O'Beirnes*. Dublin & Cork: Talbot, 1929; *Traveller's Joy*. Dublin & Cork: Talbot, 1930; *For God and Ireland*. Dublin: Talbot, 1931; *Leaves of Myrtle*. Dublin & Cork: Talbot, 1932; *The Light of Other Days*. Dublin & Cork: Talbot, [1933]; *The Marriage of Nurse Harding*. Dublin: Talbot/London: Rich & Cowan, 1935; *The White Owl*. Dublin & Cork: Talbot, 1937; *Wicklow Heather*. Dublin & Cork: Talbot, 1938; *Margaret of Fair Hill*. Dublin & Cork: Talbot, 1939; *The Weldons of Tibradden*. Dublin: Talbot, 1940; *Katherine Devoy*. Dublin: Talbot, 1941; *By Shadowed Ways*. Dublin: Talbot, 1942; *Tangled Threads*. Dublin: Talbot, 1943; *Myself—and Others. An Autobiography*. Dublin: Talbot, 1944; *The Village Mystery*. Dublin: Parkside, [1945]; *Paid in Full*. Dublin: Talbot, 1946.

SMYTH, GERARD (1951-), poet. Smyth was born in Dublin in 1951 and works there now as a journalist. He has published poems widely and has gathered them together in four collections which have received some acclaim. However, his work shows little sense of technique, and poem after poem contains such tiredly romantic writing as: when the dawn meets the sky, time hasn't changed the words of songs of long ago, I won't forget that song, the night is full of strangers, the roses in full bloom, peaceful sleep, net of tears, cruel wind, the wild Atlantic, calm before the storm, the stillness of a faded photograph, the machinery of time stands still in regions of the heart and mind, and so on. At best he seems able to offer fancies that are neither hugely individual nor accurate. His clotheslines whip the silence, his rain annoys the windows or his wind quarrels with them, and his frost sucks the air. Michael Hartnett,* however, optimistically remarks that Smyth "may do for Dublin in verse what Joyce did for it in prose."

WORKS: *The Flags Are Quiet*. Dublin: New Writers', 1969; *Twenty Poems*. Dublin: New Writers', 1970; *Orchestra of Silence*. Dublin: Gallery Books, 1971; *World Without End*. Dublin: New Writers', 1977.

Somerville and Ross— E. OE. SOMERVILLE (1858-1949) **and "MARTIN ROSS"** (1862-1915)— novelists and short story writers. The demise of the "Big House," the passing of the Ascendancy landholding class, is a prominent subject in nineteenth-century Irish fiction. No other author presents that subject in such detail and with such extraordinary vigor as the pair of writers known as Somerville and Ross. Biographical details would not lead us to expect these two eccentric ladies to produce both the best Irish novel of that century and its best series of comic stories. Edith Somerville and

Violet Martin, who employed the pseudonym Martin Ross, shared similar artistic and social interests. Somerville, born on May 2, 1858, studied art in London and on the Continent, and throughout her life continued her work as a painter. She began collaborating with Ross, her cousin, shortly after they met in 1886. Although Ross was younger, born on June 11, 1862, the literary partnership was equal; the collaboration was so perfect in fact that it is still difficult to distinguish the contributions of one from the other. Furthermore, their personal bond was so strong that the works seemed to derive from a single personality. As Somerville said, late in her life, in an essay in *Irish Writing* (1946), ". . . in all the happy years of our working and living together, there was never a break in the harmony of our work, nor a flaw in our mutual understanding."

Their first novel, *An Irish Cousin* (1889), was a nice attempt at a Gothic novel, and from the start, their skill at effective characterization is evident. In their next novel, *Naboth's Vineyard* (1891), they attempted to portray Irish village life, a subject they knew too little about to succeed.

They developed remarkably quickly as serious novelists, for their major work was published in 1894 and achieved for them a secure literary reputation. *The Real Charlotte* is generally recognized as the best Irish novel of the period. It was the first work in which they clearly aspired to artistry, and their achievement is impressive. The book is acclaimed largely for the depiction of the main character, Charlotte Mullen. She is vindictive, frustrated, and utterly destructive. In an essay in his collection, *Writers and Politics*, Conor Cruise O'Brien* remarks: "Evil has often been more dramatically exhibited, but I do not think it has ever been more convincingly worked out in humdrum action, or brought home with such a terrible cumulative effect as an element in everyday life." Such a thorough presentation of familiar life in all its facets makes the novel a masterpiece of realistic fiction. All of the characters, Charlotte's tenants and servants as well as her victims—the gentle Francie and the only man Charlotte shows any love for, Roderick Lambert—are established in such detail as to present a fully realistic world. The descriptions of Ascendancy life in the last stage of its eminence in Ireland are equally realistic. Like the novels of Jane Austen earlier, or E. M. Forster later, the atmosphere of the "Big House" engenders a whole set of values and attitudes; yet, in the presentation of that closed society, a set of universal conclusions is conveyed.

Despite the acclaim given *The Real Charlotte* by literary critics, the popular reputation of Somerville and Ross no doubt rests on their series of comic stories. In 1898, the first collection of these, *Some Experiences of an Irish R.M.*, was published. The stories center on Major Yeates, an English magistrate trying to adjust to life in Skebaun among the crafty but hilarious Irish peasants. The humor is as fast as the action: a series of encounters between landlords and tenants, masters and servants, in which roles are regularly reversed so that English naiveté is outwitted by Irish guile. Yeates' comic antagonist is a stock figure, the landlord Flurry. But the comic plots are so packed with surprises and the wit is so persistent that they surpass their formulaic structures. The first collection was so popular that two more collections followed: *Further Experiences of an Irish R.M.* (1908) and *In Mr. Knox's Country* (1915). It is difficult to account for the artistry of these comic tales, but their mischievous dissection of posturing and sophistication and their witty dialogue are strengths.

The death of Ross on December 21, 1915, was, of course, a great blow to her friend. Even after that event Somerville continued to list her cousin as co-author, believing that through spiritualist communication they remained collaborators. Several serious novels followed, the best of which are *Mount Music* (1919), on Catholic-Protestant relations; and *The Big House of Inver* (1952), an account of the decline of an aristocratic family. *The Big House* centers on the attempts of one of the ruined descendants of the Prendeville family, Shibby Pindy, to rescue the family and restore its prominence by marrying her brother to an heiress. The plot is engrossing, although the style is not consistent; comic digressions are unsuccessfully imposed on a potentially tragic plot.

The last works of Edith Somerville are less accomplished, consisting mostly of sketches and reminiscences. She died on October 8, 1949.

The best of their works, *The Real Charlotte*, has been favorably compared with some of the greatest novels of the nineteenth century—especially with *Cousine Bette* and *Middlemarch*. The praise is earned, for it well investigates the nature of malice, vividly presents an entire society, and effectively and cleverly analyzes a number of distinct characters. Somerville and Ross knew the closed society of the Big House and saw the effects of its gradual corruption. At the same time, they were able to laugh at the changes under way and to do so in a manner which has not become dated. That combination, like their successful collaboration, is rare.

Although they lived through the early years of the Irish Renaissance, they were little involved with it, preferring their quiet life outside literary circles. Their works represent the highest achievement of Anglo-Irish literature before it was transformed by Yeats,* Synge,* and Joyce.*

JAMES KILROY

WORKS: E. OE. Somerville, ed. *The Mark Twain Birthday Book*. London: Remington, 1885; E. OE. Somerville as "Geilles Herring" & Martin Ross. *An Irish Cousin*. 2 vols. London: Richard Bentley, 1889; E. OE. Somerville & Martin Ross. *Naboth's Vineyard*. London: Spencer Blackett, 1891; E. OE. Somerville & Martin Ross. *Through Connemara in a Governess Cart*. London: W. H. Allen, 1893; E. OE. Somerville & Martin Ross. *In the Vine Country*. London: W. H. Allen, 1893; E. OE. Somerville & Martin Ross. *The Real Charlotte*. 3 vols. London: Ward & Downey, 1894; Martin Ross & E. OE. Somerville. *Beggars on Horseback*. Edinburgh & London: William Blackwood, 1895; Martin Ross & E. OE. Somerville. *The Silver Fox*. London: Lawrence & Bullen, 1898; E. OE. Somerville & Martin Ross. *Some Experiences of an Irish R. M.* London: Longmans, Green, 1899; Martin Ross & E. OE. Somerville. *A Patrick's*

Day Hunt. Westminster: Archibald Constable, [1902]; E. OE. Somerville & Martin Ross. *All on the Irish Shore.* London: Longmans, Green, 1903; E. OE. Somerville. *Slipper's ABC of Fox Hunting.* London: Longmans, 1903; E. OE. Somerville & Martin Ross. *Some Irish Yesterdays.* London: Longmans, Green, 1906; E. OE. Somerville & Martin Ross. *Further Experiences of an Irish R.M.* London: Longmans, Green, 1908; E. OE. Somerville & Martin Ross. *Dan Russel the Fox.* London: Methuen, 1911; E. OE. Somerville. *The Story of the Discontented Little Elephant.* London: Longmans, Green, 1912; E. OE. Somerville & Martin Ross. *In Mr. Knox's Country.* London: Longmans, Green, 1915; E. OE. Somerville & (nominally) Martin Ross. *Irish Memories.* London: Longmans, Green, 1917; E. OE. Somerville & (nominally) Martin Ross. *Mount Music.* London: Longmans, Green, 1919; E. OE. Somerville & Martin Ross. *Stray-Aways.* London: Longmans, Green, 1920; E. OE. Somerville. *An Enthusiast.* London: Longmans, Green, 1921; E. OE. Somerville & (nominally) Martin Ross. *Wheel-Tracks.* London: Longmans, Green, 1923; E. OE. Somerville & (nominally) Martin Ross. *The Big House of Inver.* London: William Heinemann, [1925]; E. OE. Somerville & (nominally) Martin Ross. *French Leave.* London: William Heinemann, [1928]; E. OE. Somerville. *The States Through Irish Eyes.* Boston & New York: Houghton Mifflin, 1930/London: William Heinemann, [1931]; E. OE. Somerville & (nominally) Martin Ross. *An Incorruptible Irishman.* London: Ivor Nicholson & Watson, [1932]; E. OE. Somerville & (nominally) Martin Ross. *The Smile and the Tear.* London: Methuen, [1933]; E. OE. Somerville, ed. *Notes of the Horn: Hunting Verse, Old and New.* London: Peter Davies, [1934]; E. OE. Somerville & (nominally) Martin Ross. *The Sweet Cry of Hounds.* London: Methuen, [1936]; E. OE. Somerville & (nominally) Martin Ross. *Sarah's Youth.* London: Longmans, Green, [1938]; E. OE. Somerville & Boyle Townshend Somerville. *Records of the Somerville Family of Castlehaven & Drishane from 1174, to 1940.* Cork: Guy, 1940; E. OE. Somerville & (nominally) Martin Ross. *Notions in Garrison.* London: Methuen, [1941]; E. OE. Somerville & (nominally) Martin Ross. *Happy Days!* London: Longmans, Green, [1946]; E. OE. Somerville & (nominally) Martin Ross. *Maria and Some Other Dogs.* London: Methuen, [1949]. REFERENCES: Collis, Maurice. *Somerville and Ross.* London: Faber, 1968; Cronin, John. *Somerville and Ross.* Lewisburg, Pa.: Bucknell University, [1972]; Cummins, Geraldine Dorothy. *Dr. E. OE. Somerville.* London: Andrew Dakers, [1952]. (Contains Robert Vaughan's "The First Editions of Edith Oenone Somerville and Violet Florence Martin").

SPERANZA. *See* WILDE, LADY.

SQUIRES, GEOFFREY (1942-), poet. Squires was born in Derry in 1942, grew up in Raphoe, County Donegal, and studied at Cambridge. He has published a pamphlet and a small collection of poems. The dominant characteristic of his poems is brevity, and many read like the Imagist pieces of H.D. and the early Ezra Pound. If there is statement, it is either a terse, faint irony at the end, or it is implied. The great difference between the best Imagist work and that of Squires is in the quality of the language. Squires is always clear but never vivid, and so his terseness merely focuses the attentive reader on rather unremarkable prose.

In some of his poems, however, there is some slight edging towards a mild and helpful irony. There is also an awareness of levels of language, although the awareness usually consists of the poet's printing alone on some pages jargonish quotes from books like *Programming and Meta-programming in the Human Biocomputer*. Finally, there also seems to be a consistent attitude throughout his work, but these qualities do not compensate for the printing of what are the casual jottings from a writer's notebook.

WORKS: *Sixteen Poems*. Belfast: Ulsterman Publications, 1969; *Drowned Stones*. Dublin: New Writers', 1975.

STARKIE, WALTER [FITZWILLIAM] (1894-1976), autobiographer, critic, and translator. Starkie was born in Dublin on August 9, 1894. He was educated at Shrewsbury School, and Trinity College, Dublin, and was professor of language and literature at Trinity from 1926 to 1943. He was also a director of the Abbey Theatre* from 1926 to 1943, and for some years after that a rather nominal director of the Gate Theatre.* As a critic, he has published a study of Jacinto Benevente, another of Luigi Pirandello, and a translation of *Don Quixote*. He is most known, however, for his attractive studies of gypsy life in *Raggle-Taggle* and *Spanish Raggle-Taggle*, both based on his own wanderings. As A. J. Leventhal wrote of him, "He found that he could reach larger audiences by leaning his fleshy chin on his violin and bowing his way into their hearts with the throb of *Ziegeunerweisen* illustrating his comments on Romany culture. Our professor, like Borrow, found his way to Spain, but unlike him took a fiddle instead of a Bible for company. He never regretted it." Starkie spent the World War II years in Spain working for the British government, and many of his last years in Los Angeles where he was professor in residence at the University of California. He received many public honors from various governments. He died in Madrid on November 2, 1976.

WORKS: *Jacinto Benevente*. London: Humphrey Milford, 1924; *Luigi Pirandello*. London & Toronto: Dent, 1926/3d. ed., revised & enlarged, Berkeley & Los Angeles: University of California Press, 1965; *Raggle-Taggle. Adventures with a Fiddle in Hungary and Roumania*. London: J. Murray, 1933; *Spanish Raggle-Taggle. Adventures with a Fiddle in North Spain*. London: J. Murray, 1934; *Don Gypsey*. London: J. Murray, 1936; *The Waveless Plain. An Italian Autobiography*. London: J. Murray, 1938; *Grand Inquisitor, Being an Account of Cardinal Ximinez de Cisneros and His Times*. London: Hodder & Stoughton, 1940; *In Sara's Tents*. London: J. Murray, 1953; *The Road to Santiago*. London: J. Murray, 1957; *Scholars and Gypsies. An Autobiography*. London: J. Murray, [1963]; ed., with A. Norman Jeffares. *Homage to Yeats, 1865-1965*. Los Angeles: University of California Press, 1966.

STEELE, SIR RICHARD (1672-1729), playwright and journalist. Baptized at St. Bride's, Dublin, on March 12, 1672, the child of a family identified with Ballinakill, Steele later was to proclaim, "I am an Englishman born in the City of Dublin." Orphaned while young, he was supported by the Gascoignes, who were prominent in the establishment of the duke of Ormond. He was educated at Charterhouse, where he first met Joseph Addison, and at Oxford, attending Christ Church and Merton. He left without a degree in 1692 to become a Life Guard and later a Cold Stream Guard, in which he remained for thirteen years. As Captain Steele, he established in London some reputation as a wit, moralist, and writer. He supported Congreve* in the Collier controversy and published an exemplary book, *The Christian Hero* (1701). After three of his farces succeeded on stage—*The Funeral* (1702), *The Lying Lover* (1704), and *The Tender Husband* (1705)—Steele left the Army to become a courtier. He acquired several sinecures and the editorship of *The Gazette*, the official court newspaper. His career was scattered. He founded three successive periodicals, all of them successful—*The Tatler* (1709-1711), *The Spectator*, with Joseph Addison (1711-1712), and *The Guardian* (1713). The literary and financial success of *The Spectator* as it appeared daily and in later bound volumes established the genre of the urbane journalistic essay, reformist in intention but sophisticated and lively in tone, and opened the way for the newspaper. Addison moderated Steele's political enthusiasm, which emerged in *The Guardian*. Steele immersed himself in politics and controversy as a pamphleteer for the Whigs, who, on the accession of George I, knighted him and awarded him a share in the patent for the Drury Lane Theatre.

As the patent makes clear, Steele was appointed one of the managers of Drury Lane partly to carry out his well-known campaign to reform the stage from its Restoration licentiousness, but his foes were partly right in accusing him of neglecting the theatre except as a source of income. He was in continual disputes with the lord chamberlain and his fellow managers. His best known play, *The Conscious Lovers* (1723), carried out his theories of exemplary (rather than satiric) comedy, wherein the lovers are patterns of virtue, and of sentimental comedy, wherein bathos (rather than laughter) combines with the happy ending to provide delight.

Few details of his personal life are known. His personal life is speculative. An amiable and convivial man who lived by his wits and the main chance, he was impetuous and controversial. His friendships included the members of the Whig Kit-Cat Club and of Addison's "little Senate," as well as the philosopher-bishop Berkeley* and Pope and Swift.* (The relationship with Swift developed into personal and political animosity.) Little is known of his first wife. His second wife ("Prue" in *The Spectator*, the recipient of many foolish-fond notes) died in childbirth with their fifth child. He was extravagant and often in debt. Like Congreve and, later, Sheridan,* he aspired to be known as an English gentleman, although he lacked family connections and money. In ill-health, he retired to Wales in his final years, where he died on September 1, 1729.

SVEN ERIC MOLIN

WORKS: *The Letters of Richard Steele*. R. Brimley Johnson, ed. London: John Lane/New York: Dodd Mead, 1927; *The Correspondence of Richard Steele*. Rae Blanchard, ed. London: Oxford University Press, 1941; *Tracts and Pamphlets*. Rae Blanchard, ed. Baltimore: Johns Hopkins, 1944; *Occasional Verse*. Rae Blanchard, ed. Oxford: Clarendon, 1952; *The Englishman: a Political Journal*. Rae Blanchard, ed. Oxford: Clarendon, 1955; with Joseph Addison & others, *The Spectator*, Vols. 1-5, Oxford: Clarendon, 1965; *The Plays of Richard Steele*. Shirley Strum Kenny, ed. Oxford: Clarendon, 1971. REFERENCES: Connely, Willard. *Sir Richard Steele*. New York & London: Scribner's, 1934; Loftis, John. *Steele at Drury Lane*. Westport, Conn.: Greenwood, 1952; Winton, Calhoun. *Captain Steele; the Early Career of Richard Steele*. Baltimore: Johns Hopkins, 1964; Winton, Calhoun. *Sir Richard Steele, M.P.; the Later Career of Richard Steele*. Baltimore: Johns Hopkins, 1970.

STEPHENS, JAMES (1880 or 1882-1950), poet and man of letters. Stephens was in many ways the most engaging of the writers of Irish fantasy. He was witty and sympathetic, a brilliant conversationalist, and a fascinating storyteller—not only spinning tales based on Irish folklore and folklife, but also making up charming, contradictory stories about himself. Throughout his life, Stephens claimed that he was born on February 2, 1882; recently, others have proposed a birthdate of February 9, 1880, based on certain pieces of evidence. The matter remains unresolved.

There is no question about Stephens' birthplace; it was Dublin, where from 1896 to 1912 he served as a clerk-typist in the offices of several Dublin solicitors. His first story, "The Greatest Miracle," was published by Arthur Griffith* in *The United Irishman* on September 16, 1905. He sent his early pieces of writing to Griffith in envelopes without return addresses, but by 1907 they were friends. Griffith printed many of Stephens' poems, essays, and short stories in his newspaper, *Sinn Féin*. As a follower of Griffith's political views and an ardent nationalist, Stephens attended Gaelic League classes and political meetings during the period 1905-1910. His published essays in this period range from comic to serious, but they are most often passionate pleas to the Irish people: to exhibit national pride, to learn the Irish language and customs, and to remember the ancient saga heroes.

In 1907, Stephens met his friend and mentor, George Russell (AE),* who introduced him to George Moore,* W. B. Yeats,* Lady Gregory,* and other Irish writers. According to Stephens, one of the models for his early work was Lord Dunsany,* whose short stories, he explained, contained "great windy reaches, and wild flights among stars and a very youthful laughter at the gods." Another source of inspiration was Oscar Wilde's* *A House of Pomegranates*. By reading "about twenty pages" of Wilde's novel, Stephens reached his first "illuminating" conclusion: "the art of prose-writing does not really need a murder to carry it." This observation led to a second realization that a novel need not be a philosophical treatise. Stephens decided that a work of fiction did not need to be infused by its author with artificial excitement or thought, but rather that it succeeded or fell on its prose style. Having rejected murder and philosophy as necessary topics, Stephens said that he simply began writing "with the idea of doing a something which I conceived that Wilde has tried, and perhaps failed to do."

The work resulting from this challenge, *The Charwoman's Daughter* (1912), is a fantasy with a remarkably harmonious blend of disparate styles. It ranges in tone from whimsy to objectivity, sentimentality, and "philosophizing," and in approach from passages reminiscent of the nineteenth-century novelist to those peculiar to Stephens alone. At various times and in varying degrees, it is a fairy tale about two characters called the Makebelieves, a realistic look at life in the Dublin slums, and a psychological analysis of the relationship between a widowed mother and her daughter. By the end of the novel, happy endings have been provided in keeping with these genres. A mother and daughter have risen above despair through love and understanding of their life roles. Poverty, which has been described with the objectivity of a social worker and treated with the concern of a humanitarian, is no longer viewed as totally evil but more optimistically, as a spur to ambition. Even the aspects of the Märchen are satisfied: the poor but good Makebelieves find wealth and happiness.

Stephens' second novel, like his first, is a fantasy, but *The Crock of Gold* (1912) also contains philosophical debates, slapstick comedy, a romantic triangle consisting of a shepherdess and two gods, and the life stories of two prisoners. Its characters range from the mundane (shepherds) to the magnificent (Celtic gods), and its settings from an enchanted mountain to a village jail. Although Stephens rejected violence as a suitable topic for his first novel, this book opens with a robbery and two suicides, and continues with the seduction of a maiden and the abduction of two children. The work is also philosophical in tone, being in part Stephens' commentary on the Blakean notions of the enmity between Reason (male) and Emotion (female), the happy innocence of childhood, and the exploitation of men and women in a society dominated by those representing law, religion, and politics. Stephens' ability to make these divergent elements understandable, even comical, and his combination of them into a cohesive work is indicative of his literary craftsmanship.

The Demi-Gods (1914), Stephens' third novel, does not differ significantly in structure from its predecessors. Symbolism and naturalism are compounded in this story of angels who appear on earth to the bewilderment, delight, and occasional distress of a group who walk the Irish countryside. Demi-gods and tinkers converse and live together in a manner as happy as the relationship among the gods, fairies, leprecauns, and mortals in *The Crock of Gold*. The novel is narrated in the fashion of one who has lived on the road, just as *The Charwoman's Daughter* seems to be a first-hand account of life among the poor people of Dublin. *The Demi-Gods* closes with the attainment of the goals which we find in *The Crock of Gold* and

The Charwoman's Daughter: the union of man and woman, of gods and men, and of fantasy and reality.

What intervened between Stephens' third and fourth novels was an event of such impact that it changed the lives of all Irishmen—the Easter Uprising of 1916. For no major Irish writer was the impact of the Easter Uprising greater than for James Stephens. The event transformed his writing in a remarkable way—reviving old interests and kindling new abilities. Between 1915 and 1925, Stephens was registrar of the National Gallery of Ireland. He was on his way back to the National Gallery after lunch on Easter Monday 1916 when he learned of the Rising, saw a barricade, and witnessed the shooting of a man. His reactions to the event led to an elegy, *Green Branches* (1916), and a prose account, *The Insurrection in Dublin* (1916).

Beyond these works, the ten-year period after Easter 1916 became one of intense productivity for Stephens, and, it can be argued, the writing of this period was clearly influenced by an intensified patriotic feeling. He joined a class in elementary Irish at the Gaelic League and returned to his early interest in Old Irish literature. His friendship with the scholars Edmund Curtis,* Osborn Bergin (1872-1950), Richard Best (1872-1959), and Stephen MacKenna,* and his readings of the editions of the Irish Texts Society provided him with the background for *Reincarnations* (1918), a collection of poems adapted from the writings of several Gaelic poets, and for his next three books, which he later listed as his best: *Irish Fairy Tales* (1920), *Deirdre* (1923), and *In the Land of Youth* (1924).

There are certain thematic similarities between *Irish Fairy Tales* and the first three novels. Once again, fantasy (magical dwellings, shape-changing, disguised gods) is combined with reality (conflicting emotions of lovers, boasting conversations between rivals, devotion of children). What is different is the emphasis on Irish mythological figures, Fionn in particular. Fionn is an appropriate figure for a Stephens hero because he embraces two worlds. Fionn is a hero, a giant, a descendant of the gods, but he is also, like Stephens, a father, a husband, and a man who loves "the music of what happens."

The story of Deirdre, the Irish Iseult, was popular during the period of the Irish Literary Revival. Unlike his contemporaries, Stephens dealt with the Deirdre story not simply as an isolated legend, but as one of the many related tales which serve as background material in the ancient Ulster saga, *Táin Bó Cualinge* (The Cattle Raid of Cooley). His novel, like the legend, is structured around two questions: what caused the exile of the sons of Uisneac? what caused their death? His respect for his sources did not prevent him from inserting his own material, however. Stephens' Deirdre, like the heroines in his earlier works, converses with birds, hugs a shaggy mare, and loves the sunshine and peace of the Irish countryside. In his last novel, Stephens again injects his whimsical humor into four ancient tales: the

Adventures of Nera, the Vision of Angus Óg, the Tale of the Two Swine-herds, and the Wooing of Etain. The highest comic moment in the novel is a daily parade of the most beautiful women of Ireland conjured up by Angus' enthusiastic father to the boredom and depression of his mother.

Stephens wished to write a five-volume version of the *Táin*, but the task was never completed. He discontinued the project after publication of the first two volumes, *Deirdre* and *In the Land of Youth*. The task was over-whelming, the work exhausting, the critical response to his fifth novel dis-couraging, and he became too ill in mind and body to continue with the work. In his last collection of short stories, *Etched in Moonlight* (1928), which was published after *Deirdre* and *In the Land of Youth*, his mood ranged from irritability to desperation. Stephens' distinctive comic sense had left him, at least momentarily. His whimsical humor had turned sar-donic; there was no light touch to relieve the tension. He turned to fantasy one last time in *How St. Patrick Saves the Irish*, a short story written in 1928. This is the charming tale of a decision made by St. Patrick and St. Brigid that Patrick ask permission to sit in judgment in Heaven on Irish-men, thus allowing the Irish to avoid the "immovable unescapable, ter-rific" Rhadamanthus.

Stephens moved to London in 1925 and from there began a series of lecture tours in the United States which lasted until 1935. In 1927, he and James Joyce* started a friendship which, at least initially, was the result of Joyce's belief that he and Stephens shared a birthdate and other per-sonal events in common. The relationship blossomed into joint birthday parties and exchanges of gifts, and it also led to Joyce's proposal that Stephens finish *Finnegans Wake* if he could not do so.

Stephens spent the 1930s writing poetry based on his many years of reading Eastern philosophy and literature. Some readers found these works less appealing than earlier ones. The poems published in *Insurrections* (1909), for example, had a vigor and compelling anger not found in *Strict Joy* (1931). Stephens' growing depression permeated his last volume of poems, *Kings and the Moon* (1938); lost love, the coming of winter, the onset of old age became his subject matter. His final occupation was a happy one, however. He gained a new, appreciative audience through his talks on poets and poetry which began on the BBC in 1937 and continued until his death. He died in London on December 26, 1950.

In *A Short History of Irish Literature* (1967), Frank O'Connor* calls Stephens the Irish writer with the "most agile mind. He is a sort of literary acrobat, doing hair-raising swoops up in the roof of the tent." This mental agility is reflected in Stephens' ability to balance a range of emotions, sub-ject matter, and characters in his writing. His first three novels combine fantasy, philosophy, and comedy with characters including tinkers and gods, charladies and queens, warriors and philosophers, precocious chil-dren and bewildered parents. The last two cover a vast array of subjects:

love, war, heroism, betrayal, intrigue, romance, humorous events, and magical transformations of shape. Stephens is whimsical and coarse, bold and innocent, earthy and profound. His short fiction offers domestic comedy, psychological warfare, and merciless pictures of poverty, inhumanity, and madness. To describe his works as comic recalls the many forms of Irish humor—fantasy, irony, whimsy, satire, parody, word-play, among others.

Throughout his works, the contraries are to be found, but these contraries are a reflection of his life. The terrors recorded in his writing were those he knew personally: dark nights, hunger, illness, the tortuous gropings of the mind, and old age. The joys were familiar, too: childhood games, the love of a man and a woman, the pleasures of dancing, and conversation.

Stephens had a remarkable ability to marry opposites, including those of time and space—the earliest periods of mankind and the modern day, the wild country regions and the cultivated beauty of city parks—but always within an Irish setting, for he was an Irish storyteller. His stories reveal the gaiety and the loneliness of the Irish people: their estrangement from the land which was once theirs and their desire to return to an earlier, pastoral period; their animosities and suspicions; their flights of imagination and their love of words. His fantasies, especially those which were written after Easter 1916, are filled with the sunshine and thunder, lush vegetation and dirty slums, green trees and bloody combats of Ireland.

PATRICIA McFATE

WORKS: *Insurrections.* Dublin: Maunsel, 1909; *The Charwoman's Daughter.* London: Macmillan, 1912; *The Crock of Gold.* London: Macmillan, 1912; *The Hill of Vision.* New York: Macmillan, 1912; *Here Are Ladies.* London & New York: Macmillan, 1913; *The Demi-Gods.* London & New York: Macmillan, 1914; *Songs from the Clay.* London & New York: Macmillan, 1915; *Green Branches.* Dublin & London: Maunsel, 1916; *The Insurrection in Dublin.* Dublin & London: Maunsel, 1916; *Reincarnations.* London & New York: Macmillan, 1918; *Irish Fairy Tales.* London & New York: Macmillan, 1920; *Deirdre.* London & New York: Macmillan, 1923; *In the Land of Youth.* London & New York: Macmillan, 1924; *A Poetry Recital.* New York: Macmillan, 1925; *Collected Poems.* London & New York: Macmillan, 1926/2d ed., 1954; *Etched in Moonlight.* London & New York: Macmillan, 1928; *Julia Elizabeth: a Comedy in One Act.* New York: Crosby Gaige, 1929; *Theme and Variations.* New York: Fountain Press, 1930; *How St. Patrick Saves the Irish.* Privately Printed, 1931; *Strict Joy.* London & New York: Macmillan, 1931; *Kings and the Moon.* London & New York: Macmillan, 1938; *James, Seumas and Jacques: Unpublished Writings by James Stephens.* Lloyd Frankenberg, ed. London & New York: Macmillan, 1964. REFERENCES: *Letters of James Stephens.* Richard J. Finneran, ed. London & New York: Macmillan, 1974; Pyle, Hilary. *James Stephens: His Works and an Account of His Life.* London: Routledge & Kegan Paul, 1965; Martin, Augustine. *James Stephens, a Critical Study.* Dublin: Gill and Macmillan, 1977; McFate, Patricia. *The Writings of James Stephens.* [London & Basingstoke]: Macmillan, [1979].

STOKER, [ABRAHAM] "BRAM" (1847-1912), sensational novelist and theatrical manager. Stoker, author of *Dracula*, was born in Dublin on November 8, 1847. He was the son of a mild civil servant and of a Sligo woman of great energy and character who investigated Dublin's social evils with the breathless enthusiasm evinced by the television reporters of a later age, but whose reckless housekeeping kept the family in a perpetual state of bankruptcy. Stoker inherited a passion for the theatre from his father, and in his twenties combined a civil service post with unpaid service as drama critic of *The Evening Mail*. As volunteer public relations man for Henry Irving, he secured the huge success of that actor's visit to Dublin in 1876. This began a friendship with Irving which resulted in Stoker's leaving Dublin in 1878 to throw in his lot with the actor as secretary, business manager of the Lyceum Theatre in London, and what Shaw* contemptuously described as "literary henchman." He remained with Irving through thick and thin for thirty years, and was near at hand when Irving dropped dead in the hall of a Bradford hotel while on tour. In 1878, Stoker married Florence Balcombe, Oscar Wilde's* early beloved, stated by her grand-daughter to have become frigid after the birth of her only child; her frigidity is said to have propelled Stoker into womanizing and perhaps to the syphilis which caused his death on April 20, 1912. *Dracula* is the only Stoker novel which has been widely read. His large output includes other weird fiction and even nonfiction, notably *Famous Imposters* (1910), a chapter of which seriously propounds the theory that Queen Elizabeth I of England was really a man in disguise. His justly forgotten novel, *The Snake's Pass* (1891), has to do with Ireland.

ANDREW MARSH

WORKS: *Under the Sunset*. London: Sampson Low, 1882; *The Snake's Pass*. London: Sampson Low, 1891; *The Shoulder of Shasta*. Westminster: A. Constable, 1895; *The Watter's Mou*. Westminster: A. Constable, 1895; *Dracula*. Westminster: A. Constable, 1897. Translated into Irish by Sean O Cuirrin, Baile Atha Cliath: Oifig Diolta Faillseachain Rialtais, 1933. Dramatized by H. Dean & J. L. Balderston, New York: Samuel French, [1933]; *Miss Betty*. London: C. A. Pearson, 1898; *The Jewel of the Seven Stars*. London: Heinemann, 1903; *The Man*. London: Heinemann, 1905; *Personal Reminiscences of Henry Irving*. 2 vols. London: Heinemann, 1906; *Lady Athlyne*. London: Heinemann, 1908; *Snowbound, the Record of a Theatrical Touring Party*. London: Collier, 1908; *The Lady of the Shroud*. London: Heinemann, 1909; *Famous Imposters*. London: Sidgwick & Jackson, 1910; *The Lair of the White Worm*. London: William Rider, [1911]; *Dracula's Guest, and Other Weird Stories*. London: George Routledge, 1914.

STRONG, EITHNE (1923-), poet and short story writer. Mrs. Strong was born Eithne O'Connell in Glensharrold, County Limerick. She is married to Rupert Strong,* and has nine children. She has published a few fugitive short stories, and one of them, "Red Jelly"—which is a study of a chaotic and slovenly household seen through the eyes of the young daughter who is now living on her own—is extraordinarily vivid and successful. She has also published two volumes of verse. The work in her second and better volume, *Sarah, in Passing* (1974), is about liberation from domestic tyrannies. What it lacks in poetic technique it somewhat makes up by a clear and forceful statement.

WORKS: *Songs of Living*. [Dublin]: Runa, [1961]; "Red Jelly" in *Winter's Tales from Ireland: Two*. Kevin Casey, ed. Dublin: Gill & Macmillan, [1972], 95-110; *Sarah, in Passing*. Dublin: Dolmen, 1974.

STRONG, L[EONARD] A[LFRED] G[EORGE] (1896-1958), man of letters. Strong was born in Plymouth, England, on March 8, 1896, of a half Irish father and a wholly Irish mother. The summers of his childhood were spent largely in Ireland. He won an open classical scholarship to Oxford, was kept out of World War I by illness, and took his B.A. in 1920. Until 1930, he was a schoolmaster at Summer Fields School, Oxford, and then the success of one of his books persuaded him to live entirely by his writing. He was an extremely prolific and varied writer (the bibliography below is only a selected one). His poetry compels respect, and some of his fiction, admiration (his book *Travellers* of 1945, for instance, won the James Tait Black Prize). He also wrote film scripts, short and full-length plays, children's books, school books, detective stories, and unacademic literary criticism of some distinction.

Strong's serious fiction may be divided into stories with an Irish background, a Devonshire background, and a background of the Scottish Western Highlands. His finest Irish work is in two somewhat interrelated novels, *The Garden* (1931) and *Sea Wall* (1933). Both books are minor classics of modern Irish literature. They lovingly and memorably evoke that five or six miles of the eastern seacoast that stretches from Dun Laoghaire pier to Sandycove and the Forty Foot, past Bullock Harbor and Dalkey Island, around Sorrento Point, and into Killiney Bay. Anyone who knows that small picturesque portion of Ireland will recognize with startled pleasure Strong's still little-changed picture of some sixty years ago. Strong once remarked to R. L. Megroz, "I see a new novel as a landscape first, with hills and perhaps a sea-coast and bays and promontories. There are one or two clouds obscuring features of the picture. Presently the clouds begin to clear away, and then I have the main events, represented by the chief landmarks." The sense of place and a nostalgia for youth distinctively permeate these two novels, but the characterization is rather fine also—down even to the irascible pet monkey of *The Garden*. If there is any authorial forcing in the books, it is in the endings. The death of the autobiographical character in *The Garden* seems a contrived bid for poignance, perhaps appropriate thematically, but certainly disconcerting factually. The ending of *Sea Wall* has the superb idea of an airplane flight giving the hero a panoramic view of his landscape, but onto this Strong attaches a bit of thematic question-begging which hardly rises out of his narrative. Of the two books, *The Garden* is more of an essayistic evocation, while *Sea Wall* is more vigorously fictionized. It has a finely realized scene about the killing of a conger eel, as well as some boxing and swimming matches which the hero usually wins, that could come out of superior boys' fiction and that at least one critic has seen as a kind of anterior wish-fulfillment. Strong's *The Director* (1944) also has an Irish setting, and is a lesser, but worthy book. His poetry is usually fluent and graceful. At his poorest, he has the bland conventionality of the minor poet, but at his best—as in "A Young Man Drowned" or "The Door"—he is capable of a tight and memorable line. He is probably best known, albeit unfairly, for his little light verse "The Brewer's Man." In 1938, he became a director of the Methuen publishing house. He died in Guildford, Surrey, on August 17, 1958. His posthumous autobiography, *Green Memory* (1961), contains some excellent glimpses of Yeats.*

WORKS: *Dublin Days*. Oxford: Blackwell, 1921; *Doyle's Rock and Other Stories*. Oxford: Blackwell, 1925; *Difficult Love*. Oxford: Blackwell, 1927; *Dewer Rides*. London: Gollancz, 1929; *The English Captain, and Other Stories*. London: Gollancz, 1929; *The Jealous Ghost*. London: Gollancz, 1930; *Northern Lights*. London: Gollancz, 1930; *The Garden*. London: Gollancz, 1931; *The Brothers*. London: Gollancz, 1932; *Don Juan and the Wheelbarrow*. London: Gollancz, 1932; *A Letter to W. B. Yeats*. London: Leonard & Virginia Woolf, 1932. (Pamphlet); *Personal Remarks*. London: Peter Nevill, 1933. (Essays); *Sea Wall*. London: Gollancz, 1933; *Corporal Tune*. London: Gollancz, 1934; *The Seven Arms*. London: Gollancz, 1935; *Tuesday Afternoon and Other Stories*. London: Gollancz, 1935; *Call to the Swan*. London: Hamish Hamilton, 1936; *The Last Enemy*. London: Gollancz, 1936; *The Minstrel Boy, a Portrait of Tom Moore*. London: Hodder & Stoughton, 1937; *The Swift Shadow*. London: Gollancz, 1937; *The Open Sky*. London: Gollancz, 1939; *Sun on the Water, and Other Stories*. London: Gollancz, 1940; *The Bay*. London: Gollancz, 1941; *House in Disorder*. London & Redhill: Lutterworth, 1941; *John McCormack, the Story of a Singer*. London: Methuen, 1941; *John Millington Synge*. London: Allen & Unwin, 1941; *Slocombe Dies*. London: Collins, 1942; *The Unpractised Heart*. London: Gollancz, 1942; *The Director*. London: Methuen, 1944; *All Fall Down*. London: Collins, 1944; *Travellers*. London: Methuen, 1945; *The Sacred River, an Approach to James Joyce*. London: Methuen, 1949; *Darling Tom, and Other Stories*. London: Methuen, 1952; *The Hill of Howth*. London: Methuen, 1952; *The Hill of Howth*. London: Methuen, 1953; *The Writer's Trade*. London: Methuen, 1953; *Deliverance*. London: Methuen, 1955; *Dr. Quicksilver, 1660-1742. The Life and Times of Thomas Dover, M.D.* London: Andrew Melrose, 1955; *The Body's Imperfection. The Collected Poems of L. A. G. Strong*. London: Methuen, 1957; *Green Memory*. London: Methuen, 1961. (Autobiography).

STRONG, RUPERT (1911-), psychoanalyst and poet. Strong was born in London in 1911. He came to Ireland in 1937 and graduated from Trinity College. He studied psychoanalysis under Jonathan Hanaghan whose personality made a great impact upon him. He then became a practicing psychoanalyst in 1944 and has an enviable reputation for warmth and kindness. His poems are enthusiastic, occasionally witty, and his themes, sometimes on sexual passion, are refreshingly direct. Individuality, however, is small compensation for ability, and it must be said that his work generally has little poetic ability. Nevertheless, to record one dissenting vote, it might be noted that Bertrand Russell found his poems remarkable. He is married to Eithne Strong.*

WORK: *Selected Poems.* Monkstown, Dublin: Runa, 1974.

STUART, [HENRY] FRANCIS M[ONTGOMERY] (1902-), novelist. Stuart, the son of a prosperous sheep rancher originally from County Antrim, was born on April 29, 1902, in Townsville, Australia. Less than a year later, his father died, and he was brought to Ireland. He grew up in Meath, although he spent considerable time with relatives in the North of Ireland. He was educated at various preparatory schools in England, the last being Rugby which he left in 1918 without graduating. In 1920, at age eighteen, he married Iseult Gonne, the natural daughter of French deputy Lucien Millevoye and Irish nationalist Maud Gonne. During the Irish Civil War, he fought on the Republican side and was captured by Free State troops in August 1922. He was held in Maryborough Prison and later in the Curragh compound until November 1923.

The following year, the war over, he privately published a small collection of poems called *We Have Kept the Faith* (dated 1923 but actually released early in 1924), which received an award from the Royal Irish Academy and another from Harriet Monroe's Chicago journal *Poetry: A Magazine of Verse.* Strongly romantic in temper and uneven in quality, the poems occasionally touch on such typical Stuart themes as the outcast from society and the paradoxical relationship between the erotic and the religious.

While continuing to write poetry during the next several years, Stuart began to have doubts about the suitability of this literary genre to his purposes, and in the 1930s he turned to fiction. As he remarked in an interview published in *The Journal of Irish Literature* (January 1976), he had come to realize that his "real interests were far more in certain experiences —very often personal experiences, human relationships, human activities— which are certainly not best communicated through poetry." His first novel, *Women and God* (1931), was a failure critically and aesthetically, but his next two, *Pigeon Irish* (1932) and *The Coloured Dome* (1932), demonstrated surer artistry and were well received. In a letter to Olivia Shakespear (*Letters of W. B. Yeats,* Allan Wade, ed., 1955), Yeats* remarked of *The Coloured Dome* that it was "strange and exciting in theme and perhaps more personally and beautifully written than any book of our generation. . . ." In both works, the author leads his protagonists Frank Allen and Garry Delea from a life of safety and staleness through painful, isolating experiences that leave them outcasts and at the same time provide them with a depth of spiritual insight withheld from those who live conventionally. The same narrative pattern dominates all of Stuart's major

works. From 1933 through 1940, he published eight additional novels and
had two plays produced at the Abbey* (neither these nor three other plays
have been published). None of this work, however, is of compelling importance, although such books as *Try the Sky* (1933), *The Angel of Pity*
(1935), and *The White Hare* (1936) are valuable for the light they throw
on Stuart's philosophy.

In 1940, troubled by a declining career as well as by lingering financial
and marital problems, Stuart accepted a position as lecturer in English and
Irish literature at the University of Berlin, where he stayed, except for some
months in Luxembourg, for the duration of World War II. In November
1945, after the war in Europe ended, he was arrested by French occupation
forces and imprisoned first in Bregenz and later in Freiburg until July 1946.
Though no formal charges were brought against him, it seems likely that
he was detained because of a series of weekly radio broadcasts he had made
to Ireland from 1942 to 1944, in which he called for Ireland's continued
neutrality and expressed sympathy for IRA prisoners held in both the North
and South. After his release, he lived in Freiburg, Germany, until 1949
when he moved to Paris; then in 1951 he went to London, where he lived
for seven years. In 1954, following the death of Iseult, who had remained in
Ireland, he married Gertrud Meissner, whom he had met at the University
of Berlin and with whom he had been imprisoned in Germany. He returned to Ireland in 1958 and lived near Dunshaughlin in County Meath
before moving to the Windy Arbour section of Dublin in 1971.

Stuart's reputation will finally rest on the novels that appeared after the
war. The narrative pattern that informed the earlier works was largely
imaginative and not firmly rooted in lived experience. While remaining essentially the same in outline during the later period, this pattern takes on a
new and extraordinary power, for Stuart himself had now passed through
the almost ritualistic initiation he had mapped out intuitively for such early
characters as Allen and Delea.

The two novels that open his postwar career, *The Pillar of Cloud* (1948)
and *Redemption* (1949), are among Stuart's very best works and must
rank exceptionally high in Irish fiction of the period. The first of these is
set in Germany just after the war and records the spiritual journey of Irish
poet Dominic Malone, whose own suffering along with that of those close
to him results in new perceptions about the value of compassion, fraternity,
and selfless love. *Redemption*, set in postwar Ireland, focuses on Ezra
Arrigho, who has returned to his homeland after spending the war years
in Germany. He has brought with him the terrible knowledge of human
savagery, but this is a knowledge of the past, of a reality he believes he
has left behind in the blackened rubble of Germany. Subconsciously he
finds comfort in the safe, predictable life he leads in Ireland. But the delicate balance of past and present is shattered when a young woman is brutally murdered by a friend of his. Evil, he suddenly discovers, is not

something one can merely leave behind. His anguish and despair, together with the spiritual guidance of Father Mellowes, result eventually, if hesitantly, in crucial insights that are essentially the same as Dominic's.

From 1950 to 1959, Stuart produced six more novels; among the best, though they are flawed, are *The Flowering Cross* (1950) and *Victors and Vanquished* (1958). Then in 1971, after a twelve-year silence, he produced the remarkable autobiographical novel *Black List, Section H*, which Lawrence Durrell, in the *New York Times Book Review* (April 9, 1972), called "a book of the finest imaginative distinction." Here Stuart returns to his German years and traces the psychic quest of his central character H, whose unsettling and often painful experiences lead him to new depths of personal and spiritual understanding. The book also presents the clearest expression of Stuart's thoughts on the relationship between the artist and society, a subject that has long obsessed him. Since the publication of *Black List*, Stuart has produced two more novels, *Memorial* (1973) and *A Hole in the Head* (1977), both of which are interesting and valuable additions to his canon.

J. H. NATTERSTAD

WORKS: *We Have Kept the Faith*. Dublin: Oak Press, 1923 [1924]. (Poems); *Nationality and Culture*. Baile Átha Clíath: Sinn Féin Ardchomhairle, 1924. (Pamphlet); *Mystics and Mysticism*. Dublin: Catholic Truth Society of Ireland, [1929]. (Pamphlet); *Women and God*. London: Jonathan Cape, 1931. (Novel); *Pigeon Irish*. London: Gollancz/New York: Macmillan, 1932. (Novel); *The Coloured Dome*. London: Gollancz, 1932/New York: Macmillan, 1933. (Novel); *Try the Sky*. London: Gollancz/New York: Macmillan, 1933. (Novel); *Glory*. London: Gollancz/New York: Macmillan, 1933. (Novel); *Things to Live For: Notes for an Autobiography*. London: Jonathan Cape, 1932/New York: Macmillan, 1935; *In Search of Love*. London: Collins/New York: Macmillan, 1935. (Novel); *The Angel of Pity*. London: Grayson & Grayson, 1935. (Philosophy); *The White Hare*. London: Collins/New York: Macmillan, 1936. (Novel); *Racing for Pleasure and Profit in Ireland and Elsewhere*. Dublin: Talbot, 1937. (Handbook); *The Bridge*. London: Collins/Leipzig: Tauchnitz, 1937/Paris: Albatross, [1938]. (Novel); *Julie*. New York: Knopf/London: Collins, 1938. (Novel); *The Great Squire*. London: Collins, 1939. (Novel); *Der Fall Casement*, translated into German by Ruth Weiland. Hanseatische Verlag, [1940]. (Pamphlet on Sir Roger Casement); *The Pillar of Cloud*. London: Gollancz, 1948. (Novel); *Redemption*. London: Gollancz, 1949/New York: Devin-Adair, 1950. (Novel); *The Flowering Cross*. London: Gollancz/Toronto: Longmans, 1950. (Novel); *Good Friday's Daughter*. London: Gollancz/Toronto: Longmans, 1952. (Novel); *The Chariot*. London: Gollancz/Toronto: Bond Street Publishers, 1953. (Novel); *The Pilgrimage*. London: Gollancz/Toronto: Bond Street Publishers, 1955. (Novel); *Victors and Vanquished*. London: Gollancz, 1958/Cleveland: Pennington Press, 1959. (Novel); *Angels of Providence*. London: Gollancz/Toronto: Doubleday, 1959. (Novel); *Blacklist, Section H*. Carbondale, Edwardsville: Southern Illinois University Press/London, Amsterdam: Feffer & Simons, 1971. (Novel); *Memorial*. London: Martin Brian & O'Keeffe, 1973. (Novel); *A Hole in the Head*. London: Martin Brian & O'Keeffe, 1977. (Novel).   REFERENCES: Maxton, Hugh, & others. *A Festschrift for Francis Stuart on His Seventieth Birthday*. Dublin: Dolmen, 1972. (Contains a good bibliography of Stuart's book publications); Natterstad, J. H. *Francis Stuart*. Lewisburg, Pa.: Bucknell University Press, 1974; Natterstad, J. H.

"Francis Stuart: At the Edge of Recognition." *Éire-Ireland* 9 (Autumn 1974), 69-85; Natterstad, J. H., ed. "A Francis Stuart Number." *The Journal of Irish Literature* 5 (January 1976).

SULLIVAN, A[LEXANDER] M[ARTIN] (1830-1884), journalist and historian. Sullivan, the younger brother of T. D. Sullivan,* was born in Bantry, County Cork, in 1830. The brothers' careers were somewhat parallel, both being editors of *The Nation** and active in politics. A. M. was involved with Isaac Butt in the formation of the Home Rule party, and the Grattan statue in College Green was erected with money collected for him when he was in jail for his opinions on the Manchester Martyrs. His minor contribution to literature is a readable history, *The Story of Ireland*. He died on October 17, 1884, in Dublin.

WORKS: *New Ireland*. 2 vols. London: S. Low, Marston, Searle & Rivington, 1877; *A "Nutshell" History of Ireland*. London: Sampson Low, 1883; *The Story of Ireland*. Providence, R.I.: H. McElroy, 1883; *Speeches and Addresses*. 4th ed. Dublin: T. D. Sullivan, 1886.   REFERENCE: Sullivan, T. D. *A. M. Sullivan. A Memoir*. Dublin: T. D. Sullivan, 1885.

SULLIVAN, T[IMOTHY] D[ANIEL] (1827-1914), editor, politician, and poet. Sullivan was born on May 29, 1827, in Bantry, County Cork. He wrote for *The Nation** and became its editor on the retirement of his brother, A. M. Sullivan.* He was lord mayor of Dublin in 1886-1887, was associated with Parnell in the Land League agitation, and was a member of Parliament from 1880 to 1900. He published half a dozen volumes of patriotic verse, all of which is now forgotten save for the rousing "God Save Ireland." He died on March 31, 1914.

WORKS: *Dunboy and Other Poems*. Dublin: J. F. Fowler, 1861; *Green Leaves. A Volume of Irish Verses*. 2d ed. Dublin: T. D. Sullivan, 1879; *"Guilty or Not Guilty?" Speeches from the Dock*, ed., with A. M. Sullivan & D. B. Sullivan. 23d ed. Dublin: T. D. Sullivan, 1882. (This volume was more generally known as *Speeches from the Dock* and went through many editions, a recent one being edited and continued up to 1921 by Sean Ua Ceallaigh and published by Gill in Dublin in 1945); *A. M. Sullivan. A Memoir*. Dublin: T. D. Sullivan, 1885; *Lays of the Land League*. Dublin, 1887; *A Guide to Dublin*. 2d ed. Dublin: T. D. Sullivan, [1888]; *Poems:* Dublin: T. D. Sullivan, [1888]; *Prison Poems*. Dublin: Nation Office, [1888]; *A Selection from the Songs and Poems of T. D. Sullivan*. Dublin: Sealy, 1899; *Recollections of Troubled Times in Irish Politics*. Dublin: Sealy, Bryers & M. H. Gill, 1905; *Evergreen. A Volume of Irish Verses*. Dublin: Sealy, Bryers & Walker, 1907; *Bantry, Berehaven, and the O'Sullivan Sept*. Dublin: Sealy, Bryers, 1908.

SWIFT, JONATHAN (1667-1745), the great prose satirist of the English language. A hero's welcome awaited Jonathan Swift when he arrived in Dublin during the late summer of 1726. In the manner of a modern ticker-tape parade, flags, streamers, church bells, and large bonfires marked his return from England. He had earned the grudging respect of his adversary

Robert Walpole and the Whig ministers as a forceful and independent spokesman for Irish interests; he enjoyed the hospitality and attention of Alexander Pope and subsequent reunion with his beloved literary and political friends of the years 1710-1714 when he was an eloquent spokesman for Queen Anne and the Tory cause; and, not the least, he successfully arranged for the printing of his greatest work, *Gulliver's Travels*. Several months later, in a similar show of exuberant affection, Dubliners observed Swift's fifty-ninth birthday with new fires and other symbols celebrating this authentic "Hibernian Patriot" who had rallied public opinion for the cause of Irish economic and political independence in his role as M. B. Drapier of St. Francis Street. The ringing words of his Fourth Drapier Letter, addressed to the "Whole People of Ireland"—"by the Laws of God, of Nature, of Nations, and of your own Country, you are and ought to be as Free a People as your bretheren in England"—have inspired countless patriots of all nations of the world.

In our own time, as well as during the nineteenth century, Irishmen have warmly praised Swift and defended his right to the title of Irish patriot. Indeed, the great Irish poet William Butler Yeats,* who wrote his own version of Swift's Latin epitaph in 1929, and a writer "haunted," as he said, by Swift's presence and genius, argues that in the Drapier Letters Swift not only discovered his own Irishness but also "created the political nationality of Ireland." As an Irish legendary figure, a whole body of folklore—some of it humorously detrimental, even at times scurrilous—has developed around Swift, attesting to the affection and trust of his fellow countrymen. This mixture of fact and fiction has elevated the life of the dean of St. Patrick's Cathedral, Dublin, to a truly mythical status.

All of this praise and recognition was, strangely enough, for a man who could write "I do suppose nobody hates and despises this kingdom more than myself," or who refers to Ireland as "the most miserable country upon earth," or who describes the trip from England to Ireland as "a passage to the land I hate." Instead of the "fat deanery or lean bishopric" he so assiduously but vainly sought near his literary friends in England, he returned for good in 1713 as Dean of St. Patrick's to make this "wretched Dublin in Ireland" his permanent home, "a poisoned rat in a hole," as he vividly describes his situation to Bolingbroke. In fact, as early as 1709 Swift complained about the prospects of living in Ireland. A rather self-pitying letter to Esther Vanhomrigh (Vanessa), written from his country vicarage in Laracor, exhibits this incipient moroseness which he terms "discontent" and "dulness." This correspondence also documents an unsuccessful love affair poignantly expressed in Swift's memorable poem, *Cadenus and Vanessa* (1713), about the tragic insufficiency of any love relationship.

To be sure, Swift's correspondence continually reveals his talent for irony, and role-playing, traits characteristic of his most effective prose satire. This mixture of melancholy, anger, and exuberance is quite possibly the calculated stance of the satirist. In light of the many positive depictions of his Irish situation, his letters are less than a trustworthy index to his true feelings, hardly the sincere "representations of his mind," in the words of his first but severely critical biographer, Lord Orrery (John Boyle). While he is expressing deeply pessimistic attitudes to Pope and Bolingbroke, he is simultaneously corresponding with friends such as Patrick Delany, Mrs. Howard, Thomas Sheridan,* and the Achesons in the North of Ireland; clearly relishing his social life, influence, and fame in Dublin; even praising Irish weather, advocating Irish food and wine, and talking in a self-satisfied manner about his Irish life-style—all at the expense of the English counterparts. It is true, we have come to suspect his dark view of Dublin life as the deliberate self-portrait of the literary exile as well as of the artist sensitive to the expectations of his English friends. Nevertheless, Swift was not only deeply ambivalent about Ireland in general, but also about his particular relationship to the Anglo-Irish colonialists of the late seventeenth and early eighteenth centuries.

The Ireland into which Swift was born on November 30, 1667, was politically unsettled, a whipping boy of changing British governments. It was thoroughly colonized by the Stuarts, who created a Protestant ruling aristocracy amidst a relatively poor Catholic population and intimidated clergy. A native Irish rebellion in 1641 helped precipitate the English civil wars; and in 1649, sensing the political need for a foreign excursion as a show of strength, Oliver Cromwell attacked Ireland. The infamous Settlement Act of 1652 dispossessed to some degree every Irish landowner, and these lands in question were redistributed to Cromwell's sympathizers. After the Restoration of Charles II in 1660, some land reverted to the former owners; but after the Glorious Revolution of 1688, when James II made his last, desperate stand against William of Orange at the Boyne in 1690, the ownership of land was again scrambled, the bulk of the properties going to supporters of the victorious William regardless of prior claim or nationality. By 1700, England repossessed the lands to sell them to the highest bidders. Unlike the successful Scottish union with England in 1707, the Irish petition of the same year was denied and along with it great economic benefits, free trade, and representation in the English Parliament. To be sure, Dublin had a respected parliamentary government with a long history, but it was virtually powerless, able to enact only laws agreed on previously by London. Moreover, it was undemocratically self-perpetuating and inbred.

One of six sons of an English clergyman of strong Royalist sympathies, Jonathan Swift received the best education that the English governing class in Ireland could provide. Graduating from Kilkenny School, he entered Trinity College, Dublin, in 1682 and received a degree four years later. While pursuing an M.A., political uncertainties in the wake of the Revolution of 1688 forced Swift to England. The decade that followed, 1689-1699, affected his future enormously.

During most of these years, Swift was employed as secretary to Sir William Temple of Moor Park, Surrey, a retired Whig diplomat instrumental in forming the Triple Alliance (England, Holland, and Sweden) and in arranging the marriage of William and Mary. Swift read widely, tried his hand at Cowley-style Pindaric odes (which he soon gave up), and met Esther Johnson (Stella) with whom he shared love and friendship until her death in 1728. But most important, Swift began to develop his literary talents by immersing himself in editorial work on Temple's essays and letters. This experience engendered in Swift the social and intellectual attitudes characteristic of an urbane, sophisticated man of letters of the late seventeenth century. It also exposed him to the combination of aristocratic worldliness and hard-nosed antiromantic realism of the politics of the period. These two important qualities—self-assurance and a realistic view of human experience—are, of course, essential ingredients of the satiric temperament.

In 1694, failure to secure preferment in England drove Swift back to Ireland. He was subsequently ordained an Anglican priest and assumed his first parish duty as prebend of Kilroot, north of Belfast. Because of Temple's importuning and his own dissatisfaction with such a remote parish, he returned to Moor Park in 1696 and remained there until Temple's death. Little is known of these years in Kilroot, but being situated in the center of Protestant dissent seems to have inspired what for some is his most brilliant prose satire, *A Tale of a Tub*, which includes the *Battle of the Books* and the *Discourse Concerning the Mechanical Operation of the Spirit*, published in its final form in 1710, but written these last years at Moor Park. Satirizing the "numerous and gross Corruptions in Religion and Learning," the *Tale* owes much to Temple's own treatise on ancient and modern learning, a late seventeenth-century version of a perennial debate reaching back to the Renaissance. The *Battle* employs a mock-heroic framework popular with the Augustans within which Swift introduces an entertaining and skillful allegory of a bee and a spider to represent this conflict. Swift strikes a blow for "sweetness and light," that is, for the continuities and verities of traditional humanistic culture and the intangibles of faith and wisdom. As a whole, the *Tale* ridicules forms of pride, irrationality, and delusion, especially the brands revealed in the excesses of religious dissent. The mindlessness of "modern" self-importance, Swift believed, led to human folly and moral corruption—a satiric theme on which he provided many variations throughout his career. The paradox at the comic heart of this complex work is that, while Swift's own parodic art satirizes the insane world of the modern whose imagination has gotten "astride on" his better reason, he also demonstrates the extraordinary imaginative energies responsible for "modern" insanity. Although "Reason" may be "true and just," as Swift writes in his sermon *On the Trinity*, "the Reason of every particular man is weak and wavering, perpetually swayed and turned by his interests, his passions, and his vices." For some the contradiction at the conceptual core of the *Tale* marks the highpoint of Swiftian self-realization, but for others these complexities indicate confused satiric purpose, perversity, even psychic instability.

Like so many of his opinions, Swift's political attitudes during this formative period were complex and paradoxical. Under the influence of Temple, he was committed to the Whig concept of rational liberty with its scorn of political absolutism and fear of excessive reliance of the church on the state and vice versa. His *Contests and Dissensions in Athens and Rome* (1701), a response to extreme Tory partisanship, supported the principle of checks and balances in government to ensure political stability, yet tolerance of differences of opinion. Such a position he later praised under the guise of the mixed state republican government of the practical-minded and commonsensical King of Brobdingnag in Book Two of *Gulliver's Travels*. So important was this idea of rational freedom in his life that he incorporated a reference in his apologia pro vita sua, *Verses on the Death of Dr. Swift*:

> Fair *Liberty* was all his Cry;
> For her he stood prepar'd to die;
> For her he boldly stood alone;
> For her he oft expos'd his own.

Nonetheless, this political liberalism increasingly conflicted with Swift's innate conservatism and his obligation to defend the Anglican Church against Whig attempts to weaken its authority by accommodating deists, dissenters, and nonconformists of whatever stripe. Swift's *Contests and Dissensions*, written in a straightforward, impersonal manner, is an early example of his ability to deal with ideas and his delight in controversy.

In the *Sentiments of a Church-of-England Man* written about 1708, Swift argues for the independence and integrity of the Anglican Church within the framework of Whig political theory of the late seventeenth century. Its immediate impetus was the Whig desire to broaden the Church's constituency by liberalization of the Test Act, which required holders of civil and political offices to be communicants in the Anglican faith. His spokesman assumes the character of a dispassionate, detached observer of controversy, refusing to become drawn in by extremists on either Whig or Tory side. The creation of a fictional identity, independent of the author Swift, was to become stock-in-trade rhetorical strategy for Swift. Here, in a private capacity, this altruistic apologist for the Church seeks "to moderate between the Rival Powers." The speaker strikes the dominant Augustan stance of the middle way, shunning extremes and appealing to reason, tolerance, and compromise between church and state interests.

Swift's *Sentiments* and the straightforward reformist piece *A Project for the Advancement of Religion and Reformation of Manners* (1709) indicate how large the concerns of the Church loomed in Swift's consciousness during these early years of the eighteenth century. At the same time he is defending Anglican interests within the context of Whig political theory, he is approaching religious controversy in a highly oblique and ironic manner, characteristic of his most famous political and religious writings. His *Argument Against Abolishing Christianity* (1708) presents the reader with what was to become the recurring Swiftian dilemma of choosing among unsatisfactory alternatives: the abolition of religion and establishment of a thoroughgoing secular society; the maintenance of nominal Christianity that permits the pursuit of worldly interests; or the return to "real Christianity," the most radical plan, which would entail breaking "the entire frame and constitution of things, to ruin trade, extinguish arts and sciences with the professors of them . . . to turn our courts, exchanges, and shops into deserts." Like the *Tale*, the arguments and style of this brilliant polemic signal Swift's inherent skepticism of reformative impulses in general and his own in particular, and take the reader far beyond the immediate occasion of defending the Test Act. Even *Meditation Upon a Broom-stick* (1703) ironically scrutinizes "the universal Reformer and Corrector of Abuses." The satirist, like man as symbolic broom, is indeed a "topsy-turvy creature," his "Animal Faculties perpetually mounted on his Rational," revealing corruptions and stirring up a "mighty dust where there was none before; sharing deeply all the while in the very same Pollutions he pretends to sweep away."

Ironic playfulness and comic sensibility are nowhere better illustrated than in such pieces of this period as the *Bickerstaff Papers* (1708). Here Swift mocks his favorite targets, pretense, hypocrisy, and religious dissent, by means of an elaborate, zany procedure: his fictional astrologer challenges one of the day's best known practitioners, John Partridge, to a battle involving the accuracy of predictions. Lamenting the corruption of the "art" in his and others' hands, Swift's Bickerstaff predicts the exact date of Partridge's death. The joke is extended into a second installment that describes through a letter the deathbed statement of astrologer Partridge, which confesses to fraud and fakery. The third and final installment, through further extension of the logic, converts the predictable protestations of Partridge that he is indeed alive into proof that he must be dead. Beneath the comic surface is Swift's continuing attack on schemes and their perpetrators.

A number of explanations have been advanced to account for Swift's political conversion to the Tory Ministry of Bolingbroke and Harley in 1710. As we have seen, Swift's political beliefs were complex, and often his strong support of the Anglican Church against incursions on its authority and continuance, his passionate commitment to moderation in political and social realms, and his recognition of man's intellectual and moral limitations transcended party matters. Some clues appear, however, in Swift's *Journal to Stella*, a series of letters recounting his daily activities between September 1710 and June 1711. The letters are addressed both to Esther Johnson (Stella) and to her friend Rebecca Dingley, who were settled in Ireland near his vicarage. Lord Treasurer Harley had interceded for Swift in his assignment to represent the Irish bishops before Queen Anne for the purpose of securing a remission to the clergy of the First Fruits and Twentieth Parts, a tax by the Crown on clerical benefices. Despite the playful, childlike nature of this correspondence, Letter VI shows Swift relishing the attention of the Tory party, especially the assiduous cultivation of friendship by Harley himself, who according to Swift "loves the church" and "has a mind to gain me over." Among the possible reasons for Swift's embracing the new Tory government were the refusal, in 1707, of the Whig first minister, Godolphin, to honor requests for payments to the Irish clergy, the government's persecution of Henry Sacheverell for delivering a High Church sermon, and the increasing unpopularity of the War of the Spanish Succession. Whatever precisely affected his decision, Swift's temperamental conservatism, devotion to the Anglican church, and fear of Whig intentions both temporal and spiritual made the Tory cause appear increasingly the safer and more comfortable political persuasion.

At any rate, it was in this political atmosphere that Swift contributed to a series of pamphlets entitled the *Examiner*, written from November 1710 to June 1711. The pamphlets were ostensibly designed to keep politicians and the public informed about the new government and to propagandize for the Tory cause. Despite his obvious partisanship, as "Mr. Examiner" Swift professes impartiality and detachment, usually eschewing "the Violences of either Party." With his growing genius for creating fictional identities, Swift maintains a cool, reasonable mask of moderation, breaking into righteous indignation only as a calculated response to Whig provocations. His targets included political policy, the new "moneyed" class he held responsible for the long war, deism, or dissent, and individuals he personally despised, especially the Earl of Wharton, the Lord Lieutenant of Ireland, and the Duke of Marlborough, the famous Whig general of the battle of Blenheim and Ramillies, whose death Swift was to memorialize viciously in a satiric mock elegy. Swift's stance in the *Examiner* is that of the deliberate and objective observer. His best known essay of this period, *The Conduct of the Allies* (1711), still considered an effective piece of partisan propaganda, became a kind of handbook of Tory arguments, despite occasional distortion of historical fact and a blindness to English international success under the Whigs. One commentator on this Tory tract has accused Swift of advocating "a sterile past," of being a conformist not alive and responsive to a changing society. Whatever their ultimate value, Swift's major and minor Tory apologetics do reveal, in incipient form, some of the literary techniques that would characterize his great satires: a carefully created fictional identity; a detached tone hiding angry concern; joy in an occasional withering denunciation; an ability to catch the flavor and texture of mad modernism, materialist habits of mind, and banal optimism.

In the three-year period immediately before his involvement in the Tory government of Harley and Bolingbroke, Swift produced while in Ireland *The Story of the Injured Lady* (1707), an allegorical dramatization of current Irish-English relations seen in light of the union effected between England and Scotland. Since it was not published until after his death, it is not clear what Swift's intentions were in writing the piece, nor can the political effect, if any, be gauged. At this time, of course, Swift still hoped for a career in England. But his forthright pronouncements on the beleaguered Anglican Church of Ireland ("the Church in danger") would seem to rule out mere opportunism.

Swift's reputation as a so-called Irish patriot in the years 1720 to 1730 is documented and secure, but the ambivalence surrounding his attitudes toward the Irish as far back as the "Lady Injured" allegory is real and has its roots in the circumstance of his education as well as his political, religious, and literary ambitions. In a sense Swift was a colonial, born as he was into an English colony existing in Ireland for nearly five hundred years. Caution marked his Whig years in England, and opportunism can explain his Tory associations. He viewed himself as English, and, had he been accepted in England on his own terms, he might never have become a spokesman for the Irish. His return to Ireland in 1714 as Dean of St. Patrick's, rather than a joyous fulfillment of a lifelong ambition, seemed at the time more like a calamity. Swift was slow to warm to Irish causes and wrote little of consequence on those matters between 1714 and 1720. He never fully identified with "the savage old Irish," as he described the native population later to Pope. His eloquent and persuasive defense of Irish interests was largely a manifestation of his sensitive colonial pride: "Am I a Freeman in England," he complains, "and do I become a Slave in six hours, by crossing the Channel?"

However mixed his motives and intentions, Swift did react to the tangible effects of English commercial injustices. It should be remembered that he had interceded for the Irish Church with both Whig and Tory regimes, but his sentiments and emotions were apparently not fully engaged, nor was his patriotism aroused. Now that he was Dean of St. Patrick's and an Irishman, even if by default, and now that the possibility of an English career was precluded by the change to a new ruling monarchy in 1714, the repressive English laws that prevented the Irish from conducting their own political and economic affairs became for Swift an intolerable price to pay for the nominal protection provided colonials. As he does throughout his literary career, Swift again responds to practical human needs and to real, not abstract, moral issues.

The pamphlet *A Proposal for the Universal Use of Irish Manufacture* (1720) strikes a new note, moreover, by scorning automatic assumptions of English superiority and attacking greedy landlords, high rents, and Irish complacency and defeatism. Obviate the need for imports by consuming native products, he argues; "Burn everything English but their coal." The insults and aggressive attacks on both English and Irish in this tract reveal a new urgency of purpose, an immediacy of concern that belie the plain-spoken prose style, the clear, direct discourse ("Proper Words in Proper Places") appealing to men's reason and understanding that Swift advocates in *A Letter to a Young Gentleman, Lately Entered into Holy Orders* (1720).

To add insult to injury, two years later, in 1722, while the English Parliament was reaffirming its right to legislate for Ireland, King George I and the Walpole ministry granted William Wood, an English iron manufacturer, a patent to produce a copper halfpence for circulation in Ireland. The decision was controversial on a number of grounds: presumably secured by the intervention of one of George's mistresses, the agreement called for an excessive number of coins resulting in a huge profit for Wood; there were no provisions to protect against counterfeiting; and the Irish were not consulted on the matter. Over a two-year period, complaints that the debased currency would drive gold and silver from Ireland and further depress the economy grew so shrill that the English Treasury launched an official inquiry. Broadsides, ballads, poems, several by Swift, flooded the scene. In March 1724, at the height of the controversy, Swift published *A Letter to the Tradesmen, Shopkeepers, Farmers, and Common-People in General, of the Kingdom of Ireland*, by M. B. Drapier.

The full title of this first letter is significant. If Swift were indifferent to the native Irish of Roman Catholic persuasion, as has been charged, or if what interest he had shown involved essentially the fortunes of the Anglican Church and the status of English colonials, the publication in 1724 of these five successive letters (two additional ones were not printed) indisputably reflects a new nationalistic spirit and patriotic concern for what he described in the fourth letter as "the Whole People of Ireland." Despite the similarity of subject and theme, these letters differ in tone and style of expression. One and four are addressed to a cross-section of Irish society, the first playing on the prejudices, pieties, and economic self-interest of the ordinary, patriotic citizen, and the fourth dramatically asserting Irish political equality with England in unforgettable phrases. The second letter lampoons the character of Wood ("this little impudent Hard-ware-Man"), and the third, directed to a sober, educated class, sets forth political and constitutional questions. The fifth letter eloquently summarizes the issues raised and examined in the previous four.

Although his ostensible audience may have been largely Anglo-Irish and middle class, Swift's rhetorical strategies and convincingly maintained fiction of a concerned and sometimes outraged linen merchant, one M. B. Drapier, succeeded in awakening public opinion and rallying opposition to the economic and constitutional threats posed by England. Throughout his literary career, Swift often expressed doubt about the efficacy of satire and its power to reform or improve society. In September 1725, the lord lieutenant announced the cancellation of the patent and the end of the whole Wood affair. What better testimony to the force and influence of his satiric imagination? Of course, Swift was idolized for his successful challenge to Wood's halfpence, and his reputation as a local patriot was surely well deserved. His many efforts on behalf of Ireland during this period were formidable. Pope's tribute, in the Horatian poem *To Augustus*, beautifully sums up his contributions:

> Let Ireland tell how Wit upheld her cause,
> Her Trade supported, and supply'd her Laws;
> And leave on SWIFT this grateful verse ingrav'd,
> The Rights a court attacked, a Poet sav'd.

But all the polemics and mockery in the world could not halt the continuing deterioration of Ireland's economy. As Swift wrote to Pope, "the kingdom is absolutely undone, as I have been telling often in print these ten years past." In this same letter, moreover, he grimly recounts the failed harvests, starving population, and hopeless destitution brought about by crippling restraints on Irish manufacture and export and by absentee landlords draining off badly needed currency. These external conditions were exacerbated by a recalcitrant population vainly insisting on the luxury of foreign imports, refusing even to consume what they did produce.

Of these miscellaneous writings devoted to the worsening Irish scene, *A Short View of the State of Ireland* (1727) analyzes the economic and sociological causes of the malaise in a straightforward, deliberate manner. Unlike Swift's negative identification with his speaker through extended irony, in this tract when the spokesman is tempted by sarcasm he is instead overcome with emotion, confessing that "my Heart is too heavy to continue this Irony longer." Swift is, of course, presenting the facts as he saw them. Clearly, however, sympathy is mixed with anger and disappointment, a paradoxical reaction to the social and political stalemate in Ireland. *A Short View*, then, provides both the situational and emotional underpinning of Swift's best known Irish tract and greatest short satire.

An advertisement appeared in the *Dublin Intelligencer* of November 1729 announcing, in a tone of patriotic concern, a "new scheme" to alleviate the serious famine, restore a sense of national purpose, and, not the least, please the English landlords. At the center of this plan was cannibalism—the eating of a fourth of the Irish infants under two years old. The whole thought represented the basic economic goals and accompanying moral rationale of Swift's *A Modest Proposal for Preventing the Children of Poor People in Ireland from Being a Burden to Their Parents or Country, and for Making Them Beneficial to the Public* (1729).

The *Proposal* reveals Swift at not only his most complex, but also his satiric best, and it puts into sharp focus his ambivalent, often contradictory, attitudes toward Ireland. For, unlike much satire in which the satirist as spectator scorns an unsatisfactory state of affairs from an idealized and morally superior position, Swift sympathizes with the dismal circumstances of these "beggars of female sex" and "helpless infants." Like his polite, knowledgeable "proposer," skilled in statistics and economics, and desirous of putting forward "a fair, cheap, and easy method of making . . . children sound and useful members of the commonwealth," Swift's satiric objectives are equally patriotic, moral, and Christian. But distinctly unlike his "proposer," who is bent on a scheme that "as it is wholly new, so it hath something solid and real, of no expense and little trouble, full in our own power, and whereby we can incur no danger in obliging England," Swift voices self-doubts and uncertainties about his role as satirist, reformer, and Irish patriot. Swift suggests alleviating one degradation by another equally grim and savage—and thus unrelentingly exposes man's endless capacity for hypocrisy and self-deception. The ostensible target of the work is the professedly concerned narrator who is motivated by a social conscience, but whose casual references to people as commodities expose an egotism and arrogance almost beyond comprehension. This fact, however, should not blind us to Swift's desperate longing for some positive, humane act that will lessen the suffering he now identifies with. The presence of contrary attitudes characterizes irony, and the sustained ironic procedures of *A Modest Proposal* are expressive of hope and optimism as at the same time they remind us of the probability of defeat and despair. The complexity of Swift's attitude toward Ireland is, then, inseparable from his own self-scrutinizing habit of mind and realistic appraisal of the moral and corrective function of satire.

Gulliver's Travels (1726), Swift's best known and universally admired work, was written during that extraordinary four-year period when his creative energies were devoted largely to agitating and pamphleteering for the cause of Irish economic independence. It is a children's fantasy, a parody of currently fashionable travel literature, and probably the most devastating attack in English on man's pride. Like the "modest proposer," Lemuel Gulliver, a ship's surgeon, is a well-intentioned, decent, likable, educated, but often undiscriminating individual. Unlike the various personae of the pamphlets, however, Gulliver is a more complex figure, perhaps lacking the psychological density and consistency of a character in a novel, but nonetheless possessing a personality one can identify with.

His travels take him, in the phrasing of the book's formal title, into "Several Remote Nations of the World" where he meets a whole range of people, ideas, and institutions. These imaginary experiences, instead of providing a romantic escape from the world, as in the standard travel book, force the reader to confront the realities of his own physical, political, intellectual, and moral corruption.

In the *Voyage to Lilliput,* the shipwrecked Gulliver visits a nation of extraordinarily resourceful and industrious miniature people (scale 1:12) who care for his needs, provide him transportation, generally respect his desires, and, in fact, award him their highest medal of honor. But their inevitable political intrigues and pretensions, which at first appear innocent to Gulliver, show them in the end to be cruel, treacherous, and vengeful, qualities ironically accentuated by their smallness. Despite topical references to the Whig regime of Sir Robert Walpole and to recent French-English diplomacy, the satire broadens, through the use of disproportions, to emphasize disparity between man's illusions of power and importance and his moral pettiness, pomposity, fear, and paranoia. Through it all, Gulliver miraculously remains rather kindly and understanding, and his naiveté is Swift's main instrument of satire.

In Book II, the *Voyage to Brobdingnag*, Gulliver experiences a traumatic readjustment of perspectives. As a Lilliputian among giants, he begins slowly to reassess many of his opinions about the world. "Undoubtedly philosophers are right," he admits, "when they tell us, that nothing is great or little otherwise than by comparison." Although this comment marks a certain improvement in Gulliver's powers of discrimination, he continually fears of his physical well-being. Moreover, counter to his expectations, the king of Brobdingnag turns out to be fascinated by, not hostile to, this articulate *lusus naturae* (thing of nature), and enthusiastically engages Gulliver in a series of five revealing audiences devoted to an "exact account of the government of England." During the interview, Gulliver assumes the role of straightman for Swift, setting up, as it were, a variety of ideas, practices, and institutions as targets for satire. In his most fulsome panegyrical mode, Gulliver "celebrates the praise of [his] own dear native country in a style equal to its merits and felicity," only to have this wise and pragmatic king systematically demolish his opinions and veracity. In a memorable passage (with all the earmarks of Swift's style), the king denounces human nature in controlled fury: "I cannot but conclude the bulk of your natives to be the most pernicious race of little odious vermin that nature ever suffered to crawl upon the surface of the earth." Against the backdrop of his own physical vulnerability, Gulliver's frantic assertions of faith and pride in English institutions and life further deflate his pride. Far from an impossible utopia, for many readers the eminently sensible government of Brobdingnag provides a workable norm against which the follies and corruptions of England are to be measured.

The *Voyage to Laputa*, although the last to be written, appears as Book III of the *Travels* and is best described as a catchall. His main targets are theoretical, speculative science (as represented in the proceedings of the Royal Society) and ivory-tower political and economic theory. As a narrative, it is less unified than the others, comprising a long journey to the Flying Island with several sidetrips to Glubbdubdrib (to view heroes of classical and medieval history and philosophy) and to Luggnagg (to marvel at the immortals, who have escaped "that universal calamity of human nature"). In the spirit of *A Tale of a Tub*, the touch here is lighter, the satire funnier and more comic in effect than is usual in the *Travels*. Laputa itself is a brilliant set of variations on the theme of science and politics, one section in particular allegorizing the Irish-English conflicts of the 1720s. In fact, Swift's famous allegory in Book III, Chapter 3, *A Voyage to Laputa*, portrays graphically the successful resistance of the city Lindalino (Dublin) in Balnibarbi to the political oppression of Laputa, or the Flying Island (England), during the controversy over Wood's coin. (Benjamin Motte, Swift's original London publisher, omitted the four sensitive paragraphs for fear of government reprisals. All subsequent editions omitted these passages until an edition of 1899 restored the missing paragraphs.) Despite the comedy, what results is a devastating attack both on the enterprising, "projector" mentality that was so anathema to Swift and on the frenetic search for the new, the modern, and the different. It also provides one of Swift's clearest statements of faith in the notion of the "ancients," the idea of the traditional Virgilian and Horatian virtues of simplicity, frugality, and self-reliance associated with rural life and harmonious relationships between man and nature. Gulliver praises Lord Munodi, the only sane man in a land of fools, who is content with "the old forms, to live in the houses his ancestors had built, and act as they did in every part of life without innovation."

Book IV, the *Voyage to the Houyhnhnms*, the most complex and problematical, opens with a Gulliver who is thoroughly disillusioned by the experience of the immortal but decrepit Struldbrugs, at the end of Book III and by the mutiny, a breakdown of ordered society, on board his ship. The inexorable darkening of tone in this voyage has led many readers, especially Victorian critics, to condemn *Gulliver's Travels*, in the unforgettable language of the novelist Thackeray, as "filthy in word, filthy in thought, furious, raging, obscene," the production of a bitterly degenerate misanthrope. Characteristically Swift did not help matters by referring, in an often-quoted letter to Pope (September 29, 1725), to the "great foundation of misanthropy" on which his "treatise" was based, "proving the falsity of that definition *animale rationale*; and to show it should be only *rationis capax*."

Our more balanced view of Swift today, and an understanding of the rhetorical strategies of satire cannot, however, totally dispel the fears expressed by Thackeray and others that Swift's indictment of human nature in Book IV is fierce and unrelenting, living up to his own epitaph: a hauntingly accurate self-portrait of savage indignation and a lacerated heart. Such phrases do accurately represent attitudes at the end of the *Travels*, in *A Modest Proposal*, and several of the later poems, and there is no blinking this fact as the Victorians understood.

When placed in the larger context of his life, beliefs, and times, however, Swift's denunciations are the inevitable reaction of a conservative in politics and religion, an orthodox Christian humanist, to man's fallen state. Moreover, Swift's assumptions about man's corrupt nature were not unique; indeed, they were axiomatic and were shared by his fellow Scriblerians and others who dismissed the meliorist myth, which argued for man's essential goodness and perfectibility and thus society's improvement and progress. From the beginning, Swift's targets were deists, utopians, Stoics, religious enthusiasts, philosophical optimists—deluded idealists of whatever form— who denied man's pride. As he said in the undated *Of Publick Absurdityes*, "It is a mistake of wise and good men that they expect more Reason and Virtue from human nature, than . . . it is in any sort capable of." By the time of *Gulliver's Travels*, Swift had come to despise delusion in any form, even the innocent, "mistaken" brand. His attitudes and obsessions are therefore understandable, and his genius lies in compelling us to see the true nature of man and society. For Swift, the satirical outlook on life gave the sharpest focus on reality.

The interpretive crux of the fourth Voyage lies in one's reading of the Houyhnhnms, those serenely rationalistic horses who are remote and stoical but nonetheless strangely attractive. The Yahoos, the only other inhabitants in the caste society, epitomize man's unregenerate animal nature, repulsive physicality, and appetitive habits. To complicate matters, Swift's relationship to Gulliver himself, especially toward the end, is uncertain, and the question arises whether Gulliver speaks for Swift, or whether he is the object of Swift's satire, or both.

Some readers view the horses as Swift's ideal of rationality; others consider them quite the opposite—in fact, as representations of a false ideal about human nature perpetrated by the progressives, freethinkers, and sentimentalists. A close reading reveals a number of clear signals that warn against a literal reading of man as a rational animal. A number of silly scenes, when horse characteristics and rationality prove incompatible, put the reader on guard. Moreover, as one critic phrases it, "the purity of the horses is preternatural," ideal in the abstract but certainly an unlikely ideal for *human* beings. They appear as a symbol of pure reason that man cannot obtain because of his fallen and corrupt nature. In fact, after Gulliver's long litany of the wars, destruction, and chaos infecting European society, the Master Horse's reaction is: "When a creature pretending to reason could be capable of such enormities, he dreaded lest the corruption of that faculty might be worse than brutality itself." Such a response does not, however, erase the existence of the ideal, but renders it more remote.

Gulliver's experiences with the horses prove unsettling. The more he identifies with the Yahoo nature he perceives within himself, the more he tries to emulate the rational horses. His rejection of his patient family and his rescuer, Captain Pedro de Mendez, and his decision to live and converse with his own horses "at least four hours every day" can be viewed as either ludicrous or tragic. Swift refuses to provide an easy moralization, and his respect for the complexity of the human condition and recognition of man's infinite capacity for self-deception make *Gulliver's Travels* a perpetual and formidable challenge and warning to the overconfident interpreter who, like the unfortunate sailor Gulliver mentions at the beginning of Book IV, may be "an honest man . . . but a little too positive in his own opinions." Swift seems to be saying that pride may destroy the reader's humanity as it physically destroyed this sailor and mentally destroyed Gulliver.

Swift wrote some of his best poems during the 1730s, following his brilliant prose achievement as Irish apologist and engaging sea traveler to faraway places. This extraordinary literary activity should lay to rest permanently arguments for Swift's physical, mental, and literary decline during these years. *Verses on the Death of Dr. Swift, The Day of Judgement, Strephon and Chloe* (1731); *The Beasts Confession to the Priest* (1732); *An Epistle to a Lady; On Poetry: A Rapsody* (1723); *The Legion Club* (1736) surely number among his better poetic efforts. Indeed, *Verses* and *On Poetry,* in particular, would stand near the top of any list of great Augustan poems. They were so viewed in his own time and continue to inspire perceptive analyses. Moreover, criticism of Swift's verse has recently become a major industry—certainly an unlikely fulfillment of Samuel Johnson's prediction: "In the Poetical Works . . . there is not much upon which the critick can exercise his powers." Three editions (including a revision [1958] of Harold Williams's 1937 edition), a concordance, numerous books and monographs, and scores of articles and conference papers not only attest to this flourishing interest, but also immeasurably enhance our appreciation of Swift's poetic art.

Swift would have savored the irony of these recent developments, for he tended to dismiss his poetic endeavors as mere "trifles" of a "man of rhymes" (Letter to Charles Wogan, 1732). Yet, despite his playful experiments in "left-handed" composition, limericks, peasant balladry, humorous parodies, raillery, as well as some crude scatology, he produced a large body of verse demonstrating a range of feeling, ironic sophistication, skillful versification, and moral seriousness that is worthy of serious attention.

Swift's remarkably large poetic output has not enjoyed as much critical attention as has the other Augustans. He lacks Dryden's broad historical consciousness, capacity to forge meaningful analogies between Biblical narrative or prophecy, Virgilian epic practices, and the rough-and-tumble of seventeenth-century politics. He cannot match Pope's rich allusiveness, complexity of tone, verbal sonorities, and professionalism. His poetry does not have the weight and concentration and tragicomic ambivalence of Johnson's best poems.

Swift's poetic achievement is of a more paradoxical order: social while being intensely personal; at once light-textured and harshly condemnatory; didactic and moralistic through outrageously burlesque efforts; full of fun, playing all sorts of games with rhyme, rhythm, and tone at the same time that it is deadly serious satire; sporting throwaway lines, anticlimax, erratic shifts in mood and tone through carefully contrived artifice. It recoils on itself, constantly challenging its own reason for being by naming itself a fiction. In fact, his rhetorical experimentation makes his verse an ancestor, it would appear, of the "fabulator" motif in the modern novel. Some examples from *On Poetry* illustrate his comic procedures:

> And here a *Simile* comes Pat in:
> Tho' *Chickens* take a Month to fatten.

> But these are not a thousandth Part
> Of Jobbers in the Poets Art,
> Attending each his proper Station,
> And all in due Subordination;
> Thro' ev'ry Alley to be found,
> In Garrets high, or under Ground:
> And when they join their *Pericranies,*
> Out skips a *Book of Miscellanies.*
> *Hobbes* clearly proves that ev'ry Creature
> Lives in a state of War by Nature.

> So, Nat'ralists observe, a Flea
> Hath smaller Fleas that on him prey,
> And these have smaller yet to bite 'em,
> And so proceed *ad infinitum*:
> Thus ev'ry Poet in his Kind,
> Is bit by him that comes behind.

Swift's loathing of delusion in any form is often cited to explain his dislike of conventional literary forms or of traditional modes of thought and ways of feeling. Thus, he mocked the pastoral, georgic, and heroic in art, love poetry, progress poems, and laureate odes. However, any attempt to characterize Swift as an antipoetic realist, satirizing not only pride and pretension but the poetic forms that dignify them, obscures the critical norms created internally, through deliberate ironic jumbling of familiar figures, tropes, and images. Upon closer inspection this so-called realism turns out to be the product of a controlled aesthetic response involving poetic transformations, a mimetic action converting everyday actuality into high poetic seriousness.

Verses on the Death of Dr. Swift provides a fitting summary of his political, clerical, and literary careers. A combination of satiric thrusts and elegiac sentiments, the poem reviews in detail Swift's actual life and times. It compliments his friends, attacks his enemies, and creates through multiple ironies and juxtaposed speaking voices a picture of his ambivalent motives, attitudes, and commitments. Through a series of claims ranging from the purity of his satiric motives to admission of hypocrisy and vanity in fulfilling the poem's epigraph from La Rochefoucault, which states that in friends' adversities we find comfort and pleasure, Swift deliberately distorts and exaggerates the "facts" of his life. As a result, he creates, in the words of two critics, an "attractive and convincing picture" of himself. He characteristically sets the record straight by comically undercutting the self-praise so as to win the reader's assent to his real accomplishments:

> He gave the little Wealth he had,
> To build a House for Fools and Mad:
> And shew'd by one satyric Touch,
> No Nation wanted it so much:
> That Kingdom he hath left his Debtor,
> I wish it soon may have a Better.

Swift was tragically declared "of unsound mind and memory'" on August 17, 1742. On October 19, 1745, he died, leaving the greater part of his estate, as he had promised, to establish a hospital for the insane.

DONALD C. MELL

WORKS: *The Prose Works of Jonathan Swift*. Herbert J. Davis, ed. Shakespeare Head Edition. 14 vols. Oxford: Basil Blackwell, 1939-1968; *The Poems of Jonathan Swift*. Harold Williams, ed. 2d ed. 3 vols. Oxford: Clarendon, 1937/revised 1958; *Swift: Poetic Works*. Herbert J. Davis, ed. London: Oxford University Press, 1967; *A Tale of a Tub and the Battle of the Books*. A. C. Guthkelch & D. Nichol Smith, eds. 2d ed. Oxford: Clarendon, 1958. Correspondence—*Jonathan Swift: Journal to Stella*. Harold Williams, ed. 2 vols. Oxford: Clarendon, 1948; *The Correspondence of Jonathan Swift*. Harold Williams, ed. 5 vols. Oxford: Clarendon, 1963-1965.   REFERENCES: Bibliography—Teerink, Herman. *A Bibliography of the Writings of Jonathan Swift*. 2d ed., revised by A. H. Scouten. Philadelphia: University of Pennsylvania Press, 1963. Biography—Ehrenpreis, Irvin. *Swift: The Man, His Works, and the Age*. 3 vols. projected. Cambridge, Mass.: Harvard University Press, 1962—. Collections of Essays—*Jonathan Swift, 1667-1967: A Dublin Tercentenary Tribute*. Roger McHugh & Philip Edwards, eds. Dublin: Dolmen, 1967; *The World of Jonathan Swift: Essays for the Tercentenary*. Brian Vickers, ed. Cambridge, Mass.: Harvard University Press, 1968. *Fair Liberty Was All His Cry: A Tercentenary Tribute to Jonathan Swift, 1667-1745*. A. Norman Jeffares, ed. London: Macmillan, 1967; Prose—Carnochan, W. B. *Lemuel Gulliver's Mirror for Man*. Berkeley and Los Angeles: University of California Press, 1968; Clark, John R. *Form and Frenzy in Swift's "Tale of a Tub."* Ithaca: Cornell University Press, 1970; Cook, Richard. *Jonathan Swift as a Tory Pamphleteer*. Seattle: University of Washington Press, 1967; Davis, Herbert. *Jonathan Swift: Essays on His Satire and Other Studies*. New York: Oxford University Press, 1964; Harth, Phillip. *Swift and Augustan Rationalism: the Religious Background of "A Tale of a Tub."* Chicago: University of Chicago Press, 1961; Price, Martin. *Swift's Rhetorical Art: A Study in Structure and Meaning*. New Haven: Yale University Press, 1953; Quintana, Ricardo. *The Mind and Art of Jonathan Swift*. New York: Oxford University Press, 1936; Rosenheim, Edward W. *Swift and the Satirist's Art*. Chicago: University of Chicago Press, 1963. Poetry—Fischer, John I. *On Swift's Poetry*. Gainesville: University of Florida Press, 1978; Jaffe, Nora C. *The Poet Swift*.

Hanover: University Press of New England, 1977; Johnson, Maurice. *The Sin of Wit: Jonathan Swift as a Poet.* Syracuse: Syracuse University Press, 1950.

SYNGE, [EDMUND] JOHN MILLINGTON (1871-1909), playwright. Synge was born in Rathfarnham near Dublin on April 16, 1871. The youngest son of a lawyer who died the following year, he lived for most of his life with his mother, next door first to his grandmother, and later to his only sister Annie and her family. Robert, his eldest brother, became an engineer and settled in Argentina; Edward became a land agent in Wicklow and the west of Ireland; Samuel, to whom Synge was closest as a child, and who later published reminiscences of his younger brother in *Letters to My Daughter* (1932), became a medical missionary to China. Except for several brief periods, Synge spent all of his time in Ireland surrounded by family; the indomitable old women of his plays and translations owe much to his admiration for his mother, his grandmother, and elderly aunts.

Never strong as a child and solitary by temperament, Synge's self-absorption and independent critical spirit led him as a young adolescent to reject his family's evangelical teaching (inherited from a long line of clergymen) and to evolve painstakingly his own form of worship. Henceforth, a combination of nature mysticism and moral aestheticism informed all his writings and determined the course of his actions and studies. He attended school irregularly, receiving most of his education through private tuition. With a young cousin Florence Ross as companion, then as a member of the Dublin Naturalists' Field Club, he became a confirmed naturalist and later was to attribute his first religious crisis to the shock of reading Darwin when he was about fourteen. A further departure from family orthodoxy occurred in 1887 when he began studying the violin. At the same time as he attended Trinity College, Dublin, from 1889 to 1892, he was also enrolled at the Royal Irish Academy of Music, and whereas he received from Trinity merely a gentleman's or pass B.A., he won scholarships at the Academy in both counterpoint and harmony. When he joined the Academy orchestra in 1891, he decided to become a professional musician.

This ambition was encouraged by his mother's cousin, Mary Synge, a pianist who visited Dublin in 1893 and offered to accompany her relative to Germany, where he could study the German language and continue his musical education. From late July of that year, Synge boarded in Coblenz with his cousin's friends, the von Eicken sisters, the youngest of whom, Valeska, immediately became his special confidante. Here he established, for the first time outside his family circle, the easy conversational relationship he was to enjoy with women for the rest of his life.

In January, 1894, he moved to Wurzburg, studying both piano and the violin and continuing to compose privately. By spring, however, he was devoting half of his time to writing, and it is likely that when he returned to Ireland in June, he had already decided on a literary career. Later, he reasoned that extreme nervousness as a performer stimulated this change, but in his autobiography he admits that his interest in writing and languages, his devotion to nature, and his love of music had always been in uneasy balance: "I wished to be at once Shakespeare, Beethoven and Darwin; my ambition was boundless and amounted to a real torture in my life. . . . When I was fiddling I mourned over the books I wished to read; when I was reading I yearned for all manner of adventures."

Towards the end of his life, in the preface to his *Poems and Translations,* he was to commend "many of the older poets, such as Villon and Herrick and Burns," who "used the whole of their personal life as their material." From his first determination to be a writer, he seems to have consciously prepared his personality for the event. His naturalism led to an interest in Irish antiquities, which in turn encouraged him to what was then still an uncommon pursuit—the study of the Irish language. He also studied Hebrew and won prizes at Trinity College in both, but the only indication of literary ambitions (his weakest subject was English literature) was the publication in the college journal *Kottabos* in 1893 of a poem heavily influenced by his favorite poet, Wordsworth. Now, however, he resumed his writing of poetry, began a play in German, and on January 1, 1895, arrived in Paris. He joined a students' debating club which he attended faithfully for years, studied literature and languages at the Sorbonne, steeped himself in art and art history, did some tutoring in English, and in his reading ranged widely over contemporary literature, ethics, philosophy, and socialism. Except for four months in Italy in 1896 (when he again attempted to write in the language he was studying and may have first experimented with translating from the Italian), he followed this pattern for the next seven years, spending part of each winter in Paris.

Meanwhile he had fallen in love. Cherrie Matheson, a neighbor, spent several weeks of 1894 with the Synges in Wicklow, where Mrs. Synge regularly rented a house for the summer. A member of the Plymouth Brethren, Cherrie could not accept marriage with a nonbeliever, but Synge, formally proposing in both 1895 and 1896 (the second time seeking his sympathetic mother's unwilling advocacy), did not take rejection easily. Even though he contemplated marriage to at least two women students he met in Paris, his anguish and intellectual resentment over Cherrie are reflected in the arguments of his first play, *When the Moon Has Set,* which he began in 1900. The plot is forced and self-conscious—a young Irish landlord recently returned from Paris successfully woos his nursing cousin, a nun of an indeterminate religious order. In this play, however, we find clear expression of the aesthetic creed behind all of Synge's future work:

> God is in the earth and not above it. In the wet elm leaves trailing in the lane in autumn, in the deserted currents of the streams, and in the breaking out of the sap, there are joys that collect all the joy that

is in religion and art. . . . Every life is a symphony. It is this cosmic
element in the person which gives all personal art, and all sincere
life, and all passionate love a share in the dignity of the world.

More personal and even less controlled than the play is the record of his
spiritual and emotional crises entitled *Vita Vecchia* (1895-1897), a series
of fourteen poems connected by prose narrative. This, together with *Étude
Morbide* (1899), "an imaginary portrait," he soon rejected as being im-
mature, morbid, and unduly influenced by the decadent movement. All three
works were rejected for publication by Yeats* and Lady Gregory* after his
death and were not published until the Oxford edition of his collected
works (1962-1968).

Synge's political awareness increased as he studied socialism and became a close friend of the nationalist journalist and translator Stephen
MacKenna.* His courses in medieval literature and old Irish at the Sorbonne led to an interest in Celtic civilizations, but still from a European
point of view. In December 1896, he met William Butler Yeats* and Maud
Gonne, and through them many of the Irish nationalists at home and abroad.
He joined Maud Gonne's Irish League in Paris, but when he realized that
official membership in *l'Irlande Libre* meant advocating a "revolutionary
and semi-military movement," he resigned to become a passive observer.
Encouraged by MacKenna in Paris and by George Russell (AE)* in Dublin, he also briefly studied Yeats' related interest, the occult. Finally, in
May 1898, he followed Yeats' advice to seek creative inspiration in the
Aran Islands. Henceforth, his sympathies and literary ambitions sharpened
and concentrated, for in the west of Ireland he found that synthesis of
natural and supranatural and astringent reality with the shock of raw joy,
all evidence of the cosmic rhythm he sensed in music, nature, and the
human passions. On the eve of his departure from Aran for the first time,
he received an invitation to visit Lady Gregory* at Coole. Yeats also introduced him to Edward Martyn,* their colleague in the Irish Literary Theatre,*
and Synge determined to join the movement. Later that year, his first account of Aran appeared in the *New Ireland Review*.

But he did not give up Paris; rather, he settled in permanent rooms there,
continued his studies at the Sorbonne, visited Brittany, and wrote an occasional review of contemporary French and Irish writers for various journals. When he returned each summer to Ireland, he continued to join his
mother and her friends in County Wicklow, only then moving on to Aran
before returning to the Continent. Between 1898 and his last visit in the
autumn of 1902, he spent a total of four and a half months on Aran, compared with forty-three months in all living in Paris. But he had been preparing for this return to Ireland all his life, and in *The Aran Islands*, which
he later described as his "first serious piece of work," he found not only the
appropriate form through which to explore his own place in the universe

while maintaining the stance of the uninvolved though sympathetic outsider, but source material for many of his plays. Completed late in 1901 but not published until 1907, the book led to a desire to root out even more primitiveness, in visits to Mayo, Kerry, and the Blasket Islands. A happy collaboration took place in 1905 when *The Manchester Guardian,* through their mutual friend John Masefield, commissioned Synge and Jack Butler Yeats* to do a series of articles on the congested districts of the west of Ireland. Nor did he forget Wicklow, whose paths, mountains, and streams he had explored since childhood: employing the same technique of the wanderer—half drawn into the world he describes, yet distant by temperament and training—he embarked on a series of similar essays distilling the moods, sounds, colors, and movements of the people and their glens.

During the summer of 1902, Synge wrote his two one-act plays, *Riders to the Sea* (based on an incident he had heard of on Aran) and *(In) the Shadow of the Glen* (expressing many of his experiences of the atmosphere of County Wicklow). He also made the first rough draft of his two-act comedy, *The Tinker's Wedding* (originally entitled "The Movements of May," in keeping with his belief in nature's direct impact on man). Instead of going to France, he joined his new theatre colleagues in London the following January, and marked the end of his apprenticeship by moving out of his Paris flat in March 1903. When he returned to Dublin, it was apparent that his fortunes were now tied to the small company of actors led by Willie and Frank Fay who were to form the nucleus of the Irish National Theatre Society. *The Shadow of the Glen* was first produced by them in October 1903, followed by *Riders to the Sea* in February of the next year; he had written both before seeing the company perform. Now, however, he became a member of the group's Reading Committee, accompanied them on various tours, took over the rehearsal of his own plays, and assisted in revising and producing the work of others. By the time the Abbey Theatre* opened in 1904, he was established, with Yeats and Lady Gregory, as one of the leaders of the movement. *The Well of the Saints* was produced in February 1905 and *The Playboy of the Western World,* under riotous circumstances, in January 1907. His last completed play, *Deirdre of the Sorrows,* still not polished to his satisfaction, was performed in January 1910 after his death.

The first indication of the Hodgkins' disease which was to kill Synge was an enlarged gland on the side of his neck which was removed in 1897 (and which, characteristically, Synge made the occasion for an interesting essay, "Under Ether"); similar swellings recurred over the next ten years. Accustomed to walking and bicycling throughout the countryside (and in spite of the asthma he frequently suffered), Synge had an unusually strong constitution. Consequently, he experienced no pain until late in 1907. Many of his poems and translations were written after he began to realize that his illness might be fatal, but at the same time his urge towards a passionate and rich life was strengthened by his love for the Abbey actress Maire (Molly) O'Neill, the younger sister of actress Sara Allgood. For Molly, Synge wrote some of his finest poems and created the roles of Pegeen Mike in *The Playboy of the Western World* and Deirdre in his last play. Sixteen years his junior, she embodied all the qualities Synge most appreciated in life— wayward passion, artistic sensibility, a sensitive response to nature, and romantic natural beauty. He wrote to her almost daily; his letters (published in 1971) not only reveal his personal ambitions and his responses to love and nature, but also document his involvement in management and direction of the Abbey Theatre during its formative years.

These letters also throw light on the painstaking craftsmanship with which Synge honed his plays. Obsessed with the idea of perfection and the achievement of a cosmic and artistic synthesis, he refined and polished every speech and action in an effort to establish the delicate balance between reality and joy (the "romantic" and the "Rabelaisian") which he demanded of his work. "In a good play," he wrote in his preface to *The Playboy of the Western World,* "every speech should be as fully flavoured as a nut or apple," and the simile celebrates his endeavor to draw together sound and senses, light and action, meaning and color. Indeed, this very forcing of audiences to taste and directly respond to the experience before them may well be at the root of the early violent reactions to his plays. Synge's characters feel intensely, speak eloquently, and react simply and immediately to all about them. They dream and project those feelings and wishes onto the reality of their daily lives, creating an impossible tension which leads in the play to further action and in the spectator to a truth he may not be prepared to acknowledge. The world of the play is carefully established and its code and truth are undeniably familiar, while at the same time other worlds are found to be not only possible but seductively preferable. His people are rooted, as Synge felt all poetry should be, in "the clay and worms," but, like Old Mahon in *The Playboy,* they are constantly "shying clods again the visage of the stars."

Thus, in his black comedy *The Well of the Saints,* Martin Doul, "a little dark stump of a fellow looks the fool of the world," speaks persuasively of "sitting blind, hearing a soft wind turning round the little leaves of the spring and feeling the sun, and we not tormenting our souls with the sight of the grey days, and the holy men, and the dirty feet is trampling the world." So he and blind Mary turn their backs on the working, seeing world and choose probable death in the mythical south, "where the people will have kind voices maybe, and we don't know their bad looks or their villainy at all." The young lovers of *Deirdre of the Sorrows* put "a sharp end to the day is brave and glorious, as our fathers put a sharp end to the days of the kings of Ireland." As they chose life in the woods, now they seek the safety of the grave and "a story will be told forever." Even Nora of *The Shadow of the Glen* is fully aware of the choice she makes between a sheltered life with her cold, queer, unyielding husband in the lonely mist-ridden Wicklow glen, and walking the roads below with the sweetly talking Tramp: "I'm thinking it's myself will be wheezing that time with lying down under the Heavens when the night is cold, but you've a fine bit of talk, stranger, and it's with yourself I'll go." And in the rollicking, outrageous farce *The Tinker's Wedding* ("too dangerous to be performed in Dublin" for almost fifty years), young Sarah Casey falters in her ambition to be at one with the married orthodox Christian community only when drunken old Mary Byrne proves the impossibility of conforming to the priest and "his like." Only in Synge's tragic tone poem *Riders to the Sea* is there deliberate simplicity and singleness of mood and action; this distillation of the harsh fateful life on Aran reflects the greater rhythm of timeless nature.

In October 1908, while Synge was convalescing in Germany with his old friends the von Eicken sisters, his mother, whose courage and steadfastness he captured so admirably in his first tragedy, died. His own death followed on March 24, 1909, in Dublin. He was correcting the proofs of *Poems and Translations* when he entered hospital for the last time. Much of the poignancy of these late poems and of the speeches of Deirdre bear witness to his increasing appreciation of the "fiery and magnificent, and tender" popular imagination which he discovered in Ireland and celebrated so singlemindedly in his life and his works. After his death, Yeats wrote of Synge in his diaries, "He had that egotism of the man of genius which Nietzsche compares to the egotism of a woman with child. . . . In the arts he knew no language but his own."

ANN SADDLEMYER

WORKS: "Letters of John Millington Synge from Material Supplied by Max Meyerfeld," *Yale Review* (July 1924): 690-709; *Collected Works Volume I: Poems*. Robin Skelton, ed. London: Oxford University Press, 1962; *Collected Works Volume II: Prose*. Alan Price, ed. London: Oxford University Press, 1966; *Collected Works, Volumes III and IV: Plays*. Ann Saddlemyer, ed. London: Oxford University Press, 1968; *Letters to Molly: John Millington Synge to Maire O'Neill*. Ann Saddlemyer, ed. Cambridge, Mass.: Belknap, 1971; *My Wallet of Photographs*, selected by L. M. Stephens. Dublin: Dolmen, 1971; *Some Letters of John M. Synge to Lady Gregory and W. B. Yeats*. Ann Saddlemyer, ed. Dublin: Cuala, 1971; "Synge to MacKenna: The Mature Years." Ann Saddlemyer, ed. *Massachusetts Review* 5, No. 2 (Winter 1964): 279-295. REFERENCES: Bushrui, S.B., ed. *Sunshine and the Moon's Delight: A Centenary Tribute to John Millington Synge*. Gerrards Cross: Colin Smythe, 1972; Greene, David H., & Stephens, Edward M. *J. M. Synge 1871-1909*. New York: Macmillan, 1959; Gregory, Isabella Augusta. *Our Irish Theatre*. London: Putnam, 1913; Harmon, Maurice, ed. *J. M. Synge Centenary Papers 1971*. Dublin: Dolmen, 1972. Howarth, Herbert. *The Irish Writers 1880-1940*. London: Rockliff, 1958; Kilroy, James. *The 'Playboy' Riots*. Dublin: Dolmen, 1971; Price, Alan. *Synge and Anglo-Irish Drama*. London: Methuen, 1961; Saddlemyer, Ann. *J. M. Synge and Modern Comedy*. Dublin: Dolmen Press, 1968; Saddlemyer, Ann. "Synge and the Doors of Perception," *Place, Personality and the Irish Writer*. Andrew Carpenter, ed. Gerrards Cross: Colin Smythe, 1977, pp. 97-120; Skelton, Robin. *J. M. Synge and His World*.

New York: Viking/London: Thames & Hudson, 1971; Skelton, Robin. *The Writings of J. M. Synge.* New York: Bobbs-Merrill/London: Thames & Hudson, 1971; Skelton, Robin, & Saddlemyer, Ann, eds. *The World of W. B. Yeats.* Seattle: University of Washington Press, 1965; Stephens, Edward M. *My Uncle John.* Andrew Carpenter, ed. London: Oxford University Press, 1974; Synge, Samuel. *Letters to My Daughter: Memories of John Millington Synge.* Dublin: Talbot, 1932; *The Synge Manuscripts in the Library of Trinity College Dublin.* Dublin: Dolmen for the Library, 1971; Yeats, William Butler. *Autobiographies.* London: Macmillan, 1955.

TATE, NAHUM (1652-1715), poet and dramatist. Tate added nothing to Irish and little of value to English literature. His father, a Puritan divine with the remarkable name of Faithful Teate, was briefly provost of Trinity College, Dublin. His second son Nahum was born in Dublin in 1652 and received a B.A. from Trinity (about which he later wrote some deplorable verses) in 1672. He was a prolific writer of poems and plays, but much of his work was adaptation, translation, or collaboration. Sir Walter Scott called him "one of those second-rate bards, who, by dint of pleonasm and expletive, can find smooth lines if anyone will supply them with ideas." And Alexander Pope has derisively immortalized him in *The Dunciad.* Tate wrote most of the second part of Dryden's "Absalom and Achitophel," and his stage work included adaptations of Shakespeare, Chapman and Marston, Fletcher, and Webster. His happy ending version of *King Lear* is notorious; and, although Dr. Johnson liked it and it held the stage for nearly two hundred years, it gave rise to the term "Tateification," which means the debasement of a masterpiece. With Nicholas Brady he published in 1696 *A New Version of the Psalms;* but he did write the libretto for Purcell's *Dido and Aeneas,* and for that much may be forgiven. His only original poem of note is "Panacea—a Poem upon Tea." He was appointed Poet Laureate in 1692, succeeding Shadwell; Southey thought that only Shadwell was a poorer Poet Laureate than Tate. Personally he seems to have been an unprepossessing man. He died in London on July 30, 1715.

WORKS: *Poems.* 2nd ed., enlarged. London: B. Tooke, 1684; *Panacea: A Poem upon Tea.* London: J. Roberts, 1700; *Dido and Aeneas.* [London]: Boosey & Hawkes, [1961]. (Facsimile of the first edition). REFERENCES: Spencer, Christopher. *Nahum Tate.* New York: Twayne, 1972; Scott-Thomas, H. F. *The Life and Works of Nahum Tate.* 2 vols. Baltimore: Johns Hopkins University, 1932. (Doctoral dissertation).

THOMPSON, SAM (1916-1965), playwright. Thompson was a Belfast working man and, like Brendan Behan* whom he somewhat resembles, a painter. He was born on May 21, 1916, in Belfast. He was encouraged in his early writing by Sam Hanna Bell* who produced several of his early plays, such as *Brush in Hand* (1956), for radio. Thompson's first stage play, *Over the Bridge,* was a realistic study of a sectarian labor dispute. Although basically a plea for good will and religious tolerance, the play

660 TODHUNTER, JOHN

was already in rehearsal by the Ulster Group Theatre* when the theatre's directors withdrew it. The reason given was a determination "not to mount any play which would offend or affront the religious or political beliefs or sensibilities of the man in the street. . . ." However, when Thompson and friends produced it themselves at the Empire Theatre in Belfast in 1960, it had a most successful and highly acclaimed run. *Over the Bridge* is not a great play, but it is craftsmanlike and well observed; it deals with the crucial Northern problem of religious bigotry which probably only St. John Ervine* in *Mixed Marriage* had until that time put so bluntly on the stage. Thompson's later work, all unpublished, included *The Evangelist* (1963), a study of religious fanaticism, and *Cemented with Love* (1965), a television play about political chicanery. He himself was involved in union work and stood unsuccessfully for political office. He also had begun to act for the stage and for television when he died unexpectedly in Belfast on February 15, 1965, of a heart attack. Stewart Parker* described his death as "a grievous loss to Irish drama."

WORK: *Over the Bridge,* edited & introduced by Stewart Parker. Dublin: Gill & Macmillan, 1970.

TODHUNTER, JOHN (1839-1916), poet and dramatist. Todhunter was born in Dublin on December 29 or 30, 1839. He received an M.D. from Trinity College, Dublin, in 1871, and practiced medicine briefly in Dublin; he also taught English at Alexandra College. In 1874, he left for London where he became a friend of the Yeats family and a member of the Rhymer's Club. In about 1888, he directed his prolific pen toward Irish subjects, such as conventionally lamenting lyrics, retellings of portions of the Bardic tales, and a life of Sarsfield, the well-loved Irish hero who opposed the forces of William of Orange in 1690 and 1691. Stephen Gwynn* states that Todhunter's poem "Aghadoe" is deservedly found in every anthology of Irish verse, but that is a gentle and recently incorrect assessment. Todhunter was a fluent technician, but he saw the world through the eyes of previous (and mainly English) poets. Hence, his verse has a generally correct if academic dullness, and is little read today.

Todhunter's plays are neither particularly good nor modern, but they had some intellectual success in their day. *Alcestis* was done at Hengler's Circus in 1879; Beerbohm Tree appeared in *Helena in Troas* in 1886; at a minor production of *A Sicilian Idyll* in 1890, W. B. Yeats* first saw Florence Farr; J. T. Grein's Independent Theatre staged his *The Black Cat* in 1893; and in 1894, Florence Farr, with the backing of Miss A.E.F. Horniman, produced *A Comedy of Sighs* at the Avenue Theatre. This last-named play is probably Todhunter's most important contribution to Irish literature. However, the play failed so signally that Florence Farr replaced it with another new piece, Bernard Shaw's* *Arms and the Man,* and this was Shaw's first semi-success on the English stage. The curtain-raiser for both

A Comedy of Sighs and *Arms and the Man* was *The Land of Heart's Desire,* W. B. Yeats' first staged play. So, in effect, if Todhunter was himself an unsuccessful dramatist, he was something of a John the Baptist to the most notable poetic and prose dramatists in English in the twentieth century. He died on October 25, 1916, in Chiswick, England.

WORKS: *Laurella and Other Poems.* London, 1876; *Alcestis.* London, 1879; *A Study of Shelley.* London: Kegan Paul, 1880; *Forest Songs and Other Poems.* London: Kegan Paul, 1881; *The True Tragedy of Rienzi, Tribune of Rome.* London: Kegan Paul, 1881; *Helena in Troas.* London: Kegan Paul, 1886; *The Banshee, and Other Poems.* London: Kegan Paul, 1888; *A Sicilian Idyll.* London: Elkin Mathews, 1890; *The Black Cat.* London: Henry, 1893; *Three Irish Bardic Tales.* London: J. M. Dent, 1896; *Life of Patrick Sarsfield, Earl of Lucan.* London: Unwin/Dublin: Sealy, Bryers & Walker, 1901; *From the Land of Dreams.* Introduction by T. W. Rolleston. Dublin: Talbot/London: Unwin, 1918. (Irish poems); *Essays.* Foreword by Standish O'Grady. London: Elkin Mathews, 1920; *Isolt of Ireland: A Legend in a Prologue and Three Acts; and The Passion Flower.* London & Toronto: J. M. Dent, 1927; *Trivium Amoris, and the Wooing of Artemis.* London & Toronto: J. M. Dent, 1927; *Selected Poems.* E. L. Todhunter & A. P. Graves, eds. London: E. Mathews & Marrot, 1929.

TOMELTY, JOSEPH (1911-), playwright, novelist, and actor. Tomelty was born on March 12, 1911, at Portaferry near Belfast. He was a founding member, in the early 1940s, of the Group Theatre in Belfast, as well as one of its leading actors and playwrights. The Group produced some of his local Belfast comedies, such as *Barnum Was Right* and *Right Again, Barnum,* as well as his three best plays: *The End House* (1944), *All Souls' Night* (1948), and *Is the Priest at Home?* (1954). *The End House* is almost, if not quite, a Belfast equivalent of *Juno and the Paycock; All Souls' Night* is a tragedy reminiscent, if not the equal, of *Riders to the Sea;* and *Is the Priest at Home?* is a realistic but sympathetic depiction of the daily life of a cleric. Tomelty also published two worthy, if not superb, novels, *Red Is the Port Light* (1948) and *The Apprentice* (1955). He had a highly successful career as a character actor in British films and television. His versatile and talented productivity was severely truncated by an extremely serious automobile accident in 1955.

WORKS: *Red Is the Port Light.* London: Jonathan Cape, 1948; *Right Again, Barnum.* Belfast: H. R. Carter, [1950]; *The Apprentice: The Story of a Nonentity.* London: Jonathan Cape, 1953; *Mugs and Money (Barnum Was Right).* Belfast: H. R. Carter, 1953; *Is the Priest at Home?* Belfast: H. R. Carter, 1954; *All Souls' Night.* Belfast: H. R. Carter, 1955; *The End House.* Dublin: James Duffy, 1962.

TONE, [THEOBALD] WOLFE (1763-1798), patriot and autobiographer. Tone was born in Dublin on June 20, 1763, the eldest son of a coach builder of some means. While still a schoolboy, he developed a passion for military life, but his father insisted that he attend Trinity College, Dublin, where he was an able but unwilling student. In 1785, while still at Trinity, he eloped with sixteen-year-old Martha Witherington of Grafton Street and married her, spending the honeymoon in Maynooth. On graduating from Trinity, he read law in Dublin and London and was called to the Bar in 1789. "As to law, I knew exactly as much about it as I did of necromancy," Tone wrote in his *Autobiography*. Politics was his real interest, and in 1791 he was among those who formed the Society of United Irishmen, a movement uniting Catholics and Protestants to secure parliamentary reform. Although an agnostic of Protestant background, he was appointed secretary of the Catholic Committee in the following year. The Relief Act of 1793 was brought about largely through his efforts, and the Catholic Committee awarded him a gold medal and the sum of £1,500.

The concessions granted by the act were by no means adequate, and the United Irishmen began to plan a rebellion. The authorities seized some documents that revealed that Tone was in correspondence with the French, and so he sailed for America with his wife and children. He landed in Wilmington, Delaware, and had just settled to the life of an American farmer in Princeton, New Jersey, when letters arrived from the United Irishmen asking him to go to France to seek aid for Ireland. Although he could hardly speak French and had no letters of introduction, he set out immediately. Astonishingly, he succeeded in getting the French Directory to appoint General Lazarre Hoche as Commander-in-Chief of an Irish expedition. In December 1796, a large fleet with fifteen thousand soldiers aboard set sail for Ireland. Tone sailed with them as an adjutant general. Unfortunately, a hurricane prevented the soldiers from landing. A year later, the French sent their Dutch fleet, but it was defeated at sea. In 1798, the year of the Irish rebellion, two smaller fleets were defeated. Tone was aboard one of the ships of the second fleet and was captured, court-martialed, and sentenced to be hanged, in spite of his request for a soldier's death by shooting. Tone's father, aided by John Philpot Curran, tried to save him by seeking a writ of Habeas Corpus, but while this action was in progress Tone cut his own throat and died of his wounds on November 19, 1798.

If history had been otherwise, Tone might well be remembered primarily as an Irish writer. While a poor student in London, he wrote articles for money and also collaborated on a burlesque novel, *Belmont Castle*, which was a satire of current popular fiction. But, although gifted as a writer, Tone was interested in writing only as a means to communicate his political ideals. Even his *Autobiography,* which is considered an Irish classic, was written to instruct his children. This work was published in Washington in 1826 in a volume entitled *The Life of Theobald Wolfe Tone,* edited by his son William, along with Tone's diaries, autobiographical memoranda, letters, political writings, and accounts by the son of Tone's death and his family. The *Autobiography* is so engaging on Tone's early life and marriage that it is impossible to remain detached from his political beliefs. The clear strong prose is free of the verbal pomposity of John

Mitchel* and reveals an affectionate and fun-loving young man. Nevertheless, he grew fanatical and wrote, for instance, of the young French soldiers: "Many fine lads of twenty, who have sacrificed an arm or a leg to the liberty of their country. I could worship them." There are also amusing accounts of his interviews with the leaders of the French Revolution and his impressions of eighteenth-century Paris. Tone's last letters to his wife are so heart-rending in their simple courage that one cannot help wishing that he had remained living happily as an American farmer.

MARY ROSE CALLAGHAN

WORKS: *Life of Theobald Wolfe Tone . . . Written by Himself, and Continued by his Son. . . ,* William Theobald Wolfe Tone, ed. Washington: Gales & Seaton, 1826/ London: Henry Colburn, 1827/abridged by Seán O'Faoláin, London: Nelson, 1937; *The Letters of Wolfe Tone,* Bulmer Hobson, ed. Dublin: Martin Lester, [1921]; *The Best of Tone,* Proinsias Mac Aonghusa & Liam Ó Réagáin, eds. Cork: Mercier, [1972].   REFERENCES: de Blacam, A. S. *The Life Story of Wolfe Tone.* Dublin: Talbot/London: Rich and Cowan, 1935; Mac Dermot, Frank. *Theobald Wolfe Tone and his Times.* London: Macmillan, 1939/Tralee: Anvil, 1968.

TRACY, HONOR (1913-), humorist. Although an Englishwoman, Honor Tracy is best known for her humorous novels and sketches about contemporary Irish life. She was born Honor Lilbush Wingfield Tracy in Bury St. Edmunds, Suffolk, on October 19, 1913. She was educated privately in London and in Germany, and she spent two years at the Sorbonne. From 1934 to 1937, she worked for a London publisher, and from 1937 until the outbreak of the war she worked as a free-lance writer. She served for two years in the British Women's Auxiliary Air Force, and then from 1941 to 1945 was attached to the Ministry of Information as a Japanese specialist. Following the war, she was a journalist for *The Observer* and *The Sunday Times,* and a frequent contributor to the BBC Third Programme.

Her first book, *Kakemono* (1950), was a nonfictional account of her adventures in American-occupied Japan; she was later to write several books about Spain. Her identification with Ireland began with *Mind You, I've Said Nothing!* (1953), an hilarious collection of essays about the mores and manners of postwar Ireland. The wit is often astringent, but it only thinly disguises Tracy's affection for the dottier quirks of the Irish. Her first and probably best known novel, *The Straight and Narrow Path* (1956), established her as a satirical novelist of note. In this work she handled the Marian frenzy of the 1950s and the litigiousness of the Irish with a malicious tenderness. Her subsequent novels, about ten in number, are more or less in the same vein.

Tracy is an enviable stylist who satirizes both the Anglo-Irish and the Mere-Irish with equal wickedness. Her characters, although often pushed to caricature, are so gorgeously ridiculous that it is hard to read any of her novels without chuckling out loud. Nevertheless, she does not have the stature of an Evelyn Waugh, for she tilts mainly at quirks and foibles rather than at anything of significant import. Her books are pleasant reading, but neither her characters nor their adventures are very memorable.

She lives in Achill Island in County Mayo.

MARY ROSE CALLAGHAN

WORKS: *The Conquest of Violence.* Translated from Bartholomeus' *De Overwinning van het geweld.* London: G. Routledge, 1937/New York: E. P. Dutton, 1938; *Kakemono, a Sketch Book of Post-War Japan.* London: Methuen, 1950; *Mind You, I've Said Nothing! Forays in the Irish Republic.* London: Methuen, 1953; *The Deserters.* London: Methuen, 1954; *The Straight and Narrow Path.* London: Methuen/ New York: Random House, 1956; *Silk Hats and No Breakfast. Notes on a Spanish Journey.* London: Methuen, 1957/New York: Random House, 1958; *The Prospects Are Pleasing.* London: Methuen/New York: Random House, 1958; *A Number of Things.* London: Methuen/New York: Random House, 1960; *A Season of Mists.* London: Methuen/New York: Random House, 1961; *The First Day of Friday.* London: Methuen/New York: Random House, 1963; *Spanish Leaves.* London: Methuen/ New York: Random House, 1964; *Men at Work.* London: Methuen, 1966/New York: Random House, 1967; *The Beauty of the World.* London: Methuen, 1967/also published as *Settled in Chambers,* New York: Random House, 1968; *The Butterflies of the Province.* New York: Random House, 1970; *The Quiet End of Evening.* London: Eyre Methuen/New York: Random House, 1972; *Winter in Castille.* London: Eyre Methuen, 1973/New York: Random House, 1975; *In a Year of Grace.* New York: Random House, 1974/London: Eyre Methuen, 1975; *The Man from Next Door.* London: Hamilton, 1977.

TREACY, MAURA (1946-), short story writer. Treacy was born in County Kilkenny in 1946 and has published stories in the New Irish Writing page of *The Irish Press.* Her story "The Weight of the World" won the 1974 Listowel Writers' Week story competition and is included in her volume *Sixpence in Her Shoe.* The stories in this collection are largely about women from youth to old age and generally take place in rural settings. Her work is well observed and well crafted, if not, thus far, particularly exciting.

WORK: *Sixpence in Her Shoe.* Swords, County Dublin: Poolbeg, 1977.

TREVOR, WILLIAM (1928-), novelist and short story writer. William Trevor, the pseudonym of William Trevor Cox, was born in Cork on May 24, 1928, was educated at St. Columba's College, County Dublin, and Trinity College, Dublin, and now lives in Devon. A member of the Irish Academy of Letters, he has written novels, short stories, plays, and television scripts. He has received such literary awards as the Hawthornden Prize for Literature (1964), Whitbread Literary Award (1976), and the Allied Irish Banks Prize for Literature (1976).

According to Terence de Vere White* (August 10, 1976, *Irish Times* interview), Trevor is a former practicing sculptor whose writing style was influenced by a study of the Book of Kells, as well as by Joyce* and Dickens. His prizewinning novels do exhibit an intricate maze of characters and incidents. As Mark Mortimer shows in *Etudes Irlandaises,* one of his novels, *Mrs. Eckdorf in O'Neill's Hotel* (1969), recreates Dublin's atmosphere and people as successfully as Joyce ever did. The novels are psychological studies of unworthy enthusiasms and build up to Dickensian comic scenes which occur shortly before the expected catastrophes. The clothes fiasco of *The Boarding House* (1965) and the monkey business of *The Love Department* (1966), movie-style slapstick scenes, momentarily dispel the gloom of the novels in which they appear. In addition, Trevor creates believably bizarre characters, such as the lonely, garrulous Agnes Eckdorf, and his latest character, fifteen-year-old Timothy Gedge *(Children of Dynmouth,* 1976), who uncovers and spreads the town's secrets, creates suspicions in the minds of many, and willfully fantasizes his own past and future importance. Because Trevor generally focuses on the psychology of misfits, his novels are likely to gain more critical than popular approval. (In fact, they have already been praised by Graham Greene, Anthony Powell, and Evelyn Waugh.) His humorous and conventional short stories, however, will continue to reach popular audiences. They share with the novels a precise use of language and an artist's eye for character and setting.

JACK W. WEAVER

WORKS: *A Standard of Behaviour.* London: Hutchinson, 1958; *The Old Boys.* London: Bodley Head/New York: Viking, 1964; *The Boarding House.* London: Bodley Head/New York: Viking, 1965; *The Day We Got Drunk on Cake and Other Stories.* London: Bodley Head, 1967/New York: Viking, 1968; *The Love Department.* London: Bodley Head, 1966/New York: Viking, 1967; *Mrs. Eckdorf in O'Neill's Hotel.* London: Bodley Head, 1969/New York: Viking, 1970; *Miss Gomez and the Brethren.* London: Bodley Head, 1971; *Penguin Modern Stories,* with others. London: Penguin, 1971; *The Ballroom of Romance and Other Stories.* London: Bodley Head/ New York: Viking, 1972; *Going Home.* London: Samuel French, 1972. (Play); *A Night with Mrs. da Tonka.* London: Samuel French, 1972. (Play); *Elizabeth Alone.* London: Bodley Head, 1973/New York: Viking, 1974; *The Last Lunch of the Season.* London: Covent Garden Press, 1973. (Story); *Marriages.* London: Samuel French, 1974; *Angels at the Ritz and Other Stories.* London: Bodley Head, 1975; *The Children of Dynmouth.* London: Bodley Head, 1976; *Lovers of Their Time.* London: Bodley Head, 1978.   REFERENCE: Mortimer, Mark. "William Trevor in Dublin." *Etudes Irlandaises* (Lille), 4 (November 1975): 77-85.

TYNAN, KATHARINE (1861-1931), poet, novelist, and journalist. Tynan was born on January 21, 1861, in County Dublin. In 1868, she moved with her family to Whitehall, the hospitable farm in Clondalkin which was her home until her marriage. From 1869 to 1875, she attended the convent school of St. Catherine of Drogheda, her only formal education. It was during this period that she suffered from an ulcerated eye condition which, though cured, left her severely myopic.

As mistress of her father's house during the 1880s, Kate was hostess of a highly respected literary salon and met W. B. Yeats,* the great friend of her youth. Her first published poems appeared in the first offering of the Irish Literary Revival, *Poems and Ballads of Young Ireland,* in which she was the youngest collaborator. Other poems appeared in the Catholic nationalist magazine *The Irish Monthly,* and her first collection, *Louise*

de la Valliere (1885), an immediate success, established her as the most
promising young poet of the Irish Renaissance.

In 1893, she married Henry Albert Hinkson, a barrister and a classics
scholar. The Hinksons moved to England where he tutored and she began
a career in journalism in which she soon became a regular contributor to
*The Irish Statesman,** Sketch, The Illustrated London News, The English
Illustrated, The Pall Mall Gazette, The National Observer,* and, in the
United States, *The Providence* [Rhode Island] *Journal, Catholic World,*
and *The* [Boston] *Pilot.* Her journalistic pieces—some literary interviews,
but mostly articles on education, the working conditions of shopgirls, infan-
ticide, and the plight of unwed mothers—as well as the novels of social
protest she had begun to write in the 1890s, in which she celebrated the
evangelicism of the middle class, endeared her to a large reading public.

When Henry was appointed resident magistrate for County Mayo in
1911, the Hinksons returned to Ireland with their three children. Despite
the Tynan family's strong Parnellite and Republican sympathies, by 1911
both Katharine and her husband identified themselves clearly as British
subjects. As magistrate during the tragic years of the Rising and its aftermath, Hinkson evinced no discomfort at having to support pro-British
policy, and his wife retained a middle-class horror of insurrection. For her
the Rising was a "rebellion," and as such a terrible and irreconcilable embarrassment.

With the death of her husband in 1919, Mrs. Hinkson, who had always
contributed substantially to the family income, was forced to make her
living by writing. Accordingly, the last ten years of her life show an astonishing output. Since her neutrality made residence in Ireland impossible, she
lived in England and traveled extensively and intrepidly in politically chaotic
Western Europe. With her daughter Pamela as her guide and co-journalist,
she wrote articles on the countries she visited and found herself in danger
more than once. She continued to write poetry, published at least seventy
novels, and many short stories—even though she was nearly blind. She
died on April 2, 1931, in London after a brief illness.

Katharine Tynan was once considered the most promising poet of the
Irish Renaissance and during her lifetime was immensely popular. Sadly,
she ceased to develop her gifts or stifled them by directing her energies to
the mass production of works that appealed to the popular taste. (Her
oeuvre numbers 105 novels, 12 short story collections, 3 plays, 18 poetry
collections, 2 poetry anthologies, 7 books of devotions, 12 collections of
memoirs, essays, and criticism, 2 biographies, and countless uncollected
articles and stories.) One reason was surely financial necessity, but another was her latent recognition that her inner vision was limited to the
celebration of external realities, and that in celebrating these in her poetry,
she had gone as far as she could go. Despite her uniqueness among contemporary Irish writers as a spokesman of an unquestioning faith in Ca-

tholicism and the champion of the rights of women, the speed at which she was forced to work prevented her from reaching beneath the surface or beyond the middle class for her values. Consequently, the one writer to whom the most space is devoted in the British Museum Catalogue remains a minor poet, albeit of first rank, and a writer without a single epitomizing work.

When she was not being consciously professional and when she spoke most honestly from personal experience—that is, in her poetry—Katharine Tynan excelled. The early verse *(Louise de la Valliere* and *Shamrocks)* culminated in *Ballads and Lyrics* (1891), a collection of descriptive nature poetry which shows the young poet already a master of the lyric. Her poetry continued to advance: *A Lover's Breast-Knot* (1896), a celebration of marital love, was followed by her finest collection, *The Wind in the Trees* (1898), which again was almost exclusively nature poetry and evoked that of the early Wordsworth. The deft metrics of this collection were perfected in *Innocencies* (1905), a pre-Freudian celebration of the eros of motherhood. From this point on, her poetry declined noticeably. The two volumes of war poems, *The Holy War* (1916) and *Herb O'Grace* (1918), are remembered only because the first was quoted from Catholic and Anglican pulpits alike, and the second contained a single remarkable poem, "Comfort," in which a bereaved mother is comforted for her son's death by the knowledge that she will never have to share his love with a daughter-in-law.

As Tynan's poetry dwelled on what should endure, her novels, in which she was less artistically successful, showed what needed change. The earlier novels which took their themes from the journalistic pieces are the tales of the villain redeemed. These novels often testify to a strong feminism which is still compatible with motherhood and domesticity. In the later novels, many written with the younger reader in mind, she turned to historical romance and swashbuckling adventure.

Tynan's four volumes of memoirs *(Twenty-Five Years, The Middle Years, The Wandering Years,* and *The Years of Shadow)* contain sketches of literary friends and acquaintances. In addition, they present a sincere and candid self-appraisal of herself as a woman circumscribed by class values, who aspired neither to heroism nor genius, but who in fifty years of writing achieved something of substantial, though selective, worth.

M. KELLY LYNCH

WORKS: *Louise de la Valliere.* London: Kegan Paul, 1885. (Poems); *Shamrocks.* London: Kegan Paul, 1887. (Poems); *Ballads and Lyrics.* London: Kegan Paul, 1891. (Poems); *A Nun, Her Friends and Her Order.* London: Kegan Paul, 1891. (Biography of Mother Mary Xavier Fallon); *Cuckoo Songs.* London: E. Mathews & J. Lane, 1894. (Poems); *An Isle of Water.* London: A. & C. Black, 1895. (Short stories); *Miracle Plays: Our Lord's Coming and Childhood.* London: J. Lane, 1895. (Verse plays); *The Way of a Maid.* London: Lawrence & Bullen, 1895. (Novel); *A Lover's Breast-Knot.* London: E. Mathews, 1896. (Poems); *The Wind in the Trees.* London:

G. Richards, 1898. (Poems); *The Queen's Page*. London: Lawrence & Bullen, 1899. (Novel); *A Daughter of Kings*. London: Smith, Elder & Co., 1900. (Novel); *Poems*. London: Lawrence & Bullen, 1901; *The Sweet Enemy*. London: Archibald Constable & Co., 1901. (Novel); *Julia*. London: Smith, Elder & Co., 1904. (Novel); *Innocencies*. London: A. H. Bullen, 1905. (Poems); *The Story of Bawn*. London: Smith, Elder & Co., 1906. (Novel); *Her Ladyship*. London: Smith, Elder & Co., 1907. (Novel); *A Little Book of Twenty-four Carols*. Portland, Me.: T. B. Mosher, 1907. (Lyrics); *Twenty-one Poems*. Dundrum: Dun Emer, 1907. (Poems selected by W. B. Yeats); *The Lost Angel*. London: John Milne, 1908. (Stories); *Mary Grey*. London: Cassel & Co., 1908. (Novel); with Maitland, Francis—*The Book of Flowers*. London: Smith & Elder, 1909. *A Little Book for John Mahoney's Friends*. Portland, Me.: T. B. Mosher, 1909. (Poems); *Peggy the Daughter*. London: Cassell & Co., 1909. (Novel); *Betty Carew*. London: Smith, Elder & Co., 1910. (Novel); *Freda*. London: Cassell & Co., 1910. (Novel); *New Poems*. London: Sidgwick & Jackson, 1911; *The Story of Celia*. London: Smith, Elder & Co., 1911. (Novel); *Princess Katherine*. London: Ward, Lock & Co., 1912. (Novel); *Rose of the Garden*. London: Constable & Co., 1912. (Novel); *Irish Poems*. London: Sidgwick & Jackson, 1913; *A Midsummer Rose*. London: Smith, Elder & Co., 1913. (Novel); *Twenty-Five Years*. London: Smith, Elder & Co., 1913. (Memoirs); *The Wild Harp*. London: Sidgwick & Jackson, 1913. (Selection of Irish poetry edited by Katharine Tynan Hinkson); *The Flower of Peace*. London: Burn & Oates, 1914. (Devotional poetry); *Flower of Youth*. London: Sidgwick & Jackson, 1915. (War-time poems); *The Holy War*. London: Sidgwick & Jackson, 1916. (Poems); *Lord Edward*. London: Smith, Elder & Co., 1916. (A study of Edward Fitzgerald); *The Middle Years*. London: Constable & Co., 1916. (Memoirs); *Late Songs*. London: Sidgwick & Jackson, 1917. (Poems); *Herb O'Grace*. London: Sidgwick & Jackson, 1918. (Poems); *Miss Gascoigne*. London: J. Murray, 1918. (Novel); *Love of Brothers*. London: Constable & Co., 1919. (Novel); *The Man from Australia*. London: W. Collins Sons & Co., 1919. (Novel); *The Years of the Shadow*. London: Constable & Co., 1919. (Memoirs); *Denys the Dreamer*. London: W. Collins Sons & Co., 1920. (Novel); *The House*. London: W. Collins Sons & Co., 1920. (Novel); *The Second Wife*. London: John Murray, 1921. (With "A July Rose": nouvelles); *Evensong*. Oxford: Basil Blackwell, 1922. (Poems); *The Wandering Years*. London: Constable & Co., 1922. (Memoirs); *Pat, the Adventurer*. London: Ward, Lock & Co., 1923. (Novel); *They Loved Greatly*. London: E. Nash & Grayson, 1923. (Novel); *The Golden Rose*. London: E. Nash & Grayson, 1924. (Novel); *The House of Doom*. London: Eveleigh Nash & Grayson, 1924. (Novel); *Memories*. London: E. Nash & Grayson, 1924. (Essays); *Life in the Occupied Area*. London: Hutchinson & Co., 1925. (Essays); *Miss Phipps*. London: Ward, Lock & Co., 1925. (Novel); *The Moated Grange*. London: W. Collins Sons & Co., 1926. (Novel, later *The Night of Terror*); *The Face in the Picture*. London: Ward, Lock & Co., 1927. (Novel); *Twilight Songs*. Oxford: Basil Blackwell, 1927. (Poems); *Castle Perilous*. London: Ward, Lock & Co., 1928. (Novel); *The House in the Forest*. London: Ward, Lock & Co., 1928. (Novel); *Lover of Women*. London: W. Collins Sons & Co., 1928. (Novel); *A Fine Gentleman*. London: Ward, Lock & Co., 1929. (Novel); *A Most Charming Family*. London: Ward, Lock & Co., 1929. (Novel); *The Rich Man*. London. W. Collins Sons & Co., 1929. (Novel); *The River*. London: W. Collins Sons & Co., 1929. (Novel); *The Admirable Simmons*. London: Ward, Lock & Co., 1930. (Novel); *Collected Poems*. London: Macmillan, 1930; *Grayson's Girl*. London: W. Collins Sons & Co., 1930. (Novel); *The Playground*. London: Ward, Lock & Co., 1930. (Novel); *Her Father's Daughter*. London: W. Collins Sons & Co., 1930. (Novel).   REFERENCES: Alspach, Russell K. "The Poetry of Katharine Tynan Hinkson." *The Ireland America Review* 4 (1940): 121-126; Boyd, Ernest. *Ireland's Literary Renaissance*. New York: Alfred A. Knopf, 1916; Gibbon, Monk, ed. "Foreword," *Poems* [of Katharine Tynan]. Dublin: Allen Figgis, 1963; Hone, Joseph. *W. B. Yeats: 1865-1939.* London: Macmillan, 1943; Maguire, C. E. "Incense and the Breath of Spice." *Bookman* 72 (June 1931): 375-380; Rose, Marilyn Gaddis. *Katharine Tynan* [*Irish Writers Series*]. Lewisburg, Pa: Bucknell University Press, 1973; Russell, George (AE). 'Foreword," *Collected Poems* [of Katharine Tynan]. London: Macmillan, 1930; Yeats, W. B. *The Autobiography of William Butler Yeats.* London: Macmillan, 1916; Yeats, W. B. *Letters to Katharine Tynan.* Roger McHugh, ed. New York: McMullen, 1953.

ULSTER GROUP THEATRE (1940-1960). The Ulster Group Theatre was formed by three amateur companies—the Ulster Theatre, the Jewish Institute Dramatic Society, and the Northern Irish Players—joining together. The repertoire of the Group consisted of classic or foreign plays by Ibsen, Chekhov, Sheridan,* Maugham, Bridie, Shaw,* Odets, and others, as well as plays by some of the Southern Irish dramatists. This Belfast group was most successful in the production of new work from Ulster. The mainstays of its Northern repertoire were new pieces by St. John Ervine,* George Shiels,* and the actor-author Joseph Tomelty.* However, in its fifty new Ulster productions, the Group also introduced work by Jack Loudan, Hugh Quinn, John Coulter,* Patricia O'Connor, John Boyd,* Sam Hanna Bell,* and John Murphy. The theatre's final breakup was hastened by the controversy over producing Sam Thompson's* *Over the Bridge* in the late 1950s. Among the actors the theatre developed were Harold Goldblatt, J. D. Devlin, Joseph Tomelty, Stephen Boyd, and Colin Blakely.

REFERENCE: Bell, Sam Hanna. *The Theatre in Ulster.* [Dublin]: Gill & Macmillan, [1972].

ULSTER LITERARY THEATRE (1902-1934). The Ulster Literary Theatre received its original inspiration from the Irish Literary Theatre* of Yeats,* Moore,* and Martyn.* Its first organizers were Bulmer Hobson, who was a prominent nationalist in the years before the 1916 Rising, and David Parkhill, who wrote several of the theatre's early plays under the pseudonym of Lewis Purcell. Receiving no encouragement from Yeats, Hobson is reported to have said to Purcell, "Damn Yeats, we'll write our own plays."

The first production of the new group, however, in November 1902, consisted of Yeats' *Cathleen Ni Houlihan* and James Cousins'* *The Racing Lug.* Yeats' play was used on the authority of Maud Gonne who said, "Don't mind Willie. He wrote that play for me and gave it to me. It is mine and you can put it on whenever you want to." The principal actors in this first production were two visitors from the Dublin theatre group, Dudley Digges and Maire T. Quinn. The second production was not presented until early 1904 when Yeats' *Cathleen* was repeated on a bill with AE's* *Deirdre.* At this time, the group called itself the Ulster Branch of the Irish Literary Theatre, but George Roberts, the secretary of the Southern group, wrote forbidding the use of the term Irish Literary Theatre. Hence, the name was changed to the Ulster Literary Theatre. From that time, the group began to develop its own distinctively Northern repertoire and its own actors.

The first real production of the new group was on December 8, 1904, when two new Northern plays, Hobson's *Brian of Banba* and Purcell's *The Reformers,* were first produced. At about the same time, the group began publishing an interesting literary magazine, *Uladh* (or Ulster), which, unfortunately, lasted only four issues.

Many able authors, actors, and well-wishers quickly gathered around the new group. Among them were Forrest Reid* the novelist, James Winder Good the journalist, Joseph Campbell* the poet, and the two men who were to be the most popular and successful authors and actors throughout the company's existence, Rutherford Mayne* and Gerald MacNamara.*

From 1904 to its dissolution thirty years later, the group gave the first productions to over fifty new Ulster plays, including work by Joseph Campbell, Lynn Doyle,* Shan F. Bullock,* Helen Waddell,* George Shiels,* and St. John Ervine.* The most popular and frequently revived pieces were the fine Ulster comedy *The Drone* by Rutherford Mayne and the droll short satire *Thompson in Tir-na-nOg* by Gerald MacNamara. For years, the company (which in 1915 shortened its name to the Ulster Theatre) delighted Belfast with its portraits of Northern life, toured successfully in England and Ireland, and even sent a contingent as far afield as New York City. The company did not generate any masterpieces to rank with the best work of the Abbey Theatre,* nor any actors of the stature of the Fays, Sara Allgood, Maire O'Neill, Barry Fitzgerald, or F. J. McCormick.

One reason why the group was finally dissolved, after so many years of dedicated effort, was that it never succeeded, as did the Abbey group, in getting its own theatre building. Consequently, the Ulster Theatre was always limited to a handful of yearly performances by actors who necessarily had to remain amateurs. As with many theatres, even the most distinguished, the problem was always money, and, as Rutherford Mayne said, "The Ulster Theatre died as it lived—in penury."

REFERENCES: Bell, Sam Hanna. *The Theatre in Ulster.* [Dublin]: Gill & Macmillan, [1972]; McHenry, Margaret. *The Ulster Theatre in Ireland.* Philadelphia: University of Pennsylvania, 1931.

USSHER, [PERCIVAL] ARLAND (1899-), essayist. Ussher was born in Battersea, London, on September 9, 1899, into a family that had lived in Ireland for many generations. He was educated at Abbotsholme School, Derbyshire, at Trinity College, Dublin, and at St. John's College, Cambridge. He is proficient in Irish and has translated Merriman's *Midnight Court,* but is known primarily for what he describes as "philosophical belles lettres." His best books are probably *The Face and Mind of Ireland* (1949) and

Three Great Irishmen (1952). *The Face and Mind of Ireland* is half résumé of twentieth-century Irish history until about 1950 and half description of the Irish character which that history has produced. The first half will not greatly enlighten the knowledgeable, but the second half, even after thirty years, is perceptive, provocative, and relevant. An even better work is *Three Great Irishmen* which considers Shaw,* Yeats,* and Joyce.* Confirmed admirers of these three figures will find Ussher's opinions sometimes uncanonical and irritating, but the less committed general reader will find much thoughtful good sense and only occasional startling gaffes, such as the author's preference for Rosie of Somerset Maugham's *Cakes and Ale* to Molly Bloom of Joyce's *Ulysses*.

Ussher's prose has been much admired, but it seems to obfuscate more than to illuminate his thought. He is capable of the trenchant and necessarily epigrammatic insight, such as "the Irishman treats sex as the Englishman treats death." However, he usually buries his epigram in woolly prose and writes, "For it is hardly too much to say that the Irishman treats sex as the Englishman treats death." His most irritating characteristic of style is the habit of spraying parentheses and dashes through at least half of his sentences. For example, in the last paragraph on page 54 of the Gollancz edition of *The Face and Mind of Ireland*, the first sentence has a pair of dashes, the second sentence a pair of dashes, the third sentence a two-line parenthesis, the fourth sentence a pair of dashes, and so on. This habit becomes so intrusive in *Three Great Irishmen* that the general reader would be well advised to skip the material contained in parentheses and between dashes, and to return to it as one might later refer to footnotes. By the time of *Eros and Psyche* (1977), the prose has become almost too much of a chore to wade through. That fact is indeed unfortunate, for beneath the murky presentation lies one of the country's interesting minds.

WORKS: *Postscript on Existentialism and Other Essays*. Dublin: Sandymount/ London: Williams & Norgate, 1946; *The Twilight of Ideas and Other Essays*. Dublin: Sandymount, 1948; *The Face and Mind of Ireland*. London: Gollancz, 1949; *The Magic People*. London: Gollancz, 1950; *Three Great Irishmen*. London: Gollancz, 1952; *An Alphabet of Aphorisms*. [Dublin]: Dolmen, [1953]. (Pamphlet); with Carl von Metzradt, *Enter These Enchanted Woods, an Interpretation of Grimm's Fairy Tales*. [Dublin]: Sandymount, 1954/Dublin: Dolmen, 1957; *Journey Through Dread*. London: Darwen Finlayson, 1955. (Study of Kierkegaard, Heidegger, and Sartre); *The Thoughts of Wi Wong*. [Dublin]: Dolmen, 1956. (Pamphlet); *The XXII Keys of Tarot*. Dublin: Dolmen, 1957, 1969; *Spanish Mercy*. London: Gollancz, 1959; *Sages and Schoolmen*. Dublin: Dolmen, 1967; *Eros and Psyche*. Dublin: Runa Press, 1977; *From a Dead Lantern, a Journal*. Robert Nyle Parisious, ed. Dalkey, County Dublin: Cuala, 1978.

WADDELL, HELEN [JANE] (1889-1965), scholar, translator, and novelist. Waddell was born on May 31, 1889, in Tokyo. In 1900, she traveled to her father's native Ulster where she attended Victoria College and Queen's University, Belfast (B.A., 1911, in English; M.A., 1912). Care for her invalid stepmother postponed further study at Oxford until 1919, although during this time she wrote children's Bible stories for a Presbyterian weekly; wartime propaganda for *The Manchester Guardian, The Nation,* and *Blackwood's*; and a play, *The Spoiled Buddha,* produced in 1915 by the Ulster Theatre* of which her brother Sam (Rutherford Mayne)* was a member. Her rendering into verse of the 600 B.C. poems from the Court of Soo, *Lyrics from the Chinese* (1915), got flattering notices in London and Dublin.

Helen Waddell entered Oxford at thirty-one years of age. From 1920 to 1922, she taught Latin at Somerville College and in 1921 she was named Casell Lecturer for St. Hilda's College. Her witty, lucid, and popular lectures, and her scholarship in medieval Latin and French influenced the Committee of Lady Margaret Hall to give her a Susette Taylor Travelling Fellowship for two years, which she spent in Paris researching medieval French Literature for a Ph.D.

In 1923, Waddell lectured briefly at Bedford College. She never returned to Oxford to complete her residence; instead she moved to London, supporting her writing through literary odd jobs and free-lance lecturing. Her discipline led to one supremely productive decade.

In 1927, Constable published *The Wandering Scholars* (1927), a history of and translations from the Goliards, for which the Royal Society of Literature awarded her the A. C. Benson Silver Medal and elected her its first woman fellow. The book was a commercial success, bringing her speaking engagements at colleges and universities and on the BBC. For her translation of the Abbé Prévost's *The Chevalier des Grieux and of Manon Lescaut* and her *Book of Medieval Latin For Schools,* she was given an honorary D. Litt. by the University of Durham and elected (again as a first woman) to the Irish Academy of Letters in 1932. She then joined Constable and Company as a literary advisor.

After *Peter Abelard* (1933), her only novel, was published, Waddell was lionized—in Dublin as "Ulster's darling," and in London as "the most distinguished woman of her generation." *Beasts and Saints* (1934), a translation of extracts from medieval lives of the saints, and *The Desert Fathers* (1936), translations from the *Vitae Patrum,* were equally well received. In 1934, Queen's University, Belfast, and Columbia University conferred two more honorary degrees of D. Litt. A second play, *Abbé Prévost,* was produced by the Croydon Theatre in 1935.

In 1938, Waddell became the assistant editor of *The Nineteenth Century,* which published several patriotic poems which she had written in response to the war effort. During World War II, she was active in the Air-Raid Patrol and coped with the severe bombing of her own house. In her sympathy for the Free French, she translated articles by "Jacques," the pseudonym for a member of the French Resistance operating out of London, and collected them in the popular and moving *A French Soldier*

Speaks (1941). Her only scholarly work of the period was a translation of Milton's *Epitaphium Damonis* (1943).

When Waddell retired in 1945, her creative energy had been drained. Otto Kyllmann of Constable attempted to rekindle her interest by bringing out *Stories from Holy Writ* (1949), a collection of the Bible stories she had written thirty years before. Her final major contribution—a brilliant final success—was "Poetry in the Dark Ages" (1947), the W. P. Ker Memorial Lecture she delivered at the University of Glasgow.

Suffering from a progressive neurological disorder, Waddell stopped writing entirely by 1950; by 1955, she was unable to recognize her closest friends and relatives. She lingered until 1965 when she died of pneumonia.

Of Helen Waddell's major publications, three appear to be of lasting value. *The Wandering Scholars* is a study of Europe's "real" Renaissance; of the centers of learning at Chartres, Orleans, and Paris in the twelfth century and of its byproducts, the Ordo Vagorum, the rowdy, ribald, and intellectual *bohêmes* who produced, among many other works, the "Carmina Burana." Although Waddell shows that they represent a striking contrast to the traditional concept of the medieval mind, she occasionally shies from the indelicacies in their work and ascribes emotional characteristics more in keeping with a late Victorian sensibility. *Mediaeval Latin Lyrics* is a collection that explores what happened in literature between the Fall of Rome and the Cluniac Movement. Ironically, the staunch Presbyterian daughter of missionaries points out that the Protestant tradition in European literature had obscured vast traditions of Roman Catholic poetry. *Peter Abelard,* by which she is largely remembered, is flawed for the reason that Waddell was not a novelist. It suffers from a cryptographic allusiveness possible only in the fictional work of a scholar who assumes an equal interest and knowledge in his reading public. Despite its flaws and its failure to face some of the more brutal realities of the tale, the novel is a fair measure of Helen Waddell's accuracy, acumen, spirited scholarship, and love of poetry.

M. KELLY LYNCH

WORKS: trans., *Lyrics from the Chinese*, by Shih Ching. London: Constable, 1913; *The Spoiled Buddha*. Dublin: Talbot, 1919. (Play); trans., *The Hollow Field,* by M. Aymé. London: Constable, 1923; *The Wandering Scholars*. London: Constable, 1927; ed., *A Book of Medieval Latin for Schools*. London: Constable, 1929; trans., *The History of the Chevalier des Grieux and of Manon Lescaut*, by Abbé Prévost d'Exiles. London: Constable, 1931; *The Abbé Prévost*. London: Constable, 1933. (Play); trans., *Mediaeval Latin Lyrics*. London: Constable, 1933; *Peter Abelard*. London: Constable, 1933. (Novel); trans., *Beasts and Saints*. London: Constable, 1934; *New York City*. Newtown: Gregynog Press, 1935. (Poem); trans., *The Desert Fathers*. London. Constable, 1936; trans., *A French Soldier Speaks*, by Jacques (pseud.). London: Constable, 1941; trans., *Epitaphium Damonis. Lament for Damon*, by John Milton. London: Constable, 1943; *Poetry in the Dark Ages*. Glasgow: Jackson, 1947. (W. P. Ker Memorial Lecture, delivered at the University of Glasgow); *Stories from*

Holy Writ. London: Constable, 1949. (Bible stories for children); *The Princess Splendour and Other Stories.* London: Longmans Young Books, 1969. (Children's stories).   REFERENCE: Blackett, Monica. *The Mark of the Maker.* London: Constable, 1973. (Biography).

WADDELL, SAMUEL J. *See* MAYNE, RUTHERFORD.

WALL, MERVYN [EUGENE WELPLY] (1908-), novelist, playwright, and short story writer. Wall was born in Dublin on August 23, 1908, and was educated in Belvedere College, in Germany, and at the National University where he received a B.A. in 1928. After what he considered to be fourteen extremely depressing years in the Irish civil service, he was given more congenial employment by Francis MacManus* in Radio Éireann. Then, in 1957, at the instigation of Sean O'Faolain,* he became secretary of the Arts Council, a post he held until his retirement in the mid-1970s. He is married to Fanny Feehan, the music critic, and has three children.

Wall's fame rests on two inimitable books about a medieval Irish monk, *The Unfortunate Fursey* (1946) and *The Return of Fursey* (1948). The first is a sunny mélange of whimsy and satire which in tone, if not in its highly individual content, brings to mind the work of James Stephens* and George Fitzmaurice* among the Irish, and of Kenneth Grahame and J.R.R. Tolkien among the English. The lovable and ineffectual antihero of the novels moves through a malignant landscape of myth and marvels, which is peopled by an enchantingly garrulous collection of devils, witches, vampires, bishops, and Vikings. At the end of the first novel, Fursey improbably but delightfully triumphs over all. If the sequel is darker in tone and more sombre in theme, Fursey's final failure is nevertheless accompanied by a sympathetic sweetness that some of Wall's later work, probably to its detriment, lacks.

Wall's most ambitious and serious work is his prizewinning novel of 1952, *Leaves for the Burning.* This novel tells how a group of middle-aged friends makes an increasingly drunken, never-completed journey from Dublin to Sligo, to be present at the reinterment of W. B. Yeats.* The book is a sour but solid indictment of the repressive Ireland of the 1930s and 1940s. It is meticulously wrought and has a sullen power which suggests Graham Greene. Among Irish works, it is akin to the novels of Brinsley MacNamara* or John McGahern,* for its world is one which is thoroughly delineated from a very partial view.

Wall's *No Trophies Raise* (1956) is similarly glum in content, but is more intricate in plot and more farcical in tone. The smoldering dislike behind the book prevents the farce from blazing into fun, and so, despite some broadly comic invention, it remains more disturbing than satisfying in depicting its 1950s world of business and backslapping.

Wall's most recent novel, *Heritage,* has not yet been separately published, but was serialized in three issues of *The Journal of Irish Literature*

(1978-1979). It is a long (nearly 120,000 words) account of an Irish life, viewed with detachment and perhaps some puzzlement. Though the tone is muted, the prose is utterly crystalline, for Wall has one of the best commands of prose of any writer of his generation.

A collection of fugitive and rather early short stories, which are pleasant but have only minor merit, was issued in 1974 under the title *A Flutter of Wings*.

Wall's two published plays were produced with small success by the Abbey*: *Alarm among the Clerks* (1940) and *The Lady in the Twilight* (1941). The earlier work reflects Wall's never-quite-stifled resentment of the soul-deadening bureaucracy of the civil service; in content and technique it has much in common with Elmer Rice's *The Adding Machine*. The *Lady in the Twilight* is a thoughtful, complex, and thickly characterized Chekhovian study of Ireland in the 1930s. It is a highly accomplished play, and its multistranded realism is probably rivaled in Ireland only by *The Moon in the Yellow River* of Denis Johnston,* who was virtually alone among the play's defenders.

In 1962, Wall published a pamphlet of local history entitled *Forty Foot Gentlemen Only*. The work is of broad rather than local interest because it deals with the men's bathing place in Sandycove which is featured in the early pages of Joyce's* *Ulysses*.

If Wall's talents seem to outstrip his very solid achievement, the reason might be that his formative years were the 1930s and 1940s, the bleakest and most provincial years of the Free State. Even more than Brian O'Nolan,* whose comic invention he sometimes rivals, Wall seems to have been formed and, to an extent, depressed by his milieu.

WORKS: *Alarm among the Clerks*. Dublin: Richview, 1940; *The Unfortunate Fursey*. London: Pilot, 1946/New York: Crown, 1947/Dublin: Helicon, 1965; *The Return of Fursey*. London: Pilot, 1948; *Leaves for the Burning*. London: Methuen/New York: Devin-Adair, 1952; *No Trophies Raise*. London: Methuen, 1956; *Forty Foot Gentlemen Only*. Dublin: Allen Figgis, 1962. (Pamphlet); *The Lady in the Twilight*. Newark, Del.: Proscenium, 1971; *A Flutter of Wings*. Dublin: Talbot, 1974; *Heritage* in *The Journal of Irish Literature*, vols. 7 & 8 (September 1978, January 1979, May 1979).   REFERENCE: Hogan, Robert. *Mervyn Wall*. Lewisburg, Pa.: Bucknell University Press, 1972.

WALSH, EDWARD (1805-1850), translator. Walsh, one of the earliest and best translators of Irish folk poetry, was born of a County Cork soldier-father, in Londonderry, in 1805. He was taught in the hedge-schools, and his work appeared often in *The Nation*.* He had a difficult and impoverished life, being at one time schoolmaster to the convicts on Spike Island and later to paupers in a Cork Workhouse. He died at Cork in August 1850. Robert Farren* writes of him in *The Course of Irish Verse:*

> He appreciated several of the formal virtues of his originals, determined to reproduce them in translating, and did, in fact, do this

thing, in a certain degree. That is, he fits the words always to the tune, as [Thomas] Moore* did, arriving as did Moore, Callanan* and Ferguson* at the long, sinuous line; and he "vowels" well, employing cross-rhyme and assonance. His chief fault was a stiff, often bookish diction. . . .

At least a half dozen of his translations are memorable, among them "Mo Craoibhin Cno," "Have You Been at Carrick?," "The Dawning of the Day," "Brighiden ban mo Stor," and "From the Cold Sod That's O'er You."

WORKS: *Reliques of Irish Jacobite Poetry*. Dublin: Samuel J. Machen, 1844; *Irish Popular Songs*. Dublin: J. M'Glashan/London: W. S. Orr, 1847. REFERENCE: Kickham, Charles J. "Edward Walsh: A Memoir" in *The Valley Near Slievenamon*, James Maher, ed. Kilkenny: Kilkenny People, 1942, 331-354.

WALSH, JOHN EDWARD (1816-1869), author of historical sketches. Walsh was born on November 12, 1816, probably in Finglas, County Dublin. He became a barrister of some prominence and died in Paris on October 17, 20, or 25, 1869. His book *Ireland Sixty Years Ago* is made up of fictional sketches, which were originally published in *The Dublin University Magazine*. Its evocation of the Ireland of before the Act of Union is both plausible and entertaining.

WORK: *Sketches of Ireland Sixty Years Ago*. Dublin, 1847/revised ed. under the title *Ireland Ninety Years Ago*, Dublin: M. H. Gill, 1885/another revised ed. under the title *Ireland One Hundred and Twenty Years Ago*, Dillon Cosgrave, ed. Dublin & Waterford: M. H. Gill, 1911.

WALSH, MAURICE (1879-1964), novelist. Walsh was born at Ballydonoghue, a townland which lies halfway between the literary town of Listowel and the seaside resort of Ballybunion in North Kerry, on May 2, 1879. He was educated at local national schools—Liselton, Gortnaskehy, and Coolard, and later at St. Michael's College, Listowel, a classical school where the accent was on Latin and Greek. His father was a well-read farmer who transmitted a great deal of his own love of learning to his family.

To the northwest of the Walsh homestead, overlooking the mouth of the River Shannon, stood the hill of Knockanore, so-named from the Irish Cnoc an Áir (the Hill of Slaughter or as given in another version, the Hill of the Harvest) which is mentioned in the legends of the Fianna. The area is rich in folklore.

Walsh successfully stood for an examination for the civil service and subsequently spent twenty years as an excise officer in Scotland, mainly in the Highlands. There he came in contact with a life that was sib to his home experience and where also he acquired a Scottish burr which he never quite lost. He married a Scottish girl—a redhead who appears under various guises throughout his works. As a result of his excise days in Scotland, he was recognized on an international level as an authority on whisky [without the Irish *e*!].

Under the terms of the Anglo-Irish Treaty in 1922, he transferred to the Irish customs and excise. At this time, he seriously took up writing, his early works being featured in Chambers' *Journal*. His first book, *The Key Above the Door* (1926), although it failed to win a competition for which it was entered, was later published by Chambers of Edinburgh and London and sold a quarter of a million copies.

Thereafter, book after book—novels and short stories—appeared, the scene of each was laid in Scotland or in southwest Ireland. The Walsh books are of the open air, of salmon rivers, of farmlands and fairs, some with historical settings. A departure from his usual pattern was evidenced by *Thomasheen James, Man-of-No-Work,* the theme of which was provided by a rare personality who visited Walsh in his Stillorgan home and remained there for years in the nominal role of gardener. *The Quiet Man,* the famous John Ford film with a redheaded heroine and filmed mainly in the Cong area of County Galway, is based on a Maurice Walsh story from *Green Rushes.* There is now a pub of the name in Listowel. *Trouble in the Glen* was also filmed in England.

On a personal level, Walsh was delightful and cordial in every way. Sturdily built, he dressed in tweeds, sometimes with a pale green cape slung across his shoulders while his tweed hat, set at a jaunty angle, carried a brilliant salmon fly or a feather from the blackcock. His eyes, set in a bearded and fresh-complexioned face, carried more than their share of quiet merriment. His visits to his native area in North Kerry were events in the truest sense of the word as he took time out to visit old friends of his youth and "correct his perspective."

In his Stillorgan, County Dublin, home (it was named "Green Rushes" for one of his books), he held an open night once every week. These were attended by all kinds of personalities, and the conversation was vivid and far-ranging. Walsh, a fine host, was seen at his best on such occasions.

He retired from the Irish civil service in 1933, and he died in Dublin on February 18, 1964.

B R Y A N   M A c M A H O N

WORKS: *The Key Above the Door*. London & Edinburgh: Chambers, 1926; *While Rivers Run*. London & Edinburgh: Chambers, 1928; *The Small Dark Man*. London & Edinburgh: Chambers, 1929; *Blackcock's Feather*. London & Edinburgh: Chambers, 1932; *The Road to Nowhere*. London & Edinburgh: Chambers, 1934; *Green Rushes*. London & Edinburgh: Chambers, 1935; *And No Quarter*. London & Edinburgh: Chambers, 1937; *Sons of the Swordmaker*. London & Edinburgh: Chambers, 1938; *The Hill Is Mine*. London & Edinburgh: Chambers, 1940; *Thomasheen James, Man-of-No-Work*. London & Edinburgh: Chambers, 1941; *The Spanish Lady*. London & Edinburgh: Chambers, 1943; *The Man in Brown*. London & Edinburgh: Chambers, 1945; *Son of Apple*. London & Edinburgh: Chambers, 1947; *Castle Gillian*. London & Edinburgh: Chambers, 1948; *Trouble in the Glen*. London & Edinburgh: Chambers,

1950; *Son of a Tinker, and Other Tales*. London & Edinburgh: Chambers, 1951; *The Honest Fisherman, and Other Stories*. London & Edinburgh: Chambers, 1954; *A Strange Woman's Daughter*. London & Edinburgh: Chambers, 1954; *Danger under the Moon*. London & Edinburgh: Chambers, 1956; *The Smart Fellow*. London & Edinburgh: Chambers, 1964.

WEBER, RICHARD (1932-), poet. Weber was born in Dublin in 1932 and has published a few slim volumes of considerable potential. His first important collection was *Lady and Gentleman* (1963). Much of the book seems a compilation of botched opportunities, as the poet is usually working in a tight form, such as the rhyming couplet, and does not, through metrical maladroitness or laziness or ignorance, see that his flabby meters are undoing the insistence of his rhymes. In some cases, as in "The Young Poet's Letter to Olympus," the effect is to reduce a serious attempt to mere doggerel. However, there are several real successes, such as "Summa Theologica" or "An Anatomy of Love" or "The Makers" or, especially, "Morality." Weber's best known volume is *Stephen's Green Revisited* (1968), but the book is a more formally trivial and a more personally indulgent one. The title poem, for instance, contains one neatly witty idea (of ducks knowing a little Latin because they say "aqua, aqua") and a debilitating, sentimental core ("But sadness is surely the secret mother of memory"). A couple of skillful pieces, such as "Roman Elegy V" and "Religious Knowledge," and one pleasant, if not memorable, tribute to Austin Clarke* called "A Visit to Bridge House" do not quite make up for the disappointment that this poet has not matured.

WORKS: *Lady and Gentleman*. Dublin: Dolmen, 1963; *Stephen's Green Revisited*. Dublin: Dolmen, 1968; *A Few Small Ones*. Dublin: Ballyknockan, 1971.

WELDON, JOHN. *See* MacNAMARA, BRINSLEY.

WEST, ANTHONY C[ATHCOT MUIR] (1910-), novelist and short story writer. West was born in 1910 in County Down. He went to America in 1930 and spent some years wandering across the country, from New York to the Pacific Northwest, and making his living by a wide variety of temporary jobs. He returned to Europe in 1938, served in the RAF in World War II, and was a navigator in many Mosquito bombing missions over Germany. Since the war he has lived in Anglesey, North Wales, with his wife and their twelve children, and he has engaged in "creative farming" and writing.

West's early stories and what John Wilson Foster calls his best novel, *The Ferret Fancier* (1963), are so richly written and evocative that reviewers have compared him to the Dylan Thomas of "A Child's Christmas in Wales." West's great preoccupation is with the early years of puberty of a boy in a farming community in the North of Ireland. The sense of place, a ripe description of nature and landscape, and a meticulous delineation of the tortures of young sexuality are done with a poet's eye, and his early work should be lingered over and savored. West's weakness is in the progression of plot, and in both short and long works his frequently lush prose tends to bury a tenuous story. Another flaw is that his characters, other than his protagonists perhaps, are not vividly drawn. These failings keep him from being, as Foster avers, "the most fertile and originative fiction writer the North has produced since Carleton." These qualities do, as well as innumerable paragraphs of limply Lawrentian psychic probing, such as:

> The salmon made him vaguely sad, seeing it as egg in to redd, then fry, parr, smolt, and then the strong young forger in the tumbling wilderness of sea. He tried to see the shape of the symbol behind the fish as if it had some meaning for himself, some warning or conclusion or explanation for his unreconcilement with life and circumstances. He failed, vague memories defeating any symbolic recognition: the roaring weir and the ploughing salmon, the Jamesons, love's wound in graveyard days, the safety of detached innocence hazarded by overcoming experience; doubts, loneliness. O where was he now: a parr perhaps drifting down his river, unfit yet for the salt sea and waiting for mere management and strength to brave the bar: the cold courage of a fish.

West's most ambitious novel is *As Towns with Fire* (1968). It is an extremely long account of the young life of Christopher MacMannan, who is trying to be a poet and who gets caught up in World War II as a navigator. With the exception of a forty-page flashback to his youth in Ireland, the first four hundred pages flounder aimlessly through his various love affairs, little realized characters, and a good deal of philosophic discussion about life. When MacMannan joins the RAF and begins flying missions over Germany, the last two hundred pages of narrative gain much more appeal. The philosophic discussions and even all the shadowy minor characters begin to work, and one character, Jane (who is the hero's duck), becomes rather memorable. Nevertheless, despite West's usual facility with words, the book needed a drastic shaping and cutting to make it into a work of art, rather than another wayward, if very talented, amateur fiction.

WORKS: *River's End and Other Stories*. New York: McDowell, Oblonsky, 1958; *The Native Moment*. London: MacGibbon & Kee, 1961; *The Ferret Fancier*. New York: Simon & Schuster, 1963; *As Towns with Fire*. London: MacGibbon & Kee, 1968.

WHARTON, ANTHONY P. (1877-1943), playwright and novelist. Anthony P. Wharton, the pseudonym of Alister (or Alexander) McAllister, was born in Dublin in 1877, and was educated at Clongowes and at the Royal University. He achieved a considerable London success with his play *Irene Wycherley* in 1907, and some later success in 1912 with *At the Barn*.

After his World War I service during which he was wounded twice, he turned to writing novels and was most successful with a series of detective stories written under the pseudonym of Lynn Brock. In March 1943, the Abbey* presented his last play, *The O'Cuddy*. Early in April of that year, Wharton died at his home in Surrey.

WORKS: *At the Barn*. London: Joseph William/New York: Samuel French, [1912]; *Nocturne*. London: Lacy, [1913]. (One-act play); *Simon Street*. London: Lacy, [1913]. (One-act play); *Joan of Overbarrow*. London: Duckworth, 1922; *The Man on the Hill*. London: Unwin, 1923; *Be Good, Sweet Maid*. London: Unwin, 1924; *Evil Communications*. London: Unwin, 1926; *The Two of Diamonds*. London: Collins, [1926].

WHITE, JACK. *See* WHITE, W. J.

WHITE, T[ERENCE] H[ANBURY] (1906-1964), novelist and essayist. Although White, known to his friends as "Tim," was thoroughly English in his rearing and values, he spent his most productive years in Ireland in self-imposed exile during World War II, from 1939 to 1945. He was born in Bombay in 1906 of parents in the civil service whose bitter divorce was to color his adult emotional life. He was educated at Cheltenham and Cambridge, where his tutor was L. J. Potts the critic, and he took a Firsts with honors in 1929. After a brief career as a schoolmaster, he became a professional writer, living in a gamekeeper's cottage in Buckinghamshire. He was a man of many enthusiasms and a compulsive learner. "The best thing for being sad," he has Merlyn say in *The Once and Future King*, "is to learn something." He learned to fly an airplane, show horses, plow a field, fish for salmon, train hawks for hunting, and do all the field sports, all of which turned up in his writing. His hobby, listed in *Who's Who*, was "animals." In 1939, he went on a fishing trip to Ireland with his friends the David Garnetts—and stayed throughout the war. He lived at Doolistown, a farm near Trim, County Meath, and visited regularly in Dublin and in County Mayo, where he hunted and fished. He returned to England in 1945, and after the success of the musical "Camelot," which was based on his Arthuriad *The Once and Future King*, he settled on the Channel island of Alderney. Shortly after completing a successful American lecture tour in 1963 (*America at Last*, Putnam, 1965), he died of heart failure in Athens, where he is buried.

White's best known work, *The Once and Future King* (in four books, completed in 1958), concerns the boyhood, maturity, and eventual defeat of King Arthur. The story of the legendary king provided ample room for comment on personal matters, like the Lancelot-Guinevere love triangle and the clan relationship of the Orkneys, and on "the matter of Britain," or idealized conceptions of leadership and the nation, tested by reality. White based his version mainly on Thomas Malory's *Morte D'Arthur*. He deliberately kept scholarly discussion out of the work and was not directly influenced by Celtic variants of the legend. He also decided not to include the Tristan legend or the Grail quest. Rather, he deals with the Orkney clan and the revenge of Mordred on Arthur in psychological terms as an Aristotelian incest tragedy, a tragedy "of sin come home to roost." He was living in Ireland while he wrote the early versions of the last two books, later revised. He also included an impassioned fifth book, *The Book of Merlyn*, which his editor rejected; it was only recently published from the manuscript (University of Texas Press, 1977). His concern in this fifth book was influenced not by Ireland but by what the ongoing war revealed about the nature of man's self-destructiveness.

White wrote two books directly about Ireland—*The Elephant and the Kangaroo* (1948) and *The Godstone and the Blackymor* (1959). *The Elephant*, which is based on his personal experiences at Doolistown, creates the delightful fiction that the Second Flood is coming to Ireland; a Mr. White, and the aging couple he lives with, are chosen to build the ark. The ark finally flounders down the Boyne and the Liffey, bumping into all the bridges, and the book closes with a successful burlesque of Joycean prose. In a fit of remorse, White tried to stop the book's distribution in Ireland, where in Trim its satirical thrust aroused animosity. Long after he returned to England, White wrote up several of his bizarrely whimsical experiences for the most part in the west of Ireland. *The Godstone and the Blackymor* tells of his search for a talismanic stone on Inniskea, his attendance at a wake, and his climbing Croagh Patrick among other matters. White was quintessentially a foreigner, as he was aware, even though he won a Radio Éireann poetry contest in 1940 with his "Sheskin," which was a tribute to the Irish climate and countryside.

While in Ireland, White also wrote *Mistress Masham's Repose* (1946), his delightful (and neglected) novel about the thirteen-year-old Maria, who finds a hitherto unknown colony of Lilliputians on her estate, brought back by Gulliver from his first travel. Like *The Once and Future King*, it contains an eccentric wisdom figure and is concerned with growing up and the moral values that are tested by dealing with other people. Many years later, White completed a similar but deeply flawed children's book, *The Master* (1957), the setting for which first occurred to him in Ireland.

White also worked intermittently on his substantial scholarly work, *The Book of Beasts* (1954), translating medieval manuscripts in the Trinity College library, and he wrote considerable parts of his two books of eighteenth-century studies in eccentricity, *The Age of Scandal* (1950) and *The Scandalmonger* (1952). Driven in part by his loneliness, he wrote hundreds of fascinating letters (*The White/Garnett Letters*, 1968, is only a sample) and kept voluminous journals.

White was an intelligent, widely read, eccentric, lonely, charming man, nervous and driven by the need to overcome his fears, given to crazes and enthusiasms. Typically, while in Ireland he studied Irish history and Gaelic and prepared to become Catholic, only to remain the educated, agnostic Anglo-Saxon he was raised to be. A heavy drinker and suppressed homosexual, he was true to his dogs and his writing. His letters and journals have been only partly published. Sylvia Townsend Warner's *T. H. White*, while authorized by his executors, is unsympathetic in tone and rather sketchy.

SVEN ERIC MOLIN

WORKS: *The Elephant and the Kangaroo. The Godstone and the Blackymor.* London: Jonathan Cape/New York: Putnam's, 1959.

WHITE, [HEREBERT] TERENCE DE VERE (1912-), novelist and man of letters. White was born in Dublin on April 29, 1912. His father was a Protestant and his mother came from a genteel Catholic family. Both his parents kept themselves remote from the traumatic historical events of White's childhood: the 1916 Rising, the War of Independence, and the founding of the Free State. The rude nationalism of the majority meant for the de Vere Whites the emergence of a society with which they found it difficult to identify. Their son's writings have been heavily fueled by his upbringing.

White had a Catholic schooling and entered Trinity College at the age of fifteen. After a B.A. and an Ll.B., he entered the legal profession. He married in 1941 and has three children. In 1962, he became literary editor of *The Irish Times* and resigned from a senior partnership in one of Dublin's established legal firms to devote himself more fully to letters. He was literary editor of the paper until the end of 1977.

White has been active in the cultural life of Dublin for most of his life: he is on the boards of the Gate Theatre* and the National Gallery, and he is a trustee of the National Library. He is a conversationalist and after-dinner speaker of distinction. He has written extensively: ten novels, two volumes of short stories, five biographies, an autobiography, two histories, and two general interest volumes, *Ireland* and *Leinster*.

As a novelist, White moves outside the mainstream of twentieth-century Irish fiction: he writes comedies of manners. His main characters are usually society types, members of the declined Ascendancy or the professional middle classes. White's approach as a writer is to cultivate the role of the detached observer who chronicles passions and intrigue with a penetrating and ironic eye. However, his descriptive and narrative prose too often lacks genuine literary merit. In this connection, it is instructive to contrast him with Jennifer Johnston* whose treatment of the Irish gentry is so authentic. When White deals with topical subjects, the topicality is somewhat forced. In *The Distance and the Dark* (1973), the Northern Ireland troubles form the background, and both the evocation of atmosphere and the various attitudes which are voiced about violence rarely rise above the commonplace. The novel's focus is on a sensitive, unhappily married middle-aged man whose growth in self-knowledge is marked towards the novel's close by Polonius' "This above all: to thine own self be true. . . ." Instead of using this truism as a starting point to explore his hero's development, White confines himself to it, thus losing the opportunity to involve the reader imaginatively with the character's development.

The March Hare (1970) exemplifies White's strengths and weaknesses as a novelist. Set in early twentieth-century Dublin, the novel displays a good sense of period; the social and physical detail of the city are unobtrusively and interestingly presented. The comic idiom of character types is also well portrayed. The book has some serious defects, however. For example, the descriptive writing is too uniformly pedestrian, while overall credibility of plot is frequently sacrificed to the effectiveness of a single scene. As an illustration of the former, take the start of the love affair between Millie Preston and Alan Harvey. They meet at a ball where Millie's first sight of Alan brings on a "sensation as if some part of her inside had dropped, at the same time she experienced a slight weakening at the knees." Six pages later, White tells us how the occasion had affected Alan: "when he first saw her his stomach dropped and he had gone weak at the knees." With reference to credibility of plot, it is significant that White's most recent forays into fiction have been in the short story where the strength of specific scenes at the expense of the whole is of much less importance. Some of the short stories provide thinly disguised portraits of prominent Irish cultural figures.

White's first full-length work, *The Road of Excess* (1946), is a nonfictional biography of Isaac Butt, the first leader of the Irish Home Rule party at Westminster. The work is anecdotal, and Butt's historical stature is not examined in depth. The biographies White has written are not analytical, and his subjects have shifted from political figures like Butt and Kevin O'Higgins (1948) to cultural and literary figures. *Tom Moore: The Irish Poet* (1977) is his most recent work in this field. When the book's subtitle, "The Irish Poet," is considered, the lack of any critical appreciation of Moore's* verse is to be regretted.

White's autobiography, *A Fretful Midge* (1959), ranks among his best works. It gives a critically attractive picture of the birth and growth of the new Irish state, and key artistic and political personages are sharply observed in its pages. His other nonfiction includes *The Anglo-Irish* (1972), an attempt to define Ireland's most elusive social phenomenon. His *Ireland* (1968) has an interesting chapter sketching the country's literary history.

White holds a minor place in Irish letters. In future years, his works will likely appeal more to the social or literary historian than to the general reader.

MARTIN RYAN

WORKS: *The Road of Excess*. Dublin: Browne & Nolan, 1946. (Biography of Isaac Butt); *Kevin O'Higgins*. London: Methuen, 1948. (Biography); *The Story of the*

Royal Dublin Society. Tralee: Kerryman, 1955; *A Leaf from the Yellow Book, the Correspondence of George Egerton,* ed. London: Richards Press, 1958; *An Affair with the Moon.* London: Gollancz, 1959. (Novel); *A Fretful Midge.* London: Routledge & Kegan Paul, 1959. (Autobiography); *Prenez Garde.* London: Gollancz, 1961. (Novel); *The Remainderman.* London: Gollancz, 1963. (Novel); *Lucifer Falling.* London: Gollancz, 1966. (Novel); *The Parents of Oscar Wilde.* London: Hodder & Stoughton, 1967. (Biography); *Tara.* London: Gollancz, 1967. (Novel); *Ireland.* London: Thames & Hudson, 1968; *Leinster.* London: Faber, 1968; *The Lambert Mile.* London: Gollancz, 1969. (Novel); *The March Hare.* London: Gollancz, 1970. (Novel); *Mr. Stephen.* London: Gollancz, 1970. (Novel); *The Anglo-Irish.* London: Gollancz, 1972. (Nonfiction); *The Distance and the Dark.* London: Gollancz, 1973. (Novel); *The Radish Memoirs.* London: Gollancz, 1974. (Novel); *Big Fleas and Little Fleas, and Other Stories.* London: Gollancz, 1976; *Tom Moore: The Irish Poet.* London: Hamilton, 1977. (Biography); *Chimes at Midnight.* London: Gollancz, 1978. (Stories); *My Name Is Norval.* London: Gollancz, 1978. (Novel).

WHITE, W[ILLIAM] J[OHN] "JACK" (1920-), novelist, playwright, and journalist. White was born in Cork on March 30, 1920, of English parents. He was educated at Midleton College, Cork, and at Trinity College, Dublin, where he twice won the Vice-Chancellor's Prizes in both Verse and Prose. From 1942 to 1962, he was a journalist for *The Irish Times,* as well as the Irish correspondent for *The Observer* and *The Manchester Guardian.* Since 1962, he has been employed by Radio Telefis Éireann, and in 1974 he was made controller of television programs. He has written three novels, two plays, and a study of the place of Protestants in Southern Ireland, entitled *Minority Report.* The novels—*One for the Road* (1956), *The Hard Man* (1958), and *The Devil You Know* (1962)—are studies of the Dublin middle class. *One for the Road* is set during the war years and is something of a "whodunnit" involving a youngish man in the import business. *The Hard Man* has as protagonist an architect who joins the civil service, and it is a markedly more general study of business chicanery. *The Devil You Know* casts the broadest net of all, has a large and varied cast of characters, and studies the effects of love and ambition on a number of people connected with the fictional Dublin Institute for Historical Research. In all of White's novels, his characters behave with the plausibility of life, but with rather more nastiness than one expects in a novel. One senses the author's sour disillusionment with his characters and their various imbroglios and infidelities. However, all of the books are leanly written and compulsively readable, and *The Devil You Know* has some extremely clever writing ("bottle-scarred veterans," for instance), as well as some effective satire. All of the novels succeed excellently in recreating a milieu of the affluent middle-class little treated in Irish fiction until the 1950s, and one regrets that White has not continued his dissections into the more affluent and satirizable 1960s. Only one of his two plays, *The Last Eleven* (Abbey, 1968), has been published. That sad and clever drama won the Irish Life Drama Award in 1967; it is a quiet, telling study of the much diminished

congregation of a Protestant church. There is an absolutely solid craftsmanship about White's work, and the only reason he does not have a first-
rate reputation is his too meagre production.

WORKS: *One for the Road*. London: Jonathan Cape, 1956; *The Hard Man*. London: Jonathan Cape, 1958; *The Devil You Know*. London: Jonathan Cape, 1962/
reprint, Dublin: Allen Figgis, 1970; *Minority Report: The Protestant Community in
the Irish Republic*. Dublin: Gill & Macmillan, 1975; *The Last Eleven*. Newark, Del.:
Proscenium, 1978.

WILDE, LADY (ca. 1824-1896), poet and woman of letters. Lady Wilde
was born Jane Francesca Elgee in Wexford. She claimed 1826 as her birthdate, but her biographers commonly move the date back to 1824, or even
1820. As a young woman, under the pseudonymn of Speranza, she became a frequent and fervent contributor to *The Nation*.* Her patriotic
verses are generally of small merit, but they are vigorous and filled with
exhortations such as "God! Liberty! Truth!" and "Oh, courage!" and "To
Arms! To Arms! for Truth, Fame, Freedom, Vengeance, Victory!" Nevertheless, some lines are striking, such as these from "The Famine Year":

> There's a proud array of soldiers—what do they round your door?
> "They guard our master's granaries from the thin hands of the
>   poor."
> Pale mothers, wherefore weeping?—"Would to God that we were
>   dead—
> Our children swoon before us, and we cannot give them bread!" . . .
>
> Oh! we know not what is smiling, and we know not what is dying;
> But we're hungry, very hungry, and we cannot stop our crying. . . ."

Or these from "Related Souls":

> Time was not made for spirits like ours,
> Nor the changing light of the changing hours;
> For the life eternal still lies below
> The drifted leaves and the fallen snow.

Her articles for *The Nation* were as vehement as most of her verse, and
one fiery piece, "Jacta Alea Est" (The Die Is Cast), caused the July 29,
1848, issue to be immediately suppressed. When Gavan Duffy* was brought
to trial, the attorney-general accused him of writing the inflammatory piece,
but Speranza stood up in the public gallery, asserting her own authorship
and her right to be in the dock.

In 1851, she married William Wilde,* and after he was knighted they
kept virtually open house at their home in Merrion Square. After her husband's death in 1876, Lady Wilde moved to London and conducted a
somewhat raffish salon. She died on February 3, 1896, in much reduced

circumstances and during her son Oscar Wilde's* incarceration. Lady Wilde is remembered more as a fascinating and somewhat bizarre personality than as a writer. Her poems, translations, essays, and journalism have little merit, but her retellings of Irish folktales were done with simplicity and humor and with none of her usual stylistic orotundity. The best of them are absolutely enchanting.

WORKS: *Ugo Bassi: A Tale of the Italian Revolution,* by Speranza. London, 1857. (Verse); *Poems.* Dublin: James Duffy, 1864; *Driftwood from Scandinavia.* London: R. Bentley, 1884; *Ancient Legends, Mystic Charms, and Superstitions of Ireland.* 2 vols. London: Ward & Downey, 1887; *Ancient Cures, Charms and Usages of Ireland.* London: Ward & Downey, 1890; *Notes on Men, Women, and Books.* London: Ward & Downey, 1891.   REFERENCES: White, Terence de Vere. *The Parents of Oscar Wilde.* London: Hodder & Stoughton, 1967; Wyndham, Horace. *Speranza.* London: T. V. Boardman, 1951.

WILDE, OSCAR [FINGAL O'FLAHERTIE WILLS] (1854-1900), playwright, poet, and wit. Wilde was born on October 16, 1854, at 15 Westland Row, Dublin, the second son of Sir William Wilde,* eye-surgeon oculist in ordinary to the Queen, and Jane Francesca (formerly Elgee).* Sir William's first ancestor to come to Ireland was a builder from Durham whose son became agent to Lord Mount Sandford in County Roscommon, and the theory that the Wildes were descended from a Dutch officer in the army of William of Orange was a fabrication of Lady Wilde. She, too, was descended from immigrant builders, refugees from religious persecution in Scotland. The Elgees' ancestors were said to be Italians called Algeo, although Lady Wilde claimed descent from Dante.

Lady Wilde was elephantine in build and extravagant in manner, but her salon in Merrion Square was much frequented. Her husband's moral reputation (always suspect, as he had three illegitimate children) was irreparably injured when a patient alleged that he had seduced her under chloroform. The trial in 1864 was given wide publicity.

Oscar, however, does not seem to have suffered from his father's embarrassments. After school at Portora in Northern Ireland, he read a brilliant course in classics in Trinity College, Dublin; then, moving to Oxford, he took a double first and won the Newdigate Prize for a poem, "Ravenna." He was happy and successful and devoted to a beautiful Dublin girl, Florence Balcombe, who later married Bram Stoker,* author of *Dracula.* Wilde was twenty-five years of age when he took rooms with Frank Miles at 13 Salisbury Street, London, and launched himself in London.

As a poet, Wilde would have said that he had no diffidence. He sent his work to the most eminent in the land, he sighed on the doorsteps of Lily Langtry, actress, beauty, and mistress of the future Edward VII, and Ellen Terry, queen of the English stage, was another recipient of open admiration and a poem. He dressed in velvet with flowing bow tie, courtier's knee breeches, and silk stockings. His aesthetic affectations had won him some rough attentions at Oxford; in London they were part of his provocative self-advertisement. He is generally believed to have inspired Bunthorne in *Patience*, Gilbert and Sullivan's comic opera. To collect funds he made a lecture tour in America in 1882. It was a notorious success. But his first play *Vera*, staged in New York, folded after a week's run the following year.

Now a celebrity, Wilde married Constance Lloyd, the good, decorative, but not very interesting daughter of a respectable legal family in Ireland. The young couple set up house in 16 Tite Street, in circumstances of comparative luxury. Wilde was garrulous about the ardency of his passion. He had inherited a small income under his father's will, and his wife had some money, but not enough. As a result, Wilde did some lecturing, and then, in 1887, he took up the editorship of *Woman's World*, which was rather a comedown, but he invited even royalty to contribute. At this time he published the children's stories "The Happy Prince" and "The Portrait of Mr. W. H." The mystery of Shakespeare's sonnets preoccupied him for many years. It marked the first stage of his awareness of his inverted sexual nature, for which discovery Robert Ross, whom he met in 1886, is usually given responsibility. Wilde's second son, Vyvyan, was born that year; Cyril, the elder, had been born in 1885.

In 1891, Wilde met Lord Alfred Douglas, and fell under the malign influence of this petulant, selfish, and conceited son of a mad father, the marquis of Queensberry. Sulkily handsome, with a facility for writing sonnets, Douglas entered Wilde's life when his own genius was coming into full flower. Always self-confident (an inheritance from his mother), Wilde now became hubristic.

The Picture of Dorian Grey, first published in *Lippincott's*, was produced as a novel in 1891. The matrix of his later plays, sparkling with epigrams (some of which were to be put to use again), it was a scarcely veiled acknowledgment of his revolt against conventional morality. Many critics were hostile; Wilde, never loth, poured contumely on them. His four golden years had now begun. His most brilliant and characteristic essays appeared in a volume *Intentions*. Nowhere is Wilde's wit, paradox, and gracefully worn learning better in evidence than in one of them, *The Decay of the Art of Lying*. The sheer fun and intellectual impudence which was to be whipped up into comic magic in *The Importance of Being Earnest* was here in full measure. *The Soul of Man Under Socialism* was a *tour de force* and shows a side of Wilde that is not much in evidence in his writings. As a rule, he was apolitical as well as amoral, and with no inclination towards radical creeds. His life, he said, was devoted to beauty. But within the limitations of a luxury-loving and self-indulgent nature, he was essentially kind and compassionate. Remorse could be extreme and lasted a day.

Lady Windermere's Fan, produced in London early in 1892, made Wilde's reputation as a fashionable playwright. No longer attempting to emulate Racine, he correctly described his venture as "one of those modern drawing-room plays with pink lampshades." It was followed by *A Woman of No Importance*, *An Ideal Husband*, and *The Importance of Being Earnest*. (The last two were running in London's West End when Wilde was arrested in 1895.) Wit and a sure instinct for what works on the stage characterized all of Wilde's later plays, but to later tastes the sentiment was dated, the morality insincere and almost maudlin. Consequently, the play that has most of this Victorian cant, *A Woman of No Importance*, is nowadays the least often performed. The only one without any moralizing in it, *The Importance of Being Earnest*, is an established classic. As Wilde moved from one success to another in the London theatre, he attempted also to conquer Paris. *Salomé*, which he wrote in French, attracted Sarah Bernhardt's attention as an ideal vehicle. She planned to perform the play in London, but the lord chamberlain refused his license because of the representation of sacred persons on the stage.

Wilde was indignant and threatened to seek French citizenship. As his son was later to remark, it was a pity that his father did not. Infatuated with Douglas, Wilde was leading a reckless life, consorting with male prostitutes, some of them criminal. His wife, who bored him, was neglected. Lady Wilde even wrote pathetically, begging her son to take his wife to the first night of one of his plays.

Fate might have been kept at bay had Douglas not involved Wilde in his perpetual war with his father. On February 18, 1895, Queensberry left a visiting card for Wilde at his club, for all to see, addressed to "Oscar Wilde posing as a somdomite [*sic*]." Wilde issued libel proceedings. At the trial, Queensberry pleaded justification in the public interest. He was defended by Edward Carson who had been at Trinity with Wilde and was on his way to establishing a great legal and political career. The trial was a disaster for Wilde. As he knew from blackmailers that compromising letters to Douglas were available, it is extraordinary that he took the risk. He had lost all touch with reality. Douglas, seeking only to humiliate his father, must be seen as the principal agent of Wilde's downfall. In any event, after Carson had led Wilde into damaging admissions on the witness stand and after the jury had brought in a verdict of "Not guilty" against Queensberry, it was certain that Wilde would be prosecuted for homosexual offenses. The authorities would have been glad enough to let Wilde slip out of the country, and his wife prayed that he would. However, he sat irresolute in the Cadogan Hotel, and was apprehended by the police and brought to trial.

The first trial led to disagreement among the jury, and Wilde was released on bail. Friends now advised him to flee. Frank Harris for one told him a yacht was waiting to take him abroad, but Wilde could not be prevailed upon to move. His mother, who earlier had stood beside her husband in his own humiliation, urged her son to stand his trial. W. B. Yeats* remarked that "Wilde was an Irish gentleman. It was a point of honour to face the trial. It could not have occurred to him to act otherwise." He did stand trial, and he was sentenced to two years penal servitude, a term of frightful hardship for such a man. While he emerged from prison fitter than before, as events proved, he was in no other respect the better for the experience.

Had Wilde avoided his fate, only his legend would have suffered: all of his work, save one poem, had already been written. In prison he wrote *De Profundis* in the shape of a long letter to Alfred Douglas. This elaborate piece of prose had a chequered history. Douglas destroyed what he believed was the only copy, but the original was put in the safekeeping of the British Museum until 1960. Condemnatory of Douglas, the apologia is undermined by a vein of grandiloquence and an unconvincing tone of martyrdom. Wilde compares himself to Jesus Christ, and by implication, Douglas is Judas. The exercise is magnificent in its flamboyant way, but the justification rings rather hollow. After he came out of prison, Wilde struck a more genuine note of true feeling when he substituted another protagonist for himself in *The Ballad of Reading Gaol*. For all its echoes of *Eugene Aram* and *The Ancient Mariner*, this is the verse on which Wilde's status as poet most confidently rests. His other poems, even the ingenious ones like *The Sphinx*, are marred by a preciosity which frequently spoiled even his best prose. In his own words, Wilde was "a lord of language," but only when he wrote in the vein of La Rochefoucauld. He described shallowness as the supreme vice, but his cadences and purple passages all too often suggest winter gardens and hired musicians. There was some uncertainty in his taste.

But his wit and fun—he had both—were perpetual and, at his best, incomparable. In his later life, Wilde, joined by Douglas for a time, lived abroad, often penniless, always borrowing. His last years in Paris were a sad epilogue to his years of fame. His character had not been chastened by misfortune. In general, he deteriorated in health and in fortune; he had been cut by former acquaintances but some friends, notably Ross, remained staunch. His wife settled an income on him which he lost when he took up again briefly with Douglas. Constance Wilde died in 1898.

In the 1890s Wilde was associated in the public mind with John Lane's magazine *The Yellow Book* and with Aubrey Beardsley, its daring illustrator. Beardsley's illustrations for *Salomé* matched the erotic tone of the text, but Beardsley, in fact, disliked Wilde, and Wilde had no connection with Lane's publication other than as an occasional contributor. His disgrace, however, led to Beardsley's dismissal, and the magazine suffered from Wilde's connection, publicized at the trials, with Shelley, a boy in Lane's employment.

Wilde's reputation as a writer rests on a ballad, a few sparkling essays, fairy stories, *De Profundis*, and the four later plays. As plays they are not as skillfully wrought as Pinero's written at the same time or Barrie's later plays, but they survive for the greater intelligence and wit of the writer.

The Importance of Being Earnest is Wilde's sure claim to immortality. He himself said that he put his genius into his life, his talent into his work. Except for the few who inevitably found something repellent in his personality—his obesity, lardy color, and dowager mannerism (he laughed behind his hand, probably to conceal a discolored tooth)—people who heard Wilde talk came fully under his fascination. Max Beerbohm, who did not care for him, said that he had heard the table talk of Meredith, Swinburne, Gosse, James, Birrell, Balfour, Chesterton, Desmond Mac-Carthy, and Belloc—all splendid in their ways—but "Oscar was the greatest of them all—the most spontaneous and yet the most polished, the most soothing and yet the most surprising."

Wilde never exhibited his parents' interest in his own country, but his mother's career as a patriot had closed by the time he was growing up. In later years, she sought a pension for her literary work from the British government and wished for a knighthood for her son. Shaw* described Wilde as a "Merrion Square snob." Yeats, who knew him better, said: "He was not a snob. He was an Irishman; and England to an Irishman is a far strange land. To Wilde the aristocrats of England were as the nobles of Baghdad." Wilde died on November 30, 1900, in Paris, at the Hôtel D'Alsace in the Rue des Beaux Arts, where he was living at the time. He is buried in Père Lachaise.

TERENCE DE VERE WHITE

WORKS: *Complete Works of Oscar Wilde.* Vyvyan Holland, ed. London & Glasgow: Collins, 1948; *The Letters of Oscar Wilde.* Rupert Hart-Davis, ed. New York: Harcourt, Brace & World, 1962; *The Artist as Critic: Critical Writings of Oscar Wilde.* Richard Ellmann, ed. New York: Random House, 1969.   REFERENCES: Beckson, Karl, ed. *Oscar Wilde: The Critical Heritage.* New York: Barnes & Noble, 1970; Croft-Crooke, Rupert. *The Unrecorded Life of Oscar Wilde.* New York: McKay, 1972; Dougglas, Lord Alfred. *Oscar Wilde and Myself.* New York: Duffield & Co., 1914; Ellmann, Richard, ed. *Oscar Wilde: A Collection of Critical Essays.* Englewood Cliffs, N.J.: Prentice-Hall, 1969; Fido, Martin. *Oscar Wilde.* London: Hamlyn, 1973; Harris, Frank. *Oscar Wilde: Including My Memories of Oscar Wilde* by Bernard Shaw. East Lansing: Michigan State University Press, 1959; Holland, Vyvyan. *Oscar Wilde: A Pictorial Biography.* New York: Viking, 1960; Mason, Stuart. *Bibliography of Oscar Wilde.* New ed. London: Bertram Rota, 1967; Nassaar, Christopher S. *Into the Demon Universe: A Literary Exploration of Oscar Wilde.* New Haven, Conn.: Yale University Press, 1974; Pearson, Hesketh. *Oscar Wilde: His Life and Wit.* New York: Harper, 1946; Symons, Arthur. *A Study of Oscar Wilde.* London: Charles J. Sawyer, 1930.

WILDE, SIR WILLIAM (1815-1876), antiquarian and topographical writer. There have been instances where a young man's career has been hindered by the celebrity of a brilliant father; the reverse, too, can happen, and Sir William Wilde's versatility and achievements have been diminished by Oscar's* success and notoriety. However, Sir William made significant contributions to a developing specialty, aural surgery; his endeavors as assistant census connoisseur were prodigious; an enthusiastic archaeologist, his catalogue of the Royal Irish Academy's collection of antiquities has been described as "a milestone in the history of Irish Archaelogy"; and through his biographical articles (mainly of Irish medical men) and his topographical books, he has gained a place in the annals of Anglo-Irish literature.

William Wilde was born at Kilkeevin, Castlerea, County Roscommon, in 1815, the son of Dr. Thomas Wilde and his wife, Emily Fynne, a native of Ballymagibbon, near Cong, County Mayo. He took the Licentiate of the Royal College of Surgeons in Ireland in 1837 and spent the next nine months on board the "Crusader" as personal physician to a wealthy businessman who was going abroad on a health cruise. Thus, he obtained material for the two-volume *Narrative of a Voyage to Maderia, Teneriffe and along the Shores of the Mediterranean* (1839). For this work he received £250 which enabled him to study diseases of the eye and ear in London, Vienna, and Berlin.

Equipped as a specialist, Wilde set up in practice at 15 Westland Row and opened a dispensary for poor patients (the forerunner of St. Mark's Hospital) in a converted stable. Growing affluent, he moved to 21 Westland Row and later to a commodious mansion at 1 Merrion Square. Meanwhile, he had contributed biographical articles on Sir Thomas Molyneaux and Dr. R. J. Graves to the *Dublin University Magazine*, and during a brief tenure of the editorial chair of the *Dublin Journal of Medical Science* he wrote or edited other biographical articles. Later contributions to this genre were *The Closing Years of Dean Swift's Life* (1849) and a *Memoir of Gabriel Béranger* (1880).

A characteristic feature of Wilde's biographical work is its discursiveness; he lacks the true instinct of a biographer, being less interested in the man than in his achievements. His topographical works, *The Beauties of the Boyne* (1849) and *Lough Corrib, Its Shores and Islands* (1867), make more satisfactory reading.

On November 12, 1851, Wilde married Jane Francesca Elgee ("Speranza"* of *The Nation**), and they had three children, William, Oscar, and Isola. The Wildes may have seemed an ill-suited pair: he was small, untidy, and physically unprepossessing, while she was tall and striking; his mind sought facts and their collation, while hers was imaginative and fantastic. His avocations brought him in touch with many famous people. When Lord Macaulay who was then writing his *History* came to inspect the field of the Boyne, Wilde was his guide. His honors included the Order of the Polar Star bestowed by the king of Sweden and a knighthood conferred in 1864 for his work in connection with the Irish census.

If fortune had singled out Sir William Wilde in the bestowal of gifts, fate decreed that he should repay by being publicly cast down. An indiscretion with a female patient initiated a chain of events ending in a notorious libel action. His accuser won her case, although only a farthing damages, but Wilde's reputation was destroyed.

Wilde took refuge at Moytura House, overlooking Lough Corrib; soon he resumed practice. When the British Medical Association met in Dublin in 1867 (and Lister read an epoch-making paper "On the Antiseptic Principle"), Wilde acted as guide on an excursion to the Boyne Valley. He engaged in the Irish census of 1871 and rejoiced in 1874 when Oscar won the Berkeley Gold Medal at Trinity College.

Wilde's health deteriorated through 1875, and he died on April 19, 1876.

J. B. LYONS

WORKS: "Sir Thomas Molyneaux." *Dublin University Magazine* 18 (1841): 305-327, 470-489, 604-618, 744-763; "Sylvester O'Halloran." *Dublin Quarterly Journal of Medical Science* 6 (1848): 223; *The Beauties of the Boyne and Its Tributary the Blackwater.* Dublin: McGlashan, 1849/abridged, Dublin: Three Candles, 1949; *The Closing Years of Dean Swift's Life.* Dublin: Hodges & Smith, 1849; *Lough Corrib, Its Shores and Islands.* Dublin: McGlashan, 1867/3d ed., abridged, Dublin: Three Candles, 1936; *Memoir of Gabriel Beranger.* Dublin: Gill, 1880.   REFERENCES: Frogatt, P. "Sir William Wilde and the 1851 Census of Ireland." *Medical History* 9, No. 4 (1965): 302-327; Lyons, J. B. "Sir William Wilde, 1815-1876." *Journal of the Irish Colleges of Physicians and Surgeons* 5, No. 4 (1976): 147-152; de Paor, L. "Wilde the Antiquarian." *The Irish Times* 8 (September 14, 1976); White, T. deV. *The Parents of Oscar Wilde.* London: Hodder & Stoughton, 1967; Wilson, T. G. *Victorian Doctor—The Life of Sir William Wilde.* London, 1942/reprinted, Wakefield: EP Publishing Ltd., 1974.

WILLIAMS, RICHARD D'ALTON (1822-1862), poet. Williams, the natural son of Count D'Alton, was born in Dublin on October 8, 1822, and was reared in his mother's home at Grenanstown, County Tipperary. While Williams was still a schoolboy, his first published poem, "The Munster War Song," derivative of Thomas Davis'* more celebrated "Lament for Owen Roe," appeared in *The Nation.* His medical studies in Dublin were interrupted by a close association with the Young Ireland movement, and his contributions to the *Irish Tribune* led to his arrest. Defended by the better known poet Sir Samuel Ferguson,* he was acquitted of the charge of treason-felony.

Williams' poetry had three moods: patriotic, humorous, and religious. His association with St. Vincent's Hospital inspired his moving "Sister of Charity" and "The Dying Girl." Some lines in "The Dying Girl" became proverbial, particularly "Consumption has no pity/For blue eyes and golden hair."

After graduating from Edinburgh about 1850, Williams worked at Dr. Steevens' Hospital, but verses published in *The Nation* in 1851 mark his decision to emigrate to a freer world, far from "British greed" and the threat of "her dungeon bars": "Come with me o'er Ohio/Among the vines of Indiana. . . ." Upon arriving in America in 1851, he taught in a Jesuit College in Mobile and later practiced medicine in New Orleans.

He died in Thibodeaux from tuberculosis on July 5, 1862. His most famous poem of the American period was the "Song of the Irish-American Regiments."

J. B. LYONS

WORK: *The Poems of Richard D'Alton Williams,* ed. with biographical introduction by P. A. Sillard. 2d ed. Dublin: Duffy, 1901. REFERENCE: Lyons, J. B. "Medicine and Literature in Ireland." *Journal of the Irish Colleges of Physicians and Surgeons* 3, No. 1, 3-9.

WILLIAMS, RICHARD VALENTINE. *See* ROWLEY, RICHARD.

WILSON, A[NDREW] PATRICK (ca. 1880-?), playwright and producer. Wilson was probably born in Scotland or in England of Scottish parents, sometime in the 1880s. Around 1911, he appeared in Dublin and became involved in Jim Larkin's Irish Transport and General Worker's Union, and became a correspondent for the labor paper, *The Irish Worker.* Under the pseudonym of "Euchan," he engaged in an acrimonious controversy in its pages with Sean O'Casey.* At the same time, Wilson had become involved with the Abbey Theatre,* first as a student actor, then as a member of the second company, and finally as manager and chief play producer. He was a vigorous producer, doing many new plays and, in 1914, two plays of his own. The more important, *The Slough,* dealt with the 1913 Lockout and was the first Irish play to depict Dublin slum life. In the production, Wilson himself played the Jim Larkin role but apparently with little of Larkin's flamboyance. In 1915, after a terrific row with Yeats* over the staging of Synge's* *Deirdre of the Sorrows,* Wilson resigned. For a while, he managed Arthur Sinclair's Irish Players and a similar Scottish group under the name of Andrew P. Wilson. Only two minor pieces of his have been published. The date of his death is uncertain.

WORK: *Victims and Poached.* Dublin: Liberty Hall Players, ca. 1916.

WILSON, ROBERT ARTHUR (ca. 1820-1875), journalist and humorist. Wilson was born in Dunfanaghy, County Donegal, in about 1820. Under the name of Barney Maglone, he wrote popular humorous sketches. He was credited with a great mastery of languages. With his slouch hat, capacious cloak, and "necktie of pronounced hue," he was a striking figure on the streets of Enniskillen and Belfast. On April 10, 1875, he was found in his room in Belfast, dying, as one editor put it, "from the effect of his besetting sin. . . . 'Maglone' was one of the most lovable of men, but unfortunately his social qualities were his bane." He left posterity a vivid warning against his "besetting sin" in his poem "The Irish Cry," from which we extract these small gems:

There's a wail from the glen;
There's a groan from the hill;

> 'Tis the cry of the land
>   'Gainst the Fiend of the Still! . . .
>
> The living! the smitten—
>   The blasted—the seared—
> The souls by the slime of
>   The drink-snake besmeared. . . .
>
> For the sake of the soul smitten
>   Slave of the Cup—
> For the sake of his victims—
>   Up! countrymen, up! . . .

Despite the above extract, Wilson's humorous skits and verses had keen and droll power of observation, and he had the ability to have bulked much larger than the minor and forgotten figure that he is.

WORKS: *Barney Maglone's Almeynack for All Ireland,* by Ephemerides. London, 1871; *The Reliques of "Barney Maglone."* D. J. O'Donoghue, ed. Belfast: T. Dargan, 1894.

WINGFIELD, SHEILA (1906-), poet. Wingfield was born into a wealthy family in Hampshire in 1906 and through marriage became Viscountess Powerscourt. Although an active writer of poetry from childhood, her first published work did not appear until 1938 when she was thirty-two years old. Since then, she has published regularly, except for a ten-year period when illness necessitated a series of operations that rendered her an invalid.

Since Wingfield has remained somewhat outside the stream of literary activity and influences, her work has probably not received the acclaim it deserves. Most readers will probably remember her for her long, moving war poem *Beat, Drum, Beat, Heart,* which is a two thousand line comparison of the psychological and philosophical states of men at war and women in love. Her first book, *Poems,* reveals an economical, almost stark style which some reviewers have compared favorably to the early Imagist works of H.D. and Pound. *Beat, Drum, Beat, Heart* (1946), while it is more subjective than the earlier efforts, nevertheless retains much of the objective vividness and taut rigor of *Poems.* Herbert Read celebrated this volume "as the most sustained meditation on war that has been written in our time."

A Cloud Across the Sun came out in 1949, followed by *A Kite's Dinner* in 1954 which was a Poetry Book Society Choice. In 1977, *Admissions* was released, and in 1978 a selection from all the poems, 1938 to 1976, appeared under the title *Her Storms.*

G. S. Fraser classifies Wingfield as an objectivist poet, pointing out her interest "in all the wonderful, sad, and glorious detail of the world around her." She herself has insisted that "what is personally felt must be fused with what is being, and has been, felt by others. But always in terms of the factual. Nothing woolly or disembodied will do." While her poems do display a healthy respect for concrete nouns and a somewhat weaker resolve to avoid "amorphous description," few American readers would immediately comprehend the "objectivist" label Fraser assigns. Some poems do have a hard-eyed detachment and an almost brittle objectivity reminiscent of the early Ezra Pound or of H. D., particularly Wingfield's pre-1938 work. In the more ambitious pieces of some of her later work, Wingfield indulges in a romantic, highly generalized diction that does not so much bring feeling sharply into focus as it wraps it in gauze. Nevertheless, Wingfield's style never stagnates; and her thought, while always anchored to the simple things and events she knows best—country life, courage, pain, love, and even ecstasy—nearly always avoids the sentimental.

THOMAS F. MERRILL

WORKS: *Poems*. London: Cresset, [1938]; *Beat, Drum, Beat, Heart*. London: Cresset, 1946; *A Cloud Across the Sun*. London: Cresset, 1949; *Real People*. London: Cresset, 1952. (Autobiography); *A Kite's Dinner*. Poems 1938-1954. [London]: Cresset, 1954; *The Leaves Darken*. London: Weidenfeld & Nicolson, [1964]; *Sun Too Fast*. London: Bles, 1975. (Memoirs); *Admissions*. Dublin: Dolmen, 1977; *Her Storms*. Dublin: Dolmen, 1978.

WOLFE, CHARLES (1791-1823), poet. Wolfe was born in Dublin on December 14, 1791, a cousin of Wolfe Tone.* He was educated at Trinity College, Dublin. He took Holy Orders and died at Queenstown on February 21, 1823. Padraic Colum* calls him a "one-poem poet." That one good poem was "The Burial of Sir John Moore," which Byron rather overrated as "the most perfect ode in the language."

WORKS: *The Burial of Sir John Moore*. London: T. Wilson, 1825; *The Burial of Sir John Moore and Other Poems*, with memoir by C. L. Falkiner. London: Sidgwick & Jackson, 1909.

WOODS, MACDARA (1942-), poet. Woods was born in Dublin in 1942. In 1970, he published a pamphlet containing a longish poem called "Decimal D. Sec. Drinks in a Bar in Marrakesch," which was more foppish than clever. Two years later, however, his collection entitled *Early Morning Matins* showed considerable advance and contained perhaps half a dozen poems of promise. Many of his sentences are overlong and rambling, but he does use rhyme and assonance to good effect. His long poem "The Snow That Scatters the Leaves" does disintegrate technically, but a few shorter pieces, like "The Dark Sobrietee" and particularly the Auden-like "Lavender Hill," have few flaws. He is an editor of the literary magazine *Cyphers*.

WORKS: *Decimal D. Sec. Drinks in a Bar in Marrakesch*. Dublin: New Writers', 1970; *Early Morning Matins*. Dublin: Gallery Books, [1973].

WYKHAM, HELEN (ca. 1933-), novelist. Helen Wykham is the pseud-onym of Pamela Evans. She was born in about 1933, grew up in the Irish countryside, and took a degree in archaeology from Newnham College, Cambridge. She is married, has three children, and lives in a remote spot in Wales.

Wykham's first novel, *Ribstone Pippins* (1974), though marred, shows quite remarkable talent, catching beautifully and comically the intensity and sexual confusion of adolescence. Lumpy, teenage "Helen Wykham," the narrator, goes shopping with her flighty mother and sister in Brown Thomas's to prepare for a house party at the San Fes'. This turns out to be a "hissing cauldron of lust." Dominic San Fe, a debauched Heathcliff with a face "like an angel of Jaweh," seduces everyone in sight and is soon bedding Helen's attractive sister. Expeditions to the seaside, the pub, the theatre, even a picnic, are all spiced by his irrepressible appetites. Indeed, the convolutions are amazing, and so many undercurrents only distract the reader from Helen's more serious plight, the ambiguous nature of her sex-uality. A teenager with less of a flair for the absurd might have been driven insane, but Helen emerges a confirmed lesbian. Another distraction in the work is that many of the characters are mere presences and cannot be visualized in flesh and blood. Helen, her sister, and her mother are well caught, and the funniest scenes in the book rotate round them, but many of the San Fe's jell together. The prose is often dazzling; descriptions of nature leave the reader with a sense of experiencing the place described. However, too many gems appear together; in a simpler, less poetic prose they would be noticed more.

Although *Ribstone Pippins* tends to pretentiousness, it is saved by Helen's comic vision. Not so *Cavan* (1977), Wykham's second novel. With no re-deeming, believable character to filter the febrile sexuality, the novel is more than disappointing. Even the prose style seems arty and affected. Cavan, a sort of God-dolly who cannot be looked upon with the naked eye, is intro-duced, along with a cripple and his child, to the communal home of three sisters. He soon starts a sexual relationship with the youngest and prettiest. When her boyfriend objects, he is raped by Cavan. Far from disliking the experience, the boy is so transported that he falls at Cavan's feet. The cripple who witnessed it all is far from amused, but when he preaches hell-fire, Cavan heats up the poker and pierces the cripple's plastic stomach. These are only samples of the novel's tastelessness and waste of a very considerable talent.

MARY ROSE CALLAGHAN

WORKS: *Ribstone Pippins*. Dublin: Allen Figgis/London: Calder & Boyars, 1974; *Cavan*. London: Marion Boyars, 1977.

YEATS, JACK B[UTLER] (1871-1957), painter, playwright, and novelist. Yeats, who is probably Ireland's foremost modern painter, was born in

London on August 29, 1871, and died in Dublin on March 28, 1957. Like his older brother, W. B. Yeats,* he wrote his own epitaph, and it is quoted by Terence de Vere White* in *A Fretful Midge*:

> I have travelled all my life without a ticket. . . .
> When we are asked about it all in the end,
> we who travel without tickets, we can say
> with that vanity which takes the place of
> self-confidence: even though we went without
> tickets we never were commuters.

His life and work matched his epitaph for quiet and unassertive individuality and unconventionality. Neither he nor his wife Mary Cottenham White, a fellow art student whom he married in 1894, wished to be commuters or seemed to doubt that art was Jack Yeats' proper profession. He never seemed to need to adopt a flamboyant pose to convince himself that he was truly an artist. Nor did he pretend an artistic scorn for business acumen. Synge* noted in a letter to a friend that after their joint tour of the Congested Districts for the *Manchester Guardian*, "Jack Yeats, being a wiser man than I, made a better bargain." He conducted himself as a working professional, starting out as a black and white illustrator, for fifty years without spectacular success, enjoying great recognition only for the last decade and a half of his long life. His biographer, Hilary Pyle, lists sixty-two individual exhibitions of his work from 1897 to his death in 1957, and he contributed to 160 group exhibitions, during the same period. She also notes that he regularly contributed drawings to *Punch* for more than thirty years, under a pseudonym, and edited the monthly *Broadside* for more than seven years, "gathering materials and colouring his illustrations singlehanded." Pyle cites thirty books and gives the titles of more than forty "magazine articles and stories" he is known to have illustrated. Apparently, he had the work habits of a commuter.

Yeats' professed motive for becoming a painter seems to mark him as a traditionalist. Several times in his life he said that he became a painter because he was "the son of a painter." Yet he was the third, not the first, son— William Butler, Susan Mary, Elizabeth Corbett, and Robert Yeats being the elder children of the portrait painter John Butler Yeats* and Susan Pollexfen Yeats. Moreover, he spent very little of his early life with his father, being raised in Sligo by his maternal grandparents. His father deprecates his own possible influence by saying of Jack's upbringing: "I think he has received the education of a man of genius. His personality was given its full chance. It has at once the sense of expansion and the instinct for self-control. He has the habits of a man who knows his own mind" (*Christian Science Monitor*, November 20, 1920). Hilary Pyle corroborates his independence: "He worked alone," and "He continued to deny the company of other painters, living or dead . . . until the end of his life." Jack

Yeats said of himself, in à letter to his brother W.B., in 1925, "You say my painting is now 'great'. Great is a word that may mean so many different things. But I know I am the first living painter in the world. And the second is so far away that I am only able to make him out faintly. I have no modesty. I have the immodesty of the spearhead." He appears to have written with the same "immodesty," for both his plays and his nondramatic prose are expressionistic and as self-confident in their formlessness as only a man convinced of the truth and worth of his personal vision could have written.

Yeats spoke very little of aesthetic theory, convinced that too much fuss was made about it. Perhaps he formed this opinion listening to the prolonged discussions in the Bedford Park home of his youth. In a letter to Joseph Hone (March 7, 1922), he is quoted as saying "No one creates . . . the artist assembles memories." This certainly appears to be what he was doing in his own fiction of the 1930s. *Sligo*; *Sailing, Sailing Swiftly*; *The Amaranthers*; and *The Charmed Life* assemble and reassemble memories. At this time he was doing little painting, much public speaking, and some experimentation with what was for him always a mode of communication less direct, and therefore less valuable, than the visual image—the word. Now in his sixties he claimed that he wrote "to jettison some memories."

Ah, Well; *And to You Also*; and *The Careless Flower*, published in the 1940s, continue the reminiscence. His biographer speaks of Jack Yeats' conversation in this period as varying "between the charming, realistic, down-to-earth and a muddled monotone slipping from subject to subject and even with the greatest concentration from his listeners very difficult to follow. He seemed to be completely self-contained and he did not mind whether he was comprehensible or not" (p. 149). The same could be said of much of his prose. The reminiscences are stream-of-consciousness pieces, full of short tales, with very little plot or character development. There are affinities to the writing of some of his contemporaries, e.g., to Flann O'Brien's* *The Third Policeman* and to characters of Beckett* (Bowsie and Mr. No Matter resemble Vladimir and Estragon of *Waiting for Godot*). The more interesting connections, however, are to Yeats' own great paintings of this period. They are more fruitfully read as aspects of the personal vision of a powerfully original mind. While not as consciously mystical as his brother's vision and not as concerned with a formally symbolic system (although they shared some symbols like the rose, which is important in both of their works), Jack Yeats' vision was metaphysical. His work is concerned with life as flux, with randomness, and with ontological questions. The same Bowsie and Mr. No Matter of the fiction appear and reappear in the paintings and assume roles, under different names, in the plays. They seem, possibly not unlike Vladimir and Estragon, to represent Jack Yeats' own continuing explorations of the halves of the personality which so interested W.B.

The plays, collected by Robin Skelton and published in 1971, show a stronger sense of controlling form than the nondramatic pieces, while retaining their spontanaiety, love of words for their own sounds, freshness of vision, and irony. Of the nine "Plays for the Larger Theatre," three (*Harlequin's Positions*, *La La Noo*, and *In Sand*) were produced by the Abbey Theatre* or Abbey experimental theatres. Jack Yeats himself produced the "Plays for the Miniature Theatre" for the children of his neighborhood in Devon as holiday entertainments; like the later plays, they reflect his love of melodrama, pantomime, circuses, and pirate themes. This material appears in the early illustrations, such as those for the *Broadsides*, and the later paintings. There is an analogy between the early and late use of materials in his plays to their use in painting—straightforward in the early styles and transformed by his powerfully symbolic vision in the late styles. This use of material conforms to his statement of aesthetic theory, "the artist assembles memories."

Viewed as Robin Skelton views them, as anarchic drama, the later plays cast light on the intentions of the fiction, which they embody more aptly, and are clearly related both to his life and to the vision revealed in the paintings:

> Jack Yeats' drama is, one might suggest, anarchic in the proper sense. It mocks and teases notions of government and politics. It opposes materialist values. After its beginnings, it frees itself from the conventions of the drama of its time, breaks the laws of unity, and challenges all contemporary preconceptions of what is dramatic. It utilizes inconsequence and chance. . . . Belonging to no school, not even being easily allied to the Irish writers' drama of its day . . . the drama of Jack B. Yeats, especially in his major plays, *The Silencer*, *La La Noo*, and *In Sand*, is both inimitable and . . . seminal. It challenges orthodoxies and promotes questions, but does so with an affectionate humour and a dazzle of wit that few playwrights have equalled in our time, and to the question "What does it mean?" it gives the calm answer [taken from the prologue to *In Sand*, *The Green Wave*], "I think it means just to be."

So intensely individual is Yeats' vision, as it is reflected in both his painting and his writing, so profound and yet gentle is his irony and his "anarchy," that his own description of one of the characters in an early, unpublished play, *The Deathly Terrace*, might well fit him: "an Egotist steeped in generosity and seethed in affection."

NORA McGUINNESS

WORKS: *A Broadside*. Dublin: Dun Emer & Cuala, 1908-1915; *Modern Aspects of Irish Art*. Dublin: Cumann Leigheacht & Phobail, 1922; *Sligo*. London: Wishart, 1930; *Sailing, Sailing Swiftly*. London: Putnam, 1933; *The Amaranthers*. London: Heinemann, 1936; *The Charmed Life*. London: Routledge, 1938/reissued in paperback, Routledge & Kegan Paul, 1974; *Ah, Well*. London: Routledge, 1942/reissued in paperback with *And To You Also,* Routledge & Kegan Paul, 1974; *And To You Also.* London: Routledge, 1944; *The Careless Flower.* London: Pilot, 1947; *The Collected Plays of Jack B. Yeats.* Robin Skelton, ed. London: Secker & Warburg, 1971. REFERENCES: MacGowran, Jack. "Preface." *In Sand.* Dublin: Dolmen, 1964; Mac-Greevy, Thomas. *Jack B. Yeats: An Appreciation and Interpretation.* Dublin: Wadding-ton, 1945; McHugh, Roger, ed. *Jack B. Yeats: A Centenary Gathering.* Dublin: Dolmen, 1971; Marriott, E. *Jack B. Yeats: Being a True and Impartial View of His Pictorial and Dramatic Art.* London: Elkin Mathews, 1911; O'Doherty, Brian. "Humanism in Art: A Study of Jack B. Yeats." *University Review* (Summer 1955); O'Driscoll, Robert, & Lorna Reynolds, eds. *Theatre and the Visual Arts: A Centenary Celebration of Jack Yeats and John Synge.* Shannon: Irish University Press, 1972; Pyle, Hilary. *Jack B. Yeats: A Biography.* London: Routledge & Kegan Paul, 1970; Rosenthal, T. G. *Jack Yeats 1871-1957.* London: Knowledge Publications, 1966; Rothenstein. "A Visit to Jack B. Yeats." *New English Review* (July 1946); White, James, ed. *Drawings and Paintings of Jack B. Yeats.* London: Secker & Warburg, 1971; White, James. "Jack B. Yeats." *New Knowledge* (April 24, 1966).

YEATS, JOHN BUTLER (1839-1922), painter, conversationalist, and letter writer. Yeats, who was born in the Rectory of Tullylish, County Down, on March 16, 1839, was the eldest son of the Reverend William Butler Yeats and a grandson of a rector of Drumcliffe, County Sligo. A further link with Sligo was forged by his marriage to his school friend George Pollexfen's sister, Susan, in 1863. He was then a man of property, having inherited a small estate in County Kildare which brought him a modest income, as well as being an arts graduate of Trinity College, Dublin, and a law student at the King's Inns. His father-in-law, joint owner of a small shipping line and flour mill, saw him as a worthy addition to the family; however, though called to the bar in 1866 John Butler Yeats never practiced, and indecisiveness and procrastination played havoc with his career as an artist.

He claimed that through marriage with a Pollexfen he had given a voice to the sea cliffs, but he was far more than a mere transmitter of the genes of genius; a gifted portrait painter, a critic of merit, capable of highly original observations expressed epigramatically in his speech and letters, he neglected the conventional emblems of success in the pursuit of an illusory perfection. Material needs became a secondary consideration. Financial crises were circumvented with the grudging assistance of his father-in-law and by mortgaging his estate.

John and Susan Yeats had five children, one of whom died in childhood of croup. Their sons, William Butler Yeats* and Jack B. Yeats,* achieved early and increasing success as a poet and painter respectively; their daughters, Lily and Lolly, achieved eventual fulfillment in the Dun Emer Press and its successor the Cuala Press.* The family's unsettled years, with a series of homes in Dublin, Sligo, and London, doubtless had creative advantages, but Mrs. Yeats was temperamentally unsuited to an artistic milieu. While still a young woman, she had a stroke and remained in indifferent health until her death in 1900.

Writing to Sarah Purser in 1891, John Butler Yeats said that a sixteen-year-old model told him that someday he might commit suicide. "When she saw me change my mind so often and begin the picture so often and scratch out so constantly, of course she had my measure and thought me mad and on the way to disaster." He never freed himself of this obsessionalism, but had no intention of quitting a life which he continued to hope would surely someday bring recognition, however slow in coming. In 1902 he returned to Dublin where, notwithstanding his indigence, "old Mr. Yeats" commanded widespread respect and affection.

Hugh Lane and some other friends, knowing that he had never been to Italy, raised a fund to send him there, but to their surprise he elected to use the money to accompany Lily to New York, where his many acquaintances included John Quinn, a wealthy lawyer and collector. Manhattan delighted him, and he established himself there in the role of sage, growing old cheerfully and gracefully. "Young people are sad," he wrote to his daughter, "and sometimes commit suicide, but old men are naturally cheerful. Why? Because the first are oppressed by the menace of life, and of the long road before them. We are delivered from that terror." He died from heart failure on February 3, 1922.

His publications include reviews, essays, and collections of letters to family and friends, but it may be fairly said that his books are a credit to the organization of others rather than to his own unsustained ambition.

J. B. LYONS

WORKS: *Passages from the Letters of John Butler Yeats.* Ezra Pound, ed. Churchtown, Dundrum: Cuala, 1917; *Essays Irish and American,* with an Appreciation by AE. Dublin: Talbot/London: T. Fisher Unwin, 1918/reprint, Freeport, N.Y.: Books for Libraries, 1969; *Further Letters.* Lennox Robinson, ed. Dundrum: Cuala, 1920; *Early Memories: Some Chapters of Autobiography.* Dundrum: Cuala, 1923; *J. B. Yeats, Letters to his Son W. B. Yeats and Others,* ed., with a Memoir by Joseph Hone. London: Faber, 1944/New York: E. P. Dutton, 1946; *Letters from Bedford Park: A Selection from the Correspondence (1890-1901) of John Butler Yeats.* William M. Murphy, ed. Dublin: Cuala, 1972. REFERENCES: Archibald, Douglas N. *John Butler Yeats.* Lewisburg, Pa.: Bucknell University Press, 1974; Murphy, William M. *Prodigal Father, The Life of John Butler Yeats (1839-1922).* Ithaca, N.Y. & London: Cornell University Press, [1978].

YEATS, WILLIAM BUTLER (1865-1939), a foremost poet of the English-speaking world, founder of the Abbey Theatre,* dramatist, spokesman for the Irish Literary Revival, essayist, autobiographer, occultist, member of the Irish Free State Senate, and winner of the 1923 Nobel Prize for literature.

Louis MacNeice,* himself a fine poet, wrote in 1941 that if he were editing an anthology he would include sixty poems by Yeats: "There is no other poet in the language from whom I should choose so many." Throughout a long career Yeats maintained an extraordinary level of excellence, gaining in power and perception to the end. One of his many fine late poems,

"The Municipal Gallery Revisited," a valedictory on his life, his friends, and the Ireland he knew, was written after the age of seventy.

A commanding feature of Yeats' poetry is its confessional nature. The poems move from personal experience to public pronouncements or philosophic meditations. Even when based on his esoteric thought they speak to the human condition, as in the oracular "The Second Coming." Opening with a striking figure of the falcon, it reaches the dictum, so often quoted, "Things fall apart; the centre cannot hold." The imminence of the strange desert beast arouses awe and fear. We have all felt that fear; we need not know that the poem is based on a cyclical theory of history.

Yeats displays astonishing metrical skill and creates an almost magical effect through traditional symbols such as swan or unicorn, horseman or dancer. Thus, unity of being is dramatized in the conclusion of "Among School Children":

> O chestnut tree, great-rooted blossomer,
> Are you the leaf, the blossom or the bole?
> O body swayed to music, O brightening glance,
> How can we know the dancer from the dance?

Titles in *The Collected Poems* show Yeats' sense of stages in his career, but they can be misleading. "Crossways" (1889) and "The Rose" (1893) are not book titles, but were used in the 1895 *Poems*, the first to signify the many paths he had tried, and the second as "the only pathway whereon he can hope to see with his own eyes the Eternal Rose of Beauty and of Peace." Other inaccuracies will be noted later.

Despite the poet's misgivings, his early work retains considerable interest. "The Lake Isle of Innisfree" (1890) was popular from the beginning and was anthologized four years later by W. J. Paul in *Modern Irish Poets*. The rose poems and "The White Birds" rise above romantic cliché; there are also fine adaptations of the Irish song "Down by the Salley Gardens" and of Rimbaud's "When You Are Old," as well as vigorous ballads and the patriotic challenge, "To Ireland in the Coming Times."

In the beginning of this century, Yeats found that "All things can tempt me from this craft of verse"—disappointment in love, political and literary controversy. His subjects became more topical, his style more lean: "Now I may wither into the truth" ("The Coming of Wisdom with Time"). Classical terseness is found in "A Woman Homer Sung" or in the ringing conclusion of "No Second Troy": "Was there another Troy for her to burn?" Confining romantic dreams to his plays, he writes visionary poems like "The Cold Heaven" and "The Magi," and praises aristocratic virtues in "Fallen Majesty" and "That the Night Come."

The great years of 1918 to 1928 include philosophical poems, epigrams, songs, and satires. "The Wild Swan at Coole" reflects on life's transitory nature. The eulogy of Major Robert Gregory, the aviator shot down in

1918, hails him as an exemplar of Unity of Being. An expression of his ideals for womanhood is "A Prayer for My Daughter." Now truly a public man, he commemorates the victims of the Rising in "Easter 1916" and responds to the terror of war: "Now days are dragon-ridden, the nightmare / Rides upon sleep" ("Nineteen Hundred and Nineteen"), "Death" celebrates his friend Kevin O'Higgins, vice-president and minister of justice, as "A great man in his pride / Confronting murderous men" at his assassination. He contemplates legend and history in "The Tower," and in "Among School Children" he speculates on youth and age, symbol and reality. The cycles of history are evoked in "Leda and the Swan," "The Second Coming," and the ominous "Two Songs from a Play." "Sailing to Byzantium" itself is one of the "Monuments of unageing intellect" it describes. The Crazy Jane poems express desire and defiance. "The Double Vision of Michael Robartes" presents hallucinations of a Sphinx, a Buddha, and a ghostly dancer. Yeats undercuts his explanation of "The Phases of the Moon" with ironic humor when the character Aherne walks away from the tower where Yeats is studying and remarks "He'd crack his wits / Day after day, yet never find the meaning."

These are but a few of the fine poems in *The Wild Swans at Coole* (1917), *Michael Robartes and the Dancer* (1920), *The Tower* (1928), and *The Winding Stair and Other Poems* (1933).

One might expect that Yeats, after he passed sixty, would have experienced a decline in inspiration; yet during this period he explored new themes and wrote some of his finest work. There were more ballads, satires, and songs; and there emerged both a violent sexuality and a rage against infirmity and death. He celebrated the Gore-Booth sisters of County Sligo, the poet Eva and the artist-patriot Constance Markiewicz, as well as Parnell and Casement, and memorialized Lady Gregory's* estate in "Coole Park, 1929" ("They came like swallows and like swallows went") and in "Coole Park and Ballylee, 1931" ("We were the last romantics—chose for theme / Traditional sanctity and loveliness"). He glorified the Georgian Ireland of Swift* and Burke* in "Blood and the Moon" and "The Seven Sages." He pondered his own career ("Are You Content?," "What Then?," and "The Circus Animals' Desertion") and asked "Why Should Not Old Men Be Mad?" He pleaded for "An old man's eagle mind" ("An Acre of Grass"). He reached profound depths in the visionary "Byzantium" and in esoteric poems ("A Dialogue of Self and Soul," "Vacillation," "The Delphic Oracle Upon Plotinus," "The Gyres," "Meru," "Lapis Lazuli," "The Statues," "News for the Delphic Oracle"). Irish legend returned with poems on Cuchulain and "The Black Tower," his last work, one week before his death. "Under Ben Bulben," a few months earlier, epitomizes his career and much of his thought.

As a meticulous craftsman, Yeats rewrote, retitled, and rearranged many poems after publication. He defended this practice in 1908 in a quatrain he never republished. "It is myself that I remake," he asserted. We can see the poet at work in the many rough drafts he saved; an extreme example is the play *The Player Queen*, written and revised over a twenty-seven year period.

The plays, more than thirty in all, were of great importance to Yeats as experiments in theatre art and as vehicles for his thought, but they enjoyed only limited success on the stage and are now fairly seldom performed. In reaction against the realistic comedy and social drama of his time, Yeats developed a ritualistic form, later to be influenced by the Japanese Noh tradition, where masked actors, formal gestures, and choreographed actions are rendered in a style of incantation, accompanied by music and interpreted by dance. The subjects are from Irish folklore and legend, or from parable and fantasy, and the plays have close affinities to dance drama. Full appreciation depends on highly trained actors and well-schooled listeners or readers.

Though none of Yeats' prose can be neglected by the interested student, the most important works are *Autobiographies* and *A Vision*. The plural title of the autobiography is preferable, since it comprises six volumes, in different styles and with varied emphases. It is also intermittent, the periods covered being the years from childhood to 1902, then 1909, the year of Synge's* death, and, finally, an account of the Nobel Prize award. More personal testament than autobiography, it shows Yeats creating a personality and creating a philosophy, trying out theories of character and of history, preoccupations to be rendered in more schematic form in *A Vision*. His extensive miscellaneous prose reflects the same concerns, making of Yeats an eminent man of letters.

Yeats was born on June 13, 1865, at Sandymount, County Dublin, the eldest child of John Butler Yeats* and Susan Pollexfen Yeats. In the words of Sir William Wilde,* father of Oscar,* the Yeatses were "the cleverest and most spirited people I ever met." On both sides of the family there were strong personalities, and Yeats celebrated them in poems and in his autobiography, building from them a personal mythology and forming an ideal of Anglo-Irish character. In the untitled verses *"Pardon, old fathers,"* he invokes an *"Old Dublin merchant"* and an *"Old country scholar."* These were Jervis Yeats (d. 1712), first of his family in Ireland, and John Yeats (1774-1846), who had come to County Sligo as a most unconventional rector, a lover of wine and racehorses, and a friend of the patriot Robert Emmet.* With the *"Old merchant skipper"* Yeats moves to his mother's family, of which he was equally proud, the skipper being William Middleton (1770-1832) and the *"silent and fierce old man,"* Middleton's son-in-law William Pollexfen (1811-1892), the poet's grandfather, of whom Yeats wrote in his autobiography: "Even to-day when I read *King Lear* his image is always before me and I often wonder if the delight in passionate men in my plays and in my poetry is more than his memory."

To Yeats these were indeed "Half legendary men," as he wrote in another family poem, "Are You Content?" His father, a bit jealous and disdainful of the commercial bent of the Pollexfens, wrote that "In Willie's eyes they appear something grand like the figures at Stonehenge seen by moon-light." With the instinct of a poet, Yeats cherished family traditions, which included associations with Goldsmith* and Swift. In Sligo, there were many old relatives: three grandparents, a great-uncle, and a great-aunt Micky, "full of family history."

John Butler Yeats was a talented painter, known for his portraits of Synge, AE,* Lady Gregory,* and others in the Irish Revival. Of his lively personality and flair for unconventional ideas, we have some record through his letters and a brief memoir. Little is known of Yeats' mother, a quiet, sensitive woman, in later years an invalid. Her worry over her husband's impracticality and her love of Sligo led to prolonged stays in that beautiful area.

Yeats' two sisters, "Lily" (Susan Mary, 1866-1949) and "Lollie" (Elizabeth Corbet, 1868-1940), were artists. Lollie played a role in her brother's career by publishing in the Dun Emer, later Cuala Press,* about sixty titles, half by Yeats, the rest by Lady Gregory, Synge, AE, Dunsany,* Gogarty,* and others. The fourth and youngest child was "Jack"* (John Butler, 1871-1957), who made a reputation as illustrator of peasant scenes, writer of stories and plays, and painter.

The poet's early years were spent in London, except for delightful vacation visits to relatives in Sligo. Sligo is beautifully situated in a river valley, with a harbor on an inlet of the Atlantic Ocean. The steep cliff of Ben Bulben lies to the north, and on the south the hill of Knocknarea is topped by Maeve's Cairn, a huge mound of stones visible for miles, said to commemorate the Irish queen of the first century. Beneath Ben Bulben is Drumcliff, with a fine stone cross and the ruin of a round tower. Inland are the lakes and waterfalls of Yeats' poetry.

"I remember little of childhood but its pain," Yeats recalled in his autobiography, but this view should be modified by the prominence of Sligo landscape and legend in his work, as well as his memories of relatives. Fear of elders was mixed with admiration; his father could be dogmatic and domineering, but his unconventional views were stimulating. No doubt that Yeats was a shy and sensitive schoolboy in London, but the Sligo countryside had the stuff of romance—mountains and sea and the ever-changing sky, "The blue and the dim and the dark cloths / Of night and light and the half-light," as he described it in "He Wishes for the Cloths of Heaven." There were legends of chieftains, stories of seamen, superstitions, and folktales.

After the family's return to Dublin, Yeats entered the Metropolitan School of Art. Here he met the mystic poet George Russell, who took the pen name AE, and encouraged his interest in the occult. His father brought him to the Contemporary Club; members included the Gaelic scholar

Douglas Hyde* and the author Stephen Gwynn* who reported that "every one of us was convinced that Yeats was going to be a better poet than we had yet seen in Ireland."

He branched in several directions—"in a form of literature, in a form of philosophy, and a belief in nationality" ("If I were Four-and-Twenty," in *Explorations,* 1962). In literature, his earliest published verse was "Song of the Faeries" (*The Dublin University Review,* March 1885). A rarity is the pamphlet entitled *Mosada: A Dramatic Poem* (1886). In philosophy, he chaired the first meeting of the Hermetic Society on June 16, 1885; his occult studies were to continue throughout his life. In nationalism, his first essay, "The Poetry of Sir Samuel Ferguson" (*Irish Fireside,* October 9, 1886), praised the poet for recovering neglected riches of Irish lore. A month later, he had the effrontery to attack his father's friend Edward Dowden for neglecting "the interests of his own country, but more also . . . his own dignity and reputation" by ignoring Ferguson* (*The Dublin University Review,* November 1886).

Yeats had urged himself to "Hammer your thoughts into unity," seemingly impossible at the time, but by 1919 he felt that literature, philosophy, and patriotism expressed "a single conviction" which "has behind it my whole character." However, he was divided by his Anglo-Irish descent—too English for the Irish, too Irish for the English. His temperamental mixture of caution and defiance undoubtedly alienated friends, especially AE, as well as political and literary associates.

This diversity of interest is apparent in his Dublin friends at the time: the mystic AE; the romantic poet Katharine Tynan;* and the patriot John O'Leary,* a man of noble character with good literary taste. "We protest against the right of patriots to perpetrate bad verses," Yeats announced, an issue which aroused constant quarrels with patriots whose enthusiasm outran their taste.

O'Leary and Yeats, together with Douglas Hyde and Katharine Tynan, were responsible for the *Poems and Ballads of Young Ireland* (1888), of which Ernest Boyd wrote, "This slim little volume, in white buckram covers, will always be regarded with special affection by lovers of Irish literature, for it was the first offering of the Literary Revival."

With the family's removal to London began the "Four Years: 1887-1891" of *The Trembling of the Veil* (1922), a section of the autobiography filled with portraits and subtle analyses of character. Here Yeats is a master of the epigram: "the dinner table was Wilde's event," or, of Madame Blavatsky, "A great passionate nature, a sort of female Dr. Johnson." There were those psychological opposites, the strenuous William Henley and the aesthete-socialist William Morris, and, above all, the beautiful patriot Maud Gonne, whom Yeats met in 1889, wooed for years, and never forgot. "On meeting her," he wrote, "she seemed a classical impersonation of the Spring."

He continued his interest in the occult, wrote numerous book reviews, and began his study of William Blake. His first collection of verse, *The Wanderings of Oisin and Other Poems* (1889), appeared in an edition of five hundred copies and met with favorable response.

Though gradually overcoming his lack of self-confidence, Yeats was tormented by unrequited love for Maud Gonne and was divided between the comforting mysteries of the occult and the attractions of political and literary organization. His activity during the 1890s was unremitting. An important book appeared almost every year: 1891—*John Sherman and Dhoya*, two stories which illustrate his leanings toward escape and rebellion; 1892—*The Countess Kathleen and Various Legends and Lyrics*; 1893—*The Celtic Twilight*, tales and sketches of Irish folklore, as well as the three-volume edition *The Works of William Blake*, done in collaboration with Edwin J. Ellis; 1894—*The Land of Heart's Desire*, a play of enchantment produced in London in the same year; 1895—the collected and revised *Poems* and *A Book of Irish Verse*, a critical selection with an introduction attacking sentimental patriots as well as unsympathetic Anglo-Irish intellectuals who ignored Irish culture; 1897—two books of symbolic and visionary tales, *The Secret Rose* and the privately printed volume *The Tables of the Law./The Adoration of the Magi*; 1899—a third major collection of verse, *The Wind Among the Reeds*. In addition, Yeats edited or contributed to other volumes and published well over a hundred essays, in which he reported current Irish literature for two American newspapers and for the *London Bookman*.

The Irish political scene had been torn by dissension at Parnell's fall, or betrayal as his supporters would have it, when the Irish party rejected his leadership in December 1889 as a result of his involvement with the married Kitty O'Shea. The conflict between political and moral values created the antagonism so vividly depicted in Joyce's* *A Portrait of the Artist as a Young Man*. By coincidence, Yeats met Maud Gonne at Kingstown as she arrived on the boat which was bringing Parnell's body to Dublin in October 1891. Yeats, always distrustful of politics, was later to compare nationalist opinion to "the fixed ideas of some hysterical woman, a part of the mind turned into stone." In the same passage of his autobiography, he recalled nothing but the bitterness of his political involvement.

Yeats had predicted "an intellectual movement at the first lull in politics." He forthwith helped found the Irish Literary Society in London and the National Literary Society in Dublin. Here too, however, he was thwarted, for a projected series of Irish books failed, largely as a result of the selection of inferior works, insisted upon by Sir Charles Gavan Duffy,* a seventy-five-year-old patriot.

In the London Rhymers' Club Yeats found support for his aestheticism, but in his autobiography he sought an explanation for the mental, moral, and physical breakdowns of "The Tragic Generation." One of these English

Decadents was an important influence. Arthur Symons, versed in French poetry, introduced Yeats to Verlaine in Paris where Yeats first witnessed symbolic drama in a performance of *Axel's Castle*. Symons also brought Yeats in contact with George Moore* and Edward Martyn* and, through Martyn, with Lady Gregory. As if to complete the story of the beginnings of the Irish theatre, it was with Symons that Yeats visited the Aran Islands in 1896, which eventuated in enlisting Synge into the movement. Yeats tells the dramatic story of meeting Synge in Paris that December. Finding Synge to be a writer without a theme, Yeats advised him to go to the islands to "express a life that has never found expression," for "I had just come from Arran [*sic*] and my imagination was full of those gray islands, where men must reap with knives because of the stones" (Preface to Synge's *Well of the Saints*, 1905).

Another member of the Rhymers' Club, Lionel Johnson, had introduced Yeats to his cousin, Mrs. Olivia Shakespear, the "Diana Vernon" of the first draft autobiography, recently published as *Memoirs* (1972). Yeats recalled that "she was like the mild heroines of my plays," a sensitive woman trapped in a boring marriage. Still deeply in love with Maud Gonne, he confided in Mrs. Shakespear, wrote several poems to "His Beloved," and hesitantly became her lover. They remained friends up to her death in 1938.

Yeats' eagerness to combine poetry and patriotism motivated his activities in the Theosophical Society and later among the Hermetic Students of the Golden Dawn, then under the leadership of the eccentric MacGregor Mathers. The poet's experiments with visions, symbols, magic, and initiatory rites have embarrassed many admirers, but they were motivated by the desire to establish the primacy of the supernatural and the power of the poetic imagination.

When O'Leary questioned his occult interests, Yeats replied that "The mystical life is the centre of all that I do and all that I think and all that I write" (*Letters,* ed. Wade, p. 211). The Order of the Golden Dawn promoted spiritual regeneration and the perfection of society. In his study of Blake and the Rosicrucian literature, Yeats attempted to fuse esoteric doctrine with poetic symbolism. His aspirations are expressed in many essays, especially in "The Autumn of the Body" (1898); "We are, it may be, at a crowning crisis of the world, at the moment when man is about to ascend . . . the stairway he has been descending from the first days."

These ideals led to a projected "Castle of the Heroes" for adepts. Yeats also hoped to unite political factions in commemorating the centenary of the death of the patriot Wolfe Tone* in 1798. Ever alert for omens, he took as a portent his dream of a female archer shooting at a star. He felt that he had been directionless, or in the cabbalistic term of the autobiography, "Hodos Chameliontos," or "astray upon the Path of the Chamelion."

His meeting with Lady Gregory in 1896 seemed the fulfillment of some mysterious destiny. However we judge such speculations, no one can question the importance of Lady Gregory in his life. A talented woman and capable organizer, she encouraged Yeats in his hopes for an Irish theatre and came to represent the best in Anglo-Irish culture. Her modest home at Coole Park became a haven for creative spirits, serving as Yeats' own refuge for more than thirty years.

In an Irish drama that was both national and mystical, the tension between occultism and patriotism could perhaps be resolved. The theatre could become a sacred place; Yeats called some of his plays Mysteries or Moralities.

In 1894, his first stage venture brought Celtic lore to a London audience. *The Land of Heart's Desire* shared the program with an unsuccessful play by his father's friend John Todhunter* and later with Shaw's* *Arms and the Man*. With Todhunter's play withdrawn, the bill enjoyed a good run in spite of some amusement caused by Yeats' note that "the characters are supposed to speak in Gaelic." On his opening night, Shaw was booed by one person, but retorted that though he shared the opinion, "what can we do against a whole house," whereupon, as Yeats wrote in his autobiography, "Shaw became the most formidable man in modern letters." Nevertheless, Yeats was never very sympathetic to Shaw's work, and once dreamed of him as a smiling sewing-machine.

The production was managed by the actress Florence Farr, whose beauty and expressive voice entranced Yeats. She acted in his *The Countess Cathleen* in 1899, joined him in occultism, and recited his poems accompanied by a psaltery, in an attempt to revive the art of minstrelsy. She became one of Yeats' ideal characters, to be recollected after her death in the poem "All Souls' Night," along with his friends W. T. Horton and MacGregor Mathers who shared his interest in the occult.

The printed text of *The Land of Heart's Desire* (1894) is the earliest attractive Yeats first edition; the Aubrey Beardsley poster design fills the left-hand side of the cover. Beardsley, who created images of the decadent 1890s, died at the age of twenty-six in 1898; his sister Mabel is celebrated for the gallant humor with which she faced death in Yeats' "Upon a Dying Lady," published in 1917.

The idea of the Irish theatre was formulated during the first summer Yeats spent at Coole Park. (The history of the Irish theatre is well known, having been recounted with witty malice by George Moore in *Hail and Farewell* [1911-1914], by Lady Gregory in *Our Irish Theatre* [1913], and by others, notably Yeats in *Dramatis Personae* [1935], part of his autobiography.) George Moore and Edward Martyn, themselves friends and enemies ("bound one to the other by mutual contempt," Yeats wrote), joined Yeats as directors of the Irish Literary Theatre Society, projecting a series of Celtic plays each spring for three years. The first production was to be Yeats' *The Countess Cathleen* on May 8, 1899. From the start there were difficulties. Much of the financial support came from unionists, who opposed Home Rule, and Lady Gregory herself was suspected of unionist leanings. Tableaux from the play had been previewed at a seat of the enemy, the chief secretary's lodge, with Lady Fingall in the leading role. For the public performance, Moore insisted on engaging an English cast; this proved an unpopular move. There were quarrels at the London rehearsals. (Moore describes the tantrums of the leading ladies.) Before the play opened, it was attacked as unorthodox and insulting to the Irish people because of its Faustian theme. *Souls for Gold* was the title of an attack by a disaffected patriot, Frank Hugh O'Donnell, who was to follow in 1904 with a longer diatribe, *The Stage Irishman of the Pseudo-Celtic Revival*. A controversy ensued, interesting in its political and religious entanglements. Martyn threatened to withdraw support and submitted the text to a monk, who found it objectionable. The spectre of censorship infuriated Moore, but Yeats and Lady Gregory went about the task of getting two clerical votes for the play to counter the opposition. It was provisionally condemned by Cardinal Logue, who had not read it, whereupon Arthur Griffith* suggested bringing a claque to "applaud anything the Church did not like." University College students published a protest (Joyce did not sign). Yeats called the police, a tactless move, but the play went on with some hissing, "completely frustrated by enthusiastic applause which drowned their empty-headed dissension," according to Joseph Holloway,* whose diary is an almost day-by-day record of the Dublin theatre.

It was a typical Irish brouhaha, but only the first of many such conflicts, not only with the public, but also among writers, directors, and actors. Yeats, like Whistler, knew the art of making enemies.

Another absurdity was the collaboration of Yeats and Moore on the legendary *Diarmuid and Grania*, a process described by the authors of *W. B. Yeats and His World* (1971) as consisting of "stages of storm, stress, sulks and strained silences." Moore makes the unbelievable claim that Yeats and Lady Gregory proposed that Moore write the text in French, that it be translated into Irish, then retranslated by Lady Gregory into the rural dialect soon to be known as Kiltartan, and given final touches by Yeats. The celebrated actress Mrs. Patrick Campbell asked sensibly, "Oh, Mr. Yeats, why did you not do the whole play yourself?" Although it was performed with indifferent success on October 21, 1901, the text was not printed until 1951.

One moment of triumph occurred when Maud Gonne played the title role in *Cathleen Ni Houlihan* on April 2, 1902. Cathleen, the legendary figure of Ireland as the "Shan Van Vocht," or Poor Old Woman, is described in the last line of the play as "a young girl" with "the walk of a queen." A member of that audience recalled how "the tall figure straightened itself and took on beauty," and saw in that dramatic moment an augury of war (Stephen Gwynn, *Experiences of a Literary Man*).

Despite accusations of scandal and suspicions of her insincerity from O'Leary and others, Yeats had pleaded with Maud Gonne to marry him. He hoped that she would become "the fiery hand of the intellectual movement," as she did on this one evening. Harmony between such strong and divergent personalities was impossible, and Yeats sometimes realized this fact. His confessions of this hopeless love are found in the recently published *Memoirs*; such material was drastically suppressed in the autobiography.

In February 1903, Yeats was shocked to learn of Maud Gonne's marriage to John MacBride, who had led an Irish brigade against the English in the Boer War. The Boer War was England's Vietnam, in that it aroused strong opposition in England itself, both over its purpose and the way it was conducted. Though MacBride's marriage ended in separation two years later, Yeats' bitterness lasted, expressed in unpublished verses of 1909, now included in *Memoirs*. He accused her of having "taught me hate / By kisses to a clown." In "Easter 1916," he made amends to the executed patriot who "had done most bitter wrong / To some who are near my heart, / Yet I number him in my song." Unforgettable is the refrain: "A terrible beauty is born."

In the early part of the century, Yeats encountered the young James Joyce. At the age of nineteen, the arrogant Joyce accused Yeats of bringing about "The Day of the Rabblement" (1901) by catering to popular taste in the theatre, the very thing Yeats hated. A year later Joyce told Yeats, "I have met you too late," that is, too late for Yeats to be influenced by the twenty year old. Yet, in *Stephen Hero* Joyce's autobiographical counterpart intones phrases from *The Tables of the Law and The Adoration of the Magi*, phrases "heavy with incense and omens and the figures of the monk-errants." Yeats wrote that he would not have reissued them in 1904 had he not met one "who liked them very much and nothing else that I have written."

Maud Gonne's marriage shook Yeats' spirit and precipitated a crisis in his efforts to reconcile imagination and action. Though an uneasy admirer of an active life he could not espouse, he could make poetry a weapon against the world instead of an escape from the world. This attitude was reinforced by his reading of Nietzsche, his contact with the ideas of Castiglione, the success of his American lecture tour, and the necessity of fighting opponents of the theatre.

Nietzsche was to him "that strong enchanter" who "completes Blake" (*Letters*, p. 379), perhaps because he broadens Blake's satiric aphorisms into a world view. Blake and Shelley had absorbed Yeats during his early studies of poetry, but when these studies were collected in 1903 as *Ideas of Good and Evil*, he already felt Blake and Shelley to be "too lyrical, too full of aspirations after remote things." He now hoped to express himself "by that sort of thought that leads straight to action" (*Letters*, p. 379). As he wrote to AE in 1904, "Let us have no emotions, however abstract, in which there is not an athletic joy." To use the words of Denis Donoghue,* in his short study of Yeats (1971), the poet's "sense of life as action and gesture" indicates his kinship with Nietzsche, "a more telling relation than that between Yeats and Plato, Plotinus, or Blake." Yeats' father warned him: "You would be a *philosophe* and you are really a poet" (Hone, *Life*, p. 221). In writing, however, he cultivated direct utterance, abandoning the hesitation with which he had couched his earlier prose statements and turning away from wavering rhythms and vague diction in his poetry.

It was in the summer of 1903, as Yeats later remembered, that Lady Gregory read to him at Coole Park the Renaissance classic, Castiglione's *The Book of the Courtier*. This work was destined to be immensely important to his thought. He described its setting in his account of the Nobel Prize award, *The Bounty of Sweden* (1925), as "that court of Urbino where youth for certain brief periods imposed upon drowsy learning the discipline of its joy." Coole Park, with its woods and lake, its books and prints, and its Asian souvenirs (Lady Gregory's late husband had been a governor of Ceylon) became for Yeats an image of Urbino, and Lady Gregory an incarnation of the cultivated Duchess Elisabetta Gonzaga. When Lady Gregory became seriously ill in 1909, Yeats noted in his diary: "All Wednesday I heard Castiglione's phrase ringing in my memory, 'Never be it spoken without tears, the Duchess, too, is dead.' " *The Book of the Courtier*, like much of Yeats' poetry, is an elegy for past glories.

In Castiglione, Yeats found confirmation of several emerging ideas, the most important being that of Unity of Being. The key word in *The Book of the Courtier* is *sprezzatura*, which cannot be translated precisely but can be taken to mean a combination of ease and elegance, of carelessness and confidence, a product of self-discipline and the acceptance of custom. Spontaneity is central to the term. A year before encountering Castiglione's work, Yeats had written that though a line of poetry may take hours, "Yet if it does not seem a moment's thought, / Our stitching and unstitching has been naught" ("Adam's Curse"). He saw this self-confidence in Lady Gregory, in her nephews Hugh Lane and John Shawe-Taylor, in the horseman of "At Galway Races," in the imagined fisherman for whom he wished to write a poem "cold / And passionate as the dawn." Above all, it was exemplified in Lady Gregory's son Robert, who was killed in World War I, "Our Sidney and our perfect man."

The American lecture tour (November 1903 to March 1904) established Yeats' position as a commanding figure in the English-speaking literary world. He made more than forty appearances from New York City to San Francisco and Toronto. His first biographer, Joseph Hone, described his platform manner: "he was sometimes uneasy at the start, and would then stride up and down the platform in a rather surprising manner before he attained to his natural distinction of bearing, his gravity of utterance and his rhythm" (*Life*, p. 213). Here we see an actor entering upon a bravura performance. Hone characterizes his voice as "musical, touched with melancholy, the tones rising and falling in a continuous flow of sound," an effect fortunately preserved on phonograph recordings.

When Yeats returned to Ireland, he found that the theatre troubles had not abated. Moore, Martyn, and AE had dropped out, leaving the management to Yeats, Lady Gregory, and Synge. The company got its permanent home and name when two buildings on Lower Abbey Street were remodeled by the architect and diarist Joseph Holloway, through the generosity of an English patron, Miss Horniman, who in turn was to withdraw several years later, not without bitterness.

The opening program, December 27, 1904, consisted of two Yeats plays —*On Baile's Strand*, one of his best early dramas, and *Cathleen Ni Houlihan*—together with Lady Gregory's perennially popular comedy, *Spreading the News*.

A new Yeats play was produced almost every year. Already an author-director-manager, he now assumed another role as publicity agent, handling letters to the press, articles, lectures, and three theatre magazines— *Beltaine* (three issues, 1899-1900), *Samhain* (seven issues, 1901-1906 and 1908), and *The Arrow* (five issues, 1906-1907 and 1909). The first two titles are the Irish words for the seasons of production, spring and harvest, but they also suggest their significance as combative manifestos. An "irascible friend" had said that controversy had made a man of Yeats, an observation that Yeats questioned, but remembered for years, mentioning it in a 1931 reprinting of *Plays and Controversies*: "I do not agree with him, I doubt the value of the embittered controversy that was to fill my life for years, but certainly they rang down the curtain so far as I was concerned on what was called 'The Celtic Movement.' "

The Celtic Movement appealed to the public ("harps and pepperpots" was Yeats' term of contempt for the typical Irish cheap souvenir); and the major affront to the sentimental dream of Ireland was Synge's uncompromising vision. Yeats wrote to the patron and collector John Quinn, who had arranged the American lecture tour, that "Synge is invaluable to us because he has that kind of intense narrow personality which necessarily raises the whole issue." Matters reached a climax with the "Playboy Riots" of January 1907, with audience protests continuing throughout the week. Yeats called an open meeting, where he announced to the crowd, "The author of *Cathleen Ni Houlihan* addresses you." He was supported by his father, as the poet was to remember in one of his last poems, "Beautiful, Lofty Things." J. B. Yeats had been in Dublin for several years, under the patronage of Hugh Lane, doing the well-known portraits of Irish celebrities; in 1908, he was to come to New York, where he lived, ever lively, never successful, until his death in 1922.

The Collected Works in Verse and Prose (1908), in eight handsome volumes and bound in quarter vellum, included portraits by Sargent, J. B.

Yeats, and others, and contained about two thousand pages of text. It consolidated Yeats' position, though some thought his career was at an end (*Life*, p. 239). The 1,060 sets were underwritten by Miss Horniman for £1500; currently, a single set sells for about £250.

For lovers of book design, Yeats' first editions are unusually attractive, notably, the art nouveau, gold-stamped covers of the 1890s; the simple good taste of the linen bound Cuala Press* books, with title page woodcuts by Robert Gregory, T. Sturge Moore, AE, Elizabeth Yeats, and others; the blind-stamped patterns on covers of later works; the limited signed editions of *The Trembling of the Veil* and *A Vision;* and perhaps most striking of all, the bold green and gold cover of *The Tower*.

Synge's death in March 1909 ended another chapter in Yeats' career. The long fight against critics like Arthur Griffith left its mark in the bitterness of "Estrangement" and "The Death of Synge" (considerably toned down in the autobiography from the original text now in *Memoirs*). More time was now to be spent away from Dublin, though local disputes loom large in his verse. He kept his attractive London flat in Woburn Buildings, his home from 1895 to 1919. (Fortunately, this residence has been preserved.) He visited Maud Gonne in Normandy and spent summers at Coole Park. He made American tours in 1911 and 1914.

During this period, a new influence emerged—that of the brash young Ezra Pound, who undertook to convert Yeats to modernism, revised his verse, and introduced him to Japanese drama. They had met shortly after Pound's arrival in England in 1908, and Pound was to become his secretary during the winters of 1913-1914, 1914-1915, and 1915-1916. In 1913, Yeats won the *Poetry* magazine prize for "The Grey Rock," a tribute to his friends of the Rhymers' Club. Upon accepting, he made the generous suggestion that some of the money be given to Pound: "although I do not really like with my whole soul the metrical experiments he has made for you, I think those experiments show a vigorous creative mind" (*Letters*, p. 585). Pound could be exasperating, but Yeats found him "a learned companion" who "helps me to get back to the definite and concrete" (*Life,* p. 290).

Mrs. Shakespear became a link between Pound and Yeats when her daughter married Pound. Her relation to the woman Yeats married in 1917 was even closer. Miss George Hyde-Lees, whom Yeats first met in 1911, was the stepdaughter of Mrs. Shakespear's brother.

The decade after Synge's death was marked by further Dublin controversies, new directions in writing, and a turn toward reminiscence. Though topical, Yeats' verse gained a new authority. Consider his denunciation of a timid donor for Hugh Lane's projected art gallery which would bridge the River Liffey. No matter that there were problems of personality, or policy, and even of site and design; all are swept aside in the poem with its oddly archaic seventeenth-century title "To a Wealthy Man Who Promised a Second Subscription to the Dublin Municipal Gallery If It Were Proved the People Wanted Pictures" (1913). Timid dependence on "what the blind and ignorant town/Imagines best to make it thrive" is contrasted to the aristocratic indifference of Duke Ercole de l'Este of Ferrara who cared not "What th' onion-sellers thought or did" when he staged the plays of Plautus. And when Guidobaldo di Montefeltro established the court described by Castiglione, "That grammar school of courtesies/Where wit and beauty learned their trade/Upon Urbino's windy hill," he "sent no runners to and fro/That he might learn the shepherds' will." Thus, history as personal reflection is distilled into unforgettable phrases.

These may be "Poems Written in Discouragement" (the title of the 1913 limited Cuala Press* edition), but the discouragement is far from defeatist. If "Romantic Ireland's dead and gone" ("September 1913"), there's at least one voice unsilenced. In answer to his father's complaint that this poetry seemed to lack vision, Yeats replied, "I have tried for more self-portraiture . . . with a speech so natural that the hearer would feel the presence of a man thinking and feeling." The quality is rare in English poetry, but "Villon always and Ronsard at times create marvellous drama out of their own lives" (*Letters*, p. 583).

Synge was to be joined by Hugh Lane in the pantheon of heroes Yeats was creating. Lane's career is a success story with a tragic end, followed by an epilogue of controversy. It began with the sensational rise of a shrewd art dealer who had started at a pound a week, amassed considerable wealth in a few years, established the Municipal Gallery, and was knighted before his death at the age of forty in the sinking of the "Lusitania." Lane had been antagonized by authorities in London and in Dublin alike, and his bequest of thirty-nine pictures was to become a source of dispute. His intentions were debatable, for he willed them to the London National Gallery but left a codicil which gave them to Dublin. They were on loan in London at the time of his death.

The pictures exemplify Lane's extraordinary artistic taste; they include Corot and Courbet, Daumier and Degas, Manet's "Le Concert aux Tuileries," a delightful *plein air* group, a fine early impressionistic snow scene by Monet, a charming Morisot of two elegant young women in a boat, and, most striking of all, Renoir's large canvas of a colorful group of women and children in a shower, "Les Parapluies." It was one of Lane's favorites, a harmony of line and color; amazingly enough, the London National Gallery officials thought it unworthy of inclusion in their 1914 exhibit.

Lady Gregory championed the attempt to retrieve the Lane pictures for Dublin, and Yeats supported her but neither lived to see the present compromise, which involves a division into two groups, to alternate between Dublin and London every five years. (See Lady Gregory, *Hugh Lane's Life and Achievement*, 1921, and Thomas Bodkin's illustrated *Hugh Lane and His Pictures*, 1956.)

Events were turning Yeats' thoughts to concepts of personality and to family history: the ever-increasing image of Synge; the death of a favorite uncle, the eccentric horseman and astrologer, George Pollexfen, in 1910; the accounts of the Irish literary scene by George Moore, Lady Gregory, and others, between 1911 and 1914; anger at Moore's mockery. At fifty he was ready to write his *Reveries Over Childhood and Youth* (1915) and, characteristically, to have theories at hand. These theories were expressed in the puzzling poetic dialogue "Ego Dominus Tuus" and further elaborated in a forty-five page footnote to the short poem, published as *Per Amica Silentia Lunae* (1918).

To simplify drastically, the theme is one of transcendence of worldly values through conflict within oneself. In the poem, the contrast is between the worldly *Hic* and his adversary *Ille* (Pound dubbed him "Willie"). *Hic* is content with popular acclaim; *Ille* seeks his mysterious double, or anti-self, in order to achieve, not success, but vision. Dante "set his chisel to the hardest stone," says *Ille,* and his concept is modified in the title of another important collection of essays, *The Cutting of an Agate* (1912), which presents evolving views of tragic drama. As early as 1907, and again in the 1910 essay on "The Tragic Theatre," Yeats had written of the insight attained by the tragic hero. In the Japanese Noh drama to which Ezra Pound introduced him, Yeats found the purely symbolic dramatic form he had been seeking. *At the Hawk's Well* was performed privately in London in 1916 with costumes and masks by Edmund Dulac and the dance of the hawk presented by Michio Ito. This is the first of *Four Plays for Dancers,* published in 1922, with illustrations of the Dulac costumes and masks which convey something of the spirit of the performance. The illustrations are repeated in editions of *Plays and Controversies* (1923). Dulac worked with Yeats elsewhere, notably in the woodcuts for *A Vision* (1925).

As one of his most successful plays, *At the Hawk's Well* achieves the seemingly impossible union of a presumably Irish hero and an oriental form. It is a triumph of style, an abstract evocation of spiritual energy, and a worthy successor to his earlier treatment of the Cuchulain legend in the 1904 *On Baile's Strand,* a more accurate dramatization of the traditional tale.

To the influence of Pound must be added the experience of reading John Donne in the definitive 1912 edition by H.J.C. Grierson. In thanking his friend the editor, Yeats wrote: "I notice that the more precise and learned the thought the greater the beauty, the passion; the intricacy and subtleties of his imagination are the length and depths of the furrow made by his passion" (*Letters,* p. 570). He was reading Walter Savage Landor too, finding in him an admirable union of violent passion and serenity. Yeats was to become one of the first modern metaphysical poets. The conclusion of "To a Young Beauty," written in 1918, announces: "There is not a fool can call me friend,/And I may dine at journey's end/With Landor and with Donne."

The young beauty was Iseult Gonne, daughter of Maud Gonne and the French patriot Millevoye. After the execution of Maud Gonne's husband in 1916, Yeats renewed his proposals to her (she had never divorced Mac-Bride) and then proposed to her daughter before marrying Miss Hyde-Lees, who proved to be a vivacious, intelligent wife.

Yeats had received a Civil List pension of £150 per annum in 1913, and two years later he was able to do a favor for his fellow-countryman Joyce, who in the summer of 1915 had come almost penniless to neutral Switzerland for the duration of World War I. Forgetting Joyce's earlier rudeness, Yeats, at the instigation of Ezra Pound, recommended Joyce for a grant from the Royal Literary Fund. He wrote the English critic Edmund Gosse that though *Dubliners* seemed "all atmosphere perhaps" it could be "a sign of an original study of life," while the *Portrait,* then being serialized in *The Egoist,* "increases my conviction that he is the most remarkable new talent in Ireland to-day" (*Letters,* p. 599). A grant of £75 was awarded.

The opening of the world war was marked by mounting Irish tension, with three paramilitary groups active—the Ulster Volunteers, the Irish Volunteers, and the Irish Citizen Army. Many were enlisting, but the majority opposed support of England. Lady Gregory's son had joined the Air Force, and Maud Gonne was nursing the wounded. Yeats sparred with the viceroy of Ireland over political matters and impressed him enough to have him declare: "I really believe I could govern Ireland if I had Mr. Yeats' assistance." Yeats seemed not to share this opinon. When asked to write a war poem, he refused but wrote one instead explaining his refusal: "We have no gift to set a statesman right." He also refused an offer of knighthood.

With English, Irish, and American editions, private printings, theatre texts, and books with contributions or prefaces, about half of the three hundred titles published in his life appeared between 1900 and 1920. The poems are grouped under the headings *In the Seven Woods* (1904), actually published in 1903; *The Green Helmet and Other Poems* (1910); *Responsibilities* (1914); and *The Wild Swans at Coole* (1919), actually published in 1917.

After Yeats' marriage on October 21, 1917, the couple spent several years in England. (Yeats is so closely associated with Ireland that it is surprising to learn how little he actually lived there.) To his delight he discovered his wife's psychic powers and continued work on the elaborate philosophical system to be known as *A Vision* (1925). Before his marriage, he had written his father apologetically about his thought, knowing the artist's distaste for abstractions: "Much of your thought resembles mine . . . but mine is part of a religious system more or less logically worked out, a system which will I hope interest you as a form of poetry." He continued: "I find the setting it all in order has helped my verse" with "a new framework and new patterns" (*Letters,* p. 627). The same idea was apparently transmitted to his wife when the "unknown writer" of her automatic writing sent the message, "we have come to give you metaphors for poetry" (*A Vision*, 1956 ed., p. 8). Concepts from the system lie behind many magnificent poems of this time.

After his daughter's birth, in the winter of 1919-1920, he toured America, seeing his father for the last time whom he found "as full of the future as when I was a child," as he wrote Lady Gregory.

Yeats' impulse to root himself in Ireland was demonstrated by the acquisition of a Norman tower not far from Coole Park, and his purchase of a Georgian house at 82 Merrion Square, his Dublin home from 1922 to 1928. The house was only two doors away from AE's editorial office. A cartoon by Isa MacNie illustrates the Dublin anecdote that Yeats and AE, on the way to meet, crossed paths without noticing one another. Yeats, regarded by Dubliners as a snob, strides on, gazing loftily, his long black tie flowing, while AE trudges by, his bearded head bent in meditation (*The World of Yeats,* Robin Skelton and Ann Saddlemyer, eds., 1965).

From 1919 to 1923, Ireland was a battleground, first with the brutal "Black and Tans" and other English forces in their attacks on the Sinn Fein government, and then the war by the Republicans or Irregulars against the Free State. Despite atrocities, there were feats of derring-do, as in the escape of Yeats' friend and fellow senator Oliver Gogarty* (see his *An Offering of Swans,* 1923). The tragedy of these times is elevated to a philosophical level in poems such as "Meditations in Time of Civil War."

The tower, Thoor Ballylee (Irish "Tur Bail' i Liagh") with its thatched cottages, is beautifully located beside a stream, a bridge at its foot. It has now been restored. Though too damp for the family (Yeats himself was comfortably settled on an upper floor) and far from safe in time of war, as is shown in the poems, the tower was a source of poetic inspiration, with its historic traditions and symbolic associations. In "The Phases of the Moon," Robartes thinks Yeats chose it "Because, it may be, of the candle-light/From the far tower where Milton's Platonist/Sat late, or Shelley's visionary prince:/The lonely light that Samuel Palmer engraved,/An image of mysterious wisdom won by toil." Other significances are traced by T. R. Henn in *The Lonely Tower* (1950)—as an emblem of ancient ceremony, as symbol of the destructive forces of time and history, as token of night and the infinite universe beyond. In an 1899 essay, "Dust Hath Clothed Helen's Eye," Yeats had told of visiting the tower and hearing of the death there sixty years before of the beautiful Mary Hynes, subject of a romantic Gaelic poem by the blind Raftery. Yeats and his family spent only a few summers between 1919 and 1929 at Ballylee, but its associations reverberate through many poems.

Despite long-standing distrust of politics, Yeats consented to serve in the Free State Senate (1923-1928). In addressing a Celtic Festival in 1924, he expressed his doubts: "We do not believe that war is passing away, and we do not believe that the world is growing better and better." A year later, he shocked his colleagues in a debate on divorce by mentioning the private lives of Nelson, Parnell, and O'Connell, "the three old rascals" of the short poem "The Three Monuments." He concluded his speech with an angry identification of himself with the Anglo-Irish Protestant Ascendancy, the long-hated alien overlords of Ireland: "We are one of the great stocks of Europe. We are the people of Burke; we are the people of Grattan; we are the people of Swift, the people of Parnell. We have created the most of the modern literature of this country. We have created the best of its political intelligence." It was not a speech to win the audience, but such pride imparted eloquence to his writing.

Dublin gossip has it that when a journalist telephoned Yeats in 1923 to notify him that he had won the Nobel Prize, the poet's response was to ask how much money was involved. He enjoyed the ceremony with gusto, seeing in the Swedish court an embodiment of his aristocratic ideals.

The first version of *A Vision*, dated 1925, was actually issued in 1926 in a signed edition of six hundred copies. It opens with a fascinating tale by the fictional Owen Aherne, who, with Michael Robartes, had appeared in Yeats' stories years before. Aherne tells of meeting Robartes in the National Gallery and speaking about Yeats, with whom both had quarrelled, because he had not admitted that they were real persons. Robartes tells his friend about finding an old book by one Giraldus that he discovered in Cracow, with "curious allegorical figures" and "many diagrams," including one "where lunar phases and zodiacal signs were mixed with various unintelligible symbols." This text is, of course, that of *A Vision*. Finding similar signs on the Arabian desert, Robartes continued his search, meeting a man of the Judwali sect, whose leader had been Kusta ben Luka. Joining the sect, Robartes learned that though their Sacred Book had been lost, much preserved in oral tradition resembled the thought of Giraldus. After a quarrel, they agree to show the material to Yeats. In an amusing footnote, Yeats questions the accuracy of Aherne's version.

Central to *A Vision* is the lunar cycle of twenty-eight phases, representing periods of history, stages in human life, degrees of subjectivity, and types of human character, each with its Will and Body of Fate, and its true and false Mask and Creative Mind. The ideal phase, Fifteen, has no exemplar; closest are Fourteen ("Keats, Giorgione, many beautiful women") and Sixteen (Blake, and, surprisingly, Rabelais and Aretino, as well as "some beautiful women"). The intertwining gyres of human life and of history are also essential. There can be no doubt of the importance to Yeats of his system; it sums up a life of speculation and was immediately undergoing further revision. Perhaps the wisest comment upon it was made by AE when questioned by Elizabeth Yeats: "My opinion is that *anything* Willie writes will be of interest now or later on, and a book like this, which does not excite me or you, may be, possibly will be, studied later on when the psychology of the poet is considered by critics and biographers" (*Life,* p. 435). Of special interest is the passage describing Byzantium, where "religion, art and practical life were one," and "The painter and the mosaic worker, the worker in gold and silver, the illuminator of Sacred Books" were impersonally absorbed in "the vision of a whole people." Here is the germ of the magnificent "Sailing to Byzantium" and its sequel "Byzantium," the mosaics having been recalled from a visit to Palermo in 1924.

The Abbey Theatre was again a center of controversy with O'Casey's* *The Plough and the Stars,* when audiences were affronted by a less than idealistic portrayal of some patriots in the Rising. A protest was made on the fourth night, February 11, 1926, whereupon Yeats is reported to have silenced the crowd. Joseph Holloway, however, records that he could not be heard (*Joseph Holloway's Abbey Theatre,* 1967). Peter Kavanagh is probably right in assuming that the newspaper report was based on a script supplied by Yeats: "you have disgraced yourselves again. . . . Synge first and then O'Casey" (*The Story of the Abbey Theatre,* 1950).

Yeats was to meet his match when he rejected *The Silver Tassie* in 1928, commenting that though in the Irish plays "you were excited and we all caught your excitement," the fact is that "you are not interested in the Great War." O'Casey found this statement to be "impudently arrogant" (Kavanagh, pp. 139, 140). Here began O'Casey's long feud with Ireland.

For Yeats the time of farewells had come: to Merrion Square, 1928; to Ballylee, 1929; to Coole Park, 1932.

Lady Gregory's death in 1932 marked the end of an epoch. Of all the figures in the Revival, only Douglas Hyde survived Yeats. Yeats told of a Dublin sculptor who visited Coole Park at the end, gazed at the family heirlooms, then said, "All the nobility of earth." How much of my own verses has been but the repetition of those words," Yeats exclaimed (*Letters,* p. 796). The house was razed in 1941, but the beech tree remains, with its carved initials such as W.B.Y., AE, and G.B.S.

Despite ill health, Yeats' last years were vigorous ones. He found new friends (Lady Dorothy Wellesley, Ethel Mannin*), and cultivated new enemies. "And say my glory was I had such friends," he concludes in the Municipal Gallery poem, a line quoted by George McGovern in his concession speech after the 1972 presidential election in the United States. Yeats attacked modern bad taste in *On the Boiler,* published after his death. "I wonder how many friends I will have left," he mused (*Letters,* p. 910). Wide reading in philosophy (the Upanishads, Plotinus, Berkeley*) deepened his insight, though some work is marred by feverish sexuality or strident glorification of violence (he was briefly attracted to the Irish proto-fascist Blue Shirts). "You were silly like us," Auden wrote in his noble elegy, "your gift survived it all."

During the 1930s, Yeats had the energy to undertake a successful American tour in 1932, edit the idiosyncratic *Oxford Book of Modern Verse*

(1936), publish a revised edition of *A Vision* (1937), and broadcast several BBC programs. In addition, he wrote several hauntingly enigmatic plays. Most accessible are *The Words upon the Window Pane* (produced at the Abbey, November 1930), a seance invoking the ghost of Swift, and *The Resurrection* (Abbey, July 1934), on the divinity of Christ. Three fantasies—*The King of the Great Clock Tower* (Abbey, July 1934), *A Full Moon in March* (1935), and *The Herne's Egg* (1938)—were followed by the nightmare intensity of *Purgatory,* on August 10, 1938, which marked his last appearance at the Abbey Theatre. Although these dramas defy analysis, as do some of the last poems, they convey the impression of a great poet's superhuman vision of things beyond mortal understanding.

On January 4, 1939, Yeats wrote from the Riviera that though "I know for certain that my time will not be long," yet "I am happy, and I think full of an energy, of an energy I had despaired of." Then, in words which some may prefer to the dramatic epitaph, he continued, "It seems to me that I have found what I wanted. When I try to put all into a phrase I say, 'Man can embody truth but he cannot know it.' I must embody it in the completion of my life" (*Letters,* p. 922). That existential insight seems to have been demonstrated throughout his career.

Yeats died on January 28, 1939. World War II delayed the fulfillment of his desire to be buried "Under Ben Bulben" in the Drumcliff churchyard of his great-grandfather, the rector. The grave is marked with his own memorable and enigmatic words:

> Cast a cold eye
> On life, on death.
> Horseman, pass by!

RICHARD M. KAIN

WORKS: *Mosada.* Dublin: Sealy, Bryers, & Walker, 1886. (Dramatic poem); ed., *Fairy and Folk Tales of the Irish Peasantry.* London: Walter Scott/New York: Thomas Whittaker/Toronto: W. J. Gage, 1888; *The Wanderings of Oisin and Other Poems.* London: Kegan Paul, Trench, 1889; ed., *Stories from Carleton.* London: Walter Scott/New York & Toronto: W. J. Gage, [1889]; under the pseudonym of "Ganconagh," *John Sherman and Dhoya.* London: T. Fisher Unwin, 1891. (Novel); ed., *Representative Irish Tales.* 2 vols. New York & London: G. P. Putnam's Sons, The Knickerbocker Press, [1891]; *The Countess Kathleen and Various Legends and Lyrics.* London: T. Fisher Unwin, 1892/Boston: Roberts Bros., [1892]; ed., *Irish Fairy Tales.* London: T. Fisher Unwin/New York: Cassell, 1892; *The Celtic Twilight.* London: Lawrence & Bullen, 1893/New York: Macmillan, 1894. (Poems and essays); ed. with Edwin John Ellis, *The Works of William Blake.* 3 vols. London: Bernard Quaritch, 1893; *The Land of Heart's Desire.* London: T. Fisher Unwin, 1894/Chicago: Stone & Kimball, 1894/revised ed. Portland, Maine: Thomas B. Mosher, 1903. (Play); *Poems.* London: T. Fisher Unwin, 1895/revised ed. London: T. Fisher Unwin, 1899/2d revised ed. London: T. Fisher Unwin, 1901; ed., *A Book of Irish Verse.* London: Methuen, 1895; *The Secret Rose.* London: Lawrence & Bullen, 1897. (Poems); *The Tables of the Law. The Adoration of the Magi.* Privately printed, 1897/ London: Elkin Mathews, 1904. (Poems); *The Wind among the Reeds.* London: Elkin

Mathews, 1899. (Poems); ed., *Beltaine, an Occasional Publication. Number One.*
London: At the Sign of the Unicorn/Dublin: At the "Daily Express" Office, 1899; ed.,
Beltaine, Number Two. London: At the Sign of the Unicorn, 1900; ed., *Beltaine,
Number Three.* London: At the Sign of the Unicorn, 1900; *The Shadowy Waters.*
London: Hodder & Stoughton, 1900. (Play); ed., *Samhain.* [Dublin]: Sealy, Bryers &
Walker/[London]: T. Fisher Unwin, 1901. (First number of the theatre magazine);
The Celtic Twilight. Revised & enlarged. London: A H. Bullen, 1902; *Cathleen Ni
Houlihan.* London: A. H. Bullen, 1902. (Play); ed., *Samhain.* [Dublin]: Sealy, Bryers
& Walker/[London]: T. Fisher Unwin, 1902. (Second number of the theatre maga-
zine); *Where There Is Nothing.* London: A. H. Bullen, 1903. (Play, written with some
help from Lady Gregory and Douglas Hyde, and first printed as a supplement to *The
United Irishman,* Nov. 1, 1902); *Ideas of Good and Evil.* London: A. H. Bullen, 1903.
(Essays); *In the Seven Woods.* Dundrum: Dun Emer, 1903. (Poems); *The Hour-Glass.*
London: Wm. Heinemann, 1903. (Play); ed., *Samhain.* [Dublin]: Sealy, Bryers &
Walker/[London]: T. Fisher Unwin, 1903. (Third number of the theatre magazine);
The Hour-Glass and Other Plays. New York & London: Macmillan, 1904. (Contains
also "Cathleen ni Houlihan" and "The Pot of Broth"); *The Hour-Glass, Cathleen Ni
Houlihan, The Pot of Broth.* London: A. H. Bullen, 1904/Dublin: Maunsel, 1905; ed.,
Samhain. [Dublin]: Sealy, Bryers & Walker/[London]: T. Fisher Unwin, 1904.
(Fourth number of the theatre magazine); *The King's Threshold: and On Baile's
Strand.* London: A. H. Bullen, 1904. (Plays); *Twenty One Poems.* Dundrum: Dun
Emer, 1904 [actually 1905]; *Stories of Red Hanrahan.* Dundrum: Dun Emer, 1904
[actually 1905]; ed., *Some Essays and Passages by John Eglinton.* Dundrum: Dun
Emer, 1905; ed., *Samhain.* [Dublin]: Maunsel/[London]: A. H. Bullen, 1905. (Fifth
number of the theatre magazine); ed., *Sixteen Poems by William Allingham.* Dun-
drum: Dun Emer, 1905; *Poems, 1899-1905.* London: A. H. Bullen/Dublin: Maunsel,
1906; ed., *Poems of Spenser.* Edinburgh: T. C. & E. C. Jack, [1906]; ed., *The Arrow.*
(Five short pamphlets issued by the Abbey Theatre in Dublin, from October 20, 1906,
to August 22, 1909); ed., *Samhain.* Dublin: Maunsel, 1906. (Sixth number of the
theatre magazine); *The Poetical Works of William B. Yeats. Volume I, Lyrical Poems.*
New York & London: Macmillan, 1906; *Deirdre.* London: A. H. Bullen/Dublin:
Maunsel, 1907. (Play); ed., *Twenty One Poems by Katharine Tynan.* Dundrum: Dun
Emer, 1907; *The Poetical Works of William B. Yeats. Volume II, Dramatical Poems.*
New York & London: Macmillan, 1907; *Discoveries.* Dundrum: Dun Emer, 1907.
(Essays); *The Unicorn from the Stars and Other Plays,* with Lady Gregory. New York:
Macmillan, 1908. (Contains the title play by Yeats and Lady Gregory, which is a re-
working of *Where There Is Nothing,* and also "Cathleen ni Houlihan" and "The Hour
Glass"); *The Golden Helmet.* New York: John Quinn, 1908; *Poems Lyrical and
Narrative, Being the First Volume of the Collected Works in Verse and Prose of
William Butler Yeats.* Stratford-on-Avon: Shakespeare Head, 1908; *The King's Thresh-
old. On Baile's Strand. Deirdre. Shadowy Waters.* Stratford-on-Avon: Shakespeare
Head, 1908. (Vol. II of the Collected Edition); *The Countess Cathleen. The Land of
Heart's Desire. The Unicorn from the Stars.* Stratford-on-Avon: Shakespeare Head,
1908. (Vol. III of the Collected Edition); *The Hour-Glass. Cathleen Ni Houlihan.
The Golden Helmet. The Irish Dramatic Movement.* Stratford-on-Avon: Shakespeare
Head, 1908. (Vol. IV of the Collected Edition); *The Celtic Twilight and Stories of
Red Hanrahan.* Stratford-on-Avon: Shakespeare Head, 1908. (Vol. V of the Collected
Edition); *Ideas of Good and Evil.* Stratford-on-Avon: Shakespeare Head, 1908. (Vol.
VI of the Collected Edition); *The Secret Rose. Rosa Alchemica. The Tables of the
Law. The Adoration of the Magi. John Sherman and Dhoya.* Stratford-on-Avon:
Shakespeare Head, 1908. (Vol. VII of the Collected Edition); *Discoveries. Edmund
Spenser. Poetry and Tradition: & Other Essays.* Stratford-on-Avon: Shakespeare Head,

1908. (Vol. VIII of the Collected Edition); ed., *Samhain*. Dublin: Maunsel, 1908. (Seventh number of the theatre magazine); *Poetry and Ireland, Essays by W. B. Yeats and Lionel Johnson*. Churchtown, Dundrum: Cuala, 1908; ed., *Poems and Translations by John M. Synge*. Churchtown, Dundrum: Cuala, 1909; *Poems: Second Series*. London & Stratford-on-Avon: A. H. Bullen, 1909 [actually 1910]; ed., *Deirdre of the Sorrows: A Play by John M. Synge*. Churchtown, Dundrum: Cuala, 1910; *The Green Helmet and Other Poems*. Churchtown, Dundrum: Cuala, 1910; *Synge and the Ireland of his Time*. Churchtown, Dundrum: Cuala, 1911; *The Green Helmet*. Stratford-on-Avon: Shakespeare Head, 1911. (Only separate edition); *Plays for an Irish Theatre*. London & Stratford-on-Avon: A. H. Bullen, 1911. (Contains "Deirdre," "The Green Helmet," "On Baile's Strand," "The King's Threshold," "The Shadowy Waters," "The Hour-Glass," and "Cathleen ni Houlihan"); *The Countess Cathleen*, revised version. London: T. Fisher Unwin, 1912; *Poems*, revised. London: T. Fisher Unwin, 1912; *The Green Helmet and Other Poems*. New York & London: Macmillan, 1912; ed., *Selections from the Writings of Lord Dunsany*. Churchtown, Dundrum: Cuala, 1912; *The Cutting of an Agate*. New York: Macmillan, 1912. (Essays); *A Selection from the Love Poetry of William Butler Yeats*. Churchtown, Dundrum: Cuala, 1913; *Poems Written in Discouragement*. Churchtown, Dundrum: Cuala, 1913; *Responsibilities: Poems and a Play*. Churchtown, Dundrum: Cuala, 1914. (The play is a new version of "The Hour-Glass"); *Reveries over Childhood and Youth*. Churchtown, Dundrum: Cuala, 1915; *Eight Poems*. London: Morland Press, [1916]; *Responsibilities and Other Poems*. London: Macmillan, 1916; *The Wild Swans at Coole, Other Verses and a Play in Verse*. Churchtown, Dundrum: Cuala, 1917. (The play is "At the Hawk's Well"); *Per Amica Silentia Lunae*. London: Macmillan, 1918; *Nine Poems*. London: Privately printed by Clement Shorter, 1918; *Two Plays for Dancers*. Churchtown, Dundrum: Cuala, 1919. (The plays are "The Dreaming of the Bones" and "The Only Jealousy of Emer"); *The Wild Swans at Coole*. London: Macmillan, 1919; *Michael Robartes and the Dancer*. Churchtown, Dundrum: Cuala, 1920. (Poems); *Selected Poems*. New York: Macmillan, 1921; *Four Plays for Dancers*. (The plays are "At the Hawk's Well," "The Only Jealousy of Emer," "The Dreaming of the Bones," and "Calvary"); *Seven Poems and a Fragment*. Dundrum: Cuala, 1922; *The Trembling of the Veil*. London: Privately printed for subscribers by T. Werner Laurie, 1922. (Reminiscences); *Later Poems*. London: Macmillan, 1922; *Plays in Prose and Verse, Written for an Irish Theatre, and Generally with the Help of a Friend* [Lady Gregory]. London: Macmillan, 1922; *The Player Queen*. London: Macmillan, 1922; *Plays and Controversies*. London: Macmillan, 1923; *Essays*. London: Macmillan, 1924; *The Cat and the Moon and Certain Poems*. Dublin: Cuala, 1924; *The Bounty of Sweden*. Dublin: Cuala, 1925; *Early Poems and Stories*. London: Macmillan, 1925; *A Vision*. London: Privately printed for subscribers by T. Werner Laurie, 1925; *Estrangement: Being Some Fifty Thoughts from a Diary Kept by William Butler Yeats in the Year Nineteen Hundred and Nine*. Dublin: Cuala, 1926; *Autobiographies*. London: Macmillan, 1926. (Contains "Reveries over Childhood and Youth" and "The Trembling of the Veil"); *October Blast*. Dublin: Cuala, 1927. (Poems); *The Tower*. London: Macmillan, 1928. (Poems); *Sophocles' King Oedipus, a Version for the Modern Stage*. London: Macmillan, 1928; *The Death of Synge, and Other Passages from an Old Diary*. Dublin: Cuala, 1928; *A Packet for Ezra Pound*. Dublin: Cuala, 1929; *The Winding Stair*. New York: Fountain Press, 1929; *Selected Poems, Lyrical and Narrative*. London: Macmillan, 1929; *Stories of Michael Robartes and his Friends: An Extract from a Record Made by his Pupils: and a Play in Prose*. Dublin: Cuala, 1931. (The play is "The Resurrection"); *Words for Music Perhaps and Other Poems*. Dublin: Cuala, 1932; *The Winding Stair and Other Poems*. London: Macmillan, 1933; *The Collected Poems of W. B. Yeats*. New York: Macmillan, 1933;

Letters to the New Island. Horace Reynolds, ed. Cambridge, Mass.: Harvard University Press, 1934. (Collection of early essays and reviews for American newspapers); *The Words Upon the Window Pane.* Dublin: Cuala, 1934. (Play); *Wheels and Butterflies.* London: Macmillan, 1934. (Contains texts of and introductions to "The Words Upon the Window Pane," "Fighting the Waves," "The Resurrection," and "The Cat and the Moon"); *The Collected Plays of W. B. Yeats.* London: Macmillan, 1934. (Contains the texts of twenty previously printed plays and also the first printing of *Oedipus at Colonus*); ed. with F. R. Higgins, *Broadsides.* Dublin: Cuala, 1935. (Collections of poems issued in twelve monthly broadsides of 4 pages each); *A Full Moon in March.* London: Macmillan, 1935. (Contains the title play as well as a revision in verse of "The King of the Great Clock Tower" and various poems); *Dramatis Personae.* Dublin: Cuala, 1935. (Reminiscences); *Dramatis Personae 1896-1902, Estrangement, The Death of Synge, The Bounty of Sweden.* New York: Macmillan, 1936; *Modern Poetry.* London: British Broadcasting Corporation, 1936. (Lecture); ed., *The Oxford Book of Modern Verse.* Oxford: Clarendon Press, 1936; ed., and translated with Shree Purohit Swami, *The Ten Principal Upanishads.* London: Faber, [1937]; *Nine One-Act Plays.* London: Macmillan, 1937; *A Vision.* London: Macmillan, 1937. (Contains much new material); ed., with Dorothy Wellesley, *Broadsides.* Dublin: Cuala, 1937. (Issued individually throughout 1937 and as a bound volume in December 1937); *Essays, 1931 to 1936.* Dublin: Cuala, 1937; *The Herne's Egg.* London: Macmillan, 1938. (Play); *New Poems.* Dublin: Cuala, 1938; *The Autobiography of William Butler Yeats.* New York: Macmillan, 1938. (Consisting of "Reveries over Childhood and Youth," "The Trembling of the Veil," and "Dramatis Personae"); *Last Poems and Two Plays.* Dublin: Cuala, 1939. (The plays are "The Death of Cuchulain" and "Purgatory"); *On the Boiler.* Dublin: Cuala, [1939]; *Last Poems and Plays.* London: Macmillan, 1940. (The selection of poems varies from *Last Poems and Two Plays*); *If I Were Four-and-Twenty.* Dublin: Cuala, 1940; *Pages from a Diary Written in Nineteen Hundred and Thirty.* Dublin: Cuala, 1944; *Tribute to Thomas Davis.* [Cork]: Cork University Press/Oxford: B. H. Blackwell, 1947. (With a foreword by Denis Gwynn and "An Unpublished Letter" by AE); *The Poems of W. B. Yeats.* 2 vols. London: Macmillan, 1949; *The Collected Poems of W. B. Yeats.* London: Macmillan, 1950/New York: Macmillan, 1951; *Diarmuid and Grania,* with George Moore. [Dublin]: Reprinted from the *Dublin Magazine* (April-June 1951).

The Yeats bibliography is immense, as can be seen from the above compilation which only attempts to list major editions. Basic, of course, is *The Collected Poems of W. B. Yeats* (London & New York: Macmillan); the 1956 edition is the most accurate. The Macmillan London edition of *Collected Plays* (1952) is the best text. The serious student must consult *The Variorum Edition of the Poems of W. B. Yeats,* Peter Allt and Russell K. Alspach, eds. (corrected third printing, 1966), and *The Variorum Edition of the Plays of W. B. Yeats,* Russell K. Alspach, ed. (corrected second printing, 1966), in order to appreciate the poet's constant habit of revision after publication. The above volumes and all subsequent ones, unless otherwise noted, were published in London and New York by Macmillan. Much of Yeats' published prose has been collected, including *The Senate Speeches of W. B. Yeats,* Donald R. Pearce, ed. (Bloomington: Indiana University Press, 1960); *Essays and Introductions* (1961); *Mythologies* (1962); *Explorations* (1962); *Autobiographies* (1966), to which should be added the early drafts in *Memoirs,* Denis Donoghue, ed. (1972); and two volumes of *Uncollected Prose* (New York: Columbia University Press), the first edited by John P. Frayne (1970), the second by Frayne and Colton Johnson (1975). *The Letters of W. B. Yeats,* Allan Wade, ed. (1954), will be replaced by a projected exhaustive edition, which will no doubt include letters already printed in such volumes as *Letters on Poetry from W. B. Yeats to Dorothy Wellesley* (London, New York, Toronto: Oxford University Press, 1940); *Florence Farr, Bernard Shaw and W. B. Yeats,* Clifford Bax, ed. (Dublin: Cuala, 1941); and *The Correspondence of Robert Bridges and W. B. Yeats,* Richard J. Finneran, ed. (London & Basingstoke: Macmillan, 1977). REFERENCES: Yeats' complex publishing history (about 275 items during his lifetime) is given in *A Bibliography of the Writings of W. B. Yeats,* Allan Wade, ed.; revised by Russell K. Alspach (New York: Oxford University Press, 1968). There is also an extensive survey of works about Yeats by Richard J. Finneran, ed., in *Anglo-Irish Literature: A Review of Research* (New York: Modern Language Association, 1976), in which hundreds of items are discussed; and there is the enormous, nearly 800-page listing of secondary material in K.P.S. Jochum's *W. B. Yeats: A Classified Bibliography of Criticism* (Urbana: University of Illinois Press, 1977).

A definitive biography is being undertaken by F.S.L. Lyons; at present, J. B. Hone, *Life of W. B. Yeats* (1943), is basic for events; Richard Ellmann, *Yeats: The Man and the Masks* (1948), is a brilliant interpretation of dichotomies in life and thought. Micheál Mac Liammóir and Eavan Boland collaborated on the richly illustrated *W. B. Yeats and His World* (London: Thames and Hudson, 1971). A symposium and catalogue edited by Robin Skelton and Ann Saddlemyer, *The World of W. B. Yeats* (Dublin: Dolmen, 1965), has valuable accounts of the poet's backgrounds in the art world. For Sligo, see Sheelah Kirby, *The Yeats Country,* 2nd ed. (Dublin: Dolmen, 1963); for the family, William M. Murphy, *The Yeats Family and the Pol lexfens of Sligo* (Dublin: Dolmen, 1971); for the Dublin scene, Richard M. Kain, *Dublin in the Age of W. B. Yeats and James Joyce* (Norman: University of Oklahoma Press, 1962).

Yeats' painstaking craftsmanship is revealed in studies of manuscript drafts by Curtis Bradford, *Yeats at Work* (Carbondale: Southern Illinois University Press, 1965), and by Jon Stallworthy, *Between the Lines: Yeats's Poetry in the Making* (London: Oxford University Press, 1963) and *Vision and Revision in Yeats's Last Poems* (London: Oxford University Press, 1969).

Of more personal interest is E. H. Mikhail's two volume *W. B. Yeats, Interviews and Recollections* (London & Basingstoke: Macmillan, 1977).

Only a few critical studies can be mentioned. Good introductions to the poetry are by Louis MacNeice (London: Oxford, 1941) and by Donald A. Stauffer in *The Golden Nightingale: Essays on Some Principles of Poetry in the Lyrics of William Butler Yeats* (1949). T. R. Henn's *The Lonely Tower: Studies in the Poetry of W. B. Yeats* (London: Methuen, 1950) and Richard Ellmann's *The Identity of Yeats* (1954) explore aspects of thought and style.

Among numerous guides, several are outstanding: the poem-by-poem analysis of John Unterecker, *A Reader's Guide to W. B. Yeats* (New York: Noonday, 1959) and the philosophic study by B. Rajan (London: Hutchinson, 1965). Valuable collections of source materials are A. Norman Jeffares, *A Commentary on the Collected Poems of W. B. Yeats* (1968) and the companion volume on the plays by Jeffares and A. S. Knowland (1975).

Special studies are: Hazard Adams, *Blake and Yeats: the Contrary Vision* (Ithaca, N.Y.: Cornell University, 1955); Robert Beum, *The Poetic Art of William Butler Yeats* (New York: Ungar, 1969); Harold Bloom, *Yeats* (New York: Oxford, 1970), which concentrates on the influence of Shelley; Denis Donoghue, ed., *The Integrity of Yeats* (Cork: Mercier, 1964), and, with J. R. Mulryne, *An Honored Guest* (London: Arnold, 1965); Edward Engelberg, *The Vast Design: Patterns in W. B. Yeats's Aesthetic* (Toronto: University of Toronto, 1964); George M. Harper, ed., *Yeats and the Occult* (Toronto: Macmillan, 1975); Daniel A. Harris, *Yeats: Coole Park &*

Ballylee (Baltimore: Johns Hopkins University Press, 1974); Frank Kermode, *Romantic Image* (London: Routledge and Paul, 1957), on the symbol of the dancer; Giorgio Melchiori, *The Whole Mystery of Art: Pattern into Poetry in the Work of W. B. Yeats* (London: Routledge and Paul, 1960); James Rees Moore, *Masks of Love and Death: Yeats as Dramatist* (Ithaca, N.Y.: Cornell University, 1971); Thomas Parkinson, *W. B. Yeats, Self-Critic* (Berkeley: University of California, 1971); Donald Torchiana, *W. B. Yeats and Georgian Ireland* (Evanston, Ill.: Northwestern, 1966); Thomas R. Whitaker, *Swan and Shadow: Yeats's Dialogue with History* (Chapel Hill, N.C.: University of North Carolina, 1964); F.A.C. Wilson's work on Neoplatonism in *W. B. Yeats and Tradition* (London: Gollancz, 1958) and *Yeats's Iconography* (London: Gollancz, 1960).

YOUNG, AUGUSTUS (1943-), poet. Young was born in Cork in 1943. He has published one large and two small volumes of poems, as well as a slim volume of translations from the Irish. He is probably the most consistently satiric poet of his generation. His best work is witty, fluent, and usually so sharply individual in its diction that one is nonplussed at the occasional dreadful line, such as one about "pubescent grass" being scratched from the "groin of the skull." Young's chief failure is an utter lack of poetic technique to focus his wit, but his cleverness of conception and terseness of language can sometimes, as in "Inside Story," overcome his technical deficiencies.

WORKS: *Survival*. Dublin: New Writers', 1969; *On Loaning Hill*. Dublin: New Writers', 1972; *Danta Gradha: Love Poems from the Irish*. London: Menard Southampton: Advent Books, 1975; *Tapestry of Animals*. [London: Menard, 1977].

YOUNG, ELLA (1865-1951), poet and author of children's stories. Young, once called "a druidess reincarnated" by AE,* was born to a staunch Presbyterian family in County Antrim in 1865. Her family moved to Rathmines in the 1880s, and Young took her university degree in political science and law in Dublin. Like many other young scholars of her day, Young developed a consuming interest in Ireland's past. While still a college student, she had joined AE's Hermetical Society. It was he who encouraged her to pursue her interest in Irish fairy-lore and write about it. Her friends Standish James and Margaret O'Grady* introduced Young to the west of Ireland where she lived for many months over a period of years among the peasants, collecting tales and learning Irish.

Young's political sympathies were decidedly Republican. She wrote frequently for *Sinn Féin* and in 1912, rented Temple Hill, a farmhouse in Wicklow from which she ran guns and ammunition for the members of the Irish Republican Army. Although she spent most of World War I in Achill, she returned to Dublin in 1916 and resumed her gun-running from a rented room in a staunchly respectable pro-British house. At the time of the Rising, Young was blacklisted and fled to Connemara where she heard of the executions of many of her friends. She returned to Dublin in 1919 and remained through the Civil War.

In 1925, Young left for the United States on a lecturer's passport. Lecturing in the East, she gradually worked her way across the country to California where she finally settled near Berkeley, accepted a modest position at the University of California at Los Angeles, and studied Mexican and Indian folklore. She led a quiet life; she wrote, gardened, tended her cats until her death in 1951.

Although Young has published several collections of poetry, she is known primarily as a writer of children's stories, based on Celtic myth and legend, in which she often ranks with James Stephens.* *The Coming of Lugh* (1909) was quickly followed by *Celtic Wonder-Tales* (1910), a collection of fourteen stories chosen at random out of Irish mythology and ranging from tales of the fantastic Gobhaun Saor to the Etain legend. Even though these tales charm, they are somewhat restricted by Young's worshipful adherence to the traditional subject matter—something that also mars her collection of Fenian tales, *The Tangle-Coated Horse* (1929). When she used the traditional material to launch her imagination, she was at her best, as, for example, in *The Wonder-Smith and His Son* (1927). Dealing with a series of tales less circumscribed by tradition, it records the adventures of Goibniu, originally a kind of Irish Hephaestus, who came to earth as an architect, exchanged a daughter for a son, and through various wiles escaped the evil Formorian Balor. Finally, in her finest work, *The Unicorn with Silver Shoes* (1932), she takes great liberties with figures out of Celtic myth in telling of the adventures of the son of Balor, a unicorn who is calmed only by listening to epic poetry, a djinn who ends up in a Dublin zoo, and a mischievous Pooka. In the gentle irony which gives this book a refreshing freedom from sentimentality, *The Unicorn with Silver Shoes* remains one of the outstanding examples of the lyrical cadences of the Irish imagination.

M. KELLY LYNCH

WORKS: *Poems*. Tower Press Booklet No. 4. Dublin: Maunsel, 1906; *The Coming of Lugh*. Dublin: Maunsel, 1909. (Tales); *Celtic Wonder-Tales*. Dublin: Maunsel, 1910; *The Rose of Heaven*. Dublin: Colm O'Loughlin, 1918. (Poems); *The Weird of Fionavar*. Dublin: Talbot, 1922. (Poems); *The Wonder-Smith and His Son*. New York: Longmans, 1927. (Tales); *The Tangle-Coated Horse*. Dublin: Maunsel, 1929. (Tales); *The Unicorn with Silver Shoes*. New York: Longmans, 1932. (Tales); *Flowering Dusk*. New York: Longmans, 1945. (Memoirs); *Seed of the Pomegranite*. Oceano (9), 1949. (Poems privately printed in an edition of twenty copies); *Smoke of Myrrh*. Oceano (?), 1950. (Poems privately printed in an edition of twenty-five copies).

ZOZIMUS (ca. 1794-1846), ballad singer and composer. Zozimus was the public name of Michael Moran. Sometimes called "The Last Gleeman," he was a composer and singer of ballads, street songs, ranns, and quips. He was born in the Liberties of Dublin in about 1794, was blind almost from birth, and in his picturesque and tattered dress became a familiar character in a city already rich in that commodity. In *The Celtic Twilight,* W. B. Yeats* remarks that Zozimus' poem "Moses" went a little nearer poetry than much of his work, yet "without going very near." He died on April 3, 1846.

WORKS: Gulielmus Dubliniensis Humoriensis. *Memoir of the Great Original Zozimus (Michael Moran), the Celebrated Street Rhymer and Reciter, with His Songs, Sayings and Recitations.* Dublin: Carraig Books, 1976. Reprint.

CHRONOLOGY

	Political	Literary
A.D. 432	St. Patrick's mission to Ireland	
795	Viking raids on Ireland	
ca. 800		Book of Kells
841	Vikings found city of Dublin	
1014	Battle of Clontarf and death of Brian Boru	
1550		First Irish printing press set up in Dublin by Humphrey Powell
1649	Shane O'Neill dies; Cromwell comes to Ireland; massacres at Drogheda and Wexford	
1652		Nahum Tate born
1667		Jonathan Swift born
1670		William Congreve born
1672		Richard Steele born
1677		George Farquhar born
1681	Oliver Plunkett executed	
1689	Siege of Londonderry	
1690	William III wins Battle of the Boyne	
1691	Treaty of Limerick	
1694		Charles Macklin born
1695	Beginning of Penal Laws	Congreve's *Love for Love*

729

	Political	*Literary*
1700		Congreve's *The Way of the World*
1706		Farquhar's *The Recruiting Officer*
1707		Farquhar's *The Beaux Stratagem;* Farquhar dies
1709		Berkeley's *New Theory of Vision*
1715		Nahum Tate dies
1720	Act declares British Parliament to legislate for Ireland	
1724		Swift's *Drapier's Letters*
1726		Swift's *Gulliver's Travels*
1728		Oliver Goldsmith born
1729		Richard Steele dies; William Congreve dies; Swift's *A Modest Proposal*
1738		Turlough O'Carolan dies
1745		Jonathan Swift dies
1751		Richard Brinsley Sheridan born
1756		Burke's *The Sublime and the Beautiful*
1760		Arthur Murphy's *The Way to Keep Him;* MacPherson's *Ossian*
1766		Goldsmith's *The Vicar of Wakefield*
1767		Maria Edgeworth born
1770		Goldsmith's *The Deserted Village*
1773		Goldsmith's *She Stoops to Conquer*
1774		Goldsmith dies
1775		Sheridan's *The Rivals*
1776	American Declaration of Independence	
1777		Sheridan's *The School for Scandal*
1779		Thomas Moore born
1782	Grattan's Parliament	Charles Robert Maturin born
1784	Eoghan Ruadh O'Suilleabháin dies	
1785	Royal Irish Academy founded	
1789	French Revolution	Charlotte Brooke's *Reliques of Irish Poetry*
1790		Burke's *Reflections on the French Revolution*
1791	United Irishmen formed	
1792	Catholic Relief Act eases the Penal Laws	

	Political	*Literary*
1794		William Carleton born
1795	Orange Order founded in Armagh; Maynooth founded	
1796	Wolfe Tone's attempted invasion	
1797		Charles Macklin dies
1798	United Irishmen's Rising; Wolfe Tone's suicide	John Banim born
1800	United Irishmen's Rising; Wolfe ment dissolved	Edgeworth's *Castle Rackrent*
1803	Emmet's Rising	James Clarence Mangan born
1805		Brian Merriman dies
1806		Charles Lever born; Lady Morgan's *The Wild Irish Girl*
1808		Moore's *Irish Melodies*
1812		Edgeworth's *The Absentee*
1814		Thomas Davis born; Joseph Sheridan LeFanu born
1815	Battle of Waterloo	
1816		Richard Brinsley Sheridan dies; Maturin's *Bertram*
1817		Moore's *Lalla Rookh;* Edgeworth's *Ormond*
1820	Death of Henry Grattan	Maturin's *Melmoth the Wanderer*
1821		Theatre Royal, Dublin, opens
1823	Daniel O'Connell forms the Catholic Association	
1824		William Allingham born; Charles Robert Maturin dies
1825		Banims' *Tales of the O'Hara Family*
1826		Banims' *The Boyne Water*
1828	O'Connell wins Clare by-election	Charles J. Kickham born
1829	Catholic emancipation	Griffin's *The Collegians*
1830		Carleton's *Traits and Stories of the Irish Peasantry*
1835		The poet Raftery dies
1836		Mahony's *Reliques of Father Prout*
1837	Victoria ascends throne	Lover's *Handy Andy*
1839		John Butler Yeats born; Lever's *Harry Lorrequer;* Carleton's *Fardorougha the Miser*

	Political	*Literary*
1840	O'Connell founds National Repeal Association	
1841		Boucicault's *London Assurance;* Lever's *Charles O'Malley*
1842	*The Nation* founded	John Banim dies
1843	Repeal meeting banned at Clontarf	Davis et al., *The Spirit of the Nation*
1845	First of the potato famines	Thomas Davis dies
1846		Standish O'Grady born; Davis' *Collected Poems*
1847	Daniel O'Connell dies	Carleton's *The Black Prophet*
1848	Smith O'Brien's rebellion	O'Donovan's *Annals of the Four Masters*
1849		Maria Edgeworth dies; James Clarence Mangan dies
1850		Allingham's *Poems*
1852		Thomas Moore dies; George Moore born; Lady Gregory born
1854	Crimean War; Catholic University of Ireland founded	Mitchel's *Jail Journal*
1856		Oscar Wilde born; George Bernard Shaw born
1858	Fenian movement founded	Edith Somerville born
1860		Boucicault's *The Colleen Bawn*; Amanda McKittrick Ros born
1861	American Civil War	Falconer's *Peep o' Day;* O'Curry's *Manuscript Materials of Ancient Irish History*
1862		Violet Martin ("Martin Ross") born
1863		LeFanu's *The House by the Churchyard*
1864		Allingham's *Laurence Bloomfield;* Boucicault's *Arrah na Pogue;* LeFanu's *Uncle Silas*
1865	American Civil War ends	Ferguson's *Lays of the Western Gael;* W. B. Yeats born; J. O. Hannay ("George A. Birmingham") born
1867	Fenian rebellion; Manchester Martyrs executed	George Russell ("AE") born
1869	Church of Ireland disestablished	William Carleton dies; James Connolly born
1870	Gladstone's First Land Act; Butt forms Home Government Association	
1871		J. M. Synge born; Jack B. Yeats born

	Political	*Literary*
1872		LeFanu's *In a Glass Darkly;* Ferguson's *Congal;* Charles Lever dies
1874		Conal O'Riordan born
1875		Boucicault's *The Shaughraun*
1876		Forrest Reid born
1877	Parnell assumes leadership of the Irish party	
1878		O'Grady's *Bardic History of Ireland;* Daniel Corkery born; Lord Dunsany born; Oliver Gogarty born
1879	Davitt founds Land League; Land War begins; Isaac Butt dies	Kickham's *Knocknagow;* Patrick Pearse born; J. S. Starkey ("Seumas O'Sullivan") born; Maurice Walsh born
1880	Parnell elected leader of Irish Parliamentary party; boycotting of Captain Boycott; Royal University of Ireland founded	O'Grady's *History of Ireland: Cuchulain and His Contemporaries;* Sean O'Casey born
1881	Gladstone's second Land Act; Parnell imprisoned	Padraic Colum born
1882	Lord Frederick Cavendish assassinated; de Valera born; University College, Dublin, founded	Charles J. Kickham dies; James Joyce born; James Stephens born
1883		St. John Ervine born
1884	Gaelic Athletic Association founded	George Moore's *A Modern Lover*
1885		George Moore's *A Mummer's Wife*
1886	Gladstone's first Home Rule Bill defeated	George Moore's *A Drama in Muslin;* Lennox Robinson born; George Shiels born
1887	National Library of Ireland founded	
1888		*Poems and Ballads of Young Ireland*
1889		Yeats' *The Wanderings of Oisin*
1890	Parnell-O'Shea divorce case; Parnell loses control of the Irish party	Boucicault dies
1891	Parnell dies	Wilde's *The Picture of Dorian Gray;*
1892		Yeats' *The Countess Cathleen*
1893	Gladstone's second Home Rule Bill defeated; Gaelic League founded	Hyde's *Love Songs of Connacht;* Peadar O'Donnell born; Eimar O'Duffy born
1894		George Moore's *Esther Waters;* Somerville and Ross's *The Real Charlotte;* Yeats' *The Land of Heart's Desire*

	Political	*Literary*
1895		Wilde's *The Importance of Being Earnest*
1896		Austin Clarke born
1897		AE's *The Earth Breath;* Ferguson's *Lays of the Red Branch;* Ros's *Irene Iddlesleigh;* Sigerson's *Bards of the Gael and Gall;* Stoker's *Dracula;* Voynich's *The Gadfly*
1898		Shaw's *Plays, Pleasant and Unpleasant*
1899	Griffith founds *The United Irishman*	Hyde's *A Literary History of Ireland;* Martyn's *The Heather Field;* Somerville and Ross's *Some Experiences of an Irish R. M.;* Yeats' *Countess Cathleen* and *The Wind among the Reeds;* first season of Irish Literary Theatre
1900	Queen Victoria autographs the Book of Kells; Moran founds *The Leader*	Oscar Wilde dies; Paul Vincent Carroll born; Sean O'Faolain born
1901	Queen Victoria dies	Denis Johnston born
1902		AE's *Deirdre;* Lady Gregory's *Cuchulain of Muirthemne;* Francis Stuart born; Cuala Press founded
1903		George Moore's *The Untilled Field;* Yeats' *Ideas of Good and Evil;* Teresa Deevy born; Frank O'Connor born
1904	Griffith's *The Resurrection of Hungary*	Birmingham's *The Seething Pot;* Lady Gregory's *Spreading the News;* Synge's *Riders to the Sea;* Yeats' *The King's Threshold* and *On Baile's Strand;* Abbey Theatre opens; Ulster Literary Theatre founded; Patrick Kavanagh born
1905	Griffith founds Sinn Fein movement	Boyle's *The Building Fund;* Colum's *The Land;* George Moore's *The Lake;* Synge's *The Well of the Saints;* Brian Coffey born; Padraic Fallon born
1906		Joseph Campbell's *The Rush Light;* Seumas O'Kelly's *The Shuiler's Child;* Samuel Beckett born
1907		Abbey Theatre riots over Synge's *The Playboy of the Western World;* Birmingham's *The Northern Iron;* Colum's *Wild Earth;* Fitzmaurice's *The Country Dressmaker;* Joyce's *Chamber Music;* Louis MacNeice born

	Political	*Literary*
1908	Larkin forms Irish Transport & General Workers' Union; National University established	Birmingham's *Spanish Gold;* Doyle's *Ballygullion;* Dunsany's *The Sword of Welleran;* Fitzmaurice's *The Pie-dish;* Lady Gregory's *Workhouse Ward;* Mayne's *The Drone;* O'Riordan's *The Piper;* Somerville and Ross's *Further Experiences of an Irish R.M.;* Yeats' *Collected Works*
1909		Birmingham's *The Search Party;* Dunsany's *The Glittering Gates;* J. M. Synge dies; Bryan MacMahon born; W. R. Rodgers born, first production of the Cork Dramatic Society
1910		Childers' *The Riddle of the Sands;* Ervine's *Mixed Marriage;* Murray's *Birthright;* Ray's *The Casting Out of Martin Whelan;* Synge's *Deirdre of the Sorrows* and *Collected Works;* Yeats' *The Green Helmet*
1911		George Moore's first part of *Hail and Farewell*
1912	Third Home Rule bill; Ulster Covenant signed; Larkin forms Irish Labour party	Murray's *Maurice Harte;* O'Kelly's *Meadowsweet;* Stephens' *The Crock of Gold;* Mary Lavin born; Donagh MacDonagh born; Brian O'Nolan ("Flann O'Brien") born; Terence deVere White born
1913	Formation of Ulster Volunteers, Irish Volunteers, and Irish Citizen Army; the "Great Lockout" begins	AE's *Collected Poems;* Fitzmaurice's *The Magic Glasses*
1914	Outbreak of World War I; Curragh Mutiny; gun-running at Howth; Government of Ireland Act suspended	Dunsany's *Five Plays;* Ervine's *John Ferguson;* Fitzmaurice's *Five Plays;* Joyce's *Dubliners;* Yeats' *Responsibilities*
1915		AE's *Imaginations and Reveries;* MacGill's *The Rat Pit;* Somerville and Ross's *In Mr. Knox's Country;* Martin Ross dies
1916	The Easter Rising	Joyce's *A Portrait of the Artist as a Young Man;* Patrick Pearse, James Connolly, Thomas MacDonagh, and Joseph Mary Plunkett executed; Sheehy-Skeffington executed; Casement executed

	Political	*Literary*
1917	The Russian Revolution	Clarke's *The Vengeance of Fionn;* Corkery's *The Threshold of Quiet;* O'Kelly's *Waysiders;* Pearse's *Collected Works;* Yeats' *The Wild Swans at Coole*
1918	World War I ends; Sinn Fein wins majority of Irish seats in West- minster	Brinsley MacNamara's *The Valley of the Squinting Windows;* O'Duffy's *The Wasted Island;* Stephens' *Reincarnations*
1919	First Dail meets in Dublin; De Valera becomes president; Anglo-Irish War begins	Brinsley MacNamara's *The Clanking of Chains;* Benedict Kiely born
1920		Robinson's *The Whiteheaded Boy;* Yeats' *Michael Robartes and the Dancer;* Iris Murdoch born; James Plunkett born; W. J. White born
1921	Anglo-Irish War ends, and Anglo-Irish Treaty signed	Roy McFadden born; Brian Moore born
1922	Treaty approved by the Dail; establishment of Irish Free State; Civil War begins; deaths of Griffith and Collins	Reid's *Pender among the Residents;* Joyce's *Ulysses;* Yeats' *Later Poems;* the House of Maunsel ceases publication
1923	Civil War ends; Ireland joins League of Nations	O'Casey's *The Shadow of a Gunman;* Yeats receives Nobel Prize; AE founds *The Irish Statesman;* O'Sullivan founds *The Dublin Magazine;* Brendan Behan born
1924	*Freeman's Journal* ceases	Gogarty's *An Offering of Swans;* Murray's *Autumn Fire;* O'Casey's *Juno and the Paycock*; O'Flaherty's *Spring Sowing*
1925	Border between North and South confirmed	Higgins' *Island Blood;* O'Flaherty's *The Informer;* Somerville's *The Big House at Inver;* Yeats' *A Vision*
1926	de Valera founds Fianna Fail; Radio Éireann begins	Riots in the Abbey Theatre over O'Casey's *The Plough and the Stars;* O'Flaherty's *Mr. Gilhooley;* Walsh's *The Key above the Door;* Yeats' *Autobiographies*
1927	de Valera and Fianna Fail enter the Dail; Kevin O'Higgins assassinated	O'Riordan's *Soldier Born*; Aidan Higgins born; Richard Murphy born
1928		O'Casey's *The Silver Tassie;* O'Donnell's *Islanders;* O'Riordan's *Soldier of Waterloo;* Yeats' *The Tower;* Padraic O'Conaire dies; Standish O'Grady dies; Thomas Kinsella born; John B. Keane born; Hugh Leonard born; William Trevor born; the Gate Theatre opens

	Political	*Literary*
1929	Censorship of Publication Act	Johnston's *The Old Lady Says "No!"*; O'Flaherty's *The Mountain Tavern;* Brian Friel born; John Montague born
1930		Eugene McCabe born
1931	*The Irish Press* begins	Johnston's *The Moon in the Yellow River;* Manning's *Youth's the Season . . .?*; Kate O'Brien's *Without My Cloak;* O'Connor's *Guests of the Nation;* Reid's *Uncle Stephen;* Strong's *The Garden*
1932	de Valera forms Fianna Fail government	Clarke, *The Bright Temptation;* Colum's *Collected Poems;* O'Connor's *The Saint and Mary Kate;* O'Faolain's *Midsummer Night's Madness;* O'Flaherty's *Skerritt;* Lady Gregory dies; Edna O'Brien born
1933		Strong's *Sea Wall;* George Moore dies
1934		Lynch's *The Turf Cutter's Donkey;* O'Faolain's *A Nest of Simple Folk;* Joseph O'Neill's *Wind from the North;* Yeats' *The Tower*
1935		Deevy's *Katie Roche* and *The King of Spain's Daughter;* Yeats' *A Full Moon in March;* Eimar O'Duffy dies; John MacGahern born
1936	IRA declared illegal	Clarke's *The Singing Men at Cashel;* Kavanagh's *Ploughman;* Francis MacManus' *Candle for the Proud;* O'Connor's *Bones of Contention;* O'Faolain's *Bird Alone;* Sayers' *Peig;* Thomas Murphy born
1937	New constitution for the Irish Free State; Douglas Hyde the first president	Carroll's *Shadow and Substance;* Devlin's *Intercessions;* Gogarty's *As I was Going Down Sackville Street;* O'Flaherty's *Famine;* Reid's *Peter Waring*
1938		Beckett's *Murphy;* Bowen's *The Death of the Heart;* Kavanagh's *The Green Fool;* O'Riordan's *Soldier's End;* Yeats' *Purgatory*
1939	World War II begins; Ireland remains neutral	Carroll's *The White Steed;* Joyce's *Finnegans Wake;* MacNeice's *Autumn Journal;* Francis MacManus' *Men Withering;* Flann O'Brien's *At Swim Two Birds;* O'Casey's *I Knock at the Door;* W. B. Yeats dies; Amanda McKittrick Ros dies; Seamus Heaney born

	Political	*Literary*
1940	Battle of Britain	Higgins' *The Dark Breed;* O'Casey's *Purple Dust;* O'Sullivan's *Collected Poems;* Shiels' *The Rugged Path;* Wall's *Alarm among the Clerks;* Yeats' *Last Poems and Plays;* O'Faolain founds *The Bell*
1941	Pearl Harbor	Francis MacManus' *Flow on Lovely River;* Myles na Copaleen's *An Beal Bocht;* Kate O'Brien's *The Land of Spices;* Wall's *The Lady in the Twilight;* James Joyce dies; F. R. Higgins dies
1942		Kavanagh's *The Great Hunger;* Lavin's *Tales from Bective Bridge*
1943		O'Faolain's *The Great O'Neill;* O'Casey's *Red Roses for Me*
1944	D-Day	Laverty's *No More than Human;* O'Connor's *Crab Apple Jelly;* Joseph Campbell dies; Eavan Boland born
1945	End of World War II	Bowen's *The Demon Lover*
1946		Kiely's *Land Without Stars;* Mac Liammóir's *All for Hecuba;* Molloy's *The Visiting House;* Kate O'Brien's *That Lady;* Wall's *The Unfortunate Fursey*
1947		Kavanagh's *A Soul for Sale;* Donagh MacDonagh's *Happy as Larry;* Forrest Reid dies
1948	Fianna Fail defeated in general election; coalition government under John Costello	Gibbon's *Mount Ida;* Kavanagh's *Tarry Flynn;* MacMahon's *The Lion Tamer;* O'Flaherty's *Two Lovely Beasts;* Molloy's *The King of Friday's Men;* Robertson's *Field of the Stranger;* Stuart's *Pillar of Cloud;* Wall's *The Return of Fursey;* Conal O'Riordan dies
1949	Independent Republic of Éire proclaimed	Bowen's *The Heat of the Day;* McLaverty's *The Game Cock*; MacNeice's *Collected Poems;* Douglas Hyde dies; Edith Somerville dies; George Shiels dies
1950	Korean War begins	Byrne's *Design for a Headstone;* Kiely's *Modern Irish Fiction;* Macken's *Rain on the Wind;* O'Flaherty's *Insurrection;* Robertson's *Miranda Speaks*; George A. Birmingham dies; Bernard Shaw dies; James Stephens dies
1951	The Mother and Child scheme fails; Costello government falls	Beckett's *Molloy;* the Abbey Theatre fire; Liam Miller founds the Dolmen Press

	Political	*Literary*
1952		Beckett's *Waiting for Godot*; O'Connor's *Stories;* Wall's *Leaves for the Burning*
1953		Kiely's *Cards of the Gambler;* Macken's *Home Is the Hero;* Meldon's *Aisling;* Molloy's *The Wood of the Whispering;* the Pike Theatre opens
1954		O'Connor's *More Stories*
1955	Ireland enters United Nations	Brian Moore's *Judith Hearne;* O'Donnell's *The Big Window;* James Plunkett's *The Trusting and the Maimed*
1956	IRA campaign begins in the North and lasts until 1962	Behan's *The Quare Fellow;* Kinsella's *Poems;* O'Flaherty's *Stories*
1957	Sputnik I	O'Faolain's *Finest Stories;* White's *A Fretful Midge;* Lord Dunsany dies; Oliver Gogarty dies; Jack Yeats dies; First Dublin Theatre Festival; Lantern Theatre opens
1958		Behan's *Borstal Boy* and *The Hostage;* Johnston's *The Scythe and the Sunset;* Kinsella's *Another September;* O'Faolain's *Stories;* White's *The Hard Man;* Seumas O'Sullivan dies; Lennox Robinson dies
1959	de Valera becomes third president	Keane's *Sive;* Lavin's *Selected Stories;* Macken's *Seek the Fair Land;* Denis Devlin dies
1960	Irish troops engage in UN mission in the Congo; J. F. Kennedy elected president of U.S.	Clarke's *Twice Round the Black Church;* Kavanagh's *Come Dance with Kitty Stobling;* Keane's *Sharon's Grave;* MacMahon's *Song of the Anvil;* Edna O'Brien's *The Country Girls;* O'Donovan's *The Shaws of Synge Street;* Thompson's *Over the Bridge*
1961	Irish television begins with great fanfare, followed by the Cisco Kid	Clarke's *Later Poems;* MacMahon's *The Honey Spike;* Montague's *Poisoned Lands;* Thomas Murphy's *Whistle in the Dark*
1962		Friel's *Saucer of Larks;* Kinsella's *Downstream;* Macken's *The Silent People;* Edna O'Brien's *The Lonely Girl;* Flann O'Brien's *The Hard Life;* O'Donovan's *Copperfaced Jack;* Paul Smith's *The Countrywoman*
1963	Brookeborough retires as prime minister of Northern Ireland; is succeeded by Terence O'Neill; J. F. Kennedy visits Ireland	Clarke's *Collected Plays* and *Flight to Africa;* Farrell's *Thy Tears Might Cease;* McGahern's *The Barracks;* West's *The Ferret Fancier;* Teresa Deevy dies; George Fitzmaurice dies; Louis MacNeice dies

Political	*Literary*
1964	Friel's *Philadelphia, Here I Come!;* Kavanagh's *Collected Poems;* Cronin's *The Life of Riley;* Devlin's *Collected Poems;* McCabe's *The King of the Castle;* Flann O'Brien's *The Dalkey Archive;* O'Connor's *Collection Two;* Trevor's *Old Boys;* Bredan Behan dies; Daniel Corkery dies; Sean O'Casey dies; Maurice Walsh dies
1965 Sean Lemass and Terence O'Neill meet to improve North-South relations—fail utterly	Keane's *The Field;* Leitch's *The Liberty Lad;* McGahern's *The Dark;* MacNeice's *The Strings Are False;* Brian Moore's *The Emperor of Ice Cream;* Murdoch's *The Red and the Green*
1966	Boyd's *The Flats;* Heaney's *Death of a Naturalist;* Aidan Higgins' *Langrishe Go Down;* T. deV. White's *Lucifer Falling;* Frank O'Connor dies; Brian O'Nolan dies; new Abbey Theatre opens
1967	Boland's *New Territory;* Montague's *A Chosen Light;* Flann O'Brien's *The Third Policeman;* Desmond O'Grady's *The Dark Edge of Europe;* Patrick Kavanagh dies; Walter Macken dies
1968 Civil rights movement gains strength in Ulster; Bloody Sunday in Derry	Gilberts' *Ratman's Notebooks;* Paul Vincent Carroll dies; Donagh MacDonagh dies
1969 British troops assigned to Northern Ireland to maintain peace	Patrick Boyle's *All Looks Yellow to the Jaundiced Eye;* James Plunkett's *Strumpet City;* Power's *The Hungry Grass;* W. R. Rodgers dies; Beckett receives Nobel Prize
1970 IRA begins campaign of violence in the North	Brown's *Down All the Days*; Mairtin O Cadhain dies
1971 Chichester-Clark resigns as prime minister in North, is succeeded by Brian Faulkner; internment introduced in North	Kilroy's *The Big Chapel;* Lavin's *Collected Stories;* Stuart's *Black List, Section H;* St. John Ervine dies
1972 Faulkner resigns; Westminster suspends Northern Ireland constitution and rules directly	Heaney's *Wintering Out;* Jennifer Johnston's *The Captains and the Kings;* Mahon's *Lives;* Montague's *The Rough Field*
1973 Ireland enters the Common Market; coalition government; end of Vietnam War	Jennifer Johnston's *The Gates;* Leonard's *Da;* Richard Ryan's *Ravenswood*

	Political	Literary
	Political	*Literary*
1974	Sean MacBride receives Nobel Peace Prize	Clarke's *Collected Poems;* Padraic Fallon's *Poems;* R. Murphy's *High Island;* Austin Clarke dies; Padraic Fallon dies; Kate O'Brien dies
1975	Death of de Valera	Leitch, *Stamping Ground*
1976		Banville's *Dr. Copernicus;* Denis Johnston's *The Brazen Horn;* Noonan's *A Sexual Relationship;* O'Faolain's *Foreign Affairs;* Simmons' *July Garland and the Cold War*
1977	Fianna Fail returns to power; Peace women receive Nobel Prize	K. Casey's *Dreams of Revenge;* James Plunkett's *Collected Stories*

BIBLIOGRAPHY

BACKGROUND

Arnold, Bruce. *A Concise History of Irish Art.* New York & Washington: Frederick A. Praeger, 1968.

Beckett, J. C. *The Making of Modern Ireland.* New York: Alfred A. Knopf, 1966.

Carroll, Joseph T. *Ireland in the War Years, 1939-1945.* Newton Abbot: David & Charles; New York: Crane, Russak, 1975.

Connell, Kenneth Hugh. *Irish Peasant Society.* Oxford: Clarendon Press, 1968.

Craig, Maurice. *Dublin 1660-1860.* Dublin: Allen Figgis, 1969.

Croker, Thomas Crofton. *Fairy Legends and Traditions in the South of Ireland.* 3 vols. London: Murray, 1825-1828.

Cullen, L. M. *An Economic History of Ireland Since 1660.* New York: Barnes & Noble, 1973.

Curtis, Edmund. *A History of Ireland.* London: Methuen, 1950.

————. *A History of Medieval Ireland.* Dublin: Maunsel & Roberts, 1923; revised, London, 1938.

Deutsch, Richard R. *Northern Ireland 1921-1974: A Select Bibliography.* New York & London: Garland, 1975.

Dillon, Myles, ed. *Early Irish Society.* Dublin, 1954.

Edwards, R. Dudley. *Ireland in the Age of the Tudors.* London: Croom Helm; New York: Barnes & Noble, 1977.

Edwards, Ruth Dudley. *An Atlas of Irish History.* London: Methuen, 1973.

Evans, E. E. *Prehistoric and Early Christian Ireland.* London & New York, 1966.

Farrell, Brian, ed. *The Irish Parliamentary Tradition.* Dublin: Gill & Macmillan; New York: Barnes & Noble, 1973.

Kee, Robert. *The Green Flag: A History of Irish Nationalism.* New York: Delacorte Press, 1972.

Lyons, F.S.L. *Ireland Since the Famine.* London: Weidenfeld & Nicolson, 1971; revised, 1973.

Macardle, Dorothy. *The Irish Rising.* London: Gollancz, 1937.

MacCurtain, Margaret. *Tudor and Stuart Ireland.* Dublin & London, 1972.

Martin, F. X., ed. *Leaders and Men of the 1916 Rising.* Ithaca, N.Y.: Cornell University Press, [1967].

743

Moody, T. W., Martin, F. X., and Byrne, F. J., eds. *A New History of Ireland*. This
    projected series of nine volumes is appearing under the auspices of the Royal
    Irish Academy and will be published by the Clarendon Press. Volume 3, *Early
    Modern Ireland, 1534-1691*, appeared in 1976.
Murphy, John Augustine. *Ireland in the Twentieth Century*. London: Macmillan, 1975.
O'Brien, Conor Cruise. *States of Ireland*. London: Hutchinson; New York: Pantheon,
    1972.
O'Faolain, Sean. *The Irish*. West Drayton, Middlesex: Penguin, 1947.
O'Sullivan, Donal. *Irish Folk Music and Song*. Dublin: Cultural Relations Committee,
    1952.
Otway-Ruthven, A. J. *A History of Medieval Ireland*. London: Benn; New York:
    Barnes & Noble, 1968.
Praeger, Robert Lloyd. *Natural History of Ireland*. New York: Barnes & Noble, 1972.
Woodham-Smith, Cecil. *The Great Hunger*. London: Hamish Hamilton, [1962].

GENERAL LITERARY HISTORY

Best, Richard I. *Bibliography of Irish Philology and of Irish Printed Literature*. Dub-
    lin: Stationery Office, 1913.
————. *Bibliography of Irish Philology and Manuscript Literature: Publications 1913-
    1941*. Dublin: Institute for Advanced Studies, 1942.
Boyd, Ernest A. *Ireland's Literary Renaissance*. Dublin: Maunsel, 1916; Dublin: Allen
    Figgis, 1969.
Brown, Malcolm. *The Politics of Irish Literature: From Thomas Davis to W. B. Yeats*.
    Seattle: University of Washington Press, 1972.
Brown, Stephen J. *A Guide to Books on Ireland*. Part I. Dublin: Hodges Figgis, 1912;
    reprint, New York: Lema, 1970. (No Part II was ever issued.)
Cleeve, Brian. *Dictionary of Irish Writers*. 3 vols. Cork: Mercier Press, 1967, 1969,
    1971.
Costello, Peter. *The Heart Grown Brutal*. Dublin: Gill & Macmillan; Totowa, N.J.:
    Rowman & Littlefield, 1977.
de Blacam, Aodh. *Gaelic Literature Surveyed*. Dublin: Talbot Press, 1929; revised,
    1974.
Fallis, Richard. *The Irish Renaissance*. Syracuse, N.Y.: Syracuse University Press,
    1977.
Finneran, Richard, ed. *Anglo-Irish Literature, a Review of Research*. New York: Mod-
    ern Language Association of America, 1976.
Gwynn, Stephen. *Irish Literature and Drama*. New York: Nelson, 1936.
Howarth, Herbert. *The Irish Writers, 1880-1940*. London: Rockcliff, 1958.
Hyde, Douglas. *A Literary History of Ireland*. New York: Barnes & Noble, 1967.
MacDonagh, Thomas. *Literature in Ireland*. London: T. Fisher Unwin, 1916.
McKenna, Brian. *Irish Literature, 1800-1875, A Guide to Information Sources*.
    Detroit: Gale Research Co., 1978.
McSweeney, Patrick M. *A Group of Nation-Builders: O'Donovan, O'Curry, Petrie*.
    Dublin: Catholic Truth Society of Ireland, 1913.
Mercier, Vivian. *The Irish Comic Tradition*. Oxford: Clarendon Press, 1962.
O'Connor, Frank. *The Backward Look. A Survey of Irish Literature*. London: Mac-
    millan, 1967; published in the United States as *A Short History of Irish
    Literature*.
Power, Patrick C. *A Literary History of Ireland*. Cork: Mercier Press, 1969.
Rafroidi, Patrick. *L'Irlande et le Romantisme*. Paris. Editions Universitaires, 1972.

MYTHOLOGY

Gregory, Lady Augusta. *Cuchulain of Muirthemne.* London: Murray, 1902.
———. *Gods and Fighting Men.* London: Murray, 1904.
Kinsella, Thomas, trans. *The Tain.* Dublin: Dolmen Press, 1969.
Murphy, Gerard. *Saga and Myth in Ancient Ireland.* Dublin: Cultural Relations Committee, 1955.
O'Grady, Standish. *History of Ireland: Cuchulain and His Contemporaries.* London: Sampson Low, 1880.
———. *History of Ireland: The Heroic Period.* London: Sampson Low, 1878.

HISTORY AND CRITICISM OF FICTION

Brown, Stephen J. *Ireland in Fiction.* Dublin: Maunsel, 1915.
Flanagan, Thomas. *The Irish Novelists, 1800-1850.* New York: Columbia University Press, 1959.
Foster, John Wilson. *Forces and Themes in Ulster Fiction.* Totowa, N.J.: Rowman & Littlefield, 1974.
Kiely, Benedict. *Modern Irish Fiction, A Critique.* Dublin: Golden Eagle Books, 1950.
Krans, Horatio S. *Irish Life in Irish Fiction.* London: Macmillan, 1903.
Rafroidi, Patrick, and Harmon, Maurice, eds. *The Irish Novel in Our Time.* Lille: Universite de Lille, 1976.

HISTORY AND CRITICISM OF POETRY

Alspach, Russell K. *Irish Poetry from the English Invasion to 1798.* Philadelphia: University of Pennsylvania Press, 1959.
Brown, Terence. *Northern Voices: Poets from Ulster.* Totowa, N.J.: Rowman & Littlefield, 1975.
Clarke, Austin. *Poetry in Modern Ireland.* Dublin: Cultural Relations Committee, 1961.
Farren, Robert. *The Course of Irish Verse in English.* London & New York: Sheed & Ward, 1957.
Kersnowski, Frank. *The Outsiders: Poets of Contemporary Ireland.* Fort Worth, Tex.: Texas Christian University Press, 1975.
Loftus, Richard J. *Nationalism in Modern Anglo-Irish Poetry.* Madison & Milwaukee: University of Wisconsin Press, 1964.
Lucy, Sean. *Irish Poets in English.* Cork: Mercier Press, 1973.
O'Donoghue, D. J. *The Poets of Ireland, A Biographical and Bibliographical Dictionary.* Dublin: Hodges Figgis, 1912; reprint, Detroit: Gale, 1968.
Power, Patrick C. *The Story of Anglo-Irish Poetry, 1800-1922.* Cork: Mercier Press, 1967.

HISTORY AND CRITICISM OF DRAMA

Bartley, J. O. *Teague, Shenkin and Sawney. Being an Historical Study of the Earliest Irish, Welsh and Scottish Characters in English Plays.* Cork: Cork University Press, 1954.
Bell, Sam Hanna. *The Theatre in Ulster.* Dublin: Gill & Macmillan, 1972.
Clark, William S. *The Early Irish Stage. The Beginnings to 1720.* Oxford: Clarendon Press, 1955.

————. *The Irish Stage in the Country Towns, 1720-1860*. Oxford: Clarendon Press, 1965.

Duggan, G. C. *The Stage Irishman*. Dublin: Talbot Press, 1937.

Ellis-Fermor, Una. *The Irish Dramatic Movement*. London: Methuen, 1939; revised 1954.

Fay, Gerard. *The Abbey Theatre, Cradle of Genius*. London: Hollis & Carter, 1958.

Gregory, Lady Augusta. *Our Irish Theatre*. Gerrard's Cross: Colin Smythe, 1973. (The most satisfactory edition.)

Hogan, Robert. *After the Irish Renaissance*. Minneapolis: University of Minnesota Press, 1967; London: Macmillan, 1968.

————, and Kilroy, James. *The Irish Literary Theatre*. Vol 1 of *The Modern Irish Drama*. Dublin: Dolmen Press, 1975.

————. *Laying the Foundations, 1902-1904*. Vol. 2 of *The Modern Irish Drama*. Dublin: Dolmen Press, 1976.

————. *The Abbey Theatre, 1905-1909*. Vol. 3 of *The Modern Irish Drama*. Dublin: Dolmen Press, 1978.

Holloway, Joseph. *Joseph Holloway's Abbey Theatre*. Carbondale: Southern Illinois University Press, 1967.

————. *Joseph Holloway's Irish Theatre*. 3 vols. Dixon, Calif.: Proscenium Press, 1968-1970.

Kavanagh, Peter. *The Irish Theatre: Being a History of the Drama in Ireland from the Earliest Period Up to the Present Day*. Tralee: Kerryman, 1946.

————. *The Story of the Abbey Theatre*. New York: Devin-Adair, 1950.

McCann, Sean, ed. *The Story of the Abbey*. London: New English Library, 1967.

Mac Liammóir, Micheál. *Theatre in Ireland*. Dublin: Cultural Relations Committee, 1964.

Malone, Andrew E. *The Irish Drama*. London: Constable, 1929.

Nic Shiubhlaigh, Maire, and Kenny, Edward. *The Splendid Years*. Dublin: Duffy, 1955.

Ó hAodha, Micheál. *Theatre in Ireland*. Totowa, N.J.: Rowman & Littlefield, 1974.

Robinson, Lennox. *Ireland's Abbey Theatre*. London: Sidgwick & Jackson, 1951.

Simpson, Alan. *Beckett and Behan and a Theatre in Dublin*. London: Routledge & Kegan Paul, 1962.

Worth, Katharine. *The Irish Drama of Europe from Yeats to Beckett*. Atlantic Highlands, N.J.: Humanities Press, [1978].

COLLECTIONS OF CRITICISM

Carpenter, Andrew, ed. *Place, Personality & the Irish Writer*. Gerrards Cross: Colin Smythe; New York: Barnes & Noble, 1977.

Dunn, Douglas, ed. *Two Decades of Irish Writing*. Chester Springs, Pa.: Dufour, 1975.

Porter, Raymond J., and Brophy, James D., eds. *Modern Irish Literature*. New York: Iona College Press & Twayne, 1972.

Ronsley, Joseph, ed. *Myth and Reality in Irish Literature*. Waterloo, Ontario, Canada: Wilfrid Laurier University Press, 1977.

ANTHOLOGIES

General

Greene, David H. *An Anthology of Irish Literature*. New York: Modern Library, 1954.

McCarthy, Justin, and Welsh, Charles, eds. *Irish Authors and Their Writings in Ten Volumes*. Philadelphia: Morris, 1904.

Mercier, Vivian, and Greene, David H. *1000 Years of Irish Prose: The Literary Revival*. New York: Devin-Adair, 1952; New York: Grosset & Dunlap, 1961.

Read, Charles A., ed. *The Cabinet of Irish Literature*. 4 vols. London: Blackie, 1879-1880; new ed., by Katharine Tynan Hinkson, London: Gresham, 1903.

Russell, Diarmuid, ed. *The Portable Irish Reader*. New York: Viking, 1946.

Saul, George Brandon, ed. *The Age of Yeats*. New York: Dell, 1963.

Poetry

Anon., *The Spirit of the Nation, Ballads and Songs by the Writers of the Nation with Original and Ancient Music. . . .* Dublin: Duffy, 1845.

Colum, Padraic. *An Anthology of Irish Verse*. New York: Boni & Liveright, 1922.

Duffy, Charles Gavan. *The Ballad Poetry of Ireland*. Dublin: Duffy, 1845.

Fiacc, Padraic. *The Wearing of the Black: An Anthology of Contemporary Ulster Poetry*. Belfast: Blackstaff, 1974.

Greene, David, and O'Connor, Frank. *A Golden Treasury of Irish Verse, A.D. 600 to 1200*. London: Macmillan, 1967.

Hardiman, James. *Irish Minstrelsy; or, Bardic Remains of Ireland; with English Poetical Translations*. 2 vols. London: Robins, 1831; reprint, New York: Barnes & Noble, 1971.

Hewitt, John. *Rhyming Weavers and Other Country Poets of Antrim and Down*. Belfast: Blackstaff, 1974.

Hoagland, Kathleen. *1000 Years of Irish Poetry*. New York: Devin-Adair, 1947.

Kennelly, Brendan. *The Penguin Book of Irish Verse*. Harmondsworth, Middlesex: Penguin, 1970.

MacDonagh, Donagh, and Robinson, Lennox. *Oxford Book of Irish Verse*. Oxford: Clarendon Press, 1958.

Mahon, Derek. *The Sphere Book of Modern Irish Poetry*. London: Sphere Books, 1972.

Marcus, David. *Irish Poets, 1924-1974*. London: Pan Books, 1975.

Montague, John. *The Faber Book of Irish Verse*. London: Faber, 1974.

O'Reilly, John Boyle. *The Poetry and Song of Ireland*. New York: Gay Brothers, 1889.

Taylor, Geoffrey. *Irish Poets of the Nineteenth Century*. London: Routledge & Kegan Paul, 1951.

Yeats, W. B. *A Book of Irish Verse*. London: Methuen, 1895.

Fiction

Birmingham, George A. *Irish Short Stories*. London: Faber, 1932.

Casey, Kevin. *Winter's Tales from Ireland: Two*. Dublin: Gill & Macmillan, 1972.

Garrity, Devin A. *44 Irish Short Stories*. New York: Devin-Adair, 1960.

Marcus, David. *Modern Irish Love Stories*. London: Pan Books, 1974.

———. *New Irish Writing 1*. Dublin: Dolmen Press, 1970.

———. *The Sphere Book of Modern Irish Short Stories*. London: Sphere, 1972.

Martin, Augustine. *Winter's Tales from Ireland: One*. Dublin: Gill & Macmillan, 1970.

Mercier, Vivian. *Great Irish Short Stories*. New York: Dell, 1964.

O'Connor, Frank. *Modern Irish Short Stories*. London: Oxford University Press, 1957.

Drama

Barnet, Sylvan, et al. *The Genius of the Irish Theatre*. New York: New American Library, 1960.

Browne, E. Martin. *Three Irish Plays*. Harmondsworth, Middlesex, 1958.

Canfield, Curtis. *Plays of Changing Ireland*. New York: Macmillan, 1936.

———. *Plays of the Irish Renaissance*. New York: Macmillan, 1929.

Hogan, Robert. *Seven Irish Plays, 1946-1964*. Minneapolis: University of Minnesota Press, 1967.

INDEX

Numbers in italic indicate the main discussion of a topic.

Aaron Thy Brother (Conor Farrington), 234

Abbé Prévost (Helen Waddell), 672

Abbey Row, Not Edited by W. B. Yeats, The, 453

Abbey Theatre, *75-85,* 103, 123, 137, 140, 146, 153, 157, 158, 164, 165, 172, 173, 174, 175, 176, 183, 185, 192, 194, 215, 217, 219, 227, 228, 229, 230, 234, 242, 244, 252, 257, 258, 259, 267, 272, 273, 274, 278, 279, 287, 296, 299, 307, 309, 310, 314, 346, 348, 357, 372, 374, 375, 387, 389, 396, 404, 405, 406, 415, 418, 419, 420, 421, 427, 428, 429, 432, 433, 436, 437, 438, 445, 454, 476, 477, 479, 489, 490, 492, 493, 495, 496, 499, 501, 508, 511, 520, 532, 533, 534, 542, 543, 544, 557, 562, 563, 564, 565, 569, 571, 579, 580, 587, 589, 590, 593, 594, 605, 611, 623, 634, 656, 657, 670, 675, 680, 684, 693, 699, 701, 713, 720, 721

"Abbey Theatre Fire, The" (Austin Clarke), 158

Abbey Theatre Playwright's Bursary, *255*

Abbeyleix, Queens County, 96

Abbotsholme School, Derbyshire, 670

Abhráin Airt Mhic Chubthaigh (Henry Morris, ed.), 55

"Absalom and Achitophel" (John Dryden), 659

Absentee, The (Maria Edgeworth), 222

Absolute, Sir Anthony (literary character), 14

Absurd, Theatre of the, 98, 541

Accent (American magazine), 203

Account of the Drunken Sea, An (Dr. James Henry), 291

Account of the Police in the City of Canton, An (Dr. James Henry), 291

Achill Island, County Mayo, 190, 664, 726

Acres, Bob (literary character), 14

Across the Bitter Sea (Eilis Dillon), 206

Act of Union, 96, 188, 222, 268, 385, 676

Acton, Lord, 614

Acts and Monuments (Eiléan Ní Chuilleanáin), 481

Adam, Dacey (literary character), 406

Adam, Villiers de l'Isle, 460

Adam Bede (George Eliot), 462

Adam of Dublin (Conal O'Riordan), 544

Adamnan, 17, 32

Adamov, Arthur, 98

Adams, Tate, 207

"Adam's Curse" (W. B. Yeats), 712

Adding Machine, The (Elmer Rice), 675

Addison, Joseph, 107, 169, 624

Admirable Crichton, The (J. M. Barrie), 596

Admissions (Sheila Wingfield), 694

Adolf Hitler—My Part in His Downfall (Spike Milligan), 448

Advent (literary magazine), 202, 204

"Adventures in the Bohemian Jungle" (Patrick Kavanagh), 343

Adventures of Barney Mahoney, The (Mrs. T. Crofton Croker), 178

Adventures of Dr. Whitty, The (George A. Birmingham), 110

Adventures of the Black Girl in Her Search for God, The (Bernard Shaw), 593

AE (George W. Russell), 68, *85-88,* 156, 165, 170, 175, 176, 182, 183, 224, 225, 238, 239, 308, 319, 353, 362, 368, 393, 395, 407, 408, 453, 462, 501, 508, 529, 530, 536, 547, 548, 567, 569, 577, 580,

ABOUT THE EDITOR

Robert Hogan is Professor of English at the University of Delaware in Newark. His many books include *The Experiments of Sean O'Casey*, *After the Irish Renaissance*, and *Modern Irish Drama*.